Handbook of Depression and Anxiety

Medical Psychiatry

Series Editor

William A. Frosch, M.D.

Cornell University Medical College
New York, New York

1. *Handbook of Depression and Anxiety: A Biological Approach*, edited by Johan A. den Boer and J. M. Ad Sitsen

ADDITIONAL VOLUMES IN PREPARATION

Handbook of Depression and Anxiety

A Biological Approach

edited by

Johan A. den Boer

J. M. Ad Sitsen

State University of Utrecht
Utrecht, The Netherlands

Marcel Dekker, Inc. New York • Basel • Hong Kong

Library of Congress Cataloging-in-Publication Data

Handbook of depression and anxiety: a biological approach / edited by Johan A. den Boer, J. M. Ad Sitsen.
p. cm. -- (Medical psychiatry; v. 1)
Includes bibliographical references and index.
ISBN 0-8247-8858-3 (alk. paper)
1. Depression, Mental--Physiological aspects. 2. Anxiety--Physiological aspects. 3. Depression, Mental--Chemotherapy. 4. Anxiety--Chemotherapy. I. Boer, Johan A. den. II. Sitsen, J. M. A. III. Series.
[DNLM: 1. Depressive Disorder--physiopathology. 2. Depressive Disorder--drug therapy. 3. Anxiety Disorders--physiopathology. WM 171 H2363 1994]
RC537.H3377 1994
616.85'27--dc20
DNLM/DLC
for Library of Congress 93-45266
CIP

The publisher offers discounts on this book when ordered in bulk quantities. For more information, write to Special Sales/Professional Marketing at the address below.

This book is printed on acid-free paper.

MARCEL DEKKER, INC.
270 Madison Avenue, New York, New York 10016

Current printing (last digit):
10 9 8 7 6 5 4 3 2

PRINTED IN THE UNITED STATES OF AMERICA

Series Introduction

The human brain, encased in its bony skull and protected by the ethics of research, has always remained hidden from view and inaccessible to direct study. Recently, however, new imaging techniques, along with the development of our understanding of neurodevelopment, neurotransmitter and receptor physiology, and endocrinology, particularly on the molecular level, have begun to let us glimpse the rich complexity(ies) of brain function. As a result, the increasingly sophisticated view of brain biology has been accompanied by more rigorous and reliable diagnosis (by using the criteria sets of DSM-III, DSM-IIIR, and now DSM IV), larger and better genetic and epidemiologic studies, and more focused (at times even tested) therapies. In combination, these developments have given us a window into that parallel organ of interest to psychiatrists and others involved with how people behave and misbehave—the mind.

We hope this new series will introduce the reader to the newly emerging psychiatric paradigm. With the coming changes in the organization of medical care, the matters to be presented are likely to be of interest to the broader medical and health care audience.

This first volume exemplifies this wide-ranging appeal; anxiety and depression are ubiquitous; responsibility for their recognition and treatment widespread. The *Handbook of Depression and Anxiety* introduces us to the new world of psychiatry as medicine looking at disorders with emotional and behavioral symptoms. It brings us into a world of complex biology, careful description, criteria-based diagnosis, and controlled outcome studies. It is an exciting world. Welcome!

William A. Frosch

Preface

Anxiety and depression are complex emotional states in which cognitive evaluations and affective and physiological responses are involved. Considering the complexity of these emotions, which can be described in several scientific languages at different levels of analysis, there is no doubt that multiple neuronal systems in the brain are implicated in the pathophysiology of these closely related disorders.

On a phenomenological level, there is a high degree of overlap between symptoms of anxiety and depression, as well as a high degree of comorbidity. This does not imply, however, that both syndromes are merely different phenotypical expressions of a genetically based constitution sharing similar biological underpinnings. The question of whether anxiety and depression result from similar or different biological abnormalities cannot be answered using one research strategy. On one hand, psychophysiological research provides evidence suggesting that anxiety and depression are clearly distinct disorders; on the other hand, specific anxiety disorders and depressive syndromes respond to similar pharmacological interventions. Thus, these conflicting findings from different biomedical fields of research present a challenge to all of us involved in the study of these very common and often debilitating psychiatric illnesses.

According to some investigators, distinguishing different subtypes among depressive syndromes and anxiety disorders is a somewhat artificial practice. They argue that a general neurotic syndrome exists based upon a common underlying propensity toward "nervousness." Reasoning from this (dimensional) viewpoint implies that the different diagnostic categories could merely be phenotypical manifestations of an underlying vulnerability to "anxiety" or depression.

During the last decade our knowledge about the biological underpinnings of depression and anxiety disorders has increased enormously. This holds particularly true for panic disorder and obsessive compulsive disorder, and new insights are continually emerging from widely disparate fields, such as epidemiology, genetics, immunology, psychophysiology, and pharmacology. This book attempts to bring these different disciplines together. It reviews the state of the art in biological research on anxiety and depression and their interrelatedness. We consider ourselves fortunate to have succeeded in bringing together a great number of internationally renowned authors who shed light on this topic. We hope that this book will be read by scientists from many disciplines, who will be inspired by the exciting findings in fields other than their own.

During the preparation of this book we were shocked to learn of the unexpected and untimely death of Dr. Willy Haefely, who contributed an excellent chapter to this book, probably one of his last important scientific publications. Dr. Haefely was an excellent scientist, who conducted pioneering research in the field of benzodiazepines. For his family, as well as for basic research in psychiatry, his sudden death is a great loss.

Johan A. den Boer
J. M. Ad Sitsen

Contents

Contributors

James C. Ballenger, M.D. Professor and Chairman, Department of Psychiatry and Behavioral Sciences; and Director, Institute of Psychiatry, Medical University of South Carolina, Charleston, South Carolina

Richard Balon, M.D. Associate Professor, Department of Psychiatry, Wayne State University School of Medicine, Detroit, Michigan

Rosemary C. Bischoff Department of Clinical Development, CNSI, Schering AG, Berlin, Germany

Serena-Lynn Brown, M.D., Ph.D. Associate Professor, Department of Psychiatry, Director, Psychopharmacology Clinic, Albert Einstein College of Medicine/Montefiore Medical Center, Bronx, New York

Graham D. Burrows, A.O., M.D., Ch.B., B.Sc., D.P.M., F.R.A.N.Z.C.P., F.R.C.Psych. Professor and Director, Department of Psychiatry, University of Melbourne, Austin Hospital, Heidelberg, Victoria, Australia

Alexander Bystritsky, M.D. Assistant Professor and Director, Anxiety Disorders Program, Department of Psychiatry and Behavioral Sciences, UCLA School of Medicine, Los Angeles, California

Dennis S. Charney, M.D. Professor and Associate Chairman for Research, Department of Psychiatry, Yale University School of Medicine, New Haven, Connecticut

C. Robert Cloninger, M.D. Wallace Renard Professor and Head, Department of Psychiatry, Washington University School of Medicine, St. Louis, Missouri

J. F. W. Deakin, Ph.D., F.R.C.Psych. Professor, Department of Psychiatry, Manchester Royal Infirmary, Manchester, England

Pedro L. Delgado, M.D. Department of Psychiatry, Yale University School of Medicine, New Haven, Connecticut

Johan A. den Boer, M.D., Ph.D. Department of Biological Psychiatry, Academic Hospital Utrecht, State University of Utrecht, Utrecht, The Netherlands

Rainer Dorow, M.D. Head, Department of Clinical Development CV/CNS, Schering Ag, Berlin, Germany

T. Duka Schering AG, Berlin, Germany

Gerrit Glas, M.D., Ph.D. Psychiatrist, Department of Psychiatry, Academic Hospital Utrecht, Utrecht; and Professor, Department of Philosophy, State University of Leiden, Leiden, The Netherlands

Philip W. Gold, M.D. Clinical Neuroendocrinology Branch, Laboratory of Clinical Sciences, National Institute of Mental Health, National Institutes of Health, Bethesda, Maryland

Willy Haefely, M.D. F. Hoffmann-La Roche, Ltd., Basel, Switzerland

Rudolf Hoehn-Saric, M.D. Professor, Department of Psychiatry, Johns Hopkins University School of Medicine, Baltimore Maryland

Peter R. Joyce, M.B., Ch.B., Ph.D., F.R.A.N.Z.C.P. Professor, University Department of Psychological Medicine, Christchurch School of Medicine, Christchurch, New Zealand

Fiona K. Judd, M.D., D.P.M., F.R.A.N.Z.C.P. Associate Professor, Department of Psychiatry, University of Melbourne, Austin Hospital, Heidelberg, Victoria, Australia

Robert Kellner, M.D., Ph.D. Professor and Vice Chairman, Department of Psychiatry, University of New Mexico School of Medicine, Albuquerque, New Mexico

Ziad Kronfol, M.D. Associate Professor, Department of Psychiatry, University of Michigan Medical Center, Ann Arbor, Michigan

John H. Krystal, M.D. Department of Psychiatry, Yale University School of Medicine, New Haven, Connecticut

Brian E. Leonard, Ph.D., D.Sc. Professor, Department of Pharmacology, University College, Galway, Ireland

Andrew Mackinnon, Ph.D. Research Fellow, NH & MRC Social Psychiatry Research Unit, Australian National University, Canberra, Australia

S. McDonald Schering AG, Berlin, Germany

Daniel R. McLeod, Ph.D. Assistant Professor, Department of Psychiatry, Johns Hopkins University School of Medicine, Baltimore, Maryland

David Michelson, M.D. Clinical Investigator, Department of Clinical Neuroendocrinology, National Institute of Mental Health, National Institutes of Health, Bethesda, Maryland

Philip B. Mitchell, M.B., B.S., M.D., MRCPsych, F.R.A.N.Z.C.P. Associate Professor, School of Psychiatry, University of New South Wales, Sydney, Australia

Stuart A. Montgomery, B.Sc., M.D., F.R.C.Psych. Australia Academic Department of Psychiatry, St. Mary's Hospital Medical School, London, England

Charles B. Nemeroff, M.D., Ph.D. Professor and Chairman, Department of Psychiatry and Behavioral Sciences, Emory University School of Medicine, Atlanta, Georgia

Trevor R. Norman, B.Sc., Ph.D. Senior Research Fellow, Department of Psychiatry, University of Melbourne, Austin Hospital, Heidelberg, Victoria, Australia

Robert O. Pasnau, M.D. Professor and Assistant Dean, Department of Psychiatry and Behavioral Sciences, UCLA School of Medicine, Los Angeles, California

Robert Pohl, M.D. Professor, Department of Psychiatry, Wayne State University School of Medicine, Detroit, Michigan

J. M. Ad Sitsen, M.D., Ph.D. Professor of Clinical Pharmacology, Departments of Internal Medicine and Pharmacology, Academic Hospital Utrecht, State University of Utrecht, Utrecht, The Netherlands

Steven M. Southwick, M.D. Department of Psychiatry, Yale University School of Medicine, New Haven, Connecticut

Murray B. Stein, M.D. Associate Professor, Departments of Psychiatry and Pharmacology, University of Manitoba, Winnipeg, Manitoba, Canada

Robert L. Steinberg, M.D. Clinical Assistant Professor, Department of Psychiatry, Mount Sinai Medical Center, New York, New York

D. N. Stephens Schering AG, Berlin, Germany

Dragan M. Svrakic Washington University School of Medicine, St. Louis, Missouri

Dallas Treit, Ph.D. Associate Professor, Department of Psychology, University of Alberta, Edmonton, Alberta, Canada

Jonathan Tyrer, M.Sc. Department of Probability and Statistics, University of Sheffield, Sheffield, England

Peter Tyrer, M.D., F.R.C.P., F.R.C.Psych., M.F.P.H.M. Professor of Community Psychiatry, Department of Psychiatry, St. Mary's Hospital Medical School, St. Charles Hospital, London, England

Thomas W. Uhde, M.D. Chief, Section on Anxiety and Affective Disorders, Biological Psychiatry Branch, National Institute of Mental Health, National Institutes of Health, Bethesda, Maryland

Herman M. van Praag, M.D., Ph.D. Professor and Chairman, Academic Psychiatric Centre, University of Limburg, Maastricht, The Netherlands

Herman G. M. Westenberg, PhD. Associate Professor of Psychopharmacology, Department of Psychiatry, Academic Hospital Utrecht, State University of Utrecht, Utrecht, The Netherlands

Paul Willner, M.A., D.Phil. Professor, Department of Psychology, University College of Swansea, Swansea, Wales

Keith G. Wilson, Ph.D. Assistant Professor, Department of Medicine, The Rehabilitation Centre and University of Ottawa, Ottawa, Ontario, Canada

Rachel Yehuda, Ph.D. Assistant Professor, Department of Psychiatry, Mount Sinai School of Medicine and Bronx Veteran Affairs, New York, New York

Vikram K. Yeragani, M.B.B.S., F.R.C.P.(C.) Associate Professor, Department of Psychiatry, Wayne State University School of Medicine, Detroit, Michigan

Handbook of Depression and Anxiety

1

A Conceptual History of Anxiety and Depression

Gerrit Glas
Academic Hospital Utrecht, Utrecht, and
State University of Leiden, Leiden, The Netherlands

I. INTRODUCTION

For more than 2500 years, physicians have distinguished the clinical conditions that we call affective or anxiety disorder from such everyday feelings as fear, restlessness, and despondency, feelings that overwhelm each of us at one time or another.

Contrary to what might be expected, case descriptions from the past bear striking resemblances to patients encountered in modern-day clinical practice. Whomever one consults, whether it is Aristotle, Galen, Burton, or the 19th century alienists, images of a suggestive reality are evoked, images in which we can easily recognize the depressive, anxious, and melancholic individual of our own era. There are similarities in symptomatology and course, as well as in the distinction between normality and abnormality.

On the other hand, there are also considerable disparities in language and frame of reference, in conceptualization, and in interpretation. From the time of Hippocrates up until well into the 17th century, the description and interpretation of anxiety and depression were dominated by the doctrine of bodily fluids (*humores*). And, until quite recently, all manner of ideas involving neural energy overshadowed discussions of phenomena such as neurasthenia, inhibition, and motor agitation.

Traditionally, these disparities have been given particular emphasis. The undeniably impressive growth of our knowledge is seen as evidence of the superiority of contemporary explanatory models. Conversely, ideas that were current from antiquity up until the 19th century are considered to be of no more than historical interest—simply a fanciful mythology for enthusiasts. The history of medicine has become a somewhat quaint activity, pursued by a handful of specialists.

This may or may not be considered regretable. Nevertheless, these disparities once again become relevant at a certain level of discussion, as well as for clinicians and research workers. I refer here to the very foundations of medicine (i.e., the level of its basic concepts) and to the cultural and ideological strata from which these concepts derive their significance.

A consideration of the foundations of medicine helps, for example, to put into perspective the already overly strict separation of symptoms and explanatory models. Symptoms are not natural phenomena, in that they are not the invariable expressions of an unchanging biological substratum. Whatever one's concept of disease, what the patient says is always based on interpretation, at least to a certain extent. That interpretation can be colored by whatever is considered to be normal or abnormal in a particular culture. Explanatory models, on the other hand, are not simply conjured up out of the blue. They are neither arbitrary nor coincidental, but are instead meta-interpretations of a reality already interpreted by the afflicted persons and those around them. Moreover, these explanatory models are usually closely linked to whatever paradigms are currently fashionable in the various branches of science.

Accordingly, we cannot pretend that depression and anxiety are natural phenomena that have consistently been expressed and experienced in the same way down through the centuries. Concentrating purely on differences at the level of the explanatory models can easily turn the history of medicine into a study of scientific folklore. As if, with the passage of time, only the explanatory models have changed and not the phenomena themselves—*phenomena* here meaning anything that presents itself as disease. Notwithstanding the aforementioned similarities in clinical picture and course, the symptoms of anxiety and depression themselves have changed, that is, their relevance to what counts as disease and their meaning as an expression of disease.

Seen from this point of view, the study of the history of medicine suddenly becomes extremely relevant to a clear understanding of all sorts of current explanatory models. The medical history of anxiety and depression is, therefore, not simply concerned with internal scientific development. It also involves the interplay of cultural changes and psychopathological phenomena, including the scientific interpretations of such phenomena.

In this chapter several leading concepts in the history of anxiety and depression will be summarized. Instead of delving into historic detail, the emphasis will be on concepts and, particularly, on the paradigm shifts associated with the changes in conceptual content.

Anyone interested in detail is referred to the existing literature on the history of medicine, particularly to the outstanding studies of Jackson (1986) and Klibansky and associates (1964). Also of interest are the studies by Ackerknecht (1968), Beek (1969), Berrios (1988), Flashar (1966), Foucault (1965), Gardiner et al. (1937), King (1978), Leibbrand and Wettley (1961), Lewis (1934a), Roccatagliata (1986), Rosen (1969), Starobinski (1960), and Zilboorg (1941).

II. NOMENCLATURE

Before commencing with our historical review, a few comments about terminology.

First of all, it should be realized that the generally accepted distinction between anxiety and depression is of comparatively recent vintage. The first nonphobic form of anxiety to take its place in the description of disease did so as recently as the middle of the 19th century. Flemming's *Über Praecordialangst*, which dates from 1848, was cited by

Schmidt-Degenhard (1986) as the first medicopsychiatric text exclusively devoted to a nonphobic form of anxiety.

This does not mean that subtle variations in the spectrum of anxiety and depressive disorders had not been observed and described before this. Evidently, however, there was no recognition of the need for a systematic distinction between anxiety and depression. For a long time, both were encompassed by the broad concept of melancholia. Since the *Corpus Hippocraticum* (5th century BC), fear and despondency have been referred to as the prominent characteristics of melancholia.

The terms *melancholia* (Greek: *melaina cholè*, black bile) and *hypochondria* (Greek: *hypochondrios*, under the breastbone), which one is almost compelled to link together, are of ancient vintage. The same applies to the concept of *mania*. The word *depression* (Latin: *deprimere,* to press down) gradually came into use during the 18th century (Jackson, 1986; pp. 145–146).

Unlike the term *phobia* (Greek: *phobos*, fear), the term anxiety has neither Greek nor Latin origins. The word *anxiety* (German: *Angst*, worry) probably derives from the Indo-Germanic root *Angh*, which means to narrow, to constrict, or to strangulate (von Baeyer and von Baeyer-Katte, 1971; Häfner, 1971; Lewis, 1967). This root reappears in the Greek word *anchein* which means to strangle, to suffocate, or to press shut. The root *Angh* has also survived in Latin, for example, in *angor* (suffocation; feeling of entrapment) and *anxietas* (shrink back fearfully; overconcern). Fear derives from the German stem *freisa* or *frasa.* The term *panic,* on the other hand, has a Greek background, namely *Pan* or *Panikos*, the Greek god of the forest and of shepherds, who was thought to have caused panic among the Persians at Marathon.

The fields of meaning of the different terms are rather vague. This is particularly true of the term melancholia, which covers practically all forms of nonorganically determined psychopathology. In summary, however, it can be stated that despondency is an important element of meaning in the numerous terms for depression. In terms used for anxiety, the emphasis is often on a perception of tightness and constriction in the region of the chest and throat.

III. A HISTORY OF THE CONCEPTS OF ANXIETY AND DEPRESSION BASED ON THE CONCEPT OF MELANCHOLIA

A. Ancient Greece and Rome

Western psychiatry, just like somatic medicine, has its roots in Greek natural philosophy. In this philosophy, the traditional explanations of mental illness, based on the supernatural, gradually diminish in significance. Clinical observation and reasoning become established practice. Natural philosophers attempt to elucidate the universal principle behind observed phenomena. They observe heaven and earth, the orbits of heavenly bodies, and the course of the seasons, as well as the cycle of ascension, splendor, and decline in the living and the nonliving worlds. They are dissatisfied with demonological explanations of mental illness, such as those found in the works of Homer, for example.

This does not mean that moments of speculation became a thing of the past, as can be seen from the *Corpus Hippocraticum*, for example. This work consists of a series of 70 medical texts dating from the fifth century BC, which are attributed to Hippocrates and his pupils. The *Corpus* contains the earliest formulation of the theory of the four humors, or bodily fluids. This humoral theory was a modified version of the view, first encountered in the works of Empedocles, that the universe is made up of a mixture of four elements: earth, fire, air, and water. Empedocles himself was probably influenced by the pythagorean school's doctrine of the "harmony of the spheres," which placed strong emphasis on notions such as tuning and equilibrium. According to the humoral theory, disease results from a disturbance in the natural balance (*dyscrasia*) of the elements. Blood, yellow bile, black bile, and phlegm are the four bodily fluids or humors distinguished in the hippocratic texts. These fluids were considered to be influenced by the seasons. Accordingly, blood would increase in the spring, yellow bile in the summer, black bile in the fall, and phlegm in the winter. In addition, each of the humors was associated with a pair of primary qualities. Thus blood was associated with heat and wetness, yellow bile with heat and dryness, black bile with dryness and cold, and phlegm with cold and wetness (Fig. 1).

To the Greek physician, disease was caused by a disturbance in the natural balance of the bodily fluids. This balance was influenced by all sorts of factors, such as seasonal changes, climate, geographic conditions, age, mental effort, as well as eating and drinking habits. The Greeks were well aware, for example, of the link between depressive phenomena and the fall. In addition to these factors, certain people were temperamentally predisposed to melancholia. In this context, the term *temperament* refers to a person's humoral constitution. Because of an excess of black bile, or to an increased susceptibility of the black bile to heat or cold, some people could have a natural tendency toward melancholia.

This suggests that the balance between the humors reflects a much broader biopsychological and ecological equilibrium. This is indeed true. The ancient concept of disease must be seen against the contemporary background theme of the so-called macrocosm–microcosm. Mankind, as a microcosm, was part of a well-ordered universe, which the Greeks referred to as the Cosmos. This theme was to dominate the concept of disease for at least two millennia. It left no room for the principle of linear (unidirectional) causality, developed by physicists, which gradually began to dominate medi-

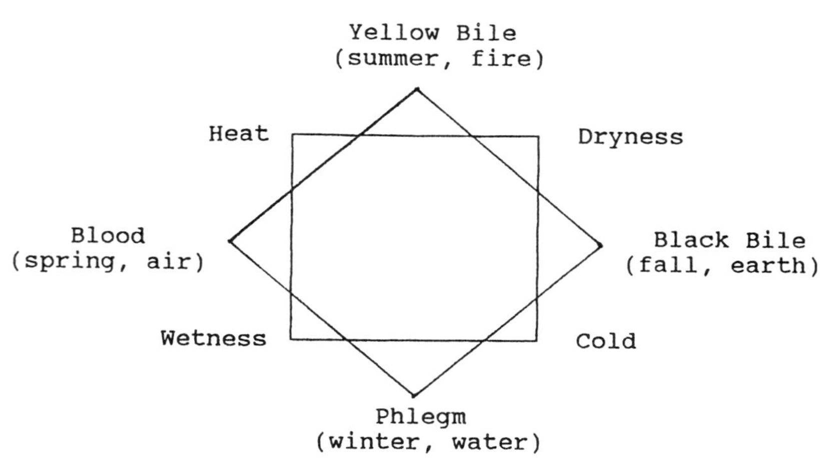

Figure 1 The four humors and their relation to the seasons, the elements, and the primary qualities.

cine in the 18th century. Nor can it be equated with the late 19th century concept of homeostasis, since this concept presupposes the idea of internal feedback, a notion that was quite foreign to the ancient Greeks. In antiquity, disease was seen as a disorder reflected on all levels of existence, rather than as the consequence of an internal disorder. The excess of black bile in melancholia was the analogue of changes in the seasons, in dietary habits, and in psychological constitution (cf. Temkin 1973; 1977, pp. 422–5). The origins and conclusion of disease were not confined to the relative isolation of the body. Instead, disease reflected changes on all sorts of levels within the macrocosm.

The 20th century reader may suspect that there are conceptual problems here; however, none seemed to exist for the Greek physician–philosopher. He seemed quite uninterested in the question of how all of these different processes interacted with one other, choosing instead to ignore the problem. Some have suggested, for example, that the Greek outlook could not accommodate a psychogenic cause of mental illness. This is factually incorrect, since the literature of that time includes many examples of scholars becoming depressed through excessive study, and of melancholics consumed by feelings of guilt, hatred, or grief over a lost love. In addition, there is also a conceptual misunderstanding here. This occurs whenever modern ways of thinking begin to dominate the interpretation of humoral pathology. The humors are then reduced to purely biological phenomena (comparable to neurotransmitters) and the lovelorn state, or that of being overworked, to mere matters of psychology. Greek physicians undeniably thought of the *melaina cholè* as a substance that was both visible and tangible, even though they had never actually seen it. Nevertheless, they persisted in associating this unseen substance with all kinds of effects at the psychological and behavioral levels. From a 20th century point of view, this association could be seen as a metaphor. To the Greek physician, however, the notion of atrabiliousness (black bitterness) was a condensation of all sorts of very real experiences and perceptions. In short, even though the emphasis lay on what is now referred to as the biological component, the psychological connotation still was implied by the terms for the bodily fluids.[1] According to Aretaeus, bile means anger and black, much or furious:

> in certain of these cases, there is neither flatulence nor black bile, but mere anger and grief, and sad dejection of mind; and these were called melancholics, because the terms bile and anger are synonymous in import, and likewise black with much and furious. (Aretaeus; via Jackson, 1986, p. 40)

For all that, black bile was the last substance to be ranked among the true bodily fluids. Initially interpreted as a breakdown product of yellow bile, black bile was first described as a natural constituent of the body in the *Corpus Hippocraticum*. Its change in status can probably be attributed to the dark-colored urine and feces observed in malaria sufferers and in patients with hepatic disease or gastric bleeding.

However, rather more than 5 centuries were to pass between this reference to black bile in the hippocratic texts and the first summarized description of its effects. This summary, which can be found in the medical works of *Galen* (131–201 AD), was to serve as a model for medical thinking for centuries to come.

Galen owed a great deal to the work of *Rufus of Ephesus* (circa 100 AD), who we must thank for a description of various melancholic delusions, among other things. One such delusion was that of being an earthen pot, another was that of lacking a head. Rufus also influenced Arabic medicine and, through it, the medicine of the Middle Ages. It was Rufus from whom the great *Ishaq ibn Imran*, of 10th century Baghdad, reputedly derived his ideas about melancholia. The latter's work was to become the direct source for *De Melancholia* by *Constantinus Africanus* (llth century), a text which enjoyed great authority during the Middle Ages and the Renaissance (Klibansky et al., 1964, pp. 82 et seq).

The distinction between the three forms of melancholia, which he may have derived from Rufus, was considered by Galen to be of particular significance. He distinguished the following forms:

1. A *generalized* form of melancholia, with the blood being full of black bile
2. A *cerebral* form of melancholia, which affected only the brain
3. An *hypochondriacal* form of melancholia involving the organs of the upper abdomen (cf. Galenus, pp. 89–94; Jackson, 1986, p. 37; Leibbrand and Wettley, 1961, pp. 122–125).

The first form, unlike the second, could be accompanied by other phenomena (e.g., discoloration of the skin, cirrhosis of the liver and the accumulation of fluid). The mental manifestations of both the generalized and the cerebral forms were due to obstructed blood vessels in the brain, as a result of a thickening of the blood. Galen suspected that this obstruction led to a blockage of the channels through which the so-called *pneuma animalis* flowed. This *pneuma* was an etherlike substance, made up of small, lightweight, highly animated particles. From ancient times until well into the 17th century, it has been associated with all kinds of mental functions, including perception and imagination. In other cases, according to Galen, black bile caused cerebral tissue damage, leading to the impairment of intellectual functions in particular. In the third form of melancholia, disease symptoms ware not interpreted as resulting from black bile, as such. Instead they were caused by a vapor emanating from this fluid, as a result of local warming in the hypochondrium. This smoky vapor, according to Galen, rose up into the brain, obscuring thought. It was this mental obscuration that explained the anxiety seen in melancholics. Galen compared it to the darkness of night, which induces an unreasoning fear in many people:

> As external darkness renders almost all persons fearful, with the exception of a few naturally audacious ones or those who were specially trained, thus the color of the black bile induces fear when its darkness throws a shadow over the area of thought [in the brain]. (Galenus, p. 93)

Apart from generating this vapor, such local warming also converted one of the other bodily fluids to black bile, thereby producing an excess. Under circumstances such as this, melancholia would be characterized by heat, rather than coldness. According to some later writers of the galenic school, this explained motor restlessness and behavioral disorders, an interpretation with which Burton concurred in 1621.

In terms of treatment, it was the distinction between the three forms of melancholia, which became of primary importance. Phlebotomy, the preeminent therapy for the generalized form, was ineffective in the treatment of the other two forms of melancholia. These required that alternative measures be taken. Mention is made of changes in eating and drinking habits, the use of emetics and laxatives, and attaining a correct balance between rest and physical exercise.

Galen was aware that, although the manifestations of anxiety and depression are tremendously varied, the heart of melancholia consists of despondency and anxiety, especially the fear of death:

> Although each melancholic patient acts quite differently than the others, all of them exhibit fear or despondency. They find fault with life and people; but not all want to die. For some the fear of death is of principal concern during melancholy. Others again will appear to you quite bizarre because they dread death and desire to die at the same time.
>
> Therefore, it seems correct that Hippocrates classified all their symptoms into two groups: fear and despondency. Because of this despondency patients hate everyone whom they see, are constantly sullen and appear terrified, like children or uneducated adults in deepest darkness. (Galenus, p. 93)

The link between melancholia and mania had already been established by Aretaeus of Cappadocia, who lived about 150 AD (cf. Leibbrand and Wettley, 1961, pp. 111–116). However, in the work of Galen, this link is conspicuous by its very absence. In the Hippocratic texts, the term *mania* was frequently used when referring to mental illness, in general, even though the link with the action of black bile had already been established. In the centuries that followed, mania and melancholia gradually became delineated as disorders having a certain periodicity, but with contrasting outward expressions. Nevertheless, we must exercise caution, and not be overhasty in identifying these ailments with the present-day, bipolar disorder. The term *melancholia* still has very wide connotations, incorporating many different forms of psychosis and all kinds of neurotic symptoms. *Mania,* on the other hand, specifically refers to the various forms of emotional restlessness and motor excitation.

In fact, mania and melancholia together encompass virtually the entire field of prolonged psychopathology, that is, chronic diseases not associated with fever. The third form of mental illness, *phrenitis,* is both acute and associated with fever. The obvious comparison here is with delirious visions and acute psychoses. Epilepsy had a place all of its own. Viewed by the Greco-Roman world as a "sacred disease," it includes forms that are transitional between classical epilepsy and melancholia.

B. The Middle Ages

During the Middle Ages, ideas about anxiety and depression actually changed very little. Scholars continued to build upon the foundations created by the hippocratic–galenic school. For many centuries, Alexandria, with its enormous library, was the center of research and contemplation. One area of Byzantine medicine, as it is known, is particularly worthy of mention in connection with the subject under discussion. This concerns the work of compilers such as *Oribasius of Pergamon* (325–403), *Alexander of Tralles* (525–605) and *Paul of Aegina* (625–690). These scholars classified existing ideas from many different sources, without adding any significant contributions of their own.

At about the same time, the work of the Greek authors began to be translated into the Semitic languages. This task was carried out by Christians who had fled the Byzantine Empire, as well as by Arab authors. This was how Arabic medicine came to assimilate its Byzantine inheritance, in addition to influences from India and even China. By the end of the first millennium, writers from the Eastern Caliphate (Baghdad), such as *Rhazes* (865–923) and *Avicenna* (980–1037), had produced medical treatises of their own. Avicenna's *Canon of Medicine*, in particular, was to dominate medical ideas for centuries to come. From Persia came another significant figure, *Ishaq ibn Imran* (early 10th century), who has been referred to previously. It was his work on melancholia that inspired the great and influential treatises on the subject by the encyclopedist *Constantinus Africanus* (1020?–1087). Originally from North Africa, Constantinus subsequently lived in Salerno and later moved to Monte Cassano. His work reflects that of

Ishaq, in that he also devoted an extraordinary amount of consideration to psychogenic causes of melancholia. Later on, famous scholars from the Western Caliphate (Spain), such as *Averroes* (1126–1198) and *Maimonides* (1135–1204), were also to exert an influence on medicine. In the late Middle Ages, however, authors dealing with melancholia mainly referred to the works of Avicenna and Constantinus (Jackson, 1986, p. 63).

In the late Middle Ages, medical knowledge was mainly concentrated in monasteries and in cathedral schools. Moreover, various university medical schools were in the ascent, the best known of these being Montpellier, Bologna, and Padua. In addition to continued classification, some scholars now began to apply morality to humoral pathology (cf. Klibansky et al., 1964, pp. 105–110). This led to melancholics being described by some as degenerate, along with phlegmatics and cholerics. Sanguinics, on the other hand, were considered to represent man, as God had intended he should be, at the Creation. Melancholia was also associated with *acedia*, a sort of listlessness and restless boredom, accompanied by a longing for change of environment. As long ago as the fourth century, Cassianus described this condition in the monks of desert monasteries, not far from Alexandria. The afternoon demon would appear around the sixth hour. It bred in the monks a loathing for their own cells, a disdain of the other brothers, and a slothful unwillingness to take part in the routine activities of monastic life. Acedia, in the guise of Sloth, was to become one of the Seven Deadly Sins of the Middle Ages (cf. Jackson, 1986, pp. 65–77; Kilbansky, et al., 1964, pp. 300 et seq).

One particular development in the continuing systematizing of humoral pathology, was an accentuation of the difference between two forms of melancholia. In addition to melancholia as a result of an excess of natural black bile, a second form was discerned, being caused by an excess of unnatural black bile. Unnatural black bile was thought to be produced by the combustion, or degeneration, of one of the four bodily fluids.

In cases of an excess of natural black bile the characteristics of the melancholic temperament became more prominent. In such patients, meditation gave way to brooding. Their previously sincere and caring attitude to life plunged into one of anxiety and gloom. They would stare at a single point, be incommunicative, and avoid all contact. Beek, whose *Waanzin in de Middeleeuwen* [Madness in the Middle Ages] is, unfortunately, not available in an English translation, summarizes the writings of many authors as follows:

> An excess of melancholic humor, which is thick and sediment-like, imparts a red color to the head. The patient also experiences a feeling of heavy-headedness. He tastes a bitter-sweet taste, the sediment of the humor. The pulse is weak and the veins full. The urine is thick and red-colored. (Beek 1969, p. 98, my translation; cf. also Klibansky et al., 1964, pp. 86–90)

Although the combustion or degeneration of black bile presents a broadly similar picture, there is the added element of a preoccupation with death:

> They become agitated about funerals. Believing that they are about to die, they lie on graves and collect the bones of the dead. The pulse is hard and tense, the urine is lead-colored and thin. (Beek, 1969, p. 98)

The picture that developed as a result of burned yellow bile was one of mania. Patients ranted, raved, and screamed all day long. Referring, once again, to Beek:

> They lie awake. They exhibit excessive movement, jumping and running around. They are reckless and quarrelsome, wanting to beat those around them, preferably with an iron bar. In the grip of the mania, they throw themselves through windows. The choleric temperament is characterized by a lack of inhibition, wild behavior, recklessness, constant motion and rage.

> Such patients have a lemon-colored complexion, their urine is thin and yellowish, the pulse hard and rapid. It is thought that sufferers do not feel the cold because the combustion of the bile keeps them warm. (Beek, 1969, p. 98)

Conversely, the combustion of blood produces feelings of happiness rather than of sadness:

> They talk and laugh the whole time, wanting to dance and make merry all whole day long. Their temperament type is one of happiness, laughter and loquacity. Their urine is thick and reddish brown. (Beek, 1969, p. 98)

Degeneration of phlegm, on the other hand:

> induces apathy, inertia and absent-mindedness. Feeling heavy-headed, these patients neither move nor laugh, nor do they feel joy. In people with this type of temperament, inertia, drowsiness and forgetfulness come to the fore. Characterized by a moist mouth and nostrils, and a pale white complexion, they are referred to as lymphatics. Believing themselves to be fish, they ask for water all day long and pine for a river, or the sea. Their pulse is small and weak, their urine pale, whitish and of medium thickness. (Beek, 1969, p.98)

In tracing the origins of melancholia, factors other than the humors (combusted or otherwise) must be taken into consideration. These were the *complexio* (the temperament and primary qualities) of the brain and the condition of the rest of the body. A brain that is overly dry, or excessively cold, has an increased susceptibility to disease. A weak heart lowers the threshold against developing melancholia. Particular and frequent mention is made of the relation between heart and head. Heart palpitations, for example, are the expression of an affection of the heart. Obviously, there is a relationship between the malfunctioning of this organ and a person's state of mlnd. After all, did not the *spiritus vitalis* ascend from the heart to the brain, where it influenced the *spiritus animalis*?

In medieval medicine, the nature of these influences was connected to the localization of functions in the different ventricles. The anterior (or lateral) ventricles were associated with imagination (*imaginatio*), the median (or third) ventricle with reasoning (*ratio*), and the posterior (or fourth) ventricle with memory (*memoria*). Melancholia was usually linked with a disorder of the middle ventricle. Conditions that involve hallucinations and delusions, such as mania and psychotic depression, were based on disturbances to the equilibrium of the anterior ventricles.

Classification was extended to include therapeutic procedures. Polypharmacy had been popular even in ancient times, with leading roles being played by black hellebore and extracts of mandragora. In addition, regulation of the so-called *non-naturalia* (external or environmental factors) remained an important part of the therapeutic arsenal. Traditionally, six such factors were identified. These were air, physical exercise and rest, waking and sleeping, food and drink, retention and excretion of body products, and the passions of the soul.

Air: The patient should be kept in a warm, moist environment, the door of his or her house should preferably face east.

Rest and exercise: The aim should be to reduce sensory excitation and to achieve relaxation. The patient should preferably be nursed in a dark room. The walls should be bare of pictures, since these might overstimulate the imagination. A not overly arduous walk, when the time is ripe, is beneficial for the maintenance of body temperature, as are massages and hot baths. An excess of body heat, however, dries out the body and causes melancholia.

Waking and sleeping: The patient should sleep neither too little nor too much.

Food and drink: This sickness can result both from overeating and from excessive fasting (as seen in the ascetics). Food must be easily digestible. Vegetables such as lentils and beans give rise to flatulence and therefore cause melancholia. Peppery spices, garlic, leeks and onions must be avoided since they can burn the humors. The same applies to both mature and salted meat, the meat of forest animals, mature cheese, vinegar and fish. A heavy wine, rich in sediment, causes sickness, whereas a light, young wine can actually raise the spirits.

Retention and excretion: Melancholia can result from the accumulation of those bodily fluids that are normally discharged, such as menstrual blood, sperm, or hemorrhoidal blood. The same is true of feces. Evacuation sometimes requires mechanical assistance, for example, in constipation, the nonappearance of menstruation, or the nonbleeding of hemorrhoids. Coitus is generally to be recommended, although men with low potency should avoid overindulgence. Bathing, whether in a herbal bath or with just plain water, is an important therapeutic agent, which can also facilitate evacuation. However, excessively hot baths can induce madness.

Finally, concerning *passions of the soul*: Excessive fear, hatred, and grief should be avoided. The same applies to excessive study and to intense preoccupation with a particular task. Nevertheless, anxious and inhibited melancholics can actually be cured by either a fierce rage or a sudden shock. Generally speaking, however, these passions should be kept under control. Discussion and philosophical reading can both be useful in calming the patient.[2]

C. Intermezzo: Melancholia as a Characteristic of Genius

We have placed great emphasis on the continuity of the medical debates concerning melancholia. This continuous dialogue spans the centuries, from ancient times up to the Middle Ages and, as we shall see, even beyond. There are, in all, three closely related concepts:

1. Natural black bile
2. The disorder of melancholia, based on either (a) an excess of natural black bile, or (b) the combustion of one of the four body humors (*melancholia adusta*)
3. A chronic predominance of natural black bile in people with a melancholic-type temperament

In spite of the allegorizing and moralizing interpretations, the concept of melancholia retained its link with humoral pathology. This doctrine, however, was not entirely undisputed in ancient times. The empirical school, for example, considered the theory of bodily fluids to be too speculative. There was also the methodist school, which sought refuge in a much simpler classification of disease (involving the *status strictus* versus *status laxus* or, in other words, the respective contraction and relaxation of the so-called internal pores). We also found that, for the temperaments, there was some doubt about the normalcy of the character variations (cf. note 1).

There is another line which, in terms of the theme of this review, is even more important. This proceeds from Plato and Aristotle, through the Florentine School of the Middle Ages (Marsilio Ficino) and Robert Burton (1621) in the Renaissance, to William James (1902) in the present century. It is a line of thought that considers the melancholic as exhibiting certain traits of genius. There is the famous opening line from the 30th book of Aristotle's *Problemata*:

> Why is it that all those who have become eminent in philosophy or politics or poetry or the arts are so clearly of an atrabilious temperament, and some of them to such an extent as to be affected by diseases caused by black bile, as is said to have happened to Heracles among the heroes? (Aristotle, Problemata, 953a 10)

Aristotle seeks a natural explanation for this "madness which comes from the gods." This is in contrast with Plato's *Phaedrus* (244b–250), which offers a mythological description. Aristotle suggests that the eminence of the poets, politicians, and philosophers in question could be ascribed to an optimum warmth of the black bile. Black bile, by its very nature, was thought to be sensitive to changes of temperature. When cooled, it brought about "apoplexy or torpor or despondency or fear." Heating induced "cheerfulness accompanied by song and frenzy and the breaking forth of sores and the like" (954a 21–26). In the case of a "man of genius," black bile, which is as such a pathogenic fluid, is in an optimum state. Such a person represents the normal within the abnormal or, in the words of Klibansky, et al. (1964, p. 40), an "eucrasia within an anomaly."

During the Renaissance, a time of revived interest in astrology, this association between melancholia and genius acquired a special meaning. In antiquity, the planet Saturn had been associated with *Kronos,* the son of *Uranus* (the god of Heaven) and *Gaia* (the Earth goddess), who had been banished to the underworld after the castration of his father. Now, Saturn gradually turned into a symbol of the ambivalence of intellectual and artistic life. According to ancient astrology, Saturn was the planet of gloom, desolation, decline, and old age. However, the neoplatonists claimed that Saturn, as the highest planet, was the planet of the elevated, of ecstatic release from earthly things and happenings (Klibansky et al., 1964, pp. 133–195). *Marsilio Ficino* (1433–1499), neoplatonist of the Florentine school as well as a priest and physician, depicted Saturn as the heavenly body the rays of which influenced the vital spirits of the brain (*spiritus animalis*), which were thought to connect the physical to the spiritual. This influence was described as a kind of saturation process, one to which those born under the sign of Saturn were especially sensitive. Although enjoying intellectual powers and creative talents far exceeding those of others, there was a tragic element to these people. They spent their lives teetering on the very brink of catastrophe, and they were especially susceptible to melancholia. Black bile was identified with the earth, including the very center of the planet itself, which meant that such people tended to have a deeply penetrating understanding of existence. The association with Saturn, the highest of the planets, meant that they aspired to higher planes of thought (Klibansky et al., 1964, pp. 241–274). The novel element here is the heightening of self-consciousness, the awareness of man's vulnerability to catastrophe and decline. Their view of life took on a nostalgic and tragic tint. This outlook was to recur in a variety of different forms in later periods, as, for example, in the Elizabethan literature of the 16th and 17th centuries (Elizabethan malady; cf. Klibansky et al., 1964, pp. 228–240).

D. The Renaissance and 17th and 18th Centuries

The Renaissance was not only an age of heightened self-awareness and the era of *Homo literatus*, with his knowledge of the classics, it was also the time of alchemy. It was this that lent impetus to the interpretation of disease in terms of chemical change, an approach that texts on the history of medicine refer to as *iatrochemistry*. Substances such as salt, sulfur, and silver became the focus of attention. Paracelsus (1493–1541) was one of the first to apply the newly gathered knowledge to medicine, in an attempt to break down the hegemony of humoral pathology. He did not, however, renounce the doctrine of the temperaments and of the elements. Melancholia now became associated with the qualities of the chemical elements, which are sharp and acidic. Thomas Willis (1621–1675), renowned for his *Two Discourses Concerning the Soul of Brutes*, expounded the theory that, in melancholia, the blood became "salinosulfureous," causing the *spiritus animalis* to adopt a different pattern of motion (Jackson, 1986, p. 112).

The high point of 17th century medical literature on melancholia, however, was Robert Burton's *The Anatamy of Melancholy*, published in 1621. This work, which may seem somewhat bizarre to the modern reader, offered a compilation of all contemporary knowledge on the subject of melancholia. Greatly indebted to ancient medicine and philosophy, Burton punctuated his arguments with references from ancient times. He subscribed to the dichotomy of the passions (derived from Thomas Aquinas), a doctrine that was generally accepted at the time. Here, the passions that predisposed one toward desire (*passiones concupiscibiles*) were distinguished from those that predisposed one toward rage (*passiones irascibiles*). "Sorrow'' and "fear,'' emotions ("perturbations'') belonging to the latter category, were described by Burton as being directed at the evil that crossed one's path. Sorrow was related to disaster in the present; fear, to disaster in the future. Burton considered sorrow to be a major cause of melancholia, as well as one of its manifestations. It was:

> an inseparable companion, the mother and daughter of melancholy, her epitome, symptom, and chief cause. (Burton 1621, p. 298)

The same was true of fear, the emotion most able to hold the imagination in thrall (Burton, 1621, p. 302). The imagination was:

> *medium deferens* of the passions, by whose means they work and produce many times prodigious effects. (Burton 1621, p. 297)

Burton went on to add, however, that the converse was also true, since imagination serves to enhance the impact of emotions.

In discussing the symptoms of melancholia, Burton considered fear and sorrow to be just some of the phenomena affecting nearly all of those suffering from this condition. Although these emotions were relatively nonspecific phenomena, this did not mean that they were unimportant.

Burton was acquainted with many of the forms of anxiety known today. He made reference to fear of death, to fear of losing those who are most important to us, and to paranoid anxiety. He also cited anxiety based on ideas and delusions of reference, fear associated with depersonalization, delusional depersonalization, and hypochondria. Other forms that are mentioned include agoraphobia (!) and many other kinds of specific phobias, such as fear of public speaking, fear of heights, claustrophobia, anticipatory fear, and hyperventilation (Burton, 1621, pp. 442–449).

The physiology of emotions was strongly emphasized in René Descartes' Les Passions *de l'Âme* [The Passions of the Soul], which was published about a quarter of a century later (Descartes, 1649; cf. Riese, 1965; Rorty, 1982). This emphasis on physiology had a distinctly mechanistic flavor, in keeping with the contemporary trend toward a general mechanization of the world view. A trend which, in medicine, would only really take off in the 18th century (*iatromechanics*; cf. King, 1978).

According to Descartes, passions not only prepare the body but also predispose the soul to desire that for which the body is being prepared. The physical manifestations of emotion, therefore, provide some degree of insight into the function of emotions.

Fear and anxiety did not rank highly among the passions (cf. *Les Passions de l' Âme*, articles 34–39, 58, 165, 174, 176). Indeed, Descartes considered the emotion of fear to be quite useless. Nevertheless, his descriptions of the processes that give rise to fear are worthy of mention, since they are representative of the 17th and 18th century mechanistic view of disease. According to Descartes, the sight of a dangerous animal caused certain particles (the "esprits animaux" or *spiritus animalis*, referred to previously) to be released by the pineal gland. Although invisible, these rapidly moving particles were quite material in nature. They traversed the neural pathways to reach the heart, the leg muscles, and the circulatory system. This gave rise to the physiological component of the "fight or flight" response. The altered distribution of blood then caused a rush of these esprits animaux to the brain. Here, the pores associated with fear were opened, directing the esprits onward, back toward the periphery. Mental influences were not, therefore, presumed to be involved in the generation of fear. Instead, fear was seen as a complex, but purely physiological, reflex.

Although emotional perception was secondary, consisting of the registration of pineal gland movements, Descartes believed that such registration had a purpose, namely evaluation. It facilitated the perception of objects in terms of their effects on us, whether beneficial or otherwise.[4] Properly employed, passions predispose the soul to desire those things that are naturally good for us. In this resigned adaptation to the eternal laws of nature, one can detect the aftereffects of the *Stoa*—aftereffects that extend to the implicit morality of certain modern-day forms of psychotherapy.

Descartes' emphasis on mechanics was not accepted by the medical world until the closing years of the 17th century. It enjoyed a brief flowering in the period about 1750, before giving way to other interpretations. Those associated with iatromechanics, as it was called, included men such as *Pitcairn, Hoffmann*, and *Boerhaave* (whose work reveals traces of a humoral pathology, interpreted from the point of view of fluid dynamics). Boerhaave and Pitcairn favored a *vasocentric* approach, seeking the origins of melancholia in the modified flow patterns and viscosity changes of liquids in the blood channels. Hoffmann was one of the first to consider a *neurocentric* approach. He considered nerves to be hollow tubes containing a flowing liquid. Under normal circumstances, this neural fluid was thin and volatile; however, if it thickened to an earthy, slimy consistency then melancholia developed. Under the influence of Isaac Newton, men such as *Mead* and *Cullen* (who was the first to use the term neurosis) speculated that this neural fluid might also have electrical properties. Cullen and others thought of this neural fluid as a tenuous, highly mobile substance, which was related to ether. This etherlike substance did not actually flow; instead it transmitted motion to the various parts of the body by means of vibration. This caused the fluid hydraulics model of mental illness to be discarded. At the time, there was only a vague notion of electrical phenomena. These were linked to the vitalistic interpretation of disease, the central concepts of which were tone and irritability. Cullen considered the irritability of the nervous system to be responsible for tissue tone (cf. Lopez Pineiro, 1983, p. 12).

Meanwhile, the clinical description of melancholia had remained virtually unchanged. Some still cited the galenic trio of generalized, cerebral, and hypochondriacal melancholia. However, there were those, such as Boerhaave, for example, who interpreted this classical triad merely as stages on a continuous scale of severity. Some authors were inclined to uncouple hypochondria from melancholia (of which it was the least serious form) and link it instead with hysteria. According to *Sydenham* and *Lorry*, for example, hysteria in women was equivalent to hypochondria in men.

The 18th century was a time bursting with tensions and contrasts, with shifts and changes. Humoralism gave way to *solidism* (the explanation of disease based on the properties of the organs and tissues). Iatrochemistry gave way to iatromechanics which, in turn, was replaced by ideas such as tone and irritability. Vasocentric views were replaced by neurocentric ones. Meanwhile, vitalistic views of disease blended with speculation on the electrical properties of neural fluids. Each of these various approaches was considered to be compatible, incompatible, or related to one other (cf. King, 1978). The rational framework of the early 18th century clearly offered medicine of that time the requisite intellectual freedom in which to forge its principal concepts.

Toward the end of the century this all began to change. Pathological anatomy had expanded enormously, and greater emphasis was being given to clinical observation and description. It was a time of sensualism and of a fascination with sensory perception. Notions such as irritability bear witness to a preoccupation with the hypersensitivity of the nervous system and of the senses. The end of the 18th century saw the final demise of humoralism. During the same period, the notion that melancholia originated in the blood, or in the functions of the liver or spleen, was also dismissed. The central nervous system replaced blood and abdominal organs. Today, the idea of temperament is all that remains of humoralism. Although it has no place in the scientific view of character and personality, it still exists as metaphorical expression for the experiences of despondent people.

E. The 19th Century: The Further Disintegration of the Concept of Melancholia

The concept of partial insanity was popular in the nosographical schemes of the 18th century and the first decades of the 19th century (Starobinski, 1960, p. 55). As has been noted, medical scholars of the late 18th century were fascinated with the sensitivity and irritability of the nervous system. This, together with the fast-growing influence of faculty psychology (which sharply distinguished between intellect, will, and imagination), may have contributed to the popularity of the concept of partial insanity. This was not particularly novel, it was more the emphasis of an element of meaning found in descriptions of melancholia dating from ancient times (e.g., those of Aretaeus and Galen). For centuries it had been observed that the thoughts and ideas of the melancholic were confined to a single theme, often to the extent that they became delusional. Melancholia was traditionally considered to be a delirium without fever, accompanied by fear, despondency, and additional phenomena, such as restlessness, insomnia, weariness, and discomfort in many parts of the body. In addition, however, frequent reference was made to the monothematic content of the melancholia sufferer's ideas and thoughts (for a review, see Jackson, 1983).

Late 18th century medicine had a neurocentric orientation, one that tended to focus on sensitivity and cognitive capabilities. This may, perhaps, have influenced the classification of mental illnesses into disorders in which the powers of judgment were completely incapacitated, and those in which this was only partly the case (partial insanity). Melancholia was considered to fall within the latter category, a view that can be found, for example, in the *Traité médico-philosophique sur l'aliénation mentale* [Medical–Philosophical Treatise on Mental Disorder] by Philippe Pinel (1745–1826; Pinel, 1801). Pinel also considered mania to belong to this "melancholia with delirium."

This (temporary) identification of melancholia with partial insanity completed the decline of a concept that, for centuries, had dominated the description of mental illness.

Melancholia was divided up, and its various parts were classified under other disorders. Several things contributed to this redistribution, such as resistance to humoral pathology and its terminology, more detailed observation (as a side effect of growing institutionalization), and rationally inspired expectations concerning psychology's ability to influence mental illness (see Porter, 1987, pp. 8–38; especially pp. 16–20).

The first line of demarcation was given with the idea of partial insanity itself, since some melancholics exhibit no signs of insanity (delirium) whatsoever. That is to say, none of their thoughts and ideas would be considered as psychotic in the modern sense. In the *Manual of Psychological Medicine*, which he wrote in collaboration with Buchnill, *D. Hack Tuke* (1827–1895) distinguished between simple melancholia, in which the intellectual powers were intact, and complicated melancholia, in which they were not. The distinction applied by *Henry Maudsley* (1935–1918) was essentially the same as Tuke's, if somewhat wider in scope. In addition to melancholia simplex (cf. Bucknill and Tuke's "simple melancholia"), he distinguished not one, but two forms of melancholia, both falling within the category of ideational insanity. These were melancholia as a form of general insanity and melancholia as a form of partial insanity. In the first instance, intellectual derangement is complete, whereas, in the latter, it is only partial. There was also a parallel distinction in mania. However, Maudsley went to great pains to emphasize the provisional nature of this classification (cf. Jackson, 1986, pp. 170–171).

Similarly, in France, the significance of the term melancholia declined considerably under the influence of a nomenclature introduced by *Jean-Etienne-Dominique Esquirol* (1772–1840) in his *Des Maladies Mentales* (1838). Since ancient times, the meaning of the term *melancholia* had encompassed both dejection and exaltation. Finding this an unsatisfactory state of affairs, Esquirol substituted the term *monamania* for melancholia. Monomania, which became an equivalent of the term partial insanity, was subdivided as follows:

1. "Monomania, properly so-called, which is indicated by a partial delirium and a gay or exciting passion"; this condition corresponded to "maniacal melancholy, maniacal fury, or . . . melancholia complicated with mania; in fine . . . (to) *amenomania*"
2. Monomania corresponding to "melancholy of the ancients, the *tristimania* of Rush and the delirium with melancholy of Pinel" (Esquirol, 1838, p. 404; English translation from Jackson, 1986, p. 152).

Esquirol borrowed the terms amenomania and tristimania from the work of *Benjamin Rush* (1745–1813), the father of North American psychiatry. It was Rush who has linked tristimania with hypochondria, alluding to the ancient hypochondriacal, form of melancholia, rather than to the diluted, 18th century meaning of the term. Confusingly, besides employing monomania in the broad aforementioned sense, Esquirol also used the term to denote the manialike form of partial delirium. In this way, monomania became the equivalent of the first form of monomania, the partial delirium with the "gay or exciting passion." The second, melancholic, form of monomania was denoted by the term *lypemania*. In addition, Esquirol distinguished mania as a generalized insanity associated with excitement and exaltation. He occasionally tended to describe lypemania, monomania (in the strict sense of the word), and mania as having progressive degrees of severity, the greatest derangement occurring in mania and the least in lypemania.

Even in ancient times, it has been frequently pointed out that melancholia and mania could occur in parallel, in sequence, and in combination. However, it was not until 1854 that cyclic mood swings were specifically identified as the distinguishing criterion of a subcategory of manic and depressive patients. In the same year, *Jules Baillarger* (1809–1890) described *la folie à double forme* [the insanity with two forms], 10 days later followed by a commentary of *Jean-Pierre Falret* (1794–1870), in which he also discussed a *folie circulaire* [circular insanity]. Some 40 years later, Kraepelin explicitly harked back to the work of these two French clinicians when he distinguished dementia praecox from manic–depressive psychosis.

Nonetheless, even by the middle of the 19th century, the terminologic distinction between affective and schizophrenic psychopathology was by no means a fait accompli. Accordingly, *Richard von Kraft-Ebing* (1840–1902) declared that there were two forms of melancholia, namely simple melancholia and melancholia with stupor. The latter form, also known as *melancholia attonita* or *melancholia stupida*, was quite different from the partial delirium of French and English psychiatry. It was related to a condition which, a few decades later, Kahlbaum was to call *catatonia*, which could also be associated with reduced consciousness. With simple melancholia, von Kraft-Ebing distinguished between a mild form of melancholia that was not associated with delusions, melancholia associated with precordial pain, and melancholia associated with delusions and hallucinations. He placed strong emphasis on psychomotor inhibition in all forms of melancholia, stating that in cases of melancholia attonita, this usually had an organic cause, such as a blockage in the motor neuron pathways. Such inhibition could, however, also be psychogenically induced. In practical terms, there were all kinds of transitional states between the two major forms of melancholia. The difference between these states lay in the relative degree to which mental and organic components were involved in the origin of the inhibition.

This shows that the 19th century ups and downs of melancholia, as a concept, were determined by a variety of different factors. In addition to the attempts to distinguish new forms and the pursuit of ever more precise classification, there were also advocates of continuity, who searched for transitional forms between the diverse clinical pictures. An extremely clear-cut example of this is provided by Wilhelm Griesinger (1817–1868) who strongly defended the concept of a unitary psychosis (*Einheitspsychose*) in his *Die Pathologie und Therapie der psychische Krankheiten für Ärtzte und Studierende* [The Pathology and Therapy of Mental Diseases for Physicians and Students]. In this work, he cited both his mentor, Zeller, and the Belgian alienist Guislain. According to Griesinger, the various clinically defined forms of mental illness could be reduced to the different stages of one and the same disease. The first of these successive "states of mental depression" was the *stadium melancholicum*, that is, the deterioration of normal emotions such as grief and jealousy. Next came *hypochondria*, the mildest form of insanity. This was followed by *melancholia in sensu stricto*, which, although not necessarily associated with psychotic phenomena, had a greater effect on the personality than did hypochondria. Finally, there was *mania*, which caused the most pronounced mental derangement of any of the conditions listed here.

F. Emil Kraepelin

The debate about the classification of mood disorders, which continued on into the 20th century, centered around the question of whether or not this group of disorders could be subdivided. However, after 1900, the matter of whether mood disorders constituted a separate category of mental illness was hardly ever discussed.

This remarkable fact can be largely traced back to the work of one man, *Emil Kraepelin* (1856–1926). It has often been pointed out that the term melancholia (along with related terms such as mania, partial delirium, and monomania) certainly cannot be identified with what we currently refer to as affective disorder. The clinical pictures concerned were always those incorporating a variety of phenomena that would currently be regarded as expressions either of schizophrenia or of a schizophreniform disorder. It is remarkable, to say the least, that this age-old intermingling of psychotic and affective symptomatology should have come to an end at the beginning of this century.

In his early years, Kraepelin worked with the neuroanatomist, Flechsig. For a lengthy period he was also a research worker in Wundt's psychological laboratory. Kraepelin cannot simply be portrayed as a materialist, or as a somatologist; his field of interest was much too comprehensive for that.[5] Nevertheless, the idea that every psychiatric clinical picture could ultimately be reduced to an organic substratum in the brain was kept alive by Kraepelin and many of his contemporaries. They were motivated by the discovery of the cause of dementia paralytica, the confrontation with many cases of alcohol dementia, and the aftermath of the theory of degeneration, formulated by Morel in the middle of the 19th century. Kraepelin accordingly established an anatomical laboratory in Heidelberg. He also brought in the histopathologist, Nissl, to assist him in the visualization of the cerebral cortex. Their collaboration eventually bore fruit, in the form of photographs (measuring from 50 to 75 cm) showing general views of the cerebral cortex (Kraepelin, 1983, p. 73).

However, it was not these efforts that ultimately contributed to the lasting topicality of Kraepelin's work. Possibly influenced by Kahlbaum, he became persuaded of the importance of systematic clinical observation and description. It was this conviction that inspired him to amass a data base of all the patients registered in Heidelberg, something that required great perseverance. This data base enabled him to follow the medical histories of his patients, in some cases for several decades. It formed the basis for the separation of manic–depressive illness ("das manisch–depressive Irresein") from schizophrenia (dementia praecox), which was first described in the fifth (1896) and sixth (1899) editions of his famous textbook (Kraepelin, 1983, pp. 68–69; cf. Kraepelin 1905; 1913). Although there was always a bias toward localization, it gradually faded into the background and made way for a more functional and strictly empirical approach, in which classification had less to do with diagnosis (i.e., the cause) and more with prognosis (cf. Berrios and Hauser, 1988). It was the course alone (rather than cause, symptoms, or periodicity) that was to prove decisive in demarcating dementia praecox from manic–depressive illness. Dementia praecox led, by definition, to personality decline (*Verblödung*; dementia), whereas manic–depressive illness did not:

> The universal experience is striking, that the attacks of manic–depressive insanity within the delimitation attempted here never led to profound dementia (Verblödung, G.G.), not even when they continue throughout life almost without interruption. Usually all morbid manifestations completely disappear; but where that is exceptionally not the case, only a rather slight, peculiar psychic weakness develops, which is just as common to the types here taken together as it is different from dementias in diseases of other kinds. (Kraepelin, 1913, p. 1185; translation from Thompson, 1987, pp. 246–247)

At the onset of the illness, it can be extremely difficult to reach a correct diagnosis. Some things to go by are age at onset (younger than 20 or beyond middle age) and a confirmed family history. There is also the premorbid character which, in manic–depressive illness, is weak, susceptible, dejected, and lacking in self-confidence (Kraepelin, 1913, p. 1387).

Meanwhile, the category of manic–depressive illness was very broad, encompassing much more than the bipolar disorder, as it is called today:

> Manic depressive insanity . . . includes on the one hand the whole domain of the so-called periodic and circular insanity, on the other hand simple mania, the greater part of the morbid states termed melancholia and also a not inconsiderable number of cases of amentia. Lastly, we include here certain slight and slightest colorings of mood, some of them periodic, some of them continuously morbid, which on the one hand are to be regarded as the rudiment of more severe disorders, on the other hand pass over without sharp boundary into the domain of personal predisposition. In the course of the years I have become more and more convinced that all the above mentioned states only represent manifestations of a single morbid process. (Kraepelin, 1913, p. 1183; translation from Thompson, 1987, p. 245)

In this definition, the bipolar disorder of our time coincides with "periodic and circular insanity." Here, manic derangement is characterized by the triad of rapid association of ideas, elated mood, and hyperactivity. Depression, on the other hand, is associated with the triad of dejection or anxious moods, inhibition of thought, and reduced spontaneity. In addition to the circular and simple disorders, amentia and milder mood disorders, Kraepelin also refers to mixed pictures. These cases exhibit some characteristics of mania and others typical of depression. He also refers to the so-called ground states (*Grundzustände*; predisposing personality traits) that form the basis for the development of mood disorders (Kraepelin, 1913, pp. 1289 et seq. resp. 1303 et seq). Kraepelin distinguished four ground states: depressive, manic, irritable (*erregbare*), and cyclothymic. Finally, a distinction was made between this group and the form of melancholia associated with a decline caused by the effects of aging (*Rückbildungsalter*; involution). In the latter event inhibition was often absent, whereas anxiety and hypochondria were more prominent. Although Kraepelin was initially inclined to keep this (involutional) melancholia separate from the others, he abandoned this line of thought following the comprehensive study of this clinical picture by Dreyfus (1907). He subsequently included this form of melancholia within *das manisch-depressive Irresein* [manic–depressive psychosis]. The debate about involutional melancholia would not be finally settled until the 1970s, when this condition became just another form of depression.

Something that is common to all forms of manic–depressive illness is the absence of an immediate cause, or at least a course that appears to be independent of any possible causes. Thereafter, a distinction should be made between psychogenic depressions and the conditions referred to in the foregoing (Kraepelin, 1913, pp. 1389–1390; cf. pp. 1369–1370). The most fundamental cause of manic–depressive psychosis is a hereditary, morbid predisposition. According to Kraepelin, of the 900 cases whom he studied in Heidelberg, he had managed to establish that about 80% involved a hereditary defect (Kraepelin, 1913, pp. 1353–1354).

Despite opposition (Hoche, 1911; Jaspers, 1953, pp. 471–479), Kraepelin's interpretations nevertheless enjoyed great authority in German-speaking regions. This is demonstrated, for example, by *Eugen Bleuler's* textbook, which was published in 1916. In describing the manic–depressive illness as a distinct disorder, this work relies heavily on the questions that Kraepelin had raised on the subject (Bleuler, 1916, pp. 345 et seq). The 13th edition of this textbook, which was published in 1975, exhibits some reservations about the heredity hypothesis and about the possibility of an airtight distinction between dementia praecox, on the one hand, and psychogenic disorders on the other. Nevertheless, it still contains references to the old kraepelinian classification (Bleuler, 1975, pp. 457 et seq).

G. Critique on Nosology: Reaction Type Versus Endogeny

The situation was different in the United States where, in the first decade of this century, *Adolf Meyer* (1866–1950) expressed doubts about the value of the course criterion. He distinguished several forms of depression, such as constitutional depression, simple melancholia proper, other forms characterized by neurasthenic malaise or hypochondriacal complaints, depressive deliria, catatonic melancholia, and the so-called delire de negation, in which the patient believes he or she is nothing (Winters, 1951, p. 566–567). This was more than just a debate about classification. Meyer was particularly uneasy about the coupling of heredity (endogeny) and manic–depressive psychosis, in the broad, kraepelinian sense. He viewed this link as nothing more than "neurologizing tautology," which might easily give rise to therapeutic nihilism. Moreover, it did not do justice to the fact that mental illness is an attempt at adaptation, a reaction to the demands of a changing situation. Only when disease is seen as an inadequate attempt at recovery, could the search for what he called "modifiable determining factors" begin. We are then "in a live field, in harmony with our instincts of action, of prevention, of modification and of an understanding doing justice to a desire for directness . . ." (Winters, 1951, p. 599).

The question remains of whether Meyer did justice to Kraepelin. In any event, Kraepelin cannot be accused of therapeutic nihilism. Under his direction, the enlarged baths at Heidelberg achieved international fame and were visited by many foreign guests. Nothing was too much trouble for him when it came to experimenting with new methods of treatment. Of greater importance is the conceptual point at issue here. According to Meyer, the debate on classification should not be short-circuited by an appeal to such ideas as endogeny and heredity, about which nothing was empirically established. He did not presume that biological processes should enjoy a privileged position in the list of determining factors for mental illness. For this reason, Meyer substituted the term manic–depressive psychosis with the etiologically neutral term *affective reaction type*. Within this reaction type, he distinguished a manic-depressive type, an anxious type, and simple depressions (Winters, 1951, p. 600).

Essentially the same view was held by Sir *Aubrey Lewis* who, in the 1930s, published an authoritative study of 61 cases investigated at the Maudsley Hospital in London (1934b; cf. 1936, 1938). According to Lewis, a total reaction of the organism is involved, even in cases in whom the illness appears to be entirely without cause. Without doubt, there were

> changes in the internal structure of the body, its chemical and vegetative regulation which play a great part in determining its course. But these are only part of the total reaction of the organism, and it is by no means in denial of their fundamental importance in the illness that one refuses them independent and preponderant significance, either aetiological or as part of the process of the illness. (Lewis, 1934b; via idem 1967, p. 113)

According to Lewis, the more closely patients were studied, the less evidence there was for a nosological distinction between autonomous (endogenous) and reactive (psychogenic; situational) depressions. Incidentally, the very same view had already been expressed 8 years earlier by Mapother, Lewis' predecessor, on the basis of impressions obtained in clinical practice.

This established the scope of a debate that, since then, has been repeated with endless variations and that, even now, continues to exert a hold on psychiatry. Ironically enough, the seeds of controversy were sown by Kraepelin, the very person who most wanted to distance himself from the speculative impetus within the debate. In spite of his empirical bias, Kraepelin continued to link the clinically descriptive course criterion with the etiological hypothesis of endogeny. Through this, the reference to heredity became an established fact.

In practical terms, Kraepelin's coupling of the course criterion with the idea of endogeny raised two mutually related issues, namely:

1. The role of exogenic (biological and nonbiological) factors in the origin of depression and
2. The demarcation of manic–depressive illness relative to psychogenic depressions and milder variants within the manic–depressive spectrum. (Kendell, 1968, p. 2; cf. Heron, 1965).

Both of these issues ultimately proved to be insoluble within the framework of the endogeny–exogeny dichotomy. In practice, it was quite impossible to distinguish, in each case, between depressions that were psychogenically induced and those in which psychological and situational factors merely played an instigating role. The responsiveness of the illness proved to be of only limited significance as a distinguishing criterion. Meanwhile, it should not be forgotten that, in Kraepelin's time, the term endogeny was also an expression of embarrassment. At the end of the 19th century, Möbius introduced the twin concepts of endogeny and exogeny. By about 1900, these concepts corresponded respectively to diseases for which causes were still unknown and those for which causes had been well defined. Causes the existence of which was (still) uncertain were described as endogenous. These were attributed, more or less out of embarrassment, to innate personal qualities (Lewis, 1971). Exogenous causes included bacteria, toxins, and tissue injury resulting from brain traumas. In 1910, Bonhoeffer devoted a monograph to these so-called exogenic reactive types, and his name has been linked to them ever since.

H. The Influence of Psychology and Psychoanalysis

After 1920, mainly because of changes in the use of the adjective *exogenous,* this debate became still more complex. Originally used only in relation to biological factors, this term was extended to include intrapsychic and situational factors as well, thereby highlighting the demarcation between depression and neurosis. New dichotomies consequently arose, such as endogenous–reactive (Lange); autonomous–reactive (Gillespie); endogenous–neurotic; psychotic–neurotic. After World War II, these were supplemented by: S (somatic) type–J (justified) type (Pollitt); and vital depression–personal depression (van Praag).

Of course, this shift in the debate cannot be dissociated from the influence of *Sigmund Freud* (1856–1939) and the psychoanalytic school. In one of his early works (Manuscript G; 1895d), Freud had already addressed the neurological explanation of melancholia. In 1917, he published an excellent, authoritative article on the link between grief and melancholia (*Trauer und Melancholie*; Freud, 1917). In this article, he stated that, unlike grief, object loss in melancholia could be coupled with unresolved feelings of ambivalence and regression of the ego. Anger at being abandoned directed itself against an ego that remained narcissistically identified with the other. The internal "other" is then destroyed. Indeed, Karl Abraham had already demonstrated self-destructive behavior and experiences in depressive patients (Abraham, 1912). A line can be traced from Freud, through Melanie Klein, to later psychoanalytic authors such as Lindemann (1944) and Bowlby (1969, 1973, 1981). Klein distinguished a depressive position as a phase in early childhood development. Lindemann wrote an influential study on the reactions to grief. Bowlby worked extensively on the relation between psychopathology and the processes of attachment and separation.

One should also mention, in passing, the influence of the theory of emotions developed by the philosopher *Max Scheler* (1874–1928). Scheler distinguished between four emotional strata: sensory feelings, physical or vital feelings, psychic feelings, and spiritual feelings (Scheler, 1916, p. 344). This theory constitutes part of Scheler's own philosophy of value. It was intended to emphasize that people are capable of experiencing more than one mood or emotion at a time. For example, someone can be in a dejected mood while at the same time being angry with his or her neighbor. *Kurt Schneider* applied this feeling theory to depression by stating that depression is based on a disorder of the vital stratum. Psychic feelings in cases of depression (such as feelings of guilt and inadequacy, for example) would then be an "understandable reaction" to this vital disorder. In other words, depressive patients would feel worthless because they believe themselves to be incapable of work, of enjoyment, and of concentration. This theory of feelings was held, albeit temporarily, in high esteem. The adjective *vital* for endogenous depression, which is still in use on the European mainland, represents the psychopathological remnant of this theory.

I. Toward the Twin Pillars of the *Diagnostic and Statistical Manual of Mental Disorders,* 3rd Edition (DSM-III)

Psychoanalysis enjoyed considerable influence for several decades, to such a degree that there was barely any perceptible movement in the classification debate. However, this began to change, with the discovery of the action of antidepressants toward the end of the 1950s. At that time, the effects of lithium had been known for 10 years, and electroconvulsive therapy (ECT) had been in use for more than 20 years. The advent of these new therapeutic drugs raised the question of whether the biological active site of these drugs could be linked with specific target symptoms of depression (or mania). Gradually, it was accepted that this was indeed true. Target symptoms, it was assumed, pointed to a given core disorder in the spectrum of depressive symptomatology. The increasing use of advanced statistical methods was also to have consequences for this debate. It enabled larger groups of patients, taken from adjacent diagnostic categories, to be investigated for clustering of symptoms (discriminant function analysis) and underlying factors or dimensions (factor analysis).

The outcome of these developments was not immediately obvious (cf. Akiskal and McKinney, 1975). In summary, the classification debate gradually split into two separate debates after 1960. These concerned (1) the distinction between manic–depressive psychosis and other forms of depression and (2) the distinction between "endogenous" and neurotic depressions. The considerable overlap between these two debates only served to complicate matters, since the classificatory status of endogenous depression was central to both.

When highlighting some moments of this debate, mention should first be made of the clinical and genetic studies of Perris (1966) and Angst (1966). Both workers found that depressives with a previous history of mania had different hereditary profiles from those with no such previous history. On the basis of these findings, they concluded that the distinction between unipolar and bipolar depressions, which was already defended on clinical grounds by Leonhard in 1959, was valid. This distinction became one of the basic assumptions of the classification of mood disorders in the *DSM-III* (American Psychiatric Association; APA, 1980) and *DSM-III (R)* (APA, 1987).

Kendell (1968), meanwhile, carried out a retrospective investigation of 1080 patients who had been admitted to the Maudsley Hospital. He could find no evidence of a bimodal distribution in the symptom profiles of a heterogeneous group consisting of manic–depressive patients, patients with neurotic depression and patients with involutional melancholia. However, just such a distribution was found in the so-called Newcastle study. Something common to both studies was the relatively high loading of a "bipolar" factor.

As Kendell himself observed, his investigation did not negate the distinction between psychotic and neurotic depression. These could represent two poles of a continuum, with the psychotic pole displaying greater homogeneity than the neurotic pole. The simple fact that the symptoms of the neurotic side are milder and fewer contributed substantially to the reduced tendency toward clustering (Kendell, 1968, 1976).

The lack of homogeneity at the neurotic depressive pole of the spectrum also found expression in the tri- and tetrapartite divisions of Klein (1974) and Paykel (1971), respectively. Klein distinguished an "endogenomorphic" depression, as well as a reactive and a (chronic) neurotic form. Paykel, on the other hand, distinguished psychotic depressives as well as three other groups, namely, anxious depressives, hostile depressives, and young depressives with personality disorder. Again, remarkably, some degree of consensus existed relative to the psychotic or endogenomorphic end of the spectrum. The limited extent of this consensus was because, for the aforementioned authors, the central issue was not bipolarity (cf. Perris, Angst, and Kendell, 1968), but rather vital phenomena and psychotic symptoms.

Therefore, it was not surprising that some workers opted not for a continuum, but for a sort of center–periphery model. Take Mendels and Cochrane (1968), for example, who observed that

> the so-called endogenous factor might represent the core of depressive symptomatology, whereas the clinical features of the reactive factor may represent phenomenological manifestations of psychiatric disorders other than depression which "contaminate" the depression syndrome.

Ultimately, however, with the advent of *DSM-III(R)*, neither the center–periphery model nor the continuum model was to gain the upper hand. Instead, the winner was a twin-pillar model, centering around the pillars of bipolar disorder and depressive disorder. In an article that appeared in 1974, Klein articulated an important consideration concerning this shift. He pointed out that endogenomorphic depressions (those that give the impression of having arisen endogenously) occur particularly frequently in the group of neurotic depressions. In addition, as a result of epidemiological studies, gradually less emphasis was placed on the heterogeneity of neurotic depressions. Conversely, greater attention was paid to the chronic course and to the degree of morbidity. Finally, there were genetic investigations, which were to undergo prodigious development in the

1980s. The evidence that these provided not only favored the further demarcation of bipolar disorder, something that had already been advocated on the basis of factorial analysis studies, but also the distinction of dysthymia (or neurotic depression) as a separate category.

In summary, it can be said that a consensus began to emerge, one in which the most important demarcation lines were those drawn between bipolar disorder and unipolar depression. In *DSM-III(R)*, within the group of unipolar depressive disorders, a subdivision was subsequently created that roughly corresponded to the distinction between endogenomorphic and chronic neurotic depression, as described by Klein. Once again, ironically enough, the old concept of melancholia was even called on for assistance, namely in the definition of the endogenomorphic (vital) form of "major depression."

It should be noted, by way of a cautionary remark, that this consensus was by no means universal. For example, it has still not been decided whether or not the categorical distinction between cyclothymia and dysthymia, on the one hand, and personality disorders, on the other, is an artifact. Besides, the debate about the demarcation between affective and anxiety disorders has become of particular relevance at the present time. Longitudinal, familial, and epidemiological studies have demonstrated that there is a high degree of comorbidity of affective and anxiety disorders, both in the course of the illness and in relatives. However, it is beyond the scope of this chapter to pursue that particular story at this point (further reading: Crowe et al., 1983; Leckmann et al., 1983; Weissman et al., 1984; van Valkenburg et al., 1984; Coryell et al., 1988; Eaton and Ritter, 1988; Hecht et al., 1989; Vollrath and Angst, 1989).

It does provide us with the opportunity of switching to a discussion of some highlights from the conceptual history of anxiety and anxiety disorders.

IV. HIGHLIGHTS FROM THE CONCEPTUAL HISTORY OF ANXIETY AND ANXIETY DISORDERS

A. The Demarcation of Agoraphobia

Before about 1850, as mentioned in Section II, anxiety was not considered to be a distinct form of psychopathology in the medical literature. This is of particular importance to the recent debate on the demarcation between affective and anxiety disorders. For hundreds of years, the symptoms of anxiety had simply been seen as part of melancholia. In the course of the past century and the present one, the various forms of anxiety came to be distinguished from depressive disorders, on a variety of grounds. In the light of the century-old merging of anxiety and depression, a reconsideration of these grounds is, therefore, a matter of considerable topical interest. What is it that explains the urge to accord the various forms of anxiety independent status within the total spectrum of psychopathological symptoms?

Historically, attention focused initially on phobias. Phobic anxiety, like other symptoms of anxiety, had been described in another terminology already in the hippocratic texts. Burton described agoraphobia, claustrophobia, and fear of public speaking. Errera (1962) cites le Camus' *Médecine de l'Esprit* [Medicine of the Mind; 1769, pp. 259–265] and de Sauvages' *Nosologie Méthodique* [Methodical Nosology; 1770–1771] as being the first medical studies in the field of phobia. The former includes a section on *Des aversions* (avoidance behavior), and the latter lists many different types of phobias. The term phobia was occasionally used in a diagnostic context even before 1850, as in the work of Benjamin Rush (1798), for example.

However, three publications that appeared about 1870 became particularly authoritative. The first of these was a short article by *Benedikt* entitled *Über Platzschwindel* [On dizziness on squares]. Here, the author focused on a form of dizziness that, because of its characteristic symptomatology and treatability, in his opinion, merited a separate classification among the various forms of giddiness (Benedikt, 1870). This article was to go down in medical history as one of the first descriptions of agoraphobia. As just noted, this is, in fact, historically inaccurate. Furthermore, the term *Platzschwindel*, was invented by Griesinger, not Benedikt. Nevertheless, by according a separate classification to the series of phenomena currently referred to as agoraphobia, Benedikt's article does mark a turning point.

Although Benedikt had observed anxiety in the patients he described, he believed this to be secondary to the dizziness:

> however, as soon as they enter a wider street or (especially) a square, they are overcome by dizziness. They either become terrified of collapsing mentally or else they are gripped by such tremendous fear that they will never dare to pass through such a place again. (Benedikt 1870, p. 488; translation by the author)

Two years later, *Westphal* (1872) challenged the view that the dizziness was of primary importance. Westphal, who was the first to use the term *agoraphobia* in a technical sense, believed that anxiety, rather than dizziness, was at the root of this phobia. It was anxiety that caused the dizziness, not the other way around. Westphal's observation was the forerunner of a debate that was to be in full swing rather more than a century later. This debate centers around the provocative role of bodily sensations and of their interpretation in the origin of panic attacks. Westphal based his hypothesis on clinical observation, rather than on theoretical considerations. He imputed Benedikt's interpretation to the incompleteness of his investigations (Westphal, 1872, p. 153).

Interestingly enough, Westphal himself was very much aware that the three patients he described were certainly not afraid of streets or squares, as such. He stressed the unfounded nature of their anxiety. Theirs was rather a fear of anxiety itself, an anxiety that only much later is linked to particular situations. Modern day authors who point out that agoraphobic anxiety is not a fear of streets or squares and that it occurs under all sorts of other circumstances find an ally in Westphal.

B. Anxiety Under Circumstances of War

In the same period *Da Costa* (1871) published an article on cardiac symptoms in exhausted infantry soldiers during the American Civil War. Da Costa, himself a cardiologist, spoke of an "irritable heart." Observations of more than 300 patients led him to believe that this condition was caused by a heightened nervous irritability of the heart. This, in turn, was caused by prior overactivity, such as long marches, for example, or physical illness. During auscultation of the heart, Da Costa heard a weak and sometimes split first sound, a pronounced second sound, and sometimes a systolic murmur. This systolic murmur has recently been related to the midsystolic "click" of mitral valve prolapse. Da Costa spoke of a sound "like the sudden motion of an only slightly elastic or cartilaginous substance" (Da Costa, 1871, p. 26).

This classic article by Da Costa continued to stir things up among cardiologists, neurologists, and psychiatrists well into the middle of this century (Skerritt, 1983). The debate became particularly intense during and after both World Wars when, once again, tens of thousands of those departing the front lines were afflicted with the syndrome described by Da Costa. Thomas Lewis gave a figure of 70,000 such cases among British soldiers in World War I, 44,000 of whom subsequently received a war pension (Lewis, 1940). In addition to a report on this subject, which he drew up for the Medical Research Committee in 1917, Lewis also published a monograph in 1940, on the same theme. By that time many agreed with Lewis that the term *irritable heart* was incorrect, since this placed a one-sided emphasis on heart palpitations and on pain in the region of the heart. This suggested, wrongly, that the complaints were cardiac in origin. However, despite this consensus, there was still no unanimity about what actually lay behind the syndrome.

This lack of unanimity was also reflected in the nomenclature. Lewis introduced the term *effort syndrome* to emphasize both the intolerance to physical exertion and the syndromal character of the picture described by Da Costa. Although the clinical picture was indeed determined by cardiac symptoms, he found that only one-sixth of the patients actually suffered from heart disease. Other terms that came into use were *soldier's heart* (MacKenzie, 1916), *war neurosis* (Mackenzie, 1920), *Da Costa syndrome* (Wood, 1941), *neurocirculatory asthenia* (Oppenheimer et al., 1918), and *heart neurosis*. Following rejection of the cardiac hypothesis, the controversy over etiology mostly centered on whether this picture was determined by psychic factors (Culpin, 1920; Wood, 1941) or whether it was a syndrome that could develop in more than one way (MacKenzie, 1916, 1920; Jones and Lewis, 1941; Jones, 1948).

MacKenzie (1920) for example, blamed the confusion surrounding the condition (which he termed *soldier's heart*) on a consideration of some individual symptoms to the exclusion of all else, and on the fact that this disorder had been named after its most prominent symptom (here, heart palpitations and pain in the region of the heart). Because of this, less prominent symptomatology tended to be disregarded. Mackenzie states that, according to the "law of associated phenomena," local disorders are usually accompanied by so-called reflex symptoms (see Sec. IV.D) in other parts of the body. Moreover, long before the formulation of the attribution theory, he already emphasized the influence of medical terms on the way in which disease is perceived. By designating the systolic murmur associated with effort syndrome as an aortic valve defect, or a mitral valve defect, physicians could turn their patients into invalids. Intolerance to exertion would then wrongly be labeled as heart disease.

The debate was settled provisionally by two collaborative studies by several of specialists from a section of the Maudsley Hospital which was rehoused at Mill Hill School during World War II. A special unit had been set up at the school for the purpose of studying patients with effort syndrome. One of these studies was a (award-winning) work by *Maxwell Jones*, who was later to achieve fame as a protagonist of the therapeutic community (Jones, 1948). In the other study, by the cardiologist *Paul Wood*, the author concluded that the symptoms of Da Costa syndrome were also prevalent in peace time and that they closely resembled the symptoms of anxiety neurosis (Wood, 1941). Although constitution, heavy exertion, and previous infectious diseases all could be precipitating factors, effort syndrome was ultimately explicable in terms of (and was maintained by) a neurotic mechanism. It affects those who, in their youth, "clung too long to their mothers' skirts" (Wood, 1941, p. 846) and who, either owing to parental overconcern or to comments by their physician, learned to interpret various (normal) physiological changes as signs of physical impotence or even of danger.

Like Mackenzie, Wood placed great emphasis on the suggestibility of the patients, particularly on their capacity to interpret, in a negative way, the normal physiological changes that occur during physical exertion. Wood's interpretation was partly based upon physiological experiments that had demonstrated that peripheral sensation in effort syndrome was founded neither upon local abnormalities, nor on a hypersensitivity of the central nervous system (such as in hyperadrenalism), nor on hyperventilation. There was, therefore, in his opinion, no specific pathophysiological mechanism that could be held responsible for the physical symptoms. However, there did exist a specific psychological mechanism, which involved the association of exertion with all sorts of imaginary physical catastrophes. Wood believed that this association was mediated by an emotion, usually anxiety, although patients were generally not consciously aware of this. The therapy, therefore, consisted of a form of psychoeducation in which people were informed of the physical manifestations of emotions and that physical sensations were not, by definition, indicative of a disorder in any particular organ.

Maxwell Jones concurred with this. He developed a form of group psychoeducation, using groups of about 100 patients, which later evolved into the first therapeutic community. The aim of this therapy was to teach patients to adopt a different attitude toward their symptoms. In addition, Jones stressed the reality of this intolerance to exertion. Extensive physiological studies failed to provide an explanation for this intolerance; therefore, he spoke of an effort phobia. Jones' investigations demonstrated namely that effort syndrome patients quit exerting themselves long before they reached their physiological limit, as expressed by a slightly smaller increase in the lactate level relative to a normal control group, following the subjective maximum of exertion.

The debate can be summarized by stating that the variation in nomenclature was determined not only by all sorts of theoretical views concerning the causation of physical sensations, but also by the immediate military importance of identifying and treating those suffering from war neurosis. Wars have contributed greatly to our knowledge, not only of anxiety disorders, but also, for example, of traumatic neuroses and terror psychoses (cf. Bonhoeffer, 1919; Kleist, 1918). In addition, they have propelled this knowledge in a specific direction. Lewis' choice of the term effort syndrome was significant, as was his involvement in the development of exercise programs to increase the exertion tolerance of the soldiers he was treating. Both can be seen as a direct reflection of the military importance of the capacity to deliver physical effort (Lewis, 1918). Lewis' effort syndrome is a splendid example of social influences affecting psychiatric diagnosis.

Subsequently, the special relation between anxiety phenomena and the heart persisted even after 1950. Even though consideration was being given, in the sidelines, to the psychiatric mode of interpretation, the somatic approach continued to play a dominant role. The 1960s saw the development of somatic concepts such as "hyperkinetic heart syndrome" and "hyperdynamic ß-adrenergic condition." Recently, the relation between anxiety disorders and mitral valve prolapse has been the subject of debate, as has the so-called fatigue syndrome (White, 1989; Wessely, 1990).

C. Anxiety Psychosis

The frequent occurrence of anxiety with psychotic symptoms did not go unnoticed by 19th century psychiatry. *Wernicke,* however, was the first to use the term *anxiety psychosis*. In Wernicke's opinion, frightening cognitions, hallucinations, delusions, and delusory ideas were the result, rather than the cause, of the emotion of anxiety. He explained the psychotic phenomena seen in anxiety psychosis by the intensity of the anxiety itself. The reverse was true of alcohol hallucinosis, in which anxiety was the result of the hallucinations. Melancholia also differed from anxiety psychosis. So-called agitated melancholia, on the other hand, which was actually a variant of anxiety psychosis, was totally unrelated to melancholia (Wernicke, 1895, p. 1020). The motor expressions that appeared in anxiety psychosis were interpreted by Wernicke as complications, rather than as a direct consequence of the anxiety.

In the ensuing debate, criticism was levelled at the term anxiety psychosis (Specht, 1907; Forster, 1910). Some questioned the worth of a classification that was based on the content of cognitions. Anxiety-dominated cognitions were not restricted to anxiety psychosis, they also occurred in a variety of other psychiatric disorders. Wernicke himself had already made a distinction between anxiety psychosis, on the one hand, and anxiety in paranoid delusions and in delusions of reference, on the other. The distinguishing criterion—namely, that the cognition in anxiety psychosis must be a direct consequence of anxiety—proved not to be unequivocally applicable in practice.

Meanwhile, Specht's interpretation differed considerably from that of Forster. *Specht* felt that anxiety psychosis was a mixed (kraepelinian) form of manic–depressive psychosis, in which motor agitation was an expression of the manic component. Like Wernicke, he drew a sharp distinction between anxiety and agitation, on the basis that the former frequently occurred in depression, whereas the latter was commonly a feature of mania. Specht's view was that anxiety psychosis involved motor agitation as an expression of the manic component, accompanied by the anxiety and inhibition of thought as a result of the depressive component. For Wernicke, anxiety was the central characteristic of anxiety psychosis; for Specht, it was agitation.

Forster, on the other hand, felt that the symptoms of anxiety psychosis could best be seen either as a variant of melancholia (melancholia agitata) or as the early stage of another disorder. Not only did Forster not want to separate anxiety from agitation, he also resisted Kraepelin's separation of manic–depressive psychosis from dementia praecox. In his opinion, anxiety was not so much an emotion that was difficult to define, but more a complex series of cognitions that cannot be expressed in words. This formal characteristic (i.e., a special type of cognitive complexity) was determined by the "fundamental disorder" which Forster placed at the level of the organic cerebral substratum (Forster, 1910, pp. 252–260).

In the ninth edition of Kraepelin's textbook, anxiety psychosis was still included under the *Emotionelle Symptomenkomplexe* [emotional symptom complexes]. It was defined as a dysphoric condition that cannot be sharply distinguished from depression. It was associated with anxiety, motor restlessness, and psychotic symptoms (Kraepelin and Lange, 1927, pp. 611 et seq). As a symptom complex, it could occur in all types of psychiatric disorders, including manic–depressive psychosis and dementia praecox. It could also be age-related, as in presenility and senility.

Two questions dominated this somewhat confusing debate surrounding anxiety psychosis. These concerned the relations between emotion and cognition, and between anxiety and (psycho)motor agitation. On the first point Wernicke considered the anxiety emotion to be dominant, whereas Forster placed the cognition in the leading role. Specht's reference to the kraepelinian idea of the manic–depressive mixed condition suggested a preference for the view that the affective component was dominant. On the second point, both Wernicke and Specht made a sharp distinction between anxiety and agitation. As a distinguishing criterion for anxiety psychosis, Wernicke emphasized the anxiety, Specht the agitation. Forster allowed anxiety, agitation, and desperation to intermingle, since he believed that there were insufficient empirical grounds for a sharp distinction between anxiety disorders, manic–depressive disorders, and psychotic disorders. The background to this was Forster's rejection of the traditional classification (derived from faculty psychology) into thinking disorders, feeling disorders, and disorders affecting the function of the will (Forster, 1910, p. 260).

In the post-1910 literature, there are two publications that are also worthy of mention. These are G.E. Störring's *Zur Psychopathologie und Klinik der Angstzustände* [On the psychopathology and treatment of anxiety states] (Störring, 1934) and K. Conrad's *Die beginnende Schizophrenie* [incipient schizophrenia] (Conrad, 1958). Although neither work includes the term anxiety psychosis, both point out the fundamental significance of anxiety in the origin of psychosis. Both go on to describe a period of depersonalization, anxiety, and anxious moods that often precedes the onset of psychosis. Conrad used the term *trema* to denote this anxious delusory mood. Störring described how this anxious delusory mood could lead to so-called objectivation of anxiety. This refers to what nowadays is called projection. Feelings of anxiety are no longer experienced internally, but transform into perceptions of a dreadful and mysteriously changed world. The background to this symptom, in the case of psychosis, is a disorder that effects the sense of identity. Psychotics are no longer able to perceive themselves as the source of meaningful experiences and activities. Feelings lose their natural bond with the I. As a consequence, they take on an enigmatic and indeterminate character. Even though the patient does not necessarily experience anxiety subjectively, the world, nevertheless, changes in an obscure way and appears to be terrifying, threatening, and gruesome. Sometimes anxiety is experienced in flashes, in which case, according to Störring, it makes sense to speak of a delusory affect, rather than of a delusory mood.

Meanwhile, with the virtual disappearance of the term anxiety psychosis from clinical usage, interest in anxiety symptoms in the context of psychosis had also faded (Schmidt-Degenhard, 1986). However, studies pertaining to the occurrence of panic attacks in schizophrenia and in schizophreniform disorders are still published from time to time.

D. Neurasthenia

In the second half of the 19th century, a new concept, *neurasthenia*, gained ground. *George M. Beard*, the American advocate of this idea, considered neurasthenia to be a functional disorder characterized by a deficiency of "nervous force." This deficiency could express itself in a multitude of symptoms, particularly at the level of the central nervous system, the digestive tract, and the reproductive tract (Beard, 1884, 1890). Although not highly prominent among these symptoms, morbid fear and phobia were nevertheless ranked among the most difficult symptoms to cure (Beard, 1884, pp. 52–53; Beard, 1890, pp. 50–67). Beard used analogies for nervous exhaustion, such as that of a furnace lacking in fuel and of a battery losing its charge (Beard, 1884, pp. 60–61). Central to the concept of neurasthenia was the lack of the strength and reserve to fight the disturbances of nervous function caused by stress. Beard's neurasthenia concept was closely linked with his vision of American society, which supposedly caused much greater overexcitation of the central nervous system than did European society. "American nervousness," one of Beard's favorite synonyms for neurasthenia, was a typical product of an industrial society in which the upper classes were doomed to a hectic lifestyle.

Beard experienced just as little difficulty with the conceptual difference between the physical depletion of energy and the psychic feeling of exhaustion as did Freud, a decade later (cf. MacMillan, 1976). He had observed that not only did neurasthenia patients tend to survive their own physicians, but that they were also capable of considerable mental effort. However, this did not cause him to reconsider the difference between subjective feelings of exhaustion and an actual deterioration in achievements resulting from a lack of physical reserves. On the contrary, he stressed that, in a functional sense, there was actually something amiss, such as a hyperemia of the cerebrum, the stomach or the prostate, for example.

Because of a lack of resistance, the functional disorder (which initially occurred locally) became transmitted to other regions of the body (irradiation). It, therefore, had no opportunity to develop into a permanent local abnormality. In Beard's opinion, this was not the case in healthy people in whom, occasionally, local overexcitation could even result in death. In neurasthenia, the local functional disorder never exceeded the threshold of intensity beyond which permanent defects could develop. Irradiation not only explained the variable and migratory course, but also the multiplicity of symptoms. Among the symptoms included by Beard were the irritable heart, all kinds of phobias, compulsions, impotence, hyperesthesia, and a huge range of physical sensations.

The irradiation of the local functional disorder occurred reflectively, and Beard thought that the sympathetic nerve played an important role here. This hypothesis of reflective nerve impulse transport was one of the three basic assumptions in Beard's concept of neurasthenia. In addition to the reflex theory, there was the idea of the electrical nature of nerve excitation and the law of conservation of energy (cf. Rosenberg, 1962).

Beard himself believed that it was openminded observation that led him to the discovery of neurasthenia, and his descriptions do indeed bear testimony to his extraordinary attention to detail. He would take even the most idiosyncratic, subjective sensations quite seriously. The fact that neurasthenia had not been previously described was, in his opinion, because neurasthenic patients are not to be found in hospitals or mental institutions. They should instead be sought elsewhere, neurasthenia being a disease of the street (Beard, 1890, pp. 25–35).

Nevertheless, Beard overestimated his inductive powers, as is demonstrated by the aforementioned three basic assumptions and the role that they played in his work. These assumptions constituted the guiding principle on which he based his attempts to forge a whole out of the positively exorbitant diversity of observations. Moreover, it was quite common in those days to think of psychic disorders in terms of an excess or a deficiency of (nervous) energy. Furthermore, as we have previously seen, ideas such as asthenia and irritability were already fashionable a century earlier (cf. Berrios, 1990; Lopez Pineiro, 1983, pp. 64 et seq). In 1848 W. B. Carpenter explicitly suggested the idea of a close relation between nervous energy and electricity. Thinkers, such as Spencer, Fechner, and Darwin, subsequently elaborated this idea still further. Meanwhile, in the therapeutic sphere, the process of "electrification" became quite popular (Russelman, 1983, pp. 119–154). Nor was Beard the first to see a connection between life-style and functional changes in the central nervous system. The previously mentioned theory of degeneration, which was very popular on the European continent at the time, provides still more far-reaching examples.

It is true to say that this fascination with the relation between nervous energy and electrical phenomena was not unconnected with developments in the natural sciences. Its origin, however, lay in the Romantic period. The intellectuals of the Romantic period are known to have been strongly captivated by the living world's organic urge to develop and evolve. Early in the 19th century, the concept of natural force encompassed not only physical forces, such as motion and heat, but also biotic and psychic forces, such as the life force, growth energy, and the urge toward further development. It is, therefore, not the case that the concept of physical energy was initially discovered by physicists and only later applied, in a metaphorical sense, to psychic symptoms. In the second half of the 19th century, the prevailing climate of thought, which was still dominated by the influence of the Romantic period, swung in a materialistic and mechanistic direction. This transformation, which was associated with such names such as *H. Helmholtz, E. du Bois-Reymond, E. W. Brücke*, and *C. Ludwig*, was triggered by the discovery of the law of conservation of energy by *Robert Mayer* in 1842. It resulted in a differentiation being made between physical and psychic force, which suddenly breathed new life into the psychophysical problem. At the end of the 19th century there was yet another swing, this time back in a (neo)romantic direction, whereby all sorts of vitalistic concepts gained ground anew. Beard's concept of "nervous force" seemed to fit in with this neoromantic pattern of a vitalistic mixture of psychic and physical forces.

In summary, it can be said that both Beard's description of neurasthenia, as well as the temporary popularity of this concept, cannot be understood from a purely medical perspective. Instead, one must consider the interaction between medical observations, theoretical opinions, philosophical traditions of thinking, and various social changes. However, that medicine concerned itself with neurasthenic patients at all was, to a great extent, a social phenomenon. When social pressure became too much for an individual's resilience, neurasthenia offered a medical excuse for taking it easy.

E. Anxiety Neurosis

The history of the classification of anxiety disorders since the time of Beard can be seen as a peeling-away of layers of the concept of neurasthenia. Anxiety neurosis was the first stratum to be laid bare under its surface. Next came all sorts of classificatory subdivisions within anxiety neurosis (Tyrer, 1984).

Kahlbaum's successor, *Hecker,* initiated the aforementioned process in a classic article on anxiety states in neurasthenia (Hecker, 1893). He had noticed that the anxiety attacks experienced by many neurasthenia sufferers were not accompanied by any subjective feeling of anxiety. There were also patients who did not show anything like the full range of physical symptoms. Hecker used the term *larvirt* (larval; larvalike) to denote this absence of a feeling of anxiety. The term *abortiv* was indicative of the interrupted, incomplete nature of the attack in terms of the somatic symptomatology. The picture described by Hecker bears a strong resemblance to the so-called limited symptom attacks in present day literature on panic disorder. Citing Lange, a Dane who had formulated an interpretation of emotions that was practically identical with that of William James, Hecker stated that the absence of subjective anxiety in the attack was based on a kind of misperception. The physical symptoms were simply not recognized as expressions of anxiety. However, it was also possible for an attack to commence with just one of the somatic symptoms, before radiating to other parts of the body. The way in which Hecker described this irradiation betrays a relation with Beard's reflex theory.

In 1895, *Sigmund Freud*, with reference to Hecker, joined the critics of Beard's broad concept of neurasthenia. However, in being more explicit about pathogenesis,

Freud went a step further than Hecker (Freud, 1895a,c). He believed that demarcation of neurasthenia was essential, since anxiety neurosis, because of its different pathogenesis, required different treatment. Neurasthenia was a disorder of the way in which the so-called somatic–sexual excitation was released, whereas anxiety neurosis was primarily a disorder in the psychic processing of such excitation. In anxiety neurosis, Freud imagined that there was a buildup of pressure on the walls of the male seminal vesicles. When this pressure exceeded a given threshold, it was transformed into somatic energy and transmitted, by neural pathways, to the cerebral cortex. Under normal conditions, sexual "fantasy groups" became charged with this energy, leading to sexual excitement (libido) and the pursuit of release. Anxiety neurosis involved a blockage in the psychic processing of this somatic sexual tension. Such a blockage might arise through abstinence, for example, or from the use of coitus interruptus, or because sexual fantasies had simply failed to take shape. Somatic sexual tension was thus deflected away from the psyche (the cortex) and directed to subcortical paths, finally expressing itself as "inadequate actions." These inadequate actions most characteristically occurred during an anxiety attack.

The pioneering article in which Freud detached anxiety neurosis from neurasthenia, includes a description of the symptomatology of the various forms of anxiety, which is still valid today (Freud, 1895a). Freud cited anxious expectation as the core symptom of anxiety neurosis. He also distinguished between specific phobias, agoraphobia, free-floating anxiety, and anxiety attacks. The latter were spontaneous in nature and were described as a purely somatic phenomenon (Freud, 1895c, pp. 368–369). The aforementioned distinctions anticipated the now generally accepted classification of specific phobias, agoraphobia, generalized anxiety, and panic disorder. Freud was not alone in anticipating *DSM-III(R)*. As the authors of *DSM-III(R)* have acknowledged, striking similarities are also to be found in the sixth edition of Kraepelin's textbook (Kraepelin, 1899; cf. Spitzer and Williams, 1985). Furthermore, it is interesting that Freud considered agoraphobia to be characterized by a fear of panic attacks, and not be fear of streets or squares per se: . . . *ce que redoute ce malade c'est l'événement d'une telle attaque* . . . [". . . what the patient fears is the occurrence of such an attack . . ."] (Freud 1895b, p. 352).

Freud's reputation was not based on his interpretations of anxiety neurosis, however. His second theory of anxiety, in which anxiety was interpreted as a signal of inner threat, would ultimately have much greater influence (Freud, 19265). This second theory had already announced its arrival by about 1895, albeit in a somatic guise. Freud asked why nonprocessed sexual excitation should express itself specifically in the form of anxiety. In answering this question, a glimpse is afforded of something that would later be more explicitly developed as a theme. Unlike real anxiety, which was based on the perception of an external threat, neurotic anxiety was a reaction to inner threat. The core of this inner threat was an inability to process "endogenously" created (sexual) excitation (Freud, 1895a, p. 338). On another occasion Freud put it as follows: "Anxiety is the sensation of the accumulation of another endogenous stimulus, the stimulus to breathing . . ." (Freud, 1894, p. 194).

It is sometimes forgotten that elements of the foregoing hypothesis also appeared in Freud's signal theory. There also, the basis of all anxiety was biological helplessness (i.e., the helplessness of the child relative to its own drive impulses (cf. Freud, 1926, p. 68). Although the signal theory also concerns the satisfying of needs, it does not relate primarily to sexual needs, but rather, to those associated with the instinct for self-preservation (cf. Freud, 1933, pp. 100–101). Object loss, the most clear-cut threat recognized by this instinct, becomes the psychological prerequisite for inducing the ego to give off a small quantum of anxiety to restore a favorable balance of pleasure and displeasure. The threat of object loss remains linked to the biological state of being at the mercy of one's drive impulses. This linkage is mediated by remembrance symbols which, by separation and birth, ultimately refer to an archaic inheritance of hereditary anxiety responses. In anxious patients, the symptom of gasping for air is no longer seen as a mitigated orgasm, but rather, as the rudiment of the cry of a newborn child (Freud, 1926, p. 168).

In a negative sense, Freud's second theory of anxiety was of great significance within the classification debate. His statement that anxiety was the "loose change" of the neurotic conflict, illustrates the nosologically nonspecific character gradually adopted by anxiety in his interpretations. This was partly why the classification of anxiety symptoms did not exactly receive top priority in the period between 1930 and 1960.

This is not meant to detract from Freud's exceptional merits. In the field of anxiety theory, these merits lay particularly in the concept of anxiety as a reaction to an inner threat. This idea, which was without precedent in Freud's days, permanently changed the face of psychiatry. Freud thereby gave a wholly individual treatment to the fundamental distinction between (objectless) anxiety and (object-linked) fear, a theme that for the rest was to find its way into psychiatry by another route.[6]

Freud's approach was not limited to the psychoanalytic school. In its interpretation of anxiety, cognitive psychology (in the style of Beck) built on Freud's pioneering concept of anxiety as an inner threat (Beck, 1976; Beck et al., 1985).

F. Clinical Studies

After 1900, despite the almost universal recognition of the central position of anxiety in psychopathology, relatively few psychiatric monographs were devoted exclusively to anxiety and anxiety disorders. One exception was the exhaustive study by Störring, mentioned previously. Several authors occupied themselves with conceptual questions, based on clinical observations. Goldstein (1929) and Kronfeld (1935) produced splendid articles that incorporated some fundamental concepts. Some other names that should be mentioned in this context are those of Hoche (1911), Kornfeld (1902), and Oppenheim (1909). Janet's *Les obsessions et la psychasthénie* [Obsessions and psychasthenia] (1903) and his *De l'angoisse à l'extase* [From anxiety to ecstasy] 1926) are worthy of special mention.

Next, reference should be made to several studies arising from particular theoretical points of view. These include not only the psychoanalytical studies by Stekel (1932), Bitter (1948), and Riemann (1961), but also the anthropological studies of von Gebsattel (1954a–c), and Tellenbach (1976). In addition, studies exclusively devoted to a particular form of anxiety, such as the innumerable publications on *Schreckneurosen* and *Schreckpsychosen* (from the German *Schreck*: terror), were carried out in the periods surrounding both World Wars (cf. Bonhoeffer, 1919; Kleist, 1918; Panse, 1952).

Seen from a broader perspective, the conceptual framework within which the debate on pathological anxiety took place was specifically determined by the intellectual legacy bequeathed by scientists and philosophers such as *Charles Darwin, W. B. Cannon, William James, Sigmund Freud*, and *Max Scheler*. It is no simple matter to illustrate just how the various interpretations and schools of thought influenced one another. Accordingly, I will restrict my discussion to two themes, the *role of bodily perceptions in the origin of anxiety* and the further determination of *the distinction between anxiety and fear*.

Relative to the first theme, there seemed to be a significant resistance amongst clinicians to the *James-Lange* theory of emotions. Bodily changes, according to this theory, instead of resulting from subjective feelings, were actually the cause of the emotional coloring of sensory perceptions. Perception became emotion through the awareness of bodily changes (cf. James, 1884, pp. 189, 204; 1890, p. 450). James himself was responsible for the subsequent confusion over whether a temporal–causal relation existed between bodily changes and emotional perceptions, or whether both occurred simultaneously. It was usually assumed (probably not entirely correctly) that James was postulating a temporal sequence between bodily changes and emotional perceptions.

Clinicians, who also adopted this interpretation, criticized him on this point by pointing out the immediacy of the experience of anxiety. According to Störring, the experience of anxiety was not mediated by prior bodily perception. However, he was not entirely logical on this point, since he consistently spoke of anxiety as a processing of, or a reaction to, sensations associated with specific organs (Störring, 1934, pp. 24, 32). Both *Kornfeld* (1902) (not to be confused with Kronfeld, who has been mentioned previously) and *Hoche* (1911) lodged objections, on descriptive grounds, against the idea of a temporal sequence between bodily change and emotional perception. Kornfeld, who himself suffered from neurasthenic complaints and panic attacks, enlivened his article with a description of one of his nightly panic attacks. On awakening, he would first experience a severe feeling of anxiety, without really knowing why he was frightened. Shortly afterward, he would become aware of bodily sensations, such as a feeling of constriction in the region of the heart, difficulty in breathing, paraesthesia and cold *akra*. This led him to conclude that a sharp distinction should be made between feelings of anxiety and the perception of bodily changes. Although Hoche thought along similar lines, like Hecker he formulated a sort of interoceptive explanation for anxiety, in which anxiety was based on the misinterpretation of bodily sensations. Kraepelin and Lange's handbook, ultimately rejected James' theory of emotions on theoretical grounds, both because of its psychophysical dualism and its disregard for central regulatory processes. An emotion, such as fear of suffocation, could be both somatic and psychological in origin. According to Kraepelin and Lange, the origin of this fear of suffocation (whether lack of oxygen, hypercapnia, acidosis, or frightening events) was irrelevant to the quality of the emotion itself. The central issue was always a threat to the patient's existence as a biological entity, rather than any perception of bodily changes (Kraepelin and Lange, 1927, p. 470). It should be noted, however, that James was too much of a Darwinist to be accused of psychophysical dualism.

In summary, it can be said that clinical psychiatrists mainly resisted the James–Lange theory because of their support for the primacy of clinical observation. Nevertheless, the antitheoretical sentiment in these convictions sometimes led to all sorts of nonexplicit theoretical views being smuggled in through the back door.

In discussing the second theme, that of the further determination of the distinction between anxiety and fear, consideration should first be given to *Kurt Goldstein's* observations of patients with organic brain damage. Most of Goldstein's patients were victims of World War I. He observed (1929) that, when faced with overly complex tasks, these patients displayed a catastrophic reaction, consisting of a wide range of physiological and psychomotor symptoms. Goldstein believed that, even though it was not subjectively experienced as such, this condition could best be interpreted as an expression of anxiety.

Although Goldstein's patients were unaware of their anxiety, the appearance of their physical symptoms coincided with the failure to accomplish their tasks. Strictly speaking, their anxiety was neither a reaction to failure nor a reaction to an awareness of failure. Anxiety—and this was the essence of Goldstein's interpretation—was quite literally the actual manifestation of failure. Goldstein concludes that, generally, anxiety was the expression of a frustrated urge for self-realization.

This reference to the urge for self-realization was particularly popular among those contemporary authors who drew their inspiration from vitalism. Although similar references can also be found in Freud's later work (Freud, 1933), it was actually the colossal presence of *Charles Darwin*, behind the scenes, that inspired this line of thought. However, Goldstein was not thinking of the survival of the species, or that of the individual, in purely darwinian terms. The urge toward self-realization was more than a purely biological reality. It also found expression, for example, in the productive creativity shown by children and adults in mastering the world. Anxiety was referred to as the *Erschütterung (des) Bestandes der Persönlichkeit* [Disruption of the stability of personality] (cf. Goldstein, 1929, pp. 415–416). Ultimately, however, Goldstein failed to fully clarify the conceptual status of the propensity for self-realization.

The task of more explicitly formulating things which Goldstein merely hinted at, fell to other authors. Here, we find a scheme in which personality was divided into an impersonal substructure and a personal superstructure. The substructure was described in vitalistic terms, whereas the superstructure was analyzed in terms derived from existentialist phenomenology. Examples of this can be found in work by *Arthur Kronfeld, Felix Krueger, Philipp Lersch*, and, to a lesser extent, *H. C. Rümke*. According to Kronfeld (1935), anxiety was based on a deterioration of the personal superstructure. In extremely succinct terms, this disintegration was expressed as psychotic anxiety. However, the type of anxiety that Kronfeld initially had in mind was existential, rather than psychotic:

> Anxiety is the mental expression of the existential annihilation of the integrity (*Einheitsform*) of the person. Its archetype is the fear of death, the anxiety related to vital destruction. (Kronfeld, 1935, p. 378; translation by the author)

Such statements only become comprehensible when it is realized that Kronfeld rejected the link between anxiety and threat. Anxiety, in the true sense of the word, is not the counterpart of safety, but of meaning, of being a person, of "one-ness," of living. The anxious person need not necessarily have a subjective awareness of this, however. Death has significance long before it becomes a subjective reality. According to Kronfeld, the biological aspect of anxiety consisted of life fleeing from death. Such flight is in vain, however, and therein lies the source of all fear of life and of anxiety about fate. Therefore, with anxiety, it is necessary to pose the question of meaning (Kronfeld, 1935, p. 384). Kronfeld's criticism of the biologically inspired interpretation of anxiety was that it failed to do this.

In uncoupling anxiety from threat, Kronfeld may have gone a little too far, but his remark that indescribable anxiety often has the quality of fear of living, receives daily confirmation from the mouths of borderline patients.

G. From Dimension to Category

The study of anxiety was not a high priority in the period from 1930 to 1960. In addition to the previously mentioned influence of psychoanalysis, which described anxiety as a nonspecific phenomenon, the assumption that anxiety occupied a low position in the hierarchy of psychiatric symptoms also had a part in this (cf. Tyrer, 1984). According to this line of thought, not only did anxiety occur in practically all psychopathological syndromes, it also marked the lower boundary of psychopathology, where this bordered on normality.

Jablensky (1985) adds to this that classification had traditionally been an area of interest for institutional psychiatry. An explanation for the relative neglect of the classification of anxiety disorders was that, as a rule, patients with neurotic anxiety were never hospitalized.

This status quo gradually changed toward the end of the 1950s. I shall summarize a number of these developments.

The psychophysiological investigation of emotions continued along the lines of the James–Lange theory. In this context, Ax (1953) attempted to draw a distinction between the emotions of anxiety and anger on the basis of their peripheral physiological symptoms.

The anxiolytic effect of benzodiazepines was discovered, resulting in a flood of research into the effects of these chemicals on the central nervous system (Sternbach, 1980).

J. Wolpe (1958) introduced systematic desensitization as a form of behavior therapy, thereby giving new impetus to the treatment of people with anxiety disorders.

The British psychiatrist M. Roth (1959) described a form of depersonalization associated with severe anxiety and phobic phenomena. This was the so-called phobic anxiety–depersonalization syndrome. Although it usually developed in the wake of a psychotrauma, this picture could sometimes occur spontaneously. The electroencephalograms (EEGs) of just under one-sixth of all patients revealed the presence of temporal–epileptic symptoms.

Finally, at the end of the 1950s, D. F. Klein (who has been referred to previously) discovered that panic attacks in agoraphobic patients could be blocked using imipramine (Klein, 1964; 1980). This marked the beginning of a great flood of experimental, pharmacological, clinical, longitudinal, epidemiological, genetic, and familial research into the existence and course of panic disorder.

With this boom in psychopharmacological research, increasingly stringent criteria for the definition of psychiatric syndromes were drawn up. This was principally for the sake of comparability between research groups. Thus, psychopharmacological and biological psychiatric research constituted a powerful impetus for the development of the *Feighner Criteria* (Feighner et al., 1972). These, together with the *Research Diagnostic Criteria* (Spitzer, et al., 1975; 1978) formed the basis of the *DSM-III(R)* (APA, 1980; 1987). The emphasis on descriptive precision led to the demarcation of various forms of anxiety and to an abandonment of the concept of neurosis, which was considered to be too vague. The "depressive neurosis" of *DSM-II* (1968) became "dysthymia" in *DSM-III*, falling under the affective disorders. Two types of hysterical neurosis, hypochondria and depersonalization, were classified under somatoform and dissociative disorders, respectively. Neurasthenic neurosis was discarded. Anxiety neurosis, phobic neurosis, and obsessive–compulsive neurosis were combined under the heading of anxiety disorders. Posttraumatic stress disorder, a newcomer, was added to the anxiety disorders. The anxiety neurosis was subsequently split up into panic disorder and generalized anxiety disorder, and the phobic neurosis was divided up into agoraphobia, simple phobias, and social phobia (cf. Spitzer and Williams, 1985).

In spite of the nontheoretical nature of *DSM-III*, this change, nevertheless, heralded in a fundamentally different approach to the psychopathology of anxiety. The *DSM-III* bade farewell, not only to the psychodynamic conflict model, but also to a broader tradition in which anxiety was associated with disorders in personality structure. It was replaced by a finely grained description and classification of more superficial symptomatology. Anxiety was no longer regarded as a consequence of the personality structure, but primarily as a symptom in itself. This resulted in a switch from the preponderantly dimensional or dispositional approach that characterized the neurosis model, to a typological or categorical approach to psychopathology.

Panic disorder represents the most outstanding example of this development, becoming "a microcosm of many of the classic controversies surrounding psychiatric research" (Gorman et al., 1989). Biological, psychoanalytic, behavioral, and cognitive explanatory models now competed for priority in this debate (cf. Tuma and Maser, 1985; Marks, 1987; Barlow, 1988; Glas, 1991). At the moment, the question of what exactly should be classified (patients? theoretical constructs? diseases?) is once again highly relevant (cf. Blashfield, 1986).

V. SUMMARY AND CONCLUSION

This chapter covers only part of the history of anxiety and depression. Although this is partly attributable to the introductory nature of this review, the main reason is that this discussion has been limited to concepts alone. Behind these concepts lie individual suffering, the often ineffective concern of those around the patient, and the numerous therapeutic efforts of physicians and paramedics. Although not covered here, this history is at least as worthy of our consideration as the one described in the foregoing.

In the Introduction, it was stated that the history of anxiety and depression should be interpreted as the interplay of cultural changes and of changes not only in psychopathological symptoms, per se, but also in their scientific interpretation. This interplay has, to some extent, been reflected in the preceding sections.

Viewed in the context of the microcosm–macrocosm theme, which was current both in antiquity and in the Renaissance, the mentally ill appeared as the personification of a disruption in the subtle balance of cosmic forces. Such people were different, but not so different that they warranted either ostracism or confinement.

The moralizing and allegorizing of humoral pathology in the Middle Ages raised the question of where disease ended and sin began. But it was difficult to know where to draw the line, as the 19th century theory of degeneration made clear. According to this theory, a transgression (because of alcoholism, for example) in one generation could lead to increasingly serious forms of psychopathology in succeeding generations.

The idea that melancholics show traits of the exceptional and of genius is a common thread running throughout history. Starting with Aristotle, it can be traced via Marsilio Ficino, through Burton and the poets of the Elizabethan era, and onward into the present century, in the work of William James. The fact that depressives' weaker perceptual defenses allow them a more adequate perception of reality may, perhaps, be a pale reflection of this very idea.

The rationalization and mechanization of the worldview in the post-Cartesian era finally resulted in a view of the mentally ill in which the irrational and uncontrollable elements of their behavior received special emphasis. The bestial side of human nature revealed itself in such people. Right up to the present day, domination and control have been key words in understanding the motivation behind medical concern for the psychiatric patient. It is this very contrast with earlier treatments that illustrates the extent to which the medical domination of previously uncontrollable emotions has become both the motive and guiding principle for current theoretical and therapeutic activity.

The current fascination of clinicians and researchers with the biological approach, therefore, comes as no surprise. Since this approach seems to bring the promise of control and of tangible results, in contrast with the unpredictable and much less concrete results obtained by psychological and social intervention.

It is appropriate to issue a warning at this point, however, since history has shown us how intractable psychopathological reality can be. It was not without reason that clinicians repeatedly demonstrated an astonishing eclecticism concerning the theoretical explanation of various insights. Clinicians showed reticence when it came to reasoning from preconceived theoretical points of view. I would remind you of the reservations expressed against the James–Lange theory of emotions. This reticence cannot simply be attributed to an antiscientific attitude. It also stems from healthy clinical skepticism. The history of the classification of anxiety and depression serves to emphasize that such skepticism was often quite appropriate. Whenever attempts were made to refine a given theory, or combination of theories, clinical reality always proved to possess an overabundance of elusiveness and unpredictability. Broadly speaking, longitudinal clinical observation advanced the classification of anxiety disorders, and especially that of mood disorders, more than did any classification based on preconceived theoretical assumptions. In view of the controversy between the unitarians and the separatists, a combination of longitudinal and interdisciplinary (biopsychosocial) research would seem to hold out particular promise for the future.

Finally, what has been said in the foregoing should also be emphasized on epistemological grounds. As scientific disciplines, neurobiology and pharmacology tackle problems abstractively and objectively. This implies that there is, by definition, a gap between the research findings in these disciplines and clinical reality. Furthermore, scientific constructs never relate to this reality in its entirety, but merely to aspects of the whole. Reification (i.e., the identification of these constructs with reality) can lead only to distortion. The conceptual history of anxiety and depression illustrates the repeated recurrence of forgotten ideas. These were eliminated in the process of abstraction, only to return through the back door. Scientific interpretations bear fruit only when the tension-filled gap separating them from clinical reality, rather than being short-circuited, is kept open.

NOTES

1. Klibansky, and associates (1964, pp. 64–66 and 98–102) point out an irregularity in the classical interpretation of melancholia; this irregularity occurs in the theory of temperaments.

In the strict *humoralist* tradition, temperaments are reduced to disturbances in the balance between the bodily fluids. These disturbances initially appear to fall within the normal range, like the usual variations of character dispositions. However, changes in interpretation over the centuries become obvious: only blood is now considered to be an integral part of the body, with the other three fluids regarded as degeneration products. The significance of these degeneration products (yellow bile, black bile, and phlegm) would, especially in the Middle Ages, take on a negative connotation, as a result of which they would be considered to be responsible for all kinds of character abnormalities and immoral behavior.

The *galenic* and *neogalenic* theories of temperament, on the other hand, were originally oriented toward the primary qualities (heat, cold, dryness, and wetness), and not so much toward the humors. The galenic temperaments are not, in fact, real temperaments, that is to say temperaments in a biological (humoral) sense, but rather, disturbances in the balance between the primary qualities. Health was considered by Galen to be an ideal state; every relative excess of a particular bodily fluid was, to his mind, a disturbance and, therefore, also a disease. Thus the galenic tradition had little influence on the development of a proper theory of temperament: it could not deal with normal variation of character dispositions.

Behind this irregularity in the theory of temperaments lies a difference of opinion about disease: the strict humoralistic tradition took a concrete and natural view of normality; whereas the galenic tradition established itself on more abstract ideas, such as the primary qualities.

2. In scholastic medicine, the emotions of anxiety and rage are diametrically opposed. In rage, heat is generated and floats to the periphery, the arms and legs display movement, the face becomes red, the pulse strengthens and the brain also comes to life again. In anxiety, the heat drains inward, peripheral parts become cold and pale, the pulse rate decreases, and the patient feels cold.

3. Plato distinguished four forms of godlike mania, namely, mania as the art of fortune telling (cf. the etymological relation between mania and *mantikè*, i.e., fortune telling); mania as ritual purification and consecration leading to the relief of disease and grief; mania in the sense of ecstasy inspired by the Muses; and finally mania in the sense of being emotionally moved by memories when looking at beautiful things.

4. Cf. Descartes, 1647, article 52: ". . . qui nous importent . . ."; and Guéroult, 1953, p. 253.

5. Kraepelin remained a dedicated experimental psychologist throughout his life. During his years in Heidelberg (1891–1903), the work that he carried out included experiments on the function of will (task performance, level of fatigue), cognitive capacities (distractibility, attention, memory, ideational association), and expressive functions (motor activity, handwriting, and language performance) (Kraepelin, 1983, p. 71). During his Münich years (1903–1922), much to his regret, he was no longer able to find the time for experimental psychology, although he did give refresher courses for colleagues (Kraepelin, 1983, pp. 144, 145, 149).

6. The distinction between objectless anxiety and object-linked fear which already had been formulated by the philosopher *Kierkegaard* (1844), was to be introduced by *Karl Jaspers* in 1946, in the fourth edition of his *Allgemeine Psychopathologie* [General Psychopathology]. In the ensuing years, it was developed as a theme in the anthropological school, which was oriented towards existential phenomenology.

REFERENCES

K. Abraham, Ansätze zur psychoanalytischen Erforschung und Behandlung des manisch–depressiven Irreseins und verwandter Zustände, *Zentralbl. Psychoanal.*, *2*: 302 (1912).

E. H. Ackerknecht, *A Short History of Medicine*, John Hopkins University Press, Baltimore (1955, revised edition 1968; reprint 1982).

H. S. Akiskal, and W.T. McKinney, Overview of recent research in depression. Integration of ten conceptual models into a comprehensive clinical frame, *Arch. Gen. Psychiatry, 32*: 285 (1975).

J. Angst, *Zur Ätiologie und Nosologie Endogener Depressiver Psychosen. Ein Genetische, Soziologische und Klinische Studie*, Monographien aus der Gesamtgebiete der Neurologie und Psychiatrie, Heft 112, Springer-Verlag, Berlin (1966).

American Psychiatric Association Committee on Nomenclature and Statistics, *Diagnostic and Statistical Manual of Mental Disorders*, 3rd ed., American Psychiatric Association, Washington, D.C. (1980).

American Psychiatric Association Committee on Nomenclature and Statistics, *Diagnostic and Statistical Manual of Mental Disorders*, 3rd ed., revised, American Psychiatric Association, Washington, D.C. (1987).

Aristoteles, Problemata, *The Complete Works of Aristotle* (J. Barnes, ed.), Princeton University Press, Princeton, p. 1319 (1984).

A. Ax, The physiological differentiation between fear and anger in humans, *Psychosom. Med., 15*: 433 (1953).

W. von Baeyer, and W. von Baeyer-Katte, *Angst,* Suhrkamp Verlag, Frankfurt (1971).

D. H. Barlow, *Anxiety and its Disorders. The Nature and Treatment of Anxiety and Panic,* Guilford Press, New York (1988).

G. M. Beard, *Sexual Neurasthenia* [nervous exhaustion]. *Its Hygiene, Causes, Symptoms, and Treatment* (A. D. Rockwell, ed.), E. B. Treat, New York (1884).

G. M. Beard, *A Practical Treatise on Nervous Exhaustion (Neurasthenia). Its Symptoms, Nature, Sequences, Treatment* (A. D. Rockwell, ed.), H. K. Lewis, London (1890).

A. T. Beck, *Cognitive Therapy and the Emotional Disorders*, New American Library, New York (1976).

A. T. Beck, G. Emery, R. L. Greenberg, *Anxiety Disorders and Phobias. A Cognitive Perspective*, Basic Books, New York (1985).

H. H. Beek, *Waanzin in de Middeleeuwen. Beeld van de Gestoorde en Bemoeienis met de Zieke*, Callenbach/De Toorts, Nijkerk/Haarlem (1969).

M. Benedikt, Über "Platzschwindel," *Allg. Wien. Med. Zeit., 15*: 488 (1870).

G. E. Berrios, Melancholia and depression during the 19th century: A conceptual history, *Br. J. Psychiatry, 153*: 298 (1988).

G. E. Berrios, Feelings of fatigue and psychopathology: A conceptual history, *Compr. Psychiatry, 31*: 140 (1990).

G. E. Berrios, and R. Hauser, The early development of. Kraepelin's ideas on classification, *Psychol. Med., 18*: 813 (1988).

W. Bitter, *Die Angstneurose. Entstehung und Heilung. Mit 2 Analysen nach Freud und Jung*, Hans Huber, Bern (1948).

R. K. Blashfield, Structural approaches to classification, *Contemporary Directions in Psychopathology. Toward the DSM-IV* (T. Millon and G. L. Klerman, eds.), Guilford Press, New York, p. 363 (1986).

E. Bleuler, *Lehrbuch der Psychiatrie*, Verlag von Julius Springer, Berlin (1916).

E. Bleuler, *Lehrbuch der Psychiatrie* (dreizehnte Auflage, neubearbeitet von Manfred Bleuler), Springer-Verlag, Berlin (1975).

K. Bonhoeffer, Die symptomatischer Psychosen im Gefolge von akuten Jufektionen und innere erkrankungen, Franz Deuticke, Leipzig und Wien (1910).

K. Bonhoeffer, Zur Frage der Schreckpsychosen, *Monatschr. Psychiatrie Neurol., 22*: 143 (1919).

J. Bowlby, *Attachment and Loss*, Vol. 1. *Attachment,* 2nd ed., Basic Books, New York (1969).

J. Bowlby, *Attachment and Loss*, Vol. 2. *Separation: Anxiety and Anger*, Penguin Books, London (1973).

J. Bowlby, *Attachment and Loss*, Vol. 3. *Loss: Sadness and Depression*, Penguin Books, London (1981).

R. Burton, *The Anatomy of Melancholy*, Vol. 1–3 (A. R. Shilleto, ed.), George Bell Sons, Lon-

don (1621; edition 1896).
K. Conrad, *Die Beginnende Schizophrenie*, Thieme, Stuttgart (1958).
W. Coryell, J. Endicott, N.C. Andreasen, M.B. Keller, P.J. Clayton, R.M.A. Hirschfeld, W.A. Scheftner, and G. Winokur, Depression and panic attacks: The significance of overlap as reflected in follow-up and family study data, *Am. J. Psychiatry, 145*: 293 (1988).
R. R. Crowe, R. Noyes, D.L. Pauls, and D. Slymen, A family study of panic disorder, *Arch. Gen. Psychiatry, 40*: 1065 (1983).
M. Culpin, The psychological aspect of the effort syndrome, *Lancet*, 2: 184 (1920).
J. M. Da Costa, On irritable heart; a clinical study of a form of functional cardiac disorder and its consequences, *Am. J. Med. Sci., 71*: 17 (1871).
R. Descartes, Les passions de l' âme, *Oeuvres de Descartes* (publiées par C. Adam and P. Tannery), Tome XI, L. Cerf, Paris, p. 327 (1649/1909).
I. E. Drabkin, Remarks on ancient psychopathology, *Isis, 46*: 223 (1955).
G. L. Dreyfus, *Die Melancholie, ein Zustandsbild des Manisch–Depressiven Irreseins. Ein Klinisch Studie* (mit einem Vorwort von Hofrat Prof. dr.'Emil Kraepelin), Verlag von Gustav Fischer, Jena (1907).
W. W. Eaton, and C. Ritter, Distinguishing anxiety and depression with field survey data, *Psychol. Med., 18*: 155 (1988).
P. Errera, Some historical aspects of the concept of phobia, *Psychiatric Q., 36*: 325 (1962).
J. E. D. Esquirol, *Des Maladies Mentales*, 2 vol., Baillière, Paris (1838).
J. P. Feighner, E. Robins, S. B. Guze, R. A. Woodruff, G. Winokur, and R. Munoz, Diagnostic criteria for use in psychiatric research, *Arch. Gen. Psychiatry, 26*: 57 (1972).
H. Flashar, *Melancholie und Melancholiker in den Medizinischen Theorien der Antike*, Walter de Gruyter and Co, Berlin (1966).
E. Forster, *Die Klinische Stellung der Angstpsychose*, S. Karger, Berlin (1910).
M. Foucault, *Madness and Civilization. A History of Insanity in the Age of Reason* (translation of *Histoire de la Folie à l'age Classique*), Random House, New York (1965/1973).
S. Freud, Draft E, *Standard Edition*, Vol. 1, p. 189 (1894).
S. Freud, Über die Berechtigung, von der Neurasthenie einen bestimmten Symptomen-komplex als 'Angstneurose' abzutrennen, *Gesammelte Werke*, Band I, p. 315 (1895a).
S. Freud, Obsessions et phobies, *Gesammelte Werke*, Band I, p. 343 (1895b).
S. Freud, Zur Kritik der Angstneurose, *Gesammelte Werke*, Band I, p. 355 (1895c).
S. Freud, Draft G, Melancholia, *Standard Edition*, Vol. 1, p. 200 (1895d).
S. Freud, Trauer und Melancholie, *Gesammelte Werke*, Band X, p. 427 (1917).
S. Freud, Hemmung, Symptom und Angst, *Gesammelte Werke*, Band XIV, p. 111 (1926),
S. Freud, Die Angst, *Gesammelte Werke*, Band XI, p. 407 (1917).
S. Freud, Neue Folge der Vorlesungen zur Einfürung in die Psychoanalyse, *Gesammelte Werke*, Band XV, p. 87 (1933).
Galenus, On the affected parts, *Galen on the Affected Parts*, translation from the Greek text with explanatory notes (R. E. Siegel, ed.), S. Karger, Basel (1976).
H. M. Gardiner, R.C. Metcalf, and J. Beebe-Center, *Feeling and Emotion. A History of Theories*, Greenwood Press, Westport (1937, repr. 1970).
G. Glas, *Concepten van Angst en Angststoornissen. Een Psychiatrische en Vakfilosofische Studie*, Swets & Zeitlinger, Amsterdam/Lisse (1991).
K. Goldstein, Zum Problem der Angst, *Allg. Ärztl. Z. Psychother. Psychische Hyg., 2*, 409 (1929).
J. K. Gorman, M.R. Liebowitz, A.J. Fyer, J. Stein, A neuroanatomical hypothesis for panic disorder, *Am. J. Psychiatry, 146*: 148 (1989).
M. Guéroult, *Descartes Selon L'Ordre des Raisons*. II. *L' âme et le Corps*, Aubier, Paris (1953).
H. Häfner, Angst, Furcht, *Historisches Wörterbuch der Philosophie*, Band I (J. Ritter ed.), Schwabe & Co., Basel, p. 310 (1971).
H. Hecht, D. von Zerssen, C. Krieg, J. Pössl, and H. U. Wittchen, Anxiety and depression: Comorbidity, psychopathology, and social functioning, *Compr. Psychiatry, 30*: 420 (1989).

E. Hecker, Ueber larvirte und abortive Angstzustände bei Neurasthenie, *Zentralbl. Nervenheilk.*, *16*: 565 (1893).
M. J. Heron, A note on the concept endogenous–exogenous, *Br. J. Med. Psychol.*, *38*: 241 (1965).
A. E. Hoche, Pathologie und Therapie der nervösen Angstzustände, *Dtsch. Z. Nervenheilk.*, *41*: 194 (1911).
A. Jablensky, Approaches to the definition and classification of anxiety and related disorders in European psychiatry, *Anxiety and the Anxiety Disorders* (A. H. Tuma and J. Maser, eds.), Lawrence Erlbaum Assoc., Hillsdale, N.J., p. 735 (1985).
S. W. Jackson, Melancholia and partial insanity, *J. Hist. Behav. Sci.*, *19*: 173 (1983).
S. W. Jackson, *Melancholia and Depression. From Hippocratic Times to Modern Times*, Yale University Press, New Haven (1986).
W. James, What is an emotion? *Mind*, *9*: 188 (1884).
W. James, *Principles of Psychology*, 2 vols., Dove, New York (1890).
W. James, *The Varieties of Religious Experience. A Study in Human Nature*, Longmans, Green Co. (1902; repr. by Penguin Books, 1982).
P. Janet, *Les Obsessions et la Psychasthénie*, Alcan, Paris (1903).
P. Janet, *De L'Angoisse à L'Extase*, Alcan, Paris (1926).
K. Jaspers, *Allgemeine Psychopathologie* (sechste unveränderte Auflage), Springer-Verlag, Berlin (1953).
M. Jones, Physiological and psychological responses to stress in neurotic patients, *J. of Ment. Sci.*, *94*: 392 (1948).
M. Jones, and A. Lewis, Effort syndrome, *Lancet*, *1*: 813 (1941).
R. E. Kendell, *The Classification of Depressive Illness*, Oxford University Press, London (1968).
R. E. Kendell, The classification of depressions: a review of contemporary confusion, *Br. J. Psychiatry*, *129*: 15 (1976).
S. Kierkegaard, *The Concept of Anxiety. A Simple Psychologically Orienting Deliberation on the Dogmatic Issue of Hereditary Sin* (Translation of Begrebet Angest, ed. and transl. by R. Thomte, in collaboration with A. B. Anderson), Princeton University Press, Princeton (1844/1980).
L. S. King, *The Philosophy of Medicine. The Early Eighteenth Century*, Harvard University Press, Cambridge, Mass. (1978).
D. F. Klein, Delineation of two drug-responsive anxiety syndromes, *Psychopharmacologia*, *5*: 397 (1964).
D. F. Klein, Endogenomorphic depression. Conceptual and terminological confusion, *Arch. Gen. Psychiatry*, *31*: 447 (1974).
D. F. Klein, Anxiety reconceptualized, *Compr. Psychiatry*, *21*: 411 (1980).
K. Kleist, Schreckpsychosen, *Allg. Z. Psychiatr.*, *75*: 432 (1918).
R. Klibansky, E. Panofsky, and F. Saxl, *Saturn and Melancholy. Studies in the History of Natural Philosophy, Religion and Art*, Thomas Nelson Sons, London (1964; Kraus Reprint, Nendeln/Liechtenstein, 1979).
S. Kornfeld, Zur Pathologie der Angst, *Jahrb. Psychiatr. Neurol.*, *22*: 411 (1902).
E. Kraepelin, *Psychiatrie. Ein Lehrbuch für Studirende und Aertzte* (sechste, vollständig umgearbeitete Auflage), Johann Ambrosius Barth, Leipzig (1899).
E. Kraepelin, *Einführung in die Psychiatrische Klinik. Zweiunddreissig Vorlesungen* (zweite, durchgearbeitete Ausgabe), Verlag von Johann Ambrosius Barth, Leipzig (1905).
E. Kraepelin, *Psychiatrie. Ein Lehrbuch für Studierende und Ärzte* (achte, volständig umgearbeitete Auflage), Verlag von Johann Ambrosius Barth, Leipzig (1913).
E. Kraepelin, *Lebenserinnerungen* (herausgegeben von H. Hippius, G. Peters, and D. Ploog), Springer-Verlag, Berlin (1983).
E. Kraepelin, and J. Lange, *Psychiatrie*. Band I (neunte Auflage), Johann Ambrosius Barth, Leipzig (1927).
A. Kronfeld, Über Angst, *Ned. Tijdschr. Psychol.*, *3*: 366 (1935).

J. F. Leckman, M. M. Weissman, K. R. Merikangas, D. L. Pauls, and B. A. Prusoff, Panic disorder and major depression. Increased risk of depression, alcoholism, panic, and phobic disorders in families of depressed probands with panic disorder, *Arch. Gen. Psychiatry, 40*: 1055 (1983).

W. Leibbrand, and A. Wettley, *Der Wahnsinn. Geschichte der abendländischen Psychopathologie*, Verlag Karl Alber, Freiburg/München (1961).

A. J. Lewis, Melancholia: A historical review, *J. Ment. Sci., 80*: 1 (1934a).

A. J. Lewis, Melancholia: A clinical survey of depressive states. *J. Ment. Sci., 80*: 277 (1934b). Reprinted in A. J. Lewis, *Inquiries in Psychiatry. Clinical and Social Investigations*, Routledge and Kegan Paul, London, p. 118 (1967).

A. J. Lewis, Melancholia: A prognostic study, *J. Ment. Sci., 82*: 488 (1936).

A. J. Lewis, States of depression: Clinical and aetiological differentiation, *Br. Med. J., 2*: 875 (1938).

A. Lewis, Problems presented by the ambigous word "anxiety" as used in psychopathology, *Isr. Ann. Psychiatry Relat. Discipl., 5*: 105 (1967).

A. Lewis, Endogenous and exogenous: A useful dichotomy? *Psychol. Med., 1*: 191 (1971).

T. Lewis, The tolerance of physical exertion, as shown by soldiers suffering from so-called "irritable heart," *Br. Med. J., 1*: 363 (1918).

T. Lewis, *Soldier's Heart and the Effort Syndrome*, 2nd ed., Shaw, London (1940).

E. Lindemann, Symptomatology and management of acute grief, *Am. J. Psychiatry, 101*: 141 (1944).

J. López Pineiro, *Historical Origins of the Concept of Neurosis* (transl. by D. Berrios), Cambridge University Press, Cambridge (1983).

J. MacKenzie, The soldier's heart. *Br. Med. J., 1*: 117 (1916).

J. MacKenzie, The soldier's heart and war neurosis: A study in symptomatology, *Br. Med. J., 1*: 491, 530 (1920).

M. B. MacMillan, Beard's concept of neurasthenia and Freud's concept of the actual neuroses, *J. Hist. Behav. Sci., 12*: 376 (1976).

I. M. Marks, *Fears, Phobias and Rituals: Panic, Anxiety, and Their Disorders*, Oxford University Press, New York (1987).

J. Mendels, and C. Cochrane, The nosology of depression: the endogenous-reactive concept, *Am. J. Psychiatry, 124* (May Suppl.): 1 (1968).

B. S. Oppenheimer, S. A. Levine, R. A. Morrison, M. A. Rothschild, W. St. Lawrence, and F. N. Wilson, Report on Neurocirculatory Asthenia and Its Management, *Military Surgeon, 42*: 409, 711 (1918).

H. Oppenheim, Zur Psychopathologie der Angstzustände, *Berl. Klin. Wochenschr., 46*: 1293 (1909).

F. Panse, *Angst und Schreck in Klinisch-Psychologischer und Sozialmedizinischer Sicht. Dargestellt an Hand von Erlebnisberichten aus dem Luftkrieg*, Georg Thieme Verlag, Stuttgart (1952).

E. S. Paykel, Classification of depressed patients: A cluster analysis derived grouping, *Br. J. Psychiatry, 118*: 275 (1971).

C. Perris, (ed.), A study of bipolar (manic–depressive) and unipolar recurrent depressive psychosis, *Acta Psychiatr. Scand., 42* (Suppl. 194) (1966).

P. Pinel, *Traité Médico-philosophique sur L'Aliénation Mentale*, Paris (1801).

Phaedrus, Plato, *The Collected Dialogues of Plato* (E. Hamilton and H. Cairns, eds.), Princeton University Press, Princeton, p. 475 (1961).

R. Porter, *A Social History of Madness. Stories of the Insane*, Weidenfeld and Nicolson, London (1987).

F. Riemann, *Grundformen der Angst und die Antinomien des Lebens*, Ernst Reinhardt Verlag, München/Basel (1961).

W. Riese, *La Théorie des Passions à la Lumière de la Pensée Médicale du XVIIe Siècle*, S. Karger, Basel (1965).

V. Rippere, Behavioral treatment of depression in historical perspective, *Contributions to Medi-*

cal Psychology, Vol. 2 (S. Rachman, ed.), Pergamon Press, Oxford, p. 31 (1980).
G. Roccatagliata, *A History of Ancient Psychiatry*, Greenwood Press, New York (1986).
A. O. Rorty, From passions to emotions and sentiments, *Philosophy, 57*: 157 (1982).
G. Rosen, *Madness in Society. Chapters in the Historical Sociology of Mental Illness*, Harper & Row, New York (1969).
C. E. Rosenberg, The place of George M. Beard in nineteenth century psychiatry, *Bull. Hist. Med., 36*: 245 (1962).
M. Roth, The phobic anxiety-depersonalization syndrome, *Proc. Roy. Soc. Med., 52*: 587 (1959).
G. H. E. Russelman, *Van James Watt Tot Sigmund Freud. De Opkomst van Het Stuwmodel van de Zelfexpressie*, Van Loghum Slaterus, Deventer (1983).
B. Rush, On the different species of phobia (1798), *Three Hundred Years of Psychiatry 1535–1860* (R. Hunter, and I. McAlpine, eds.), Oxford University Press, Oxford, pp. 669 (1963).
M. Scheler, *Der Formalismus in der Ethik und die Materiale Wertethik* II.V. *Materiale Wertethik und Eudaimonismus*, Halle (1913/1916).
M. Schmidt-Degenhard, Angst—problemgeschichtliche und klinische Aspekte, *Fortschr. Neurol. Psychiatr., 54*: 321 (1986).
P. Skerritt, Anxiety and the heart—a historical review, *Psychol. Med., 13*: 17 (1983).
G. Specht, Ueber Angstaffekt im manisch-depressiven Irresein, *Centralbl. Nervenheilk. Psychiatr., 30*: 529 (1907).
R. L. Spitzer, and J.B.W. Williams, Proposed revisions in the *DSM-III* classification of anxiety disorders based on research and clinical experience, *Anxiety and the Anxiety Disorders* (A.H. Tuma, and J. Maser, eds.), Lawrence Erlbaum Assoc., Hillsdale, N.J., p. 759 (1985).
R. L. Spitzer, J. Endicott, E. Robins, et al., Preliminary Report of the Reliability of Research Diagnostic Criteria Applied to Psychiatric Case Records, *Predictability in Psychopharmacology: Preclinical and Clinical Correlations* (A. Sudilovsky, S. Gershon, and B. Beer, eds.), Raven Press, New York (1975).
R. L. Spitzer, J. Endicott, and E. Robins, Research diagnostic criteria: Rationale and reliability, *Arch. Gen. Psychiatry*, 35: 773 (1978).
J. Starobinski, *Geschichte der Melancholiebehandlung von den Anfängen bis 1900*, Geigy, Basel (1960).
W. Stekel, *Nervöse Angstzustände und Ihre Behandlung*, Urban und Schwarzenberg, Wien (1932).
L. H. Sternbach, The benzodiazepine story, *Benzodiazepines. Today and Tomorrow* (R. G. Priest, H. Vianna Filho, R. Amrein and M. Skreta, eds.), MTP Press, Lancaster, p. 5 (1980).
G. E. Störring, *Zur Psychopathologie und Klinik der Angstzustände*, Abhandlungen aus der Neurologie, Psychiatrie, Psychologie und ihren Grenzgebieten. Beihefte zur Monatschrift für Psychiatrie und Neurologie, Heft 72, 50 Karger, Berlin (1934).
H. Tellenbach, *Melancholie. Problemgeschichte, Endogenität, Typologie, Pathogenese, Klinik* (dritte erweiterte Auflage), Springer-Verlag, Berlin (1976).
O. Temkin, *Galenism. Rise and Decline of a Medical Philosophy*, Cornell University Press, Ithaca (1973).
O. Temkin, Health and disease, *The Double Face of Janus and Other Essays in the History of Medicine*, Johns Hopkins University Press, Baltimore, p. 419 (1977).
C. Thompson, (ed.), *The Origins of Modern Psychiatry*, John Wiley & Sons, Chichester (1987).
A. H. Tuma, and J. Maser (eds.), *Anxiety and the Anxiety Disorders*, Lawrence Erlbaum Assoc., Hillsdale, N.J. (1985).
P. J. Tyrer, Classification in anxiety, *Br. J. Psychiatry, 144*: 78 (1984).
C. VanValkenburg, H. S. Akiskal, V. Puzantian, and T. Rosenthal, Anxious depressions. Clinical, family history, and naturalistic outcome—comparisons with panic and major depressive disorders, *J. Affective. Disord., 6*: 67 (1984).
M. Vollrath, and J. Angst, Outcome of panic and depression in a seven-year follow-up: Results of the Zürich study, *Acta Psychiatr. Scand., 80*: 591 (1989).
E. von Gebsattel, Freiherr von, Anthropologie der Angst, *Prolegomena Einer Medizinischen Anthropologie. Ausgewählte Aufsätze*, Springer-Verlag, Berlin, p. 378 (1954a).

E. von Gebsattel, Freiherr von, Zur Psychopathologie der Phobien. Die psychasthenische Phobie, *Prolegomena einer Medizinischen Anthropologie. Ausgewählte Aufsätze*, Springer-Verlag, Berlin, p. 42 (1954b).

E. von Gebsattel, Freiherr von, Die Welt des Zwangskranken, *Prolegomena einer Medizinischen Anthropologie. Ausgewählte Aufsätze*, Springer-Verlag, Berlin, p. 743 (1954a).

M. M. Weissman, J. F. Leckman, K. R. Merikangas, G. D. Gammon, and B. A. Prusoff, Depression and anxiety disorders in parents and children, *Arch. Gen. Psychiatry, 41*: 845 (1984).

C. Wernicke, Die Angstpsychose, *Allg. Z. Psychiatr., 51*: 1020 (1895).

S. Wessely, Old wine in new bottles: Neurasthenia and "ME," *Psychol. Med., 20*: 35 (1990).

C. Westphal, Die Agoraphobie, eine neuropathische Erscheinung, *Arch. Psychiatr. Nervenkrankh., 3*: 138 (1872).

P. White, Fatigue syndrome: Neurasthenia revived, *Br. Med. J., 298*: 1199 (1989).

E. E. Winters, (ed.), *The Collected Papers of Adolf Meyer*, Vol. 2, Johns Hopkins Press, Baltimore (1951).

J. Wolpe, *Psychotherapy by Reciprocal Inhibition*, Stanford University Press, Stanford (1958).

P. Wood, Da Costa's syndrome (or effort syndrome), *Br. Med. J., i,* 767, 805, 845 (1941).

G. Zilboorg, *A History of Medical Psychology*, Norton Company, New York (1941).

2

On the Comorbidity of Anxiety and Depression

Robert O. Pasnau and Alexander Bystritsky
UCLA School of Medicine, Los Angeles, California

I. INTRODUCTION

In this chapter, the authors describe the concept of *comorbidity* as contrasted with the concepts of *primary* and *secondary* as applied to psychiatric illness. Although the idea of comorbidity has valuable clinical relevance, and the concepts of primary and secondary are more difficult to define when dealing with comorbid conditions, both sets of concepts may lead to more precise treatment approaches. Studies of patients suffering from panic disorder with comorbid depression reveal marked deterioration in physical health, social condition, and overall level of psychosocial adjustment. Patients with primary depression complicated by anxiety pose more difficulties in treating both sets of symptoms. Patients with primary anxiety with secondary depression pose not only greater risk from suicide, but they also are more refractory to treatment. The authors also review the literature on the several types of mixed anxiety and depressive states, including panic disorder, obsessive–compulsive disorder, and generalized anxiety disorder with major depression.

II. THE CONCEPT OF COMORBIDITY

Dictionary definitions of *morbidity* refer to "the relative incidence of disease" which, according to Winokur, is not terribly useful in studying psychiatric syndromes. He writes: "It is entirely possible that the word comorbidity, as it is widely used in psychiatry, is in fact describing multiformity of a disease or the existence of two syndromes in the same individual, which is an aspect of multiformity" (Winokur, 1990).

Feinstein has also written extensively about the use of comorbidity in explaining complex clinical presentations. He defines *comorbidity* as a term that refers "to any distinct additional clinical entity that has existed or that may occur during the clinical course of a patient who has the index disease under study" (Feinstein, 1970). According to Winokur, this expands the concept of comorbidity to *cosyndromal,* a term that in our view is probably more useful.

Some rating scales and diagnostic instruments use the temporal criterion for determining which is primary and which is secondary by attempting to determine which condition came first. (By using the Research Diagnostic Criteria (RDC), for example, the interviewer is permitted to decide whether the depression was preceded by another disorder. This can lead to a fair degree of unreliability. On the other hand, patients' memories are also very uncertain guides to precise relationships. Family members' verifications are usually not sought. Winokur suggests that instead of relying on temporal sequences, we should add the concepts of "chronic" versus "acute" course.

> Let us assume that we are studying one illness that is generally chronic, anxiety disorder, and another illness that is generally episodic, unipolar depression. The following set of rules might be used. These have never been tested, but it would be interesting to see if they presented some possibility for better precision.
>
> 1. If anxiety disorder is first and depression is second in onset, then the depression is secondary. This implies a clear and unequivocal estimation.
> 2. If depression is first and separated from anxiety by 2 years, the depression is primary.
> 3. If depression and anxiety disorder first occur within 2 years of each other, the chronic illness takes precedence so anxiety is primary and the depression is secondary. (We invoked chronicity as an alternative because the temporal relationship is unclear.)
> 4. If anxiety disorder is first and remits, which occurs occasionally, and depression supervenes after no less than 2 years of a lack of anxiety symptoms, the depression is primary. This is an unusual but possible occurrence. (Winokur, 1990)

For most clinical psychiatrists, this discussion may seem to have only minor importance. Yet, it is the study of comorbidity, which is greater than chance would predict, that demonstrates the importance of secondary or primary. For example, the lifetime prevalence for a major depressive episode is 6%, and the lifetime prevalence for panic attack is 10%. If the coexistence of panic and depressive episodes were purely coincidental, the comorbidity should be about 10% of the individuals with major depression or 6% of the individuals with panic episodes. In fact, the comorbidity is between 40 and 65 (Regier et al., 1988).

This leads to three possible conclusions:

1. A unitary theory holding that depression and anxiety are variants of the same disorder.
2. A pluralistic model that depression and anxiety are distinct disorders.
3. A third model that anxiety–depression (comorbid depression and anxiety) is a separate entity.

It is possible that any of the three may be valid in any individual patient. It is the responsibility of the clinician to identify these interrelations and to formulate a treatment strategy based on some underlying assumptions about them. Most experts subscribe to the pluralistic model, but the research is not at all clear, as we will describe later.

III. PREVALENCE OF DEPRESSIVE AND ANXIETY DISORDERS

The current prevalence of depressive and anxiety disorders is found in Table 1. It reveals that the current prevalence for any affective disorder is 5.1%; the current prevalence for any anxiety disorder is 7.3% (Regier et al., 1988).

Table 1 Current Prevalence[a]

Depressive disorders	%	Anxiety disorders	%
Major depressive episode	2.2	Panic disorder	0.5
Bipolar	0.4	Phobias	6.2
Dysthymia[b]	3.3	Any anxiety disorder	7.3
Any affective disorder	5.1		

[a] Current state comorbidity of anxiety and depression across all studies is 25–40%.
[b] 25% had double depression within the past 6 months; 50% have a lifetime diagnosis of double depression.
Source: Regier et al., 1988.

The lifetime prevalence of depressive and anxiety disorders is shown in Table 2. It shows that the lifetime prevalence for any affective disorder is 8%; the lifetime prevalence for any anxiety disorder is 15% (Regier et al., 1988).

IV. THE PROBLEM OF SYMPTOM OVERLAP

One of the major problems in discussing comorbidity of anxiety and depression is the problem of overlapping symptoms in the two conditions. This becomes very important when studying the treatment outcomes of various modalities on the target symptoms of anxiety and depression. For instance, some of the depression scales that are used to measure degree of depression contain many anxiety items. Failure to correct for this could lead to the conclusion that antianxiety medications were useful in treating depression as well, even if this were not true.

Table 3 illustrates the common more or less specific symptoms and the overlapping ones in anxiety and depression.

A more useful approach is to focus on the symptoms that distinguish anxiety from depression. Diurnal variation of mood, early-morning awakening, psychomotor retardation, and delusions are rarely encountered in any of the anxiety disorders. On the other hand, severe agoraphobia, depersonalization, derealization, and perceptual distortions are

Table 2 Lifetime Prevalence[a]

Depressive disorders	%	Anxiety disorders	%
Major depressive episode		Panic disorder	2
Any episode	6	Panic symptoms	10
Unipolar only	5	Phobias	13
Bipolar	1	Any anxiety disorder	15
Dysthymia[b]	3		
Without major depression	2		
Any affective disorder	8		

[a] Current state comorbidity of anxiety and depression across all studies is 25–40%.
[b] 25% had double depression within the past 6 months; 50% have a lifetime diagnosis of double depression.
Source: Regier et al., 1988.

Table 3 Symptom Overlap of Anxiety and Depression

Depression	Symptom overlap	Anxiety
Depressed mood	Sleep disturbance	Trembling
Depressed interest	Psychomotor agitation	Muscle tension
Psychomotor retardation	Fatigue	Dyspnea
Appetite disturbance	Worry/guilt	Sweating
Helplessness	Concentration difficulty	Dry mouth
Hopelessness	Suicidal ideation	Nausea

very characteristic symptoms in anxiety disorder patients, rarely seen in depressives. With this in mind, it is clinically relevant to consider the symptoms usually associated with mental exhaustion as *depressive*, and to consider the symptoms usually associated with mental excitation as *anxious*.

V. COMORBID ANXIETY AND DEPRESSIVE COMBINATIONS

Several types of mixed anxiety-depressive states frequently coexist and have been described in the literature. They include panic disorder and primary and secondary major depression, obsessive compulsive disorder and major depression, and generalized anxiety disorder and major depression.

A. Panic Disorder (with or Without Agoraphobia) and Major Depression

Early descriptive and psychometric studies pointed out that panic attacks are frequent symptoms in depressed patients (Gurney et al., 1972; Derogatis et al., 1972) Paradoxically, these studies also showed that the presence of panic attacks is a major differentiating factor between anxious and depressive patients.

In a study of 63 patients with panic disorder, researchers found that 63% experienced at least one episode of major depression at some time during the course of their illness. This finding serves as a reminder that depressive illness occurs in most patients with panic disorder. Patients with longer duration of illness, early onset depression, melancholic depression, or family histories of anxiety or depression had an increased likelihood of having experienced recurrent depression. Patients with recurrent depression scored approximately twice as high on two independent measures of social anxiety and avoidance. Those patients diagnosed with comorbid social phobia had a statistically significant increase in longitudinal likelihood of major depression compared with patients without this comorbid diagnosis. This suggests either that social anxiety and avoidance predispose to recurrent depression or, alternatively, that these represent the outcome of recurrent depressive episodes or longer duration of panic disorder. Not surprisingly, recurrent depression was associated with a longer duration of illness and an earlier age of onset of the first depressive episode. The authors speculated that the increased risk for suicidal ideation and attempts seen in patients with early-onset panic disorder may be mediated through an increased likelihood of recurrent or early-onset depression. This hypothesis remains to be tested in future studies (Stein et al., 1990).

A study of the comorbidity of depression, agoraphobia, and panic disorder refutes the view that panic disorder is an integral component of agoraphobia. Rather, the findings indicate that panic disorder is more closely associated with depression. These findings were based on an analysis of the comorbidity of these three disorders in a random sample of 3258 individuals from the general population. With use of the Diagnostic Interview Schedule, researchers identified 416 persons (12.8%) with one or more of the three disorders. The relation between depression, agoraphobia, and panic disorder seemed to account for the high comorbidity of agoraphobia and panic. Overall, first symptoms for agoraphobia appeared at a much earlier age (early teens) than first symptoms for either major depression or panic disorder (both at approximately age 20). These results do not support the view that depression is a precursor to anxiety disorders. The association between panic disorder and agoraphobia is relatively weak compared with the association between panic disorder and depression. In no case did agoraphobia and panic disorder occur without the presence of minor depression. These findings also show that patients with anxiety disorders are much more likely to seek treatment if they are also suffering from depression (Thompson et al., 1989).

The interpretation of the foregoing study should be viewed with caution because of the retrospective nature of the diagnostic instrument. As noted by Winokur, people forget or selectively recall recent life experiences. However, this study casts serious doubt on the view that panic disorder is an essential component of, and leads to, agoraphobia. There may be several other pathways to agoraphobia other than as the avoidance of panic. This, together with the finding that panic disorder and depression are highly related, indicates that further research on the relationship of all these disorders is preferable to studying two and excluding the third.

Patients with comorbid panic and depression present very special challenges to the clinician. These individuals suffer more, are more difficult to treat, and have poorer treatment outcomes than either noncomorbid group. These findings are the preliminary results from the Harvard Anxiety–Panic Disorder Research Project (HARP). This study is a prospective, naturalistic study of 800 individuals with a current or past history of panic disorder interviewed at 6-month intervals for 2 1/2 years. Of the 182 comorbid patients, 89 (49%) had primary depression, 58 (32%) had primary panic disorder, and 35 (19%) developed both disorders within 3 months of each other.

The findings revealed that panic patients with comorbid major depression, as compared with panic patients without major depression,

1. Attained a lower level of education
2. Were more likely to have one or more other comorbid anxiety disorders
3. Were more likely to still be suffering from anxiety symptoms
4. Were more likely to have been hospitalized
5. Were more likely to have made a suicide attempt or gesture
6. Had poorer emotional health overall
7. Had poorer physical health overall
8. Were more likely to miss time at work
9. Had a less active social life
10. Had poorer functioning on all domains of social functioning and the Global Assessment Scale

These findings are supportive of the clinical observations that whether or not this group is suffering from a separate disorder, there is no doubt that they represent a very special subset of anxiety disorder patients and pose difficulties in designing treatment strategies to alleviate their suffering (Keller, 1991).

Studies with similar findings have been reported in a 7-year follow-up study done in Zurich. Patients suffering from both panic and depression were more severely ill than those with panic or depression only. Patients with both panic and depression shared higher treatment rates and lifetime suicide attempts. The investigation covered an initial patient diagnosis in 1979, with two follow-up diagnoses in 1981 and 1986. The follow-up diagnoses included pure panic, pure depression, and comorbid conditions. Data from all three interviews showed a clear preponderance of comorbid cases. Longitudinal analysis found a greater severity in the nixed panic and depression group than in the panic or depression groups. This severity was shown in elevated treatment rates. Patients with comorbidity sought treatment twice as often as those with depression or panic alone. Nearly one-third reported at least one suicide attempt. These results support Keller's view that panic disorder without depression and panic disorder with depression differ considerably in the severity of subjective suffering (Vollrath and Angst, 1989).

Studies on lifetime occurrence of panic attacks and major depression confirm concomitant occurrence of panic and major depression. Furthermore, longitudinal studies of agoraphobia and panic attacks have revealed that 41–91% of panic and agoraphobia patients had previous or concomitant diagnosis of major depression (Cloninger et al., 1981; Munjack and Moss, 1981; Breier et al., 1984; Bowen and Kohout, 1979). Our own studies support these findings (Fogelson et al., 1988). These studies permit us to conclude that approximately 65–75% of panic patients have experienced past or present episodes of major depression.

Many family studies (Munjack and Moss, 1981; Bowen and Kohout, 1979; Leckman et al., 1983; Crowe et al., 1980, 1983; Harris et al., 1983), have shown a familiar relation between panic and depression. Munjack and Moss and Leckman et al. found that patients with both of these disorders have first-degree relatives at a markedly increased risk of major depression, panic disorder, phobia, and alcoholism. From genetic and family data, some scientists propose that anxiety and depression share diatheses (Mountjoy and Roth, 1982; Hoehn-Saric, 1982). However, Dealy et al. (1981) and the reports of Crowe's group noted earlier, contradict this hypothesis.

Nonetheless, family studies have thrown some light on the significance of overlap symptoms. Patients with panic attacks that occur within depressive episodes suffer from more severe depressive symptoms and are more likely to have an endogenous or agitated depression than depressed patients without panic attacks. Results from a 2-year follow-up family study of 469 patients from the Collaborative Program on the Psychobiology of Depression indicated that depressed patients with panic attacks also were less likely to recover during the follow-up period than those depressed patients without panic attacks. Depressed patients with panic experienced significantly higher levels of depressive symptoms during the final 6 months of the 2-year follow-up and were more likely to show inpairment in each of the psychosocial areas of functioning than were the depressed patients without panic. These variables included an impaired relation with spouse, an impaired relation with friends, and an overall psychosocial impairment. Patients with panic disorder and secondary depression, who made up the third comparison group, had the worst outcome in these areas. When panic attacks occurred only within depressive episodes, they were not associated with significant increases in familial loading for anxiety disorders, primary depression, or mania. However, in the patients with panic disorder, familial loading was significantly lower for primary affective disorder and substantially higher for the major anxiety disorders. Overall, the family data supported the hypothesis that a patient presenting with a panic attack and depression probably has one of two separate disorders. Panic attacks may mark a severe and genetically significant form of depression (Coryell et al., 1988).

Numerous biological studies have attempted to distinguish panic disorder, agoraphobia, and major depression. However, such endeavors have been very difficult. Patients with both conditions exhibit noradrenergic hyperactivity (Easton and Sherman, 1976; Charney et al., 1981, 1984; Lake et al., 1982; Esler et al., 1982). Furthermore, the serotonergic system seems to play a major role in both panic disorder (Kahn et al., 1988; Charney and Heninger, 1986a,b) and depression (Cohn and Wilcox, 1985; Feighner et al., 1986). Both conditions demonstrate abnormal thyroid-stimulating hormone responses to thyrotropic-releasing hormones (Loosen and Prange, 1982; Roy-Byrne et al., 1986a), blunted growth hormone response to clonidine, and blunted adrenocorticotropic hormone responses to corticotropin-releasing factor (Siever and Uhde, 1984; Charney and Heninger, 1986a,b; Von Bardeleben and Holsboer, 1988; Roy-Byrne et al., 1986b; Gold et al., 1986). At the same time, the dexamethasone suppression test (DST) does not seem to be promising in differentiating these states (Coryell et al., 1989). The several abnormalities found in major depressive patients, but not in panic disorder patients, include increased imipramine binding, decreased rapid eye movement (REM) latency, and positive response to sleep deprivation (Heninger et al., 1988; Dube et al., 1983; Uhde et al., 1986). Some of these findings, however, have already been questioned (Fogelson et al., 1988; Stavraki and Bargo, 1986). Studies on the provocation of panic using yohimbine or sodium lactate have thus far failed to differentiate between panic disorder and depression (Liebowitz et al., 1985; McGrath et al., 1985). However, some of these studies produced limited success in separation of these two disorders. (Buller et al., 1989)

Treatment strategies also fail to differentiate between panic and depression. Both conditions seem to be responsive to cognitive behavioral strategies (Beck and Emery, 1984). However, the emphasis of this treatment is different with the inclusion of more relaxation and with introceptive exposure techniques in the treatment of panic patients (Barlow and Craske, 1989). Pharmacological treatment has been marginally helpful in distinguishing between these conditions. Tricyclic antidepressants, monamine oxidase inhibitors, fluoxetine, and some benzodiazepines appear to be effective in both conditions (Coplan and Gorman, 1990). However, benzodiazepines appear to be very weak antidepressants (Lesser et al., 1988). At the same time, some recent studies indicate that at least some patients with panic disorder may require milder doses of antidepressants (Fogelson et al., 1988; Bystritsky et al., 1991).

Some of the treatment questions can be answered by attempting to separate primary depression with secondary panic, and primary panic disorder with secondary depression. It does appear to be clinically useful to make this distinction. Studies show that approximately one-third of patients with panic disorder develop a secondary major depression, approximately one-third of patients with panic disorder have had a previous major depression or a concomitant one, approximately one-third of patients with primary major depression develop panic attacks, and approximately one-half of patients with atypical depression develop panic attacks (Lesser et al., 1988).

There is only one study of a group of patients with primary major depression and secondary panic disorder. The findings were that, after 6 weeks of treatment, patients with panic attacks had a better global response to phenelzine than to amitriptyline. The researchers also reported that the panic attacks and anxiety symptoms responded better to phenelzine, but the depression responded equally to amitriptyline (Lesser, 1991).

In one controlled study of atypical major depression, patients with panic attacks ($N = 60$) responded better than those without panic attacks ($N = 59$) to both imipramine and phenelzine compared with placebo. They also found a trend for superiority of phenelzine over imipramine in both groups (Liebowitz et al., 1988). However, a study reported 2 years later failed to replicate the previous finding that the presence of panic attacks is associated with a better response to medications. They did find that phenelzine was superior to imipramine, independent of the presence of panic attacks (Lesser, 1991).

A great deal more has been learned about secondary depression in panic disorder patients. As noted earlier, most studies suggest that when there is secondary major depression, the panic disorder symptoms are more severe and the outcome is less favorable, compared with panic disorder without depression. Several studies suggest that secondary depression and agoraphobia independently contribute to the severity of the panic disorder. The findings from the Cross-National Collaborative Panic study, a multiple medication, double-blind study reveal that in primary panic disorder with severe secondary depression, antidepressants are preferable to benzodiazepines. However, in most panic disorder patients with secondary depression, antidepressants and benzodiazepines are equally effective. Alprazolan was shown to have a more rapid onset of action (Lesser et al., 1988).

B. Obsessive–Compulsive Disorder and Depression

The interrelationship between obsessive compulsive disorder (OCD) and major depression is much less analyzed. Several studies have revealed that approximately one-third of OCD patients also have major depression (Karno et al., 1988). At the same time, other descriptive studies report that up to 80% of OCD patients have depressive symptoms (Rassmussen and Tsuang, 1986). Research on lifetime occurrence of depression and OCD are practically nonexistent. In our clinic, we frequently observe depression occurring prior, concurrently, and after the first onset of OCD. Thus, we suggest that the temporary interaction between these disorders may be somewhat similar to that of panic disorder.

Currently there have been no biological studies attempting to differentiate between OCD and major depression. Contemporary treatment approaches to OCD emphasizes serotonergic medications, such as clomipramine, fluoxetine, fluvoxamine, and sertraline (Greist, 1990). All of these medications are potent antidepressants. The relation between antidepressive and antiobsessional effects of these drugs needs further clarification (Marks et al., 1988). Our own studies suggest that when mixed conditions of OCD and major depression occur, it presents a more severe illness that is more difficult to treat (Fogelson et al., 1988).

C. Generalized Anxiety and Depression

Approximately 80% of generalized anxiety disorder (GAD) patients report depressive symptoms (Dubovsky, 1990). Current studies give little support for the existence of separate diagnosis of GAD (Mullaney, 1984). Generalized anxiety disorder often combines either with depression or with other anxiety disorders such as panic disorder or OCD. It may occur either as a prodrome or as a sequela of these conditions. Descriptive studies and family studies do not provide consistent, strong separation for anxiety and depressive symptoms. Most of our depression scales include an exorbitant number of questions addressing anxiety (Lesser et al., 1988). Mullaney et al. (1984) have also shown that symptoms usually attributed to generalized anxiety could not be used to differentiate between anxiety and depression. As we noted earlier, we have found it useful in our clinic to base our selection of psychopharmacological treatment on either the presence of the symptoms of mental exhaustion and use antidepressants, or the symptoms of mental excitation and use antianxiety agents, or if both sets of symptoms are present, use both.

Treatments have also failed to differentiate between GAD and depression. Previously, it was commonly held that patients with depression responded more favorably to antidepressants and those with GAD responded better to benzodiazepines. Current studies support effectiveness of tricyclics in GAD (Liebowitz et al., 1988) and benzodiazepines in depression (Lesser et al., 1984; Tiller et al., 1989). Monoamine oxidase inhibitors are helpful in the treatment of so-called atypical or anxious depression (Liebowitz et al., 1984). Recently introduced buspirone has a neurochemical action relatively similar to other serotonergic antidepressants and may act as an effective antidepressant (Rickels, 1990).

VI. IN CONCLUSION: THE HIGH MORBIDITY OF COMORBIDITY

In summary, the authors of this chapter have attempted to demonstrate that the contemporary scientific literature is largely confusing and incomplete in terms of separating anxiety and depressive conditions. It suggests a large overlap between obsessive–compulsive disorder, panic disorder, generalized anxiety disorder, agoraphobia, and depression.

The conclusions from the treatment outcome studies reveal that panic disorder and major depression show considerable comorbidity, regardless of which disorder is primary. No studies have compared treatment results between antidepressants and benzodiazepines in patients with primary depression and secondary panic disorder. No controlled studies were found to assess the combination of antidepressants and benzodiazepines in treating comorbid conditions, even though case reports indicate that this may be useful and is safe. There is a lack of studies using cognitive, behavioral, or interpersonal psychotherapies alone or in combination with medications to assess their value in comorbid conditions. Case reports, anecdotal evidence, and naturalistic studies all suggest that antidepressants are the treatment of choice for patients who have primary depression and secondary panic. When atypical major depression presents with panic choice. The literature suggests the possibility of common biological pathways that result in unspecific, even though effective, biological and psychological treatment.

Perhaps the most important finding of the many studies reviewed in this chapter is that patients who have both anxiety and depression tend to be sicker, more disabled, more chronic, more unhappy, and much more difficult to treat.

REFERENCES

D. H. Barlow, and M. G. Craske, *Mastery of Your Anxiety and Panic*, Graywind Publications, Albany New York (1989).

A. T. Beck, and G. Emery, *Anxiety and Phobias: A Cognitive Approach*, Basic Books, New York (1984).

R. C. Bowen, and J. Kohout, The relationship between agoraphobia and primary affective disorders, *Can. J. Psychiatry, 24*:317 (1979).

A. Breier, D. S. Charney, and G. R. Heninger, Major depression in patients with agoraphobia and panic disorder, *Arch. Gen. Psychiatry, 41*:1129 (1984).

R. Buller, U. Von Bardeleben, W. Maier, et al., Specificity of lactate response in panic disorder, panic with concurrent depression and major depression, *J. Affective Disord., 16*:109 (1989).

A. Bystritsky, A. Ackerman, and R. O. Pasnau, Low dose desipramine treatment of cocaine-related panic attacks, *J. Nerv. Ment. Dis. 179*: 755 (1991).

D. S. Charney, D. B. Menkes, and G. R. Heninger, Receptor sensitivity and the mechanism of action of antidepressant treatment: Implications for the etiology and therapy of depression, *Arch. Gen. Psychiatry, 38*:1160 (1981).

D. S. Charney, G. R. Heninger, and A. Breiser, Noradrenergic function and panic anxiety effects of yohimbine in healthy subjects and patients with agoraphobia and panic disorder, *Arch. Gen. Psychiatry, 41*:751 (1984).

D. S. Charney, and G. R. Heninger, Abnormal regulation for noradrenergic function in panic disorders, *Arch. Gen. Psychiatry, 43*:1042 (1986a).

D. S. Charney, and G. R. Heninger, Serotonergic function in panic disorders, *Arch. Gen. Psychiatry, 43*:1059 (1986b).

C. R. Cloninger, R. L. Martin, P. Clayton, et al., A blind follow-up and family study of anxiety neurosis: Preliminary analysis of the St Louis 500, *Anxiety: New Research and Chancing Concepts* (D. F. Klein, J. Rabkin ed.), Raven Press, New York (1981).

J. B. Cohn, and C. Wilcox, A comparison of fluoxetine, imipramine and placebo in patients with major depressive disorder, *J. Clin. Psychiatry, 46*(sec 2):26 (1985).

J. D. Coplan, and J. M. Gorman, Treatment of anxiety disorder in patients with mood disorders, *J. Clin. Psychiatry, 51*(suppl):9 (1990).

W. Coryell, J. Endicott, N. C. Andreason, et al., Depression and panic attacks: The significance of overlap as reflected in follow-up and family studies data, *Am. J. Psychiatry, 145*:293 (1988).

W. Coryell, R. Noyes, and J. Schlechte, The significance of HPA axis disturbance in panic disorder, *Biol. Psychiatry, 25*: 989 (1989).

R. R. Crowe, D. L. Pauls, D. J. Slymen, et al., A family study of anxiety neurosis: Morbidity in families of patients with and without mitral valve prolapse, *Arch. Gen. Psychiatry, 37*:77 (1980).

R. R. Crowe, R. Noyes, D. L. Pauls, et al., A family study of panic disorder, *Arch. Gen. Psychiatry, 40*:1065 (1983).

R. S. Dealy, D. M. Ishiki, D. H. Avery, et al., Secondary depression in anxiety disorders, *Compr. Psychiatry, 22*:612 (1981).

L. R. Derogatis, R. S. Lipman, L. Cove, et al., Factorial invariance of symptom dimensions in anxious and depressive neuroses, *Arch. Gen. Psychiatry, 27*:659 (1972).

S. Dube, N. Jumar, E. Ettedgui, et al., Cholinergic REM induction response separation of anxiety and depression, *Biol. Psychiatry, 20*:408 (1983).

S. L. Dubovsky, Generalized anxiety disorder: New concepts and psychopharmacologic therapies, *J. Clin. Psychiatry*, 51(suppl)9:3 (1990).

J. D. Easton, and D. G. Sherman, Somatic anxiety attacks and propranolol, *Arch. Neurol., 33*:689 (1976).

M. Esler, J. Turbott, R. Schwarrta, et al., The peripheral functions of norepinephrine in depressive illness, *Arch. Gen. Psychiatry*, 39:295 (1982).

J. Feighner, C. Hendrickson, L. Miller, et al., Double-blind comparison of doxepin versus bupropion in outpatients with a major depressive disorder, *J. Clin. Psychopharmacol. 6*:27 (1986).

A. Feinstein, The pre-therapeutic classification of comorbidity in chronic disease, *J. Chronic Dis. 23*:455 (1970).

D. L. Fogelson, A. Bystritsky, and N. Sussman, Interrelationships between major depression and the anxiety disorders: Clinical relevance, *Psychiatr. Ann., 18*:158 (1988).

P. W. Gold, D. L. Loriaux, and A. Roy, Responses to corticotropin-releasing hormone in the hypercortisolisn of depression and Cushing's disease: Pathophysiologic and diagnostic implications, *N. Engl. J. Med., 314*:1329 (1986).

J. H. Greist, Treatment of obsessive compulsive disorder: Psychotherapies, drugs, and other somatic treatment, *J. Clin. Psychiatry*, 51(suppl8):44 (1990).

C. Gurney, M. Roth, R. F. Garside, et al., Studies in the classification of affective disorders: The relationship between anxiety states and depressive illness, *Br. J. Psychiatry*, 121:162 (1972).

E. L. Harris, R. Noyes, R. R. Crowe, et al., Family study of agoraphobia, *Arch. Gen. Psychiatry, 40*:1061 (1983).

G. R. Heninger, D. S. Charney, L. H. Price, L.H., α^2-Adrenergic receptor sensitivity in depression: The plasma MHPG, behavioral and cardiovascular responses to yohimbine, *Arch. Gen. Psychiatry, 45*: 718 (1988).

R. Hoehn-Saric, Comparison of generalized anxiety disorder with panic disorder patients, *Psychopharmacol. Bull., 18:104* (1982).

R. S. Kahn, H. M. Van Praag, S. Wetzler, et al., Serotonin and anxiety revisited, *Biol. Psychiatry, 23*:189 (1988).

M. Karno, J. M. Golding, S. B. Sorenson, and H. A. Burnam, The epidemiology of obsessive–compulsive disorder in five U.S. communities. *Arch. Gen. Psychiatry, 45*:1094 (1988).

M. B. Keller, "The Comorbidity Factor;" Presented at the 1991 Annual Meeting of the American Psychiatric Association, New Orleans, May 12 (1991).

C. R. Lake, D. Pickar, M. Ziegler, et al., High plasma norepinephrine levels in patients with major affective disorder, *Am. J. Psychiatry, 139:1315* (1982).

J. F. Leckman, M. M. Weissman, K. R. Merikangas, et al., Panic disorder increases risk of major depression, alcoholism, panic and phobic disorders in affectively ill families, *Arch. Gen. Psychiatry*, 40:1055 (1983).

I. M. Lesser, R. T. Rubin, J. C. Pecknold, et al., Secondary depression in panic disorder and agoraphobia. I: Frequency, severity and response to treatment, *Arch. Gen. Psychiatry, 45*:427 (1988).

I. M. Lesser, "Panic Disorder and Depression: Treatment Strategies." Presented at the 1991 Annual Meeting of the American Psychiatric Association, New Orleans, May 12, (1991)

M. R. Liebowitz, F. M. Quitkin, J. W. Stewart, et al., Phenelzine vs imipramine in atypical depression, *Arch. Gen. Psychiatry*, 41:669 (1984).

H. R. Liebowitz, J. M. Gorman, A. J. Fyer, et al., Lactate provocation of panic attacks, *Arch. Gen. Psychiatry, 42*:709 (1985).

M. R. Liebowitz, A. J. Fyer, J. M. Gorman, et al., Tricyclic therapy of the *DSM-III* anxiety disorders: A review with implications for further research, *J. Psychiatr. Res.*, 22 (suppl.1):7 (1988).

P. T. Loosen, and A. J. Prange, Serum thyrotropin response to thyrotropin-releasing hormone in psychiatric patients: A review, *Am. J. Psychiatry*, 139:405 (1982).

I. M. Marks, M. Basoglu, J. Lelliott, et al., Clomipramine self-exposure and therapist-aided exposure in obsessive–compulsive ritualizers, *Br. J. Psychiatry, 152*:522 (1988).

P. J. McGrath, J. W. Stewart, W. M. Harrison, et al., Lactate infusion in patients with depression and anxiety, *Psychopharmacol. Bull., 21*:555 (1985).

C. O. Mountjoy, and M. Roth, Studies in the relationship between depressive disorders and anxiety states, *J. Affective Disord., 4*:149 (1982).

I. A. Mullaney, The relationship between anxiety and depression: A review of some principal component analytic studies, *J. Affective Disord. 7:139* (1984).

D. J. Munjack and H. B. Moss, Affective disorder and alcoholism in families of agoraphobics, *Arch. Gen. Psychiatry, 38*:869 (1981).

S. A. Rassmussen, and M. T. Tsuang, Clinical characteristics and family history, *DSM-III Obsessive Compulsive Dis., 3*:317 (1986).

D. A. Regier, J. H. Boyd, J. D. Burke, et al, One-month prevalence of mental disorders in the United States, *Arch. Gen. Psychiatry, 45*:977 (1988).

K. Rickels, Buspirone in clinical practice, *J. Clin. Psychiatry*, 51(suppl9): 51 (1990).

P. P. Roy-Byrne, T. W. Uhde, D. R. Rubinow, et al., Reduced TRH and prolactin responses to TRH in panic disorder, *Am. J. Psychiatry, 143*:503 (1986a).

P. P. Roy-Byrne, T. W. Uhde, R. M. Post, et al., The corticotropin-releasing hormone stimulation test in patients with panic disorder, *Am. J. Psychiatry, 143*:896 (1986b).

S. J. Siever, and T. W. Uhde, New studies and perspectives on the noradrenergic receptor system in depression: Effects of the alpha-2 adrenergic agonist clonidine, *Biol. Psychiatry, 19*:131 (1984).

C. Stavraki, and B. Bargo, The relationship of anxiety and depression: A review of the literature, *Br. J. Psychiatry, 149*:7 (1986).

M. B. Stein, M. E. Tancer, and T. W. Uhde, Major depression in patients with panic disorder: Factors associated with course and recurrence, *J. Affective Disord., 19*:287 (1990).

A. H. Thompson, R. C. Bland, and H. T. Orn, Relationship and chronology of depression, agoraphobia, and panic disorder in the general population, *J. Nerv. Ment. Dis., 177*:456 (1989).

J. Tiller, I. Schweitzer, K. Maguire, et al., Is Diazepam an antidepressant? *Br. J. Psychiatry, 155*: 483 (1989).

T. W. Uhde, P. Roy-Byrne, J. C. Gillin, et al., The sleep of patients with panic disorder: A preliminary report, *Psychiatr. Res., 12*:251 (1986).

M. Vollrath, and J. Angst, Outcome of panic and depression in a seven-year follow-up: Results of the Zurich study, *Acta Psychiatr. Scand., 80*:591 (1989).

U. Von Bardeleben, and F. Holsboer, Human corticotropin releasing hormone: Clinical studies in patients with affective disorders, alcoholism, panic disorder and in normal controls, *Prog. Neuropsychopharmacol. Biol., 12*:165 (1988).

G. Winokur, The concept of secondary depression and its relationship to comorbidity, *Psychiatric Clin. North Am., 13:567* (1990).

3

The Epidemiology of Depression and Anxiety

Peter R. Joyce
Christchurch School of Medicine, Christchurch, Zew Zealand

I. INTRODUCTION

In psychiatric epidemiology the principal concern is the distribution of disorders in populations, rather than of disorders in individuals. This includes the distributions between populations and within populations over time. Thus, any epidemiological study must not only define caseness, but also the population at risk. One of the key concepts of epidemiology is that of the risk factor, and basic measures are rates and associations. Over the past decade, interest and research into the epidemiology of depression and anxiety has continued to increase, and there are many reviews of these areas (Hirschfield and Cross, 1982; Weissman et al., 1984; Weissman, 1988; Marks, 1986). As in many areas of research, developments have often been linked to advances in methodology, with the most important factors in this area being sampling, design, caseness, and methods of analysis.

Progress in the epidemiology of depressive and anxiety disorders requires the use of criteria for caseness. This may be achieved either by using symptom counts and the use of cutoff points on a symptom count distribution, or by the use of categorical diagnoses, which will often include not only symptoms, but duration and persistence of symptoms and exclusion criteria. Several studies have examined the relations between depressive symptoms and depressive diagnoses and, although there is obviously overlap, about a third of those identified as a clinical case do not self-report high symptoms, and many who score high on self-report symptoms either meet criteria for no psychiatric disorder or for a disorder other than depression (Myers and Weissman, 1980).

One of the advantages of using diagnostic categories is that they enhance communication between clinicians and epidemiologists and epidemiological findings are more relevant to clinicians. Thus, post-World War II psychiatric epidemiology studies in the United States, which used symptom counts and impairment scales, could not be related to developments in clinical psychiatry. However, it must be remembered that the use of diagnostic categories could obscure relation between risk factors and the disorders of interest, if the same risk factors apply to subjects with subthreshold symptom clusters. Furthermore, reliability of diagnoses in community samples is usually lower than in clinical samples because of the many cases that are near the threshold, as well as the lower base rate of the disorders. In many situations, dimensional measures may produce findings with more statistical power than categorical measures. Furthermore, although at the clinical interface, diagnostic systems that categorize and subtype appear to have a face validity, epidemiological studies can at times cast doubt on the validity of these discrete diagnostic categories. Thus, despite the face validity of dividing the old categories of phobic neurosis into agoraphobia, social phobia, and simple phobia; of dividing anxiety neurosis into panic disorder and generalized anxiety; and of associating panic and agoraphobia, there is an alternative view, which is supported in part by some epidemiological data, that suggest that there may be a general neurotic syndrome and that the discrete diagnostic categories are mere surface manifestations of a common underlying propensity toward nervousness or neuroticism (Andrews et al., 1990).

Within the psychiatric literature several prevalence rates are commonly reported. There is the *point prevalence*, which is the proportion of people in a population who have the disorder of interest at a given point in time. Point prevalence rates have been especially used in studies reporting depressive and anxiety symptoms. There are *period prevalence* rates, which are the proportion of people with the disorder within a given period of time. Commonly used period prevalences are 1 month, 6 months, and 1 year. Studies using different diagnostic interviews tend to publish different periods, thus, studies using the Present State Examination (PSE) typically report a 1-month prevalence, whereas the Diagnostic Interview Schedule (DIS) can report on any period prevalence, and many studies report the 6-month prevalence. The Composite International Diagnostic Interview (CIDI), although incorporating all PSE items, will be able to report on any period prevalence in a manner similar to the DIS and may be an appropriate interview schedule for future community surveys (Robins et al., 1988).

Finally, there are *lifetime prevalence* rates or morbid risk, which define the likelihood of developing a disorder in a lifetime. There is a difference between lifetime prevalence and *morbid risk* in that lifetime prevalence is usually estimated up to the age at which the subject is interviewed, whereas morbid risk makes an adjustment for the fact that some individuals who have not developed the disorder of interest to date may develop the disorder over the rest of their lifetime. Morbid risk has been especially used in genetic studies, whereas lifetime prevalence has been used more in epidemiological studies. Although lifetime prevalence rates are convenient to use in some situations, there are debates about the accuracy of lifetime diagnoses, especially for depressive and anxiety disorders (Parker, 1987; Harrington et al., 1988; Bromet et al., 1986).

Over the past 10 years the most extensive psychiatric epidemiology studies of depressive and anxiety disorders ever undertaken have been completed. These studies were sponsored by the National Institute of Mental Health (NIMH) in the United States, and are called the Epidemiologic Catchment Area (ECA) program and have been described as a landmark in the development of psychiatric knowledge (Freedman, 1984). In the ECA program over 17,000 adults from five communities in the United States were interviewed with the DIS. Studies using comparable methodology were then completed in Edmonton, Canada (Bland, et al., 1988), Puerto Rico (Canino et al., 1987), Taiwan (Hwu et al., 1989) and Christchurch, New Zealand (Wells et al., 1989). These studies

Table 1 The 6-Month Prevalence (%) of Affective and Anxiety Disorders in Various Centers That Have Completed Community Studies Using the Diagnostic Interview Schedule

	Affective and anxiety disorders				
Center	Mania	MDD	Phobia	Panic	OCD
Christchurch	0.1	5.3	7.5	1.1	1.0
Edmonton	0.1	3.2	5.1	0.7	1.6
New Haven	0.8	3.5	5.9	0.6	1.4
Baltimore	0.4	2.2	13.4	1.0	2.0
St. Louis	0.7	3.2	5.4	0.9	1.3
Piedmont	0.2	2.0	13.7	0.7	2.2
Los Angeles (Mexican)	0.1	3.0	7.3	1.0	0.6
Los Angeles (non-Hispanic whites)	0.5	3.7	6.1	1.0	0.9
Puerto Rico	0.3	3.0	6.3	1.1	1.8

in adults have stimulated a series of epidemiological studies in children and adolescents (Whitaker et al., 1990; Boyle et al., 1987), and the child version of the DIS has also been administered to school-age children in the context of longitudinal child development studies (McGee et al., 1990).

Although there had been many previous studies on the epidemiology of depressive disorders, the ECA and related studies provided the first extensive prevalence data on anxiety disorders as defined by the *Diagnostic and Statistical Manual of Mental Disorders,* 3rd ed. (*DSM-III*). In general, the prevalence rates were about as expected, except for obsessive–compulsive disorder (OCD) and to a smaller degree, phobic disorders, for which rates were higher than expected, and the prevalence for major depression was lower in the ECA studies than in many previous epidemiological studies of depression. The most marked of these discrepancies was that the prevalence rates of OCD were 40–50 times higher than earlier studies had suggested (Marks, 1986). These higher rates for OCD have been replicated in an epidemiological study of adolescents (Whitaker et al., 1990). Table 1 shows the 6-month prevalence rates of the major affective and anxiety disorders, as determined in the ECA and comparable studies.

II. PREVALENCE AND RISK FACTORS FOR SPECIFIC DEPRESSIVE AND ANXIETY DISORDERS

A. Bipolar Affective Disorder

The findings from the ECA and related studies on the epidemiology of bipolar affective disorder were very much in keeping with the psychiatric literature available at the time. Across the five ECA sites, the lifetime prevalence of bipolar affective disorder was 0.8% and a further 0.5% met criteria for bipolar II disorder (i.e., hypomania plus major depression). The 1-year prevalence rates were 0.7% and 0.3%, respectively, for bipolar and bipolar II disorders. That most people who ever met criteria for bipolar disorder were cases in the past year emphasizes the recurrent and chronic nature of bipolar disorders (Weissman et al., 1988). The ratio of bipolar I and II disorders to major depression was 1:5. This ratio is lower than previously generally accepted, but some studies, such as the Amish (Egeland and Hostetter, 1983), find that the bipolar/nonbipolar ratio may be nearer 1:1. However, the Amish may be a special group, and the bipolar/nonbipolar ratio depends on the prevalence of both bipolar disorder and major depression, and the Amish may have especially low rates of nonbipolar depression. The bipolar/nonbipolar ration also depends on the ascertainment of past hypomanic episodes, which tends to have a lower reliability than past major depressive episodes or full manic episodes.

Consistent with previous findings on bipolar disorder, there was little difference between men and women in prevalence rates. Bipolar subjects are more likely to be never married, to be separated or divorced, to be financially dependent, to live in urban environments, and to be in prison (Weissman et al., 1991). The mean age of onset was 18.0 years (Weissman et al., 1991), which is younger than the mean age of 25–38 usually reported from clinical samples, but is consistent with the findings that the most common age of onset is between 15 and 19 years (Joyce, 1984).

One of the more intriguing and challenging findings from the ECA studies is that there is evidence for secular changes in the rates of mania (and major depression), such that more recent birth cohorts appear to be at greater risk of suffering from this disorder (Lasch et al., 1990). This is consistent with one family study, that reported that rates of bipolar disorder, schizoaffective disorder, and unipolar depression are increasing across generations in relatives of probands with bipolar disorder (Gershon et al., 1987). That birth-cohort changes appear to be occurring in bipolar disorder (which has such a high genetic contribution to its etiology), as well as major depression, suggests that to fully understand these secular changes will require a greater appreciation of genetic–environmental interactions in the etiology of affective disorders.

B. Major Depression

Across the five ECA sites, the lifetime prevalence for major depressive disorder was 4.9%, with rates across the five sites varying from 3.0 to 5.9%. The 1-year prevalence was 2.7% across the five sites. Compared with the ECA sites, the Taiwan study (Hwu, et al., 1989) reported even lower lifetime and 1-year rates for major depression. In Christchurch (Wells et al., 1989; Oakley-Browne et al., 1989), the lifetime and 1-year rates were higher at 12.6% and 6.7%, respectively. The higher rates in Christchurch were due to higher rates in older women and younger men, rather than consistently across all age and sex groups (Oakley-Browne et al., 1989).

Studies using the Schedule for Affective Disorders and Schizophrenia (SADS) have usually reported rates more in line with the Christchurch prevalences. For instance, a community survey in Florence, using the SADS, reported a 1-year prevalence of 1.5% for bipolar I and II disorders and a rate of 6.3% for major depression (Faravelli et al., 1990). In an early review, it was concluded that with new diagnostic techniques, such as the SADS, the point prevalence for nonbipolar major depression was about 3% in men and between 5 and 9% in women (Boyd and Weissman, 1982). These discrepancies raise the issue of whether the five site ECA prevalences for nonbipolar major depression are underestimates.

One of the most consistent findings over time on the epidemiology of nonbipolar major depression has been that women are more at risk than men, generally in a ratio of about 2:1 (Weissman et al., 1984). There have been ongoing debates about whether this gender difference is a genuine difference in rate, whether it reflects differential reporting of symptoms or, if true, whether the difference arises because of biological or psychosocial factors (Wilhelm and Parker, 1989). Angst and co-workers (Angst and Dobler-Mikola, 1984) have suggested that the sex difference is not genuine and arises from applying the same diagnostic criteria to men and women and that, if a criteria, such as impaired functioning, is used, the differences between the genders disappear. However, recent work, applying varying diagnostic criteria across over 2000 relatives of the affectively disordered probands in the NIMH Collaborative Study of the Psychobiology of Depression, did not support this hypothesis and concluded that there is a true difference in the rate of major depression between the sexes (Young et al., 1990).

In recent years, one of the most challenging ideas about the epidemiology of depression has been the observation that the prevalence of major depression is increasing and that the onset of depression is occurring at a younger age (Klerman, 1988; Klerman and Weissman, 1989). Support for this increasing rate of depression comes from cross-sectional community studies (Klerman, 1988; Joyce et al., 1990), longitudinal community studies (Hagnell et al., 1982; Murphy, 1986), and family studies (Gershon et al., 1987; Klerman et al., 1985; Lavori et al., 1987). It is of considerable interest that the rates of depression appear to be increasing faster in young men than in young women, and that the differences in the prevalences between the sexes are thus decreasing (Joyce et al., 1990; Murphy, 1986). Given that depressive disorders are an important risk factor for suicide, although tempered by the observations that substance use disorders are also important risk factors in the young (Rich, et al., 1986), it is noteworthy that there are increasing rates of suicide, which are especially increasing in the young and in young men particularly (Asgard, et al., 1987; Klerman, 1987; Skegg and Cox, 1991). Although these studies support the view that rates of depression and suicide have increased in recent birth cohorts, and consequently, have prompted the question of why rates have been increasing over the past 30 years, there is evidence with suicide that the rates of suicide were unusually low from the 1940s to 1960s (Monk, 1987); if this is true, then the question becomes: What were the protective factors against the development of suicide and of depression for those in adulthood over the earlier years of this century?

Although there is growing evidence for the role of genetic factors as risk factors for major depression, most epidemiological studies of depression have studied psychosocial risk factors; the current status of these factors has been reviewed (O'Connell and Mayo, 1988). Early influential work was done by George Brown and colleagues on working-class women, who found that risk factors for depression included loss of a mother in childhood, having three or more young children, lack of paid employment, and lack of a confidant (Brown and Harris, 1978). Subsequent studies have not replicated the risk factors suggested by Brown, except for the absence of a supportive partner. In general, people who are single, separated, or divorced have higher rates of depressive disorders. However, it is likely that it is the quality, rather than a simple presence or absence, of intimate relationships that is the important aspect of the risk factor (Wilhelm and Parker, 1988; Hickie et al., 1991).

Studies examining the adult impact of loss of a parent in childhood have not consistently found that loss is a risk factor for adult depression (Tennant, 1988). However, studies that examine the enduring quality of child–parent relationships, using measures such as the Parental Bonding Instrument, have consistently found that a perceived parental relationship of low care and overprotection increases the risk of suffering from depression in adult life (Parker, 1983). As increasing data emerge on depression in childhood and adolescence (Fleming and Offord, 1990; Angold, 1988; Harrington et al., 1990), an important question to be asked will be whether exposure to a parental rearing style of low care and high protection increases the risk of early-onset depression, but not late-onset depression. Phrased in other terms, does exposure to a low-care and high-protection style of parenting leave an individual forever vulnerable to depression, or if it has not developed by a certain age (e.g., 30 years), does the importance of this risk factor decrease over time?

Perhaps the strongest risk factor for a further episode of depression is a past episode, and given the increasing evidence that many who suffer depression in childhood or adolescence will have further episodes of depression in adulthood (Harrington et al., 1990), then adult studies may need to pay particular attention to the early experience of depressive states when looking at the adult risk factors.

In recent years, there have been suggestions and some data that childhood sexual abuse will increase the risk of adult depression (Mullen et al., 1988). What remains to be resolved is how much the sexual abuse itself predisposes to later depression, or how much it is the general adverse family environment that is the risk factor. Ongoing studies that inquire about sexual abuse and measure the quality of parent-child relationships should he able to resolve this question.

Although much has been made of having young children at home as being a risk factor for depression, two New Zealand studies found no evidence for this. Thus, in a study of urban and rural women in and around Dunedin, which used a General Health Questionnaire screening followed by interviews using the PSE, having young children was not a risk factor for depression (Romans-Clarkson, et al., 1988). In Christchurch women, interviewed by lay interviewers using the DIS, having young children, again, was not a risk factor for depression (Oakley-Browne, submitted). The consistency of these two New Zealand studies, which used different methods for case ascertainment, perhaps raises questions about whether young children could be a risk factor in some cultures, but not others, and, if this is true, whether it is only a risk factor if children lead to isolation, rather than integration of mothers with their surrounding communities.

Another proposed risk factor for major depression has been living in an urban, rather than rural, environment. Two of the ECA sites have data on this issue. In Durham, major depression was more prevalent in the urban sample, but in St. Louis, major depression was less common in the urban sample (Weissman et al., 1991). In Dunedin women, there was no difference in the prevalence of depression between those from urban and rural samples (Romans-Clarkson et al., 1990). Results from the ECA study support that the unemployed have higher rates of depression; however, they acknowledge that this does not imply a causal relationship (Weissman et al., 1991).

C. Panic Disorder

The diagnostic separation of panic disorder from generalized anxiety disorder first officially occurred with the publication of *DSM-III* in 1980. This development occurred because of the influential work of Donald Klein, who claimed that panic was a discrete disorder that responded to antidepressant drugs, such as imipramine, whereas generalized anxiety responded to benzodiazepines. Although there is still argument about the validity of this separation of panic from generalized anxiety, it has been widely adopted. However, when examining studies on the epidemiology of panic disorder, it is often unclear in pre-1980 studies on anxiety disorders about what combination of panic and generalized anxiety constituted anxiety neurosis. Early studies on the epidemiology of anxiety disorders found a current prevalence of 2–5%, with women having higher rates than men (Marks and Lader, 1973).

The most definitive data on the epidemiology of panic have been collected as part of the ECA and related studies. However, all these data have been collected using the DIS, and the reliability of the diagnosis of panic with the DIS is very low. This low reliability arises because of low reliability in answering the question on whether the person has ever had three panic attacks in a 3-week period and despite high reliability for whether panic attacks have ever occurred (Robins, 1989). Despite this difficulty with the reliability of the diagnosis of panic disorder, the 6-month prevalence for panic disorder across the five ECA sites, Edmonton, Puerto Rico and Christchurch was within the range of 0.7–1.1%. These prevalences are consistent with results from other methods.

In the ECA study, the lifetime prevalence of panic disorder was 1.6%, of whom about one-third also had agoraphobia and two thirds did not have agoraphobia. However, the lifetime prevalence of panic attacks was about 6%, with the major reason for subjects not meeting criteria being not having had three attacks in 3 weeks (Eaton, et al., 1991). Across the ECA and related studies, women were about twice as likely to suffer from panic attacks or disorder than men.

Two of the most notable findings from the ECA results on panic disorder and panic attacks are the associations with treatment-seeking and with suicide attempts. Thus, people with panic disorder or attacks are six times more likely to have attempted suicide than people without any psychiatric disorder (Weissman et al., 1989). Even allowing for comorbidity with major depression or other psychiatric disorders, the adjusted odds ratio for a suicide attempt in uncomplicated panic disorder is 5.4, which compares with 5.1 for uncomplicated major depression and 14.3 for those with panic plus major depression (Johnson, et al., 1990). The second important finding is that people with panic are higher users of health services than any other diagnostic group, including schizophrenia, and that they frequently present with physical health symptoms (Eaton, et al., 1991; Boyd, 1986).

D. Phobic Disorders

In the ECA study, phobic disorders were the most common mental disorders, with lifetime, 1-year and 1-month prevalences of 14.2, 9.7, and 6.7%. Simple phobias were most common, followed by agoraphobia, with social phobia the least common. For simple and agoraphobia, the prevalence rates are about twice as high in women as in men, whereas for social phobia there was a male excess (Eaton, et al., 1991). Phobic disorders were more common under the age of 65, were more common in blacks than whites, and rates varied across sites. Phobic disorders were associated with higher rates of health and mental health service use, but not to the degree associated with panic disorder.

In *DSM-III(R)*, agoraphobia was moved from being considered as primarily a phobic disorder to being a subtype of panic disorder, because of clinical observations that agoraphobia usually arose secondary to panic attacks and that agoraphobia in the absence of panic was rare. Given the ECA data, Weissman has questioned this clinical observation, as she noted that about one-third of agoraphobic subjects had neither panic symptoms nor major depression (Weissman and Merikangas, 1986). In a similar analysis of data from the Christchurch Psychiatric Epidemiology study we found that, if the agoraphobic avoidance was limited to one phobic stimulus, then about 50% had neither panic symptoms nor major depression; however, if the phobic avoidance was more extensive and involved two or more phobic situations, then agoraphobia, in the absence of other psychopathology, was not found. These findings are more consistent with the clinical observations and suggest that, if agoraphobia without panic or depression exists, the extent of phobic avoidance will not be extensive (Joyce et al., 1989).

E. Obsessive-Compulsive Disorder

Before the 1980s, obsessive–compulsive disorder was believed to be a rare mental disorder with a prevalence of 0.1% (Marks, 1986), but epidemiological studies during the past decade, including the ECA and related studies, have found it to be surprisingly common (Whitaker et al., 1990). The ECA studies also confirmed that it is a disorder of early onset, with two-thirds of cases having an onset before 25 years and that it usually runs a chronic course. There is a slight female preponderance, but there do not appear to be clear associations with education, marital status, household size, nor current unemployment. As with all the anxiety disorders, rates of comorbidity, are high and three-quarters of people with OCD will at some time suffer from another disorder, most commonly major depression, other anxiety disorders, or substance abuse or dependence. Although comorbid panic or phobia will often precede the onset of OCD, major depression and substance abuse will more often develop after the onset of OCD (Karno and Golding, 1991).

III. CLINICAL IMPLICATIONS OF EPIDEMIOLOGICAL FINDINGS

A. Health Service Use

Most epidemiological studies of depressive and anxiety disorders find that the majority of cases identified are not receiving treatment. Thus, in the ECA study it was found that, although 65–70% of people with a mental disorder in the past 6 months have visited a health professional, only 15–20% had a visit for mental health reasons and only 8–12% had seen a mental health specialist, as opposed to a general medical provider. The likelihood of having received treatment did vary by site, gender, age, and diagnosis. For affective disorders 16–19% had seen a mental health specialist, and the comparable figure for anxiety disorders was 7–15% (Shapiro et al., 1984). However, within the anxiety disorders there are marked differences in rates; those with panic attacks (Klerman et al., 1991) and panic disorder are more likely to have utilized health services than those with any psychiatric diagnosis, whereas those with simple phobia are least likely to have used health services (Boyd, 1986). Comparable figures have been found in other studies from other countries that have a different system for the organization of health services. Thus, in the Christchurch (New Zealand) epidemiology study, 40% of those with an affective disorder and 36% of those with an anxiety disorder had seen a health professional for mental health reasons in the past 6 months, and only 13–14% had seen a mental health specialist (Hornblow et al., 1990).

For over a decade Goldberg (Goldberg and Huxley, 1980) and colleagues in Manchester, England, have been studying the pathways and filters to psychiatric care. One of the consistent findings has been that presenting with somatic symptoms predicts nonrecognition and longer delays in getting to psychiatric care (Gater and Goldberg,

1991). In the Netherlands, 68% of cases of depression and 50% of cases of anxiety were recognized by the general practitioner. However, if the primary presenting complaint was somatic, rather than psychological, only 23% of cases were recognized by the general practitioner (Ormel et al., 1991).

B. Are Community and Clinical Cases Similar?

As the results from epidemiology studies continue to find rates of anxiety and affective disorders in considerable excess of those who are treated, the question has rightly been asked as to whether the cases seen in clinical settings are similar or dissimilar to those found in community surveys. Thus, it has been suggested that community cases of depression, as opposed to clinic cases, have fewer symptoms, have less severe symptoms, have different symptoms, are of shorter duration, are less incapacitating, are more environmentally and less biologically caused, and are more responsive to psychotherapies than to pharmacotherapies. None of these suggestions has been unequivocally confirmed, and considerable further work is required on this issue (Costello, 1990). It is also necessary to determine the extent to which comorbid axis I or axis II disorders determine who gets to treatment, rather than just the features of the primary disorder.

C. Implications of Nonrecognition and Nontreatment

Given that high rates of nonutilization and nonrecognition of depressive and anxiety disorders have been found in most epidemiological studies, one important question becomes the implication of this. Relatively few studies have as yet adequately addressed this question. However, there is increasing evidence that depression in the community, especially in older subjects, is associated with increased mortality (Bruce and Leaf, 1989). Also, major depression is frequently not recognized in nursing homes, and those with major depression have an increased risk of death over 1 year (Rovner et al., 1991). Nonrecognition of depression is also common in medical settings, and there is increasing evidence that depression increases mortality and morbidity in acute medical illness (Silverstone, 1990). The challenge for the future is to establish whether treatment of these depressive disorders can reduce mortality.

Finally, it is well established that depression, and perhaps panic, are important risk factors for suicide. One study, which has not received the attention it should have, has shown that by systematically educating all general practitioners about the recognition and management of depression, it is possible to lower the suicide rate in a population (Rutz, et al., 1989). There must be few other areas of medicine where it has been demonstrated that better recognition and treatment will affect mortality. In the depressive and anxiety disorders, the morbidity is also substantial, and it is thus pleasing to note that in several countries, including the United States and United Kingdom, concerted efforts are being made to improve the recognition and management of depression in primary care and other medical settings.

REFERENCES

G. Andrew, Stewart, A. Morris-Yates, P. Holt, and S. Henderson, Evidence for a general neurotic syndrome, *Br. J. Psychiatry, 157*: 6 (1990).

A. Angold, Childhood and adolescent depression: I. Epidemiological and aetiological aspects, *Br. J. Psychiatry, 152*: 601 (1988).

J. Angst, and A. Dobler-Mikola, Do the diagnostic criteria determine the sex ratio in depression? *J. Affective Disord., 7*: 189 (1984).

U. Asgard, P. Nordstrom, and G. Raback, Birth cohort analysis of changing suicide risk by sex and age in Sweden 1952 to 1981, *Acta Psychiatr. Scand., 76*: 456 (1987).

R. C. Bland, H. Orn, and S. C. Newman, Lifetime prevalence of psychiatric disorders in Edmonton, *Acta Psychiatr. Scand., 77*: 24 (1988).

J. H. Boyd, Use of mental health services for the treatment of panic disorder, *Am. J. Psychiatry, 143*: 1569 (1986).

J. H. Boyd, and M. M. Weissman, *Epidemiology, Handbook of Affective Disorders* (E. S. Paykel, ed.), Churchill-Livingstone, New York, p. 109–125. (1982).

M. H. Boyle, D. R. Offord, H. G. Hoffman, G. P. Catlin, J. A. Byles, D. T. Cadman, J. W. Crawford, P. S. Links, N. I. Rae-Grant, and P. Szatmari, Ontario Child Health Study, I. Methodology, *Arch. Gen. Psychiatry, 44*: 826 (1987).

E. J. Bromet, L. O. Dunn, M. M. Connell, M. A. Dew, and H. C. Schulberg, Long-term reliability of diagnosing lifetime major depression in a community sample, *Arch. Gen. Psychiatry, 43*: 435 (1986).

G. W. Brown, and T. Harris, *Social Origins of Depression: A Study of Psychiatric Disorders in Women*, Tavistock, London (1978).

M. L. Bruce, and P. J. Leaf, Psychiatric disorders and fifteen-month mortality in a community sample of older adults, *Am. J. Public Health, 79*: 727 (1989).

G. J. Canino, B. R. Bird, P. E. Shrout, M. Rubio-Stipec, M. Bravo, R. Martinez, M. Sesman, and L. M. Guevara, Prevalence of specific psychiatric disorders in Puerto Rico, *Arch. Gen. Psychiatry, 44*: 727 (1987).

C. G. Costello, The similarities and dissimilarities between community and clinic cases of depression, *Br. J. Psychiatry, 157*: 812 (1990).

W. W. Eaton, A. Dryman, and M. M. Weissman, Panic and phobia, *Psychiatric Disorders in America: The Epidemiologic Catchment Area Study* (L. N. Robins and D. A. Regier, eds.), Free Press, New York, p. 53–80. (1991).

J. A. Egeland, and A. M. Hostetter, Amish study, I: Affective disorders among the Amish, 1976–1980, *Am. J. Psychiatry, 140*: 56 (1983).

C. Faravelli, B. G. Degl'Innocenti, L. Aiazzi, G. Incerpi, and S. Pallanti, Epidemiology of mood disorders: A community survey in Florence, *J. Affective Dis., 20*: 135 (1990).

J. E. Fleming, and D. R. Offord, Epidemiology of childhood depressive disorders: A critical review, *J. Am. Acad. Child Adolesc. Psychiatry, 29*: 571 (1990).

D. X. Freedman, Psychiatric epidemiology counts, *Arch. Gen. Psychiatry, 41*: 931 (1984).

R. Gater, and D. Goldberg, Pathways to psychiatric care in South Manchester, *Br. J. Psychiatry, 159*: 90 (1991).

E. Gershon, J. Hamovit, J. Guroff, and J. Nurnberger, J., Birth-cohort changes in manic and depressive disorders in relatives of bipolar and schizoaffective patients, *Arch. Gen. Psychiatry, 44*: 314 (1987).

D. Goldberg, and P. Huxley, *Mental Illness in the Community: The Pathway to Psychiatric Care.* London, Tavistock (1980).

O. Hagnell, J. Lanke, B. Rorsman, and L. Ojesjo, Are we entering an age of melancholy? Depressive illnesses in a prospective epidemiological study over 25 years: the Lundby Study, Sweden, *Psychol. Med., 12*: 279 (1982).

R. Harrington, H. Fudge, M. Rutter, A. Pickles, and J. Hill, Adult outcomes of childhood and adolescent depression. I. Psychiatric status, *Arch. Gen. Psychiatry, 47*: 465 (1990).

R. Harrington, J. Hill, M. Rutter, K. John, H. Fudge, M. Zoccolillo, and M. Weissman, The assessment of lifetime psychopathology: A comparison of two interviewing styles, *Psychol. Med., 18*: 487 (1988).

I. Hickie, G. Parker, K. Wilhelm, and C. Tennant, Perceived interpersonal risk factors of nonendogenous depression, *Psychol. Med., 21*: 399 (1991).

R. Hirschfield, and C. K. Cross, Epidemiology of affective disorders, *Arch. Gen. Psychiatry, 39*: 67 (1982).

A. R. Hornblow, J. A. Bushnell, J. E. Wells, P. R. Joyce, and M. A. Oakley-Browne, Christchurch psychiatric epidemiology study: Use of mental health services, *N. Z. Med. J., 103*: 415 (1990).

H.-G. Hwu, E.-K. Yeh, and L.-Y. Chang, Prevalence of psychiatric disorders in Taiwan defined by the Chinese Diagnostic Interview Schedule, *Acta Psychiatr. Scand., 79*: 136 (1989).

J. Johnson, M. M. Weissman, and G. L. Klerman, Panic disorder, comorbidity, and suicide attempts, *Arch. Gen. Psychiatry, 47*: 805 (1990).

P. R. Joyce, Age of onset in bipolar affective disorder and misdiagnosis as schizophrenia, *Psychol. Med., 14*: 145 (1984).

P. R. Joyce, J. A. Bushnell, M. A. Oakley-Browne, J. E. Wells, and A. R. Hornblow, The epidemiology of panic symptomatology and agoraphobic avoidance, *Compr. Psychiatry, 30*: 303 (1989).

P. R. Joyce, M. A. Oakley-Browne, J. E. Wells, J. A. Bushnell, and A. R. Hornblow, Birth cohort trends in major depression: increasing rates and earlier onset in New Zealand, *J. Affective Dis., 18*: 83 (1990).

M. Karno, J. M. Golding, Obsessive compulsive disorder, *Psychiatric Disorders in America: The Epidemiologic Catchment Area Study* (L. N. Robins and D. A. Regier, eds.), Free Press, New York, pp. 204–219 (1991).

G. L. Klerman, Clinical epidemiology of suicide, *J. Clin. Psychiatry, 48 (Suppl12)*: 33 (1987).

G. L. Klerman, P. W. Lavori, J. Rice, T. Reich, J. Endicott, N. C. Andreasen, M. B. Keller, and R. M. A. Hirschfield, Birth-cohort trends in rates of major depressive disorder among relatives of patients with affective disorder, *Arch. Gen. Psychiatry, 42*: 689 (1985).

G. L. Klerman, The current age of youthful melancholia: evidence for increase in depression among adolescents and young adults. *Br. J. Psychiatry, 152*: 4 (1988).

G. L. Klerman, and M. M. Weissman, Increasing rates of depression, *JAMA, 261*: 2229 (1989).

G. L. Klerman, M. M. Weissman, R. Ouellette, J. Johnson, and S. Greenwald, Panic attacks in the community. Social morbidity and health care utilization, *JAMA, 265*: 742 (1991).

K. Lasch, M. Weissman, P. Wickramaratne, and M. L. Bruce, Birth-cohort changes in the rates of mania, *Psychiatry Res., 33*: 31 (1990).

P. W. Lavori, G. L. Klerman, M. B. Keller, T. Reich, J. Rice, and J. Endicott, Age–period–cohort analysis of secular trends in onset of major depression: Findings in siblings of patients with major affective disorder, *J. Psychiatr. Res., 21*: 23 (1987).

I. Marks, and M. Lader, Anxiety states (anxiety neuroses): A review, *J. Nerv. Ment. Dis., 156*: 3 (1973).

T. M. Marks, Epidemiology of anxiety, *Soc. Psychiatry, 21*: 167 (1986).

R. McGee, M. Feehan, S. Williams, F. Partridge, P. A. Silva, and J. Kelly, *DSM-III* disorders in a large sample of adolescents, *J. Am. Acad. Child Adolesc. Psychiatry, 29*: 611 (1990).

M. Monk, Epidemiology of suicide, *Epidemiol. Rev., 9*: 51 (1987).

P. E. Mullen, S. E. Romans-Clarkson, V. A. Walton, and G. P. Herbison, Impact of sexual and physical abuse on women's mental health, *Lancet, 1*: 841 (1988).

J. M. Murphy, Trends in depression and anxiety: Men and Women, *Acta Psychiatr. Scand., 73*: 113 (1986).

J. K. Myers, and M. M. Weissman, Screening for depression in a community sample: The use of a self-report scale to detect the depressive syndrome, *Am. J. Psychiatry, 137*: 1081 (1980).

M. A. Oakley-Browne, P. R. Joyce, J. E. Wells, J. A. Bushnell, and A. R. Hornblow, Christchurch Psychiatric Epidemiology Study, Part II: Six month and other period prevalences for specific psychiatric disorders, *Aust. N. Z. J. Psychiatry, 23*: 327 (1989).

M. A. Oakley-Browne, P. R. Joyce, J. E. Wells, J. A. Bushnell, and A. R. Hornblow, Sociodemographic risk factors for depression, (submitted).

R. A. O'Connell, and J. A. Mayo, The role of social factors in affective disorders: A review, *Hosp. Commun. Psychiatry, 39*: 842 (1988).

J. Ormel, M. W. J. Koeter, W. van den Brink, and G. van de Willige, Recognition, management, and course of anxiety and depression in general practice, *Arch. Gen. Psychiatry, 48*: 700 (1991).

G. Parker, Are the lifetime prevalence estimates in the ECA study accurate? *Psychol. Med., 17*: 275 (1987).

G. Parker, Parental "affectionless control" as an antecedent to adult depression. A risk factor delineated, *Arch. Gen. Psychiatry, 40*: 956 (1983).

C. L. Rich, D. Young, and R. C. Fowler, San Diego suicide study: I. Young vs old subjects, *Arch. Gen. Psychiatry, 43*: 577 (1986).

L. N. Robins, Diagnostic grammar and assessment: Translating criteria into questions, *Psychol. Med., 19*: 57 (1989).

L. N. Robins, J. K. Wing, H. U. Wittchen, J. E. Helzer, T. F. Babor, J. Burke, A. Farmer, A. Jablenski, R. Pickens, D. A. Regier, N. Sartorius, and L. H. Towle, The composite international diagnostic interview: An epidemiologic instrument suitable for use in conjunction with different diagnostic systems and in different cultures, *Arch. Gen. Psychiatry, 45*: 1069 (1988).

S. E. Romans-Clarkson, V. A. Walton, and G. P. Herbison, Marriage, motherhood and psychiatric morbidity in New Zealand, *Psychol. Med., 18*: 983 (1988).

S. E. Romans-Clarkson, V. A. Walton, G. P. Herbison, and P. E. Mullen, Psychiatric morbidity among women in urban and rural New Zealand: Psychosocial correlates, *Br. J. Psychiatry, 156*: 84 (1990).

B. W. Rovner, P. S. German, L. J. Brant, R. Clark, L. Burton, and M. F. Folstein, Depression and mortality in nursing homes, *JAMA 265*: 993 (1991).

W. Rutz, L. von Korring, and J. Walinder, Frequency of suicide in Gotland after systematic postgraduate education of general practitioners, *Acta Psychiatr. Scand., 80*: 151 (1989).

S. Shapiro, E. A. Skinner, L. G. Kessler, M. Von Korff, P. S. German, G. L. Tischler, P. J. Leaf, L. Beeham, L. Cottler, and D. A. Regier, Utilization of health and mental health services. Three epidemiologic catchment area sites, *Arch. Gen. Psychiatry, 41*: 971 (1984).

P. H. Silverstone, Depression increases mortality and morbidity in acute life-threatening medical illness, *J. Psychosomatic Res., 34*: 651 (1990).

K. Skegg, and B. Cox, Suicide in New Zealand 1957–1986: The influence of age, period and birth-cohort, *Aust. N. Z. J. Psychiatry, 25*: 181 (1991).

C. Tennant, Parental loss in childhood: its effect in adult life, *Arch. Gen. Psychiatry, 45*: 1045 (1988).

M. M. Weissman, The epidemiology of anxiety disorders: Rates, risks and familial patterns, *J. Psychiat. Res., 22*(Suppl. 1): 99 (1988).

M. M. Weissman, M. L. Bruce, P. J. Leaf, L. P. Florio, and C. Holzer, Affective disorders, *Psychiatric Disorders in America: The Epidemiologic Catchment Area Study* (L. N. Robins, and D. A. Regier, eds), Free Press, New York, pp. 53 (1991).

M. M. Weissman, G. L. Klerman, J. S. Markowitz, and R. Ouellette, Suicidal ideation and suicide attempts in panic disorder and attacks, *N. Engl. J. Med., 321*: 1209 (1989).

M. M. Weissman, P. J. Leaf, C. E. Holzer, J. K. Myers, and G. L. Tischler, The epidemiology of depression: An update on sex differences in rates, *J. Affective Disord., 7*: 179 (1984).

M. M. Weissman, P. J. Leaf, G. L. Tischler, D. G. Blazer, M. Karno, and M. L. Bruce, Affective disorders in five United States communities, *Psychol. Med., 18*: 141 (1988).

M. M. Weissman, and K. R. Merikangas, The epidemiology of anxiety and panic disorders: An update, *J. Clin. Psychiatry, 47*(Suppl 6): 11 (1986).

J. E. Wells, J. A. Bushnell, A. R. Hornblow, P. R. Joyce, and M. A. Oakley-Browne, Christchurch Psychiatric Epidemiology Study, Part I: Methodology and lifetime prevalences for specific psychiatric disorders, *Aust. N. Z. J. Psychiatry, 23*: 315 (1989).

A. Whitaker, J. Johnson, D. Shaffer, J. A. Rapport, K. Kalikow, B. T. Walsh, M. Davis, S. Braiman, and A. Dolinsky, Uncommon troubles in young people: Prevalence estimates of selected psychiatric disorders in a nonreferred adolescent population, *Arch. Gen. Psychiatry, 47*: 487 (1990).

K. Wilheim, G. Parker, Are sex differences in depression really necessary? *Psychol. Med., 19*: 401 (1989).

K. Wilheim, G. Parker, The development of a measure of intimate bonds, *Psychol. Med., 18*: 225 (1988).

M. A. Young, L. F. Fogg, W. A. Scheftner, M. B. Keller, and J. A. Fawcett, Sex differences in the lifetime prevalence of depression: Does varying the diagnostic criteria reduce the female/male ratio? *J. Affective Disord., 18:* 187 (1990).

4

The Genetics of Anxiety and Depression

Andrew Mackinnon
Australian National University, Canberra, Australia

Philip B. Mitchell
University of New South Wales, Sydney, Australia

I. INTRODUCTION

That psychological distress and psychiatric disorders arise from constitutional factors that are heritable is a classic concept, in existence before even elementary laws of genetics were formulated. The first major descriptions of the role of inheritance in depression and mania derive from the writings of 19th century European and British psychiatrists. Particularly influential were the treatises of the French alienists Morel and Moreau (Dowbiggen, 1985). Kraepelin (1921) was adamant about the central role of genetic factors in his "manic–depressive insanity," demonstrating "hereditary taint" in about 80% of the cases that he observed.

The progress made in genetic research throughout this century can be described as exponential: large and significant developments have been followed by larger and more important ones. Almost universally acknowledged is recent progress in molecular genetics: recombinant DNA techniques give us the promise of mapping the human genome and, thereby, precisely locating and perhaps modifying individual genes that play a significant role in particular disorders. Less glamorous, but also of considerable importance to psychiatry, are parallel advances in statistical genetics, with the development of more sophisticated models, underpinned by improvements in numerical methods and computing power: statistical techniques that produce efficient parameter estimates and often have associated significance tests have become available for most models appropriate in genetics. Computers are now powerful enough to allow the implementation of iterative techniques for parameter estimation when, as is usually the case, no analytic solution exists for these models.

The aim of this chapter is, first, to present the evidence that affective and anxiety disorders have a substantial genetic substrate. Although not excluding other causal factors, the role of gene action for all affective disorders and most anxiety disorders should now be beyond question. Current and future questions concern the specific nature of genetic involvement, the mechanisms of gene action, and the interaction of genetic and other etiological factors.

Although recent reviews in this area have been optimistic about the prospects for rapid advancement of knowledge, this enthusiasm needs to be tempered. Psychiatric disorders differ in several important aspects from those diseases whose etiology is fully understood. The final part of this review examines some limitations of current approaches and suggests some future directions.

A. Phenotypic Preliminaries

As the goal of genetics is to establish the relationship between genotype and phenotype, the definition of the disorder under study is a crucial first step in any genetic study. Psychiatric disorders are characterized by variable age of onset and, frequently, remitting and relapsing courses. Thus, phenotypic definitions should be in terms of lifetime prevalence. When persons who have not passed through the risk period for the disorder are included in a study, corrections for age should be made.

The primary interest in psychogenetics is in disorders as they present clinically. This poses problems, as psychiatric diagnoses rely on symptoms and signs, with no biologically based or other objective tests available to support clinical judgment. Operational criteria such as the *Diagnostic and Statistical Manual of Mental Disorders*, 3rd ed., revised (*DSM-III-R*, American Psychiatric Association, 1987), ICD (*ICD-10*; World Health Organization, 1990) and the Research Diagnostic Criteria (RDC) (Spitzer et al., 1977) help to increase the reliability of current studies. Such criteria cannot, however, be applied retrospectively to earlier studies. In addition, some relevant studies were carried out before the introduction of internationally accepted definitions, or make distinctions not incorporated into these schemes. Thus, although complying with the scope of *DSM-III-R* definitions of mood and anxiety disorders, it is necessary to examine studies in which criteria for diagnosis may have varied significantly from standards currently in use.

1. Affective Disorders

Genetic studies of depression predate the existence of widely accepted classification schemes and standardized measurement techniques. Accepting variations in operationalizing the concepts underlying the disorder, depression has been studied as one of three major phenotypes: bipolar disorder, unipolar depression, and minor or neurotic depression. Following the presumption that minor disorders are reactive or personality-related and, therefore, substantially environmental in etiology, whereas the major ones are biologically based, the principal focus of genetic research has been on these more severe disorders.

The term *unipolar depression* refers to episodes of endogenous depression in European psychiatry. In North America, unipolar depression refers to episodes of nonbipolar major depression, without further specification of a particular subtype. The North American definition will be used in this chapter. *Bipolar disorder* has been further subdivided as, for instance, by the RDC into bipolar I (BPI) (history of both depressive disorder and frank mania) and bipolar II (BPII) (involving milder mood elevation) disorders.

Most of the genetic studies of depression do not use the subdivided into "endogenous" or "neurotic" (nonendogenous) forms, instead using the "umbrella" concept of *major depression*. There are undoubtedly limitations to the use of these subtypes with their uncertain boundaries. It is possible that the very heterogeneous populations incorporated under the rubric major depression may include an excess number of those with a *sporadic* (or nongenetic) form of the illness.

As the concepts of endogenous and neurotic forms of depression have been particularly influential in Western Europe (including the United Kingdom), it is not surprising that most studies of that dichotomy—with the exception of Winokur's group in the United States—have arisen from that region. Although there have been many attempts to refine the concept of *endogenous depression* or *melancholia* (e.g., Parker et al., 1990) the definition of *neurotic depression* has been even more ambiguous (for review see Winokur, 1987).

Regardless of the method of diagnosis employed, researchers must make decisions such as the inclusion of subjects with psychotic symptoms, the combined or separate analysis of individuals with BPI and BPII, and the combination of subjects with bipolar and unipolar disorder. Although not able to be applied retrospectively, current statistical techniques enable analyses to be repeated with varying category boundaries. The collection of appropriate information means that different classification schemes can be applied to the same subjects. These techniques permit any sensitivity to particular classifications or boundaries to be identified.

2. *Anxiety Disorders*

The disorders embraced under this category by *DSM-III-R* and *ICD-10* are symptomatically more heterogeneous than mood disorders. They include panic disorder, agoraphobia, social and other phobias, obsessive–compulsive disorder, and generalized anxiety disorder. However, some of these distinctions, such as that between generalized anxiety disorder and panic disorder, are relatively recent and, consequently, are absent from earlier studies.

Although determining whether any of these disorders share a common genetic etiology is an important research question, most studies have focused on one disorder; therefore, each will be considered separately.

3. *Other Phenotypes*

In addition to clinical syndromes, the genetic analysis of other phenotypes could yield information in this field. Variation in psychopathological traits in normal persons, although much studied in behavior genetic analyses of personality, is an area that has not been integrated into genetic psychiatry. These measures are usually derived from self-report inventories. Although they are necessarily imperfectly related to clinical definitions and reflect normal, subclinical variation, data on these traits are much easier to obtain, so that a number of large and methodologically sophisticated studies have been undertaken.

B. Genetic Models

The simplest patterns of heritability are Mendelian. When the occurrence of a disorder fails to conform to any Mendelian pattern, parameters may be introduced to reflect reduced penetrance of the genotype, reflecting the concept that not all individuals with the pathogenic genotype may exhibit the disorder.

It is apparent that psychiatric disorders do not display simple Mendelian patterns of segregation. Quantitative models of transmission of these disorders have, therefore, relied on the abstraction of a continuous latent variable, referred to as *liability*. All genetic and environmental factors that influence expression of the disorder do so through their effect on liability. Individuals whose liability exceeds a threshold value exhibit the disorder, whereas those whose liability is below the threshold do not (Fig. 1a).

Liability to express a particular disorder is generally assumed to be normally distributed in the population. Although this can be derived from the central limit theorem when a large number of factors independently influence liability, the choice of distribution is primarily a matter of statistical convenience. It is possible that a continuous quantity, such as a biological marker or psychometric scale, could be found to index liability; however, this is not a requirement for the development of genetic liability models: liability is an essentially theoretical construct.

Two main forms of *liability-threshold* models have been applied to psychiatric disorders: are multifactorial polygenic (MFP) model and the single major locus (SML) model.

1. Multifactorial Polygenic Model

In this model numerous genetic and environmental factors are assumed to make small, additive contributions to liability. This model is basically an adaptation of the principles of genetics of continuous variables applied to a dichotomous outcome (see Falconer, 1981). The model can be modified to incorporate multiple thresholds. This enables models to be tested in which different disorders are hypothesized to be mild and severe expressions of the same liability (Reich et al., 1979). The threshold model implies that all individuals whose liability is greater than this value will be diagnosed as having the disease, and no persons whose liability is less than this value will be so diagnosed. This "hard" threshold can be replaced with a "penetrance function," typically logistic in form, that relates the value of liability to the *probability* of receiving a diagnosis (Eaves, 1987a).

2. Single Major Locus

As its name suggests, this model posits the existence of a single gene responsible for all genetic variation in liability. The distribution of liability under this model will be a mixture of three normal distributions, each corresponding to random environmental influences on liability about the three genotypes dd, dD, and DD (see Fig. 1b). An important characteristic of this is that it allows for the possibility of individuals who lack the disorder-related genotype (see dd in Fig. 1b) showing the disorder. Although the mean liability of these individuals will be lower than for the other genotypes, variability owing to environmental factors means that some individuals with this genotype may still exceed the threshold. Such cases are referred to as phenocopies or sporadic cases. This model can also be modified to incorporate multiple thresholds.

3. Mixed Models

The SML model implies that, when the effect of the major locus is removed, all covariation between relatives can be accounted for by the covariation of environmental factors. It may be more plausible to consider that a major locus may operate against a background of polygenic influences. Schematically such a mixed model has the same form as the SML model shown in Figure 1b. However, a different pattern of covariation of liability between relatives is predicted under the different models. The mixed model may be used as a base against which tests of no SML effect or no MFP effect can be examined.

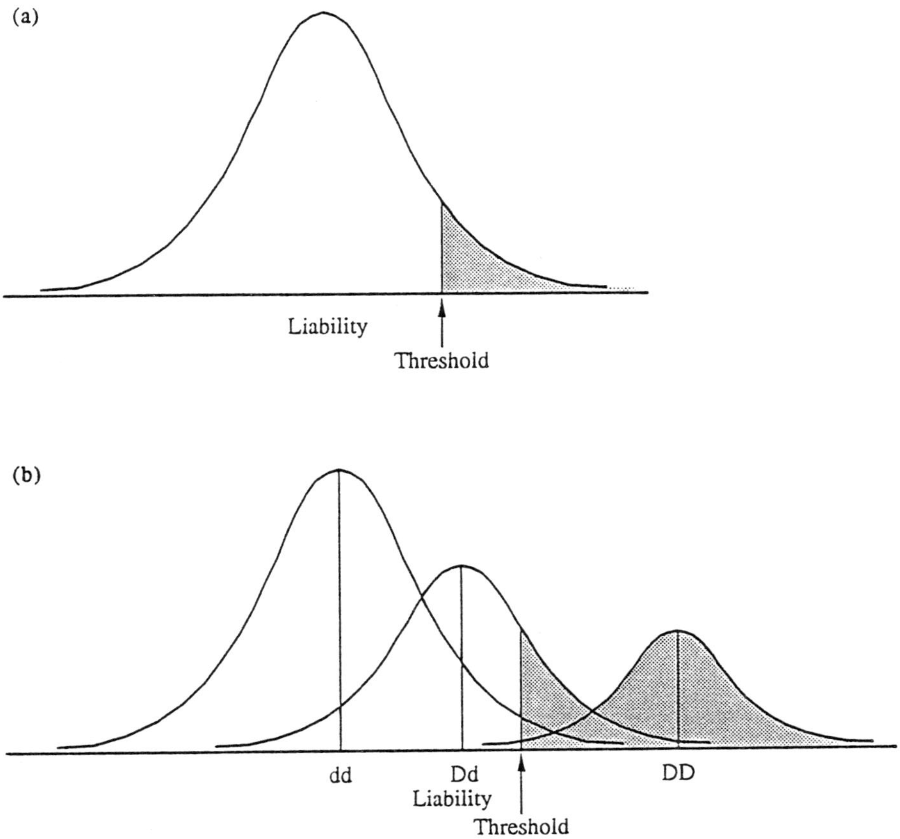

Figure 1 (a) Multifactorial polygenic model showing the distribution of liability to a disorder in the population. Individuals above the threshold have the disorder. The proportion of affected individuals is shaded on the diagram. (b) Single major locus model in which the gene D increases liability to the disorder.

C. Research Designs

All genetic analyses rely on the collection of information from pedigrees with known patterns of genetic covariation. Environmental covariation is also controlled in certain designs. Three types of studies are found in the psychiatric literature.

1. Family Studies

***Demonstration of Familiality*.** Investigation of the patterns of illness among family members is the most common type of investigation. The basic aim of such studies is to demonstrate that the disorder concerned is familial, having a higher prevalence in relatives of ill individuals than in the general population.

Families are recruited into studies through an affected proband. Prevalence rates for relatives of different degrees of genetic similarity may then be compared with prevalence rates for the same disorder in the population. Prevalence rates for psychiatric disorder vary according to the methods used to diagnose the disorder and recruitment methods. Consequently, these studies can be methodologically strengthened by the addition of families recruited through a control proband: if ill probands are recruited from inpatient psychiatric units, age- and sex-matched controls might be recruited from medical or surgical wards. Higher prevalence rates in the families of ill probands are indicative of familiality. This is a necessary, but not sufficient, condition to demonstrate genetic transmission, because shared environmental exposure tends to covary with degree of genetic similarity.

Segregation Analysis. The segregation analytic approach goes beyond the calculation of prevalence rates in families by attempting to model the segregation of the disorder in pedigrees with multiply affected members. The aim is to demonstrate whether or not the observed pattern of transmission is consistent with one or more genetic models of the type discussed in the foregoing. In addition to these general classes of gene action, specific models, such as sex-linked transmission, may be tested.

Linkage Analysis. Linkage analysis is a technique designed to locate the position on a chromosome of a single locus responsible for a disorder. Genes that are on different chromosomes or physically distant from another on the same chromosome have a 50% probability of recombining at meiosis. As the distance between genes on a chromosome decreases, the probability that they will remain together after meiosis increases. Linkage analysis relies on the cosegregation of the putative genetic locus of a disorder with marker genes that are known to control a measurable trait and for which the mode of inheritance is known. Statistically, the demonstration of linkage involves the estimation of the recombination fraction using maximum likelihood techniques and the comparison of this likelihood with the likelihood calculated under the assumption of no linkage (a recombination fraction of 0.5). The likelihood ratio expressed logarithmically is referred to as the *lod score*. Lods greater than 3 (1000:1) are taken to support linkage, lods between 2 and –2 are inconclusive, and lods less than –2 are taken as evidence excluding linkage (Ott, 1985).

Three approaches to the choice of which genes or chromosomal regions to examine have been used:

1. The identification of candidate sites at the region of related chromosomal abnormalities
2. Candidate genes for proteins (e.g., enzymes, receptors) that may bear some a priori theoretical relevance of the etiology of the condition
3. Genome scanning

The recent development of detailed genome-mapping libraries (e.g., Stephens et al., 1990) now make it feasible to test for linkage to most chromosomal regions.

Regions explored in previous studies have been limited by the then available technologies. These have included classic markers [i.e., color blindness or enzyme deficiencies (e.g., G6PD), blood group proteins, and HLA antigens]. These markers cover only about 20% of the human genome.

Recombinant DNA technology has developed a new generation of markers not necessarily related to measurable traits or disorders. Restriction fragment length polymorphisms (RFLPs) result from the breaking of DNA at specific sites by restriction enzymes. The length of the fragments is determined by the inherited spacing of these sites along the DNA chain. Because of their numbers, wide distribution throughout the genome, and genetic variability, RFLPs are replacing classic markers in linkage studies. The RFLPs enable linkage analyses along the entire genome to be undertaken (Donis-Keller et al., 1989). The recent development of AC repeats (Weber, 1990) has introduced even more statistically powerful forms of DNA polymorphisms.

Other Methods. Several other methods have been proposed for testing linkage, most notably the sib pair method and extensions to it (see, e.g., Weeks and Lange, 1988). Although offering a nonparametric approach, independent of the genetic model underlying the disease, these methods have been eschewed because of their low power.

2. *Twin Studies*

The classic twin design relies on the comparison of monozygotic (MZ) twins, who are genetically identical, with dizygotic (DZ) twins, who share, on average, half their genes. Studies use twins who have been raised together.

In most studies of illness, twins are ascertained through an affected proband. The concordance rates for MZ and DZ twins are calculated and compared statistically. Significantly higher concordance in MZ than in DZ twins is evidence for a genetic effect. This ratio is also a function of the prevalence of the disorder. Thus Gottesman and Carey (1983) have argued that concordance rates should be transformed into tetrachoric correlations. These correlations are essentially correlations in normally distributed liability estimated from the twofold table recording concordance between twins. Although this approach relies on a separate estimate of prevalence, it enables the model-fitting approach, described later, to be applied to liability of the disorder concerned.

Twins may also be selected randomly (specifically, unconditioned on a proband with the disorder) from sources such as twin registries. This allows the direct estimation of heritabilities and other sources of variation, but is generally suitable only for traits that are common or continuously distributed in the population.

Advances in the analysis of twin data have centered on unconditioned designs using continuous variables. Approaches focusing on between and within twin-pair sums of square and intraclass correlation coefficients calculated from analysis of variance allowed the estimation of the effect of environmental and genetic factors, the latter being expressed as one of several heritability indices (Jinks and Fulker, 1970). Modern practice includes the calculation of between-twin correlations of dichotomous and polychotomous variables as tetrachoric and polychoric correlations, an approach concordant with the polygenetic liability models. A model-fitting approach allows the estimation and fit of modeling, including additive and dominant genetic terms (VA and VD), as well as terms for the common or shared environment (EC), and the unique environment of each twin (ES). Estimates of these quantities are not independent, and models containing all sources of variation cannot be fitted simultaneously (Grayson, 1989; Martin et al., 1988). Multivariate extensions of the basic twin design have also been developed (see Boomsma et al., 1989). This development is interesting because it allows the relation between variables, such as illness, personality, and life events, to be modeled and apportioned between genetic and environmental sources.

Dissociating genetic and environmental components using twin data relies on mathematical modeling, rather than controlled manipulation of an experimental nature. So that valid conclusions are drawn from the comparison of twins reared together, several assumptions must be met: MZ twins must be treated no more similarly than DZ twins relative to environmental determinants of the trait being measured. Assortative mating is assumed to be absent. It is also assumed that there is no correlation or interaction between the genotype and the environment. Many of the assumptions of the twin model can at least be partially tested using the data collected in a study or by examining independent evidence (see Eaves et al., 1989).

Along with other disciplines, psychiatry has had a long-standing fascination with MZ twins reared apart. Genetically identical individuals who have not shared an environment appear to offer the means of directly estimating genetic effects. Quite apart from the rarity of such twins, the age and circumstances surrounding the separation, degree of contact, and correlations between the environments of twins make the interpretation of data gathered from such pairs far more ambiguous than is often believed.

3. Adoption Studies

Studying adoptees seems to offer the opportunity to break the nexus between genetic and environmental transmission of disorders. Two major designs have been used. The proband may be the adoptee, in which case the prevalence of the disorder in the biological parents is compared between affected and unaffected children. Alternatively, the families may be recruited through biological parents. Here, prevalence of the disorder in adoptees with affected and unaffected biological parents is compared. This design may be expanded to include the status of the adoptive parents, so the well and ill biological parents are "crossed" with well and ill adoptive parents.

Although embraced enthusiastically by several authors (see, e.g., Tsuang and Faraone, 1990), adoption studies have several limitations. These designs may incorporate control groups; however, findings of higher levels of psychopathology in adoptees than in control groups (Rosenthal et al., 1975) must question the generalizability of findings to other groups. It is also likely that the environments of biological and adoptive parents are different. This will vary according to the country and time at which the adoptions occurred. In many instances, diagnoses of the biological parents must be made from incomplete information collected before they have passed through the period of risk for the disorder. Information concerning fathers is usually absent. In most developed countries, the practical difficulties in undertaking these studies is increasing, with the number of adoptions decreasing and strengthened privacy laws limiting access to essential information. Nevertheless, adoption studies can make a contribution in demonstrating that familiality of disorders is due to genetic, rather than environmental, factors.

4. Diagnostic Procedures

Genetic research shares with other investigations the need for reliable diagnoses. Methods, such as structured interviews, that increase reliability, therefore, will not be discussed in this chapter. The requirement of most genetic research for lifetime diagnoses of disorders in relatives of probands can raise difficulties. Most methods of analysis require the identification of both affected and unaffected family members. Optimally, all sources of information should be used; interviews with each family member, the examination of medical records, and interviews with informants. The difficulty of personally interviewing all family members (termed the family study method) has led to the use of interviews of relatives as a means of diagnosing family members (the family history method). Unfortunately, this approach has been shown to be associated with high rates of false-negative results in pedigrees (Andreasen et al., 1986; Mendlewicz et al., 1975); thus, the family history approach is to be preferred.

II. AFFECTIVE DISORDERS

A. Family Studies

Leonhard (1979), who distinguished patients with bipolar disorder (manic and depressive episodes) from those with monopolar (unipolar) depression, mainly on phenomenological grounds, noted that bipolar patients had a higher frequency of mania among their close relatives than did those with only episodes of depression—an observation previously made by Kallmann (1953). As the more recent studies have used the bipolar–unipolar dichotomy of Leonhard, this division is reflected here. Older studies using the terms "manic–depressive illness" or "affective disorder" are difficult to interpret and, therefore, will not be dealt with in detail.

1. Studies of Families with a Unipolar Depressed Proband

Familial Aggregation Studies. Recent studies of the rates of the various affective disorders in relatives of unipolar probands are summarized in Table 1. These should be compared with the reported rates in relatives of control probands outlined in Table 2. The morbid risk of unipolar depression ranges from 9.3 to 29.4%—rates consistently higher than the 4.6–5.9% found in control families and the 3.7–7.6% reported in the Epidemiological Catchment Area (ECA) study (Robins et al., 1984). Rates for bipolar disorder range from 1.0 to 4.5%. These figures are moderately higher than the

Table 1 Rates of Affective Illness in First-Degree Relatives of Unipolar Probands

	Morbid risk%					
Ref.	N	SA	BP	UP	All affective	Cyclothymia
Baron et al., 1982	144[a]	4.6	2.2	17.7	19.9	
Gershon et al., 1982	138[a]	0.7	2.9	16.6	19.5	0.0
Winokur et al., 1982	305[a]		1.0	11.2	12.2	
Coryell et al., 1984	572[a]		BPI 0.2 BPII 2.6 2.8	29.4	32.2	
Fieve et al., 1984	265[a]		4.3	9.7	14.0	
Weissman et al., 1984a[b]	974		BPI 0.8–1.5			0.6–0.7
Tsuang et al., 1985b[b]	482		2.5	9.3	11.8	
Rice et al., 1987	823[a]		1.1			
Andreasen et al., 1987[b]	1171	0.5	BPI 0.6 BPII 2.9 3.5	28.4		0.3
Stancer et al., 1987[b]	344		1.4	24.4	24.3	

[a] Age-corrected relatives at risk.
[b] Raw percentage figures—not morbid risk.
N, sample size; SA, schizoaffective disorder; BP, bipolar disorder; UP, unipolar disorder.
Source: Adapted from Gershon, 1990.

Table 2 Rates of Affective Illness in First-Degree Relatives of Normal Probands

		Morbid risk%				
Ref.	N	SA	BP	UP	All affective	Cyclothymia
Gershon et al., 1982	217[a]	0.5	0.5	5.8	6.3	0.8
Winokur et al., 1982	344[a]		0.2	4.6	4.8	
Weissman et al., 1984a[b]	521	0.2	BPI 0.2 BPII 1.1 1.3	5.9		0.0

[a] Age-corrected relatives at risk.
[b] Raw percentage figures—not morbid risk.
N, sample size; SA, schizoaffective disorder; BP, bipolar disorder; UP, unipolar disorder.
Source: Adapted from Gershon, 1990.

0.2–1.3% found in the families of control probands (see Table 2) and the 0.6–1.1% reported in the ECA study (Robins et al., 1984). Those studies that have subdivided bipolar subjects into BPI and BPII (Coryell et al., 1984; Andreasen et al., 1987) suggest that the increased bipolar rates may be due to mainly higher prevalences of BPII—an entity with characteristics that overlap bipolar and unipolar disorder. There have been few studies of schizoaffective disorders in unipolar families. With the exception of the Baron et al. (1982) study, the morbid risk of schizoaffective illness (0.5–0.7%) is little different from the 0.2–0.5% in controls. Cyclothymia does not seem to appear more commonly in these families. The total risk of affective disorder of 14.0–32.3%, however, is clearly higher than that observed in control pedigrees (4.8–6.3%).

The presence of assortative mating could be a partial explanation for elevated prevalence in offspring. Evidence for assortative mating is equivocal. In some studies, spouses have been found to have higher rates of affective disorders (see, e.g., Baron et al., 1981b), but in others (Gershon et al., 1975; Waters et al. 1988), no evidence for elevated prevalence or family history of affective disorder was observed. Some cases of depression in spouses could be reactive to the disorder in their partner. More recent studies have excluded families with assortative mating.

Mode of Transmission. There have been a limited number of studies of the mode of transmission of unipolar depression. Such studies have been complicated by the demonstration of a cohort effect (i.e., increased rates of illness and an earlier age of onset in successive cohorts; see, e.g., Klerman et al., 1985; Price et al., 1987; Reich et al., 1987).

The findings of these studies have been inconsistent. Crowe et al. (1981) and Price et al. (1987) found evidence for SML inheritance. Crowe and associates' study found that major depression, alcoholism, and drug dependency were the inherited spectrum of a major gene. Price's investigation, although favoring SML over MFP, was not without some statistical ambiguities. Additionally, there was no evidence for a major gene effect if the proband had coexisting panic disorder. Tanna et al. (1979), however, found no evidence for a SML mode of inheritance. On the other hand, Merikangas et al. (1985) found no evidence for a MFP model.

Two studies have examined for a sex effect in the inheritance of major depression. Reich et al. (1987) found higher rates of depression in female relatives. Faraone et al. (1987) found no support for X-linked transmission as an explanation for the increased female prevalence. They interpreted their negative findings as indicating that nongenetic factors are responsible for the robust finding of the increased risk for major depression among females.

Factors Associated with Increased Familial Risk for Unipolar Depression. Several studies have identified a series of features in unipolar-depressed probands associated with increased familial risk. These features are as follows:

1. *Early age of onset* (< *30 years*) (Pollitt, 1972; Weissman et al., 1986; Mendlewicz and Baron, 1981; Bland et al., 1986; and Kupfer et al., 1989). However, there has been one important negative finding. Reich et al. (1987) found no effect of age of onset when they took into account the cohort of birth.
2. *Unipolar depression with anxiety disorder or secondary alcoholism* (Weissman et al., 1986) was reported as being independent of the age of onset.
3. *Recurrent depression* has been reported as being associated with increased familial risk by Bland et al. (1986) and Kupfer et al. (1989). The latter group reported morbid risks in relatives of 20.7% for depression, 15.4% for alcoholism, and 1.1% for bipolar disorder.
4. *Increased number of depressive symptoms* (Klein, 1990).

Subtypes of Unipolar Depression. Endogenous versus neurotic. Although there have been a reasonable number of twin studies, there have been few family investigations of neurotic depression. Stenstedt (1966) investigated the relatives of probands with neurotic depression. He found that 4.8% of the parents and siblings of these patients had *affective disorder*—a broad term incorporating manic–depressive psychosis and neurotic depression. This rate of 4.8% was less than the 6.1% found in the relatives of those with involutional melancholia, and 10.2% in the families of patients with manic–depressive psychosis.

In 1982, Perris et al. similarly examined the morbid risk for affective disorder in the relatives of probands with neurotic–reactive depression. They found a 12.1% morbid risk in the parents and 6.7% in siblings. This compared with 22.8% of parents and 15.5% of siblings in the relatives of unipolar probands (using the European definition).

McGuffin and Bebbington (McGuffin et al., 1988a,b; Bebbington et al., 1991) examined the relevance of both the endogenous–neurotic division and life events in a genetic study undertaken in an inner-London community. With use of the Present State Examination (PSE)-derived CATEGO diagnoses, they examined the character of depression in relatives of probands with CATEGO categories indicative of endogenous or neurotic depression. They reported that in relatives of neurotic depressives there was a 23.1% morbid risk for any form of depression and a 6.8% risk of depression requiring inpatient treatment. Although relatives of those with a more endogenous pattern of depression demonstrated *no difference* in their morbid risk for depression per se (25.9%), there was a higher rate of depressed individuals requiring inpatient treatment (15.2%) in these families. This suggested that endogenous depression was not associated with an increased genetic risk for depression itself, but did increase the likelihood of a more severe depression requiring hospitalization.

Interestingly, these researchers found no relation between antecedent stress (life events) and a familial risk of depression. (They had postulated that depression that was not precipitated by life events would more likely be genetic). Their finding, however, is consistent with the more recent literature on endogenous depression, which was tended to find no difference in previous life events between these subjects and patients with neurotic depression (Paykel, 1982). They did find, however, familial aggregation of life events in some families with depression, a result that is difficult to explain in terms of genetic factors. In an earlier study, Pollitt (1972) reported a higher familial risk among families of depressed probands with psychological compared with physical precipitants.

Several other studies have examined whether endogenous depression is more familial. Although Leckman et al. (1984) found higher rates of endogenous depression in the relatives of endogenous-depressed probands, most other studies have not (e.g., Andreasen et al., 1986). Zimmerman et al. (1986) compared familial rates of major depression in endogenous and nonendogenous probands, but could not demonstrate a difference. Weissman et al. (1986) found that any difference in rates did not persist after controlling for factors such as age of onset. Price et al. (1984) reported findings akin to those of McGuffin et al. (1988a); that is, although finding no more depression in the families of endogenous depressed probands, they reported that more had received electroconvulsive therapy (ECT) than among the relatives of nonendogenous patients.

Delusional depression. There have been several investigations of rates of depression in the relatives of delusionally depressed probands; however, the results have been ambiguous. Weissman et al. (1984b) found bipolar disorder to be six times as frequent in the relatives of delusional probands when compared with the relatives of nondelusional major-depressed patients or controls.

Price et al. (1984) and Andreasen et al. (1986), however, found no more affective illness in these families. Lykouras et al. (1987) found no increase in rates of psychotic illness in the relatives of delusionally depressed probands. Lykouras et al. (1987) found the mode of transmission of illness in families of delusional depressives to be multifactorial.

Linkage Studies in Unipolar Disorder. Unlike the situation with bipolar disorder (see following), there have been relatively few linkage studies of unipolar pedigrees. Many of these investigations have arisen from Winokur's research group, reflecting their interest in validating their familial subtyping system. This system (Winokur et al., 1982) divides unipolar depression into familial pure depressive disease, depressive spectrum disease, and sporadic depressive disease.

There have been several positive linkage findings reported between Winokur's subtypes of unipolar depression and a series of non-HLA blood group markers. Depressive spectrum disorder has been found in sibship pair analyses to be linked to the marker C3 and HP (Tanna et al., 1976) and ORM (Hill et al., 1988). Familial pure depressive disorder has also been examined in sibship pair analyses and reported to be linked to MNS (Hill et al., 1988; Tanna et al., 1989) and ABO and IGK (Tanna et al., 1989). Using the lod score method, Tanna et al. (1977) reported loose linkage to G_C. However, all of these studies have arisen from Winokur's own group.

The studies examining linkage to histocompatibility (HLA) markers have examined either bipolar families only, or combinations of bipolar and unipolar pedigrees. In a sibship pair analysis (with additional pedigrees to their original 1980 study) Weitkamp and Stancer (1989) found a significant increase in HLA haplotype sharing between affected relatives *only* in unipolar subjects.

In the only study of unipolar pedigrees examining linkage to RFLP markers, Neiswanger et al. (1990) reported no linkage to chromosomal regions 11p15 or Xq28.

1. Studies of Families with a Bipolar Disorder Proband

Familial Aggregation Studies. Table 3 summarizes recent studies examining the diagnostic spectrum found in families of bipolar disorder probands. Earlier studies have been well outlined by Nurnberger and Gershon (1984).

Three of the studies have examined rates of schizoaffective disorder, finding indications of an increased morbid risk in bipolar families (0.7–1.5% compared with 0.2–0.5% in controls; see Table 2). It should be noted that these studies have used the

Table 3 Rates of Affective Illness in First-Degree Relatives of Bipolar Probands

	Morbid risk%					
Ref.	N	SA	BP	UP	All affective	Cyclothymia
Baron et al., 1982	135[a]	1.5	14.5	16.3	30.3	
Gershon et al., 1982	598[a]	1.2	8.0	14.9	22.9	BPI Proband
						2.7
						BPII Proband
						2.6
Winokur et al., 1982	196[a]		1.5	12.8	14.3	
Coryell et al., 1984	389[a]		BPI proband			
			BPI 0.6			
			BPII 2.9			
			5.4	22.7	28.1	
			BPII proband			
			BPI 0.9			
			BPII 9.8			
			11.7	21.4	33.1	
Fieve et al., 1984	1309[a]			9.0	15.6	
Weissman et al., 1984a[b]	508			14.3		
Tsuang et al., 1985[b]	218			7.8	10.6	
Rice et al., 1987	557[a]					
Andreasen et al., 1987[b]	836		BPI proband			
		0.4	BPI 3.9			
			BPII 4.2			
			8.1	22.8		
			BPII proband			
		0.4	BPI 1.1			
			BPII 8.2			
			9.3	26.2		
Stancer et al., 1987[b]	277		4.4	18.7	24.6	

[a] Age-corrected relatives at risk.
[b] Raw percentage figures—not morbid risk.
N, sample size; SA, schizoaffective disorder; BP, bipolar disorder; UP, unipolar disorder.
Source: Adapted from Gershon, 1990.

RDC definition of this disorder—many such patients would be diagnosed as psychotically manic or depressed under other classificatory systems or in clinical practice.

Bipolar disorder is clearly increased, with rates of 1.5–14.5% compared with 0.2–1.3% in controls. Three studies (Coryell et al., 1984; Weissman et al., 1984a; Andreasen et al., 1987) have investigated the heritability of the BPI and BPII subtypes. For families of bipolar I probands, there would appear to be increased rates of both BPI and BPII disorders. The two studies that have examined families of BPII probands indicate a higher risk of BPII, but the BPI rates appear similar to those in control families and general population samples.

Unipolar depression definitely occurs more frequently in these pedigrees, with rates of 7.8–22.8%, higher than the rates of 4.6–5.9% found in control pedigrees. Two studies have examined rates of cyclothymia, suggesting that this is increased, with morbid risks of 2.6–3.0% compared with up to 0.8% in controls

Overall, rates of affective disorder are clearly increased in the families of bipolar probands, with rates of 7.8–30.8% compared with 4.8–6.3% in control pedigrees. These figures indicate a strong genetic diathesis to a spectrum of affective disorders in families of bipolar probands. This spectrum would appear to include at least bipolar disorder, unipolar depression, and schizoaffective disorder, with the possible addition of cyclothymia.

Cohort effect. As with unipolar depression, there is apparently also a cohort effect for bipolar disorder. Gershon et al. (1987) have reported that, among relatives of probands with bipolar and schizoaffective disorder, rates of bipolar, schizoaffective, and unipolar disorders were higher in controls born after 1940 than in earlier cohorts. This increase has not been seriously addressed in linkage studies for which it may be a significant confounding factor.

The genetic relation between bipolar I and bipolar II. A few investigations have addressed the issue of the genetic relation between BPI and BPII disorders. Coryell et al. (1984) reported that BPII probands were more likely to have BPII relatives than were BPI or major-depressed probands. That group also found that BPII probands were slightly more likely than major-depressed, and slightly less likely than BPI probands, to have relatives with BPI illness. Similar findings have been reported by Gershon et al. (1982) and Fieve et al. (1984). Such studies indicate the necessity to treat BPII disorder as a different threshold of affective illness for prevalence studies, and segregation and linkage analyses.

Early-onset bipolar disorder. Although there is some consistency in the finding that early onset unipolar depression is more likely to be genetic in its causation, findings have been less consistent for bipolar disorder. In 1981, Taylor and Abrams reported that those bipolar probands with the onset of their disorder before 30 years of age had three times the morbidity risk for affective disorder in their first-degree relatives, compared with those of later-onset probands. They also had more bipolar relatives. Gershon et al. (1982), however, did not replicate these findings. Strober and coauthors' 1988 report of higher familial aggregation rates in adolescent BPI probands than in adults suggests that adolescent onset may indicate a greater likelihood of a genetic etiology.

The Mode of Transmission of Bipolar Disorder. Studies using pedigree segregation analysis for families with bipolar disorder have been of two major forms (Faraone et al., 1990). Some have used polarity-specific thresholds (i.e., they have assumed that the two disorders are different phenotypic manifestations of the same single gene), with bipolar disorder being the more severe form and unipolar disorder the milder form. Other analyses have not assumed different thresholds for bipolar and unipolar disorders, either considering only bipolar relatives to be ill (e.g., Rice et al., 1987) or assuming those with *either* bipolar or unipolar disorder to be affected.

Table 4 outlines pedigree segregation analyses of families of bipolar probands, including both those studies that have used polarity-specific thresholds, and those that have not.

Table 4 Pedigree Segregation Analyses of Bipolar Disorder Probands

Study	Model tested	Support for model
Analyses using polarity-specific thresholds		
Gershon et al., 1975	SML	Yes
	MFP	Yes
Gershon et al., 1976	SML	Yes/No (two different data sets)
	MFP	Yes/No (two different data sets)
Smeraldi et al., 1977	MFP	Yes
Van Eerdewegh et al., 1980[a]	SML (X-chromosome)	Yes/No (two different data sets
Baron et al., 1981	SML	Yes
	MFP	No
Gershon et al., 1982	MFP	Yes
Tsuang et al., 1985a	SML	Yes
Price et al., 1985[a]	SML	Yes
	MFP	No
Tsuang et al., 1985b	MFP	Yes
Cox et al., 1989	SML	No
	MFP	No
Analyses without polarity-specific thresholds		
Mendlewicz and Rainer, 1974	SML	Yes
Leckman and Gershon, 1977[a]	SML	Yes/No (five different data sets)
	MFP	Yes/No (five different data sets)
Van Eerdewegh et al., 1980[a]	SML (X-chromosome)	Yes/No (three different data sets)
Crowe and Smouse, 1977	SML	Yes
	SML (X-chromosome)	Yes
Bucher et al., 1981	SML	No (three different data sets)
	SML (X-chromosome)	No (three different data sets)
Goldin et al., 1983	SML	No
	SML (X-chromosome)	No
Smeraldi et al., 1984	SML	Yes
	MFP	Yes
Shaughnessy et al., 1985	Mixed	Familial transmission. Unable to distinguish between SML and MFP models.
Rice et al., 1987[a]	Mixed	Some evidence for presence of SML on multifactorial background

[a] Modeling includes assessment of effect of sex.
Source: Modified from Faraone et al., 1990.

Those analyses that have incorporated an assessment of the effect of gender are indicated. The studies have largely employed different pedigree data sets (for more details, see Faraone et al., 1990).

As indicated in these tables, the results of the analyses have been conflicting, with no consistent evidence for either a single major locus or a multifactorial mode of inheritance. Similarly, ambiguous findings are reported, irrespective of whether polarity-specific thresholds have been employed. Even when SML inheritance has been supported, some analyses have been consistent with a dominant (autosomal or X-linked) model and others with recessive inheritance.

The comprehensive study of Rice et al. (1987) is worthy of particular note. This NIMH Collaborative Program study of the families of 187 bipolar probands tested a mixed model. That model gave evidence for the presence of a major locus when controlling for the effects of birth cohorts and age of onset. The results of that study were tempered, however, when comparing the mixed model with a more general transmission model.

It is apparent that no definitive conclusions can be drawn from these studies. Although by no means clearly supportive of SML inheritance, such conflicting results cannot exclude this possibility. Genetic heterogeneity, phenocopies, and incomplete penetrance may significantly reduce the potential of these statistical methods to demonstrate a major locus effect. It is unlikely that further developments in segregation analysis techniques will be able to discriminate satisfactorily between SML and MFP inheritance.

Linkage Studies in Bipolar Disorder. As outlined in the preceding discussion, there is currently inconclusive evidence concerning the mode of transmission of this condition. Linkage studies, therefore, are currently being employed mainly to clarify if there is a major gene for this condition. As discussed previously, the first step in linkage analysis is the selection of the region of the chromosome to be scanned for linkage.

Cytogenetic studies indicating a potential site of the gene(s) for bipolar disorder. Use of chromosomal abnormalities detected in cytogenetic studies has been a useful means of identifying the region of the disease gene for at least two major inherited disorders in recent years. First, the demonstration of a translocation in the X chromosome in a female presenting with Duchenne's muscular dystrophy (an X-linked disorder; therefore, normally only manifesting in males) indicated the potential region of the disease gene, which was thereafter soon identified. Second, the identical brain pathology of demented Down syndrome sufferers and Alzheimer's disease patients suggested undertaking linkage studies at the trisomy 21 site. This strategy led to the first of the positive linkage studies to this chromosome in familial Alzheimer's disease.

Although there have been no consistent chromosomal abnormalities demonstrated in bipolar disorder, the following reports in recent years may provide clues to the possible site of the gene(s):

1. *Chromosome 11*: Smith et al. (1989) reported a family with a cosegregation of a balanced 9/11 chromosomal translocation with affective disorder. The breakpoint in this pedigree was at 11q22.3. In 1990, St. Clair et al. detailed a pedigree with an association of a balanced translocation—t(1:11)(q43, q21)—with psychiatric illness presenting variably as schizophrenia, schizoaffective disorder, and recurrent major depression. Intriguingly, these reports related to contiguous regions on the long arm of chromosome 11.

2. *Chromosome 15*: Kerbeshian et al. (1990) described a case report of a patient with "atypical" bipolar disorder, autism, and profound mental retardation. Cytogenetic studies demonstrated a deletion of 15q12.
3. *Chromosome 21*: El-Badramany et al. (1989) have detailed a family with bipolar disorder and a deletion of the short arm of chromosome 21. However, only two members of the pedigree were affected.
4. *X Chromosome*: In 1986, Reiss et al. described a family with an association between fragile X (either clinical status or carrier) and major affective disorders. Mendlewicz and Hirsch (1991), more recently, reported another fragile X family in which there was an association between bipolar disorder and this syndrome.

In addition to the well-known previously reported linkage with X-linked traits or disorders (see the following), there have been several recent reports of bipolar disorder being associated with other clinical disorders:

1. *Thalassemia minor*: Joffe et al. (1986) described a family in which thalassemia minor and bipolar disorder–unipolar depression were associated. This is of interest as the ß-globin gene (which is defective in thalassemia minor) is located on the short arm of chromosome 11.
2. *Stuttering*: Hays and Field (1989) reported an association between stuttering and bipolar disorder in three pedigrees. Stuttering, however, is usually thought to be inherited by multifactorial polygenic inheritance.

The following linkage studies are considered in historical order. The initial linkage studies, stimulated by reports of an association between color blindness and bipolar disorder, focused on the X chromosome. The discovery of the highly polymorphic HLA antigenic system on chromosome 6 in the 1970s stimulated much research into potential associations with a range of disorders, including the affective illnesses. Finally, the development of RFLPs was recognized by Botstein (1980) as providing the means for potentially examining linkage to any region of the human genome. Although initial RFLP studies have focused on particular candidate genes, comprehensive genome-scanning studies are now in progress (Leboyer and McGuffin, 1991; Paratkis et al., 1991). The recent development of CA repeat markers has provided a significant refinement of the RFLP technology (Weber et al., 1990).

Studies of linkage to the X chromosome. The first report of linkage to the X chromosome was that of Winokur et al. (1969). That group reported a significant association between bipolar disorder and color blindness (an X-linked trait). Consistent with this apparent X-linkage, they were unable to find evidence of father-to-son transmission in their pedigrees.

Since that original study, the major confirmatory studies have derived from the research group under Mendlewicz in Belgium. In 1974, Mendlewicz and Fleiss reported tight linkage to both protan (CBP) and deutan (CBD) color blindness, which are both now recognized to be in close proximity in chromosomal region Xq28. This report appeared to be confirmed by a 1980 study by Mendlewicz et al. in which tight linkage to *glucose-6-phosphate dehydrogenase* (G6PD) deficiency was reported, as G6PD is located about 3 centimorgans (cM) from CBP and CBD. Further reports (e.g., Mendlewicz and Fleiss, 1974) of loose linkage to the Xg blood group marker (also on the X chromosome) were claimed as being confirmatory of the original findings, as was this group's report of linkage to factor IX on the same chromosome (Mendlewicz et al., 1987). The other major positive report of X-linkage has been from Baron et al. (1987). That study of five Israeli pedigrees found very significant evidence of linkage to Xq28 markers, particularly CBD and CBP.

There have been, however, a large number of equivocal findings. Moreover, there have been some significant findings clearly excluding linkage to the Xq28 region. Foremost among this has been the report of Berrettini et al. (1990). This report, arising from Gershon's group (which also reported the only other definite rejection of linkage to this region (Gershon et al., 1979), examined linkage to RFLP markers for Xq28 in nine bipolar pedigrees.

Recently, there have been several serious criticisms of the studies arising from the Mendlewicz group. In 1987, Suarez et al. criticized the 1987 report which claimed linkage to factor IX for not including any correction for penetrance or age of onset. More recently, Vassart et al., 1991 (the authors included some of the initial collaborators in the Mendlewicz et al., 1987, paper) emphasized that factor IX is not linked to the factor VIII-G6PD-color blindness cluster at region Xq28, but is, in fact, sited at Xq27. They also noted that one of the families in the 1987 paper was a fragile X pedigree (with all mood disordered individuals in that pedigree having that chromosomal abnormality), which meant that it was not a suitable pedigree for inclusion in such a study.

Gershon (1991) reevaluated Mendlewicz's previous studies of linkage to color blindness and the Xg blood group. Subsequent to the original reports it was recognized that Xg is at the tip of short arm of the X chromosome, whereas the color blindness genes are located at the tip of the long arm. This would mean logically that a single locus for bipolar disorder could not be linked to both regions. Reanalysis by Gershon of these studies demonstrated apparent close linkage between the two markers, a logically impossible outcome. Gershon interpreted this result as indicating systematic genotyping errors in Mendlewicz's reports.

There are two possible interpretations of the current literature related to the X chromosome. Either there is genetic heterogeneity, with a small number of X-linked pedigrees with a locus at Xq28 or, alternatively, there is no linkage, with the Baron et al. (1987) finding representing a chance result—an unlikely proposition, as Baron et al. reported very high lod scores. Baron et al. (1990a) have recently reanalyzed the data of their 1987 paper by estimating the level of diagnostic uncertainty and examining various definitions of the bipolar spectrum. They still found strong evidence for linkage—particularly to color blindness, with each of those models. This reanalysis would appear to confirm the validity of the initial report. The most parsimonious explanation of the current literature is that only a small proportion of bipolar families have a responsible gene on the X chromosome.

Studies of linkage to the HLA region on chromosome 6. The initial interest in a potential association between bipolar disorder and the HLA region on the short arm of chromosome 6 derived from an association study published by Shapiro et al. in 1976. That investigation found an altered frequency of four HLA antigens in patients with affective disorder, and particularly in those with bipolar disorder. Subsequent association studies (Fieve et al., 1984; Biederman et al., 1987; Payami et al., 1989) have had variable findings, with those positive studies finding associations with *different* HLA antigens from those identified in the original report.

Sibship studies have been also variable in their findings. The major positive study has been that of Weitkamp et al. (1981), but their methodology has been criticized (Goldin et al. 1982). A more recent reanalysis by Weitkamp et al. (1989), including new pedigrees, confirmed the original findings, but found that the association was more marked in unipolar siblings. Linkage studies (e.g., Waters et al., 1988) have been virtually unanimous in their negative results, with the exception of the investigation of Turner and King (1981, 1983). Overall, these results indicate that it is highly unlikely that there is a gene responsible for bipolar disorder in the HLA region of chromosome 6.

Studies of linkage to chromosomal region 11p15 and other autosomal chromosomal regions using RFLP markers. The first report of significant evidence of linkage of RFLP markers to bipolar disorder was that of Egeland et al. (1987). This study investigated linkage of markers on the short arm of chromosome 11 (region 11p15)—specifically the oncogene c-Harvey-*ras* (*HRAS* 1) and insulin (*INS*)—in a large bipolar pedigree in the Old Order Amish community. This was a family with demonstrated autosomal dominant inheritance with reduced penetrance. Examining linkage to those with either bipolar disorder or unipolar disorder depression, the authors demonstrated tight linkage to *HRAS* 1 and loose (albeit impressive) linkage to *INS*. As outlined in Kidd et al. (1987), the chromosome 11p15 markers were among the original markers tested when this research group commenced a limited genome scanning study in the mid-1980s.

The only confirmatory report has been an association study by Leboyer et al. (1990). This French group examined tyrosine hydroxylase (*TH*) RFLP alleles in a group of bipolar patients and a group of controls. *TH* is situated adjacent to *INS* in 11p15 and is of theoretical interest as it is the rate-limiting enzyme in the catecholaminergic metabolic pathway. Leboyer et al. demonstrated a significant difference in the frequency of *TH* alleles in the patient and control groups—a finding suggestive, although not confirmative, of linkage between *TH* and bipolar disorder.

There has, however, been a failure to replicate these positive reports using either the lod score method (Hodgkinson et al., 1987; Detera-Wadleigh et al., 1987; Gill et al., 1988; Wesner et al., 1990; and Mitchell et al., 1991) or association studies (Todd and O'Malley, 1989; Korner et al., 1990). More significantly, a revision and reanalysis of the Old Amish pedigree (which was originally undertaken to further identify the putative gene on 11p15) found a reduced statistical likelihood of linkage (Kelsoe et al., 1989). The family was reanalyzed after addition of genotypes from some previously untyped members, inclusion of two new presentations of illness in the original "core" pedigree, and the inclusion of two lateral "extensions" of this original family. The first two changes led to a reduction of the likelihood of linkage, whereas the inclusion of the lateral extensions, in fact, led to *exclusion* of close linkage. It is theoretically possible that this reduced significance of linkage with the inclusion of the lateral extensions may have been due to genetic heterogeneity—it is possible that a Mennonite with a family history of bipolar disorder may have been married to one of these extensions. However, it is now considered most likely that the original positive linkage findings to chromosome 11p15 in the original core pedigree was due to chance.

There have been only a few RFLP linkage studies examining other chromosomal regions. Holmes et al. (1991) have excluded linkage to the dopamine D_2 receptor, a finding that was replicated by Mitchell et al. (1992), who also excluded linkage to the D_1 receptor. Paratkis and associates (1991) have recently reported preliminary findings from the ongoing genome-scanning study of the Old Order Amish pedigree. They have excluded linkage to approximately one-third of the human genome.

3. The Future of Linkage-Studies of Affective Disorder

Linkage studies will continue to dominate research in severe psychiatric disorders. In view of the previous pattern of discovery and reversal of linkage findings it is critical that linkage be optimized.

Resolving the Inconsistencies in the Linkage Studies of Bipolar Disorder. Gershon (1991) has suggested four possible sources of error in linkage studies:

1. *Genetic heterogeneity*. There may be different major genes responsible for this condition in different pedigrees. This is a well-recognized phenomenon in many other genetic disorders.
2. *Type I error*. Positive findings may represent chance findings where there is no "true" association. Edwards and Watt (1989) have commented that this is more likely when multiple markers are tested. They argue that allowance for multiple testing should be considered when determining the lod score necessary to indicate significance. Ott (1989) has also argued that testing of multiple parameters (such as varying levels of penetrance) maximizes the chance of demonstrating linkage. Lod scores, he suggests, should, therefore, be at least 3.5 to be considered indicative of close linkage.
3. *Random procedural errors in diagnosis or genotyping*. These errors would be more likely to reduce the chance of being able to demonstrate linkage rather than produce spurious positive evidence (Clerget-Darpoux, 1991; Martinez et al., 1989).
4. *Nonrandom (or systematic) errors in diagnosis or genotyping*. It is essential to carry out these procedures blindly to exclude this possibility. Gershon (1991) has suggested that this may explain the bizarre apparent linkage of bipolar disorder to both color blindness and Xg, as has been reported by Mendlewicz's group.

Methodological Improvements. Suggestions for such improvements have been made by Merikangas et al. (1989) and Baron et al. (1990b). The recommendations of these authorities can be synthesized and summarized as follows:

1. *Assessment of pedigrees*: The means of ascertainment should be clearly described. Large dense pedigrees are to be preferred to maximize the chances of a monogenic mode of inheritance. There should be a systematic evaluation of spouses (and their relatives) marrying into the pedigree. Pedigrees with bilineal transmission or assortative mating should be excluded.
2. *Diagnosis*: Standardized diagnostic criteria with documented reliability must be employed, preferably using multiple diagnostic systems. Standardized assessment procedures [such as SADS-L; CIDI (Robins et al., 1988)] should be used. Clinical information should be based on multiple sources (e.g., direct interview, information from other family members, and hospital records). Blindness between the diagnostic and genotyping procedures must be maintained. Longitudinal follow-up to confirm diagnosis is preferred.
3. *Linkage markers*: Genotyping reliability should be monitored. Candidate genes and random genome scanning can be studied concurrently.
4. *Statistical analyses*: Realistic estimates of penetrance and other parameters should be used. Allowances for variable age of onset and any cohort effect should be incorporated into the analysis. Diagnostic boundaries should be varied, moving from narrow to broad, and Baron et al. (1990a) have also argued that estimates

of diagnostic uncertainty and *penetrance free* models of analysis (in which unaffecteds in the risk period are identified as *unknown*) should be employed.

5. *Replication*: Independent replication is essential. Pedigrees in which positive linkage is demonstrated should be scrutinized by extending these, when possible, and ensuring that the maximal proportion has been genotyped.

Alternative Approaches to Segregation Analyses of Bipolar Disorder. Current methods for determining the mode of transmission (i.e., SML vs MFP inheritance) have proved unsatisfactory. An alternative approach to distinguishing monogenic from polygenic inheritance has recently been proposed by Risch (1990a). As yet, this has not been applied to bipolar disorder, although it appears to be of use in analyzing the inheritance of schizophrenia—a condition analogous to bipolar disorder in its genetic complexity. Risch has refined the ratio lambda, which was originally devised by Penrose (1953). Lambda is the ratio of the "risk (of the disorder) of relatives of a proband" versus "population prevalence of a trait." This method uses the principle that lambda decreases with the degree of the relation between probands and relative. Risch (1990a) applied this technique to published prevalence studies for schizophrenia and demonstrated that these figures best fitted an epistatic (interaction of genes) model of two or three major loci. This technique has undoubted relevance to the analysis of the inheritance of bipolar disorder. A similar hypothesis of oligenic inheritance for bipolar disorder would support current attempts to find genes through linkage analyses, although larger numbers of families than used hitherto may be necessary to be confident about the outcome of such studies.

4. Summary

A pejorative review of this area might claim that beyond demonstrating familiality, little else has been revealed by family studies of affective disorder. This state of affairs reflects the time at which this review is compiled: the inconclusive results of segregation analyses reflect their lack of power to distinguish between models that predict similar results. Recent linkage studies have confidently *excluded* certain sites for linkage. There is considerable frustration in not having available the outcome of those studies currently in progress that will provide more definitive answers to the single-locus question.

B. Twin Studies

1. Bipolar, Unipolar Disorder, and Major Depression

Unlike family studies, a review of twin studies cannot assemble sufficient data to warrant the separate consideration of these diagnostic categories. Therefore, severe affective disorders are considered together.

Twin studies were one of the earliest methods by which the heritability of depression was demonstrated and quantified. Table 5 shows concordance rates and heritabilities presented by Tsuang and Faraone (1990) for 12 studies of major depression, together with two others: Harvald and Hauge, (1965) and McGuffin et al., (1991). Although most studies were undertaken before 1960, later investigations have generally recruited much larger numbers of twins.

These studies differ widely in the manner in which cases were ascertained and diagnoses made. The earlier studies (Luxenburger, 1928; Rosanoff et al., 1935; Slater and Shields, 1953) relied on hospital records for the recruitment of twin pairs. Some recent studies, notably those carried out in Scandinavia by Torgersen (1986) and Bertelsen et

Table 5 Concordance Rates and Heritabilities for Major Depression Derived From Twin Studies

		Concordance		Heritability	
Study	Diagnosis	MZ	DZ	H	G
Luxenburger, 1928, 1930	MD	0.80	0.00	0.80	
Rosanoff et al., 1935	MD	0.69–0.82	0.23–0.37	0.77	0.45
Slater and Shields, 1953	MD	0.57–0.73	0.19–0.32	0.60	0.47
Kallmann, 1953, 1954	MD	1.00	0.26	0.59	
Da Fonseca, 1963	MD	0.60	0.31	0.42	0.33
Harvald and Hauge, 1965	MD	0.67	0.05	0.65	
Kringlen, 1967	MD	0.33–0.50	0.00	0.50	
	BP	0.67–0.80	0.00	0.80	
Pollin et al., 1969	MD	0.04–0.08	0.00	0.08	
Allen et al., 1974	MD	0.33–0.50	0.00	0.50	
	UP	0.40–0.57	0.00	0.57	
	BP	0.20–0.33	0.00	0.33	
Bertelsen et al., 1977	MD	0.67	0.20	0.59	0.61
	UP	0.43	0.18	0.30	
	BP	0.62	0.08	0.59	
Torgersen, 1986	MD	0.38–0.56	0.12–0.22		0.56
	UP	0.30–0.47	0.14–0.24		
	BP	1.00	0.00		
McGuffin and Katz, 1991	MD	0.68	0.43	0.44	0.43
	UP	0.53	0.28	0.35	0.51

MD, mood disorder; BP, bipolar disorder; UP, unipolar disorder; H, Holzinger's heritability; G, Smith's heritability (heritability of liability to the disorder). Except for Kallman (1953, 1954), DZ twins are same sex pairs.
Source: Adapted from Tsuang and Faraone, 1990.

al. (1977) have been able to recruit twins from systematic twin and psychiatric registers.

The studies also vary considerably in the criteria used for diagnosis and, therefore, in the nature of the concordance reported. Studies such as Luxenburger's have been reported to have classified relatively minor mood disorders, mixed and other conditions as concordant for mood disorder (Kringlen, 1967). Although the availability of the data of some studies, such as that of Maudsley twins reported by Slater and Shields (1953), is detailed enough to allow reclassification and reanalysis (see Tsuang and Faraone, 1990; McGuffin et al., 1991), generally this is not the case.

Twins are shared by some of the studies. Both Pollin et al. (1969) and Allen et al. (1974) used medical records from the US Veterans Administration; however, the latter study conducted a more exhaustive search for cases than did the former. Failure to detect cases could explain why the former study reported considerably lower concordance than most other twin studies.

Three of the larger studies warrant particular attention. Bertelsen et al. (1977) interviewed 133 twins from 220 potential cases identified through the Danish Psychiatric Twin Register. Although standardized diagnostic criteria were not used, subjects had to have been hospitalized as the result of a mood disorder to qualify as cases. This study demonstrated a gradient of heritability declining from bipolar disorder with manic episodes (BPI) (0.77), through bipolar disorder with hypomania (BPII) (0.68), to unipolar disorder (0.41 for three or more episodes and 0.22 for fewer than three episodes). This supports the concept of bipolar disorder as a biological disorder, principally genetic in etiology, with less severe depressive disorders as correspondingly less genetically and more environmentally determined.

Bertelsen et al. (1977) also examined the extent to which polarity "breeds true." Of 32 concordant MZ pairs, 14 were concordant for bipolar disorder and 11 for unipolar disorder. They demonstrated that the seven pairs in which one twin had unipolar and the other had bipolar disorder were significantly fewer than would be predicted if both disorders shared the same genotype.

Torgersen (1986) undertook a similar register-based study of Norwegian twins. A version of the Present State Examination (Wing et al., 1974) modified for lifetime symptoms was used to interview 299 twin pairs. The *DSM-III* diagnoses were derived from records of the interview. Like Bertelsen et al.'s study, Torgersen also found a decreasing gradient of heritability from bipolar disorder, through psychotic major depression, nonpsychotic major depression, to dysthymic disorder and depressive adjustment disorder.

McGuffin and coworkers' (1991) recent study is unique in using the formal model-testing approach described earlier on a relatively large twin sample ascertained through the Maudsley Twin Register. Some of these twins have previously been included in studies reported by Da Fonseca (1963) and Slater and Shields (1953). A lifetime version of the PSE supplemented by questions that allowed *DSM-III* classifications to be made was used to interview 67 probands and 81 cotwins. Liability models involving the unique environment (ES) only, followed by the addition of either additive genetic effects (VA) or common environment effects (EC) were fitted to the concordance data for hospital-treated depression and *DSM-III* major affective disorder. Models involving only ES provided a poor fit in both cases. The addition of terms for either VA or EC improved fit significantly, but only in the major affective disorder did the fit of an unsaturated model (including ES and VA) approach acceptable levels. Parameters may be estimated for models containing all three terms, but fit cannot be evaluated, as these models are saturated and perfectly fit the data.

Penetrance. Special twin-based designs can be used to investigate specific research questions. Bertelsen and Gottesman (1986) compared the prevalence of bipolar disorder in the offspring of discordant twins. They found that 24.7% of the offspring of unaffected and 20.7% of the offspring of affected MZ twins were cases, compared with 2.1% and 14% of the offspring of DZ twins. This demonstrates the extent to which the genotype for the disorder may be transmitted, but remain unexpressed.

Concordance in Dizygotic Twins. Consistent with findings for many psychological traits, concordance between DZ twins is lower than would be expected under an additive genetic model: if depression is as heritable as suggested by MZ twin concordance, then DZ concordance should not be zero, as shown for most studies in Table 5. For traits, notably extraversion, this has been taken as evidence for the influence of one twin on the other (see Eaves et al., 1989). Alternative explanations focus on intra- and interloci interaction (dominance and epistasis). Because twins form a very restricted pedigree, there are only very limited possibilities to test for dominance in the twin design. Nevertheless, this level of concordance suggests that factors, whether genetic or environmental, in addition to additive gene action may influence depression in twins and, presumably, other kinships.

Other Sources of Variation in Twin Studies. Although not the major concern of this chapter, the fitting of variance components to twin data reveals other interesting characteristics of the etiology of depression. This approach has been taken by only a few researchers (e.g., Torgersen, 1986, McGuffin et al., 1991); however, Faraone et al., (1988, cited by Tsuang and Faraone, 1990) have estimated variance components from five other studies. These studies show VA accounting for 33–64% of the total variance. Common environment accounted for between 21 and 61% of the variance with ES from between nil and 23%. With the exception of Torgersen's study, Tsuang and Faraone (1990) report that estimates of heritability and common environment fall within 1 standard error of each other between studies, indicating substantial consensus.

When it is realized that ES includes any variability caused by unreliability in measurement of the phenotype, these figures invite closer scrutiny. Studies of reliability of lifetime diagnoses suggest that structured interviews may have only moderate reliability (see, e.g., Helzer et al., 1977). Thus, these low figures seem somewhat implausible as estimates of the total proportion of unique effects on twin data variance.

The magnitude of the EC effect is also surprising when compared with other twin research into personality, cognitive, and intellectual characteristics. This research has uniformly demonstrated low or no common environmental effects (Plomin and Daniels, 1987). The existence of significant EC effects implicates a narrow range of environmental determinants of depression, namely, those within families. Such factors could include adverse social experience, poor parenting, or exposure to causal agents in the physical environmental. Although some of these factors have been associated with depression, the magnitude of these effects has been much lower than is implied by these twin studies and has not been uniquely associated with bipolar and severe unipolar disorder. For instance, Parker (1983) demonstrated an association between adverse parenting and depression, but this effect is unique to neurotic depression and was not found in cases of endogenous depression.

Assortative mating (see foregoing) is one explanation for the high values of EC. In a twin study assortative mating acts to increase the genetic similarity of DZ twins and will increase their concordance for heritable conditions. This acts to inflate the EC effect, but at the expense of the genetic component. An alternative explanation is that the common environment effect observed is that of paths to treatment (in the form of hospitalization) is a source of the EC effect.

Summary. If the principal objective is to demonstrate that a genetic effect of some sort exists, then these studies must indicate the robustness of such an effect to considerable differences in definitions of the disorder and large variations in ascertainment strategies. More specific assertions need to be made with care: most of these studies are based on small numbers. Although the concordance of MZ twins may be statistically greater than for DZ twins, point estimates of heritabilities carry wide confidence intervals. Evidence to support the differential heritability of bipolar and unipolar disorder and sex differences has been discussed in several reports, but few of these observations have been supported by formal model testing. The principal reason for this is small sample sizes. Nevertheless, the primary contribution of the twin study—to demonstrate that familiality is at least partially due to genetic, rather than environmental, factors—stands.

2. *Minor Depressive Disorder*

Disorders such as neurotic or reactive depression, dysthymia, cyclothymia, cyclothymic personality disorder fall into this category. Two types of study of minor mood disorder have been reported: (1) those in which probands have been ascertained as having a severe disorder, but in which less severe diagnoses for cotwins were recorded; and (2) those in which ascertainment also occurred on the basis of minor disorders.

Minor Depression in Cotwins of Severely Depressed Probands. Studies of this type enable examination of the concept that minor disorders that are less severe, genetically-identical forms of severe disorders. Although not examined using formal models, such as multiple threshold liability models, Kallman (1954) reported that in 17 of 42 DZ twins and 1 of 2 MZ twins discordant for manic depression, the cotwin had a cycloid personality type (a mild tendency to emotional instability). Given that 55 DZ and 57 MZ pairs were studied, using a broader definition of concordance, the increased concordance of DZ twins was taken to imply lower heritability.

Kringlen (1967) reanalysed Da Fonseca's (1959) study, broadening the definition of manic depression to include cotwins with a hypomanic or depressive personality as concordant. Concordance of both MZ and DZ twins was increased and, thus, no significant change in heritability was noted.

As part of his study of twins from the Norwegian Twin Register, Torgersen (1986) reported concordance for bipolar disorder in three cotwins of four probands with the disorder. Only one cotwin with bipolar disorder was ascertained from 102 probands with major depression and none with a less severe illness. Of 33 MZ and 59 DZ probands with major depression, 21% of MZ and 15% of DZ cotwins had minor depressive disorder, suggesting low heritability.

Twin Studies with Probands with Minor Depressive Disorder. Among probands with affective disorders in Torgersen's twin study, 16 MZ and 19 DZ twins met the *DSM-III* criteria for dysthymia. Strict concordance for dysthymia was low (MZ/DZ = 19%:5%) leading to a heritability estimate of 19%. Broadening criteria to include either more severe illness or depressive adjustment disorder had little influence on heritability.

Shapiro (1970) identified 30 twin pairs on the Danish Twin Registry who had been hospitalized, but who failed to meet the criteria for inclusion in the study of Bertelsen and associates (1977), reported in Table 5. Strict concordance for hospitalized depression was low (MZ/DZ = 22:0%) and not significantly different between zygosities, leading to a heritability of 28%. Broadening the definition of disorder to include other nonendogenous disorders increased concordance to 56:14% increasing heritability to 58%. Englund and Klein (1990) reanalysed Shapiro's data classifying twins' disorders according to the RDC criteria for major or definite minor depression and Winokur's neurotic–reactive criteria. This led to increased concordance for both zygosities with a significantly higher concordance for MZ twins. In addition to demonstrating the heritability of neurotic depression, Englund and Klein's analysis shows that the definition of the disorder may be critical in determining its heritability.

3. *Studies Using Self-Report Inventories*

A different stream of evidence about the genetic basis of minor depression comes from the analysis of self-report questionnaires. Relatively little attention has been paid to these studies in the psychiatric literature, presumably because there is no specific relation between inventory scores and clinical disorders. Symptom inventories record mood and symptoms present over a brief period, rather than lifetime prevalence. Nevertheless, this group of studies eliminates the confounding factor of hospitalization or treatment-seeking inherent in studies using these sources to ascertain probands. This is particularly important for minor disorders for which a large proportion of sufferers do not seek treatment. Inventory studies have generally studied a much larger number of twins, providing reasonably accurate point estimates and the power to reject incorrect models of transmission. In addition, one large data set has been the subject of a number of state-of-the-art analyses that demonstrate possible future approaches to modeling twin data as well as throwing light onto the role of genes in minor mental disorders.

The Australian Twins Study. A study of Australian twins undertaken by Jardine and co-workers (1984) is important for several reasons. Data were collected from a registry-derived sample of 3810 twin pairs. Since the original publication of the results of the study, the data have been subjected to additional analyses by other researchers. Thus, examination of the findings of this study constitute not only a contribution to the understanding of the genetic basis of anxiety and depression, but also demonstrate the applicability of multivariate modeling to twin studies and genetics.

Among a number of questionnaires, respondents completed the neuroticism scale of the Eysenck Personality Questionnaire (EPQ) (Eysenck and Eysenck, 1975) and the Delusions–Symptoms–States Inventory Anxiety and Depression Scales (DSSI/sAD) (Bedford et al., 1976). In studies of the general community and the twins sampled by Jardine et al., most respondents report no symptoms, with the proportion of respondents with scores of 4 or greater on either scale ranging from 5 to 15% according to the particular study. Symptoms recorded by the DSSI cannot be dismissed as simply reflecting common distress. Rather, the DSSI can be characterized as a high-threshold instrument in which elevated scores are consistent with the diagnosis of affective disorders, such as depression, dysthymia, or one of the anxiety disorders.

In the original analysis of the Australian twin data, Jardine et al. reported univariate genetic analyses of each scale, together with a multivariate analysis including both scales and the EPQ neuroticism scale. In the univariate cases, models containing terms for unique variance and additive genetic variance provided a good fit to the data. Models including shared environment or dominant components either did not fit the data or did not result in significant improvements in the fit of the models. The heritability of depression was 0.36 for females and 0.32 for males, with similar results for the other scales. Although it was shown that substantially the same genes were involved for males and females, genetic effects were consistently larger for females. A factor analysis fitted common and specific genetic and individual environmental factors to the two symptom scales and neuroticism. On the genetic side of the model, the common factor had uniform loadings of about 0.30, with considerably smaller loadings on the specific factors. In contrast, although loadings on the environment common factor were only slightly lower than for the genetic common factor, loadings on the specific environmental factors were slightly larger than those on the common factor. This pattern may be interpreted as suggesting that a common set of genes underlies responses to all three scales, but environmental factors are largely unique to each scale.

Kendler et al. (1986) refined the foregoing analyses by working at the level of the items of the DSSI scales. Univariate analyses were carried out on 13 of the items (the item relating to suicidal ideation was not included because of low frequency of endorsement). Polychoric correlations between twins were calculated for each item as a function of sex and zygosity. Genetic analyses of these correlations showed that the additive gene plus unique environment model provided the best fit for seven items and an adequate fit for five others. Significant dominance variance was found for two items relating to feelings of panic and having a pounding heart. Replacing gene action with a parameter for the shared environment provided an equally good or adequate fit for four items, three of which concerned depression symptoms.

The polychoric correlations were subsequently subjected to phenotypic and genetic factor analyses (Kendler et al., 1987). A phenotypic analysis is identical with a normal factor analysis. One major depression–distress and two smaller factors concerned with general anxiety and insomnia were found. Subsequent genetic analyses compared the fit of models in which genetic and specific environment factors common to items or shared between items were specified. The best-fitting model had three genetic and three environmental factors. A genetic factor accounted for 27% of the total variance and had loadings for both anxiety and depression items. Genetic components specific to each item accounted for an average of 8% of the variance. The largest environmental factor related to depression, rather than to anxiety items, and item-specific loadings accounted for 28% of the variance. This analysis implies that the symptoms of depression and anxiety are underpinned by a common genetic background, with their differential manifestation controlled by environmental factors: Kendler et al. found little evidence for genes that are specifically related to depression or to anxiety.

An alternative approach was demonstrated by Eaves et al. (1987), who simultaneously fitted a measurement model to the six depression symptoms and compared the fit of the MFP, SML, and a mixed model of the latent trait underlying the items. Compared with standard classification procedures, for which the manner in which symptoms are combined to make a diagnosis is prescribed, the fitting of a latent trait model to the symptoms shows the contribution of each symptom to the underlying dimension of depression in terms of its discriminatory power and where it lies along the dimension. The model fitting a single locus was rejected. Both the mixed and polygenic models fitted the data: the major locus in the mixed model accounted for 7% of the variance, whereas, under the polygenic model, 51% of the variance of the latent trait was accounted for genetically. Although unable to discriminate between these two models, this approach demonstrates that no single gene has an outstanding effect on depressive symptoms as measured by the DSSI.

Other Inventory Studies. Andrews and his colleagues undertook a multiwave study including the same questionnaires as Jardine and associates, but completed five times at intervals of 4 months. Correlations for neuroticism and the DSSI anxiety and depression scales averaged over five occasions were comparable with those reported for the larger, single-wave study (see Andrews et al., 1990a); models including only an additive genetic term provided the best fit for symptom measures (Mackinnon et al., 1990). Although not meeting diagnostic criteria, the use of an inventory collected over 16 months approaches the duration required for *DSM-III-R* dysthymia, strengthening the conclusion that the heritabilities found for this inventory relate to clinically significant distress.

Other studies using different inventories have reported broadly similar results to the Australian study. Vandenburg (1967) reported correlations based on depression scores from the Minnesota Multiphasic Personality Inventory (MMPI). The MZ correlation of 0.44 and DZ correlation of 0.14 led to a heritability estimate of 0.60. Using a sample of 92 twin pairs, Wierzbicki (1986) calculated a heritability of only 0.23 for the depression scale of the MMPI, although two depression subscales—the DR and D30—had higher estimates of 0.41 and 0.43, respectively.

Clifford et al. (1984) used the Middlesex Hospital Questionnaire in a study of 572 twins and their first-degree relatives. Heritability of the depression scale estimated using the classic method from twin data alone was 0.01 for males and 0.67 for females. In a model including first-degree relatives and taking twin cohabitation effects into account, heritability dropped to 0.13. One explanation for this low result is that the model used effectively takes any correlation between DZ twins in excess of siblings as evidence for a shared environment effect. As such, this estimate might be regarded as defining a lower bound on the heritability of this scale.

In a multivariate analysis of the Centre for Epidemiology Studies depression scale (CES-D) on a sample of 771 female twins, Silberg et al. (1990) found a genetic depression factor that accounted for 13% of the total item variance.

The variability in the foregoing studies might be attributed to sampling variation; however, these studies suggest that the item content of inventories is a critical determinant of observed correlations and gender effects: For instance, although the DSSI is essentially unifactorial, Silberg et al. were able to extract four factors, relating to positive affect, somatization, and interpersonal sensitivity, as well a depression factor, from the CES-D.

4. *Gene–Environment Interaction*

Although the concept that genes and the environment may act together to produce disorders is a popular one (see, for instance, the "stress-diathesis" model of Slater and Slater, 1944) few studies exist that directly investigate this phenomenon. Gene–environment interaction and correlation can be detected in twin data, but the usual procedure is to attempt to reduce any effect by rescaling the variable concerned (Eaves et al., 1989).

A recent analysis of adverse life events and depressive symptoms in 824 female twins by Kendler et al. (1991) may be seen as an innovation in this area. Twins were divided into high- and low-stress environments, according to their exposure to life events. Structural equation modeling showed that genetic or familial environmental factors (CE) player a greater role in depression in high-stress than in low-stress environments. Although some evidence in favor of a gene–environment, rather than a CE–environment interaction was found, the models lacked power to discriminate between these explanations. Evidence for this interaction was found only when stress was based on life events, independently of the individuals themselves.

In retrospect it may be unfortunate that Kendler et al. used the CES-D as a measure of depressive symptoms, finding an even lower estimate of heritability (15%) than did Silberg et al. (1990). The use of an inventory measuring a more heritable depressive trait may have produced more definitive results. This study also indicates the large samples that are required if tests of more than simple hypotheses are undertaken using twins.

5. *Summary*

When taken without interpretation, the data from twin studies suggest a U-shaped curve of heritability; with bipolar disorder being highly heritable and genetic influence declining as unipolar disorders are considered. Studies of less severe disorders, classified variously as neurotic depression, cyclothymia, or dysthymia, have been reported to have little or no genetic basis. Self-reported symptoms obtained using checklists, reflecting presumably lower, subclinical levels of depression, have been shown to have heritabilities of between 20 and 60%. It must be noted that agreement between studies diminishes as less severe disorders are considered: this is probably due to the use of differing definitions and scales. Parallel with this relationship, severe depression is associated with environmental influences shared by twin pairs. Such influences are not significant for minor depressive symptoms for which common environment terms have not been significant and environmental determinants unique to each twin are preponderant.

C. Adoption Studies

Adoption studies of mood disorders are fewer than family or twin studies and do not have their long history. Mendlewicz and Rainer (1977) carried out the first adoption study of bipolar disorder. Twenty-nine adoptees, ascertained from medical records of outpatient and inpatient clinics were probands, and psychopathology in their biological and adoptive parents was compared with that of parents in three control groups: (1) parents of bipolar individuals who were not adopted, (2) biological and adoptive parents of healthy adoptees, and (3) parents of individuals who had contract poliomyelitis in childhood or adolescence.

They found an excess of psychopathology in the biological parents of affected adoptees compared with their adoptive parents. Similar levels of psychopathology were found in the biological parents of nonaffected adoptees and nonadoptees. Although the total prevalence of psychopathology was slightly greater for the biological parents of normal adoptees than in their adoptive parents, this was due to cases of alcoholism and sociopathy, rather than affective disorders. Parents of children with poliomyelitis had the same level of disorder as adoptive parents, indicating the comparability of adoptive parents of affected children with other parents raising an ill child.

Mendlewicz and Rainer found that cases of unipolar disorder in biological parents almost always preceded the occurrence of bipolar disorder in their children while always following it in adoptive parents. They speculated that cases of unipolar depression in adoptive parents might be a reactive, less severe form of the disorder. This study supports the notion that familial aggregation of bipolar disorder is the result of genetic, rather than social transmission.

Cadoret (1978) compared adoptees whose biological mothers had a mood disorder with a control group of adoptees with healthy mothers. Although 3 of 8 adoptees in the first group, compared with 4 of 43 in the control group, were diagnosed with a mood disorder, this difference was not significant. Failure to achieve significance could have resulted from low power owing to small numbers of affected parents or that the sample of adoptees was relatively young and thus may not have passed through the period of risk.

Von Knorring et al. (1983) took advantage of Swedish social welfare records to compare the biological parents of 56 affected adoptees and 115 matched controls. Little evidence for genetic transmission of affective disorders was found with nonsignificant excess of affective disorder in biological, compared with adoptive, parents. Although this study is unique in including details of fathers' as well as mothers' histories, the reliance on medical records for diagnostic information may have led to underdiagnosis of mood disorders.

Similar positive, but nonsignificant, results were obtained by Cadoret et al., (1985) in a study of 443 adoptees containing 48 individuals who met criteria for a lifetime diagnosis of major depressive disorder. Interestingly, Cadoret et al. found stronger, significant associations between depression in adoptees and psychiatric disorder and social problems in the adoptive family.

Wender et al. (1986) carried out a study in which 71 adoptees with a history of affective disorder were individually matched with a control adoptee on the basis of sex, age, time spent with biological mother, age at transfer, and socioeconomic status of the adoptive parents. Psychiatric histories of relatives were accessible by the cross-matching of Danish population registries and psychiatric records. An excess of bipolar and unipolar depression was found in the biological relatives of affected, compared with control adoptees. This difference was not maintained for neurotic depression and affect reaction. No significant differences were found between the two groups for adoptive relatives. Thus, like Mendlewicz and Rainer (1977), this study supports a genetic basis for mood disorders, particularly in severe forms.

1. Summary

None of the studies is inconsistent with the notion of a genetic basis for mood disorders; however, statistically reliable evidence is equivocal. The small number of studies involved makes the identification of trends impossible. Nevertheless, the only study using an homogeneous group of probands (that of Mendlewicz and Rainer) found strong evidence for genetic effects. Similar results were obtained in Wender and associates' study when comparison was restricted to severe disorders. In this light, the results may be seen as supporting the results of family and twin studies.

Adoption studies provide the opportunity to examine gene–environment interaction. Only Cadoret et al. (1985) have presented formal models relating pathology in biological parents and the environmental adversity. Failure to find evidence of a genetic effect in their data reduces the interest of this approach.

III. ANXIETY DISORDERS

Anxiety disorders have not been as widely studied as mood disorders. In addition to a paucity of information, the situation is further complicated by variations in their classification. Although anxiety disorders as classified by *DSM-III-R* are considered here, many studies predate the introduction of *DSM-III* (1980) and record diagnoses of anxiety neurosis or other categories that accord poorly with current *DSM-III* nomenclature.

The small number of family studies of anxiety neurosis have recorded prevalence in first-degree relatives of 3–49% (Alanen, 1966; Brown, 1942; Cohen et al., 1951; McInnes, 1937; Noyes et al., 1978; Pauls et al., 1979; Wheeler, 1948). These studies clearly indicate a familial tendency, the variability in rates probably reflects the lack of operationalized diagnostic criteria. Details of those investigations where specific diagnoses were made are considered in the following.

A. Phobic Disorders

1. Agoraphobia

In the first major familial aggregation study of this disorder, Solyom et al. (1974), found no increase in agoraphobia in families of agoraphobia probands. They did, however, demonstrate an increase in phobic disorders in their mothers and an increase in total psychiatric disorder in both parents. These findings would appear to indicate a nonspecific inheritance of neurotic tendency. Buglass et al. (1977) similarly found no increase in agoraphobia in these families and did not find increased levels of any disorders.

Munjack and Moss (1981) also found no increased risk of agoraphobia, but did find increased rates of depression and alcoholism.

Harris et al. (1983) studied the families of 20 agoraphobic probands, 20 panic disorder probands, and 20 controls. They identified similarly high rates of all anxiety disorders in families of agoraphobics and panic disorder patients (32 and 33%, respectively). These rates were elevated compared with families of control probands (15%). There was no specific increase in the rate of agoraphobia among the relatives of agoraphobics compared with controls, unlike the increased rated demonstrated by Noyes et al. (1978). They found a definite increased rate of alcoholism in the relatives of agoraphobics when compared with controls.

Moran and Andrews (1985) studied families of 60 agoraphobic probands. The morbid risk of agoraphobia in the 232 relatives was 12.5%, which is higher than the ECA community epidemiological figures of 4.1% (Robins et al., 1984). The risk for females was three times that for male relatives.

Carey and Gottesman (1981a) conducted a self-report study of phobias in families in a sample unselected for disorders. Using respondents judged to have an agoraphobic condition as probands, significantly higher prevalence of agoraphobia and phobias was reported by relatives than in the families of nonphobic probands.

Carey and Gottesman also report concordance rates for twins from the Maudsley register. Most probands were agoraphobics or severe social phobics. Only when concordance was broadened to include phobic symptoms and features, whether or not treated, were MZ twins clearly more concordant than DZ twins.

Torgersen (1983) was able to extract a number of twins with agoraphobia or social phobia, diagnosed according to *DSM-III* criteria from his study of Norwegian twins. None of the cotwins of 12 MZ and 18 DZ probands with agoraphobia and social phobia were strictly concordant. When concordance was broadened to include other *DSM-III* anxiety disorders, concordance was 42% and 11% for MZ and DZ twins, respectively.

2. *Other Phobias*

There have been few studies of the heritability of other phobic disorders. Fyer et al. (1990) investigated the relatives of simple phobics. They demonstrated that simple phobia occurs in 31% of the relatives of simple phobic probands, compared with 11% of the relatives of controls. There was no difference in the rates of depression or other anxiety disorders. Specifically, there was no evidence for increased rates of other phobic disorders, suggesting a genetic specificity for simple phobics.

Twin studies conducted using self-report questionnaires of fears have found moderate heritability (Rose and Ditto, 1983). Multivariate analyses of such data by Phillips et al. (1987) showed that a genetic, rather than social, model could account for patterns of parent–child transmission. Specificity of the object of fear was also analyzed by Phillips et al. They concluded that both a general tendency toward a fearful reaction and fear of specific objects were separately transmitted. Marks (1986) has reported strong familial transmission of blood phobia.

These studies give equivocal support for a familial tendency for agoraphobia, and suggest increased rates for other conditions such as depression and alcoholism. Twin studies suggest that any genetic component is a general neurotic one, rather than related to agoraphobia specifically. Other phobias present an intriguing picture: there is some evidence for the transmission of phobias to specific objects, with subsidiary evidence for genetic, rather than social, transmission. The numbers of families and twin pairs studied is small, and a definitive statement about heritability would be premature.

B. Panic Disorder

Pauls et al. (1980) undertook pedigree analysis in 19 pedigrees with panic disorder, finding suggestive evidence that the condition was transmitted as an autosomal dominant trait. These results must be regarded as preliminary because of the small number of families involved. Crowe et al. (1983) in a further preliminary analysis, could not exclude SML or MFP models.

The investigations of Crowe et al. (1983) and Noyes et al. (1986) both indicate a familial tendency for panic disorder, but not generalized anxiety disorder (GAD) or agoraphobia, in these families. However, families of agoraphobic probands (Noyes et al., 1986) appear to have higher rates of both agoraphobia and panic disorder than do families of control probands.

Although the study of Leckman et al. (1983) indicated significant overlap in the genetics of depression and anxiety disorders, Noyes et al. found no increase in the rate of depression in the relatives of agoraphobics or panic disorder patients. Weissman et al. (1984c) investigated the children of depressed probands with or without panic disorder. They found that panic disorder or agoraphobia in addition to depression in the proband conferred an additional risk of depression and an anxiety disorder in the children.

The only two linkage studies in panic disorder have derived from Crowe's group in the United States. Crowe et al. (1987) investigated 26 panic disorder pedigrees, testing 29 red cell antigens and protein polymorphisms as genetic markers. They excluded linkage to 18 loci, but found evidence suggestive of linkage to α-haptoglobin (located in chromosomal region 16q22) with a lod score of 2.27. In 1990, however, the same group (Crowe et al., 1990) analyzed 10 new pedigrees alone and in combination with the previous 26. On this occasion, they demonstrated exclusion of close linkage to α-haptoglobin, a finding that suggests that the earlier result reflected a type I error.

No twin study has been undertaken specifically into panic. Torgersen (1983) presented concordance rates for probands with panic disorder and agoraphobia with panic attacks. Concordance for cotwins with anxiety disorders with panic attacks was 31% for MZ and 0% for DZ twins. Broadening concordance to include all anxiety disorders produced concordance of 46% and 25%, respectively.

Martin et al. (1988) undertook a multivariate analysis of the EPQ neuroticism scale and two items from the DSSI relating to panic ("Recently I have been breathless or had a pounding of my heart." and "Recently, for no good reason, I have had feelings of panic."). Data came from the Australian twin study discussed earlier. For males, genetic effects in common could explain 34% of the variance of the heart pounding and 56% for feeling of panic. A substantial proportion of this shared variation could be attributed to dominant, rather than additive, gene action. Although 33 and 42% of the variance could be attributed to genetic variation in females, very little was in common with neuroticism. This analysis suggests that panic is substantially heritable and, for males, related to neuroticism. However, the relation between these two items and panic disorder must be uncertain and, at very least, of low specificity.

C. Obsessive–Compulsive Disorder

Rates of obsessive–compulsive disorder (OCD) vary between 2 and 10% of first-degree relatives (Brown, 1942; Kringlen, 1965; Rosenberg, 1967). Higher rates of 20–37%

were reported by Lewis (1935). The published studies all have examined raw prevalence figures: there have been no age-corrected studies of morbid risk, and no pedigree segregation analyses.

Young and associates (1971) calculated the heritability of eight obsession-related items from the Middlesex Hospital Questionnaire as 0.43 on a sample of 32 twins. Clifford and colleagues (1984) calculated similar heritabilities from the trait and symptom scales of the Brief Leyton Obsessional Inventory as 0.47 and 0.44. As the result of multivariate genetic analysis of these two scales and EPQ neuroticism, Clifford et al. concluded that the genetic transmission of obsessive tendencies involved a general neurotic tendency as well as specific obsessional genetic factors.

Marks et al. (1969) calculated the chance of finding a concordant MZ twin pair as 1:6 million to 1:800 million, based on prevalence rate of 0.05% and 1:120 to 1:200 live births being MZ twins. Thus the existence of even a small number of reliably diagnosed twins has been taken as evidence for nonindependence in the etiology of the disorder. This reasoning alone does not exclude environmental transmission.

Twin studies of clinically defined OCD have principally comprised individual case reports or very small numbers (see Black, 1974; Carey and Gottesman, 1981b). Considerable doubt exists about the nature of the diagnoses made in several of these studies, with speculation that the literature may be biased in the reporting of concordant MZ cases. Nevertheless, concordance is greater for MZ than DZ twins.

Carey and Gottesman reported the largest single twin study of OCD involving 15 MZ and 15 DZ pairs derived from the Maudsley Twin Register. Although MZ concordance was not significantly greater than DZ, MZ/DZ concordance ranges from 33:7% for treated conditions involving obsessional symptoms to 87:47% for both treated and untreated obsessional symptoms or features.

Even though total numbers are small and doubts must remain about ascertainment bias and diagnostic validity, the likelihood of familial aggregation and the higher concordance in MZ than DZ twins suggests that genetic factors are involved in this disorder.

D. Generalized Anxiety Disorder

There has been only one study of the families of generalized anxiety disorder (GAD) probands. Noyes et al. (1987) studied relatives of 20 probands with agoraphobia and 20 control probands. They reported the following findings. There was a morbid risk of 19.5% for GAD among first-degree relatives of GAD probands and 30.1% for any disorder. All anxiety disorders were more frequent in relatives of GAD probands than in those of controls, and specifically, GAD was more frequent in relatives of GAD probands than in controls. Additionally, panic disorder and agoraphobia combined were less frequent in the relatives of GAD probands than among those of probands with panic disorder. These findings are consistent with the clinical separation of GAD and panic disorder as distinct disorders. No twin study focusing on GAD has been undertaken. Torgersen's (1983) study of anxiety disorders recorded this diagnoses, but too few cases were observed to allow comment. Andrews et al. (1990a) study included diagnoses of GAD. It is dealt with below.

E. A General Neurotic Syndrome

A recurrent finding for both family and twin studies is the lack of specificity of transmission. Prevalence for individual disorders in relatives of probands may not be raised, but increased prevalence has frequently been observed for a broader spectrum of anxiety disorders. Similarly, in twin studies, although concordance for specific anxiety disorders is often low, broadening the definition of the disorder considered often increases concordance beyond what would be predicted on the basis of the necessarily increased prevalence of a broader category of disorders alone. This has led to the suggestion that the heritable component of anxiety disorders is shared, whereas other, possibly environmental, factors determine the nature of the disorder.

A twin study by Andrews et al. (1990a) provides support for this view. They studied 446 twin pairs unselected for mental illness. Lifetime diagnoses for *DSM-III-R* anxiety disorders, dysthymia, and major depressive episode were made for each twin using a standardized interview. Phenotypically, substantial correlations in liability, ranging from 0.41 to 0.77, were observed between all disorders (Andrews et al. 1990b). It also was demonstrated that a single common factor model provided a good fit to the correlations. The number of cases of each disorder detected preclude the testing of a multivariate model involving a genetic common factor. Cotwins had elevated numbers of diagnoses, with concordance for any disorder being significantly greater for MZ than DZ twins. The breakdown of individual diagnoses is striking in showing the lack of specific concordance among twins who had any anxiety disorder. When specific concordance was observed, it was often because one twin had multiple diagnoses, with the cotwin having just one of these disorders.

This study suggests a common heritable tendency to neurotic disorders, rather than to specific disorders. It is consistent with analyses self-report symptoms in the Australian twins study of Kendler et al. (1987). Their conclusion was that a common set of genes was responsible for symptoms of anxiety and depression and neuroticism.

Torgersen's analyses of his Norwegian twin study also support this view, with specific concordance being low, whereas broader concordance was greater with the pattern of MZ/DZ concordance supporting a heritable factor. A point of divergence from the results of Andrews et al. and Kendler et al. is that later analyses presented by Torgersen (1985) reveal a differentiation between genetic factors underlying anxiety disorders and those associated with neurotic depression. It is possible that the manner in which symptoms were recorded and assembled into diagnoses in these studies might account for this difference.

The postulation of a common genetic background for anxiety disorders does not preclude the existence of genes specific to individual disorder. Strongest evidence for this proposition comes from the studies of phobias to specific objects (see Marks, 1986).

1. Summary

Although there are some dissenting studies, most support the notion that these disorders are at least moderately heritable. The evidence also points to the polygenic inheritance of a general tendency toward neurotic illness. Together the studies reviewed have the limitations of being very small, often lacking appropriate control groups or using historically collected data that may be unreliable or unsuitable for making diagnoses concordant with current classification schemes. Family aggregation has generally been demonstrated, but in the absence of adoption studies or segregation analyses, the attribution of transmission to gene action relies on solely twin studies. Twin studies do support the role of genes, but the extent to which recruitment biases and the violation of the assumptions of the twin method might be responsible for differences in MZ/DZ concordance is unclear. Although demonstrating that concordance is significantly greater in MZ than DZ twins, the only twin studies to formally model transmission concern self-report inventories, rather than the clinically defined disorders.

IV. CONCLUSION

A. Mood Disorders

1. Severe Disorders

This section must be dominated by current efforts to locate a single gene responsible for bipolar disorder. Rather than join arguments about the probable outcome of such studies, we prefer to consider the implications of these outcomes (see later discussion) and reflect on whether the focus on linkage has overshadowed lines of investigation that might otherwise have been undertaken.

2. Minor Disorders

Overshadowed by severe disorders, the heritability of minor depression has been dismissed as negligible by several reviewers (see, e.g., Tsuang and Faraone, 1990). This chapter has attempted to demonstrate that heritability is an increasing function of more reliable diagnosis and better classification, together with systematic ascertainment: too many studies of minor disorders have relied on hospital and treatment recruitment and diagnosis, in spite of the fact that many sufferers of minor disorders do not seek treatment. The use of appropriate inventories on community samples reinforces the view that these disorders are at least moderately heritable.

There is no suggestion that a single gene contributes an outstanding proportion of the variance in these cases: a polygenic model appears to fit the data.

B. Anxiety Disorders

Although evidence in support of a genetic basis for anxiety disorders has been amassed, few could be satisfied with the fragmented state of genetic knowledge concerning these disorders. The small samples and unsystematic ascertainment strategies of some studies, together with the evolving nature of the classification of these disorders, argue strongly for a large, systematic genetic investigation of these disorders. Given the apparent nonspecificity of their heritability, such a study should cover the range of anxiety disorders, rather than focus on one disorder. Screening for other disorders, principally minor depressive disorders, should be included. Both family and twins studies could make contributions. The use of a twin design is attractive because of the ability to disaggregate familial environmental causes from genetic ones. Such a study could well be buttressed by the inclusion of first-degree relatives. Because a significant proportion of suffers do not seek treatment, it is important that a family study method be adopted, regardless of the type of study undertaken.

Linkage studies of anxiety disorders would appear to be premature. The successful outcome of linkage studies in other psychiatric disorders may well prove to be an impetus to their use in anxiety disorders. The identification of a locus responsible for bipolar disorder could provide a candidate locus for linkage studies of anxiety disorders.

C. Implications of Different Genetic Models for Psychiatric Research

Arguments about the likelihood of the existence of a major locus for bipolar disorder (or any of the disorders considered here) are somewhat pointless in view of the large collaborative studies now under way in Europe and the United States. Rather than speculate on the outcome of this research, it is useful to consider the ramifications of support for the three possible outcomes of gene searching. These apply to genetic studies of all psychiatric disorders.

1. Single Major Locus

In both bipolar disorder and schizophrenia, the search for the single causal gene has become a Holy Grail. It is easy to see why: such a gene marks unequivocally the beginning of the biological pathway that leads to the disorder. Its discovery almost terminates the work of the geneticist, leaving other biologically oriented psychiatrists to elucidate this path. The existence of such gene could well allow the testing of individuals at risk and the identification of carriers, thereby giving a much sounder basis for genetic counseling in psychiatry. The ultimate promise of genetically based treatments and prevention is foreshadowed.

Even, if as seems highly likely, the disorder is genetically heterogeneous such that no single locus is responsible for all observed cases, the impact of such a finding is not greatly diminished. The foregoing remarks apply in full to that proportion of cases having the gene. Furthermore, the ability to differentiate the etiology of a phenomenologically homogeneous disorder would be useful in many areas of research outside genetics. For instance, in research into environment–social causes of a disorder, the separation of those cases known to have a specific genetic etiology could markedly increase the power and clarity of analyses.

2. Polygenetic Etiology

Compared with the ramifications of the discovery of a major locus, the conclusion that a polygenetic model accounts for a disorder seems a very poor second prize. It is possible that disorders, such as bipolar disorder, are still mediated by a single biological pathway under polygenic control, but the MPF model opens the possibility of complex biological etiology. The role for genetics research would be likely to accord with the more recent twin research, which has focused on measurement and environmental interaction. Certainly, the role of genetics in counseling and cure would be diminished.

Although not providing the categorical simplicity of a single major locus, MPF implies a continuum from those with a low loading of liability-increasing genes to those with a high load of such genes. The identification of individuals in these categories might allow some etiological differentiation of psychiatric disorders for research purposes.

3. A Middle Pathway

It is principally conceptual tractability that divides genetic models into one gene or many genes. An intriguing possibility is that a small (countable) number of genes may be responsible for a disorder (cf. Risch, 1990b). Such genes might act in an essentially additive manner, resulting in a model directly comparable with the MPF liability model. Alternatively, interactive effects may be involved. A preliminary point of evidence for interaction comes from the low concordance observed between DZ twins (see foregoing). Interaction has been considered in terms of inter- and intraloci effects. Theoretically, these can be shown to account for little genetic variance (see Eaves, 1987b). Another possibility is extragenetic interaction. Lykken (1981) coined the term *emergenesis* to describe interactions between gene products that produce certain outcomes. He gives the hypothetical example of a protein assembled from 12 polypeptides coded for by 12 genes on separate chromosomes. Even if the genes are common, transmission of all 12 required to produce the protein will be rare. When the path from the genotype to phenotype is as long as is acknowledged for mood and behavior disorders, stages at which such interactive effects could be present must abound (e.g., a disorder could occur as the joint occurrence of neurotransmitter *and* receptor site irregularities, both genetically determined). Speculation should not run too far ahead of data. Suffice it to say that, although conceptually plausible, the specification and testing of these models would represent a major challenge for psychiatric genetics. If either type of oligogenetic effect is present, then presently used techniques could detect at least the main effect of such genes. However, the small size of such effects and the low power of the analyses imply the need for extremely large samples.

4. *The Environment and Genetic Research*

Apart from the attribution of variance components to unique and shared environmental sources in the classic twin method, far too little attention has been paid to role of environmental factors in genetic research. Stress diathesis concepts, in which a genetic disposition to a disorder is manifest as the result of exposure to an environmental stressor, are classic, but serious studies of the concept are few. The work of Kendler and his colleagues has broken ground in this area, but there is little work that involves clinical levels of disorder.

D. The Future of Research Methodologies

1. *Family Studies*

Although the need to simply demonstrate elevated prevalence in families has passed, ascertainment of family pedigrees can be expected to form the mainstay of genetic studies in the near future. Most current developments center around methodological improvements or means of enhancing the orthodox lod score methods by the techniques outlined earlier. Some researchers, such as Risch (1990b), have suggested alternative techniques to "cut the Gordian knot in the linkage analyses of complex human traits" (Ott, 1990). Risch (1990b) and Bishop and Williamson (1990) have suggested focusing on pairs of affected relatives of different degrees of relationship and investigating the power of such data under different modes of inheritance to find, by linkage analyses, the genes contributing to these complex disorders. Risch advocates using *identity by descent*, whereas Bishop and Williamson recommend *identity by state*.

The use of families to examine the relation between genes and the environment has been disappointing. This is partially because of negative findings (see Bebbington et al., 1991), but also because these studies cannot unravel gene–environment covariation as can twin studies.

2. *Twins Research*

The principal work of twin studies has been to apportion familial variation between genetic and environmental sources. That most twin studies have focused on reporting heritability values that have little scientific use beyond demonstrating that a trait is more or less genetic (Wilson, 1982) might lead to the suggestion that this type of study has played its role and is of historical importance only. Certainly, there is no need for another study demonstrating heritability of severe affective disorder, although a large and methodological twin study of anxiety disorders (and perhaps minor depressive disorders) could well be justified.

The usefulness of twins in genetic research is more likely to come from the ability to fit complex models to twin data. This arises because of the relative ease with which twins can be recruited and the fact that twinship is a relatively simple pedigree. Specialized twin designs enable specific questions to be answered. The use of MZ twins also provides a unique method of partialing out genetic variance from experimental designs.

3. Adoption Studies

As was suggested earlier, although adoption studies have made a contribution to defining familial transmission as genetic transmission, practical difficulties may see the end of this approach.

4. The Curse of Numbers

A common requirement of projected familial- and twin-based research is the need for large sample sizes. Except in the analyses of subclinical traits, this speaks to the desirability of multiple site and international cooperation. The requirements for the application of standardized diagnostic systems and the collection of symptom information at the atomistic level so those new standards of classification can be applied are also essential.

E. Concluding Remarks

As the genes for "this" disease or "that" medical disorder are found, the failure of genetics to provide similar simple and conclusive explanations for psychiatric conditions may be seen as reflecting a lack of success of this enterprise. Psychiatric disorders may well be the most difficult areas for the application of genetic techniques, involving problems of diagnosis and definition, etiological heterogeneity, incomplete and variable expression genotypes. Scientific problems are compounded by the practical problems of case and pedigree ascertainment. Viewed in this light, progress made thus far is remarkable: a genetic basis has been soundly established for affective disorders, with similar conclusions provisionally applying to anxiety disorders. The next few years should see a definitive answer to the question of a major gene for bipolar disorder.

REFERENCES

Y. O. Alanen, The family in the pathogenesis of schizophrenia and neurotic disorders, *Acta Psychiatr. Scand., 6*(Suppl. 189): 42 (1966).

M. G. Allen, S. Cohen, W. Pollin, and S. I. Greenspan, Affective illness in Veterans twins, *Am. J. Psychiatry, 131*: 1234 (1974).

American Psychiatric Association, *Diagnostic and Statistical Manual of Mental Disorders, 3rd ed. revised,* American Psychiatric Association, Washington, D. C. (1987).

N. C. Andreasen, W. Scheftner, T. Reich, R. M. A. Hirschfeld, J. Endicott, and M. B. Keller, The validation of the concept of endogenous depression: A family study approach, *Arch. Gen. Psychiatry, 43*: 246 (1986).

N. Andreasen, J. Rice, J. Endicott, W. Coryell, W. M. Grove, and T. Reich, Familial rates of affective disorder, *Arch. Gen. Psychiatry, 44*: 461 (1987).

G. Andrews, G. Stewart, R. Allen, and A. S. Henderson, The genetics of six neurotic disorders: A twin study, *J. Affective Disord., 19*: 23–29 (1990a).

G. Andrews, G. Stewart, A. Morris-Yates, P. Holt, and S. Henderson, Evidence for a general neurotic syndrome, *Br. J. Psychiatry, 157*: 6 (1990b).

M. Baron, J. Klotz, J. Mendlewicz, and J. Rainer, Multiple-threshold transmission of affective disorders, *Arch. Gen. Psychiatry, 38*: 79 (1981a).

M. Baron, J. Mendlewicz, R. Gruen, L. Asnis, and R. R. L. Fieve, Assortative mating in affective disorders, J. *Affective Disord., 3*: 167–171 (1981b).

M. Baron, r. Gruen, L. Asnis, and J. Kane, Schizoaffective illness, schizophrenia and affective disorders: Morbidity risk and genetic transmission, *Acta Psychiatr. Scand., 65*: 253 (1982).

M. Baron, N. Risch, R. Hamburger, B. Mandel, S. Kushner, M. Newman, D. Drumer, and R. H. Belmaker, Genetic linkage between X-chromosome markers and bipolar affective illness, *Nature, 326*: 289 (1987).

M. Baron, R. Hamburger, L. A. Sandkuyl, N. Risch, B. Mandel, J. Endicott, R. H. Belmaker,and J. Ott, The impact of phenotypic variation on genetic analysis: application of X-linkage in manic–depressive illness, *Acta Psychiatr. Scand., 82*: 196 (1990a).

M. Baron, J. Endicott, and J. Ott, Genetic linkage in mental illness, *Br. J. Psychiatry, 157*: 645(1990b).

P. Bebbington, R. Katz, P. McGuffin, The familial aggregation of affective disorders: Relation to symptom severity and social provocation, *The New Genetics of Mental Illness* (P. McGuffin and R. Murray, eds.), Butterworth–Heinemann, Oxford, pp. 130–145 (1991).

A. Bedford, G. A. Foulds, and B. F. Sheffield, A new personal disturbance scale (DSSI/sAD), *Br. J. Soc. Clin. Psychol., 15*: 387 (1976).

W. H. Berrettini, L. R. Goldin, J. Gelernter, P. V. Gejman, E. S. Gershon, and S. Detera-Wadleigh, X-chromosome markers and manic–depressive illness: Rejection of linkage to Xq28 in nine bipolar pedigrees, *Arch. Gen Psychiatry, 47*: 366 (1990).

A. Bertelsen and I. I. Gottesman, Offspring of twin pairs discordant for psychiatric illness, *Acta Genet. Med. Gemellol. (Roma), 35*: 310 (1986).

A. Bertelsen, B. Harvald, and M. Hauge, A Danish twin study of manic–depressive disorders, *Br. J. Psychiatry, 130*: 330 (1977).

J. Biederman, M. Keller, P. Lavori, J. Harmatz, D. Knee, D. Dubey, and E. Yunis, HLA haplotype A26-B38 in affective disorders: Lack of association, *Biol. Psychiatry, 22*: 221 (1987).

D. T. Bishop, and J. A. Williamson, The power of identity-by-state methods for linkage analysis, *Am. J. Hum. Genet., 46*: 254 (1990).

A. Black, The natural history of the obsessional states, *Obsessional States* (H. R. Beech, ed.), Methuen, London, pp. 20–54 (1974).

R. C. Bland, S. C. Newman, and H. Orn, Recurrent and nonrecurrent depression, *Arch. Gen. Psychiatry, 43*: 1085 (1986).

D. I. Boomsma, N. G. Martin, and M. C. Neale, Genetic analysis of twin and family data: Structural modelling using LISREL, *Behav. Genet., 19(1)*: whole issue, (1989).

D. Botstein, Construction of a genetic linkage map in man using restriction fragments length polymorphisms, *Am. J. Hum. Genet., 32*: 314 (1980).

F. Brown, Heredity in the psychoneuroses, *Proc. R. Soc. Med., 35*: 785 (1942).

K. D. Bucher, R. C. Elston, R. Green, P. Whybrow, J. Helzer, T. Reich, P. Clayton, and G. Winokur, The transmission of manic depressive illness: II. Segregation analysis of three sets of family data, *J. Psychiatr. Res., 16*: 65 (1981).

D. Buglass, J. Clarke, A. S. Henderson, N. Kreitman, and A. S. Presley, A study of agoraphobic housewifes, *Psychol. Med., 7*: 73 (1977).

R. J. Cadoret, Evidence for genetic inheritance in primary affective disorder in adoptees, *Am. J. Psychiatry, 135*: 463 (1978).

R. J. Cadoret, T. W. O'Gorman, E. Heywood, and E. Troughton, Genetic and environmental factors in major depression, *J. Affective Disord., 9*: 155 (1985).

G. Carey, and I. I. Gottesman, Defining cases by genetic criteria, *What is a case?* (J. K. Wing, P. Bebbington, and L. N. Robins, eds.), Grant McIntyre, London, pp. 29–41 (1981a).

G. Carey, and I. I. Gottesman, Twin and family studies of anxiety, phobic and obsessive disorders, *Anxiety: New Research and Changing Concepts* (D. F. Klein and J. Rabkin, eds.) Raven Press, New York, pp. 117-136 (1981b).

F. Clerget-Darpoux, The uses and abuses of linkage analysis in neuropsychiatric disorder, *The New Genetics of Mental Illness* (P. McGuffin and R. Murray, eds.), Butterworth–Heineman, Oxford, pp. 44–57 (1991).

C. A. Clifford, R. M. Murray, and D. W. Fulker, Genetic and environmental influences on obsessional traits and symptoms, *Psychol. Med., 14*: 791 (1984).

M. E. Cohen, D. W. Badal, A. Kilpatrick, E. W. Reed, and P. White, The high familial prevalence of neurocirculatory asthenia (anxiety neurosis, effort syndrome), *Am. J. Hum. Genet., 3*: 126 (1951).

W. Coryell, J. Endicott, T. Reich, N. Andreasen, and M. Keller, A family study of bipolar II disorder, *Br. J. Psychiatry, 145*: 49 (1984).

N. Cox, T. Reich, J. Rice, R. Elston, J. Schober, and B. Keats, Segregation and linkage analyses of bipolar and major depressive illnesses in multigenerational pedigrees, *J. Psychiatr. Res., 23*: 109 (1989).

R. R. Crowe, and R. E. Smouse, The genetics implications of age-dependent penetrance in manic–depressive illness, *J. Psychiatr. Res., 13*: 273 (1977).

R. R. Crowe, K. K. Namboodiri, H. B. Ashby, and R. C. Elston, Segregation and linkage analysis of a large kindred of unipolar depression, *Neuropsychobiology, 7*: 20 (1981).

R. R. Crowe, R. Noyes, Jr., D. L. Pauls, and D. Slymen, A family study of panic disorder, *Arch. Gen. Psychiatry, 40*: 1065 (1983).

R. R. Crowe, R. Noyes, Jr., A. F. Wilson, R. C. Elston, and L. Ward, A linkage study of panic disorder, *Arch. Gen. Psychiatry, 44*: 933 (1987).

R. R. Crowe, R. Noyes, Jr., S. Samuelson, R. Wesner, and R. Wilson, Close linkage between panic disorder and α-haptoglobin excluded in 10 families, *Arch. Gen. Psychiatry, 47*: 377 (1990).

A. F. Da Fonseca, Analise Heredo-Clina das Perturbacoes, Afestivas (Estudio de 60 pares de gemeos, e sues congangiun neos), Imopresna Protuguesa, Proto, (1959).

A. F. Da Fonseca, Affective equivalents, *Br. J. Psychiatry, 109*: 464 (1963).

S. D. Detera-Wadleigh, W. H. Berrettini, and R. Goldein, Close linkage of c-Harvey-*ras*-1 and insulin gene to affective disorder is ruled out in three North American pedigrees, *Nature, 325*: 806 (1987).

H. Donis-Keller, C. Helms, and C. Green, A human genome linkage map with more than 500 RFLP loci and average maker spacing of 6 centimorgans, *Cytogenet. Cell Genet., 51*: 991 (1989).

I. Dowbiggen, Degeneration and hereditarianism in French mental medicine, *The Anatomy of Madness*. Vol 1 (W. F. Bynum, R. Porter, and M. Shepherd, eds.), Tavistock, London, p. 188 (1985).

L. J. Eaves, Including the environment in models for genetic segregation, *J. Psychiatr. Res, 21*: 639 (1987a).

L. J. Eaves, Dominance alone is not enough, *Behav. Genet., 8*: 27 (1987b).

L. J. Eaves, Eysenck, H. J., and N. G. Martin, *Genes, Culture and Personality*, Academic Press, London (1989).

L. J. Eaves, N. G. Martin, A. C. Heath, and K. S. Kendler Testing genetic models for multiple systems: An application to the genetic analysis of liability to depression, *Behav. Genet., 17*: 331 (1987).

J. H. Edwards, and D. C. Watt, Caution in locating the gene(s) for affective disorder, *Psychol. Med., 19*: 273 (1989).

J. A. Egeland, D. S. Gerhard, D. L. Pauls, J. N. Sussex, K. K. Kidd, C. Allen, A. M. Hostetter, and D. E. Housman, Bipolar affective disorders linked to DNA markers on chromosome 11, *Nature, 325*: 783 (1987).

M. H. El-Badramany, T. I. Farag, S. A. Al-Awadi, I. M. Hammad, A. Abdelkader, and D. S. K. Murthy, Familial manic-depressive illness with deleted short arm of chromosome 21: Coincidental or causal? *Br. J. Psychiatry, 155*: 856 (1989).

S. A. Englund, and D. N. Klein, The genetics of neurotic–reactive depression: A reanalysis of Shapiro's (1970) twin study using diagnostic criteria, *J. Affective Disord., 18*: 247 (1990).

H. J. Eysenck, and S. B. G. Eysenck, *Manual of the Eysenck Personality Questionnaire*, Digits, San Diego (1975).

D. S. Falconer, *Quantitative Genetics*, 2nd ed., Longman, London (1981).

Faraone, S. V., M. J. Lyons, and M. T. Tsuang, Sex differences in affective disorder: Genetic transmission, *Genet. Epidemiol. 4*: 331 (1987).

S. V. Faraone, M. J. Lyons, J. Pepple, and M. T. Tsuang, Twin studies of affective disorders (1988). Manuscript cited in M. T. Tsuang and S. V. Faraone, *The Genetics of Mood Disorders*, Johns Hopkins University Press, Baltimore (1990).

S. V. Faraone, W. S. Kremen, and M. T. Tsuang, Genetic transmission of major affective disorders: Quantitative models and linkage analyses, *Psychol. Bull., 108*: 109 (1990).

R. R. Fieve, R. Go, D. L. Dunner, and R. Elston, Search for biological/genetic markers in a long-term epidemiological and morbid risk study of affective disorders, *J. Psychiatr. Res., 18*: 425 (1984).

A. J. Fyer, S. Mannuzza, M. S. Gallops, L. Y. Martin, C. Aaronson, J. M. Gorman, M. R. Liebowitz, and D. F. Klein, Familial transmission of simple phobias and fears, *Arch. Gen. Psychiatry, 47*: 252 (1990).

E. S. Gershon, Genetics, Manic–Depressive Illness. (F. K. Goodwin, K. R. Jamison, eds.), Oxford University Press, New York, 1990.

E. S. Gershon, Marker genotyping errors in old data on X-linkage in bipolar illness, *Biol. Psychiatry, 29*: 721 (1991).

E. S. Gershon, M. Baron, and J. F. Leckman, Genetics models of the transmission of affective disorders, *J. Psychiatr. Res. 12*: 301 (1975).

E. S. Gershon, W. E. Bunney, Jr., J. F. Leckman, M. Van Eerdewegh, and B. A. DeBauche, The inheritance of affective disorders: A review of data and of hypotheses, *Behav. Genet., 6*: 227 (1976).

E. S. Gershon, D. L. Dunner, L. Sturt, and F. K. Goodwin, Assortative mating in the affective disorders, *Biol. Psychiatry, 7*: 63 (1981).

E. S. Gershon, S. D. Targum, S. Matthysse, and W. E. Bunney, Jr., Color blindness not closely linked to bipolar illness: Report of a new pedigree series, *Arch. Gen. Psychiatry, 36*: 1423 (1979).

E. S. Gershon, J. Hamovit, J. J. Guroff, E. Dibble, J. F. Leckman, W. Sceery, S. D. Targum, J. I. Nurnberger, L. R. Goldin, and E. W. Bunney, Jr., A family study of schizoaffective, bipolar I, bipolar II, unipolar, and normal control probands, *Arch. Gen. Psychiatry, 39*: 1157 (1982).

E. S. Gershon, C. R. Merril, L. R. Goldin, L. E. DeLisi, W. H. Berrettini, and J. I. Nurnberger, The role of molecular genetics in psychiatry, *Biol. Psychiatry, 22*: 1388 (1987).

M. Gill, P. McKeon, and P. Humphries, Linkage analysis of manic depression in an Irish family using h-*ras* 1 and *INS* DNA markers, *J. Med. Genet., 25*: 634 (1988).

L. R. Goldin, F. Clergex-Darpoux, and E. S. Gershon, Relationship of HLA to major affective disorder not supported, *Psychiatr. Res., 7*: 29 (1982).

L. R. Goldin, E. S. Gershon, S. D. Targum, R. S. Sparkes, and M. McGinniss, Segregation and linkage analyses in families of patients with bipolar, unipolar and schizoaffective mood disorders, *Am. J. Genet., 35*: 274 (1983).

I. I. Gottesman, and G. Carey, Extracting meaning and direction from twins data, *Psychiatr. Dev., 1*: 35 (1983).

D. A. Grayson, Twins raised together: Minimizing shared environmental variance, *Behav. Genet. 19*: 593 (1989).

B. Halvard, and M. Hauge, Hereditary factors elucidated by twin studies, *Genetics and Epidemiology of Chronic Diseases* (D. V. Neel, M. W. Shaw, and W. J. Schure, eds.), PSPHEW, Washington, D. C. (1965).

E. L. Harris, R. Noyes, Jr., R. R. Crowe, and D. R. Chaudhry, Family study of agoraphobia, *Arch. Gen. Psychiatry, 40*: 1061–1064 (1983).

P. Hays, and L. L. Field, Postulated genetic linkage between manic-depression and stuttering, *J. Affective Disord., 16*: 37 (1989).

J. E. Helzer, P. J. Clayton, R. Pambakian, T. Reich, R. A. Woodruff, and M. A. Reveley, Reliability of psychiatric diagnosis. II. The test/retest reliability of diagnostic classification. *Arch. Gen. Psychiatry, 34*: 136 (1977).

E. M. Hill, A. F. Wilson, R. C. Elston, and G. Winokur, Evidence for possible linkage between genetic markers and affective disorders, *Biol. Psychiatry, 24*: 903 (1988).

S. Hodgkinson, R. Sherrington, and M. Gurling, Molecular genetic evidence for heterogeneity in manic depression, *Nature, 325*: 805 (1987).

D. Holmes, J. Brynjolfsson, P. Brett, D. Curtis, H. Petursson, R. Sherrington, and H. Gurling, No evidence for a susceptibility locus predisposing to manic depression in the region of the dopamine (D^2) receptor gene, *Br. J. Psychiatry, 158*: 635 (1991).

R. Jardine, N. G. Martin, and A. S. Henderson, Genetic covariation between neuroticism and the symptoms of anxiety and depression, *Genet. Epidemiol., 1*: 89 (1984).

J. L. Jinks, and D. W. Fulker, Comparison of the biometrical, genetical, MAVA, and classical approaches to the analysis of human behavior, *Psychol. Bull., 73*: 311–349 (1970).

R. T. Joffe, Horvath, and I. Tarvydas, Bipolar affective, disorder and thalassemia minor [letter], *Am. J. Psychiatry, 143*: 933 (1986).

F. J. Kallmann, *Heredity in Health and Mental Disorder*, W. W. Norton, New York (1953).

F. J. Kallmann, Genetic principles in manic–depressive psychosis, *Depression* (P. H. Hoch and J. Zubin, eds.), Grune and Stratton, New York (1954).

J. R. Kelsoe, E. I. Ginns, J. A. Egeland, D. S. Gerhard, A. M. Goldstein, S. J. Bale, D. L. Pauls, R. T. Long, K. K. Kidd, G. Conte, D. E. Housman, and S. A. Paul, Revaluation of the linkage relationship between chromosome 11p loci and the gene for bipolar affective disorder in the Old Order Amish, *Nature, 342*: 238 (1989).

K. S. Kendler, A. C. Heath, N. G. Martin, and L. J. Eaves, Symptoms of anxiety and depression in a volunteer twin population: The etiologic role of genetic and environmental factors, *Arch. Gen. Psychiatry, 43*: 213 (1986).

K. S. Kendler, A. C. Heath, N. G. Martin, and L. J. Eaves, Symptoms of anxiety and symptoms of depression: Same genes, different environments? *Arch. Gen. Psychiatry, 44*: 451 (1987).

K. S. Kendler, M. C. Neale, A. C. Heath, R. C. Kessler, and L. J. Eaves, Life events and depressive symptoms: a twin study perspective, *The New Genetics of Mental Illness* (P. McGuffin and R. Murray, eds.), Butterworth–Heineman, Oxford, pp. 146–164 (1991).

L. Kerbeshian, L. Burd, T. Randall, J. Martsolf, and S. Jalal, Autism, profound mental retardation and atypical bipolar disorder in a 33 year-old female with a deletion of 15q12, *J. Ment. Defic. Res., 34*: 205 (1990).

J. R. Kidd, J. A. Egeland, A. J. Pakstis, C. M. Castiglione, B. A. Pletcher, L. A. Morton, and K. K. Kidd, Searching for a major genetic locus for affective disorder in the Old Order Amish, *J. Psychiatr. Res., 21*: 577 (1987).

D. N. Klein, Symptom criteria and family history in major depression, *Am. J. Psychiatry, 147*: 850 (1990).

G. L. Klerman, P. W. Lavori, J. Rice, T. Reich, J. Endicott, N. C. Andreasen, M. B. Keller, and R. M. A. Hirschfield, Birth-cohort trends in rates of major depressive disorder among relatives of patients with affective disorder, *Arch. Gen. Psychiatry, 42*: 689 (1985).

J. Korner, J. Fritze, and P. Propping, RFLP alleles at the tyrosine hydroxylase locus: No association found to affective disorders, *Psychiatry. Res., 33*: 275 (1990).

E. Kraepelin, *Manic depressive insanity and paranoia* (M. Barclay, transl.), Churchill–Livingstone, Edinburgh (1921).

E. Kringlen, Obsessional neurosis: A long-term follow-up, *Br. J. Psychiatry, 111*: 709 (1965).

E. Kringlen, *Heredity and Environment in the Functional Psychoses*, Universitetforlaget, Oslo (1967).

D. J. Kupfer, E. Frank, L. L. Carpenter, and K. Neiswanger, Family history in recurrent depression, *J. Affective Disord., 17*: 113 (1989).

M. Leboyer, A. Malafosse, S. Boularand, D. Campion, F. Gheysen, D. Samolyk, B. Henriksson, R. E. Denise, A. des Lauriers, J.-P. Lepine, E. Zarifian, F. Clerget-Darpoux, and J. Mallet, Tyrosine hydroxylase polymorphisms associated with manic-depressive illness, *Lancet, 335*: 1219 (1990).

M. Leboyer, and P. McGuffin, Collaborative strategies in the molecular genetics of the major psychoses, *Br. J. Psychiatry, 158*: 605 (1991).

J. F. Leckman, and E. S. Gershon, Autosomal models of sex effect in bipolar-related major affective illness, *J. Psychiatr. Res., 13*: 237 (1977).

J. F. Leckman, M. M. Weissman, K. R. Merikangas, D. L. Pauls, and B. A. Prusoff, Panic disorder and major depression, *Arch. Gen. Psychiatry, 40*: 1055 (1983).

J. F. Leckman, M. M. Weissman, B. A. Prusoff, K. A. Caruso, K. R. Merikangas, D. L. Pauls, and K. K. Kidd, Subtypes of depression, *Arch. Gen. Psychiatry, 41*: 833 (1984).

K. Leonhard, *The Classification of Endogenous Psychoses* (Robins E., ed., R. Berman, trans.), Irvington, New York (1979).

A. J. Lewis, Problems of obsessional illness, *Proc. R. Soc. Med., 29*: 325 (1935).

H. Luxenburger, Vorlaufiger bericht uber psychiatrishce serinumtersuchungen an zwillinger, *Z. Gesamte Neurol. Psychiatr., 116*: 297 (1928).

H. Luxenburger, Psychiatrish–neurologisch zwillingspathologie, *Zentralbl. Gesamte Neurol. Psychiatr., 56*: 145 (1930).

D. T. Lykken, Research with twins: The concept of emergenesis, *Psychophysiology, 19*: 361 (1981).

L. Lykouras, D. Vassilopoulos, A. Voulgari, C. Stefanis, and D. Malliaras, Delusional depression: Further evidence for genetic contribution, *Psychiatr. Res., 21*: 277 (1987).

A. J. Mackinnon, A. S. Henderson, and G. Andrews, A twin study of the lability of trait neuroticism and neurotic symptoms, *Psychol. Med., 20*: 581 (1990).

I. M. Marks, Genetics of fear and anxiety disorder, *Br. J. Psychiatry, 149*: 406 (1986).

I. M. Marks, M. Crowe, E. Drewe, J. Young, and W. G. Dewhurst, Obsessive–compulsive neurosis in identical twins, *Br. J. Psychiatry, 115*: 991 (1969).

N. G. Martin, R. Jardine, G. Andrews, and A. C. Heath, Anxiety disorders and neurotisicm: Are there genetic factors specific to panic? *Acta Psychiatr. Scand., 77*: 698 (1988).

M. Martinez, M. Khlat, M. Leboyer, and F. Clerget-Darpoux, Performance of linkage analyses under misclassification error when the genetic model is unknown, *Genet. Epidemiol. 6*: 253–258 (1989).

P. McGuffin, R. Katz, J. Aldrich, P. E. Bebbington, The Camberwell Collaborative Depression Study II. The investigation of family members, *Br. J. Psychiatry, 152*: 766 (1988a).

P. McGuffin, R. Katz, P. E. Bebbington, The Camberwell Collaborative Depression Study III: Depression and adversity in the relatives of depressed probands, *Br. J. Psychiatry, 152*: 775 (1988b).

P. McGuffin, R. Katz, and J. Rutherford, Nature, nurture and depression: A twin study, *Psychol. Med., 21*: 329 (1991).

R. G. McInnes, Observations of heredity in neurosis, *Proc. R. Soc. Med., 30*: 895 (1937).

J. Mendlewicz, and M. Baron, Morbidity risks in subtypes of unipolar depressive illness: Differences between early, and late onset forms, *Br. J. Psychiatry, 139*: 463 (1981).

J. Mendlewicz, and J. L. Fleiss, Linkage studies with X-chromosome markers in bipolar (manic–depressive) and unipolar (depressive) illness, *Biol. Psychiatry, 9*: 261 (1974).

J. Mendlewicz, and D. Hirsch, Bipolar manic depressive illness and the fragile X syndrome [letter], *Biol. Psychiatry, 29*: 295 (1991).

J. Mendlewicz, and J. D. Rainer, Morbidity risk and genetic transmission in manic–depressive illness, *Am. J. Hum. Genet. 26*: 692 (1974).

J. Mendlewicz, and J. D. Rainer, Adoption study supporting genetic transmission in manic–depressive illness, *Nature, 268*: 327 (1977).

J. Mendlewicz, J. L. Fleiss, M. Cataldo, and J. D. Rainer, Accuracy of the family history method in affective illness, *Arch. Gen. Psychiatry, 32*: 309 (1975).

J. Mendlewicz, P. Linkowski, and J. Wilmotte, Linkage between glucose-6-phosphate dehydrogenase deficiency and manic–depressive psychosis, *Br. J. Psychiatry, 137*: 337 (1980).

J. Mendlewicz, P. Simon, S. Sevy, F. Charon, H. Brocas, S. Legros, and G. Vassart, Polymorphic DNA marker on X-chromosome and manic depression, *Lancet, 1*: 1230 (1987).

K. R. Merikangas, M. M. Weissman, and D. L. Pauls, Genetic factors in the sex ratio of major depression, *Psychol. Med., 15*: 63 (1985).

K. R. Merikangas, A. Spence, D. J. Kupfer, Linkage studies of bipolar disorder, methodologic and analytic issues, *Arch. Gen. Psychiatry, 46*: 1137 (1989).

P. Mitchell, B. Waters, N. Morrison, J. Shine, J. Donald, and J. Eisman, Close linkage of bipolar disorder to chromosome 11 markers is exluded in two large Australian pedigrees, *J. Affective Disord., 21*: 23 (1991).

P. Mitchell, L. Selbie, B. Waters, J. Donald, C. Vivero, M. Tully, and J. Shine, Exclusion of close linkage between bipolar disorder and D^1 and D^2 dopamine receptor gene markers, *J. Affective Disord.,* in press (1992).

C. Moran, and G. Andrews, The familial occurrence of agoraphobia, *Br. J. Psychiatry, 146*: 262 (1985).

D. J. Munjack, and H. B. Moss, Affective disorder and alcoholism in families of agoraphobics, *Arch. Gen. Psychiatry, 38*: 869 (1981).

K. Neiswanger, S. A. Slaugenhaupt, H. B. Hughes, E. Frank, D. R. Frankel, M. J. McCarty, A. Chakravarti, G. S. Zubenko, D. J. Kupfer, and B. B. Kaplan, Evidence against close linkage of unipolar affective illness to human chromosome 11p markers *HRASI* and *INS* and chromsome Xq marker *DXS52*, *Biol. Psychiatry, 28*: 63 (1990).

R. Noyes, Jr., J. Clancy, R. Crowe, P. R. Hoenk, and D. J. Slymen, The familial prevalence of anxiety neurosis, *Arch. Gen Psychiatry, 35*: 1057 (1978).

R. Noyes, Jr., R. R. Crowe, E. L. Harris, B. Hamra, C. M. McChesney, and D. R. Chaudry, Relationship between panic disorder and agoraphobia, *Arch. Gen. Psychiatry, 43*: 227 (1986).

R. Noyes, Jr., C. Clarkson, R. R. Crowe, W. R. Yates, and C. M. McChesney, A family study of generalized anxiety disorder, *Am. J. Psychiatry, 144*: 1019 (1987).

J. I. Nurnberger, and E. S. Gershon, Genetics of affective disorders, *Neurobiology of Mood Disorders* (R. M. Post and J. C. Ballenger, eds.), Williams & Wilkins, Baltimore, p. 76 (1984).

J. Ott, *Analysis of Human Genetic Linkage*, Johns Hopkins University Press, Baltimore (1985).

J. Ott, "Linkage Analysis—Potential Problems Introduced by the Practice of Maximising the Lod Score Over a Wide Range of Parameters Including Disease Classification," Proceedings of The First World Congress in Psychiatric Genetics, Cambridge, England (1989).

J. Ott, Cutting a Gordian Knot in the linkage analysis of complex human traits, *Am. J. Hum. Genet., 46*: 219 (1990).

A. J. Paratkis, J. R. Kidd, C. M. Castiglione, and K. K. Kidd, Status of the search for a major genetic locus for affective disorder in the Old Order Amish, *Hum. Genet., 87*: 475 (1991).

G. Parker, *Parental Overprotection*, Grune & Stratton, New York (1983).

G. Parker, D. Hadzi-Pavlovic, P. Boyce, K. Wilhelm, H. Brodaty, P. Mitchell, I. Hickie, and K. Eyers, Classifying depression by mental state signs, *Br. J. Psychiatry, 157*: 55 (1990).

D. L. Pauls, R. Noyes, and R. R. Crowe, The familial prevalence in second degree relatives in anxiety neurosis, *J. Affective Disord., 1*: 279, (1979).

D. L. Pauls, K. D. Bucher, R. R. Crowe, and R. Noyes, Jr., A genetic study of panic disorder pedigrees, *Am. J. Hum. Genet., 32*: 639 (1980).

H. Payami, C. Dubay, and C. Valenzuela, HLA may be involved in resistance and susceptibility to affective disorders, *Genet. Epidemiol. 6*: 293 (1989).

E. S. Paykel, Life events and early environment, *Handbook of Affective Disorders* (E. S. Paykel, ed.), Churchill–Livingstone, Edinburgh, p. 146 (1982).
L. S. Penrose, The genetical background of common diseases, *Acta Genet.,* *4*: 257 (1953).
C. Perris, H. Perris, U. Ericsson, and L. Von Knorring, The genetics of depression, *Arch. Psychiatr. Nervenkr.,* *232*: 137 (1982).
K. Phillips, D. W. Fulker, and R. J. Rose, Path analysis of seven fear factors in adult twin and sibling pairs and their parents, *Genet. Epidemiol.* *4*: 345 (1987).
R. Plomin, and D. Daniels, Why are children in the same family so different from one another? *Behav. Brain Sci.,* *10*: 1 (1987).
W. Pollin, M. G. Allen, A. Hoffer, J. R. Stabenau, and Z. Hrubec, Psychopathology in 15,909 pairs of Veteran twins: Evidence for a genetic factor in the pathogenesis of schizophrenia and its relative absence in psychoneurosis, *Am. J. Psychiatry,* *126*: 597 (1969).
J. Pollitt, The relationship between genetic and precipitating factors in depressive illness, *Br. J. Psychiatry,* *121*: 67 (1972).
L. H. Price, J. C. Nelson, D. S. Charneym, and D. M. Quinlan, Family history in delusional depression, *J. Affective Disord.,* *6*: 109 (1984).
R. A. Price, K. K. Kidd, E. S. Gershon, B. A. Prusoff, M. M. Weissman, and L. R. Goldin, Multiple threshold models for affective disorders: The Yale–NIMH collaborative family study, *J. Psychiatr. Res.,* *19*: 533 (1985).
R. A. Price, K. K. Kidd, and M. M. Weissman, Early onset (under age 30 years) and panic disorder as markers for etiologic homogeneity in major depression, *Arch. Gen. Psychiatry,* *44*: 434 (1987).
T. Reich, J. W. James, and C. Morris, The use of multiple thresholds in determining the mode of transmission of semi-continuous traits, *Ann. Hum. Genet.,* *42*: 371 (1979).
T. Reich, P. Eerdewegh, J. Rice, J. Mullaney, J. Endicott, and G. L. Klerman, The familial transmission of primary major depressive disorder, *J. Psychiatr. Res.,* *21*: 613 (1987).
A. L. Reiss, C. Feinstein, K. E. Toomey, B. Goldsmith, K. Rosenbaum, and M. A. Caruso, Psychiatric disability associated with the fragile X chromosome, *Am. J. Med. Genet.,* *23*: 393 (1986).
J. Rice, T. Reich, N. Andreasen, J. Endicott, M. Van Eerdewegh, R. Fishman, R. M. A. Hirschfeld, and G. L. Klerman, The familial transmission of bipolar illness, *Arch. Gen. Psychiatry,* *44*: 441 (1987).
N. Risch, Linkage strategies for genetically complex traits. I. Multilocus models, *Am. J.Hum. Genet.,* *46*: 222–228 (1990a).
N. Risch, Linkage strategies for genetically complex traits. II. The power of affected relative pairs, *Am. J. Hum. Genet.,* *46*: 229 (1990b).
L. N. Robins, J. E. Helzer, M. Weissman, H. Orvaschel, E. Gruenberg, J. D. Burke, Jr., and D. A. Regier, Lifetime prevalence of specific psychiatric disorders in three sites. *Arch. Gen. Psychiatry,* *41*: 949 (1984).
L. N. Robins, J. Wing, H. U. Wittchen, J. E. Helzer, T. F. Babor, J. Burke, A. Farmer, A. Jablenski, R. Pickens, D. A. Regier, N. Sartorius, and L. H. Towle, The Composite International Diagnostic Interview, *Arch. Gen. Psychiatry,* *45*: 1069 (1988).
A. J. Rosanoff, L. M. Handy, and I. Rosanoff Plesset, The etiology of manic–depressive syndromes with special reference to their occurrence in twins, *Am. J. Psychiatry,* *91*: 725 (1935).
R. J. Rose, and W. B. Ditto, A developmental-genetic analysis of common fears from early adolescence to early adulthood, *Child Dev.,* *54*: 361 (1983).
C. M. Rosenberg, Familial aspects of obsessional illness, *Br. J. Psychiatry,* *113*: 405 (1967).
D. Rosenthal, P. H. Wender, S. S. Kety, F. Schulsinger, J. Welner, and R. Reider, Parent–child relationships and psychopathological disorder in the child, *Arch. Gen. Psychiatry,* *32*: 466 (1975).
R. W. Shapiro, E. Bock, O. J. Rafaelsen, L. P. Ryder, and A. Svejgaard, Histocompatibility antigens and manic–depressive disorders, *Arch. Gen. Psychiatry,* *33*: 823 (1976).

R. W. Shapiro, A twin study of non-endogenous depression, *Acta Jutlandica, 42*: 1–179, (1970).
R. Shaughnessy, S. C. Greene, G. N. Pandey, and E. Dorus, Red-cell lithium transport and affective disorders in a multigeneration pedigree: Evidence for genetic transmission of affective disorders, *Biol. Psychiatry, 20*: 451 (1985).
J. L. Silberg, A. C. Heath, R. Kessler, M. C. Neale, J. M. Meyer, L. J. Eaves, and K. S. Kendler, Genetic and environmental effects on self-reported depressive symptoms in a general twin population, *J. Psychiatr. Res., 24*: 197 (1990).
E. Slater, and J. Shields, *Psychotic and Neurotic Illness in Twins*, Medical Research Current Special Report, Series No. ZN8. HMSO, London (1953).
E. Slater, and P. Slater, A heuristic theory of neurosis, *J. Neurol. Psychiatry, 7*: 49 (1944).
E. Smeraldi, F. Negri, and A. M. Melica, A genetic study of affective disorders, *Acta Psychiatr. Scand., 56*: 382 (1977).
E. Smeraldi, A. Petroccione, M. Gasperini, F. Macciardi, and A. Orsini, The search for genetic homogeneity in affective disorders, *J. Affective Disord., 7*: 99 (1984).
M. Smith, J. Wasmuth, D. McPherson, C. Wagner, D. Grandy, O. Civelli, S. Potkin, and M. Litt, Cosegregation of an 11q22.3-9p22 translocation with affective disorder: Proximity of the dopamine D^2 receptor gene relative to the translocation breakpoint, *Am. J. Hum. Genet., 45*: A220 (1989).
L. Solyom, P. Beck, C. Solyom, and R. Hugel, Some etiological factors in phobic neuroses, *Can. Psychiatr. Assoc. J., 19*: 69 (1974).
R. L. Spitzer, J. Endicott, and E. Robins, *Research Diagnositic Criteria RDC for a Selected Group of Functional Disorders*, 3rd ed., New York State Psychiatric Institute, New York (1977).
D. St. Clair, D. Blackwood, and W. Mint, Association within a family of a balanced translocation with major mental illness, *Lancet, 336*: 13 (1990).
H. C. Stancer, E. Persad, D. K. Wagener, and T. Jorna, Evidence for homogeneity of major depression and bipolar affective disorder, *J. Psychiatr. Res., 21*: 37 (1987).
A. Stenstedt, Genetics of neurotic depression, *Acta Psychiatr. Scand., 42*: 392 (1966).
J. C. Stephens, M. L. Cavanaugh, M. I. Gradie, M. L. Mador, and K. K. Kidd, Mapping the human genome: Current status, *Science, 250*: 237 (1990).
M. Strober, W. Morrell, J. Burroughs, C. Lampert, H. Danforth, and R. Freeman, A family study of bipolar I disorder in adolescence, *J. Affective Disord., 15*: 255 (1988).
B. K. Suarez, C. L. Hampe, and A. F. Wright, Linkage analysis in manic–depressive illness [letter], *Lancet, 2*: 345 (1987).
V. L. Tanna, G. Winokur, R. C. Elston, and R. C. P. Go, A linkage study of pure depressive disease: The use of the sib-pair method, *Biol. Psychiatry, 11*: 767 (1976).
V. L. Tanna, R. C. P. Go, G. Winokur, and R. C. Elston, Possible linkage between group-specific component (G_c protein) and pure depressive disease, *Acta Psychiatr. Scand., 55*: 111 (1977).
V. L. Tanna, R. C. P. Go, G. Winokur, and R. C. Elston, Possible linkage between alpha-haptoglobin (Hp) and depression spectrum disease, *Neuropsychobiology, 5*: 102 (1979).
V. L. Tanna, A. F. Wilson, G. Winokur, and R. C. Elston, Linkage analysis of pure depressive disease, *J. Psychiatr. Res., 23*: 99 (1989).
M. A. Taylor, and R. Abrams, Early-and late-onset bipolar illness, *Arch. Gen. Psychiatry, 38*: 58 (1981).
R. D. Todd, and K. L. O'Malley, Population frequencies of tyrosine hydroxylase restriction fragment length polymorphisms in bipolar affective disorder, *Biol. Psychiatry, 25*: 626 (1989).
S. Torgersen, Genetic factors in anxiety disorders, *Arch. Gen. Psychiatry, 40*: 1085 (1983).
S. Torgersen, Hereditary differentiation of anxiety and affective neuroses, *Br. J. Psychiatry, 146*: 530 (1985).
S. Torgersen, Genetic factors in moderately severe and mild affective disorders. *Arch. Gen. Psychiatry, 43*: 222 (1986).

M. T. Tsuang, and S. V. Faraone, *The Genetics of Mood Disorders*, Johns Hopkins University Press, Baltimore (1990).

M. T. Tsuang, K. D. Bucher, J. A. Fleming, and S. V. Faraone, Transmission of affective disorders: An application of segregation analysis to blind family study data, *J. Psychiatr. Res., 19*: 23 (1985a).

M. T. Tsuang, S. V. Faraone, and J. A. Fleming, Familial transmission of major affective disorders: Is there evidence supporting the distinction between unipolar and bipolar disorders? *Br. J. Psychiatry, 146*: 268 (1985b).

W. J. Turner, and S. King, Two genetically distinct forms of bipolar affective disorder, *Biol. Psychiatry, 16*: 417 (1981).

W. J. Turner, and S. King, BPD_2 an autosomal dominant form of bipolar disorder, *Biol. Psychiatry, 18*: 63 (1983).

S. G. Vandenburg, Hereditary factor in normal personality (As measured by inventories), *Recent Developments in Biological Psychiatry* (J. Wortis, ed.), Plenum Press, New York, pp. 65–104 (1967).

M. M. Van Eerdewegh, E. S. Gershon, and P. M. Van Eerdewegh, X-chromosome threshold models of bipolar manic-depressive illness, *J. Psychiatr. Res., 15*: 215 (1980).

G. Vassart, and P. Simon, Manic–depression locus on X-chromosome [letter], *Lancet, 338*: 821 (1991).

A. L. Von Knorring, C. R. Cloninger, M. Bohman, and S. Sigvardsson, An adoption study of depressive disorders and substance abuse, *Arch. Gen. Psychiatry, 40*: 943 (1983).

B. Waters, I. Marchenko, N. Adams, D. Smiley, and D. Kalin, Assortative mating for major affective disorder, *J. Affective Disord., 5*: 9 (1983).

B. Waters, D. Sengar, I. Marchenko, G. Rock, Y. Lapierre, C. Foster-Gibson, and N. E. Simpson, A linkage study of primary affective disorder, *Br. J. Psychiatry, 152*: 560 (1988).

J. L. Weber, Human DNA polymorphisms based on length variations in simple-sequence tandem repeats, *Genome Analysis,* Vol. 1: *Genetic and Physical Mapping*, Cold Spring Harbour Press, Cold Spring Harbor, N. Y., p. 159 (1990).

D. E. Weeks, and K. Lange, The affected–pedigree–member method linkage analysis, *Am. J. Hum. Genet., 42*: 315 (1988).

M. M. Weissman, E. S. Gershon, K. K. Kidd, B. A. Prusoff, J. F. Leckman, E. Dibble, J. Hamovit, D. Thompson, D. L. Pauls, and J. J. Guroff, Psychiatric disorders in the relatives of probands with affective disorders, *Arch. Gen. Psychiatry, 41*: 13 (1984a).

M. M. Weissman, B. A. Prusoff, and K. R. Merikangas, Is delusional depression related to bipolar disorder? *Am. J. Psychiatry, 141*: 892 (1984b).

M. M. Weissman, J. F. Leckman, K. R. Merikangas, G. D. Gammon, and B. A. Prusoff, Depression and anxiety disorders in parents and children, *Arch. Gen. Psychiatry, 41*: 845 (1984c).

M. M. Weissman, K. R. Merikangas, P. Wickramaratne, K. K. Kidd, B. A. Prusoff, J. F. Leckman, and D. L. Pauls, Understanding the clinical heterogeneity of major depression using family data, *Arch. Gen. Psychiatry, 43*: 430 (1986).

L. R. Weitkamp, and H. C. Stancer, Analysis of the Toronto–Rochester depression study follow-up data confirms an HLA-region gene contribution to susceptibility to affective disorder, *Genet. Epidemiol., 6*: 305 (1989).

L. R. Weitkamp, H. C. Stancer, E. Persad, C. Flood, and S. Guttormsen, Depressive disorders and HLA: A gene on chromosome 6 that can affect behaviour, *N. Engl. J. Med., 305*: 1301 (1981).

P. H. Wender, S. S. Kety, D. Rosenthal, F. Schulsinger, J. Ortmann, and I. Lunde, Psychiatric disorders in the biological and adoptive families and adopted individuals with affective disorders, *Arch. Gen. Psychiatry, 43*: 923 (1986).

R. B. Wesner, W. Scheffner, P. J. Palmer, P. R. Crowe, and G. Winokur, The effect of comorbidity and penetrance on the outcome of linkage analysis in a bipolar family, *Biol. Psychiatry, 27*: 241 (1990).

E. O. Wheeler, P. D. White, E. Reed, and M. E. Cohen, Familial incidence of neurocirculatory asthenia, *J. Clin. Invest., 27*: 562 (1948).

M. Wierzbicki, Similarity of monozygotic and dizygotic twins in level and lability of subclinically depressed mood, *J. Clin. Psychol., 42*: 577 (1986).

S. R. Wilson, Heritability, *J. Appl. Probab., 19A*: 71 (1982).

J. K. Wing, J. E. Cooper, and N. Sartorius, *The Measurement and Classification of Psychiatric Symptoms*, Cambridge University Press, Cambridge (1974).

G. Winokur, The development and validity of familial subtypes in primary unipolar depression, *Pharmacopsychiatry, 15*: 142 (1982).

G. Winokur, Family (genetic) studies in neurotic depression, *J. Psychiatr. Res., 21*: 357 (1987).

G. Winokur, and V. L. Tanna, Possible role of X-linked dominant factor in manic depressive disease, *Dis. Nerv. Syst., 30*: 89 (1969).

G. Winokur, M. T. Tsuang, and R. R. Crowe, The Iowa 500: Affective disorder in relatives of manic and depressed patients, *Am. J. Psychiatry, 139*: 209 (1982).

World Health Organization. *ICD-10 1990 Draft of the Chapter V: Categories F00-F99, Mental and Behavioural Disorders (Including Disorders of Psychological Development. Diagnostic Criteria for Research*) (WHO/MNH/MEP/87.1 Rev 2), World Health Organization, Division of Mental Health, Geneva (1990).

J. P. R. Young, G. W. Fenton, and M. H. Lader, The inheritance of neurotic traits: A twin study of the Middlesex Hospital Questionnaire, *Br. J. Psychiatry, 119*: 393 (1971).

M. Zimmerman, W. Coryell, B. Pfohl, and D. Stangi, The validity of four definitions of endogenous depression, *Arch. Gen. Psychiatry, 43*: 234 (1986).

5

Depression and Anxiety: Is There a Common Etiology?

Rudolf Hoehn-Saric and Daniel R. McLeod
Johns Hopkins University School of Medicine, Baltimore, Maryland

I. INTRODUCTION

Since the early part of the century, psychiatrists have debated whether pathological anxiety and depression constitute different aspects of the same disorder (Lewis, 1934) or distinct, although often overlapping, conditions (Roth et al., 1982). For the first assumption to be correct, biological mechanisms that underlie the two disorders should be identical and should show quantitative, but not qualitative, differences. For the second assumption to be correct, the biological mechanisms responsible for anxiety should differ distinctly from those seen in depression. The debate over which of the two assumptions is correct remains unresolved. This chapter will briefly review clinical and laboratory data on anxiety and depression and try to point out similarities and differences between the two groups of disorders. The reviewed studies suggest that biological mechanisms and, therefore, etiology not only differ between anxiety and depressive disorders, in general, but also between subgroups of anxiety and depressive disorders. In some cases, however, mechanisms that are disturbed in anxiety disorders appear also to be disturbed in depression, or at least may induce disturbances found in depression.

II. ANXIETY AND DEPRESSION: NORMAL AND ABNORMAL

When we discuss anxiety and depression we need to distinguish normal affective responses from exaggerated affective responses as seen in emotionally labile personality disorders, and from clearly defined clinical anxiety and depressive disorders. As affects, anxiety and depression are experienced in everyday life and serve important biological functions. Normal anxiety is a warning system that alerts a person to potential dangers. As it is future-oriented, anxiety helps us to focus on potentially dangerous situations and to formulate plans to deal with them. Moreover, since anxiety is an unpleasant emotion from which we like to escape, it motivates us to master or avoid anxiety-provoking situations. Depression, on the other hand, is oriented toward the past. A depressed person perceives that an irreparable internal or external loss has occurred. The biological usefulness of depression is less obvious than that of anxiety. In phylogenic development, depression may have been useful as an energy-saving response to situations in which active-coping mechanisms were exhausted (Seligman, 1975). In everyday life, the perception of imminent, but potentially correctable, danger often coexists or, more likely, alternates with the perception of hopelessness. Therefore, distressed persons often experience feelings of both anxiety and depression. An exaggeration of normal anxiety and depression can be observed in neurotic patients who exhibit emotional lability. The coexistence of anxiety and depression is also a common feature in chronic anxiety states and in pathological depressions. Numerous studies have shown that anxiety disorders may contain an element of depression and vice versa (Rickels and Schweizer, 1990; Clayton et al., 1991; Coryell et al., 1988). Therefore, many anxiety rating scales contain subscales of depression, and depression scales also include subscales describing psychic and somatic symptoms of anxiety (e.g., Hamilton, 1959; 1960). Rating instruments that measure both mood states simultaneously have been useful in the recognition of how clinicians have separated nonpsychotic anxiety patients from nonpsychotic depressive patients. Studies that employed comprehensive scales found that patients who were given the diagnosis of anxiety neurosis differed from those diagnosed with depressive neurosis, primarily in the severity ratings of depression (Hoehn-Saric, 1983; Lipman, 1982). As expected, patients with depressive neurosis scored higher on ratings of depression, but ratings of anxiety were comparably elevated in groups of patients who were diagnosed by clinicians as having either anxiety neurosis or depressive neurosis (Hoehn-Saric, 1983). Thus, patients with depressive neurosis were as anxious, but were more depressed than patients with anxiety neurosis. Not all anxiety and depressive disorders exhibit mixed features. Some patients with anxiety disorders are free of clinically significant depression, and some patients with depressive disorders do not experience significant levels of anxiety. However, many patients, estimated to be between 20 and 90% of surveyed patient populations (Wetzler and Katz, 1989), experience both anxiety and depression. Mixed anxiety–depressive disorders appear to have a more protracted course and a poorer response to treatment than “pure” anxiety or depressive disorders (Coryell et al., 1988).

III. CLINICAL STUDIES: LONGITUDINAL SURVEYS AND FAMILY STUDIES

Soon after the advent of *the Diagnostic and Statistical Manual of Mental Disorders*, 3rd ed. (*DSM-III*; American Psychiatric Association, 1980), it became clear that not all patients could be categorized according the guidelines of the manual (Detre, 1985; Roth et al., 1982; Tyrer, 1989). One way to overcome the confines of *DSM-III* without violating its spirit was to introduce the concept of comorbidity. This conceptual change stimulated research on the comorbidity of anxiety and depressive disorders. The term *comorbidity*, however, is poorly defined and is used differently in different studies. In some studies this term indicates that anxiety and depressive symptoms coexist simultaneously. In other studies, however, the term states that one condition frequently follows the other. Earlier studies on comorbidity were mostly descriptive; more recent studies have tried to explore biological relations between disorders that frequently show comorbidity. Some investigators have proposed that anxiety and depression are biologically separate disorders (Roth et al., 1982). If this is true, we should find little overlap in their clinical pictures. It is also conceivable that symptoms of anxiety and depression represent different aspects of the same disorder (Lewis, 1934). Here, symptoms of anxiety and depression could occur simultaneously or alternate. A third possibility is that one condition, such as anxiety, induces changes that lead to another condition, such as depression. In this model, pathological depression is the consequence of pathological anxiety and should not lead to anxiety disorders. Finally, comorbidity may be the final common pathway of two originally independent conditions. This model applies to conditions, such as dementia, but does not seem to apply to anxiety and depressive disorders.

Two epidemiological studies followed patients with initial diagnoses of anxiety, depressive disorder, or mixed anxiety–depressive disorder over several years (Kendell, 1974; Angst et al., 1990). At follow-up examinations, these studies showed that patients who originally had suffered from anxiety disorders often subsequently developed depressive disorders. Patients who initially were diagnosed as having depressive disorders without anxiety, however, rarely developed an anxiety disorder. Thus, whereas depression maintained a diagnostic stability over time, this was not true for anxiety disorders. It is unclear whether all anxiety disorders show comorbidity with depression. Results of most studies suggest that panic disorder and depression are frequently associated or that depression emerges in the course of a panic disorder (Leckman et al., 1990). Data on comorbidity in generalized anxiety disorder (GAD) patients are less consistent. Breslau and Davis (1985) reported a high incidence of major depression in surveyed mothers who carried the primary diagnosis of generalized anxiety disorder. Noyes et al. (1987) diagnosed a large number of GAD patients who had "secondary" depression. Angst et al. (1990), on the other hand, rarely found coexisting depression in their GAD groups. The differences in the findings of the three research groups may be explained by differences in their patient populations, diagnostic criteria, and methods of assessment.

Results of family studies have been more informative than those of longitudinal studies. Noyes et al. (1987) and Crowe et al. (1980) demonstrated that the risk of having an anxiety neurosis was six times higher in relatives of probands with that disorder than in relatives of controls. The specificity of transmission of anxiety disorders is also suggested by the work of Cloninger et al. (1981) and Dealy et al. (1981), whose studies showed that relatives of probands with anxiety disorders, but not depressive disorders, exhibited an increased risk of anxiety neurosis. The results of the foregoing studies suggest that anxiety and depressive disorders have different etiologies and, therefore, probably different biological mechanisms. Noyes et al. (1987) found that relatives of patients with GAD had an increased occurrence of generalized anxiety, but not panic disorder. These results suggest that it may not be possible to speak about the etiology of anxiety in general, but rather about each specific type of anxiety disorder. The same is probably true for depression (Goodwin and Jamison, 1990). Merikangas (1990), who reviewed recent family and genetic studies, came to the conclusion that "pure" anxiety neurosis and panic disorder tend to break through to a substantial degree. However, probands who suffered from major depressive disorder concomitantly with an anxiety disorder had an increased familiar loading of affective disorders. Twin studies also support the hypothesis that pure depression and mixed anxiety–depression are etiologically similar disorders, whereas pure anxiety disorders differ etiologically from depressive and mixed disorders (Torgersen, 1990).

Other studies, however, have yielded less clear results. Angst et al. (1990) found that parents of patients with pure anxiety or depressive disorders and mixed anxiety–depressive disorder had comparable histories of anxiety and depressive disorders. Studies of panic disorder patients not only showed a greater increase of panic disorder, but also an increased prevalence of major depression among relatives (Maier et al., 1988). This finding led some investigators to believe that a common teleological factor exists in the expression of at least some anxiety and depressive disorders (Angst et al., 1990; Maier et al., 1988). Obviously, further studies are needed to explain these discrepancies.

In summary, longitudinal studies indicate that it is more likely that anxiety disorders lead to depression than vice versa. Family studies suggest that pure anxiety disorders cluster in families. On the other hand, mixed anxiety–depressive disorders are associated with a higher incidence of depressive disorders in relatives of probands, and tend, etiologically speaking, to resemble depressive disorders. However, present data are sufficiently discrepant to warrant further research in familiar incidence of anxiety and depressive disorders. Obviously, many questions will remain unanswered until genes associated with specific disorders are identified.

IV. IMAGING STUDIES

Several studies have identified areas in the brain where damage frequently is associated with depression. These studies have shown positive correlations between the proximity of the lesions to the left frontal pole and the level of depression. The closer the lesion was to the frontal pole, the more severe it was (Starkstein and Robinson, 1989). Patients who were anxious and depressed frequently had more cortical lesions, whereas patients who had major depression without anxiety suffered more frequently from a subcortical (basal ganglia) stroke (Starkstein et al., 1990). Not all studies reviewed by Goodwin and Jamison (1990, p. 504), however, are consistent with the findings of the foregoing authors.

Imaging studies of neurologically normal patients often, but not always, have found differences among anxious, depressed, and normal subjects. Cerebral blood flow studies in depressed patients, using the ^{133}Xe inhalation method, gave mixed results. Three studies reported reduced blood flow, whereas four other studies reported no differences at all (Goodwin and Jamison, 1990, p. 518).

Single-photon emission computed tomography (SPECT) studies that measure cerebral blood perfusion suggest that cortical blood flow is lowered in depressed patients (Rush et al., 1982). Cerebral blood flow and glucose metabolism are closely related. The findings by Baxter et al. (1987; 1989) that glucose metabolism, measured by positron emission tomography (PET) scans, is lowered in patients with major depression confirm the findings of some SPECT scan studies. Moreover, these studies suggest the presence of differences in brain metabolism among depressive subgroups. Decreased glucose metabolism in the left anterior dorsal prefrontal cortex was identified in all depressive subgroups, whereas more global abnormalities in metabolism were specific for the bipolar group. With use of the same method, Post et al. (1987) found no significant changes in glucose metabolism in the temporal lobes, but recently, Amsterdam and Mozley (1992) noticed asymmetry in the temporal pole perfusion in SPECT-scanned patients with major depression.

Studies of anxiety and anxiety disorders also have found increased or decreased general cerebral perfusion or metabolism, depending on the method of scanning and the state of the patient. It appears that mild levels of anxiety produce an increase of cerebral blood flow, in general, and in the frontal lobes specifically, whereas higher levels of anxiety lead to decreased blood flow (Wilson and Mathew, 1993). We (Machlin, et al., 1991) observed hyperfrontality in, but at the same time a negative correlation, between levels of frontal cerebral perfusion and levels of anxiety in SPECT scans of highly anxious, obsessive–compulsive patients. The global decrease of cerebral blood flow observed during high levels of anxiety may be a consequence of hyperventilation and sympathetically induced vasoconstriction. This mechanism, however, does not explain regional change. Xenon-133 inhalation studies showed little difference in cerebral blood flow between GAD patients and controls at rest. The reactivity of the GAD patients to challenges that increase cerebral blood flow, however, appears to be diminished (Wilson and Mathew, 1993). The PET scan studies examining cerebral glucose metabolism in GAD patients revealed a lower absolute metabolic rate in the basal ganglia and white matter, and a relative increase of metabolism in the occipital lobe, right posterior temporal lobe, and right precentral gyrus (Wu et al. 1991). Oxygen-15 has been used as a tracer in PET studies of normal persons anticipating a painful electric shock (Reiman et al., 1989) and in panic disorder patients in whom panic attacks had been induced by means of sodium lactate infusion (Reiman et al., 1989). Increased cerebral blood flow in the temporal lobes was found in both groups of subjects. The same group (Reiman et al., 1984) also found differences in blood flow between the right and left parahippocampal gyri of panic disorder patients. This finding was confirmed by Nordahl et al. (1990), who used cerebral glucose metabolism as their measure. However, in contrast to Reiman et al. (1984; 1989), the latter group found no differences in global metabolism between panic disorder patients and controls.

Results of psychometric studies support some findings of imaging studies. Taylor and Abrams (1987) found that many melancholia patients performed poorly on tests that assessed frontal lobe function and right hemisphere function. This corresponds to the hyperfrontality found in many imaging studies of depressed patients. Cognitive performance in normal subjects follows the well-known Yerkes–Dodson law (Yerkes and Dodson, 1908); namely, that the quality of performance during anxiety changes is an inverted U-shaped function of increasing anxiety. Under moderate levels of anxiety, performance improves, but beyond a certain level, it declines again. This pattern of performance change corresponds to the changes in brain perfusion reported by Gur et al. (1988), who found cerebral perfusion increases during mild anxiety, but decreases during higher levels.

In summary, imaging studies are still difficult to interpret owing to differences in techniques, patient selection, the state of the patient during the scan, and the few patients examined in each study. Available data suggest, however, that differences in cerebral blood flow and metabolism exist between patients with depression and anxiety. In depression, cerebral blood flow and metabolism, in general, and in the frontal lobes particularly, tend to be diminished. In anxiety, overall blood flow and metabolism are increased or decreased, depending on the level of anxiety. Anticipatory anxiety and severe panic anxiety are associated with increased activity in the temporal lobes; panic disorder, in the absence of a panic attack, is associated with changes in the parahippocampal gyri; and obsessive–compulsive disorder is associated with hyperfrontality. Differences in glucose metabolism between unipolar and bipolar depression have also been reported. Thus, imaging studies suggest a diversity in the etiology not only of anxiety and depression in general, but of subdisorders as well.

V. PSYCHOPHYSIOLOGICAL STUDIES

In contrast with regular electroencephalographic (EEG) studies, which have shown little specific change in anxiety and depression, sleep studies suggest the existence of different mechanisms for anxiety and depression. In depressed patients, Reynolds and Kupfer (1987) have found interruptions in sleep throughout the night, early morning awakening, and a shortened rapid eye movement (REM) latency. Anxiety disorder patients also show sleep disturbances, particularly during their first night in the sleep laboratory, whereas dysthymic patients tend to experience hypersomnia (Akiskal et al., 1984). These findings suggest that hyperarousal in novel situations is associated with anxiety, but not with depression. Reynolds et al. (1983) compared the sleep pattern of GAD patients with those of depressed patients and found impairment of sleep continuity and reduction of delta sleep in both groups. Patients with GAD differed from depressed patients in exhibiting greater reduction of stage 1 sleep and REM percentage, whereas patients with primary depression exhibited shorter REM latency. Papadimitrion et al. (1988) were able to differentiate GAD patients from patients with primary depression by means of sleep records, even when depression coexisted with GAD. Unlike patients with either GAD or depression, panic disorder patients tend to exhibit increased delta sleep (Hauri et al., 1986). Panic disorder patients also experienced insomnia characterized principally by difficulty initiating or maintaining sleep (Mellman and Uhde, 1989). The REM abnormalities, however, were not a consistent feature in panic disorder patients. Sleep deprivation studies further support the difference between anxiety and depression. Sleep deprivation in depression leads to a transitory improvement, whereas sleep deprivation in panic disorder often exacerbates the patient's condition (Roy-Byrne et al., 1986).

Studies of the peripheral autonomic nervous system have been less specific in differentiating anxiety and depression. Electrodermal activity, which reflects sympathetically controlled sweat gland activity, is often decreased in depressed persons (Christie et al., 1980). Cardiovascular activity corresponds to anxiety levels, rather than to presence or absence of depression. In studies conducted before *DSM-III* classification, patients with agitated depression exhibited levels of basal forearm blood flow, heart rate, and blood pressure similar to those of chronic anxiety patients. In both groups, measured levels were higher than in normal controls. Patients with "nonagitated depression," however, had values similar to normals (Kelly, 1980). Thus, peripheral autonomic states reflect nonspecific states of central nervous system arousal that are also seen in sedation threshold measures. A higher sedation threshold, as measured by the amount of amobarbital sodium (Amytal Sodium) necessary to induce stage 1 sleep, was found in anxiety neurotics and in patients with agitated depression (Shagass, 1954). A lower sedation threshold was found in patients with retarded depression.

Acute anxiety is associated with hyperarousal and autonomic excitation. Under acute stress a person exhibits increased muscle tension, heart rate, blood pressure, skin conductance, and gastrointestinal motility (Ursin et al., 1978). Chronic anxiety disorder patients differ little from nonanxious persons during rest (for review see Hoehn-Saric and McLeod, 1993). Under mild stress, panic disorder, but not generalized anxiety or obsessive–compulsive disorder patients, tend to show increased autonomic responses

(Hoehn-Saric et al., 1989, 1991). In addition, some anxiety disorders are characterized by autonomic responses that are specific to the disorder. For instance, panic attacks are associated with a paroxysmal, but short-lasting, increase in skin conductance, heart rate, and forearm blood flow that can be attributed to sympathetic excitation (Lader and Mathews, 1970). On the other hand, fainting at the sight of blood in a blood injury phobic patient is caused by a parasympathetically activated decrease in heart rate, along with a simultaneous drop in blood pressure secondary to sympathetic inhibition (Marks, 1988; Wallin and Sundlof, 1982).

In summary, sleep studies provide good evidence of different biological mechanisms in anxiety and depressive disorders. Measures of central or peripheral levels of arousal and measures of the peripheral autonomic system, however, reflect levels of arousal, anxiety, and agitation, irrespective of the presence or absence of depression. In some disorders, for instance, panic disorder or blood injury phobia, disorder-specific autonomic manifestations occur that are not present in other anxiety or depressive disorders.

VI. NEUROHORMONAL MANIFESTATIONS AND REACTION PATTERNS

Various abnormalities in neurohumoral levels and in responses to specific challenges have been described in depression and in anxiety disorders. For a short while, it appeared that the challenge studies would have diagnostic and prognostic value in depression and anxiety disorders. Unfortunately, neurohormonal manifestations lack specificity. Changes in the hypothalamic–pituitary–adrenal (HPA) axis, leading to hypercortisolemia and nonsuppression of cortisol in the dexamethasone suppression test, are found in approximately 50% of patients with major depression (Goodwin and Jamison, 1990, p. 448). The test, however, gives false-positive results in alcohol withdrawal, psychotropic drug withdrawal, acute weight loss, or physical exercise, and is frequently positive in schizophrenia and in dementias (Lamberts, 1986). It also has been found positive, although to a lesser degree, in anxiety disorders. Heninger (1990) reported that, in the studies he had surveyed, panic disorder patients had a median nonsuppression rate of 18%, which places them between the rate of normal persons (approximately 10%) and those of major depression.

Hospitalized panic disorder patients were more frequently nonsuppressed, which suggests that nonsuppression is linked to the severity of the disorder. Nonsuppression has also been reported in GAD and in obsessive–compulsive disorder (Lamberts, 1986). Interestingly, in one study of generalized anxiety patients, the nonsuppression normalized after successful nondrug behavioral treatment (Tiller et al., 1988).

Results of recent studies that examined the response of the HPA axis to corticotropin-releasing hormone indicate a diminished corticotropin (ACTH) response in major depression and panic disorder as compared with normal subjects (Heninger, 1990, p. 388). Since corticotropin-releasing hormone is under partial control of the noradrenergic system, the effect of challenges on the system are reflected in the cortisol response. The cortisol response to the α_2-noradrenergic agonist clonidine and to the α_2-noradrenergic antagonist yohimbine were similar in both disorders. Thus, overactivity of the HPA axis occurs in subsets of depressive and anxiety disorders and, therefore, lacks specificity.

The serotonergic system is even more complex and less well understood than the noradrenergic and HPA systems. Challenge studies of the serotonergic system are also difficult to interpret. An infusion of the serotonin precursor tryptophan induced a normal prolactin response in panic patients, but a blunted response in major depression (Charney and Heninger, 1986; Heninger et al., 1984).

The same group (Heninger, 1990, p. 393) reported that prolactin responses to the serotonin 1c agonist *m*-chlorophenylpiperazine(mCPP) (Curzon and Kennett, 1990) were normal in both conditions. Kahn et al. (1990) found, however, that small doses of mCPP caused anxiety and, compared with normals, heightened cortisol secretion in panic disorder, but not in major depression. The authors interpreted their findings as evidence for a postsynaptic serotonin oversensitivity in panic disorder, but not in depression. Their study did not rule out a subsensitivity of the serotonergic system in depression. mCPP also caused transitory increases in obsessive–compulsive symptoms, without a differential effect on hormonal levels in patients with obsessive–compulsive disorder (Murphy et al., 1989).

In summary, results of neurohormonal studies have shown abnormalities in the HPA axis that lack sensitivity and specificity. Challenge studies of the serotonergic system suggest differences between panic disorder and major depression, but now available data are insufficient to be integrated into an overall theory of anxiety or depression.

VII. EFFECTS OF PHARMACOLOGICAL INTERVENTIONS

Anxiety disorders differ from depressive disorders in their response to some, but not all, psychopharmacological interventions. Medications that act through the benzodiazepine–γ-aminobutyric acid (GABA) receptor lower anxiety, particularly the physiological manifestations of anxiety, but generally are not effective in the treatment of depression per se, except by lowering anxiety in agitated depression (Schatzberg and Cole, 1978). Antidepressants that block the reuptake of norepinephrine or serotonin reduce depression and block panic attacks, but have no acute effect on generalized anxiety (Hoehn-Saric et al., 1988; Kahn et al., 1986). Prolonged administration of some, but not all, antidepressants also decrease generalized anxiety. Imipramine, a serotonin as well as norepinephrine reuptake-blocking antidepressant has been effective in reducing psychic symptoms of generalized anxiety when given regularly for several weeks. Similar effects have also been observed with serotonin reuptake blockers given to panic disorder (den Boer and Westenberg, 1990) and obsessive compulsive disorder (Hoehn-Saric et al., 1991a) patients. In both conditions, coexisting generalized anxiety decreased after several weeks of regular treatment. Not all antidepressants, however, have anxiolytic effects. Antidepressants that probably exert their effects through the dopaminergic system (such as bupropion) have not been anxiolytic (Sheehan et al., 1983). It is of interest that the predominantly psychic obsessive–compulsive symptoms respond to serotonin, but not norepinephrine reuptake-blocking drugs (Leonard et al., 1989). The former class of drugs may exercise antiobsessional effects by decreasing frontal lobe functions (Hoehn-Saric et al., 1990, 1991b). Since psychic symptoms of anxiety often have ruminative qualities, it is possible that serotonin reuptake blockade on frontal lobe functions has a beneficial effect not only on obsessive–compulsive symptoms, but on the psychic, ruminative manifestations in other anxiety and possibly depressive disorders.

The development and application of receptor-specific drugs will enhance our understanding of biological mechanisms of anxiety and depression. Clonidine, a fairly specific α_2-noradrenergic agonist, for instance, blocks panic attacks and has a stabilizing effect on fluctuations in anxiety. However, after an initially sedating effect, it has only a modest effect on generalized anxiety and has no effect on depression (Hoehn-Saric et al.,

1981). Particularly interesting are drugs that affect specific serotonergic receptors. Although a general blockade of serotonin reuptake suppresses panic attacks, relieves depression, decreases obsessive–compulsive symptoms and, after prolonged administration, decreases psychic symptoms of generalized anxiety, specific serotonin receptor agonists and antagonists have either anxiety-inducing or anxiolytic (Kahn, 1993) effects and may lower depression (Klieser and Strauss, 1988).

In summary, pharmacotherapeutic interventions suggest complex, but different, mechanisms for anxiety and depressive disorders. Moreover, mechanisms differ in subgroups of the disorders. Some symptoms of anxiety and depression are ameliorated by the same medication. This may indicate overlapping mechanisms in certain disorders. On the other hand, many drugs have a broad spectrum of actions and may affect two independent mechanisms. Systematic investigations of the disorders with receptor-specific drugs promise to widen our understanding of these disorders.

VIII. CONCLUSIONS

The degree to which the etiology and underlying brain mechanisms in anxiety and depression overlap remains unknown. Anxiety and depression are complex emotions that involve affective and physiological responses, as well as cognitive evaluations, elaborations, and learning. Obviously, such elaborate responses must involve multiple systems in the brain, from the nuclei of the brain stem to the limbic system and the frontal–temporal cortices. Mechanisms of normal anxiety and depression probably differ substantially from those of pathological anxiety and depression. In addition, subgroups of the disorders exhibit unique characteristics that suggest separate etiologies and mechanisms.

Our knowledge of brain physiology and neurochemistry has greatly advanced during the last decade. Several theories of anxiety involving the locus coeruleus–noradrenergic system, the raphe nuclei (Redmond, 1979; Goodwin and Jamison, 1990, p. 417; Kahn and Moore, 1993), other brain stem nuclei that are linked with autonomic functions (Hsiao and Potter, 1990), and the septohippocampal system (Gray, 1982) have been proposed, but they explain only some aspects of anxiety. No comparably explicit theories of depression, except for exhaustion of the noradrenergic and possibly other neurotransmitter systems in "learned helplessness" conditions (Maier, 1984) have been developed. Pharmacological probes suggest, however, that certain neurotransmitter systems are intimately involved in anxiety and depression. The GABAergic system has been linked predominantly with anxiety (Hoehn-Saric, 1982), although some evidence suggests that it may also be involved in depression (Paul, 1988). The noradrenergic and serotonergic systems are involved in the biology of anxiety and depression, but the exact mechanisms are still unknown. Recently, the corticotropin-releasing hormone has been suggested as a neurotransmitter that affects and possibly links mechanisms involved in anxiety and depression. When given intrathecally, corticotropin-releasing hormone induces reactions that are comparable with those seen in animals during acute stress. The same hormone also controls the HPA axis, which is often disturbed in depression (Pihoker and Nemeroff, 1993).

The fact that anxiety and depression are affected by the same neurotransmitter systems does not mean that the mechanisms underlying the two disorders are identical. The effects of neurotransmitter systems are complex. They vary according to location in the brain and the neuronal state, and are modified through interactions with other neurotransmitters and modulators. Moreover, prolonged stimulation, or the absence of stimulation, may induce yet poorly understood alterations in brain function.

Animals studies, for instance, suggest that acute stress can be effectively ameliorated with benzodiazepines, but that prolonged stress responds better to antidepressants (Maier, 1984). It is unclear whether changes induced by chronic stress (e.g., learned helplessness) present a model for depression that explains the epidemiological observation that depression often follows anxiety, but not vice versa. These changes may simply represent exhaustion or learning that is unrelated to human depression.

At present, clinical, epidemiological, and laboratory studies give us better clues than neurochemical studies to the etiology of anxiety and depressive disorders. Clinical and family studies indicate that pure anxiety and pure depression may be distinctly different conditions, whereas states that combine severe anxiety and depression are more likely to be variants of a depressive disorder. Imaging studies, sleep studies, and psychological tests also favor different mechanisms for anxiety and depression. With the exception of sleep studies, neurohormonal and psychophysiological studies are less helpful, since they seem to differentiate arousal states rather than anxiety and depression and, therefore, are nonspecific in differentiating the two affective states. They do suggest, however, that subgroups of anxiety and depressive disorders may have different etiologies.

Definite answers about the etiology of anxiety and depressive disorders will not be forthcoming until we have obtained clearer genetic information and have developed better pharmacological, neurophysiological, and imaging techniques. It will also be fruitful to focus on the physiopathology of brain units responsible for certain manifestations of the disorders, such as arousal, surges of anxiety, physiological response patterns, pathological fixation of cognitive states, levels of concentration, and mood states. An understanding of the interactions of these units in the different subdisorders will permit us to develop composite models of the disorders and to understand their etiologies through knowledge of which units cause the primary disturbances and which units respond secondarily to the disturbance.

REFERENCES

H. S. Akiskal, H. Lemmi, H. Dickson, et al., Chronic depression. Part 2. Sleep EEG differentiation of primary dysthymic disorders from anxious depression, *J. Affective Disord., 6*: 287 (1984).

American Psychiatric Association, *Diagnostic and Statistical Manual of Mental Disorders, 3rd ed.,* American Psychiatric Association, Washington, D. C. (1980).

J. D. Amsterdam, and P. D. Mozley, Temporal lobe asymmetry with iofetamine (IMP) SPECT imaging in patients with major depression, *J. Affective Disord., 24*: 43 (1992).

J. Angst, M. Vollrath, K. R. Merikangas, et al., Comorbidity of anxiety and depression in the Zurich Cohort Study of Young Adults, *Comorbidity of Mood and Anxiety Disorders* (J. D. Maser and C. R. Cloninger, eds.), American Psychiatric Press, Washington, D. C., p. 123 (1990).

L. R. Baxter, Jr., M. E. Phelps, J. C. Mazziotta, et al., Local cerebral glucose metabolic rates in obsessive–compulsive disorder: A comparison with rates in unipolar depression and in normal controls, *Arch. Gen. Psychiatry, 44*: 211 (1987).

L. R. Baxter, Jr., J. M. Schwartz, M. E. Phelps, et al., Reduction of prefrontal cortex glucose metabolism common to three types of depression, *Arch. Gen. Psychiatry, 46*: 243 (1989).

N. Breslau, and G. C. Davis, Further evidence on the doubtful validity of generalized anxiety disorder, *Psychiatr. Res., 16*: 177 (1985).

D. S. Charney, and G. R. Heninger, Serotonin function in panic disorder: The effect of intravenous tryptophan in healthy subjects and in panic disorder patients before and during alprazolam treatment, *Arch. Gen. Psychiatry, 43*: 1059 (1986).

M. J. Christie, B. C. Little, and A. M. Gordon, Peripheral indices of depressive states, *Handbook of Biological Psychiatry.* Part II: *Brain Mechanisms and Abnormal Behavior Psychophysiology* (H. M. Van Praag, M. H. Lader, O. J. Raphaelsen, et al., eds.), Marcel Dekker, New York, p. 145 (1980).

P. J. Clayton, W. M. Grove, W. Coryell, et al., Follow-up and family study of anxious depression, *Am. J. Psychiatry, 148*: 1512 (1991).

C. R. Cloninger, R. L. Martin, S. B. Guze, et al., A blind follow-up and family study of anxiety neuroses: Preliminary analysis of the St. Louis 500, *Anxiety: New Research and Changing Concepts* (D. F. Klein and J. Rabkin, eds.), Raven Press, New York, p. 137 (1981).

W. Coryell, J. Endicott, N. C. Andreasen, et al., Depression and panic attacks: The significance of overlap as reflected in follow-up and family study data, *Am. J. Psychiatry, 145*: 293 (1988).

R. R. Crowe, D. L. Pauls, D. J. Slymen, et al., A family study of anxiety neurosis: Morbidity risk in families of patients with and without mitral valve prolapse, *Arch. Gen. Psychiatry, 37*: 77 (1980).

G. Curzon, and G. A. Kennett, m-CPP: A tool for studying behavioural responses associated with 5- HT 1c receptors, *TIPS, 11*: 181 (1990).

R. S. Dealy, D. M. Ishiki, D. H. Avery, et al., Secondary depression in anxiety disorders, *Compr. Psychiatry, 22*: 612 (1981).

J. A. den Boer, and H. G. M. Westenberg, Serotonin function in panic disorder: A double-blind controlled study with fluvoxamine and ritanserin, *Psychopharmacology, 102*: 85 (1990).

T. Detre, Is the grouping of anxiety disorders in *DSM-III* based on shared beliefs or data? *Anxiety and Anxiety Disorders* (A. H. Tuma and J. D. Maser, eds.), Lawrence Erlbaum, Hillsdale, N. J., p. 783 (1985).

F. K. Goodwin, and K. R. Jamison, *Manic-Depressive Illness*, Oxford University Press, New York (1990).

J. A. C. Gray, *The Neuropsychology of Anxiety*, Oxford University Press, New York (1982).

R. C. Gur, R. E. Gur, B. E. Skolnick, et al., Effect of task difficulty on regional blood flow: Relationship with anxiety and performance, *Psychophysiology, 25*: 392 (1988).

M. Hamilton, The assessment of anxiety states by rating, *Br. J. Med. Psychol., 32*: 50 (1959).

M. Hamilton, A rating scale for depression, *J. Neurol. Neurosurg. Psychiatry, 23*: 56 (1960).

P. J. Hauri, C. L. Ravaris, and M. J. Friedman, Sleep laboratory evaluations and double-blind medication trials in patients with panic disorder, Paper presented at the panic disorder biological research workshop (Sponsored by the Upjohn Co., Kalamazoo, Michigan), Washington, D. C., April (1986).

G. R. Heninger, A biological perspective on comorbidity of major depressive disorders and panic disorders, *Comorbidity of Mood and Anxiety Disorders* (J. D. Maser and C. R. Cloninger, eds.), American Psychiatric Press, Washington, D. C., p. 381 (1990).

G. R. Heninger, D. S. Charney, and D. E. Steinberg, Serotonin function in depression: Prolactin responses to intravenous tryptophan in depressed patients and healthy subjects, *Arch. Gen. Psychiatry, 41*: 398 (1984).

R. Hoehn-Saric, Neurotransmitters in anxiety, *Arch. Gen. Psychiatry, 39*: 735 (1982).

R. Hoehn-Saric, Affective profiles of chronically anxious patients, *Hillside J. Clin. Psychiatry, 5*: 43 (1983).

R. Hoehn-Saric, and D. R. McLeod, Somatic manifestations of anxiety, *Biology of Anxiety Disorders: Recent Developments*, (R. Hoehn-Saric and D. R. McLeod, eds.), American Psychiatric Press, Washington, D. C., p. 177 (1993).

R. Hoehn-Saric, A. Merchant, M. Keyser, et al., Effects of clonidine on anxiety disorders, *Arch. Gen. Psychiatry, 38*: 1278 (1981).

R. Hoehn-Saric, J. R. Lipsey, and D. R. McLeod, Apathy and indifference in patients on fluvoxamine and fluoxetine, *J. Clin. Psychopharmacol., 10*: 343 (1990).

R. Hoehn-Saric, G. J. Harris, G. D. Pearlson, et al., Effect of fluoxetine on regional cerebral blood flow in obsessive-compulsive patients, *Am. J. Psychiatry, 148*: 1243 (1991a).

R. Hoehn-Saric, G. J. Harris, G. D. Pearlson, et al., A fluoxetine induced frontal lobe syndrome in an obsessive-compulsive patient, *J. Clin. Psychiatry, 52*: 131 (1991b).

R. Hoehn-Saric, D. R. McLeod, and W. D. Zimmerli, Differential effects of alprazolam and imipramine in generalized anxiety: Somatic vs psychic symptoms, *J. Clin. Psychiatry, 49*: 293 (1988).

R. Hoehn-Saric, D. R. McLeod, and W. D. Zimmerli, Somatic manifestations in women with generalized anxiety disorder: Physiological responses to psychological stress, *Arch. Gen. Psychiatry, 46*: 1113 (1989).

R. Hoehn-Saric, D. R. McLeod, and W. D. Zimmerli, Psychophysiological response patterns in panic disorder, *Acta Psychiatr. Scand., 83*: 4 (1991).

J. K. Hsiao, and W. Z. Potter, Mechanisms of action of antipanic drugs, *Clinical Aspects of Panic Disorder* (J. C. Ballenger, ed.), Wiley-Liss, New York, p. 297 (1990).

R. J. Kahn, D. M. McNair, R. S. Lipman, et al., Imipramine and chlordiazepoxide in depressive and anxiety disorders: II. Efficacy in anxious outpatients, *Arch. Gen. Psychiatr., 43*: 79 (1986).

R. S. Kahn and C. Moore, Serotonin in the pathogenesis of anxiety, *Biology of Anxiety Disorders: Recent Developments* (R. Hoehn-Saric and D. R. McLeod, eds.) American Psychiatric Press, Washington, D. C., p. 61 (1993).

R. S. Kahn, S. Wetzer, G. M. Asnis, et al., Serotonin receptor sensitivity in major depression, *Biol. Psychiatry, 28*: 358 (1990).

D. Kelly, *Anxiety and Emotions*, Charles C Thomas, Springfield, IL, p. 141 (1980).

R. E. Kendall, The stability of psychiatric diagnoses, *Br. J. Psychiatry, 124*: 352 (1974).

E. Klieser, and W. H. Strauss, Study to establish the indication for the selective S_2 antagonist ritanserin, *Pharmacopsychiatry, 21*: 391 (1988).

M. H. Lader, and A. Mathews, Physiological changes during spontaneous panic attacks, *J. Psychosom. Res., 14*: 377 (1970).

S. Lamberts, Neuroendocrine aspects of the dexamethasone suppression test in psychiatry, *Life Sci., 39*: 91 (1986).

J. F. Leckman, M. M. Clubb, and D. L. Pauls, Comorbidity of panic disorder and major depression: A review of epidemiological and genetic data, *Clinical Aspects of Panic Disorder* (J. C. Ballenger, ed.), Wiley-Liss, New York, p. 141 (1990).

H. L. Leonard, S. E. Swedo, J. L. Rapoport, et al., Treatment of obsessive-compulsive disorder with clomipramine and desimipramine in children and adolescents, *Arch. Gen. Psychiatry, 46*: 1088 (1989).

A. Lewis, Melancholia: A clinical survey of depressive states, *J. Ment. Sci., 80*: 1 (1934).

R. S. Lipman, Differentiating anxiety and depression in anxiety disorders: Use of rating scales, *Psychopharmacol. Bull., 18*: 69 (1982).

S. R. Machlin, G. J. Harris, G. D. Pearlson, et al., Elevated medial frontal-cerebral blood flow in obsessive-compulsive patients: A SPECT study, *Am. J. Psychiatry, 148*: 1240 (1991).

S. F. Maier, Learned helplessness and animal models of depression, *Prog. Neuropsychopharmacol. Biol. Psychiatry, 8*: 435 (1984).

W. Maier, R. Buller, and J. Hallmayer, Comorbidity of panic disorder and major depression: Results from a family study, *Panic and Phobias* (I. Hand and H.-U. Wittchen, eds.), Springer-Verlag, Berlin, p. 180 (1988).

I. M. Marks, Blood-injury phobia: A review, *Am. J. Psychiatry, 145*: 1207 (1988).

J. D. Maser, and C. R. Cloninger, *Comorbidity of Mood and Anxiety Disorders*, American Psychiatric Press, Washington, D. C. (1990).

T. A. Mellman, and T. W. Uhde, Electroencephalographic sleep in panic disorder, *Arch. Gen. Psychiatry, 46*: 178 (1989).

K. R. Merikangas, Comorbidity for anxiety and depression: Review of family and genetic studies, *Comorbidity of Mood and Anxiety Disorders* (J. D. Maser and C. R. Cloninger, eds.). American Psychiatric Press, Washington, D. C., p. 331 (1990).

D. L. Murphy, J. Zohar, M. Benkelfat, et al., Obsessive–compulsive disorder as a 5-HT subsystem-related behavioural disorder, *Br. J. Psychiatry, 155*(Suppl. 8): 15 (1989).

T. E. Nordahl, W. E. Semple, M. Gross, et al., Cerebral glucose metabolic differences in patients with panic disorder, *Neuropsychopharmacology, 3*: 261 (1990).

R. Noyes, Jr., C. Clarkson, R. R. Crowe, et al., A family study of generalized anxiety, *Am. J. Psychiatry, 144*: 1019 (1987).

G. N. Papadimitriou, P. Linkowski, M. Kerkhofs, et al., Sleep EEG recordings in generalized anxiety disorder with significant depression, *J. Affective Disord., 15*: 113 (1988).

S. M. Paul, Anxiety and depression: A common neurobiological substrate? *J. Clin. Psychiatry, 49*: (Suppl. 10): 13 (1988).

C. Pihoker, and C. B. Nemeroff, The role of corticotropin releasing factor in the pathophysiology of anxiety disorders, *Biology of Anxiety Disorders: Recent Developments* (R. Hoehn-Saric and D. R. McLeod, eds.), American Psychiatric Press, Washington, D. C., p. 103 (1993).

P. M. Post, L. E. DeLisi, H. H. Holcomb, et al., Glucose utilization in the temporal cortex of affectively ill patients: Positron emission tomography, *Biol. Psychiatry, 22*: 545 (1987).

D. E. Redmond, New and old evidence for the involvement of a brain NE system in anxiety, *Phenomenology and Treatment of Anxiety* (W. E. Fann, I. Karacan, A. D. Pokorny, et al., eds.), Spectrum Publications, New York, p. 153 (1979).

E. M. Reiman, M. E. Raichle, F. K. Butler, et al., A focal brain abnormality in panic disorder, a severe form of anxiety, *Nature, 310*: 683 (1984).

E. M. Reiman, M. J. Fusselman, P. T. Fox, et al., Neuroanatomical correlates of anticipatory anxiety, *Science, 243*: 1071 (1989).

E. M. Reiman, M. E. Raichle, E. Robins, et al., Neuroanatomical correlates of a lactate-induced anxiety attack, *Arch. Gen. Psychiatry, 46*: 493 (1989).

C. F. Reynolds, and D. J. Kupfer, Sleep research in affective illness: State of the art circa 1987, *Sleep, 10*: 199 (1987).

C. F. Reynolds III, D. H. Shaw, T. F. Newton, et al., EEG sleep in outpatients with generalized anxiety: A preliminary comparison with depressed outpatients, *Psychiatr. Res., 8*: 81 (1983).

K. Rickels, and E. Schweizer, The clinical course and long-term management of generalized anxiety disorder, *J. Clin. Psychopharmacol., 10*: 101S (1990).

M. Roth, C. Q. Mountjoy, and D. Caetano, Further investigations into the relationship between depressive disorders and anxiety states, *Pharmacopsychiatry, 15*: 135 (1982).

P. P. Roy-Byrne, T. W. Uhde, and R. M. Post, Effects of one night's sleep deprivation on mood and behavior in patients with panic disorder: Comparison with depressed patients and normal controls, *Arch. Gen. Psychiatry, 43*: 895 (1986).

A. J. Rush, M. S. Schlesser, E. Stokely, et al., Cerebral blood flow in depression and mania, *Psychopharmacol. Bull., 18*: 6 (1982).

A. F. Schatzberg, and J. O. Cole, Benzodiazepines in depressive disorders, *Arch. Gen. Psychiatry, 35*: 1359 (1978).

D. V. Sheehan, J. Davidson, T. Manschreck, et al., Lack of efficacy of a new antidepressant (buproprion) in the treatment of panic disorder with phobias, *J. Clin. Psychopharmacol., 3*: 28 (1983).

M. E. P. Seligman, Depression and learned helplessness, *Research in Neurosis: Symposium Organized by the Interdisciplinary Society of Biological Psychiatry*, Bohn, Scheltema & Holkema, Amsterdam, p. 72 (1975).

C. Shagass, The sedation threshold: A method for estimating tension in psychiatric patients, *EEG Clin. Neurophysiol., 6*: 221 (1954).

S. E. Starkstein, and R. G. Robinson, Affective disorders and cerebral vascular disease, *Br. J. Psychiatry, 154*: 170 (1989).

S. E. Starkstein, B. S. Cohen, P. Fedoroff, et al., Relationship between anxiety disorders and depressive disorders in patients with cerebrovascular injury, *Arch. Gen. Psychiatry, 47*: 246 (1990).

M. A. Taylor, and R. Abrams, Cognitive impairment patterns in schizophrenia and affective disorder, *J. Neurol. Neurosurg. Psychiatry, 50*: 895 (1987).

J. W. G. Tiller, N. Biddle, K. P. Maguire, et al., The dexamethasone suppression test and plasma dexamethasone in generalized anxiety disorder, *Biol. Psychiatry, 23*: 261 (1988).

S. Torgersen, A twin-study perspective of the comorbidity of anxiety and depression, *Comorbidity of Mood and Anxiety Disorders* (J. D. Maser and C. R. Cloninger, eds.), American Psychiatric Press, Washington, D. C., p. 367 (1990).

P. Tyrer, *Classification of Neurosis,* John Wiley & Sons, New York (1989).

H. Ursin, E. Baade, and S. Levine, *Psychobiology of Stress*, Academic Press, New York (1978).

G. Wallin, and G. Sundlof, Sympathetic outflow of muscles during vasovagal syncope, *J. Auton. Nerv. Syst., 6*: 287 (1982).

S. Wetzler, and M. M. Katz, Problems with the differentiation of anxiety and depression, *J. Psychiatr. Res., 23*: 1 (1989).

W. H. Wilson, and R. J. Mathew, Cerebral blood flow in anxiety disorders, *Biology of Anxiety Disorders: Recent Developments* (R. Hoehn-Saric and D. R. McLeod, eds.), American Psychiatric Press, Washington, D. C., p. 1 (1993).

J. C. Wu, M. S. Buchsbaum, T. G. Hershey, et al., PET in generalized anxiety disorder, *Biol. Psychiatry, 29*: 1181 (1991).

R. M. Yerkes, and J. D. Dodson, The relation of strength of stimulus to rapidity of habit formation, *J. Comp. Neurol. Psychiatry, 18*: 458 (1908).

6

The Measurement of Depression and Anxiety

Robert Kellner
University of New Mexico School of Medicine, Albuquerque, New Mexico

I. INTRODUCTION

Depression and anxiety are affective states that share some clinical features. The aim of the present chapter is to survey psychometric issues in measurement of these disorders, the various methods of measurements, and recommendations for the choice of scales.

The measurements of generalized anxiety and depressive states have many features in common. The measurement of anxiety is somewhat more complex because of the various kinds of anxiety disorders, such as situational fears, phobias, and panic attacks. The measurement of anxiety is discussed, therefore, in somewhat greater detail.

The psychometrics of generalized anxiety and depressive states are similar to those of other distress scales. Unless otherwise indicated, the term *distress* applies in this chapter to either generalized anxiety or depression.

II. VALIDITY

Validity is a property of test, and the term expresses the degree to which the test actually measures what it purports to measure (Anastasi, 1982). Cronbach (1970, p. 121) has argued that a test that helps make one decision may have no value at all for another. There are many valid scales of depression and of anxiety; validation studies suggest that some measures that are appropriate for some situations are unsuitable for others.

Cronbach also proposed that, with many psychological scales, the interpretation of the test results is as important as the validity of the scale. There are several different components of validity (Cronbach, 1970, pp. 121–150; Feinstein, 1987, pp. 190–224). The concepts of validity and reliability as they apply to the measurements of distress have been discussed in several previous articles (Kellner, 1971; Kellner and Uhlenhuth, 1988, 1991; Carrol et al., 1973; Snaith, 1991). In this chapter, the main components that are pertinent to the measurement of anxiety and depression will be discussed.

A. Measurement of Trait and State

The concept of trait stems from Spearman's work (Spearman, 1927). In the measurements of distress it is important to distinguish between a trait and a state; two concepts that were derived from factor analytical studies (Cattell and Scheier, 1958). Depression and anxiety as *traits* are dispositions to respond in a certain way. The manifestation of the trait will change temporarily with circumstances, but there is a tendency for these features of the personality to endure. Depression or anxiety as *states* are temporary and changeable phenomena; in some patients preponderantly endogenous factors influence the course of the state, in others the state tends to change when a person's circumstances change. Scales that purport to measure a trait are analogous to a tape measure, whereas scales that measure a state of anxiety are analogous to a thermometer (Kellner, 1971a,b). In a group of patients undergoing treatment, state measures tend to change, whereas trait measures change substantially less (Bedford et al., 1978; 1979).

State scales are focused on the present or on the recent past with instruction such as, "describe how you have felt today," or "during the past week," whereas, in a trait measure, the subject is instructed to describe how he or she generally feels. Trait scales tend to be influenced by a patient's recall and interpretation of the past and, in turn, these may be influenced by the current emotional state of the patient. Thus, even a valid trait scale may be biased if administered in the course of a depressive or anxiety state.

B. Concepts of Validity

1. Face Validity

Face validity, the apparent validity of a test, has been derided as being the equivalent of "faith validity." The judgment by an observer is inadequate if it is used as the sole criterion of validity, yet face validity is a pertinent feature of an anxiety or depression scale. It is difficult to imagine a scale with adequate content validity in which an expert would not recognize the items as being appropriate to the measurement of the affective disorder. Most items of currently used anxiety scales and depression scales clearly describe manifestations of the corresponding syndrome. Earlier scales contained items that were found to be associated with the disorder; for example, anxiety scales included items measuring defensiveness.

2. Content Validity

Content validity is the result of a "systematic evaluation of a test" content to determine whether each item covers a representative sample of the behavioral domain that it measures (Anastasi 1982, p. 131). Content validity is relatively simple when the test measures skills, such as spelling or achievement tests in mathematics. In the measurement of clinical syndromes, content validation is more complicated because the item may measure a behavior or symptom of a syndrome, such as obsessive features or weight gain in depression, which may occur only in a few individuals. Moreover, the item may represent a symptom that occurs frequently in the syndrome, but that belongs to a different construct because of common co-occurrence of the two constructs; this issue is discussed further in the section on construct validity.

3. Concurrent Validity

Concurrent validation is a procedure by which the test is compared with an established standard; for example, a test is introduced to replace a more cumbersome method

(Cronbach, 1970, p. 122). The term is used to emphasize that little time has elapsed between the two tests to distinguish it from predictive validity, although some authors use the two terms synonymously. There are various ways of determining concurrent validity. For example, changes in a self-rated anxiety state scale could be correlated with observer ratings of behaviors that are indicative of anxiety, or a self-rating scale of a depressive state would be the correlation of the scale scores with the ratings of expert raters using a validated observer depression-rating scale (Fava et al., 1986).

4. Predictive Validity

The criterion of predictive validity makes it possible to predict the subject's future performance (Lehmann, 1968). An example would be a scale of trait anxiety that would predict which subjects would need antianxiety drugs on follow-up, on the assumption that a scale of trait anxiety predicts the occurrence of anxiety states. A test of predictive validity would not be necessary for a state measure, although it can be assumed that subjects who score above a cutoff point on a state anxiety scale would be more prone to recurrences than subjects who score low. Predictive validity is important in some branches of psychometrics; for example, in the measurement of skills in vocational counseling. For the measurement of state anxiety and state depression other methods of validation are more important.

5. Construct Validity

Cronbach (1971) argues that, whereas predictive validity can be established by a single experiment, construct validity is established by a process that is the same as that by which scientific theories are developed; it depends on reasoning and numerous observations. Construct validation is usually involved whenever a test is to be interpreted as a measure of some attribute or quality that is not operationally defined (Cronbach and Meehl, 1956).

Most authors agree that anxiety and depression are valid constructs; the present volume is an affirmation of this belief. In the choice of scales, scale construction, and the modification of existing scales, the problem is no longer whether anxiety and depression are valid constructs. Moreover, most commonly used anxiety and depression scales had numerous validation procedures of various kinds and have adequate construct validity. There is, however, incomplete agreement on the boundaries of the construct and on which of the phenomena of anxiety or depression the scale should include in the measurement.

It could be argued that most anxiety symptoms or most features of depression should be contained by a scale that measures that syndrome. This is not always feasible; for example, contemporary diagnostic and statistical manuals—such as the *Diagnostic and Statistical Manual of Mental Disorders,* 3rd ed., revised (*DSM-III-R*; American Psychiatric Association, 1987) or the *International Classification of Diseases and Causes of Death*, 10th ed. (*ICD*-10; WHO, 1990)—recognize various diagnostic categories of anxiety disorders, including different categories of phobias, panic disorder, and generalized anxiety disorder. Some of these categories require specific scales. There is a consistent association of anxiety and depression, on one hand, and somatic complaints, on the other (Kellner, 1988). There is no agreement about whether the common somatic symptoms of anxiety states or depressive states should be represented in the corresponding scale, or whether somatic symptoms should constitute a separate scale. The coexistence of anxiety and depression is discussed later. Other constructs frequently coexist with anxiety and depression, a phenomenon that has been described by the term *comorbidity* (Maser and Cloninger, 1990; Wittchen and Essau, 1991). There is no conclusive agreement on the extent to which items other than core symptoms should be represented in a depression or anxiety scale (Carroll et al., 1973).

An example of the difficulties of limiting the boundaries of a construct is the Hamilton Depression Rating Scale (HAM-D) (Hamilton, 1960). The HAM-D is one of the most commonly used observer rating scales of depression and is the most commonly used scale of depression in drug trials in English-speaking countries. The scale has 21 items, and each is rated on a 3-point, 4-point, or 5-point–rating scale; in other words, the rater has 3, 4, or 5 choices for rating. The decision on the number of cues for rating was made by Hamilton and was based on clinical impressions; to my knowledge, the relative sensitivity (see later discussion) of these different methods of scoring has not been empirically tested. Three items of the scale are for the rating of insomnia, three items rate anxiety (anxiety psychic, agitation, anxiety somatic), four items deal with somatic symptoms, and one each with hypochondriasis and depersonalization–derealization. Thus, ten of the items could be symptoms measuring a coexisting anxiety state. One item deals with insight and one each with paranoid symptoms and compulsive symptoms, symptoms that could belong to another construct. Thus, only 5 of the 21 items deal with symptoms that are largely limited to depressive states. The scale has been useful in determining the frequency of phenomena that occur in depressed patients, but it is not a pure measure of depressive mood. Hamilton recommended that only 17 items should be included in the score if the severity of depression is being measured and deleting items that occur infrequently or those that were included for reasons other than measurement of severity. Such a change increases the sensitivity of the scale in discriminating between patients and nonpatient controls (Fava et al., 1982).

Another example of blurred boundaries of a construct is the Hamilton Anxiety Rating Scale (HAM-A), the most commonly used anxiety scale in drug trials with antianxiety drugs. The scale consists of 13 categories of symptoms and 1 category of rating of observed behavior, each rated by the interviewer on a 5-point scale. The scale contains three items that describe categories of symptoms and signs of generalized anxiety: anxious mood, tension, and behavior at interview. Another item deals with fears and phobias. Insomnia and intellectual difficulty are not specific to anxiety states and occur also in depression and other psychiatric disorders. One item is depressed mood; although a frequent symptom of anxiety states, it may be argued that it is not part of the anxiety construct, but a symptom of comorbidity. Seven items deal with various categories of somatic symptoms, such as cardiovascular symptoms, somatic sensory symptoms, and genitourinary symptoms. Thus, out of 14 items only 3 deal with symptoms of a generalized anxiety state, and many of the symptoms, including the somatic symptoms, could be manifestations of a coexisting depression. A shorter scale, the Clinical Anxiety Scale, which was derived from the HAM-A, has only six items and has a higher correlation with global anxiety ratings than the HAM-A (Snaith et al., 1982).

In a study of generalized anxiety in the presence of other disorders, for example, in one of the phobic disorders or a study of anxiety in one of the psychophysiological disorders (such as nonulcer dyspepsia or the irritable bowel syndrome), the use of the total HAM-A score would be an inappropriate measure of anxiety. Some items of the HAM-A would not measure anxiety, but the symptoms of the coexisting disorder; the scale would have to be modified by deleting the item with the common content to avoid spurious associations. Thus, although the HAM-A effectively measures the severity of the clinical *anxiety syndrome* (as Hamilton intended and the studies described later show), even the psychic factor of this scale cannot be considered a pure measure of the generalized anxiety construct.

6. Construct Boundaries of Anxiety and Depression

The measurement of anxiety and that of depression is complicated by a consistent and robust correlation of these two constructs, regardless of whether the symptoms are rated by an observer or whether self-rating scales are used. This issue is discussed in several chapters of this volume. Because of this coexistence, depression should be rated jointly with anxiety when either syndrome is rated. To measure the affect of anxiety, as opposed to the syndrome of an anxiety state, the items that are shared with the depression scale (such as insomnia and somatic symptoms) should be eliminated from the total scores of both scales, otherwise the correlation would be artificially high because of the common content of the scales. Alternatively, scales that have no common content should be used (Lipman et al., 1968; Kellner, 1987; Fava et al., 1986).

There are several scales in which the items are limited to generalized anxiety, and scales in which cognitive anxiety or cognitive depression and somatic symptoms are rated separately. For example, in the Rating Scale of Depression, Anxiety and Somatic Symptoms (Kellner, 1986, 1988), items that have common content are not scored. A scale derived from the Hamilton Anxiety Rating Scales, the Clinical Anxiety Scale (Snaith et al., 1982) is limited to psychic anxiety. The Montgomery–Asberg Depression Rating Scale (MADRS), except for one item (affective), is limited to items of psychic depression (Montgomery and Asberg, 1979).

III. RELIABILITY

If a child receives an IQ score of 110 on Monday and an IQ score of 80 when retested on Friday, it is obvious that little or no confidence can be put in either score (Anastasi, 1982, p. 26). *Reliability* is a property of a measure or scale that describes the extent to which the errors or unwanted fluctuation in a test score affect the measurement. In other words, reliability means the extent to which the score can be trusted.

Reliability is expressed as a correlation coefficient of two test scores gathered under various conditions, which will be described later. A high correlation of two test scores, such as +0.95, indicates the two scores were almost identical and—assuming that the results were truly independent and not biased—the scale is highly reliable. If the correlation is low, for example, such as +0.40, this indicates that there were large differences between the two scores and, unless one of the tests was carried out in most unusual circumstances that interfered with test taking or rating, the scale is unreliable. Such a scale should be used only if there are adequate empirical reasons that support the usefulness of the scale; for example, it has been shown that the scale is valid, but is strongly influenced by the mood of the tester on the day of testing.

A. Test–Retest Reliability

A common method of testing reliability, particularly of self-rating scales, is test–retest reliability. This is determined by having a group of people repeating the identical scale or test on a second occasion.

Reliability is a desirable property of a personality inventory or a trait scale. The test–retest correlation should be adequate after a time interval of at least a few weeks.

A test–retest correlation coefficient under +0.80 indicates that the scale is likely to include elements of a state measure or that the scale is unstable for other reasons, such as poor comprehension of the items by some of the subjects (Kellner and Uhlenhuth, 1991).

Test–retest reliability is inappropriate in patients who have acute psychiatric disorders and in those who are undergoing treatment. For example, in a group of new depressed patients, the test–retest correlation may be low for various reasons. Improvement is likely with the passage of time and a low test–retest correlation may be caused by different degrees of improvement among the patients. A trait scale may have a low test–retest reliability for other reasons. Self-description, self-esteem, and recall tend to vary with the affective state of the patient, so a low test–retest correlation may reflect actual differences in self-reports by the patient on two different occasions and not a low reliability of the trait scale.

Many of the scales that have been frequently used in research in psychology and psychiatry have low test–retest reliabilities, even when only a few days or a week separate testing. For example, the test–retest correlation for the Minnesota Multiphasic Personality Inventory (MMPI) scale 6 (PA) ranges from +0.05 to +0.81 and for scale 8 (Sc) ranges from -0.3 to +0.89 (Dahlstrom and Welch 1960). Yet the MMPI is supposed to be a personality inventory that measures stable traits. The reliability of some of the scales is so low that a person could not be identified by a repeat test. The MMPI was also used at one time in outcome studies both in drug treatment and in psychotherapy, and these results explain, in part, that the MMPI scores could not discriminate between the groups that had active treatment and a control (Kellner, 1967, 1971a,b).

Test–retest reliability of distress scales or state scales has to be interpreted with caution. Some authors have argued that the test–retest reliability is inappropriate for a state measure or a problem list (Mooney and Gordon, 1950; Knowles, 1963; Crown and Crisp, 1966). State scale purports to measure changes. A high test–retest reliability may suggest that a trait is being measured, that changes in the patient's state are not reflected in the test score and, therefore, may indicate that the scale is inadequately sensitive to measure changes. In practice, however, a high test–retest reliability of a state scale has not been found to be a problem because of other ways of testing sensitivity of state measures (Spielberger and Krasner, 1988).

The conventional test–retest reliability can be used for state measures with certain precautions. It is an appropriate test when used in a group of nonpatients. If administered to psychiatric patients, they should have chronic disorders, have had treatment for some time, and be unlikely to change in the interval between test and retest. Under these circumstances, some state measures, particularly scales consisting of symptoms, show high test–retest reliability (Fava et al., 1986).

Scales consisting of symptoms tend to be more stable than scales consisting of statements of well-being (such as calm or relaxed) that are scored when the subject fails to endorse them. These scales seem to be liable to change with minor fluctuations in mood and show low test–retest correlations (Fava et al., 1986).

B. Interrater Reliability

Interrater reliability is expressed as a correlation coefficient of the scores of two raters using independently the same rating scale with the same group of patients. The correlation expresses the extent to which the ratings of two raters are similar. Usually, the two raters interview the same patient together; both raters are present during the interview and rate the patient independently. The test of the reliability of the scale is more rigorous if two raters interview the patient separately. This is likely to reduce the correlation because the patient may not give the same history to the two interviewers.

Alternatively, both raters may rate a patient from a videotape; in this situation, however, the raters may not have the adequate opportunity needed to explore the patient's symptoms for accurate rating.

The training of raters in the use of a scale as well as tests of interrater reliability are likely to induce a greater uniformity among raters. Theoretically, this should enhance the sensitivity of the rating scales if more than one rater participates in an experiment or study, for example, in a drug trial. To my knowledge, however, the enhancement of sensitivity by training of raters has not been demonstrated empirically.

C. Intrarater Reliability

The intrarater reliability is a test–retest reliability of the individual rater using the same rating scale. Raters tend to differ in skills and the rating–rerating correlation differs among raters. If such reliability is explored, it would be inappropriate for the rater to rate the same patient after a time interval because the patient's state may have changed, and this may be the reason for a low rerating correlation. An appropriate method would be for the rater to rate a group of patients from a videotape on two occasions after a lengthy time interval and to correlate the scores on two occasions. This will reveal the extent to which the rater will achieve the same score on different occasions with the same individual. This method of testing a rater's performance appears to be desirable, but as with interrater reliability, the value of this procedure has not been tested empirically.

D. Scorer Reliability

In scales in which scoring consists not merely of a count of check marks and in which scoring depends in part on interpretations, the scoring method as well as various scorers' performances need to be tested for scorer reliability. The principles and the methods are the same as those for intrarater reliability. For example, the same expert is given a number of Rorschach protocols after, say, 1 year, and some of these protocols the rater had scored previously. The rater is unlikely to remember which he or she has scored before and what the diagnosis was on the previous occasion. The correlation expresses the extent to which the rater has given the protocol the same diagnosis as on the previous occasion (or to the extent to which he or she rated the trait that is being measured). Some studies with expert raters have shown extremely low reliability. For example, in one study, the expert agreed with himself in no more than in 50% of cases (Little and Schneideman, 1959).

In other examples of a rating in which scorer reliability may be important is the Gottschalk and Gleser scale. The patient's verbal behavior is scored from an audiotape; the scale yields a score for anxiety and hostility. A similar method is the Zeitbinde Video-Analyse (Renfordt et al., 1978), using segments of video tapes. These are interesting techniques, but there is no conclusive evidence yet that they offer advantages over conventional rating scales.

E. Split-Half Reliability

The split-half reliability is determined from a single administration when the scores of two halves of the tests are being correlated (Anastasi, 1982). The aim is to examine whether the test has an internal consistency, whether the randomly chosen halves, which can be selected by various methods, are equivalent.

The split-half reliability is appropriate only if the items are psychometrically equivalent. For example, a scale that has items of cognitive or psychic anxiety as well as somatic symptoms would be unsuitable (unless both groups of symptoms were evenly divided in the two halves) because there are large differences among patients with affective disorder in the ratios of somatic symptoms to cognitive symptoms of anxiety or depression (Kellner et al., 1972).

One method to test the reliability of a state measure is the split-half reliability of changes. This means that reliability is expressed as a correlation coefficient of the changes that have occurred in each half. Some depression and anxiety state scales have shown adequate split-half reliability of changes (Kellner, 1987). This method is also appropriate only if the items are deemed to be psychometrically equivalent and if there is an adequate number of items. The usefulness of this method for the testing of reliability of state scales has not been adequately demonstrated.

F. Alternate-Form Reliability

Alternate-form applies only to scales and tests that have alternate forms. This method was designed to prevent an artificially high reliability because the subject may remember how he scored on a previous occasion. The alternate-form reliability is not pertinent for the present chapter because the commonly used scales for depression and anxiety have no alternate forms.

IV. SENSITIVITY

The term *sensitivity* has two meanings in psychometrics; one is borrowed from medical epidemiology, which means the proportion of actual cases detected; for example, patients with tuberculosis identified by a screening test. When the term is used for a psychiatric diagnostic or screening scale, the term means the proportion of true cases who score above the cutoff score. *Specificity* means the proportion of normal persons (e.g., free of tuberculosis) with negative results on the test. For a psychiatric diagnostic-screening scale, it means the proportion of normal persons who score below the cutoff. Another property of the test is the overall *misclassification rate*, which is the sum of false-negative and false-positive results, meaning the percentage of patients classified by the test as normal and the number of normal subjects classified by the test as patients.

A. Sensitivity of a Screening Device

Most of the studies of sensitivity and specificity dealt with psychological inventories that were administered to a group of patients and to a random control group. The misclassification rate for inventories such as Taylor Manifest Anxiety Scale (TMAS) (Taylor, 1953), Zung Self-rating Depression Scale (SDS) (Zung, 1965), the Symptom Rating Test (SRT) (Kellner and Sheffield, 1973), the Hopkins Symptom Checklist (SCL) (Derogatis et al., 1974), and the General Health Questionnaire (GHQ) ranged from 8.5

to 27.4, with the GHQ having generally the lowest and the SDS the highest (Goldberg, 1972, pp. 5, 23, 80, 83). A more recent study showed a high sensitivity as well as high specificity for the Mental Health Inventory and for the Somatic Symptom Inventory (Weinstein et al., 1989).

The determination of sensitivity and specificity of a scale in psychology or psychiatry is a complex procedure. In any one study, the scales depend on the properties of the screening device, on the prevalence of the disease or disorder, and on the method of study. When comparing the test scores of psychiatric patients and nonpatient control groups, there is a tendency to measure extreme cases, which makes the task for the screening device easier; subjects in the community are less ill, and many are mild cases (Goldberg, 1972). If the screening test is validated in the community, the criterion of caseness depends on the diagnosis by an expert; whether a person has or has not a psychiatric disorder varies with the diagnostic criteria the expert uses; moreover, the cutoff point of the expert may be different from that of the screening device.

The severity of symptoms also influences misidentification rates in another way: When patients and nonpatient controls are being compared, some of the patients have mild disorders or have already recovered; conversely, in a random group of controls, there is a substantial proportion of subjects with psychopathology. So the misclassification rate may not necessarily be caused by the deficiency of the screening device, but may be caused by an actual overlap: some of the patient group should score in the normal range, and some of the controls should score as cases. A method by which the actual overlap can be avoided is to select as patients a group in which all individuals are found to be depressed in a clinical interview and, from the control group, all persons who are depressed have been excluded (Goldberg, 1972, p. 73). By this method, however, the misclassification rate would apply only to the more severe cases of depression.

B. Sensitivity of Change Measures

1. Meaning and Evolution of the Term

The other meaning of the term sensitivity stems from research in clinical psychopharmacology. Sensitivity is a term describing a scale's characteristic to discriminate between the effects of a drug and of a placebo. A more detailed definition is as follows: *sensitivity* is a characteristic of a scale to discriminate at a significant level between the effects of a psychotropic drug and placebo (or between the effects of two drugs or two or more doses of the same drug) in a double-blind drug trial. The rest of the chapter will deal with this second meaning of the term.

The concept of sensitivity evolved by several stages. It consisted initially of the comparison of the performance of various scales in the same drug trial (Lipman et al., 1965), of surveys of drug trials comparing the sensitivity of scales (Kellner, 1971a,b; McNair, 1974; Uhlenhuth et al., 1982; Glass et al., 1987) and, finally, the empirical modification of scales to enhance sensitivity (Kellner, 1986, 1987; Kellner et al., 1978). The main conclusions from these studies are summarized in the next section.

2. Studies in Sensitivity

In psychometrics, a high correlation of two scales is usually regarded as evidence that two scales measure the same factor and that they are interchangeable. There are several published studies showing that in distress scales, a high correlation does not necessarily indicate the same sensitivity. For example, one scale could be measuring a trait that is stable and is unlikely to change with treatment; thus, the scale will have a lower sensitivity; the other scale could be a sensitive state scale. Two scales may be highly correlated, but one of the scales is unreliable; its score may change substantially with treatment, but it contains too many errors and random fluctuations, both in the drug group and in the placebo group, for the scale to be sensitive. An example of such a dissociation between correlation and sensitivity comes from a crossover trial with chlordiazepoxide in anxious patients; two scales that differed substantially in sensitivity (the Hamilton Anxiety Rating Scale and an absolute global rating scale) were highly correlated ($+0.90$; $p < 0.001$). Conversely, the correlation was low between two scales (somatic well-being and global scale)

Uhlenhuth et al. (1982) and Glass et al. (1987) surveyed drug trials with anxious patients in which a benzodiazepine was compared with placebo and in which more than one outcome measure was used; the authors carried out meta-analyses, and only those pairs of scales were considered that had been used in an adequate number of drug trials so that the difference in sensitivity between the two scales could be statistically evaluated. They found that physicians' global rating was more sensitive than the rating of target symptoms, the total score of the Hopkins Symptom Checklist (SCL) (Lipman et al., 1968), and the Clyde Mood Scale. The Hamilton Anxiety Rating Scale (HAM-A) was significantly more sensitive than the total score of the SOL. The total scores of the SCL and its anxiety and somatic scales were equally sensitive; the HAM-A was more sensitive than any of the SCL scales. There was no evidence from the data that physicians' recognition of side effects helped make observer ratings more sensitive. Sedative effects appeared to affect adversely the sensitivity of patient ratings. Comparisons between other pairs of scales showed trends, but the number of pairs appeared to have been inadequate for the results to reach significant levels. These results apply to benzodiazepines; it is not certain whether the results would be the same in anxious patients in trials with other classes of psychotropic drugs.

3. *The Relation of Sensitivity to Validity*

Fisher (1976) has argued that sensitivity is not necessarily equivalent to validity in the sense of detecting specifically antianxiety effects. He pointed out that the two concepts are equivalent when the drug is effective and when no biases are operating that change the meaning of the measure.

Tests of sensitivity should not replace conventional validation procedures. A scale could be sensitive and yet lack construct validity. A theoretical case would be as follows: A class of long acting sedative drugs, believed to be antidepressants, are taken by the patients once in 24 h before retiring. This would ensure good sleep, but would have no antidepressant effect. A depression scale that has several sleep items in which the scores for sleep disturbance items represent a substantial proportion of the total score would yield significant differences between drug and placebo, yet only the sleep items would have changed significantly. This would be an example of a sensitivity scale that would not be a valid depression-rating scale. Another theoretical case is that of a depression scale in which only the anxiety items are sensitive. This scale could be highly sensitive, yet not be a valid scale of depressed mood.

Sensitivity of a distress scale is, however, an important additional validation procedure. The scale is not validated against an expert's judgment, but against the responses to a chemical substance of a certain dose that can be varied by the experimenter, a situation that is unique in clinical psychometrics.

It could be argued that, if one scale discriminates between a drug and placebo, whereas another scale fails to do so, this does not indicate which of the two is valid. If the drug tested were no better than placebo, the scale that *failed* to discriminate would be the valid test, whereas the other scale would have given a misleading result. Therefore, the drugs used in studies on the sensitivity of scales should not be experimental drugs, but must be of proved efficacy.

The use of sensitivity as the only measure of validity might yield an anxiety scale that detects differences between a class of drugs (such as the benzodiazepines) and placebo, but may not measure adequately changes in the syndrome of anxiety, a situation similar to the hypothetical example of sedative antidepressants described earlier. In other words, the scale may detect only the benzodiazepine effects, which may not be identical with antianxiety effects. This is theoretically possible, but, to my knowledge, this has not yet happened. Most scales used in research in therapeutics that were found to be sensitive to drug effects had series of other tests of validity and reliability and appear to compare favorably with other scales and inventories used in psychometrics (Gleser, 1975). For example, the Symptom Questionnaire, which evolved on the basis of several modifications to achieve greater sensitivity, was also found to have concurrent validity with other independent criteria, such as a high correlation with cortisol levels (Kellner, 1987; Willis et al., 1987). Moreover, surveys of sensitivity that included drug trials with various classes of drugs, including antidepressants (Kellner, 1971a,b; McNair, 1974) yielded results similar to those with antianxiety drugs (Kellner and Uhlenhuth 1988).

4. Response Bias and Response Set

A response set or response bias is a person's tendency to respond in a certain way that influences the results of the test and makes the results less accurate. For example, a person may habitually choose the middle of the scale (central tendency), or is more likely to check "Yes" than "No" (yay sayer), or may distort his or her replies in a socially desirable way.

The studies of response bias and response set have been reviewed by Guilford (1954), Cronbach (1946; 1950), and Kellner (1971a,b). A response set makes a test less sensitive, since a very strong response set would prevent changes altogether. It can be assumed that a sensitive scale of depression or anxiety that discriminates effectively between two treatments is not materially affected by response set.

5. The Importance of Sensitivity

There are certain situations for which the sensitivity of the scale is unimportant. In a multicentered drug trial, in which an effective drug is compared with placebo, the conventional scales used are likely to discriminate robustly between a drug and placebo. In such a situation, minor differences that may reach a statistical level of significance may not be clinically relevant. Only when a sample is small in relation to the drug–placebo difference does the sensitivity of the scale become important.

Even the most sensitive scale will fail to reveal meaningful data adequately if the design of the study is inappropriate. The design of various studies in therapeutics is beyond the scope of the present chapter. In a poorly designed experiment, the sensitivity of the scale is only a small fraction of the total variance.

There are numerous situations in clinical psychopharmacology when the number of subjects in the experiment is necessarily small; for example, the number of suitable patients with a certain diagnosis to be studied is small. It has been shown in drug trials in clinical pharmacology that commonly used scales may be adequate to detect differences between a drug and placebo when the sample is of conventional size; if the sample is smaller, only the most sensitive scales will continue to discriminate between the treatment effects, whereas less sensitive scales will fail to do so (Kellner et al., 1968, 1979). There are some situations in which the sensitivity of the scale may be crucial. For example, when the difference between effects of two treatments is small, such as in a comparison of two drugs when different blood levels of a drug are correlated with changes in anxiety or depression in one individual.

Thus, sensitivity should not be considered synonymous with validity. It is, however, an important property when changes are being measured. A scale that repeatedly fails to discriminate between the responses of an active psychotropic drug and to those of placebo may be valid, but is of less value in the evaluation of short-term changes of anxiety and depression than a scale that consistently discriminates between the effects of two treatments.

V. ITEMS AND CUES

Items of a scale refer to the symptom or behavior that is being rated (for example, sad or hopeless), and *cues* describe the responses that are available to the rater, such as "Not at all," "A little," and "Severe." The length of a scale refers to the number of cues; for example, a Likert-type scale with three items, such as "Not at all," "A little," "A lot," will be referred to as a 3-point (short) scale, whereas a scale with seven to ten cues, ranging from "Not at all" to "Extremely" is referred to as a 7-point or 10-point (long) scale.

A. The Number of Items and Cues

The optimum number of items and the optimum number of cues depend on several factors. They vary with the person rating, mainly, whether it is a rating or self-rating scale; on the verbal skills of the subject; on his or her meticulousness; the nature of the study, for example, whether the measurement is carried out only once or twice, or whether frequent ratings are needed; and on the nature of the construct (e.g., trait or state) that is being measured.

A large number of items have advantages in some types of research. For example, when comparing depressed patients with a nondepressed group, a large number of symptoms and behaviors would yield more extensive comparisons than a scale with only a few items. Increasing the number of items, however, beyond a certain point does not improve the validity of a scale, may detract from its construct validity (which will be discussed in the following), and makes the measurement more time-consuming. A large number of items, if administered in conjunction with other lengthy scales, might impair a patient's concentration and attention.

1. Number of Items

In an anxiety scale that uses Likert scales for self-rating, the optimum number of items appears to be fewer than 20. The extensively validated State–Trait Anxiety Inventory (STAI) (Spielberger, 1983) has 20 items, but several are not specific for anxiety. Items such as "I tire quickly," "I feel like crying," would be as suitable or more suitable for a depression scale. If the number of items is large, some of the adjectives to describe mood are, by necessity, synonymous; also, it is difficult to find an adequate number of symptoms and adjectives that are meaningful to subjects with poor verbal skills.

Substantially more research has been done to determine the optimal properties of a state scale because of studies of sensitivity in drug trials. These studies suggest that the structure of rating and self-rating scales affects their sensitivity.

Surveys of drug trials have shown that global scales that contain only one item are sensitive (Kellner, 1971a,b; Uhlenhuth et al., 1982; Glass et al., 1987). The Brief Psychiatric Rating Scale (Overall and Gorham, 1962) has one item of anxiety and one of depressive mood, and both are sensitive long scales (Overall and Hollister 1986).

The Covi Anxiety Rating Scale has only three items, each rated by an observer on a 5-point scale (Covi and Lipman 1984), and the similar Raskin Depression Scale (Raskin et al., 1969) have been used as outcome measures in a few studies, and they discriminated between drug treatments. Similarly, the Brief Depression Rating Scale (a part of the Rating Scale of Depression, Anxiety and Somatic Symptoms; Kellner, 1986) has only three items that measure cognitive (or psychic) depression; these items have discriminated sensitively between drug and placebo and between two doses of the same drug, as well as between populations (Fava et al., 1986). Thus, there is evidence that a scale consisting of only one or a few items can be sensitive. Increasing the number of items beyond a certain point may decrease construct validity and may reduce sensitivity. In a Likert-type anxiety- or depression-rating or self-rating scale, five to seven items combine adequate construct validity, brevity, and sensitivity.

2. Number of Cues

In self-rating scales that measure current state, the optimal number of cues for self-rating probably varies between two and four, provided that the scale has several items. In the General Health Questionnaire (GHQ) (Goldberg, 1972) which purports to identify psychiatric illness, the subjects rate each symptom on a 4-point Likert scale, but the best sensitivity and specificity is achieved by dichotomizing the scale and using only two scores: 0 for either of the two left-hand columns and 1 for either of the two right-hand columns. The GHQ has one of the lowest misclassification rates when psychiatric patients (most of whom are anxious and depressed) are searched for in a random population. An anxiety self-rating state scale and depression self-rating scale that has only two cues, "Yes" or "No" (thus, only two scores), for each item is more sensitive than scales that contain more cues (Kellner, 1987). Apparently, decreasing the number of cues or scores for each item reduces errors or enhances the incisiveness in some other way. When the number of cues decreases, the number of items must increase to maintain the scale's sensitivity. To choose an extreme example, if there is only one item, such as in a global scale of depression, two cues, "Yes" and "No," would yield clearly inadequate information and would make it an insensitive scale. In a drug trial with the Symptom Questionnaire (Kellner et al., 1979), which has only two cues, reducing the number of items made the scale less sensitive.

3. Type of Cues

The choice of cues influences the properties of the scale, such as the ability to discriminate between groups, its ability to measure changes, and its sensitivity in drug trials. Sheffield and Kellner (1970) compared several kinds of cues in a study in which nonpsychotic psychiatric outpatients were administered the Symptom Rating Test. Each symptom was measured by five different 5-point Likert scales. The patients rated themselves when they first came to the clinic and after 1 month of drug treatment and supportive psychotherapy. The scale scores were compared with the scores of a group of random employees. The scales compared were two scales of intensity of symptoms, two scales of frequency of symptoms, and one scale of duration of symptoms. These scales differ in their ability to discriminate between the two groups as well as measuring significant changes after 1 month of treatment.

The most sensitive scale was one of intensity of symptoms with items such as "Slight," "Unpleasant," "Distressing." This scale discriminated between patients and random employees and, both before and after treatment, also measured significantly a change in scores after 1 month of treatment of the patients. The least sensitive scale was a scale of duration of symptoms describing whether the symptom lasted "Only for a short time" or "Most of the day."

VI. MODIFICATION OF EXISTING SCALES

A. Enhancing Sensitivity by Item and Cue Modification

The sensitivity of a scale can be systematically improved. Because the criterion is external and objective, each modification of the scale can be repeatedly tested against a drug and placebo difference in double-blind drug trials. My colleagues and I carried out several studies with the aim of constructing scales suitable for the measurement of changes in distress in experiments in therapeutics, such as drug trials. The steps in the development of these scales are described elsewhere (Kellner et al., 1978; Kellner, 1992). We carried cut item and cue analyses in a series of small crossover drug trials. We retained items and cues that were sensitive and deleted the others. We also retained a few items that were not highly sensitive, but needed to be included in the scale because they clearly belonged to the factor of anxiety or depression. In several studies, the final form of the Symptom Questionnaire (SQ) discriminated between a psychotropic drug and placebo, whereas several other scales in the same trial failed to do so (Kellner, 1987). The SQ has also been found to be more sensitive in controlled studies of psychological treatments (Nettleton, 1989; Neidhardt et al., 1992).

In conjunction with the development of the SQ, observer rating scales were developed (the Brief Rating Scales of Depression, Anxiety and Somatic Symptoms; (RDAS) with the same aims as for the self-rating scales. The scales were sensitive as well as valid and reliable (Kellner, 1986, 1992).

B. Methods of Scoring

The scoring of self-rating scales of distress differs substantially. On some scales (e.g., the SQ and GHQ) the total score of the scale is the number of symptoms the patient has endorsed; the rating of intensity or severity is not taken into account. Other scales depend on a sum of ratings for each symptom. The last method is the most common and is used in most observer rating scales.

Methods differ substantially in the number of items, manner of cues, and methods of scoring, yet may yield comparative results. The reason for the similarity, in spite of the substantial differences among the scales, is caused by the strong correlation of self-rated severity or frequency of symptoms, on one hand, and number of symptoms endorsed, on the other (Kellner, 1967).

The use of a product of several scales to measure one symptom or behavior has a logical appeal. One would expect that a compound score consisting of the product of scores of intensity, frequency, and duration (e.g., of depressed mood) would be a more effective measure than one scale of intensity alone. For example, a patient who rated himself as feeling severely depressed most days and most of the day would merit a lower score than a patient who rated herself as feeling severely depressed only for a few days and the depression lasted for a short time. This, however, was not found to be true; one sensitive scale discriminated as effectively between groups and was as sensitive as a compound scale (Kellner, 1967). This would suggest that either using multiple scales for each symptom increases the opportunity for error, or the product score would have to be empirically derived from psychiatric patients at various stages of their illness and from normal subjects to improve on the discriminating power and sensitivity of a compound scale.

C. Refining Construct Validity

The Symptom Checklist-90 (SCL-90) (Derogatis et al., 1976) belongs to the most commonly used self-rating scales of distress in the United States. The SCL-90 anxiety scale contains items such as "Feeling that familiar things seem strange or unreal" (derealization), "Feeling pushed to get things done" (obsessional trait), and "Heart pounding or racing" (a somatic symptom). The scales of the SCL-90 are based on factor analyses; the anxiety scale does not measure merely cognitive anxiety; this may not be a desirable goal unless the aim is to measure specifically cognitive anxiety, rather than an anxiety factor or the clinical syndrome of anxiety.

Many scales have items that they share with scales that purport to measure another construct. For example, several scales measuring depression contain sleep disturbance, somatic symptoms, anxiety symptoms, or items describing general distress such as "feeling upset" In the MMPI, the same item may occur in up to four different scales.

If a clinical syndrome is being measured, the boundaries of the syndrome can be adequately determined by factor analytic studies. If, however, the investigator chooses to study anxiety separately from depression, items that are shared by the two scales should be considered as separate measurements. For example, if anxiety and depression are measured simultaneously and both scales have a sleep item, sleep should be measured separately and not included in the anxiety or depression score. This has been done in a later edition of the Symptom Checklist-90, otherwise there would be a spurious correlation between anxiety and depression if the patient reported sleep disturbance. In the Brief Rating Scale of Depression (Kellner, 1986), items that pertain to sleep, somatic symptoms, and anxiety (which all belong to the clinical syndrome of depression), are excluded from the total score if anxiety and somatic symptoms are rated in addition to the rating of depression.

It soon became apparent in these studies that the most sensitive and suitable rating scale had a structure different from that of a self-rating scale of distress. These differences are described in the next section.

D. Difference Between Rating and Self-Rating Scales

There is evidence from published drug trials, as well as from our studies, to suggest that to optimally achieve sensitivity, the structure of a self-rating scale needs to differ from that of an observer rating scale.

1. *Self-Rating Scales*

The optimal number of items and cues for self-rating scales of depression state or anxiety state varies with scoring method and the type of scale. About seven items, and perhaps fewer, are adequate if a Likert-type scale is used for self-rating; the usual number of cues is four or five. Long self-rating scales, which contain more cues for each symptom, are of no advantage, and there is some decrease in sensitivity (Kellner et al., 1978). If there are only two self-rating cues available, then the number of items needs to be increased; for example, in the SQ (which has only two cues), the sensitivity decreased when the number of items decreased (Kellner et al., 1979).

2. *Observer Rating Scales*

Trained raters are apparently more skilled than patients in handling long scales. Increasing the number of items for each scale, while decreasing the number of items, made observer rating scales of anxiety and depression more sensitive (Kellner, 1992).

VII. SPECIAL METHODS

This review has dealt with the measurement of generalized anxiety and depressive states and trials. The evaluation of specific anxiety syndromes, such as agoraphobia, social phobia, and panic attacks, requires different methods because scales of generalized anxiety do not adequately measure the salient features of these syndromes. These methods have been reviewed comprehensively by Marks and Mathews (1978). Several authors have used special methods in outcome studies of these syndromes, which appear to be appropriate for measurement (Falloon et al., 1977; 1981; Gelder and Marks, 1966; James et al., 1983; Mavisskalian and Perel, 1985; Nay 1977; Noyes et al., 1984; Zitrin et al., 1983).

A. Target Symptoms

The use of target symptoms as outcome criteria has been described by several authors. The method was first proposed by Freyhan (1959), and the rationale has been discussed by Battle et al. (1966). The technique of the rating and self-rating of target symptoms has been reviewed elsewhere (Kellner, 1971a,b). Target symptoms may be chosen by the investigator; for example, "anxious mood," "tension," or may be chosen by the patients who list their most troublesome symptoms. Target symptoms chosen by physicians tend to be less sensitive than other criteria (Uhlenhuth et al., 1982), whereas three main complaints as selected by the patients (Battle et al., 1966) are sensitive to treatment effects in outcome research in psychotherapy (Kellner et al., 1968; Kellner, 1987; Hoehn-Saric et al., 1964). There are inadequate numbers for comparison of the most sensitive choice of target symptoms. The few comparisons that are available suggest that target symptoms chosen by the patient are somewhat more sensitive than target symptoms chosen by the investigator.

B. Physiological Measures in Anxiety and Depression

There are numerous publications on the physiology of anxiety and many measures of physiological activity change at times of anxiety (Cattell, 1966, p. 35). The correlation of physiological measurements with self-rating scales of anxiety has been inconsistent (Kraus, 1961), largely because the kinds of physiological responses at times of stress differ substantially from one person to another (Lacey and Lacey, 1958). The average for a group of people of one type of response (such as heart rate or galvanic skin response) is an inadequate measure of arousal (Lader, 1975; Tyrer, 1976), and the correlates with psychic anxiety are low. However, physiological changes are an important research topic; they may have a place in outcome studies of treatment if a specific physiological response is a pertinent outcome criterion.

Physiological measurements in depression pose special problems. The physiological changes are not of the same magnitude as those in anxiety, hostility, or other adrenergic–sympathetic arousal, and depression is more difficult to change adequately in experimental situations. Although measurable physiological changes occur in depression in a substantial proportion of patients, it is impractical to attempt to measure these changes as a part of measurement of depression unless it is a specific goal of the experiment.

C. The Rating of Phobias and Panic Attacks

The rating and self-rating of changes in phobias and panic attacks are different from those of the measurement of generalized anxiety or depressive states. For example, for a patient who has only a moderate level of generalized anxiety, but experiences several attacks of severe panic during the study period, the use of a conventional anxiety scale is an inadequate measure of change. In patients who are phobic, it is essential to rate changes in the severity of the symptoms experienced in the phobic situation, as well as the degree of avoidance. When the conventional self-rating scales of anxiety are used, they must be considered as supplementary criteria. If the investigator is interested in the severity of the generalized anxiety, apart from the phobia, the instructions may need to be modified, such as "Describe how you felt when you were not in the situation which scares you." If generalized anxiety is rated by an observer, the rater needs to specify that he or she wants to know how the patient felt when away from the phobic situation.

Some of the main methods that have been used are reviewed here. The rating and self-rating of phobias were reviewed comprehensively by Marks and Mathews (1978).

1. Agoraphobia and Specific Phobias

In the rating of phobias it is essential to measure the degree of avoidance. For example, a measure of anxiety would yield misleading results if a severe agoraphobic had not even approached the feared situation. Several methods have been used to measure avoidance. One of the methods is a diary in which the patient reports how often he or she has exposed himself or herself to the threatening situation. Another method, which is more reliable, but makes greater demands on the investigator, is the observation of the patient in the phobic situation. In a study of the treatment of agoraphobia, the patients were asked to walk unaccompanied along a standard course in a crowded urban center. Apart from the rating of the patients' behavior (with failure to complete the course having the worst rating), the patient also self-rated his or her anxiety (Mavisskalian and Perel, 1985). In another study (James et al., 1983) the patients were observed in the situations they had avoided in the past. In some specific phobias, such as animal phobias, the subjects can be observed during exposure to evaluate the effects of treatment. For example, subjects who are afraid of snakes are asked to pick up a nonpoisonous snake from an aquarium, or those who are afraid of rats are asked to pick up a laboratory rat. Various methods have been used to rate fear during exposure, for example, self-rating with a "fear thermometer," a graphic scale of fear that the subject fills in after exposure.

Phobic anxiety and phobic avoidance correlate highly; hence, combining anxiety and avoidance in one scale is often adequate (Marks and Mathews, 1978). In evaluating outcome, particularly on follow-up, the distinction should be made between the patient's ability to perform the feared task when asked to do so, as opposed to spontaneous frequency of exposure.

The Brief Standard Self-Rating Scale for Phobic Patients by Marks and Mathews (1978) is a self-rating scale that has been used to compare research results across centers. The main target phobia is self-rated on a 9-point broken graphic scale (Gelder and Marks, 1966); a 9-point global rating scale reflects both distress and avoidance; a fear questionnaire in which 17 different phobias are each self-rated on 9-point broken graphic scales completes the scale. This scale also includes a brief scale of anxiety and depression, consisting of six items, each self-rated on 9-point scales. The scales have been sensitive to treatment effects.

Various other methods have been used to measure changes in phobias. These include multiple assessment of emotion and behavior, such as generalized anxiety, avoidance, and impairment and fear–phobia inventories (Zitrin et al., 1983; Noyes et al., 1984).

2. *Social Phobias*

Methods of rating social phobias have been described by Falloon et al. (1977, 1981). Generalized anxiety and tension were self-rated; the observer and patient rated the target problem on a global scale; self-reports included a social questionnaire with self-ratings of fear and avoidance of social situations; and self-image was self-rated on semantic differential scales. The rater and the patient's partner rated overt anxiety, competence of performance, and pulse rate. The patient's partner made these ratings also in real-life situations.

3. *Spontaneous Panic Attacks*

Most patients with panic attacks are also phobic, but the rating of spontaneous panic attacks is of interest in therapeutics. The separate rating of panic attacks has been used in only a few outcome studies. In compliant patients, a diary in which the patient records the frequency, duration, and severity of the attacks, as well as the precipitating event or situation, is a useful record of progress. The patient should report all attacks, not only the truly spontaneous ones. In patients who are agoraphobic and have attacks only outside the home, the recording of panic attacks alone is misleading, and the rating methods described for phobias need to be used. When self-rating scales of generalized anxiety are used, they may need to be modified, similarly to those described for use in the measurements of phobias.

D. Special Situations

There are numerous research situations that require a special design to test a hypothesis concerning anxiety or depression. In several of these situations, it is inappropriate to use a standard scale of depression or anxiety, without making modifications. For example, when frequent ratings are desirable, such as the measurement of changes from one day to the next, it seems important to keep self-rating scales brief and simple so as not to burden the subjects and to enhance compliance. Brief scales of a few items appear adequate. With educated and compliant subjects, visual analogue self-rating scales are economical and sensitive (Aitken, 1969; Zealley and Aitken, 1969). Patients prefer broken (or segmented) graphic scales (Eastwood et al., 1984). In double-blind drug trials with the average psychiatric outpatient population, scales with verbal cues (broken, segmented, or box scales) tended to be somewhat more sensitive than the visual analogue scales (Kellner et al., 1978).

When using measurements more than once a week, such as every day, a change needs to be made in the instructions for self-ratings. In a state scale the patient usually is instructed to rate the way he or she felt during the past *week*. If daily self-ratings are needed the instructions need to be changed: "Describe how you have felt today," and usually the patient is advised to fill in the scale in the evening and to record the exact time. There may be other situations when even more frequent fluctuations are being measured; for example, after various time intervals following the ingestion of a drug or in the measurements of diurnal variations. In this situation the instructions need to be changed. For example, "Describe how you feel *now*," or "Describe how you have felt during the past hour," or "Please answer these questions each day (say) at 8:00 am and 6:00 pm.

VIII. SURVEYS OF RATING AND SELF-RATING SCALES

Several scales have been discussed in the present chapter. Numerous other scales are listed and discussed in several surveys of published anxiety and depression scales. These include Borkovec et al. (1977), Lader and Marks (1971), McNair (1974), Carroll et al. (1973), Snaith (1981), Murphy (1986), Raskin (1986), Waskow and Parloff (1975), Wetzel et al. (1982), and Kellner and Uhlenhuth (1988, 1991). Descriptions of scales are contained in a symposium edited by Guy (1976). Several authors have written surveys describing the scales used in their respective countries; for example, Fahndrich et al. (1986) in German-speaking countries, Bobon (1986) in French-speaking countries, and Codignola and Mantorani (1975) in Italy. Scales that have been used in geriatric patients are discussed in a volume edited by Crook and associates (1983). Rating scales for children have been reviewed by Raskin (1986). All the editions of the Mental Measurement yearbooks (Conoley and Kramer 1989) describe anxiety as well as depression self-rating scales with comments by experts. In a comprehensive volume of rating and self-rating scales of depression that are in use worldwide, the contributors describe depression as well as several subscales of anxiety (Sartorius and Ban 1986). A list of depression scales is contained in Beckham and Leber (1985); the authors also list selected rating scales that pertain to various features that are associated with depression. A symposium on psychotherapy research measures lists several rating and self-rating methods, which include anxiety and depression (Waskow and Parloff, 1975). To attempt to survey all these scales is a lengthy undertaking, yet the list of surveys in this section is not exhaustive. When it comes to the choice of scales, researchers and clinicians do not lack tools, but they may have difficulties selecting the most suitable ones.

IX. THE CHOICE OF SCALES

There are no simple rules for choosing scales. Several scales have been discussed in this chapter but that does not mean that they are the most suitable. The choice of scales will depend on the properties of the scale, on the kind of study being conducted, and on the investigator's preferences. Any recommendation is inevitably influenced by the reviewer's experience and his or her interpretation of previous research, as well as his or her personal bias.

The investigator should use a scale that has been commonly used in his or her country. The investigator as well as the readers are likely to be familiar with the scale and usually adequate normative data are available.

The inclusion of a frequently used scale is useful because it allows a rough comparison of the severity of the disorder compared with that in other studies. The investigator should not rely on standard scales alone. A practical approach is to survey previous similar studies and choose a scale that has previously yielded a meaningful and significant result. Such a search will increase the likelihood that the scale is adequately sensitive for the particular study or experiment. In other words, it would be taking a risk to limit oneself to a commonly used scale when a previous similar study or experiment has yielded incisive data with a special scale. For example, if, in a previous study of self-rated anxiety as related to changes in stress hormone level, the authors reported a satisfactory correlation with a particular scale, this scale would need to be included in the design, in addition to whatever other scales the investigator wishes to use.

Global scales rated by the observer as well as by the patient are valid, but somewhat less sensitive than other scales for the use of outcome studies such as drug trials. Because of their simplicity and economy, they should be additional measures. In a parallel, between-subjects trial, absolute global scales (with cues such as "Not depressed," "Slightly," "Moderately," "Severely," and so on) are somewhat more sensitive than relative scales (which compare the present state to another state with cues such as "Better," "Same," and "Worse") (Kellner et al., 1972).

If the measurement of anxiety or depression is the main or a crucial aspect of the study, the investigator may choose more than one rating or self-rating scale measuring the same construct. Scales differ in psychometric properties, and the use of more than one scale yields additional information (Fava et al., 1986). This is also a way to cross-validate the results. Sometimes it adds interest to the study if the investigator also includes either a lesser-known scale, a scale that may not have been adequately researched, or even an experimental scale.

If the effects of two or more similar treatments are being compared, or if the samples are small, or if minor changes need to be measured accurately, it is important to include among the measurements a scale of high sensitivity. Such choices and other reasons for choosing specific scales have been discussed in previous sections of this chapter.

X. SUMMARY AND MAIN CONCLUSION

This chapter contains a review of the literature on the principles of measuring depression and anxiety. The psychometrics of the measurements of depressive states and generalized anxiety are similar and the principles are those of the measurement of distress.

Scales of depression and anxiety differ in their time focus. State anxiety scales, or scales of depressive states purport to measure temporary distress; the questions are focused on the present or on the recent past. Trait scales purport to measure a long-lasting disposition; and these measure the ways the subject generally feels.

The various methods of validation have been discussed. The commonly used scales in research on depression and anxiety have adequate validity. There is incomplete agreement on the boundaries of the constructs; for example, some anxiety scales include somatic symptoms, others include associated symptoms (for example, depressive symptoms that are common in the clinical syndrome of generalized anxiety), other scales are derived from factor analyses and some others are limited to items of cognitive or psychic anxiety.

The test–retest reliability is appropriate for trait scales. For state scales the method is appropriate when used in nonpatients or in chronically anxious or depressed patients who are unlikely to change during the interval between the two tests. Other methods of testing reliability of state scales have been proposed, but their usefulness has not been adequately demonstrated.

The term *sensitivity* has two meanings in psychometrics. In epidemiology the term means the proportion of persons with a psychiatric disorder who are identified by the score on the scale. The sensitivity of the scale depends on several factors apart from the properties of the scale; these include the prevalence of the disorder and the diagnostic criteria used to determine which subject is deemed to have a psychiatric disorder. If a clinic population is being compared with a random nonpatient control group, the sensitivity and misclassification rate, in part, depend on the composition of the two samples.

In clinical psychopharmacology, sensitivity means the scale's ability to discriminate between an active psychotropic drug and placebo in a double blind trial. It is one of the methods of validation; it is assumed that a scale that repeatedly discriminates significantly between, say, an active antianxiety drug and placebo is a more valid and sensitive measure of change in anxiety than a scale that fails to do so in the same trials. The use of insensitive scales may yield misleading results; they may fail to detect existing differences between the effects of two treatments.

Surveys as well as drug trials designed to compare sensitivity show that there are consistent differences in sensitivity among commonly used distress scales. There is evidence to suggest that there are several scales that are more sensitive than the commonly used ones. Some of the most sensitive scales have not been compared with the others in an adequate number of drug trials to allow a meta-analysis of the results.

Items of a scale are the symptoms or behaviors that are rated, and *cues* indicate the responses available to the rater, such as adjectives "Slight" and "Severe." Scales vary greatly in the number of items, number of cues, and in the method of scoring. There is some evidence to suggest that for self-rating scales many items with only two cues (such as "Yes" and "No"), or only two scores for each item, increases the sensitivity of the scale for detecting drug–placebo differences. Numerous cues decreases the sensitivity of a self-rating scale. Some observer rating scales have a high interrater correlation and are sensitive, even when the number of cues is large; it is unknown whether a large number of cues in observer rating scales is advantageous in group research. In research with large groups when Likert-type of cues are used, few items are adequate both for rating and self-rating scales.

Scales that measure generalized anxiety are inadequate to measure certain other anxiety syndromes, for example, phobias; the methods designed for these syndromes are discussed. Various special situations are described; for example, when daily self-ratings are desirable; in these situations either special methods of measurement need to be used or commonly used scales need to be modified in order to yield meaningful results.

In research in anxiety and depression, it is of advantage to choose scales that have been most incisive in previous studies with a similar purpose and design. When the measurement of anxiety or depression is the main or a crucial feature of the study, it may be advantageous to use, in addition to the main scale, another scale that has different psychometric properties; the result from the second scale may serve as a cross-validation of the results.

ACKNOWLEDGMENTS

This chapter is based on several previously published surveys by the author and his colleagues; these articles are referenced throughout the chapter. I should like to thank my colleagues for their contribution to this work, to the original research, as well as for the joint authorship of previous similar surveys; in particular, to Drs. Brian Sheffield, E. H. Uhlenhuth, Giovanni Fava, Richard Glass, and George Simpson.

REFERENCES

R. C. B. Aitken, Measurement of feelings using visual analogue scales, *Proc. R. Soc. Med., 62*: 989 (1969).

American Psychiatric Association, *Diagnostic and Statistical Manual of Mental Disorders*, 3rd ed., revised *(DSM-III-R)*, American Psychiatric Association, Washington, D.C., (1987).

A. Anastasi, *Psychological Testing*, 5th ed., Macmillan Publishing, New York (1982).

C. C. Battle, S.D. Imber, R. Hoehn-Saric, A.R. Stone, E.R. Nash, and J.D. Frank, Target complaints as criteria of improvement. *Am. J. Psychother., 20*: 184 (1966).

E. E. Beckhan, and W. R. Leber (eds.), *Handbook of Depression, Treatment. Assessment, and Research,* Brooks-Cole, Pacific Grove, CA (1985).

A. Bedford, A. Edington, A., and R. Kellner, Changes in self-rating of symptoms: A comparison of questionnaire graphic scales with test cards, *Br. J. Psychiatry, 134*: 108 (1979).

A. Bedford, D. McIver, and P.R. Pearson, A further test of Foulds' personality and personal illness differentiate in psychiatric group, Psychol. Med., 8: 467 (1978).

D. Bobon, Systems and scales for the assessment of depression in French-speaking countries, *Assessment of Depression* (N. Sartorius and T.A. Ban, eds.), Springer-Verlag, New York, pp. 9–18, (1986).

T. D. Borkovec, T.C. Weerts, and D.A. Bernstein, Assessment of anxiety, *Handbook of Behavioral Assessment*, (A.R. Ciminero, K.S. Calhoun, and H.E. Adams, eds.), John Wiley & Sons, New York, pp. 367–428 (1977).

B. J. Carroll, J.M. Fielding, and T.G. Blashki, Depression rating scales, *Arch. Gen. Psychiatry, 28*: 361 (1973).

R. B. Cattell, Patterns of change: Measurement in relation to state-dimension, trait change, lability, and process concepts, *Handbook of Multivariate Experimental Psychology*, Rand McNally, Chicago (1966).

R. B. Cattell, and I.H. Scheier, The nature of anxiety: A review of thirteen multivariate analyses comprising 814 variables, *Psychol. Rep., 4*: 351 (1958).

E. Codignola, and G. Mantovani, *Rating Scales*, Schering Corp., Kenilworth, N.J. (1975).

J. C. Conoley, and J.J. Kramer, *Buros l0th Mental Measurements Yearbooks*, University of Nebraska, Lincoln (1989).

L. Covi, and R.S. Lipman, Primary depression or primary anxiety? A possible psychometric approach to a diagnostic dilemma, *Clin. Neuropharmacol., 7*(Suppl 1): S501 (1984).

L. J. Cronbach, Response sets and test validity, *Educ. Psychol. Meas., 6*: 475 (1946).

L. J. Cronbach, Further evidence on response sets and test design, *Educ. Psychol. Meas., 10*: 3 (1950).

L. J. Cronbach, *Essentials of Psychological Testing*, 3rd ed., Harper & Row, New York (1970).

L. J. Cronbach, Test validation, *Educational Measurement*, (R.L. Thorndike, ed.), American Council on Education, Washington, D.C., (1971).

L. J. Cronbach, and P.E. Meehl, Construct validity in psychological tests, *Minnesota Studies in the Philosophy of Science,* Vol. 1 (H. Feigl, and M. Scriven eds.), University of Minnesota Press, Minneapolis, pp. 174–204, (1956).

T. Crook, S. Ferris, and R. Bartus, *Assessment in Geriatric Psychopharmacology*, Mark Powley Associates, New Canaan, (1983).

S. Crown, and A. H. Crisp, A short clinical diagnostic self-rating scale for psychoneurotic patients, *Br. J. Psychiatry, 112*: 917 (1966).

W. B. Dahlstrom, and G.S. Welsh, *An MMPI Handbook*, University of Minnesota Press, Minneapolis (1960).

L. R. Derogatis, R.S. Lipman, K. Rickels, E. H. Uhlenhuth, and L. Covi, The Hopkins Symptom Check List (HSCL): A self-report symptom inventory, *Behav. Sci., 19*: 1 (1974).

L. R. Derogatis, R.S. Lipman, and L. Covi, An outpatient psychiatric rating scale: Preliminary report, *ECDEU Assessment Manual for Psychopharmacology, Revised, 1976*, U.S. Department of Health, Education, and Welfare, Rockville, Md., p. 320 (1976).

M. R. Eastwood, J. L. Whitton, and P. M. Kramer, A brief instrument for longitudinal monitoring of mood states, *Psychiatry Res., 11*: 119 (1984).

E. Fahndrich, H. Helmchen, and M. Linden, Standardized instruments used in the assessment of depression in German-speaking countries, *Assessment of Depression* (N. Sartorius and T.A. Ban, eds.), Springer-Verlag, New York, pp. 1–8 (1986).

I. R. H. Falloon, G.G. Lloyd, and R.E. Harpin, The treatment of social phobia, *J. Nerv. Ment. Dis., 169*: 180 (1981).

I. R. H. Falloon, P. Lindley, R. McDonald, and I.M. Marks, Social skills training of outpatient groups: A controlled study of rehearsal and homework, *Br. J. Psychiatry, 131*: 599 (1977).

G. A. Fava, R. Kellner, F. Munari, and L. Pavan, The Hamilton Depression Rating Scale in normals and depressives, *Acta Psychiatr. Scand., 66*: 26 (1982).

G. A. Fava, R. Kellner, J. Lisansky, S. Park, G.I. Perini, and M. Zielezny, Rating depression in normals and depressives: Observer versus self-rating scales, *J. Affective Disord., 11*: 29 (1986).

A. R. Feinstein, *Cernimetrics,* Yale University Press, New Haven (1987).

S. Fisher, Measurement of anxiety in outpatient trials: Detection of bias in patient and doctor ratings, *Psychopharmacol. Bull., 12*: 17 (1976).

F. A. Freyhan, Therapeutic implications of differential effects of new phenothiazine compounds, *Am. J. Psychiatry, 115*: 577 (1959).

M. G. Gelder, and I.M. Marks, Severe agoraphobia: A controlled prospective trial of behaviour therapy, *Br. J. Psychiatry, 112*: 309 (1966).

R. M. Glass, E.H. Uhlenhuth, and R. Kellner, The value of self-report assessment in studies of anxiety disorders, *J. Clin. Psychopharmacol. 7*: 215 (1987).

G. C. Gleser, Evaluation of psychotherapy outcome by psychological tests, *Psychotherapy Change Measures* (I.E. Waskow and M.B. Parloff, eds.), National Institute of Mental Health, Rockville, Md., pp. 32–39, (1975).

D. P. Goldberg, *The Detection of Psychiatic Illness by Questionnaire*, Oxford University Press, London (1972).

J. P. Guilford, *Psychometric Methods*, 2nd ed., McGraw-Hill, London (1954).

W. Guy, *EODEU Assessment Manual for Psychopharmacology*, revised, U.S. Department of Health, Education, and Welfare, Rockville, Md., (1976).

M. A. Hamilton, A rating scale for depression, *J. Neurol. Neurosurg. Psychiatry, 23*: 56 (1960).

R., Hoehn-Saric, J.D. Frank, S.D. Imber, E.H. Nash, A.R. Stone, and C. C. Battle, Systematic preparation of patients for psychotherapy—1. Effects on therapy behaviour and outcome, *J. Psychiatr. Res., 2*: 267 (1964).

J. E. James, B.A.M. Hampton, and S.A. Larsen, The relative efficacy of imaginal and in vivo desensitization in the treatment of agoraphobia, *J. Behav. Ther. Exp. Psychiatry, 14*: 203 (1983).

R. Kellner, The Assessment of Changes in the Symptoms of Neurotic Adults, Ph.D. thesis, University of Liverpool (1967).

R. Kellner, Improvement criteria in drug trials with neurotic patients. Part I, *Psychol. Med. 1*: 416 (1971a).

R. Kellner, Improvement criteria in drug trials with neurotic patients, Part II, *Psychol. Med. 2*: 73 (1971b).

R. Kellner, The brief depression rating scale, *Assessment of Depression* (N. Sartorius and T.A. Ban, eds.), Springer-Verlag, New York, pp. 179–187 (1986).

R. Kellner, A symptom questionnaire. *J. Clin. Psychiatry, 48*: 268 (1987).

R. Kellner, Anxiety, somatic sensations and bodily complaints, *Handbook of Anxiety. Vol. 2, Classification, Etiological Factors and Associated Disturbances* (R. Noyes, M. Roth, and G.D. Burrows, eds.), Elsevier Science Publishers, New York, pp. 213–237 (1988).

R. Kellner, The development of sensitive scales for research in therapeutics, *Research Designs and Methods in Psychiatry* (M. Fava and J.F. Rosenbaum, eds.), Elsevier, Amsterdam (1992).

R. Kellner, and B.F. Sheffield, A self-rating scale of distress, *Psychol. Med., 3*: 88 (1973).

R. Kellner, and E.H. Uhlenhuth, The assessment of changes in anxiety in therapeutics, *Handbook of Anxiety, Vol. 2: Classification, Etiological Factors and Associated Disturbances* (R. Noyes, M. Roth and G.D. Burrows, eds.), Elsevier Science Publishers, New York, pp. 189–211 (1988).

R. Kellner, and E.H. Uhlenhuth, The rating and self-rating of anxiety, *Br. J. Psychiatry, 159*: 15 (1991).

R. Kellner, A.V. Kelly, and B.F. Sheffield, The assessment of changes in anxiety in a drug trial. A comparison of methods, *Br. J. Psychiatry, 114*: 863 (1968).

R. Kellner, G.M. Simpson, and W.W. Winslow, The relationship of depressive neurosis to anxiety and somatic symptoms, *Psychosomatics 13*: 358 (1972).

K. Kellner, B. F. Sheffield, and G. M. Simpson, The value of self-rating scales in drug trials with nonpsychotic patients, *Prog NeuroPsychopharmacol., 2*: 197 (1978).

R. Kellner, R.T. Rada, T. Andersen, and D. Pathak., The effects of chlordiazepoxide on self-rated depression, anxiety and well-being. *Psychopharmacology, 64*: 185 (1979).

J. B. Knowles, Rating methods and measurement of behaviour, *Methods of Psychiatric Research* (P. Sainsbury and N. Kreitman, eds.), Oxford University Press, London, pp. 74–84 (1963)

M. S. Kraus, The measurement of transitory anxiety, *Psychol. Rev., 68*: 178 (1961).

J. I. Lacey, and B.C. Lacey, Verification and extension of the principle of autonomic response—stereotypy, *Am. J. Psychol., 71*: 50 (1958).

M. Lader, *The Psychophysiology of Mental Illness,* Routlege and Kegan Paul, London (1975).

M. Lader, and I. Marks, *Clinical Anxiety*, Grune & Stratton, New York (1971).

H. E. Lehmann, The place and purpose of objective methods in psychopharmacology, *Drugs and Behavio*r (R. Uhr and J.G. Miller, eds.), John Wiley & Sons, New York, pp. 107–127 (1960).

R. S. Lipman, J.0. Cole, L.C. Park, and K. Rickels, Sensitivity of symptom and nonsymptom-focused criteria of outpatient drug efficacy, *Am. J. Psychiatry, 122*: 24 (1965).

R. S. Lipman, L. Covi, K. Rickels, E.H. Uhlenhuth, and R. Lazar, Selected measures in outpatient evaluation, *Psychopharmacology: A Review of Progress. 1957–1967* (D.H. Efron, ed.), U.S. Govt. Printing Office: Washington, D.C., pp. 249–254 (1968).

I. M. Marks, and A. Mathews, Case histories and shorter communication: Brief standard self-rating for phobic patients, *Behav. Res. Ther., 17*: 263 (1978).

J. D. Maser, and C.R. Cloninger, Comorbidity of anxiety and mood disorders: Introduction and overview, *Comorbidity of Mood and Anxiety Disorders*, (J.D. Maser and C.R. Cloninger, eds.), American Psychiatric Press, Washington, D.C., pp. 3-12 (1990).

M. Mavisskalian, and J. Perel, Imipramine in the treatment of agoraphobia: Dose–response relationships, *Am. J. Psychiatry, 142*: 1032 (1985).

D. M. McNair, Self-evaluation of antidepressants, *Psychopharmacologia, 37*: 281 (1974).

S. A. Montgomery, and M. Asberg, A new depression scale designed to be sensitive to change, *Br. J. Psychiatry, 134*: 382 (1979)

R. L. Mooney, and L. V. Gordon, *Mooney Problem Check List, 1950 revision*, Psychological Corporation, New York (1950).

J. M. Murphy, *Psychiatric Instrument Development for Primary Care Research: Patient Self-Report Questionnaire*, Division of Biometry and Epidemiology, National Institute of Mental Health, Alcohol, Drug Abuse, and Mental Health Administration, Rockville, Md. (1986).

W. R. Nay, Analogue measures, *Handbook of Behavioral Assessment* (A.R. Ciminero, K.S. Calhoun, and H.E. Adams, eds.), John Wiley & Sons, New York (1977).

J. Neidhardt, B. Krakow, R. Kellner, and D. Pathak, The effects of one session of treatment of chronic nightmares, Sleep Res. Abstr. (in press; 1992).

C. S. Nettleton, Coping with disability: The psychological consequences of central nervous system injury, Doctoral dissertation, University of New Mexico (1989).

R. Noyes, D.J. Anderson, J. Clancy, R.R. Crowe, D.J. Slymen, M.M. Ghoneim, and J.V. Hinrichs, Diazepam and propranolol in panic disorder and agoraphobia. *Arch. Gen. Psychiatry, 41*: 287 (1984).

J. E. Overall, and L.B. Hollister, Assessment of depression using the Brief Psychiatric Rating Scale, *Assessment of Depression* (N. Sartorius and T.A. Ban, eds.), Springer-Verlag, New York, pp. 159–178 (1986).

J. E. Overall, and D.R. Gorham, The brief psychiatric rating scale. *Psychol. Rep., 10*: 799 (1962).

A. Raskin, Sensitivity to treatment effects of evaluation instruments completed by psychiatrists, psychologists, nurses, and patients, *Assessment of Depression* (N. Sartorius and T.A. Ban, eds.), Springer-Verlag, New York, pp. 367–376 (1986).

A. Raskin, J. Schulterbrandt, N. Rectig, et al., Replication of factors of psychopathology in interview, ward behaviour, and self report ratings of hospitalized depressives, *J. Nerv. Ment. Dis., 148*: 87 (1969).

E. Renfordt Fortschritte in der klinisch-psychopharmakologischen Forschung durch fernsehtechnische Hilfsmittel, *Pharmakonsychiatria, 11*: 266 (1978).

N. Sartorius, and T.A. Ban, *Assessment of Depression,* Springer-Verlag, New York (1986).

B. F. Sheffield, and R. Kellner, The temporal stability of self-ratings of neurotic symptoms, *Br. J. Soc. Clin. Psychol., 9*: 46 (1970).

R. P. Snaith, Rating scales, *Br. J. Psychiatry, 138*: 512 (1981).

R. P. Snaith, Measurement in psychiatry, *Br. J. Psychiatry, 159*: 78 (1991).

R. P. Snaith, S. J. Baugh, A. D. Calyden, A. Husain, and M. A. Sipple, The Clinical Anxiety Scale: An instrument derived from the Hamilton Anxiety Scale, *Br. J. Psychiatry, 141*: 518 (1982).

C. Spearman, *The Abilities of Man*, Macmillan, New York (1927).

C. D. Spielberger, *Manual for the State-Trait Anxiety Inventory,* revised ed., Consulting Psychologists Press, Palo Alto (1983).

C. D. Spielberger, and S.S. Krasner, The assessment of state and trait anxiety, *Handbook of Anxiety, Vol. 2: Classification. Biological Factors and Associated Disturbances*, (R. Noyes, M. Roth, and G.D. Burrows, eds.), Elsevier Science Publishers, New York, pp. 31–51 (1988).

J. A. Taylor, A personality scale of manifest anxiety, J. *Abnorm. Soc. Psychol., 48*: 285 (1953).

P. Tyrer, *The Role of Bodily Feelings in Anxiety*, Oxford University Press, London (1976).

E. H. Uhlenhuth, R.M. Glass, S.J. Haberman, and R. Kellner, Relative sensitivity of clinical measures in trials of antianxiety agents, *The Behavior of Psychiatric Patients: Quantitative Techniques for Evaluation*, (E.I. Burdock, A. Sudilovsky, and S. Gershon. eds.), Marcel Dekker, New York, pp. 393–409 (1982).

I. E. Waskow, and M.B. Parloff (Eds.), *Psychotherapy Change Measures*, National Institute of Mental Health, Rockville, Md., (1975).

M. C. Weinstein, D. M. Berwick, P. A. Goldman, J. M. Murphy, and J. A. Barsky, A comparison of three psychiatric screening tests using receiver operating characteristic (ROC) analysis, *Med. Care, 27*: 593 (1989).

R. D. Wetzel, C.R. Cloninger, and S.B. Guze, The assessment of patients with neurosis, *The Behavior of Psychiatric Patients* (E.I. Burdock, A. Sudilovsky, and S. Gershon, eds.), Marcel Dekker, New York, p. 439 (1982).

L. Willis, P. Thomas, P.J. Garry, and J.S. Goodwin, A prospective study of response to stressful life events in initially healthy elders, *J. Gerontol., 42*: 627 (1987).

H. U. Wittchen, G.A. Essau, and J.C. Krieg, Anxiety disorders: Similarities and differences of comorbidity in treated and untreated groups, *Br. J. Psychiatry, 159*(suppl. 12): 23 (1991).

World Health Organization, *International Classification of Diseases,* l0th ed. (ICD-10), World Health Organization, Geneva (1990).

A. K. Zealley, and R.C.B. Aitken, Measurement of mood, *Proceed. Roy. Soc. Med., 62*: 993 (1969).

C. M. Zitrin, D.F. Klein, M.G. Woerner, and D.C. Ross, Treatment of phobias, *Arch. Gen. Psychiatry, 40*: 125 (1983).

W. W. K. Zung, A self-rating depression scale, *Arch. Gen. Psychiatry, 12*: 63 (1965).

7

The Psychophysiology of Depression and Anxiety

Murray B. Stein
University of Manitoba, Winnipeg, Manitoba, Canada

Keith G. Wilson
The Rehabilitation Centre and University of Ottawa, Ottawa, Ontario, Canada

Thomas W. Uhde
National Institute of Mental Health, National Institutes of Health, Bethesda, Maryland

I. INTRODUCTION

In this chapter, we set out to review the psychophysiology of anxiety and depression. We soon discovered that this was a monumental task, for several reasons. First, there is a long and rich tradition of psychophysiology in anxiety and depression, extending back at least a century. It seemed to us that a history of psychophysiological research was not what the readers of this book would be interested in, but rather, they would be looking for an update on current thinking in this area. Consequently, we have, with some exceptions, limited our review to the literature of the past 25 years, with the most attention paid to studies done even more recently using modern diagnostic criteria, such as the *Diagnostic and Statistical Manual of Mental Disorders*, 3rd ed. (*DSM-III*; American Psychiatric Association, 1980) or *DSM-III-R* (American Psychiatric Association, 1987).

Once the chronologic parameters had been delimited, we found ourselves with two remaining problems. One problem was how to define *psychophysiology*. In the classic sense, psychophysiology has referred to the measurement of things such as heart rate, galvanic skin responses (GSR), or electrodermal activity (EDA) and, in the past quarter century, electrophysiological responses, such as P^3 and other components of the electroencephalographic (EEG) responses to specific stimuli. Given, that technology has advanced considerably in recent years, however, we began to wonder if psychophysiology now included more sophisticated EEG measures, such as computed topographic EEG mapping (sometimes known as brain electrical activity mapping, or BEAM), and polysomnographic (sleep) studies (which offer the wonderful opportunity to study physiology when cognitive influences are at a minimum). If we were to include a review of those technologies, should we not then include a review of the most novel "psychophysiological" techniques; that is, brain-imaging techniques, such as positron emission tomography (PET) and single-photon emission computerized tomography (SPECT). We dealt with this problem somewhat arbitrarily by stopping just short of reviewing the brain-imaging studied that have involved the measurement of cerebral blood flow or cerebral glucose metabolism (i.e., PET and SPECT), but decided to include those studies that have analyzed brain electrical activity (such as computerized quantitative EEG).

Having made that decision, we were still faced with the problem of which depressive disorders and which anxiety disorders to include in the review. Particularly with the anxiety disorders, for which some very different disorders (e.g., panic disorder and obsessive–compulsive disorder) are included in the category, would it make sense to review the literature for each and every anxiety disorder? Again, here, we took a conservative middle-of-the-road approach, and elected to focus, in large part, on panic disorder and agoraphobia, which have been by far the best studied of the anxiety disorders. In some places, however, when the topic was of sufficient interest and there was sufficient literature to make a review worthwhile (e.g., the sleep of patients with posttraumatic stress disorder), we went ahead and included this in the chapter.

When all was said and done, we found ourselves with a fairly comprehensive, very current review of the psychophysiology of depression and anxiety. Where the review is less than comprehensive, we are satisfied that we have referred the reader to a more complete treatise on the topic in question. Whenever possible, we have attempted to compare and contrast findings between depression and anxiety, and when it seemed relevant, between the different anxiety disorders. The chapter begins with a review of the literature on electrodermal activity in depression and anxiety, proceeds to cover the subject of cardiovascular activity, moves on to an assessment of EEG studies, and concludes with a review of sleep physiology in these disorders.

II. ELECTRODERMAL ACTIVITY

Studies of electrodermal activity (EDA) have a long history in psychopathology research, and they continue to occupy an important position in the psychophysiological assessment of mood and anxiety disorders. Typically, EDA is measured as changes in skin conductance from sites on the palms of the hands or the phalanges of the fingers, areas that have dense distributions of eccrine sweat glands. The accumulation of sweat in these glands and the corresponding hydration of the skin result in increased electrical conductivity, which is the basic phenomenon of interest in the measurement of EDA (Fowles, 1986).

The secretory activity of the eccrine sweat glands is regulated by the sympathetic branch of the autonomic nervous system. However, the innervation is somewhat atypical for autonomic effector organs, because the postganglionic transmitter is acetylcholine, rather than norepinephrine. Although there is a sparse representation of adrenergic fibers (Shields et al., 1987), under normal circumstances, the mediation of sweating is primarily a cholinergic phenomenon (Fowles, 1986).

There are several features of EDA that have been the subject of empirical investigation, but three characteristics in particular have been examined most extensively in studies of psychiatric patients. These are (1) the background, or tonic level of skin conductance; (2) the occurrence of "nonspecific" ED fluctuations, and (3) the elicitation and habituation of ED "orienting responses." In practice, these measures all tend to be moderately correlated with one another (Wilson, 1987), although they are usually viewed as indexes of different psychophysiological processes. For example, the tonic level of skin conductance is thought to be related to the number of active sweat glands (Venables and Christie, 1973), and it has often been interpreted as an index of the global state of activation of the sympathetic nervous system.

Nonspecific ED fluctuations have also been related to the construct of activation or arousal. As the name implies, *nonspecific fluctuations* are defined as phasic changes in skin conductance that do not appear to be evoked by a specific eliciting stimulus. In many cases, in fact, there may *be* an eliciting stimulus, in the sense that covert mental activity seems to be associated with nonspecific fluctuations in resting normal subjects (Nikula, 1991). From the perspective of most research investigations, however, these fluctuations have been typically interpreted as spontaneous or nonspecific discharges of the sympathetic nervous system.

In contrast with nonspecific fluctuations, *orienting responses* are phasic increases in skin conductance that are evoked by the presentation of a discrete stimulus. The typical experimental paradigm has involved the repeated presentation of simple stimulus, such as a tone or flash of light. Under these conditions, the initial presentations of the stimulus characteristically evoke an ED orienting response, which habituates over successive trials.

Following the tradition established by Sokolov (1963), the occurrence of an orienting response indicates that a subject has discriminated the presence of a novel or significant stimulus, while *habituation* can be viewed as a process of learning to ignore. In this context, most recent research on orienting has adopted an attentional or information-processing perspective. For example, Öhman (1979) considers the orienting response as a "call for processing resources," which serves to redirect the subject's attention toward an analysis of novel or unexpected events. In fact, recent studies that have combined ED recording with concurrent measures of attentional resource allocation have found that, within limits, the magnitude of the ED orienting response is indeed correlated with the extent to which a subject's attention is drawn toward the eliciting stimulus (Filion et al., 1991; Siddle, 1991).

From a consideration of the various physiological and psychological mechanisms that contribute to ED phenomena, it is clear that the global finding of differences between a psychiatric group and a control group may actually be due to one or more of several different factors. These include (1) factors related to differences in physiological state (e.g., level of activation or arousal of the sympathetic nervous system, (2) biochemical factors related to cholinergic neurotransmission, and (3) cognitive factors related to attention and information processing. In fact, each of these mechanisms has been invoked in the past to explain anomalies in EDA that have been found in various clinical groups.

Finally, each of these ED measures shows a moderate degree of temporal stability in studies of test–retest reliability, with correlations generally ranging from 0.50–0.90, depending on the length of the interval between sessions (Freixa i Baqué, 1982). In research that has been undertaken with identical twins, the magnitude of the within-pair correlations for measures of ED response amplitude and habituation are also at about the same level as their respective retest reliabilities (Lykken et al., 1988). Hence, within the normal population, individual differences in EDA reflect a relatively stable psychophysiological trait, which has a substantial genetic determination. When generalized to the clinical context, it is possible that some aspects of EDA may provide potential biological markers for identifying individuals who may have an increased genetic risk for specific psychiatric disorders (Iacono, 1985).

A. Electrodermal Activity in Depression

1. Comparisons of Patients and Normal Controls

Lader (1975) has reviewed the early literature pertaining to EDA in clinical depression and notes that, although there have been inconsistencies in the results across studies, the most common finding—that of generally lower levels of EDA in depressed patients—was reported as early as the 1920s (Richter, 1928). The results of six recent studies are summarized in Table 1. Each of these investigations employed contemporary diagnostic criteria to screen patients and also reported overall comparisons between a depressed group (without necessarily addressing diagnostic subtypes) and a group of nondepressed control subjects. As is evident in Table 1, all six studies found lower EDA among the patients in at least one measure. Tonic conductance levels were consistently low in each of the five studies for which they were reported, whereas orienting responses recorded to the presentations of discrete auditory stimuli were significantly smaller (or habituated faster) among the patients in each of the four reports that included an orienting paradigm.

Table 1 Electrodermal Activity in Depressed Patients and Control Subjects

Study	No. of patients	Stimuli	No. of controls	SCL[a]	NSFs[b]	Response to stimuli[a]
Bernstein et al. (1988)	39 major depression, 11 minor depression (RDC)		50			
Carney et al. (1981)	15 primary affective disorder (Feighner)		15	P<C		
Dawson et al. (1985)	20 major depression (RDC and *DSM-III*)	Verbal stimuli (auditory)	20	P<C		P<C
Iacono et al. (1983)	24 unipolar and 24 bipolar major depression in remission (RDC)	86-dB tones	46	P<C	NS	P<C
Thorell et al. (1987a)	50 major depression, 9 dysthymia (*DSM-III*)	90-dB tones	59	P<C	NS	P<C
Ward and Doerr (1986)	50 major depression (RDC and *DSM-III*)		71	P<C		

[a] P, patients; C, control; SCL, skin conductance level.
[b] NSFs, nonspecific fluctuations; NS, nonsignificant.

Nonspecific fluctuations have not always been presented, but they appear to be less sensitive in distinguishing between patients and controls.

In some laboratories, the differentiation in EDA between depressed patients and control subjects has been quite marked. Ward and Doerr (1986), for example, have suggested that the tonic skin conductance level could actually be considered as a potentially useful diagnostic screening test for depression. They were able to identify cutoff scores that discriminated depressed patients from normal controls with a sensitivity and specificity of about 90%. For phasic response measures, Berstein et al. (1988) found that 78% of their sample of depressed patients showed a complete failure to produce an orienting response to the initial tone presentations in a habituation series, compared with 15% of control subjects. Iacono et al. (1983) reported nonresponse rates of 58% and 54% among patients with histories of unipolar and bipolar depression, respectively, but only 24% in control subjects. Furthermore, low EDA has characterized depressed patients in these studies, even when attempts have been made to raise it by using respiratory maneuvers (Iacono et al., 1983; Storrie et al., 1981), loud noises (Iacono et al., 1984), or task instructions that require the subjects to respond in some way to the stimulus presentations (Bernstein et al., 1988; Dawson et al., 1985).

2. Clinical Correlates of Low Electrodermal Activity in Depression

Despite that most recent studies have found that a pattern of low EDA is associated with depression, that is not always true. Toone and associates (1981) failed to find any EDA differences between a group of 11 depressed patients and 22 control subjects, although they speculated that their patients may have been less severely depressed than patients in other reports.

Furthermore, several studies have found that low EDA is characteristic of only certain subtypes of depressed patients. The distinction between unipolar and bipolar depression does not appear to be a major distinguishing factor in this context (Iacono et al., 1983; Williams et al., 1985), although certain clinical features of the depressive syndrome have been related to low EDA by several investigators. Lader and Wing (1969) provided the most striking evidence of this in a study of depressed patients who could be classified as "agitated" or "retarded." Compared with control subjects, agitated patients had *higher* tonic skin conductance levels, *more* nonspecific fluctuations, and *more* frequent orienting responses to tones, whereas only the retarded patients showed the pattern of lower EDA on all measures. However, subsequent research has shown more mixed results at least for the status of agitated patients. For example, Dawson et al. (1985) and Lapierre and Butter (1980) both found that depressed patients have lower skin conductance levels than control subjects, regardless of their presentation as agitated or retarded. Nevertheless, other investigators have confirmed that, within samples of depressed patients as a whole, those with the most pronounced degrees of retardation tend to have the lowest levels of EDA (Bernstein et al., 1988; Noble and Lader, 1971; Thorell et al., 1987a; Williams et al., 1985).

These findings have led to some speculation that perhaps low EDA may be a psychophysiological correlate of the "endogenous" subtype of depression. Unfortunately, the conclusions here appear to depend on the definition of the endogenous syndrome that one employs. Not all systems identify the same patients (Zimmerman et al., 1986), and some may be more related to EDA than others. For example, patients identified as having "psychotic" endogenous depressions have been reported to have fewer nonspecific fluctuations and small orienting responses than normal control subjects, whereas those with "neurotic" depressions were found to show the opposite pattern of increased activity (Byrne, 1975). Comparisons of endogenous and nonendogenous depressed patients defined by the Newcastle criteria (Carney et al., 1965) have usually found that endogenous depressives have lower EDA (Mirkin and Coppen, 1980; Noble and Lader, 1972; Thorell et al., 1987a). However, endogenous subtyping with the Research Diagnostic Criteria (Spitzer et al., 1977) or the melancholia criteria of the *DSM-III* (American Psychiatric Association, 1980) have yielded few significant results (Thorell et al., 1987a; Ward and Doerr, 1986; Williams et al., 1985). Hence, it appears that some of the clinical characteristics of endogenous depression (e.g., psychomotor retardation) may be related to EDA, whereas others (e.g., early-morning awakening, diurnal variation; Thorell et al., 1987a) are probably not.

Recently, an association has been drawn between EDA and the specific clinical symptom of suicidal behavior. Thorell (1987) divided his sample of 59 patients into subgroups of 25 suicidal (those with prominent suicidal ideation or a history of suicide attempts, most of which involved nonviolent methods such as overdoses or superficial slashing), and 34 nonsuicidal subjects, and found that the suicidal group displayed fewer nonspecific fluctuations, smaller initial orienting response magnitudes, and more rapid habituation. However, these findings were not replicated in subsequent research (Keller et al., 1991). Rather, Keller et al. (1991) found that only patients who had made *violent* suicide attempts showed low EDA, compared with nonsuicidal patients, and then only the speed of habituation showed the effect. Edman et al. (1986) also found that violent suicide attempters showed faster habituation than patients who had made nonviolent suicide attempts. Thus, there have been discrepancies across studies, particularly for the ED status of patients who have made nonviolent attempts. There has been somewhat greater consistency in classifying patients who have used violent methods as "fast habituators." Importantly, this finding also seems to extend to patients who eventually go on to complete suicide in the future. When the reports of Edman et al. (1986) and Keller et al. (1991) are considered together, a total of nine patients who had participated in studies of EDA did kill themselves at later points in time. Eight of the nine had been classified as fast habituators at the time of their initial ED testing.

3. Electrodermal Activity and the Clinical Course of Depression

Given that within the general population, EDA reflects a relatively stable psychophysiological characteristic, with a significant degree of genetic determination, there has been some speculation that low EDA may represent a potential trait marker for clinical mood disorders (Iacono, 1985). One necessary condition that such a trait marker must satisfy is that it should be observable, regardless of the patient's current clinical status. Three studies have, in fact, examined EDA in depressed patients immediately before and after treatments with electroconvulsive therapy (Dawson et al., 1985; Noble and Lader, 1971a) or antidepressant medication (Storrie et al., 1981). In each case, the treatments were associated with clear clinical improvement, but no increase in ED measures. As noted by Storrie et al. (1981), the tonic skin conductance level and phasic responses to respiratory maneuvers remained lower for patients than for control subjects, even after treatment.

This line of research has been pursued further by Iacono and his colleagues (Iacono et al., 1983, 1984). They studied both unipolar and bipolar patients who had histories of recurrent depressions, but who were in clinical remission at the time of testing. Compared with control subjects, both clinical groups had lower skin conductance levels, smaller orienting responses to tones, and higher proportions of electrodermally unresponsive subjects. In addition, the ED measures showed generally stable retest reliability 1 year later (Iacono et al., 1984).

This work clearly suggests that low EDA is separable from a patient's current clinical status, but the validity of these measures as genetic or trait markers for depression remains questionable owing to the results of two recent studies. First, Thorell and d'Elia (1988) have reported long-term follow-up data (median = 2 years) for patients who were tested both when depressed and when in remission. Their results show unequivocal increases in tonic conductance levels, nonspecific fluctuations, and orienting response magnitudes and habituation rates, which became comparable with those of control subjects for all but the most unresponsive individuals. Second, Zahn et al. (1989) have employed a "high-risk" method, studying the children of patients with bipolar disorder. Presumably, these children should be at increased genetic risk for depression, but they did not show reduced levels of EDA. In fact, these subjects had *increased* numbers of nonspecific fluctuations during a mild stress task.

In summary, then, there is little firm evidence that reduced levels of EDA are characteristic of an increased genetic risk for mood disorders. Nevertheless, it does occur in substantial numbers of depressed patients. Low EDA does not seem to vary with the individual's clinical status of remission and relapse, at least over the short term. Rather, it may remain as a residual effect of a depressive episode, which eventually normalizes in some patients over periods of months or years.

4. The Psychophysiological Basis of Low Electrodermal Activity in Depression

As a final comment, it is worthwhile to review current thinking on the nature of the biological mechanism by which EDA is reduced in depressed patients. Although many studies have included patients who were in treatment with antidepressant medications (some of which have prominent anticholinergic effects) at the time of testing, comparisons of medicated and unmedicated patients have uniformly found that similar patterns hold, regardless of medication status (Bernstein et al., 1988; Storrie et al., 1981; Thorell et al., 1987b; Ward and Doerr, 1986; Williams et al., 1985). Hence, we can be relatively certain that low EDA is not a side effect of pharmacotherapy.

Referring back to Table 1, it is also apparent that reduced EDA occurs with both tonic conductance levels and with phasic orienting responses to discrete stimuli, as well as with responses to purely physiological manipulations, such as respiratory maneuvers. Hence, it represents a relatively global deficit in those patients for whom it occurs. This has prompted some investigators to conclude that low EDA in depression is primarily a biological phenomenon, rather than a psychological one, related to, for example, a failure to attend or orient to environmental events (Bernstein et al., 1988; Iacono et al., 1984). This is an important conclusion, because it suggests that ED nonresponding in depressed patients may be fundamentally different than in other patient groups with whom nonresponding has been documented. In fact, Bernstein et al. (1988) have presented interesting data that this is indeed true. These investigators found that schizophrenic patients also showed high rates of electrodermal nonresponding in an orienting paradigm, but with important qualitative differences from that of depressed patients. Specifically, unresponse schizophrenic patients could be induced to show substantially increased ED activity by enhancing the signal value of the eliciting stimuli. The depressed subjects, however, continued to show low EDA, even under these conditions.

Such dissociation suggests that low EDA in depression does not reflect a deficit in the cognitive or information-processing substrate of ED responding (e.g., a failure to orient). Rather, Bernstein et al. (1988) propose that those depressed patients with low EDA may be exhibiting a psychophysiological manifestation of reduced cholinergic activity. This conclusion is somewhat paradoxical; most evidence for a cholinergic involvement in depression indicates supersensitivity of cholinergic mechanisms, rather than reduced activity (Dilsaver, 1986; Janowsky and Risch, 1986). Although it could be possible for reduced cholinergic activity to lead to a compensatory supersensitivity of the receptors, attempts to reconcile this paradox will represent an important direction for ED research in the future. Studies that combine ED assessment with other paradigms that presumably reflect cholinergically mediated behavior (e.g., reduced REM sleep latencies, response to cholinergic agonists) should help to clarify further the underlying biological mechanism contributing to low EDA in depression.

B. Electrodermal Activity in Anxiety Disorders

Studies of peripheral psychophysiological measures have a particular relevance for the anxiety disorders, in part because many of the clinical symptoms of anxiety pertain directly to uncomfortable bodily sensations. The importance of these symptoms are reflected in our current diagnostic nosologies. For example, in the *DSM III-R* (American Psychiatric Association, 1987), diagnostic criteria for generalized anxiety disorder include symptom clusters of motor tension and autonomic hyperactivity; posttraumatic stress disorder involves persistent symptoms of increased arousal; and panic disorder is characterized by the sudden and unexpected occurrence of a range of bodily symptoms, including heart palpitations, sweating, trembling, and dizziness. Hence, implicit in the study of peripheral measures in patients with anxiety disorders is the effort to determine the mechanisms that contribute directly to the development of these physical symptoms. In its strongest form, this line of research speculates that the prominence and persistence of such symptoms can be attributed to an underlying biological disorder that leads to dysfunctional regulation of the autonomic nervous system. For some investigators, EDA has provided a key index within this perspective.

1. Comparisons of Patients and Normal Controls

Conditions of chronic anxiety have been characterized as disorders of "overarousal," at least since the writing of Malmo and his colleagues in the 1950s (Malmo, 1957). Controlled studies of EDA in clinically anxious patients have been available for almost as long. Unfortunately, the early research in this area was not conducted with the same diagnostic standards as those currently employed; consequently the diagnostic categories do not correspond precisely to those that are used today. In particular, the diagnosis of "anxiety states" comprises subgroups of patients who would likely receive diagnoses of panic disorders or generalized anxiety disorder based on the *DSM-III-R*.

Table 2 summarizes the results of 15 studies of EDA that have compared groups of clinically anxious patients with normal control subjects. As is evident from an inspection of Table 2, a few generalizations emerge. First, the occurrence of frequent nonspecific fluctuations through the course of an experimental session appears to be the most robust ED parameter differentiating anxious patients from controls, and was found in 10 of 14 studies that reported this measure. Second, tonic skin conductance levels have also been higher in the patients in several investigations, although the available data are by no means consistent.

Table 2 Electrodermal Activity in Patients with Anxiety Disorders and Control Subjects

Study	No. of patients	Stimuli	No. of controls	SCL	NSFs	Response to stimuli
Bond et al. (1974)	30 anxiety states	30	Psychological stress task	P>C	NS	P<C in SCL increment under stress
Chattopadhyay et al. (1980)	12 anxiety states	12 "low-threat" +	Light flashes	NS	P>C	NS
		12 "high-threat"		NS	P>C	NS
Goldstein (1964)	21 clinically anxious women	21	Sustained white noise	NS		
Hart (1974)	18 anxiety neurosis or anxiety states	18	50-, 75-, 100-, dB tones (intermixed)	NS	P>C	NS
Hoehn-Saric et al. (1989)	20 women with GAD	20	Cognitive stress task	P<C under stress	P<C under stress	
Hoehn-Saric et al. (1991)	18 panic disorder	18	Cognitive stress task	NS	NS	
Horvath and Meares (1979)	10 anxiety states	15	100-dB tone	P>C	P>C	P>C
Lader (1967)	18 anxiety with depression	75	100-dB tones		P>C	P>C
	16 anxiety states				P>C	P>C
	19 agoraphobia				P>C	P>C
	18 social phobia				P>C	P>C
	19 simple phobia				NS	NS
Lader and Wing (1964)	20 anxiety states	20	100dB tones	P>C	P>C	P>C
Orr and Pitman (1987)	20 GAD (some patients also met *DSM-III* criteria for other anxiety disorders)	20	86-dB tone	—	P>C	NS
Raskin (1975)	30 "chronically anxious"	30	100-dB tones	P>C	P>C	P>C
Roth et al. (1990)	17 PD	14	100-dB tone	P>C	P>C	P>C
	21 PD (*DSM-III*)	15	75-dB tone			NS
Roth et al. (1986)	37 PD (*DSM-III*)	19	75-dB tones	P>C	P>C	P>C
Wing (1964)	20 anxiety states	20	Psychological stress task	NS	NS	P>C in time to recover from stress

P, patients; C, controls; PD, panic disorder; GAD, generalized anxiety disorder; SCL, skin conductance level; NSFs, nonspecific fluctuations; NS, nonsignificant.

Third, although there is clearly a paucity of research that has directly compared patients with different anxiety disorders, the finding of elevated rates of nonspecific fluctuations has characterized most studies of anxious patients, regardless of their specific diagnoses. One important exception, here, has been the group of simple phobics studied by Lader (1967), who were comparable with control subjects in all measures of EDA.

Fourth, the data for phasic ED response and habituation measures have also been mixed. Habituation is a particularly important construct in the psychophysiology of anxiety, because it occupies a central place in the biological model of panic attacks that has been proposed by Lader and Mathews (1968). According to this model, habituation is viewed as an index of central inhibitory control over autonomic arousal responses. If habituation is deficient in patients with panic attacks, there will be no "dampening down" of arousal responses that might occur commonly through the course of normal interactions with the environment. In this event, there would be a cumulative upward spiraling of autonomic activation, which at an extreme could be experienced as panic.

In fact, not all habituation studies of EDA have found support for this hypothesis. The most relevant work has been conducted by Roth and his colleagues (Roth et al., 1986, 1990), who investigated habituation in patients diagnosed with agoraphobia or panic disorder according to *DSM-III* criteria. In their first study, Roth et al. (1986) found equivocal evidence for a specific slowing of habituation in response to 75-dB tones. Although the patients had more responses overall, they did not differ from control subjects in various measures of response magnitude and decrement over trials. In their later work, Roth et al. (1990) examined habituation to two tone intensities—75 dB and 100 dB—and found that patients habituated more slowly than controls only under the high-intensity condition. Hence, it appears that habituation differences are more pronounced with particularly intense stimuli (Öhman, 1981), which helps explain some of the discrepancies across studies that are evident in Table 2. In other contexts, stimuli of very high intensity are sometimes thought to evoke "defense reflexes," rather than orienting responses (Sokolov, 1963), with the former being more resistant to habituation. Thus, it may be that anxious patients have a lower threshold for this type of response (Hart, 1974).

Finally, two recent studies by Hoehn-Saric and associates (1989, 1991) are also worthy of note, in part because their findings go against the general trend of most of the EDA research with anxious patients. These investigators have conducted psychophysiological studies of patients with generalized anxiety disorder (Hoehn-Saric et al., 1989) and panic disorder (Hoehn-Saric et al., 1991) that involved participation in psychological stress tasks. In both studies, there were no resting baseline differences between patients and control subjects in either tonic skin conductance levels or nonspecific fluctuations. Under stress, however, the patients with generalized anxiety disorder actually showed *smaller* elevations in these measures than did controls (Hoehn-Saric et al., 1989), whereas panic disorder patients showed levels of stress-induced reactivity comparable with control subjects (Hoehn-Saric et al., 1991). Nevertheless, in both studies, Hoehn-Saric and associates noted an apparent reduction in the variability of skin conductance activation under stress, in the sense that, compared with their respective control groups, both patient groups showed a lower range of skin conductance levels through the course of the experimental protocol.

Hoehn-Saric et al. (1989, 1991) interpret these findings as a reflection of diminished flexibility of autonomic response, which may or may not occur within a context of globally elevated activation levels. Although their results, particularly for nonspecific fluctuations, stand out to some extent from other studies of EDA in anxious patients, they do attest to the limits to which conclusions of elevated EDA in anxiety disorders can be generalized.

In summary, then, the weight of evidence indicates that patients with chronic anxiety conditions (other than simple phobias) often show elevations in one or more measures of EDA. However, this is certainly not so for every patient, nor has it been found in every study. For some EDA parameters, such as habituation indexes, it is still unclear whether patient–control differences are best viewed as a main effect of anxiety per se, or a more complex interaction of patient characteristics with specific features of the experimental protocol and stimulation procedures.

2. *Clinical Correlates of Electrodermal Activity in the Anxiety Disorders*

Relatively little is known about the clinical correlates of elevated EDA in patients with anxiety disorders. Lader (1967) reported data from a mixed group of 71 patients with anxiety states, agoraphobia, social phobias, and combined anxiety and depression. He found that patients who had many nonspecific fluctuations and slowly habituating ED responses tended to suffer from more frequent panic attacks, more severe generalized anxiety, and more overt anxiety during the testing session itself. However, the overall magnitude of these correlations was modest (0.27–0.58). Furthermore, Roth et al. (1988, 1990) failed to find any significant correlations between ED measures and clinical variables in two groups of patients with panic attacks.

Lader's (1967) study is also noteworthy because it included a separate group of patients who were clearly considered to suffer concurrently from anxiety and depressive disorders. In clinical practice, comorbidity among these syndromes is quite common. For example, 30–60% of patients with a primary anxiety disorder will meet diagnostic criteria for dysthymia or a major depressive episode at some point in their lives (Sanderson et al., 1990; Stein and Uhde, 1988, 1991). Yet, from a psychophysiological perspective, the patterns of EDA that are most characteristic of these syndromes are the *opposites* of one another: low in depression; high in anxiety. In Lader's (1967) mixed group, EDA was comparable with that of patients with other anxiety disorders. Hence, although the research base is small, comorbidity between anxiety and depressive disorders may show a greater resemblance in ED measures to anxiety without depression, rather than vice versa.

3. *Electrodermal Activity and the Clinical Course of Agoraphobia*

As with low EDA in depression, the common observation of elevations in some aspects of EDA in patients with anxiety disorders encourages the speculation that these measures may offer a potential biological risk marker for susceptibility to anxiety or panic. However, this hypothesis seems untenable in light of findings by Roth et al. (1988). These investigators have reported short-term follow-up data for a group of 23 agoraphobic patients whom they had also examined before treatment (Roth at al., 1986). At pretreatment, the patients had higher resting skin conductance levels than control subjects and more frequent nonspecific fluctuations. These measures tended to normalize with treatment and, for some conditions, they reached levels comparable with those of controls.

4. *The Psychophysiological Basis of Elevated Electrodermal Activity in Anxiety*

The traditional view of ED measures in the anxiety disorders has been that they reflect a heightened level of sympathetic nervous system activation (Lader, 1967). However, as Roth et al. (1986, 1990) point out, it does not follow that the results of laboratory investigations necessarily imply that patients are chronically hyperaroused in other contexts. For people with prominent panic-related anticipatory anxiety, the unusual and confining circumstances of the psychophysiology laboratory may itself be anxiety-provoking, and thus promote increased sympathetic activity in a state-related, rather than trait-related, way. As yet, there are apparently no studies of ambulatory monitoring of EDA among patients in their natural environments.

It is also possible that cognitive factors contribute to increased EDA in some patients. As noted earlier, the occurrence of nonspecific fluctuations in normal subjects tends to be associated with covert mental activity—"arousing thoughts" (Nikula, 1991). If patients are experiencing frequent anxiety-related cognitions in the laboratory, this might be expected to increase their rates of nonspecific fluctuations. The same may be true of findings of slow habituation. Raskin (1975) conducted postexperimental interviews with anxious patients participating in her habituation study, and found that those who were most electrodermally responsive were more likely to attribute special significance to the tone presentations (e.g., that the stimuli might be harmful in some way). Thus, patient–control differences in EDA may not be entirely due to differences in biology alone.

Regardless of mechanisms, however, the data on EDA in anxiety is of considerable interest when viewed in conjunction with comparable work that has been conducted in the study of depression. Both bodies of literature are relatively large and, despite a lack of complete consistency, there are several broad trends that are evident in both areas. These trends are quite different for the two groups of disorders, suggesting that for EDA, more so than for most psychophysiological measures, the story that emerges is truly a "tale of two syndromes" (Stein and Uhde, 1988)

III. CARDIOVASCULAR ACTIVITY

The regulation of cardiovascular activity involves a complex interaction of several mechanisms, so that a global finding of differences in cardiovascular function between a group of psychiatric patients and a control group really provides only a starting point in the effort to identify a biological substrate to the disorder. The most commonly assessed component of cardiovascular activity in studies of depression and anxiety has been heart rate, which is influenced by several factors, both intrinsic and extrinsic (Siddle and Turpin, 1980). *Intrinsic* factors refer to autoregulatory mechanisms within the heart and vasculature themselves, whereas *extrinsic* influences integrate changes in cardiovascular performance with changes in the metabolic demands of the tissues. The most important of these extrinsic factors is the neural input to the heart.

The heart is innervated by both the sympathetic and parasympathetic divisions of the autonomic nervous system. In general, these branches tend to perform antagonistically to one another. The sympathetic input increases the heart rate and the force of myocardial contractions, primarily as a result of noradrenergic stimulation of ß-adrenergic receptors. Parasympathetic (vagal) activity, on the other hand, produces the reverse pattern of reduced heart rate and myocardial contractility by cholinergic effects on cardiac muscarinic receptors (Larsen et al., 1986).

In addition to these neural factors, there are also humoral influences of circulating catecholamines that act as cardiac stimulants to increase the rate and force of the heart's action. Furthermore, other peripheral mechanisms, such as the level of activity of arterial baroreceptors and chemoreceptors, introduce feedback loops into the cardiovascular control system that result in reflexive heart rate changes in response to alterations in blood pressure and chemical composition. In this complex system, the biological significance of findings of differential heart rates in patients with depressive or anxiety disorders can remain obscure, even if reliable.

Besides heart rate, other cardiovascular measures have been reported occasionally in studies of psychiatric populations. In depression and anxiety disorders, blood pressure and forearm blood flow, in particular, have been the subjects of some investigation. Although blood pressure is a familiar measure because of its routine clinical use, its physiological basis is actually complexly determined by a combination of cardiac output and peripheral resistance—both of which can be influenced by neural and humoral (including hormonal) factors (Larsen et al., 1986). Forearm blood flow is also related to peripheral resistance, and represents the amount of blood that can be "trapped" in the forearm by an occluding cuff. A major determinant of this will be the state of relative vasodilation or vasoconstriction of the arteries subserving blood flow to the muscles. This state is also complexity determined. For example, even predominantly sympathetic effects can result in vasoconstriction owing to the stimulation of α-adrenergic receptors by norepinephrine, or to vasodilation owing to the stimulation of $ß_2$-receptors by epinephrine (Larsen et al., 1986). Cholinergic transmission also affects the tone of the blood vessels supplying the skeletal muscles in the direction of vasodilation.

Of course, the overall purpose of the cardiovascular system is not to provide a vehicle for studying emotional states, but rather, to provide the body with an appropriate supply of nutrient-rich oxygenated blood. This functional distinction is worth remembering when considering cardiovascular studies of psychiatric patients. As we shall see, heart rate and other cardiovascular measures have, indeed, been found in many investigations to differ between such patients and control subjects, but at least nine conceptually distinct issues are relevant to the interpretation of these findings. These include differences in (1) fitness levels and the efficiency of the heart as a pump; (2) motor activity levels (resulting in a greater metabolic demand by the musculature); (3) perceived stress, which may produce an exaggerated cardiac response that is disproportionate to metabolic demand (Langer et al., 1985); (4) the levels of circulating catecholamines; (5) the density and sensitivity of transmitter receptor sites, which can change over time as a function of the concentration and length of exposure to receptor agonists; (6) sympathetic neural regulation; (7) parasympathetic neural regulation; (8) the presence of extraneous variables that affect the function of the cardiovascular system (e.g., smoking, caffeine, medications, or other), and; (9) subject characteristics that may be associated with differential cardiovascular performance (e.g., age and sex). No studies of either depressed or anxious patients have attempted to evaluate or control for all of these factors, so the available data are necessarily incomplete. Nevertheless, they are instructive and, particularly in the case of the anxiety disorders, they have generated a great deal of recent interest.

A. Cardiovascular Activity in Depression

The literature pertaining to cardiovascular psychophysiology in depression in relatively small. Much of the relevant data comes from the same studies discussed earlier for EDA in investigations that included multiple measures. In addition, there is a body of work that has recorded the response of the cardiovascular system to various biochemical provocations. Although it is beyond the scope of the present review to address the results of these challenge studies, their findings for tonic baseline levels of heart rate and blood pressure are relevant to this discussion.

1. Comparisons of Depressed Patients and Controls

Despite an early report by Goldstein (1965) that depressed patients had increased systolic blood pressures at rest, recent research has typically shown that both supine and standing blood pressure levels are comparable with those of normal control subjects (Charney et al., 1982; Esler et al., 1982; Lake et al., 1982; Roy et al., 1985; Rudhorfer et al., 1985; Siever et al., 1984; Veith et al., 1983). This has been true even of those studies in which plasma norepinephrine was elevated in the patients (Esler et al., 1982; Lake et al., 1982; Roy et al., 1985).

Heart rate, on the other hand, has sometimes told a different story, because several studies have found the resting tonic heart rates of depressed patients to be significantly higher than those of control subjects (Abramson et al., 1989; Dawson et al., 1985; Iacono et al., 1983; Kelly and Walter, 1969; Lader and Wing, 1969; Lahmeyer and Bellur, 1987; Lake et al., 1982; Siever et al., 1984). However, the importance of this finding is tempered by several factors. For example, some of these studies have included patients who were currently in treatment with tricyclic antidepressants, which are known to elevate heart rate (Dawson et al., 1977; Iacono et al., 1983). Furthermore, several other investigators have failed to find any heart rate differences between depressed patients and control subjects, indicating that the results are not very robust (Byrne, 1975; Esler et al., 1982; Rudhorfer et al., 1985; Veith et al., 1983). Finally, even several of those studies that have found elevated heart rates have noted that this is characteristic of only *some* depressed patients.

2. Clinical Correlates of Cardiovascular Activity in Depression

In general, the subgroup of depressed patients who have most often been found to have elevated heart rates is the same subgroup who have been found to have elevated EDA—those with symptoms of agitation or comorbid anxiety disorders (Abramson et al., 1989; Kelly and Walter, 1969; Lader and Wing, 1969). Patients with primarily retarded clinical presentations (Lader and Wing, 1969), or with depression uncomplicated by a concurrent panic disorder (Abramson et al., 1989), have usually been found to have tonic heart rates that are comparable with those of control subjects. The one exception is the group of nonagitated depressed patients studied by Kelly and Walter (1969). These patients had higher resting heart rates than controls, but similar levels of forearm blood flow. However, both measures were still significantly lower than those of patients with psychomotor agitation. Nevertheless, there was also evidence from this study that depressed patients, as a whole, may show low reactivity in some cardiovascular measures under conditions of modest laboratory stress. Specifically, the challenge of performing mental arithmetic under conditions of harassment provoked smaller elevations in forearm blood flow among both agitated and nonagitated depressed patients.

Other investigators have examined the association of clinical variables with measures of cardiovascular performance using correlational designs. Noble and Lader (1971b) and Bruno et al. (1983) have each reported studies in which various parameters of cardiovascular activity were correlated with Hamilton Scale (1960) scores within groups of depressed patients. Noble and Lader (1971b) found that the clinical symptoms of loss of interest and retardation were associated with low forearm blood flow and reactivity. In this report, heart rate itself showed no significant correlations with any individual symptoms, including clinician ratings of anxiety and agitation. Bruno et al. (1983) reported a more complex study, in which the effects of anxiety and psychomotor retardation were partialed out statistically before entering total Hamilton scores into a series of correlations involving forearm blood flow and cardiac preejection period. This latter measure is derived from systolic time intervals in the electrocardiograph (ECG), and it is sometimes employed as a noninvasive index of myocardial contractility. In a sample of unipolar patients, the overall severity of depression correlated negatively with the tonic baseline level of forearm blood flow, and positively with the cardiac preejection period.

3. *Psychophysiological Mechanisms of Cardiovascular Changes in Depression*

Bruno et al. (1983) argued that their measure of forearm blood flow was most likely to reflect sympathetic cholinergic influences on the vasculature, whereas preejection period is more likely to be influenced by ß-adrenergic activity. Hence, they suggested that the autonomic correlates of the severity of depression include decreases in central sympathetic cholinergic outflow (and possibly increases in α-adrenergic activity as well), combined with decreases in cardiac ß-adrenergic effects. However, such conclusions can be offered only tentatively. In other studies, significant cardiovascular findings have been accompanied by a range of concurrently monitored physiological effects, including high plasma norepinephrine levels (Lake et al., 1982), a reduced heart rate response to clonidine (Siever et al., 1984), and a smaller cardioacceleratory response to movements during sleep (Lahmeyer and Bellur, 1987). The former results have been interpreted as reflecting a possible deficit in central noradrenergic inhibitory mechanisms, resulting in increased sympathetic output (Siever et al., 1984). The sleep findings, on the other hand, have been taken as evidence of a cholinergic contribution to heart rate elevations in depression—vagal withdrawal (Lahmeyer and Bellur, 1987). Thus, there may be several distinct mechanisms, both adrenergic and cholinergic, that contribute to the differences in cardiovascular function that have sometimes been observed between depressed patients and control subjects. Unfortunately, however, the relevant findings reflect a relatively isolated series of individual reports, and many other studies have simply found no significant difference between depressed patients and controls in any aspect of cardiovascular activity. This lack of consistency across studies, combined with the complexity of the control mechanisms that regulate the cardiovascular system, make it difficult to arrive as yet at any definitive conclusions about depression based on the available evidence from cardiovascular psychophysiology.

B. Cardiovascular Activity in Anxiety

Interest in the regulation of the cardiovascular system in patients with anxiety disorders has increased greatly over the last decade, spurred by the development of sophisticated new technologies for investigating cardiovascular response to biochemical and pharmacological provocations, as well as by advances in ambulatory monitoring techniques that have taken psychophysiological assessment beyond the confines of the laboratory. However, a unique association between the experience of anxiety and the action of the heart has been drawn throughout history. In the medical literature of the 19th and early 20th centuries, diagnostic terms such as "irritable heart syndrome," "neurocirculatory asthenia," and "soldier's heart" emphasized the importance of the link between cardiovascular symptoms and anxiety, if not an outright identification between them (Skerritt, 1983).

In the modern psychophysiological literature, a renewed interest in this link emerged from a report by Lader and Mathews (1970), who presented data from a small series of patients who happened to experience spontaneous panic attacks while taking part in psychophysiological studies. Among the dramatic physiological changes associated with these attacks were rapid, large-magnitude increases in heart rate. These observations provided a new perspective on the psychophysiology of panic, as well as on the phenomenology of the patient's experience. Sensations of palpitations and a racing heart are among the most common symptoms reported by people with panic disorder, and the cognitive interpretation that one is having a heart attack or other acute medical crisis is the most frequent conclusion at which they arrive to explain the initial occurrence of these symptoms (Breier et al., 1986). Not surprisingly, then, the literature relevant to cardiovascular psychophysiology in anxiety is a rich and rapidly expanding one.

1. Comparisons of Patients and Controls

Resting Measures. Even before Lader and Mathews (1970) reported their observations of spontaneous panic, several investigators had undertaken studies of the cardiovascular system in groups of anxious psychiatric patients. In the 1930s, White and Gildea (1937) reported that anxious patients had higher heart rates than control subjects, both at rest and during the performance of a cold pressor test. In the 1940s, it was reported that patients with "anxiety neurosis" also differed from controls in their response to physical exercise, reaching higher heart rates and levels of blood lactate during the performance of standard exercise tests (Cohen et al., 1947). By the mid-1970s, many reports of carefully conducted psychophysiology experiments involving large groups of patients had appeared in the literature. For the most part, their findings tended to confirm that an important component of the physiological profile of the "anxiety states" was an elevated tonic heart rate (Bond et al., 1974; Kelly and Walter, 1968, 1969; Wing, 1964), often accompanied by a markedly increased level of forearm blood flow (Kelly et al., 1971; Kelly and Walter, 1968, 1969). Even at this time, the findings were not always unanimous (Goldstein, 1965; Hart, 1974), although they were consistent enough to suggest that patients with chronic anxiety conditions are characterized by a "persistent arousal of the defense reaction" (Kelly and Walter, 1968), regardless of whether they were placed in an overtly anxiety-producing situation (Barlow, 1988).

In the years following the publication of the *DSM-III*, however, findings have been more variable concerning whether patients with anxiety disorders (most commonly, panic disorder and agoraphobia) have shown elevations in cardiovascular measures at rest. About half of the relevant laboratory studies through the 1980s and early 1990s have found that patients with panic disorder or agoraphobia, with panic attacks, had higher tonic resting heart rates than control subjects (Aronson et al., 1989; Castellani et al., 1988; Ehlers et al., 1986; Freedman et al., 1984; Hoehn-Saric et al., 1991; Holden and Barlow, 1986; Liebowitz et al., 1985; Michelson and Mavissakalian, 1985; Nesse et al., 1984; Nutt, 1989; Roth at al., 1986; Uhde et al., 1989; Yeragani et al., 1989, 1990a), whereas the remainder—which includes many reports from the same laboratories—have not (Cameron et al., 1990; Charney et al., 1984, 1987; Cowley et al., 1987; Gaffney et al., 1988; Stein and Uhde, 1991; Villacres et al., 1987; Weissman et al., 1987; Woods et al., 1987, 1988; Yeragani et al., 1990b). Blood pressure has also been measured in many of these studies, and despite occasional findings that patients have had elevated systolic (Cowley et al., 1987; Hoehn-Saric, 1991; Uhde et al., 1989; Woods et al., 1987; Yeragani et al., 1987b, 1989) or diastolic blood pressures (Cowley et al., 1987; Liebowitz et al., 1985; Uhde et al., 1989; Yeragani et al., 1987c, 1989), 1990b) most reports have found that patients and control subjects have been comparable on these measures. Interestingly, forearm blood flow, which provided some of the clearest differentiation between patients and controls in Kelly's research (Kelly et al., 1971; Kelly and Walter, 1968, 1969) has largely been abandoned as a variable of interest in more recent studies (although it would be expected to correlate with measures of heart rate and blood pressure).

Ambulatory monitoring has provided another perspective on tonic cardiovascular function in patients with panic attacks. In studies of this type, the background heart rates of these patients as they go through the daily routines of their lives has uniformly been comparable with those of control subjects (Cameron et al., 1987; Freedman et al., 1985; Pauli et al., 1991; Taylor et al., 1987). Thus, it no longer seems tenable to consider people with panic disorder to be in a state of "chronically" high cardiovascular activation, although in some circumstances—including many laboratory settings—they do exhibit elevated baseline heart rates and blood pressures.

Patients with panic disorder or agoraphobia also seem more likely to show these baseline elevations than patients with other types of anxiety disorders. In a direct comparison of panic patients with those suffering from generalized anxiety disorder, Rapee (1986) found the panic patients to have higher baseline heart rates. Moreover, Öst (1987) has provided comparative data on a large series of agoraphobics, social phobics, claustrophobics, dental phobics, blood phobics, and animal phobics. He reported that the group with agoraphobia had heart rates in the laboratory that were significantly higher than those of patients in all other groups.

Response to Tasks. Given this apparent propensity to show increased cardiovascular activity in some situations, and particularly during panic attacks themselves, several investigators have attempted to identify the autonomic mechanisms that may contribute to such effects by examining cardiovascular responses to various challenges. Some of these have been primarily physical in nature. For example, Gaffney et al. (1988) and Taylor et al. (1987) compared patients with panic disorder with normal control subjects on the cardiovascular response to physical exercise. Their findings largely confirmed those that had been reported for anxiety neurosis in the 1940s, in the sense that the patients had either greater heart rate responses to a standard level of exercise (Taylor et al., 1987), or achieved maximal heart rates at lower workloads (Gaffney et al., 1988). However, Gaffney et al. (1988) have argued that this, in itself, may not reflect an inherent dysfunction in autonomic regulation, but rather, may be related to lower fitness levels among the patients.

Other studies have examined the cardiovascular response to orthostatic challenges, such as changes in posture from supine to standing, which elicit reflexive, autonomically mediated alterations in heart rate and blood pressure. The results of these studies have usually found larger responses to sustained quiet standing among symptomatic patients with panic disorder in either heart rate (Taylor et al., 1987; Stein and Uhde, 1992) or the product of heart rate and mean blood pressure (an index of cardiac load; Weissman et al., 1987; Yeragani et al., 1990b). Weissman et al. (1987) considered that their findings suggested an exaggerated sympathetic response to changes in posture, although they were unable to identify whether the mechanisms mediating that response might be a transient increase in central output, a generalized elevation of adrenergic tone, or an increase in peripheral responsiveness.

Yeragani et al. (1990a), on the other hand, have recently found that the heart rate response to standing did *not* differ between a group of patients with panic disorder and a group of normal controls. Nevertheless, they did find that the patients had decreased variability in R-R intervals, which was particularly pronounced when standing. Because heart rate variability measures of this type are thought to reflect parasympathetic influences on the heart, these investigators suggested that vagal withdrawal may represent another factor contributing to exaggerated orthostatic responses in patients with panic disorder. Interestingly, these same investigators (Yeragani et al., 1991) recently added a comparison group of depressed patients, and found that they had normal indexes of cardiac vagal function. This latter study suggests that abnormalities in cardiac vagal tone (if that is indeed what is being measured) may be unique to that disorder.

Most recently, we (Stein et al., 1992) found exaggerated heart rate responses to standing in 20 patients with panic disorder, compared with 20 age- and sex-matched normal controls. We were unable to find any differences in plasma norepinephrine responses between the two diagnostic groups, again raising the possibility that abnormalities in vagal tone in the patients with panic disorder might account for the findings.

A second group of laboratory investigations has examined the pattern of physiological response to conditions of psychological stress. Cardiovascular reactions to psychological stress have been studied extensively among normal subjects in recent years, and the physiological mechanisms underlying stress-induced increases in heart rate and blood pressure are relatively well known, at least at the peripheral level. They tend to reflect a prominent ß-adrenergic stimulation of the myocardium, with an additional contribution of vagal withdrawal (Grossmand and Svebak, 1987; Langer et al., 1985; Obrist, 1981).

Surprisingly, however, relatively few recent studies have examined the cardiovascular response to psychological stress among anxious patients identified according to modern diagnostic criteria. In the pre-*DSM-III* literature, patients with chronic anxiety states were usually found to have markedly elevated baselines for cardiovascular measures. During the performance of challenging tasks, control subjects tended to either reach levels comparable with those of the patients, as was found with forearm blood flow by Kelly and Walter (1968, 1969), or to reach levels that were somewhat lower, as was often observed with heart rate (Bond et al., 1974; Kelly and Walter, 1968, 1969; Wing, 1964). The blood flow findings seemed to reflect the operation of a "ceiling" effect, whereby both groups approached maximal levels of response (Lader, 1975). With heart rate, it appears that baseline differences were carried over to the stress period, so that, although both patients and controls showed heart rate increases during task performance, patients maintained faster rates overall. When expressed as a change from baseline, however, the *control* subjects sometimes showed the greater degree of reactivity (Kelly and Walter, 1968, 1969).

A noteworthy aspect of these early studies is that they generally failed to find evidence that patients with chronic anxiety states would show an elevated or exaggerated cardiovascular response to stress. Although their absolute levels of heart rate may have been higher, the extent of stress-induced change was not. Only recently has this issue been reexamined with patients diagnosed according to *DSM-III-R* criteria. Hoehn-Saric et al. (1989) found that patients with generalized anxiety disorder were similar to control subjects in resting heart rate and blood pressure, and also showed increases of a comparable magnitude during the performance of psychological tasks. However, in a later experiment using the same procedures, patients with panic disorder showed a different pattern (Hoehn-Saric et al., 1991). At rest, panic patients had higher heart rates and systolic blood pressures than control subjects. In response to the psychological challenges, heart rate rose in a similar way for both groups, but systolic blood pressure increased significantly more in the patients. In summary, then, despite considerable interest in the role of cardiovascular activity in the etiology and maintenance of anxiety and panic disorders, this isolated finding by Hoehn-Saric et al. (1991) appears to provide the only evidence to date for a differentially elevated level of reactivity in a patient sample in response to a standardized psychological laboratory challenge.

Behavioral Approach Tests. A third line of psychophysiological research has investigated the cardiovascular response of agoraphobic patients under conditions of "real-life" stress, by recording heart rate and blood pressure in behavioral approach tests. In these ambulatory-monitoring procedures, the patients are taken through a series of stations, such as shopping malls or crowded areas, that would normally elicit fear in people with agoraphobic concerns. Presumably, these situations are relatively innocuous for control subjects, whose heart rates would be expected to rise above resting baseline levels only as a result of the increased motor activity associated with walking through the stations.

Despite that behavioral approach tests differ markedly in their emotional salience for agoraphobics and controls, the results of studies that have employed these procedures have shown some parallels to those of laboratory stress experiments. That is, most investigations have found that the patients had higher baseline heart rates before the tests, which remained elevated through the course of the procedure. The amount of change provoked by the tests, however, has usually been comparable for both groups (Holden and Barlow, 1986; Michelson et al., 1990b; Roth et al., 1986). The one exception, is a report by Woods et al. (1987), who monitored heart rate during an extended supine baseline and during behavioral approach tests that were tailored individually to be maximally fear-inducing for each patient. In fact, this procedure actually provoked situational panic attacks for most of them. With this procedure, Woods et al. (1987) found no baseline differences in heart rate between the patients and matched controls, but a greater heart-rate increase for the agoraphobics during exposure to the feared situations.

Summary. Over the last decade, enough evidence has accumulated to draw into question the notion that anxious patients are chronically in a state of high cardiovascular activation. Although those with panic disorder and agoraphobia have frequently had elevated resting heart rates in the laboratory, this has not always been true. Furthermore, studies of ambulatory monitoring provide no evidence that tonic heart rates are differentially increased among these patients during the normal course of their lives. Perhaps the most parsimonious interpretation of the discrepant results in this area is that offered by Roth et al. (1986), who suggested that increased autonomic activation at rest in agoraphobic patients could reflect a phobic response to the test situation itself. In this sense, a visit to the psychophysiology laboratory may be similar in many ways to participation in a behavioral approach test. This would also explain why several investigators have found that patients and control subjects show similar patterns of heart-rate change in behavioral approach tests—baseline measures in the patients have already been elevated owing to anticipatory anxiety, so that further increases elicited by the tests are mainly due to motor activity for *both* patients and controls. Thus, it is likely that globally heightened cardiovascular activity in panic disorder is dependent on the capacity of specific situations to elicit anticipatory fear. It should also be recognized, however, that for individuals with pervasive anticipatory anxiety who dread the imminent occurrence of the next sudden panic attack, such situations may, in fact, be relatively common.

Nevertheless, there is also evidence from investigations of orthostatic responses that some patients with panic attacks may suffer from dysfunctional regulation of the autonomic nervous system. Unfortunately, the extent to which orthostatic reflexes themselves might be influenced by chronic anxiety states is unclear. Hence, the significance of these findings as reflecting potentially causal factors in the etiology of panic attacks remains to be determined.

Finally, the hypothesis that patients with anxiety disorders might be inherently hyperreactive in cardiovascular responses to psychosocial stress generally has received little empirical attention in the recent literature. As with the behavioral approach tests, most of the available studies have suffered from the interpretive problem of elevated prestress baselines that carry over in to the stress protocol. Again, this calls into question the validity of the baseline measures as reflecting "no-stress" resting conditions for the patients. Although they have sometimes been found to have higher heart rates and blood pressures than control subjects during psychological tasks, baseline elevations suggest that these responses may comprise additive effects of pretask anticipatory anxiety plus responses to the stressor itself. No studies have yet employed procedures to minimize initial baseline differences (Zahn, 1986), as has been done by Woods et al. (1987) for agoraphobic-specific behavioral testing. This approach would be necessary before it could be concluded that patients with panic attacks show exaggerated cardiovascular responses to stress, other than in circumstances that access their specific anxiety-related concerns.

2. *Clinical Correlates of Cardiovascular Activity in Panic Disorder and Agoraphobia*

Several studies have reported significant correlations between resting measures of cardiovascular activity and self-report ratings of state anxiety (cf. Aronson et al., 1989; Kelly et al., 1971; Kelly and Walter, 1968) or agoraphobic fears (Roth et al., 1988), but they have usually been modest in magnitude and not always confirmed by other investigators (cf. Roth et al., 1986; Yeragani et al., 1989). In general, Lang's (1968) discussion of physiological, self-report, and behavioral indexes of anxiety as comprising three loosely intercorrelated systems continues to provide an important conceptual framework recognizing the potential for independence among these measures.

A more recent interest of relevance to the cardiovascular psychophysiology of anxiety has been the effort to evaluate the cardiovascular changes that take place during panic attacks themselves, and to determine the extent of their association with tonic or "background" levels of cardiovascular activation.

As noted earlier, the physiological correlates of the spontaneous panic attacks that were captured serendipitously by Lader and Mathews (1970) included rapid increases in heart rate. For some time, this was thought to provide part of the biological signature of the spontaneous panic attack. It also appears that such heart rate changes can be induced in the laboratory. For example, although sodium lactate infusions result in substantial heart-rate increases for both patients with panic disorder and control subjects, people who actually panic during these infusions are more likely to experience abrupt surges in heart rate, which seem to parallel their subjective reports of a sudden crescendo of symptoms (Gorman et al., 1987).

Studies involving ambulatory monitoring, however, have provided a picture of panic attacks that is more subtle than can be explained on the basis of sudden surges in heart rate alone. Margraf (1990) has recently reviewed the findings of ten studies in which naturally occurring panic attacks were recorded by ambulatory electrocardiographic monitoring. On average, heart rate during panic attacks has usually been higher than during nonanxious control periods, but there is a wide range of variability across attacks, even within the same subjects. Many attacks occur without any changes in heart rate at all. In general, then, the results of these ambulatory monitoring studies suggest that the typical panic attack in the natural environment tends to be of a lower intensity than those that have been recorded in the laboratory, with a psychophysiological profile that is much less dramatic (Margraf, 1990). The fact that some attacks occur *without* heart rate changes argues for the importance of central factors in the experience of panic, with peripheral indexes that are not always consistent.

Another line of research has attempted to determine the extent to which increased baseline levels of activation, as reflected in elevated heart rate, contributes to the likelihood of having a panic attack. This work stems from initial observations by Liebowitz et al. (1984, 1985) that patients who experienced panic during sodium lactate infusions were more fearful and had higher heart rates than nonpanicking patients *before* the administration of the infusion. This seemed to suggest that panic attacks might involve a combination of high-baseline activation, followed by the triggering of panic. Liebowitz et al. (1985) proposed that the specific trigger for panic might involve the discharge of central noradrenergic neurons in the locus coeruleus. On the other hand, Margraf et al., (1986) have argued that these findings actually point to the importance of peripheral factors in the etiology of lactate-induced panic attacks. In their view, when the induced peripheral physiological changes are added to an already elevated baseline, the experience may become intolerable for some patients. Their panic, according to this model, is a phobic response to the perception of strong bodily sensations, regardless of how they are caused, which the patients tend to interpret as being potentially threatening or dangerous (Clark, 1986; Margraf et al., 1986).

Thus, the association between elevated cardiovascular activity and the likelihood of experiencing panic is of some theoretical importance. The issue has subsequently been addressed in depth by Cowley et al. (1987) and Yeragani and colleagues (Yeragani et al., 1987a,b, 1988), in the context of sodium lactate infusions, and also by Yeragani (1987a) who examined panic attacks that were elicited occasionally during placebo infusions. The results of these studies were similar in that patients with panic disorder were *not* found to have higher preinfusion heart rates than control subjects, although they did have higher blood pressures and self-ratings of anxiety or panic symptoms. However, the baseline blood pressure elevations characterized both patients who panicked during the infusions and those who did not. Thus, the cardiovascular effects of biochemical provocations may indeed add to those of preexisting baseline differences, but the pattern of such differences has not always been consistent across studies; nor are baseline elevations in cardiovascular function necessarily specific to those patients who go on to experience panic.

Finally, studies of naturally occurring panic attacks show that they frequently happen within a context of low background heart rates, and even during periods of relaxation and sleep (Cohen et al., 1985; Margraf et al., 1987; Mellman and Uhde, 1989). Apparently, only the particular case of situational attacks, which are associated with entry into fear-inducing environments, are linked reliably to elevated baseline heart rates before the point of panic (Margraf et al., 1987). In these cases, it is possible that the heightened level of activation that accompanies entry into the feared situation may serve to prime the individual to have an attack, or perhaps contribute to its severity once initiated. In general, however, discrete panic attacks can be superimposed on any background level of cardiovascular activity.

3. *Cardiovascular Activity and the Clinical Course of Panic Disorder and Agoraphobia*

Lang's (1968) three-systems model, with its emphasis on multidimensional assessment of behavioral, cognitive–affective, and psychophysiological components of emotion, has had a significant influence on the field of behavior therapy. As a result, there has been considerable interest among behavioral researchers in using psychophysiological measures—and heart rate in particular—as indexes of the course and outcome of treatments for the anxiety disorders. Much that is known about the effects of treatment on cardiovascular function comes from studies of ambulatory heart rate during the performance of behavioral approach tests before and after the implementation of psychological or behavioral interventions. The actual treatments that have been used in these studies have included relaxation training, cognitive therapy, and paradoxical interventions, but most commonly they have involved some type of method that calls for exposure to feared situations, either by "flooding" or graduated exposure in vivo.

A central question is whether these interventions effect any overall change in psychophysiological measures. In fact, although negative results have been reported occasionally (Mavissakalian, 1987; Telch et al., 1985; Vermilyea et al., 1984), it seems reasonably certain that the most common behavioral treatments for agoraphobia do bring about reliable reductions in heart rate in behavioral approach tests (Holden and Barlow, 1986, Öst et al., 1984; Mavissakalian and Michelson, 1982; Michelson and Mavissakalian, 1985; Michelson et al., 1985, 1990a,b; Roth et al., 1988). A stronger formulation of this question is whether these interventions bring the agoraphobics' situationally induced heart-rate increases down to the level of nonanxious control subjects. This is less clear, in large part, because few treatment studies have included a nonclinical comparison group that underwent psychophysiological assessment according to the same schedule as the patients. It is also a stringent criterion of outcome. Studies of behavioral and self-report measures of change indicate that not all agoraphobic patients are helped by behavior therapy; about 60–65% are reported to make clinically significant gains (Jacobson et al., 1988; Jansson and Öst, 1982), and many of these may continue to struggle with some residual symptoms of anxiety. Not surprisingly, then, comparisons of treated patients and normal controls have produced mixed results. Holden and Barlow (1986), for example, found that heart rate during a behavioral approach test decreased over time for *both* patients and controls, but the patients remained higher at all assessment points. On the other hand, Michelson and Mavissakalian (1985) and Michelson et al. (1990a) reported that patients treated with exposure or relaxation had heart rates comparable with control subjects on posttreatment behavioral approach tests, even though they had been significantly higher before treatment.

Middleton (1990) has recently taken a different approach to the assessment of cardiovascular function following treatment, by focusing on the status of panic disorder patients who had experienced a complete remission of symptoms with cognitive therapy. A small sample of 12 patients, all of whom had been panic-free for at least 4 months, were examined in a series of tests that included orthostatic challenges similar to those employed by Weissman et al. (1987) and Yeragani et al. (1990b). Middleton (1990) found that the remitted patients actually had lower resting heart rates than a group of matched control subjects, but slightly higher systolic blood pressures. The patients had a normal heart rate response during 10 min of quiet standing, but they differed from control subjects in their pattern of change in systolic blood pressure; whereas the control subjects had a modest increase, the patients showed a drop.

This pattern is quite different from that reported by Weissman et al. (1987), who found that patients with panic attacks had an exaggerated increase in the cardiovascular response to standing. Middleton (1990) suggested that recovered panic patients may have undergone a long-term readjustment of cardiovascular function, either because of a centrally mediated disturbance of cardiovascular control, or because of peripheral changes that might be induced by states of chronic anxiety. Whatever their cause, Middleton's findings are of particular interest because they underscore the difficulty in drawing general conclusions about cardiovascular function in anxious patients who are actively symptomatic.

In addition to using heart rate assessment to gauge the overall outcome of therapy, behavioral researchers have also been interested in evaluating the patterns of change that take place during treatment. If behavioral, self-report, and psychophysiological response systems are correlated only loosely, then it stands to reason that they may change at different rates, and perhaps even in different directions (Rachman and Hodgson, 1974). Indeed, there is some evidence that with exposure therapy, behavioral changes take place relatively early in the course of treatment, followed by declines in anxiety self-reports and, finally, by decreases in heart rate during behavioral approach tests (Mavissakalian and Michelson, 1982).

The potential for the different components of the three-systems model to change either in parallel with one another, or in different directions, has been termed *synchrony–desynchrony* by Rachman and Hodgson (1974). Desynchrony is now a well-documented phenomenon, with the most common form being patients who make clear treatment gains on self-report scales and behavioral measures of avoidance, while showing *increased* heart rate responses in test situations (Barlow et al., 1980; Himadi et al., 1985; Mavissakalian, 1987; Mavissakalian and Michelson, 1982). Conceptually, that a patient shows a desynchronous pattern of heart-rate changes suggests that the test situation continues to evoke some aspect of a latent fear response, even if the patient does not report (or is not aware of) a subjective sense of anxiety. Hence, some investigators have attempted to evaluate the relevance of the synchrony–desynchrony dimension to more global measures of psychosocial outcome.

These efforts have produced mixed results. In several studies, Michelson and colleagues have found that agoraphobic patients who made synchronous changes across response systems from pre- to posttreatment showed greater overall improvement than patients classified as having made desynchronous changes (Michelson and Mavissakalian, 1985; Michelson et al., 1985, 1990b). However, other studies have failed to replicate that finding (Mavissakalian, 1987; Vermilyea et al., 1984), noting instead that desynchronizers were just as likely as synchronizers to make treatment gains on outcome measures that were not related specifically to heart rate itself.

Another psychophysiological dimension of individual differences that has occasionally been related to treatment outcome is simply the magnitude of the heart rate response observed during a pretreatment behavioral approach test. In several reports, a large initial cardiovascular response has been associated with good outcome (Craske et al., 1987; Roth et al., 1988; Vermilyea et al., 1984). Although perhaps counterintuitive, there are, in fact, several reasons why a large initial response might have positive implications for behavioral based treatments. First, it indicates that in vivo exposure is a relevant technique for activating the patient's fear in the physiological response system (Craske et al., 1987; Lang, 1979). Second, it may demonstrate a willingness on the patients's part to become engaged in the exposure process, even in the face of physiological discomfort

(Craske et al., 1987). Some patients, for example, may drop out of a behavioral approach test as soon as they feel their heart rate start to rise, whereas others may engage in "functional avoidance" by using cognitive strategies that distract them from their anxiety (Craske et al., 1987; Foa and Kozak, 1986). Such patients are likely to show comparatively small heart-rate responses. However, they may also fail to benefit from a form of therapy that depends for its efficacy on physiological activation, habituation, and complete "emotional processing" of all the relevant elements of fear signals—including psychophysiological ones (Foa and Kozak, 1986; Rachman, 1980).

Although initial cardiovascular reactivity is conceptually different from the notion of synchrony–desynchrony (which is concerned with patterns of change over time), in practice they are not orthogonal dimensions (Craske et al., 1987). Heart rate during behavioral approach tests shows only moderate test–retest stability (Holden and Barlow, 1986), so that patients with very high initial heart rates are likely to show some "synchronous" decline simply on the basis of regression to the mean (and vice versa for those with very low heart rates initially). Furthermore, as with synchrony–desynchrony, several investigators have failed to find any relation between pretreatment cardiovascular reactivity and outcome (Mavissakalian, 1987; Michelson et al., 1990a,b). Hence, it appears that neither dimension reflects a powerful predictor of change in response to behavioral interventions, although they may each be tapping into some aspects of the patients' anxiety experience that can only be accessed by psychophysiological means. Further research will be required to establish the independence of these measures and their ultimate significance for the process of clinical change. However, both constructs have strong conceptual bases and at least some empirical support as relevant dimensions in the assessment of panic disorder and agoraphobia.

4. Psychophysiological Mechanisms of Elevated Cardiovascular Activity in Panic Disorder and Agoraphobia

Studies of cardiovascular activity in panic disorder and agoraphobia can be classified into three general categories: (1) those that are concerned with the physiological regulation—and possible dysregulation—of basic cardiovascular function; (2) those that employ cardiovascular measures as indexes of the psychophysiological component of the fear response; and (3) those that investigate the physiological bases of panic attacks themselves.

Studies of the first type are relatively few, but the results of orthostatic challenges do suggest that a subset of actively symptomatic patients show an exaggerated cardiovascular response to prolonged standing. The reasons for this exaggerated response are not clear as yet, but both adrenergic (central and peripheral) factors (Weissman et al., 1987) and vagal withdrawal (Yeragani et al., 1990b) have been discussed as possible mediating mechanisms. This pattern does not characterize panic disorder patients in remission (Middleton, 1990), so its etiological significance for the initial development of panic states remains obscure.

The second type of investigation is probably most relevant to the clinical presentation of anticipatory anxiety, and it includes most behavioral studies of heart rate during behavioral approach tests. As a component of the fear response, the traditional view of the fight-or-flight reaction—and particularly the latter in agoraphobia—may be applicable as a model for elaborating the psychophysiological mechanisms that underlie situationally provoked increases in heart rate. Recent research in the psychophysiology of stress indicates that heart rate responses of this type are driven primarily by the sympathetic nervous system by ß-adrenergic stimulation of the myocardium (Langer et al., 1985; Obrist, 1981; Sherwood et al., 1986), albeit with a secondary contribution of vagal withdrawal (Grossman and Svebak, 1987). These cardiovascular adjustments are in excess of the actual metabolic demands of the body at the time they occur, although it is believed that they serve a preparatory function to the ready the musculature for vigorous physical activity (i.e., escape; Sherwood et al., 1986). In agoraphobia, ß-adrenergic blockers do attenuate the heart-rate response in flooding sessions, but paradoxically, this may diminish the therapeutic effectiveness of exposure (Hafner and Milton, 1977).

If tonic heart rate is linked in this way to anticipatory anxiety, then the view that patients with panic disorder and agoraphobia are constantly in a state of high activation is probably mistaken. Rather, these states appear to be provoked by particular situations. Such situations may occur very often in the patients' lives, however, and there is some evidence that peripheral adrenergic receptors are down-regulated (Cameron and Nesse, 1988; Cameron et al., 1990; Nesse et al., 1984), as might be expected if there are frequent episodic elevations in the levels of circulating catecholamines. As Middleton (1990) has suggested, an extended history of panic and anticipatory anxiety may result in some long-term readjustments of the cardiovascular system.

Nevertheless, these mechanisms appear to hold only a rather tenuous relation to panic attacks themselves. Naturally occurring panic attacks are quite variable in their peripheral manifestations. From the perspective of cardiovascular psychophysiology, attacks that are characterized by dramatic and abrupt increases in heart rate seem to have little in common with attacks that involve no change in heart rate at all. The fact that patients report some comparability of experience across episodes that vary markedly in their pattern of peripheral expression suggests that central factors, rather than peripheral ones, are fundamentally implicated in the phenomenon of panic. However, it remains a matter of debate about whether these "central factors" constitute a dysfunction in the central regulation of the autonomic nervous system, or whether they are psychological, and reflect a phobic fear of a broad array of bodily changes that may normally take place during periods of anxiety.

Further studies of the cardiovascular system may be of some relevance in this context, especially for clarifying the mechanisms that contribute to heart rate increases in that majority of panic attacks in which such increases are observed. For example, the biological mechanisms that cause the heart rate to accelerate during sodium lactate infusions still have not been identified satisfactorily. ß-adrenergic blockers do not stop the heart rate from increasing during sodium lactate infusions; nor do they protect patients from experiencing panic under these conditions (Gorman et al., 1983). Vagal tone, on the other hand, has been reported to diminish with lactate among normal subjects (George et al., 1989), but evidence that it is responsible for panic-related tachycardia is still lacking (Gorman et al., 1987), but worthy of further study (Stein et al., 1992). Clearly, then, there is much that has yet to be learned about the role of the cardiovascular system in panic attacks and panic disorder.

In summary, the cardiovascular system has constituted a major focus in the psychophysiological approach to the study of anxiety. A well-developed body of knowledge has accrued that, if not always consistent, attests to the continuing recognition of the importance of the link between anxiety and the heart within both biological and behavioral traditions. Cardiovascular studies of depressed patients have occasionally shown some parallels with those of anxious patients, in the sense that several investigations have reported a pattern of elevated heart rate in this group as well. However, this pattern, and the conditions under which it occurs, has been studied much less intensively in depression. It is not clear whether it is typical of depression per se, or rather, confined to that substantial subgroup of depressed patients who suffer concurrently from prominent symptoms of anxiety.

IV. ELECTROENCEPHALOGRAPHY

Ever since a link between brain dysfunction and psychiatric disorder has been proposed, investigators have sought to uncover such evidence in patients with mental illness. Early studies, making use of the technology available at the time, scrutinized the electroencephalograms (EEGs) of patients with mental illness. Not surprisingly, given the myriad of neuropsychological deficits attributed to that disorder at one time or another, schizophrenia has received the most attention by those interested in the study of EEGs and evoked potentials in psychiatric illness (Blackwood et al., 1987; Roth et al., 1980; Shagass et al., 1977). A smaller body of data does exist, however, for depressive and anxiety disorders, and these will be reviewed here.

As has been noted by others (Berenbaum et al., 1990), much of this literature is beset with methodological and analytical difficulties. These problems include the use of nonstandardized techniques that have rendered replication studies across sites nearly impossible, variable approaches to dealing (or not dealing, in some cases) with artifact, and the failure to control for attentional or cognitive effects at the time of testing. Nonetheless, some fairly consistent findings have arisen, whereas others have failed to stand the test of time.

A. Electroencephalography in Depression

The simplest method of EEG analysis, visual inspection, has generally failed to find gross evidence of EEG abnormalities in patients with affective illness (Abrams and Taylor, 1979). In contrast, studies that use power spectral analysis—wherein EEG spectra of various frequencies (e.g., alpha, beta, delta, and theta) are summed and usually expressed as a proportion of total EEG power—have more frequently detected abnormalities (Knott and Lapiere, 1987; Perris, 1975).

Topographic power-spectral studies (Duffy, 1982, 1989) have also suggested abnormalities in EEG left–right symmetry or frontotemporal power distribution in patients with major depression (Pockberger et al., 1985), although not unanimously so (Guidi et al., 1989). The major shortcomings of these topographic EEG studies are twofold: the very small sample sizes used, and perhaps, more importantly, the frequent failure to correct for multiple statistical comparisons. In some cases, investigators have made well over a hundred multiple comparisons, and declared one or two isolated findings as signifying something important—when, clearly, the odds were high that such differences would be found on the basis of chance alone. Evoked potential studies—for which a distinct component of an EEG response to a specific sensory stimulus (e.g., auditory, visual) is isolated and measured—have been no less confusing and contradictory (Blackwood et al., 1987; Khanna et al., 1989; Guidi et al., 1989; Vasile et al. 1992). Overall, the evidence in favor of genuine electrophysiological abnormalities in depression, distinct from possible abnormalities attributable to depressive correlates, such as attentional difficulties, is far from persuasive. It is unlikely, given the clinical heterogeneity of the depressive syndrome, that definitive EEG abnormalities in depression are likely to be elicited in the near future without currently available technologies.

B. Electroencephalography in Anxiety

As part of an effort to document a biological basis for some anxiety disorders, considerable energy has been expended on the study of the EEG in patients with anxiety disorders. In this section, we will review only studies that have examined patients with well-defined anxiety syndromes. Thus, much of the older literature that has reported on heterogeneous groups of anxious patients will not be referred to here. Similarly, electroencephalographic correlates of anxiety in normal volunteers will not be examined in this section.

1. Electroencephalographic Findings in Obsessive–Compulsive Disorder

Several recent studies have examined the EEGs of patients with obsessive–compulsive disorder (OCD) defined according to contemporary criteria. Because of the hypothesized connection between OCD and temporal lobe epilepsy, based largely on interictal characteristics of patients with temporal lobe epilepsy that overlap somewhat with those of OCD (Bear and Fedio, 1977), investigators have been particularly vigilant for possible temporal lobe abnormalities. Rapoport and colleagues (1981) examined the EEGs of nine adolescents with OCD and found no abnormalities. Insel et al. (1983) found only 2 of 18 patients with OCD to have nonspecific EEG abnormalities, a rate likely no higher than in the general population. Jenike and Brotman (1984) found that 4 of 12 patients with OCD had temporal lobe EEG abnormalities, but only 1 of these responded to anticonvulsant medication [Joffe and Swinson (1988) later replicated this when they found no response to carbamazepine in patients with OCD].

Studies of evoked potentials in patients with OCD have been interesting, with one series of studies (Beech et al., 1983; Cieselski et al., 1981) showing abnormalities in P^{300} that were interpreted to be consistent with a state of hyperarousal. Other investigators have similarly found abnormalities in somatosensory evoked potentials in patients with OCD (Shagass et al., 1984). That study once again related the findings to generalized cortical hyperexcitability or hyperarousal. Given the similarities between these studies and the positive findings, it is surprising that more research initiatives in this area have not been apparent in recent years.

2. Electroencephalographic Findings in Panic Disorder

Panic disorder (PD) has been hypothesized to involve a functional abnormality of temporolimbic structures (Reiman et al., 1984; Stein and Uhde, 1989). Several cases have been reported of disturbances in the temporal lobes leading to the phenomenological manifestations of panic attacks (Wall et al., 1985; Ghadirian et al., 1986; Devinsky et al., 1989; George et al., 1990). In addition, patients with PD exhibit numerous psychosensory symptoms similar to those seen in temporal lobe epilepsy (Boulenger et al., 1986). Furthermore, investigators have reported EEG abnormalities in some cases of panic attacks associated with atypical features (Edlund et al., 1987). Nonetheless, routine EEG studies in patients with PD have failed to reveal characteristic abnormalities (Stein and Uhde, 1989; Lepola et al., 1990).

Two studies have applied quantitative EEG techniques to the study of patients with panic disorder. Knott et al. (1981) examined occipital EEG during lactate infusion among six patients with panic disorder (all of whom panicked during the infusion). A slight decrease in alpha-power and a large increase in delta-power were observed during panic. More recently, we (Newman et al., 1992) have examined the EEG using computerized quantitative techniques in seven medication-free patients with panic disorder and seven healthy control subjects. Patients with panic disorder had globally reduced alpha-amplitude, compared with control subjects; this difference was most notable occipitally, in the slow alpha (8.6–10.5 Hz) range. Left–right power asymmetries reported in some studies of depressed patients were not apparent in this study.

In summary, the EEG findings in the anxiety disorder have been quite unimpressive. Visual inspection of EEGs has failed to find any substantive evidence of epileptiform abnormalities, and this is also true for major depression. There are too few quantitative EEG studies and there is sufficient variance in methodology between studies to render premature any comments about quantitative EEGs in depression versus anxiety. Finally, it is our belief that further EEG studies of attentional correlates are needed, and that these may shed further light on differentiating characteristics of anxiety and depressive syndromes.

V. SLEEP PHYSIOLOGY

Of all the biological and physiological measures that have been surveyed in psychiatric research, the study of sleep in depression has probably been the most extensively studied. The characteristics of sleep and the nature of sleep abnormalities in patients with affective illness has been the subject of an excellent review (Reynolds, 1989), and we will not duplicate that effort here. Rather, this section will briefly examine the existing sleep findings in patients with depression, but focus in more detail on the considerably less-studied phenomenology of sleep in patients with anxiety disorders.

In humans, sleep is traditionally divided into rapid eye movement (REM) and non-REM sleep. These broad divisions are further characterized into 4 stages: stage 1 sleep, which is usually a brief transition phase into stage 2 sleep, which occupies much of the night. The deeper stages of sleep, stages 3 and 4, are known together as *slow-wave sleep* (SWS) or *delta-sleep*. Throughout the night, the individual cycles from lighter (predominantly stage 2) sleep through to deeper sleep (stages 3 and 4), interrupted at times by periods of REM sleep during which the eyes move rapidly, but skeletal muscles are atonic. For a complete description of sleep and sleep stages, the reader is referred to the comprehensive textbook on this subject (Carskadon and Dement, 1989).

Mental health researchers have been particularly interested in the study of *sleep architecture* in psychiatric disorders. Sleep architecture refers to the structure and distribution of the various components of sleep throughout the night. Sleep architecture and other physiological measures during sleep are studied polysomnographically in the sleep laboratory. Polysomnographic capabilities differ from laboratory to laboratory, but generally comprise a minimal set of EEG measures to enable determination of sleep staging, electro-oculographic (EOG) leads to detect nonphasic eye movements during REM, and a chin electromyographic (EMG) lead to discern muscle tone and movement, and a single-lead electrocardiographic (ECG) recording. Depending on the specific interests of the sleep laboratory, additional polysomnographic measures might include chest and abdominal wall movements, expired CO^2 measurements, pulse-oximetry, more extensive EEG and ECG montages, and leg EMG leads. In recent years, as improved technology for ambulatory monitoring has been developed, some sleep recordings are being carried out in the patient's home, not in the sleep laboratory. Although this technique offers the obvious advantage of recording physiological parameters in the subjects' usual sleep environment, this technology has yet to be widely adopted for psychiatric research. For most of the studies described herein, unless otherwise specified, the data described have been acquired in a traditional hospital-based sleep laboratory.

A. Sleep in Depression

Patients with major depressive illness frequently report experiencing disturbed sleep, and, indeed, this is a hallmark of this disorder and a major component of the diagnostic criteria for depression (American Psychiatric Association, 1987). Clinically, sleep in depressive illness is generally characterized by decreased sleep [although some patients, particularly those with atypical depression, may experience hypersomnia (Akiskal and Lemmi, 1989)], poor quality of sleep, and, in some patients, early-morning awakenings.

Polysomnographic findings in depression that have been well replicated in many laboratories include the following: Shortened REM latency (time from sleep onset until the beginning of the first REM period) has been consistently observed in patients with major depression (Benca et al., 1992; Thase and Kupfer, 1987), but it is not a unique characteristic of that disorder. For example, approximately 50% of studies have found shortened REM latency in patients with schizophrenia (Keshavan et al., 1990; Ganguli et al., 1987; Reynolds et al., 1987). Gillin et al. (1990) have also reported lower REM latency in some alcoholics with secondary depression, suggesting that reduced REM latency may be a feature of the depressive state, rather than a unique feature of major depressive illness. That observation becomes very important when we attempt to interpret REM latency data from patients with anxiety disorders who have varying degrees of depressive symptoms at the time of polysomnographic assessment.

Other reliable and predictable sleep EEG findings in depression include disturbances in sleep continuity (including decreased total sleep and frequent awakenings); diminished delta (slow-wave) sleep, particularly in the first NREM period compared with the second NREM period, known as the *delta sleep ratio* (Kupfer et al. 1990); increased REM density during the first REM sleep period; and an increased duration of the first REM period (Reynolds, 1989). Many of these more recently defined measurements have not been directly studied in patients with anxiety disorders, but, when these data are available, they will be discussed in the following section.

Overall it would appear that sleep difficulties are a major component of the depressive syndrome, and that, to a large degree, these are reflected in a variety of polysomnographic abnormalities in depressed patients.

B. Sleep in Anxiety

As any clinician knows, anxious patients frequently describe problems with their sleep. Surprisingly, in contrast with the diagnostic criteria for the mood disorders (American Psychiatric Association, 1987), the diagnostic criteria for the anxiety disorders almost uniformly (with the exception of the criteria for posttraumatic stress disorder; PTSD) fail to include mention of sleep disturbances. This is despite the fact that insomnia is a complaint of between 40 and 80% of patients with anxiety disorders (Mellman and Uhde, 1989b). In one study conducted in three separate clinics specializing in the treatment of anxiety disorders, it was found that 67% of patients with panic disorder complained of recurrent insomnia, compared with 35% of healthy controls (Mellman and Uhde 1989b).

Compared with the multitude of sleep EEG studies that have been performed in depressed patients, the study of EEG sleep in patients with anxiety disorders has been less intensively investigated. Currently, there have been only a few studies of sleep in patients with generalized anxiety disorder (Reynolds et al., 1983; Papadimitriou et al., 1988) and obsessive-compulsive disorder, several in posttraumatic stress disorder, and a handful in panic disorder (see Sec. IV.B.2). The remainder of this discussion will focus on the two disorders for which a reasonable body of data has accrued: namely, posttraumatic stress disorder and panic disorder.

1. Sleep in Posttraumatic Stress Disorder

Perturbed sleep is an almost uniform finding in patients who suffer from posttraumatic stress disorder (PTSD). This disorder is a sequela of either acute or chronic emotional trauma, best-described in Vietnam war combat veterans and prisoners of war, but also increasingly recognized in survivors of other traumata, such as rape and sexual abuse. Interference with sleep is so common and so prominent in patients with PTSD that one author has referred to sleep disturbance as the "hallmark" of PTSD (Ross et al., 1989).

Glaubman et al. (1990) reported a case–control study of sleep in patients with PTSD. They found that their patients with PTSD had evidence of a disturbance in sleep maintenance (increased arousals, decreased delta-sleep) and sleep efficiency. These findings are compatible with those reviewed by Ross et al. (1989) in terms of non-REM abnormalities. Because none of their subjects experienced nightmares, however, they were unable to comment on the hypothesized REM component of the PTSD sleep disturbance.

Dagan and colleagues (1991) recorded *increased* arousal thresholds from delta-sleep in 19 war veterans with PTSD. Given that PTSD patients are reported to experience increased arousals from sleep, this finding is somewhat unexpected. As the authors suggest, however, this may represent an "adaptive mechanism" that develops many years after the traumatic event(s). This finding remains to be replicated and its significance further evaluated.

Rosen et al. (1991) surveyed 42 survivors of the Nazi holocaust, 37 depressed patients, and 54 healthy subjects of similar age, all living in the community, using the Pittsburgh Sleep Quality Index (PSQI; Buysse et al., 1989). The PSQI is a self-rating instrument designed to measure sleep quality and other subjective sleep parameters in psychiatric disorders. As expected, the survivors had significantly reduced sleep quality, sleep latency, sleep duration, and sleep efficiency, than the healthy control group (Rosen et al., 1991), as well as increased sleep disturbance. The depressed patients, in contrast, reported significantly more impairment on almost all measures, except for the sleep disturbance subscale (which measures nocturnal events such as nightmares). The survivors had significantly more awakenings from bad dreams than the depressed patients. These observations are confirmatory of the profound sleep disturbance that can persist in survivors of major trauma, here, even 45 years after the event. The findings also support the magnitude of REM disturbance (herein characterized as nightmares) in this population.

Although the clinical phenomenology of the sleep disturbance in PTSD has become better delineated in recent years, the polysomnographic study of EEG sleep in PTSD remains in its infancy. A major problem in the elucidation of EEG sleep abnormalities unique to PTSD is the frequent comorbidity seen in patients with PTSD. This comorbidity includes, but is not limited to, substance abuse (e.g., Kauffman et al., 1987) and major depression. Thus, many of the existing sleep EEG studies in PTSD are potentially influenced by these confounding factors.

Ross et al. (1989) reviewed the status of sleep abnormalities in patients with PTSD. They focused particularly on the potential importance of REM dysregulation in PTSD as being a central contributant to both daytime (i.e., flashbacks) and nighttime (i.e., posttraumatic anxiety dreams) symptomatology. Given that noradrenergic dysfunction is strongly suspected to play a role in PTSD (Southwick et al., 1993), along with the likelihood that this same system is aberrantly regulated in another disorder of REM, namely, narcolepsy, it is compelling to speculate that CNS noradrenergic and REM dysfunction may be critical components of the pathophysiology of PTSD.

Even though this hypothesis is indeed appealing, data is lacking. In fact, Mellman and colleagues (1991) presented two cases in whom symptoms of PTSD and narcolepsy diverged over time. Future studies should attend carefully, however, to the cooccurrence of PTSD and other REM-related disorders such as narcolepsy. Furthermore, given the association between the histocompatibility (HLA)-DR2 antigen and narcolepsy (Langdon et al., 1984), a study of the prevalence of this particular HLA haplotype in a series of patients with posttraumatic stress disorder would be of considerable interest.

In summary, from the handful of polysomnographic studies of patients with posttraumatic stress disorder that have been performed, it would appear that there is little overlap with the most characteristic sleep EEG features of melancholic major depression; namely, reduced REM latency and increased REM density. It is hoped that future studies will focus on PTSD patients with and without concurrent major depression to delineate features of PTSD that are unique to that syndrome. Such studies should pay careful attention to the possible role of abnormalities in REM regulation in the pathophysiology of PTSD.

2. Sleep in Panic Disorder

Many patients with panic disorder report disturbances in their sleep. The current literature on sleep in panic disorder has recently been reviewed in detail by Mellman and Uhde (1990) and, therefore, we will simply reiterate some of their conclusions as they relate to the comparison of sleep in anxious and depressed patients.

Four studies have now examined the EEG sleep of patients with the exclusive diagnosis of panic disorder (with or without agoraphobia) (Uhde et al., 1984; Hauri et al., 1989; Mellman and Uhde, 1989; Stein et al., 1993). The consensus that has arisen from these studies is that patients with panic disorder do *not* display the classic abnormalities in sleep architecture that are seen in melancholic patients. In fact, objective EEG sleep findings in panic disorder appear to be limited to fairly unimpressive disturbances in sleep initiation (prolonged time to sleep onset) and sleep efficiency (Mellman and Uhde, 1990).

An interesting feature of patients with panic disorder that may further distinguish them from patients with major depression is their response to sleep deprivation. Several investigators have reported that a subgroup of depressed patients experience an impressive, albeit transient, improvement in their mood immediately following one night of sleep deprivation (for review see Leibenluft and Wehr, 1992). In the sole study of its kind that we are aware of, Roy-Byrne and colleagues (1986) deprived 12 patients with panic disorder of a single night's sleep. In marked contrast to the pattern of improvement usually seen in at least a subgroup of patients with major depression, a subgroup of the patients with panic disorder reported a worsening of anxiety symptoms, with 40% experiencing a panic attack the following day. Thus, although in need of replication and extension to examine other anxiety disorders, this study would suggest that the response to sleep deprivation may be a pathophysiological feature that will be of further value in the study of differences between depressed and anxious patients.

VI. CONCLUSIONS

What emerges most clearly from the large body of literature that we have reviewed in this chapter is how much more work remains to be done in elucidating and, ultimately, understanding the meaning of the psychophysiological findings in depression in anxiety. Several areas seem most promising for future research studies: the further analysis of EDA in various depressive and anxiety disorders and the further study of sleep in depressive and anxiety disorders. The existing EDA studies in depressive and anxiety disorders are globally supportive of pronounced differences in response patterns between the two syndromes. Similarly, the typical disturbances in REM latency and REM density seen in endogenous depression are generally not seen in any of the anxiety disorders. Furthermore, particularly for polysomnographic measures, there is evidence to suggest that the anxiety disorders may, in some ways, differ markedly from one another (e.g., PTSD versus panic disorder).

Outstanding shortcomings in the study of the psychophysiology of these disorders include the following: (1) the failure to standardize paradigms across laboratories, making the comparison of findings between studies nearly impossible; (2) the relative neglect that has heretofore been paid to factors such as cognitions at the time of testing, which might potentially impinge on psychophysiological findings; and (3) the infrequency with which comorbid conditions (e.g., depression in patients with anxiety disorders and, conversely, anxiety in patients with depression) are considered as covariates for the various psychophysiological measures being reported. These methodological inadequacies are being increasingly addressed in the modern literature, which, we are hopeful, will lead us farther along the path toward a genuine understanding of the psychophysiology of depression and anxiety.

REFERENCES

R. Abrams and M. A. Taylor, Differential EEG patterns in affective disorder and schizophrenia. *Arch. Gen. Psychiatry*, *36*:1355 (1979).

L. Abramson, M. S. Keshavan, and N. Sitaram, Elevated sleep and waking heart rates in anxious depressions, *Biol. Psychiatry, 26*: 496 (1989).

H. S. Akiskal, and H. Lemmi, Sleep in dysthymic, hypethymic, and related conditions, *Principles and Practice of Sleep Medicine* (M. H. Kryger, T. Roth, and W. C. Dement, eds.), W. B. Saunders, Philadelphia, pp. 416–419 (1989).

American Psychiatric Association, *Diagnostic and Statistical Manual of Mental Disorders*, 3rd ed., American Psychiatric Association, Washington, D.C. (1980).

American Psychiatric Association, *Diagnostic and Statistical Manual of Mental Disorders*, 3rd ed., revised, American Psychiatric Association, Washington, D.C. (1987).

J. G. Arena, E. B. Blanchard, F. Andrasik, P. A. Cotch, and P. E. Myers, Reliability of psychophysiological assessment, *Behav. Res. Ther., 4*: 447 (1983).

T. A. Aronson, I. Carasiti, D. McBane, and P. Whitaker-Azmitia, Biological correlates of lactate sensitivity in panic disorder, *Biol. Psychiatry, 26*: 463 (1989).

D. H. Barlow, *Anxiety and its Disorders: The Nature and Treatment of Anxiety and Panic,* Guilford Press, New York (1988).

D. H. Barlow, M. R. Mavissakalian, and L. D. Schofield, Patterns of desynchrony in agoraphobia: A preliminary report, *Behav. Res. Ther., 18*: 441 (1980).

D. M. Bear, and P. Fedio, Quantitative analysis of interictal behavior in temporal lobe epilepsy. *Arch. Neurol., 34*: 454 (1977).

H. R. Beech, K. T. Ciesielki, and P. K. Gordon, Further observations of evoked potentials in obsessional patients, *Br. J. Psychiatry, 142*: 605 (1983).

R. M. Benca, W. H. Obermeyer, R. A. Thisted, and J. C. Gillin, Sleep and psychiatric disorders: A meta-analysis, *Arch Gen. Psychiatry, 49*: 651 (1992).

S. A. Berenbaum, K. Kerns, and M. A. Taylor, A neuropsychological perspective on comorbid disorders, *Comorbidity of Mood and Anxiety Disorders* (J.D. Maser and C.R. Clonger, eds.), American Psychiatric Press, Washington, D.C., pp. 563–584 (1990).

A. S. Bernstein, J. A. Riedel, G. Flemming, D. Seidman, H. Steele, J. Connolly, and J. Lubowsky, Schizophrenia is associated with altered orienting activity; depression with electrodermal (cholinergic?) deficit and normal orienting response, *J. Abnorm. Psychol., 97*: 3 (1988).

D. H. R. Blackwood, I. J. Whalley, J. E. Christie, I. M. Blackburn, D. M. St. Claire, and A. McInnes, Changes in auditory P[3] event-related potential in schizophrenia and depression, *Br. J. Psychiatry, 150*: 154 (1987).

A. J. Bond, D. C. James and M. H. Lader, Physiological and psychological measures in anxious patients, *Psychol. Med., 4*: 364 (1974).

J.-P. Boulenger, L. M. Bierer, T. W. Uhde, E. K. Silberman, and R. M. Post, Psychosensory phenomena in panic and affective disorder. *Biological Psychiatry 1985* (C. Shagass et al., eds.), Elsevier Science Publishing, New York, pp. 462–465, (1986).

A. Breier, D. S. Charney, and G. R. Heninger, Agoraphobia with panic attacks: Development, diagnostic stability, and course of illness, *Arch. Gen. Psychiatry, 43*: 1029 (1986).

R. L. Bruno, S. J. Myers, and A. H. Glassman, A correlational study of cardiovascular autonomic functioning and unipolar depression, *Biol. Psychiatry, 18*: 227 (1983).

D. J. Buysse, C. F. Reynolds III, T. H. Monk, et al., The Pittsburgh Sleep Quality Index: A new instrument for psychiatric practice and research, *Psychiatry Res., 28*: 193 (1989).

D. J. Byrne, A psychophysiological distinction between types of depressive states, *Aust. N. Z. J. Psychiatry, 9*: 181 (1975).

O. G. Cameron, M. A. Lee, G. C. Curtis, and D. S. McCann, Endocrine and physiological changes during "spontaneous" panic attacks, *Psychoneuroendocrinology, 12*: 321 (1987).

O. G. Cameron, and R. M. Nesse, Systemic hormonal and physiological abnormalities in anxiety disorders, *Psychoneuroendocrinology, 13*: 287 (1988).

O. G. Cameron, C. B. Smith, M. A. Lee, P. J. Hollingsworth, E. M. Hill, and G. C. Curtis, Adrenergic status in anxiety disorders: Platelet α 2-adrenergic receptor binding, blood pressure, pulse, and plasma catecholamines in panic and generalized anxiety disorder patients and in normal subjects, *Biol. Psychiatry, 28*: 3 (1990).

M. W. P. Carney, M. Roth, and R. F. Garside, The diagnosis of depressive syndromes and the prediction of ECT, *Br. J. Psychiatry, 111*: 659 (1965).

R. M. Carney, B. A. Hong, S. Kulkarni, and A. Kapila, A comparison of EMG and SCL in normal and depressed subjects, *Pavlov. J. Biol. Sci., 16*: 212 (1981).

M. A. Carskadon, and W. C. Dement, Normal human sleep: An overview, *Principles and Practice of Sleep Medicine* (M. H. Kryger, T. Roth, and W. C. Dement, eds.), W. B. Saunders, Philadelphia, pp. 3–13 (1989).

S. Castellani, M. A. Quillen, D. A. Vaughan, M. A. Hund, L. Ho, M. G. Ziegler, and W. R. Levine, TSH and catecholamine response to TRH in panic disorder, *Biol. Psychiatry, 24*: 87 (1988).

D. S. Charney, G. R. Heninger, and A. Breier, Noradrenergic function in panic anxiety: Effects of yohimbine in healthy subjects and patients with agoraphobia and panic disorder, *Arch. Gen. Psychiatry, 41*: 751 (1984).

D. S. Charney, G. R. Heninger, D. E. Sternberg, K. M. Hafstad, S. Giddings, and D. H. Landis, Adrenergic receptor sensitivity in depression: Effects of clonidine in depressed patients and healthy subjects, *Arch. Gen. Psychiatry, 39*: 290 (1982).

D. S. Charney, S. W. Woods, W. K. Goodman, and G. R. Heninger, Neurobiological mechanisms of panic anxiety: Biochemical and behavioral correlates of yohimbine-induced panic attacks, *Am. J. Psychiatry, 144*: 1030 (1987).

P. Chattopadhyay, E. Cooke, B. Toone, and M. Lader, Habituation of physiological responses in anxiety, *Biol. Psychiatry, 15*: 711 (1980).

K. T. Cieselski, H. R. Beech, and P. K. Gordon, Some electrophysiological observations in obsessional states, *Br. J. Psychiatry, 138*: 479 (1981).

D. M. Clark, A cognitive approach to panic, *Behav. Res. Ther., 24*: 461 (1986).

M. E. Cohen, F. Consolazio, and R. E. Johnson, Blood lactate response during moderate exercise in neurocirculatory asthenia, anxiety neurosis, or effort syndrome, *J. Clin. Invest., 26*: 339 (1947).

D. S. Cowley, T. S. Hyde, S. R. Dager, and D. L. Dunner, Lactate infusions: The role of baseline anxiety, *Psychiatry Res., 21*: 169 (1987).

M. C. Craske, W. C. Sanderson, and D. H. Barlow, How do desynchronous response systems relate to the treatment of agoraphobia: A follow-up evaluation, *Behav. Res. Ther., 25*: 117 (1987).

Y. Dagan, P. Lavie, and A. Bleich, Elevated awakening thresholds in sleep stage 3–4 in war-related posttraumatic stress disorder, *Biol. Psychiatry, 30*: 618 1991.

M. E. Dawson, A. M. Schell, J. R. Braaten, and J. J. Catania, Diagnostic utility of autonomic measures for major depressive disorders, *Psychiatry Res., 15*: 261 (1985).

O. Devinsky, S. Sato, W. Theodore, and R. Porter, Fear episodes due to limbic seizures with normal scalp ictal EEG: A subdural electrographic study, *J. Clin. Psychiatry, 50*: 28 (1989).

S. C. Dilsaver, Pathophysiology of "cholinoceptor supersensitivity" in affective disorder, *Biol. Psychiatry, 21*: 813 (1986).

F. H. Duffy, Topographic display of evoked potentials: Clinical applications of brain electrical activity mapping (BEAM), *Ann. N. Y. Acad. Sci., 388*: 183 (1982).

F. H. Duffy, Topographic mapping of brain electrical activity: Clinical applications and issues, *Topographic Brain Mapping of EEG and Evoked Potentials* (K. Maurer, ed.), Springer-Verlag, Heidelberg, pp. 19–52 (1989).

M. J. Edlund, M. E. McNamara, and R. P. Millman, Sleep apnea and panic attacks, *Compr. Psychiatry, 32*: 130 (1991).

G. Edman, M. Asberg, S. Levander, and D. Schalling, Skin conductance habituation and cerebrospinal fluid 5-hydroxyindoleacetic acid in suicidal patients, *Arch. Gen. Psychiatry, 43*: 586 (1986).

A. Ehlers, J. Margraf, W. T. Roth, C. B. Taylor, R. J. Maddock, J. Sheikh, M. L. Kopell, K. L. McClenahan, D. Gossard, G. H. Blowers, W. S. Agras, and B. S. Kopell, Lactate infusions and panic attacks: Do patients and controls respond differently? *Psychiatry Res., 17*: 295 (1986).

M. Esler, J. Turbott, R. Schwartz, P. Leonard, A. Bobik, H. Skews, and G. Jackman, The peripheral kinetics of norepinephrine in depressive illness, *Arch. Gen. Psychiatry, 39*: 295 (1982).

D. L. Filion, M. E. Dawson, A. M. Schell, and E. A. Hazlett, The relationship between skin conductance orienting and the allocation of processing resources, *Psychophysiology, 28*: 410 (1991).

E. B. Foa, and M. S. Kozak, Emotional processing of fear: Exposure to corrected information, *Psychol. Bull., 99*: 20 (1986).

D. C. Fowles, The eccrine system and electrodermal activity, *Psychophysiology: Systems, Processes, and Applications* (M. G. H. Coles, E. Donchin, and S. W. Porges, eds.), Guilford Press, New York, p. 51 (1986).

R. R. Freedman, P. Ianni, E. Ettedgui, R. Pohl, and J. M. Rainey, Psychophysiological factors in panic disorders, *Psychopathology, 17* (Suppl. 1): 66 (1984).

R. R. Freedman, P. Ianni, E. Ettedgui, and N. Puthezhath, Ambulatory monitoring of panic disorder, *Arch. Gen. Psychiatry, 42*: 244 (1985).

E. Freiza i Baqué, Reliability of electrodermal measures: A compilation, *Biol. Psychol., 14*: 219 (1982).

F. A. Gaffney, B. J. Fenton, L. D. Lane, and C. R. Lake, Hemodynamic, ventilatory, and biochemical responses of panic patients and normal controls with sodium lactate infusion and spontaneous panic attacks, *Arch. Gen. Psychiatry, 45*: 53 (1988).

R. Ganguli, C. F. Reynolds, D. J. Kupfer, EEG sleep in young, never-medicated schizophrenics: A comparison with delusional and nondelusional depressives and with healthy controls, *Arch. Gen. Psychiatry, 44*: 36 (1987).

D. T. George, D. J. Nutt, W. V. Walker, S. W. Porges, B. Adinoff, and M. Linnoila, Lactate and hyperventilation substantially vagal tone in normal volunteers, *Arch. Gen. Psychiatry, 46*: 153 (1989).

M. S. George, S. McLeod-Bryant, R. B. Lydriard, J. E. Kurent, and J. Zealberg, Panic attacks and agoraphobia asociated with a giant right cerebral arteriorenous malformation, *Neuropsychiatry Neuropsychol. Behav. Neurol., 3*: 206 (1990).

A. M. Ghadirian, S. Gauthier, and S. Bertrand, Anxiety attacks in a patient with a right temporal lobe meningioma, *J. Clin. Psychiatry, 47*: 270 (1986).

J. C. Gillin, T. L. Smith, M. Irwin, D. F. Kripke, S. Brown, and M. Shuckit, Short REM latency in primary alcoholic patients with secondary depression, *Am. J. Psychiatry, 147*: 106 (1990).

H. Glaubman, M. Mikulciner, A. Porat, et al., Sleep of chronic posttraumatic patients, *J. Traum. Stress 3*: 255 (1990).

I. B. Goldstein, Physiological responses in anxious women patients: A study of autonomic activity and muscle tension, *Arch. Gen. Psychiatry, 10*: 382 (1964).

I. B. Goldstein, The relationship of muscle tension and autonomic activity to psychiatric disorders, *Psychosom. Med., 27*: 39 (1965).

J. M. Gorman, M. Davies, R. Steinman, M. R. Liebowitz, A. J. Fyer, J. Coromilas, and D. F. Klein, An objective marker of lactate-induced panic, *Psychiatry Res., 22*: 341 (1987).

J. M. Gorman, G. F. Levey, M. R. Liebowitz, P. McGrath, I. L. Appleby, D. J. Dillon, S. O. Davies, and D. F. Klein, Effect of acute ß-adrenergic blockade on lactate-induced panic, *Arch. Gen. Psychiatry, 40*: 1079 (1983).

P. Grossman, and S. Svebak, Respiratory sinus arrhythmia as an index of parasympathetic cardiac control during active coping, *Psychophysiology, 24*: 228 (1987).

L. Grunhaus, S. Gloger, B. Birmacher, C. Palmer, and M. Ben-David, Prolactin response to the cold pressor test in patients with panic attacks, *Psychiatry Res., 8*: 171 (1983).

M. Guidi, O. Scarpino, and F. Angeleri, Topographic EEG and flash visual evoked potentials in elderly subjects, depressed patients, and demented patients. *Psychiatry Res., 29*: 403 (1989).

J. Hafner, and F. Milton, The influence of propranolol on the exposure in vivo of agoraphobics, *Psychol. Med., 7*: 419 (1977).

J. D. Hart, Physiological responses of anxious and normal subjects to simple signal and nonsignal auditory stimuli, *Psychophysiology, 11*: 443 (1974).

P. J. Hauri, M. Friedman, and C. L. Ravaris, Sleep in patients with spontaneous panic attacks, *Sleep, 12*: 232 (1989).

W. G. Himadi, R. Boice, and D. H. Barlow, Assessment of agoraphobia: Triple response measurement, *Behav. Res. Ther., 23*: 311 (1985).

R. Hoehn-Saric, D. R. McLeod, and W. D. Zimmerli, Somatic manifestations in women with generalized anxiety disorder: Psychophysiological responses to psychological stress, *Arch. Gen. Psychiatry, 46*: 1113 (1989).

R. Hoehn-Saric, D. R. McLeod, and W. D. Zimmerli, Psychophysiological response patterns in panic disorder, *Acta Psychiatr. Scand., 83*: 4 (1991).

A. E. Holden, and D. H. Barlow, Heart rate and heart rate variability recorded in vivo in agoraphobics and nonphobics, *Behav. Ther., 17*: 26 (1986).

T. Horvath, and R. Meares, The sensory filter in schizophrenia: A study of habituation, arousal, and the dopamine hypothesis, *Br. J. Psychiatry, 134*: 39 (1979).

W. G. Iacono, Psychophysiological markers of psychopathology: A review, *Can. Psychol., 26*: 96 (1985).

W. G. Iacono, D. T. Lykken, L. J. Peloquin, A. E. Lumry, R. H. Valentine, and V. B. Tuason, Electrodermal activity in euthymic unipolar and bipolar affective disorders: A possible marker for depression, *Arch. Gen. Psychiatry, 40*: 557 (1983).

W. G. Iacono, D. T. Lykken, K. P. Haroian, L. J. Peloquin, R. H. Valentine, and V. B. Tuason, Electrodermal activity in euthymic patients with affective disorders: One-year retest stability and the effects of stimulus intensity and significance, *J. Abnorm. Psychol., 93*: 304 (1984).

T. R. Insel, E. F. Donnelly, M. L. Lalakea, I. S. Alterman, and D. L. Murphy, Neurological and neuropsychological studies of patients with obsessive–compulsive disorder. *Biol. Psychiatry, 18*: 741 (1983).

N. S. Jacobson, L. Wilson, and C. Tupper, The clinical significance of treatment gains resulting from exposure-based interventions for agoraphobia: A re-analysis of outcome data, *Behav. Ther., 19*: 539 (1988).

D. S. Janowksy, and S. C. Risch, Adrenergic–cholinergic balance and affective disorders, *Depression: Basic Mechanisms, Diagnosis, and Treatment* (A. J. Rush and K. Z. Altshuler, eds.), Guilford Press, New York, p. 84 (1986).

L. Jansson, and L.-G. Öst, Behavioral treatments for agoraphobia: An evaluative review, *Clin. Psychol. Rev., 2*: 311 (1982).

L. Jansson, A. Jerremalm, and L.-G. Öst, Follow-up of agoraphobic patients treated with exposure in vivo or applied relaxation, *Br. J. Psychiatry, 149*: 486 (1986).M. A. Jenike, and A. W. Brotman, The EEG in obsessive-compulsive disorder. *J. Clin. Psychiatry, 45*: 122 (1984).

R. T. Joffe, and R. P. Swinson, Carbamazepine in obsessive-compulsive disorder. *Biol. Psychiatry, 22*: 1169 (1987).

C. D. Kauffman, C. Reist, A. Djenderedjian, et al., Biological markers of affective disorders and posttraumatic stress disorder: A pilot study with desipramine, *J. Clin. Psychiatry, 48*: 366 (1987).

F. Keller, M. Wolfersdorf, R. Straube, and G. Hole, Suicidal behaviour and electrodermal activity in depressive inpatients, *Acta Psychiatr. Scand., 83*: 324 (1991).

D. H. W. Kelly, and C. J. S. Walte, The relationship between clinical diagnosis and anxiety, assessed by forearm blood flow and other measurements, *Br. J. Psychiatry, 114*: 611 (1968).

D. Kelly, and C. J. S. Walter, A clinical and physiological relationship between anxiety and depression, *Br. J. Psychiatr., 115*: 401 (1969).

D. Kelly, N. Mitchell-Heggs, and D. Sherman, Anxiety and the effects of sodium lactate assessed clinically and physiologically, *Br. J. Psychiatry, 119*: 129 (1971).

M. S. Keshavan, F. Reynolds, D. J. Kupfer, EEG in schizophrenia: A critical review, *Compr. Psychiatry, 31*: 34 (1990).

S. Khanna, C. R. Mukundan, and S. M. Channabasavanna, Middle latency evoked potentials in melancholic depression, *Biol. Psychol., 25*: 494 (1989).

V. I. Knott, and Y. D. Lapierre, Electrophysiological and behavioral correlates of psychomotor responsivitity in depression, *Biol. Psychol., 22*: 313 (1987).

W. Knott, R. Chaudry, and Y. LaPierre, Panic induced by sodium lactate: Electrophysiological correlates, *Prog. Neuropsychopharmacol. Biol. Psychiatry, 5*: 511 (1981).

D. J. Kupfer, and E. Frank, EEG sleep changes in recurrent depression. *New Directions in Affective Disorders* (B. Lerer and S. Gershon, eds.). Springer-Verlag, New York, pp. 225–228 (1989).

D. J. Kupfer, E. Frank, M. S. McEachran, V. J. Grochocinski, delta Sleep ratio: A biological correlate of early recurrence in unipolar affective disorder, *Arch. Gen. Psychiatry, 47*: 1100 (1990).

M. H. Lader, Palmar skin conductance measures in anxiety and phobic states, *J. Psychosom. Res., 11*: 271 (1967).

M. H. Lader, *The Psychophysiology of Mental Illness*, Routledge and Kegan Paul, London (1975).

M. H. Lader, and A. M. Mathews, A physiological model of phobic anxiety and desensitization, *Behav. Res. Ther., 6*: 411 (1968).

M. H. Lader, and A. Mathews, Physiological changes during spontaneous panic attacks, *J. Psychosom., Res., 14*: 377 (1970).
M. H. Lader, and L. Wing, Habituation of the psycho-galvanic reflex in patients with anxiety states and in normal subjects, *J. Neurol. Neurosurg. Psychiat., 27*: 210 (1964).
M. H. Lader, L. Wing, Physiological measures in agitated and retarded depressed patients, *J. Psychiatr. Res., 7*: 89 (1969).
H. W. Lahmeyer, and S. N. Bellur, Cardiac regulation and depression, *J. Psychiatr. Res., 21*: 1 (1987).
C. R. Lake, D. Pickar, M. G. Ziegler, S. Lipper, S. Slater, and D. L. Murphy, High plasma norepinephrine levels in patients with major affective disorder, *Am. J. Psychiatry, 139*: 1315 (1982).
P. J. Lang,. Fear reduction and fear behavior: Problems in treating a construct, *Research in Psychotherapy* (J. M. Shlien, ed.), American Psychological Association, Washington, D.C., p. 90 (1968).
P. J. Lang, A bio-informational theory of emotional imagery, *Psychophysiology, 16*: 495 (1979).
N. Langdon, K. I. Walsh, M. Van Dam, R. W. Vaughan, and D. Parkes. Genetic markers in narcolepsy, *Lancet, 2*: 1178 (1984).
A. W. Langer, J. A. McCubbin, C. M. Stoney, J. S. Hutcheson, J. D. Charlton, and P. A. Obrist, Cardiopulmonary adjustments during exercise and an aversive reaction time task: Effects of beta adrenoceptor blockade, *Psychophysiology, 22*: 59 (1985).
Y. D. Lapierre, and H. J. Butter, Agitated and retarded depression: A clinical psychophysiological evaluation, *Neuropsychobiology, 6*: 217 (1980).
P. B. Larsen, N. Schneiderman, and R. D. Pasin, Physiological bases of cardiovascular psychophysiology, *Psychophysiology: Systems, Processes, and Applications* (M. G. H. Coles, E. Donchin, and S. W. Porges, eds.), Guilford Press, New York, p. 122 (1986).
P. Lavie, A. Hefez, G. Halperin, and D. Enoch. Long-term effects of traumatic war-related events on sleep, *Am. J. Psychiatry, 136*: 175 (1979).
E. Leibenluft, and T. A. Wehr, Is sleep deprivation useful in the treatment of depression? *Am. J. Psychiatry, 149*: 159 (1992).
U. Lepola, U. Nousiainen, M. Puranen, X. Kiekkinen, R. Rimon, EEG and CT findings in patients with panic disorder, *Biol. Psychiatry, 28*: 721 (1990).
M. R. Leibowitz, A. J. Fyer, J. M. Gorman, D. Dillon, I. L. Appleby, G. Levy, S. Anderson, M. Levitt, M. Palij, S. O. Davies,and D. F. Klein, Lactate provocation of panic attacks: I. Clinical and behavioral findings. *Arch. Gen. Psychiatry, 41*: 764 (1984).
M. R. Liebowitz, J. M. Gorman, A. J. Fyer, M. Levitt, D. Dillon, G. Levy, I. L. Appleby, S. Anderson, M. Palij, S. O. Davies, and D. F. Klein, Lactate provocation of panic attacks II. Biochemical and physiological findings, *Arch. Gen. Psychiatry, 42*: 709 (1985).
D. T. Lykken, W. G. Iacono, K. Haroian, M. McGue, and T. J. Bouchard, Habituation of the skin conductance response to strong stimuli: A twin study, *Psychophysiology, 25*: 4 (1988).
R. B. Malmo, Anxiety and behavioral arousal, *Psychol. Rev., 64*: 276 (1957).
J. Margraf, Ambulatory psychophysiological monitoring of panic attacks, *J. Psychophysiol., 4*: 315 (1990).
J. Margraf, A. Ehlers, and W. T. Roth, Sodium lactate infusions and panic attacks: A review and critique, *Psychosom. Med., 48*: 23 (1986).
J. Margraf, C. B. Taylor, A. Ehlers, W. T. Roth, and W. S. Agras, Panic attacks in the natural environment, *J. Nerv. Ment. Dis., 175*: 558 (1987).
M. Mavissakalian, Trimodel assessment in agoraphobia research: Further observations on heart rate and synchrony-desynchrony, *J. Psychopathol. Behav. Assoc., 9*: 89 (1987).
M. Mavissakalian, and L. Michelson, Patterns of psychophysiological change in the treatment of agoraphobia, *Behav. Res. Ther., 20*: 347 (1982).
T. A. Mellman, and T. W. Uhde, Electroencephalographic sleep in panic disorder: A focus on sleep-related panic attacks, *Arch. Gen. Psychiatry, 46*: 178 (1989a).

T. A. Mellman, and T. W. Uhde, Sleep panic attacks: New clinical findings and theoretical implications, *Am. J. Psychiatry, 146*: 1204 (1989b).

T. A. Mellman, and T. W. Uhde, Sleep in panic and generalized anxiety disorders, *Neurobiology of Panic Disorder*, (J. C. Ballenger, ed.), Alan R. Liss, New York, pp. 365–376 (1990).

T. A. Mellman, R. E. Ramsay, and S. G. Fitzgerald, Divergence of PTSD and narcolepsy associated with military trauma, *J. Anxiety Disord., 5*: 267 (1991).

L. Michelson, and M. Mavissakalian, Psychophysiological outcome of behavioral and pharmacological treatments of agoraphobia, *J. Consult. Clin. Psychol., 53*: 229 (1985).

L. Michelson, M. Mavissakalian, and K. Marchione, Cognitive and behavioral treatments of agoraphobia: Clinical, behavioral, psychophysiological outcomes, *J. Consult. Clin. Psychol., 53*: 913 (1985).

L. Michelson, K. Marchione, M. Greenwald, L. Glanz, S. Testa, and N. Marchione, Panic disorder: Cognitive-behavioral treatment, *Behav. Res. Ther., 28*: 141 (1990a).

L. Michelson, M. Mavissakalian, K. Marchione, R. F. Ulrich, N. Marchione, and S. Testa, Psychophysiological outcome of cognitive behavioral and psychophysiologically-based treatments of agoraphobia, *Behav. Res. Ther., 18:* 51 (1990b).

H. C. Middleton, Cardiovascular dystonia in recovered panic patients, *J. Affect. Disord., 19*: 229 (1990).

A. M. Mirkin, and A. Coppen, Electrodermal activity in depression: Clinical and biochemical correlates, *Br. J. Psychiatry, 137*: 93 (1980).

R. M. Nesse, O. G. Cameron, C. G. Curtis, D. S. McCann, and M. J. Huber-Smith, Adrenergic function in patients with panic anxiety, *Arch. Gen. Psychiatry, 41*: 771 (1984).

F. X. Newman, M. B. Stein, J. R. Trettau, R. Coppola, and T. W. Uhde, Quantitative EEG effects of caffeine in panic disorder, *Psychiatry Res.* (*Neuroimaging*), *45*: 105 (1992).

R. Nikula, Psychological correlates of nonspecific skin conductance responses, *Psychophysiology, 28*: 86 (1991).

P. Noble, and M. Lader, The symptomatic correlates of the skin conductance changes in depression, *J. Psychiatr. Res., 9*: 61 (1971a).

P. Noble, and M. Lader, Depressive illness, pulse rate and forearm blood flow, *Br. J. Psychiatry, 119*: 261 (1971b).

P. Noble, and M. Lader, A physiological comparison of "endogenous" and "reactive" depression, *Br. J. Psychiatry, 120*: 541 (1972).

D. J. Nutt, Altered central α_2-adrenoceptor sensitivity in panic disorder, *Arch. Gen. Psychiatry, 46*: 165 (1989).

P. A. Obrist, *Cardiovascular Psychophysiology: A Perspective*, Plenum Press, New York (1981).

A. Öhman, The orienting response, attention, and learning: An information-processing perspective, *The Orienting Reflex in Humans* (H. D. Kimmel, E. H. Van Olst, and J. F. Orlebeke, eds.), Lawrence Erlbaum, Hillsdale, N.J., p. 443 (1979).

A. Öhman, Electrodermal activity and vulnerability to schizophrenia: A review, *Biol. Psychol., 12*: 87 (1981).

S. P. Orr, and R. K. Pitman, Electrodermal psychophysiology of anxiety disorder: Orienting response and spontaneous fluctuations, *Biol. Psychiatry, 22*: 653 (1987).

L.-G. Öst, Age on onset in different phobias, *J. Abnorm. Psychol., 96*: 223 (1987).

L.-G. Öst, A. Jerremalm, and L. Jansson, Individual response patterns and the effects of different behavioral methods in the treatment of agoraphobia, *Behav. Res. Ther., 22*: 697 (1984).

G. N. Papadimitriou, M. Kerkhofs, C. Kempenaers, and J. Mendlewicz, EEG sleep studies in patients with generalized anxiety disorder, *Psychiatry Res. 26*: 183 (1988).

P. Pauli, C. Marquardt, L. Hartl, D. O. Nutzinger, R. Hölzl, and F. Strian, Anxiety induced by cardiac perceptions in patients with panic attacks: A field study, *Behav. Res. Ther., 29*: 137 (1991).

C. Perris, EEG techniques in the measurement of the severity of the depressive syndromes, *Neuropsychobiology, 1*: 16 (1975).

H. Pockberger, H. Petsche, P. Rappelsberger, B. Zidek, and H. G. Zapotoczky, Ongoing EEG in depression: A topographic spectral analytical pilot study, *Electroenchephalogr. Clin. Neurophysiol., 61*: 349 (1985).

S. J. Rachman, Emotional processing. *Behav. Res. Ther., 18*: 51 (1980).

S. J. Rachman, and R. Hodgson, Synchrony and desynchrony in fear and avoidance, *Behav. Res. Ther., 12*: 311 (1974).

R. Rapee, Differential response to hyperventilation in panic disorder and generalized anxiety disorder, *J. Abnorm. Psychol., 95*: 24 (1986).

J. Rapoport, R. Elkins, D. H. Langer, et al., Childhood obsessive–compulsive disorder, *Am. J. Psychiatry, 138*: 12 (1981).

M. Raskin, Decreased skin conductance response habituation in chronically anxious patients, *Biol. Psychol., 2*: 309 (1975).

E. M. Reiman, M. E. Raichle, F. K. Butler, P. Herscovitch, and E. Robins, A focal brain abnormality in panic disorder, *Nature, 310*: 683 (1984).

C. F. Reynolds, Sleep in affective disorders. *Principles and Practice of Sleep Medicine* (M. H. Kryger, T. Roth, and W. C. Dement, eds.), Philadelphia, Saunders, pp. 413 (1989).

C. F. Reynolds, and D. J. Kupfer, Sleep research in affective illness: State of the art circa 1987 (state-of-the-art), *Sleep, 10*: 199 (1987).

C. F. Reynolds, D. H. Shaw, T. F. Newton, P. A. Coble, and D. J. Kupfer, EEG sleep in outpatients with generalized anxiety: A preliminary comparison with depressed outpatients, *Psychiatry Res., 8*: 81 (1983).

C. R. Richter, The electrical skin resistance: Diurnal and daily variation in normal and psychopathic persons, *Arch. Neurol. Psychiatry, 19*: 488 (1928).

J. Rosen, C. F. Reynolds, A. L. Yeager, R. R. Houck, and L. F. Hurwitz, Sleep disturbances in survivors of the Nazi holocaust, *Am. J. Psychiatry, 148*: 62 (1991).

R. J. Ross, W. A. Ball, K. A. Sullivan, et al., Sleep disturbance as the hallmark of posttraumatic stress disorder, *Am. J. Psychiatry, 146*: 697 (1989).

W. T. Roth, T. B. Horvath, A. Pfefferbaum, and B. S. Kopell, Event-related potentials in schizophrenics, *Electroencephalogr. Clin. Neurophysiol., 48*: 127 (1980).

W. T. Roth, M. J. Telch, C. B. Taylor, J. A. Sachitano, C. C. Gallen, M. L. Kopell, K. L. McClenahan, W. S. Agras, and A. Pfefferbaum, Autonomic characteristics of agoraphobia with panic attacks, *Biol Psychiatry, 21*: 1133 (1986).

W. T. Roth, M. J. Telch, C. B. Taylor, and W. S. Agras, Autonomic changes after treatment of agoraphobia with panic attacks, *Psychiatry Res., 24*: 95 (1988).

W. T. Roth, A. Ehlers, C. B. Taylor, J. Margraf, and W. S. Agras, Skin conductance habituation in panic disorder patients, *Biol. Psychiatry, 27*: 1231 (1990).

A. Roy, D. Pickar, M. Linnoila, and W. Z. Potter, Plasma norepinephrine level in affective disorders, *Arch. Gen. Psychiatry, 42*: 1181 (1985).

P. P. Roy-Byrne, T. W. Uhde, and R. M. Post, Effects of one night's sleep deprivation on mood and behavior in panic disorder, *Arch. Gen. Psychiatry, 43*: 895 (1986).

M. V. Rudorfer, R. J. Ross, M. Linnoila, M. A. Sherer, and W. Potter, Exaggerated orthostatic responsivity of plasma norepinephrine in depression, *Arch. Gen. Psychiatry, 42*: 1186 (1985).

W. C. Sanderson, P. A. DiNardo, R. M. Rapee, and D. H. Barlow, Syndrome comorbidity in patients diagnosed with *DSM-III-R* anxiety disorder, *J. Abnorm. Psychol., 99*: 308 (1990).

C. Shagass, R. A. Roemer, J. J. Straumanis, and R. C. Josiassen, Distinctive somatosensory evoked potential features in obsessive-compulsive disorder, *Biol. Psychiatry, 19*: 1507 (1984).

C. Shagass, J. J. Straumanis, R. A. Roemer, and M. Amadeo, Evoked potentials of schizophrenics in several sensory modalities, *Biol. Psychiatry, 12*: 221 (1977).

A. Sherwood, M. T. Allen, P. A. Obrist, and A. W. Langer, Evaluation of beta-adrenergic influences on cardiovascular and metabolic adjustments to physical and psychological stress, *Psychophysiology, 23*: 89 (1989).

S. A. Shields, K. A. MacDowell, S. B. Fairchild, and M. L. Campbell, Is mediation of sweating cholinergic, adrenergic, or both? A comment on the literature, *Psychophysiology, 24*: 312 (1987).

D. A. T. Siddle, Orienting, habituation, and resource allocation: An associative analysis, *Psychophysiology, 28*: 245 (1991).

D. A. T. Siddle, and G. Turpin, Measurement, quantification, and analysis of cardiac activity, *Techniques in Psychophysiology* (I. Martin and P. H. Venables, eds.), John Wiley & Sons, Chichester, p. 139 (1980).

L. J. Siever, T. W. Uhde, D. C. Jimerson, C. R. Lake, E. R. Silberman, R. M. Post, and D. L. Murphy, Differential inhibitory noradrenergic responses to clonidine in 25 depressed patients and 25 normal control subjects, *Am. J. Psychiatry, 141*: 733 (1984).

P. W. Skerritt, Anxiety and the heart —a historical review, *Psychol. Med., 13*: 17 (1983).

E. N. Sokolov, *Perception and the Conditional Reflex,* Pergamon Press, Oxford (1963).

S. M. Southwick, J. H. Krystal, A. Morgan, D. Johnson, L. M. Nagy, A. Nicolaou, G. R. Heninger, D. S. Charney, Abnormal noradrenergic function in posttraumatic stress disorder, *Arch. Gen. Psychiatry, 50*: 266 (1993).

R. L. Spitzer, J. Endicott, and E. Robins, *Research Diagnostic Criteria (RDC) for a Selected Group of Functional Disorders*, Biometrics Research, New York State Psychiatric Institute (1977).

M. B. Stein, M. W. Enns, and M. H. Kryger, Sleep in nondepressed patients with panic disorder: II. Polysomnographic assessment of sleep architecture and sleep continuity, *J. Affect. Disord., 28*: 1 (1993).

M. B. Stein, M. Tancer, and T. W. Uhde, Major depression in patients with panic disorder: Factors associated with course and recurrence, *J. Affective Disord., 11*: 105 (1990).

M. B. Stein, and T. W. Uhde, Panic disorder and major depression: A tale of two syndromes, *Psychiatr. Clin. North Am., 11*: 441 (1988).

M. B. Stein, and T. W. Uhde, Endocrine, cardiovascular, and behavioral effects of intravenous protirelin in patients with panic disorder, *Arch. Gen. Psychiatry, 48*: 148 (1991).

M. B. Stein, and T. W. Uhde, Infrequent occurrence of EEG abnormalities in panic disorder, *Am. J. Psychiatry, 146*: 517 (1989).

M. B. Stein, M. E. Tancer, and T. W. Uhde, Physiologic and plasma norepinephrine responses to orthostasis in patients with panic disorder and social phobia. *Arch. Gen. Psychiatry, 49:* 311 (1992).

M. C. Storrie, H. O. Doerr, and M. H. Johnson, Skin conductance characteristics of depressed subjects before and after therapeutic intervention, *J. Nerv. Ment. Dis., 69*: 176 (1981).

C. B. Taylor, R. King, A. Ehlers, J. Margraf, D. Clark, C. Hayward, W. T. Roth, and S. Agras, Treadmill exercise test and ambulatory measures in panic attacks, *Am. J. Cardiol., 60*: 48J-52J (1987).

M. J. Telch, W. S. Agras, C. B. Taylor, W. T. Roth, and C. C. Gallen, Combined pharmacological and behavioral treatment for agoraphobia, *Behav. Res. Ther., 23*: 325 (1985).

M. E. Thase, and D. J. Kupfer, Current status of EEG sleep in the assessment and treatment of depression, *Advances in Human Psychopharmacology, Vol. 4* (G. D. Burrows, and J. S. Werry, eds.), JAI Press, Greenwich, pp. 93–148 (1987).

L.-H. Thorell, Electrodermal activity in suicidal and nonsuicidal depressive patients and in matched healthy subjects, *Acta Psychiatr. Scand., 76*: 420 (1987).

L.-H. Thorell, and G. d'Elia, Electrodermal activity in depressive patients in remission and in matched healthy subjects, *Acta Psychiatr. Scand., 78*: 247 (1988).

L.-H. Thorell, B. F. Kjellman, and G. d'Elia, Electrodermal activity in relation to diagnostic subgroups and symptoms and depressive patients, *Acta Psychiatr. Scand., 76*: 693 (1987a).

L.-H. Thorell, B. F. Kjellman, and G. d'Elia, Electrodermal activity in antidepressant medicated and unmedicated depressive patients and in matched healthy subjects, *Acta Psychiatr. Scand., 76*: 684 (1987b).

B. K. Toone, E. Cooke, and M. H. Lader, Electrodermal activity in the affective disorders and schizophrenia, *Psychol. Med., 11*: 497 (1972).

T. W. Uhde, P. P. Roy-Byrne, J. C. Gillin, W. Mendelson, J.-P. Boulenger B. J. Vittone, and R. M. Post, The sleep of patients with panic disorder, *Psychiatry Res., 12*: 251 (1984).

T. W. Uhde, M. B. Stein, B. J. Vittone, L. J. Siever, J.-P. Boulenger, E. Klein, and T. A. Mellman, Behavioral and physiologic effects of short-term and long-term administration of clonidine in panic disorder, *Arch. Gen. Psychiatry, 46*: 170 (1989).

R. G. Vasile, F. H. Duffy, G. McAnulty, J. J. Mooney, K. Bloomingdale, and J. J. Schildkraut, Abnormal flash visual evoked response in melancholia: A replication study. *Biol Psychiatry 31*: 325–336 (1992).

R. C. Veith, M. A. Raskind, R. F. Barnes, G. Gumbrecht, J. L. Ritchie, and J. B. Halter, Tricyclic antidepressants and supine, standing, and exercise plasma norepinephrine levels, *Clin. Pharmacol. Ther., 33*: 763 (1983).

P. H. Venables, and M. J. Christie, Mechanisms, instrumentation, recording techniques, and quantification of responses, *Electrodermal Activity in Psychological Research* (W. F. Prokasy and D. S. Raskin, eds.), Academic Press, New York, p. 1 (1973).

J. A. Vermilyea, R. Boice, and D. H. Barlow, Rachman and Hodgson (1974) a decade later: How do desynchronous response systems relate to the treatment of agoraphobia? *Behav. Res. Ther., 25*: 319 (1984).

E. C. Villacres, M. Hollifield, W. J. Katon, C. W. Wilkinson, and R. C. Veith, Sympathetic nervous system activity in panic disorder, *Psychiatry Res., 21*: 313 (1987).

L. M. Wall, M. Tuchman, and D. Mielke, Panic attacks and temporal lobe seizures associated with a right temporal lobe arteriovenous malformation: case report. *J. Clin. Psychiatry, 46*: 143 (1985).

N. G. Ward, and H. O. Doerr, Skin conductance: A potentially sensitive and specific marker for depression, *J. Nerv. Ment. Dis., 174*: 553 (1986).

N. J. Weissman, M. K. Shear, R. Kramer-Fox, and R. B. Devereux, Contrasting patterns of autonomic dysfunction in patients with mitral valve prolapse and panic attacks, *Am. J. Med., 67*: 880 (1987).

B. V. White, and E. F. Gildea, "Cold pressor test" in tension and anxiety: A cardiochronographic study, *Arch. Neurol. Psychiatry, 38*: 964 (1937).

K. M. Willimas, W. G. Iacono, and R. A. Remick, Electrodermal activity among subtypes of depression, *Biol. Psychiatry, 20*: 158 (1985).

K. G. Wilson, Electrodermal lability and simple reaction time, *Biol. Psychol., 24*: 275 (1987).

L. Wing, Physiological effects of performing a difficult task in patients with anxiety states.

S. W. Woods, D. S. Charney, W. K. Goodman, and G. R. Heninger, Carbon dioxide-induced anxiety: Behavioral, physiologic, and biochemical effects of carbon dioxide in patients with panic disorders and healthy subjects, *Arch. Gen. Psychiatry, 45*: 43 (1988).

S. W. Woods, D. S. Charney, C. A. McPherson, A. H. Gradman, and G. R. Heninger, Situational panic attacks: Behavioral, physiologic, and biochemical characterization, *Arch. Gen. Psychiatry, 44*: 365 (1987).

V. K. Yeragani, R. Balon, R. Pohl, A. Ortiz, P. Weinberg, and J. M Rainey, Do higher preinfusion heart rates predict laboratory-induced panic attacks? *Biol. Psychiatry, 22*: 554 (1987a).

V. K. Yeragani, R. Pohl, R. Balon, and P. Sherwood, Lactate infusions: The role of baseline anxiety and autonomic measures, *Psychiatry Res., 22*: 263 (1987b).

V. K. Yeragani, R. Pohl, J. M. Rainey, R. Balon, A. Ortiz, H. Lycaki, and S. Gershon, Preinfusion heart rates and laboratory-induced panic anxiety, *Acta Psychiatr. Scand., 75*: 51 (1987c).

V. K. Yeragani, J. M. Rainey, R. Pohl, R. Balon, R. Berchou, S. Jolly, and H. Lycaki, Preinfusion anxiety and laboratory induced panic attacks in panic disorder patients, *J. Clin. Psychiatry, 49*: 302 (1988).

V. Yeragani, R. Balon, and R. Pohl, Lactate infusions in panic disorder patients and normal controls: Autonomic measures and subjective anxiety, *Acta Psychiatr. Scand., 79*: 32 (1989).

V. K. Yeragani, R. Balon, R. Pohl, C. Ramesh, D. Glitz, P. Weinberg, and B. Merlos, Decreased R-R variance in panic disorder patients, *Acta Psychiatr. Scand., 81*: 554 (1990a).

V. K. Yeragani, P. C. Meiri, R. Pohl, R. Balon, N. Desai, and S. Golec, Heart rate and blood pressure changes during postural change and isometric handgrip exercise in patients with panic disorder and normal controls, *Acta Psychiatr. Scand., 81*: 9 (1990b).

V. K. Yeragani, R. Pohl, R. Balon, C. Ramesh, D. Glitz, I. Jung, and P. Sherwood, Heart rate variability in patients with major depression. *Psychiatry Res.,* (1991).

T. P. Zahn, Psychophysiological approaches to psychopathology, *Psychophysiology: Systems, Processes, and Applications,* (M. G. H. Coles, E. Donchin, and S. W. Porges, eds.), Guilford Press, New York, pp. 508 (1986).

T. D. Zahn, J. I. Nurnberger, and W. H. Berrettini, Electrodermal activity in young adults at genetic risk for affective disorder, *Arch. Gen. Psychiatry, 46*: 1120 (1989).

V. P. Zarcone, K. L. Benson, and P. A. Berger, Abnormal rapid eye movement latencies in schizophrenia, *Arch. Gen. Psychiatry, 44*: 45 (1987).

M. Zimmerman, W. Coryell, B. Pfohl, and D. Stangl, The validity of four definitions of endogenous depression, *Arch. Gen. Psychiatry, 43*: 234 (1986).

8

Animal Models of Anxiety and Anxiolytic Drug Action

Dallas Treit
University of Alberta, Edmonton, Alberta, Canada

I. INTRODUCTION

A. Animal Models and Anxiolytic Drugs

Animal models of anxiety attempt to represent some aspect of the etiology, symptomatology, or treatment of human anxiety disorders, to facilitate the scientific study of these disorders (Marks, 1987; Mineka, 1985). Within this broad context, animal models of anxiolytic drug action can be viewed as treatment models concerned with the pharmacological control of human anxiety disorders. In particular, these animal models are used to identify novel anxiolytic compounds and to study the mechanisms whereby these compounds produce their anxiolytic effects (Treit, 1985a). Animal models of anxiolytic drug action have been useful in the preclinical testing of benzodiazepine-type anxiolytics, in studying the functional relevance of the benzodiazepine receptor system, and in characterizing the effects of benzodiazepine antagonists (e.g., Ro 15–1788; flumazenil), partial agonists (e.g., CGS 9896), and inverse agonists (e.g., B-CCM). (For recent reviews see Crawley, 1985; File, 1984, 1985, 1987; Gardner, 1988; Lal and Emmett-Oglesby, 1983; Lister, 1990; Shephard, 1986; Thiebot, 1983; Thiebot et al., 1988; Treit, 1985a.)

In spite of their proven usefulness, however, animal models of anxiolytic drug action have two important limitations, which are outlined in the following paragraphs and will serve as the focus of the present review. The first limitation is that the validation of these models has depended primarily on their relative sensitivity to one class of clinically proven and widely prescribed anxiolytic compounds: the benzodiazepines. The successful introduction of nonbenzodiazepine anxiolytics (e.g., buspirone; Skolnick et al., 1984) into recent clinical practice presents a particular challenge to the validity of these tests as general models of antianxiety drug effects; it is unclear whether or not and to what extent current animal models of anxiolytic drug effects are also sensitive to nonbenzodiazepine anxiolytics such as buspirone (Chopin and Briley, 1987; Gardner, 1986; Traber and Thomas, 1987).

In addition to influencing the validation of animal tests, the preeminence of benzodiazepine anxiolytics in clinical practice and research during the last 30 years has naturally shaped the study of the mechanisms of anxiolytic drug action. Since the discovery in 1977 of benzodiazepine binding sites in the brain (Braestrup and Squires, 1977), and their functional association with γ-aminobutyric acid (GABA) receptors and a chloride ionophore, the GABA–benzodiazepine receptor complex has been a dominant focus for the study of the mechanisms of anxiolytic drug action (for recent reviews see Brier and Paul, 1990; Haefely, 1990; Hommer et al., 1987). Nevertheless, novel anxiolytics, such as buspirone, do not appear to interact primarily at this receptor complex. Instead, the evidence suggests that buspirone-type anxiolytics interact with a subset of serotonergic targets: the serotonin (5-HT_{1A}) receptor sites (Peroutka, 1985). Whether or not buspirone-type anxiolytics work through a mechanism of action that is ultimately distinct from benzodiazepine-type anxiolytics is an issue of both theoretical and practical importance, but the resolution of this question will depend, in part, on the relative sensitivity of current animal models to both benzodiazepine and nonbenzodiazepine anxiolytics.

The second limitation of current animal models of anxiolytic drug action is that pharmacological validation of these models has often taken precedence over behavioral or physiological validation; the degree to which these models mimic some aspect of either the symptomatology or etiology of human anxiety has been of secondary interest, in spite of the fact that antianxiety drug effects, by definition, must be measured against a baseline of anxiety.

Validation of animal models of anxiolytic drug action typically proceeds along three lines: correlation, isomorphism, and homology (Treit, 1985a). A correlational model is validated on pharmacological grounds alone. At a minimum, the correlational model must be sensitive to the effects of clinically proved, anxiolytic agents. In addition, the relative potency of anxiolytic compounds in the model should be comparable with their relative potency in treating human anxiety. Finally, the model should be selectively sensitive to anxiolytic agents, so that anxiolytics can be distinguished from nonanxiolytics. Although these pharmacological criteria have the virtues of being objective and testable, and may be adequate if the purpose of the test is exclusively the detection of anxiolytic agents (e.g., screening tests), they may not be sufficient if the purpose of the test is to understand the mechanisms whereby drugs reduce anxiety or fear. In the latter, some degree of behavioral isomorphism or homology relative to anxiety or fear is desirable. *Isomorphism* implies that the animal's anxiety response is in some way similar to a human anxiety response (e.g., fleeing), and *homology* implies that the cause of the anxiety response in the animal (e.g., the threat of an aversive stimulus) is sufficient to cause an anxiety response in humans. Although isomorphism and homology are difficult to validate empirically, some functional similarity between the animal model and human anxiety is a logical requirement if the animal model is used for studying the mechanisms of antianxiety drug action (Treit, 1985a).

It should be emphasized that isomorphism and homology are reasonable criteria only insofar as they are viewed as analogies used to search for the actual causes of human anxiety disorders and their associated symptomatologies. These animal analogues are needed because the actual causes of human anxiety disorders are largely unknown, and even the proper classification of the symptomatology of human anxiety is somewhat controversial. Although some clinicians argue that many of the diverse symptoms of human anxiety reflect a single, general neurotic disorder (Tyrer, 1986, 1990), others, for example, the *Diagnostic and Statistical Manual of Mental Disorders*, 3rd ed., revised, (*DSM-III-R*, 1987) specifically separate anxiety into different subtypes: generalized anxiety disorder, panic disorder, agoraphobia, simple phobia, social phobia, obsessive–compulsive disorder, and posttraumatic stress disorder. Without a general consensus on the appropriate classification of human anxiety, as either a unitary phenomenon, or a group of separate phenomena with different etiologies, it is difficult to determine the face validity of any particular animal model of anxiety. If one uses *DSM-III-R* as the most widely accepted classification system, most existing animal models weakly resemble phobic disorders, insofar as a particular set of stimuli is sufficient to elicit *fear* reactions (e.g., avoidance). Whether these fear reactions in animals express a subjective anxiety that is similar to that experienced by anxious humans, or lie on the same continuum as abnormal human anxiety reactions are difficult, and perhaps unresolvable questions. For animal models of anxiolytic drug action, however, the one, simplifying assumption is that aversive stimulation, real or anticipated, can produce anxietylike states in humans and infrahumans, and these should be diminished by antianxiety agents. Beyond this minimal level of isomorphism and homology, present animal models of anxiolytic drug action cannot pretend to even partially mimic the complexity of human anxiety disorders. On the other hand, the methodological and ethical problems associated with the scientific study of anxiety in humans are formidable. Thus, methodological rigor and precision are important advantages of animal models of anxiety that may ultimately facilitate our understanding of the etiology, symptomatology, and treatment of human anxiety disorders (Roth, 1990).

Initially, many pharmacologists chose to study the effects of anxiolytic agents using the traditional aversive-learning paradigms originally developed by psychologists (e.g., conditioned suppression, active avoidance, and punishment). This seemed reasonable because most aversive-learning paradigms tend to use painful stimuli (e.g., foot-shock) to elicit fear or conflict in experimental animals, and aversive stimulation, or its anticipation, has long been a pivotal construct in many theoretical accounts of clinical anxiety (Marks, 1987; Treit, 1985a). In particular, paradigms such as the punishment or conflict tests have made many significant contributions to the study of anxiolytic drugs and, generally, satisfy the criteria of correlation, isomorphism, and homology (Treit, 1985a). However, the training procedures involved in these tests are often time-consuming, and complex control procedures are sometimes needed to separate antianxiety drug effects from possible side effects on sensory, motor, or associative processes (for detailed discussions of these issues see Thiebot et al., 1985; Treit, 1985a; Treit et al., 1981).

For the most part, this review will be restricted to a consideration of models that involve animals' *prepared*, or unlearned, reactions to aversive or novel stimuli. The following section will provide a rational for this choice of models. (For comprehensive reviews of models based on punished operant responding, interoceptive stimulus discrimination, and conditioned emotional responding, see Davis, 1990; Lal and Emmett-Oglesby, 1983; Pollard and Howard, 1990; Treit, 1985a).

B. Prepared Fear Reactions

In the early 1970s, Seligman (1971) and others suggested a new approach to the study of aversive learning, and one that is adopted here for its implications for animal models of anxiolytic drug action. What Seligman suggested, essentially, is that animals are biologically "prepared" to learn or respond to events that are relevant to the species' survival, but are relatively "unprepared" to learn about events that are not relevant to the species' survival. For example, rats may be biologically prepared to associate quickly a taste with a subsequent sickness (taste aversion), but are unprepared to learn about an association between taste and shock (Garcia and Koelling, 1966). Similarly, rats readily learn to avoid shock when the avoidance response (jumping) is compatible with their natural tendency to stay close to the walls of the environment (thigmotaxis), but are reluctant to make the same response (jumping) when it is incompatible with their thigmotaxic bias (jumping near the center of the environment; Treit and Fundytus, 1988b). Operationally, then, *preparedness* defines a continuum that runs from reflexive reactions, or extremely rapid (prepared) learning, to slower (unprepared) learning, to extremely difficult, unreliable (contraprepared) learning (Seligman, 1971).

From a clinical standpoint, Seligman's most important proposal is that there may be a number of striking similarities between prepared forms of aversive learning in animals and specific human anxieties, such as phobic disorders. First, it has been argued that human phobias are acquired extremely rapidly (Seligman, 1971), and may be more resistant to extinction than classically conditioned fears to neutral objects (Ohman, 1986). Second, the range of stimuli associated with human phobias is statistically constrained, in the sense that a disproportionate number of humans are afraid of objects such as snakes, spiders, or dogs (Marks, 1987). Third, in spite of their prevalence, these specific fears are infrequently paired with unconditioned aversive events, such as pain or trauma, whereas many other objects, such as electrical outlets, hot irons, glass, and knives are paired in this way, sometimes repeatedly, but do not reliably produce phobias. Thus, there are many similarities between human phobias and prepared fear conditioning in animals (Seligman, 1971).

Although human phobias have been characterized as irrational, it has been argued, within an evolutionary context, that these irrational fears could represent phylogenetically old adaptations to real dangers (Marks, 1987; Ohman, 1986). For example, specific phobias of snakes might have been an adaptive advantage to many early mammals, the chief predators of which, it has been speculated, were reptilian (Ohman et al., 1985). Although the genetic evidence for these speculations is tenuous (Marks, 1987), one might expect some evolutionary continuity for certain fears and phobias, even in mammals as different as rats, monkeys, and humans. Furthermore, there is some provocative behavioral evidence that the acquisition of fears in both monkeys (Cook and Mineka, 1990; Mineka, 1985; Mineka et al., 1980) and humans (Ohman et al., 1985) is more robust when it involves biologically relevant stimuli, such as snakes, than more neutral stimuli, such as flowers (but see McNally, 1987).

The implications for psychopharmacologists of this theoretical viewpoint are threefold. First, the speed and reliability of animals' prepared reactions to aversive or novel stimuli may be useful for the development of rapid, screening tests of anxiolytic compounds. Second, the neural substrates of biologically prepared fear reactions may be less complex, and more directly related to anxiety than the neural substrates of more general, learned adaptations. Therefore, models based on prepared fear reactions may be advantageous for studying the neural mechanisms of antianxiety drug action. Third, to the extent that human fears and phobias have been shaped by evolutionary pressures shared by other mammals, the prepared fear reactions of lower animals could represent biologically relevant models of human anxiety. Although a detailed evaluation of this general hypothesis is beyond the scope of the present review (for relevant discussions see Marks,

1987; Lister, 1990; Treit, 1985a), the construct of biological preparedness sets a broad rationale for the potential utility of many of the models that are reviewed in the following sections.

II. EFFECTS OF ANXIOLYTIC DRUGS ON PREPARED FEAR REACTIONS

The models reviewed in the following sections are grouped into two categories. The first category involves animals' untrained reactions to stress stimuli that do not explicitly involve pain or discomfort (e.g., exposure to a novel test chamber). The second category involves animals' untrained reactions to stress stimuli that are explicitly associated with pain or discomfort (e.g., exposure to electric foot-shock). Although clear distinctions between these two categories of stress stimuli are occasionally difficult to make, the two serve as a convenient, if somewhat arbitrary, organizational dichotomy.

First, each of the models will be evaluated in terms of their selective sensitivity to standard anxiolytic agents (e.g., benzodiazepines), and the relation of these models to the constructs of preparedness and human anxiety will be discussed. Second, the neuropharmacological specificity of anxiolytic effects in these models will be assessed (e.g., by examining benzodiazepine agonist–antagonist interactions). Finally, the effects of standard anxiolytics in these models will be compared with those of putative 5-HT_{1A} agonists [e.g., buspirone, ipsapirone, gepirone, 8-hydroxy-2-(di-*n*-propylamino)tetralin; 8-OH-DPAT]. Comparable effects of benzodiazepine and 5-HT_{1A} agonists would support the validity of a test as a general model of antianxiety drug effects. Because dose is thought to be a critical determinant of the effects of 5-HT_{1A} compounds in these animal models (e.g., Solderpalm et al., 1989b), the values of this variable will be noted in the text. [See Peroutka (1985) for a detailed discussion of the pharmacological specificity of these agents for the 5-HT_{1A} receptor subtype.]

A. Models Based on Reactions to Nonpainful Stressors

1. Light–Dark Exploration

Crawley and her associates (Blumstein and Crawley, 1983; Crawley and Goodwin, 1980; Crawley, 1981, 1985; Crawley et al., 1984) developed a model of anxiolytic drug action that appears to be based on the natural tendency of rodents to avoid brightly lit areas of a compartmentalized test chamber. Mice are placed on the brightly lit side of a two-compartment chamber, and the number of transitions between the light and dark sides, as well as time spent on the two sides, are recorded. A variety of benzodiazepine anxiolytics, including diazepam, clonazepam, flurazepam, and chlordiazepoxide, produced dose-dependent increases in the number of light–dark transitions, whereas antidepressants (clorgiline and butriptyline) and an antipsychotic (chlorpromazine) did not increase transitions. The relative potency of anxiolytics in increasing mouse "exploratory" transitions agreed well with their relative potency in the clinical treatment of human anxiety (Crawley, 1981).

A nonspecific stimulatory effect of anxiolytics on mouse general activity did not appear to explain these increases in light–dark transitions because anxiolytic-treated mice in a uniformly lit, undifferentiated chamber were not significantly more active than vehicle-treated mice (Crawley and Goodwin, 1980).

Although in these early studies the rodents' avoidance of the brightly lit side of the light–dark chamber was not significantly affected by anxiolytic agents, later studies have shown that standard anxiolytics do increase exploratory activity in the lit section of light–dark test chambers or, conversely, decrease exploration in the dark chamber, whereas several nonanxiolytic agents do not produce this pattern of results (Costall, et al., 1988a,b, 1989, 1987; Kilfoil et al., 1989). This suggests that light intensity aversively modulates rodent exploration, suppressing exploration in the brightly lit compartment, and this suppression is antagonized by standard anxiolytics.

Crawley et al. (1984) showed that the anxiolytic effect of diazepam on light–dark transitions could be counteracted by the coadministration of benzodiazepine receptor antagonists flumazenil (Ro 15–1788), CGS 8216, B-CCM, and FG-7142. When administered alone, none of these antagonists produced intrinsic effects on light–dark transitions, except B-CCM, which also reduced general activity at higher doses. Similarly, Belzung et al. (1987) were able to reverse the anxiolytic effect of chlorazepate on light–dark transitions and exploration in the light chamber by coadministering flumazenil. These agonist–antagonist interactions suggest that the enhancement of rodent exploration in the light–dark chamber by benzodiazepine anxiolytics is mediated by central benzodiazepine receptor systems.

Several researchers have examined the effects of putative 5-HT_{1A} agonists in the light–dark exploration test. Pich and Samanin (1986) showed that 0.1 mg/kg of buspirone increased light–dark transitions, without significantly affecting locomotor activity, suggesting an anxiolytic effect. However, when compared with diazepam, the magnitude of the effect of buspirone on light–dark transitions was small, and the active dose range extremely narrow. Similar results have been reported by Carli et al., (1989). More recently, Fernandez-Guasti and Lopez-Rubalcava (1990) found that ipsapirone (2.5–5.0 mg/kg) and indorenate (5.0–10.0 mg/kg) increased light–dark transitions, at doses that did not increase motor activity. Furthermore, the nonspecific serotonergic antagonists pindolol (2.0 mg/kg), alprenolol (5.0 mg/kg), and metitepine (methiothepin; 0.25 mg/kg) blocked the anxiolytic effect of ipsapirone and indorenate, without affecting motor activity.

With use of a decrease in rodent exploration of the dark chamber as the index of an antianxiety effect, Kilfoil et al. (1989) reported that 0.1–10.0 mg/kg buspirone was anxiolytic in this test. Although this interpretation is compromised because doses of buspirone between 1.0 and 10.0 mg/kg also reduced locomotor activity and shuttles, the lower dose data (0.1–0.3 mg/kg) probably represent an anxiolytic effect. Costall et al. (1989) also found that low doses of buspirone (0.25 and 1.0 mg/kg) produced an anxiolytic effect, increasing rodent exploration of the light chamber, and the magnitude of this effect was comparable with that of diazepam. Finally, Onaivi and Martin (1989) showed that higher doses of buspirone (1.0–5.0 mg/kg) enhanced rodent exploration of the light chamber in a manner comparable with that of diazepam.

Costall et al. (1988b) found that infusion of buspirone (10 and 20 ng) into the dorsal raphe nucleus increased exploration in the light chamber, and Carli et al. (1989) found that infusion of buspirone (1.0–10 μg) into the median raphe nucleus increased exploratory transitions. Unfortunately, doses above 1 μg in the Carli study also enhanced motor activity, complicating the interpretation of the higher-dose data. In general, however, these studies show that rodent exploration in the light–dark chamber can be enhanced by centrally administered buspirone.

Although the basic anxiolytic effect of buspirone and ipsapirone on rodent exploration in the light–dark paradigm is reasonably robust across test conditions, the effect of the selective 5-HT_{1A} agonist 8-OH-DPAT in this test appears to be more labile. Carli and Samanin (1988) found that peripherally injected 8-OH-DPAT did not significantly increase rodents' light–dark transitions across a range of doses from 0.125 to 2.0 mg/kg. However, in animals stressed by 48 h of water deprivation, 1.0 mg/kg 8-OH-DPAT significantly increased light–dark transitions. When infused into the median raphe nucleus, 8-OH-DPAT (5 μg) significantly increased light–dark transitions in nondeprived rats. Thus, the anxiolytic effect of 8-OH-DPAT in this test seems to depend on prior stress level when administered peripherally, but not when administered centrally into the median raphe nucleus.

In summary, the light–dark exploratory test seems to be sensitive the anxiolytic effect of 5-HT_{1A} agonists (buspirone, ipsapirone, indorenate, and 8-OH-DPAT). Only in a few cases, however, is the magnitude of this effect comparable with that of benzodiazepines.

2. *Social Interaction*

The social interaction test, developed by File and colleagues, is also based on rodents' apparent aversion to bright light and unfamiliar surroundings (for reviews see File, 1984, 1985, 1987). Pairs of rats are placed in an open arena, and the time they spend in active social interaction (e.g., sniffing, grooming) is measured. Under bright lights or in an unfamiliar test environment, social interaction is suppressed relative to low light–familiar conditions, and this suppression is the index of anxiety (File and Hyde, 1978). Several anxiolytic agents, including chlordiazepoxide, diazepam, and flurazepam, administered subacutely, all antagonized the suppression of social interaction under unfamiliar, high-light conditions, without producing concomitant changes in motor activity. In contrast, nonanxiolytic agents, such as the neuroleptics haloperidol and thioridazine, and CNS stimulants, such as caffeine and amphetamine, did not produce these selective effects on social interaction (File and Hyde, 1978, 1979).

By using a modified procedure in which novelty of the partner is the primary anxiogenic stimulus, Gardner and Guy (1984) found increases in social interaction after acute administration of chlordiazepoxide, diazepam, oxazepam, loprazolam, nitrazepam, flurazepam, and flunitrazepam, at doses that did not significantly affect ambulation. Social interaction in this modified test was not selectively affected by other centrally active agents, including phentolamine, trazodone, nortriptyline, metergoline, propranolol, amphetamine, and chlorpromazine. Although there are some exceptions (File, 1985), the results generally suggest that social interaction under conditions of novelty is selectively sensitive to the effects of benzodiazepine-type anxiolytics.

In File's original version of the social interaction test, the benzodiazepine receptor antagonist, flumazenil produced an intrinsic anxiogenic effect on social interaction, which could be reversed with subacute chlordiazepoxide (File and Pellow, 1984b). Other antagonists presumed to act at different sites on the GABA–benzodiazepine receptor complex also induced an increase in anxiety (e.g., B-CCE, B-CCP, FG-7142, picrotoxin, and pentylenetetrazol; File and Pellow, 1983, 1984a,b, 1985). With the modified social interaction test, Bold et al. (1985) found that flumazenil completely reversed the anxiolytic effect of chlordiazepoxide on social interaction; flumazenil had no effect in this test when administered alone. Thus, there is some neuropharmacological evidence that the benzodiazepine receptor complex mediates the anxiolytic and the anxiogenic effects of drugs on rodent social interaction. Moreover, Primus and Kellogg (1991) have recently reported that the function of the GABA–benzodiazepine receptor complex is selectively altered in rats exposed to the unfamiliar condition of the social interaction test.

Although there has been one report that buspirone (0.25–2.5 mg/kg) failed to produce a full, benzodiazepinelike profile in the social interaction test (File, 1984), other studies have generally shown that 5-HT_{1A} agonists produce effects comparable with those of benzodiazepines. Guy and Gardner (1985) showed that buspirone (5–20 mg/kg) significantly increased social interaction, at doses that did not significantly affect motor activity, and the magnitude of this anxiolytic effect was similar to that of benzodiazepines. Cutler (1991) gave buspirone in drinking fluid to female mice for several days (2.3–2.6 mg/kg per day). After 5–7 days, there was a reliable increase in the social interaction of these chronically treated mice. Using acute administration, Dunn et al. (1989) showed that buspirone (5.0–10.0 mg/kg) and gepirone (5–10 mg/kg) produced significant increases in social interaction, although buspirone also reduced motor activity. Another 5-HT_{1A} agonist, 8-OH-DPAT (0.125–0.25 mg/kg), enhanced social interaction without producing a concomitant change in motor activity. Finally, Higgins et al. (1988) found that buspirone (40–200 ng), ipsapirone (200 ng), and 8-OH-DPAT (20–100 ng), microinjected into the dorsal raphe nucleus, all produced significant increases in social interaction, with little change in locomotor activity.

Thus, the social interaction test, like the light–dark exploration test, is sensitive to both benzodiazepine and 5-HT_{1A} agonists. These tests may also be analogous to human anxiety insofar as avoidance of novel social or environmental stimuli is common in both rodents and humans.

3. Elevated Plus-Maze

In the elevated plus-maze, two adjacent arms are enclosed with walls, and two are open. Rodents on their first exposure to the maze normally avoid the open arms, restricting most of their activity to the closed arms. The total number of arm crosses, regardless of whether they are into open or closed arms, serves as an inbuilt control for nonspecific changes in motor activity. An antianxiety effect is indicated by an increase in the proportion of activity in the open arms of the maze (i.e., an increase in the percentage of time spent in the open arms, or an increase in the percentage of crosses into the open arms; for a review of procedures and methods, see Pellow, 1986).

A variety of standard anxiolytic agents have been found to increase the proportion of activity in the open arms, including chlordiazepoxide, diazepam, alprazolam, adinazolam, and phenobarbital. Conversely, agents that are not broadly useful in the treatment of human anxiety did not increase open-arm activity (e.g., amphetamine, caffeine, imipramine, mianserin, amitriptyline, pargyline, clorgiline, and haloperidol; Handley and Mithani, 1984; Lister, 1987; Pellow, 1986; Pellow et al., 1985; Pellow and File, 1986; Soderpalm et al., 1989a).

No one has yet investigated whether the anxiolytic effect of benzodiazepines in the elevated plus-maze can be reversed with benzodiazepine receptor antagonists, such as flumazenil. However, the putative anxiogenic effects (i.e., a decrease in the proportion of open-arm activity) of ß-carboline "inverse agonists" can be reversed with full benzodiazepine agonists (Pellow, 1986; Rago et al., 1988). Thus, although the neuropharmacological specificity of the anxiolytic effects of benzodiazepines in the plus-maze test requires further study, the test appears to be sensitive to the effects of both anxiolytic and putative anxiogenic agents that apparently act at the benzodiazepine receptor complex.

Although there are some reports that 5-HT_{1A} agonists can have clear, benzodiazepinelike effects in the elevated plus-maze, the effects of 5-HT_{1A} agonists in this test are often equivocal. Pellow and File (1986) found no evidence for an anxiolytic effect of buspirone (0.5 and 20 mg/kg) in the elevated plus-maze. In fact, there was a reduction in the proportion of open-arm activity. However, analysis of covariance suggested that this might be attributed to a concomitant reduction in total arm activity (i.e., behavioral sedation). Critchley and Handley (1987a,b) also found that buspirone (0.25–5.0 mg/kg) depressed both the proportion of open-arm activity and total activity. Pellow and associates (1987), however, showed that buspirone (0.5–8.0 mg/kg) decreased open-arm activity *without* significantly suppressing total-arm activity, suggesting an anxiogeniclike effect.

Ipsapirone failed to produce a significant anxiolytic effect in the plus-maze test at doses of 2.5–10.0 mg/kg (Pellow et al., 1987). Similar to buspirone, ipsapirone actually decreased the proportion of open-arm activity, although in this case total arm activity was also decreased. Pellow et al. (1987) found that 8-OH-DPAT (0.0625–0.25 mg/kg) had no significant effect on open-arm activity, whereas Critchley and Handley (1987a,b) found that 8-OH-DPAT (0.15–1.0 mg/kg) produced a significant reduction in the proportion of open-arm activity, at doses (0.15–0.25) that had no significant effect on total-arm activity (i.e., an anxiogenic effect).

One of the more systematic studies of the effects of 5-HT_{1A} agonists in the elevated plus-maze was conducted by Moser (1989). Neither chronic (16 days, 1 mg/kg, subcutaneously) nor acute treatment with buspirone (0.25–1.0 mg/kg) produced an anxiolyticlike effect in the plus-maze. Acute treatments produced nonsignificant decreases in the proportion of open-arm activity, and significant decreases in total-arm activity. Other 5-HT_{1A} agonists [ipsapirone, 0.15–10 mg/kg; (-) MDL 72832, 0.05–0.8 mg/kg; (+) MDL 72832, 0.4–3.2 mg/kg; and 8-OH-DPAT] in a subsequent study (Moser et al., 1990) produced similar suppressive effects on the percentage of open-arm activity and total-arm activity. Moser concluded that the plus-maze test is either insensitive to certain classes of anxiolytics, or is measuring a process in rodents that is unrelated to human anxiety.

However, the suggestion that the plus-maze test is insensitive to the anxiolytic effects of 5-HT_{1A} agents should be tempered by the results of several studies showing good sensitivity. In contrast with their other findings, Moser et al. (1990) showed that a highly specific 5-HT_{1A} ligand, MDL 73005 EF (0.06–0.25 mg/kg), did produce significant, anxiolyticlike effects in the plus-maze. Similarly, Critchley and Handley (1987a) noted that ipsapirone (0.25–2.5 mg/kg) significantly increased the proportion of rats' open-arm activity, without affecting their total-arm activity, a finding that has been replicated by Graeff et al. (1990) at an equivalent dose range (i.e., 0.5–2.5 mg/kg). Furthermore, Dunn et al. (1989) showed that buspirone (0.5–1.0 mg/kg), gepirone (1.0–2.5 mg/kg), and 8-OH-DPAT (0.1–0.2 mg/kg) all significantly increased open-arm activity at doses that did not affect total activity. Soderpalm et al. (1989b) also found a specific increase in open-arm activity with buspirone (32–128 nmol/kg), gepirone (32–128 nmol/kg), ipsapirone (32–512 nmol/kg), and 8-OH-DPAT (50–200 nmol/kg). The effective doses in this study were extremely low (e.g., equivalent to 12 μg/kg of buspirone), and Soderpalm et al. (1989b) suggested that dose may be a significant factor in determining the anxiolytic profile of 5-HT_{1A} agonists in the elevated plus-maze. Finally, Kostowski and associates (1989) found that 2.5 μg of buspirone, microinjected in the dentate gyrus of the hippocampus, increased open-arm activity in the plus-maze. These authors suggested that the effects of peripherally injected 5-HT_{1A} agonists in the plus-maze may depend on dose-related changes in the relative activity of pre- and postsynaptic 5-HT systems (cf. Moser, 1989; Moser et al., 1990). In any case, the positive effects of 5-HT_{1A} agonists in these studies suggest that it may be premature to conclude that the plus-maze test is insensitive to the anxiolytic effects of 5-HT_{1A} agonists, or is inappropriate as a model of human anxiety.

B. Models Based on Reactions to Painful Stressors

1. Ultrasonic Distress Vocalization

This section will deal with the effects of anxiolytic agents on ultrasonic distress vocalizations elicited in adult rats by either electric foot-shock of high-intensity acoustic stimuli, or elicited in preweanling rats by separation from mother and littermates. Although the latter procedure does not explicitly involve a painful stressor, for the purposes of continuity it will be included in this section.

Rat pups separated from their mother and littermates emit high-frequency (30–50 kHz) distress calls, which in turn, elicit retrieval behavior from the mother (Noirot, 1972). Distress calls are infrequent just after birth, increase up to maximal levels at about 10 days of age, and then decrease to minimal levels at about 17 days of age. The eliciting stimulus (separation), under certain conditions (e.g., dependency) would seem capable of producing fear or anxiety in humans. An anxiolytic drug effect in this response system is indicated by a significant reduction in high-frequency vocalization in the absence of behavioral sedation (Engel et al., 1987; Gardner, 1985a,b; Insel et al., 1986).

Gardner (1985a,b) found that chlordiazepoxide and diazepam inhibited ultrasonic vocalization in rat pups at doses that did not generally disrupt behavior, whereas muscimol, chlorpromazine, yohimbine, morphine, amphetamine, amitriptyline, haloperidol, naloxone, clonidine, and prazosin did not selectively suppress vocalization. A possible false-positive result was given with metergoline, which inhibited ultrasounds at doses that were not behaviorally impairing, as did morphine in a subsequent study (Carden and Hofer, 1990). Benton and Nastiti (1988) found that ultrasonic calling in mouse pups was inhibited by benzodiazepine anxiolytics and provided evidence that this inhibition was not related to drug-induced decreases in body temperature. However, in this study, meprobamate registered as a false negative result and amitriptyline as a false-positive result. Thus, as a screening test for anxiolytic agents, ultrasonic vocalization appears to be only partially selective, and care must be taken to separate general behavioral impairments from specific suppression of ultrasonic vocalization.

However, the neuropharmacological specificity of the effects of benzodiazepine anxiolytics in this model appears to be clear, since several studies have shown that the inhibitory effect of these anxiolytics on ultrasonic vocalization can be blocked by the benzodiazepine receptor antagonist, flumazenil (Carden and Hofer, 1990; Gardner and Budhram, 1987; Insel et al., 1986). These data, combined with evidence of decreased in vivo binding to brain benzodiazepine receptors during social isolation (Insel, 1989), suggest that this receptor complex is involved in the modulation of distress vocalizations in the rat pup.

Ultrasonic vocalization elicited in adult rats by electric foot-shocks can be selectively inhibited by low doses of diazepam and alprazolam. Desipramine, imipramine, and haloperidol did not selectively suppress shock-elicited vocalizations, although other nonanxiolytic agents (chlorpromazine and morphinelike substances) did (Cuomo et al., 1988; Tonoue et al., 1986, 1987). The inhibitory effect of diazepam on shock-elicited vocalization was blocked by flumazenil and CGS-8216, benzodiazepine receptor antagonists (Cuomo, 1988; Tonoue et al., 1987). When using a different eliciting stimulus, Kaltwasser (1991) found that ultrasonic vocalization induced in adult rats by high-intensity acoustic stimuli was suppressed by flunitrazepam and diazepam, but not by nonanxiolytic agents maprotiline or FG-7142.

Hard and Engel (1988) found that 7.5, 15, and 30 μg/kg of 8-OH-DPAT significantly inhibited separation vocalization in preweanling rats, without affecting motor activity, and Benton and Nastiti (1988) showed that ipsapirone (2.5–5.0 mg/kg) inhibited ultrasonic calling in mouse pups. Similarly, Kehne et al. (1991) found that buspirone and MDL 73005 EF (0.31–5.0 mg/kg) suppressed ultrasonic vocalization in preweanling rats at doses (0.63–5.0 mg/kg) that did not disrupt motor coordination on an inclined screen test. Rowan et al. (1990) found that 2 mg/kg of buspirone selectively suppressed shock-elicited vocalization in adult rats, and Kaltwasser (1991) showed that ipsapirone (5.0 mg/kg) suppressed both acoustic-induced and shock-induced vocalization in adult rats. These data suggest that 5-HT_{1A} agonists may have effects on ultrasonic distress vocalizations that are similar to those of benzodiazepine anxiolytics. The similarity of these drug effects, along with ethological data reviewed earlier, suggest that ultrasonic vocalizations elicited in preweanling rats by separation, and in adult rats by electric shock or acoustic startle stimuli, are unconditioned fear reactions that may provide useful animal models of anxiety (Kaltwasser, 1990).

2. *Freezing and Thigmotaxis*

Two of the most common reactions of rodents to any sudden, novel, or noxious stimulus are freezing and thigmotaxis. *Freezing* is normally defined as a completely rigid, immobile body posture (Blanchard and Blanchard, 1971), and *thigmotaxis* is the tendency of rodents to stay in close contact with the perimeters of the environment (Barnett, 1963; Treit and Fundytus, 1988b). It has been speculated that these behaviors may have adaptive value in the wild, since it may be more difficult for predators to attack an immobile, thigmotaxic rodent than a rodent that is moving out in the open (Barnett, 1963; Grossen and Kelley, 1972). Within the present context, freezing and thigmotaxis are prepared fear reactions, and are seen in a variety of species, including humans under extreme conditions (Roth, 1990). Although the pharmacological assessment of these behaviors as animal models of anxiety is not extensive, there are some relevant studies that are reviewed below.

Treit and Fundytus (1988b) found that rats' tendency to stay near the perimeters of a novel environment (thigmotaxis) was suppressed by standard anxiolytic agents (diazepam, chlordiazepoxide, and pentobarbital), with a relative potency that was similar to their relative potency in the treatment of human anxiety. Furthermore, when drug effects on general activity were factored out using analysis of covariance, this antithigmotaxis effect showed some degree of drug-class specificity, since *d*-amphetamine, morphine, or chlorpromazine did not reduce thigmotaxis independently of their effects on general activity. Similar antithigmotaxic effects have been reported for chlordiazepoxide (Bruhwyler, 1990), at doses as low as 0.1 mg/kg. Although the neuropharmacological specificity of these effects has not been tested with benzodiazepine antagonists, it would be of interest to determine whether 5-HT_{1A} agonists (e.g., buspirone) have antithigmotaxic effects that are similar to those of benzodiazepines.

Several studies have shown that rats' freezing behavior is suppressed by benzodiazepine anxiolytics, such as diazepam and midazolam (Conti et al., 1990; Fanselow and Helmstetter, 1988; Korte et al., 1990), whereas nonanxiolytic agents, such as haloperidol, B-CCE, and MK-801, do not generally suppress freezing (Conti et al., 1990). However, *d*-amphetamine has registered as a false-positive result in this test (Conti et al., 1990) and chlordiazepoxide as a false-negative one (Fanselow and Helmstetter, 1988). Furthermore, it is very difficult in this test to separate drug effects on general activity from drug effects that are specific to freezing behavior (Conti et al., 1990). Nevertheless, it is noteworthy that both buspirone (1.25–5.0 mg/kg) and ipsapirone 2.5–12.5 mg/kg) have suppressed freezing behavior in rats (Conti et al., 1990; Korte et al., 1990). These preliminary results, in combination with other studies that have examined the effects of benzodiazepine and serotonergic drugs on rats' antipredator defense responses (Blanchard et al., 1990), support the potential usefulness of these simple behaviors as animal models of anxiety and anxiolytic drug action.

3. Conditioned Taste Aversion

One of the best-known examples of prepared aversive learning is the conditioned taste aversion effect. Rats rapidly learn to avoid a novel-tasting solution (CS) that has previously been paired with an aversive interoceptive stimulus (US), even when there is a long delay between the CS and the US. On the other hand, rats are relatively unprepared to learn about a taste CS that has been paired with an aversive exteroceptive stimulus such as electric foot-shock (Garcia and Koelling, 1966). Presumably, a bias toward associating novel tastes with subsequent illness may be an adaptive advantage for the rat in its natural environment.

Several studies have shown that anxiolytic agents, such as chlordiazepoxide, diazepam, lorazepam, oxazepam, phenobarbital, and meprobamate, can antagonize conditioned taste aversions (Concannon and Freda, 1980; Ervin and Cooper, 1988; Jolicoeur et al., 1980; Riley and Lovely, 1978; Roache and Zabik, 1986; Rondeau et al., 1981). Nonanxiolytic agents, including amphetamine, chlorpromazine, morphine, naloxone, imipramine, atropine, and caffeine, do not antagonize taste aversions (Ervin and Cooper, 1988). The relative potency of anxiolytics in antagonizing taste aversions is similar to their relative potency in the treatment of human anxiety (Ervin and Cooper, 1988).

Although anxiolytics consistently antagonize taste aversions in single-bottle tests, where the sole source of fluid is the one associated with sickness, these drugs only inconsistently antagonize taste aversions in two-bottle tests, where water is also available during the test period (Delameter and Treit, 1988; Ervin and Cooper, 1988; Roache and Zabik, 1986). Some authors have argued that dipsogenic effects could contribute to the antagonism of taste aversions by anxiolytics in the single-bottle tests (e.g., Treit, 1985a), whereas others have provided evidence that dipsogenic effects do not account for this antagonism (Ervin and Cooper, 1988; Ervin et al., 1987).

Ervin and Cooper (1988) could not antagonize taste aversions in single-bottle tests with dipsogenic agents (e.g., isoproterenol), or with additional fluid deprivation. On this basis, they suggested that anxiolytic drugs do not act through homeostatic drinking mechanisms to increase fluid intake in single-bottle tests of taste aversion. Nevertheless, it is still possible that benzodiazepine-type anxiolytics increase fluid intake by modulating palatability mechanisms that are independent of anxiolytic mechanisms and homeostatic drinking mechanisms (Berridge and Treit, 1986; Cooper, 1980; Cooper and Yerbury, 1988; Parker, 1991; Treit and Berridge, 1990; Treit et al., 1987). Another complication is that anxiolytic agents themselves are capable of producing taste aversions, and with repeated injection, can potentiate the taste aversion induced with lithium chloride (e.g., Delameter and Treit, 1988; Neisewander et al., 1990).

Thus, as a simple screening device, the single-bottle taste aversion test appears able to separate anxiolytic from nonanxiolytic agents, but as a model for studying the mechanisms of antianxiety drug action it is somewhat more complicated. Like all tests that are based on a conflict between avoidance of an aversive stimulus and acquisition of a rewarding stimulus, antiaversive drug effects can be confounded with proreward drug effects (Treit, 1985a). Future studies should continue to address this issue, as well as establish the neuropharmacological specificity of the effects of benzodiazepines in the taste aversion test.

With these caveats in mind, it is interesting that buspirone (0.5–5.0 mg/kg) significantly antagonized taste aversions in the single-bottle test at doses (1 and 5 mg/kg) that did not affect unconditioned fluid consumption (Ervin et al., 1987). These preliminary results suggest that conditioned taste aversion may indeed be sensitive to the anxiolytic effects of drugs, regardless of their initial site of action (benzodiazepine versus 5-HT_{1A} receptor).

4. Shock-Probe Burying

Rats shocked from an electrified probe that is attached to the wall of a test chamber characteristically spray bedding material toward or over the probe, with rapid, alternating movements of the forepaws (i.e., *burying* behavior; Pinel and Treit, 1978). Rats appear to rapidly associate the shock with the probe, and will bury the probe even after long delays between shock and test (Pinel and Treit, 1978). These and other data (reviewed in Treit, 1985a) suggest that burying behavior may represent a prepared fear reaction to aversive or threatening stimuli (for reviews see Pinel and Treit, 1983; Treit, 1985a). A reduction in the duration of this burying response in the absence of a decrease in general activity is often used as the index of an anxiolytic drug effect (e.g., Treit et al., 1981).

Several investigators have shown that low doses of standard anxiolytic agents (e.g., chlordiazepoxide, diazepam) reduce the amount that rats bury the shock probe, without suppressing general activity (Beardslee et al., 1990; Blampied and Kirk, 1983; Rohmer et al., 1990; Treit, 1985a,b, 1987, 1990; Treit and Fundytus, 1988a; Treit et al., 1986, 1981; Tsuda et al., 1988). Chlordiazepoxide has also been reported to abolish the shock-induced elevations in plasma corticosterone and epinephrine that occur during the burying test (De Boer et al., 1990). The effects of anxiolytic compounds on probe-burying can be distinguished from those of several nonanxiolytic agents (Beardslee et al., 1990; Rohmer et al., 1990; Treit, 1987; Treit et al., 1981; Tsuda et al., 1988), although the drug class-specificity of the test is sensitive to procedural variations (Broekkamp et al., 1986; Craft et al., 1988; Njung'e and Handley, 1991; Treit, 1990; Treit et al., 1981). The suppression of burying behavior by benzodiazepine anxiolytics does not appear to be secondary to analgesia (Treit, 1985c), or to associative deficits (Blampied and Kirk, 1983), and can be blocked with benzodiazepine receptor antagonists such as flumazenil (Treit, 1987). In addition, putative anxiogenic agents, such as yohimbine and B-CCE, have been reported to increase the duration that rats bury the probe (Tsuda et al., 1988, 1989).

In a preliminary study (Treit and Fundytus, 1988a), the effects of chlordiazepoxide and buspirone (0.05–1.0 mg/kg) were compared in the shock probe-burying test. Both anxiolytic agents decreased the amount of time rats buried the probe, and concurrently increased the number of contact-induced probe shocks rats received. These bidirectional, anxiolytic drug effects increased as a function of drug dose and were independent of changes in general activity (Treit and Fundytus, 1988a). At higher doses (e.g., 8–64 mg/kg), at which general activity is suppressed, buspirone does not produce selective effects on either probe-avoidance (Meert and Colpaert, 1986) or probe-burying (Craft et al., 1988).

More recently, Korte and Bohus (1990) found that ipsapirone (2.5–10 mg/kg) produced substantial reductions of probe-burying behavior, in the absence of effects on general activity. Stress-induced tachycardia observed in the presence of the shock probe was also attenuated by ipsapirone. Similar results have been found in an extensive series of experiments by Fernandez-Guasti and colleagues (Fernandez-Guasti and Picazo, 1990; Fernandez-Guasti et al., 1992). These researchers found dose-dependent decreases in the burying behavior of both male and female rats after the administration of buspirone (2.5–5.0 mg/kg), ipsapirone (5.0–10.0 mg/kg), and indorenate (2.5–5.0 mg/kg). Furthermore, the anxiolytic effect of ipsapirone and indorenate on the burying behavior of mice was attenuated by the serotonergic antagonists pindolol, alprenolol, and metitepine (methiothepin; Fernandez-Guasti et al., 1992). Taken together, these results suggest that the shock probe-burying test may provide a useful method for studying the anxiolytic action of 5-HT_{1A} agonists.

5. Fear-Potentiated Startle

Brown and associates (1951) showed that the magnitude of rats' startle reflex to an acoustic stimulus could be potentiated by presenting the acoustic startle stimulus together with a cue (e.g., light) that had previously been paired with shock (for a review see Davis, 1986). Although the acoustic startle reflex itself could be considered a prepared fear reaction, its potentiation by the conditioned light stimulus appears to follow the general laws of classic conditioning. In this sense, the fear-potentiated startle paradigm represents a mixture of natural and acquired fear-responding. An anxiolytic drug effect in this paradigm is most clearly indicated by a specific reduction of potentiated startle (i.e., a reduction of startle on light–noise trials versus a reduction of startle on noise-alone trials, Davis, 1986).

Several standard anxiolytic agents, including diazepam, flurazepam, and midazolam produced selective, dose-dependent reductions of fear-potentiated startle (Davis, 1979; Hijzen and Slangen, 1989), whereas several nonanxiolytic agents, including cinanserin, *p*-chloroamphetamine, and imipramine, did not block potentiated startle (Casella and Davis, 1985; Davis et al., 1988). However, a false-positive result has been reported for morphine (Davis, 1986). In one study (Berg and Davis, 1984), the inhibitory effect of diazepam on potentiated startle was attenuated by the benzodiazepine receptor antagonist, flumazenil, and in another study (Hijzen and Slangen, 1989), a benzodiazepine receptor inverse agonist with putative anxiogenic properties (DMCM), was reported to enhance potentiated startle. Taken together, these data suggest that potentiated startle is sensitive to both anxiolytic and anxiogenic ligands acting at the benzodiazepine receptor.

Kehne and colleagues (1988) reported that systemically administered buspirone (0.6–5.0 mg/kg) and gepirone (1.25–10.0 mg/kg) each blocked potentiated startle, as did intraventricular administration of 200 μg of buspirone. Mansbach and Geyer (1987) found that buspirone (1.25–5.0 mg/kg), gepirone (3.0–10.0 mg/kg), ipsapirone (1.0–10.0 mg/kg), and 8-OH-DPAT (0.125 and 0.5 mg/kg) blocked potentiated startle after systemic administration. Davis et al. (1988) did not find that 8-OH-DPAT (2.5–10.0 mg/kg) blocked potentiated startle, in contrast to Mansbach and Geyer (1987). Mansbach and Geyer suggested that differences in the doses of 8-OH-DPAT used in the two studies, or differences in methodology, may account for this discrepancy. In general, however, the results from these studies show that the fear-potentiated startle paradigm is sensitive to several putative 5-HT_{1A} agonists, and the magnitude of their effects is similar to those of full benzodiazepine agonists.

IV. SUMMARY AND CONCLUSIONS

In summary, five of the eight models reviewed in this chapter show reasonably good sensitivity to both benzodiazepine and 5-HT_{1A} agonists: light–dark exploration, social interaction, ultrasonic vocalization, shock probe-burying, and fear-potentiated startle. Two of the remaining tests (freezing and taste aversion) also show positive effects, although 5-HT_{1A} agonists have been tested only once in each case. The plus-maze test shows reliable sensitivity to benzodiazepine agonists, but variable sensitivity to 5-HT_{1A} agonists. Although all of the models were sensitive to both benzodiazepine and 5-HT_{1A} agonists, it was apparent that the effects of 5-HT_{1A} agonists in these tests were sometimes more variable than the effects of standard anxiolytics, especially in the elevated plus-maze. Furthermore, there were a few instances in which 5-HT_{1A} agonists produced effects opposite those of standard anxiolytics, suggestive of an anxiogenic action. There are several possible explanations for these inconsistencies that have implications for animal models of anxiety and anxiolytic drug action.

A particular drug or drug class may have very reliable effects in an animal model of anxiety, but unless the drug or drug class also has reliable, antianxiety effects in humans, the ultimate pharmacological validation of the model is incomplete. Conversely, a drug that has inconsistent or unreliable anxiolytic effects in humans cannot be used to invalidate an animal model of anxiety. Variation in the clinical effectiveness of 5-HT_{1A} anxiolytics (e.g., buspirone) might account for some of the variation in the effects of these agents in animal models of anxiolytic drug action. There is little clinical evidence that 5-HT_{1A} agonists, other than buspirone, produce reliable antianxiety effects in humans, and even the effects of buspirone may be somewhat more variable than the effects of standard anxiolytics, such as the benzodiazepines. Although buspirone has been anxiolytic in several clinical studies (e.g., Wheatley, 1982) there are some exceptions (e.g., Olajide and Lader, 1984; Sheehan et al., 1990). Buspirone's onset of action is slower than benzodiazepines (Wheatley, 1982), and buspirone may be more effective in female than in male patients (Sheehan et al., 1988). Buspirone may not be effective in patients with a previous history of benzodiazepine use (Pecknold, 1985; Sheehan et al., 1988; 1990). These clinical data are very limited, but, if anxious humans respond more variably to buspirone than to standard anxiolytics, one might expect the effects of 5-HT_{1A} agonists in animal models of anxiolytic drug action to be more variable than the effects of standard anxiolytics.

Pharmacological variables may account for some of the variation in the effects of 5-HT_{1A} agonists in animal studies. The route of administration, for example, appears to be an important variable. Whereas direct administration of 5-HT_{1A} agonists into the CNS resulted in reliable, anxiolyticlike effects in a variety of animal models (Carli et al., 1989; Carli and Samanin, 1988; Costall et al., 1988b; Higgins, 1988; Kehne et al., 1988; Kostowski et al., 1989), peripheral administration resulted in less reliable effects (e.g., Moser, 1989; Soderpalm et al., 1989b).

In peripherally administered 5-HT_{1A} agonists, there was some tendency for lower doses to result in a greater proportion of positive (i.e., anxiolytic) effects. By using peripherally administered buspirone as the standard, 13 of the 20 instances in which buspirone showed an anxiolytic effect involved doses between approximately 0.05 and 5.0 mg/kg, whereas five of the eight instances in which buspirone failed to show an anxiolytic effect involved doses between approximately 0.5 and 64.0 mg/kg. Since motoric side effects of buspirone have been noted at doses as low as 1 mg/kg (e.g., Moser, 1989; Soderpalm et al., 1989b), it seems possible that some of the failures to detect anxiolytic effects with buspirone may have been the result of motor impairments. Furthermore, it has been argued that low doses of 5-HT_{1A} agonists preferentially activate specific subpopulations of 5-HT receptors (e.g., autoreceptors on cell bodies of the raphe nuclei; Kostowski et al., 1989; Traber and Thomas, 1987). To the extent that activation of specific receptors by low doses of 5-HT_{1A} agonists might mediate anxiolysis, one might expect more variability in the anxiolytic effects of higher doses of 5-HT_{1A} agonists (cf. Moser, 1989; Soderpalm et al., 1989b).

Variation in the effects of buspirone in animal models of anxiolytic drug action could also reflect differences in the degree to which the models exclusively represent fear or anxiety. Some models undoubtedly contain other motivational elements in addition to fear and, to the extent that 5-HT_{1A} agonists, such as buspirone, are truly anxioselective (Skolnick et al., 1984), their effects in certain models may be diminished compared with those of benzodiazepines. As mentioned in an earlier review, the anticonflict effect of benzodiazepines may involve both an antifear effect, and a proreward effect (Treit, 1985a). An anxiolytic drug without proreward effects might not be expected to produce as robust an anticonflict effect as the benzodiazepines. Behavior in an elevated plus-maze may involve a conflict between fear of heights and the rewarding aspects of exploring a novel environment (Widgiz and Beck, 1990). If benzodiazepines enhance the rewarding aspects of exploration, but 5-HT_{1A} agonists do not, here again, we might expect less robust effects of 5-HT_{1A} agonists in this test. These theoretical considerations are admittedly speculative, but if there is some variation in the extent to which animal models reflect a simple state of anxiety, and some variation in the degree to which drugs selectively affect clinical anxiety, one might not expect all anxiolytic agents to have uniform effects in animal models.

A related possibility is that different animal models represent qualitatively different types of anxiety or fear, only some of which are reliably inhibited by 5-HT_{1A} agonists. Thus, we might suppose that the social interaction test primarily reflects a type of social phobia, which is reliably suppressed by 5-HT_{1A} agonists, whereas the elevated plus-maze reflects a type of acrophobia, which is not as reliably suppressed by 5-HT_{1A} agonists. This would imply that animal fears can be pharmacologically dissected which, in turn, would support and direct the pharmacological dissection of human anxiety. Although these speculations seem to be consistent with some of the animal data reviewed in this chapter, there is as yet no clinical evidence that specific anxiety disorders are differentially affected by benzodiazepine or 5-HT_{1A} anxiolytics (Montgomery and Fineberg, 1989).

Thus, several factors, including clinical effectiveness, route of administration, dose, and model type, may alter the correspondence between the effects of benzodiazepines and 5-HT_{1A} agonists in animal models of anxiety. Indeed, the influence of these factors may have shaped some of the early literature in this area (e.g., Gardner, 1986), in which inconsistencies were more apparent than similarities. Future studies should elucidate the relative importance of each of these factors. On the whole, however, the data summarized in the present review suggest that there is a fairly impressive correspondence between the effects of benzodiazepine anxiolytics and 5-HT_{1A} agonists on animals' prepared fear reactions. This correspondence supports the view, elaborated in the introduction, that biologically prepared fear reactions may provide useful animal models of anxiety and anxiolytic drug action. Further evidence of the usefulness of these models comes from recent studies revealing a correspondence between the effects of anxiolytic drugs and the effects of specific lesions of the limbic system on animals' prepared fear reactions (e.g., Davis, 1986, 1990; Treit, 1991; Treit and Pesold, 1990). Future studies along these lines promise to shed further light on the neutral bases of anxiety and anxiolytic drug action, and ultimately facilitate our understanding of the biological basis of human anxiety and its pharmacological control.

ACKNOWLEDGMENTS

This work was supported by grants from NSERC and PMHAC. I thank M. L. Spetch for her helpful comments and suggestions. Reprint requests should be sent to Dallas Treit, Department of Psychology, University of Alberta, Edmonton, Alberta, Canada T6G 2E9.

REFERENCES

S. A. Barnett, *The Rat: A Study in Behavior*, Metheun, London (1963).

S. L. Beardslee, E. Papadakis, D. J. Fontana, and R. L. Commissaris, Antipanic drug treatments: Failure to exhibit anxiolytic-like effects on defensive burying behavior, *Pharmacol. Biochem. Behav., 35*: 451 (1990).

C. Belzung, R. Misslin, E. Vogel, R. H. Hood, and G. Chapouthier, Anxiogenic effects of methyl-*b*-carboline-3-carboxylate in a light/dark choice situation, *Pharmacol. Biochem. Behav., 28*: 29 (1987).

D. Benton, and K. Nastiti, The influence of psychotropic drugs on the ultrasonic calling of mouse pups, *Psychopharmacology, 95*: 99 (1988).

W. K. Berg, and M. Davis, Diazepam blocks fear-enhanced startle elicited electrically from the brainstem, *Physiol. Behav., 32*: 333 (1984).

K. C. Berridge, and D. Treit, Chlordiazepoxide directly enhances positive ingestive reactions in the rat, *Pharmacol. Biochem. Behav., 24*: 217 (1986).

N. M. Blampied, and R. C. Kirk, Defensive burying: Effects of diazepam and oxprenolol measured in extinction, *Life Sci., 33*: 695 (1983).

R. J. Blanchard, and D. C. Blanchard, Defensive reactions in the albino rat, *Learn. Motiv., 21*: 351 (1971).

D. C. Blanchard, R. J. Blanchard, and R. J. Rodgers, Pharmacological and neural control of antipredator defense in the rat, *Aggresive Behav., 16*: 165 (1990).

L. K. Blumstein, and J. N. Crawley, Further characterization of a simple, automated exploratory model for the anxiolytic effects of benzodiazepines, *Pharmacol. Biochem. Behav., 18*: 37 (1983).

J. M. Bold, C. R. Gardner, and R. J. Walker, Central effects of nicotinamide and inosine which are not mediated through benzodiazepine receptors, *Br. J. Pharmacol., 84*: 689 (1985).

C. Braestrup, and R. F. Squires, Pharmacological characterization of benzodiazepine receptors in rat brain characterized by high-affinity [^{3}H]diazepam binding, *Proc. Natl. Acad. Sci. USA, 74*: 3804 (1977).

A. Breier, and S. M. Paul, The GABA/benzodiazepine receptor: Implications for the molecular basis of anxiety, *J. Psychiat. Res., 24*: 91 (1990).

C. L. Broekkamp, H. W. Rijk, D. Joly-Gelouin, and K. L. Lloyd, Major tranquilizers can be distinguished from minor tranquilizers on the basis of effects on marble burying and swim-induced grooming in mice, *Eur. J. Pharmacol., 126*: 223 (1986).

J. S. Brown, H. I. Kalish, and I. E. Farber, Conditioned fear as revealed by magnitude of startle response to an auditory stimulus, *J. Exp. Psychol., 41*: 317 (1951).

J. Bruhwyler, Anxiolytic potential of a microgram dose of chlordiazepoxide in the open-field test, *Eur. J. Pharmacol., 187*: 547 (1990).

S. E. Carden, and M. A. Hofer, Independence of benzodiazepine and opiate action in the suppression of isolation distress in rat pups, *Behav. Neurosci., 104*: 160 (1990).

M. Carli, and R. Samanin, Potential anxiolytic properties of 8-hydroxy-2-(di-*n*-propylamino)tetralin, a selective serotonin 1A receptor agonist, *Psychopharmacology, 94*: 84 (1988).

M. Carli, C. Prontera, and R. Samanin, Evidence that central 5-hydroxytryptaminergic neurons are involved in the anxiolytic activity of buspirone, *Br. J. Pharmacol., 96*: 829 (1989).

J. V. Cassella, and M. Davis, Fear-enhanced acoustic startle is not attenuated by acute or chronic imipramine treatment in rats, *Psychopharmacology, 87*: 278 (1985).

P. Chopin, and M. Briley, Animal models of anxiety: The effect of compounds that modify 5-HT neurotransmission, *Trends Pharmacol. Sci., 8*: 383 (1987).

J. T. Concannon, and J. Freda, Modulation of conditioned taste aversion by sodium pentobarbital, *Pharmacol. Biochem. Behav., 13*: 761 (1980).

L. H. Conti, C. R. Maciver, J. W. Ferkany, and M. E. Abreu, Footshock-induced freezing behavior in rats as a model for assessing anxiolytics, *Psychopharmacology, 102*: 492 (1990).

M. Cook, and S. Mineka, Selective associations in the observational conditioning of fear in rhesus monkeys, *J. Exp. Psychol. Anim. Behav. Proc., 16*: 372 (1990).

S. J. Cooper, Benzodiazepines as appetite-enhancing compounds, *Appetite, 1*: 7 (1980).

S. J. Cooper, and R. E. Yerbury, Clonazepam selectively increases saccharin ingestion in a two-choice test, *Brain Res., 456*: 173 (1988).

B. Costall, C. A. Hendrie, M. E. Kelly, and R. J. Naylor, Actions of sulpiride and tiapride in a simple model of anxiety in mice, *Neuropharmacology, 26*: 195 (1987).

B. Costall, A. M. Domeney, P. A. Gerrard, M. E. Kelly, and R. J. Naylor, Zacopride: Anxiolytic profile in rodent and primate models of anxiety, *J. Pharm. Pharmacol., 40*: 302 (1988a).

B. Costall, M. E. Kelly, R. J. Naylor, and E. S. Onaivi, Actions of buspirone in a putative model of anxiety in the mouse, *J. Pharm. Pharmacol., 40*: 494 (1988b).

B. Costall, B. J. Jones, M. E. Kelly, R. J. Naylor, and D. M. Tomkins, Exploration of mice in a black and white test box: Validation as a model of anxiety. *Pharmacol. Biochem. Behav., 32*: 777 (1989).

R. M. Craft, J. L. Howard, and G. T. Pollard, Conditioned defensive burying as a model for identifying anxiolytics, *Pharmacol. Biochem. Behav., 30*: 775 (1988).

J. N. Crawley, Neuropharmacologic specificity of a simple animal model for the behavioral actions of benzodiazepines, *Pharmacol. Biochem. Behav., 15*: 695 (1981).

J. N. Crawley, Exploratory behavior models of anxiety in mice, *Neurosci. Biobehav. Rev., 9*: 37 (1985).

J. Crawley, and F. K. Goodwin, Preliminary report of a simple animal behavior model for the anxiolytic effects of benzodiazepines, *Pharmacol. Biochem. Behav., 13*: 167 (1980).

J. N. Crawley, P. Skolnick, and S. M. Paul, Absence of intrinsic antagonist actions of benzodiazepine antagonists on an exploratory model of anxiety in the mouse, *Neuropharmacology, 23*: 531 (1984).

M. A. E. Critchley, and S. L. Handley, 5-HT 1A ligand effects in the X-maze anxiety test, *Br. J. Pharmacol., 92*: 660P (1987a).

M. A. E. Critchley, and S. L. Handley, Effects in the X-maze model of agents acting at 5-HT 1 and 5-HT 2 receptors, *Psychopharmacology, 93*: 502 (1987b).

V. Cuomo, R. Cagiano, M. A. De-Salvia, M. A. Maselli, G. Renna, and G. Racagni, Ultrasonic vocalization in response to unavoidable aversive stimuli in rats: Effects of benzodiazepines, *Life Sci., 43*: 485 (1988).

M. G. Cutler, An ethological study of the effects of buspirone and the 5-HT_3 receptor antagonist, BRL 43694 (granisetron) on behaviour during social interactions in female and male mice, *Neuropharmacology, 30*: 299 (1991).

M. Davis, Diazepam and flurazepam: Effects on conditioned fear as measured with the potentiated startle paradigm, *Psychopharmacology, 62*: 1 (1979).

M. Davis, Pharmacological and anatomical analysis of fear conditioning using the fear-potentiated startle paradigm, *Behav. Neurosci., 100*: 814 (1986).

M. Davis, Animal models of anxiety based on classical conditioning: The conditioned emotional response (CER) and the fear-potentiated startle effect, *Pharmacol. Ther., 47*: 147 (1990).

M. Davis, J. V. Cassella, and J. H. Kehne, Serotonin does not mediate anxiolytic effects of buspirone in the fear-potentiated startle paradigm: Comparison with 8-OH-DPAT and ipsapirone, *Psychopharmacology, 94*: 14 (1988).

S. F. De Boer, J. L. Slangen, and J. van der Gugten, Plasma catecholamine and corticosterone levels during active and passive shock-prod avoidance behavior in rats: Effects of chlordiazepoxide, *Pharmacol. Biochem. Behav., 47*: 1089 (1990).

Diagnostic and Statistical Manual of Mental Disorders, 3rd ed. revised, American Psychiatric Association, Washington, D.C., p. 235 (1987).

A. R. Delamater, and D. Treit, Chlordiazepoxide attenuates shock-based and enhances LiCl-based fluid aversions, *Learn. Motiv., 19*: 221 (1988).

R. W. Dunn, R. Corbett, and S. Fielding, Effects of 5-HT_{1A} receptor agonists and NMDA receptor antagonists in the social interaction test and the elevated plus maze, *Eur. J. Pharmacol., 169*: 1 (1989).

J. Engel, E. Hard, and A. S. Lindh, Effects of diazepam, ethanol and Ro 15–1788 on ultrasonic vocalization, locomotor activity and body righting in the neonatal rat, *Alcohol Alcoholism [Suppl.], 1*: 709 (1987).

G. N. Ervin, and B. R. Cooper, The use of conditioned taste aversion as a conflict model: Effects of anxiolytic drugs, *J. Pharmacol. Exp. Ther., 245*: 137 (1988).

G. N. Ervin, F. S. Soroko, and B. R. Cooper, Buspirone antagonizes the expression of conditioned taste aversion in rats, *Drug Dev. Res., 11*: 87 (1987).

M. S. Fanselow, and F. J. Helmstetter, Conditioned analgesia, defensive freezing, and benzodiazepines, *Behav. Neurosci., 102*: 233 (1988).

A. Fernandez-Guasti, and C. Lopez-Rubalcava, Evidence for the involvement of the 5-HT_{1A} receptor in the anxiolytic action of indorenate and ipsapirone, *Psychopharmacology, 101*: 354 (1990).

A. Fernandez-Guasti, E. Hong, and C. Lopez-Rubalcava, Species differences in the mechanism through which the serotonergic agonists indorenate and ipsapirone produce their anxiolytic action, *Psychopharmacology, 107*: 61 (1992).

A. Fernandez-Guasti, and O. Picazo, The actions of diazepam and serotonergic anxiolytics vary according to the gender and the estrous cycle phase, *Pharmacol. Biochem. Behav., 37*: 77 (1990).

S. E. File, The contribution of behavioral studies to the neuropharmacology of anxiety, *Neuropharmacology, 26*: 877 (1987).

S. E. File, The validation of animal tests of anxiety—pharmacological implications, *Pol. J. Pharmacol. Pharm., 36*: 505 (1984).

S. E. File, Animal models for predicting clinical efficacy of anxiolytic drugs: Social behaviour, *Neuropsycholobiology, 13*: 55 (1985).

S. E. File, and J. R. G. Hyde, Can social interaction be used to measure anxiety? *Br. J. Pharmacol., 62*: 19 (1978).

S. E. File, and J. R. G. Hyde, A test of anxiety that distinguishes between the actions of benzodiazepines and those of other minor tranquilisers and stimulants, *Pharmacol. Biochem. Behav., 11*: 65 (1979).

S. E. File, and S. Pellow, Anxiogenic action of a convulsant benzodiazepine: Reversal by chlordiazepoxide, *Brain Res., 278*: 370 (1983).

S. E. File, and S. Pellow, The anxiogenic action of FG 7142 in the social interaction test is reversed by chlordiazepoxide and Ro 15–1788 but not by CGS 8216, *Arch. Int. Pharmacodyn. Ther., 271*: 198 (1984a).

S. E. File, and S. Pellow, The anxiogenic action of Ro 15–1788 is reversed by chronic, but not by acute, treatment with chlordiazepoxide, *Brain Res., 310*: 154 (1984b).

S. E. File, and S. Pellow, The anxiogenic action of RO 5–4864 in the social interaction test: Effect of chlordiazepoxide, RO 15–1788 and CGS 8216, *Naunyn Schmiedebergs Arch. Pharmacol., 328*: 225 (1985).

J. Garcia and R. Koelling, Relation of cue to consequence in avoidance learning, *Psychon. Sci., 4*: 123 (1966).

C. R. Gardner, Inhibition of ultrasonic distress vocalizations in rat pups by chlordiazepoxide and diazepam, *Drug Dev. Res., 5*: 185 (1985a).

C. R. Gardner, Distress vocalization in rat pups. A simple screening method for anxiolytic drugs, *J. Pharmacol. Methods, 14*: 181 (1985b).

C. R. Gardner, Recent developments in 5-HT-related pharmacology of animal models of anxiety, *Pharmacol. Biochem. Behav., 24*: 1479 (1986).

C. R. Gardner, Functional in vivo correlates of the benzodiazepine agonist–inverse agonist continuum, *Prog. Neurobiol., 31*: 425 (1988).

C. R. Gardner, and P. Budhram, Effects of agents which interact with central benzodiazepine binding sites on stress-induced ultrasounds in rat pups, *Eur. J. Pharmacol., 134*: 275 (1987).

C. R. Gardner, and A. P. Guy, A social interaction model of anxiety sensitive to acutely administered benzodiazepines, *Drug Dev. Res., 4*: 207 (1984).

F. G. Graeff, E. A. Audi, S. S. Almeida, E. O. Graeff, and M. H. L. Hunziker, Behavioral effects of 5-HT receptor ligands in the aversive stimulation, elevated plus-maze and learned helplessness tests, *Neurosci. Biobehav. Rev., 14*: 501 (1990).

N. E. Grossen, and M. J. Kelley, Species-specific behavior and acquisition of avoidance behavior in rats, *J. Comp. Physiol. Psychol., 81*: 307 (1972).

A. P. Guy, and C. R. Gardner, Pharmacological characterisation of a modified social interaction model of anxiety in the rat, *Neuropsychobiology, 13*: 194 (1985).

W. E. Haefely, The GABAa-benzodiazepine receptor: Biology and pharmacology, *Handbook of Anxiety,* Vol. 3 (G. D. Burrows, M. Roth, and R. Noyes, Jr., eds.), Elsevier, Amsterdam, p. 165 (1990).

S. L. Handley, and S. Mithani, Effects of alpha-adrenoreceptor agonists and antagonists in a X-maze-exploration model of fear motivated behaviour, *Naunyn-Schmiedebergs Arch. Pharmacol., 327*: 1 (1984).

E. Hard, and J. Engel, Effects of 8-OH-DPAT on ultrasonic vocalization and audiogenic immobility reaction in pre-weaning rats, *Neuropharmacology, 27*: 981 (1988).

G. A. Higgins, A. J. Bradbury, B. J. Jones, and N. R. Oakley, Behavioural and biochemical consequences following activation of $5HT_1$-like and GABA receptors in the dorsal raphe nucleus of the rat, *Neuropharmacology, 27*: 993 (1988).

T. H. Hijzen, and J. L. Slangen, Effects of midazolam, DMCM and lindane on potentiated startle in the rat, *Psychopharmacology, 99*: 362 (1989).

D. W. Hommer, P. Skolnick, and S. M. Paul, The benzodiazepine/GABA receptor complex and anxiety, *Psychopharmacology: The Third Generation of Progress* (H. Y. Meltzer, ed.), Raven Press, New York, p. 977 (1987).

T. R. Insel, Decreased in vivo binding to brain benzodiazepine receptors during social isolation, *Psychopharmacology, 97*: 142 (1989).

T. R. Insel, J. L. Hill, and R. B. Mayor, Rat pup ultrasonic isolation calls: Possible mediation by the benzodiazepine receptor complex, *Pharmacol. Biochem. Behav., 24*: 1262 (1986).

F. B. Jolicoeur, M. J. Wayner, A. D. Merkel, D. B. Rondeau, and R. B. Mintz, The effects of various barbiturates on LiCl induced taste aversion, *Pharmacol. Biochem. Behav., 12*: 613 (1980).

M. T. Kaltwasser, Startle-inducing acoustic stimuli evoke ultrasonic vocalization in the rat, *Pharmacol. Biochem. Behav., 48*: 13 (1990).

M. T. Kaltwasser, Acoustic startle induced ultrasonic vocalization in the rat: A novel animal model of anxiety? *Behav. Brain Res., 43*: 133 (1991).

J. H. Kehne, J. V. Cassella, and M. Davis, Anxiolytic effects of buspirone and gepirone in the fear-potentiated startle paradigm, *Psychopharmacology, 94*: 8 (1988).

J. H. Kehne, T. C. McCloskey, B. M. Baron, E. M. Chi, B. L. Harrison, J. P. Whitten, and M. G. Palfreyman, NMDA receptor complex antagonists have potential anxiolytic effects as measured with separation-induced ultrasonic vocalizations, *Eur. J. Pharmacol., 193*: 283 (1991).

T. Kilfoil, A. Michel, D. Montgomery, and R. L. Whiting, Effects of anxiolytic and anxiogenic drugs on exploratory activity in a simple model of anxiety in mice, *Neuropharmacology, 28*: 901 (1989).

S. M. Korte, and B. Bohus, The effect of ipsapirone on behavioral and cardiac responses in the shock-probe/defensive burying test in male rats, *Eur. J. Pharmacol., 181*: 307 (1990).

S. M. Korte, J. M. Koolhaas, T. Schuurman, J. Traber, and B. Bohus, Anxiolytics and stress-induced behavioral and cardiac responses: A study of diazepam and ipsapirone (TVX Q 7821), *Eur. J. Pharmacol., 179*: 393 (1990).

W. Kostowski, A. Plaznik, and R. Stefanski, Intra-hippocampal buspirone in animal models of anxiety, *Eur. J. Pharmacol., 168*: 393 (1989).

H. Lal, and M. W. Emmett-Oglesby, Behavioral analogues of anxiety. Animal models, *Neuropharmacology, 22*(12B): 1423 (1983).

R. G. Lister, Ethologically-based animal models of anxiety disorders, *Pharmacol. Ther., 46*: 321 (1990).

R. G. Lister, The use of a plus-maze to measure anxiety in the mouse, *Psychopharmacology, 92*: 180 (1987).

R. S. Mansbach and M. A. Geyer, Blockade of potentiated startle responding in rats by 5-hydroxytryptamine 1A receptor ligands, *Eur. J. Pharmacol., 156*: 375 (1987).

I. M. Marks, *Fears, Phobias, and Rituals*, Oxford University Press, New York (1987).

R. J. McNally, Preparedness and phobias: A review, *Psychol. Bull., 101*: 283 (1987).

T. F. Meert, and F. C. Colpaert, The shock probe conflict procedure. A new assay responsive to benzodiazepines, barbiturates and related compounds, *Psychopharmacology, 88*: 445 (1986).

S. Mineka, Animal models of anxiety-based disorders: Their usefulness and limitations, *Anxiety and Anxiety Disorders* (A. H. Tuma and J. D. Maser, eds.), Lawrence Erlbaum, Hillsdale, N. J., p. 199 (1985).

S. Mineka, R. Keir, and V. Price, Fear of snakes in wild- and lab-reared rhesus monkeys, *Anim. Learn. Behav., 8*: 653 (1980).

S. A. Montgomery, and N. Fineberg, Is there a relationship between serotonin receptor subtypes and selectivity of response in psychiatric illnesses? *Br. J. Psychiatry, 155*(suppl. 8): 63 (1989).

P. C. Moser, An evaluation of the elevated plus-maze test using the novel anxiolytic buspirone, *Psychopharmacology, 99*: 48 (1989).

P. C. Moser, M. D. Tricklebank, D. N. Middlemiss, A. K. Mir, M. F Hibert, and J. R. Fozard, Characterization of MDL 73005EF as a 5-HT 1A selective ligand and its effects in animal models of anxiety: Comparison with buspirone, 8-OH-DPAT and diazepam. *Br. J. Pharmacol., 99*: 343 (1990).

J. L. Neisewander, S. A. McDougall, S. L. Bowling, and M. T. Bardo, Conditioned taste aversion and place preference with buspirone and gepirone, *Psychopharmacology, 100*: 485 (1990).

K. Njung'e, and S. L. Handley, Evaluation of marble-burying behavior as a model of anxiety, *Pharmacol. Biochem. Behav., 38*: 63 (1991).

E. Noirot, Ultrasounds and maternal behavior in small rodents, *Dev. Psychobiol., 5*: 371 (1972).

A. Ohman, Face the beast and fear the face: Animal and social fears as prototypes for evolutionary analyses of emotion, *Psychophysiology, 23*: 123 (1986).

A. Ohman, U. Dimberg, and L. G. Ost, Animal and social phobias: Biological constraints on learned fear responses, *Theoretical Issues in Behavior Therapy* (S. Reiss and R. R. Bootzin, eds.), Academic Press, New York, p. 123 (1985).

D. Olajide, and M. Lader, A double-blind comparison of buspirone and diazepam in outpatients with chronic anxiety states, Abstract at C.I.N.P. meeting, Florence, (1984).

E. S. Onaivi, and B. R. Martin, Neuropharmacological and physiological validation of a computer-controlled two-compartment black and white box for the assessment of anxiety, *Prog. Neuropsychopharmacol. Biol. Psychiatry, 13*: 963 (1989).

L. A. Parker, Chlordiazepoxide nonspecifically enhances consumption of saccharin solution, *Pharmacol. Biochem. Behav., 38*: 375 (1991).

J. C. Pecknold, P. Familamiri, H. Chang, R. Wilson, J. Alarcia, and D. J. McClure, Buspirone: Anxiolytic? *Prog. Neuropsychopharmacol. Biol. Psychiatry, 9*: 639 (1985).

S. Pellow, Anxiolytic and anxiogenic drug effects in a novel test of anxiety: Are exploratory models of anxiety in rodents valid? *Methods Find. Expl. Clin. Pharmacol., 8*: 557 (1986).

S. Pellow, and S. E. File, Anxiolytic and anxiogenic drug effects on exploratory activity in an elevated plus-maze: A novel test of anxiety in the rat, *Pharmacol. Biochem. Behav., 24*: 525 (1986).

S. Pellow, P. Chopin, S. E. File, and M. Briley, Validation of open:closed arm entries in an elevated plus-maze as a measure of anxiety in the rat, *J. Neurosci. Methods, 14*: 149 (1985).

S. Pellow, A. L. Johnston, and S. E. File, Selective agonists and antagonists for 5-hydroxytryptamine receptor subtypes, and interactions with yohimbine and FG 7142 using the elevated plus-maze test in the rat, *J. Pharm. Pharmacol., 39*: 917 (1987).

S. J. Peroutka, Selective interaction of novel anxiolytics with 5-hydroxytryptamine 1A receptors, *Biol. Psychiatry, 20*: 971 (1985).

E. M. Pich, and R. Samanin, Disinhibitory effects of buspirone and low doses of sulpiride and haloperidol in two experimental anxiety models in rats: Possible role of dopamine, *Psychopharmacology, 89*: 125 (1986).

J. P. J. Pinel, and D. Treit, Burying as a defensive response in rats, *J. Comp. Physiol. Psychol., 92*: 708 (1978).

J. P. J. Pinel, and D. Treit, The conditioned defensive burying paradigm and behavioral neuroscience, *Behavioral Approaches to Brain Research* (T. Robinson, ed.), Oxford Press, Oxford, p. 212 (1983).

G. T. Pollard, and J. L. Howard, Effects of drugs on punished behavior: Pre-clinical test for anxiolytics, *Pharmacol. Ther., 45*: 403 (1990).

R. J. Primus, and C. K. Kellogg, Experience influences environmental modulation of function at the benzodiazepine (BZD)/GABA receptor chloride channel complex, *Brain Res., 545*: (1991).

L. Rago, R. A. Kiivet, J. Harro, and M. Pold, Behavioral differences in an elevated plus-maze: Correlation between anxiety and decreased number of GABA and benzodiazepine receptors in mouse cerebral cortex, *Naunyn-Schmiedebergs Arch. Pharmacol., 337*: 675 (1988).

A. L. Riley, and R. H. Lovely, Chlordiazepoxide induced reversal of an amphetamine-established aversion: Dipsogenic effects, *Physiol. Psychol., 6*: 488 (1978).

J. D. Roache, and J. E. Zabik, Effects of benzodiazepines on taste aversions in a two-bottle choice paradigm, *Pharmacol. Biochem. Behav., 25*: 431 (1986).

J. G. Rohmer, G. Di Scala, and G. Sandner, Behavioral analysis of the effects of benzodiazepine receptor ligands in the conditioned burying paradigm, *Behav. Brain Res., 38*: 45 (1990).

D. B. Rondeau, F. B. Jolicoeur, A. D. Merkel, and M. J. Wayner, Drugs and taste aversion, *Neurosci. Biobehav. Rev., 5*: 279 (1981).

M. Roth, Anxiety disorders—normal, pathological and episodic: A dilemma for aetiology, *Hand-*

book of Anxiety, Vol. 3 (G. D. Burrows, M. Roth, and R. Noyes, Jr., eds.), Elsevier, Amsterdam, p. 439 (1990).

M. J. Rowan, W. K. Cullen, and B. Moulton, Buspirone impairment of performance of passive avoidance and spatial learning tasks in the rat, *Psychopharmacology, 100*: 393 (1990).

M. E. P. Seligman, Phobias and preparedness, *Behav. Ther., 2*: 307 (1971).

D. V. Sheehan, A. B. Raj, K. H. Sheehan, and S. Soto, Is buspirone effective for panic disorder? *J. Clin. Psychopharmacol., 10*: 3 (1990).

D. V. Sheehan, A. B. Raj, K. H. Sheehan, and S. Soto, The relative efficacy of buspirone, imipramine and placebo in panic disorder: A preliminary report, *Pharmacol. Biochem. Behav., 29*: 815 (1988).

R. A. Shephard, Neurotransmitters, anxiety and benzodiazepines: A behavioral review, *Neurosci. Biobehav. Rev., 10*: 449 (1986).

P. Skolnick, S. M. Paul, and B. A. Weissman, Preclinical pharmacology of buspirone hydrochloride, *Pharmacotherapy, 4*: 308 (1984).

B. Soderpalm, E. Eriksson, and J. A. Engel, Anticonflict and rotarod impairing effects of alprazolam and diazepam in rat after acute and subchronic administration, *Prog. Neuropsychopharmacol. Biol. Psychiatry, 13*: 269 (1989a).

B. Soderpalm, S. Hjorth, and J. A. Engel, Effects of 5-HT_{1A} receptor agonists and L-5-HTP in Montgomery's conflict test, *Pharmacol. Biochem. Behav., 32*: 259 (1989b).

M. H. Thiebot, Behavioral models of anxiety in animals, *Encephale, 9(4 Suppl. 2)*: 167B (1983).

M. H. Thiebot, P. Soubrie, and P. Simon, Is delay of reward mediated by shock-avoidance behavior a critical target for anti-punishment effects of diazepam in rats? *Psychopharmacology, 87*: 473 (1985).

M. H. Thiebot, P. Soubrie, and D. Sanger, Anxiogenic properties of beta-CCE and FG 7142: A review of promises and pitfalls, *Psychopharmacology, 94*: 452 (1988).

T. Tonoue, Y. Ashida, H. Makino, and H. Hata, Inhibition of shock-elicited ultrasonic vocalization by opioid peptides in the rat; a psychotropic effect, *Psychoneuroendocrinology, 11*: 177 (1986).

T. Tonoue, H. Iwasawa, and H. Naito, Diazepam and endorphin independently inhibit ultrasonic distress calls in rats, *Eur. J. Pharmacol., 142*: 133 (1987).

J. Traber, and G. Thomas, 5-HT 1A receptor-related anxiolytics, *Trend. Pharmacol. Sci., 8*: 432 (1987).

D. Treit, Animal models for the study of anti-anxiety agents: A review, *Neurosci. Biobehav. Rev., 9*, 203 (1985a).

D. Treit, Evidence that tolerance develops to the anxiolytic effect of diazepam in rats, *Pharmacol. Biochem. Behav., 22*: 383 (1985b).

D. Treit, The inhibitory effect of diazepam on defensive burying: Anxiolytic vs. analgesic effects, *Pharmacol. Biochem. Behav., 22*: 47 (1985c).

D. Treit, Ro 15–1788, CGS 8216, picrotoxin, and pentylenetetrazol: Do they antagonize anxiolytic drug effects through an anxiogenic action? *Brain Res. Bull., 19*: 401 (1987).

D. Treit, A comparison of anxiolytic and nonanxiolytic agents in the shock-probe/burying test for anxiolytics, *Pharmacol. Biochem. Behav. 36*: 203 (1990).

D. Treit, A comparison of the effects of septal lesions and anxiolytic drugs on defensive behavior in rats, *Psychol. Rec., 41*: 217 (1991).

D. Treit, and K. C. Berridge, A comparison of benzodiazepine, serotonin, and dopamine agents in the taste-reactivity paradigm, *Pharmacol. Biochem. Behav., 37*: 451 (1990).

D. Treit, and M. Fundytus, A comparison of buspirone and chlordiazepoxide in the shock-probe/burying test for anxiolytics, *Pharmacol. Biochem. Behav., 30*: 1071 (1988a).

D. Treit, and M. Fundytus, Thigmotaxis as a test for anxiolytic activity in rats. *Pharmacol. Biochem. Behav., 31*: 959 (1988b).

D. Treit, and C. Pesold, Septal lesions inhibit fear reactions in two animal models of anxiolytic drug action, *Physiol. Behav., 47*: 365 (1990).

D. Treit, J. P. J. Pinel, and H. C. Fibiger, Conditioned defensive burying: A new paradigm for the study of anxiolytic agents, *Pharmacol. Biochem. Behav., 15*: 619 (1981).

D. Treit, V. M. Lolordo, and D. E. Armstrong, The effects of diazepam on "fear" reactions in rats are modulated by environmental constraints on the rat's defensive repertoire, *Pharmacol. Biochem. Behav., 25*: 561 (1986).

D. Treit, K. C. Berridge, and C. E. Shultz, The direct enhancement of positive palatability by chlordiazepoxide is antagonized by Ro 15–1788 and CGS 8216, *Pharmacol. Biochem. Behav., 26*: 709 (1987).

A. Tsuda, Y. Ida, and M. Tanaka, The contrasting effects of diazepam and yohimbine on conditioned defensive burying in rats, *Psychobiology, 16*: 213 (1988).

A. Tsuda, Y. Ida, H. Nishimura, and M. Tanaka, Anxiogenic effects of B-CCE as measured in two different conditioning paradigms, *Psychobiology, 17*: 202 (1989).

P. J. Tyrer, Classification of anxiety disorders: A critique of *DSM-III, J. Affective Disord., 11*: 99 (1986).

P. J. Tyrer, The division of neurosis: A failed classification, *J. R. Soc. Med., 83*: 614 (1990).

Wheatley, D., Buspirone: Multicenter efficacy study, *J. Clin. Psychiatry, 43*: 92 (1982).

S. L. M. Widgiz, and C. H. M. Beck, The effects of diazepam on the exploratory behaviour of rats in an elevated runway: Evidence for biphasic effects of benzodiazepines, *Behav. Brain Res., 40*: 109 (1990).

9

Theories on the Etiology of Anxiety Disorders

Fiona K. Judd, Trevor R. Norman, and Graham D. Burrows
University of Melbourne, Austin Hostpital, Heidelberg, Victoria, Australia

I. INTRODUCTION

There has been a dramatic increase in interest in the anxiety disorders over the past decade. Epidemiological studies have demonstrated that these disorders are common (Robins et al., 1984). They persist without treatment and result in significant disability. The development of operationalized diagnostic criteria has led to the delineation of specific syndromes (American Psychiatric Association; APA, 1987). Panic disorder and obsessive–compulsive disorder have been most studied.

Early studies focused on the possible role of psychodynamic factors in the etiology of anxiety disorders. Over the past decade, cognitive and biological factors have been most studied. In this chapter, we examine several theories of the etiology of anxiety disorders, with particular emphasis on panic and obsessive–compulsive disorders (OCD).

II. PSYCHODYNAMIC THEORIES

Freud's earliest extended discussions of anxiety focus on his attempts to distinguish neurasthesia from anxiety neurosis. Neurasthesia and anxiety neurosis were grouped together as "Aktual neurosis" (Freud, 1962), caused by "sexual noxae." Freud suggested that, in the anxiety neurosis, physical sexual tension that cannot be discharged psychically as affect is transformed into anxiety (Freud, 1966).

About 1900, Freud focused his attention on mental phenomena, such as forgetting, dreams, parapraxes, and jokes. He described three sources of anxiety: somatic, e.g., difficulty in breathing in heart or lung disease, determines the anxiety (Freud, 1953); aktual neurotic and psychoneurotic (repressed libido, psychosexual excitation) are transformed into anxiety (Freud, 1953). Here, the clear distinction between somatic and psychic libido is no longer maintained.

With the report of the case of "Little Hans" came a broadening of Freud's views on anxiety at the dynamic level (Freud, 1955). The transformation of repressed affect came to be viewed as the major cause for anxiety. Freud distinguished realistic anxiety, a manifestation of the ego's self-preservative instincts, from neurotic anxiety (Freud, 1963). During the last 20 years of his life, Freud extensively revised his theory of anxiety. With the introduction of the ego–id–superego model Freud proposed that "the ego is the actual seat of anxiety" (Freud, 1961). He described three kinds of anxiety: neurotic, moral, and real, corresponding to the three kinds of dangers the ego faces—from the id, from the superego, and from the external world. Anxiety was seen as a danger, its main function being to motivate the ego to employ repression and other defensive mechanisms to control the underlying drives and affects. Anxiety was now the cause of repression, rather than the result of it. If the defenses are successful, anxiety is contained or dispelled, but, depending on the nature of the defenses employed, the individual may develop a variety of psychoneurotic symptoms. The frequent presence of anxiety in association with other neurotic symptoms indicates that the auxiliary defenses themselves are often not totally effective, although generally keeping the affect within tolerable limits. If repression fails to function adequately, or if other defenses are not used, anxiety will be the only symptom and clinically may be manifest as anxiety or panic attacks.

Following Freud's work, various analytical approaches have emphasized different kinds of anxiety, resulting in differences of opinion about its nature. Thus, the genesis of anxiety may be attributed to diverse factors, such as birth trauma, the early relationship between mother and child with the transmission of mother's anxiety to her infant, or existential issues. Currently, there is no single agreed psychodynamic view of anxiety.

III. FAMILY BACKGROUND AND CHILD–PARENT RELATIONSHIP

Early family background and child–parent relationships have been examined in a variety of studies of patients with agoraphobia. Snaith (1968) found that the families of patients with agoraphobia were less stable than those of other phobic patients. Buglass et al. (1977) noted stepparents, stepsiblings, and adopted siblings were more common in families of agoraphobic patients than in those of control subjects. Bowlby (1973) suggested agoraphobic families were characterized by maternal overprotection and lack of maternal affection. Parker (1979), in a controlled study using the Parental Bonding Instrument (PBI), found that agoraphobic subjects reported significantly less maternal care. Patients were unlikely to report "optimal parenting" (high care–low protection) and much more likely to report "affectionless control" (low care–high protection). In a replication study, Silove (1986) found agoraphobics scored their parents as less caring and more overprotective than parents of controls. Maternal overprotection has been confirmed by some other (Solyom et al., 1976; Burns and Thorpe, 1977) but not all (Snaith et al., 1971; Arrindell et al., 1983) studies.

The finding of a history of pathogenic parenting in those with anxiety disorders may indicate that this is a causal developmental factor. Alternatively, the association may be noncausal. One suggested link is that the child may, as a consequence of premorbid characteristics or early signs of anxiety, elicit anomalies in care and overprotection from parents.

IV. SEPARATION ANXIETY AND ANXIETY DISORDERS

Several lines of evidence suggest a link between separation anxiety and panic or phobic disorders. Klein (1981), noting that parents with agoraphobia are often dependent and intolerant of being alone, suggested that agoraphobia may be a form of separation anxiety. Patients with agoraphobia report a higher incidence of separation anxiety in childhood and school phobia than do normal controls (Klein, 1981; Berg et al., 1974; Tyrer and Tyrer, 1974) and patients with simple phobia (Klein et al., 1983; Zitrin et al., 1983). Second, family studies have demonstrated children of adult probands with agoraphobia and panic attacks have higher rates of school phobia and separation anxiety (Berg et al., 1976; Weissman et al., 1984). Third, both school phobia and agoraphobia respond to treatment with imipramine (Gittelman-Klein and Klein, 1973, 1980). By contrast, generalized anxiety disorder (GAD) and parental psychopathology in general are not associated with separation anxiety in offspring (Gittleman and Klein, 1985).

V. PARENTAL SEPARATION AND LOSS

Empirical data investigating Bowlby's suggestion that early exposure to parental separation (death, loss, desertion) or threat of such separation are developmental stressors predisposing to the development of anxiety in adulthood are contradictory. Early studies (Buglass et al., 1977; Solyom et al., 1974; Shafar, 1976) did not find an increased rate of parental loss or separation in childhood, whereas Silove (1986), in a controlled study, reported a trend for more childhood losses and major separations. Torgersen (1986) found a trend for patients with panic disorder and agoraphobia to be more likely to report parental death in childhood than those with GAD. Rutter (1972) has noted that "although bond disruption is a potent source of short-term distress, it is not a particularly important factor in the development of serious long-term disturbance of any type." However, he has highlighted that long-term effects of separation in animals are dependent on whether separation leads to a disturbed relationship after reunion, with persistence of emotional disturbance reflecting dysfunction in ongoing parenting, rather than separation per se (Rutter, 1985).

VI. LIFE EVENTS AND ANXIETY DISORDERS

Despite a vast literature concerning life events and psychiatric illness, little definitive information about the link between life events and anxiety disorders is available. The relation between anxiety symptoms (measured by questionnaire) and life events (measured by questionnaire or interview) has been evaluated in several studies (Lauer, 1973; Miller et al., 1976; Sarason et al., 1978; Flannery, 1986). All but one (Flannery, 1986) found a positive correlation between life events and anxiety. All these studies were retrospective and, thus, prone to a variety of methodological problems (Tennant, 1983).

Studies assessing the relation between life events and onset of anxiety disorders have demonstrated a strong association between onset of anxiety disorder and life event threat, particularly events implying danger or demand performance (Barrett, 1979; Finlay-Jones and Brown, 1981).

Roth (1959) first noted the high incidence of threatening events before the onset of phobic disorders (mostly agoraphobia with panic attacks). Since that time, although clinicians have repeatedly noted the association (Buglass et al., 1977; Shafar, 1976; Sheehan et al., 1981), few studies systematically evaluating the role of life events in the etiology of agoraphobia have been reported. Interpersonal problems are a commonly reported precipitating event. Bowen and Kohout (1979) found 76% of agoraphobics who identified a precipitating event described this as rejection or loss in an interpersonal relationship. Shafar (1976) found interpersonal difficulties were the primary precipitant in onset or aggravation of phobic disorders. Physiological disturbance is also commonly identified as a precipitant to onset of panic attacks, with onset being linked to serious illness (Shafar, 1976), childbirth, surgical operations (McGennis et al., 1977), and endocrinological changes, such as hypothyroidism (Liebowitz and Klein, 1979).

Roy-Byrne et al. (1986), who used a life event inventory, compared the number, type, and effect of life events in the year preceding onset of panic attacks in patients with a Research Diagnostic Criteria (RDC) diagnosis of panic disorder, with 44 matched control subjects. Compared with controls, patients had significantly more events, events were more typically distressing, and they had a more adverse impact. In particular, events reported by patients were more frequently viewed as uncontrollable, undesirable, or causing lowering of self-esteem. Franklin and Andrews (1989), using a life event inventory, compared life events in the 12 months preceding onset of illness in patients with agoraphobia, with matched controls. Patients reported a significant excess of life events in the year before onset of illness.

Similarly anecdotal reports and clinical experience suggest an association between life events and onset of OCD. In a controlled study, McKeon et al. (1984) found patients reported twice as many events as did controls. Differences were particularly evident for the 6 months before onset of symptoms. For posttraumatic stress disorder (PTSD), the causal link with life events is clear. By definition (APA, 1987) the disorder follows a psychologically distressing event outside the range of usual human experience. However, as with the other anxiety disorders, the mechanism by which the life event leads to anxiety remains to be elucidated. As the life events associated with other anxiety disorders include a variety of events, both noxious and positive, but often of the type coped with by others, the mechanisms leading to the development of PTSD may be different.

VII. COGNITIVE MODELS OF ANXIETY STATES

Cognitive models propose that it is not events per se but a person's expectations and interpretations of events that produce anxiety. Generally, the important cognitions relate to perceived physical or psychosocial danger. Beck (1976) proposes that in anxiety states, individuals systematically overestimate danger in a given situation. As a result, responses inherited from our evolutionary past, which were originally designed to protect us from harm in a primitive environment, are automatically activated. These responses include changes in autonomic arousal, with preparation for flight-or-fight; inhibition of current behavior; and vigilance and selective scanning of the environment for possible sources of danger. When these responses are activated by misperception, rather than realistic threat, they are inappropriate to the situation and often are interpreted as a further source of threat, which then tends to maintain or exacerbate the anxiety reaction.

Beck and associates (1985) have formulated a cognitive model of generalized anxiety in which they suggest that individuals experience pervasive anxiety because their beliefs about themselves make them prone to interpret a wide range of situations as threatening. The suggested beliefs or dysfunctional assumptions in individuals with generalized anxiety generally include issues of acceptance, competence, responsibility, or control. Once the individual develops anxiety, attention and behavioral changes maintain the symptoms. In situations perceived as being dangerous, the individual selectively attends to aspects of the situation that indicate danger.

The cognitive model of panic formulated by Clark (1986) proposes that individuals experience panic attacks as a result of their interpretation of a range of bodily sensations in a catastrophic fashion. Sensations misinterpreted are those that occur in a normal anxiety response (e.g., palpitations, breathlessness, dizziness). Patients with panic perceive these sensations as indicative of immediate impending physical or mental disaster (e.g., heart attack, cessation of breathing, collapse). Both external (e.g., a situation in which panic previously occurred) or internal (e.g., thoughts, images, bodily sensations) stimuli can provoke attacks. Stimuli interpreted as threatening lead to a state of apprehension, associated with a range of bodily sensations. Catastrophic interpretation of these sensations leads to increased apprehension. Escalation of this cycle results in a panic attack. Once initiated, the panic disorder is maintained by two factors. Hypervigilance and focus of attention on bodily sensations causes patients to notice sensations that most people are not aware of. These sensations are then interpreted as evidence of serious physical or mental disease. Second, avoidance of situations that initiate symptoms (e.g., exercise) maintains the patient's negative interpretations by reinforcing the belief that had they not avoided the situation, the catastrophe they fear would have occurred.

Rachman's (1978) psychological model of obsessions highlight's the functional significance of overt and covert compulsions, or neutralizing behaviors. In this model, obsessions (intrusive thoughts, impulses, images) are involuntary and accompanied by increased anxiety; overt and covert compulsions are neutralizing behaviors that are voluntary and are carried out to reduce anxiety. The cognitive model (Salkovskis, 1985) built on this analysis, sees intrusive thoughts per se as a normal phenomenon. The environment is full of a wide range of potential triggering stimuli for intrusive thoughts. If an individual believes that odd thoughts with an unpleasant content can occur and have no further implications, the sequence leading to the development of obsessional thoughts and behavior does not progress. If an individual believes the thoughts might have important implications, then automatic thoughts will arise as a function of the strength of the beliefs.

The sequence suggested to occur in obsessional patients is as follows: Environmental stimuli trigger intrusive thoughts. Obsessional patients take steps, overt and covert, to avoid such stimuli. When avoidance fails or is not possible, triggering stimuli are encountered and intrusive thoughts, experienced as ego dystonic, occur. These are followed by automatic thoughts, usually concerning some combination of blame, threat, and loss. These thoughts result in mood disturbance which, in turn, leads to neutralizing responses. Neutralizing has three main consequences: reduced discomfort, allowing the development of obsessional behavior as a strategy for coping with stress; nonpunishment, which is a powerful reinforcer; the performance or completion of neutralizing is a powerful and unavoidable triggering stimulus.

These cognitive models have resulted in the development of treatment programs that have been shown to be effective in the management of these disorders (Clark et al., 1985; Salkovskis and Warwick, 1985).

VIII. PERSONALITY

The literature on the relation between personality and anxiety states is limited. In addition, most studies suffer from methodological problems, most notably use of the case–control design. Patients with anxiety disorders are identified when they present for treatment, personality is then assessed concomitantly. This method results in several problems: it does not allow determination of whether personality predated illness; personality traits may be exacerbated by illness; illness may distort the individual's view of premorbid personality. Studies that use dimensional measures of personality have generally suggested high neuroticism and low extroversion among anxious patients.

Kerr et al. (1970) found patients with panic–anxiety–depersonalization state had high levels of neuroticism (measured by the Maudsley Personality Scale), but these high scores decreased to almost normal after successful treatment. These patients also have low levels on the extroversion scale, which remained stable at follow-up. Subsequently, Hoehn-Saric (1981), who used the same scale, found high neuroticism in patients with both panic attacks and generalized anxiety.

Extroversion scores were lower than normal in both groups, but more so in the group with generalized anxiety. Roth et al. (1972) found that anxious, compared with depressed, patients more often reported premorbid personality traits of social anxiety, hypersensitivity to criticism, dependence, immaturity, hysteria, and anergia.

Tyrer et al. (1983), who used a personality assessment that yields four personality diagnoses (sociopathic, passive dependent, anacastic, and schizoid), studied 316 patients with various neurotic disorders. Patients with phobic anxiety and obsessive neurosis were significantly more likely to have personality disorders, especially of the passive-dependent type than those with depressive neurosis. Koenigsberg et al. (1985) found relatively high rates of personality diagnosis (*DSM-III*) among patients with phobic (48%) and panic disorders (50%). The most common personality diagnoses were dependent, avoidant, borderline, and histrionic. Similarly, Mavissakalian and Hanann (1986) found avoidant, dependent, and histrionic were the most frequent personality diagnoses in patients with agoraphobia and panic attacks who have an axis II disorder (*DSM-III* criteria).

Reich et al. (1987) noted that dependent personality disorder was the most frequent diagnosis in their patients with panic disorder, whereas the most frequently noted cluster of diagnoses was cluster C (dependent, avoidant, compulsive, passive–aggressive). Patients with phobic avoidance had significantly more dependent personality and cluster C diagnoses than those without phobic avoidance.

It is often assumed that individuals with compulsive personality disorder develop obsessive–compulsive disorder, but little data exist to support this. Rasmussan and Tsuang (1986) found patients with OCD had a wide range of personality disorder diagnoses. Less than half satisfied criteria for compulsive personality disorder. Joffe et al. (1988) compared personality disorder diagnoses in patients with OCD and a group of age- and sex-matched patients with major depressive disorder. There were no significant differences between the groups relative to frequency or type of personality disorder diagnoses. A mixed personality disorder with avoidant, dependent, and passive–aggressive factors was the most common diagnosis in the OCD group. Recently, Baer et al. (1990) have used the Structured Interview for the *DSM-III* personality disorders to assess 96 patients with OCD. Fifty patients met criteria for at least one personality disorder. Mixed, dependent, and histrionic personality disorders were most frequently diagnosed. Only six patients met the diagnostic criteria for compulsive personality disorder.

IX. PSYCHOPHYSIOLOGICAL THEORIES

Peripheral physiological variables have been studied in a variety of anxiety disorders. Commonly measured autonomic variables include heart rate, systolic and diastolic blood pressure, vascular resistance, pulse volume, skin temperature and blood flow, and skin resistance and conductance. Musculoskeletal measures include respiratory rate and depth and electromyogram (EMG) at various sites.

The relation between the emotion anxiety and its physiological concomitants is yet to be elucidated. James (1884) and Lange (1885) independently suggested that emotions were secondary to the perception of bodily changes. Whether physiological changes are the antecedents or consequences of the emotional aspects of anxiety remains unclear.

Patients with anxiety disorders show increased levels of arousal, as measured by heart rate (Lader and Wing, 1964), forearm blood flow (Kelly and Walter, 1968), skin conductance (Lader, 1967), and EMG activity and respiratory rate (Goldstein, 1964). The EEG studies have consistently shown reduced alpha-activity (Strauss, 1945) and higher proportion of beta-activity (Brazier et al., 1945). Physiological changes in patients with panic disorder have been studied during and between panic attacks. During spontaneous panic attacks, increase in heart rate and forearm blood flow and decrease in skin conductance have been recorded (Lader and Mathews, 1970). Before the onset of panic, finger temperature increases, followed by cooling at the beginning of the attack itself (Freedman et al., 1985). Between attacks, Freedman et al. (1985) found no differences in tonic heart rate and finger temperature (relative to ambient) between patients with panic disorder and normal controls. By contrast, Roth et al. (1986) found patients with agoraphobia with panic had higher tonic levels of skin conductance and heart rate than normal controls.

Psychophysiology provides methods of assessment of the concomitants of anxiety. It may also aid in efforts to determine the cause of anxiety.

Further work is required to study patterns of psychophysiological response in the various anxiety disorders. Ideally, this requires the study of multiple physiological measures, both in vivo and in the laboratory, together with behavioral and cognitive variables.

X. ANIMAL MODELS

Animal experiments have suggested a relation between stress responses, the production of fear and anxiety, and cerebral noradrenergic systems.

Available data are preliminary, and results are conflicting. In a series of monkey experiments, Redmond and Huang (1979) found electrical stimulation of the locus coeruleus produced the same behavioral changes as threatening stimuli. Similar effects were found with the α_2-adrenergic agonist piperoxane. Destruction of the locus coeruleus reduced naturally occurring fear reactions. In contrast, Crow et al. (1978) failed to produce an anxiolytic response following production of specific lesions in the locus coeruleus and ascending noradrenergic pathways. Injection of norepinephrine into the ventricles or amygdala has also been reported to be anxiolytic (Margules, 1971).

In laboratory animals tricyclic antidepressants (TCAs) and monoamine oxidase inhibitors (MAOIs) have primary effects on both serotonin and noradrenergic function (Charney et al., 1981). Short- and long-term administration of TCAs and MAOIs decrease rat brain norepinephrine turnover and locus coeruleus firing rate. Long-term treatment with TCA and MAOI reduce postsynaptic ß-adrenergic receptor function.

Experimental evidence also suggests that overactivity of serotonergic pathways, particularly the ascending dorsal raphe system, may contribute to the production of pathological anxiety. Inhibitors of serotonin (5-Hydroxytryptamine; 5HT) synthesis produce anxiolytic effects in animal tests (Tenen, 1967) that are reversed by injection of the serotonin precursor 5-hydroxytryptophan (Wise et al., 1972). Carbachol stimulation of the dorsal raphe produces an anxiety response that is reversed by benzodiazepines (Stein et al., 1973). Direct application of chlordiazepoxide into the dorsal raphe nucleus produces an anxiolytic profile (Thiebot et al., 1980). Chronic administration of benzodiazepines enhances serotonin synthesis (Rastogi et al., 1978).

XI. CATECHOLAMINES AND ANXIETY

Several studies suggest a role for catecholamines in the etiology of anxiety states; particularly panic disorder. Hyperactivity of the noradrenergic system has been proposed. Evidence comes from the measurement of monoamines and metabolites, neuroendocrine response to adrenergic challenge, and responses to pharmacological treatment.

A. Panic Disorder

Plasma epinephrine and norepinephrine levels have been reported to be elevated in patients with panic attacks, compared with a control group (Ballenger et al., 1984; Cameron et al., 1984). By contrast, Schneider et al. (1987) found no differences in plasma epinephrine, norepinephrine, or dopamine in agoraphobic patients compared with controls. No difference in baseline urinary 3-methoxy-4-hydroxyphenylethylene glycol (MHPG) levels in panic patients compared with normal controls has been reported (Clow et al., 1988). On the other hand, Hamlin et al., (1983) reported lower 24-h urinary MHPG output in panic patients compared with controls. Sheehan and associates (1984) finding of higher baseline urinary MHPG output for patients with agoraphobia and panic than in normal controls is consistent with the hypothesized adrenergic hyperactivity in anxiety disorders, but not with other published reports.

Monoamine responses to a variety of challenge tests have been studied. Yohimbine, an α_2-antagonist increases norepinephrine release and, when administered to humans, produces behavioral and physiological changes consistent with an anxiety state (Holmberg and Gershon, 1961). Yohimbine administration increases plasma MHPG levels (Charney et al., 1982). Significantly higher MHPG increases have been demonstrated in patients with frequent panic attacks, compared with controls (Charney et al., 1984). Charney and Heninger (1985a,b) have demonstrated that the MHPG rise induced by yohimbine is significantly diminished by alprazolam, but not by imipramine. The different effects may reflect the different mechanisms of action of these drugs in treating panic—imipramine by affecting noradrenergic turnover and alprazolam by a benzodiazepine-sensitive noradrenergic receptor.

Intravenous infusion of the α_2-agonist clonidine produces a decrease in plasma MHPG, greater in patients with agoraphobia with panic attacks than in controls (Charney and Heninger, 1986a).

Infusion of the ß-receptor agonist isoproterenol causes acute anxiety attacks (Easton and Sherman, 1976) and increased mean plasma epinephrine and norepinephrine in patients compared with controls (Nesse et al., 1984).

Radiological binding sites in peripheral cell membranes have been used as a model of the corresponding central receptor site. Relatively few studies of adrenergic receptors have been described. Studies of platelet α_2-receptor binding have used a variety of radioligands, including the agonist clonidine and the antagonists yohimbine and rauwolsine (α-yohimbine). The number of clonidine-binding sites for patients was no different from controls, whereas the number of yohimbine-binding sites was significantly reduced in patients, compared with controls (Cameron et al., 1984). A further study found no difference in number of rauwolsine-binding sites between patients and controls (Norman et al., 1987).

The responsiveness of ß-adrenergic receptors has been studied by the lymphocyte cyclic-AMP response to isoproterenol stimulation. Lower responses were found in anxious patients than in controls (Lima and Turner, 1983). Lymphocyte ß-adrenergic binding has been measured in panic patients compared with controls. Patients had a significantly lower number of binding sites (lower B_{max}) and higher affinity of binding (lower K_d) than controls (Brown et al., 1988).

Tests of neuroendocrine function have been used as a measure of monitoring brain monoamine function in a variety of psychiatric disorders. The effect of pharmacological agents on cortisol and growth hormone have been studied in patients with panic attacks.

The release of growth hormone is under the influence of both α- and ß-adrenergic receptors. Infusion of α-agonists (e.g., methoxamine, phenylephrine, clonidine) stimulate the release of growth hormone (Checkley, 1980). This response can be blocked by α-blocking drugs, such as phentolamine. α-Blockade also inhibits the response of growth hormone to physiological stimuli, such as hypoglycemia (Checkley, 1980). An inhibitory influence of ß-receptors is proposed (Checkley, 1980). Similarly, α- and ß-adrenergic responses are involved in regulation of corticotropon (ACTH) and, thus, cortisol secretion. Checkley (1980) has described an excitatory mechanism involving α-adrenoreceptors and an inhibitory mechanism involving ß-adrenoreceptors in controlling ACTH secretion.

Blunted growth hormone (Charney and Heninger, 1986a; Nutt, 1989) and cortisol response (Charney and Heninger, 1986a) to clonidine in patients compared with controls has been noted. On the other hand, yohimbine administration produced a significantly higher cortisol response in panic patients than controls (Charney et al., 1987a). Nutt (1989) suggests the subsensitive neuroendocrine response in panic patients indicates diminished postsynaptic receptor function.

A primary source of evidence for the biological nature of panic has been the response of the disorder to pharmacological treatment. Most tricyclic antidepressants have been effective in the treatment of panic attacks (Judd et al., 1990). The mechanism of action of these drugs remains speculative. Extended TCA administration causes a down-regulation of ß-adrenergic receptors, as a consequence of their effect on presynaptic α_2-adrenergic autoreceptors (Charney et al., 1981). The effect on α_2-receptors is more likely to be important than ß-adrenergic effects. Support for this is derived from studies showing antipanic effects of the α_2-agonist clonidine (Charney and Heninger, 1986a; Uhde et al., 1989), the relative lack of effect of ß-blockers in the treatment of panic attacks (Noyes et al., 1984), and the failure of prior treatment with propranolol to block lactate-induced panic attacks (Gorman et al., 1983).

B. Obsessive–Compulsive Disorder

Growth hormone response to clonidine is blunted in patients with OCD (Insel et al., 1984). Successful treatment of OCD with oral clonidine (Knesevick, 1982) and with a combination of clonidine and antidepressants (Lipsedge and Protheroe, 1987) has been reported. Infusion of intravenous clonidine has also been reported to diminish OC symptoms (Hollander et al., 1988).

XII. SEROTONIN AND ANXIETY

The possible role of serotonin in the etiology of panic and obsessive–compulsive disorders has been the focus of considerable research interest over the past decade.

A. Panic Disorder

Few studies of serotonin and its metabolites have been reported. Evans et al. (1985) found significantly reduced plasma 5-HT concentration in patients with agoraphobia with panic attacks, compared with controls. There are no published cerebrospinal fluid (CSF) studies in panic disorder.

Serotonin facilitates the release of several pituitary hormones, notably prolactin, growth hormone, and ACTH. The most commonly used challenge agents are *meta*-chlorophenylpiperazine (MCPP), a 5-HT receptor agonist; ritanserin a 5-HT_2 antagonist; the 5-HT-releasing agent fenfluramine; and the 5-HT precursors, L-tryptophan and 5-hydroxytryptophan. In general, results of these challenge paradigms in the study of panic disorder have been disappointing. Charney et al. (1986b, 1987b) found no difference in endocrine response to either L-tryptophan or MCPP between panic patients and normal controls. In contrast, Kahn et al. (1988) found an augmented cortisol response to MCPP in panic disorder patients compared with controls. The differences found by the two groups may be accounted for by both the dose and route of administration of the dose. The data support a serotonin receptor hypersensitivity in panic.

Most studies of the serotonergic system in panic disorders have used blood platelets, which possess 5-HT_2 receptors and a specific high-affinity binding site for [^{3}H]imipramine. Studies of platelet serotonin uptake have shown a significant increase compared with normal controls (Norman et al., 1986). This finding has been replicated by the Melbourne group (Norman et al., 1989a,b), who also found serotonin uptake was unchanged by 8 weeks of treatment with diazepam or alprazolam (Norman et al., 1988). In contrast, Pecknold and colleagues (1988) reported decreased platelet serotonin uptake in panic disorder, similar to that observed in depression. Differences between results are difficult to reconcile, as patient selection criteria were similar for the two studies, but may be explained by different assay methods.

Several studies of the [^{3}H]imipramine-binding site in panic disorder have been carried out. A decrease in number of binding sites on the platelet membrane in patients with panic attacks was first reported by Lewis and co-workers (1985). Subsequent studies have not repeated this observation and have found no difference between patients and controls.

The efficacy of antidepressants in alleviating panic may be due to their effect on serotonergic pathways. Long-term administration of tricyclic antidepressants leads to a reduction in the number of 5-HT_2 receptors (Peroutka and Snyder, 1980). Some tricyclics are potent serotonin-uptake blockers, and MAOIs enhance the availability of serotonin.

Antiphobic efficacy has been demonstrated for zimelidine, a potent and specific serotonin-uptake inhibitor (Evans et al., 1986; Kahn et al., 1984). den Boer and Westenberg (1988) found fluvoxamine, a specific 5-HT-reuptake inhibitor, to be a potent antipanic agent. Specific benefit in reducing panic was found for fluvoxamine, but not for maprotiline (a specific norepinephrine-uptake inhibitor). Consistent with a serotonergic hypothesis, 5-hydroxytryptophan has been found to be effective in reducing anxiety symptoms, particularly panic attacks (Kahn and Westenberg, 1985). Antipanic effect has also been demonstrated for trazodone, which has activity both as an inhibitor of 5-HT reuptake and as a direct agonist of postsynaptic 5-HT receptors (Mavissakalian et al., 1987).

B. Obsessive–Compulsive Disorder

Direct biochemical investigation of serotonin in patients has also provided evidence for abnormalities, but the limited studies available are equivocal. Measurements of CSF levels of the serotonin metabolite 5-hydroxyindoleacetic acid (5-HIAA) have shown no difference or perhaps slightly raised concentrations in OCD patients compared with controls (Insel et al., 1985; Thoren et al., 1980). On the other hand, Insel et al. (1985) came to the opposite conclusion on the basis of studies with the specific serotonin-reuptake inhibitor zimeldine. This drug significantly decreased 5-HIAA levels in CSF.

A variety of neuroendocrine challenges have been reported in OCD. Blunted plasma prolactin response to MCPP has been demonstrated in two studies (Zohar et al., 1987; Hollander et al., 1988). In a third study, this patient–control difference was found only in female patients (Charney et al., 1988). The blunted prolactin response to MCPP suggests some patients may have reduced postsynaptic 5-HT sensitivity. Blunted prolactin response to fenfluramine has been demonstrated in patients with OCD when compared with controls (Hollander et al., 1989), but in a second study, the patient–control difference was evident only for females (Hewlett et al., 1989).

Other studies have focused on the blood platelet as a model of central serotonergic neurons. In one study, platelet [^{3}H]imipramine-binding was decreased in OCD patients compared with controls (Weizman et al., 1986). These results are in accord with those of Insel et al. (1985), who also showed a decreased B_{max} of [^{3}H]imipramine binding, although the difference was not statistically significant. Both groups reported no changes in platelet serotonin uptake in OCD patients, compared with controls. These findings suggest that serotonin abnormalities are important in the etiology of OCD. It seems unlikely that changes in [^{3}H]imipramine binding are an adaptive down-regulation to excessive serotonin production, since similar findings were noted in both adolescent and adult OCD patients (Weizman et al., 1986).

Oral MCPP has been reported to produce an acute exacerbation of OC symptoms (Zohar et al., 1987). By contrast, Charney et al. (1988) found no consistent effect on OC symptoms following intravenous administration of MCPP. Following treatment with clomipramine, Zohar et al. (1988) found the behavioral hypersensitivity noted before treatment was blunted. Benkelfat et al. (1989) found the addition of metergoline, a 5-HT antagonist, caused modest exacerbation of OC symptoms in OC patients who were improved with clomipramine. The efficacy of drug treatments of OCD has also been taken as evidence of a biological basis to the disorder. In particular, the tricyclic antidepressant clomipramine appears to be unique in its effect on obsessive–compulsive symptoms. Several double-blind, placebo-controlled studies have shown clomipramine to be more effective than a placebo in relieving symptoms of the disorder, which were unrelated to its effect on coexisting depressive symptoms. Furthermore, other antidepressants (imipramine, desipramine, nortriptyline, amitriptyline, clorgiline) are not as effective as clomipramine in treating OCD symptoms (McTavish and Benfield, 1990). The relative serotonergic specificity of clomipramine, compared with other antidepressants, coupled with the relative lack of efficacy of desipramine, a drug with predominant noradrenergic effects, suggests a role for serotonin in the etiology of OCD. Indeed the "serotonin hypothesis" of OCD has provided the major impetus for research into the psychobiological basis of the disorder and novel treatment approaches.

Nontricyclic selective serotonin-reuptake inhibitors, such as zimeldine (Kahn et al., 1984), fluoxetine (Turner et al., 1985), and fluvoxamine (Jenike et al., 1990a), all have proved effective in OCD. Sertraline, the most potent serotonin-reuptake blocker in clinical use, also appears to be of benefit in OCD. One negative study (Jenike et al., 1990b) and one positive study (Chouinard et al., 1990) have been reported. However, the study of Jenike and colleagues (1990b) reported data for a small group of patients, who formed one center of the multicenter trial reported by Chouinard et al. (1990).

Treatment augmention strategies also support the role of 5-HT in OCD. In case reports, Hollander et al. (1990) found the addition of fenfluramine to the serotonin-reuptake blockers fluoxetine, fluvoxamine, or clomipramine, reduced obsessions and compulsions. In an open study, Markovitz et al. (1990) found the addition of buspirone to fluoxetine to be superior to fluoxetine alone. Of interest, in an earlier study, buspirone alone was ineffective in patients with OCD (Jenike and Baer, 1988).

XIII. NEUROIMAGING STUDIES AND ANXIETY

Over the past two decades, advances in anatomical and functional brain imaging have led to considerable progress in understanding brain structure and function. In anxiety research, most studies have used computed tomography (CT) and magnetic resonance imaging (MRI) to provide anatomical information and positron emission tomography (PET) to evaluate brain function. The latter technique enables researchers to measure and image regional blood flow, oxygen and glucose metabolism, protein synthesis, and neurotransmitters–neuroreceptor systems.

A. Panic Disorder

During the latter part of the 1980s, a series of PET studies of panic disorder patients have been published. Reiman et al. (1984) first demonstrated that patients with panic disorder who were vulnerable to lactate-induced panic could be distinguished from other panic patients and normal controls by an abnormal asymmetry (L < R) of blood flow in the posterior parahippocampal region. In an extension of this study, these workers demonstrated that patients who were vulnerable to lactate-induced panic had several abnormalities in the nonpanic state: an abnormal asymmetry (L < R) of blood flow, blood volume, and the metabolic rate for oxygen in the parahippocampal region; an abnormally high metabolic rate for oxygen in the whole brain; and a mild, but abnormal, degree of hyperventilation (determined by arterial blood samples) (Reiman et al., 1986). The authors suggested the abnormal asymmetry was related to increased blood flow and metabolism in the right parahippocampal region, rather than decreased measurements in the left. Subsequently, Reiman et al. (1989a) have demonstrated that lactate-induced panic is associated with significant increases in blood flow bilaterally in the temporal cortex; bilaterally in the insular cortex, claustrum, or lateral putamen; bilaterally in the superior colliculus, in the left anterior cerebellar vermis. Lactate infusion was not associated with changes in blood flow in nonpanicking patients and normal control subjects. Most recently, Reiman et al. (1989b) have demonstrated changes accompanying a normal form of anxiety. Normal volunteers in the anticipation of painful shock had significant increases in subjective and physiological measures of anxiety and in blood flow in the same bilateral regions of temporopolar cortex. Reiman et al. (1989a) suggest that, although temporopolar cortex appears to be involved in both lactate-induced panic and normal anxiety, these forms of anxiety are distinguished by the processes involved in their generation—these authors speculate that antipanic interventions may exert their therapeutic effects by correcting the parahippocampal abnormality that appears to mediate vulnerability to panic attacks.

B. Obsessive–Compulsive Disorder

One CT study in OCD has shown increased ventricular size (Behar et al., 1984). A subsequent study, which used a more sensitive measure of ventricular volume, failed to find ventricular enlargement, but found caudate nuclei volume was reduced in patients compared with normal controls (Luxenberg et al., 1988). One MRI study of patients with OCD has been reported (Garber et al., 1989). No differences in gross structural brain defects were found between patients and controls. Comparisons of T1 values (spin-lattice relaxation time) between eight specific regions for patients and controls were made. The T1 of right-side frontal white matter was prolonged in patients, compared with controls. As no morphological measurements were performed, the findings of Luxenberg et al. (1988) could not be confirmed.

Although one of the newest brain-imaging techniques to be used with OCD, PET has been most extensively employed in this disorder. Studies have been reported from three different laboratories. Baxter and colleagues have reported two PET studies (1987, 1988) of patients with OCD. They have found significantly elevated absolute glucose metabolic rates for the whole cerebral hemispheres, caudate nuclei, and orbital gyri in patients compared with normal controls. Two separate groups at the NIMH have performed similar studies independently (Nordahl et al., 1989; Swedo et al., 1989a). Nordahl and colleagues (1989) found higher regional brain metabolic rates in orbital gyri in patients compared with normal controls, but similar rates in caudate nuclei for patients and controls. The other group (Swedo et al., 1989a) reported increased glucose metabolism in the left orbital and right sensorimotor regions and bilaterally in the anterior cingulate gyri and lateral prefrontal areas for patients, compared with controls.

Different methods used in these PET studies make them difficult to compare. The perturbed brain processes that may be reflected by abnormal glucose metabolic rates demonstrated by PET in OCD are unknown.

XIV. GENETIC STUDIES AND ANXIETY DISORDERS

Traditionally, genetic factors in psychiatric disorders have been investigated by family, twin, and adoption studies, or by attempts to find genetic linkage or association between a disorder and known genetic markers. For anxiety disorders, the latter two methods have received little attention. Most evidence comes from family and twin methods, but both have their limitations. Families share environments, not just genes. At best, family studies can estimate "familiality" and not "heritability." Twin data may be biased by the effects of pre- and perinatal insult and shared postnatal environment.

A. Panic Disorder

Several family studies of patients with panic disorder have been reported (Crowe et al., 1983; Noyes et al., 1986; Pauls et al., 1979). These suggest the incidence of panic in first-degree relatives is approximately 20%. In addition, Noyes and colleagues demonstrated (Harris et al., 1983) that the risk of panic in first-degree relatives of probands with GAD was similar to the risk of controls.

Only one twin study of panic disorder has been performed (Torgersen, 1983). Of 318 nonpsychotic twin probands, 29 twins were diagnosed as having panic disorder or agoraphobia with panic. Results showed 4 of 13 monozygotic (MZ) cotwins, but none of the 16 dizygotic (DZ) cotwins, had panic. Although this study could be interpreted as demonstrating increased concordance for panic in MZ pairs, the lack of any concordant DZ twins (who have half their genes in common) questions the genetic implications of the study (Judd et al., 1987). One linkage study (Crowe et al., 1987) that obtained a lod score of 2.23 for linkage between a gene for panic disorder and the α-haptoglobin locus suggested a gene of importance for the development of panic anxiety might be located on chromosome 16. Subsequently, this linkage has been excluded (Crowe et al., 1990).

B. Obsessive–Compulsive Disorder

Early studies of obsessive traits and symptoms among relatives of probands with OCD found widely ranging results.

Two family studies, which used structured interviews, standardized diagnostic criteria, and direct interviews, have been reported (Pauls et al., 1988; Swedo et al., 1989b). Both studies found that between 21 and 25% of nuclear family members of OC probands also suffer from OCD. Of note, Swedo and colleagues (1989b) found the symptom pattern of the proband and the affected relative were often different, thus giving no evidence that ill parents provided a model for children to develop ritual behaviors.

Rasmussen and Tsuang (1984), in a review of the obsessive–compulsive literature in twins, found that of 51 MZ twin pairs in which at least one twin had OCD, 32 (63%) pairs were concordant for obsessive–compulsive symptoms. The authors noted that such data are subject to report bias, as discordant twins are less likely to be reported, and that there was some uncertainty about diagnostic accuracy and zygosity of the samples. Torgersen's study (1983) did not report OCD in either MZ or DZ cotwins. Taken together, family and twin data suggest a genetic component to the etiology of OCD, but the relative contributions of genetic and environmental factors remain to be untangled.

C. Generalized Anxiety Disorder

One published family study of GAD shows a frequency of GAD of 20% among first-degree relatives of probands, compared with 4% among controls (Noyes et al., 1987). The only twin study of GAD (Torgersen, 1983) shows a similar frequency of anxiety disorders among cotwins of MZ and DZ probands, 17 and 20%, respectively. Thus, GAD seems to show familial transmission, and this is likely to be predominantly environmental.

XV. CONCLUSIONS

The range of theories on the etiology of anxiety disorders is vast. Historically the focus has moved from a variety of psychological theories to consider a range of possible biological causes. Clinical experience suggests that frequently a variety of factors are important in the onset and maintenance of these disorders. Further research is required to clarify the relative roles of these disparate factors.

REFERENCES

American Psychiatric Association, *Diagnostic and Statistical Manual of Mental Disorders*, 3rd ed., revised (*DSM-III-R*), American Psychiatric Association, Washington, D.C. (1987).

W. A. Arrindell, P. M. G. Emmelkamp, A. Monsma, and E. Brilman, The role of perceived parental rearing experiences in the etiology of phobic disorders: A controlled study, *Br. J. Psychiatry, 143*: 183 (1983).

L. Baer, M. A. Jenike, J. N. Ricciardi, A. D. Holland, R. J. Seymour, W. E. Minichiello, and L. Buttolph, Standardised assessment of personality disorders in obsessive compulsive disorder, *Arch. Gen. Psychiatry, 47*: 826 (1990).

J. C. Ballenger, G. A. Peterson, M. Larcia, A. Hucek, C. R. Lok, D. Jimerson, D. J. Cox, C. Trockman, J. R. Shipe, and C. Wilkinson, A study of plasma catecholamines in agoraphobia and the relationship of serum tricyclic levels to treatment response, *Biology of Agoraphobia* (J. Ballenger, ed.), American Psychiatric Press, Washington, D.C., p. 27 (1984).

J. E. Barrett, The relationship of life events to the onset of neurotic disorders, *Stress and Mental Disorders* (J. E. Barrett, R. M. Rose, and G. L. Klerman, eds.), Raven Press, New York, p. 87 (1979).

L. R. Baxter, M. E. Phelps, J. C. Mazziotta, B. H. Guze, J. M. Schwartz, and C. E. Selin, Local cerebral glucose metabolic rates in obsessive–compulsive disorder: A comparison with rates in unipolar depression and in normal controls, *Arch. Gen. Psychiatry, 44*: 211 (1987).

L. R. Baxter, J. M. Schwartz, J. C. Mazziotta, M. E. Phelps, J. J. Pahl, B. H. Guze, and L. Fairbanks, Cerebral glucose metabolic rates in nondepressed patients with obsessive–compulsive disorder, *Am. J. Psychiatry, 145*: 1560 (1988).

A. T. Beck, *Cognitive Therapy and the Emotional Disorders*, International Universities Press, New York (1976).

A. T. Beck, G. Emery, and R. L. Greenberg, *Anxiety Disorders and Phobias*, Basic Books, New York (198?).

D. Behar, J. L. Rapoport, C. J. Berg, M. B. Denckla, L. Mann, C. Cox, P. Fedio, T. Zahn, and M. G. Wolfman, Computerised tomography and neuropsychological test measures in adolescents with OCD, *Am. J. Psychiatry, 141*: 363 (1984).

C. Benkelfat, D. L. Murphy, J. Zohar, J. L. Hill, G. Grover, and T. R. Insel, Clomipramine in obsessive–compulsive disorder, *Arch. Gen. Psychiatry, 46*: 23 (1989).

I. Berg, I. Marks, R. McGuire, and M. Lipsedge, School phobia and agoraphobia, *Psychol. Med., 4*: 428 (1974).

I. Berg, A. Butler, and G. Hall, The outcome of adolescent school phobia, *Br. J. Psychiatry, 120*: 80 (1976).

R. C. Bowen, and J. Kohout, The relationship between agoraphobia and primary affective disorders, *Can. J. Psycholog. 24*: 317 (1979).

J. Bowlby, *Attachment and Loss*, Vol. 2. *Separation Anxiety and Anger*, Basic Books, New York (1973).

M. A. B. Brazier, J. E. Finesinger, and S. Cobb, A contrast between the electroencephalograms of 100 psychoneurotic patients and those of 500 normal adults, *Am. J. Psychiatry, 101*: 443 (1945).

S. L. Brown, D. S. Charney, S. W. Woods, G. R. Heninger, and J. Tallman, Lymphocyte–adrenergic receptor binding in panic disorder, *Psychopharmacology, 94*: 24 (1988).

D. Buglass, J. Clark, and A. S. Henderson, A study of agoraphobia housewives, *Psychol. Med., 7*: 73 (1977).

L. E. Burns, and G. L. Thorpe, The epidemiology of fears and phobias (with particular reference to the National Survey of Agoraphobia), *J. Int. Med. Res. 5* (Suppl. 5): 1 (1977).

O. G. Cameron, C. B. Smith, P. J. Hollingsworth, R. M. Nesse, and G. C. Curtis, Platelet α_2-adrenergic receptor binding and plasma catecholamines before and during imipramine treatment in patients with panic anxiety, *Arch. Gen. Psychiatry, 41*: 1144 (1984).

D. S. Charney, and G. R. Heninger, Noradrenergic function and the mechanisms of action of antianxiety treatment I. The effect of long term alprazolam treatment, *Arch. Gen. Psychiatry, 42*: 458 (1985a).
D. S. Charney, and G. R. Heninger, Noradrenergic function and the mechanisms of antianxiety treatment. II. The effect of long-term imipramine treatment, *Arch. Gen. Psychiatry, 42*: 473 (1985b).
D. S. Charney, and G. R. Heninger, Abnormal regulation of noradrenergic function in panic disorder. Effects of clonidine on patients with agoraphobia and panic disorder, *Arch. Gen. Psychiatry, 43*: 1042 (1986a).
D. S. Charney, and G. R. Heninger, Serotonin function in panic disorders. The effects of intravenous tryptophan in healthy subjects and patients with panic disorder before and during alprazolam treatment, *Arch. Gen. Psychiatry, 43*: 1059 (1986b).
D. S. Charney, D. B. Menkes, and G. R. Heninger, Receptor sensitivity and the mechanism of action of antidepressant treatment. Implications for the etiology and therapy of depression, *Arch. Gen. Psychiatry, 38*: 1160 (1981).
D. S. Charney, G. R. Heninger, and D. E. Sternberg, Assessment of adrenergic autoreceptor function in humans: Effects of oral yohimbine, *Life Sci., 30*: 2033 (1982).
D. S. Charney, G. R. Heninger, and A. Breier, Noradrenergic function in panic anxiety. Effects of yohimbine in healthy subjects and patients with agoraphobia and panic disorder, *Arch. Gen. Psychiatry, 41*: 751 (1984).
D. S. Charney, S. W. Woods, W. K. Goodman, and G. R. Heninger, Neurobiological mechanisms of panic anxiety: Biochemical and behavioral correlates of yohimbine induced anxiety, *Am. J. Psychiatry, 144*: 1030 (1987a).
D. S. Charney, S. W. Woods, W. K. Goodman, and G. R. Heninger, Serotonin function in anxiety II. Effects of the serotonin agonist MCPP in panic disorder patients and healthy subjects, *Psychopharmacology, 92*: 14 (1987b).
D. S. Charney, W. K. Goodman, L. H. Price, S. W. Woods, S. A. Rasmussen, and G. R. Heninger, Serotonin function in obsessive–compulsive disorder. A comparison of the effects of tryptophan and *m*-chlorophenylpiperazine in patients and healthy subjects, *Arch. Gen. Psychiatry, 45*: 177 (1988).
S. A. Checkley, Neuroendocrine tests of monoamine function in man: A review of basic theory and its applications to the study of depressive illness, *Psychol. Med., 10*: 35 (1980).
G. Chouinard, W. Goodwin, and J. Greist, Results of a double-blind placebo-controlled trial of a new serotonin uptake inhibitor, sertraline, in the treatment of obsessive–compulsive disorder, *Psychopharmacol. Bull., 26*: 279 (1990).
D. M. Clark, A cognitive approach to panic, *Behav. Res. Ther., 24*: 461 (1986).
D. M. Clark, P. M. Salkovskis, and A. J. Chalkley, Respiratory control as a treatment of panic attacks, *J. Behav. Ther. Exp. Psychiatry, 16*: 23 (1985).
A. Clow, V. Glover, M. W. Weg, P. L. Walker, D. V. Sheehan, D. B. Carr, and M. Sandler, Urinary catecholamine metabolite and tribulin output during lactate infusion, *Br. J. Psychiatry, 152*: 122 (1988).
T. J. Crow, J. F. W. Deakin, S. W. File, A. Longden, and S. Wendlandt, The locus coeruleus noradrenergic system—evidence against a role in attention, habituation, anxiety and motor activity, *Brain Res., 155*: 249 (1978).
R. R. Crowe, R. Noyes, D. L. Pauls, and D. Slymen, A family study of panic disorder, *Arch. Gen. Psychiatry, 40*: 1065 (1983).
R. R. Crowe, R. Noyes, A. F. Wilson, R. C. Elston, and L. J. Ward, A linkage study of panic disorder, *Arch. Gen. Psychiatry, 44*: 933 (1987).
R. R. Crowe, R. Noyes, S. Samuelson, R. Wesner, and R. Wilson, Close linkage between panic disorder and α-haptoglobin excluded in 10 families, *Arch. Gen. Psychiatry, 47*: 377 (1990).
J. A. den Boer, and G. M. Westenberg, Effect of a serotonin and noradrenaline uptake inhibitor in panic disorder; a double-blind comparative study with fluvoxamine and maprotiline, *Int. Clin. Psychopharmacol., 3*: 59 (1988).

J. D. Easton, and D. G. Sherman, Somatic anxiety attacks and propranolol, *Arch. Neurology, 33*: 689 (1976).

L. Evans, P. Schnider, L. Ross-Lee, B. Wiltshire, M. Eadie, J. Kenardy, and H. Hoehy, Plasma serotonin levels in agoraphobia, *Am. J. Psychiatry, 142*: 267 (1985).

L. Evans, J. Kenardy, P. Schneider, and H. Hoey, Effect of a selective serotonin uptake inhibitor in agoraphobia with panic attacks, *Acta. Psychiatr. Scand., 73*: 49 (1986).

R. Finlay-Jones, and G. W. Brown, Types of stressful life event and the onset of anxiety and depressive disorders, *Psychol. Med., 11*: 803 (1981).

R. B. Flannery, Jr., Major life events and daily hassles in predicting health status; methodological enquiry, *J. Clin. Psychol., 42*: 485 (1986).

J. A. Franklin, and G. Andrews, Stress and the onset of agoraphobia, *Aust. Psychol., 24*: 203 (1989).

R. R. Freedman, P. Ianni, E. Ettedgui, and N. Puthezhath, Ambulatory monitoring of panic disorder, *Arch. Gen. Psychiatry, 42*: 244 (1985).

S. Freud (1900), The interpretation of dreams, *Standard Edition, 4 and 5*, Hogarth Press, London, p. 236 (1953).

S. Freud (1909), Analysis of a phobia in a five-year old boy, *Standard Edition 10*, Hogarth Press, London, p. 35 (1955).

S. Freud, The ego and the id. *Standard Edition 19*, Hogarth Press, London, p. 57 (1961).

S. Freud (1898), Sexuality in the etiology of the neuroses, *Standard Edition 3*, Hogarth Press, London, p. 279 (1962).

S. Freud (1917), Introductory lectures on psychoanalysis, *Standard Edition 15 and 16*, Hogarth Press, London, p. 392 (1963).

S. Freud (1894), "Draft E," How anxiety originates, *Standard Edition 1*, Hogarth Press, London, p. 194 (1966).

J. Garber, J. V. Anath, L. Chiu, V. J. Griswold, and W. H. Oldendorg, Magnetic resonance study of obsessive compulsive disorder, *Am. J. Psychiatry, 146*: 1001 (1989).

R. Gittelman-Klein, and D. F. Klein, School phobia. Diagnostic considerations in the light of imipramine effects, *J. Nerv. Ment. Dis., 156*: 199 (1973).

R. Gittelman-Klein, and D. F. Klein, Separation anxiety in school refusal and its treatment with drugs, *Out of School* (L. Hersov, and I. Berg, eds.), John Wiley and Sons, London, p. 321 (1980).

R. Gittelman, and D. F. Klein, Childhood separation anxiety and adult agoraphobia, *Anxiety and the Anxiety Disorders* (A. M. Tuma and J. D. Maser, eds.), Lawrence Erlbaum, Hillsdale, N. J., p. 389 (1985).

I. B. Goldstein, Physiological responses in anxious women patients. A study of autonomic activity and muscle tension, *Arch. Gen. Psychiatry, 10*: 382 (1964).

J. M. Gorman, G. F. Levy, M. R. Liebowitz, P. McGrath, I. L. Appleby, D. J. Dillon, S. O. Davies, and D. F. Klein, Effects of acute ß-adrenergic blockade on lactate-induced panic, *Arch. Gen. Psychiatry, 40*: 1079 (1983).

C. L. Hamlin, R. B. Lydiard, D. Martin, C. A. Dackis, A. G. Pottash, D. Sweeney, and M. S. Gold, Urinary excretion of noradrenaline metabolite decreased in panic disorder, *Lancet, 2*: 740 (1983).

E. L. Harris, R. Noyes, R. R. Crowe, and D. R. Chaudry, Family study of agoraphobia. Report of a pilot study, *Arch. Gen. Psychiatry, 40*: 1061 (1983).

W. A. Hewlett, W. S. Agras, and S. Berman, Fenfluramine stimulation of hormone release in obsessive compulsive disorder, *Soc. Neurosci. 1122*: abstr. 449.4 (1989).

R. Hoehn-Saric, Characteristics of chronic anxiety patients, *Anxiety, New Research and Changing Concepts* (D. F. Klein, and J. Rabkin, eds.), Raven Press, New York, p. 399 (1981).

E. Hollander, M. Fay, B. Cohen, R. Campeas, J. M. Gorman, and M. R. Liebowitz, Serotonergic and noradrenergic sensitivity in obsessive–compulsive disorder: Behavioural findings, *Am. J. Psychiatry, 145*: 1015 (1988).

E. Hollander, C. DeLaria, F. Schneier, J. Hatterer, L. Papp, and M. R. Liebowitz, Neuroendocrine sensitivity in obsessive compulsive disorder, *Am. Psychiatr. Assoc., 187*: abstr. 344 (1989).

E. Hollander, C. M. De Caria, F. R. Schneier, H. A. Schneier, M. R. Liebowitz, and D. F. Klein, Fenfluramine augmentation of serotonin reuptake blockage antiobsessional treatment, *J. Clin. Psychiatry, 51*: 119 (1990).

G. Holmberg, and S. Gershon, Autonomic and psychic effects of yohimbine hydrochloride, *Psychopharmacologia, 2*: 93 (1961).

T. R. Insel, E. A. Mueller, J. C. Gillin, L. J. Siever, and D. L. Murphy, Biological markers in obsessive–compulsive and affective disorders, *J. Psychiatr. Res., 18*: 407 (1984).

T. Insel, E. Mueller, and I. Alterman, Obsessive–compulsive disorder and serotonin: Is there a connection? *Biol. Psychiatry, 20*: 1174 (1985).

W. James, *Mind, 9*: 188 (1884).

M. A. Jenike, and L. Baer, An open trial of buspirone in obsessive–compulsive disorder, *Am. J. Psychiatry, 145*: 1285 (1988).

M. Jenike, S. Hyman, L. Baer, A. Holland, W. E. Minichiello, L. Buttolph, P. Summergrad, R. Seymour, and J. Ricciardi, A controlled trial of fluvoxamine in obsessive–compulsive disorder: Implications for a serotonergic theory, *Am. J. Psychiatry, 147*: 1209 (1990a).

M. Jenike, L. Baer, P. Summergrad, W. E. Minichiello, A. Holland, and R. Seymour, Sertraline in obsessive–compulsive disorder: A double-blind comparison with placebo, *Am. J. Psychiatry, 147*: 923 (1990b).

R. T. Joffe, R. P. Swinson, and J. J. Regan, Personality features of obsessive compulsive disorder, *Am. J. Psychiatry, 145*: 1127 (1988).

F. K. Judd, G. D. Burrows, and D. A. Hay, Panic disorder: Evidence for genetic vulnerability, *Aust. N. Z. J. Psychiatry, 21*: 197 (1987).

F. K. Judd, T. R. Norman, and G. D. Burrows, Pharmacotherapy of panic disorder, *Int. Rev. Psychiatry, 2*: 399 (1990).

R. Kahn, H. Westenberg, and J. Jolles, Zimelidine treatment of obsessive–compulsive disorder, *Acta Psychiatr. Scand., 69*: 259 (1984).

R. S. Kahn, and H. G. M. Westenberg, L-5-Hydroxtryptophan in the treatment of anxiety disorder, *J. Affective Disord., 8*: 197 (1985).

R. S. Kahn, G. M. Asnis, S. Wetzler, and H. M. van Praag, Neuroendocrine evidence for serotonin hypersensitivity in panic disorder, *Psychopharmacology, 96*: 360 (1988).

D. H. W. Kelly, and C. J. S. Walter, The relationship between clinical diagnosis and anxiety, assessed by forearm blood flow and other measurements, *Br. J. Psychiatry, 114*: 611 (1968).

T. A. Kerr, K. Schapira, M. Roth, and R. F. Garside, The relationship between the Maudsley Personality Inventory and the course of affective disorders, *Br. J. Psychiatry, 116*: 11 (1970).

D. F. Klein, Anxiety reconceptualised, *Anxiety: New Research and Changing Concepts* (D. F. Klein and J. Rabkin, eds.), Raven Press, New York, p. 235 (1981).

D. Klein, C. Zitrin, M. Woerner, and D. Ross, Treatment of phobias II: Behaviour therapy and supportive psychotherapy: Are there any specific ingredients? *Arch. Gen. Psychiatry, 40*: 139 (1983).

J. W. Knesevick, Successful treatment of obsessive compulsive disorder with clonidine hydrochloride, *Am. J. Psychiatry, 139*: 364 (1982).

H. W. Koenigsberg, R. D. Kaplan, M. M. Gilmore, and A. M. Cooper, The relationship between syndrome and personality disorder in *DSM-III*: Experience with 2,462 patients, *Am. J. Psychiatry, 142*: 207 (1985).

M. H. Lader, Palmar skin conductance measures in anxiety and phobic states, *J. Psychosom. Res., 11*: 271 (1967).

M. Lader, and A. Mathews, Physiological changes during spontaneous panic attacks, *J. Psychosom. Res., 14*: 377 (1970).

M. H. Lader, and L. Wing, Habituation of the psycho-galvanic reflex in patients with anxiety

states and in normal subjects, *J. Neurol. Neurosurg. Psychiatry, 27*: 210 (1964).
C. G. Lange, Om Sindsvevagelser, Copenhagen (1885).
R. H. Lauer, The Social Readjustment Scale and anxiety: A cross-cultural study, *J. Psychosom. Res., 17*: 171 (1973).
D. A. Lewis, R. Noyes, W. Coryell, and J. Clancy, Tritiated imipramine binding to platelets is decreased in patients with agoraphobia, *Psychiatry Res., 16*: 1 (1985).
M. R. Liebowitz, and D. F. Klein, Clinical Psychiatric Conferences: Assessment and treatment of phobic anxiety, *J. Clin. Psychiatry, 40*: 486 (1979).
D. R. Lima, and P. Turner, Propranolol increases reduced beta-receptor function in severely anxious patients, *Lancet 2*: 1505 (1983).
M. S. Lipsedge, and W. Protheroe, Clonidine and clomipramine in obsessive compulsive disorder, *Am. J. Psychiatry, 144*: 965 (1987).
J. S. Luxenberg, S. E. Swedo, M. F. Flament, R. P. Friedland, J. Rapoport, and S. I. Rapoport, Neuroanatomical abnormalities in obsessive–compulsive disorder detected with quantitative x-ray computed tomography, *Am. J. Psychiatry, 145*: 1089 (1988).
A. McGennis, G. Nolan, and M. Hartman, The role of a self help association in agoraphobia: One year's experience with Out and About, *Ir Med J., 70*: 10 (1977).
J. McKeon, B. Roa, and A. Mann, Life events and personality traits in obsessive–compulsive neurosis, *Br. J. Psychiatry, 144*: 185 (1984).
D. McTavish, and P. Benfield, Clomipramine: An overview of its pharmacological properties and a review of its therapeutic use in obsessive–compulsive disorder and panic disorder, *Drugs, 39*: 136 (1990).
D. L. Margules, alpha- And beta-adrenergic receptors in the amygdala—reciprocal inhibitors and facilitators of punished operant behaviour, *Eur. J. Pharmacol., 16*: 21 (1971).
P. J. Markovitz, S. J. Stagno, and J. R. Calabrese, Buspirone augmentation of fluoxetine in obsessive compulsive disorder, *Am. J. Psychiatry, 147*: 798 (1990).
M. Mavissakalian, and M. S. Hanann, *DSM-III* personality disorder in agoraphobia, *Compr. Psychiatry, 27*: 471 (1986).
M. Mavissakalian, J. Perel, K. Bowler, and R. Dealy, Trazadone in the treatment of panic disorder and agoraphobia with panic attacks, *Am. J. Psychiatry, 144*: 785 (1987).
P. McMiller, J. G. Ingham, and S. Davidson, Life events, symptoms and social support, *J. Psychosom. Res., 20*: 515 (1976).
R. M. Nesse, O. G. Cameron, G. C. Curtis, D. S. McCann, and M. J. Huber-Smith, Adrenergic function in patients with panic anxiety, *Arch. Gen. Psychiatry, 41*: 771 (1984).
T. E. Nordahl, C. Benkelfat, W. E. Semple, M. Gross, A. C. King, and R. M. Cohen, Cerebral glucose metabolic rates in obsessive–compulsive disorder, *Neuropsychopharmacology, 2*: 23 (1989).
T. R. Norman, F. K. Judd, M. Gregory, R. H. James, N. M. Kimber, I. M. McIntyre, and G. D. Burrows, Platelet serotonin uptake in panic disorder, *J. Affective Disord., 11*: 69 (1986).
T. R. Norman, N. M. Kimber, F. K. Judd, G. B. Burrows, and I. M. McIntyre, Platelet ^{3}H-rauwolscrine binding in patients with panic attacks, *Psychiatry Res., 22*: 43 (1987).
T. R. Norman, M. S. Gregory, F. K. Judd, G. D. Burrows, and I. M. McIntyre, Platelet serotonin uptake in panic disorder: Comparison with normal controls and the effect of treatment, *Aust. N. Z. J. Psychiatry, 22*: 390 (1988).
T. R. Norman, M. S. Gregory, F. K. Judd, G. D. Burrows, and I. M. McIntyre, Platelet serotonin uptake in panic disorder: A replication, *Psychiatry Res., 30*: 63 (1989a).
T. R. Norman, D. M. Sartor, M. S. Gregory, F. K. Judd, G. D. Burrows, and I. M. McIntyre, Platelet serotonin uptake and [^{3}H]imipramine binding in patients with panic attacks, *J. Affective Disord., 17*: 77 (1989b).
R. Noyes, D. J. Anderson, J. Clancy, R. R. Crowe, D. J. Slymen, M. M. Choneim, and J. V. Hinrichs, Diazepam and propranolol in panic disorder and agoraphobia, *Arch. Gen. Psychiatry, 41*: 287 (1984).
R. Noyes, R. R. Crowe, E. L. Harris, B. J. Hamra, C. M. McChesney, and D. R. Chaudry,

Relationship between panic disorder and agoraphobia. A family study, *Arch. Gen. Psychiatry, 43*: 227 (1986).

R. Noyes, C. Clarkson, and R. R. Crowe, A family study of generalised anxiety disorder, *Am. J. Psychiatry, 144*: 1019 (1987).

D. J. Nutt, Altered central β_2-adrenoreceptor sensitivity in panic disorder, *Arch. Gen. Psychiatry, 46*: 165 (1989).

G. Parker, Reported parental characteristics of agoraphobics and social phobias, *Br. J. Psychiatry, 135*: 555 (1979).

D. L. Pauls, R. Noyes, and R. R. Crowe. The familial prevalence in second-degree relatives of patients with anxiety neurosis (panic disorder), *J. Affective Disord., 1*: 279 (1979).

D. L. Pauls, C. L. Raymond, and C. R. Hurst, "Transmission of OCD and Related Behaviours," Proceedings of the 43rd Annual Meeting of the Society of Biologic Psychiatry, Montreal (1988).

J. C. Pecknold, B. Suranyi-Cadotte, H. Chang, and N. P. V. Nair, Serotonin uptake in panic disorder and agoraphobia, *Neuropsychopharmacology, 1*: 173 (1988).

S. J. Peroutka, and S. H. Snyder, Longterm antidepressant treatment decreases spiroperidol labelled serotonin receptor binding, *Science, 210*: 88 (1980).

S. J. Rachman, An anatomy of obsessions, *Behav. Anal. Mod., 2*: 253 (1978).

S. A. Rasmussen, and M. T. Tsuang, Epidemiology of obsessive compulsive disorder: A review, *J. Clin. Psychiatry, 45*: 450 (1984).

S. A. Rasmussen, and M. T. Tsuang, Clinical characteristics and family history in *DSM-III* obsessive compulsive disorder, *Am. J. Psychiatry, 143*: 317 (1986).

R. B. Rastogi, Y. D. Lapierre, and R. L. Singhal, Synaptosomal uptake of norepinephrine and 5-hydroxytryptamine and synthesis of catecholamines during benzodiazepine treatment, *Can. J. Physiol. Pharmacol., 56*: 777 (1978).

D. E. Redmond, and Y. H. Huang, New evidence for a locus coeruleus—norepinephrine connection with anxiety, *Life Sci., 25*: 2149 (1979).

J. Reich, R. Noyes, Jr., and E. Troughton, Dependent personality disorders associated with phobic avoidance in patients with panic disorder, *Am. J. Psychiatry, 142*: 207 (1987).

E. M. Reiman, M. E. Raichle, F. K. Butler, R. Herscovitch, and E. Robins, A focal brain abnormality in panic disorder, a severe form of anxiety, *Nature, 310*: 683 (1984).

E. M. Reiman, M. E. Raichle, E. Robins, F. K. Butler, P. Herscovitch, P. Fox, and J. Perlmutter, The application of positron emission tomography to the study of panic disorder, *Am. J. Psychiatry, 143*: 469 (1986).

E. M. Reiman, M. E. Raichle, E. Robins, M. A. Mintun, M. J. Fusselman, P. T. Fox, J. L. Price, and K. A. Hackman, Neuroanatomical correlates of a lactate induced anxiety attack, *Arch. Gen. Psychiatry, 29*: 493 (1989a).

E. M. Reiman, M. J. Fusselman, P. T. Fox, and M. E. Raichle. Activation of temporal cortex in the production of anticipatory anxiety, *Science, 243*: 1071 (1989b).

L. N. Robins, J. E. Helzer, M. M. Weissman, H. Orvaschel, E. Gruenberg, J. D. Burke, and D. A. Regier, Lifetime prevalence of specific psychiatric disorders in three sites, *Arch. Gen. Psychiatry, 41*: 949 (1984).

M. Roth, The phobic anxiety depersonalisation syndrome, *Proc. R. Soc. Med., 52*: 587 (1959).

M. Roth, C. Gurney, R. F. Garsdie, and T. A. Kerr, Studies in the classification of affective disorders: The relationship between anxiety states and depressive illness—I, *Br. J. Psychiatry, 121*: 147 (1972).

W. T. Roth, M. J. Telch, C. B. Taylor, J. A. Sachitano, C. G. Gallen, M. L. Kopell, K. L. McClenahan, W. S. Agras, and A. Pfefferbaum, Autonomic characteristics of agoraphobia with panic attacks, *Biol. Psychiatry, 21*: 1133 (1986).

P. P. Roy-Byrne, M. Geraci, and T. W. Uhde, Life events and the onset of panic disorder, *Am. J. Psychiatry, 143*: 1424 (1986).

M. Rutter, *Maternal Deprivation Reassessed*, Penguin, Harmondsworth (1972).

M. Rutter, Resilience in the face of adversity, *Br. J. Psychiatry, 147*: 598 (1985).

P. M. Salkovskis, Obsessional-compulsive problems: A cognitive-behavioural analysis, *Behav. Res. Ther., 25*: 571 (1985).

P. M. Salkovskis, and H. M. C. Warwick, Cognitive therapy of obsessive-compulsive disorder—treating treatment failures, *Behav. Psychother., 13*: 243 (1985).

I. G. Sarason, J. H. Johnson, and J. M. Siegel, Assessing the impact of life changes. Development of the life experiences survey, *J. Consult. Clin. Psychol., 46*: 932 (1978).

P. Schneider, L. Evans, L. Ross-Lee, B. Wiltshire, M. Eadie, J. Kenardy, and H. Hoey, Plasma biogenic amine levels in agoraphobia with panic attacks, *Pharmacopsychiatry, 20*: 102. (1987).

S. Shafar, Aspects of phobic illness—a study of 90 personal cases, *Br. J. Med. Psychol., 49*: 221 (1976).

D. V. Sheehan, K. E. Sheehan, and W. E. Minichello, Age of onset of phobic disorders: A reevaluation, *Comp. Psychiatry, 22*: 544 (1981).

D. V. Sheehan, J. H. Coleman, D. J. Greenblatt, K. S. Jones, P. H. Levine, P. J. Orsulak, M. Peterson, J. J. Schildkraut, E. Vlogara, and D. Watkins, Some biochemical correlates of panic attacks with agoraphobia and their response to a new treatment, *J. Clin. Psychopharmacol., 4*: 66 (1984).

D. Silove, Perceived parental characteristics and reports of early parental deprivation in agoraphobic patients, *Aust. N. Z. J. Psychiatry, 20*: 365 (1986).

R. P. Snaith, A clinical investigation of phobias, *Br. J. Psychiatry, 114*: 673 (1968).

R. P. Snaith, S. N. Ahmed, S. Mehta, and M. Hamilton, A clinical investigation of phobias, *Psychol. Med., 1*: 143 (1971).

L. Solyom, P. Beck, C. Solyom, and R. Hugel, Some aetiological factors in phobic neurosis, *Can. Psychiatry Assoc. J., 19*: 69 (1974).

L. Solyom, M. Silbersfeld, and C. Solyom, Maternal overprotection in the aetiology of agoraphobia, *Can. Psychiatry Assoc. J., 21*: 109 (1976).

L. Stein, C. D. Wise, and B. D. Berger, Anti anxiety action of benzodiazepines: Decrease in activity of serotonin neurons in the punishment system, *The Benzodiazepines* (S. Garattini, E. Mussini, and L. O. Randall, eds.), Raven Press, New York, p. 299 (1973).

H. Strauss, Clinical and electroencephalographic studies: The electroencephalogram in psychoneurotics, *J. Nerv. Ment. Dis., 101*: 19 (1945).

S. E. Swedo, M. B. Schapiro, C. L. Grady, D. L. Cheslow, H. L. Leonard, A. Kumar, R. Friedland, S. I. Rapoport, and J. Rapoport, Cerebral glucose metabolism in childhood-onset obsessive-compulsive disorder, *Arch. Gen. Psychiatry, 46*: 518 (1989a).

S. E. Swedo, J. L. Rapoport, H. Leonard, M. Lenanc, and D. Cheslow, Obsessive compulsive disorders in children and adolescents, *Arch. Gen. Psychiatry, 46*: 335 (1989b).

S. S. Tenen, The effects of *p*-chlorophenyalanine, a serotonin depletor, on avoidance acquisition, pain sensitivity and related behaviour in the rat, *Psychopharmacologia, 10*: 204 (1967).

C. Tennant, Life events and psychological morbidity: The evidence from prospective studies, *Psychol. Med. 13*: 483 (1983).

M. Thiebot, A. Jobert, and P. Soubrie. Conditioned suppression of behaviour—its reversal by intraraphe microinjection of chlordiazepoxide and GABA, *Neurosci. Lett., 16*: 213 (1980).

P. Thoren, M. Asberg, L. Bertilsson, B. Mellstrom, F. Sjoqvist, and L. Traskman, Clomipramine treatment of obsessive-compulsive disorder II. Biochemical aspects, *Arch. Gen. Psychiatry, 37*: 1289 (1980).

S. Torgersen, Genetic factors in anxiety disorders, *Arch. Gen. Psychiatry, 40*: 1085 (1983).

S. Torgersen, Childhood and family characteristics in panic and generalised anxiety disorders, *Am. J. Psychiatry, 143*: 630 (1986).

S. Turner, R. Jacob, and D. Beidel, Fluoxetine treatment of obsessive-compulsive disorder, *J. Clin. Psychopharmacol., 5*: 207 (1985).

P. Tyrer, and S. Tyrer, School refusal, truancy and adult neurotic illness, *Psychol. Med., 4*: 416 (1974).

P. Tyrer, P. Casey, and J. Gall, Relationship between neurosis and personality disorder, *Br. J. Psychiatry, 142*: 404 (1983).

T. W. Uhde, M. B. Stein, B. J. Vittone, L. J. Siever, J.-P. Boulenger, E. Klein, and T. A. Mellman, Behavioural and physiologic effects of short-term and long-term administration of clonidine in panic disorder, *Arch. Gen. Psychiatry, 46*: 170 (1989).

M. M. Weissman, J. F. Leckman, K. R. Merikangas, G. D. Gammon, and B. A. Prusoff, Depression and anxiety disorders in parents and children. Results from the Yale Family Study, *Arch. Gen. Psychiatry, 41*: 845 (1984).

A. Weizman, M. Carmi, H. Hermesh, A. Shahar, A. Apter, S. Tyano, and M. Rehavi, High affinity imipramine binding and serotonin uptake in platelets of eight adolescent and ten adult obsessive–compulsive patients, *Am. J. Psychiatry, 143*: 335 (1986).

C. D. Wise, B. D. Berger, and L. Stein, Benzodiazepines—anxiety-reducing activity by reduction of serotonin turnover in the brain, *Science, 177*: 180 (1972).

C. M. Zitrin, D. F. Klein, M. G. Woerner, and D. C. Ross, Treatment of phobias I. Comparison of Imipramine hydrochloride and placebo. *Arch. Gen. Psychiatry, 40*: 125 (1983).

J. Zohar, E. A. Mueller, T. R. Insel, R. C. Zohar-Kadouch, and D. L. Murphy, Serotonergic responsivity in obsessive compulsive disorder. Comparison of patients and healthy controls, *Arch. Gen. Psychiatry, 44*: 946 (1987).

J. Zohar, T. R. Insel, R. C. Zohar-Kadouch, J. L. Hill, and D. L. Murphy, Serotonergic responsitivity in obsessive compulsive disorder, *Arch. Gen. Psychiatry, 45*: 167 (1988).

10

The Provocation of Anxiety States in Humans and Its Possible Significance for the Pathogenesis of These Disorders

Richard Balon, Robert Pohl, and Vikram K. Yeragani
Wayne State University School of Medicine, Detroit, Michigan

I. INTRODUCTION

Some of the first biological studies of anxiety disorders measured various physiological and biochemical variables, an approach that laid the theoretical basis for certain provocative techniques used today. The most relevant early study was the finding that anxiety patients had higher blood lactate concentrations than normal controls after moderate exercise (e.g., Cohen and White, 1950).

Another approach has been the monitoring of spontaneously occurring attacks of anxiety. This monitoring confirmed the presence of major physiological changes—heart rate increase and finger temperature changes—during self-reported panic attacks (Freedman et al., 1985; Taylor et al., 1986). However, some of these changes did not correlate well with subjective anxiety, as demonstrated in our laboratory study (Balon et al., 1988a). In addition, the number and character of variables that can be measured during monitoring of spontaneous anxiety attacks is limited. It is interesting that monitoring of spontaneous panic attacks also suggests that many of these attacks have specific causes, in contrast with the belief that these attacks generally occur without clear precipitant (Freedman et al., 1985).

Anxiety frequently has an episodic character, and there has been an interest in provoking these episodes in a controlled laboratory setting. Some of these techniques were inspired by the observation that certain behavioral patterns of fear in animals were associated with the release of epinephrine from adrenal glands, and that these changes are reproducible by epinephrine administration. Although epinephrine was used to reproduce the symptoms of irritable heart in anxiety patients in 1919 (Wearn and Sturgis, 1919), the use of provocative models had not been systematically pursued until about 20 years ago. Over the past two decades, sodium lactate has been the most frequently studied provocative agent (Cowley and Arana, 1990). However, a large variety of other substances have also been used. These include ß-carbolines (Dorow et al., 1983), caffeine (Charney et al., 1985), carbon dioxide (Cohen and White, 1950), cholecystokinin-tetrapeptide (Bradwejn et al., 1990), epinephrine (Lindeman and Finesinger, 1938), norepinephrine (Pyke and Greenberg, 1986), fenfluramine (Targum and Marshall, 1989), isoproterenol (Balon et al., 1988b), *m*-chlorophenylpiperazine (Charney et al., 1987), and yohimbine (Charney et al., 1982a). The most recent development has been coupling of these provocation methods with other more advanced research tools, such as positron emission tomography (Reiman et al., 1989) and cerebral blood flow (Mathew and Wilson, 1990a). In this chapter, we review the most frequently used provocative models and their significance for pathogenesis of anxiety disorders.

II. SODIUM LACTATE

A. Early Studies

In 1967 Pitts and McClure (1967) reported that, in a double-blind study, 13 of 14 patients with anxiety neurosis and 2 of 10 healthy controls developed anxiety attacks during the infusion of 0.5 M sodium lactate. The anxiety attacks developed very rapidly, over a few minutes. Patients and controls did not significantly differ in their response to lactate infusions with added calcium chloride, and none of the subjects had anxiety attacks during glucose in saline infusion. Pitts and McClure (1967) hypothesized that the lactate ion produced the hypocalcemic anxiety symptoms in human beings. Their finding was soon replicated by Fink and co-workers (Fink et al., 1969), who reported sodium lactate-induced anxiety attacks in five of five patients and one of five controls.

However, Pitts and McClure's theory about the specificity of lactate ion in the etiology of anxiety was soon criticized by Grosz and Farmer (1969, 1972) and Grosz alone (Grosz, 1973). They observed that high levels of lactate and anxiety symptoms do not necessarily occur together, and that infused sodium lactate becomes rapidly converted to sodium bicarbonate and, thus, leads to metabolic alkalosis. They also demonstrated that a significant portion of symptoms can be produced by an infusion of another alkalinizing agent, sodium bicarbonate (Grosz and Farmer, 1972). These authors' case is weakened by the fact that they did not study patients with panic attacks.

Other early studies include the work of Kelly and associates (1971), who reported panic attacks in 16 of 20 patients with chronic anxiety neurosis, and 1 of 10 controls during an infusion with 0.5 M sodium lactate. They also reported that one patient panicked during the saline lead-in infusion, but not during the lactate infusion. Forearm blood flow and heart rate were higher during the lactate than during the saline infusion. Bonn and colleagues (1971, 1973) reported that they infused 66 subjects with sodium lactate (1 M). They used a separate saline infusion (1 week between infusions) as a control condition. They emphasized the striking hypophosphatemia during lactate infusions, and reported that propranolol could not modify the symptoms produced by lactate. This is the only group that has used sodium lactate infusions as a treatment for intractable anxiety. They used a twice-weekly "flooding" with sodium lactate (i.e., repeated induction of panic) in 33 subjects for treatment of intractable anxiety, and they reported marked improvement. Appleby et al. (1981) reported that 16 of 25 panic disorder patients and none of 16 healthy controls panicked during lactate infusion. They also studied various biochemical indexes and found that epinephrine was a promising index of lactate-induced stress. Rainey et al. (1984a) reported that lactate and isoproterenol induced panic more frequently in panic disorder patients than in controls. Patients differed from controls on various psychophysiological measures (finger temperature, skin conductance) at various points throughout the experimental sessions. These early studies established the sodium lactate infusions (either 0.5 or 1 M) as a reliable method of provocation of panic.

B. Studies Focused on Reliability and Validity

The provocation of panic attacks in patients with defined anxiety neurosis or panic disorder have been reproduced in various laboratories around the world, under various conditions, and with different concentrations of sodium lactate (0.5 M and 1 M solution) (Pitts and McClure, 1967; Fink et al., 1969; Kelly et al., 1971; Bonn et al., 1971; Liebowitz et al., 1984a, 1985a; Carr et al., 1986a; Ehlers et al., 1986; Knott and Lapierre, 1986; Balon et al., 1988b; Clow et al., 1988; Gaffney et al., 1988; Aronson et al., 1989a). Cowley et al. (1987b) demonstrated similar response to lactate in nine patients with infrequent panic attacks who did not meet the *Diagnostic and Statistical Manual of Mental Disorders*, 3rd ed. (*DSM-III*) criteria for panic disorder, whereas Targum (1991) reported that patients with a low frequency of panic attacks (one or fewer attacks per month) did not react positively to lactate infusion. Panic disorder patients always respond quite differently from healthy controls (70–100% patients showed a panic response, compared to 0–40% controls). Overall, lactate-induced panic has a sensitivity of 67% and specificity of 89% in differentiating patients with panic disorder from nonpsychiatric controls (Cowley and Arana, 1990). However, others argue that patients and controls respond to lactate similarly (Ehlers et al., 1986), suggesting that response to lactate is not a marker of a person's proneness to panic.

Liebowitz et al. (1984a) reported that both lactate-induced panic attacks and those that occurred naturally were symptomatically similar. Balon and co-workers (1988d) compared the phenomenology of panic attacks during lactate and placebo (dextrose) infusions in 12 panic disorder patients. Patients rated both dextrose (presumably spontaneous) and lactate attacks between moderately and very much similar to their usual attacks. Lactate attacks were rated slightly more similar, possibly because attacks were rated as more severe and were associated with more somatic symptoms of anxiety. Aronson et al., (1989a) also noted a high degree of similarity between lactate-induced and naturally occurring panic attacks.

Several studies address the question of the diagnostic specificity of lactate infusions. Only 1 of 7 obsessive–compulsive disorder and 26 of 48 panic disorder patients panicked during sodium lactate infusion, in a study by Gorman et al. (1985a). Similarly, only 1 of 15 patients with social phobia and 10 of 20 panic disorder patients panicked during lactate infusions in a blind study by Liebowitz et al. (1985b). Lactate induced flashbacks in all seven patients with posttraumatic stress disorder, six of whom also met criteria for panic disorder in a study by Rainey et al. (1987). Lactate also induced a panic attack in six of these posttraumatic stress disorder patients. Cowley et al. (1988) reported that patients with generalized anxiety disorder reacted more like panic disorder patients during lactate infusions. Cowley and associates' conclusion was criticized by Liebowitz and Hollander (1989) who pointed out that only 1 out of 9 generalized anxiety patients panicked with lactate in the Cowley et al. (1988) study compared with 9 of 22 panic disorder patients.

Alcoholic patients with panic disorder have fewer panic attacks in response to lactate than the nonalcoholic patients with panic disorder (George et al., 1989a). Cowley et al. (1989b) reported a significantly higher rate of lactate-induced panic in alcoholics with panic attacks than in alcoholics without panic attacks. Alcoholic patients with panic attacks were similar to nonalcoholic patients with panic attacks in their response to lactate.

Bulimic patients have also been studied. In a study by George et al. (1987), none of the bulimic patients experienced a panic attack during a lactate infusion. Four of 18 bulimics (1 of them had a history of panic disorder) compared with none of 11 controls panicked during lactate infusions in a study by Lindy et al. (1988). Four of eight bulimics infused with lactate had panic attacks in a study by Pohl et al. (1989). All of the bulimics who panicked with lactate in this study had concurrent panic attacks.

Cowley and coauthors (1986) reported similar rates of panic response to lactate in patients with both primary depression and secondary panic attacks and patients with panic disorder. The same authors (Cowley et al., 1987a) found that patients with major depression without panic attacks had a much lower response to lactate than did panic disorder patients. McGrath et al. (1988) reported significantly higher response to lactate in depressed patients with panic attacks than in depressed patients without panic attacks. These findings were confirmed by Cowley et al. (1989a), Buller et al. (1989), and Targum (1990).

Thus, lactate-induced panic seems to be associated with a recent history of panic attacks, rather than the diagnosis of panic disorder. Lactate has a moderate sensitivity and good specificity in distinguishing subjects with panic attacks from controls and from patients without coexisting panic attacks (Cowley and Arana, 1990).

C. Studies Focused on Etiology

Various theories of the etiology of panic hypothesize involvement of the noradrenergic and serotonergic systems. Noradrenergic theories often focus on either α- or ß-receptor systems. Other theories suggest abnormalities in chemoreceptor sensitivity and sudden changes in peripheral biochemistry, such as acute respiratory alkalosis. Several challenge studies focused on the possible etiology of lactate-induced panic were done during 1980s.

1. Noradrenergic Mechanism

The involvement of a noradrenergic mechanism in the etiology of lactate-induced panic has been entertained by several authors (Gorman et al., 1983; Liebowitz et al., 1985a, 1986a; Pohl et al., 1987; Aronson et al., 1989a,b).

Liebowitz et al. (1985a, 1986a) hypothesized that lactate-induced panic involves central noradrenergic discharge, with inconsistent peripheral manifestation, and that peripheral catecholamine surge is not the mechanism of lactate-induced panic. Lactate-induced panic attacks in their study were regularly accompanied by biological changes consistent with hyperventilation and central noradrenergic activation (elevated heart rate and lowered Pco_2 and bicarbonate levels). Elevations of plasma norepinephrine and cortisol were irregular, and changes in lactate, pyruvate, pH, phosphate, epinephrine, and diastolic blood pressure were not consistent during panic attacks. The findings on epinephrine levels during lactate infusions in various studies have been contradictory (Appleby et al., 1981; Liebowitz et al., 1985a; Carr et al., 1986a).

Rick and coauthors (1985) reported supportive animal data that racemic sodium lactate decreases the density of α_1-adrenergic receptors in rat brain membranes in vitro. Patients who panicked during lactate infusions showed a higher mean plasma 3-methyl-4-hydroxyphenylethylene glycol (MHPG; a major metabolite of peripheral and CNS norepinephrine) and higher anxiety ratings at baseline in a study by den Boer et al. (1989). On the other hand, Pohl et al. (1987) did not find plasma MHPG elevation at baseline, nor during lactate or isoproterenol infusions, in panic disorder patients and controls. Carr et al. (1986a) also found neither a significant increase of MHPG during lactate-induced panic nor correlations between various biochemical and neuroendocrine variables and lactate-induced panic.

Urinary output of homovanillic acid and 4-hydroxy-3-methoxymandelic acid (catecholamine metabolites) was decreased in patients with panic attacks and in controls during lactate infusions in a study by Clow et al. (1988). The urinary output of tribulin, an endogenous monoamine oxidase inhibitor and benzodiazepine receptor-binding inhibitor, was increased in this study.

Propranolol, a ß-receptor-blocking agent, does not block panic attacks or lengthen the time to panic during lactate infusions (Gorman et al., 1983). This finding casts doubt on a ß-adrenergic hypothesis of panic as an explanation for lactate-induced panic. Intravenous propranolol reduces lactate-induced anxiety only negligibly, whereas intravenous diazepam is quite effective (Aronson et al., 1989a,b). On the other hand, panic disorder patients have a lower lymphocyte ß-adrenergic receptor-binding [^{3}H]dihydroalprenolol) at the baseline, a finding of relative ß-adrenergic receptor down-regulation. The lactate infusion was not found to affect differentially any physiological or biochemical measure in nine patients and nine controls in this study.

Several studies have focused on the response to lactate after successful treatment with various medications and its significance for the etiology of panic anxiety. Rifkin (1981) demonstrated blockade of lactate-induced panic with tricyclic antidepressants. In a study by Fyer et al. (1985), 7 of 13 patients panicked with lactate before treatment with tricyclic antidepressants, none of them panicked with lactate while treated, and 3 of 13 panicked after the treatment was stopped. This suggests that lactate vulnerability can exist in clinically well, unmedicated patients and may be a trait characteristic. Successful alprazolam therapy also blocked lactate vulnerability in a study by Liebowitz et al. (1986b). Gorman et al. (1987a) reported a detailed analysis of patients reinfused after the treatment with various antipanic medications. They suggested that the nine symptoms that responded to drug therapy were associated with hyperventilation, and that antipanic drugs may have a specific effect in blunting hyperventilation. Yeragani et al. (1988a) also reported that tricyclic antidepressants appeared to increase the threshold for lactate-induced panic. These studies demonstrated the successful blockade of lactate-induced panic. Sunderland and co-workers (1989) presented interesting supportive animal data in their study with ten macaque monkeys infused with sodium lactate before and after treatment with alprazolam, imipramine, or placebo. Both drugs blocked the lactate-induced endogenous distress, but only alprazolam significantly reduced the conditioned situational anxiety, whereas imipramine-treated monkeys still exhibited behavioral disturbances. None of the above mentioned treatment studies provide any definitive clues to the etiology of lactate-induced panic. The successful blockade can be explained by several mechanisms (e.g., a decrease in the respiratory rate and blockade or down-regulation of various receptors).

Findings linking the mechanism of lactate-induced panic to noradrenergic systems are weak. Other provocative techniques seem to be better-suited to address the involvement of the α-adrenergic (yohimbine) or the ß-adrenergic (isoproterenol) system in the etiology of panic anxiety. The involvement of another neurotransmitter, serotonin, in the etiology of lactate-induced panic was suggested by Lingjaerde (1985). He theoretized that lactate may stimulate serotonin reuptake in central serotonergic neurons and, thereby, induce anxiety by reducing the inhibitory serotonergic influence on the locus coeruleus.

2. *Neuroendocrine Findings*

Various endocrine glands are involved in central and peripheral neurotransmitter regulation. The abnormalities of the hypothalamopituitary–adrenal (HPA) axis during stress led several authors to study the abnormalities of this axis during lactate-induced panic.

Levin et al. (1987) later on measured cortisol and corticotropin (adrenocorticotropic hormone; ACTH) during lactate-induced panic and did not find elevation of either hormone. Plasma ß-endorphin decreased slightly, but significantly, during lactate infusions in panic disorder patients, depressed patients, and controls (Dager et al., 1989). This findings suggests that the HPA axis is not activated by lactate-induced panic, as ACTH and ß-endorphin arise from the same precursor molecule in the anterior pituitary gland and are released concurrently into the blood. Appleby et al. (1981) and Carr et al. (1986a) also did not find evidence for pituitary–adrenal activation during lactate-induced panic. Untreated and treated panic disorder patients do not have a plasma vasopressin response to lactate different from normal subjects (Carr et al., 1986b), a finding suggestive of intact posterior pituitary function in these patients. den Boer et al. (1989) also did not find a single neuroendocrine variable (cortisol, ß-endorphin) to correlate with lactate-induced panic.

Thus, the neuroendocrine findings during lactate-induced panic do not support any single hypothesis for induction of such panic.

3. *Respiratory and Biochemical Findings*

Shortness of breath and hyperventilation are frequent symptoms of spontaneous and lactate-induced panic attacks (Gorman et al., 1988a,b). Lactate is metabolized to bicarbonate and then to carbon dioxide and water. Carbon dioxide then easily passes the blood–brain barrier. Centrally perceived hypercarbia may cause hyperventilation and panic (Sandberg and Liebowitz, 1990). However, D-lactate, which is poorly metabolized to carbon dioxide, does induce panic (Gorman et al., 1990a). The role of carbon dioxide in the induction of anxiety and in etiology of panic attacks will be discussed in detail later.

Panicking patients have a lower P_{CO_2} than nonpanicking patients during lactate infusions (Liebowitz et al., 1985a). Carbon dioxide pressure decreases during the lactate infusion (Gorman et al., 1986) and lactate causes metabolic alkalosis. However, metabolic and respiratory alkalosis develops in all subjects during lactate infusions, whereas only hyperventilation-induced hypocapnia differentiates panickers and nonpanickers. Patients who had an acute panic attack during lactate infusions had greater increase in minute ventilation over baseline than nonpanicking patients or controls in a study by Gorman et al. (1988a). Gaffney et al. (1988) similarly described hyperventilation during lactate-induced panic, together with hypernatremia, hypocalcemia, and decreased bicarbonate levels. They suggested that sodium lactate produces panic by mimicking the physiology of spontaneous panic. Gorman et al. (1989a), in a study to address the proposed theory of Grosz and Farmer (1972), infused panic patients with lactate and with sodium bicarbonate, a sodium lactate metabolite. They reported a similar rate of panic during both infusions, although lactate appeared to be a stronger stimulus. Lactate induced a decrease in P_{CO_2} in panickers and nonpanickers, whereas bicarbonate decreased P_{CO_2} only in panickers. D-Lactate also produces hypocapnia (Gorman et al., 1990b). Venous carbon dioxide pressure normalizes after treatment with tricyclic antidepressants (Gorman et al., 1985b). These findings suggest a ventilatory dysregulation as a possible cause of panic anxiety.

The role of lactate-induced hypocalcemia was initially suggested by Pitts and McClure (1967). This was later confirmed, in part, by Fink and associates (1969). Fyer et al. (1984) obtained serial ionized calcium measurements during lactate infusions of 22 panic disorder patients who panicked during the infusion, 11 panic patients who did not panic, and 6 controls. There was a significant decrease of calcium in all groups. However, there was no relation between the rate or magnitude of calcium decrease and the occurrence of panic during the infusion. Ionized calcium levels significantly decrease during lactate infusions (Liebowitz et al. 1985a), but panicking patients do not have lower ionized calcium levels than nonpanicking patients do. Ionized calcium also decreases during infusion of D-lactate (Gorman et al., 1990a). Considered together, these data do not support a decrease in calcium as a sufficient cause of lactate-induced panic.

A significant decrease in plasma inorganic phosphate during lactate infusions was observed by Liebowitz et al. (1985a). However, no consistent change in phosphate levels accompanied lactate-induced panic. Inorganic phosphate also decreased nonsignificantly during lactate infusions in a study by Gaffney et al. (1988) and significantly in a study by Aronson et al. (1990b). Inorganic phosphate also decreases during D-lactate infusions (Gorman et al., 1990a). A significantly lower inorganic phosphate level at baseline was associated with patients who panicked during the subsequent lactate infusion when compared with nonpanicking patients (Gorman et al., 1986). This finding was later confirmed by Balon and co-workers (1988d), but not by Griez and associates (Bass et al., 1988). Hyperventilation is the most probable cause of phosphate decrease during the infusions. Baseline hypophosphatemia suggest an abnormal metabolic state.

Other biochemical changes, such as an alteration in the body's $NAD^+/NADH$ ratio are speculative and were discussed by other authors (Liebowitz et al., 1985a).

4. *Hypoglycemia*

Gorman et al. (1984a,b) addressed the popular idea that hypoglycemia causes panic attacks. They infused two sets of panic disorder patients with 0.5 M sodium lactate, and they did not find any evidence of low blood sugar levels during lactate-induced panic attacks (1984a) nor significant changes in insulin levels (1984b).

5. *Neuroanatomical Hypotheses*

Some authors tried to explain the etiopathogenesis of panic by localizing anatomical correlates of lactate-induced panic; thereby, identifying the brain region responsible for panic anxiety. Knott and Lapierre (1986) examined the effect of lactate-induced panic on brain stem auditory-evoked potentials. Their finding of a prolonged III–V interpeak interval in patients with agoraphobia with panic attacks during the infusion is suggestive of hyperactivity of brain stem noradrenergic nuclei. Stewart et al. (1988), using dynamic single-photon computed axial tomography found that lactate markedly raised hemispheric blood flow levels in both controls and patient nonpanickers, whereas panickers experienced a minimal increase or a decrease in hemispheric blood flow. Reiman et al. (1989) reported that lactate-induced panic was associated with significant blood flow increases bilaterally in the temporal poles; insular cortex, claustrum or lateral putamen; superior colliculus; and in or near the left anterior cerebellar vermis, as shown by positron emission tomography. Gorman et al. (1989b) proposed a neuroanatomical model of panic disorder, allocating the acute panic attack to the brain stem, anticipatory anxiety to the limbic system, and phobic avoidance to the prefrontal cortex.

6. Cognitive Theories

Many authors (e.g., Ackerman and Sachar, 1974; Margraf et al., 1986) have suggested that lactate produces panic through conditioning and cognitive mechanisms. According to this theory, the large volume of hypersomatic fluid infused produces various symptoms and cues panic. Peskind et al. (1990) were able to produce panic symptomatology in panic disorder patients by infusing them with hypertonic saline (3% NaCl). They suggested that the rapidly increased sodium or osmolality may be involved in panic induction. This study apparently did not require any lactate being metabolized during infusion. On the other hand, Gorman et al. (1990a) infused patients with sodium D-lactate, which is poorly metabolized. D-Lactate produced panic, and also hypocapnia and alkalosis, thereby indicating hyperventilation. Even though lactate metabolism may not be necessary for panic induction, D-lactate may work through some other, as yet unknown, mechanism. Lactate appears to cross the blood–brain barrier, and lactate concentration in cisternal fluid increased three times during the intravenous lactate infusion of baboons (Dager et al., 1990).

The perception of various cues may be influenced by the severity of anxiety, especially before the infusion. Some authors, therefore, have focused on the role of baseline anxiety on subsequent response to lactate. Liebowitz (1985a) found a greater baseline autonomic arousal in subsequent panickers. Cowley et al. (1987c) reported that patients who had a typical panic attack with lactate had higher baseline symptom ratings, but these did not fully account for differences in response to lactate. They felt that baseline measures may influence how a patient reaches the threshold for panic. Yeragani et al. (1988b) also reported that patients who panicked during lactate infusion had higher preinfusion anxiety scores. This was also observed by Aronson and associates (1989a). Yeragani et al. (1988c) studied the effects of infusion-induced panic anxiety on subsequent preinfusion anxiety and infusion-induced panic attacks during repeated infusions. Although there was a decrease of preinfusion anxiety from one infusion to the next, there was no evidence of either a significant decrease or increase in the frequency of subsequent panic attacks. In a study by Targum (1991) patients with high frequency of panic attacks (at least one attack a week) reacted positively to lactate infusions, whereas patients with low frequency of panic attacks (one or fewer a month) did not respond to lactate infusions. The author felt that the current heightened anticipatory state (influenced by recent spontaneous attacks), rather than a putative underlying trait, predominates in the provocation of panic.

Many other hypotheses of panic etiology have been tested. There is no support for the involvement of endogenous opiates in the pathogenesis or control of panic attacks (Liebowitz et al., 1984b). Cowley and Dunner (1988) found a lack of significant association between lactate response and presenting clinical variables. Patients with a panic response to lactate were more likely to report a definite history of panic attacks in at least one first-degree relative in this study. Balon et al. (1989) found a higher prevalence of anxiety disorders among first-degree relatives of controls who panicked during lactate infusion than in those who did not panic. Two of these controls subsequently developed panic attacks and, in one of them, panic attacks began soon after the infusion (Balon et al., 1988c). Both of these findings (Cowley and Dunner, 1987; Balon et al., 1989) suggest some genetic vulnerability to lactate-induced panic. George et al. (1989b) reported a marked reduction of parasympathetic nervous activity (vagal tone) in six healthy volunteers during lactate administration and hyperventilation. They hypothesized that this facilitates sympathetic activity (tachycardia).

D. Summary

Sodium lactate is a specific and reliable provocative technique of panic attacks, similar to naturally occurring panic attacks, and accompanied by similar physiological changes. Lactate-induced panic is blocked by antipanic drug treatment. The presented studies clearly demonstrate that the pathogenesis of lactate-induced panic is still unknown (see also Sandberg and Liebowitz, 1990). Various theories of lactate-induced panic, such as hypocalcemia, hypophosphatemia, hypoglycemia, hypersensitive ß-adrenergic receptors, sudden shifts in pH, alkalosis, stimulation of central noradrenergic centers, decreased α_1-adrenergic receptor density, endogenous opioid dysregulation, reduction of inhibitory serotonergic influence on the locus coeruleus, hypothalamopituitary–adrenal axis stimulation, decrease in parasympathetic activity (vagal tone), increase in tribulin, alteration of $NAD^+/NADH$ ratio, hyperventilation, chemoreceptor sensitivity, carbon dioxide sensitivity, fluid expansion, and cognitive theories (nonspecific stress, interceptive phobic cues; van den Hout et al., 1987) have been entertained. Ventilatory dysregulation (stimulation of ventilation) and cognitive misinterpretation of peripheral cues may be the most plausible explanations at present.

III. CARBON DIOXIDE

Shortness of breath is one of the prominent symptoms of panic attacks. Accompanying hyperventilation leads to an increased exhalation of carbon dioxide and lowering of arterial concentration of carbon dioxide. Therefore, one would assume that an increased inhalation of carbon dioxide would decrease anxiety.

Carbon dioxide reduces anxiety in some studies. Griez and van den Hout (1982) reported that double inhalation of a mixture of 35% carbon dioxide and 65% oxygen reduced anxiety level in 12 healthy volunteers. These authors also used this technique, together with exposure, in the treatment of "phobophobia" (Griez and van den Hout, 1983a). Wolpe (1987) strongly advocated the use of carbon dioxide inhalation in the treatment of anxiety.

However, most studies report an anxiogenic effect from inhaled carbon dioxide. Cohen and White (1950) found that the rebreathing technique, which increases carbon dioxide levels, produced anxiety attacks in anxiety neurosis patients. In another study (Gorman et al., 1984c) 7 of 12 panic disorder patients panicked during an increased ventilation, stimulated by 5% carbon dioxide, and 3 of them also during room-air hyperventilation. The rate of carbon dioxide-induced panic was similar to the rate of lactate-induced panic in this study. Gorman et al. (1988b) later expanded their sample to 31 patients and reported that 39% of them panicked with 5% carbon dioxide and 23% with room-air hyperventilation. They also administered 7% carbon dioxide to some subjects who did not panic during the 5% carbon dioxide challenge. Most of the 5% carbon dioxide nonpanickers (panic disorder and other anxiety disorders) panicked with 7% carbon dioxide. The 5% carbon dioxide inhalation technique provoked panic in 8 of 14 panic disorder patients in a study by Woods et al. (1988).

van den Hout and Griez (1984) demonstrated that inhalation of 35% carbon dioxide and 65% oxygen resulted in autonomic symptoms highly reminiscent of natural or lactate-induced panic in normal subjects. If carbon dioxide inhalation was preceded by intake of a ß-blocker (60 mg of propranolol), fewer symptoms occurred than if preceded by a placebo. The same procedure provoked short-lived autonomic panic symptoms in both panic disorder patients and normal controls (Griez et al., 1987), but high subjective anxiety was elicited only in patients. Other researchers (van den Hout et al., 1987; Fyer et al., 1987) also reported that this procedure provoked higher anxiety in panic patients than in controls. Zandbergern et al. (1990) reported significantly higher anxiety during 35% carbon dioxide challenge in panic disorder patients, when compared with the response during this challenge in normal persons and during hyperventilation in both patients and normal subjects. They suggested that panic disorder patients are specifically hypersensitive to an increase in carbon dioxide pressure.

Anxiety ratings increased markedly during rebreathing both in patients and controls in study by Woods et al. (1986), and anxiety increases were significantly greater in patients than in healthy subjects. Ventilatory response to carbon dioxide was similar in patients and controls. On the other hand, Lousberg and associates (1988) reported that panic patients showed significantly higher ventilatory response than normal controls using the same rebreathing technique.

The role of carbon dioxide as a laboratory model for initiating panic has thus been clearly established. As with lactate, several studies tried to address the diagnostic specificity of carbon dioxide challenge (Gorman et al., 1988b, 1990b; Rapee et al., 1986; Harrison et al., 1989). Patients with other anxiety disorders such as social phobia, generalized anxiety disorder, and obsessive–compulsive disorder did not panic, whereas 39% panic disorder patients panicked during 5% carbon dioxide challenge in a study by Gorman et al. (1988b). Nine of 14 women with premenstrual dysphoria without panic disorder panicked during 35% carbon dioxide challenge, compared with none of 12 controls (Harrison et al., 1989).

Patients with social phobia were the most frequently studied group besides panic disorder patients. All three patients with social phobia and 67% panic disorder patients panicked during subsequent challenge with 7% carbon dioxide in the aforementioned study by Gorman et al., (1988b). On the other hand, 36% of social phobics, compared with 50% of panic disorder patients, panicked during 35% carbon dioxide challenge in a study by Gorman et al. (1990b). This finding was obscured by poor differentiation between groups (patients and controls). The difference in the frequency of panic between patients with social phobia and panic disorder patients was even larger—18.7 vs 62.5%—during single inhalation of 50% carbon dioxide in a study by Rapee et al. (1986). Carbon dioxide thus seems to be less panic disorder-specific than lactate. The sensitivity to carbon dioxide in panic disorder patients may be concentration-dependent, and Gorman et al. (1990b) suggest that increasing the dose of carbon dioxide may compromise diagnostic specificity. Further studies are necessary to elucidate the sensitivity and specificity of this technique.

A. Studies Focused on Etiology

Results of animal studies present some theoretical basis of the carbon dioxide mechanism of anxiety induction. Garcia de Yebenes Prous and associates (1977) found an increased synthesis of brain monoamines in male albino rats exposed to various concentrations of carbon dioxide. Hypercapnia also caused a rapid increase in the firing rate of the locus coeruleus neurons of rats (Elam et al., 1981).

Gorman et al. (1984c) theorized that the similarity in response to lactate and carbon dioxide in their patients was suggestive of the involvement of carbon dioxide (lactate→bicarbonate→carbon dioxide) in the triggering of anxiety by stimulation of the locus coeruleus. Carbon dioxide-induced panic was associated with an exaggerated ventilatory response and increases in plasma norepinephrine and diastolic blood pressure (Gorman et al., 1988b), suggesting that patients may have hypersensitive carbon dioxide receptors. On the other hand, the complex physiological and biochemical measurements (MHPG, plasma cortisol, prolactin, growth hormone) obtained in a study by Woods et al. (1988) did not elucidate the anxiogenic effect of carbon dioxide, and Gorman et al. (1990b) were not able to find a significant group difference in anxiety level, physiological measures, or biochemical measures in response to 35% carbon dioxide. However, 35% carbon dioxide may be too high a dose (Gorman et al., 1990b).

Several studies also reported on the effect of treatment on carbon dioxide-induced anxiety and its relation to etiology. Venous pH, venous carbon dioxide pressure, and bicarbonate were normalized in panic patients after treatment with tricyclic antidepressants or clonidine (Gorman et al., 1985b). Beckett and colleagues (1986) reported blockade of rebreathing-induced panic attack with clonazepam in a patient with panic disorder. Alprazolam markedly attenuated anxiety increases during rebreathing of 5% carbon dioxide in eight panic disorder patients (Woods et al., 1986). These authors hypothesized that alprazolam may antagonize carbon dioxide-induced anxiety by decreasing noradrenergic function through stimulation of benzodiazepine receptors located on noradrenergic neurons. Pretreatment with alprazolam, but not with clonidine, significantly reduced the rebreathing-induced increase in anxiety (Woods et al., 1989). The anxiogenic effect of rebreathing 5% carbon dioxide was significantly reduced in six patients after long-term imipramine treatment (Woods et al., 1990), a finding consistent with an increase of noradrenergic function in carbon dioxide-induced anxiety.

Other authors have suggested other physiological, behavioral, and cognitive explanations of carbon dioxide-induced panic. Griez and van den Hout (1983b) reported that carbon dioxide produces largely sympathomimetic responses in the cardiovascular system of healthy subjects. van den Hout and Griez (1985) indicated that the occurrence of peripheral panic symptoms in healthy volunteers after carbon dioxide inhalation in their study could be attributed to the sudden decrease in arterial P_{CO_2}. These authors (Griez et al., 1988) also suggested that hypocarbia alone is not sufficient to provoke anxiety in patients. van den Hout et al. (1987) observed a decrease in anxiety with the increased number of carbon dioxide challenges and suggested that their data support a behavioral account of the anxiogenic effect of carbon dioxide. Subjects with panic attacks who were given no explanation reported a greater proportion of catastrophic cognition and greater panic than those with panic attacks who received a full explanation (Rapee et al., 1986). Another possible contribution of psychological factors to the laboratory induction of panic was presented in a study by Sanderson and coauthors (1989). Patients who believed that they had control over carbon dioxide administration reported a smaller amount of anxiety and less intense anxiety than the patients who believed that they could not control the carbon dioxide administration. Both groups went through the same procedure.

The etiology of carbon dioxide-induced panic remains unknown. The hypersensitivity of carbon dioxide receptors, an increase in noradrenergic function, or cognitive misinterpretation of peripheral symptoms induced by carbon dioxide are the most plausible explanations. It is interesting that benzodiazepines, respiratory depressants, and various breathing techniques, are effective in treatment of panic.

B. Summary

Carbon dioxide is a valid and relatively convenient model of panic anxiety. It provokes anxiety similar to naturally occurring panic, and its anxiogenic effect is successfully blocked by antianxiety agents. The specificity of this model may be dose- or concentration-dependent. The etiology remains unknown.

IV. YOHIMBINE

Yohimbine, an indole alkaloid chemically known as 17α-hydroxyyohimban-16α–carboxylic acid methyl ester, is an α_2-adrenergic antagonist. Yohimbine interacts with adrenoceptors that are selectively stimulated by clonidine, an α_2-adrenergic agonist; however, radioligand and pharmacological studies also suggest that it can interact with α_1-receptors. It has been well established that α_2-adrenoceptors regulate sympathetic flow in intact animals and humans. α_2-Agonists, such as clonidine, reduce sympathetic outflow and blood pressure, whereas α_2-antagonists, such as yohimbine, increase sympathetic outflow (Goldberg and Robertson, 1983).

Increased noradrenergic function may play a pivotal role in the pathophysiology of anxiety states. The nucleus locus coeruleus (LC) is a collection of noradrenergic neurons in the brain stem, and electric stimulation of this nucleus in monkeys results in fearful behaviors, whereas destruction of this nucleus reduces such responses (Redmond et al., 1976a,b). The same investigators have demonstrated that activation of LC by yohimbine produces an increase in LC firing and produces fearful behaviors. These behaviors were also blunted or reversed by clonidine (Redmond, 1979).

In humans, yohimbine produces symptoms of anxiety and an increase in heart rate and blood pressure (Holmberg and Gershon, 1961). Evidence suggests that yohimbine administration in humans results in an increase in plasma MHPG, the principal metabolite of CNS norepinephrine (Charney et al., 1982a). Charney and associates (1983) gave 30 mg of yohimbine to ten healthy subjects, and this resulted in increases in subjective anxiety, blood pressure, and plasma MHPG. In this study, both diazepam and clonidine significantly antagonized yohimbine-induced anxiety. When given alone, only clonidine significantly decreased plasma MHPG and blood pressure, but diazepam did not.

In another study, Charney et al., (1984b) administered 20 mg of yohimbine orally to 20 healthy controls and 39 drug-free patients with agoraphobia and panic attacks. This resulted in a significantly greater anxiety and somatic symptoms, such as palpitations, hot and cold flashes, restlessness, and tremors, in patients compared with the effects in controls. There were also significant correlations between patient-rated anxiety and nervousness, the frequency of reported panic attacks, and the yohimbine-induced rise in plasma MHPG. These investigators also found that patients with frequent panic attacks had a significantly higher plasma MHPG response to yohimbine than did normal persons. Gurguis and Uhde (1990) recently reported their findings for 7 normal controls and 11 panic disorder patients. Panic disorder patients had a greater anxiogenic response to 20 mg of yohimbine. Yohimbine increased plasma MHPG levels in both groups, but there was a trend toward a greater increase in panic disorder patients. In patients, there was also a significant positive correlation between yohimbine-induced increases in MHPG and ratings of anxiety.

There is evidence suggesting that opiate abstinence syndrome in laboratory animals is associated with noradrenergic hyperactivity (Aghajanian, 1978). This syndrome is similar to the stimulation of the locus coeruleus, resulting in fearlike behaviors. Charney and Redmond (1983) have reported that methadone withdrawal in patients addicted to methadone is also associated with increased levels of free plasma MHPG. Clonidine has been reported to be effective in the treatment of such conditions (Gold et al., 1978). Charney and colleagues (1982b) have reported on withdrawal symptoms, related to abrupt discontinuation of tricyclics, that result in an increase in anxiety. This state is also associated with increased plasma and urinary MHPG levels.

The foregoing reports suggest that clonidine, which decreases sympathetic outflow, might be useful to treat anxiety. In fact, several reports suggest such effects of clonidine (Hoehn-Saric et al., 1981; Ko et al., 1983). Ko et al. (1983) reported that clonidine and imipramine were equally effective in decreasing the number of panic attacks and also blocked panic in response to known phobic stimuli. In this study, free plasma MHPG levels were decreased to a greater extent in patients who responded to clonidine than in those patients who did not respond. Charney and Heninger (1986) have reported on the effects of clonidine in 21 healthy subjects and 26 drug-free panic disorder patients. Clonidine produced significantly greater decreases in plasma MHPG levels, in sitting and standing diastolic blood pressure, and significantly smaller increases in growth hormone levels and drowsiness in patients.

Some tricyclic antidepressants are effective in the treatment of panic disorder (Zitrin et al., 1980). Evidence suggests that tricyclics decrease levels of free plasma MHPG (Charney et al., 1981). Charney and Redmond (1983) speculate that the decrease in norepinephrine turnover may be related to their antianxiety effect. These authors also reported (1985a) that alprazolam treatment of panic disorder patients was associated with a decrease in baseline MHPG levels and a blunting of the yohimbine-induced increase. They speculated that the antipanic mechanism of action of alprazolam may be due to an interaction between benzodiazepine-sensitive and noradrenergic neural systems.

Charney and Heninger (1986) also speculated that the regulation of noradrenergic activity is aberrant in some patients with panic disorder, and the increased dynamic range of noradrenergic activity observed as an increased sensitivity to both yohimbine and clonidine may be due to abnormalities in regulatory input to noradrenergic neurons or dysfunction in the α_2-adrenergic receptor–effector-coupling mechanism. Rasmussen et al. (1987) found that yohimbine, administered to 12 drug-free patients with obsessive–compulsive disorder and 12 healthy subjects had no significant effect on obsessive–compulsive symptoms. The behavioral and MHPG responses were similar in the two groups. This lends some support to the specificity of the anxiogenic responses in panic disorder patients.

In summary, yohimbine appears to be a specific anxiogenic agent, and the yohimbine model of anxiety has helped understand the pathophysiology of anxiety to a considerable extent. However, it should also be noted that there are some inconsistencies with this model. Some studies did not find a baseline difference in the levels of MHPG between panic disorder patients and controls (Hamlin et al., 1983). Lactate-induced panic and caffeine-induced anxiety are not accompanied by increases in plasma free MHPG (Charney et al., 1984a; Carr et al., 1986b; Pohl et al., 1987). Although the yohimbine model of anxiety is very attractive, it is also possible that the increase in sympathetic flow can result in symptoms of anxiety through an additional ß-adrenergic mechanism, as isoproterenol induces symptoms of panic anxiety in patients with a hyperdynamic ß-adrenergic state (Frolich et al., 1969) and also in patients with a *DSM-III* diagnosis of panic disorder (Pohl et al., 1988a).

V. CAFFEINE

Caffeine, 1,3,7-trimethylxanthine, is a widely used psychotropic substance. Caffeine is associated with an increase in self-rated symptoms of anxiety in several studies (Lee et al., 1985; Boulenger et al., 1984). Caffeine, in doses 600 mg/day has been reported to result in caffeinism, characterized by anxiety, sleep disturbances, and nervousness (Greden, 1974). Caffeine is also known to produce symptoms of panic anxiety in patients with anxiety disorders (Charney et al., 1985).

Boulenger et al. (1984) studied caffeine consumption in 30 patients with panic disorder, 23 patients with major depressive disorder, and 53 normal controls matched for sociocultural background. They found that patients with panic disorder, but not depressed patients or normal controls, had levels of self-rated anxiety and depression that correlated with their degree of caffeine consumption. They also found that panic disorder patients had an increased sensitivity to the effects of 1 cup of coffee. Furthermore, patients with panic disorder reported the discontinuation of coffee intake because of untoward side effects more frequently than controls. In another study, Lee et al. (1985) administered a caffeine questionnaire to 43 patients with *DSM-III* anxiety disorders and 124 medical inpatients. Eighty-four percent of anxious patients were low-caffeine consumers, compared with 41% of medical inpatients. Patients who reported becoming anxious in response to drinking coffee had higher anxiety subscale scores on SCL-90-R than those who did not.

Uhde et al. (1984), under double-blind conditions, administered three doses of oral caffeine (240, 480, and 720 mg) to eight normal controls and two panic patients. The subjects maintained a caffeine-free diet for at least 1 week before the study. There was a dose-related increase in measures of anxiety state in all subjects. Two normal controls developed unequivocal panic attacks after receiving 720 mg of caffeine.

Charney and associates (1984a) have reported on the effects of oral administration of 10 mg/kg of caffeine in 11 healthy subjects. There were robust increases in subject-rated anxiety and nervousness, small increases in blood pressure, and a decrease in heart rate. There were no consistent changes in plasma MHPG levels or significant relation between the MHPG levels and ratings of anxiety. Charney and co-workers (1985) also reported on administration of caffeine (10 mg/kg) to 17 healthy subjects and 21 patients with panic disorder. They found that patients had a significantly greater anxiogenic response, compared with controls, and the levels of anxiety were significantly correlated with plasma caffeine levels in patients. Caffeine did not significantly alter the levels of MHPG in patients or controls. Caffeine increased plasma cortisol levels equally in both groups.

Recently, Mathew and Wilson (1990b) studied the effects of 250 mg of caffeine in eight patients with generalized anxiety disorder, nine patients with panic disorder, and nine normal controls. The anxiety disorder patients did not show any evidence of increased anxiety and panic after caffeine. Both patients and controls who received caffeine had significant decreases in cerebral blood flow. These changes in cerebral blood flow were unrelated to changes in mood, autonomic activity, or carbon dioxide levels. These authors conclude that the caffeine-induced change in cerebral blood flow is largely caused by the vascular effect of the drug, unrelated to changes in mood and peripheral physiological responses. This study suggests that small doses of caffeine may not induce symptoms of panic anxiety.

Recent studies on the mechanism of action of caffeine have focused on its antagonism of the effects of adenosine. Caffeine reverses adenosine-induced vasodilation (Berne et al., 1983), renal constriction (Osswald, 1983), and spontaneous neuronal firing (Phillips and Wu, 1983). There are two basic subtypes of adenosine receptors, A_1 and A_2.

Both adenosine receptors are blocked by caffeine and other xanthine derivatives (Shimizu, 1983; Snyder and Sklar, 1984). The A_1 adenosine receptor has been implicated in the regulation of taste sensitivity, and a recent study of DeMet et al. (1989) is very interesting in this regard. These authors tried to measure the adenosine receptor sensitivity based on the action of specific receptor blockers to potentiate the ability to detect threshold quinine concentrations. They compared gustatory adenosinergic responses to caffeine challenges in 17 normal controls, 10 patients with panic disorder, and 5 patients with posttraumatic stress disorder. Panic disorder patients had an exaggerated response to the caffeine challenge that was not found in normal controls or posttraumatic stress disorder patients. The authors suggest that A_1 adenosine receptor upregulation might produce an increased sensitivity to caffeine.

Several mechanisms may be involved in the anxiogenic response to caffeine. These include inhibition of phosphodiesterase (Butcher and Sutherland, 1962), increased brain catecholamine activity (Berkowitz et al., 1970), and antagonism of benzodiazepine and adenosine receptor function (Marangos et al., 1979; Snyder and Sklar, 1984). Caffeine anxiogenic effect thus may be related to several neurobiological systems, namely noradrenergic, dopaminergic, adenosinergic, and even GABAergic. Alprazolam blocks caffeine-induced anxiety (Uhde, 1990). Findings from study by Orlikov and Ryzov (1991) on increased kynurenine (metabolite of tryptophan) during caffeine-induced anxiety in 15 male volunteers suggests the possibility of serotonergic system involvement. The caffeine model of anxiety, although inconclusive as to the mechanism of its anxiogenic effects, appears to be a useful research tool.

VI. ISOPROTERENOL

The role of catecholamines in anxiety has been of interest since the beginning of this century, when Cannon demonstrated that fear and rage in cats was accompanied by the release of epinephrine from the adrenals (Cannon, 1929). In early studies in humans, epinephrine reproduced the symptoms of "irritable heart," a syndrome with functional cardiac symptoms and anxiety (Wearn and Sturgis, 1919). In another study, subcutaneous injections of epinephrine produced "cold" anxiety in many individuals, "as if" they were afraid, but provoked intense emotional states characterized by anxiety, crying, sobbing, and sighing in individuals predisposed by hyperthyroidism, emotional instability, psychoneurosis, or excitement (Marañon, 1924). In subsequent studies, epinephrine provoked anxiety attacks in patients with anxiety disorders, but not in subjects with other psychiatric disorders (Lindemann, 1935; Lindemann and Finesinger, 1938). Norepinephrine also induces anxiety attacks in panic disorder patients (Pyke and Greenberg, 1986).

Isoproterenol is a sympathomimetic amine, structurally very similar to epinephrine. Unlike epinephrine, isoproterenol lacks α-adrenoceptor agonist effects and acts almost exclusively on ß-adrenoceptors. In early uncontrolled studies, isoproterenol provoked intense anxiety states in 9 of 14 patients with a history of anxiety symptoms (Frohlich et al., 1969), and produced anxiety attacks in 5 subjects with a history of panic attacks (Easton and Sherman, 1976). In both studies, the anxiety states quickly subsided after intravenous injections of the ß-blocker propranolol.

The foregoing catecholamine studies suggest a ß-receptor model for panic. Many of the symptoms of panic, such as heart palpitations and tremulousness, also point to the ß-adrenergic system. The following section reviews more recent studies of isoproterenol in panic disorder. There is also a discussion of the relation of a ß-receptor model to the pharmacology of many antidepressants, the yohimbine model, and the noradrenergic theory of anxiety. In addition, the following inconsistencies in the model are briefly discussed: (1) ß-Blockers appear to be a mediocre treatment for panic. (2) Isoproterenol may not cross the blood–brain barrier. (3) Serotonergic drugs appear to be effective treatments for panic disorder.

A. Isoproterenol Infusions in Panic Disorder Patients

In a large study, 86 panic disorder patients and 45 nonpsychiatric controls were infused with isoproterenol at a rate of 1 μg/min for up to 20 min (Pohl et al., 1988a). Subjects also received placebo infusions under double-blind conditions. Using the Panic Description Scale (Rainey et al., 1984b), panic disorder patients became much more anxious during isoproterenol infusions and were much more likely to panic than were normal controls (66 vs 9%). Only 16% of the panic disorder patients had an attack during the placebo infusion, and none of the controls panicked with placebo. Panic disorder patients who panicked with isoproterenol rated the similarity of the attack as between "moderately" and "very much" like previous attacks, and the panic attacks were rated as moderately severe.

A greater proportion of women panic disorder patients panicked during this experiment than did men, but this difference could be accounted for by dosage. The fixed dosage of 1 μg/min did not take weight into account, so that women received a higher dose of isoproterenol per kilogram. Once weight was accounted for, there was no gender difference. Moreover, stratification of weight-adjusted dosage demonstrated that the frequency of panic attacks induced in patients was dose-dependent; 55% of those given a mean of 8.2 ±1.8 μg min^{-1} kg^{-1} panicked, while 79% of those given 18.5 ±3.2 μg min^{-1} kg^{-1} isoproterenol panicked.

In a follow-up experiment, 14 of the patients in this study were reinfused with isoproterenol and placebo after treatment with tricyclic antidepressants (Pohl et al., 1990). Thirteen of these patients panicked before treatment, and only 2 after treatment. There was a significant decrease in anxiety as measured by the Panic Description Scale during posttreatment infusions, and patients were able to tolerate longer infusions posttreatment. Although there was no control group of patients treated with placebo, the results of this study suggest that tricyclic antidepressants block isoproterenol-induced anxiety.

Blood pressure data obtained in this study may provide a clue to how tricyclic antidepressants work. Isoproterenol infusions increase systolic blood pressure, and this effect appears to be mediated primarily by $ß_1$-receptor mechanisms. For example, $ß_2$-blockade has no or little effect on isoproterenol-induced increases in systolic blood pressure, whereas $ß_1$-blockers strongly antagonize this effect (Brodde et al., 1988; Pringle et al., 1988). Although isoproterenol infusions increased systolic blood pressure in both controls and panic disorder patients before treatment, tricyclic antidepressant treatment abolished this increase (Pohl et al., 1990). On the other hand, isoproterenol-induced decreases in diastolic blood pressure are mediated by $ß_2$-receptors; $ß_1$-blockers do not prevent this decrease, and $ß_2$-4 and nonselective blockers prevent or strongly antagonize this decrease (Brodde et al., 1988; Arnold et al., 1985; Motomura et al., 1990; Vincent et al., 1982). In panic disorder patients, there is no change in isoproterenol-induced decreases in diastolic blood pressure after treatment (Pohl et al., 1990).

Thus, after treatment, isoproterenol continues to decrease diastolic blood pressure, but does not increase systolic blood pressure. These blood pressure findings are consistent with animal studies that show selective $ß_1$-receptor down-regulation after tricyclic antidepressant treatment in the CNS (Minneman et al., 1979, 1982) and in the heart (Keith et al., 1986; Nomura et al., 1982), and suggest ß$_1$-receptor down-regulation may be a possible mechanism of action for tricyclic antidepressants.

B. ß-Adrenergic Model of Panic Anxiety

The anxiogenic effects of isoproterenol in panic disorder patients suggests that ß-adrenoceptors may play a role in the pathophysiology of panic. This hypothesis provides an explanation for the mechanism of action of almost all antidepressants, because most down-regulate ß-receptors (Vetulani et al., 1976; Bannerjee et al., 1977). Since ß$_2$-receptors are not affected by antidepressants, this hypothesis would specifically implicate ß$_1$-receptors. How does this hypothesis fit in with other major theories of anxiety?

The noradrenergic theory of anxiety is perhaps the most studied. The locus coeruleus is a noradrenergic nucleus with the most norepinephrine-containing neurons in the brain; drugs that decrease LC firing decrease anxiety, whereas most drugs that increase LC firing increase anxiety (Redmond, 1979). Norepinephrine stimulates both α- and ß-adrenoceptors. Although the noradrenergic theory has focused on α-adrenergic receptors, norepinephrine-containing efferent axons from the LC affect postsynaptic ß-receptors that are widely distributed throughout the cerebrum, limbic system, cerebellum, and spinal cord (Grant and Redmond, 1981). Stimulation of the LC in monkeys results in fearlike behavior, and these effects are almost completely blocked by the ß-blocker propranolol, suggesting that postsynaptic ß-adrenergic receptors are essential for LC-mediated anxiety (Huang et al., 1977).

Yohimbine, an α_2-autoreceptor blocker, induces more anxiety in panic disorder patients than in controls (Charney et al., 1984b). Yohimbine blocks α_2-autoreceptors and increases norepinephrine release, thereby stimulating α- and ß-receptors. Research to date has focused on the α-receptor, because yohimbine causes an abnormally greater MHPG response in frequent panickers (Charney et al., 1984b). However, it is unclear how this is related to the known treatment effects of antidepressants, because imipramine treatment does not diminish this yohimbine-induced increase in plasma MHPG levels (Charney and Heninger, 1985b) and clonidine produces abnormal decreases in plasma MHPG in panic patients (Charney and Heninger, 1986). The yohimbine model of anxiety is also consistent with ß-receptor model, since norepinephrine is a strong ß$_1$-agonist. A ß$_1$-theory also explains the initial increase in anxiety seen in panic disorder patients treated with tricyclic antidepressants, since there is an initial increase in available norepinephrine, whereas ß-receptor down-regulation is a chronic effect. The initial stimulation seen with tricyclic antidepressants is more pronounced with desipramine, a more selectively noradrenergic drug, than with imipramine (Pohl et al., 1988b).

It is now apparent that highly selective serotonergic drugs are also effective for panic disorder (Schneider et al., 1990; Gorman et al., 1987b; Kahn et al., 1988). Moreover, these drugs also cause an initial-stimulating effect that may be more pronounced in panic disorder patients than in depressed patients (Kahn et al., 1988). This has led to theories of anxiety that focus exclusively on the serotonergic system. The relation between serotonergic theories and the noradrenergic theory of anxiety is unknown, but it seems unlikely that only one or the other is "correct." More likely, the two systems interact, and a greater understanding of these interactions would help us understand the disorders of interest. Although reports on fluoxetine's effect on ß-receptors are mixed (Wong et al., 1985; Wamsley et al., 1987; Byerley et al., 1988; Manier et al., 1989), ß-receptor down-regulation is serotonin-dependent (Sulser, 1984), and fluoxetine shortens the amount of time required for desipramine-induced decreases in ß-receptor density (Baron et al., 1988). Destruction of part of the serotonergic system increases norepinephrine turnover within the LC (Pujol et al., 1978), and stimulation of the serotonin system decreases LC firing typically observed with noxious stimuli. Direct application of serotonin on the LC suppresses LC firing (Segal, 1979). Fluvoxamine, a highly serotonergic, fluoxetinelike antidepressant, blunts yohimbine-induced anxiety in PTSD patients (Goddard et al., 1990). These findings taken together suggest that serotonergic systems modulate the release of norepinephrine.

One inconsistency in a ß-adrenergic model is that ß-blockers are relatively ineffective for panic anxiety (Noyes, 1982), although they are effective for performance anxiety. However, this finding might be explained by the up-regulation of ß-receptors that occurs when ß-blockers are given for an extended time. The ß-blocker propranolol increases peripheral ß-receptor function in severely anxious patients (Lima and Turner, 1983), and panic disorder patients may experience early improvement with propranolol that is not sustained (Noyes et al., 1984; Pohl et al., 1988). ß-Blocker use for performance anxiety is generally episodic, and since the drugs are only given before scheduled public performances, ß-receptor up-regulation would not occur.

Although modest amounts of tritiated epinephrine, which is structurally closely related to isoproterenol, crosses into the hypothalamus (Weil-Malherbe et al., 1959), and isoproterenol has central nervous system effects (Marley and Key, 1963; Goldstein and Munoz, 1961), isoproterenol (and epinephrine) do not readily cross the blood–brain barrier, and some of the central effects may be mediated by isoproterenol's peripheral effects. If isoproterenol exerts its anxiogenic effects outside of the CNS, there are several possible explanations. One is the possibility that, since provocative models of anxiety all have peripheral effects and symptoms, drug-induced anxiety is a function of the psychological effects that occur secondary to a provocative infusion (i.e., cognitive perceptions of the experience). Effective treatments may block some peripheral effects of anxiogenic infusions. Another potential hypothesis is that panic disorder is a peripheral disease of autonomic arousal, and that the subjective symptoms of anxiety, like many of the phobic symptoms, are a secondary phenomenon. It is also possible that peripheral sympathetic activation has reflex CNS effects on the LC. Studies that examine the effect of different treatments on provocative models of anxiety may help resolve these issues.

C. Summary

Isoproterenol is another reliable model of anxiety induction. As with the other provocation techniques, it induces anxiety similar to the naturally occurred panic, and its effects are blocked by antianxiety treatment. The relation of this model to CNS hypotheses of anxiety is unknown.

VII. CONCLUSION

The five provocative strategies discussed in this chapter all have been replicated as a method for inducing anxiety in panic disorder patients. They all provoke anxiety that is similar to naturally occurring panic anxiety, and they all have some threshold specificity. The methods have varied, but all share some possible common pathophysiology or mechanism: all may affect the noradrenergic system, and all could potentially be explained by cognitive misinterpretation of peripheral symptoms. Arguing against the latter is that many of the techniques occasionally provoke signs of anxiety in normal controls, and normal controls with family history of anxiety disorders may be at greater risk for this.

They are all reversed by clinical treatment and, thus, clinically validated. As Woods et al. (1986) pointed out, all these provocation techniques appear to constitute useful neurobiological probes into the pathophysiology of panic anxiety. However, even though our knowledge of the biology of anxiety has increased enormously, the etiology of panic is still an enigma. These provocative techniques seem to be also an effective model for the development and testing of more specific and effective treatments.

REFERENCES

S. H. Ackerman, and E. J. Sachar, The lactate theory of anxiety: A review and reevaluation, *Psychosom. Med., 36*: 69 (1974).

G. K. Aghajanian, Tolerance of locus ceruleus neurons to morphine and suppression of withdrawal response by clonidine, *Nature, 276*: 186 (1978).

I. L. Appleby, D. F. Klein, E. J. Sachar, and M. Levitt, Biochemical indices of lactate-induced panic: Preliminary report, *Anxiety: New Research and Changing Concepts* (D. F. Klein and J. G. Rabkin, eds.), Raven Press, New York, p. 411 (1981).

J. M. O. Arnold, P. C. O'Connor, J. G. Riddell, D. W. G. Harron, R. G. Shanks, and D. G. McDevitt, Effects of the beta 2-adrenoceptor antagonist ICI 118,551 on exercise tachycardia and isoprenaline-induced ß-adrenoceptor responses in man, *Br. J. Clin. Pharmacol., 19*: 619 (1985).

T. A. Aronson, P. Whitaker-Azmitia, and I. Caraseti, Differential reactivity to caltate infusions: The relative role of biological, psychological, and conditioning variables, *Biol. Psychiatry, 25*: 469 (1989a).

T. A. Aronson, I. Caraseti, D. Mc Bane, and P. Whitaker-Azmitia, Biological correlates of lactate sensitivity in panic disorder, *Biol. Psychiatry, 26*: 463 (1989b).

R. Balon, A. Ortiz, R. Pohl, and V. K. Yeragani, Heart rate and blood pressure during placebo associated panic attacks, *Psychosom. Med., 50*: 434 (1988a).

R. Balon, R. Pohl, V. K. Yeragani, J. M. Rainey, and P. Weinberg, Lactate- and isoproterenol-induced panic attacks in panic disorder patients and controls, *Psychiatry Res., 23*: 153 (1988b).

R. Balon, R. Pohl, V. K. Yeragani, J. M. Rainey, and R. Berchou, Follow-up study of control subjects with lactate- and isoproterenol-induced panic attacks, *Am. J. Psychiatry, 145*: 238 (1988c).

R. Balon, V. K. Yeragani, and R. Pohl, Phenomenological comparison of dextrose, lactate, and isoproterenol associated panic attacks, *Psychiatry Res., 26*: 43 (1988d).

R. Balon, V. K. Yeragani, and R. Pohl, Relative hypophosphatemia in patients with panic disorder, *Arch. Gen. Psychiatry, 45*: 294 (1988e).

R. Balon, M. Jordan, R. Pohl, and V. K. Yeragani, Family history of anxiety disorders in control subjects with lactate-induced panic attacks, *Am. J. Psychiatry, 146*: 1304 (1989).

S. P. Bannerjee, L. S. Kung, S. J. Riggi, and S. K. Chanda, Development of beta-adrenergic receptor subsensitivity by antidepressants, *Nature, 268*: 455 (1977).

B. M. Baron, A. M. Ogden, B. W. Siegel, J. Stegeman, R. C. Ursillo, and M. W. Dudley, Rapid down regulation of beta-adrenoceptors by co-administration of desipramine and fluoxetine, *Eur. J. Pharmacol., 154*: 125 (1988).

C. Bass, W. N. Gardner, E. Griez, H. Pols, and J. M. Gorman, Blood gas changes and hypophosphatemia in lactate-induced panic [letters], *Arch. Gen. Psychiatry, 45*: 95 (1988).

A. Beckett, S. M. Fishman, and J. Rosenbaum, Clonazepam blockade of spontaneous and CO_2 inhalation-provoked panic in a patient with panic disorder, *J. Clin. Psychiatry, 47*: 475 (1986).

B. A. Berkowitz, J. H. Tarver, and S. Spector, Release of norepinephrine in the central nervous system by theophylline and caffeine, *Eur. J. Pharmacol., 10*: 64 (1970).

R. M. Berne, H. R. Winn, R. M. Knabb, S. W. Ely, and R. Rubio, Blood flow regulation by adenosine in heart, brain and skeletal muscle, *Regulatory Function of Adenosine* (R. M. Berne, T. W. Rall, and R. Rubio, eds.), Martinus Nijhoff, The Hague, p. 293 (1983).

J. A. Bonn, J. Harrison, and W. L. Rees, Lactate-induced anxiety: Therapeutic application, *Br. J. Psychiatry, 119*: 468 (1971).

J. A. Bonn, J. Harrison, and L. Rees, Lactate infusion in the treatment of "free-floating" anxiety, *Can. Psychiatr. Assoc. J., 18*: 41 (1973).

J. Boulenger, T. W. Uhde, E. A. Wolff, and R. M. Post, Increased sensitivity to caffeine in patients with panic disorders, *Arch. Gen. Psychiatry, 41*: 1067 (1984).

J. Bradwejn, D. Koszycki, and G. Meterissian, Cholecystokinin-tetrapeptide induces panic attacks in patients with panic disorder, *Can. J. Psychiatry, 35*: 83 (1990).

O. E. Brodde, A. Daul, A. Wellstein, D. Palm, M. C. Michel, and J. J. Beckeringh, Differentiation of $beta_1$- and $beta_2$-adrenoceptor-mediated effects in humans, *Am. J. Physiol., 254*: H199 (1988).

R. Buller, U. von Bardeleben, W. Maier, and O. Benkert, Specificity of lactate response in panic disorder, panic with concurrent depression and major depression, *J. Affective Disord., 16*: 109 (1989).

R. W. Butcher, and E. W. Sutherland, Adenosine 3′, 5′, phosphate in biological materials, *J. Biol. Chem., 237*: 1244 (1962).

W. F. Byerley, E. J. McConnell, R. T. McCabe, T. M. Dawson, B. I. Grosser, and J. K. Wamsley, Decreased beta-adrenergic receptors in rat brain after chronic administration of the selective serotonin uptake inhibitor fluoxetine, *Psychopharmacology, 94*: 141 (1988).

W. B. Cannon, *Bodily Changes in Pain, Hunger, Fear, and Rage: An Account of Recent Researchers into the Function of Emotional Excitement*, 2nd ed., Appleton-Century-Crofts, New York (1929).

D. B. Carr, D. V. Sheehan, O. S. Susman, J. H. Coleman, D. J. Greenblatt, G. R. Heninger, K. J. Jones, P. H. Levine, and W. D. Watkins, Neuroendocrine correlates of lactate-induced anxiety and their response to chronic alprazolam therapy, *Am. J. Psychiatry, 143*: 483 (1986a).

D. B. Carr, S. M. Fishman, N. W. Kasting, and D. V. Sheehan, Vasopressin response to lactate infusion in normals and patients with panic disorder, *Funct. Neurol. 1*:123 (1986b).

D. S. Charney, and G. R. Heninger, Noradrenergic function and the mechanism of action of antianxiety treatment. I. The effect of long-term alprazolam treatment, *Arch. Gen. Psychiatry, 42*: 458 (1985a).

D. S. Charney, and G. R. Heninger, Noradrenergic function and the mechanism of action of antianxiety treatment. II. The effect of long-term imipramine treatment, *Arch. Gen. Psychiatry, 42*: 473 (1985b).

D. S. Charney, and G. R. Heninger, Abnormal regulation of noradrenergic function in panic disorders. Effects of clonidine in healthy subjects and patients with agoraphobia and panic disorder, *Arch. Gen. Psychiatry, 43*: 1042 (1986).

D. S. Charney, and D. E. Redmond, Neurobiological mechanisms in human anxiety. Evidence supporting central noradrenergic hyperactivity, *Neuropharmacology, 22*: 1531 (1983).

D. S. Charney, G. R. Heninger, D. E. Sternberg, and R. H. Roth, Plasma MHPG in depression. Effects of acute and chronic desipramine treatment, *Psychiatry Res., 5*: 217 (1981).

D. S. Charney, G. R. Heninger, and D. E. Sternberg, Assessment of adrenergic autoreceptor function in humans. Effects of oral yohimbine, *Life Sci., 30*: 2033 (1982a).

D. S. Charney, G. R. Heninger, and D. E. Sternberg, Abrupt discontinuation of tricyclic antidepressant drugs. Evidence for noradrenergic hyperactivity, *Br. J. Psychiatry, 141*: 377 (1982b).

D. S. Charney, G. R. Heninger, and D. E. Redmond, Yohimbine induced anxiety and increased noradrenergic function in humans. Effects of diazepam and clonidine, *Life Sci., 33*: 19 (1983).

D. S. Charney, M. P. Galloway, and G. R. Heninger, The effects of caffeine on plasma MHPG, subjective anxiety, autonomic symptoms and blood pressure in healthy humans, *Life Sci., 35*: 135 (1984a).

D. S. Charney, G. R. Heninger, and A. Breier, Noradrenergic function in panic anxiety. Effects of yohimbine in healthy subjects and patients with agoraphobia and panic disorder, *Arch. Gen. Psychiatry, 41*: 751 (1984b).

D. S. Charney, G. R. Heninger, and P. I. Jatlow, Increased anxiogenic effects of caffeine in panic disorders, *Arch. Gen. Psychiatry, 42*: 233 (1985).

D. S. Charney, S. W. Woods, W. K. Goodman, and G. R. Heninger, Serotonin function in anxiety. II. Effects of the serotonin agonist MCPP in panic disorder patients and healthy subjects, *Psychopharmacology, 92*: 14 (1987).

A. Clow, V. Glover, M. W. Weg, P. L. Walker, D. V. Sheehan, and M. Sandler, Urinary catecholamine metabolite and tribulin output during lactate infusion, *Br. J. Psychiatry, 152*: 122 (1988).

M. E. Cohen, and P. D. White, Life situations, emotions and neurocirculatory asthenia (anxiety neurosis, neurasthenia, effort syndrome), *Proc. Assoc. Res. Nerv. Ment. Dis., 29*: 832 (1950).

D. S. Cowley, and G. W. Arana, The diagnostic utility of lactate sensitivity in panic disorder, *Arch. Gen. Psychiatry, 47*: 277 (1990).

D. S. Cowley, and D. L. Dunner, Response to sodium lactate in panic disorder: Relationship to presenting clinical variables, *Psychiatry Res., 25*: 253 (1988).

D. S. Cowley, S. R. Dager, and D. L. Dunner, Lactate-induced panic in primary affective disorder, *Am. J. Psychiatry, 143*: 646 (1986).

D. S. Cowley, S. R. Dager, and D. L. Dunner, Lactate infusions in major depression without panic attacks, *J. Psychiatr. Res., 21*: 243 (1987a).

D. S. Cowley, S. R. Dager, S. I. Foster, and D. L. Dunner, Clinical characteristics and response to sodium lactate of patients with infrequent panic attacks, *Am. J. Psychiatry, 144*: 795 (1987b).

D. S. Cowley, T. S. Hyde, S. R. Dager, and D. L. Dunner, Lactate infusions: The role of baseline anxiety, *Psychiatry Res., 21*: 169 (1987c).

D. S. Cowley, S. R. Dager, J. McClennan, P. R. Roy-Byrne, and D. L. Dunner, Response to lactate infusions in generalized anxiety disorder, *Biol. Psychiatry, 24*: 409 (1988).

D. S. Cowley, S. R. Dager, and D. L. Dunner, Lactate response in patients with primary major depression, *Psychiatry Res., 27*: 357 (1989a).

D. S. Cowley, C. F. Jensen, D. Johannessen, L. Parker, S. R. Dager, and R. D. Walker, Response to sodium lactate infusion in alcoholics with panic attacks, *Am. J. Psychiatry, 146*: 1479 (1989b).

S. R. Dager, D. S. Cowley, D. M. Dorsa, and D. L. Dunner, Plasma beta-endorphin response to lactate infusion, *Biol. Psychiatry, 25*: 243 (1989).

S. R. Dager, J. M. Rainey, M. A. Kenny, A. A. Artu, G. D. Metzger, and D. W. Bowden, Central nervous system effects of lactate infusion in primates, *Biol. Psychiatry, 27*: 193 (1990).

E. DeMet, M. K. Stein, C. Tran, A. Chicz-DeMet, C. Sangdal, and J. Nelson, Caffeine taste test for panic disorder, *Psychiatry Res., 30*: 231 (1989).

J. A. den Boer, H. G. M. Westenberg, A. A. Klompmakers, and L. E. M. van Lint, Behavioral biochemical and neuroendocrine concomitants of lactate-induced panic anxiety, *Biol. Psychiatry, 26*: 612 (1989).

R. Dorow, R. Horowski, G. Paschelke, M. Amin, and C. Braestrup, Severe anxiety induced by FG 7142, a beta-carboline ligand for benzodiazepine receptors, *Lancet, 2*: 98 (1983).

J. D. Easton and D. G. Sherman, Somatic anxiety attacks and propranolol, *Arch. Neurol., 33*: 689 (1976).

A. Ehlers, J. Margraf, W. A. Roth, C. B. Taylor, R. J. Maddock, J. Sheik, M. L. Kopell, K. L. McClenahan, D. Gossard, G. H. Blowers, W. S. Agras, and B. S. Kopell, Lactate infusions and panic attacks: Do patients and controls respond differently? *Psychiatry Res., 17*: 295 (1986).

M. Elam, T. Yao, P. Thoren, and T. H. Svensson, Hypercapnia and hypoxia: Chemoreceptor-mediated control of locus coeruleus neurons and splanchnic, sympathetic nerves, *Brain Res., 222*: 373 (1981).

M. Fink, M. A. Taylor, and J. Volavka, Anxiety precipitated by lactate, *N. Engl. J. Med., 281*: 1429 (1969).

R. R. Freedman, P. Ianni, E. Etteggui, and N. Puthezhath, Ambulatory monitoring of panic disorder, *Arch. Gen. Psychiatry, 42*: 244 (1985).

E. D. Frolich, R. C. Tarazi, and H. P. Dustan, Hyperdynamic beta adrenergic circulatory state, *Arch. Intern. Med., 123*: 1 (1969).

A. J. Fyer, J. M. Gorman, M. R. Liebowitz, M. Levitt, E. Danielson, J. Martinez, and D. F. Klein, Sodium lactate infusion, panic attacks, and ionized calcium, *Biol. Psychiatry, 19*: 1437 (1984).

A. J. Fyer, M. R. Liebowitz, J. M. Gorman, S. O. Davies, and D. F. Klein, Lactate vulnerability of remitted panic patients, *Psychiatry Res., 14*: 143 (1985).

M. R. Fyer, J. Uy, J. Martinez, R. Goetz, D. F. Klein, A. J. Fyer, M. R. Liebowitz, and J. Gorman, CO_2 challenge of patients with panic disorder, *Am. J. Psychiatry, 144*: 1080 (1987).

F. A. Gaffney, B. J. Fenton, L. D. Lane, and C. R. Lake, Hemodynamic, ventilatory, and biochemical responses of panic patients and normal controls with sodium lactate infusion and spontaneous panic attacks, *Arch. Gen. Psychiatry, 45*: 53 (1988).

J. Garcia de Yebenes Prous, A. Carlsson, and M. A. Mena Gomez, The effect of CO_2 on monoamine metabolism in rat brain, *Naunyn Schmiedebergs Arch. Pharmacol., 301*: 11 (1977).

D. T. George, T. D. Brewerton, and D. C. Jimerson, Comparison of lactate-induced anxiety in bulimic patients and healthy controls, *Psychiatry Res., 21*: 213 (1987).

D. T. George, D. J. Nutt, R. P. Waxman, and M. Linnoila, Panic response to lactate administration in alcoholic and nonalcoholic patients with panic disorder, *Am. J. Psychiatry, 146*: 1161 (1989a).

D. T. George, D. J. Nutt, W. V. Walker, S. W. Porges, B. Adinoff, and M. Linnoila, Lactate and hyperventilation substantially attenuate vagal tone in normal volunteers. Possible mechanism of panic provocation? *Arch. Gen. Psychiatry, 46*: 153 (1989b).

A. W. Goddard, D. S. Charney, G. R. Heninger, and S. W. Woods, Effects of fluvoxamine on yohimbine anxiety, *New Research Program and Abstracts*, American Psychiatric Association 143rd Annual Meeting New York, American Psychiatric Association, Washington, D.C., p. 161 (1990).

M. S. Gold, D. E. Redmond, Jr., and H. D. Kleber, Clonidine blocks acute opiate withdrawal symptoms, *Lancet, 2*: 599 (1978).

M. R. Goldberg, and D. Robertson, Yohimbine: A pharmacological probe for study of the alpha 2-adrenoceptor, *Pharmacol. Rev., 35*: 143 (1983).

L. Goldstein, and C. Munoz, Influence of adrenergic stimulant and blocking drugs on cerebral and electrical activity in curarized animals, *J. Pharmacol. Exp. Ther., 132*: 345 (1961).

J. M. Gorman, G. F. Levy, M. R. Liebowitz, P. McGrath, I. L. Appleby, D. J. Dillon, S. O. Davies, and D. F. Klein, Effect of acute beta-adrenergic blockade on lactate-induced panic, *Arch. Gen. Psychiatry, 40*: 1079 (1983).

J. M. Gorman, J. M. Martinez, M. R. Liebowitz, A. J. Fyer, and D. F. Klein, Hypoglycemia and panic attacks, *Am. J. Psychiatry, 141*: 101 (1984a).

J. M. Gorman, M. R. Liebowitz, J. Stein, A. J. Fyer, and D. F. Klein, Insulin levels during lactate infusions, *Am. J. Psychiatry, 141*: 1621 (1984b).

J. M. Gorman, J. Askanazi, M. R. Liebowitz, A. J. Fyer, J. Stein, J. M. Kinney, and D. F. Klein, Response to hyperventilation in a group of patients with panic disorder, *Am. J. Psychiatry, 141*: 857 (1984c).

J. M. Gorman, M. R. Liebowitz, A. J. Fyer, D. Dillon, S. O. Davies, J. Stein, and D. F. Klein, Lactate infusions in obsessive–compulsive disorder, *Am. J. Psychiatry, 142*: 864 (1985a).

J. M. Gorman, A. J. Fyer, D. C. Ross, B. S. Cohen, J. M. Martines, M. R. Liebowitz, and D. F. Klein, Normalization of venous pH, Pco_2, and bicarbonate levels after blockade of panic attacks, *Psychiatry Res., 14*: 57 (1985b).

J. M. Gorman, B. S. Cohen, M. R. Liebowitz, A. J. Fyer, D. Ross, S. O. Davies, and D. F. Klein, Blood gas changes and hypophosphatemia in lactate-induced panic, *Arch. Gen. Psychiatry, 43*: 1067 (1986).

J. M. Gorman, M. R. Liebowitz, D. Dillon, A. J. Fyer, B. S. Cohen, and D. F. Klein, Antipanic drug effects during lactate infusion in lactate-refractory panic patients, *Psychiatry Res., 21*: 205 (1987a).

J. M. Gorman, M. R. Liebowitz, A. J. Fyer, D. Goetz, R. B. Campeas, M. R. Fyer, S. O. Davies, and D. F. Klein, An open trial of fluoxetine in the treatment of panic attacks, *J. Clin. Psychopharmacol., 7*: 329 (1987b).

J. M. Gorman, R. R. Goetz, J. Uy, D. Ross, J. Martinez, A. J. Fyer, M. R. Liebowitz, and D. F. Klein, Hyperventilation occurs during lactate-induced panic, *J. Anxiety Disord., 2*: 193 (1988a).

J. M. Gorman, M. R. Fyer, R. Goetz, J. Askanazi, M. R. Liebowitz, A. J. Fyer, J. Kinney, and D. F. Klein, Ventilatory physiology of patients with panic disorder, *Arch. Gen. Psychiatr., 45*: 31 (1988b).

J. M. Gorman, D. Battista, R. R. Goetz, D. J. Dillon, M. R. Liebowitz, A. J. Fyer, J. P. Kahn, D. Sandberg, and D. F. Klein, A comparison of sodium bicarbonate and sodium lactate infusion in the induction of panic attacks, *Arch. Gen. Psychiatry, 46*: 145 (1989a).

J. M. Gorman, M. R. Liebowitz, A. J. Fyer, and J. Stein, A neuroanatomical hypothesis for panic disorder, *Am. J. Psychiatry, 146*: 148 (1989b).

J. M. Gorman, R. R. Goetz, D. Dillon, M. R. Liebowitz, A. J. Fyer, S. Davies, and D. F. Klein, Sodium D-lactate infusion of panic disorder patients, *Neuropsychopharmacology, 3*: 181 (1990a).

J. M. Gorman, L. A. Papp, J. Martinez, R. R. Goetz, E. Hollander, M. R. Liebowitz, and F. Jordan, High-dose carbon dioxide challenge test in anxiety disorder patients, *Biol. Psychiatry, 28*: 743 (1990b).

S. J. Grant, and D. E. Redmond, Jr., Pharmacology of clonidine, *The Neuroanatomy and Pharmacology of the Nucleus Locus Coeruleus* (H. Lal and S. Fielding, eds.), Alan R. Liss, New York, p. 5 (1981).

J. F. Greden, Anxiety or caffeinism: A diagnostic dilemma, *Am. J. Psychiatry, 131*: 1089 (1974).

E. Griez, and M. A. van den Hout, Effects of carbon dioxide-oxygen inhalations on subjective anxiety and some neurovegetative parameters, *J. Behav. Ther. Exp. Psychiatry, 13*: 27 (1982).

E. Griez, and M. A. van den Hout, Treatment of phobophobia by exposure to CO_2-induced anxiety symptoms, *J. Nerv. Ment. Dis., 171*: 506 (1983a).

E. Griez, and M. A. van den Hout, Carbon dioxide and anxiety: Cardiovascular effects of a single inhalation, *J. Behav. Ther. Exp. Psychiatry, 14*: 297 (1983b).

E. J. L. Griez, H. Lousberg, M. A. van den Hout, and G. M. van der Molen, CO_2 vulnerability in panic disorder, *Psychiatry Res., 20*: 87 (1987).

E. Griez, J. Zandbergen, H. Lousberg, and M. van den Hout, Effects of low pulmonary CO_2 on panic anxiety, *Compr. Psychiatry, 29*: 490 (1988).

H. J. Grosz, and B. B. Farmer, Blood lactate in the development of anxiety symptoms, *Arch. Gen. Psychiatry, 21*: 611 (1969).

H. J. Grosz, and B. B. Farmer, Pitts' and McClure's lactate–anxiety study revisited, *Br. J. Psychiatry, 120*: 415 (1972).

H. J. Grosz, Lactate-induced anxiety: Hypothesis and experimental model, *Br. J. Psychiatry, 122*: 116 (1973).

G. N. M. Gurguis, and T. W. Uhde, Plasma 3-methoxy-4-hydroxyphenylethylene glycol (MHPG) and growth hormone responses to yohimbine in panic disorder patients and normal controls, *Psychoneuroendocrinology, 15*: 217 (1990).

C. L. Hamlin, R. B. Lydiard, D. Martin, C. A. Dackis, A. C. Pottash, D. Sweeney, and M. S. Gold, Urinary excretion of noradrenaline metabolite decreased in panic disorder, *Lancet, 2*: 740 (1983).

W. M. Harrison, D. Sandberg, J. M. Gorman, M. Fyer, J. Nee, J. Uy, and J. Endicott, Provocation of panic with carbon dioxide inhalation in patients with premenstrual dysphoria, *Psychiatry Res., 27*: 183 (1989).

G. Hibbert, and D. Pilsbury, Hyperventilation: Is it a cause of panic attacks? *Br. J. Psychiatry, 155*: 805 (1989).

R. Hoehn-Saric, A. F. Merchant, M. L. Keyser, and V. K. Smith, Effects of clonidine on anxiety disorders, *Arch. Gen. Psychiatry, 38*: 1278 (1981).

G. Holmberg, and S. Gershon, Autonomic and psychic effects of yohimbine hydrochloride, *Psychopharmacologia, 2*: 93 (1961).

Y. H. Huang, J. W. Maas, and D. E. Redmond, Jr., Evidence for noradrenergic specificity of behavioral effects of electrical stimulation of the nucleus locus ceruleus, *Soc. Neurosci. Abstr., 3*: 251 (1977).

R. S. Kahn, H. M. van Praag, S. Wetzler, G. M. Asnis, and G. Barr, Serotonin and anxiety revisited, *Biol. Psychiatry, 23*: 189 (1988).

R. A. Keith, B. B. Howe, and A. I. Salama, Modulation of peripheral beta 1 and alpha 2 receptor sensitivities by the administration of the tricyclic antidepressant imipramine alone and in combination with alpha 2 antagonists to rats, *J. Pharmacol. Exp. Ther., 236*: 356 (1986).

D. Kelly, N. Mitchell-Heggs, and D. Sherman, Anxiety and the effects of sodium lactate assessed clinically and physiologically, *Br. J. Psychiatry, 119*: 129 (1971).

V. J. Knott, and Y. D. Lapierre, Effects of lactate-induced panic attacks on brain stem auditory evoked potentials, *Neuropsychobiology, 16*: 9 (1986).

G. N. Ko, J. D. Elsworth, R. H. Roth, B. G. Rifkin, H. Leigh, and D. E. Redmond, Jr., Panic induced elevation of plasma MHPG levels in phobic–anxious patients. Effects of clonidine and imipramine, *Arch. Gen. Psychiatry, 40*: 425 (1983).

M. A. Lee, O. G. Cameron, and J. F. Greden, Anxiety and caffeine consumption in people with anxiety disorders, *Psychiatry Res., 15*: 211 (1985).

A. P. Levin, A. R. Doran, M. R. Liebowitz, A. J. Fyer, J. M. Gorman, D. F. Klein, and S. M. Paul, Pituitary adrenocortical unresponsiveness in lactate-induced panic, *Psychiatry Res., 21*: 23 (1987).

M. R. Liebowitz, and E. Hollander, Lactate-induced anxiety [editorial], *Biol. Psychiatry, 25*: 669 (1989).

M. R. Liebowitz, A. J. Fyer, J. M. Gorman, D. Dillon, I. L. Appleby, G. Levy, S. Anderson, M. Levitt, M. Palij, S. O. Davies, and D. F. Klein, Lactate provocation of panic attacks. I. Clinical and behavioral findings, *Arch. Gen. Psychiatry, 41*: 764 (1984a).

M. R. Liebowitz, J. M. Gorman, A. J. Fyer, D. J. Dillon, and D. F. Klein, Effects of naloxone on patients with panic attacks, *Am. J. Psychiatry, 141*: 995 (1984b).

M. R. Liebowitz, J. M. Gorman, A. J. Fyer, M. Levitt, D. Dillon, G. Levy, I. L. Appleby, S. Anderson, M. Palij, S. O. Davies, and D. F. Klein, Lactate provocation of panic attacks. II. Biochemical and physiological findings, *Arch. Gen. Psychiatry, 42*: 709 (1985a).

M. R. Liebowitz, A. J. Fyer, J. M. Gorman, D. Dillon, S. Davies, J. M. Stein, B. S. Cohen, and D. F. Klein, Specificity of lactate infusions in social phobia versus panic disorders, *Am. J. Psychiatry, 142*: 947 (1985b).

M. R. Liebowitz, J. M. Gorman, A. Fyer, D. Dillon, M. Levitt, and D. F. Klein, Possible mechanisms for lactate's induction of panic, *Am. J. Psychiatry, 143*: 495 (1986a).

M. R. Liebowitz, A. J. Fyer, J. M. Gorman, R. Campeas, A. Levin, S. R. Davies, D. Goetz, and D. F. Klein, Alprazolam in the treatment of panic disorder, *J. Clin. Psychopharmacol., 6*: 13 (1986b).

D. R. Lima, and P. Turner, Propranolol increases reduced beta-receptor function in severely anxious patients, *Lancet, 2*: 1505 (1983).

E. Lindemann, The psychopathological effect of drugs affecting the vegetative system, *Am. J. Psychiatry, 91*: 983 (1935).

E. Lindemann, and J. Finesinger, The effect of Adrenalin and mecholyl in states of anxiety in psychoneurotic patients, *Am. J. Psychiatry, 95*: 353 (1938).

D. C. Lindy, B. T. Walsh, J. M. Gorman, S. R. Roose, M. Gladis, M. J. Devlin, and A. H. Glassman, Lactate infusions in patients with bulimia, *Psychiatry Res., 26*: 287 (1988).

O. Lingjaerde, Lactate-induced panic attacks: Possible involvement of serotonin reuptake stimulation, *Acta Psychiatr. Scand., 72*: 206 (1985).

H. Lousberg, E. Griez, and M. A. van den Hout, Carbon dioxide chemosensitivity in panic disorder, *Acta Psychiatr. Scand., 77*: 214 (1988).

D. H. Manier, D. D. Gillespie, and F. Sulser, Dual aminergic regulation of central beta adrenoceptors: Effect of "atypical" antidepressants and 5-hydroxytryptophan, *Neuropsychopharmacology, 2*: 89 (1989).

P. J. Marangos, S. M. Paul, A. M. Parma, F. K. Goodwin, P. Syapin, and P. Skolnick, Purinergic inhibition of diazepam binding to rat brain (in vitro), *Life Sci., 2*: 851 (1979).

G. Marañon, Contribution a l'Etude de l'action Emotive de l'adrenaline, *Rev. Fr. Endocrinol., 2*: 301 (1924).

J. Margraf, A. Ehlers, and W. T. Roth, Sodium lactate infusions and panic attacks: A review and critique, *Psychosom. Med., 48*: 23 (1986).

E. Marley, and B. J. Key, Maturation of the electrocorticogram and behaviour in the kitten and guinea-pig and the effect of some sympathomimetic amines, *Electroencephalogr. Clin. Neurophysiol., 15*: 620 (1963).

R. J. Mathew, and W. H. Wilson, Cerebral blood flow in anxiety and panic, *Neurobiology of Panic Disorder* (J. C. Ballenger, ed.), Alan R. Liss, New York, p. 281 (1990a).

R. J. Mathew, and W. H. Wilson, Behavioral and cerebrovascular effects of caffeine in patients with anxiety disorders, *Acta Psychiatr. Scand., 82*: 17 (1990b).

P. J. McGrath, J. W. Stewart, M. R. Liebowitz, J. M. Markowitz, F. M. Quitkin, D. F. Klein, and J. M. Gorman, Lactate provocation of panic attacks in depressed outpatients, *Psychiatry Res., 25*: 41 (1988).

K. P. Minneman, M. D. Dibner, B. B. Wolfe, and P. B. Molinoff, beta 1 And beta 2-adrenergic receptors in rat cerebral cortex are independently regulated, *Science, 20*: 866 (1979).

K. P. Minneman, B. B. Wolfe, and P. B. Molinoff, Selective changes in the density of $beta_1$-adrenergic receptors in rat striatum following chronic drug treatment and adrenalectomy, *Brain Res., 252*: 309 (1982).

S. Motomura, H. R. Zerkowski, A. Daul, and O. E. Brodde, On the physiologic role of beta-2 adrenoceptors in the human heart: In vitro and in vivo studies, *Am. Heart J., 119*: 608 (1990).

Y. Nomura, H. Kajiyama, and K. Oki, Influence of repeated administration of desmethylimipramine of beta-adrenergic and muscarinic cholinergic receptors and Ca^{2+} binding to sarcoplasmic reticulum in the rat heart, *J. Pharmacol. Exp. Ther., 223*: 834 (1982).

R. Noyes, Jr., Beta-blocking drugs and anxiety, *Psychosomatics, 23*: 155 (1982).

R. Noyes, Jr., D. J. Anderson, J. Clancy, R. R. Crowe, D. J. Slymen, M. M. Ghoneim, and J. V. Hinrichs, Diazepam and propranolol in panic disorder and agoraphobia, *Arch. Gen. Psychiatry, 41*: 287 (1984).

A. Orlikov, and I. Ryzov, Caffeine-induced anxiety and increase of kynurenine in plasma of healthy subjects. A pilot study, *Biol. Psychiatry, 29*: 391 (1991).

H. Osswald, *Adenosine and Renal Function. Regulatory Function of Adenosine* (R. M. Berne, T. W. Rall, and R. Rubio, eds.), Martinus Nijhoff, The Hague, p. 399 (1983).

E. R. Peskind, C. F. Jensen, R. C. Veith, J. Hughes, D. S. Cowley, P. Roy-Byrne, and M. Raskind, Hypertonic saline infusion induces panic in patients with panic disorder, *Abstract of Panels and Posters of the 29th Annual Meeting of the American College of Neuropsychopharmacology*, p. 129 (1990).

J. W. Phillips, and P. H. Wu, The role of adenosine in central neuromodulation, *Regulatory Function of Adenosine* (R. M. Berne, T. W. Rall, and R. Rubio, eds.), Martinus Nijhoff, The Hague, p. 419 (1983).

F. N. Pitts, and J. N. McClure, Lactate metabolism and anxiety neurosis, *N. Engl. J. Med., 277*: 1329 (1967).

R. Pohl, E. Ettedgui, M. Bridges, H. Lycaki, D. Jimerson, I. Kopin, and J. M. Rainey, Plasma MHPG levels in lactate and isoproterenol anxiety states, *Biol. Psychiatry, 22*: 1127 (1987).

R. Pohl, V. K. Yeragani, R. Balon, J. M. Rainey, H. Lycaki, A. Ortiz, R. Berchou, and P. Weinberg, Isoproterenol induced panic attacks, *Biol. Psychiatry, 24*: 891 (1988a).

R. Pohl, V. K. Yeragani, R. Balon, and H. Lycaki, The jitteriness syndrome in panic disorder patients treated with antidepressants, *J. Clin. Psychiatry, 49*: 100 (1988b).

R. Pohl, R. Balon, and V. K. Yeragani, Performance anxiety and panic disorder, *J. Clin. Psychopharmacol., 8*: 225 (1988).

R. Pohl, V. K. Yeragani, R. Balon, and H. Lycaki, Lactate and isoproterenol infusions in bulimic patients, *Neuropsychobiology, 22*: 225 (1989).

R. Pohl, V. K. Yeragani, and R. Balon, Effects of isoproterenol in panic disorder patients after antidepressant treatment, *Biol. Psychiatry, 28*: 203 (1990).

T. H. Pringle, J. G. Riddell, and R. G. Shanks, Characterization of the beta-adrenoceptors which mediate the isoprenaline-induced changes in finger tremor and cardiovascular function in man, *Eur. J. Clin. Pharmacol., 35*: 507 (1988).

J. F. Pujol, P. Keane, A. McRae, B. D. Lewis, and B. Renaud, Biochemical evidence for serotonergic control of the locus ceruleus, *Interactions Between Putative Neurotransmitters in the Brain* (S. Garratini, et al., eds.), Raven Press, New York, p. 401 (1978).

R. E. Pyke, and H. S. Greenberg, Norepinephrine challenges in panic patients, *J. Clin. Psychopharmacol., 6*: 279 (1986).

J. M. Rainey, C. E. Frohman, R. R. Freedman, R. B. Pohl, E. Ettedgui, and M. Williams, Specificity of lactate infusion as a model of anxiety, *Psychopharmacol. Bull., 20*: 45 (1984a).

J. M. Rainey, E. Ettedgui, R. Pohl, R. Balon, P. Weinberg, S. Yelonek, and R. Berchou, The beta-receptor: Isoproterenol anxiety states, *Psychopathology, 17* (suppl 3): 40 (1984b).

J. M. Rainey, A. Aleem, A. Ortiz, V. Yeragani, R. Pohl, and R. Berchou, A laboratory procedure for the induction of flashbacks, *Am. J. Psychiatry, 144*: 1317 (1987).

R. Rapee, R. Mattick, and E. Murrell, Cognitive mediation in the affective component of spontaneous panic attacks, *J. Behav. Ther. Exp. Psychiatry, 17*: 245 (1986).

S. A. Rasmussen, W. K. Goodman, S. W. Woods, G. R. Heninger, and D. S. Charney, Effects of yohimbine in obsessive compulsive disorder, *Psychopharmacology, 93*: 308 (1987).

D. E. Redmond, New and old evidence for the involvement of a brain norepinephrine system in anxiety, *Phenomenology and Treatment of Anxiety* (W. E. Fann, I. Karacan, A. D. Pokorny, and R. L. Williams, eds.), Spectrum Press, New York, p. 153 (1979).

D. E. Redmond, Jr., Y. H. Huang, D. R. Snyder, J. W. Mass, and J. Baulu, Behavioral changes following lesions of the nucleus locus ceruleus in macaca arctoides, *Neurosci. Abstr., 1*: 472 (1976a).

D. E. Redmond, Jr., Y. H. Huang, D. R. Snyder, and J. W. Mass, Behavioral effects of stimulation of the nucleus locus ceruleus in the stump-tailed monkey (*Macaca arctoides*), *Brain Res., 116*: 502 (1976b).

S. Rick, H. Beckman, and W. E. Muller, DL-Sodium lactate reduces alpha$_1$-adrenergic receptor binding in rat and mouse brain, *Psychiatry Res., 16*: 241 (1985).

A. Rifkin, D. F. Klein, D. Dillon, and M. Levitt, Blockade by imipramine or desipramine of panic induced by sodium lactate, *Am. J. Psychiatry, 138*: 676 (1981).

E. M. Reiman, M. E. Reichle, E. Robins, M. A. Mintun, M. J. Fusselman, P. T. Fox, J. L. Price, and K. A. Hackman, Neuroanatomical correlates of a lactate-induced anxiety attack, *Arch. Gen. Psychiatry, 46*: 493 (1989).

D. P. Sandberg, and M. R. Liebowitz, Potential mechanisms for sodium lactate's induction of panic, *Neurobiology of Anxiety* (J. C. Ballenger, ed.), *Frontiers of Clinical Neuroscience*, Vol. 8, Alan R. Liss, New York, p. 155 (1990).

W. C. Sanderson, R. M. Rapee, and D. H. Barlow, The influence of an illusion of control on panic attacks induced via inhalation of 5.5% carbon dioxide-enriched air, *Arch. Gen. Psychiatry, 46*: 157 (1989).

F. R. Schneider, M. R. Liebowitz, S. O. Davies, J. Fairbanks, E. Hollander, R. Campeas, and D. F. Klein, Fluoxetine in panic disorder, *J. Clin. Psychopharmacol., 10*: 119 (1990).

M. Segal, Serotonergic innervation of the locus coeruleus from the dorsal raphe and its actions on responses to noxious stimuli, *J. Physiol., 286*: 401 (1979).

H. Shimizu, Adenosine receptors associated with adenylate cyclase system, *Physiology and Pharmacology of Adenosine Derivatives* (J. W. Daly, Y. Kuoda, J. W. Phillips, H. Shimizu, and M. Ui, eds.), Raven Press, New York, p. 31 (1983).

S. Snyder, and P. Sklar, Behavioral and molecular actions of caffeine. Focus on adenosine, *J. Psychiatr. Res., 18*: 91 (1984).

R. S. Stewart, M. D. Devous, A. J. Rush, L. Lane, and F. J. Bonte, Cerebral blood flow changes during sodium-lactate-induced panic attacks, *Am. J. Psychiatry 145*: 442 (1988).

F. Sulser, Regulation and function of noradrenaline receptor systems in the brain: Psychopharmacological aspects, *Neuropharmacology, 23*: 255 (1984).

G. Sunderland, S. Friedman, and L. A. Rosenblum, Imipramine and alprazolam treatment of lactate-induced acute endogenous distress in nonhuman primates, *Am. J. Psychiatry, 146*: 1044 (1989).

S. D. Targum, Differential responses to anxiogenic challenge studies in patients with major depressive disorder and panic disorder, *Biol. Psychiatry, 28*: 21 (1990).

S. D. Targum, Panic attack frequency and vulnerability to anxiogenic challenge studies, *Psychiatry Res., 36*: 75 (1991).

S. D. Targum, and L. E. Marshall, Fenfluramine provocation of anxiety in patients with panic disorder, *Psychiatry Res., 28*: 295 (1989).

C. B. Taylor, J. Sheikh, W. S. Agras, W. T. Roth, J. Margraf, A. Ehlers, R. J. Maddock, and D. Gossard, Ambulatory heart changes in patients with panic attacks, *Am. J. Psychiatry, 143*: 478 (1986).

T. W. Uhde, Caffeine provocation of panic: A focus on biological mechanisms, *Neurobiology of Anxiety* (J. C. Ballenger, ed.), *Frontiers of Clinical Neuroscience*, Vol. 8, Alan R. Liss, New York, p. 219 (1990).

T. W. Uhde, J. P. Boulenger, D. C. Jimerson, and R. M. Post, Caffeine: Relationship to human anxiety, plasma MHPG and cortisol, *Psychopharmacol. Bull., 20*: 426 (1984).

M. A. van den Hout, and E. Griez, Panic symptoms after inhalation of carbon dioxide, *Br. J. Psychiatry, 144*: 503 (1984).

M. A. van den Hout, and E. Griez, Peripheral panic symptoms occur during changes in alveolar carbon dioxide, *Compr. Psychiatry, 26*: 381 (1985).

M. A. van den Hout, G. M. van der Molen, E. Griez, H. Lousberg, and A. Nansen, Reduction of CO_2-induced anxiety in patients with panic attacks after repeated CO_2 exposure, *Am. J. Psychiatry, 144*: 788 (1987).

J. Vetulani, R. J. Stawarz, J. V. Dingel, and F. Sulser, A possible common mechanism of action of antidepressant treatments. Reduction in the sensitivity of the noradrenergic cyclic AMP generating system in limbic forebrain, *Naunyn Schmiedebergs Arch. Pharmacol., 293*: 109 (1976).

H. H. Vincent, A. J. Man in't Veld, F. Boomsma, G. J. Wenting, and M. A. D. H. Schalekemp, Elevated plasma noradrenaline in response to beta-adrenoceptor stimulation in man, *Br. J. Clin. Pharmacol., 13*: 717 (1982).

J. K. Wamsley, W. F. Byerley, R. T. McCabe, E. J. McConnell, T. W. Dawson, and B. I. Grosser, Receptor alterations associated with serotonergic agents: An autoradiographic analysis, *J. Clin. Psychiatry, 48* (suppl): 19 (1987).

J. Wearn, and C. Sturgis, Studies on epinephrine: Effects of the injection of epinephrine in soldiers with "irritable heart," *Arch. Intern. Med., 24*: 247 (1919).

N. Weil-Malherbe, J. Axelrod, and R. Tomchick, Blood–brain barrier for Adrenaline, *Science, 129*: 1226 (1959).

J. Wolpe, Carbon dioxide inhalation treatments of neurotic anxiety, *J. Nerv. Ment. Dis., 175*: 129 (1987).

D. T. Wong, L. R. Reid, F. P. Bymaster, and P. G. Threlkeld, Chronic effects of fluoxetine, a selective inhibitor of serotonin uptake on neurotransmitter receptors, *J. Neural. Transm., 64*: 251 (1985).

S. W. Woods, D. S. Charney, J. Loke, W. K. Goodman, D. E. Redmond, and G. R. Heninger, Carbon dioxide sensitivity in panic anxiety, *Arch. Gen. Psychiatry, 43*: 900 (1986).

S. W. Woods, D. S. Charney, W. K. Goodman, and G. R. Heninger, Carbon dioxide-induced anxiety, *Arch. Gen. Psychiatry, 45*: 43 (1988).

S. W. Woods, J. H. Krystal, G. R. Heninger, and D. S. Charney, Effects of alprazolam and clonidine on carbon dioxide-induced increases in anxiety ratings in healthy human subjects, *Life Sci., 45*: 233 (1989).

S. W. Woods, D. S. Charney, P. L. Delgado, and G. R. Heninger, The effect of long-term imipramine treatment on carbon dioxide-induced anxiety in panic disorder patients, *J. Clin. Psychiatry, 51*: 505 (1990).

V. K. Yeragani, R. Pohl, R. Balon, J. M. Rainey, R. Berchou, and A. Ortiz, Sodium lactate infusions after treatment with tricyclic antidepressants: Behavioral and physiological findings, *Biol. Psychiatry, 24*: 767 (1988a).

V. K. Yeragani, J. M. Rainey, R. Pohl, R. Balon, R. Berchou, S. Jolly, and H. Lycaki, Preinfusion anxiety and laboratory-induced panic attacks in panic disorder patients, *J. Clin. Psychiatry, 49*: 302 (1988b).

V. K. Yeragani, R. Balon, J. M. Rainey, A. Ortiz, R. Berchou, H. Lycaki, and R. Pohl, Effects of laboratory-induced panic–anxiety on subsequent provocative infusion, *Psychiatry Res., 23*: 161 (1988c).

J. Zandbergen, H. H. A. Lousberg, H. Pols, C. de Loof, and E. J. L. Griez, Hypercarbia versus hypocarbia in panic disorder, *J. Affective Disord., 18*: 75 (1990).

C. M. Zitrin, D. F. Klein, and M. G. Woerner, Treatment of agoraphobia with group exposure in vivo and imipramine, *Arch. Gen. Psychiatry, 37*: 63 (1980).

11

Pharmacological Treatment of Panic Disorder

James C. Ballenger
Medical University of South Carolina, Charleston, South Carolina

I. INTRODUCTION

The remarkable advances in the panic disorder field over the past 25 years have resulted in several effective treatments for this condition. This chapter will focus on pharmacological treatments and related issues, although limited attention will be given to treatments combining drugs and behavioral therapies. The four primary classes of drugs used in the treatment of panic disorder (PD) are the monoamine oxidase inhibitor (MAOI) antidepressants and the traditional tricyclic antidepressants (TCAs; Table 1), the selective serotonin-reuptake inhibitors (SSRIs; Table 2), and the benzodiazepines (BZs; Table 3). The various drugs within these classes that have been studied in clinical trials will be reviewed. Briefly, information will be provided on dosing strategies, length of treatment, side effects, and advantages and disadvantages of the different drugs. Following this, a review will be provided on short-term versus long-term treatment and issues related to discontinuation of pharmacotherapy.

II. TRICYCLIC ANTIDEPRESSANTS

The TCAs and the MAOIs were first used in the treatment of PD in the early 1960s. Perhaps the best and most rigorously studied of the TCAs is imipramine. In over a dozen double-blind, placebo-controlled trials (Ballenger et al., 1977; Klein, 1964; Klein and Fink, 1962; Zitrin et al., 1980; Marks et al., 1983; Sheehan et al., 1980; Zitrin et al., 1983), as well as several open trials (Ballenger et al., 1984; Lydiard and Ballenger, 1988; Mavissakalian and Michelson, 1982; Mavissakalian et al., 1983; McNair and Kahn, 1981), imipramine has consistently demonstrated its superiority to placebo in the treatment of panic disorder. The onset of action for imipramine is relatively slow. Generally, 4–6 weeks and, for some patients, 12–24 weeks of treatment with imipramine at

Table 1 Tricyclic and Monoamine Oxidase Inhibitor Antidepressants in the Treatment of Panic Disorder

Pros	Cons
Single daily dose	Hyperstimulatory reaction
Antidepressant	Delayed onset
Generics available	Anticholinergic symptoms
Well-studied	Orthostatic hypotension
More antiphobic (?): MAOIs only	Sexual effects
	Dangerous with overdoses
	Weight gain
	Dietary restrictions: MAOIs only

Table 2 Selective Serotonin Reuptake Inhibitors in Panic Disorder

Pros	Cons
Less weight gain	Slow onset (less than TCAs/MAOIs?)
Less postural hypotension	"Hyperstimulation": slow initial titration
Less anticholinergic side effects	Nausea
Less risk with overdose	Frequent sexual side effects
Antidepressant	Public concern (suicidality)
Once-daily dosing	Cost

Table 3 Benzodiazepines in Panic Disorder

Pros	Cons
Rapid onset	Dependence/withdrawal
Well tolerated	Sedation
Reduce anticipatory anxiety	Multiple daily dosing
Some generics available	Cognitive effects

adequate doses is necessary to achieve clinically significant improvement. Once therapeutic doses have been attained, imipramine is generally effective, with 70–90% of patients experiencing moderate or marked improvement (Ballenger, 1986).

Other TCAs have not been studied as extensively as imipramine, although experience with the SSRIs is accumulating rapidly. Clorimipramine has been efficacious in agoraphobia with panic attacks in open and controlled trials (Amin et al., 1977; Beaumont, 1977; Carey et al., 1975; Escobar and Landbloom, 1976; Gloger et al., 1981; Grunhaus et al., 1984; Karabanow, 1977; Waxman, 1975). Den Boer compared clomipramine with fluvoxamine in a double-blind trial (den Boer et al., 1987) and determined both drugs to be effective in the treatment of PD. In addition, nortriptyline, amitriptyline, and doxepin (Lydiard and Ballenger, 1987) have been effective in the treatment of PD. Maprotiline was also demonstrated useful in PD (Lydiard, 1987; Muskin and Fyer,

1981); however, in a study by den Boer and Westenberg (den Boer and Westenberg, 1988), maprotiline was significantly less effective than fluvoxamine. This suggests that the medications that act on the serotonergic system may be more effective than those for which action is selectively confined to the noradrenergic system. There is also some evidence indicating the superiority of zimelidine to placebo in the treatment of PD (Evans et al., 1986). Gorman et al. (1987) have also shown fluoxetine to be useful for this indication. In Europe experience with the SSRIs, most extensively fluvoxamine, suggests they are at least as effective as traditional antidepressants, but that they may have an earlier onset of action and fewer side effects (see Table 2),

Bupropion was ineffective in a trial by Sheehan et al. (1983). Trazodone was effective in a small study conducted by Mavissakalian et al. (1987). This was not confirmed, however, by Charney's study (Charney et al., 1987), which demonstrated less positive results. The conflicting results of the Mavissakalian and Charney studies point to the need for additional clinical trials to fully determine the usefulness of trazodone in the treatment of PD.

Considerable controversy remains concerning the usefulness of combined treatment (i.e., drugs with some form of behavioral therapy). Mavissakalian et al. (1983) studied agoraphobic patients who were treated with imipramine alone or imipramine plus self-exposure homework. The results of this study demonstrated limited differences between the groups in terms of outcome, although there was some evidence favoring combined treatment. This is generally consistent with the bulk of the available evidence (Mavissakalian, 1990a).

A. Dosing Strategies

In a study conducted by Mavissakalian and Perel (1985), a definite correlation was demonstrated between dose and improvement. Patients in this study who received less than 150 mg/day showed little to no improvement, comparable with the results seen in the placebo patients. In contrast, the group of patients who were maintained on more than 150 mg/day had a significantly higher rate of improvement. Zitrin et al. (1978, 1980, 1983) have found that most patients require 150–200 mg/day for clinically significant improvement, whereas others improve on as little as 25 mg/day, and still others need as much as 200–300 mg/day.

Along these same lines, two studies investigated the optimal serum level of tricyclic necessary to achieve clinical improvement. Ballenger et al. (19B4) studied two groups of 18 patients for 12 weeks. The serum level of imipramine plus its principal metabolite desipramine was maintained between 100 and 150 ng/ml in the first group and between 200 and 250 ng/ml in the second group. In addition to drug treatment, patients were seen weekly in group sessions for support and self-exposure instruction. Surprisingly, there was little difference in response between the two groups, although some outcome measures actually favored the lower serum range. Approximately 75% of the patients in both groups achieved an excellent response, with marked reduction in symptoms and in work and social disability. The results of this study would indicate that patients can be treated effectively at lower serum levels of imipramine, in the 100–150 ng/ml range.

Mavissakalian et al. (1984) subsequently demonstrated a significant relationship between plasma imipramine (not desipramine) and reduction in symptoms in a group of 15 PD patients. These results were replicated in a further study (Mavissakalian, 1990b), again suggesting a threshold level for imipramine in the 125 ng/ml range. Additional studies are needed to determine if there is an optimal dose or serum level for the TCAs necessary to achieve clinically significant results.

B. Dosing Issues

In the clinical setting, imipramine is usually initiated at 10 mg/day for 2 days, with subsequent increases at 10 mg/day every 3–4 days. Clinical experience indicates that if the patient reaches 50 mg/day through gradual increases, higher doses can be tolerated without much difficulty (Ballenger, 1991). If the patient remains unimproved after reaching doses of 150 mg/day, increases should continue over a 4 to 8-week period, until a maximum dose of 300 mg/day has been attained.

The importance of initial low doses and gradual increases cannot be overemphasized. Panic patients are, for the most part, extremely reluctant to begin medication treatment. Concerns include worry over becoming drug-dependent or "addicted"; plus irrational fears that the medication may exacerbate their condition or even kill them; and fear of side effects. Gradually increasing the dose is also very helpful in reducing side effects to a minimum.

C. Advantages and Disadvantages

The TCAs afford the patient once-a-day dosing and, unlike the MAOIs, have no dietary restrictions (see Table 1). They may offer increased protection against recurrent depression and do not put the patient at risk for developing dependence. The biggest drawback to the use of the TCAs, MAOIs, and, perhaps to a smaller extent, the SSRIs, is their delayed onset of action. In most patients, 4–12 weeks are required to achieve clinically significant improvement.

In addition, side effects, particularly the hyperstimulatory response to TCAs and MAOIs can limit their usefulness. About 20–30% of panic patients experience an amphetaminelike reaction, which they describe as feeling like they are "coming out of their skin." In addition, they experience more severe tachycardia and palpitations and increased panic attacks. As mentioned, these reactions are minimized if treatment is initiated at lower doses and increased gradually.

When medication treatment is being discussed, patients should be educated about the potential development of these side effects. However, at the same time, the patient should be reassured that these side effects are generally transient and are not dangerous. The patient should be encouraged to call their physician to discuss management of these symptoms. If relief is not obtained by slowing the increases in dose or transiently reducing the dose, the addition of benzodiazepines or ß-blockers may be helpful. This reaction, although bothersome, generally resolves in 2–3 weeks. Availability of the physician during this time is critical in convincing the patient to remain medication compliant.

About one-third of patients treated long-term with the TCAs also experience significant weight gain (Noyes et al., 1989). This is probably true with the MAOIs, but may be less true with the SSRIs. Other side effects include orthostatic hypotension and sexual side effects. If either have been administered for several months and is suddenly stopped, the patient may develop gastrointestinal distress, a rebound effect (Schatzberg and Ballenger, 1991). A recent study by Taylor et al. (1990) showed mild elevations in blood pressure, although the significance of this is uncertain.

III. MONOAMINE OXIDASE INHIBITOR ANTIDEPRESSANTS

The MAOIs have also been extensively studied for the treatment of PD. The first studies of the MAOIs were conducted in Australia, England, and Canada in the early 1960s, about the same time that imipramine was being studied in the United States. These early studies demonstrated the effectiveness of the MAOIs for this condition (Kelly et al., 1970; King, 1962; Kline, 1967; Sargant, 1962; West and Dally, 1959).

Of the MAOIs, the most frequently studied has been phenelzine. Five placebo-controlled trials with phenelzine (Ballenger et al., 1977; Mountjoy et al., 1977; Sheehan et al., 1980; Solyom et al., 1973, 1981; Tyrer et al., 1973) confirmed its efficacy for this condition. These trials are not as conclusive as those conducted with the TCAs due to the relatively small number of patients studied, relatively low doses used, and mixed diagnoses of the patient population.

The study by Ballenger and Sheehan (Ballenger et al., 1977; Sheehan et al., 1980), however, provides the most definitive results. This trial compared phenelzine, imipramine, and placebo in agoraphobic patients with panic attacks. Patients received phenelzine 45 mg/day, imipramine 150 mg/day, or placebo for 12 weeks, along with self-exposure instruction and group therapy. Although significant improvement was achieved by the placebo group, patients in both the phenelzine and imipramine groups showed superior efficacy with greater reduction in phobic anxiety and fears, agoraphobic avoidance, work and social disability, and general anxiety. The phenelzine-treated patients showed significantly greater improvement than the imipramine-treated patients on the two physician- and patient-rated behavioral scales that evaluated severity of phobic and avoidance symptoms and performance in work and social situations. Approximately 75% of the patients in the phenelzine group demonstrated clinically significant results, with marked improvement or alleviation of symptoms. Some of the patients on active drug continued to show improvement following the study as medication was increased, making it difficult to determine if the phenelzine–imipramine difference was dose-related.

Three open studies have subsequently demonstrated the efficacy of phenelzine. In a study conducted by Buiges and Vallejo (1987), PD patients with and without panic attacks were treated with phenelzine at a mean dose of 55 mg/day. Patients in this study experienced almost total relief from panic symptoms. A second study compared phenelzine at a mean dose of 53 mg/day, with lorazepam, alprazolam, and imipramine, combined with self-exposure homework for 12 weeks (Ballenger et al., 1987; Howell et al., 1987). Excellent results were obtained overall, with marginal superiority demonstrated for phenelzine. Sheehan (1986) compared alprazolam, imipramine, phenelzine, and placebo. All drugs were effective, with comparable rates of response.

Iproniazid has also been studied in a double-blind, placebo-controlled trial of 60 outpatients for 8 weeks (Lipsedge et al., 1973). Results showed that iproniazid was significantly more effective in decreasing anxiety, but not phobic avoidance.

Compelling evidence points to the usefulness of the MAOIs in the treatment of PD. However, additional controlled studies are necessary, particularly with the new reversible MAOIs which may have fewer side effects and may not require special dietary restrictions.

A. Dosing Strategies

Phenelzine treatment is generally initiated at doses of 15 mg/day, with 15 mg/day increases every 3–4 days, until a total dosage of 60 mg/day is attained. Patients are instructed to take phenelzine on rising and at lunch, to reduce the chances of developing insomnia. Treatment should be maintained at 45–60 mg/day for 8–12 weeks. However, if improvement is not seen at this dose, phenelzine can be increased to 75–90 mg/day.

B. Advantages/Disadvantages

Similar to the TCAs, the MAOIs appear to provide prophylaxis against depression with no risk of medication dependence (see Table 1). The MAOIs are known for the strict dietary restrictions necessary to minimize the chances of a tyramine-induced hypertensive episode. Many common foods and medicines must be avoided while taking an MAOI, including some cheeses, aged meats, red wine, and caffeine products. These restrictions are problematic for some patients and have limited the usefulness of the MAOIs.

The most common side effects seen with the MAOIs include insomnia; hence, the dosing regimen described earlier, and weight gain. The MAOIs, like the TCAs, also have delayed onset of action and generally require 8–12 weeks to achieve clinically significant improvement. Other side effects include postural hypotension and sexual difficulties.

Currently, there are at least two reversible MAOIs being studied in the United States and Europe for the treatment of PD. If they are as effective as predicted, they could represent significant advances because special diets will probably not be required and there should be little if any risk of hypertensive or hyperpyrexic tyramine reactions.

IV. BENZODIAZEPINES

More recently, clinical trials have been conducted with the high-potency benzodiazepines (BZs). Alprazolam has been studied most extensively and rigorously and has been demonstrated to be effective in the treatment of PD.

Chouinard et al. (1982) conducted the first double-blind trial comparing alprazolam with placebo in patients with PD and generalized anxiety disorder. Of the 14 patients studied, 8 had a moderate or excellent response to alprazolam administered at a mean dose of 2.06 mg/day. Subsequently, 12 controlled studies, 9 of which were placebo-controlled, have replicated the efficacy of alprazolam in this condition.

The Cross-National Phase I trial reported by Ballenger et al. (1988) is one of the largest studies performed on panic disorder to date. Alprazolam was compared with placebo, without behavioral therapy, in 526 patients. The study definitively demonstrated the superiority of alprazolam over placebo, with approximately 50% of the alprazolam patients showing marked improvement, and an additional 40% with moderate improvement with the medication alone, without behavioral treatment. Alprazolam was successful in reducing both spontaneous and situational PAs, with approximately 60% of the patients experiencing complete cessation of PAs at the end of the 8-week trial. Alprazolam also reduced phobias, phobic anxiety, anticipatory anxiety, and work, family, and social disabilities to the almost normal range in the 8-week period. Improvement with alprazolam was sustained without loss of efficacy, even while dosage was reduced over the next 6–23 months following the study. Recent data suggest that 6 mg may be more effective than 2 mg, especially for complete resolution of PAs and reduction of phobic behavior (Lydiard et al., 1992; Uhlenhuth et al., 1989). However, the lower dose was effective in a smaller percentage of patients, and again, reduced all of the psychopathological features of PD, although to a somewhat smaller degree.

The Cross National Phase II trial was even larger, and compared alprazolam, imipramine, and placebo in 1168 patients (Cross National Collaborative Panic Study, Second Phase Investigators, 1992; Rosenberg et al., 1991). This study essentially replicated the results of the earlier trial, confirming the efficacy of alprazolam, as well as imipramine. Although imipramine was slower in achieving therapeutic efficacy, with significant improvement not seen until week 4 of treatment, by week 8, both alprazolam and imipramine were comparable in effectiveness.

Two additional studies deserve comment. In a study by Liebowitz et al. (1986), 30 patients were treated with alprazolam for 12 weeks. Results demonstrated 65% of the subjects had significant clinical improvement, with best results seen in reduction of PAs, and more variable results for anticipatory anxiety and phobic avoidance. Alexander and Alexander (1986) treated 27 PD patients in a private practice setting, 23 of whom also suffered from agoraphobia, with alprazolam, at a mean dose of 2.2 mg/day, a relatively low dose. In this study, 85% of the patients experienced complete resolution of PAs. In addition, 21 of the 23 agoraphobic patients also experienced resolution of their phobic avoidance behavior. These studies demonstrate the effectiveness of alprazolam in the treatment of PD, with effectiveness comparable with the TCAs and MAOIs.

Comparison studies have been conducted with alprazolam and other psychopharmacological treatments for PD, including antidepressants (Ballenger et al., 1987; Charney et al., 1986; Rizley et al., 1986; Sheehan et al., 1983), ibuprofen (Sheehan et al., 1984), adinazolam (Pyke and Greenberg, 1989), propranolol (Munjack et al., 1989), diazepam (Dunner et al., 1986), lorazepam (Charney and Woods, 1989), and clonazepam (Tesar et al., 1987). All of these studies have confirmed the comparable efficacy of alprazolam in the treatment of PD as well as its rapid onset of action.

In addition to alprazolam, clonazepam has also been demonstrated to be particularly effective in panic disorder. Tesar and Rosenbaum (1986) treated ten PD patients, described as treatment-resistant, with clonazepam. Treatment-resistant was defined for the purposes of this study as patients having received traditional treatments, including alprazolam, without achieving clinically significant results. In this study 70% of the patients experienced total resolution of their panic symptomatology on clonazepam, with the remaining 30% having some relief from their symptoms (Tesar and Rosenbaum, 1986). Tesar (1990) subsequently conducted a retrospective study of 50 treatment-resistant patients. This study also indicated good results with clonazepam, with 90% of the patients demonstrating efficacy equivalent to other traditional drugs prescribed for long-term treatment (Pollack et al., 1986). Tesar then treated 72 PD patients, with or without agoraphobia, with alprazolam, clonazepam, or placebo for 6 weeks (Tesar et al., 1987). Alprazolam and clonazepam were comparable in terms of efficacy, with patients on both drugs experiencing rapid relief in the first week of treatment, which continued throughout the 6 weeks of the study. Side effects most frequently reported were sedation and ataxia, which were not sufficiently bothersome to interfere with study results and, by the end of the trial, had for the most part resolved.

Diazepam, when administered at high doses, roughly ten times that used with alprazolam, was also effective (Dunner et al., 1986). Lorazepam also has demonstrated efficacy in open studies (Howell et al., 1987; Rickels and Schweizer, 1986; Schweizer et al., 1987). In a double-blind, placebo-controlled trial with lorazepam and alprazolam, as well as behavioral therapy, the two drugs were shown to be equally effective, with significant clinical improvement in panic symptoms. The patients receiving alprazolam, however, tended to rate themselves as more improved (Charney and Woods, 1989). Bronazepam (Beaudry et al., 1984) and oxazepam (Fogelson, 1988) have also been effective for this indication.

A. Dosing Strategies

Patients usually begin alprazolam treatment at doses of 0.25 or 0.5 mg, three times a day. The medication is then increased by 1 tablet every 4–6 days, as needed and tolerated. If side effects, primarily sedation, are particularly bothersome, the patient should be maintained for a longer period before the next increase is implemented. Some patients respond to relatively low doses of 1.5–2.0 mg/day (Lydiard et al., 1992); however, 3–6 mg/day appears to be effective for most patients, with others requiring as much as 6–10 mg/day. The acute response generally lasts only 4–6 h; therefore, alprazolam must be administered multiple times a day in most patients.

B. Advantages and Disadvantages

One of the greatest advantages to using the BZs is their rapid onset of action, with significant relief occurring in the first week of treatment (see Table 3). In addition, the BZs are well tolerated, often more so than the other agents traditionally used for this condition. They are also effective in reducing the anticipatory anxiety associated with PD.

The most frequently reported side effects include sedation, ataxia, and sexual difficulties at higher doses. As mentioned earlier, it is also necessary to administer this medication multiple times a day to provide continuous antianxiety coverage. The BZs have also received recent negative publicity concerning their risk for developing dependence and a withdrawal syndrome on termination. Clinical experience shows, however, that if the BZs are tapered gradually and flexibly and the patient is educated about what to anticipate during discontinuation, most patients can tolerate the transient recurrence of the mild-to-moderate symptoms, if they occur, without major difficulties (Fontaine et al., 1984; Pecknold, 1990).

C. Short- Versus Long-Term Treatment

The length of time that PD patients have been ill when presenting for treatment, generally a decade or longer, implies that PD is a chronic condition, requiring long-term treatment in most patients. The treatment model proposed by Ballenger (1991) divides treatment into three phases, beginning with the acute phase, which typically takes place over months 1–3 of treatment. The goal of the initial phase of treatment is significant reduction in many of the panic symptoms. After an initial positive response has been achieved, the patient is entered into a maintenance phase of treatment, usually over months 3–12 of treatment. During this period, the initial improvement is expanded, hopefully with subsequent restoration of the patient's self-esteem and full return to normal activities of life. The final stage of treatment, generally occurring 8–12 months after treatment initiation and perhaps 6 months after recovery is the taper or discontinuation period. This phase of treatment should be accomplished slowly and gradually to reduce the chances of relapse or development of a withdrawal syndrome. Some patients discover that after several months off medicine, their symptoms return (relapse). Collaboratively, the patient and physician must then make a decision about reinstituting psychopharmacological treatment, either with the patient's original medicine or another drug. However, many times the relapse is not severe enough to require medication treatment, in which event, reassurance by the clinician is adequate.

Data concerning long-term versus short-term treatment of PD patients are limited. However, a recent study by Curtis et al. (1990) demonstrated that 8 months of treatment with alprazolam and imipramine was superior to 2 months of treatment. Also a study by Fyer et al. (1989) provides additional evidence of the need for long-term treatment. Patients in this study were treated with alprazolam or imipramine for 6 months, with 50–55% of all patients experiencing total resolution of panic symptomatology at 8 weeks. Eight weeks after discontinuation of the medication, 44% of the imipramine and 55% of the alprazolam patients had recurrent panic, although the alprazolam patients had been tapered at a much more rapid rate than is currently recommended. Only 21% of the imipramine and 14% of the alprazolam patients were able to discontinue medication and remain well.

Further clarification has been provided for long-term outcome, in a follow-up study 3–6 years after patients were briefly treated with alprazolam or imipramine. This study included 423 patients, 75% of whom responded that they had not been taking the drugs continuously. The study asked how many subjects were currently taking the drug, and approximately 55% of the total responded affirmatively, with 23.4% taking a benzodiazepine, 11.7% an antidepressant, 9% taking both, or 11.2% taking a different medication. Of the 423 patients, only 18.2% had been continuously well. During follow-up an additional 12.7% recovered and remained well. Of the remaining subjects, 23.6% experienced subclinical symptoms alternating with periods of total recovery, 26.8% suffered from subclinical symptoms continuously, and 18% had clinically severe PD for the entire follow-up period (Katschnig et al., 1988).

V. DISCONTINUATION

There are several valid reasons for discontinuing effective medication treatment. However, the physician should carefully consider whether the patient is at a point in treatment where taper or discontinuation is appropriate and if the reasons expressed for terminating medication are good ones. It is certainly appropriate to reassess the patient's continued need for medication treatment following successful pharmacotherapy that has allowed the patient to regain and maintain pre-illness levels of functioning. The most important reason is that perhaps continued treatment is no longer needed. Side effects that cannot be tolerated or managed are also good reasons for considering termination or a change in medication. The patient's wish to become pregnant is also an appropriate reason for terminating pharmacotherapy.

Although not as appropriate as those outlined in the preceding paragraph, the following issues have some merit and should receive collaborative consideration by the physician and patient. The expense associated with medication treatment is an issue. Some patients may be bothered by self-esteem issues associated with their perceived need for medication and their feelings about a lack of control of their illness. Another issue that sometimes surfaces includes the development of a substance abuse problem, in which case it would probably be more appropriate to treat the PD with one of the antidepressants, as opposed to the benzodiazepines.

Probably the least appropriate reasons for terminating treatment include the following. Patients and family members may express undue concern over potentially harmful long-term effects of the drugs. This concern can be allayed through reassurance, backed up by clinical data, that there is little to no evidence of adverse physical effects associated with long-term treatment with the MAOIs, TCAs, SSRIs, or BZs, except the risk of withdrawal symptoms with the BZs (Rickels et al., 1990). Panic disorder patients, as a general rule, are extremely reluctant to begin and then continue medication treatment, expressing worry over becoming "addicted" or "dependent" on the drugs. Again, reassurance and education that there is no evidence of patients becoming addicted or drug abusers (Rifkin et al., 1989; Katschnig et al., 1989) may be adequate to ensure that the patient remains medication compliant. The fear of becoming addicted may be confused with concerns about physiological dependence or development of withdrawal symptoms on discontinuation. If the taper and the complex discontinuation process are properly managed (Ballenger, 1992), difficulties with the withdrawal syndrome can be minimized (see the following section). These all represent generally poor reasons for terminating medication treatment, but are issues that may necessitate considerable reassurance by the physician to convince the patient that the drug is needed and in most patients, if taken correctly, is effective.

A. Discontinuation Process

The decision to terminate medication treatment should be a collaborative one between the physician and patient. Also, timing is critical. To enhance the patient's chances of remaining well, discontinuation should not be undertaken during a stressful or difficult time. In addition, it has been shown that patients fare better if the medicine is tapered slowly, gradually, and flexibly (Pecknold, 1990; Pecknold et al., 1988). Education is important, and discontinuation should be discussed early in treatment, with careful explanation of possible outcomes and management of symptoms. If the taper is then conducted slowly in a flexible individualized fashion, and if the patient has been adequately educated and supported, most individuals can tolerate the discontinuation process without undue difficulty.

B. Discontinuation Outcomes

What actually happens when the medication is discontinued? Ideally, the patient will remain well, functioning at a pre-illness level. However, some patients may experience transient withdrawal symptoms, including the recurrence of panic symptomatology. In most patients, these symptoms generally resolve relatively quickly, within 1–3 weeks. There also exists the possibility that the patient may experience rebound panic, generally associated with symptoms more severe than those experienced pretreatment. Again, this condition is transient and should resolve within 2 weeks.

The least desirable outcome is relapse. The patient may find that, after an adequate reassessment period without medicine (3 weeks to allow transient withdrawal symptoms to resolve), they remain symptomatic or are becoming increasingly symptomatic. The physician and patient will then need to determine together if any treatment should be reinstated. Severity of symptoms and the patient's tolerance of these symptoms are obviously critical factors in making this decision.

REFERENCES

P. E. Alexander, and D. D. Alexander, Alprazolam treatment for panic disorders, *J. Clin. Psychiatry, 47*: 301 (1986).

M. M. Amin, T. A. Ban, J. C. Pecknold, and A. Klinger, Chlorimipramine (Anafranil) and behavior therapy in obsessive compulsive and phobic disorders, *J. Int. Med. Res., 5*: 33 (1977).

J. C. Ballenger, Pharmacotherapy of the panic disorders, *J. Clin. Psychiatry, 47*(6): 27 (1986).

J. C. Ballenger, Long-term pharmacologic treatment of panic disorder, *J. Clin. Psychiatry, 52*(2): 18 (1991).

J. C. Ballenger, Medication discontinuation in panic disorder, *J. Clin. Psychiatry, 53*–(3S): 26 (1992).

J. C. Ballenger, G. D. Burrows, R. L. DuPont, Jr., I. M. Lesser, R. Noyes, J. C. Pecknold, A. Rifkin, and R. P. Swinson, Alprazolam in panic disorder and agoraphobia: Results from a multicenter trial. I: Efficacy in short-term treatment, *Arch. Gen. Psychiatry, 45*: 413 (1988).

J. C. Ballenger, E. F. Howell, M. Laraia, and R. B. Lydiard, "Comparison of Four Medicines in Panic Disorder," Presented at 140th Annual Meeting of the American Psychiatric Association, Chicago, May 14, 1987.

J. C. Ballenger, G. A. Peterson, M. Laraia, A. Hucek, C. R. Lake, D. Jimerson, D. J. Cox, C. Trockman, J. Shipe, Jr., and C. Wilkinson, A study of plasma catecholamines in agoraphobia and the relationship of serum tricyclic levels to treatment response, *Biology of Agoraphobia* (J. C. Ballenger, ed.), American Psychiatric Association Press, Washington, D.C. (1984).

J. C. Ballenger, D. V. Sheehan, and G. Jacobsen, Antidepressant treatment of severe phobic anxiety, *Abstracts of the Scientific Proceedings of the 130th Annual Meeting of the American Psychiatric Association*, Toronto, May, 1977.

P. Beaudry, R. Fontaine, and G. Chouinard, Bromazepam, another high-potency benzodiazepine for panic attacks [letter], *Am. J. Psychiatry, 141*: 464 (1984).

G. Beaumont, A large open multicentre trial of clomipramine (Anafranil) in the management of phobic disorders, *J. Int. Med. Res., 5*: 116 (1977).

J. Buiges, and J. Vallejo, Therapeutic response to phenelzine in patients with panic disorder and agoraphobia with panic attacks, *J. Clin. Psychiatry, 48*: 55 (1987).

M. S. Carey, R. Hawkinson, A. Kornhaber, and C. S. Wellish, The use of clomipramine in phobic patients: Preliminary research report, *Curr. Ther. Res., 17*: 107 (1975).

D. S. Charney, and S. W. Woods, Benzodiazepine treatment of panic disorder: A comparison of alprazolam and lorazepam, *J. Clin. Psychiatry, 50*: 418 (1989).

D. S. Charney, S. W. Woods, W. K. Goodman, B. Rifkin, M. Kinch, B. Aiken, L. M. Quadrino, and G. R. Heninger, Drug treatment of panic disorder: The comparative efficacy of imipramine, alprazolam, and trazodone, *J. Clin. Psychiatry, 47*: 580 (1986).

G. Chouinard, L. Annable, R. Fontaine, and L. Solyom, Alprazolam in the treatment of generalized anxiety and panic disorders: A double-blind, placebo-controlled study. *Psychopharmacology, 77*: 229 (1982).

Cross-National Collaborative Panic Study, Second Phase Investigators, Drug treatment of panic disorder: Comparative efficacy of alprazolam, imipramine and placebo, *Br. J. Psychiatry, 160*: 191 (1992).

G. C. Curtis, J. Massana, C. Udina, and J. L. Ayuso-Gutierrez, "Maintenance drug therapy of panic disorder," *New Research Programs and Abstracts,* NR 304, p. 154, Presented at the 143rd Annual Meeting of the American Psychiatric Association, New York, May 12–17, 1990

J. A. den Boer, and H. G. M. Westenberg, Effect of a serotonin and noradrenaline uptake inhibitor in panic disorder; a double blind comparative study with fluvoxamine and maprotiline, *Int. Clin. Psychopharmacol., 3*: 59 (1988).

J. A. den Boer, H. G. M. Westenberg, W. D. F. Kamerbeek, W. M. A. Verhoeven, and R. S. Kahn, Effect of serotonin uptake inhibitors in anxiety disorders: A double-blind comparison of clomipramine and fluvoxamine, *Int. Clin. Psychopharmacol, 2*: 21 (1987).

D. L. Dunner, D. Ishiki, D. H. Avery, L. G. Wilson, and T. S. Hyde, Effect of alprazolam and diazepam on anxiety and panic attacks in panic disorder: A controlled study, *J. Clin. Psychiatry, 47*: 458-460 (1986).

J. I. Escobar, and R. P. Landbloom, Treatment of phobic neurosis with chlorimipramine: A controlled clinical trial, *Curr. Ther. Res., 20*: 680 (1976).

L. Evans, J. Kenardy, P. Schneider, and H. Hoey, Effect of a selective serotonin uptake inhibitor in agoraphobia with panic attacks: A double-blind comparison of zimeldine, imipramine and placebo, *Acta Psychiatr. Scand., 73*: 49 (1986).

D. L. Fogelson, Lorazepam and oxazepam in the treatment of panic disorder [letter], *J. Clin. Psychopharmacol., 8*: 150 (1988).

R. Fontaine, G. Chouinard, and L. Annable, Rebound anxiety in anxious patients after abrupt withdrawal of benzodiazepine treatment, *Am. J. Psychiatry, 141*: 848 (1984).

A. J. Fyer, M. R. Liebowitz, J. M. Gorman, D. Goetz, and D. F. Klein, "Comparative discontinuation of alprazolam and imipramine in panic patients," *Abstracts of Panels and Posters, 27th Annual Meeting of the American College of Neuropsychopharmacology*, p. 145 December 11–16, 1988, San Juan, Puerto Rico.

S. Gloger, L. Grunhaus, B. Birmacher, and T. Troudart, Treatment of spontaneous panic attacks with chlorimipramine, *Am. J. Psychiatry, 138*: 1215 (1971).

J. Gorman, M. R. Liebowitz, A. J. Fyer, D. Goetz, R. B. Compeas, M. R. Fyer, S. O. Davies, and D. F. Klein, An open trial of fluoxetine in the treatment of panic attacks, *J. Clin. Psychopharmacol., 7*: 329 (1987).

L. Grunhaus, S. Gloger, and B. Birmacher, Chlorimipramine for panic attacks in patients with mitral valve prolapse, *J. Clin. Psychiatry, 45*: 25 (1984).

E. F. Howell, M. T. Laraia, J. C. Ballenger, and R. B. Lydiard, "Lorazepam Treatment of Panic Disorder," Presented at the 140th Annual Meeting of the American Psychiatric Association, Chicago, May 9–15, 1987.

O. Karabanow, Double-blind controlled study in phobias and obsessions, *J. Int. Med. Res. 5*: 42 (1977).

H. Katschnig, J. Stolk, G. L. Klerman, J. C. Ballenger, M. Amering, A. Briggs, R. Buller, O. Cassano, M. Garvey, M. Roth, and C. Solyom, "Long-Term Follow-up of Panic Disorder. I: Clinical Outcome of a Large Group of Patients Participating in an International Multicenter Clinical Drug Trial," Presented at the 27th Annual Meeting of the American College of Neuropsychopharmacology, December 11–16, 1988, San Juan, Puerto Rico.

D. Kelly, W. Guirguis, E. Frommer, N. Mitchell-Heggs, and W. Sargent, Treatment of phobic states with antidepressants. A retrospective study of 246 patients, *Br. J. Psychiatry, 116*: 387 (1970).

A. King, Phenelzine treatment of Roth's calamity syndrome, *Med. J. Aust., 1*: 879 (1962).

D. F. Klein, Delineation of two drug-responsive anxiety syndromes, *Psychopharmacologia, 53*: 397 (1964).

D. F. Klein, and M. Fink, Psychiatric reaction patterns to imipramine, *Am. J. Psychiatry, 119*: 432 (1962).

N. Kline, Drug treatment of phobic disorders, *Am. J. Psychiatry, 123*: 1447 (1967).

M. R. Liebowitz, A. J. Fyer, J. M. Gorman, R. Campeas, A. Levin, S. Davies, D. Goetz, and D. F. Klein, Alprazolam in the treatment of panic disorders, *J. Clin. Psychopharmacol., 6*: 13 (1986).

M. S. Lipsedge, J. Hajioff, P. Huggins, L. Napier, J. Pearce, D. F. Pike, and M. Rich, The management of severe agoraphobia: A comparison of iproniazid and systematic desensitization, *Psychopharmacologia, 32*: 67 (1973).

R. B. Lydiard, Successful utilization of maprotoline in a patient intolerant of tricyclics, *J. Clin. Psychopharmacol, 7*: 113 (1987).

R. B. Lydiard, and J. C. Ballenger, Antidepressants in panic disorder and agoraphobia, *J. Affective Disord., 13*: 153 (1987).

R. B. Lydiard, and J. C. Ballenger, Panic-related disorders: Evidence for efficacy of the antidepressants, *J. Anxiety Disord., 2*: 77 (1988).

R. B. Lydiard, I. M. Lesser, J. C. Ballenger, R. T. Rubin, M. Laraia, and R. DuPont, A fixed-dose study of alprazolam 2 mg, alprazolam 6 mg and placebo in panic disorder, *J. Clin. Psychopharmacol.* 1992; *12*(2): 96–103.

I. M. Marks, S. Gray, D. Cohen, R. Hill, D. Mawson, E. Ramm, and R. Stern, Imipramine and brief therapist-aided exposure in agoraphobics having self-exposure homework, *Arch. Gen. Psychiatry, 40*: 153 (1983).

M. Mavissakalian, Differential efficacy between tricyclic antidepressants and behavior therapy of panic disorder, *Clinical Aspects of Panic Disorder* (J. C. Ballenger, ed.), Wiley–Liss, New York, pp. 195–210 (1990a).

M. Mavissakalian, Relationship of dose/plasma concentrations of imipramine to the treatment of panic disorder with agoraphobia, *Clinical Aspects of Panic Disorder*, (J. C. Ballenger, ed.), Wiley–Liss, New York, pp. 211–218 (1990b).

M. Mavissakalian, and L. Michelson, Agoraphobia: Behavioral and pharmacological treatment, preliminary outcome, and process findings, *Psychopharmacol. Bull., 18*: 91 (1982).

M. Mavissakalian and J. Perel, Imipramine in the treatment of agoraphobia: Dose-response relationship, *Am. J. Psychiatry, 142*: 1032 (1985).

M. Mavissakalian, L. Michelson, and R. S. Dealy, Pharmacological treatment of agoraphobia. Inipramine versus imipramine with programmed practice, *Br. J. Psychiatry, 143*: 348 (1983).

M. Mavissakalian, J. M. Perel, and L. Michelson, The relationship of plasma imipramine and *N*-desmethylimipramine to improvement in agoraphobia, *J. Clin. Psychopharmacol., 4*: 36 (1984).

M. Mavissakalian, J. Perel, K. Bowler, and R. Dealy, Trazodone in the treatment of panic disorder and agoraphobia with panic attacks, *Am. J. Psychiatry, 144*: 785 (1987).

D. M. McNair, and R. J. Kahn, Imipramine compared with a benzodiazepine for agoraphobia, *Anxiety: New Research and Changing Concepts* (D. F. Klein and J. G. Rabkin, eds.), Raven Press, New York (1981).

C. Q. Mountjoy, M. Roth, R. F. Garside, and I. M. Leitch, A clinical trial of phenelzine in anxiety depressive and phobic neuroses, *Br. J. Psychiatry, 131*: 486 (1977).

D. J. Munjack, B. Crocker, D. Cabe, D. McDowell, R. Palmer, and M. Leonard, Alprazolam, propranolol, and placebo in the treatment of panic disorder and agoraphobia with panic attacks, *J. Clin. Psychopharmacol., 9*: 22 (1989).

P. R. Muskin, and A. J. Fyer, Treatment of panic disorder, *J. Clin. Psychopharmacol., 1*: 81 (1981).

R. Noyes, Jr., M. J. Garvey, B. L. Cook, and L. Samuelson, Problems with tricyclic antidepressant use in patients with panic disorder or agoraphobia: Results of a naturalistic follow-up study, *J. Clin. Psychiatry, 50*: 163 (1989).

J. C. Pecknold, "Discontinuation Reactions to Alprazolam in Panic Disorder," Presented at the Panic Conference, Carlsbad, California, November 27–30, 1990.

J. C. Pecknold, R. P. Swinson, K. Kuch, and C. P. Lewis, Alprazolam in panic disorder and agoraphobia: Results from a multicenter trial, III: Discontinuation effects, *Arch. Gen. Psychiatry, 45*: 429 (1988).

M. H. Pollack, G. E. Tesar, J. F. Rosenbaum, and S. A. Spier, Clonazepam in the treatment of panic disorder and agoraphobia: A one year follow-up, *J. Clin. Psychopharmacol., 6*: 302 (1986).

R. E. Pyke, and H. S. Greenberg, Norepinephrine challenges in panic patients, *J. Clin. Psychopharmacol, 6*: 279 (1986).

K., Rickels, and E. E. Schweizer, Benzodiazepines for treatment of panic attacks: A new look, Psychopharmacol. Bull., 22: 93 (1986).

K. Rickels, E. Schweizer, W. G. Case, and D. J. Greenblatt, Long-term therapeutic use of benzodiazepines. I: Effects of abrupt discontinuation, *Arch. Gen. Psychiatry, 47*: 899 (1990).

A. Rifkin, S. Doddi, B. Karajgi, N. Hasan, and L. Alvarez, Benzodiazepine use and abuse by patients at outpatient clinics, *Am. J. Psychiatry, 146*: 1331 (1989).

R. Rizley, R. J. Kahn, D. M. McNair, and L. M. Frankenthaler, A comparison of alprazolam and imipramine in the treatment of agoraphobia and panic disorder, *Psychopharmacol. Bull., 22*: 167 (1986).

R. Rosenberg, J. O. Ottosson, P. Bech, and M. Mellergard (eds.), Alprazolam, imipramine and placebo treatment of panic disorder in Scandinavia, *Acta Psychiatr. Scand. [Suppl.] 364*: (1991).

W. Sargant, The treatment of anxiety states and atypical depressions by the monoamine oxidase inhibitor drugs, *J. Neuropsychiatry, 3*: 96 (1962).

A. F. Schatzberg, and J. C. Ballenger, Decisions for the clinician in the treatment of panic disorder: When to treat, which treatment to use, and how long to treat, *J. Clin. Psychiatry, 52*: 26 (1991).

E. E. Schweizer, I. Fox, and W. G. Case, "Alprazolam Versus Lorazepam in the Treatment of Panic Disorder," Presented at the New Clinical Drug Evaluation Unit Meeting, Key Biscayne, Florida, May 1987.

D. V. Sheehan, "Tricyclic Antidepressants in the Treatment of Anxiety Disorders," Presented at the 139th Annual Meeting of the American Psychiatric Association, Washington, D.C., May 1986.

D. V. Sheehan, J. Ballenger, and G. Jacobsen, Treatment of endogenous anxiety with phobic, hysterical and hypochondriacal symptoms, *Arch. Gen. Psychiatry, 37*: 51 (1980).

D. V. Sheehan, J. B. Claycomb, and O. S. Surman, "The Relative Efficacy of Alprazolam, Phenelzine, and Imipramine in Treating Panic Attacks and Phobias," Presented at the Symposium on the Biology of Panic-Related Anxiety Disorders, Boston, Mass. November 1983.

D. V. Sheehan, J. H. Coleman, D. J. Greenblatt, K. J. Jones, P. H. Levine, P. J. Orsulak, M. Peterson, J. J. Schildkraut, E. Vzagara, and D. Watkins, Some biochemical correlates of panic attacks with agoraphobia and their response to a new treatment, *J. Clin. Psychopharmacol., 4*: 66 (1984).

L. Solyom, G. F. D. Heseltine, D. J. McClure, C. Solyom, B. Ledwidge, and G. Steinberg, Behavior therapy versus drug therapy in the treatment of phobic neurosis, *Can. Psychiatr. Assoc. J., 18*: 25 (1973).

C. Solyom, L. Solyom, Y. LaPierre, J. Pecknold, and L. Morton, Phenelzine and exposure in the treatment of phobias, *Biol. Psychiatry, 16*: 239 (1981).

C. B. Taylor, C. Hayward, R. King, A. Ehlers, J. Margraf, R. Maddock, D. Clark, W. T. Roth, and W. S. Agras, Cardiovascular and symptomatic reduction effects of alprazolam and imipramine in patients with panic disorder: Results of a double-blind, placebo-controlled trial, *J. Clin. Psychopharmcol., 10*: 112 (1990).

G. E. Tesar, High-potency benzodiazepines for short-term management of panic disorder: The US experience, *J. Clin. Psychiatry, 51*(5 Suppl.): 4 (1990).

G. E. Tesar, and J. F. Rosenbaum, Successful use of clonazepam in patients with treatment-resistant panic disorder, *J. Nerv. Ment. Dis. 174*: 477 (1986).

G. E. Tesar, J. F. Rosenbaum, M. H. Pollack, J. B. Herman, G. S. Sachs, E. M. Mahoney, L. S. Cohen, M. McNamara, and S. Goldstein, Clonazepam versus alprazolam in the treatment of panic disorder: Interim analysis of data from a prospective double-blind, placebo-controlled trial, *J. Clin. Psychiatry, 48*(10 Suppl): 16 (1987).

P. Tyrer, J. Candy, and D. Kelly, A study of the clinical effects of phenelzine and placebo in the treatment of phobic anxiety. *Psychopharmacologia, 32*: 237 (1973).

E. H. Uhlenhuth, W. Matuzas, R. M. Glass, and C. Easton, Response of panic disorder to fixed dose of alprazolam or imipramine, *J. Affective Disord., 17*: 261 (1989).

D. Waxman, An investigation into the use of Anafranil in phobic and obsessional disorders, *Scott. Med. J., 20*: 61 (1975).

E. D. West, and P. J. Dally, Effects of iproniazid in depressive syndromes, *Br. Med. J., 1*: 1491 (1959).

C. M. Zitrin, D. F. Klein, and M. G. Woerner, Behavior therapy, supportive psychotherapy, imipramine, and phobias, *Arch. Gen. Psychiatry, 35*: 307 (1978).

C. M. Zitrin, D. F. Klein, and M. G. Woerner, Treatment of agoraphobia with group exposure in vivo and imipramine, *Arch. Gen. Psychiatry, 37*: 63 (1980).

C. M. Zitrin, D. F. Klein, M. G. Woerner, and D. C. Ross, Treatment of phobias. I. Comparison of imipramine hydrochloride and placebo. *Arch. Gen. Psychiatry, 40*: 125 (1983).

12

Animal Models of Depression

Paul Willner
University College of Swansea, Swansea, Wales

I. INTRODUCTION

Animal models of depression are used for a variety of purposes: as screening tests in antidepressant discovery and development programs; as simulations for investigating aspects of the neurobiology of depression; and as experimental models within which to study the mechanisms of action of antidepressant drugs (Jesberger and Richardson, 1985; Henn and McKinney, 1987; McKinney, 1984; Willner, 1984, 1990). These various functions have different, and to some extent, conflicting requirements. Although the only essential requirement for antidepressant-screening tests is that they make accurate predictions of antidepressant activity, they should also be cheap, robust, reliable, and easy to use (Danysz et al., 1991; Willner, 1991a); for all of these subsidiary reasons, a screening test should be as simple as possible and should respond rapidly to antidepressant treatment. However, a simulation of depression aims to mimic aspects of the clinical situation, and from this perspective should embody a degree of complexity, to permit investigation of the validity of the model. In addition, if a model is to be used to investigate antidepressant actions, a slow onset over several weeks of continued treatment, comparable with the clinical time course, is highly desirable. These tensions have led to a situation in which the models used routinely as antidepressant-screening tests are of limited or minimal validity as simulations of depression (cf. Willner, 1984).

This chapter is primarily concerned with evaluating the suitability of the available models as research tools and with reviewing their contribution (actual and potential) to an understanding of the biological basis of depressive disorders. Clearly, the contribution of animal models to psychobiology must, to a large extent, depend on their validity. A general methodology has, therefore, been developed for assessing the validity of animal models, which has been applied not only to animal models of depression (Willner 1984, 1986, 1991a), but also to a wide range of other psychiatric disorders (Ellenbroek and Cools, 1990; Goudie, 1991; Green and Hodges, 1991; Montgomery, 1991; Sarter et al., 1992). This method consists of the application of three sets of relatively independent criteria that assess *predictive validity* (the extent to which the model responds appropriately to drugs that are clinically effective and those that are not), *face validity* (the degree of symptomatic resemblance between the model and the clinical condition), and *construct validity* (the theoretical rationale underlying the model).

A. Predictive Validity

The concept of predictive validity implies that manipulations known to influence the pathological state should have similar effects in the model. In practice, the predictive validity of animal models of depression is determined largely by their response to antidepressant drugs. A valid test should be sensitive and specific: it should respond to effective antidepressants and should fail to respond to ineffective agents. Positive responses should occur at sensible doses and should be demonstrable with a range of structurally diverse compounds.

Although the basic requirement for predictive validity is that a putative animal model of depression should respond to antidepressant drugs, in fact, some 30% of depressed patients fail to do so. Nevertheless, currently, a model that did not respond to tricyclics would not be taken seriously, and this situation is unlikely to change in the absence of well-established therapies for tricyclic-resistant depressions. The position in relation to monoamine oxidase inhibitors (MAOIs) is more forgiving: a failure to respond to MAOIs is not usually considered to invalidate an animal model of depression (provided that the model does respond to tricyclics). However, this situation could change if it should be established that selective MAO-A inhibitors are as efficacious as tricyclics.

Beyond the classic antidepressants (tricyclics and MAOIs) are a wide range of newer compounds for which antidepressant activity has been claimed, ranging from reasonably well-established antidepressants (e.g., selective serotonin [5-HT] or norepinephrine [NE] uptake inhibitors), through compounds that are probably effective (e.g., α_2-antagonists; 5-HT_1 agonists), to compounds of uncertain status (e.g., phosphodiesterase inhibitors, calcium antagonists, anticonvulsants). Even for the specific 5-HT-uptake inhibitors, of which the antidepressant efficacy is beyond doubt, it is still uncertain whether their spectrum of activity is identical with that of the tricyclics. Therefore, although a well-rounded description of an animal model of depression should include an account of its pharmacological profile broader than that provided by its response to traditional antidepressants, the contribution of these newer compounds to validation is limited.

To some extent, similar uncertainties exist in relation to drugs that are ineffective as antidepressants. The drugs that most commonly elicit false-negative responses in animal models of depression are psychomotor stimulants, anticholinergics, and opiates. However, before the development of antidepressants, drugs from all three of these classes were regularly prescribed for the relief of depression (see Willner, 1985). Some recent studies have confirmed that certain opiates (e.g., buprenorphine) have antidepressant activity (Emrich et al., 1983), but anticholinergics and stimulants have never been properly assessed, as their use was discontinued before the introduction of blind clinical trials. Again, the uncertain status of these compounds undermines, to some extent, their value as definitive standards.

Finally, it has recently become clear that the response to antidepressant drugs is insufficient to define an animal model of depression, since antidepressants are active in at least some animal models of anxiety, following long-term treatment (Bodnoff et al., 1988; Fontana et al., 1989) and, indeed, are increasingly seen as the drugs of choice in many forms of anxiety. Therefore, it is crucial for establishing the predictive validity of an animal model of depression to demonstrate that the model does not respond to benzodiazepines.

B. Face Validity

Face validity refers to a phenomenological similarity between the model and the disorder modeled. In the paper that first considered the problem of validating animal models, and so formed a starting point for subsequent research, McKinney and Bunney (1969) proposed that an animal model should resemble the condition modeled in terms of its etiology, symptomatology, treatment, and biological basis. However, in a second important theoretical contribution, Abramson and Seligman (1978) pointed out that not all symptoms carry equal weight: a valid animal model should demonstrate a resemblance to the clinically defined core symptoms of the disorder, rather than the subsidiary symptoms. Furthermore, not all of the symptoms of depression can be modeled in animals; symptoms that can only be known by subjective verbal report (such as excessive guilt, feelings of worthlessness, or thoughts of suicide) are in principle excluded (Willner, 1984, 1990). A DSM-III-R (*Diagnostic and Statistical Manual of Mental Disorders*, 3rd ed., revised) diagnosis of major depression requires the presence of at least one of two core symptoms: loss of interest or pleasure (*anhedonia*) and depressed mood. Of these two core symptoms, anhedonia can be modeled in animals, but depressed mood cannot. Therefore, in assessing the face validity of animal models of depression, anhedonia assumes a central position.

The subsidiary symptoms of depression that are amenable to modeling in animals include psychomotor change, decreased persistence, decreased sexual activity, and disturbances of sleep or food intake. However, psychomotor, sleep, and appetite changes may be in either direction, so that, for example, both decreases and increases in locomotor activity may be claimed as support for the validity of a model. This lack of precision and the fact that the clinical phenomena of psychomotor retardation and agitation are considerably more complex than gross changes in locomotor activity and, indeed, may coexist (Nelson and Charney, 1981), suggest that simulations in which a change in locomotor activity is the major, or only, behavioral feature should not be taken too seriously. Unfortunately, it is precisely these behaviors that feature most prominently in most animal models of depression (Willner, 1991b).

Little attention has been paid to the question of subtypes of depression in the development of animal models, which have tended to focus either on an undifferentiated depressive state or on the principal subtype of major depression, melancholia. Some other well-defined subtypes of depression have been largely ignored. Delusional depression is one example. This condition is difficult to translate into behavioral terms, being differentiated from nondelusional depression only by a greater association with psychomotor agitation (Nelson and Charney, 1981). However, delusional depressions are pharmacologically distinct, being unresponsive to tricyclic antidepressants, but responsive to electroconvulsive therapy (ECT) or to tricyclic–neuroleptic combinations (Nelson, 1987). The challenge of developing an animal model that responds to ECT, but not to tricyclics, has not yet been met. Bipolar disorder is another well-defined diagnostic category for which no animal models are available. Here, the depressive episodes appear to be identical with those of unipolar endogenous depression, but episodes of mania are interspersed. Although there are several animal models of mania (see Lyon, 1991), the alternation of depressive-like and manic-like behaviors in an animal model has not yet been systematically addressed. Indeed, the episodic nature of unipolar depression is itself another area that has not been explored in animal models.

In *DSM-III* (although not in *DSM-III-R*), the defining symptom of melancholia was anhedonia, which is readily modeled as a decrease in sensitivity to rewards. In many empirical studies, psychomotor retardation has emerged as the symptom most characteristic of melancholia, whereas psychomotor agitation tends to be more closely associated with psychotic features, such as delusions of guilt (Nelson and Charney, 1981). Nevertheless, there is considerable overlap between these two groups of symptoms, and agitated melancholias are not uncommon. Unlike nonmelancholic depressions, melancholia is characterized by a decrease in the latency to enter the first period of rapid eye movement (REM) sleep (Kupfer and Thase, 1983) and an increased secretion of cortisol, usually detected by the dexamethasone suppression test (DST; Carroll, 1982). In a valid simulation of melancholia, these biological markers might be expected to coexist alongside a decreased sensitivity to reward.

It is widely believed that because the pharmacotherapy of depression requires long-term drug treatment, the validity of an animal model is called into question by a rapid antidepressant response. In fact, the clinical requirement for long-term treatment may be more apparent than real: there is some evidence of very early antidepressant responses in clinical studies designed explicitly to detect them (e.g., Frazer et al., 1985; see also Willner, 1989a). The real test for a simulation of depression is that tolerance must not develop to the antidepressant response: irrespective of how it responds to brief antidepressant treatment, the model must respond to long-term treatment. This test has not been universally applied to animal models of depression, but in general, those models to which the test has been applied have passed it. Indeed, it is usually found that if a test does respond rapidly to antidepressants, the response is potentiated by extended treatment (Willner, 1989a), although tolerance to antidepressant effects has been reported in some behavioral paradigms (Cuomo et al., 1983; Niesink and van Ree, 1982). However, an extended time course becomes a critical feature if the model is to be used to investigate the physiological mechanisms of antidepressant action, and even longer durations are necessary if the focus of the investigation is the reversal of behavioral abnormalities by antidepressants, rather than simply their prophylaxis.

C. Construct Validity

To evaluate the theoretical rationale of an animal model, we require a theoretical account of the disordered behavior in the model, a theoretical account of the disorder itself, and a means of bringing the two theories into alignment. This can be done only if the clinical theory occupies an appropriate framework, which uses terms and concepts applicable also to subhuman species. However, the evaluation of animal models of depression is intrinsically limited by the rudimentary state of biologically oriented theories of depression. Although there is an extensive literature describing neurochemical abnormalities or biochemical markers associated with depression, there is little in this literature that can be used to provide theoretical standards against which to validate animal models. For example, even the most basic questions of whether the level of activity in monoaminergic systems is elevated or decreased in depression remain controversial (Willner, 1985). As a result, the construct validity of the reserpine model, which is based on the assumption that monoaminergic transmission is decreased, is difficult to assess (Bourin et al., 1983). [The fact that this model has minimal predictive validity or face validity (Willner, 1984) is beside the point.]

Similar problems arise in relation to modeling the etiology of depression. It is now clear that a variety of different factors are implicated in the etiology of depression: *psychological* factors include undesirable life events, chronic mild stress, adverse childhood experiences, and personality traits, such as introversion and impulsiveness; *biological* factors include genetic influences, and a variety of physical illnesses and medications (see Akiskal, 1985, 1986; Willner, 1985 for reviews). However, there is little theoretical understanding of the processes by which these factors influence the physiological processes underlying mood. In certain cases, the immediate precipitant of a depression may be clearly identified: for example, seasonal affective disorder and postpartum depression. More usually, the pathogenesis of depression is better understood as the result of an accumulation of several different risk factors (see e.g., Akiskal, 1985; Aneshensel and Stone, 1982; Brown and Harris, 1978). This point has been largely overlooked in the construction of animal models of depression which, in general, have assumed a single causal factor. This may be counterproductive, since few of the identified etiological factors appear sufficiently potent to precipitate depression in an otherwise risk-free individual.

Although attempts to assess the theoretical rationale of animal models are limited by this lack of theoretical structure at the clinical level, several generalizations are possible. The major group of animal models of depression are based on responses to stressors of various kinds and are usually justified by reference to the role of stressful life events in the etiology of depression (Lloyd, 1980; Brown and Harris, 1978, 1988). However, if very severe acute stress is used (e.g., Weiss et al., 1982), there is a clear onus on the user to justify the relevance of these procedures to depression, rather than, for example, to posttraumatic stress disorder. Furthermore, the adverse consequences of life events endure for a prolonged period of 6–12 months, in part by exacerbating ongoing life difficulties (Brown, 1989; Brown and Harris, 1988). Thus, life events should not be viewed as acute stressors (indeed, in the case of bereavement, a diagnosis of depression is explicitly excluded during the period of immediate loss); from this perspective, it may be more appropriate to use chronic stress regimens, rather than acute stressors, to model the etiological role of life events. Other factors have been identified that confer a long-lasting vulnerability to depression, in particular, an inadequate level of social support, which to a large extent arises from inadequate socialization (Aneshensel and Stone, 1982; Brown, 1989; Brown and Harris, 1978, 1988: see Willner, 1989b). From these starting points, several animal models of depression have been developed that are based on the adverse effects of social isolation. However, with the exception of some of the primate studies (see later discussion), these models have largely ignored both the complexity of childhood social deprivation phenomena and the mediation of their effects through later social relationships.

Although assessment of the theoretical rationale of animal models of depression is limited by the paucity of theory, construct validity can also be evaluated at the level of constructs. This approach is best exemplified by the extensive experimental analysis of whether *learned helplessness* is an appropriate term to describe the impairments of escape learning that follow exposure to inescapable electric shock (Seligman, 1975). The term learned helplessness implies that the animals perform poorly because they have learned that their responses are ineffective in controlling their environment (Seligman, 1975). However, inescapable shock has a variety of other, simpler effects that could also explain many of the behavioral impairments, such as decreased locomotor activity (Glazer and Weiss, 1976; Anisman et al., 1979) and analgesia (Lewis et al., 1980). To demonstrate that inescapable shock does, additionally, cause "cognitive" impairments, Jackson et al. (1978) assessed performance accuracy using a maze task, in which performance would be independent of factors influencing motor speed. As predicted, accuracy was reduced in animals previously subjected to unavoidable shock, confirming the presence of a cognitive component to the pattern of impairment. However, subsequent work showed that this cognitive impairment arose from an increase in distractibility, rather than from a learning disability (Minor et al., 1984). So inescapable shock does cause cognitive impairment, but at the level of attentional processes, rather than helplessness.

Anhedonia is another construct that has been subjected to this kind of experimental attention. Here, the question is whether the performance of rewarded behavior is suppressed because the animal is insensitive to rewards or for some other reason and, again, the problem is best illustrated by a case study. Prolonged sequential exposure to a variety of mild stressors causes an antidepressant-reversible decrease in the consumption of dilute sucrose solutions, which is hypothesized to reflect a decrease in their reward value (Willner et al., 1987, 1991). Initial studies showed that in contrast with the decreased intake of dilute solutions of sucrose or saccharin, chronic mild stress did not decrease intake of plain water, food pellets, or concentrated sucrose solutions; thus, the effects are not simply nonspecific changes in consummatory behavior (Muscat and Willner, 1992). Next, an extensive series of experiments was conducted in which place conditioning was used to measure rewarding effects. In this paradigm, animals display a preference for a distinctive environment in which they have previously received rewards (Carr et al., 1989). Chronic mild stress attenuated or abolished place preferences established with a variety of natural or drug rewards; by contrast, drug-induced place aversions were unaffected by chronic mild stress (Papp et al., 1991, 1992, 1993). Consequently, the effect is properly described as anhedonia (decreased sensitivity to rewards), rather than being a nonspecific motivational impairment or a failure of associative learning. Finally, chronic mild stress also causes an increase in the threshold for brain stimulation reward (Moreau et al., 1992). Together, these results support the position that decreases in sucrose intake provide a simple means of detecting anhedonia.

These examples of successful experimental analyses of construct validity contrast sharply with a third example, the *behavioral despair* test (Porsolt et al., 1979). This term was introduced to describe the immobility seen in rats or mice forced to swim in a confined space; it was assumed that when the animals adopted an immobile posture, they had "despaired" of escaping. Unfortunately, this interpretation is not susceptible to experimental analysis. Consequently, although the test continues to be very widely used, the name "behavioural despair" has been largely abandoned, and replaced instead by the theoretically neutral term *the forced swim test.*

II. MODELS OF MELANCHOLIA

In previous reviews, animal models of depression have been classified according to their level of validity (Willner, 1984) or the inducing conditions used (Willner, 1990). An attractive alternative classification could be based on the subtype of depression modeled. The art of modeling has not yet progressed to the point where this is entirely feasible. However, several models include anhedonia as one of their features. In *DSM-III*, anhedonia was assumed to be the defining symptom of melancholia. A weaker position is adopted by *DSM-III-R*, in which anhedonia is one option for defining melancholia. Nevertheless, it seems that anhedonia might provide a useful starting point for modeling melancholia in animals and, therefore, the first section of this review considers together those models in which anhedonia has been demonstrated. Also included are two models (submissive behavior and the forced swim test) in which anhedonia has not been demonstrated, but which appear to be conceptually related to one or more of the anhedonia models.

A. Acute Stress: The Learned Helplessness Model(s)

The learned helplessness paradigm is based on the observation that animals exposed to uncontrollable stress (usually electric shocks) are subsequently impaired in learning to escape shock; this effect is not seen in animals exposed to comparable, or indeed, identical, patterns of controllable shock. The protective effect of control appears to result from lower levels of fear (Jackson and Minor, 1988), which raises important questions about the relation between depression and anxiety. Seligman (1975) proposed that exposure to uncontrollable stress provides the basis, in animals as in people, for learning that stress is uncontrollable (helplessness), and that this learning has a number of debilitating consequences, including depression. However, this interpretation has been the subject of considerable controversy in both the human (Abramson et al., 1978, 1989) and the animal literature (Weiss et al., 1982; Minor et al., 1984, 1988) and is probably incorrect (see foregoing and Willner, 1986, 1990). Nevertheless, the learning difficulties that follow exposure to uncontrollable shock are reversed with reasonable selectively by subchronic (3–7 days) treatment with tricyclic or atypical antidepressants (Sherman et al., 1982). Serotonin-uptake inhibitors also appear to be effective, but only within a limited dose range (Martin et al., 1989), as well as several other potential antidepressants such as 5-HT_{1A} agonists (Giral et al., 1988) and ß-agonists (Martin et al., 1986a), although some of these effects have been disputed (Christensen and Geoffroy, 1991). There are few if any false-negative responses, neuroleptics, stimulants, sedatives, and anxiolytics being ineffective (Sherman et al., 1982; Porsolt et al., 1991).

The learned helplessness paradigm shows many symptomatic parallels to major depression—so much so that it has been suggested that rodents subjected to uncontrollable shock could meet *DSM-III* diagnostic criteria (Weiss et al., 1982). However, the learned helplessness paradigm is implemented in a variety of different ways in different laboratories, and the version of the paradigm giving rise to the broadest range of symptoms (Weiss et al., 1982) uses extremely high shock levels (4–6 ma) which are of doubtful relevance to depression: the effects of this regimen largely dissipate within 2–3 days, and the effects of antidepressant pretreatment have not been studied using this procedure. The effects of antidepressants have typically been studied using shocks of a considerably lower intensity (1.0–1.5 ma), which cause a far less pervasive pattern of behavioral impairment; paradoxically, however, these effects are of longer duration, making it possible to interpose subchronic drug treatment (typically for 3–5 days) between the initial uncontrollable shock session and the learning test. A further problem is that different components of the learned helplessness syndrome may be related to different aspects of the induction procedure. For example, a long-term (7 weeks) suppression of home-cage locomotor activity has been reported following a single shock session (Desan et al., 1988), but this effect is unrelated to shock controllability; hence, it is clearly distinct from other learned helplessness phenomena (Woodmansee et al., 1991). It is clear that the learned helplessness paradigm should more correctly be considered a mixture of paradigms, and care should be taken in generalizing conclusions among them.

Among the consequences of low-intensity uncontrollable (but not controllable) shock is a poor performance of rewarded behavior which, as noted earlier, may be of particular relevance to melancholia. One manifestation of this effect in mice is a long-lasting decrease in responding for brain stimulation reward, which is specific to certain electrode placements and, therefore, suggests a subsensitivity within part of the brain mechanism of reward, rather than, for example, a motor impairment (Zacharko et al., 1983, 1987). Normal sensitivity to brain stimulation reward was restored by chronic, but not acute, treatment with tricyclic antidepressants (Zacharko et al., 1983; Zacharko and Anisman, 1991). Interestingly, a long-lasting anhedonia is seen only if the animals are tested in the immediate aftermath of stress; otherwise, the effect dissipates rapidly (Zacharko et al., 1983). A related observation is that, following an initial exposure to severe stress, behavioral deficits may be reinstated by mild stressors that are without effect in normal animals (Anisman and Zacharko, 1982). These studies suggest that it may be possible to develop conditioning models to explain how the risk of depression is elevated for several months in the aftermath of a stressful life event.

Another important observation is that uncontrollable electric shock has variable behavioral effects (most of which are antidepressant-reversible) in different inbred mouse strains. To take an extreme example, in the C57BL/67 strain, uncontrollable shock severely impaired subsequent learning to escape shock, but had no effect on responding for brain stimulation reward, whereas the DBA/2J strain showed exactly the opposite pattern of deficits (Shanks and Anisman, 1988; Zacharko et al., 1987). These studies may provide a starting point from which to investigate the physiological mechanisms underlying individual differences in responses to stress.

There is a relatively extensive literature dealing with the neurochemical bases of stress-induced motor inactivation (see Maier, 1984; Willner, 1985). Briefly, the debilitating effect of uncontrollable stress on later performance may be reversed by agonists at dopamine (DA), α_1- and ß-adrenergic receptors, or by anticholinergic drugs; conversely, helplessness may be simulated pharmacologically by drugs that reduce DA or NE function, or by drugs that increase cholinergic function (Anisman and Zacharko, 1982; Willner, 1985). The α_1- and ß-adrenergic antagonists (as well as the opiate antagonist naloxone) also block the therapeutic effect of tricyclics (Martin et al., 1986b). In contrast, studies of the role of 5-HT in learned helplessness are inconsistent (Brown et al., 1982; Sherman and Petty, 1980; Anisman et al., 1979; Christensen and Geoffroy, 1991); and although some 5-HT agonists may reverse learned helplessness, 5-HT lesions did not prevent the action of tricyclic antidepressants in this model (Soubrie et al., 1986).

B. The Forced Swim and Tail Suspension Tests

In the forced swim test, rats or mice are forced to swim in a confined space in two tests, usually spaced 24 h apart. The onset of immobility in the second test is delayed by pretreatment with a wide variety of antidepressants, usually administered in a subacute treatment schedule consisting of three injections in 24 h. Effective agents include tricyclics, MAOIs, most atypical antidepressants, ECS, and REM sleep deprivation (Porsolt, 1981; Borsini and Meli, 1988; Porsolt et al., 1991). The test is not usually sensitive to 5-HT uptake inhibitors (Borsini and Meli, 1988), although activity of these compounds has sometimes been reported (e.g., van der Heyden, 1991). There have also been a variety of other negative reports; nevertheless, some 90% of clinically active antidepressants are active in the forced swim test, with the proportion rising in studies using chronic drug treatment (Borsini and Meli, 1988; Porsolt et al., 1991). That the forced swim test responds to acute drug treatment has been a frequent, but unjustified, source of criticism. Although small antidepressant effects may be present after a single high dose, larger effects are observed after chronic treatment at lower doses. These changes cannot be explained simply by the elevation of brain drug concentrations (reviewed by Willner, 1989).

On the negative side, although the test successfully discriminates antidepressants from neuroleptics and anxiolytics (Porsolt et al., 1977), false-positive responses have been reported for stimulants, convulants, anticholinergics, antihistamines, pentobarbital, opiates, a variety of brain peptides, and several other drugs (Borsini and Meli, 1988; Porsolt et al., 1991). Some false-positive responses have been reported to disappear if chronic drug treatment is used, or the duration of the test is prolonged (Kitada et al., 1981; Kawashima et al., 1986), but the generality of these effects has not been established.

Even though the predictive validity of the forced swim test may be better than has sometimes been assumed, its face and construct validity are minimal. The only symptomatic resemblance to depression is an inability or reluctance to maintain effort. The theoretical rationale of this test derives entirely from its supposed relation to learned helplessness. However, the relation between the two models is unclear. Prior inescapable, but not escapable, shock has increased immobility in the forced swim test (Nomura et al., 1982; Weiss et al., 1981), but in view of the consistent finding of decreased motor activity following inescapable shock (see Anisman and Zacharko, 1982), it would be surprising were this not so. The reciprocal finding has not been demonstrated: forced swimming did not impair subsequent escape performance in a shock avoidance task in which performance deficits are typically seen following inescapable shock (O'Neill and Valentino, 1982).

Nevertheless, the two tests do seem to share similar physiological substrates. Similar to learned helplessness, immobility in the swim test is also reversed by stimulating DA or α_1-adrenergic receptors or by anticholinergics, and potentiated by treatments that decrease the activation of DA or NE systems or increase cholinergic transmission. Similarly, the therapeutic actions of antidepressants in this model are blocked by DA receptor antagonists and by treatments that reduce NE function, including neurotoxic destruction of the ascending NE pathways and α_1-receptor antagonists (see Borsini and Meli, 1988; Willner, 1990). Also, as in the learned helplessness test, impairment of 5-HT transmission neither increases immobility (Porsolt et al., 1979; Plaznik et al., 1985a,b) nor blocks its reversal by antidepressants (Araki et al., 1985; Borsini et al., 1981; Kitada et al., 1981); nevertheless, 5-HT$_{1A}$ agonists do appear to be effective in this test (van der Heyden et al., 1991).

Several variants of the forced swim test have been proposed. One of these, the tail suspension test, has been claimed to be ethically superior to the forced swim test, as stress levels appear to be reduced (Steru et al., 1985; Porsolt et al., 1986). In this model, mice suspended by the tail show a temporal pattern of struggling, followed by immobility, similar to that seen in the forced swimming test. Antidepressants, at strikingly low doses, have been shown to increase the duration of mobility and, also, in an automated version of the test, to increase the power of the movements (although the latter effect is rather less convincing). Effective agents include tricyclics, MAOIs, and atypical antidepressants; the latter include mianserin and, significantly, 5-HT-uptake inhibitors, which are usually ineffective in the forced swim test. Immobility was also reduced by stimulant drugs, but was potentiated by neuroleptics or anxiolytics (Steru et al., 1985; Porsolt et al., 1986). Although it is tempting to see the tail suspension test as a more sensitive version of the forced swim test, there are subtle differences between them, which are not yet understood. In particular, 5-HT_{1A} agonists are active in the forced swim test, but are ineffective in the tail suspension test (Porsolt et al., 1991).

C. Chronic Stress Models

Repeated presentation of the same stressor usually leads to adaptation. However, adaptation can be prevented by presenting a variety of stressors in an unpredictable sequence. Katz and colleagues showed that 3 weeks of exposure to electric shocks, immersion in cold water, immobilization, reversal of the light–dark cycle, and a variety of other stressors, caused a decrease in the activating effect of acute stress in an open-field test. However, the activating effect of acute stress was maintained in animals receiving daily antidepressant treatment during the chronic stress period; the effects of administering antidepressants after exposure to stress have not been studied in this model. A variety of antidepressant drugs, as well as ECS, prevented the effect of chronic stress, but the MAOI tranylcypromine was ineffective; various nonantidepressants failed to prevent the effect of stress. In addition to causing changes in open-field activity, chronic stress also increased plasma corticosteroid levels. This effect showed the same spectrum of pharmacological sensitivity, with the exception that an anticholinergic agent was also effective (Katz et al., 1981: see Willner, 1990 for review). Similar effects have also been reported in mice; corticosteroid levels and the response to an acute stress were normalized by tricyclic antidepressants, though not by fluoxetine (Soblosky and Thurmond, 1986).

A further effect observed in rats after chronic stress was a failure to increase fluid consumption when saccharin was added to the drinking water, suggesting that chronic stress might cause anhedonia; this deficit was partially restored by imipramine (Katz, 1982). The chronic stress model has been used very little since the original series of publications, in part because the levels of severity employed raise serious ethical problems. However, a variant of the model has been devised that employs very mild stressors, such as periods of food and water deprivation, small temperature reductions, changes of cage mates, and other similarly innocuous manipulations. Over a period of weeks of exposure to the mild stress regimen, rats gradually reduced their consumption of a preferred dilute sucrose solution and, in untreated animals, this deficit persisted for several weeks following the cessation of stress (Willner et al., 1987, 1991). As discussed earlier (see Sec. I.C), a variety of studies have been performed to confirm that these effects reflect a generalized insensitivity to reward; in particular, chronic mild stress also impairs responsiveness to reward as assessed by place conditioning (Papp et al., 1991, 1992, 1993) and intracranial self-stimulation (ICSS) (Moreau et al., 1991). Studies of the effects of the individual elements of the chronic mild stress regimen revealed that one element, social housing (in animals usually housed individually) was particularly potent, but no individual element (including social housing) was either necessary to induce anhedonia nor sufficient to maintain anhedonia for a prolonged period (Muscat and Willner, 1992).

Antidepressant treatment had no effect on sucrose consumption in nonstressed animals, but following the reduction of sucrose intake by stress, normal behavior was restored by chronic treatment (2–5 weeks) with tricyclic antidepressants, a specific 5-HT-uptake inhibitor (fluoxetine), a specific NE-uptake inhibitor (maprotiline), and mianserin; chlordiazepoxide was ineffective (Willner et al., 1987; Muscat et al., 1990, 1992; Sampson et al., 1991). Fluoxetine, maprotiline, and mianserin (but not chlordiazepoxide) also restored the rewarding properties of food, as assessed in the place-conditioning paradigm (Muscat et al., 1992; Cheeta et al., 1992). The reversal of an established behavioral deficit during the continued presence of the stressor is an important feature of this model: if, as seems likely, chronic stress does play a role in the etiology of melancholia (e.g., Aneshensel and Stone, 1982; Monroe et al., 1985; Rodgers, 1991), its continued presence during antidepressant therapy would usually be the norm.

Studies of the neural basis of the chronic mild stress-induced anhedonia have focused on the mesolimbic DA system. Animals subjected to chronic mild stress show an increase in DA release within the nucleus accumbens (Willner et al., 1991; Stamford et al., 1991), accompanied by a decrease in the sensitivity of postsynatic D_2 receptors in the same area (Papp et al., 1993). The effects of antidepressants appear to be mediated by an increase in D2 receptor sensitivity, as antidepressant effects were reversed, following successful treatment by single low doses of dopamine antagonists (Muscat et al., 1990, 1992; Sampson et al., 1991). It is now well established that chronic treatment with antideprpssants increases functional responses to dopamine agonists (see Willner, 1989a), but a dopaminergic mechanism of antidepressant action runs counter to the established wisdom, and requires clinical investigation.

D. Submissive Behavior

Parallels have often been noted between depressive and submissive behaviors (Price, 1972; Gardner, 1982); recently, several laboratories have attempted to model depression by using animals of low social rank. Social defeat is a potent stressor, and repeated defeat is a form of chronic stress; also, responsiveness to a sucrose reward in individually housed rats was suppressed following periods of paired housing (Muscat and Willner, 1992). Therefore, it seems appropriate to view submission models, potentially, as models of melancholia.

In one such study, a single defeat by a dominant male was reported to cause a gradual increase over weeks in passive behavior in response to a mild stressor, which could be antagonized by clomipramine; defeated animals also had higher immobility times in the forced swim test (Korte et al., 1991). In a chronic version of a similar procedure, mice were housed in social contact, but were physically separated except for one daily 3-min encounter. Again, increased immobility in the forced swim test was observed in repeatedly defeated animals, and this effect was prevented by chronic treatment with imipramine (Kudryatseva et al., 1991). In this study, imipramine did not normalize social behavior in the defeated animals (Kudryatseva et al., 1991), although in other studies, chronic administration of antidepressant drugs has increased success in dyadic encounters between singly housed treated and untreated rats (Willner et al., 1981; Mitchell and Redfern, 1992a). Finally, a procedure has been described in which rats are housed in threes, and antidepressants are administered chronically to the middle-ranking animal. Animals treated for 2 weeks with either clomipramine or mianserin gradually assumed the dominant rank (Mitchell and Redfern, 1992b).

A major advantage of the submission models is that, similar to the chronic mild stress procedure, they employ realistic and ecologically relevant inducing conditions. However, even though the parallels between depression and submissive behavior are intuitively appealing, there has been little clinical investigation of this hypothesis. Also, the relation between social dominance and social competition is potentially problematic: in group-housed rats competing for limited access to a high-incentive reward, the performance of subordinate animals was improved by acute or chronic anxiolytic treatment (Gentsch et al., 1990; Joly and Sanger, 1991), suggesting that the social competition test models anxiety, rather than depression. In contrast, diazepam, administered briefly or long-term, did not increase aggressive behavior in dyadic encounters (Mitchell and Redfern, 1992a); further studies will be necessary to confirm the ineffectiveness of anxiolytics in social dominance tests. Finally, perhaps surprisingly, other than reports relating low status to blood levels of 5-HT (Raleigh et al., 1984) and some endocrinological observations (Henry and Stephens, 1977), there is at present little information concerning the brain mechanisms associated with loss of rank.

E. Withdrawal from Chronic Psychomotor Stimulants

Several studies have reported that responding for ICSS was reduced in the days following withdrawal from chronic amphetamine treatment. In these studies, amphetamine was administered to rats for between 4 and 10 days, typically using several administrations each day, at increasing doses (Leith and Barrett, 1976; Simpson and Annau, 1977; Barrett and White, 1980; Kokkinidis and Zacharko, 1980). The threshold for ICSS was elevated following amphetamine withdrawal, confirming that the rate reduction reflects a subsensitivity to brain stimulation reward, rather than a depression of motor activity (Cassens et al., 1981; Leith and Barrett, 1980). After 14 days of amphetamine treatment, the decreased sensitivity to ICSS did not recover during 18 days of further testing (Leith and Barrett, 1980). In a single pharmacological study, this effect was alleviated by 2 days of imipramine or amitriptyline treatment, and with continued treatment, normal responding was restored (Kokkinidis et al., 1980).

In a variant of this procedure, animals self-administer cocaine, rather than being administered amphetamine (Koob, 1989). In these experiments, the threshold for brain stimulation reward, administered through electrodes in the posterior lateral hypothalamus, was obtained using a discrete trial procedure (Kornetsky and Esposito, 1981), which is sensitive to changes in reward value, but not to changes in motor performance (Markou et al., 1989). Following 24 h of cocaine self-administration, ICSS thresholds were elevated for several hours (Koob, 1989). Acute administration of the dopamine (DA) agonist bromocriptine restored ICSS thresholds to normal (Markou and Koob, 1989). Conventional antidepressants have not been tested in this paradigm.

It has frequently been assumed that stimulant drug treatment is a form of stress, since, in many respects, stimulant treatment and stress appear to be interchangeable (Post, 1975; Antelman et al., 1980). These similarities are thought to arise because, similar to stimulant drugs, stressors activate the mesolimbic and mesocortical DA projections (Blanc et al., 1980). Independent of a relation to stress, there is an obvious parallel between the effects of stimulant withdrawal and the depressions that frequently follow the cessation of extended stimulant use (Watson et al., 1972), although, in the animal model, the time course is rather more compressed.

As the stimulant withdrawal models are based exclusively on changes in ICSS behavior, their construct validity depends largely on the assumption that brain stimulation reward activates natural reward pathways (Hoebel, 1976). Although early studies suggested that ICSS had unusual properties compared with natural rewards (for example, rapid extinction), it was later recognized that these properties derive from differences in the experimental procedures typically employed (such as the delay of reinforcement); when such extraneous factors are equated, ICSS appears very comparable with a high-incentive, natural reward presented under conditions of low drive (e.g., Gibson et al., 1965). These parallels, together with the observation that responding for ICSS performance is influenced by many of the factors that control responding for natural rewards, have justified the assumption that the ICSS electrode directly stimulates the neural substrates that are activated indirectly by natural rewards (Hoebel, 1976). A degree of caution is required because, although people implanted with ICSS electrodes report a variety of pleasurable sensations, they also report other reasons for stimulating, such as curiosity (Valenstein, 1973; Atrens, 1984). Nevertheless, the commonality of anatomical substrate between ICSS and other types of reward supports the use of this procedure as an animal model of hedonic behavior (see also Koob, 1989; Wise, 1989).

F. Neonatal Antidepressant Treatment

Neonatal treatment with the tricyclic antidepressant clomipramine has recently been reported to cause a spectrum of symptoms reminiscent of depression, including decreases in sexual and aggressive behavior, a shortening of REM sleep latency, and subsensitivity to ICSS (Vogel et al., 1990). Treated animals were also hyperactive in some tests. Animals were typically tested when mature, at ages that varied between tests. Most of the behavioral and sleep abnormalities were present on first testing at approximately 3 months; however, the ICSS abnormalities were absent at 4–5 months, but present at 6–8 months. ICSS was not tested in older animals, but some other abnormalities appeared to normalize at about 11 months (Vogel et al., 1990). These effects are probably not specific to clomipramine, as another group has reported that neonatal treatment with either desipramine or zimeldine caused increased immobility in the forced swim test in adult rats (Hilakivi and Hilakivi, 1987).

As yet, information concerning the pharmacological responsiveness of this model is minimal: some effects of imipramine and REM sleep deprivation have been reported, but the numbers of subjects tested were too few to allow reliable conclusions to be drawn (Vogel et al., 1990). Although this model appears to have good face validity, in terms of the range of symptoms displayed and the insidious onset of anhedonia, the extent to which the symptoms can be reversed by antidepressants is uncertain, and the mechanisms by which neonatal clomipramine has adverse effects in mature animals are unknown. In particular, it is unclear what, if any, is the relation between neonatal clomipramine and the etiology of depression in humans. Nevertheless, these studies raise the disconcerting possibility that a breast-fed infant could develop a susceptibility to melancholia by ingesting tricyclic antidepressants prescribed to the nursing mother for the relief of postpartum depression.

G. Selective Breeding for Muscarinic Hypersensitivity

The Flinders Sensitive Line (FSL) rat is the result of selective breeding for sensitivity to the hypothermic effect of cholinergic agonists. Although bred for cholinergic hypersensitivity, FSL animals also show several other pharmacological abnormalities, including serotonergic hypersensitivity and dopaminergic hyposensitivity (Overstreet and Janowsky, 1991). Relative to the control Flinders Resistant Line, FSL animals have several characteristics reminiscent of depression, including cholinergic supersensitivity, increased REM sleep, and reduced locomotor activity. The FSL animals also show greater immobility in the forced swim test (Overstreet and Janowsky, 1991) and a greater vulnerability to the suppressive effect of chronic mild stress on responsiveness to sweet reward (Pucilowski et al., 1993). However, FSL animals behave normally in the elevated plus maze, a putative animal model of anxiety (Overstreet, 1991). Behavior in the forced swim test was normalized by chronic treatment with a high dose of imipramine, and partly reversed by desipramine or sertraline (Overstreet, 1991).

III. OTHER MODELS

As might be expected, the absence of (demonstrated) anhedonia defines a diverse group of models, which in this review is also relatively small. However, the size of this section is artificially reduced by concentrating on behaviorally defined models, thereby excluding several screening tests that are based on pharmacological interactions of antidepressants with drugs of other classes, such as reserpine, amphetamine, yohimbine, or clonidine (see Willner, 1984; Porsolt et al., 1991).

A. Separation Models

The presumed etiological role in depression of loss events and, particularly, loss of a loved one, has led to the development of several animal models of depression based on separation phenomena. The most familiar of these models involve nonhuman primates, either infants isolated from their parents, or juveniles isolated from their peer group. The separation response consists of an initial stage of *protest*, characterized by agitation, sleeplessness, and distress calls; followed by *despair*, characterized by a decrease in activity, appetite, play, and social interaction, and the assumption of a hunched posture and "sad" facial expression (see Suomi, 1976; Henn and McKinney, 1987). These symptoms are strikingly similar to those of "anaclitic depression" in institutionalized children (Robertson and Bowlby, 1952). However, although parental loss in childhood, and loss events such as bereavement in adults, are implicated in the etiology of depression, they also increase the risk of a variety of other psychiatric and nonpsychiatric disorders (Brown et al., 1973; Schmale, 1973). The nature of the separation response is sensitive to the environment in which the experiments are carried out (e.g., Reite et al., 1981; Suomi, 1976), and the incidence of "depressive" behaviors may, in some experiments, be as low as 15% (Lewis et al., 1976).

The few pharmacological studies that have used these models have not been impressive. Very few published studies have attempted to use antidepressant treatments to modify primate separation behavior, and because of the expense of using primates, the size of experimental groups in most studies has usually been too small to provide reliable data. Chronic desmethylimipramine (DMI) (Hrdina et al., 1979), imipramine (Suomi et al., 1978), oxaprotiline (McKinney and Kraemer, 1989), and ECS (Lewis and

McKinney, 1976) have been reported to reverse some, but not all, of the effects of separation in monkeys. Trifluoperazine, amphetamine, and diazepam did not affect responses to social isolation in chimpanzees (Menzel et al., 1963; Turner et al., 1969), but some therapeutic effects of chlorpromazine were seen in rhesus monkeys (McKinney et al., 1973). Depressive-like behaviors in singly housed rhesus monkeys are associated with decreased concentrations of NE in the cerebrospinal fluid, with relatively little effect on DA or 5-HT (Kraemer et al., 1989). Following a return to social housing, NE levels normalize, but the animals remain hypersensitive to pharmacological challenges of the noradrenergic system (Kraemer et al., 1984a,b).

Although the evolutionary proximity of primates has led some authors to consider primate separation models to be of particular importance (e.g., Everitt and Keverne, 1979), they have produced remarkably little of value. Precisely because of their evolutionary proximity, the use of primates sacrifices many of the advantages of animal models, such as the easing of ethical constraints and the possibility of testing adequately sized groups of subjects.

In fact, separation phenomena of protest followed by despair are present, to some extent, in many other species, including cats, dogs, rodents, and precocial birds (McKinney and Bunney, 1969; Katz, 1981), and several of these phenomena have also been used as the basis for the development of animal models of depression. One of these, the reactivation of distress calling in 1-week old chicks, appears to perform relatively well as an antidepressant screening test (Lehr, 1989). Chronic (4–6 weeks) isolation of adult rats causes a disruption of cooperative social behavior (Berger and Schuster, 1982) reminiscent of the poor social performance of depressed people (Lewinsohn, 1974). The impairment of social cooperation was reversed by chronic treatment with either imipramine or fluoxetine, and the effect of imipramine in this model was abolished by the 5-HT antagonist metergoline (Willner et al., 1989).

B. Olfactory Bulbectomy

The other major animal model of depression is based on the destruction of the olfactory bulb in rats. Bulbectomized animals display a variety of behavioral changes, including irritability, hyperactivity, and an impairment of passive avoidance learning (Cairncross et al., 1979). They also show an elevation of circulating corticosteroid levels (as do stressed animals), which appears to be an increased corticosteroid response to stress, rather than an increase in basal levels (Broekkamp et al., 1986). These changes are reversed by antidepressants, the most specific effect being the reversal of the passive avoidance learning deficit (Cairncross et al., 1979; Van Riezen and Leonard, 1990). However, even though all tricyclic and atypical antidepressants appear to be effective in this test, MAOIs are not (Jesberger and Richardson, 1986). Whereas repeated administration of tricyclics is necessary to normalize behavior in this model, 5-HT-uptake inhibitors act after acute treatment (Lloyd et al., 1982; Joly and Sanger, 1986). The implication that the model involves primarily serotonergic mechanisms is supported by the observation that the effects of subchronic treatment with imipramine and mianserin were reversed by brief administration of metergoline (Broekkamp et al., 1980).

Although pharmacologically specific for antidepressants, the face validity of the olfactory bulbectomy model is slight. Unlike the stress models, the bulbectomized rat resembles an agitated, rather than a retarded depression, but beyond hyperactivity, it is difficult to discern any further points of behavioral resemblance. Nevertheless, bulbectomized rats do resemble depressed humans on a surprisingly wide range of peripheral neurochemical and immunological markers, such as abnormalities of platelet 5-HT transport and neutrophil phagocytosis (Leonard, 1991).

C. Waiting Behavior

To the extent that they appear to involve serotonergic mechanisms, two final models may be related to olfactory bulbectomy. These are two paradigms in which antidepressants increase the ability of rats to withhold responses. In one paradigm (DRL-72), premature responding delays the delivery of reward; the ability of drugs to improve performance in this model has been claimed to be an efficient antidepressant screening test (Seiden et al., 1985), although this has been disputed (Pollard and Howard, 1986). In the second paradigm, a larger reward may be earned by waiting; again, the improvement of performance in this model appears to be a specific property of a wide range of antidepressants (Bizot et al., 1988a). The 5-HT_1 agonists are antidepressant-like in both of these waiting paradigms (Bizot et al., 1988b; Archer, 1991), and in the DRL-72 test, antidepressant effects were blocked by a 5-HT antagonist (Marek et al., 1989). The relevance of these behaviors to depression is unclear. Clinical evidence strongly suggests that similar disorders of 5-HT function cut across diagnostic boundaries, and are expressed as "pathologically impulsive behavior," rather than as any particular disorder (Soubrie, 1986; Willner, 1989b). The inability to withhold responses in the two waiting models may constitute instances of impulsive behavior, and as such, the effect of antidepressants in these paradigms may not relate specifically to depression.

IV. SOME LIKELY FUTURES

Animal models of depression have traditionally been defined primarily by their responsiveness to antidepressant drugs and, in consequence, this term encompasses a range of different procedures that are difficult to subsume within a simple conceptual structure. Previous reviews (e.g., Willner, 1990) have suggested that a broad distinction can be made between two groups of models, which is preserved in the present review. There are various, partially overlapping, ways of defining the two groups: by etiology, symptomatology, and physiological basis. Thus, one group of models, here defined as models of anhedonia (although this is not demonstrated for the forced swim test or submissive behavior models) are brought about largely by stress (even though this is difficult to argue in the neonatal antidepressant model) and reflect primarily impairments of catecholaminergic transmission (to the extent that the physiological substrates are known). The second group (other models) may involve aspects of impulsive behavior; may be related to social isolation; and may reflect impairments of 5-HT primarily. The tentative nature of the generalizations is all too obvious. However, they do provide hypotheses that bring animal models into contact with traditional monoamine theories of depression and suggest ways in which those theories might be tested and amplified (Willner, 1985, 1990). It does seem important that the diversity of depressive symptomatology is matched by a similar diversity in the phenomenology expressed in animal models, and this consideration may justify the continued use of models that have little face or construct validity.

Although the etiology of depression probably involves multiple factors, animal models have tended to be unifactorial. An interesting recent development is that symptoms characteristic, or at least reminiscent, of depression may be generated in animal models in various ways. Thus, anhedonia is subject to genetic influences (strain differences in the anhedonic effects of uncontrollable shock or chronic mild stress: Zacharko and Anisman, 1991; Pucilowski et al., 1993); epigenetic influences (neonatal antidepressant treatment: Vogel et al., 1990); acute severe stress (uncontrollable shock: Zacharko and Anisman, 1991); chronic mild stress (Willner et al., 1991); and psychomotor stimulant withdrawal (Koob, 1989). Similarly, immobility time in the forced swim test is increased by genetic influences (strain differences: Overstreet and Janowsky, 1991); epigenetic influences (neonatal antidepressant treatment: Hilakivi and Hilakivi, 1987); acute stress (defeat or uncontrollable shock: Korte et al., 1991; Weiss et al., 1982); and chronic stress (defeat: Kudryatseva et al., 1991). Studies of combinations of etiological factors are clearly warranted: an understanding of the manner in which different factors interact to generate depression-like symptoms in animals models would be of considerable interest to both basic researchers and clinicians.

The greatest immediate contribution of animal models of depression is likely to be in relation to the elucidation of the mechanisms of action of antidepressant drugs. Thirty years of clinical experience has given rise to two widely accepted axioms: that only rarely do antidepressants cause discernible clinical improvement within the first 2 weeks of treatment, and that they are devoid of mood-elevating effects in normal human subjects. The clinical requirement for chronic treatment regimens has led to a considerable literature describing the effects of chronic antidepressant administration in normal animals, and numerous changes in pre- or postsynaptic receptor function, or both, have been reported, in a variety of systems. These descriptive studies are an essential first step toward establishing mechanisms of antidepressant action. However, the inability to determine which of the many effects of antidepressants are responsible for their therapeutic actions constitutes a fundamental limitation of this approach, which has not been widely recognized. The development of chronic animal models, in which an abnormal state is induced and maintained for a prolonged period during which "therapy" can be administered, provides a powerful methodology for investigating these problems.

Finally, although this review has not been concerned with the problem of screening for antidepressant activity, it is clear that some of the models discussed could profitably be incorporated into antidepressant screening programs. It has traditionally been a major consideration in the design of antidepressant screening tests that they respond to acute or subacute drug administration. As a direct consequence, they are incapable, by virtue of their design, of responding to the major current challenge of discovering new antidepressants that have a shorter onset of action. By contrast, it is implicit in their protracted time course that chronic realistic animal models do have the capacity to detect a rapidly acting novel antidepressant. In fact, most pharmaceutical companies have now abandoned the high-volume, random-screening approach in favor of the development of a few compounds specifically designed to meet predetermined pharmacological criteria. In such a program, the place of behavioral screening methods shifts from the discovery phase to the development phase, and the logistical disadvantages of using complex, chronic models are small, relative to the costs of testing an ineffective drug in the clinic.

REFERENCES

L. Y. Abramson, and M. E. P. Seligman, Modeling psychopathology in the laboratory: History and rationale, *Psychopathology: Experimental Models* (J. D. Maser and M. E. P. Seligman, eds.), Freeman, San Francisco, 1–26 (1978).

L. Y. Abramson, M. E. P. Seligman, and J. D. Teasdale, Learned helplessness in humans: Critique and reformulation, *J. Abnorm. Psychol., 87*: 49 (1978).

L. Y. Abramson, G. Metalsky, and L. B. Alloy, Hopelessness depression: A theory-based subtype of depression, *Psychol. Rev., 96*: 358 (1989).

H. S. Akiskal, Interaction of biologic and psychologic factors in the origin of depressive disorders, *Acta Psychiatr. Scand., 71*: 131 (1985).

H. S. Akiskal, A developmental perspective on recurrent mood disorders: A review of studies in man, *Psychopharmacol. Bull., 22*: 579 (1986).

C. S. Aneshensel, and J. D. Stone, Stress and depression: A test of the buffering model of social support, *Arch. Gen. Psychiatry, 39*: 1392 (1982).

H. A. Anisman, and R. M. Zacharko, Depression: The predisposing influence of stress, *Behav. Brain Sci., 5*: 89 (1982).

H. Anisman, J. Irwin, and L. S. Sklar, Deficits of escape performance following catecholamine depletion: Implications for behavioural deficits induced by uncontrollable stress, *Psychopharmacology, 64*: 163 (1979).

S. M. Antelman, A. J. Eichler, C. A. Black, and D. Kocan, Interchangeability of stress and amphetamine sensitization, *Science, 207*: 329 (1980).

H. Araki, K. Kazuaki, Y. Uchiyama, and H. Aihara, Involvement of amygdaloid catecholaminergic mechanism in suppressive effects of desipramine and imipramine on duration of immobility in rats forced to swim, *Eur. J. Pharmacol., 113*: 313 (1985).

T. Archer, Animal models and drug screens for depression: Pragmatism and the validity requirement, *Animal Models in Psychopharmacology* (B. Olivier, J. Mos, and J. Slangen, eds.), Birkhauser, Basel, pp. 243–250 (1991).

D. M. Atrens, Self-stimulation and psychotropic drugs: A methodological and conceptual critique, *Animal Models in Psychopathology* (N. S. Bond, ed.), pp. 227–256, Academic Press, Sydney, (1984).

R. J. Barrett, and D. K. White, Reward system depression following chronic amphetamine: Antagonism by haloperidol, *Pharmacol. Biochem. Behav., 13*: 555 (1980).

B. D. Berger, and R. Schuster, An animal model of social interaction: Implications for the analysis of drug action, *Behavioral Models and the Analysis of Drug Action*, M. Y. Spiegelstein and A. Levy, eds.), Elsevier, Amsterdam, pp. 415–428 (1982).

J. C. Bizot, M. H. Thiebot, C. Le Bihan, P. Soubrie, and P. Simon, Effects of imipramine-like drugs and serotonin uptake blockers on delay of reward in rats: Possible implication in the behavioral mechanism of action of antidepressants, *J. Pharmacol. Exp. Ther., 286*: 1144 (1988a).

J. C. Bizot, M. H. Thiebot, and A. J. Puech, Effects of 5-HT-related drugs on waiting capacities in rats, *Psychopharmacology, 96*: S5 (1988b).

G. Blanc, D. Herve, H. Simon, A. Lisoprawski, J. Glowinski, and J. P. Tassin, Response to stress of mesocortical frontal dopaminergic neurons in rats after long-term isolation, *Nature, 284*: 265 (1980).

S. R. Bodnoff, B. Suranyi-Codotte, D. H. Aitken, R. Quirion, and M. Y. Meaney, The effects of chronic antidepressant treatment in an animal model of anxiety, *Psychopharmacology, 95*: 298 (1988).

F. Borsini, and A. Meli, Is the forced swimming test a suitable model for revealing antidepressant activity, *Psychopharmacology, 94*: 147 (1988).

F. Borsini, G. Bendotti, V. Velkov, R. Rech, and R. Samanin, Immobility test: Effects of 5-hydroxytryptaminergic drugs and role of catecholamines in the activity of some antidepressants, *J. Pharm. Pharmacol., 33*: 33 (1981).

M. Bourin, M. Poncelet, R. Chermat, and P. Simon, The value of the reserpine test in psychopharmacology, *Arzneimittelforschung, 33*: 1173 (1983).

C. L. Broekkamp, D. Garrigou, and K. G. Lloyd, Serotonin-mimetic and antidepressant drugs on passive avoidance learning by olfactory bulbectomized rats, *Pharmacol. Biochem. Behav., 13*: 643 (1980).

C. L. Broekkamp, W. T. O'Connor, J. A. D. M. Tonnaer, H. W. Rijk, and A. M. L. Van Delft, Corticosterone, choline acetyltransferase and noradrenaline levels in olfactory bulbectomized rats in relation to changes in passive avoidance acquisition and open field activity, *Physiol. Behav., 37*: 429 (1986).

G. W. Brown, A psychosocial view of depression, *Community Psychiatry* (D. H. Bennett and H. Freeman, eds), Churchill-Livingstone, London, pp. 71–114 (1989).

G. W. Brown, and T. Harris, *Social Origins of Depression*, Tavistock, London (1978).

G. W. Brown, and T. Harris, *Life Events and Illness*, Guilford Press, New York (1988).

G. W. Brown, F. Sklair, T. O. Harris, and J. L. T. Birley, Life events and psychiatric disorders. I. Some methodological issues, *Psychol. Med., 3*: 74 (1973).

L. Brown, R. A. Rosellini, O. B. Samuels, and E. P. Riley, Evidence for a serotonergic mechanism of the learned helplessness phenomenon, *Pharmacol. Biochem. Behav., 17*: 877 (1982).

K. D. Cairncross, B. Cox, C. Forster, and A. F. Wren, Olfactory projection systems, drugs and behaviour: A review, *Psychoneuroendocrinology, 4*: 253 (1979).

G. D. Carr, H. C. Fibiger, and A. G. Phillips, Conditioned place preference as a measure of drug reward, *The Neuropharmacological Basis of Reward* (J. M. Liebman and S. J. Cooper, eds.), Oxford University Press, Oxford pp. 264-319 (1989).

B. J. Carroll, The dexamethasone suppression test for melancholia, *Br. J. Psychiatry, 140*: 292 (1982).

G. P. Cassens, C. Actor, M. Kling, and J.J. Schildkraut, Amphetamine withdrawal effects threshold of intracranial self-stimulation, *Psychopharmacology, 73*: 318 (1981).

S. Cheeta, C. L. E. Broekkamp, and P. Willner, Reversal of stress-reduced antidomia by inanserin and its (+)-enantiomer, *J. Psychopharmacol,* Abst., 55.

A. V. Christensen, and M. Geoffroy, The effect of different serotonergic drugs in the learned helplessness model of depression, *Animal Models in Psychopharmacology* (B. Olivier, J. Mos, and J. Slangen, eds.), Birkhauser, Basel, pp. 205-209 (1991).

V. Cuomo, R. Cagiano, N. Brunello, R. Fumagalli, and G. Racagni, Behavioural changes after acute and chronic administration of typical and atypical antidepressants in rat: Interactions with reserpine, *Neurosci. Lett., 40*: 315 (1983).

W. Danysz, T. Archer, and C. J. Fowler, Screening for new antidepressant compounds, *Behavioural Models in Psychopharmacology: Theoretical, Industrial and Clinical Perspectives* (P. Willner, ed.), Cambridge University Press, Cambridge, pp. 126–156 (1991).

P. H. Desan, L. H. Silbert, and S. F. Maier, Long-term effects of inescapable stress on daily running activity and antagonism by desipramine, *Pharmacol. Biochem. Behav., 30*: 21 (1988).

B. A. Ellenbroek, and A. R. Cools, Animal models with construct validity for schizophrenia, *Behav. Pharmacol., 1*: 469 (1990).

H. M. Emrich, P. Vogt, and A. Herz, Possible antidepressant effects of opioids: Action of buprenorphine, *Ann. N. Y. Acad. Sci., 398*: 108 (1983).

B. J. Everitt, and E. B. Keverne, Models of depression based on behavioural observations of experimental animals, *Psychopharmacology of Affective Disorders* (E. S. Paykel and A. Coppen, eds.), Oxford University Press, Oxford, pp. 41–59 (1979).

D. J. Fontana, T. J. Carbary, and R. L. Commisaris, Effects of acute and chronic anti-panic drug administration on conflict behavior in the rat, *Psychopharmacology, 98*: 157 (1989).

A. Frazer, I. Lucki, and M. Sills, Alterations in monoamine-containing neuronal function due to administration of antidepressants repeatedly to rats, *Acta Pharmacol. Toxicol., 56* (Suppl. 1), 21 (1985).

R. Gardner, Mechanisms in manic–depressive disorder: An evolutionary model, *Arch. Gen. Psychiatry, 39*: 1436 (1982).

C. Gentsch, M. Lichsteiner, and H. Feer, Competition for sucrose-pellets in triads of male Wistar rats: Effects of acute and subchronic chlordiazepoxide, *Psychopharmacology, 100*: 530 (1990).

W. E. Gibson, L. D. Reid, M. Sakai, and P. B. Porter, Intracranial reinforcement compared with sugar-water reinforcement, *Science, 148*: 1357 (1965).

P. Giral, P. Martin, P. Soubrie, and P. Simon, Reversal of helpless behaviour in rats by putative $5HT_{1A}$ agonists. *Biol. Psychiatry, 23*: 237 (1988).

H. I. Glazer, and J. M. Weiss, Long-term interference effect: An alternative to "learned helplessness," *J. Exp. Psychol. Anim. Behav. Proc., 2*: 201 (1976).

A. Goudie, Animal models of drug abuse and dependence, *Behavioural Models in Psychopharmacology: Theoretical, Industrial and Clinical Perspectives* (P. Willner, ed.), Cambridge University Press, Cambridge, pp. 453–484 (1991).

S. Green, and H. Hodges, Animal models of anxiety, *Behavioural Models in Psychopharmacology: Theoretical, Industrial and Clinical Perspectives* (P. Willner, ed.), Cambridge University Press, Cambridge, pp. 21–49 (1991).

F. A. Henn, and W. T. McKinney, Animal models in psychiatry, *Psychopharmacology: The Third Generation of Progress* (H. Y. Meltzer, ed.), Raven Press, New York, pp. 697–704 (1987).

J. P. Henry, and P. M. Stephens, The social environment and essential hypertension in mice: Possible role of the innervation of the adrenal cortex, *Hypertension and Brain Mechanisms* (W. DeLong, A. P. Provoost, and A. P. Shapiro, eds.), Elsevier, New York, pp. 263–276, (1977).

L. A. Hilakivi, and I. Hilakivi, Increased adult behavioural "despair" in rats neonatally exposed to desipramine or zimelidine: An animal model of depression, *Pharmacol. Biochem. Behav., 28*: 267 (1987).

B. G. Hoebel, Brain-stimulation reward and aversion in relation to behaviour, *Brain-Stimulation Reward* (A. Wauquier and E. Rolls, eds.), North Holland/American Elsevier, New York, pp. 331-372 (1976).

P. D. Hrdina, P. Von Kulmiz, and R. Stretch, Pharmacological modification of experimental depression in infant macaques, *Psychopharmacology, 64*: 89 (1979).

R. L. Jackson, and T. R. Minor, Effects of signaling inescapable shock on subsequent escape learning: Implications for theories of coping and "learned helplessness," *J. Exp. Psychol. Anim. Behav. Proc., 14*: 390 (1988).

R. L. Jackson, S. F. Maier, and P. M. Rapoport, Exposure to inescapable shock produces both activity and associative deficits in rats, *Learn. Motiv., 9*: 69 (1978).

J. A. Jesberger, and J. S. Richardson, Animal models of depression: Parallels and correlates to severe depression in humans, *Biol. Psychiatry, 20*: 764 (1985).

J. A. Jesberger, and J. S. Richardson, Effects of antidepressant drugs on the behavior of olfactory bulbectomized and sham-operated rats, *Behav. Neurosci., 100*: 256 (1986).

D. Joly, and D. J. Sanger, The effects of fluoxetine and zimelidine on the behavior of olfactory bulbectomized rats, *Pharmacol. Biochem. Behav., 24*: 199 (1986).

D. Joly, and D. J. Sanger, Social competition in rats: A test sensitive to acutely administered anxiolytics, *Behav. Pharmacol., 2*: 205 (1991).

R. J. Katz, Animal models and human depressive disorders, *Neurosci. Biobehav. Rev., 5*: 231 (1981).

R. J. Katz, Animal model of depression: Pharmacological sensitivity of a hedonic deficit, *Pharmacol. Biochem. Behav., 16*: 965 (1982).

R. J. Katz, K. A. Roth, and B. J. Carroll, Acute and chronic stress effects on open field activity in the rat: Implications for a model of depression, *Neurosci. Biobehav. Rev., 5*: 247 (1981).

K. Kawashima, H. Araki, and H. Aihara, Effect of chronic administration of antidepressants on duration of immobility in rats forced to swim, *Jpn. J. Pharmacol., 40*: 199 (1986).

Y. Kitada, T. Miyauchi, A. Satoh, and S. Satoh, Effects of antidepressants in the rat forced swimming test, *Eur. J. Pharmacol., 72*: 145 (1981).

L. Kokkinidis, and R. M. Zacharko, Response sensitization and depression following long-term amphetamine treatment in a self-stimulation paradigm, *Psychopharmacology, 68*: 73 (1980).

L. Kokkinidis, R. M. Zacharko, and P. A. Predy, Post-amphetamine depression of self-stimulation responding from the substantia nigra: Reversal by tricyclic antidepressants, *Pharmacol. Biochem. Behav., 13*: 379 (1980).

G. F. Koob, Anhedonia as an animal model of depression, *Animal Models of Depression* (G. F. Koob, C. L. Ehlers, and D. J. Kupfer, eds.), Birkhauser, Boston, pp. 162–183.

C. Kornetsky, and R. U. Esposito, Reward and detection thresholds for brain stimulation: Dissociative effects of cocaine, *Brain Res., 209*: 496 (1981).

S. M. Korte, J. Smit, G. A. H. Bouws, J. M. Koolhaas, and B. Bohus, Neuroendocrine evidence for hypersensitivity in serotonergic neuronal system after psychosocial stress of defeat, *Animal Models in Psychopharmacology* (B. Olivier, J. Mos, and J. Slangen, eds.), Birkhauser, Basel, pp. 199–203 (1991).

G. W. Kraemer, M. H. Ebert, C. R. Lake, and W. T. McKinney, Hypersensitivity to *d*-amphetamine several years after early social deprivation in rhesus monkeys, *Psychopharmacology, 82*: 266 (1984a).

G. W. Kraemer, M. H. Ebert, C. R. Lake, and W. T. McKinney, Cerebrospinal fluid measures of neurotransmitter changes associated in the pharmacological alteration of the despair response to social separation in rhesus monkeys, *Psychiatry Res., 11*: 303 (1984b).

G. W. Kraemer, M. H. Ebert, D. E. Schmidt, and W. T. McKinney, A longitudinal study of the effect of different rearing conditions on cerebrospinal fluid norepinephrine and biogenic amine metabolism in rhesus monkeys, *Neuropsychopharmacology, 2*: 175 (1989).

N. N. Kudryatseva, I. V. Bakshtanovskaya, and L. A. Koryakina, Social model of depression in mice of C57BL/6J strain, *Pharmacol. Biochem. Behav., 38*: 315 (1991).

D. J. Kupfer, and M. E. Thase, The use of the sleep laboratory in the diagnosis of affective disorders, *Psychiatr. Clin. North Am., 6*: 3 (1983).

E. Lehr, Distress-call reactivation in isolated chicks: A behavioural indicator with high selectivity for antidepressants, *Psychopharmacology, 97*: 145 (1989).

N. J. Leith, and R. J. Barrett, Amphetamine and the reward system: Evidence for tolerance and post-drug depression, *Psychopharmacology, 46*: 19 (1976).

N. J. Leith and R. J. Barrett, Effects of chronic amphetamine or reserpire on self-stimulation: Animal model of depression? *Psychopharmacology, 72*: 9 (1980).

B. Leonard, The olfactory bulbectomized rat as a model of depression, *Eur. Neuropsychopharmacol., 1*: 297 (1991).

P. M. Lewinsohn, A behavioral approach to depression, *The Psychology of Depression: Contemporary Theory and Research* (R. J. Friedman and M. M. Katz, eds.), Winston/Wiley, New York, pp. 157–185 (1974).

J. K. Lewis, and W. T. McKinney, Effects of electroconvulsive shock on the behaviour of normal and abnormal rhesus monkeys, *Behav. Psychiatry, 37*: 687 (1976).

J. K. Lewis, W. T. McKinney, L. D. Young, and G. W. Kraemer, Mother–infant separation in rhesus monkeys as a model of human depression: A reconsideration, *Arch. Gen. Psychiatry, 33*: 699 (1976).

J. W. Lewis, J. T. Cannon, and J. C. Liebeskind, Opioid and nonopioid mechanisms of stress-induced analgesia, *Science, 208*: 623 (1980).

C. Lloyd, Life events and depressive disorder reviewed, *Arch. Gen. Psychiatry, 37*: 529 (1980).

K. G. Lloyd, D. Garrigou, C. L. E. Broekkamp, The action of monoaminergic, cholinergic and GABAergic comopunds in the olfactory bulbectomized rat model of depression, *New Vistas in Depression* (S. Z. Langer, R. Takahashi, T. Segawa, and M. Briley, eds.), Pergamon Press, New York, pp. 179–186 (1982).

M. Lyon, Animal models of mania and schizophrenia, *Behavioural Models in Psychopharmacology: Theoretical, Industrial and Clinical Perspectives* (P. Willner, ed.), Cambridge University Press, Cambridge, pp. 253–310 (1991).

S. F. Maier, Learned helplessness and animal models of depression, *Prog. Neuropsychopharmacol. Biol. Psychiatry, 8*: 435 (1984).

G. J. Marek, A. Li, and L. S. Seiden, Selective 5-hydroxytryptamine-2 antagonists have antidepressant-like effects on differential-reinforcement-of-low-rate 72-s schedule, *J. Pharmacol. Exp. Ther., 250*: 60 (1989).

A. Markou, and G. F. Koob, Bromocriptine reverses post-cocaine anhedonia in a rat model of cocaine withdrawal, *Am. Coll. Neuropsychopharmacol. Abstr.* No. 157 (1989).

A. Markou, S. J. Hanley, A. K. Chehade, and G. F. Koob, Effects of performance and reward manipulations on current-intensity thresholds and other measures derived from a discrete-trial self-stimulation procedure in rats, *Soc. Neurosci. Abstr., 15*: 35 (1989).

P. Martin, P. Soubrie, and P. Simon, Shuttle-box deficits induced by inescapable shocks in rats: Reversal by the beta-adrenoreceptor stimulants clenbuterol and salbutamol, *Pharmacol. Biochem. Behav., 24*: 177 (1986a).

P. Martin, P. Soubrie, and P. Simon, Noradrenergic and opioid mediation of tricyclic-induced reversal of escape deficits caused by inescapable shock pretreatment in rats, *Psychopharmacology, 90*: 90 (1986b).

P. Martin, A. M. Laporte, P. Soubrie, S. El Mestikawy, and S. Hamon, Reversal of helpless behaviour by serotonin reuptake inhibitors, *Behavioural Pharmacology of 5HT* (P. Bevan, A. R. Cools, and T. Archer, eds.), Laurence Erlbaum, New York, pp. 231–234 (1989).

W. T. McKinney, Animal models of depression: An overview, *Psychiatr. Dev., 2*: 77 (1984).

W. T. McKinney, and W. E. Bunney, Animal model of depression: Review of evidence and implications for research, *Arch. Gen. Psychiatry, 21*: 240 (1969).

W. T. McKinney, and G. W. Kraemer, Effects of oxaprotiline on the response to peer separation in rhesus monkeys, *Biol. Psychiatry, 25*: 818 (1989).

W. T. McKinney, L. D. Young, and S. J. Soumi, Chlorpromazine treatment of disturbed monkeys, *Arch. Gen. Psychiatry, 29*: 490 (1973).

E. W. Menzel, R. K. Davenport, and C. M. Rogers, Effects of environmental restriction upon the chimpanzee's responsiveness to objects, *J. Comp. Physiol. Psychol., 56*: 78 (1963).

T. R. Minor, R. L. Jackson, and S. F. Maier, Effects of task-irrelevant cues and reinforcement delay on choice-escape learning following inescapable shock: Evidence for a deficit in selective attention, *J. Exp. Psychol. Anim. Behav. Proc., 10*: 543 (1984).

T. R. Minor, M. A. Pelleymounter, and S. F. Maier, Uncontrollable shock, forebrain norepinephrine, and stimulus selection during choice-escape learning, *Psychobiology, 16*: 135 (1988).

P. J. Mitchell, and P. H. Redfern, Acute and chronic antidepressant drug treatments induce opposite effects in the social behaviour of rats, *J. Psychopharmacol., 6*: 214 (1992a).

P. J. Mitchell, and P. H. Redfern, Chronic treatment with clomipramine and mianserin increases the hierarchical position of subdominant rats housed in triads, *Behav. Pharmacol., 3*: 239 (1992b).

S. M. Monroe, M. E. Thase, M. Hersen, J. M. Himmelhoch, and A. S. Bellack, Life events and the endogenous–nonendogenous distinction in the treatment and posttreatment course of depression, *Compr. Psychiatry, 26*: 175 (1985).

A. M. J. Montgomery, Animal models of eating disorders, *Behavioural Models in Psychopharmacology: Theoretical, Industrial and Clinical Perspectives* (P. Willner, ed.), Cambridge University Press, Cambridge, pp. 177–214 (1991).

J.-L. Moreau, F. Jenck, J. R. Martin, P. Mortas, and W. E. Haefely, Antidepressant treatment prevents chronic unpredictable mild stress-induced anhedonia as assessed by ventral tegmental self-stimulation behavior in rats, *Eur. Neuropsychopharmacol., 2*: 43 (1992).

R. Muscat, and P. Willner, Suppression of sucrose drinking by chronic mild unpredictable stress: A methodological analysis, *Neurosci. Biobehav. Rev., 16*: 507 (1992).

R. Muscat, D. Sampson, and P. Willner, Dopaminergic mechanism of imipramine action in an animal model of depression, *Biol. Psychiatry, 28*: 223 (1990).

R. Muscat, M. Papp, and P. Willner, Reversal of stress-induced anhedonia by the atypical antidepressants, fluoxetine and maprotiline, *Psychopharmacology, 109*: 433 (1992).

J. C. Nelson, The use of antipsychotic drugs in the treatment of depression, *Treating Resistant Depression* (J. Zohar, and R. H. Belmaker, eds.), PMA Corp., New York, pp. 131–146 (1987).

J. C. Nelson, and D. S. Charney, The symptoms of major depression, *Am. J. Psychiatry, 138*: 1 (1981).

R. J. M. Niesink, and J. M. van Ree, Antidepressant drugs normalize the increased social behaviour of pairs of male rats induced by short term isolation, *Neuropharmacology, 21*: 1343 (1982).

A. Nomura, J. Shimizu, H. Kamateni, M. Kinjo, M. Watanabe, and T. Nakazawa, Swimming mice: In search of an animal model for human depression, *New Vistas in Depression* (S. Z. Langer, R. Takahashi, T. Segawa, and M. Briley, eds.), Pergamon Press, New York, pp. 203–210 (1982).

K. A. O'Neill, and D. Valentino, Escapability and generalization: Effect on behavioural despair, *Eur. J. Pharmacol., 78*: 379 (1982).

D. H. Overstreet, A behavioral, psychopharmacological and neurochemical update on the Flinders Sensitive Line rat, a potential genetic animal model of depression, *Behav. Genet., 21*: 67 (1991).

D. H. Overstreet, and D. S. Janowsky, A cholinergic supersensitivity model of depression, *Neuromethods*, Vol 20: *Animal Models in Psychiatry* (A. Boulton, G. Baker, and M. Martin-Iverson, eds.), Birkhauser, Basel, pp. 81–114 (1991).

M. Papp, P. Willner, and R. Muscat, An animal model of anhedonia: Attenuation of sucrose consumption and place preference conditioning by chronic unpredictable mild stress, *Psychopharmacology, 104*: 255 (1991).

M. Papp, S. Lappas, R. Muscat, and P. Willner, Attenuation of place preference conditioning but not place aversion conditioning by chronic mild stress, *J. Psychopharmacol., 6*: 352 (1992b).

M. Papp, R. Muscat, and P. Willner, Subsensitivity to rewarding and locomotor stimulant effects of a dopamine agonist following chronic mild stress, *Psychopharmacology, 110*: 152 (1993).

A. Plaznik, W. Danysz, and W. Kostowski, Mesolimbic noradrenaline but not dopamine is responsible for organization of rat behavior in the forced swim test and an anti-immobilizing effect of desipramine, *Pol. J. Pharmacol. Pharm., 37*: 347 (1985a).

A. Plaznik, W. Danysz, and W. Kostowski, A stimulatory effect of intraaccumbens injections of noradrenaline on the behavior of rats in the forced swim test, *Psychopharmacology, 87*: 119 (1985b).

G. T. Pollard, and J. L. Howard, Similar effects of antidepressant and non-antidepressant drugs on behavior under an interresponse-time > 72-s schedule, *Psychopharmacology, 89*: 253 (1986).

R. D. Porsolt, Behavioural despair, *Antidepressants: Neurochemical, Behavioural and Clinical Perspectives* (S. J. Enna, J. B. Malick, and E. Richelson, eds.), Raven Press, New York, pp. 121–139 (1981).

R. D. Porsolt, M. LePichon, and M. Jalfre, Depression: A new animal model sensitive to antidepressant treatment, *Nature, 266*: 730 (1977).

R. D. Porsolt, A. Bertin, M. Blavet, M. Deniel, and M. Jalfre, Immobility induced by forced swimming in rats: Effects of agents which modify central catecholamine and serotonin activity, *Eur. J. Pharmacol., 57*: 201 (1979).

R. D. Porsolt, R. Chermat, P. Simon, and L. Steru, The tail suspension test: Computerized device for evaluating psychotropic activity profiles, *Psychopharmacology, 89*: S28 (1986).

R. D. Porsolt, A. Lenegre, and R. A. McArthur, Pharmacological models of depression, *Animal Models in Psychopharmacology* (B. Olivier, J. Mos, and J. L. Slangen, eds.), Birkhauser, Basel, pp. 137–159 (1991).

M. D. Post, Cocaine psychoses: A continuum model, *Am. J. Psychiatry, 132*: 225 (1975).

J. S. Price, Genetic and phylogenetic aspects of mood variation, *Int. J. Ment. Health, 1*: 124 (1972).

O. Pucilowski, D. S. Overstreet, A. Rezvani, and D. S. Janowsky, Chronic mild stress-induced anhedomia: Greater effect in a genetic rat model of depression, *Physiol. Behav.* (in press, 1993)

M. J. Raleigh, M. T. McGuire, G. L. Brammer, and A. Yuwiler, Social and environmental influences on blood serotonin concentrations in monkeys, *Arch. Gen. Psychiatry, 139*: 679 (1984).

M. Reite, R. Short, C. Seiler, and J. D. Pauley, Attachment, loss and depression, *J. Child Psychol. Psychiatry, 22*: 141 (1981).

J. Robertson, and J. Bowlby, Responses of young children to separation from their mothers, *Cour Centre Int. Enfance, 2*: 131 (1952).

B. Rodgers, Models of stress, vulnerability and affective disorder, *J. Affective Disord., 21*: 1 (1991).

D. Sampson, R. Muscat, and P. Willner, Reversal of antidepressant action by dopamine antagonists in an animal model of depression, *Psychopharmacology, 104*: 491 (1991).

M. Sarter, J. Hagan, and P. Dudchenko, Behavioral screening for cognition enhancers: From indiscriminate to valid testing, *Psychopharmacology*, *107*: 114, 461 (1992).

A. H. Schmale, Adaptive role of depression in health and disease, *Separation and Depression* (J. P. Scott and E. Senay, eds.), Am. Assoc. Adv. Sci., Washington, D.C., pp. 187–214 (1973).

L. S. Seiden, J. L. Dahms, and R. A. Shaughnessy, Behavioral screen for antidepressants: The effects of drugs and electroconvulsive shock on performance under a differential-reinforcement-of-low-rate schedule, *Psychopharmacology, 86*: 55 (1985).

M. E. P. Seligman, *Helplessness: On Depression, Development and Death*, Freeman, San Francisco (1975).

N. Shanks, and H. Anisman, Stressor-provoked behavioral changes in six strains of mice, *Behav. Neurosci., 102*: 894 (1988).

A. D. Sherman, and F. Petty, Neurochemical basis of the action of antidepressants on learned helplessness, *Behav. Neural. Biol., 30*: 119 (1980).

A. D. Sherman, J. L. Sacquitne, and F. Petty, Specificity of the learned helplessness model of depression, *Pharmacol. Biochem. Behav., 16*: 449 (1982).

D. M. Simpson, and Z. Annau, Behavioural withdrawal following several psychoactive drugs, *Pharmacol. Biochem. Behav., 7*: 59 (1977).

J. S. Soblosky, and J. B. Thurmond, Biochemical and behavioral correlates of chronic stress: Effects of tricyclic antidepressants, *Pharmacol. Biochem. Behav., 24*: 1361 (1986).

P. Soubrie, Reconciling the role of central serotonin neurons in human and animal behaviour, *Behav. Brain Sci., 9*: 319 (1986).

P. Soubrie, P. Martin, S. El Mestikawy, M. H. Thiebot, P. Simon, and M. Hamon, The lesion of serotonergic neurons does not prevent antidepressant-induced reversal of escape failures produced by inescapable shocks in rats, *Pharmacol. Biochem. Behav., 25*: 1 (1986).

J. A. Stamford, R. Muscat, J. J. O'Connor, J. J. Patel, W. J. Wieczorek, Z. L. Kruk, and P. Willner, Voltammetric evidence that subsensitivity to reward following chronic mild stress is associated with increased release of mesolimbic dopamine, *Psychopharmacology, 105*: 275 (1991).

L. Steru, R. Chermat, B. Thierry, and P. Simon, The tail suspension test: A new method for screening antidepressants in mice, *Psychopharmacology, 85*: 367 (1985).

S. J. Suomi, Factors affecting responses to social separation in rhesus monkeys, *Animal Models in Human Psychobiology* (G. Serban and A. Kling, eds.), Plenum Press, New York, pp. 9–26 (1976).

S. J. Suomi, S. F. Seaman, J. K. Lewis, R. B. DeLizio, and W. T. McKinney, Effects of imipramine treatment on separation-induced social disorders in rhesus monkeys, *Arch. Gen. Psychiatry, 35*: 321 (1978).

C. Turner, R. Davenport, and C. Rogers, The effect of early deprivation on the social behaviour of adolescent chimpanzees, *Am. J. Psychiatry, 125*: 1531 (1969).

E. S. Valenstein, *Brain Control: A Critical Examination of Brain Stimulation and Psychosurgery*, John Wiley and Sons, New York (1973).

J. A. M. van der Heyden, B. Olivier, and T. J. J. Zethof, The behavioural despair model as a predictor of antidepressant activity: Effects of serotonergic drugs, *Animal Models in Psychopharmacology* (B. Olivier, J. Mos, and J. Slangen, eds.), Birkhauser, Basel, pp. 211–215 (1991).

H. Van Riezen, and B. E. Leonard, Effects of psychotropic drugs on the behaviour and neurochemistry of olfactory bulbectomized rats, *Psychopharmacology of Anxiolytics and Antidepressants* (S. E. File, ed.), Pergamon Press, New York, pp. 231–250 (1990).

G. Vogel, D. Neill, M. Hagler, and D. Kors, A new animal model of endogenous depression: A summary of present findings, *Neurosci. Biobehav. Rev., 14*: 85 (1990).

R. Watson, E. Hartman, and J. J. Schildkraut, Amphetamine withdrawal: Affective state, sleep patterns and MHPG excretion, *Am. J. Psychiatry, 129*: 263 (1972).

J. M. Weiss, P. A. Goodman, B. G. Losito, S. Corrigan, J. M. Charry, and W. H. Bailey, Behavioural depression produced by an uncontrollable stressor: Relationship to noreprinephrine, dopamine, and serotonin levels in various regions of rat brain, *Brain Res. Rev., 3*: 167 (1981).

J. M. Weiss, W. H. Bailey, P. A. Goodman, L. J. Hoffman, M. J. Ambrose, S. Salman, and J. M. Charry, A model for neurochemical study of depression, *Behavioural Models and the Analysis of Drug Action* (M. Y. Spiegelstein and A. Levy, eds.), Elsevier, Amsterdam, pp. 195–223 (1982).

P. Willner, The validity of animal models of depression, *Psychopharmacology, 83*: 1 (1984).

P. Willner, *Depression: A Psychobiological Synthesis*, John Wiley & Sons, New York (1985).

P. Willner, Validating criteria for animal models of human mental disorders: Learned helplessness as a paradigm case, *Prog. Neuropsychopharmacol. Biol. Psychiatry, 10*: 677 (1986).

P. Willner, Sensitization to the actions of antidepressant drugs, *Psychoactive Drugs: Tolerance and Sensitization* (M. W. Emmett-Oglesby and A. J. Goudie, eds.), Humana Press, Clifton, N. J., pp. 407–459 (1989a).

P. Willner, Towards a theory of serotonergic dysfunction in depression, *Behavioural Pharmacology of 5-HT* (T. Archer, P. Bevan, and A. Cools, eds.), Lawrence Erlbaum, New York, pp. 157–178 (1989b).

P. Willner, Animal models of depression: An overview, *Pharmacol. Ther., 45*: 425 (1990).

P. Willner, Behavioural models in psychopharmacology, *Behavioural Models in Psychopharmacology: Theoretical, Industrial and Clinical Perspectives* (P. Willner, ed.), Cambridge University Press, Cambridge, pp. 3–18 (1991a).

P. Willner, Animal models as simulations of depression, *Trends Pharmacol. Sci., 12*: 131 (1991b).

P. Willner, A. Theodorou, and A. M. J. Montgomery, Subchronic treatment with the tricyclic antidepressant DMI increases isolation-induced fighting in rats, *Pharmacol. Biochem. Behav., 14*: 475 (1981).

P. Willner, A. Towell, D. Sampson, S. Sophokleous, and R. Muscat, Reduction of sucrose preference by chronic mild unpredictable stress, and its restoration by a tricyclic antidepressant, *Psychopharmacology, 93*: 358 (1987).

P. Willner, D. Sampson, G. Phillips, R. Fichera, P. Foxlow, and R. Muscat, Effects of isolated housing and chronic antidepressant treatment on cooperative social behaviour in rats, *Behav. Pharmacol., 1*: 85 (1989).

P. Willner, D. Sampson, M. Papp, G. Phillips, and R. Muscat, Animal models of anhedonia, *Animal Models of Psychiatric Disorders*, Vol 3, *Anxiety, Depression and Mania* (P. Soubrie, ed.), S. Karger, Basel, pp. 71–99 (1991).

R. A. Wise, The brain and reward, *The Neuropharmacological Basis of Reward* (J. M. Liebmann and S. J. Cooper, eds.), Oxford University Press, Oxford, pp. 377–424 (1989).

W. W. Woodmansee, L. H. Silbert, and S. F. Maier, Stress-induced changes in daily activity in the rat are modulated by different factors than are stress-induced escape-learning deficits, *Soc. Neurosci. Abstr., 17*: 146 (1991).

R. M. Zacharko, and H. Anisman, Stressor-provoked alterations of intracranial self-stimulation in the mesocortiolimbic dopamine system: An animal model of depression, *The Mesolimbic Dopamine System, From Motivation to Action* (P. Willner, and J. Scheel-Kruger, eds.), John Wiley & Sons, Chichester, pp. 411–442 (1991).

R. M. Zacharko, W. J. Bowers, L. Kokkinidis, and H. Anisman, Region-specific reductions of intracranial self-stimulation after uncontrollable stress: Possible effects on reward processes, *Behav. Brain Res., 9*: 129 (1983).

R. M. Zacharko, G. T. Lalonde, M. Kasian, and H. Anisman, Strain specific effects of inescapable shock on intracranial self-stimulation from the nucleus accumbens, *Brain Res., 426*: 164 (1987).

13

The Pathogenesis of Depression: Reconsideration of Neurotransmitter Data

Serena-Lynn Brown
Albert Einstein College of Medicine/Montefiore Medical Center, Bronx, New York

Robert L. Steinberg
Mount Sinai Medical Center, New York, New York

Herman M. van Praag
University of Limburg, Maastricht, The Netherlands

I. THE MONOAMINE HYPOTHESIS

With the discovery several decades ago that both the tricyclic antidepressants (TCAs) and the monoamine oxidase (MAO) inhibitors provide clinical efficacy in the treatment of depression (Kuhn, 1958), the "monoamine hypothesis of depression" was proposed (Bunney and Davis, 1965; Schildkraut, 1965). According to this hypothesis, monoamines (MAs), and particularly norepinephrine (NE), are deficient in depression, and the TCAs and the MAO inhibitors exert their therapeutic action by increasing synaptic availability of the monoamines, either through blockade of presynaptic uptake (the TCAs) or through inhibiting degradation of the neurotransmitters (the MAO inhibitors). van Praag and Leijnse (1963a, b) and, subsequently, Maas (1975) extended this hypothesis to include the important role of a proposed deficiency of serotonin (5-hydroxytryptamine; 5-HT), in this disorder.

Over the next 25 years, research into the biology of depression proliferated. As the role of the monoamines in depression was investigated further, several problems with the monoamine hypothesis emerged: (1) There is a significantly delayed onset of clinical response after antidepressant treatment. Although MAO inhibition and the NE or 5-HT-uptake blockade effects of the antidepressants occur within hours of initial administration, clinical improvement usually requires between 1 and 4 weeks of treatment (Iversen and Mackay, 1979; Oswald et al., 1972; Stahl, 1984). (2) Several drugs that appear to have no effect on monoamine reuptake, such as iprindole (Gluckman and Baum, 1969; Lahti and Maickel, 1971) are nevertheless, effective antidepressants (Zis and Goodwin, 1979; Sugrue, 1983a, b). (3) Compounds that are effective monoamine reuptake inhibitors, such as amphetamines and cocaine, do not possess effective antidepressant properties (Heninger and Charney, 1982; Overall et al., 1962; Post et al., 1974; Sugrue, 1983a).

Such clinical data suggest that the therapeutic efficacy of antidepressant treatment (TCAs, MAO inhibitors, atypical antidepressants, and electroconvulsive therapy; ECS) may not be elucidated by examination of the short-term effects of these compounds on NE or 5-HT availability. Therefore, more recently, investigators have focused on specific receptor changes over time induced by long-term administration of various antidepressants, with emphasis on the noradrenergic and, more recently, the serotonergic system. This review will generally focus on human clinical data involving both monoamine metabolism and receptor function in depression, except when no such data are available and animal data may be suggestive of future directions in human research.

II. THE SEROTONIN SYSTEM

In this section we will review the large body of data published over the last several decades implicating 5-HT in the pathogenesis of depression. Although, originally, the 5-HT hypothesis of depression proposed a hypofunction of this system, subsequent research made it unclear whether the 5-HT dysfunction in depression was related to hypofunction or hyperfunction of this system. Thus, recent investigations in this area have focused more on receptor subtypes and complex interactions between these and other transmitter systems.

A. Biochemical Data

Several measures of presynaptic 5-HT functioning have been examined in depression.

1. Postmortem Brain Studies

Postmortem brain studies have provided data suggesting that central nervous system (CNS) metabolism of 5-HT may be reduced in the midbrain raphe nuclei (the major loci of 5-HT-containing neuronal cell bodies) of depressed patients who died of natural causes, and of suicide victims (Beskow et al., 1976; Birkmayer and Riederer, 1975; Bourne et al., 1968; Cochran et al., 1976; Lloyd et al., 1974; Shaw et al., 1967). However, other investigators have not been able to confirm these findings (Cheetham et al., 1989; Grahame-Smith, 1989).

Several groups of investigators have examined [^{3}H]imipramine binding in postmortem brain specimens of depressed persons (who died either from natural causes or as a consequence of suicide) and normal controls, and have shown a reduction in the number of [^{3}H]imipramine binding sites in the depressed group, unrelated to age, delay of assay, and type of terminal illness or cause of death (Langer et al., 1981a, b). Perry et al. (1983), Stanley et al. (1982), and Stanley and Mann (1983) have also reported a decrease in presynaptic [^{3}H]imipramine-binding sites in the hippocampus and occipital cortex of suicide victims. These findings, however, were not replicated by Meyerson et al. (1982). Gross-Isseroff et al. (1989) have also demonstrated region-specific differences in [^{3}H]imipramine binding in postmortem brain specimens of suicide victims without history of schizophrenia, alcoholism, or drug abuse. They found increased binding compared with normal controls in areas of the hippocampal formation and decreased binding in the claustrum and some cortical regions, with no differences between controls and suicide victims in prefrontal cortex binding, as have been shown by other investigators (Stanley et al., 1982).

2. Cerebrospinal Fluid 5-Hydroxyindoleacetic Acid Studies

Pretreatment. Most, but not all investigators have found decreased postprobenecid 5-hydroxyindoleacetic acid (5-HIAA) accumulation in cerebrospinal fluid (CSF) of depressed patients compared with normal persons, suggesting decreased CNS 5-HT metabolism (Bowers, 1974a; Goodwin et al., 1977; Sjostrom, 1973; van Praag et al., 1970, 1973a,b), particularly in those patients meeting criteria for "endogenous" or "vital" depression (Goodwin et al., 1977; van Praag and Korf, 1971).

Posttreatment. Interestingly, decreased CSF 5-HIAA is also consistently demonstrated in depressed patients after long-term administration of antidepressant medications, including the TCAs, such as amitriptyline, imipramine, nortriptyline, and clomipramine (chlorimipramine); atypical antidepressants, such as the selective 5-HT uptake blocker zimelidine; or MAO inhibitors, such as phenelzine (Asberg et al., 1975; Bertilsson et al., 1976; Bowers, 1974b; Bowers and Kupfer, 1971; Kupfer and Bowers, 1972; Mendlewicz et al., 1982; Papeschi and McClure, 1971; Post and Goodwin, 1974; Siwers et al., 1976; Traskman et al., 1979). This [further] decrease in CSF 5-HIAA may arise as a compensation for enhanced 5-HT neurotransmission across the synapse. Electroconvulsive shock (ECS) therapy has not been shown to produce consistent changes in CSF 5-HIAA (Abrams et al., 1976; Ashcroft et al., 1966; Bowers et al., 1969; Nordin et al., 1971).

3. Platelet Studies: Serotonin Uptake

Over the last several decades, the human blood platelet, which is a neuroectodermal derivative, has emerged as a peripheral model for the study of the transport, storage, metabolism, and release of 5-HT by serotonergic nerve endings (Sneddon, 1973; Stahl, 1977).

Pretreatment. Investigators have consistently demonstrated that platelet 5-HT uptake is reduced in unmedicated depressed patients (Born et al., 1980; Coppen et al., 1978; Faludi et al., 1988; Hallstrom et al., 1976; Meltzer et al., 1981; Mirkin and Coppen, 1980; Mulgirigama, 1976; Scott et al., 1979; Suranyi-Cadotte et al., 1985; Tuomisto, 1974; Tuomisto and Tukiainen, 1976; Tuomisto et al., 1979; Wood et al., 1983a). Rausch et al. (1988) have shown that one ECS treatment significantly increases platelet 5-HT uptake to normal levels.

More recently, Quintana (1989) has found two separate affinity states of the platelet 5-HT transport system, which differ significantly in a group of unmedicated depressed patients and a group of normal controls, with a greater gap between these two states for depressives than for the normal controls. When the depressed patients were treated for 2 months with imipramine, the kinetic constants of both transports normalized, with a decrease between the kinetic gap.

There are accumulating data suggesting that circadian rhythmicity may be a prominent factor influencing 5-HT uptake dynamics in depressed patients (Humphries et al., 1985; Modai et al., 1986; Oxenkrug et al., 1978; Rausch et al., 1982; Wirz-Justice and Puhringer, 1978). Other investigators have reported seasonal variations in platelet 5-HT uptake in normal and depressed patients (Arora et al., 1984; Egrise et al., 1986; Malmgren et al., 1989; Swade and Coppen, 1981). This will be discussed later.

Posttreatment. Data on the effects of antidepressant treatment on 5-HT uptake have generally shown that TCAs, zimelidine, and lithium cause a further decrease in platelet 5-HT uptake after several weeks of treatment (Coppen and Wood, 1980; Coppen et al.,

1981; Meltzer et al., 1981, 1983a; Ross et al., 1980; Willner, 1985). On the other hand, some investigators have reported no significant change in or normalization of 5-HT uptake after antidepressant treatments, such as TCAs, atypical antidepressants, ECS, and lithium (Born et al., 1980; Giret et al., 1980; Healy and Leonard, 1987; Meltzer et al., 1981; Suranyi-Cadotte et al., 1985; Tuomisto et al., 1979; Wood et al., 1983b).

4. Platelet Studies: Tritiated Imipramine Binding

Pretreatment. Most investigators have found a consistent and significant decrease in platelet [^{3}H]imipramine binding in unmedicated depressed patients when compared with controls (Asarch et al., 1980; Baron et al., 1983, 1986; Briley et al., 1980; Coppen and Wood, 1980; Kaplan and Mann, 1982; Langer and Raisman, 1983; Lewis and McChesney, 1985; Paul et al., 1981; Raisman et al., 1981, 1982; Roy et al., 1987a; Slotkin et al., 1989; Stanley and Mann, 1983; Suranyi-Cadotte et al., 1983, 1985; Wood et al., 1983a). Roy et al. (1987a) have found this decreased density of binding sites only in depressed women. Several other investigators, however, have failed to find differences in platelet [^{3}H]imipramine binding between depressives and controls (Carstens et al., 1986; Egrise et al., 1986; Tang and Morris, 1985; Whitaker et al., 1984). In addition, measurement of 5-HT-binding sites with [^{3}H]paroxetine (thought to be a more specific and potent 5-HT reuptake inhibitor than [^{3}H]imipramine) also revealed no differences in binding sites between depressives and normal controls (D'haenen et al., 1988).

Posttreatment. The few studies of the effects of chronic antidepressant treatment or ECS on platelet [^{3}H]imipramine binding in humans have produced variable results; consequently, they are inconclusive (Cowen et al., 1986; Langer and Raisman, 1983; Langer et al., 1986; Suranyi-Cadotte et al., 1985).

5. Postsynaptic Studies

Postsynaptic 5-HT parameters in depression have received much less attention, principally because of the difficulties involved in examining these in vivo. Several postmortem brain studies of suicide victims have demonstrated increased density of postsynaptic 5-HT_2 receptors, along with reduced density of presynaptic imipramine-binding sites in frontal cortex (Stanley and Mann, 1983; Stanley et al., 1982; Mann et al., 1986). McKeith et al. (1987) have reported similar results with postmortem binding studies of individuals with well-documented affective disorder.

Pretreatment. The 5-HT_2 receptor sites have also been identified on human blood platelets, with increase in receptor density, but no differences in affinity reported for depressives compared with normal controls in [^{3}H]ketanserin-binding studies (Biegon et al., 1987).

Posttreatment. Long-term TCA treatment (Fuxe et al., 1982; Peroutka and Snyder, 1980; Stockmeier and Kellar, 1986; Stolz et al., 1983), treatment with MAO inhibitors (Kellar et al., 1981; Koshikawa et al., 1985; Peroutka and Snyder, 1980), and treatment with atypical antidepressants (Fuxe et al., 1982; Peroutka and Snyder, 1980; Stolz et al., 1983) have consistently caused a decrease in postsynaptic 5-HT_2 receptor binding. In contrast, ECS treatment has caused an increase in 5-HT_2 receptor binding (Kellar et al., 1981; Vetulani et al., 1981; Stockmeier and Kellar, 1986).

In general, no change has been seen in 5-HT_1 receptor binding with the administration of a wide range of TCA and atypical antidepressant medications (Blackshear and Sanders-Bush, 1982; Fuxe et al., 1982; Lucki and Frazer, 1982; Peroutka and Snyder, 1980; Stolz et al., 1983) and ECS (Bergstrom and Kellar, 1979), although MAO inhibitors (Lucki and Frazer, 1982; Peroutka and Snyder, 1980) and two atypical antidepressants, mianserin (Segawa et al., 1982) and zimelidine (Fuxe et al., 1979, 1981), have caused decreased binding to these receptors.

In summary, it appears that postsynaptic 5-HT_2 receptor indices may be increased in depression, with decrease after a variety of antidepressant treatments.

6. *Treatment Studies*

Treatment studies involving depressed patients generally have shown the following: (1) Both of the 5-HT precursors 5-hydroxytryptophan (5HTP) and L-tryptophan may have antidepressant effects (van Praag, 1983, 1984). (2) The 5-HT-depleting agents, such as *p*-chlorophenylalanine, may have depressogenic effects (Shopsin et al., 1976). (3) Selective 5-HT uptake inhibitors, such as fluvoxamine, fluoxetine, clomipramine, and zimelidine, which presumably enhance 5-HT activity, possess antidepressant efficacy (Benfield and Ward, 1986; Carlsson et al., 1981; Chouinard, 1985; Dick and Ferrero, 1983; Dominguez et al., 1985; Stark and Hardison, 1985). (4) Lithium augments clinical response to TCAs, MAO inhibitors, or a combination of the two (Frazer and Jauher, 1985; Nelson and Mazure, 1986; Price et al., 1983; Price et al., 1985a). Although some investigators believe that this may occur by increasing 5-HT neurotransmission (de Montigny et al., 1981), others have suggested that lithium may exert its primary serotonergic effects at the presynaptic level, with secondary effects on postsynaptic parameters resulting from the increased availability of 5-HT (Price et al., 1990). Electrophysiological single-cell recording studies have generally suggested that most antidepressant treatments enhance 5-HT neurotransmission (Blier et al., 1987). Finally, Delgado et al. (1990), found that after rapid tryptophan depletion, patients in antidepressant-induced remission from depression experienced a relapse of depressive symptoms, with gradual return to remission following resumption of regular food intake. Such findings may suggest that some antidepressants may require 5-HT availability to exert their therapeutic actions.

In summary, many antidepressant treatments appear to cause an increase in 5-HT activity.

B. Neuroendocrine Challenge Data

Another strategy for studying neurotransmitter receptor systems in psychiatric disorders has been developed. This is the *neuroendocrine challenge* or *neuroendocrine probe* paradigm, which provides a "window" on central monoamine function, enabling investigators to evaluate receptor function indirectly in vivo. This paradigm involves the administration of a specific monoaminergic agent (generally an agonist or antagonist), either orally or intravenously, with subsequent measurements of a function or functions under control of that particular monoaminergic system. In terms of probing the 5-HT system, certain hormones under serotonergic control, including cortisol, prolactin, and growth hormone, or physiological measures, such as temperature regulation, are often measured. It is believed that the magnitude of the response is an indicator of the functional status of the monoaminergic system and provides an indirect measurement of receptor sensitivity or function.

This technique has been used increasingly in the study of depression and anxiety (Charney et al., 1982a), as well as schizophrenia (Murphy et al., 1986).

Neuroendocrine challenge studies conducted on depressed patients are limited in number and have provided variable results. Challenge tests examining the 5-HT system have generally used the 5-HT precursors L-tryptophan and 5-hydroxytryptophan (5-HTP), both thought to cause an increase in 5-HT synthesis and function and, therefore, both expected to produce an elevated release of the aforementioned hormones. However, neither L-tryptophan nor 5-HTP are 5-HT-selective. Both influence catecholamine (CA) metabolism significantly and differentially (van Praag et al., 1987a,b). High doses of L-tryptophan diminish tyrosine influx into the CNS and thereby decrease norepinephrine and dopamine synthesis. 5-Hydroxytryptophan, however, increases both 5-HT and NE synthesis. The 5-HTP is decarboxylated to 5-HT by the nonspecific enzyme, aromatic amino acid decarboxylase and, therefore, 5-HTP may be converted to 5-HT in catecholaminergic neurons, ultimately acting as a false transmitter. Catecholamine metabolism is thought to increase as a consequence. The net effect of increased CA synthesis and false-transmitter production is probably increased CA function.

1. Studies with L-Tryptophan

Pretreatment. Depressed patients have been reported to show a blunted release of prolactin in response to administration of high doses of intravenous L-tryptophan, interpreted as indicative of subsensitive postsynaptic 5-HT receptors (Charney et al., 1984b; Heninger et al., 1984), but some investigators have found no significant change in the prolactin response to considerably lower doses of L-tryptophan (Charney et al., 1982a; Glass et al., 1980; Handwerger et al., 1975; Kato et al., 1987; Westenberg et al., 1982). Other data also suggest that recent weight loss in depression may play a role in the prolactin response. Depressed patients who have lost more than 3 kg of body weight show no decrease in prolactin response, but depressed patients who have not lost that amount of weight have an attenuation of prolactin release. These data suggest possible receptor supersensitivity owing to reduced 5-HT function secondary to lower dietary tryptophan intake (Deakin et al., 1990; Delgado et al., 1990). Another confounding variable here is that significant sex differences have been noted for the prolactin response, with females showing greater responses than males (Deakin et al., 1990; Delgado et al., 1990).

Depressed individuals also show a blunted release of growth hormone in response to administration of high doses of intravenous L-tryptophan, not explained by differences from controls in sex, age, or basal growth hormone levels (Deakin et al., 1990).

Posttreatment. Chronic treatment with amitriptyline or desipramine (Charney et al., 1984b), tranylcypromine (Price et al., 1985b), and fluvoxamine (Price et al., 1989a) has produced an enhanced prolactin response to L-tryptophan in depressed patients when compared with normal controls, possibly because of the enhancement of postsynaptic 5-HT receptor sensitivity. Prolonged treatment with the tetracyclic antidepressant mianserin (Cowen, 1988), or with the atypical triazolopyridine antidepressant trazodone (Price et al., 1988), however, does not produce a change in prolactin response to L-tryptophan in depressives. The prolactin response to L-tryptophan has been significantly enhanced after short-term, but not long-term, lithium treatment in depressed patients (Price et al., 1989b), whereas both short-term and long-term lithium treatment cause an enhanced prolactin response in normal controls (Glue et al., 1986). However, Cowen et al. (1989) have reported enhanced prolactin response to L-tryptophan after both short-term and long-term addition of lithium to tricyclic antidepressants in depressed patients. This might suggest one reason why lithium shows its primary antidepressant efficacy in patients pretreated with antidepressants, but is not as effective an antidepressant alone.

2. Studies with 5-Hydroxytryptophan

Pretreatment. Intravenous administration of high doses of 5-HTP after pretreatment with a peripheral decarboxylase inhibitor appears to cause an increased release of prolactin in normal subjects, although data on depressed patients are not yet available (Lancranjan et al., 1977; van Praag, 1983).

In depressed patients, oral 5-HTP has been reported to produce significantly enhanced serum cortisol levels, which has been interpreted as a possible consequence of 5-HT postsynaptic receptor hypersensitivity (Meltzer, 1984; Meltzer et al., 1983b). Koyama et al. (1987) have shown that the enhanced serum cortisol response to 5-HTP is significantly and negatively correlated with CSF 5-HIAA levels, but not with CSF levels of homovanillic acid (HVA), 3-methoxyphenylglycol (MHPG), or 3,4-dihydroxyphenylacetic acid (DOPAC), suggesting that this elevated cortisol response may be directly related to decreased presynaptic brain 5-HT metabolism.

On the other hand, it has been reported that there is no change in plasma cortisol levels in depressed patients after administration of L-tryptophan and 5-HTP (Westenberg et al., 1982). A possible explanation for such a discrepancy in data involves differences in the 5-HTP doses used; thus, the higher doses of 5-HTP may have produced increased synthesis of NE, thereby inhibiting cortisol (van Praag et al., 1987b).

One early preliminary report that 5-HTP produces a blunted growth hormone (GH) response in depressed patients (Takahashi et al., 1976) could not be confirmed by a more recent study that demonstrated no changes in plasma GH after administration of either L-tryptophan or 5-HTP in depressed patients (Westenberg et al., 1982).

Posttreatment. Meltzer (1984) has further attempted to assess the effects of various antidepressant compounds on the cortisol response to 5-HTP in depressed patients. Whereas his group found an enhanced cortisol response to 5-HTP after a 3- to 5-week course of treatment with lithium or MAO inhibitors, and after treatment with 5-HT reuptake inhibitors, they also showed that the cortisol response was reduced after the same period of treatment with TCAs (Meltzer, 1989; Meltzer et al., 1984). These data are contradictory and appear to be uninterpretable at this time.

3. *Studies with Fenfluramine*

Pretreatment. Fenfluramine, a 5-HT releaser and reuptake inhibitor, has also been used as a neuroendocrine challenge agent in the study of depression. Siever et al. (1984a) have found blunted prolactin responses to fenfluramine in a subset of depressed patients, unrelated to status of illness (acute episode versus remission). More recently, Coccaro et al. (1989) have demonstrated reduced prolactin responses to fenfluramine in a subgroup of patients with major affective and/or personality disorder, associated with a history of suicide attempts.

4. *Studies with* m-*Chlorophenylpiperazine*

Pretreatment. The 5-HT direct agonist *m*-chlorophenylpiperazine (MCPP) induces an increase in levels of prolactin and cortisol in animals, an effect that is blocked by the 5-HT antagonist metergoline, thereby suggesting that the effect of MCPP on cortisol and prolactin is mediated by the 5-HT system (Kahn et al., 1990). Neuroendocrine challenge studies using low-dose MCPP have shown no significant cortisol release in unmedicated depressives compared with normal controls (Kahn et al., 1990).

5. *Studies with Serotonin$_{1A}$ Agents*

Pretreatment. Lesch et al. (1990a) found a decreased corticotropin (adrenocorticotropic hormone; ACTH) and cortisol response to ipsapirone, a selective 5-HT$_{1A}$ receptor ligand, in unmedicated depressives compared with normal controls, thereby supporting the hypothesis of a disintegrated 5-HT and hypothalamic–pituitary–adrenal axis (HPA) system interaction in this disorder.

Posttreatment. Rausch et al. (1990) have shown a correlation between severity of depression and cortisol levels after challenge with gepirone, a 5-HT_{1A} agonist, in depressed subjects. After chronic gepirone administration, desensitization occurs, with attenuation of this response. Lesch et al. (1990b) have also reported that prolonged amitriptyline treatment causes attenuation of 5-HT_{1A}-mediated hypothermia in depressed patients, compared with controls.

6. Summary of Neuroendocrine Challenge Data

Because of the limited number of neuroendocrine challenge studies and the variability of the results obtained, few definitive conclusions can be drawn about 5-HT status in depressed patients. van Praag et al. (1987b) reviewed the present state of 5-HT challenge studies, delineating two major pitfalls: nonselectivity of the challengers generally employed and noncomparability of studies because of variations in dosages and route of administration of the challenging agents.

The prolactin studies and the cortisol studies just summarized give contradictory results. The prolactin data suggest that 5-HT receptors may be hyposensitive in depressed patients (as expressed by blunted prolactin responses to L-tryptophan), and antidepressant treatments, including TCAs, MAOIs, lithium, and ECS, may enhance 5-HT receptor sensitivity, as expressed by augmentation of prolactin response to 5-HT agonists. However, the cortisol data suggest the opposite, namely, increased sensitivity of postsynaptic 5-HT receptors in depressed patients (as expressed by enhanced cortisol response to 5-HTP). Here, TCAs reduced the cortisol response to 5-HTP. A possible explanation for this contradiction between the results of the prolactin and the cortisol studies could be that when different 5-HT precursors that might possess differential effects on both serotonergic and catecholaminergic function are used, results may reflect effects on multiple receptor types. A second possible explanation is that, in depression, 5-HT receptor subtypes may be differentially affected. Finally, challenge studies of 5-HT_{1A} receptors are promising, but require more data before conclusions can be drawn.

C. Conclusions

Currently, both *5-HT hypofunction* and *5-HT hyperfunction* theories of depression have been proposed. Evidence for 5-HT hypofunction includes the following:

1. Data suggesting decreased CNS 5-HT synthesis and metabolism in depression (as reflected in lowered concentrations of 5-HT and 5-HIAA in postmortem brain and CSF studies)
2. Increased 5-HT receptor sensitivity, neurotransmission, and function in depressives after antidepressant treatment (as expressed by an enhanced prolactin respose, and data from electrophysiological and behavioral studies)
3. Antidepressant effects shown by 5-HT precursors that increase 5-HT synthesis or function and by selective 5-HT-reuptake inhibitors, as well as augmentation of antidepressant treatment by lithium
4. Depressogenic effects shown by 5-HT-depleting agents
5. Recent data suggesting decreased sensitivity of 5-HT_{1A} receptors in depressed patients, with further decrease following antidepressant treatment.

Evidence also exists for the 5-HT hyperfunction hypothesis of depression, which suggests that 5-HT neurotransmission is enhance in depression, presumably as a consequence of hypersensitive postsynaptic 5-HT receptors. If such hypersensitivity is primary, it might account for a (compensatory) decrease in brain 5-HT metabolism found in unmedicated depressed patients, although the opposite mechanism is also possible. Evidence supporting 5-HT hyperfunction includes the following:

1. Data suggesting that platelet 5-HT uptake is decreased in depressed patients, which increases the availability of 5-HT at the synapse (if brain and platelets are comparable) and thereby serves to enhance 5-HT neurotransmission
2. The fact that antidepressant treatment produces further decreases in presynaptic 5-HT availability (as reflected in further decreases in CSF 5-HIAA, and normalized platelet uptake found in several studies)
3. The demonstration of increased binding to postsynaptic 5-HT_2 receptors in the frontal cortex of suicide victims
4. The demonstration of decreased binding to postsynaptic 5-HT_2 receptors after chronic antidepressant treatment

III. THE NOREPINEPHRINE SYSTEM

As is true for the history of research into the role of 5-HT in the pathogenesis of depression, early theoreticians proposed a linear model of NE hypofunction in this disorder. As more has become known about this system, and as research methods have become more sophisticated, investigators have developed a more complex and dynamic schema for interpreting the role of NE in depression, involving receptor subtypes and the use of the neuroendocrine challenge paradigm.

A. Biochemical Data

1. Studies of Plasma, Cerebrospinal Fluid, and Urinary Metabolites

Several investigators have demonstrated decreased levels of urinary 3-methoxy-4-hydroxyphenylglycol (MHPG; the primary NE metabolite) in depression, although others have reported no abnormality or increased levels of MHPG in depressed patients (Lingjaerde, 1983). Data on plasma, CSF, and urinary MHPG are diverse, and it has been suggested that such measures may not consistently distinguish depressives from controls, although they may distinguish specific depressive subtypes (Siever et al., 1986).

2. Adrenergic Receptor Studies

Both α-adrenergic and ß-adrenergic receptors regulate the function of cyclic adenosine monophosphate (cAMP), thought to be a "second messenger" at the postsynaptic receptor. In recent years the monoamine hypothesis of depression has been extended to include both α-adrenergic and ß-adrenergic dysfunction in this disorder.

β-Adrenergic Receptors. Pretreatment. Unmedicated depressed patients have decreased lymphocyte ß-adrenergic sensitivity, involving both decreased receptor binding and decreased isoproterenol-stimulated increase in cAMP synthesis (Extein et al., 1979; Halper et al., 1988; Pandey et al., 1979). More recent data from Magliozzi et al. (1989) suggest that decreased lymphocyte ß-adrenergic binding may be due to greater differences between depressed females and female controls, with differences in binding between depressed males and controls not reaching statistical significance.

Posttreatment. Several studies have demonstrated that long-term antidepressant treatment consistently results in the further decrease in sensitivity of ß-adrenergic receptors, both in vitro in rats (Bergstrom and Kellar, 1979; Cowen, 1990; Sugrue, 1983b), and in vivo on human lymphocyte ß-adrenergic receptors (Extein et al., 1979; Mann et al., 1985; Pandey et al., 1979), although neither bupropion, a newer antidepressant compound with proven clinical efficacy (Ferris and Beaman, 1983), nor ECS (Cooper et al., 1985; Mann et al., 1990) demonstrate this effect. This is shown both in a decrease in receptor binding (B_{max}) without change in affinity (K_d), and in a decreased isoproterenol-stimulated increase in cAMP synthesis when compared with normal subjects.

α-Adrenergic Receptors: α_1. α_1-Adrenergic receptors also increase postsynaptic cAMP concentration after stimulation by NE. α_2-receptors, which had formerly been identified as inhibitory and presynaptic, have more recently been shown to be located both presynaptically and postsynaptically.

Pretreatment. Several studies on postsynaptic α_1-receptors in unmedicated depressed patients have produced contradictory results, and there are as yet no good receptor-binding data (Willner, 1985).

Posttreatment. Several investigators have indirectly demonstrated an increase in the sensitivity of postsynaptic α_1-receptors after extended antidepressant treatment, as shown through the enhancement of α_1-mediated behavioral responses. Interestingly, however, no consistent changes in α_1-receptor binding have been demonstrated after long-term antidepressant treatment, so that the molecular basis for such behavioral changes remains unclear (Charney et al., 1981a, b; Menkes et al., 1983; Sugrue, 1983b; Vetulani et al., 1984).

α-Adrenergic Receptors: α_2. Pretreatment. Kanof et al. (1988) have found no differences in platelet α_2-receptor sensitivity between actively depressed and remitted depressed patients, with no correlation between symptom severity and platelet α_2-receptor sensitivity. This is in contrast to findings by Healy et al. (1985) of higher platelet α_2-adrenergic receptor density in endogenously versus reactively depressed patients, and data from Roy and Kafka (1989) suggesting increased binding, but decreased platelet α_2-receptor sensitivity in depressed patients compared with normal controls. Southwick et al. (1990) have reported that platelet α_2-receptor-binding in depressed persons is significantly influenced by comorbid diagnoses, with decreased binding in depressed patients with concurrent borderline personality disorder, and increased binding in depressed patients compared with controls.

Posttreatment. Some investigators have demonstrated decreased presynaptic α_2-inhibitory autoreceptors in unmedicated depressed patients, compared with controls, with a further decrease after long-term treatment with many, although not all, antidepressants. Specifically, this has been shown directly in platelets by a decrease in B_{max} without change in K_d, indirectly by hormonal alterations in neuroendocrine challenge studies, and indirectly by changes in α_2-mediated behavioral responses (Charney et al., 1982b; Garcia-Sevilla et al., 1981). Brief but not long-term ECS treatment has also decreased platelet α_2-receptor densities (Cooper et al., 1985). These data, in contrast with those discussed in the foregoing, may suggest a possible supersensitivity of these receptors in depression, although this does not explain the further down-regulation of these receptors by antidepressant medications. However, other researchers have found either increased or unchanged numbers of platelet α_2-receptors in depressives compared with normal controls (Healy et al., 1983; Siever et al., 1984b,c; Stahl et al., 1983; Wolfe et al., 1989).

α-Adrenergic Receptors: *Summary*. Thus, it appears that (1) unmedicated depressed individuals do not show consistent changes in α_1-adrenergic receptor binding. (2) Unmedicated depressed individuals demonstrate a decrease in binding in ß-adrenergic and, possibly, α_2-adrenergic receptors. (3) Long-term antidepressant treatment causes a decrease in number or density of α_2-adrenergic and ß-adrenergic receptors. (4) Chronic antidepressant treatment causes an increase in number or density of α_1-adrenergic receptors, as demonstrated by behavioral studies, but not yet shown in receptor-binding experiments.

B. Neuroendocrine Challenge Data

Pretreatment. Studies of the α_2-adrenergic system have involved the use of yohimbine, an α_2-receptor antagonist that increases noradrenergic function, and clonidine, an α_2-receptor agonist that decreases noradrenergic function. Although investigators have not shown differences between depressed patients and normal controls in measures of presynaptic α_2-activity (i.e., plasma NE metabolite levels), differences in postsynaptic α_2-sensitivity have been demonstrated in depressed patients.

Specifically, yohimbine causes significantly increased cortisol response, but no change in plasma MHPG response in depressives versus normal controls, suggesting a hyposensitivity of postsynaptic α_2-adrenergic receptors in depression (Heninger et al., 1988; Price et al., 1986). Clonidine induces a greater decrease in plasma cortisol levels in depressed than in normal individuals (Siever et al., 1984c), whereas growth hormone response to clonidine (a postsynaptic response) is attenuated in depressives compared with normal controls (Charney et al., 1982b; Lesch et al., 1990c; Siever et al., 1982). Other studies have shown reduced clonidine-induced decreases in plasma MHPG and heart rate in depressive patients compared with normal subjects, again suggesting hyposensitivity of the α_2-adrenergic system (Siever et al., 1984b). Such findings are in contrast with data, discussed earlier, demonstrating decrease in α_2-adrenergic receptors after long-term antidepressant treatment, which would suggest hypersensitivity of α_2-receptors in depression (Heninger et al., 1988). Thus, the meaning of such studies now remains unclear.

C. Conclusions

Similar to results of studies on 5-HT and depression, investigators studying the role of NE and depression have either concluded that central NE deficiency triggers depression (Schildkraut, 1965), or that NE hyperfunction is related to depression (Koslow et al., 1983; Lake et al., 1982).

Plasma, urine, and CSF NE metabolite studies have provided results too variable to be interpreted. Receptor-binding studies provide contradictory evidence that does not support either an NE hyperfunction or an NE hypofunction hypothesis of depression. No consistent changes have been identified in α_1-adrenergic receptor binding in unmedicated depressives. Although decreased ß-adrenergic and, possibly, α_2-adrenergic receptor binding has been found in unmedicated depressives, long-term antidepressant treatment also causes a decrease in number or density of α_2-adrenergic and ß-adrenergic receptors; hence, these data are not now clear and cannot be interpreted as evidence for either hypothesis.

Siever and Davis (1985) have suggested that, because of such confusing results, it might be more helpful to conceptualize neurotransmitter systems as "poorly regulated," rather than postulating exposure to "too much" or "too little" neurotransmitter. They have proposed that the NE system can be characterized by specific abnormalities of regulation in depression and, therefore, to understand results involving NE in depression, one must have a dynamic view of the neurotransmitter system and its functioning.

IV. THE DOPAMINE SYSTEM

Very little work has yet been done on the role of DA in the etiology and pathogenesis of depression. Several areas of research have yielded some data that appear to be of pertinence to this topic:

1. The CSF concentration of homovanillic acid (HVA), the primary metabolite of DA, is decreased in depressed individuals compared with normal controls (Willner, 1985), although these results have been contested (Gjerris et al., 1987). Data on the effects of chronic antidepressant treatment on CSF HVA levels are inconsistent (Potter et al., 1985). Interestingly, decreased CSF HVA levels in depressives correlate with degree of psychomotor retardation (Papeschi and McClure, 1971). van Praag and Korf (1975) have reported more pronounced motor retardation and inertia in depressives with low CSF HVA levels, with improvement in motor functioning and level of initiative, but not in mood after administration of L-dopa.
2. The CSF 5-HIAA and HVA levels have been shown to correlate with severity of depression (Roy et al., 1985). Other investigators have suggested that CSF 5-HIAA may regulate the CSF HVA level in a facilitatory manner, thus offering one explanation for this correlation (Agren et al., 1986).
3. Studies have consistently shown an association between Parkinson's disease and depression, thereby suggesting that decreased DA may play some role in the pathogenesis of depression (Birkmayer and Birkmayer, 1987; Robins, 1976).
4. Agents that affect DA functional activity possess antidepressant effects. For instance, tricyclic antidepressants possess some DA reuptake-blocking effects, with reversal of effects seen with DA antagonists (Friedman et al., 1977; Muscat et al., 1990).
5. The DA reuptake inhibitor nomifensine (Kinney, 1985), the DA agonists bromocriptine (Sitland-Marken et al., 1990) and piribedil (Joffe et al., 1986; Post et al., 1978), and the DA-releasing stimulants methylphenidate and methamphetamine (Sitland-Marken et al., 1990), all have demonstrated antidepressant effects.
6. Few neuroendocrine challenge studies have been conducted in this area. In the only study applicable to this chapter, Ansseau et al. (1988) found that GH response to apomorphine, a dopaminergic agonist, was blunted in depressives compared with normal subjects. Interestingly, these investigators found no correlation between blunted GH responses to both apomorphine and clonidine in these subjects, suggesting that disturbances in NE and DA systems in depression may be independent of each other.
7. Several investigators have proposed dopaminergic involvement in depression: (1) It has been proposed that central DA dysfunction may play an important role in seasonal affective disorder, with phototherapy and summer light facilitating DA neurotransmission in this disorder (Arbisi et al., 1989). (2) In contrast with other researchers, Skutsch (1985) has proposed an increase of dopaminergic activity in bipolar disorder, with hyposensitivity to ambient temperature change, so that DA does not become suppressed. He also proposes that lower estrogen, with a consequent increase in dopaminergic activity at the anterior pituitary, may be involved in the pathogenesis of unipolar depression. (3) van Praag et al. (1991) have proposed that the mobilization and direction of goal-directed behaviors, or the incentive system, an important psychopathological dimension in depression, as well as many other psychiatric disorders, is mediated by DA, and thus DA dysfunction is implicated in the drive reduction seen in depression.

V. THE HYPOTHALAMIC–PITUITARY–ADRENAL AXIS

Several investigators have examined HPA axis dysregulation in depression. Both 5-HT and NE have a major role in the regulation of the hypothalamic–pituitary–adrenal (HPA) axis. Serotonin stimulates secretion of corticotropin-releasing factor (CRF), and adrenocorticotropin hormone (ACTH), and is required for the inhibition by corticosteroids of CRF and ACTH, whereas NE inhibits CRF and also can stimulate ACTH secretion (Maes et al., 1989).

Most research to date has focused on the role of NE in HPA axis dysfunction in depression. Hyperactivity of this system has consistently been demonstrated. Hypercortisolemia and increased plasma and urinary epinephrine, NE, and MHPG levels have been found in depressed compared with normal individuals (Carroll et al., 1981; Davis et al., 1988; de Villiers et al., 1987; Maas et al., 1987; Roy et al. 1988).

The dexamethasone suppression test (DST) is based on the fact that many (although not all) endogenously depressed individuals will fail to show suppression of plasma cortisol after dexamethasone administration (Carroll, 1982). Conflicting data have emerged from studies in this area. For instance, a significant correlation between postdexamethasone plasma cortisol levels and basal plasma and CSF levels of the primary NE metabolite 3-methoxy-4-hydroxyphenylglycol (MHPG) in depressives has been repeatedly identified (Jimerson et al., 1983; Rubin et al., 1985; Roy et al., 1988), although some investigators have not been able to replicate these findings (Maes et al., 1987; Stokes et al., 1987). In contrast, Lu et al. (1986) have reported a significant negative correlation between CSF NE and predexamethasone plasma cortisol in depressed patients who were dexamethasone suppression test-positive.

It should be noted that several different hypotheses have been proposed for the DST data, speculating on whether the primary defect exists at the level of the neurotransmitter or in the HPA axis itself, or whether such parallel stimulation of the HPA axis and the NE system is dependent or independent, but this issue remains to be resolved.

It has been suggested that the primary defect in depression involves hypersecretion of corticotropin-releasing hormone (CRH), thereby causing the hypercortisolemia seen in depression. Roy et al. (1987a,b) have found that the CSF CRH level is significantly correlated with urinary NE and its metabolites, suggesting the involvement of CRH in the dysregulation of the NE system found in depression. Others have hypothesized that hyperactivity of the HPA axis in depression occurs secondary to either decreased NE inhibitory control (Schlesser et al., 1980), or to excitation from increased noradrenergic activity (Jimerson et al., 1983; Rosenbaum et al., 1983). Such differing hypotheses are possible because of the dual effects NE appears to exert on different hormones in the HPA axis.

Because central 5-HT neurons stimulate ACTH and cortisol, an important role for 5-HT in the HPA hyperactivity seen in depression remains an important consideration. Little work has yet focused on this interaction.

In one study, Maes et al. (1989) have found decreased postdexamethasone plasma L-tryptophan and tyrosine levels in depressed compared with normal individuals. They thus suggest that this difference in precursor levels might cause altered central serotonergic and noradrenergic control over the HPA axis, and might be indicative of altered neurotransmitter function in this disorder.

Finally, one other abnormal endocrinological finding in some depressives is the blunting of thyroid-stimulating hormone (TSH) response after administration of thyroid-releasing hormone (TRH) (Loosen and Prange, 1982). This may be a trait, rather than state, marker, since continued TSH blunting after clinical improvement is related to relapse. This measure is also independent of blunted DST suppression (Joyce, 1985). The meaning of such studies still remains unclear.

In summary, recent work in the endocrinology of depression has focused on interrelationships between neurotransmitter dysfunction and HPA and thyroid axis dysfunction. Although the most consistent findings have associated hypercortisolemia and increased NE function, much of the data are contradictory, probably because of methodological problems (e.g., central versus peripheral samples).

VI. CIRCADIAN RHYTHMS IN DEPRESSION

Biological rhythms have been implicated in the pathophysiology of depression because of certain clinical features, such as the presence of early-morning awakening, diurnal mood variation, seasonal patterns of recurrence, and the overall cyclicity of the disorder seen in some depressions (Goodwin et al., 1982; Hallonquist et al., 1986; Czeisler et al., 1987). Recently, with the introduction of seasonal affective disorder into the *DSM-III-R* (American Psychiatric Association, 1987), and with the development of new and radically different forms of treatment, such as phototherapy, there has been increasing interest in disturbances of biological rhythms in depression (Rosenthal et al., 1984; Blehar and Rosenthal, 1989).

Most researchers agree that there are two main oscillators, or rhythmic processes, in humans (Czeisler et al., 1987). The so-called strong oscillator has a free-running period of slightly longer than 24 h, and is entrained to a 24-h cycle by various environmental cues, such as the light of dawn. It is believed to control body temperature, REM sleep, plasma cortisol, and melatonin secretion. The strong oscillator is then entrained by, or coupled to, a weak oscillator, that controls the sleep–wakefulness rhythm, or the behavioral rest–activity cycle, which is apparently strongly influenced by various social and environmental cues. Most hypotheses of circadian rhythm dysfunction in depression focus on a form of desynchronization of these rhythms, in which the oscillators are entrained ineffectively to external cues or to each other (Papolos, 1991).

Over the years, there has been extensive evidence of a phase advance in several circadian rhythms in some, but not all, depressed patients. It is suggested that certain circadian rhythms occur earlier, relative to night and day, in depressed patients than in normal persons. Rhythms that are thought to be phase-advanced include REM sleep (decreased latency and increased length of the first REM period), temperature, cortisol secretion, and production of neurotransmitter metabolites of 5-HT, dopamine, and NE, which have led to the elaboration of a phase advance theory of depression (Goodwin et al., 1982; Hallonquist et al., 1986; Czeisler et al., 1987).

However, Souêtre et al. (1989) have found that reduced amplitude of circadian rhythms of body temperature, TSH, NE, cortisol, and melatonin secretion, is a more consistent finding than phase advance in endogenous depressives. These investigators have reported that most of these abnormal rhythms normalize upon recovery from depression. They suggest that these reduced amplitudes may be indicative of an overall weakness in entrainment processes in depressed individuals.

Various neurotransmitter systems are influenced by circadian processes. These include the 5-HT-uptake dynamics and seasonal variations in platelet 5-HT uptake noted earlier, as well as diurnal rhythms in α-adrenergic, ß-adrenergic, cholinergic, dopaminergic, opiate, and benzodiazepine receptor number in female hamsters (Goodwin et al., 1982).

Because of the influence of light on melatonin production, there has been interest in the relation of melatonin to seasonal disorders, such as some forms of depressive illness (Frazer et al., 1986; Grasby and Cowen, 1987). Some, but not all (Zetin et al., 1987) studies have shown decreased nocturnal melatonin levels in depressed patients. However, these studies have generally not been controlled for potentially confounding variables, such as age and stage of the menstrual cycle. Interestingly, melatonin is synthesized from 5-HT by *n*-acetylation, and its secretion from the pineal gland is regulated by ß-adrenergic receptors on pineal cells. Furthermore, there is evidence that melatonin is involved in the coupling or synchronization of circadian rhythms (Redman et al., 1983).

Several treatments that are based on directly addressing circadian rhythm disturbances in patients have been tried, with some success. These include advancing the time of sleep relative to the REM–temperature–cortisol cycle (Goodwin et al., 1982), sleep deprivation or disruption (Goodwin et al., 1982; Wehr et al., 1987), and the use of phototherapy (Wehr et al., 1986).

Finally, antidepressant drugs and lithium lengthen and phase-delay circadian systems in animals (Goodwin et al., 1982), suggesting that their mechanism of action may be related to effects on circadian systems.

Circadian rhythm disturbances do not necessarily result in mood disturbances, but may do so only in predisposed individuals. For example, transcontinental air travel, being blind (where light effects cannot regulate internal synchronization of circadian rhythms), and isolation experiments exposing patients to abnormal day lengths, do not necessarily lead to significant mood disturbance (Hallonquist et al., 1986).

In summary, disruptions in circadian rhythms seem to be an important part of the changes seen in depression. Abnormalities found include phase-advance and reduced amplitude of some circadian rhythms. Efforts to correct these disturbances have proved promising in the treatment of some depressed patients. Future research into the role of neurotransmitters in depression will need to take into account these disturbances in order to paint a more complete picture of the pathogenesis of depression.

VII. SEROTONIN–NOREPINEPHRINE AND SEROTONIN–DOPAMINE INTERACTIONS

Years of investigations have demonstrated multiple abnormalities in both the serotonergic and the noradrenergic systems in depressed individuals. The etiological role and the relation between such dysfunctions is still unclear, however. In spite of the fact that some recent research has focused on the response of depressed and even previously treatment-resistant depressed patients to "selective" 5-HT agents (Asberg et al., 1986; Charney et al., 1990; Schatzberg et al., 1987), most data now suggest that a mixed treatment that augments both 5-HT and NE availability may provide more efficacy in the treatment of depression (van Praag et al., 1987a). Thus, it would appear that Maas' original hypothesis concerning separate serotonergic and noradrenergic subtypes of depression (Maas, 1975), might be too simplistic, since the pathogenesis of this complex disease is unlikely to be explained by abnormalities occurring individually in one neurotransmitter system alone.

The classic monoamine hypothesis of depression initially proposed that decreased availability of NE and hypofunction of the noradrenergic system are causally related to depressive illness. With advances in molecular research techniques, this hypothesis has been modified to include the function of specific NE receptors. Sulser (1987) has proposed that primary hypersensitivity of ß-adrenergic receptors may be causally related to depression, and that the efficacy of antidepressant treatments is related to the ability to down-regulate these receptors. Charney et al. (1981b) have also suggested that antidepressant treatments, as one common pathway, decrease ß-adrenergic receptor sensitivity and function. Given that this is so, the question then becomes the nature of the role that 5-HT might play in these processes.

There is an increasing body of data showing anatomical as well as functional interactions between 5-HT neurons originating in the midbrain raphe and cerebral cortex and NE neurons in the locus coeruleus (Dahlstrom and Fuxe, 1964; Levitt and Moore, 1978; Morrison et al., 1982). At the same time, evidence of certain mutual modulation effects between these two systems has been well documented (Brunello et al., 1982; Janowsky et al., 1982; Dumbrille-Ross and Tang, 1983; Nimgaonkar et al., 1985; Scott and Crews, 1985, 1986).

Taking the anatomical data a step further, Sulser (1986, 1987) has proposed that an intact 5-HT system is required not only for the proper functioning of ß-adrenergic receptors, but also for the down-regulation of the density of these receptors by antidepressant treatments, citing data that suggest that lesions in serotonergic pathways can prevent ß-adrenergic down-regulation by antidepressants.

Other investigators have shown that selective 5-HT agents can indirectly stimulate the NE system by other anatomical pathways, subsequently causing ß-adrenergic receptor down-regulation in discrete brain regions (Wamsley et al., 1987). Kellar and Stockmeier (1986) have found that, although most antidepressant treatments may require the presence of intact serotonergic neurons to mediate down-regulation of ß-adrenergic receptors, ECS can cause decreases in ß-adrenergic receptor binding even after lesioning of serotonergic neurons, suggesting that the influence of serotonergic axons on ß-adrenergic receptors may be complex, and may extend beyond a simple effect on down-regulation by antidepressant medications. Price et al. (1990) have also suggested that, while it appears that lithium's enhancement of the efficacy of primary antidepressants is serotonergically mediated, its effects on other systems, including NE, through alteration of cellular ion transport mechanisms or secondary-messenger interactions, may be critical to understanding its complete mechanism of action. Finally, Asnis et al. (1990) have recently found a significant inverse relation between cortisol release in response to 0.75 mg intramuscular desipramine (a NE agonist) and cortisol release in response to 0.25 mg/kg oral MCPP (a 5-HT agonist) in normal, depressed, and panic disordered individuals, thus again suggesting that fluctuations in one neurotransmitter system may influence the function of others.

Therefore, it appears that an indirect, but critical, role of 5-HT in antidepressant treatments may be to mediate or transduce the antidepressant effects on the NE system. In addition, recent evidence indicates that increased NE function may also increase 5-HT raphe nuclei function (Marwaha and Aghajanian, 1982). Sulser's "serotonin–norepinephrine link" hypothesis of affective disorders (Sulser, 1987) proposes that there are many steps in noradrenergic information flow involving multiple feedback loops with multiple aminergic systems, including 5-HT. The functioning of the noradrenergic system acts as an oscillator that leads to adaptation or amplification of important vital functions. Disturbances in any one of the steps regulating noradrenergic function (e.g., 5-HT function) can lead to pathophysiological manifestations seen in depression. This recent revision of the original amine hypothesis of depression may serve as an important stimulus for the further study of biological substrates in the pathogenesis of depression.

Finally, there is a significant body of anatomical data taken from animal models that demonstrates complex interactions between the 5-HT and the DA systems. The raphe nuclei, the substantia nigra, and the striatum are interconnected by afferents from each area (Fibiger and Miller, 1977; Priestley et al., 1981), while 5-HT terminals have been found in rat caudate and neostriatum (Ternaux et al., 1977). Physiological studies have found possible 5-HT inhibition of central DA neuron function (Jenner et al., 1983), with serotonergic antagonists increasing and 5-HT agonists decreasing dopaminergically mediated activity (Korsgaard et al., 1985). Further elucidation of such 5-HT–DA interactions may also provide critical information for understanding the role of neurotransmitter dysfunction in depression.

In conclusion, then, it would appear that the 5-HT, NE, and DA systems are functionally and anatomically interconnected in a complex manner, making it overly simplistic to attribute the pathogenesis of a multidimensional disease, such as depression, to dysfunction in one particular neurotransmitter.

VIII. DISCUSSION

Data presented in the foregoing show the impossibility of creating a unifying theory to explain the pathogenesis of depression through the dysfunction of any single neurotransmitter. Because of this, we have suggested that 5-HT, NE, and DA dysfunctions may be better related to certain psychopathological dimensions, rather than to depression per se (Brown and van Praag, 1991; van Praag et al., 1987c, 1991).

For example, we have extensively reviewed a large body of data (Brown et al., 1990) suggesting the following: (1) a high correlation has been consistently demonstrated between decreased measures of central 5-HT function and history of suicide attempts, particularly those that involve a violent component. This has been shown across psychiatric diagnoses. (2) Several studies have found a strong negative correlation between measures of central 5-HT function and violence. Thus, disordered aggression regulation (both inwardly and outwardly directed) has proved to be a major dimension in depression, with the possibility that disordered 5-HT metabolism is more directly related to the dimension of aggression dysregulation than to the nosological category of depression itself (van Praag et al., 1991).

Other data reviewed elsewhere (Brown et al., 1990; Kahn et al., 1988, 1990) have suggested a dysregulation of 5-HT function in anxiety, which is a second important psychopathological dimension occurring in depression, as well as other psychiatric disorders. In addition, impulsivity has been suggested as a third dimension, seen across psychiatric diagnoses, in which abnormal 5-HT function has also been found.

Although the data concerning psychopathological dimensions related to noradrenergic and dopaminergic function are less clear-cut, we have, nonetheless, suggested, from preliminary evidence, that disordered NE metabolism may be more directly related to the psychopathological dimension of hedonic function, or the ability to experience pleasure, whereas disordered DA metabolism may be more directly related to the mobilizing and directing of goal-directed behaviors, or an incentive system (van Praag et al., 1991). Such disturbances are not specific for depression, but are also found in other psychiatric and neurological disorders, thus possibly explaining the nosological nonspecificity of monoamine disturbances. Clearly, understanding the interaction between disturbances in serotonergic, noradrenergic, and dopaminergic function will be critical to mapping the disturbances in psychopathological dimensions that characterize different types of depressive disorder.

We have recently proposed a two-tier approach to classification of psychiatric illness, incorporating both nosological diagnosis and evaluation of dysfunction along the psychological dimensions outlined earlier (van Praag, 1991). We have suggested that such an approach may allow a better understanding of biological disturbances as they occur in behavioral disorders.

Cloninger (1986, 1987) has proposed a dimensional approach for the biological study of personality disorders, in which specific dimensions of personality, rather than psychopathological dimensions, have been linked to particular monoaminergic systems. Although Cloninger's approach differs somewhat from our own, it certainly appears that such a way of conceptualizing psychiatric disorders may allow us to finally begin to make some sense of a huge and disparate body of biological data. In addition, this approach may also increase the sophistication of our current taxonomy.

REFERENCES

R. Abrams, W. B. Essman, M. A. Taylor, and M. Fink, Concentration of 5-hydroxyindoleacetic acid, homovanillic acid, and tryptophan in the cerebrospinal fluid of depressed patients before and after ECT, *Biol. Psychiatry, 11*: 85 (1976).

H. Agren, I. N. Mefford, M. V. Rudorfer, M. Linnoila, and W. Z. Potter, Interacting neurotransmitter systems. A nonexperimental approach to the 5HIAA–HVA correlation in human CSF, *J. Psychiatr. Res., 20*: 175 (1986).

American Psychiatric Association, *Diagnostic and Statistical Manual of Mental Disorders*, 3rd ed., revised, American Psychiatric Association, Washington, D.C. (1987).

M. Ansseau, R. von Frenckell, J. L. Cerfontaine, P. Papart, G. Franck, M. Timsit-Berthier, V. Geenen, and J. J. Legros, Blunted response of growth hormone to clonidine and apomorphine in endogenous depression, *Br. J. Psychiatry, 153*: 65 (1988).

P. A. Arbisi, R. A. Depue, M. R. Spoont, A. Leon, and B. Ainsworth, Thermoregulatory response to thermal challenge in seasonal affective disorder: A preliminary report, *Psychiatry Res., 28*: 323 (1989).

R. C. Arora, L. Kriegel, and H. Y. Meltzer, Seasonal variation of serotonin uptake in normal controls and depressed patients, *Biol. Psychiatry, 19*: 795 (1984).

K. B. Asarch, J. C. Shih, and A. Kulcsar, Decreased ^{3}H-imipramine binding in depressed males and females, *Commun. Psychopharmacol., 4*: 425 (1980).

M. Asberg, V. A. Ringberger, F. Sjoqvist et al., Monoamine metabolites in cerebrospinal fluid and serotonin uptake inhibition during treatment with chlorimipramine, *Clin. Pharmacol. Ther., 21*: 201 (1975).

M. Asberg, B. Eriksson, B. Martensson et al., Therapeutic effects of serotonin uptake inhibitors in depression, *J. Clin. Psychiatry, 46*, (Suppl. 4): 23 (1986).

G. W. Ashcroft, T. B. B. Crawford, D. Eccleston et al., 5-Hydroxyindole compounds in the cerebrospinal fluid of patients with psychiatric or neurological diseases, *Lancet, 2*: 1049 (1966).

G. M. Asnis, S. Wetzler, W. C. Sanderson, R. S. Kahn, W. K. Bajwa, A. Ryes-Garza, and H. M. van Praag, "Serotonin, norepinephrine and hormones: A bidirectional interaction?" XXth International Congress of the International Society of Psychoneuroendocrinology, Buffalo, New York (1990).

M. Baron, A. Barkai, R. Gruen et al., ^{3}H-imipramine platelet binding sites in unipolar depression, *Biol. Psychiatry, 18*: 1403 (1983).

M. Baron, A. Barkai, R. Gruen et al., Platelet ^{3}H-imipramine binding in affective disorders: Trait versus state characteristics, *Am. J. Psychiatry, 143*: 711 (1986).

P. Benfield, and A. Ward, Fluvoxamine: A review of its pharmacodynamic and pharmacokinetic properties, and therapeutic efficacy in depressive illness, *Drugs, 32*: 313 (1986).

D. A. Bergstrom, and K. J. Kellar, Effect of electroconvulsive shock on monoaminergic receptor binding sites in rat brain, *Nature, 278*: 464 (1979).

L. Bertilsson, M. Asberg, and P. Thoren, Differential effect of chlorimipramine and nortriptyline on cerebrospinal fluid metabolites of serotonin and noradrenaline in depression, *Eur. J. Clin. Pharmacol., 21*: 194 (1976).

J. Beskow, C. G. Gottfries, B. E. Roos, and D. B. Winblad, Determination of monoamine and monoamine metabolites in the human brain: Postmortem studies in a group of suicides and in a control group, *Acta Psychiatr. Scand., 53*: 7 (1976).

A. Biegon, A. Weizman, L. Karp et al., Serotonin 5-HT_2 receptor binding on blood platelets—a peripheral marker for depression? *Life Sci., 41*: 2485 (1987).

W. Birkmayer, and J. D. Birkmayer, Dopamine action and disorders of neurotransmitter balance, *Gerontology, 33*: 168 (1987).

W. Birkmayer, and P. Riederer, Biochemical post-mortem findings in depressed patients, *J. Neural Transm., 37*: 95 (1975).

M. A. Blackshear, and E. Sanders-Bush, Serotonin receptor sensitivity after acute and chronic treatment with mianserin, *J. Pharmacol. Exp. Ther., 221*: 303 (1982).

M. C. Blehar, and N. E. Rosenthal, Seasonal affective disorders and phototherapy: Report of a National Institute of Mental Health-sponsored workshop, *Arch. Gen. Psychiatry, 46*: 469 (1989).

P. Blier, C. de Montigny, and Y. Chaput, Modifications of the serotonin system by antidepressant treatments: Implications for the therapeutic response in major depression, *J. Clin. Psychopharmacol., 7* (Suppl. 6): 24S (1987).

P. Blier, C. de Montigny, Y. Chaput, A role for the serotonin system in the mechanism of action on antidepressant treatments: Preclinical evidence, *J. Clin. Psychiatry, 5* (Suppl. 4): 14 (1990).

G. V. R. Born, G. Grignani, and K. Martin, Long-term effect of lithium on the uptake of 5-hydroxytryptamine by human platelets, *Br. J. Clin. Pharmacol., 9*: 321 (1980).

H. R. Bourne, W. E. Bunney, Jr., and R. W. Colburn, Noradrenaline, 5-hydroxytryptamine and 5-hydroxyindoleacetic acid in hindbrains of suicidal patients, *Lancet, 2*: 805 (1968).

M. B. Bowers, Lumbar CSF 5-hydroxyindoleacetic acid and homovanillic acid in affective syndromes, *J. Nerv. Ment. Dis., 158*: 325 (1974a).

M. B. Bowers, Amitriptyline in man: Decreased formation of central 5-hydroxyindoleacetic acid, *Clin. Pharmacol. Ther., 15*: 167 (1974b).

M. B. Bowers, and D. J. Kupfer, Central monoamine oxidase inhibition and REM sleep, *Brain Res., 35*: 561 (1971).

M. B. Bowers, G. R. Heninger, and F. A. Gerbode, Cerebrospinal fluid 5-hydroxyindoleacetic acid and homovanillic acid in psychiatric patients, *Int. J. Neuropharmacol., 8*: 255 (1969).

M. S. Briley, S. Z. Langer, R. Raisman, et al., Tritiated imipramine binding sites are decreased in platelets of untreated depressed patients, *Science, 209*: 303 (1980).

S. L. Brown, M. L. Korn, and H. M. van Praag, Serotonin in depression and anxiety, *Serotonin: From Cell Biology to Pharmacology and Therapeutics* (R. Paoletti, P. M. Vanhoutte, N. Brunello, F. M. Maggi, eds.), Brunner/Mazel, New York, p. 487 (1990).

S. L. Brown, and H. M. van Praag (eds.), *The Role of Serotonin in Psychiatric Disorders*, Brunner/Mazel, New York (1991).

N. Brunello, M. L. Barbaccia, D. M. Chuang, and E. Costa, Down-regulation of beta-adrenergic receptors following repeated injections of desmethylimipramine: Permissive role of serotonergic axons, *Neuropharmacology, 21*: 1145 (1982).

W. E. Bunney, and J. M. Davis, Norepinephrine in depressive reactions: A review, *Arch. Gen. Psychiatry, 13*: 483 (1965).

A. Carlsson, C. G. Gottfries, G. Holmberg et al., Recent advances in the treatment of depression, *Acta Psychiatr. Scand. [Suppl] 290*: 1 (1981).

B. J. Carroll, The dexamethasone suppression test for melancholia. *Br. J. Psychiatry, 140*: 292 (1982).

B. J. Carroll, M. Feinberg, J. F. Greden et al., A specific laboratory test for the diagnosis of melancholia: Standardization, validation, and clinical utility, *Arch. Gen. Psychiatry, 38*: 15 (1981).

M. Carstens, A. Engelbrecht, V. Russell et al., Imipramine binding sties on platelets of patients with major depressive disorder, *Psychiatry Res., 18*: 333 (1986).

D. S. Charney, G. R. Heninger, D. E. Sternberg, D. E. Redmond, J. F. Leckman, J. W. Maas, and R. H. Roth, Presynaptic adrenergic receptor sensitivity in depression. The effect of long-term desipramine treatment, *Arch. Gen. Psychiatry, 38*: 1334 (1981a).

D. S. Charney, D. B. Menkes, and G. R. Heninger, Receptor sensitivity and the mechanism of action of antidepressant treatment: Implications for the etiology and therapy of depression, *Arch. Gen. Psychiatry, 38*: 1160 (1981b).

D. S. Charney, G. R. Heninger, J. F. Reinhard et al., The effect of IV L-tryptophan on prolactin, growth hormone, and mood in healthy subjects, *Psychopharmacology, 78*: 38 (1982a).

D. S. Charney, G. R. Heninger, D. E. Sternberg et al., Adrenergic receptor sensitivity in depression: Effects of clonidine in depressed patients and healthy subjects, *Arch. Gen. Psychiatry, 39*: 290 (1982b).

D. S. Charney, G. R. Heninger, and A. Breier, Noradrenergic function in panic anxiety: Effects of yohimbine in healthy subjects and patients with agoraphobia and panic disorder, *Arch. Gen. Psychiatry, 41*: 751 (1984a).

D. S. Charney, G. R. Heninger, and D. E. Sternberg, Serotonin function and mechanism of action of antidepressant treatment, *Arch. Gen. Psychiatry, 41*: 359 (1984b).

D. S. Charney, J. H. Krystal, P. L. Delgado, and G. R. Heninger, Serotonin-specific drugs for anxiety and depressive disorders, *Annu. Rev. Med., 41*: 437 (1990).

S. C. Cheetham, M. R. Crompton, C. Czudek et al., Serotonin concentrations and turnover in brains of depressed suicides, *Brain Res., 502*: 332 (1989).

G. Chouinard, A double-blind controlled clinical trial of fluoxetine and amitriptyline in the treatment of outpatients with major depressive disorder, *J. Clin. Psychiatry, 46*: 32 (1985).

C. R. Cloninger, A unified biosocial theory of personality and its role in the development of anxiety states, *Psychiatr. Dev., 3*: 167 (1986).

C. R. Cloninger, A systematic method for clinical description and classification of personality variants, *Arch. Gen. Psychiatry, 44*: 573 (1987).

E. F. Coccaro, L. J. Siever, H. M. Klar, G. Maurer, K. Cochrane, T. B. Cooper, R. C. Mohs, and K. L. Davis, Serotonergic studies in patients with affective and personality disorders: Correlates with suicidal and impulsive aggressive behavior, *Arch. Gen. Psychiatry, 46*: 587 (1989).

E. Cochran, E. Robins, and S. Grote, Regional serotonin levels in brain: A comparison of depressive suicides and alcoholic suicides with controls, *Biol. Psychiatry, 11*: 283 (1976).

S. J. Cooper, J. G. Kelly, and D. J. King, Adrenergic receptors in depression: Effects of electroconvulsive therapy, *Br. J. Psychiatry, 147*: 23 (1985).

A. Coppen, and K. M. Wood, Peripheral serotonergic and adrenergic responses in depression. *Acta Psychiatr. Scand. [Suppl.] 280*: 21 (1980).

A. Coppen, C. Swade, and K. Wood, Platelet 5-hydroxytryptamine accumulation in depressive illness, *Clin. Chim. Acta, 87*: 165 (1978).

A. Coppen, C. Swade, and K. Wood, The action of antidepressant drugs on 5-hydroxytryptamine uptake by platelets—relationship to therapeutic effect, *Acta Psychiatr. Scand., [Suppl.] 290*: 236 (1981).

P. J. Cowen, Prolactin response to tryptophan during mianserin treatment, *Am. J. Psychiatry, 145*: 740 (1988).

P. J. Cowen, Antidepressants: Current concepts of mode of action, *Int. Clin. Psychopharmacol., 5*(Suppl. 3): 45 (1990).

P. J. Cowen, D. P. Geaney, M. Schachter et al., Desipramine treatment in normal subjects. Effects on neuroendocrine responses to tryptopan and on platelet serotonin 5HT-related receptors, *Arch. Gen. Psychiatry, 43*: 61 (1986).

P. J. Cowen, S. L. McCance, P. R. Cohen, and D. L. Julier, Lithium increases 5-HT-mediated neuroendocrine responses in tricyclic resistant depression, *Psychopharmacology, 99*: 230 (1989).

C. A. Czeisler, R. E. Kronauer, J. J. Mooney et al., Biologic rhythm disorders, depression, and phototherapy. *Psychiatr. Clin. North Am., 4*: 687 (1987).

A. Dahlstrom, and K. Fuxe, Evidence for the existence of monoamine-containing neurons in the central nervous system: I. Demonstration of monoamines in the cell bodies of brain stem neurons, *Acta Physiol. Scand., [Suppl.] 232*: 1 (1964).

J. M. Davis, S. H. Koslow, R. D. Gibbons et al., Cerebrospinal fluid and urinary biogenic amines in depressed patients and healthy controls, *Arch. Gen. Psychiatry, 45*: 705 (1988).

J. F. W. Deakin, I. Pennell, A. J. Upadhyaya, and R. Lofthouse, A neuroendocrine study of 5HT function in depression: Evidence for biological mechanisms of endogenous and psychosocial causation, *Psychopharmacology, 101*: 85 (1990).

P. L. Delgado, D. S. Charney, L. H. Price et al., Serotonin function and the mechanism of antidepressant action: Reversal of antidepressant-induced remission by rapid depletion of plasma tryptophan, *Arch. Gen. Psychiatry, 47*: 411 (1990).

C. de Montigny, F. Grunberg, A. Mayer, and J.-P. Duschenes, Lithium induces rapid relief of depression in tricyclic antidepressant drug non-responders, *Br. J. Psychiatry, 138*: 252 (1981).

A. S. de Villiers, V. A. Russell, M. E. Carstens et al., Noradrenergic function and hypothalamic–pituitary–adrenal axis activity in primary unipolar major depressive disorder, *Psychiatry Res., 22*: 127 (1987).

A. S. de Villiers, V. A. Russell, and M. E. Carstens, Noradrenergic function and hypothalamic–pituitary–adrenal axis activity in adolescents with major depressive disorder, *Psychiatry Res., 27*: 101 (1989).

H. D'haenen, M. De Waele, and J. E. Leysen, Platelet ^{3}H-paroxetine binding in depressed patients, *Psychiatry Res., 26*: 11 (1988).

P. Dick, and E. Ferrero, A double-blind comparative study of the clinical efficacy of fluvoxamine and chlorimipramine, *Br. J. Clin. Pharmacol., 15*: 419s (1983).

R. A. Dominguez, B. J. Goldstein, A. F. Jacobson, and R. M. Steinbrook, A double-blind placebo-controlled study of fluvoxamine in depression, *J. Clin. Psychiatry, 46*: 84 (1985).

A. Dumbrille-Ross, and S. W. Tang, Noradrenergic and serotonergic input necessary for imipramine induced changes in beta but not S2 receptor densities, *Psychiatry Res., 9*: 207 (1983).

D. Egrise, M. Rubinstein, A. Schoutens et al., Seasonal variation of platelet serotonin uptake and ^{3}H-imipramine binding in normal and depressed subjects, *Biol. Psychiatry, 21*: 283 (1986).

I. Extein, J. Tallman, C. C. Smith, and F. K. Goodwin, Changes in lymphocyte beta-adrenergic receptors in depression and mania, *Psychiatry Res., 1*: 191 (1979).

G. Faludi, I. Magyar, and K. Tekes et al., Measurement of ^{3}H-serotonin uptake in blood platelets in major depressive episodes, *Biol. Psychiatry, 23*: 829 (1988).

R. M. Ferris, and O. J. Beaman, Bupropion: A new anti-depressant drug, the mechanism of action of which is not associated with down-regulation of postsynaptic beta adrenergic, serotonergic (5-HT_2), alpha-2-adrenergic, imipramine and dopaminergic receptors in brain, *Neuropharmacology, 22*: 1257 (1983).

H. C. Fibiger, and J. J. Miller, An anatomical and electrophysiological investigation of the serotonergic projection from the dorsal raphe nucleus to the substantia nigra in the rat, *Neuroscience, 2*: 975 (1977).

A. Frazer, R. Brown, J. Kocsis et al., Patterns of melatonin rhythms in depression, *J. Neural Transm., 21*(Suppl.): 269 (1986).

A. A. Frazer, and P. Jauher, Lithium in severe depression, *Br. J. Psychiatry, 147*: 324 (1985).

E. Friedman, F. Fung, and S. Gershon, Antidepressant drugs and dopamine uptake in different brain regions, *Eur. J. Pharmacol. 42*: 47 (1977).

K. Fuxe, S.-O. Ogren, and L. F. Agnati, The effects of chronic treatment with the 5-hydroxytryptamine uptake blocker zimelidine on central 5-hydroxytryptamine mechanism. Evidence for the induction of a low affinity binding site for 5-hydroxytryptamine, *Neurosci. Lett., 14*: 307 (1979).

K. Fuxe, S.-O. Ogren, L. F. Agnati et al., Long-term treatment with zimelidine leads to a reduction in 5-hydroxytryptamine neurotransmission within the central nervous system of the mouse and rat, *Neurosci. Lett., 21*: 57 (1981).

K. Fuxe, S.-O. Ogren, L. F. Agnati et al., Effects of subchronic antidepressant drug treatment on central serotonergic mechanism in the male rat, *Typical and Atypical Antidepressants: Molecular Mechanisms* (E. Costa and G. Racagni, eds.), Raven Press, New York, p. 91. (1982).

J. Garcia-Sevilla, A. Zis, P. Hollingsworth, J. Greden, and C. Smith, Platelet alpha-2 adrenergic receptors in major depressive disorder, *Arch. Gen. Psychiatry, 38*: 1327 (1981).

M. Giret, J. M. Launay, C. Dreux et al., Modifications of biochemical parameters in blood platelets of schizophrenic and depressive patients, *Neuropsychobiology, 6*: 290 (1980).

A. Gjerris, L. Werdelin, O. J. Rafaelsen, C. Alling, and N. J. Christensen, CSF dopamine increased in depression: CSF dopamine, noradrenaline and their metabolites in depressed patients and in controls, *J. Affective Disord., 13*: 279 (1987).

A. R. Glass, R. C. Smallridge, M. Schaaf, and R. C. Dimond, Absent prolactin response to L-tryptophan in normal and acromegalic subjects, *Psychoneuroendocrinology, 5*: 261 (1980).

M. I. Gluckman, and T. Baum, The pharmacology of iprindole, a new antidepressant, *Psychopharmacologia (Berl.), 15*: 169 (1969).

P. W. Glue, P. J. Cowen, D. J. Nutt, T. Kolakowska, and D. G. Grahame-Smith, The effect of lithium on 5-HT mediated neuroendocrine responses and platelet 5-HT receptors, *Psychopharmacology, 90*: 398 (1986).

F. Goodlet, S. E. Mreylees, and M. F. Sugrue, Effects of mianserin, a new antidepressant, on the in vitro and in vivo uptake of monoamines, *Br. J. Pharmacol., 61*: 307 (1977).

F. K. Goodwin, R. Rubovits, D. Jimerson, R. M. Post, Serotonin and norepinephrine subgroups in depression, *Sci. Proc. Am. Psychiatr. Assoc., 130*: 108 (1977).

F. K. Goodwin, A. Wirz-Justice, and T. A. Wehr, Evidence that the pathophysiology of depression and the mechanism of action of antidepressant drugs both involve alterations in circadian rhythms, *Adv. Biochem. Psychopharmacol., 32*: 1 (1982).

D. G. Grahame-Smith, Studies in vivo on the relationship between brain tryptophan, brain 5-HT synthesis and hyperactivity in rats treated with a monoamine oxidase inhibitor and L-tryptophan, *J. Neurochem., 18*: 1053 (1971).

D. G. Grahame-Smith, Serotonin function in affective disorders, *Acta Psychiatr. Scand. [Suppl.] 350*: 7 (1989).

P. M. Grasby, and P. J. Cowen, The pineal and psychiatry: Still fumbling in the dark? *Psychol. Med., 17*: 817 (1987).

R. Gross-Isseroff, M. Israeli, and A. Biegon, Autoradiographic analysis of tritiated imipramine binding in the human brain post mortem: Effects of suicide, *Arch. Gen. Psychiatry, 46*: 237 (1989).

J. D. Hallonquist, M. A. Goldberg, and J. S. Brandes, Affective disorders and circadian rhythms, *Can. J. Psychiatry, 31*: 259 (1986).

C. O. S. Hallstrom, C. M. B. Pare, W. L. Rees et al., Platelet uptake of 5-hydroxytryptamine and dopamine in depression, *Postgrad. Med. J., 52* (Suppl.): 40 (1976).

J. P. Halper, R. P. Brown, J. A. Sweeney, J. H. Kocsis, A. Peters, and J. J. Mann, Blunted beta-adrenergic responsivity of peripheral blood mononuclear cells in endogenous depression. Isoproterenol dose-response studies, *Arch. Gen. Psychiatry, 45*: 241 (1988).

S. Handwerger, J. W. Plank, H. E. Lebovitz et al., Failure of 5-hydroxytryptophan to stimulate prolactin and growth hormone secretion in man, *Horm. Metab. Res., 7*: 214 (1975).

D. Healy, and B. E. Leonard, Monoamine transport in depression: Kinetics and dynamics, *J. Affective Disord., 12*: 91 (1987).

D. Healy, P. Carney, and B. Leonard, Monoamine-related markers of depression-changes following treatment, *J. Psych. Res., 17*: 251 (1983).

D. Healy, P. Carney, A. O'Halloran, and B. Leonard, Peripheral adrenoceptors and serotonin receptors in depression, *J. Affective Disord., 9*: 285 (1985).

G. R. Heninger, and D. S. Charney, The monoamine receptor sensitivity hypothesis of antidepressant drug action, *Psychopharmacol. Bull., 18*: 130 (1982).

G. R. Heninger, D. S. Charney, and D. E. Sternberg, Serotonergic function in depression, *Arch. Gen. Psychiatry, 41*: 398 (1984).

G. R. Heninger, D. S. Charney, and L. H. Price, α_2-Adrenergic receptor sensitivity in depression: The plasma MHPG, behavioral, and cardiovascular responses to yohimbine, *Arch Gen. Psychiatry, 45*: 718 (1988).

L. Humphries, P. Shirley, M. Allen et al., Daily patterns of serotonin uptake in platelets from psychiatric patients and control volunteers, *Biol. Psychiatry, 20*: 1073 (1985).

L. L. Iversen, and A. V. P. Mackay, Pharmacodynamics of antidepressants and antimanic drugs, *Psychopharmacology of Affective Disorders* (E. S. Paykel and A. Coppen, eds.), Oxford University Press, New York, p. 60 (1979).

A. Janowsky, F. Okada, D. Manier et al., Role of serotonergic input in the regulation of the beta-adrenergic receptor-coupled adenylate cyclase system, *Science, 218*: 900 (1982).

P. Jenner, M. Sheehy, and C. D. Marsden, Noradrenaline and 5-hydroxytryptamine modulation of brain dopamine function. Implications for the treatment of Parkinson's disease, *Br. J. Clin. Pharmacol., 15*: 277S (1983).

D. C. Jimerson, T. R. Insel, V. I. Reus, and I. J. Kopin, Increased plasma MHPG in dexamethasone-resistant depressed patients, *Arch. Gen. Psychiatry, 40*: 173 (1983).

R. T. Joffe, R. M. Post, J. C. Ballenger, R. Rebar, R. Rakita, and P. W. Gold, Neuroendocrine effects of the dopamine agonist piribedil in depressed patients, *Clin. Neuropharmacol., 9*: 448 (1986).

P. R. Joyce, Neuroendocrine changes in depression, *Aust. N. Z. J. Psychiatry, 19*: 120 (1985).

R. S. Kahn, G. M. Asnis, S. Wetzler, and H. M. van Praag, Neuroendocrine evidence for serotonin receptor hypersensitivity in panic disorder, *Clin. Psychopharmacol., 96*: 360 (1988).

R. S. Kahn, S. Wetzler, G. M. Asnis, D. Papolos, and H. M. van Praag, Serotonin receptor sensitivity in major depression, *Biol. Psychiatry, 28*: 358 (1990).

P. D. Kanof, C. A. Johns, M. Davidson et al., Platelet alpha$_2$-adrenergic receptor function in psychiatric disorders, *Psychiatry Res., 23*: 11 (1988).

R. D. Kaplan, and J. J. Mann, Altered platelet serotonin uptake kinetics in schizophrenia and depression, *Life Sci., 31*: 583 (1982).

Y. Kato, Y. Nakai, H. Imura et al., Effect of 5-hydroxytryptophan (5-HTP) on plasma prolactin levels in man, *J. Clin. Endocrinol. Metab., 38*: 695 (1974).

K. J. Kellar, and C. A. Stockmeier, Effects of electroconvulsive shock and serotonin axon lesions on beta-adrenergic and serotonin-2 receptors in rat brain, *Electroconvulsive Therapy: Clinical and Basic Research Issues* (S. Malitz and H. A. Sackeim, eds.), *Ann. N. Y. Acad. Sci., 462*: 76 (1986).

K. J. Kellar, C. S. Cascio, J. A. Butler, and R. N. Kurtzke, Differential effects of electroconvulsive shock and antidepressant drugs on serotonin-2 receptors in rat brain, *Eur. J. Pharmacol., 69*: 515 (1981).

J. L. Kinney, Nomifensine maleate: A new second-generation antidepressant, *Clin. Pharm., 4*: 625 (1985).

S. Korsgaard, J. Gerlach, and E. Christenson, Behavioral aspects of serotonin–dopamine interactions in the monkey, *Eur. J. Pharmacol., 118*: 245 (1985).

F. Koshikawa, N. Koshikawa, and J. D. Stephenson, Effects of antidepressant drug combinations on cortical $5HT_2$ receptors and wet-dog shakes in rats, *Eur. J. Pharmacol., 118*: 273 (1985).

J. H. Koslow, J. W. Maas, C. L. Bowden et al., CSF and urinary biogenic amines and metabolites in depression and mania, *Arch. Gen. Psychiatry, 40*: 999 (1983).

T. Koyama, M. T. Lowy, and H. Y. Meltzer, 5-Hydroxytryptophan-induced cortisol response and CSF 5-HIAA in depressed patients, *Am. J. Psychiatry, 144*: 334 (1987).

R. Kuhn, The treatment of depressive states with G-22355 (imipramine), *Am. J. Psychiatry, 115*: 459 (1958).

D. J. Kupfer, and M. B. Bowers, REM sleep and central monoamine oxidase inhibition, *Psychopharmacologia, 27*: 182 (1972).

T. A. Lahti, and R. P. Maickel, The tricyclic antidepressants—inhibition of norepinephrine uptake as related to potentiation of norepinephrine and clinical efficacy, *Biochem. Pharmacol., 20*: 482 (1971).

C. R. Lake, D. Pickar, M. Ziegler et al., High plasma norepinephrine levels in patients with major affective disorder, *Am. J. Psychiatry, 139*: 1315 (1982).

I. Lancranjan, A. Wirz-Justice, W. Puhringer and E. Del Pozo, Effect of L-5-hydroxytryptophan infusion on growth hormone and prolactin secretion in man, *J. Clin. Endocrinol. Metab., 45*: 588 (1977).

S. Z. Langer, and R. Raisman, Binding of ^{3}H-imipramine and ^{3}H-desipramine as biochemical tools for studies in depression, *Neuropharmacology, 22*: 407 (1983).

S. Z. Langer, E. Zarifian, M. Briley et al., High affinity binding of (^{3}H)imipramine in brain and platelets and its relevance to the biochemistry of affective disorders, *Life Sci., 29*: 211 (1981a).

S. Z. Langer, F. Javoy-Agid, R. Raisman et al., Distribution of specific high affinity binding sites for (^{3}H)imipramine in human brain, *J. Neurochem., 37*: 267 (1981b).

S. Z. Langer, D. Sechter, H. Loo, R. Raisman, and E. Zarifian, Electroconvulsive shock therapy and maximum binding of platelet tritiated imipramine binding in depression, *Arch. Gen. Psychiatry, 43*: 949 (1986).

K. P. Lesch, S. Mayer, J. Disselkamp-Tietze, A. Hoh, M. Weismann, M. Osterheider, and H. M. Schulte, $5\text{-}HT_{1A}$ receptor responsivity in unipolar depression: Evaluation of ipsapirone-induced ACTH and cortisol secretion in patients and controls, *Biol. Psychiatry, 28*: 620 (1990a).

K. P. Lesch, J. Disselkamp-Tietze, and A. Schmidtke, $5\text{-}HT_{1A}$ receptor function in depression: Effect of chronic amitriptyline treatment, *J. Neural Transm. Gen. Sect., 80*: 157 (1990b).

K. P. Lesch, G. Laux, and T. Mueller, $alpha_2$-Adrenoceptor responsivity in depression: Effect of chronic treatment with moclobemide, a selective MAO-A-inhibitor, versus maprotiline, *J. Neural Transm. 32* (Suppl.): 457 (1990c).

P. Levitt, and R. Y. Moore, Noradrenaline neuron innervation of the neocortex in the rat, *Brain Res., 139*: 219 (1978).

D. A. Lewis, and C. McChesney, Tritiated imipramine binding distinguishes among subtypes of depression, *Arch. Gen. Psychiatry, 42*: 485 (1985).

O. Lingjaerde, The biochemistry of depression: A survey of monoaminergic, neuroendocrinological, and bio-rhythmic disturbances in endogenous depression, *Acta Psychiatr. Scand., [Suppl.] 302*: 36 (1983).

K. G. Lloyd, I. J. Farley, J. H. N. Deck, and O. Horneykiewicz, Serotonin and 5-hydroxyindoleacetic acid in discrete areas of the brainstem of suicide victims and control patients, *Adv. Biochem. Psychopharmacol., 11*: 387 (1974).

P. T. Loosen, and A. J. Prange, Serum thyrotropin response to thyrotropin-releasing hormone in psychiatric patients: A review, *Am. J. Psychiatry, 139*: 405 (1982).

R.-B. Lu, S.-L. Ho, B. T. Ho et al., Correlations between plasma cortisol and CSF catecholamines in endogenous depressed dexamethasone nonsuppressors, *J. Affective Disord., 10*: 177 (1986).

I. Lucki, and A. Frazer, Prevention of the serotonin syndrome in rats by repeated administration of monoamine oxidase inhibitors but not tricyclic antidepressants, *Psychopharmacology, 77*: 205 (1982).

J. W. Maas, Biogenic amines and depression: Biochemical and pharmacological separation of two types of depression, *Arch. Gen. Psychiatry, 32*: 1357 (1975).

J. W. Maas, S. H. Koslow, J. Davis et al., Catecholamine metabolism and disposition in healthy and depressed subjects, *Arch. Gen. Psychiatry, 44*: 337 (1987).

M. Maes, M. de Ruyter, and E. Suy, Cortisol response to dexamethasone and noradrenergic function in depression, *Acta Psychiatr. Scand. 75*: 171 (1987).

M. Maes, R. Vandevelde, and E. Suy, Influences on cortisol and noradrenergic turnover of healthy controls and depressed patients during L-tryptophan loading, *J. Affective Disord., 17*: 173 (1989).

J. R. Magliozzi, D. Gietzen, R. J. Maddock, D. Haack, A. R. Doran, T. Goodman, and P. J. Weiler, Lymphocyte beta-adrenoreceptor density in patients with unipolar depression and normal controls, *Biol. Psychiatry, 26*: 15 (1989).

R. Malmgren, A. Åberg-Wistedt, and B. Martensson, Aberrant seasonal variations of platelet serotonin uptake in endogenous depression, *Biol. Psychiatry, 25*: 393 (1989).

J. J. Mann, R. P. Brown, J. P. Halper, J. A. Sweeney, J. H. Kocsis, P. E. Stokes, and J. P. Bilezikian, Reduced sensitivity of beta-adrenergic receptors in patients with endogenous depression and psycho-motor agitation, *N. Engl. J. Med., 313*: 715 (1985).

J. J. Mann, J. C. Mahler, P. J. Wilner, J. P. Halper, R. P. Brown, K. S. Johnson, J. H. Kocsis, and J. S. Chen, Normalization of blunted lympocyte beta-adrenergic responsivity in melancholic inpatients by a course of electroconvulsive therapy, *Arch. Gen. Psychiatry, 47*: 461 (1990).

J. J. Mann, M. Stanley, P. A. McBride, and B. S. McEwen, Increased serotonin-2 and beta-adrenergic receptor binding in the frontal cortices of suicide victims, *Arch. Gen. Psychiatry, 43*: 954 (1986).

J. J. Mann, V. Arango, P. M. Marzuk et al., Evidence for the 5-HT hypothesis of suicide: A review of post-mortem studies, *Br. J. Psychiatry, 155*(Suppl. 8): 7 (1989).

J. Marwaha, and G. K. Aghajanian, Relative potencies of alpha-1 and alpha-2 antagonists in the locus coeruleus, dorsal raphe and dorsal lateral geniculate nuclei: An electrophysiological study, *J. Pharmacol. Exp. Ther., 222*: 287 (1982).

I. G. McKeith, E. F. Marshall, I. N. Ferrier et al., 5-HT receptor binding in post-mortem brain from patients with affective disorder, *J. Affective Disord., 13*: 67 (1987).

H. Y. Meltzer, Serotonergic function in the affective disorders: The effect of antidepressants and lithium on the 5-hydroxytryptophan-induced increase in serum cortisol, *Ann. N. Y. Acad. Sci., 430*: 115 (1984).

H. Y. Meltzer, Serotonergic dysfunction in depression, *Br. J. Psychiatry, 155*(Suppl. 8): 25 (1989).

H. Y. Meltzer, R. C. Arora, R. Baber, and B. J. Tricou, Serotonin uptake in blood platelets of psychiatric patients, *Arch. Gen. Psychiatry, 38*: 1322 (1981).

H. Y. Meltzer, R. C. Arora, and P. Goodnick, Effect of lithium carbonate on serotonin uptake in blood platelets of patients with affective disorders, *J. Affective Disord., 5*: 215 (1983a).

H. Y. Meltzer, B. J. Tricou, A. Robertson, and M. Lowy, Hormone response to 5-hydroxytryptophan, *Psychiatry Res., 10*: 151 (1983b).

H. Y. Meltzer, M. Lowy, A. Robertson et al., Effect of 5-hydroxytryptophan on serum cortisol levels in major affective disorders: III. Effect of antidepressants and lithium carbonate, *Arch. Gen. Psychiatry, 41*: 391 (1984).

J. Mendlewicz, R. M. Pinder, S. M. Stulemeijer, and R. Van Dorth, Monoamine metabolites in cerebrospinal fluid of depressed patients during treatment with mianserin or amitriptyline, *J. Affect. Disord. 4*: 219 (1982).

D. B. Menkes, G. K. Aghajanian, and D. W. Gallager, Chronic antidepressant treatment enhances agonist affinity of brain alpha-1 adrenoceptors, *Eur. J. Pharmacol., 87*: 35 (1983).

L. R. Meyerson, L. P. Wennogle, M. S. Abel et al., Human brain receptor alterations in suicide victims, *Pharmacol. Biochem. Behav., 17*: 59 (1982).

A. M. Mirkin, and A. Coppen, Electrodermal activity in depression: Clinical and biochemical correlates, *Br. J. Psychiatry, 137*: 93 (1980).

I. Modai, R. Malmgren, M. Asberg, and H. Bering, Circadian rhythm of serotonin transport in human platelets, *Psychopharmacology, 88*: 493 (1986).

J. H. Morrison, S. L. Foote, M. E. Molliver et al., Noradrenergic and serotonergic fibers innervate complementary layers in monkey primary visual cortex: An immunohistochemical study, *Proc. Natl. Acad. Sci. USA, 79*: 2401 (1982).

L. D. Mulgirigama, Significance of uptake studies with biogenic amines, *Research and Clinical Investigation in Depression* (J. E. Murphy, ed.), Cambridge Medical Publications, Northampton, England, p. 10 (1976).

D. L. Murphy, E. A. Mueller, N. A. Garrick, and C. S. Aulakh, Use of serotonergic agents in the clinical assessment of central serotonin function, *J. Clin. Psychiatry, 47*(Suppl.): 9 (1986).

R. Muscat, D. Sampson, and P. Willner, Dopaminergic mechanism of imipramine action in an animal model of depression, *Biol. Psychiatry, 28*: 223 (1990).

J. C. Nelson, and C. M. Mazure, Lithium augmentation in psychotic depression refractory to combined drug treatment, *Am. J. Psychiatry, 143*: 363 (1986).

V. L. Nimgaonkar, F. K. Goodwin, C. L. Davies, and A. R. Green, Down-regulation of beta-adrenoceptors in rat cortex by repeated administration of desipramine, electroconvulsive shock and clenbuterol requires 5HT neurons but not 5HT, *Neuropharmacology, 24*: 279 (1985).

G. Nordin, J. O. Ottosson, and B. E. Roos, Influence of convulsive therapy on 5-hydroxyindoleacetic acid and homovanillic acid in cerebrospinal fluid in endogenous depression, *Psychopharmacologia, 20*: 315 (1971).

I. Oswald, V. Brezinova, and D. L. F. Dunleavy, On the slowness of action of tricyclic antidepressant drugs, *Br. J. Psychiatry, 120*: 673 (1972).

J. E. Overall, L. E. Hollister, A. D. Pokorny et al., Drug therapy in depressions: Controlled evaluation of imipramine, isocarboxazid, dextroamphetamine, amobarbital, and placebo, *Clin. Pharmacol. Ther., 3*: 16 (1962).

I. M. Oxenkrug, J. Prakhje, and J. N. Mikhalenko, Disturbed circadian rhythms of 5-hydroxytryptamine uptake by blood platelets in depressive psychoses, *Act. Nerv. Super., 20*: 66 (1978).

G. N. Pandey, M. W. Dysken, D. L. Garver, and J. M. Davis, beta-Adrenergic receptor function in affective illness, *Am. J. Psychiatry, 136*: 675 (1979).

R. Papeschi, and D. J. McClure, Homovanillic and 5-hydroxyindoleacetic acid in cerebrospinal fluid of depressed patients, *Arch. Gen. Psychiatry, 25*: 354 (1971).

D. P. Papolos, Serotonin, seasonality, and mood disorders. *The Role of Serotonin in Psychiatric Disorders* (S. L. Brown, and H. M. van Praag, eds.), Brunner/Mazel, New York, p. 260. (1991).

S. M. Paul, M. Rehavi, K. C. Rice et al., Does high affinity (^{3}H)imipramine binding label serotonin reuptake sites in brain and platelet? *Life Sci. 28*: 2753 (1981).

S. J. Peroutka, and S. H. Snyder, Long term antidepressant treatment decreases spiroperidol-labelled serotonin receptor binding, *Science, 210*: 88 (1980).

E. K. Perry, E. F. Marshall, G. Blessed et al., Decreased imipramine binding in the brains of patients with depressive illness, *Br. J. Psychiatry, 142*: 188 (1983).

R. M. Post, and F. K. Goodwin, Effects of amitriptyline and imipramine on amine metabolites in the cerebrospinal fluid of depressed patients, *Arch. Gen. Psychiatry, 30*: 234 (1974).

R. M. Post, J. Kopin, and F. K. Goodwin, The effects of cocaine in depressed patients, *Am. J. Psychiatry, 131*: 511 (1974).

R. M. Post, R. H. Gerner, J. S. Carman et al., Effects of a dopamine agonist piribedil in depressed patients: Relationship of pretreatment homovanillic acid to antidepressant response, *Arch. Gen. Psychiatry, 35*: 609 (1978).

W. Z. Potter, M. Scheinin, R. N. Golden et al., Selective antidepressants and cerebrospinal fluid, *Arch. Gen. Psychiatry, 42*: 1171 (1985).

L. A. Price, Y. Conwell, and J. C. Nelson, Lithium augmentation of combined neuroleptic–tricyclic treatment in delusional depression *Am. J. Psychiatry, 140*: 318 (1983).

L. A. Price, D. S. Charney, and G. R. Heninger, Efficacy of lithium–tranylcypromine treatment in refractory depression, *Am. J. Psychiatry, 142*: 619 (1985a).

L. H. Price, D. S. Charney, and G. R. Heninger, Effects of tranylcypromine treatment on neuroendocrine, behavioral, and autonomic responses to tryptophan in depressed patients, *Life Sci., 37*: 809 (1985b).

L. H. Price, D. S. Charney, A. L. Rubin, and G. R. Heninger, $alpha_2$-Adrenergic receptor function in depression: The cortisol response to yohimbine, *Arch. Gen. Psychiatry, 43*: 849 (1986).

L. H. Price, D. S. Charney, and G. R. Heninger, Effects of trazodone treatment on serotonergic function in depressed patients, *Psychiatry Res., 24*: 165 (1988).

L. H. Price, D. S. Charney, and P. L. Delgado, Effects of desipramine and fluvoxamine treatment on the prolactin response to tryptophan: Serotonergic function and the mechanism of antidepressant action, *Arch. Gen. Psychiatry, 46*: 625 (1989a).

L. H. Price, D. S. Charney, P. L. Delgado, and G. R. Heninger, Lithium treatment and serotoninergic function: Neuroendocrine and behavioral responses to intravenous tryptophan in affective disorder, *Arch. Gen. Psychiatry, 46*: 13 (1989b).

L. H. Price, D. S. Charney, P. L. Delgado, and G. R. Heninger, Lithium and serotonin function: Implications for the serotonin hypothesis of depression, *Psychopharmacology, 100*: 3 (1990).

J. V. Priestley, P. Somogyi, and A. C. Cuello, Neurotransmitter-specific projection neurons revealed by combining PAP immunohistochemistry with retrograde transport of HRP, *Brain Res.*, 231 (1981).

J. Quintana, Platelet serotonin uptake dynamic changes in depression: Effects of long-term imipramine treatment and clinical recovery, *J. Affective Disord., 16*: 233 (1989).

R. Raisman, D. Sechter, M. S. Briley et al., High affinity ^{3}H-imipramine binding in platelets from untreated and treated depressed patients compared to healthy volunteers, *Psychopharmacology, 75*: 368 (1981).

R. Raisman, M. S. Briley, F. Bouchami et al., ^{3}H-imipramine binding and serotonin uptake in platelets from untreated depressed patients and control volunteers, *Psychopharmacology, 77*: 332 (1982).

J. L. Rausch, N. S. Shah, E. A. Burch, and A. G. Donald, Platelet serotonin uptake in depressed patients: Circadian effect, *Biol. Psychiatry, 17*: 121 (1982).

J. L. Rausch, C. L. Rich, and S. C. Risch, Platelet serotonin transport after a single ECT, *Psychopharmacology, 95*: 139 (1988).

J. L. Rausch, S. M. Stahl, and R. L. Hauger, Cortisol and growth hormone responses to the 5-HT_{1A} agonist gepirone in depressed patients, *Biol. Psychiatry, 28*: 73 (1990).

J. Redman, S. Armstrong, and K. T. Ng, Free running activity rhythms in the rat: Entrainment by melatonin, *Science, 219*: 1089 (1983).

A. H. Robins, Depression in patients with parkinsonism, *Br. J. Psychiatry, 128*: 141 (1976).

A. H. Rosenbaum, T. Maruta, A. F. Schatzberg et al., Toward a biochemical classification of depressive disorders: VII. Urinary free cortisol and urinary MHPG in depressions, *Am. J. Psychiatry, 140*: 314 (1983).

N. E. Rosenthal, D. A. Sack, J. C. Gillin et al., Seasonal affective disorder: A description of the syndrome and preliminary findings with light therapy, *Arch. Gen. Psychiatry, 41*: 72 (1984).

S. B. Ross, B. Aperia, J. Beck-Friis et al., Inhibition of 5-hydroxytryptamine uptake in human platelets by antidepressant agents in vivo, *Psychopharmacology, 67*: 1 (1980).

A. Roy, and M. S. Kafka, Platelet adrenoceptors and prostaglandin responses in depressed patients, *Psychiatry Res., 30*: 181 (1989).

A. Roy, D. Pickar, M. Linnoila, A. R. Doran, P. Ninan, and S. M. Paul, Cerebrospinal fluid monoamine and monoamine metabolite concentrations in melancholia, *Psychiatry Res., 15*: 281 (1985).

A. Roy, D. Everett, D. Pickar, and S. M. Paul, Platelet tritiated imipramine binding and serotonin uptake in depressed patients and controls: Relationship to plasma cortisol levels before and after dexamethasone administration, *Arch. Gen. Psychiatry, 44*: 320 (1987a).

A. Roy, D. Pickar, M. Linnoila et al., Cerebrospinal fluid corticotropin-releasing hormone in depression: Relationship to noradrenergic function, *Psychiatry Res., 20*: 229 (1987b).

A. Roy, D. Pickar, J. De Jong et al., Norepinephrine and its metabolites in cerebrospinal fluid, plasma and urine: Relationship to hypothalamic–pituitary–adrenal axis function in depression, *Arch. Gen. Psychiatry, 45*: 849 (1988).

A. Roy, J. De Jong, and M. Linnoila, Cerebrospinal fluid monoamine metabolites and suicidal behavior in depressed patients: A 5-year follow-up study, *Arch. Gen. Psychiatry, 46*: 609 (1989a).

A. Roy, D. Pickar, and J. De Jong, Suicidal behavior in depression: Relationship to noradrenergic function, *Biol. Psychiatry, 25*: 341 (1989b).

L. Rubin, L. Price, D. Charney, and G. Heninger, Noradrenergic function and the cortisol response to dexamethasone in depression, *Psychiatry Res., 15*: 5 (1985).

A. F. Schatzberg, E. Dessain, P. O'Neil et al., Recent studies on selective serotonergic antidepressants: Trazodone, fluoxetine, and fluvoxamine, *J. Clin. Psychopharmacol., 7*(Suppl. 6): 44S (1987).

J. J. Schildkraut, The catecholamine hypothesis of affective disorders: A review of supporting evidence, *Am. J. Psychiatry, 122*: 509 (1965).

M. A. Schlesser, G. Winokur, and B. M. Sherman, Hypothalamic–pituitary–adrenal axis activity in depressive illness, *Arch. Gen. Psychiatry, 37*: 737 (1980).

J. A. Scott, and F. T. Crews, Increase in serotonin-2 receptor density in rat cerebral cortex slices by stimulation of beta-adrenergic receptors, *Biochem. Pharmacol., 34*: 1585 (1985).

J. A. Scott, and F. T. Crews, Down-regulation of serotonin-2, but not of beta-adrenergic receptors during chronic treatment with amitriptyline is independent of stimulation of serotonin-2 and beta-adrenergic receptors, *Neuropharmacology, 25*: 1301 (1986).

M. Scott, H. W. Reading, and J. B. Loudon, Studies on human platelets in affective disorders, *Psychopharmacology, 60*: 131 (1979).

T. Segawa, T. Mizuta, and M. Uehara, Role of the central serotonergic system as related to the pathogenesis of depression: Effect of antidepressants on rat central serotonergic activity, *New Vistas in Depression* (S. Z. Langer, R. Takahashi, T. Segawa, M. Briley, eds.), Pergamon Press, New York, p. 3 (1982).

D. M. Shaw, F. E. Camps, and E. G. Eccleston, 5-Hydroxytryptamine in the hindbrain of depressive suicides, *Br. J. Psychiatry, 113*: 1407 (1967).

B. Shopsin, E. Friedman, and S. Gershon, Parachlorophenylalanine reversal of tranylcypromine effects in depressed patients, *Arch. Gen. Psychiatry, 33*: 811 (1976).

L. J. Siever, and K. L. Davis, Overview: Toward a dysregulation hypothesis of depression, *Am. J. Psychiatry, 142*: 1017 (1985).

L. J. Siever, T. W. Uhde, E. K. Silberman et al., The growth hormone response as a probe of noradrenergic receptor responsiveness in affective disorder patients and controls, *Psychiatry Res., 6*: 171 (1982).

L. J. Siever, D. L. Murphy, S. Slater et al., Plasma prolactin changes following fenfluramine in depressed patients compared to controls: An evaluation of central serotonergic responsivity in depression, *Life Sci., 34*: 1029 (1984a).

L. J. Siever, T. W. Uhde, D. C. Jimerson et al., Differential inhibitory noradrenergic responses to clonidine in 25 depressed patients and 25 normal control subjects, *Am. J. Psychiatry, 141*: 733 (1984b).

L. J. Siever, T. W. Uhde, D. C. Jimerson et al., Plasma cortisol responses to clonidine in depressed patients and controls: Evidence for a possible alteration in noradrenergic–neuroendocrine relationships, *Arch. Gen. Psychiatry, 41*: 63 (1984c).

L. J. Siever, E. F. Coccaro, E. Benjamin et al., Adrenergic and serotonergic receptor responsiveness in depression, *Ciba Found. Symp., 123*: 148 (1986a).

L. J. Siever, T. W. Uhde, D. C. Jimerson et al., Indices of noradrenergic output in depression, *Psychiatry Res., 19*: 59 (1986b).

P. A. Sitland-Marken, B. J. Wells, J. H. Froemming, C. C. Chu, and C. S. Brown, Psychiatric applications of bromocriptine therapy, *J. Clin. Psychiatry, 51*: 68 (1990).

B. Siwers, V. A. Ringberger, R. Tuck, and F. Sjoqvist, Initial clinical trial based on clinical methodology of zimelidine (a serotonin uptake inhibitor) in depressed patients, *Clin. Pharmacol. Ther., 21*: 194 (1976).

R. Sjostrom, 5-Hydroxyindole acetic acid and homovanillic acid in cerebrospinal fluid in manic–depressive psychosis and the effect of probenecid treatment, *Eur. J. Clin. Pharmacol., 6*: 75 (1973).

G. M. Skutsch, Manic–depression: A multiple hormone disorder? *Biol. Psychiatry, 20*: 662 (1985).

T. A. Slotkin, W. L. Whitmore, G. A. Barnes et al., Reduced inhibitory effect of imipramine on radiolabeled serotonin uptake into platelets in geriatric depression, *Biol. Psychiatry, 25*: 687 (1989).

J. M. Sneddon, Blood platelets as a model for monoamine-containing neurons, *Prog. Neurobiol., 1*: 151 (1973).

E. Souêtre, E. Salvati, J.-L. Belugou et al., Circadian rhythms in depression and recovery: Evidence for blunted amplitude as the main chronobiological abnormality, *Psychiatry Res., 28*: 263 (1989).

S. M. Southwick, R. Yehuda, E. L. Giller, Jr., and B. D. Perry, Platelet alpha-2 adrenergic receptor binding sites in major depressive disorder and borderline personality disorder, *Psychiatry Res., 34*: 193 (1990).

S. M. Stahl, The human platelet, *Arch. Gen. Psychiatry, 34*: 509 (1977).

S. M. Stahl, Regulation of neurotransmitter receptors by desipramine and other antidepressant drugs: The neurotransmitter receptor hypothesis of antidepressant action. *J. Clin. Psychiatry, 45*: 37 (1984).

S. Stahl, P. Lemoire, R. Ciaranello, and P. Berger, Platelet alpha-2 adrenergic receptor sensitivity in major depressive disorder, *Psychiatry Res., 10*: 157 (1983).

M. Stanley, and J. J. Mann, Increased serotonin-2 binding sites in frontal cortex of suicide victims, *Lancet, 1*: 214 (1983).

M. Stanley, J. Virgilio, and S. Gershon, Tritiated imipramine binding sites are decreased in the frontal cortex of suicides, *Science, 216*: 1337 (1982).

P. Stark, and C. D. Hardison, A review of multicenter controlled studies of fluoxetine vs. imipramine and placebo in outpatients with major depressive disorder, *J. Clin. Psychiatry, 46*: 53 (1985).

C. A. Stockmeier, and K. J. Kellar, In vivo regulation of the serotonin-2 receptor in rat brain, *Life Sci., 38*: 117 (1986).

P. E. Stokes, J. W. Maas, and J. M. Davis, Biogenic amine and metabolite levels in depressed patients with high versus normal hypothalamic–pituitary–adrenocortical activity, *Am. J. Psychiatry, 144*: 868 (1987).

J. F. Stolz, C. A. Marsden, and D. N. Middlemiss, Effect of antidepressant treatment and subsequent withdrawal on 3H-5-hydroxytryptamine and ^{3}H-spiperone binding in rat frontal cortex and serotonin receptor mediated behaviour, *Psychopharmacology, 80*: 150 (1983).

M. F. Sugrue, Chronic antidepressant therapy and associated changes in central monoaminergic receptor functioning, *Pharmacol. Ther., 21*: 1 (1983a).

M. F. Sugrue, Do antidepressants possess a common mechanism of action? *Biochem. Pharmacol., 32*: 1811 (1983b).

F. Sulser, Update on neuroreceptor mechanisms and their implication for the pharmacotherapy of affective disorders, *J. Clin. Psychiatry, 47*(Suppl.): 13 (1986).

F. Sulser, Serotonin–norepinephrine receptor interactions in the brain: Implications for the pharmacology and pathophysiology of affective disorders, *J. Clin. Psychiatry, 48*(Suppl.): 12 (1987).

B. E. Suranyi-Cadotte, P. L. Wood, G. Schwartz, and N. P. V. Nair, Altered platelet ^{3}H-imipramine binding in schizoaffective and depressive disorders, *Biol. Psychiatry, 18*: 923 (1983).

B. E. Suranyi-Cadotte, R. Quirion, N. P. Nair et al., Imipramine treatment differentially affects platelet ^{3}H-imipramine binding and serotonin uptake in depressed patients, *Life Sci., 36*: 795 (1985).

C. Swade, and A. Coppen, Seasonal variation in biochemical factors related to depressive illness, *J. Affective Disord., 2*: 249 (1981).

S. Takahashi, R. Takahashi, and I. Masamura, Measurement of 5-hydroxyindole compounds during 5-HTP treatment in depressed patients, *Folia Psychiatr. Neurol. Jpn., 30*: 463 (1976).

S. Tang, and J. Morris, Variation in human platelet ^{3}H-imipramine binding, *Psychiatry Res., 16*: 141 (1985).

J. P. Ternaux, F. Hery, S. Bourgoin, J. Adrien, J. Glowinski, and M. Hamon, The topographical distribution of serotonergic terminals in the neostriatum of the rat and the caudate nucleus of the cat, *Brain Res., 121*: 311 (1977).

L. Traskman, M. Asberg, L. Bertilsson et al., Plasma levels of chlorimipramine and its desmethyl metabolite during treatment of depression, *Clin. Pharmacol. Ther., 26*: 600 (1979).

J. Tuomisto, A new modification for studying 5-HT uptake by blood platelets: A re-evaluation of tricyclic antidepressants as uptake inhibitors, *J. Pharm. Pharmacol., 26*: 92 (1974).

J. Tuomisto, and E. Tukiainen, Decreased uptake of 5-hydroxytryptamine in blood platelets from depressed patients, *Nature, 266*: 596 (1976).

J. Tuomisto, E. Tukiainen, and U. G. Ahlfors, Decreased uptake of 5-hydroxytryptamine in blood platelets from patients with endogenous depression, *Psychopharmacology, 65*: 141 (1979).

H. M. van Praag, In search of the mode of action of antidepressants: 5-HTP/tyrosine mixtures in depressions, *Neuropharmacology, 22*: 433 (1983).

H. M. van Praag, Studies in the mechanism of action of sevotonin precursors in depression, *Psychopharmacol. Bull., 20*: 599 (1984).

H. M. van Praag, Two-tier diagnosing in psychiatry, *Psychiatry Res., 34*: 1 (1991).

H. M. van Praag, and J. Korf, Endogenous depressions with and without disturbances in the 5-hydroxytryptamine metabolism: A biochemical classification? *Psychopharmacologia, 19*: 148 (1971).

H. M. van Praag, and J. Korf, Central monoamine deficiency in depressions: Causative or secondary phenomenon? *Pharmacopsychiatr. Neuropsychopharmacol., 8*: 322 (1975).

H. M. van Praag, and B. Leijnse, Die bedeutung dermonoamineoxydasehemmung als antidepressives Prinzip I, *Psychopharmacologia, 4*: 1 (1963a).

H. M. van Praag, and B. Leijnse, Die bedeutung dermonoamineoxydasehemmung als antidepressives Prinzip II, *Psychopharmacologia, 4*: 91 (1963b).

H. M. van Praag, J. Korf, and J. Puite, 5-Hydroxyindoleacetic acid levels in the cerebrospinal fluid of depressive patients treated with probenecid, *Nature, 225*: 1259 (1970).

H. M. van Praag, J. Korf, and T. Schut, Cerebral monoamines and depression. An investigation with the probenecid technique, *Arch. Gen. Psychiatry, 28*: 827 (1973a).

H. M. van Praag, F. Flentge, J. Korf et al., The influence of probenecid on the metabolism of serotonin, dopamine and their precursors in man, *Psychopharmacologia, 33*: 141 (1973b).

H. M. van Praag, R. Kahn, G. M. Asnis et al., Therapeutic indications for serotonin potentiating compounds: A hypothesis, *Biol. Psychiatry, 22*: 205 (1987a).

H. M. van Praag, C. Lemus, and R. Kahn, Hormonal probes of central serotonergic activity: Do they really exist? *Biol. Psychiatry, 22*: 86 (1987b).

H. M. van Praag, R. Kahn, G. M. Asnis, S. Wetzler, S. L. Brown, A. Bleich, and M. Korn, Denosologization of biological psychiatry, or the specificity of 5-HT disturbances in psychiatric disorders. *J. Affective Disord., 13*: 1 (1987c).

H. M. van Praag, S. L. Brown, G. M. Asnis, R. S. Kahn, M. L. Korn, J. M. Harkavy-Friedman, and S. Wetzler, Beyond serotonin: A multi-aminergic perspective on abnormal behavior, *The Role of Serotonin in Psychiatric Disorders* (S. L. Brown and H. M. van Praag, eds.), Brunner/Mazel, New York, p. 302 (1991).

J. Vetulani, Complex action of antidepressant treatment on central adrenergic system: Possible relevance to clinical effects, *Pharmacopsychiatry, 17*: 16 (1984).

J. Vetulani, U. Lebrecht, and A. Pilc, Enhancement of responsiveness of the central serotonergic system and serotonin-2 receptor density in rat frontal cortex by electroconvulsive shock treatment, *Eur. J. Pharmacol., 76*: 81 (1981).

J. K. Wamsley, W. F. Byerley, R. T. McCabe et al., Receptor alterations associated with serotonergic agents: An autoradiographic analysis, *J. Clin. Psychiatry, 48*: 19 (1987).

T. A. Wehr, F. M. Jacobsen, D. A. Sack, J. Arendt, L. Tamarkin, and N. E. Rosenthal, Phototherapy of seasonal affective disorder, *Arch. Gen. Psychiatry, 43*: 870 (1986).

T. A. Wehr, and D. A. Sack, Sleep disruption: A treatment of depression and a cause of mania, *Psychiatr. Ann., 17*: 654 (1987).

H. G. M. Westenberg, H. M. van Praag, J. T. V. M. de Jong, and J. H. H. Thyssen, Postsynaptic serotonergic activity in depressive patients: Evaluation of the neuroendocrine strategy, *Psychiatry Res., 7*: 61 (1982).

P. M. Whitaker, J. J. Warsh, H. C. Stancer et al., Seasonal variation in platelet ^{3}H-imipramine binding: Comparable values in control and depressed populations, *Psychiatry Res., 11*: 127 (1984).

P. Willner, Antidepressants and serotonergic neurotransmission: An integrative review, *Psychopharmacology, 85*: 387 (1985).

P. Willner, *Depression: A Psychobiological Synthesis*, Wiley-Interscience, New York (1985).

A. Wirz-Justice, and W. Puhringer, Seasonal incidence of an altered diurnal rhythm of platelet serotonin in unipolar depression, *J. Neural Transm., 42*: 45 (1978).

N. Wolfe, A. J. Gelenberg, and R. B. Lydiard, alpha 2-Adrenergic receptor sensitivity in depressed patients: Relation between ^{3}H-yohimbine binding to human platelet membranes and clonidine-induced hypotension, *Biol. Psychiatry, 25*: 382 (1989).

P. L. Wood, B. E. Suranyi-Cadotte, G. Schwartz, and N. P. V. Nair, Platelet ^{3}H-imipramine binding and red blood cell choline in affective disorders: Indications of heterogenous pathogenesis, *Biol. Psychiatry, 18*: 715 (1983a).

K. Wood, C. Swade, M. Abou-Saleh et al., Drug plasma levels and platelet 5-HT uptake inhibition during long-term treatment with fluvoxamine or lithium in patients with affective disorders, *Br. J. Clin. Pharmacol., 15*: 365s (1983b).

M. Zetin, S. Potkin, and M. Urbanchek, Melatonin in depression, *Psychiat. Ann., 17*: 676 (1987).

Z. P. Zis, and F. K. Goodwin, Novel antidepressants and the biogenic amine hypothesis of depression: The case for iprindole and mianserin, *Arch. Gen. Psychiatry, 36*: 1097 (1979).

14

The Pharmacological Treatment of Depression and Its Problems

J. M. Ad Sitsen
Academic Hospital Utrecht, State University of Utrecht, Utrecht, The Netherlands

Stuart A. Montgomery
St. Mary's Hospital Medical School, London, England

I. INTRODUCTION

The pharmacological treatment of depression stems from the serendipitous discovery of the antidepressant action of two drugs, iproniazid and imipramine.

In 1951, iproniazid, a substance closely related to the well-known tuberculostatic drug isoniazid, was clinically tested for antitubercular activity. The drug clearly showed such antitubercular effects, but the patients felt disproportionally well. Soon its potential as a psychotropic drug was recognized and formal clinical trials proved its antidepressant efficacy. Its actions were ascribed to its monoamine oxidase (MAO)-inhibiting property, but other factors also may be at work, since some of the most potent MAO inhibitors have weak or no antidepressant activity (Lehmann and Kline, 1983). Nevertheless, since the discovery of the antidepressant activity of iproniazid, many other MAO inhibitors have been developed and successfully used in the treatment of depressed patients.

The discovery, in 1952, by Delay and Deniker of the antipsychotic properties of chlorpromazine revived the interest of research workers in the laboratories of J. R. Geigy in Basel in a recently abandoned line of research; namely, investigations on iminodibenzyl derivatives—chemically related to chlorpromazine—as potential antihistaminics, sedatives, analgesics, or drugs for the treatment of Parkinson's disease. Kuhn tested some of the compounds as potential antipsychotics in patients with various psychiatric disorders, among them some with endogenous depression. One of these compounds—now known as imipramine—led to the unexpected discovery of its therapeutic value in the treatment of depression (Sulser and Mishra, 1983). Imipramine was the first tricyclic antidepressant and is still one of the mainstays of the psychopharmacological treatment of depression. Many other tricyclic antidepressants were to follow.

The discovery of the antidepressant activity of the monoamine oxidase inhibitors and the tricyclic compounds sparked an intense interest for their mechanism of action that continues to the present day. A great deal of both preclinical and clinical research is directed at elucidating the molecular events in the brain that cause the antidepressant effects.

At the same time that the treatment of depression underwent important changes because of the introduction into clinical psychiatric practice of the antidepressants, the diagnosis of depression changed concurrently. Diagnostic criteria were defined and subsequently refined and redefined. This process still continues. In clinical research, depression is currently usually diagnosed according to the *Diagnostic and Statistical Manual of Mental Disorders*, 3rd ed., revised edition (*DSM-III-R*; American Psychiatric Association, 1987). For issues concerning the diagnosis of depression reference is made to Chapter 2 of this handbook.

II. OVERVIEW OF ANTIDEPRESSANT DRUGS

A. Tricyclic Antidepressants

1. Pharmacology

At the time the favorable clinical effects of imipramine in depression were discovered, relatively little was known about the pharmacology of this compound. Research soon revealed that imipramine and related compounds in vitro in peripheral organs potently inhibited the uptake of norepinephrine and serotonin into the presynaptic nerve terminals (Glowinski and Axelrod, 1964; Lidbrink et al., 1971). It had also been observed that imipramine could antagonize the effects of reserpine in animals. Therefore, it appeared logical to conclude that imipramine—and the tricyclic antidepressants in general—inhibited the reserpine-induced depressive syndrome in animals and relieved human depression by enhancing noradrenergic or serotonergic, or both, neural transmission through blockade of their reuptake into the presynaptic nerve terminals. Schildkraut (1965) based his monoamine hypothesis of depression on these observations. The subsequent development of antidepressant agents that did not cause inhibition of monoamine uptake in presynaptic nerve terminals (e.g., mianserin, trazodone) and were clinically as effective as imipramine and amitriptyline prompted reconsideration of Schildkraut's monoamine hypothesis of depression. It is now generally agreed that "the real cause" of depression is unknown, and that antidepressant drugs cause a multitude of changes in the functioning of neurotransmitter receptors in the central nervous system, in particular on long-term administration (Leonard, 1991), which—if any—of these changes should be held responsible for the therapeutic action is still uncertain.

The tricyclic antidepressants have many pharmacological properties in common, but clinically relevant differences do exist. The tertiary amine tricyclic drugs (e.g., amitriptyline, imipramine, clomipramine, doxepin) inhibit the neuronal uptake of serotonin more than do the secondary amine drugs (e.g., desipramine, nortriptyline) that preferentially enhance noradrenergic neurotransmission. However, in vivo to some extent, the tertiary amines are metabolized to secondary amines, which blurs any specificity of action.

The choice of a tertiary or secondary amine tricyclic antidepressant does affect the spectrum of side effects because the tertiary amines have the greatest affinity for muscarinic, histamine H_1, and α_1-adrenergic receptors and, consequently, the greatest anticholinergic, antihistaminergic (and presumably by the latter mechanism) sedative, and orthostatic hypotensive properties (Potter et al., 1991).

2. Pharmacokinetics

The tricyclic antidepressants are usually administered orally. Their bioavailability is low and variable owing to often extensive first-pass metabolism. The metabolism of the tricyclic antidepressants varies widely between individuals, resulting in pronounced interindividual differences in the steady-state plasma levels from standard doses of tricyclic antidepressants (Hammer and Sjöqvist, 1967). Therefore, the doses must be tailored carefully to the needs of each individual patient. Plasma assays are available for tricyclic antidepressants, and the pharmacokinetics of this class of drugs have been investigated extensively. The usefulness of plasma level monitoring is disputed, since a narrow range of plasma levels for optimum therapeutic response is accepted only for nortriptyline (Montgomery et al., 1978; Kragh-Sörensen et al., 1976). The value of plasma level monitoring with amitriptyline is also disputed, although there is strong evidence of the disadvantage of its active metabolite nortriptyline (Montgomery et al., 1979). For imipramine and desipramine, high plasma levels are advocated by some (Rudorfer and Potter, 1987), but not by others (Montgomery et al., 1983), and doses to achieve high levels are not widely accepted in Europe. The high levels of imipramine are, in any event, associated with an increased level of cardiotoxicity and convulsions, and rather than risk these side effects, European practice is to use safer drugs. Plasma level monitoring may be useful if there is a lack of therapeutic response or suspected toxicity.

A relatively recent development is the demonstration of the influence that the sparteine–debrisoquine oxidation polymorphism has on the elimination of most tricyclic antidepressants. A simple phenotype test can now identify poor metabolizers of sparteine or debrisoquine, who, when taking standard doses of tricyclic antidepressants may develop higher than expected, and sometimes even toxic, blood levels (Gram, 1991).

3. Clinical Efficacy

The introduction into clinical psychiatry of the tricyclic antidepressants in the late 1950s and following years represented a major advance in the treatment of depression. The earliest reports on their antidepressant efficacy stemmed mainly from uncontrolled studies in clinical practice, but later they have been thoroughly evaluated, and their efficacy has been established in placebo-controlled clinical trials.

It has been suggested that patients with preponderantly biological symptoms of depression (*endogenous depression*) respond better to treatment with tricyclic antidepressants than other depressed patients. This, however, is subject to debate, and it is currently generally accepted that the tricyclic antidepressants are effective across a wide range of depressed patients. There is some suggestion of a relative lack of response in delusional depressives, although this has not been properly investigated. Some suggest the use of electroconvulsive treatments preferentially for these patients (Khan et al., 1987).

Tricyclic antidepressants give recovery or marked improvement in approximately 65% of cases and, therefore, show a lack of efficacy in 30–40% of patients (Klerman and Cole, 1965; Montgomery, 1990a). Consequently, a major goal in clinical research with antidepressant drugs has been to develop biochemical tests or to identify pathophysiological factors that predict whether particular patients will respond to treatment. The impaired suppression of plasma cortisol levels in response to the administration of dexamethasone and the subnormal plasma thyroid-stimulating hormone (TSH) response to thyrotropin-releasing hormone (TRH) have been extensively investigated as such a test or factor. However, these tests have yielded insufficiently consistent results to allow them to be used as predictors of response to antidepressant therapy (Gitlin et al., 1984; Kirkegaard, 1981).

In view of the observation that a substantial proportion of depressed patients do not respond or respond insufficiently to treatment with tricyclic antidepressants, means have been sought for enhancing the antidepressant effectiveness of these drugs. This topic will be discussed in Section III of this chapter.

Depression associated with other conditions may require a more selective approach. For example, there is now good evidence that the depressive symptoms associated with obsessive–compulsive disorder do not respond to noradrenergic antidepressants (e.g., desipramine and nortriptyline; Thoren et al., 1980; Goodman et al., 1990), but do respond to potent serotonergic antidepressants, such as clomipramine or the selective serotonin reuptake inhibitors (Montgomery, 1991a). Depression associated with panic disorder responds well to the tricyclic antidepressants clomipramine, imipramine and, probably, others, although panic disorder without associated depression appears to respond only to serotonergic antidepressants (den Boer and Westenberg, 1988).

4. *Side-Effects*

The tricyclic antidepressants have many and varied side effects, ranging in severity from troublesome to dangerous. These often compromise treatment by the patient's failure to comply with taking medication. Many patients who stop medication do not restart and suffer a relapse, and they are often lost to further follow-up and treatment. Many of the side effects are extensions of the pharmacological actions. Dry mouth, impaired accommodation, difficulty in micturition, increased sweating, constipation, sexual dysfunction, and tachycardia, all are anticholinergic effects. Postural hypotension also occurs, probably as an extension of the adrenolytic effects. These can have serious consequences, such as fractures resulting from falls in the elderly (Glasman and Bigger, 1981; L'Orme, 1984). Tremors, sedation, confusion, and weight gain occur frequently. Changes of clinical laboratory values, such as liver enzyme levels and, rarely, blood dyscrasias, have been observed (Pollack and Rosenbaum, 1987). The incidence of convulsions is sufficiently high enough to cause concern (Montgomery, 1990a), with reports of convulsions caused by tricyclic antidepressants frequently above the 0.5% level, which is the maximum tolerated for a new antidepressant.

5. *Interactions*

The continued use of alcohol, barbiturates, or other hepatic microsomal enzyme-inducing agents enhances the metabolic breakdown of the tricyclic antidepressants, thereby reducing the plasma concentrations, whereas neuroleptic drugs, cimetidine, or fluoxetine can increase the plasma levels by inhibiting these enzymes (Simpson and Singh, 1990). The combination of tricyclic antidepressants and monoamine oxidase inhibitors has been reported to produce dangerous hypertensive crisis and is contraindicated in most countries (White and Simpson, 1984). There is thought to be a particular danger with the combination of clomipramine and tranylcypromine for which a several deaths attributed to the neuroleptic malignant syndrome have been reported.

6. *Other Aspects*

The older tricyclic antidepressants include imipramine, amitriptyline, nortriptyline, desipramine, and clomipramine. These drugs are effective antidepressants, but their safety and side effects leave a great deal to be desired. Presumably, for this reason, other tricyclic antidepressants have been developed, such as maprotiline, dothiepin, doxepin, and lofepramine. Except for lofepramine, these newer drugs differ little from the classic tricyclic antidepressants in their clinical effects. Lofepramine is the only tricyclic antidepressant with significantly improved safety in overdose (Cassidy and Henry, 1987).

B. Monoamine Oxidase Inhibitors

1. Pharmacology

Monoamine oxidase (MAO) is an enzyme present in many tissues including the central nervous system, in the liver, in adrenergic nerve terminals, and in the gut wall. It is concerned with the metabolic breakdown of norepinephrine, serotonin, tyramine, and other amines that are widely distributed in the body as neurotransmitters, or taken in food and drink, or as drugs.

Monoamine oxidase inhibitors (MOAIs) inhibit the action of MAO, leading to a rapid elevation of brain monoamine concentrations, which fits nicely with the monoamine hypothesis of depression, referred to earlier. However, their action is not always confined to MAO in its different forms. The MAOIs also inhibit hydroxylases in the liver. The three classic MAOIs currently marketed as antidepressant drugs—phenelzine, isocarboxazid, and tranylcypromine—irreversibly inhibit both the A and the B form of MAO (see following discussion). The inhibition of the metabolic breakdown of tyramine in some types of food has been associated with hypertensive reactions, thereby necessitating strict adherence to dietary restrictions. Studies in the last decade have revealed that there are two major isoenzymes of MAO, MAO-A and MAO-B. These isoenzymes act preferentially on different monoamines, (i.e., MAO-A more actively metabolizes serotonin and norepinephrine, and MAO-B preferentially deaminates phenylethylamine and dopamine; Murphy et al., 1987). There is now substantial evidence that MAO-A inhibition is associated with the antidepressant action of the MAO. Low doses of deprenyl that selectively inhibit MAO-B do not produce antidepressant effects (Youdim and Finberg, 1983). Higher doses of deprenyl act on both isoenzymes and have clear antidepressant action (Mann et al., 1989).

2. Pharmacokinetics

In contrast with initial data suggesting that acetylation was a major metabolic pathway for the degradation of the hydrazine MAOIs, phenelzine and isocarboxazid, later studies showed that this is not so and that acetylation plays only a minor role in the metabolism of the hydrazine MAOIs. In humans, phenelzine is rapidly converted to phenylacetic acid with ring hydroxylation, and acetylated metabolites are undetectable in plasma or urine (Robinson et al., 1978, 1985). Phenelzine exhibits nonlinear pharmacokinetics, which makes the choice of dose critical. The brief metabolic half-life does not correlate with the longer pharmacodynamic half-life that has been reported (Robinson et al., 1985), presumably because of its irreversible binding to MAO. According to Kurtz (1990) pharmacokinetic studies indicate that MAOIs are cleared rapidly from the systemic circulation, whereas their pharmacological effects persist much longer. The irreversible inhibition means that the pharmacodynamic effects of MAOIs will persist for as long as 2 weeks after the drug is discontinued.

3. Clinical Efficacy

The older nonspecific MAOIs were introduced into psychiatric practice when the required testing of new drugs was less stringently delineated than it is today. Although they were reported to be more effective than placebo, the precise role that MAOIs should play in the treatment of depressive illness is still being defined. They are less effective than the tricyclic antidepressants in major depression and have largely been replaced (Pare, 1985; Montgomery, 1990a). Their efficacy, however, is rated as similar to that of the tricyclic antidepressants by others (Murphy et al., 1987).

In the recent past, attempts have been made to identify a group of patients who respond particularly well to MAOIs. These patients would have a so-called atypical depression and be categorized by reactive mood, rejection sensitivity, and vegetative atypical features, such as overeating, oversleeping, and lethargy (Quitkin et al., 1984). Two recent studies suggest that MAOIs may be particularly effective for these anxious or atypically depressed patients (Liebowitz et al., 1988; Quitkin et al., 1988).

Reversible Inhibitors of Monoamine Oxidase. Drugs that selectively and reversibly inhibit MAO-A such as moclobemide, brofaromine, and toloxatone, are now becoming available (Laux et al., 1991; Kurtz, 1990). The pharmacokinetics of the reversible MAO-A inhibitors have been extensively studied. Recently, Laux et al. (1991) gave a brief but relevant overview indicating that the bioavailabilities of moclobemide and toloxatone range from 0.5 to 0.8. Maximum plasma levels are reached after 30 min to several hours (in particular brofaromine and climoxatone being absorbed slowly). Plasma elimination half-lives of these drugs range from approximately 2h (moclobemide, toloxatone) to about 12–14 h (brofaromine, climoxatone). Elimination is almost exclusively by hepatic metabolism.

Moclobemide is now freely available, although there are lingering doubts about its efficacy. There is also some question about the correct dose, which has led to the use of high doses that could be expected to compromise the selectivity. There is increasing evidence that brofaromine and moclobemide may have a role in the treatment of social phobia and panic disorder.

4. Side Effects

The side effects of the MAOIs are manifold and include orthostatic hypotension, weight gain, sexual dysfunction, and insomnia. Less common side effects include myoclonic twitching during sleep onset, joint pains and, rarely, pyridoxine deficiency with neuropathy. The initially observed hepatotoxicity of iproniazid, and to a smaller extent, other MAOIs appeared less cumbersome in daily clinical practice than anticipated (Kurtz, 1990). As yet, it is still too early to evaluate the full side effect profile of the new, selective MAO-A inhibitors, such as moclobemide and brofaromine.

5. Interactions

Interactions of MAOIs occur both with food, in particular food rich in tyramine, and with other drugs. Tyramine is an amine that releases norepinephrine from presynaptic nerve terminals. When available in sufficient amounts, this can elevate blood pressure to dangerous levels. Under normal conditions, the tyramine contained in food is broken down by MAO in the gut wall and liver, but when MAO is inhibited by MAOIs, the tyramine is free to exert its hypertensive effects, and a hypertensive crisis may follow. This potentially dangerous reaction that can be prevented only by dietary restrictions led many clinicians to prefer safer antidepressants (Montgomery, 1990a).

Although MAO-A is the preponderant form of MAO in the human intestine, and the pressor response after oral administration of tyramine in healthy volunteers treated with MAO-A inhibitors is enhanced (Bieck et al., 1991), nevertheless, there is some evidence that the reversible MAO-A inhibitors moclobemide and brofaromine can safely be used without dietary restrictions (Bonetti et al., 1991; Möller, 1991). Presumably, the main reason is that the tyramine content of many European foodstuffs has been overestimated.

More dangerous than the interaction with dietary tyramine is the concomitant use of MAOIs and over-the-counter cough mixtures containing directly or indirectly acting sympathomimetic drugs and several other drugs (narcotics, antihypertensives, insulin, anesthetics), including the 5-HT-reuptake inhibitors (e.g., fluvoxamine, fluoxetine) (Montgomery, 1991a; Kurtz, 1990). Serious adverse reactions, including rapid death from hyperthermia, have been reported with a combination of MAOIs and clomipramine or the new 5-HT-reuptake inhibitors (Blackwell, 1991; Committee on Safety of Medicines, 1989).

C. Specific Serotonin Reuptake Inhibitors

1. Pharmacology

The neurotransmitter serotonin is now the focus of psychopharmacological research. Numerous receptor subtypes have been discovered, and their functional roles are being delineated. This development has led to the design of drugs that selectively and specifically interfere with serotonin metabolism or serotonin receptor subtypes. The drugs selectively inhibiting the reuptake of serotonin are now reaching the market: drugs such as fluvoxamine, fluoxetine, paroxetine, sertraline, and citalopram, are now widely available (Montgomery, 1991a). Their main pharmacological action is the inhibition of serotonin reuptake in presynaptic nerve terminals. Chronic treatment of rats appears to induce subsensitivity of β-adrenergic receptors in forebrain, a neurochemical alteration believed to be a common feature of efficacious antidepressant treatments. Serotonin-reuptake inhibitors show up in animal tests for antidepressant drugs. In humans, serotonin-reuptake inhibitors reduce the transport of [^{3}H]-serotonin into the platelets of control subjects (Leonard, 1990).

2. Pharmacokinetics

The selective serotonin-reuptake inhibitors are well absorbed after oral administration, with peak plasma levels occurring at 1 to several hours after drug ingestion. Fluoxetine is an exception because its maximum plasma level does not occur until 6–7 h after drug administration (Lemberger, 1990). Fluvoxamine is extensively metabolized, and its major metabolites are inactive in inhibiting the reuptake of serotonin and norepinephrine. Its elimination half-life is approximately 15 h. Fluoxetine has a half-life of 1–3 days, its major metabolite, norfluoxetine, is pharmacologically active and has an even longer half-life of 7–15 days. These pharmacokinetics are not significantly altered in healthy elderly subjects or in patients with renal impairment, but they may be prolonged in patients with hepatic insufficiency. It is excreted primarily by the renal system following its degradation to more polar metabolites in the liver (Lemberger, 1990). Citalopram has a half-life of 36 h, and undergoes minimal first-pass metabolism in humans. Its metabolites have the same specificity for serotonin as the parent compound, but they are less potent. A prolonged half-life and reduced metabolism have been observed in elderly patients. Sertraline is rather slowly absorbed from the gastrointestinal tract, peak plasma levels occurring 6–8 h after an oral dose. It has a half-life of 24 h (its less potent desmethyl metabolite approximately 36 h) which is unchanged in the elderly. Paroxetine is completely and rapidly absorbed after oral administration, it has a half-life of approximately 20 h. Paroxetine is extensively metabolized in the liver, the metabolites being inactive. Elderly patients may develop higher plasma levels than younger patients given the same dose (for review and references, see Boyer and Feighner, 1991).

3. *Clinical Efficacy*

The efficacy of the selective serotonin reuptake inhibitors (SSRIs) is well established in large placebo and reference antidepressant-controlled studies (Stark and Hardison, 1985; Dunbar et al., 1991; Montgomery, 1990b, 1991a; Amin et al., 1984). These studies are sufficiently large to allow determination of efficacy in subgroups, such as the predominantly anxious, and in severe and moderate depression, separately. In general there is little to choose in efficacy between the specific serotonin-reuptake inhibitors and reference tricyclic antidepressants. However, there are claims that the SSRIs are associated with superior efficacy compared with imipramine in severe depression (Montgomery, 1992; Mendlewicz, 1992), although these claims are disputed by some (Danish University Antidepressant Group, 1986, 1990). There are some suggestions that the SSRIs may be more effective in treating the anxiety symptoms associated with depression (Montgomery et al., 1989).

Fluvoxamine, paroxetine, and fluoxetine, all have shown evidence of better efficacy than the reference compounds on the anxiety or agitation items of depression scales, despite the lack of sedation characteristic of these antidepressants. Claims have also been made for superior efficacy of SSRIs in reducing suicidal thoughts faster than reference tricyclic antidepressants (Wakelin, 1988; Montgomery et al., 1981). The evidence from the placebo-and reference-controlled studies suggests that the onset of antidepressant action is as fast or faster than the tricyclic antidepressants, although there have been isolated reports of slower latency. Fixed-dose, placebo-controlled studies have enabled the identification of the minimum effective dose for citalopram and paroxetine and to substantially lower the dose of fluoxetine from that originally proposed.

In view of the specificity of the SSRIs, the identification of patients with a "serotonin-deficient" depression would be very useful: these patients could be expected to benefit most from this class of antidepressant drugs. However, the existence of such a subgroup of depressed patients is however controversial (Westenberg and Verhoeven, 1988; Davis et al., 1988). The evidence is clear that the SSRIs have a broad spectrum of action across the range of depressed patients.

4. *Side Effects*

The serotonin-reuptake inhibitors have little or none of the side effects associated with the tricyclic antidepressants. They are better tolerated and more acceptable to patients than the older tricyclic antidepressants. They lack the hypotensive, anticholinergic, and cardiotoxic effects of the tricyclic compounds and, therefore, are probably relatively safe in overdose (Montgomery, 1990a). In addition, they are not sedative, which makes them useful for patients who are trying to continue at work. The disadvantage of this aspect, however, is that the sleeping problems are not improved and may even worsen.

Characteristic side effects of the serotonin-reuptake inhibitors, expected from the pharmacological activity, relate to anxiety and gastrointestinal disturbance. An increase in nervousness is reported in some patients early in treatment (Montgomery, 1990a). Most often this effect subsides rapidly and, in the placebo and reference-controlled studies, an advantage is seen with the anxiety and agitation items at the end of the acute treatment. Gastrointestinal discomfort, nausea and, in extreme cases, vomiting can occur. Weight loss is reported with some compounds, but not apparently with paroxetine. Blurred vision, which has occasionally been reported with the serotonin-reuptake inhibitors, is probably mediated through serotonergic innervation of the eye (Moro et al., 1981). Adverse effects on sexual function have been reported and include anorgasmia and delayed orgasm (Herman et al., 1990). As with other antidepressants, the side effects are dose-related and the advantage of identifying the minimum effective dose is that the side effects can be minimized.

5. *Interactions*

Data about the use of selective serotonin-reuptake inhibitors in combination with other drugs is emerging. Single-dose interaction studies with paroxetine and several commonly prescribed drugs, such as digoxin, cimetidine, and warfarin, have been performed (Bannister et al., 1989). Cimetidine impairs the first-pass metabolism, leading to a buildup of higher drug levels, and coadministration with warfarin may increase bleeding tendency. The meaning of these findings for daily clinical practice is not entirely clear. Dangerous reactions may occur owing to interactions between monoamine oxidase inhibitors and SSRI's with the rapid development of potentially lethal hyperthermia.

The combination of tricyclic antidepressants and fluoxetine is likely to raise the plasma levels of both drugs, since they inhibit the metabolism of each other (Rudorfer and Potter, 1989). Because fluoxetine has a long half-life, clinicians will need to take this into account in choosing the appropriate dose of a tricyclic antidepressant following treatment with fluoxetine.

6. *Other Aspects*

Attempts at identifying patients with a dysfunction in the serotonin system have been disappointing. The hope that SSRIs might be indicated, in particular, in patients with a serotonin-type depression, has not been fulfilled (Montgomery, 1990a).

The selective effect of SSRIs is most clearly seen in the treatment of obsessive–compulsive disorder, in which condition, conventional tricyclics, with the exception of clomipramine, are apparently ineffective. Antiobsessional efficacy is seen with fluvoxamine, sertraline, and fluoxetine at doses very similar to those established for the treatment of depression. When major depression and obsessive compulsive disorder overlap, the depression only responds to the same serotonergic drugs, which suggests that the depression is part of the obsessive–compulsive disorder, rather than a separate disorder.

Some selectivity is also seen in the treatment of panic disorder, with pure panic disorder responding best to the serotonergic drugs (den Boer and Westenberg, 1988). This selectivity, however, is lost when panic overlaps with major depression and when a variety of antidepressants appear to be effective.

Fluoxetine is apparently effective in bulimia, although the studies are small. The possible indication of weight loss still requires evidence of efficacy in the long-term, in view of reports of breakthrough weight gain.

Fluvoxamine has some positive evidence of efficacy in addictive behaviors, in particular, alcoholism. There are positive reports of the usefulness of the SSRIs citalopram and fluvoxamine in treating the depressive symptoms associated with dementia. Fluvoxamine has additionally some data suggesting an improvement in cognitive dysfunction in alcoholic memory-defect states.

D. Serotonin Serotonin$_{1A}$ Receptor Agonists

1. Pharmacology

Although initial screening tests with buspirone revealed a psychopharmacological profile consistent with that of an antipsychotic, clinical studies in schizophrenic patients were disappointing, as most patients exhibited a deterioration, rather than an improvement of their symptoms (Sathananthan et al., 1975). Indications of efficacy against anxiety neurosis suggested that buspirone was an atypical anxiolytic, nonbenzodiazepine in structure and pharmacology. Subsequent investigations indicated that buspirone has high affinity for serotonin 5-HT$_{1A}$ receptors, which may explain its anxiolytic activity. Meanwhile, several other drugs have been developed that also act through this particular subset of serotonin receptors (Traber and Glaser, 1987). These compounds, gepirone, ipsapirone, tandospirone, and others, act as full agonists at the 5-HT$_{1A}$ cell body autoreceptor, but as partial agonists at postsynaptic 5-HT$_{1A}$ receptor sites in the hippocampus (Traber and Glaser, 1987; Yocca, 1990). In animal studies, the acute anxiolytic effect of 5-HT$_{1A}$ agonists is apparently caused by their interaction with the cell-body autoreceptors, thereby decreasing 5-HT neurotransmission (Eison et al., 1986). Long-term administration of these compounds can induce adaptive changes in 5-HT$_{1A}$ receptors, of which the meaning is as yet unclear (Cowen, 1991).

2. Pharmacokinetics

Buspirone is rapidly absorbed after oral administration, peak plasma levels occurring at about 1 h after dosing. It is extensively metabolized, with less than 1% of administered dose excreted unchanged. In addition to the oxidative dealkylation that yields 1-(2-pyrimidinyl) piperazine, buspirone also undergoes hydroxylation. The elimination half-life of the parent compound is approximately 2.4 h, whereas that of the 5-hydroxy metabolite is 4.8 h (Goa and Ward, 1986).

The metabolite 1-(2-pyrimidinyl)piperazine is also formed from other azapirones acting at 5-HT$_{1A}$ receptors, such as gepirone and ipsapirone (Fuller, 1991). It has little affinity at 5-HT$_{1A}$ receptors, but has relatively high affinity for α_2-adrenergic receptors and acts at these receptors as an antagonist. This may explain antidepressant effects that are now emerging from clinical studies, in addition to the anxiolytic effects of these drugs. This explanation, however, is not generally accepted (Lucki, 1991). Extensive pharmacokinetic data on the other azapirones that are still in clinical development are not yet available.

3. Clinical Efficacy

Buspirone is now marketed as an anxiolytic drug, and the anxiolytic potential of the related azapirones is being investigated. Meanwhile, evidence is emerging (Lucki, 1991) that this class of compounds also possesses antidepressant properties (Heller et al., 1990; Jenkins et al., 1990; Rausch et al., 1990; Rickels et al., 1990), but it must be added that as yet none of these drugs is marketed for the indication depression.

The antidepressant activity of buspirone was studied in patients meeting *DSM-III* criteria for major depressive disorder with concomitant symptoms of anxiety. Twenty-nine percent of buspirone- and 40% of placebo-treated patients discontinued treatment before 8 weeks. Seventy percent of buspirone and 35% of placebo patients ($p < 0.01$) were rated moderately or markedly improved after 8 weeks of therapy. Buspirone was found to be safe and well tolerated at doses of up to 90 mg/day (Rickels et al., 1990). Clinical investigations with other azapirones, ipsapirone and gepirone, suggest similar efficacy in patients with major depression (Jenkins et al., 1990; Heller et al., 1990). However, further clinical experience is needed before a final judgment on the merits of this new class of antidepressants can be given.

4. *Side Effects*

Buspirone and related compounds may well be a useful addition to the antidepressant armamentarium because the experience to date with buspirone indicates that this compound is without significant sedative, cognitive, or convulsant effects and does not interfere with psychomotor function (Montgomery, 1990a). Main side effects of buspirone include dizziness, restlessness, nausea, and headache. High doses may cause sedation, dysphoria, and increased prolactin and growth hormone levels. Withdrawal symptoms appear not to occur (Goa and Ward, 1986). Ipsapirone and gepirone cause essentially similar side effects. These drugs are generally well tolerated, the main side effects with ipsapirone being dizziness, dazedness, and uncertain feelings in the legs, and with gepirone, dizziness, nausea, headache, and drowsiness.

5. *Interactions*

Relatively little is now known on the possibilities of adverse drug interactions with buspirone and other azapirones. Buspirone does not exhibit interaction with alcohol. In view of its metabolic pathways, increased blood levels are to be expected with concomitant use of drugs that inhibit cytochrome-P450 oxidases, such as cimetidine, erythromycin and others (Goa and Ward, 1986).

E. Other Antidepressant Drugs

In addition to the classes that have been reviewed in the foregoing, several of other antidepressant drugs are available that are less easy to categorize. Therefore, they are individually discussed in this section.

1. *Mianserin*

Mianserin is a tetracyclic antidepressant and, as such, structurally distinct from the classic tricyclic antidepressants and other compounds reviewed in the preceding sections. It was one of the first of the so-called second-generation antidepressants (Zis and Goodwin, 1979). The precise mechanisms underlying the antidepressant efficacy of mianserin are unknown, but it is highly likely that mianserin enhances noradrenergic neurotransmission by rapidly raising synaptic levels of norepinephrine. Unlike tricyclic antidepressants, however, in vivo it is not an inhibitor of norepinephrine and probably releases norepinephrine by antagonism at presynaptic α_2-adrenoceptors. Mianserin also blocks α_1-adrenoceptors, which may, at least in part, explain the postural hypotension that is sometimes observed in susceptible patients after the initial doses of mianserin. It also affects serotonergic systems in the brain. It does not inhibit the reuptake of serotonin, but is a potent antagonist at all three major subclasses of serotonin receptor: 5-HT_1, 5-HT_2, and 5-HT_3 (Hoyer, 1988a,b; Schmidt and Peroutka, 1989). It is most potent at the 5-HT_{1C} and 5-HT_2 sites, its potency at 5-HT_3 receptors is intermediate, and it has its least (but still appreciable) affinity for the lA, lB, and lD receptor subtypes. Although the 5-HT_2 receptor may be intimately involved in depression (Meltzer, 1989), highly selective 5-HT_2 antagonists, such as ritanserin, are not noted for their antidepressant properties, which seem to be confined to compounds with additional effects. Mianserin is a moderately potent antagonist at presynaptic serotonin autoreceptors, which in humans, are of the 5-HT_{1D} subtype and may, thereby, raise synaptic leads of 5-HT by a process akin to elevation of the norepinephrine levels. The functional significance of the 5-HT_3 antagonistic properties is not yet clear, since 5-HT_3 antagonists, such as ondansetron, are unproved antidepressant or anxiolytic agents. The histamine H_1 receptor-blocking properties of mianserin may explain its sedative action. Unlike the tricyclic antidepressants, mianserin is devoid of anticholinergic activity. After oral administration mianserin is rapidly absorbed, the absolute bioavailability being approximately 25%. Is main metabolites are 8-hydroxymianserin and 8-hydroxy-desmethylmianserin. The average half-life of elimination is 32 h. The clinical antidepressant efficacy of mianserin has been established in several placebo-controlled clinical trials. This assessment is supported by the reference-controlled studies, of which there are a sufficient number to establish equivalent efficacy (for references see Vinar et al., 1991; Carman et al., 1991). Mianserin exerts sedative effects, which may be advantageous in patients perceiving their disturbed sleep as a problem. Mianserin has been compared with the reference tricyclic antidepressant amitriptyline and found to have significantly less cardiotoxicity. This is also exemplified by mianserin's relative safety after overdosage (Cassidy and Henry, 1987). Clinically relevant drug–drug interactions with mianserin are not known.

2. *Trazodone*

Trazodone is structurally unrelated to the tricyclic antidepressants and has complex effects on the serotonergic system of the central nervous system. At low doses, it acts as a serotonin antagonist, but after higher doses, it is a modest inhibitor of serotonin reuptake. In the periphery trazodone acts as a α_1-adrenoceptor antagonist and partial serotonin agonist. It has some affinity to histamine H_1-receptors. The main metabolite of trazodone, *m*-chlorophenylpiperazine, has serotonergic effects that may contribute to the pharmacological profile of trazodone in vivo. Trazodone is well absorbed after oral administration, and it is eliminated in a biphasic manner with half-lives of 1 and 8–14 h, respectively. Recent reviews indicate that the clinical antidepressant efficacy of trazodone equals that of standard antidepressants such as amitriptyline, imipramine, and other tricyclic antidepressants (Feighner and Boyer, 1988; Fabre, 1989; 1990).

Its main side effects include drowsiness, dizziness, headache, nausea, and postural hypotension. Anticholinergic side effects are less common than with the tricyclic antidepressants. Priapism is a rare, but very serious, side effect of trazodone. Overdosage has only relatively rarely resulted in deaths when trazodone was taken as a single drug, suggesting that it is safer than the tricyclic antidepressants (Pinder, 1988).

Interactions of trazodone with MAO inhibitors are predicted by an animal model. Clinical evidence suggests that trazodone antagonizes the hypotensive properties of clonidine and α-methyldopa and that it increases the plasma levels of phenytoin and digoxin (for references see Blackwell, 1987).

3. *Tianeptine*

Tianeptine is an intriguing antidepressant because its pharmacological profile is rather different. Tianeptine shows up in several animal models considered predictive of antidepressant activity in humans and has been reported to *increase* (rather than to decrease) the presynaptic uptake of serotonin after single and repeated administration, without affecting postsynaptic serotonergic systems. This effect may be regionally specific (Mennini et al., 1987). The small increase in serotonin uptake in platelets in humans is consistent with the preclinical profile of tianeptine (Kato and Weitsch, 1988). Also, in a number of other effects, both in animals and in humans (in particular electroencephalographic effects), tianeptine is radically different from other antidepressants (for references see Vinar et al., 1991).

Tianeptine shows no affinity for α_1-adrenergic, H_1-histaminic, or muscarinic receptors. Neither tianeptine itself nor two active metabolites have effects on catecholamine uptake, release, or neurotransmitter binding.

The clinical efficacy of tianeptine is reported to be equivalent to that of imipramine, amitriptyline, and other standard antidepressant drugs. It produces few anticholinergic effects and does not impair vigilance. Side effects occur probably at a lower frequency than with tricyclic antidepressants and include irritability, changes in blood pressure, convulsions, sleep disturbance, and gastrointestinal symptoms (Marey et al., 1991).

4. Amoxapine

Amoxapine is a tricyclic antidepressant that is chemically related to the antipsychotic agent loxapine. Like conventional tricyclic antidepressants, it blocks the presynaptic neuronal uptake of norepinephrine and, to a smaller extent, of serotonin. In addition, it has some dopamine receptor-blocking activity, similar to the antipsychotic drugs. It has little anticholinergic effects. In animals it has similar but milder effects on the heart than the classic tricyclic antidepressants.

Amoxapine is rapidly and virtually completely absorbed when administered orally, peak plasma concentrations occurring after 1–2 h. Aromatic hydroxylation in the liver produces two metabolites, of which 8-hydroxyamoxapine is pharmacologically similar, but the 7-hydroxy metabolite has antipsychotic activity. The elimination half-life of amoxapine is approximately 8 h, whereas that of 8-hydroxyamoxapine is about 30 h. Therefore, accumulation of the 8-hydroxy metabolite will occur.

In clinical trials, amoxapine has been compared with amitriptyline and imipramine and with other antidepressant drugs. Amoxapine was as effective as the reference drugs, but in some studies, the therapeutic effects of amoxapine were measurable earlier (at 1 or 2 weeks) (Coccaro and Siever, 1985; Jue et al., 1982; McNair et al., 1984).

Side effects of amoxapine are mild anticholinergic effects (such as dry mouth, blurred vision, and constipation), sedation, convulsions, hypotension, and minor electrocardiographic changes. The dopamine receptor antagonism results in hyperprolactinemia, which may lead to galactorrhea, amenorrhea, and impotence. Extrapyramidal effects are uncommon, but serious if they occur (Thornton and Stahl, 1984). There have been no reports of adverse interactions with chloral hydrate, orphenadrine, hypnotics, α-methyldopa, reserpine, or anxiolytic drugs (Jue et al., 1982).

5. Bupropion

Bupropion is chemically related to anorectic drugs such as diethylpropion. It has a relatively selective action on dopamine reuptake in presynaptic nerve terminals and a direct agonist effect on dopamine receptors. It does not release catecholamines or produce down-regulation of postsynaptic receptors. It has no significant effect on serotonergic, histamine, or cholinergic receptors and lacks effects on growth hormone, prolactin, and response to TRH (Blackwell, 1987).

Bupropion is rapidly absorbed, with peak plasma levels within 2 h and its half-life is approximately 12 h. It is extensively metabolized in the liver to three active metabolites (for references see Blackwell, 1987). Bupropion is equally as effective as standard antidepressants in major depression. Its dose range is narrow, which may require therapeutic drug monitoring (Preskorn, 1991), and its onset of action slow.

It is not recommended for patients predisposed to seizures, but is useful in patients with heart disease or those who gain weight easily. Bupropion has few anticholinergic side effects and does produce some stimulation, including excitement, palpitations, tremor, agitation, and such. Skin rashes and gastrointestinal side effects have also been reported. It seems to be relatively safe at overdosage.

Interactions with alcohol or benzodiazepines are not a problem, and bupropion has safely been used with antiarrhythmic, antihypertensive, and analgesic drugs (Preskorn and Othmer, 1984; Blackwell, 1987; James and Lippmann, 1991).

6. *Viloxazine*

Viloxazine is a bicyclic compound that inhibits the neuronal uptake of norepinephrine, without affecting the uptake of serotonin. It has little effect on adrenoceptors, dopamine receptors, or cholinergic receptors and has little sedative or cardiac depressant activity. It is well absorbed and has an elimination half-life of 2–5 h necessitating more than once-daily administration (Blackwell, 1987). The clinical efficacy of viloxazine seems to be comparable with that of the tricyclic antidepressants, although in placebo-controlled clinical trials its performance was not always unequivocal (for references see *Drug Ther. Bull.,* 1990).

Unwanted effects include mainly gastrointestinal symptoms such as nausea and vomiting. Occasionally hypotension and tachycardia and migraine headaches may occur. Most cases of overdosage recover without serious complications. Adverse interactions are not a serious clinical problem (Blackwell, 1987).

7. *Antipsychotics*

In the literature reports are appearing that suggest that drugs, such as flupenthixol and sulpiride, compounds usually classified as antipsychotics, exert antidepressant actions. Open, uncontrolled (e.g., Budde, 1992), single-blind, comparative studies (e.g., Dwivedi et al., 1990), or double-blind, comparative clinical trials (e.g., Hamilton et al., 1989) should not be accepted as proof of antidepressant activity of such antipsychotic drugs. Only double-blind, placebo-controlled clinical trials in well-defined patient populations can provide unequivocal proof of such effectiveness. Such studies, however, are scarce (Gruber and Cole, 1991). Mindham et al. (1991) conducted a relatively small study in 51 patients with moderate depressive states in which dothiepin, diazepam and sulpiride were compared with placebo. All four groups improved nonsignificantly on the Montgomery Åsberg Depression Rating Scale over a 4-week period, although there was a trend for the sulpiride group to do better. Thioridazine has been investigated in placebo-controlled studies in depressed patients with inconsistent results (Fann et al., 1974; De Jonghe et al., 1976).

Until further evidence from more rigorously designed clinical trials comparing an antidepressant and an antipsychotic drug with placebo is presented, the antidepressant effectiveness of antipsychotic compounds, such as flupenthixol and sulpiride, should be considered as unproven.

8. *Nefazadone*

There has been a theoretical basis for developing 5-HT antagonists as antidepressants since the reports that TCAs down-regulate 5-HT_2 receptors. Most 5-HT_2 antagonists appear to have potent effects on 5-HT_{1c} receptors that are similar. Since 5-HT_{1c} receptors have been shown to provoke anxiety, the differentiation may be important.

Nefazadone is an analogue of trazodone, which is reported to be more selective as a 5-HT_2 antagonist but is also reported to have 5-HT reuptake inhibitory properties.

Nefazadone has a short half-life of approximately 3 h and has two active metabolites, hydroxy nefazadone and mCPP, both of which also have short half-lives.

A dose regimen of twice daily or three times daily has been shown to be effective in depression. Significant clinical efficacy was seen with nefazadone in a number of placebo-controlled trials, particularly with higher doses (D'Amico et al., 1990; Mendels et al., 1991). The side effects of nausea and other fastic symptoms are fairly typical of drugs with serotonin reuptake inhibiting properties. Nefazodone is also associated with some sedation. Nefazadone is licensed for the treatment of depression in some countries in Europe.

9. Venlafaxine

Venlafaxine has potent serotonin and noradrenaline reuptake inhibitor properties. It is reported to be associated with rapid β-adrenoreceptor down-regulation, which is regarded as an important marker of antidepressant activity (Sulser 1984). Venlafaxine has undoubted antidepressant efficacy and has been approved by the FDA. There are four positive placebo-controlled studies and a number of reference controlled studies where venlafaxine was shown to have a clinical advantage.

Rapid onset of action and an early statistically significant antidepressant effect compared with placebo was reported on the MADRS at 4 days in an in-patient study and a clinically relevant difference was reported at 1 week (Montgomery, 1991). In comparing different regimens both low, moderate, and high doses were shown to have antidepressant efficacy compared with placebo, but the higher dose showed a significant advantage compared with both placebo and low dose early in treatment.

It appears that the more rapid antidepressant effect is seen best when the dose is escalated rapidly to 200 mg or more. Rapid dose escalation is unfortunately associated with a higher side effect profile, particularly nausea. Venlafaxine appears to be associated with rises in blood pressure but at doses of 200 mg these rises are in line with those seen with imipramine. The relative short half-life makes a twice daily dose regimen necessary.

10. Mirtazapine

Mirtazapine, an analogue of mianserin, has presymaptic α_2 antagonist properties but it also has marked antagonism at 5-HT_{1c}, 5-HT_2, and 5-HT_3 receptors, which mechanisms have all been proposed as having anxiolytic or antidepressant effects. Mirtazapine has undoubted antidepressant efficacy, shown in placebo-controlled studies, with approximate equivalent efficacy to reference antidepressants amitriptyline, clomipramine, doxepin, trazodone, and maprotiline (Bremner and Panagides, 1992; de Jongh, 1992).

A half-life of approximately 30 h makes mirtazapine suitable for once daily dosing. Mirtazapine appears to be well tolerated with significantly fewer anticholinergic side effects compared with TCAs. The main side effects are dry mouth and transient somnolence in the first week of treatment.

III. TREATMENT-RESISTANT DEPRESSION

Despite the advances in the psychopharmacological treatment of depression there is a consistent literature indicating that between 20 and 40% of depressed patients either do not, or insufficiently, respond to adequate treatment with antidepressant drugs. These patients are generally considered as cases of *treatment-resistant depression*. In this section the concept of treatment-resistant depression and treatment approaches for this type of patient are discussed.

The first problem in treatment-resistant depression is the problem of definition. When is a patient considered to be *resistant* to treatment? The current scientific literature on treatment-resistant depression shows clearly that there is neither agreement on what this condition is, nor on how it should be treated (Remick, 1989; Nierenberg, 1990; Nierenberg and Amsterdam, 1990; Nierenberg and White, 1990; Guscott and Grof, 1991).

Although it is generally recognized that there is a group of depressed patients who are clearly more treatment-resistant than others and might be absolutely refractory, virtually all these patients are only relatively resistant to treatment. Usually, treatment-resistant depression is likely to be due to variables involving the diagnostic and treatment process, rather than the patient (Guscott and Grof, 1991). This is supported by the data reported by Remick (1989). Only 8 of 114 patients referred for treatment-resistant depression exhibited "absolute" treatment-resistant depression after 1 year of extensive psychopharmacological, psychological, and somatic treatments.

Interestingly, little systematic research has been conducted in the field of treatment-resistant depression. Several treatment strategies have been tried. If the patient is being treated with a tricyclic antidepressant, it may be helpful to undertake plasma level monitoring, since there is evidence that high plasma levels of some tricyclic antidepressants (e.g., nortriptyline, amitriptyline) are associated with poorer response. The use of augmentation strategies has not been adequately investigated with properly controlled studies, although there is some evidence of increased response with adjunctive lithium. The use of thyroid hormone adjunctive therapy is not thought to be as potent. Various combinations of lithium and L-tryptophan have been employed, but without sufficient controls to allow proper assessment (Nierenberg and Amsterdam, 1990). The problem with the combination treatment models is the substantial increase in side effects, without necessarily any increase in efficacy. Adequate controlled trials are needed so that proper assessment of the risks and benefits of proposed combinations can be made. Many of the strategies are aimed at increasing serotonergic function, and it may be simpler and safer to switch to potent serotonergic drugs.

IV. DEPRESSION, SUICIDE, AND OVERDOSE OF ANTIDEPRESSANT DRUGS

Depression severely compromises the quality of life and is associated with excessive mortality. Despite the significant improvements in the quality of life of depressed patients since the introduction of antidepressant drugs in the 1950s, suicide is still a major problem in depression. It is estimated that approximately 15% of depressives eventually kill themselves (for references see Montgomery, 1990a). Reports of lethal antidepressant drug overdoses started appearing as early as 1959. In particular, the tricyclic antidepressants are extremely toxic in overdose. Thus, the clinician faces a dilemma in the treatment of depression, since many of the drugs used in the treatment of the illness can result in as fatal an outcome as the disease itself. A related issue that should be considered is the question of whether or not suicidal behavior is promoted by treatment with antidepressants (i.e., by antidepressants in general or by some antidepressants in particular; Montgomery and Pinder, 1987).

People who commit suicide use the means available, among which drugs, in particular prescribed antidepressant drugs, are common. Therefore, the toxicity of antidepressants is a major issue in the treatment of depressed patients with antidepressants. The benefits and risks of such treatment should be carefully weighed against each other and against the risks of the disease itself as well. Crome and Newman (1979) reported a death rate of 3.3% following tricyclic antidepressant overdose, and a later survey indicated a death rate of 2.2% (Frommer et al., 1987). An important issue in this context is the relative toxicity of antidepressants in overdose. Some measure of this relative toxicity can be derived from mortality statistics. From one published survey (Cassidy and Henry, 1987), it appears that the older tricyclic antidepressants are most toxic, followed in order of toxicity by monoamine oxidase inhibitors and tricyclic and other antidepressants introduced after 1974. Further analysis—also pursued by Montgomery and Pinder (1987)—reveals differences between individual antidepressants within the indicated groups. Although the two independent surveys used different patient data bases and the results have been expressed in different ratios (i.e., numbers of fatal overdoses per million prescriptions and per million patients, respectively), the conclusions are remarkably consistent. Desipramine, dothiepin, and amitriptyline appear to be the most dangerous in overdose when compared with other antidepressants. The "old" tricyclic antidepressants have a significantly higher ratio of deaths per million prescriptions than the mean for all antidepressants, whereas drugs introduced after 1973 have a significantly lower ratio than the overall mean. The MAO inhibitors as a group are not significantly different from the overall mean. The drugs with the lowest fatality indexes are those atypical antidepressants, such as mianserin, introduced after 1973. The new serotonin-reuptake inhibitors are by and large lacking in cardiotoxic effects and, although they have not yet been available for sufficiently long to establish their safety in clinical use, they are likely to be rather safe in overdose (Montgomery, 1990a). The notion that these differences in fatality rates reflect differences in inherent toxicity is supported by a significant correlation between ranking of fatal toxicity index (number of deaths per million prescriptions) and median lethal dose (LD_{50}) values (Molcho and Stanley, 1992).

An oddity in these analyses is that clomipramine, which is known to be a rather toxic antidepressant, appears to be rather low in the toxicity index, which suggests that some antidepressants may have a protective effect by reducing the suicidal urges. Other antidepressants, on the other hand, may induce suicidal behavior. A large study of long-term treatment with maprotiline compared with placebo found that maprotiline was associated with a significantly higher suicide rate than placebo. This suggests that maprotiline is able to provoke suicide attempts, despite its efficacy as an antidepressant. Similarly, in the large surveillance study of Inman (1988), there were significantly more suicide attempts associated with amitriptyline than with mianserin, suggesting a differential ability to provoke attempts. This raises the possibility that other antidepressants, such as desipramine and amitriptyline, may provoke suicide attempts, and the high lethality index may reflect a combination of inherent toxicity and provocation potential.

In the large placebo-controlled studies of the newer drugs, there is evidence that suicidal thoughts in depression fluctuate during placebo treatment and that there are fewer emerging suicidal thoughts during treatment with the specific serotonin-reuptake inhibitors, fluoxetine, fluvoxamine, and paroxetine, than are seen with placebo, which suggests a protective effect with these antidepressants.

The suicide rate in major depression can probably most effectively be reduced by recognizing the illness and treating it energetically using full doses of safer antidepressants (Montgomery, 1991b).

V. LONG-TERM AND PROPHYLACTIC TREATMENT OF DEPRESSION

The more careful follow-up studies have found that depression is a highly recurrent disorder, with some 80% embarking on a recurrent debilitating course. The placebo-controlled studies have uniformly reported that approximately 50% of patients relapse if their treatment is stopped soon after apparent symptomatic response, both in first-time and in recurrent depression. This has led to firm recommendations that all antidepressant treatments should be continued for some 4 months after apparent response, to consolidate response and avoid relapse. This is referred to as the continuation phase of treatment.

The efficacy of antidepressants in this continuation phase is good, although the studies are sparse. There is convincing evidence from placebo-controlled studies of efficacy in continuation treatment for the tricyclic antidepressants, amitriptyline and imipramine, for maprotiline, and for the specific serotonin reuptake inhibitors sertraline, paroxetine, and citalopram (Montgomery, 1989; Montgomery et al., 1991b; Montgomery and Rasmussen, 1992). The relapse rate is reduced by between two and three times that seen with placebo.

In recurrent depression a different therapeutic aim is the reduction of subsequent new episodes of depression. This prophylactic or recurrence prevention efficacy is tested following the successful continuation treatment period. Prophylactic efficacy is established for imipramine in full doses, phenelzine, and for fluoxetine, sertraline, and paroxetine (Prien et al., 1984; Prien and Kupfer, 1986; Frank et al., 1990; Montgomery et al., 1988; Doogan and Caillard, 1992; Montgomery and Dunbar, in press).

These studies demonstrated that the chances of a new episode of depression are reduced by a factor of two or three over that seen on placebo. The longest of these studies compared imipramine and placebo for 3 years, after which the remaining patients receiving imipramine were rerandomized to active treatment or placebo. The recurrence rate for placebo in the following period of 3 to 5 years was similar in number and timing to that seen in the first 3 years, which suggests that the rate of recurrence in untreated patients is high and constant. This reinforces the recommendations that, for best effect, prophylactic antidepressant treatment should be continued for life. Simply because a patient has had successful prophylactic treatment for 3 years does not mean that they are no longer at risk if treatment is discontinued. The risk of recurrence will remain as high as originally predicted, and if patients wish to discontinue prophylactic treatment, as they sometimes do, the frequency of follow-up should be increased.

The early criteria for prophylactic studies required that the individual had three or more prior episodes. Most of the recent studies have used the criterion of two or more episodes in 5 years and, for this group, a high-recurrence rate is predicted. However, since better tolerated antidepressant drugs are now available that have proved prophylactic efficacy, it may be appropriate to offer this option of prophylaxis to patients after their second episode of depression, since the risk and damage of each episode of depression is profound. With bipolar affective disorder, the efficacy of lithium in reducing subsequent episodes of illness is well established. The consistency with which the prophylactic effects of lithium have been observed by many different investigators allows the conclusion that, in bipolar disorder, lithium is the treatment of choice for prophylaxis (Jefferson and Greist, 1990; Montgomery, 1990a). There are some studies indicating that carbamazepine may have efficacy in bipolar disorder, suggesting that it be used as second-line treatment. Carbamazepine appears effective in a slightly different group of patients with more schizoaffective features, and there have been suggestions that adjunct treatment of carbamazepine and lithium may be effective in those resistant to lithium treatment alone. Finally, there are reports that rapid cycling may be induced in patients with bipolar disorder by stopping lithium treatment. The implication of this is that once the treatment is started, it should be continued.

VI. LITHIUM

In the treatment of depression, lithium has a special place distinguishing it from regular antidepressant drugs such as the tricyclic antidepressants, the MAO inhibitors, and the specific serotonin-reuptake inhibitors. It is used mainly for the prophylactic treatment, rather than for the acute treatment of depression and, in particular, in the treatment of bipolar disorder.

A. Pharmacology

The pharmacology of lithium has been extensively investigated, but the mechanism of action of its mood-stabilizing effect remains largely unknown. Lithium is the lightest of the alkali metals and shares some characteristics with those of sodium and potassium. However, unlike sodium and potassium, it has a relatively small gradient of distribution across biological membranes. Although it can replace sodium ions in supporting a single action potential in a nerve cell, it is not an adequate "substrate" for the sodium pump, and it cannot, therefore, maintain membrane potentials (Baldessarini, 1990). In animal brain tissue, lithium at concentrations ranging from 1 to 10 mEg/L inhibits the calcium-dependent release provoked by depolarization from nerve terminals of norepinephrine and dopamine, but not of serotonin (Baldessarini and Vogt, 1988). Lithium may even enhance the release of serotonin, especially in the hippocampus. In recent years, research has focused on the interference of lithium with metabolism of membrane phosphatidylinositides, which results from activation of receptors for several of neurohormones. At a concentration of 1 mM, lithium inhibits the hydrolysis of inositol-1-phosphate in brain (and other tissues), which may lead to depletion of phosphatidylinositides of cells (such as neurons in the brain) that are stimulated intensely and that are insulated from exogenous sources of inositol. This might reduce the responsiveness of the affected neurons to neurotransmitter-mediated stimuli (Casebolt and Jope, 1989). The meaning of these effects for the antidepressant (and antimanic) effects of lithium treatment in patients remains to be established.

B. Pharmacokinetics

The pharmacokinetics of lithium has been the focus of extensive investigations. Absorption of lithium is rapid and almost complete within 8 h following an oral dose, with peak plasma levels occurring after 30 min to 4 h. Slow-release preparations of lithium reduce the rate of absorption and minimize early peaks in plasma concentration of this ion. Lithium is not protein bound and is distributed in the total body water, shifting slowly into cells (which may explain its slow onset of action). The volumes of distribution vary widely between individual patients, from 0.4 to 1.4 l/kg body weight (Mason et al., 1978). Lithium concentrations in the cerebrospinal fluid peak 24 h later than those in the extracellular fluid and, generally, reach a level only 50% of that in plasma. Metabolism of lithium does not occur, and virtually all of the ion is excreted by the kidneys. Renal clearance of lithium varies between 10 and 40 ml/min and is correlated with creatinine clearance. The elimination half-time ranges from approximately 24 to 48 h (Mason et al., 1978; Hollister, 1987; Baldessarini, 1990).

C. Clinical Efficacy

Lithium is accepted as first line treatment in the prophylactic treatment of bipolar illness in which the individual has suffered from a single episode or more of mania or hypomania. The place of lithium in the prophylaxis of unipolar disorder is more controversial, with a major negative study from the National Institute of Mental Health (NIMH; Prien et al., 1984). A metanalysis of the data from a variety of studies (Fieve and Peselow, 1983; Schou, 1979) suggests that lithium may be effective, but its high level of toxicity, renal damage, and teratogenicity makes it unacceptable as a first-line treatment. The problem with these metanalyses is the confusion of the withdrawal effects of lithium, which are well known. These metanalyses also did not distinguish between continuation treatment and prophylactic treatment.

There is some evidence that lithium has a direct antidepressant effect, although the studies that reported an effect are mainly early and methodologically flawed. Compared with tricyclic antidepressants, and more particularly, the newer antidepressants, lithium is too toxic to be considered for the short-term treatment of depression, even if the efficacy were better established. There is a narrow index between therapeutic efficacy and toxicity, and the plasma levels of lithium, therefore, have to be monitored. Early reports showed that to achieve efficacy in mania and the prophylaxis of bipolar disorder, levels should be maintained between 0.8 and 1.2 mEq/L, but these levels are now thought to be too high in view of the toxicity of lithium. Reports of the efficacy of lithium at lower levels have led to suggestions that plasma levels should be monitored to vary between 0.6 and 0.8 mEg/L, although the study of Gelenburg et al. (1989) suggests that higher levels may be associated with greater efficacy.

The usual starting dose of lithium carbonate is 800–1200 mg/day and, after steady-state levels have been reached (i.e., after 4 to sometimes even as many as 8 days), dose adjustments are made based on lithium plasma levels. It has generally been agreed that the interval between dosing and plasma sampling is to be 12 h (Jefferson and Greist, 1990).

D. Side Effects

Lithium therapy is often associated with side effects that to some extent, are related to the plasma concentration. Nevertheless, they can only partially be prevented by means of strict control of plasma levels. Lithium treatment may adversely affect thyroid and kidney function. Pretreatment testing of relevant laboratory parameters, therefore is considered very useful.

The most prominent side effects that may occur during lithium therapy include the following: dysarthria, ataxia, and neuromuscular irritability are early signs of impending intoxication. Lack of spontaneity, dysphoria, marked mental confusion, nausea, diarrhea, edema, weight gain, and tremor are common side effects. If necessary, dosage reductions should be initiated. Abnormal thyroid function tests may occur in 5 to 15% of patient's receiving long-term lithium therapy. However, clinical symptoms (relatively often hypothyroidism with goiter, but thyrotoxicosis also occurs) are rare. Hypothyroidism may have to be treated with thyroid hormone supplements. Lithium therapy can cause impaired renal concentrating ability, a modest reduction in glomerular filtration rate, increased urine volumes (sometimes to the extent of nephrogenic diabetes insipidus), and morphological abnormalities such as focal interstitial fibrosis, tubular atrophy and glomerular sclerosis (Hetmar et al., 1987). Periodic monitoring of kidney function is mandatory in patients receiving long-term lithium therapy. Maintaining the lowest effective plasma lithium level will do much to reduce the renal toxicity of lithium treatment (Jefferson and Greist, 1990; Baldessarini, 1990; Hollister, 1987).

E. Interactions

Lithium interactions have been described both with other drugs and with diet. The combined use of lithium and other antidepressants only slightly increases the toxicity of lithium itself. Neurotoxicity and the neuroleptic malignant syndrome may occur with the combination of lithium and antipsychotic drugs, which should prompt caution in the use of these drugs together, particularly when large doses are used (Jefferson and Greist, 1990).

Increased lithium plasma levels may result from concomitant use of thiazide (and possibly potassium-sparing) diuretics and nonsteroidal anti-inflammatory drugs owing to decreased lithium clearance. Nevertheless, lithium can safely be used with these drugs if the daily dose of lithium is reduced (Jefferson et al., 1987). Carbamazepine may enhance the neurotoxicity of lithium (Hollister, 1987).

The excretion of lithium is linked to that of sodium, which means that if sodium intake is reduced, renal retention of sodium *and* lithium is increased, and lithium plasma levels will rise, with the possibility of toxicity. In case of a low-sodium diet or increased sodium loss by nonrenal routes (e.g., sweating), the dosage of lithium may have to be adjusted (Jefferson and Greist, 1990).

F. Teratogenicity

The risk of malformation, especially cardiovascular abnormalities, such as the Ebstein anomaly, is increased by the use of lithium during the first trimester of pregnancy. Consequently, its use should be avoided during this period (Hollister, 1987; Jefferson and Greist, 1990) and in all those not taking effective contraceptive precautions.

The renal clearance of lithium increases during pregnancy and reverts to a lower rate immediately after delivery. Special care and more frequent monitoring of lithium concentrations at these times is necessary. Lithium is transferred to breast-fed infants through breast milk. Therefore, breast-feeding is discouraged if the mother is taking lithium (Hollister, 1987).

VII. SUMMARY AND CONCLUSION

The greatest problem with depression is the failure to treat. Between 60 end 70% of those suffering from depression at a level that impairs their function and with features predicting response, do not attend for treatment (Robins and Regier, 1990). Undoubtedly, the stigma of the diagnosis of depression is one factor, as indeed is the failure to convince the public at large that depression is a readily treated illness, with a high response rate.

Depression is common—one in ten new attenders in primary care—yet about half of those who attend for treatment are recognized by their physician as suffering from depression (Freeling et al., 1985). Physicians are easily sidetracked by the presence of somatic complaints, and are often afraid of inquiring after psychological illness, particularly in the elderly and in the chronically depressed. The evidence is that the medical services carry an undue burden of chronic attenders and hospital admissions, which may well be avoided by paying more attention to diagnosis and treatment of depression. Antidepressants are effective, the major differences between them relating to their side effects and tolerability profiles. The newer antidepressants are preferred because of their favorable side effect profile and patients find them more acceptable. If used properly, in appropriate doses, antidepressants can generally shorten the episode, reduce the relapse rate, and substantially reduce the rate of subsequent new depressive episodes.

REFERENCES

American Psychiatric Association, *Diagnostic and Statistical Manual of Mental Disorders, 3rd ed., revised*, American Psychiatric Association, Washington D.C. (1987).

M. M. Amin, J. V. Anath, B. S. Coleman et al., Fluvoxamine: Antidepressant effects confirmed in a placebo controlled international study, *Clin. Psychopharmacol., 7*: 317 (1984).

R., Baldessarini, Drugs and the treatment of psychiatric disorders, *The Pharmacological Basis of Therapeutics,* 8th ed. (A. G. Gilman, T. W. Rall, A. S. Nies, and P. Taylor, eds.), Pergamon Press, New York, p. 383 (1990).

R. Baldessarini, and M. Vogt, Release of ^{3}H-dopamine and analogous monoamines from rat striatal tissue, *Cell. Mol. Neurobiol., 8*: 205 (1988).

S. J. Bannister, V. P. Houser, J. D. Hulse, J. C. Kisicki, and J. G. C. Rasmussen, Evaluation of the potential for interactions of paroxetine with diazepam, cimetidine, warfarin and digoxin, *Acta Psychiatr. Scand., 80*: 102 (1989).

P. R. Bieck, K.-H. Antonin, and R. Schulz, Clinical pharmacology of selective and reversible MAO-A inhibitors: Comparison with the first generation of MAO inhibitors, *Biological Psychiatry*, Vol. 1 (G. Racagni, N. Brunello, and T. Fukuda, eds.), Elsevier, Amsterdam, p. 406 (1991).

B. Blackwell, Newer Antidepressant drugs, *Psychopharmacology: The Third Generation of Progress* (H. Y. Meltzer ed.), Raven Press, New York, p. 1041 (1987).

B. Blackwell, Monoamine oxidase inhibitor interactions with other drugs, *J. Clin. Psychopharmacol., 11*: 55 (1991).

E. P. Bonetti, R. Scherschlicht, and M. Da Prada, Safety of the RIMA antidepressant moclobemide: minimal interactions with dietary tyramine and 5-HT uptake blockers, *Biological Psychiatry*, Vol. 1 (G. Racagni, N. Brunello, and T. Fukuda, eds.), Elsevier, Amsterdam, p. 390 (1991).

W. F. Boyer, and J. P. Feighner, Pharmacokinetics and drug interactions, *Selective Serotonin Reuptake Inhibitors Perspectives in Psychiatry*, Vol. 1 (J. P. Feighner and W. F. Boyer, eds.), Wiley, Chicester, p. 81 (1991).

J. D. Bremner and J. Panagides, Remergon efficacy in major depressive episode: A randomized, double-blind, placebo and amitriptyline controlled study. *Clin. Neuropharmacol. 15*(Suppl.1 part B) 136B (1992).

G. Budde, Efficacy and tolerability of flupenthixol decanoate in the treatment of depression and psychosomatic disorders: a multicenter trial in general practice, *Prog. Neuropsychopharmacol. Biol. Psychiatry, 16*: 677 (1992).

J. S. Carman, H. Ahdieh, E. Wyatt-Knowles, E. Warga, and J. Panagides, A controlled study of mianserin in moderately to severely depressed outpatients, *Psychopharmacol. Bull., 27*: 135 (1991).

T. L. Casebolt, and R. S. Jope, Long-term lithium treatment selectively reduces receptor-coupled inositol phospholipid hydrolysis in rat brain, *Biol. Psychiatry, 25*: 329 (1989).

S. Cassidy, and J. Henry, Fatal toxicity of antidepressant drugs in overdose, *Br. Med. J., 295*: 1021 (1987).

E. F. Coccaro and L. J. Siever, Second generation antidepressants: A comparative review, *J. Clin. Pharmacol., 25*: 241 (1985).

Committee on Safety of Medicines, Fluvoxamine and fluoxetine—interactions with monoamine oxidase inhibitors, lithium and tryptophan, *Curr. Probl.*, 26: (1989).

P. J. Cowen, Serotonin receptor subtypes: Implications for psychopharmacology, *Br. J. Psychiatry, 159*(Suppl. 12): 7 (1991).

P. Crome, and B. Newman, Fatal tricyclic antidepressant poisoning, *J. Royal Soc. Med.. 72*: 649 (1979).

M. F. D'Amico, D. L. Roberts, D. S. Robinson, U. E. Schwiderski, J. Copp. Placebo-controlled close-ranging trial designs in phase II development of nefazodone, *Psychopharmacol. Bull. 26*: 147 (1990).

Danish University Antidepressant Group, Citalopram: Clinical effect profile in comparison with clomipramine. A controlled multicentre study, *Psychopharmacology, 90*: 131 (1986).

Danish University Antidepressant Group, Paroxetine: A selective serotonin reuptake inhibitor showing better tolerance, but weaker antidepressant effect than clomipramine in a controlled multicentre study, *J. Affective Disord., 18*: 289 (1990).

J. M. Davis, S. H. Koslow, R. D. Gibbons, J. W. Maas, C. L. Bowden, R. Casper, I. Hanin, J. I. Javaid, S. S. Chang, and P. E. Stokes, Cerebrospinal fluid and urinary biogenic amines in depressed patients and healthy controls, *Arch. Gen. Psychiatry, 45*: 705 (1988).

G. D. de Jongh, Remergon efficacy in major depressive episode: A brief overview of the principal clinical trials data. *Clin. Neuropharmacol. 15*(Suppl.1 part B) 238B (1992).

F. E. R. E. De Jonghe, H. F. A. Schalken, and H. J. van der Helm. Thioridazine in the treatment of depressive patients, *Acta Psychiatr. Scand., 53*: 271 (1976).

J. A. den Boer, and H. G. M. Westenberg, Effect of a serotonin and a noradrenaline uptake inhibitor in panic disorder: A double-blind comparative study with fluvoxamine and maprotiline, *Int. Clin. Psychopharmacol., 3*: 59 (1988).

D. P. Googan, and V. Caillard, Sertraline in the prevention of depression, *Br. J. Psychiatry, 160*: 217 (1992).

Drug. Ther. Bull., Update of antidepressants: Lofepramine, amoxapine and viloxazine, *28*: 82 (1990).

G. C. Dunbar, J. B. Cohn, L. F. Fabre et al, A comparison of paroxetine, imipramine and placebo in depressed outpatients, *Br. J. Psychiatry, 159:* 394 (1991).

V. S. Dwivedi, A. B. Berger, T. K. Khong, B. A. Hamilton, P. G. Jones, and P. Brantingham, Depression in general practice: A comparison of flupenthixol dihydrochloride and dothiepin hydrochloride, *Curr. Med. Res. Opin., 12*: 191 (1990).

A. S. Eison, M. S. Eison, M. Stanley, and L. A. Riblet, Serotonergic mechanisms in the behavioural effects of buspirone and gepirone, *Pharmacol. Biochem. Behav., 24*: 701 (1986).

L. F. Fabre, United States experience and perspectives with trazodone, *Clin. Neuropharmacol., 12*(Suppl. 1): S11 (1989).

L. F. Fabre, Trazodone dosing regimen: Experience with single daily administration, *J. Clin. Psychiatry, 51*(Suppl.): 23 (1990).

W. E. Fann, C. R. Lake, and L. F. Majors. Thioridazine in neurotic, anxious and depressed patients, *Psychosomatics 15*: 117 (1974).

J. P. Feighner, and W. F. Boyer, Overview of USA controlled trials of trazodone in clinical depression, *Psychopharmacology, 95*(Suppl.): S50 (1988).

R. R. Fieve, and E. D. Peselow, Lithium: Clinical applications, *Drugs in Psychiatry*, Vol. 1, *Antidepressants*, (G. D. Burrows, T. R. Norman, and B. Davies, eds.), Elsevier, Amsterdam, p. 277 (1983).

E. Frank, D. J. Kupfer, J. M. Perel, C. Cornes, D. B. Jarrett, A. G. Mallinger, M. E. Thase, A. B. McEachran, and V. J. Grochocinski, Three-year outcomes for maintenance therapies in recurrent depression, *Arch. Gen. Psychiatry, 47*: 1093 (1990).

P. Freeling, B. M. Rao, E. S. Paykel, L. I. Sireling, and R. H. Burton, Unrecognised depression in general practice, *Br. Med. J., 290*: 1880 (1985).

D. A. Frommer, K. W. Kulig, J. A. Marx, and B. Rumack, Tricyclic antidepressant overdose, *JAMA, 257*: 521 (1987).

R. W. Fuller, Role of serotonin in therapy of depression and related disorders, *J. Clin. Psychiatry, 52*(Suppl): 52 (1991).

A. J. Gelenberg, J. M. Kane, and M. B. Keller, Comparison of standard and low serum levels of lithium for maintenance treatment of bipolar disorders, *N. Engl. J. Med., 321*: 1489 (1989).

M. J. Gitlin, H. Gwirtsman, L. Fairbanks, H. A. Sternbach, P. I. Cedars, and R. H. Gerner, Dexamethasone suppression test and treatment response, *J. Clin. Psychiatry, 45*: 387 (1984).

A. H. Glasman, and J. T. Bigger, Cardiovascular effects of therapeutic doses of tricyclic antidepressants—a review, *Arch. Gen. Psychiatry, 38*: 815 (1981).

J. Glowinski, and J. Axelrod, Inhibition of uptake of tritiated-noradrenaline in the intact rat brain by imipramine and structurally related compounds, *Nature, 203*: 1318 (1964).

K. L. Goa, and A. Ward, Buspirone: A preliminary review of its pharmacological properties and therapeutic efficacy as an anxiolytic, *Drugs, 32*: 114 (1986).

W. K. Goodman, L. H. Price, P. L. Delgado, J. Palumbo, J. H. Krystal, L. M. Nagy, S. A. Rasmussen, G. R. Heninger, and D. S. Charney, Specificity of serotonin reuptake inhibitors in the treatment of obsessive compulsive disorder: Comparison of fluvoxamine and desipramine, *Arch. Gen. Psychiatry, 47*: 577 (1990).

L. F. Gram, Plasma/serum concentration of antidepressants and clinical response: State of the art, *Biological Psychiatry*, Vol. 1 (G. Racagni, N. Brunello, and T. Fukuda, eds.), Elsevier, Amsterdam, p. 359 (1991).

A. J. Gruber and J. O. Cole, Antidepressant effects of flupenthixol, *Pharmacotherapy, 11*: 450 (1991).

R. Guscott, and P. Grof, The clinical meaning of refractory depression: A review for the clinician, *Am. J. Psychiatry, 148*: 695 (1991).

B. A. Hamilton, P. G. Jones, A. N. Hoda, P. M. Keane, I. Majid, and S. I. A. Zaidi, Flupenthixol and fluvoxamine in mild to moderate depression: A comparison in general practice, *Pharmatherapeutica, 5*: 292 (1989).

W. Hammer, and F. Sjöqvist, Plasma levels of monomethylated tricyclic antidepressants during treatment with imipramine-like compounds, *Life Sci., 6*: 1895 (1967).

A. H. Heller, M. Beneke, B. Kuemmel, D. Spencer, and N. M. Kurtz, Ipsapirone: Evidence for efficacy in depression, *Psychopharmacol. Bull., 26*: 219 (1990).

J. B. Herman, A. W. Brotman, M. H. Pollack, W. E. Falk, J. Biederman, and J. F. Rosenbaum, Fluoxetine-induced sexual dysfunction, *J. Clin. Psychiatry, 51*: 25 (1990).

O. Hetmar, C. Brun, L. Clemmesen, J. Ladefoged, S. Larsen, and O. J. Rafaelsen, Lithium: Long-term effects on the kidney, 2. structural changes, *J. Psychiatr. Res., 21*: 279 (1987).

L. E. Hollister, Psychiatric disorders, *Drug Treatment,* 3rd ed. (T. M. Speight, ed.), Williams & Wilkins, Baltimore, p. 1137 (1987).

D. Hoyer, Functional correlates of serotonin 5-HT_1 recognition sites, *J. Receptor Res., 8*: 59 (1988a).

D. Hoyer, Molecular pharmacology and biology of 5-HT_{1C} receptors, *Trends Pharmacol. Sci., 9*: 89 (1988b).

W. H. Inman, Blood disorders and suicide in patients taking mianserin or amitriptyline, *Br. J. Clin. Pharmacol., 26*: 90 (1988).

W. A. James, and S. Lippmann, Bupropion: Overview and prescribing guidelines in depression, *South. Med. J., 84*: 222 (1991).

J. W. Jefferson, and J. H. Greist, The clinical application of lithium, *Pharmacotherapy of Depression—Applications for the Outpatient practitioner* (J. D. Amsterdam, ed.), Marcel Dekker, New York, p. 111 (1990).

J. W. Jefferson, J. H. Greist, D. L. Ackerman, and J. A. Carroll, *Lithium Encyclopedia for Clinical Practice*, 2nd ed., American Psychiatric Press, Washington D.C. (1987).

S. W. Jenkins, O. S. Robinson, L. F. Fabre, Jr., J. J. Andary, M. E. Messina, and L. A. Reich, Gepirone in the treatment of major depression, *J. Clin. Psychopharmacol., 10*: 77S (1990).

S. G. Jue, G. W. Dawson, and R. N. Brogden, Amoxapine: A review of its pharmacology and efficacy in depressed states, *Drugs, 24*: 1 (1982).

G. Kato, and A. F. Weitsch, Neurochemical profile of tianeptine, a new antidepressant drug. *Clin. Neuropharmacol., 11*(Suppl. 2): S43 (1988).

A. Khan, S. Cohen, M. Stowell et al., Treatment options in severe psychotic depression, *Convulsive Ther., 3*: 93 (1987).

C. Kirkegaard, The thyrotropin response to thyrotropin-releasing hormone in endogenous depression, *Psychoneuroendocrinology, 6*: 189 (1981).

G. L. Klerman, and J. O. Cole, Clinical pharmacology of imipramine and related antidepressant compounds, *Pharmacol. Rev., 17*: 101 (1965).

P. Kragh-Sørensen, C. E. Hansen, P. C. Baastrup and E. F. Hvidberg, Self-inhibiting action of nortriptyline's antidepressive effect at high plasma levels. A randomised double-blind study controlled by plasma concentrations in patients with endogenous depression, *Psychopharmacologia, 46*: 305 (1976).

N. M. Kurtz, Monoamine oxidase inhibiting drugs, *Pharmacotherapy of Depression—Applications for the Outpatient Practitioner* (J. D. Amsterdam, ed.), Marcel Dekker, New York, p. 93 (1990).

M. E. L'Orme, Antidepressants and heart disease, *Br. Med. J., 289*: 1 (1984).

G. Laux, M. P. Schoerlin, W. Classen, T. Becker, K. P. Lesch, and G. Carl, Pharmacokinetics of reversible MAO-A inhibitors (RIMA), *Biological Psychiatry*, Vol. 1 (G. Racagni, N. Brunello, and T. Fukuda, eds.), Elsevier, Amsterdam, p. 372 (1991).

H. E. Lehmann, and N. S. Kline, Clinical discoveries with antidepressant drugs, *Discoveries in Pharmacology* (M. J. Parnham and J. Bruinvels, eds.), Elsevier, Amsterdam, p. 209 (1983).

L. Lemberger, The clinical pharmacology and pharmacokinetic aspects of selective serotonin reuptake inhibitors, *Clin. Neuropharmacol., 13*(Suppl. 2): 283 (1990).

B. Leonard, The effect of serotonin reuptake inhibitors on some peripheral markers of the serotonergic system in depressed patients, *Clin. Neuropharmacol., 13*(Suppl. 2): 287 (1990).

B. E. Leonard, New antidepressants: Chemical diversity but unity of action? *Biological Psychiatry*, Vol. 1 (G. Racagni, N. Brunello, and T. Fukuda, eds.), Elsevier, Amsterdam, p. 311 (1991).

P. Lidbrink, G. Jonsson, and K. Fuxe, The effect of imipramine-like drugs and antihistamine drugs on uptake mechanisms in the central noradrenaline and 5-hydroxytryptamine neurons, *Neuropharmacology, 10*: 521 (1971).

M. R. Liebowitz, F. M. Quitkin, J. W. Stewart, P. J. McGrath, W. M. Harrison, J. S. Markowitz, J. G. Rabkin, E. Tricamo, D. M. Goetz, and D. F. Klein, Antidepressant specificity in atypical depression, *Arch. Gen. Psychiatry, 45*: 129 (1988).

I. Lucki, Behavioral studies of serotonin receptor agonists as antidepressant drugs, *J. Clin. Psychiatry, 52*(Suppl): 24 (1991).

J. J. Mann, S. F. Aarons, P. J. Willner, J. G. Keilp, J. A. Sweeney, T. Pearlstein, A. J. Frances, J. H. Kocsis, and R. P. Brown, A controlled study of the antidepressant efficacy and side effects of (–)-deprenyl: A selective monoamine oxidase inhibitor, *Arch. Gen. Psychiatry, 46*: 45 (1989).

C. Marey, H. Ganry, B. Delalleau and A. Kamoun, Effets therapeutiques de la tianeptine chez des patients deprimés et anxieux avec ou sans alcoolisme associé. *Presse Med., 20*: 1828 (1991).

R. W. Mason, E.G. McQueen. P. J. Keary, and N. James, Pharmacokinetics of lithium: Elimination half-time, renal clearance and apparent volume of distribution in schizophrenia, *Clin. Pharmacokinet., 3*: 241 (1978).

D. M. McNair, R. J. Kahn, L. M. Frankenthales, and L. L. Faldetta, Amoxapine and amitriptyline. II. Specificity of cognitive effects during brief treatment of depression, *Psychopharmacology, 83*: 134 (1984).

H. Y. Meltzer, Serotonergic function in depression, *Br. J. Psychiatry, 155*(Suppl. 8): 25 (1989).

J. Mendels, F. Reimherr, D. Roberts, et al., A double-blind comparison of high dose netazadone, low dose netazadone, and placebo in the treatment of depressed outpatients. *Eur. Neuropsychopharmacol, 1*: 451 (1992).

J. Mendlewicz, Efficacy of fluvoxamine in severe depression, *Drugs, 43*(Suppl. 2): 32 (1992).

T. Mennini, E. Mocaer and S. Garattini. Tianeptine: A selective enhancer of serotonin uptake in rat brain, *Naunyn Schmiedebergs Arch. Pharmacol., 336*: 478 (1987).

R. H. S. Mindham, T. C. Jerram, H. L. Cole, A. G. Oswald, and S. Khan. A comparison of sulpiride, dothiepin, diazepam and placebo in the treatment of depressed out-patients, *J. Psychopharmacol., 5*: 259 (1991).

A. Molcho, and M. Stanley, Antidepressants and suicide risk: Issues of chemical and behavioral toxicity, *J. Clin. Psychopharmacol., 12*(Suppl. 3): 13 (1992).

H.-J. Möller, General efficacy and safety of brofaromine in depression, *Biological Psychiatry*, Vol. 1 (G. Racagni, N. Brunello, and T. Fukuda, eds.), Elsevier, Amsterdam, p. 410 (1991).

S. A. Montgomery, Prophylaxis in recurrent unipolar depression: A new indication for treatment studies, *J. Psychopharmacol., 3*: 47 (1989).

S. A. Montgomery, Anxiety and Depression, Wrightson Biomedical Publishing, Petersfield (1990a).

S. A. Montgomery, Clinical efficacy of 5-HT uptake inhibitors, *Clin. Neuropharmacol., 13*(Suppl. 2): 285 (1990b).

S. A. Montgomery, Clinical significance of 5-HT uptake inhibitors, *Hum. Psychopharmacol., 6*(Suppl. 3): S3 (1991a).

S. A. Montgomery, The separate diagnostic status of obsessive–compulsive disorder, *Serotonin Related Psychiatric Syndromes: Clinical and Therapeutic Links* (G. B. Cassano and H. S. Akiskal, eds.), R. Soc. Med. Lond., p. 67 (1991b).

S. A. Montgomery, and G. Magui, Clinical aspects of onset of action of antidepressant efficacy, *Biological Psychiatry,* Vol. 1 (G. Racagai, N. Brunello, and T. Fuleuda, eds.), Elsevier, Amsterdam, p. 343 (1991).

S. A. Montgomery, The advantages of paroxetine in different subgroups of depression, *Int. Clin. Psychopharmacol., 6*(Suppl. 4): 91 (1992).

S. A. Montgomery, and G. Dunbar, Paroxetine is better than placebo in relapse prevention and the prophylaxis of recurrent depression, (in press).

S. A. Montgomery, and R. M. Pinder, Do some antidepressants promote suicide? *Psychopharmacology, 92*: 265 (1987).

S. A. Montgomery, and J. G. Rasmussen, Citalopram 20 mg, citalopram 40 mg and placebo in the prevention of relapse of major depression, *Int. Clin. Psychopharmacol., 6*(Suppl. 5): 63 (1992).

S. A. Montgomery, R. Braithwaite, S. Dawling, and R. McAuley, High plasma nortriptyline levels in the treatment of depression, *Clin. Pharmacol. Ther., 23*(Suppl. 3): 309 (1978).

S. A. Montgomery, R. McAuley, S. J. Rani, D. B. Montgomery, R. Braithwaite and S. Dawling, Amitriptyline plasma concentrations and clinical response, *Br. Med. J., 1*: 230 (1979).

S. A. Montgomery, R. McAuley, S. J. Rani, D. Roy, and D. B. Montgomery, A double blind comparison of zimeldine and amitriptyline in endogenous depression, *Acta Psychiatr. Scand.,* [Suppl.] 290: 314 (1981).

S. A. Montgomery, D. Roy, S. Wynne-Willson, C. Robinson, and D. B. Montgomery, Plasma levels and clinical response with imipramine in a study comparing efficacy with mianserin and nomifensine, *Br. J. Clin. Pharmacol., 15*: 205S (1983).

S. A. Montgomery, H. Dufour, S. Brion, J. Gailledreau, X. Laguielle, G. Ferrey, P. Moron, N. Parant-Lucena, L. Singer, J. M. Danion, J. N. Beuzen, and M. A. Pierredon, The prophylactic efficacy of fluoxetine in unipolar depression, *Br. J. Psychiatry, 152*(Suppl.3): 69 (1988).

S. A. Montgomery, N. Fineberg. D. Baldwin, and D. Montgomery, 5-HT uptake in the treatment of anxiety, agitation and suicidal thoughts, *Psychiatry A World Perspective 3* (C. N. Stefanis, A. D. Rabavilas, C. R. Soldatos, eds.), Elsevier, Amsterdam, p. 301 (1989).

D. B. Montgomery, D. Baldwin, M. Green, T. Bullock, and S.A. Montgomery, Pharmacotherapy in the prevention of suicidal behaviour, *Biological Psychiatry*, Vol. 1 (G. Racagni, N. Brunello, and T. Fukuda, eds.), Elsevier, Amsterdam, p. 125 (1991a).

S. A. Montgomery, D. P. Doogan, and R. Burnside, The influence of different relapse criteria on the assessment of long-term efficacy of sertraline, *Int. Clin. Psychopharmacol., 6*(Suppl. 2): 37 (1991b).

F. Moro, U. Scapagnini, S. Scaletta, and F. Drago, Serotonin nerve endings and regulation of pupillary diameter, *Ann. Ophthalmol., 13*: 487 (1981).

D. L. Murphy, C. S. Aulakh, N. A. Garrick, and T. Sunderland, Monoamine oxidase inhibitors as antidepressants: Implications for the mechanism of action and the psychobiology of the affective disorders and some related disorders, *Psychopharmacology: The Third Generation of Progress* (H. Y. Meltzer, ed.), Raven Press, New York, p. 545 (1987).

A. A. Nierenberg, Methodological problems in treatment resistant depression research, *Psychopharmacol. Bull., 26*: 461 (1990).

A. A. Nierenberg, and J. D. Amsterdam, Treatment-resistant depression. *J. Clin. Psychiatry, 51*(Suppl): 39 (1990).

A. A. Nierenberg, and K. White, What next? A review of pharmacologic strategies for treatment resistant depression, *Psychopharmacol. Bull., 26*: 429 (1990).

C. M. B. Pare, The present status of monoamine oxidase inhibitors, *Br. J. Psychiatry, 146*: 576 (1985).

R. M. Pinder, The benefits and risks of antidepressant drugs, *Hum. Psychopharmacol., 3*: 73 (1988).

M. H. Pollack, and J. F. Rosenbaum, Management of antidepressant-induced side effects: A practical guide for the clinician, *J. Clin. Psychiatry, 48*: 3 (1987).

W. Z. Potter, M. V. Rudorfer, and H. Manji, The pharmacologic treatment of depression, *N. Engl. J. Med., 325*: 633 (1991).

S. H. Preskorn, Should bupropion dosage be adjusted based upon therapeutic drug monitoring? *Psychopharmacol. Bull., 27*: 637 (1991).

S. H. Preskorn, and S. C. Othmer, Evaluation of bupropion hydrochloride: The first of a new class of atypical antidepressants. *Pharmacotherapy, 4*: 20 (1984).

R. F. Prien, and O. J. Kupfer, Continuation drug therapy for major depressive episodes: How long should it be maintained? *Am. J. Psychiatry, 40*: 18 (1986).

R. F. Prien, O. J. Kupfer, P. A. Mansky, J. G. Small, V. B. Tuason, C. B. Voss, and W. E. Johnson, Drug therapy in the prevention of recurrences in unipolar and bipolar affective disorders. Report of the NIMH collaborative Study Group comparing lithium carbonate, imipramine and a lithium carbonate–imipramine combination, *Arch. Gen. Psychiatry, 41*: 1096 (1984).

F. M. Quitkin, W. Harrison, M. Liebowitz, P. McGrath, J. G. Rabkin, J. Stewart, and J. Markowitz, Defining the boundaries of atypical depression, *J. Clin. Psychiatry, 45*: 19 (1984).

F. M. Quitkin, J. W. Stewart, P. J. McGrath, M. R. Liebowitz, W. M. Harrison, E. Tricamo, D. F. Klein, J. G. Rabkin, J. S. Markowitz, and S. G. Wagner, Phenelzine versus imipramine in the treatment of probable atypical depression: Defining syndrome boundaries of selective MAOI responders, *Am. J. Psychiatry, 145*: 306 (1988).

J. L. Rausch, R. Ruegg, and F. G. Moeller, Gepirone as a 5-HT_{1A} agonist in the treatment of major depression, *Psychopharmacol. Bull., 26*: 169 (1990).

R. A. Remick, Treatment resistant depression, *Psychiatr. J. Univ. Ottowa, 14*: 394 (1989).

K. Rickels, J. Amsterdam, C. Clary, J. Hassman, J. London, G. Puzzuoli, and E. Schweizer, Buspirone in depressed outpatients: A controlled study, *Psychopharmacol. Bull., 26*: 163 (1990).

L. N. Robins, and D. A. Regier, *Psychiatric Disorders in America: The Epidemiologic Catchment Area Study,* Free Press, New York, 1990.

D. S. Robinson, T. B. Cooper, S. R. Jindal, J. Corcella, and T. Lutz, Pharmacokinetics and metabolism of phenelzine, *J. Clin. Psychopharmacol., 5*: 333 (1985).

D. S. Robinson, A. Nies, C. L. Ravaris, J. O. Ives, and D. Bartlett, Clinical pharmacology of phenelzine, *Arch. Gen. Psychiatry, 35*: 629 (1978).

M. V. Rudorfer, and W. Z. Potter, Combined fluoxetine and tricyclic antidepressants, *Am. J. Psychiatry, 146*: 562 (1989).

M. V. Rudorfer, and W. Z. Potter, Pharmacokinetics of antidepressants, *Psychopharmacology: the Third Generation of Progress* (H. Y. Meltzer, ed.), Raven Press, New York, p. 1353 (1987).

G. L. Sathananthan, I. Sangvi, N. Phillips, and S. Gershon, MJ 9022: Correlation between neuroleptic potential and stereotype, *Curr. Ther. Res., 18*: 701 (1975).

J. J. Schildkraut, The catecholamine hypothesis of affective illness: A review of supporting evidence, *Am. J. Psychiatry, 122*: 509 (1965).

A. W. Schmidt, and S. J. Peroutka, Antidepressant interactions with 5-hydroxytryptamine$_3$, receptor binding sites, *Eur. J. Pharmacol., 163*: 397 (1989).

M. Schou, Lithium as a prophylactic agent in unipolar affective illness, *Arch. Gen. Psychiatry, 36*: 849 (1979).

G. M. Simpson, and H. Singh, Tricyclic antidepressants, *Pharmacotherapy of Depression—Applications for the Outpatient Practitioner* (J. D. Amsterdam, ed.), Marcel Dekker, New York, p. 75 (1990).

P. Stark, and C. D. Hardison, A review of multicentre controlled studies of fluoxetine vs imipramine and placebo in outpatients with major depressive disorder, *J. Clin. Psychiatry, 46*: 53 (1985).

F. Sulser, Regulation and function of noradrenaline receptor systems in brain: Psychopharmacological aspects. *Neuropharmacology 23*: 255 (1984).

F. Sulser, and R. Mishra, The discovery of tricyclic antidepressants and their mode of action, *Discoveries in Pharmacology* (M. J. Parnham and J. Bruinvels, eds.), Elsevier, Amsterdam, p. 233 (1983).

P. Thoren, M. Åsberg, B. Cronholm, L. Jernestedt, and L. Traskman, Clomipramine treatment of obsessive compulsive disorder. A controlled clinical trial, *Arch. Gen. Psychiatry, 37*: 1281 (1980).

J. E. Thornton and S. M. Stahl, Case report of tardive dyskinesia and parkinsonism associated with amoxapine therapy, *Am. J. Psychiatry, 141*: 704 (1984).

J. Traber, and T. Glaser, 5-HT_{1A} receptor anxiolytics, *Trends Pharmacol. Sci.. 8*: 432 (1987).

O. Vinar, D. F. Klein. W. Z. Potter, and E. M. Gause, A survey of psychotropic medications not available in the United States, *Neuropsychopharmacology, 5*: 201 (1991).

J. Wakelin, The role of serotonin in depression and suicide, *Adv. Biol. Psychiatry, 17*: 70 (1988).

H. G. M. Westenberg, and W. M. A. Verhoeven, CSF monoamine metabolites in patients and controls: Support for a bimodal distribution in major affective disorders, *Acta Psychiatr. Scand., 78*: 541 (1988).

K. White, and G. Simpson, The combined use of MAOIs and tricyclics, *J. Clin. Psychiatry, 45*: 67 (1984).

F. Yocca, Neurochemistry and neurophysiology of buspirone and gepirone: Interactions at presynaptic and postsynaptic 5-HT_{1A} receptors, *J. Clin. Psychopharmacol., 10*: 6S (1990).

M. B. Youdim, and J. P. Finberg, Implications of MAO-A and MAO-B inhibition for antidepressant therapy, *Mod. Probl. Pharmacopsychiatry, 19*: 63 (1983).

A. P. Zis, and F. K. Goodwin, Novel antidepressants and the biogenic amine hypothesis of depression. The case for iprindole and mianserin, *Arch. Gen. Psychiatry, 36*: 1097 (1979).

15

Effect of Antidepressants on Specific Neurotransmitters: Are Such Effects Relevant to the Therapeutic Action?

Brian E. Leonard
University College, Galway, Ireland

I. INTRODUCTION

The ancients postulated that melancholia was caused by an excess of "black bile," and despite the failure of investigators to identify the nature of this substance in the intervening 2000 years, the search for its identity continues. The importance of such a search lies in its emphasis on the biochemical basis of affective disorders and, in recent years, there have been a plethora of studies to suggest that such disorders arise as a consequence of the malfunctioning of one or more neuronal pathways in limbic regions of the brain. Neurons containing norepinephrine and serotonin (5-hydroxytryptamine; 5-HT) as neurotransmitters have been considered as the major candidates that are functionally abnormal in the affective disorders (Asberg et al., 1977). It must be emphasized, however, that other transmitters and neuromodulators, such as neuropeptides and prostaglandins, may also be involved (Emrich et al., 1979). For technical reasons, largely related to the difficulty involved in quantifying these substances in the body fluids of patients, their precise role is uncertain. By contrast, several studies have shown correlations between the response of depressed patients to antidepressants, or electroconvulsive therapy (ECT), and the return of peripheral noradrenegic and serotonergic receptor sensitivity to control values (Tuomisto et al., 1979). Nevertheless, it still remains to be shown that changes in noradrenergic and serotonergic receptor function in the membrane of peripheral blood cells correlates with similar changes in the brain. Thus, despite the primacy of theories concerning the role of 5-HT and norepinephrine in the etiology of depressive illness, 20 years of experimental and clinical studies have provided little in the way of firm supportive evidence. It is possible that the application of imaging techniques, such as positron emission tomography (PET) and single-photon emission computed tomography (SPECT) that enables the receptor-binding sites to be visualized and quantified in the brain of a patient, will help to solve the problem.

The monoamine theory of depression postulated that the symptoms of the illness arise as a consequence of a defect in the availability of serotonin or norepinephrine, or both. Direct evidence from the analysis of the body fluids of non–drug-treated depressed patients is equivocal, but indirect investigations of changes in the densities or functional activities of peripheral receptors of the noradrenergic and serotonergic system provide more compelling evidence (Leonard, 1982; 1986; 1989). The studies of van Praag and his associates (1970, 1973, 1979, 1982) and Asberg and colleagues (1973, 1976a,b) suggested that there could be a subgroup of depressed patients whose depressive symptoms were primarily related to a deficit in the availability of serotonin. Asberg et al. (1976b) further suggested that such patients, who were identified as having a markedly reduced concentration of the main serotonin metabolite, 5-hydroxyindolacetic acid (5-HIAA) in the cerebrospinal fluid (CSF), were more prone to violent suicidal attempts than those depressed patients not suffering from such a severe serotonin deficit. If such a subgroup of depressed patients exists, it would seem reasonable to speculate that antidepressants that selectively facilitate central serotonergic transmission should be particularly beneficial to such a patient group. In an attempt to test this hypothesis, Montgomery (1982) studied the response of a group of depressed patients, either with or without low CSF 5-HIAA concentrations, following the administration of a selective serotonin (zimelidine) or norepinephrine (maprotiline) reuptake inhibitor. The results of this double-blind study showed that the response to treatment was uncorrelated with the biochemical status of the patient. This study, and those of Veith et al. (1983) and Potter et al. (1985), in which the concentrations of metabolites in the urine were used to assess the neurotransmitter status, raised serious doubts concerning the relation between the CSF amine metabolite concentrations and the response of the depressed patient to a selective amine-reuptake inhibitor. Despite these clinical observations, a plethora of antidepressants with profiles that show a high degree of selectivity for the serotonergic or noradrenergic systems have been developed in recent years. There would appear to be no clinical evidence to suggest that these drugs are more effective, or have a faster onset of action, than the older nonspecific tricyclic antidepressants. Their major advantage is apparently a reduction in their anticholinergic effects and relative lack of cardiovascular toxicity in overdose.

The purpose of this chapter is to critically assess the evidence concerning the relation between the specificity of antidepressants in modulating neurotransmitter systems and their therapeutic activity. This poses the question whether all antidepressants, including electroconvulsive shock (ECS), have a common mode of action. If so, is this common action a reflection of adaptational changes in several interconnecting neurotransmitter systems, as has been critically considered by Charney and co-workers (1990) and by Leonard (1992), or does the site of action of antidepressants lie at the intercellular level, as has been recently postulated by Perez et al. (1991)?

II. EVIDENCE FOR NEUROTRANSMITTER ABNORMALITIES IN DEPRESSED PATIENTS: WHAT CHANGES DO ANTIDEPRESSANTS CAUSE TO NEUROTRANSMITTER FUNCTION?

Despite the advances that have been made in recent years in developing animal models of depression (see Leonard, 1989; Willner, 1985 for reviews), the depressed human being is the only animal that, in the final analysis, must be investigated if one is to understand the biochemical basis of the condition. There are three major approaches to understanding the biochemical etiology of depression: (1) analysis of postmortem brain of depressed suicide victims for neurotransmitters and their metabolites, (2) analysis of cerebrospinal fluid and urine from depressed patients, and (3) investigation of peripheral markers of neurotransmitter receptors by studying blood cells (e.g., platelets, lymphocytes). Of these three main approaches, the investigations of peripheral markers of neurotransmitter receptors have recently proved to be particularly useful as indexes of the clinical state of the patient and, therefore, will now be considered in more detail. A critical assessment of the postmortem and cerebrospinal fluid changes in neurotransmitter metabolites in depressed patients, and in those who had been given antidepressants, has been published recently (Leonard, 1992).

III. PERIPHERAL AMINE RECEPTORS AND AMINE TRANSPORT SITES

A. Adrenergic System

The results of experimental studies on the chronic effects of antidepressant drugs on postsynaptic adrenoceptors have led to a greater insight into the adaptive changes that occur following drug administration and have also enriched the methods that have been developed for the selection of new putative antidepressants (Olpe, 1982). However, has such an approach led to a greater understanding of the state-dependent biochemical changes that might occur in the depressed patient? If antidepressants decrease the functional activity of the adrenoceptor-linked cyclase system, then it may be postulated that this receptor–enzyme complex is hyperactive in the untreated patient. Furthermore, as the activity of the postsynaptic receptor system reflects changes in the concentration of neurotransmitters in the synaptic cleft, it must also be assumed that the mechanisms governing the release of the neurotransmitter are abnormal in the depressed patient. As the release of norepinephrine from the terminal is regulated, at least partially, by the presynaptic α_2-adrenoceptors (Stärke, 1977; Stärke et al., 1989), it seems likely that the activity of this receptor system is also abnormal.

Although there is broad agreement that chronic antidepressant treatment attenuates postsynaptic adrenoceptor activity in the limbic cortex of the rat brain, presumably as a consequence of a decrease in the activity of the inhibitory α_2-adrenoceptors that are located presynaptically, the results of studies on changes in monoamine receptor activities on the lymphocyte and platelet membrane are equivocal. Thus, different groups of investigators have found that the density of α_2-adrenoceptors (which are presumed to be similar to the presynaptic α_2-adrenoceptors on the neuronal membrane) is unchanged, decreased, or increased on the platelet membrane of untreated depressed patients (see Healy et al., 1983, for a review of literature). Garcia-Sevilla and colleagues (1981), who showed that the α_2-adrenoceptor density was increased on the platelet membrane of untreated depressives, also reported that the density of these receptors returned to control value following effective antidepressant treatment, thereby suggesting that the change in α_2-adrenoceptor density was a state-dependent marker. These findings have been largely replicated in a more extensive study by Healy et al. (1983, 1985) and by Garcia-Sevilla (1990). Studies of the changes in ß-adrenoceptors on lymphocytes of depressives have yielded equivocal results, with Pandey and colleagues (1979) showing a diminished response of the receptor-linked isoproterenol (isoprenaline)-stimulated cyclase in untreated patients, which presumably reflects a diminished ß-receptor activity, whereas Healy et al.

(1983) and Butler and Leonard (1986) have shown an increased ß-receptor density. Undoubtedly, one of the main difficulties in drawing any firm conclusions from such findings lies in the heterogeneous population of patients used (some studying manic–depressives during the depressive phase of the illness, whereas other studies were of postpartum or endogenously depressed patients), the differences in the techniques used to assess the density of the adrenoceptors, and the possible effects of circadian fluctuation on changes in the receptor sensitivity. Another possible explanation for the variation in the results could be associated with a variation in the nutritional status of the patients during the different phases of the study. It is well known that anorexia and a loss in body weight are frequent symptoms of depression; increased appetite is generally taken to be a sign of clinical improvement, and many of the conventional (tricyclic) antidepressants increase body weight as a consequence of the changes in the intermediary metabolism of carbohydrates that they induce. There is clinical evidence that an inverse relation exists between platelet α_2-adrenoceptor density and the plasma catecholamine concentrations (Davies et al., 1982). Fasting has also been shown to induce a fall in the concentration of plasma norepinephrine (Jung et al., 1980), whereas Luck et al. (1983) have shown that, in a group of malnourished patients with anorexia nervosa, the plasma norepinephrine concentrations were significantly lower than in age- and sex-matched controls; the decrease in plasma norepinephrine was associated with a rise in the platelet α_2-adrenoceptor density. It may be concluded that the nutritional status of the depressed patient must be critically assessed and taken into account when attempts are made to correlate changes in the adrenoceptor density with the psychiatric status of the patient. In the studies of changes in platelet adrenoceptor activity in the depressed patient, already referred to, such factors as the loss in body weight and nutritional status of the patient before and following therapy have largely been ignored.

One of the major problems that arises when attempts are made to interpret the changes in tritiated ligand binding to the platelet or lymphocyte membrane concerns the relevance of such ligand-binding data to the functional role of the receptor. Apart from the study by Kafka et al. (1981), none of the platelet α_2-receptor-binding studies concurrently measured the response mediated by the receptor. α_2-Adrenoreceptors, by modulating the release of norepinephrine, indirectly inhibit cyclic adenosine monophosphate (cAMP) synthesis at the postsynaptic receptor site, whereas prostaglandin E_1 (PGE_1) has the opposite effect. Thus the inhibition by norepinephrine of PGE_1-stimulated cAMP synthesis, can be used as an index of responsiveness of the α_2-receptor (Kafka et al., 1977). Whereas two earlier studies reported no difference in the inhibition by norepinephrine of prostaglandin E_1 (PGE_1)-stimulated cAMP synthesis (Murphy et al., 1974; Wang et al., 1974), Siever et al. (1984) have shown that, in a group of 23 selected depressives, although the α_2-receptor density was increased before treatment, the PGE_1-stimulated cAMP response and its inhibition by norepinephrine were significantly reduced compared with the controls. Thus there was an apparent dissociation between the α_2-receptor-binding data (suggesting increased numbers of receptors) and the functional changes which suggested hyposensitivity of the receptors. These changes were not correlated with the plasma norepinephrine concentrations, which did not differ significantly from the controls. The results of such studies emphasize the need for caution when extrapolating from ligand-binding sites (which reflect membrane regions that may not be associated with physiologically active receptor sites) to physiologically responsive receptors sites. Whether changes in platelet membrane receptors are a true reflection of those occurring in the brain remains an open question, but detailed studies by Checkley

(1980) on the neuroendocrine responsiveness to different adrenoceptor agonists in depressed patients suggest that central adrenoceptors are functionally subnormal in the untreated patient. This implies that the changes in α_2-responsiveness on the platelet membrane may be a reflection of similar changes in the brain. Another important factor that is often ignored when interpreting the changes in platelet α_2-adrenoceptor density in depressed patients concerns the nature of the radioactive ligands used to identify the adrenoceptor. Thus, the earlier studies generally used [^{3}H]dihydroergocryptine, which is an antagonist that binds to both α_1- and α_2-adrenoceptors, or [^{3}H]-WB4101, which is relatively selective for α_1-receptors. The introduction of [^{3}H]clonidine as a ligand for the α_2-receptors has led to more consistent results, as has the more recently introduced highly selective antagonist [^{3}H]rauwolscine (α-yohimbine). Results using [^{3}H]rauwolscine have tended to confirm the view that the density of the α_2-adrenoceptors on the platelet membrane are unchanged in untreated severely depressed patients (see Butler and Leonard, 1986 for discussion).

B. Serotonergic System

It is well established that many effective antidepressants impede the reuptake of [^{3}H]serotonin into cortical synaptosomes from rat brain and into platelets of nondepressed subjects who have received a single dose of antidepressant, such as clomipramine or zimelidine. Such findings imply that the transport system governing the uptake of serotonin into the synaptosome and platelet may provide a useful model of the nerve terminal in the brain of the depressed patient. Several investigators have found that the transport of [^{3}H]serotonin into the platelets of depressed patients is reduced before treatment, but returns to normal following effective therapy, irrespective of the presumed mechanism of action of the antidepressant (i.e., whether a specific norepinephrine- or serotonin-uptake inhibitor); ECT has also been equally as effective as antidepressants in normalizing serotonin uptake (Healy et al., 1983, 1985; Born et al., 1980; Tuomisto et al., 1979).

The sensitivity of the serotonin receptor on the platelet membrane also appears to be subnormal in the untreated patient and returns to control values following effective drug treatment (Healy et al., 1985). There is experimental evidence to suggest that the serotonin receptor on the platelet membrane is of the 5-HT$_2$ type (Lampugunani et al., 1982), which is widely distributed in limbic regions of the brain and the activity of which is increased following long-term antidepressant treatment. These findings, therefore, suggest that the sensitivity of 5-HT receptors is decreased in the untreated patients and returns to normal values following effective treatment. Brusov et al. (1989), in a study of platelet shape change velocity in a population of drug-free bipolar and unipolar depressed women, found that the 5-HT$_2$ receptors sensitivity was enhanced initially and normalized following effective antidepressant treatment. These authors suggest that the up-regulation of the 5-HT$_2$ receptors is a consequence of reduced presynaptic serotonergic activity, possibly caused by a reduction in the number of functioning nerve terminals in the untreated depressed state. The reason for the differences in the findings of Brusov et al. (1989) and Healy et al. (1983, 1985) are currently unclear.

More recently, Arora and Meltzer (1989), who used [^{3}H]lysergic acid diethylamide (LSD) as the ligand to determine the density of 5-HT$_2$ receptors on the platelet membranes of depressed patients, reported that the density of these receptors was increased in comparison with age- and sex-matched controls. However, the increase in 5-HT$_2$ receptor density was increased in female depressed patients only; no changes were reported in the male depressives, neither in the density of the [^{3}H]imipramine-binding sites nor rate of uptake of [^{3}H]serotonin into the platelets of either the male or female patients. Clearly, there is a major discrepancy in these findings and those of many other investigators, who used the more specific 5-HT$_2$ receptor ligand, [^{3}H]ketanserin, to label the receptor sites.

Other investigators have failed to find changes in peripheral serotonin receptor sensitivity in depressed patients. Thus, Wood et al. (1984) reported no difference in the serotonin-induced aggregation response in the platelets obtained from drug-free depressed patients and their controls. The reason for the difference in the findings of Wood et al. (1984) and Healy et al. (1983) is uncertain, apart from the different methods used to prepare the platelet-rich plasma. The question also arises concerning the relevance of platelet serotonin receptors and those found in the brain. Thus, although central 5-HT$_2$-type receptors have a high affinity for [^{3}H]spiperone, Schacter and Grahame-Smith (1982) failed to show that this ligand could bind to the human platelet membrane.

Leysen et al. (1981), however, have convincingly argued that both the ligand-binding sites and the platelet aggregation responses are mediated by 5-HT$_2$-type receptors. In addition to their ability to transport and store 5-HT, catecholamines are also found in platelets, but the evidence for the existence of a high-affinity transport site for the uptake of these amines is lacking. Nevertheless, Omenn and Smith (1978) have suggested that dopamine is transported into the platelet by the 5-HT-uptake site, whereas norepinephrine appears to be taken up by a process of passive diffusion. Platelets, therefore, may be used as a model for serotonergic and possibly dopaminergic nerve terminals (Stahl and Meltzer, 1978). By using ^{3}H- or ^{14}C-labeled amines, it is possible to assess differences between depressed patients and controls in the transport of these amines. Furthermore, as the transport of 5-HT into platelets has kinetic characteristics similar to those reported for synaptosomes (Shaskin and Snyder, 1970), it is also possible to determine the effects of various drug treatments on 5-HT transport in patients (Ghose, 1982).

An indication of the accuracy of platelet 5-HT uptake in reflecting such a process in the human brain is difficult to obtain. Nevertheless, Paul et al. (1981) compared the [^{3}H]serotonin uptake and [^{3}H]imipramine binding under similar experimental conditions in a synaptosomal fraction from rat brain and in human platelets. These investigators showed that, for a series of antidepressants, there was an excellent correlation (r = 0.99) between the ability of these compounds to inhibit 5-HT uptake and in their efficacies in displacing [^{3}H]imipramine from its binding site. Electrolytic lesions of the raphe nuclei of rats also resulted in a decreased hypothalamic [^{3}H]imipramine binding that paralleled the reduced [^{3}H]serotonin uptake into the hypothalamus, whereas an irreversible inhibitor of [^{3}H]imipramine binding, 2,8-dinitroimipramine, produced a dose-dependent decrease in [^{3}H]serotonin uptake, without affecting the uptake of [^{3}H]norepinephrine or [^{3}H]dopamine. Paul et al. (1981) concluded that [^{3}H]imipramine selectively labels 5-HT-uptake sites in both the brain and platelets. Therefore, it would seem reasonable to use studies of changes in platelet function in depressed patients to gain an insight into possible alterations in central neurotransmitter processes in these patients before and during treatment.

Several studies have shown that the transport of [^{3}H]serotonin into the platelets of depressed patients is reduced (Coppen et al., 1978; Tuomisto et al., 1979; Scott et al., 1979; Born et al., 1980; Healy et al., 1983, 1985). There is evidence from some of these studies that the [^{3}H]serotonin uptake returns to control values following recovery, suggesting that this uptake is a state-dependent marker of depression (Tuomisto et al., 1979; Born et al., 1980; Healy et al., 1983, 1985). Coppen et al. (1978), however, showed that the uptake rate was still impaired following clinical recovery, although other studies from this research group showed that patients with an affective disorder who responded to lithium showed a normalization in their platelet [^{3}H]serotonin-uptake rate (Wood et al., 1985). It is possible that the differences reported in the [^{3}H]serotonin uptake by different investigators could, at least partly, be ascribed to the presence or absence of aggressive features associated with the illness. Thus, Modai et al. (1989) found that, in a mixed group of 34 adolescent patients with schizophrenia, borderline personality disorder, and unipolar depression, a reduction in platelet [^{3}H]serotonin uptake was correlated with violent suicide attempts, which was independent of the category of psychiatric disorder.

Even though the reason for the abnormal [^{3}H]serotonin transport into platelets of depressed patients is uncertain there is a suggestion that, in patients with the premenstrual syndrome, a serum factor may be involved in decreasing serotonin transport. Thus, Ashby et al. (1990) reported that an aqueous fraction of plasma from patients with premenstrual syndrome inhibited the uptake of [^{3}H]serotonin into platelets and also into synaptosomes from rat brain. Although the nature of this inhibitory factor has yet to be determined, Faull et al. (1982) has provided experimental evidence to suggest that a ß-carboline may be responsible; several groups of investigators have shown that ß-carbolines decrease [^{3}H]serotonin uptake in various tissues with a high degree of specificity (Kellar et al., 1976; Kari et al., 1979). Such substances have also been implicated in the etiology of anxiety and depression (Skolnick et al., 1984; Huttenen et al., 1985). More recently, Nemeroff and co-workers (1990) have suggested that an α_1-acid glycoprotein, which is raised in the plasma of untreated depressed patients, might be the factor responsible for modulating serotonergic function in the platelets of depressed patients. However, Healy et al. (1991) could find no evidence to support the view that this glycoprotein interferes with the serotonin transporter site in depressed patients, hence the precise role of this factor remains uncertain.

C. Amine Uptake Sites

There is good experimental evidence to suggest that tricyclic antidepressants bind specifically, and with high affinity, to platelet and neuronal membranes. These binding sites are associated with, but probably not identical to, the transport site for 5-HT and norepinephrine (Paul et al., 1980, 1981; Rehavi et al., 1978, 1981, 1992). Tricyclic antidepressants have been shown to have a high affinity for the [^{3}H]imipramine or [^{3}H]desipramine binding sites, whereas other centrally acting drugs, such as phentolamine or chlorpromazine, have only a low affinity for these sites. The physiological relevance of these binding sites is the subject of debate. If these sites function as presynaptic receptors controlling the uptake of 5-HT or norepinephrine, is there an endogenous ligand for these sites? Alternatively, does the [^{3}H]imipramine-binding site reside on the 5-HT carrier mechanism and alter the uptake of 5-HT by allosteric conformational changes that are not physiologically relevant? Such questions, together with those suggesting that the imipramine-binding sites in the cortex are heterogeneous and involve selective-binding sites for [^{3}H]cocaine and [^{3}H]norzimelidine (see review by Davis, 1984), can only be answered by more detailed biochemical and pharmacological studies.

During the period 1980–1987, some 36 studies have been undertaken into the density of [^{3}H]imipramine-binding sites on the platelet membranes of untreated depressed patients (see Langer and Schoemaker, 1988 for review). Twenty-three of these studies showed that there was a decrease in the density of the imipramine-binding sites, varying from 10 to 54%; one study showed a 9% increase in the number of binding sites, whereas 12 of the studies reported no change. It seems probable that several experimental and clinical variables contribute to the variability reported, for example, the method used to isolate the platelets and the preparation of the platelet membranes, or the duration of the washout period before blood was taken from those patients that had been on antidepressant therapy. It is well known, that some tricyclic antidepressants (e.g., clomipramine) will decrease the density of the platelet imipramine-binding sites in healthy volunteers (Poirer et al., 1987), whereas amitriptyline increases the number of sites (Braddock et al., 1984), and maprotiline has no effect (Poirer et al., 1987). Wennogle and Meyerson (1985) studied the effects of 21 selective serotonin-uptake inhibitors on the high-affinity imipramine-binding site on the human platelet membrane and showed that such drugs fall into three groups that either attenuate, increase, or do not affect the dissociation of imipramine from the platelet membranes; the presence or absence of sodium ions markedly affected the ability of a drug to displace imipramine from its binding site. Hrdina (1989) has critically assessed the importance of the sodium dependency of [^{3}H]imipramine binding to intact platelets as a measure of those imipramine-binding sites that are relevant to serotonin uptake in patients with affective disorders. In general, it would appear that a washout period of 4 weeks is necessary to ensure that the changes in platelet imipramine binding are not affected by the antidepressant that has been administered to the patient.

Paul (1986) reported that the decreased [^{3}H]imipramine binding to the platelet membrane of depressives is influenced by the hypercortisolemia often found in these patients. In many studies, a parallel decrease in [^{3}H]imipramine binding and 5-HT uptake has been observed (Briley et al., 1980; Coppen et al., 1978; Tuomisto and Turkiainen, 1976; Healy et al., 1983, 1985), but it would seem that the two systems are differently controlled, particularly as the activity of the [^{3}H]serotonin uptake system appears to normalize following effective treatment. Differences between the imipramine-binding sites and the 5-HT transport sites probably reside in the differences in genetic control over such sites. Most studies in which changes in [^{3}H]imipramine binding were investigated in depressed patients suggests that this is a trait, rather than a state, marker of the illness (Paul et al., 1981), although some studies have shown that the imipramine-binding sites return to normal on clinical recovery (Suranyi-Cadotte et al., 1982). By contrast, Gay and co-workers (1983) studied a group of depressives who were treated with ECT or maprotiline and showed that, independently of their clinical response to treatment, the [^{3}H]imipramine-binding sites remained low, which favors a trait marker of depression. Overall, the evidence would suggest that the [^{3}H]imipramine-binding site is a trait marker of depression, which may be useful in the evaluation of the vulnerability of a person to the illness. Whether changes in [^{3}H]imipramine binding are unique for depression still remains an open question, however. The results for changes in the density of these binding sites on platelet membranes from schizophrenics are so far inconclusive (Arora and Meltzer, 1982; Modai et al., 1989). It would be of particular value to study changes in this system in other groups of patients in whom there has been shown to be a decrease in 5-HT transport, for example in Huntington's chorea (McLean and Nihei, 1977) and Down syndrome (Bayer and McCoy, 1974; Boullin and O'Brien, 1971).

Recently, a highly specific ligand for the serotonin transport site [^{3}H]paroxetine has been introduced, which may help clarify the situation concerning the relation between the changes in the serotonin transporter and the vulnerability to depression (Marcursson et al., 1989). However, in a recent study by Lawrence et al. (1989) on [^{3}H]paroxetine-labeled serotonin-uptake sites in six discrete regions of brains from depressed suicide victims, no changes could be detected. The action of antidepressants on the binding of selective radioligands to the serotonin transport site will be considered in more detail in the next section of this review.

D. Do Antidepressants Act by Changing Endogenous Endocoids in the Depressed Patient?

Several groups of investigators have produced evidence to indicate that the plasma and brain contain factors that affect the action of serotonin on the platelet membranes (Brusov et al., 1989) and the transport of serotonin into synaptosomes (Rehavi et al., 1987). Thus, Brusov et al. (1989) showed that, in a population of drug-free bipolar and unipolar depressed women, a concentration of serotonin sufficient to induce half-maximal shape change in the platelet, a measure of 5-HT$_2$ receptor function, was significantly lower than that of age-matched controls. Chronic antidepressant treatment resulted in a normalization of the 5-HT$_2$ receptor function. Similar changes have been reported by Healy et al. (1983, 1985). Such changes in serotonin receptor sensitivity that are associated with effective antidepressant treatments have been attributed to a change in the concentration of an endogenous peptide(s) (Barbaccia et al., 1985)—which other investigators have reported as being present in bovine forebrain and that inhibits both [^{3}H]mianserin and [^{3}H]ketanserin binding to 5-HT$_2$ receptors (Roth et al., 1985). McAdams et al. (1992) have recently shown that the aggregatory response of platelets to serotonin was reduced by a plasma factor that occurred only in those patients who were depressed or had not responded to antidepressant treatment. This factor(s) would also inhibit the aggregatory response when incubated with platelets from control subjects. Once the patients recovered, the patients' plasma no longer affected the serotonin-induced aggregation. In these same patients, the plasma also inhibited the uptake of [^{3}H]serotonin into the platelets. Although it is uncertain whether the factor, or factors, that suppress 5-HT$_2$ receptor function and [^{3}H]serotonin transport are the same, the results do suggest that such a factor(s) is only present while the symptoms of depression persist, which then raises the possibility that antidepressants produce their beneficial effects by changing the endogenous concentration of some endocoid.

Other investigators have studied changes in [^{3}H]serotonin uptake into platelets from depressed patients and found evidence that bovine brain and human platelet extracts contain substances that inhibit both serotonin uptake and [^{3}H]imipramine binding (Tang et al., 1990). Some of the endogenous substances responsible for the inhibition of [^{3}H]serotonin uptake were recognized by rabbit antibodies against imipramine, thereby suggesting that they may possess structures similar to those identified by the antibodies. An aqueous plasma fraction from patients with premenstrual syndrome was also shown by Ashby et al. (1990) to inhibit platelet serotonin uptake. Although the precise identity of the factor, or factors, responsible for those effects is unknown, there is evidence that α_1-acid glycoprotein, which is present in higher concentration in the depressed patient and normalizes following effective treatment, is one possible cause of these changes in serotonin function (Nemeroff et al., 1990).

One may speculate that antidepressant treatments produce their beneficial effects not necessarily by specifically modulating deranged neurotransmitter systems, but rather, by counteracting the adverse effects of endogenous endocoids (Leonard, 1993). Could this be the "black bile" that has preoccupied clinicians over the last 2000 years?

IV. CHRONIC EFFECTS OF ANTIDEPRESSANTS ON NEUROTRANSMITTER FUNCTION

In the last decade, there has been a major switch in research emphasis from the pre- to the postsynaptic neurons relative to the mode of action of antidepressant drugs. The initial studies of Vetulani et al. (1976) and Banerjee et al. (1977) indicated that various long-term antidepressant treatments changed the number and responsiveness of postsynaptic ß-adrenoceptors, whereas brief treatments were without effect. These findings were of considerable conceptual value because they established for the first time a single biochemical event that could be specifically induced by both pharmacological and nonpharmacological treatments, irrespective of the acute effects of the treatments. Subsequent studies have shown that, in addition to tricyclic antidepressants, MAOIs, ECT, and atypical antidepressants, such as iprindole and mianserin, also reduced the functional activity of the ß-adrenoceptor. On the other hand, barbiturates, anticonvulsants, benzodiazepines, antihistamines, and butyrophenones had no effect. This subject has been critically reviewed by Sulser (1983). Interestingly, chlorpromazine has an "antidepressant" profile in this biochemical model. Although this may be an example of a false-positive response, it should be remembered that this drug was at one time suggested to have antidepressant properties (Overall et al., 1966).

Although the effects of antidepressant treatments on the functional activity of cortical ß-adrenoceptors has been of value in studying known antidepressants, it remains to be established whether this will provide a completely reliable model for the selection of novel antidepressants. The specific serotonin-uptake inhibitor fluoxetine, which has been an effective antidepressant in several clinical studies, does not change the density or functional activity of cortical ß-adrenoceptors (Mishra et al., 1980). Relatively high doses of other novel nontricyclic antidepressants, such as trazodone (Clements-Jewery, 1978) and bupropion (Ferris et al., 1983), however, have decreased the cortical ß-receptor density. Moreover, studies on the effect of the triazolobenzodiazpine, alprazolam, on the functional activity of cortical adrenoceptors suggests that this atypical antidepressant may have a neurochemical profile similar to the tricyclic antidepressants (Sethy and Hodges, 1982).

A. Changes in Brain Noradrenergic Receptors

Whereas most clinically effective antidepressants decrease the density of cortical ß-adrenoceptors in the rat, there is experimental evidence to show that the tetracyclic antidepressant, mianserin, does not affect the density of these receptors, neither does it affect the isoproterenol (isoprenaline)-stimulated accumulation of cAMP in rat brain (Mishra et al., 1980; Mann and Enna, 1982). More recently, however, Pilc and Enna (1987) showed that mianserin prevented or reversed the supersensitivity of cortical ß-adrenoceptors caused by the neurotoxin 6-hydroxydopamine or by reserpine. A somewhat similar effect has been reported to occur for the novel triazolobenzodiazepine, alprazolam (Sethy and Hodges, 1982). These results indicate that antidepressant-induced alterations in ß-adrenoceptor activity may be a function of receptor sensitivity at the time of drug administration.

Because of the well-established finding that most clinically effective antidepressants reduce the functional responsiveness of the ß-adrenoreceptors in rat brain, it has been suggested that changes in the postsynaptic receptors must reflect an increase in neurotransmitter release, presumably as a consequence of a decrease in the sensitivity of the noradrenergic autoreceptors. This hypothesis is supported by the finding that mianserin (Fludder and Leonard, 1979) and tricyclic antidepressants (Crews and Smith, 1978) decrease the sensitivity of the noradrenergic autoreceptors following extended treatment. Because the autoreceptors inhibit the release of norepinephrine, the blockade or desensitization of these receptors by prolonged drug treatment would facilitate transmission and, thereby, decrease the sensitivity of the postsynaptic receptor sites. This simple hypothesis has been challenged by the observation that not all antidepressants that decrease the functional activity of postsynaptic ß-receptors, decrease the density of the presynaptic autoreceptors (Sugrue, 1981). Furthermore, the results of experiments in which the density of α_2-adrenoceptors, presumed to be similar to the noradrenergic autoreceptors, were determined using [^{3}H]clonidine are conflicting, with both a decrease (Smith et al., 1981) and an increase in receptor density being reported following the prolonged administration of antidepressants.

The confusion that arises when attempting to interpret the mode of action of antidepressants from the changes they produce in the density of cortical adrenoceptors in rats is partly due to the failure to distinguish between ligand-binding sites and functional receptors. As Sulser (1982) has emphasized, to qualify as a receptor, the dual function of *recognition and response* must be demonstrated. Consequently, irrespective of its affinity and number of specific sites, a binding site for a ligand cannot be designated a receptor unless a close relation between occupancy and biological response can be demonstrated; this has been considered in detail by Goodford (1984). Furthermore, it must be emphasized that changes in sensitivity reflect the functional responsiveness of the cell to a neurotransmitter, and the number of receptors as determined by ligand-binding studies need not necessarily parallel the changes in cellular responsiveness. This is not surprising, since not all receptors need be occupied for an optimal response to be elicited. Presumably, all receptors would be occupied by a ligand and, therefore, incorrect conclusions could be drawn concerning the relation between receptor number and the subsequent physiological response of the cell. So far only those studies in which the changes in receptor-linked adenylate cyclase activity have been monitored, after chronic antidepressant treatment, appear to have addressed this question rigorously.

B. Changes in Brain Serotonin Receptors

Several studies have shown that chronic antidepressant treatment results in an increased responsiveness of serotonin receptors in rat brain. Such an effort occurs following the repeated administration of tricyclic antidepressants, mianserin, adinazolam, ECT, MAOIs (particularly the MAO-A inhibitor, clorgyline, but not the MAO-B inhibitor, deprenyl), and such specific serotonin-uptake inhibitors as zimelidine and indalpine (De Montigny et al., 1984).

In a detailed study of a variety of serotonin-reuptake inhibitors, monoamine oxidase inhibitors, and tricyclic antidepressants, this group of investigators made an electrophysiological assessment of the effects of the various antidepressant treatments on the efficacy of serotonergic transmission in rat brain (Blier et al., 1988). The result of this study showed that the different types of antidepressants all enhanced serotonergic neurotransmission by different mechanisms, namely, by sensitizing the forebrain neurons (presumably 5-HT_2 receptors) to the transmitter (e.g., tricyclic antidepressants), by increasing the quantity of neurotransmitter that is available for release (e.g., MAO inhibitors), or by desensitizing the serotonin autoreceptors (e.g., serotonin-uptake inhibitors). These changes in rat brain appear to simulate the functional change in serotonin receptor responsiveness in platelets from depressed patients in whom the aggregation response to serotonin is reduced to approximately 50% of the control value before the start of treatment, but returned to control values following effective drug treatment (Healy et al., 1983).

Despite the observation that chronic antidepressant treatment facilitates serotonergic neurotransmission, as shown by electrophysiological studies, the potent serotonin-uptake inhibitor fluoxetine decreases the binding of [^{3}H]serotonin to cortical membranes of the rat brain (Wong and Bymaster, 1981). Other investigators have also shown that the density of postsynaptic 5-HT_2 receptors were decreased following the chronic administration of tricyclic antidepressants and mianserin; the serotonin autoreceptors were desensitized by these chronic antidepressant treatments (Schoups and De Potter, 1988; Peroutka and Snyder, 1979). Thus, there would appear to be a disparity between the decrease in the number of postsynaptic serotonergic receptors and an increase in serotonergic transmission. Kendall and Nahorski (1985) showed that chronic, but not acute, treatment of rats with imipramine and iprindole caused a reduction in serotonin-stimulated [^{3}H]inositol phosphate accumulation into brain slices, the extent of the decrease exceeding that of the decrease in the density of 5-HT_2-binding sites. This could suggest that the action of the antidepressants lies at a point distal to the 5-HT_2 receptor. In contrast with the findings of Kendall and Nahorski (1985), Osborne (1988) showed that in vitro three tricyclic antidepressants and mianserin, but not the MAO inhibitors pargyline and nialamide, stimulated [^{3}H]inositol accumulation into rat brain slices in a concentration-dependent manner. One possible explanation for these effects is that the antidepressants, because of their lipophilicity, penetrate the neuronal membrane and then influence phosphatidylinositol hydrolysis.

C. The Link Between the Noradrenergic and Serotonergic System

The ability of most antidepressants to modulate ß-adrenoceptor and 5-HT_2 receptor function in rat cortex following chronic administration, suggests that there might be an interaction between these types of receptors. Several studies have suggested such interconnections between the serotonergic and noradrenergic systems. Thus, Brunello and colleagues (1982) showed that lesions of central serotonergic tracts prevent the reduction in the density of cortical ß-adrenoceptors by repeatedly administered desipramine. In vitro studies have also shown that stimulation of ß-receptors in cortical slices is associated with an increase in the density of 5-HT_2 receptors (Scott and Crews, 1986), whereas a_2-receptor antagonists can enhance the desensitization of both ß-adrenoceptors and 5-HT_2 receptors by antidepressants (Crews et al., 1983). Further studies by Scott and Crews (1986) showed that the concurrent administration of a 5-HT_2 receptor antagonist, nefazadone, did not prevent the reduction in cortical ß-adrenoceptors caused by chronic amitriptyline treatment, thereby suggesting that enhanced serotonergic transmission is not necessary for the reduction in the density of 5-HT receptors caused by antidepressants. Furthermore, these investigators found that depletion of central stores of norepinephrine and serotonin by reserpine increased the density of cortical and hippocampal ß-adrenoceptors, without affecting the density of 5-HT_2 receptors, thereby showing that the 5-HT_2 receptor number is not regulated by the availability of serotonin. Additional experimental evidence showing that the decrease in the density of 5-HT_2 receptors by amitriptyline is independent of the change in ß-adrenoceptor density was presented by Scott and Crews (1986) when they found that the decrease in the ß-receptor density by amitriptyline could be prevented by the concurrent administration of the ß-receptor antagonist, propranolol; in this experiment the decrease in the density of 5-HT_2 receptors was not prevented by propranolol treatment.

Heal and colleagues (1990) studied the effects of serotonergic lesions with 5,7-dihydroxytryptamine, or by the serotonin-depleting agent *p*-chlorophenylalanine, on the behavioral effects of the specific α_2-receptor agonist clonidine. Clonidine-induced hypoactivity was enhanced following the serotonergic lesion, but not after serotonin-induced depletion. In addition, the serotonergic lesion attenuated the adaptive change that occurs after repeated desipramine administration, without affecting the adaptive change to electroconvulsive shocks. These results suggest that either serotonin, or a peptide cotransmitter contained within serotonergic neurons, modulates noradrenergic function. Thus, there is experimental evidence to suggest that both the serotonergic and noradrenergic systems must be intact to ensure optimal adaptive changes in transmitter receptor function that appear to be an essential correlate of antidepressant activity. Nevertheless, there would appear to be a concordance between the results of the ligand-binding studies and electrophysiological studies concerning the interdependence of the noradrenergic and serotonergic systems. Thus, Gravel and De Montigny (1987) showed that prior lesioning of central noradrenergic neurons with 6-hydroxydopamine failed to enhance the responsiveness of hippocampal pyramidal neurons to microiontophoretically applied serotonin, without affecting their responsiveness to norepinephrine or acetylcholine. From such studies, it would appear that the integrity of the noradrenergic system is required for antidepressants to modify central serotonergic neurotransmission.

Several studies have been undertaken recently to characterize further the role of serotonin in the regulation of the norepinephrine-coupled adenylate cyclase system in the rat cortex. Gillespie et al. (1988) found that although serotonin in vitro did not affect the maximum binding of [^{3}H]dihydroalprenolol in cortical tissue, it did abolish the increase in ß-receptor density and the marked increase in isoproterenol-stimulated cAMP synthesis in cortical membrane preparations after selective lesions with 5,7-dihydroxytryptamine. These investigators also showed that the changes in the ß-receptor density were restricted to the low-affinity conformation state for the agonist, the increase in the density of this subpopulation of ß-adrenoceptors occurring approximately 11 days after the lesions of the serotonergic system by 5,7-dihydroxytryptamine. The selective 5-HT_2 receptor antagonist ritanserin did not mimic the effects of the serotonergic neurotoxin. In this, and in other studies in which the effects of mianserin and the serotonin-uptake inhibitor fluoxetine were investigated (Manier et al., 1989; Sulser, 1987), the pivotal role of serotonin in the dual regulation of the linked serotonin–norepinephrine ß-adrenoceptor-coupled adenylate cyclase system has been demonstrated in which norepinephrine regulates the population of ß-adrenoceptors in the antagonist high-affinity state, whereas serotonin regulates those in the low-affinity conformation.

Perhaps some attention should also be directed to the effect of long term antidepressant administration and ECT on the guanosine triphosphate (GTP) activation of adenylate cyclase. Menkes et al. (1983) showed that such treatments facilitate cyclase activation by promoting the interaction of the regulatory and catalytic subunits of the enzyme. Such findings suggest a mechanism for the changes in the sensitivity to various neurotransmitters, including norepinephrine and serotonin, seen after repeated antidepressant administration. More recently, Nestler et al. (1989) showed that repeated antidepressants and ECT stimulated the translocation of cAMP-dependent protein kinase from the cytosol to the nucleus, which may be the ultimate step in the adaptational process to antidepressant treatments. Although the precise mechanism whereby this occurs is unclear, Brunello and colleagues (1990) and Perez et al. (1991) have demonstrated that repeated tricyclic antidepressant treatment elicits specific changes in the phosphorylation system associated with a crude microtubule fraction in rat cortex and hippocampus. This is a conceptually exciting finding, as it demonstrates how chronic antidepressant treatment may affect the mechanisms involved in protein synthesis, not only in the brain, but also in other tissues in which monoamines play an important physiological role (e.g., platelets). In short, all antidepressant treatments work by normalizing the synthesis of those proteins that are involved in the release and reuptake of the neurotransmitters that may be concerned in affective behavior.

In their study, Perez and co-workers (1991) attempted to locate the action of antidepressants on subcellular processes by investigating the changes in cAMP-binding proteins in rat cerebral cortex after the administration of antidepressants that were selective for the norepinephrine (+ oxaprotiline) or serotonin (fluoxetine) uptake processes. These investigators found that chronic administration of either of these drugs induced an increase in the photoactivated incorporation of 8-N^3-[^{32}P]cAMP into a protein band with an apparent molecular mass of 52,000 in both soluble and crude microtubule fractions. These effects were not found after acute administration nor following chronic treatment with isomers (e.g., oxaprotiline) that lacked antidepressant activity. The results suggest that modification in cAMP-binding proteins may be related to the adaptive changes elicited by prolonged antidepressant treatments and provide evidence for a specific intracellular target for the action of antidepressant drugs.

From such studies and those of others in which the effects of nontricyclic antidepressants, such as pargyline and nomifensine, were found to have qualitative effects on corticol ß- and 5-HT_2 receptors similar to the tricyclic antidepressants (Paul et al., 1988), it may be concluded that chronically administered antidepressants cause interdependent adaptive changes in both 5-HT_2 and ß-adrenoceptor changes in the rat cortex, which may give an insight into their common mechanism of action in the depressed patient. Furthermore, although such changes in receptor function may be important in explaining how all antidepressants appear to cause adaptation in both the noradrenergic and serotonergic systems, the more recent discovery that antidepressants have specific target sites in the coupling mechanism between the receptor and the secondary messenger system, and in the translation of information from the secondary messenger to various intercellular processes, lends further support to the hypothesis that all antidepressants have a common mechanism of action at the subcellular level.

D. Antidepressants and the γ-Aminobutyric Acid System

Despite the convincing experimental evidence that most antidepressants have qualitatively similar effects on the serotonergic and noradrenergic systems following their chronic administration, effects which are in accord with the view that these drugs exert their antidepressant action by initiating adaptive changes in these neurotransmitter systems, unequivocal evidence from clinical studies that such events occur in the brain of the depressed patients following effective treatment is lacking. Most antidepressants in clinical use affect a number of neurotransmitter receptors in addition to those of norepinephrine and serotonin (Green and Nutt, 1983) and we must consider the possibility that other neurotransmitter systems, such as the γ-aminobutyric acid (GABAergic) system, may be deranged in depression and, therefore, could be the site of action of antidepressants (Table 1).

There is evidence to suggest, for example, that the concentration of GABA is decreased in the biological fluids of depressed patients (Kasa et al., 1982; Petty and Sherman, 1981), whereas Pilc and Lloyd (1984) showed that tricyclic antidepressants, an MAO inhibitor, and the nontricyclic antidepressants viloxazine and citalopram, increased the number of $GABA_B$ receptor sites in the frontal cortex and hippocampus of the rat. More extensive studies were later published by Lloyd et al. (1985), in which a wide variety of antidepressants and ECT had qualitatively similar effects in increasing the density of $GABA_B$ receptors in the frontal cortex of the rat brain. Novel GABAmimetic drugs that may have antidepressant properties (e.g., progabide and fengabine) also caused similar changes in the $GABA_B$ receptor density. No changes were observed after administration of various neuroleptics or anticonvulsants, which suggests that a modulation of the GABAergic system may play a role in the mechanism of action of antidepressants. However, not all investigators have observed an increase in the $GABA_B$ receptor density after repeated antidepressant treatment (Cross et al., 1988a,b).

There is evidence that $GABA_B$ receptors may act as heteroceptors on serotonergic terminals in limbic regions of the rat brain. Gray et al. (1986) have shown that chronic administration of the GABAmimetic agent progabide increases the head twitch response induced by serotonin in rodents; the density of cortical 5-HT_2 receptors was also shown

Table 1 Type of Radioligands Used to Identify Monoamine Transport Sites in Brain

Monoamine	Radioligands
Serotonin	[^{3}H]imipramine
	[^{3}H]cyanoimipramine
	[^{3}H]nitroimipramine
	[^{3}H]paroxetine
	[^{3}H]indalpine
	[^{3}H]norzimelidine
	[^{3}H]citalopram
Norepinephrine	[^{3}H]desipramine
	[^{3}H]mazindol
Dopamine	[^{3}H]nomifensine
	[^{3}H]threo-($\pm$) - methylphenidate
	[^{3}H]cocaine
	[^{3}H]mazindol
Epinephrine	[^{3}H]desipramine

Source: After Langer and Schoemaker, 1988.

to increase under these experimental conditions. Accordingly, it may be hypothesized that functional changes in the GABAergic system are closely interrelated to those in the serotonergic and noradrenergic systems in the limbic regions of the brain.

E. Relevance of Tritiated Antidepressant-Binding Sites to the Mode of Action of Antidepressants

Receptor-binding studies using ^{3}H-labeled antidepressants have now been used for several years in an attempt to identify and characterize the interaction of these drugs with specific synaptic sites within the brain. Studies with ^{3}H-antidepressants known to inhibit the uptake of serotonin or norepinephrine have resulted in the identification of high-affinity-binding sites for these drugs that are associated with the macromolecular complex of the serotonin and norepinephrine transport site. Some of the ^{3}H-ligands that have been used to identify the high-affinity transport sites for serotonin, norepinephrine, dopamine, and epinephrine are listed in Table 2.

The most extensive experimental and clinical studies have been undertaken using [^{3}H]imipramine. It would appear that the relevance of the ^{3}H-antidepressant ligands for the norepinephrine, dopamine, and epinephrine transport sites as markers of psychiatric and neurological disease is less well established (see Langer and Schoemaker, 1988 for review).

Most investigators have concentrated their attention on the high-affinity-binding sites on the neurotransmitter transporters and have ignored the possible importance of the low-affinity sites. By contrast, Biegon and Samuel (1979) reported that both imipramine and desipramine show saturable, low-affinity binding, but have markedly different high-affinity-binding profiles. There has been considerable controversy over whether the action of the tricyclic antidepressants on low- or high-affinity-binding sites is of relevance to the therapeutic effects of these drugs. As Biegon and Samuel (1979) have postulated, in depressed patients, relatively large doses of the drugs given over prolonged periods are necessary for clinical improvement to occur. Under such conditions, it is likely that the drugs are present in the brain in the micromolar range, rather than the nanomolar range which is relevant to the high-affinity sites.

In the more recent study, Biegon (1984) reported that [^{3}H]nortriptyline which shows specificity for high-affinity sites on noradrenergic and serotonergic nerve terminals when present in the nanomolar range, binds in the low-affinity micromolar range to unidentified sites. This investigator has also shown that both secondary (e.g., desipramine and nortriptyline) and tertiary (e.g., amitriptyline and imipramine) antidepressants interact with this low-affinity site and displace each other (Biegon, 1990); these antidepressants bind with different affinities to the high-affinity sites situated on noradrenergic and serotonergic terminals. Furthermore, autoradiographic localization of the low-affinity-binding sites reveal a distribution pattern that is quite distinct to the high-affinity sites, the highest degree of low-affinity binding being in the cortical and hippocampal regions (Biegon, 1990). Therefore, it would appear that the occupancy of the low-affinity sites by tricyclic antidepressants may be of relevance to the therapeutic action of these drugs. Hrdina (1987) has also shown that nontricyclic antidepressants, such as fluoxetine and iprindole, increase the low-affinity imipramine sites in frontal cortex of the rat brain. Furthermore, the cortex and hippocampus are brain regions where both chronic antidepressant and ECS treatments have been shown to produce a desensitization of ß-adrenoceptors (Biegon and Israeli, 1986). Thus, there would appear to be a neuroanatomical link between the

Table 2 Effect of Repeated Administration of Antidepressants on the Density of Biogenic Amine Receptors in Rat Brain

	Receptor Type					
Antidepressant	5-HT$_1$ Ligand: 5[^{3}H]HT	5-HT$_2$ β-Adrenergic [^{3}H]Spiperone	β-Adrenergic [^{3}H]WB4101[a]	Muscarinic [^{3}H]DHA[b]		Dopaminergic [^{3}H]QNB[c]
Tricyclic antidepressants						
Amitriptyline	→	↓	→	↓	→	→
Imipramine	→	↓	→	↓	→	→
Desipramine	→	↓	→	↓	→	→
Atypical antidepressants						
Iprindole	→↓	→	↓	→	→	
Fluoxetine	→	↓	→	→	→	→
Monoamine oxidase inhibitors						
Pargyline	↓	↓	→	↓	→	→
Serotonin antagonists						
Methysergide	→	→	→	→	→	→
Neuroleptics						
Chlorpromazine	→	→	→	→	→	↑

→ No change relative to controls; ↓ decrease; ↑ increase relative to controls
[a] WB4101, α-antagonist; dimethyoxphenoxyethylamine methyl benzodioxan
[b] DHA, β-antagonist; dihydroalprenolol
[c] QNB, muscarinic antagonist; quinuclidinyl benzilate
Source: Data summarized in Ankier and Leonard, 1987.

changes in ß-adrenoceptor function and low-affinity antidepressant-binding sites following prolonged drug treatment that may be crucial to the understanding of the mode of action of these drugs.

Hrdina and co-workers (1990), in a very extensive study of the binding of [^{3}H]imipramine and the highly selective serotonin-uptake inhibitor [^{3}H]paroxetine in rat brain, showed that the binding of the latter ligand was heterogeneous and selectively labeled those brain regions known to contain serotonergic terminals, axons, and cell bodies. The binding of [^{3}H]paroxetine was abolished by the serotonergic neurotoxin *p*-chloroamphetamine. Conversely, [^{3}H]imipramine binding was more diffuse and only partially affected by the *p*-chloroamphetamine-induced lesion. These findings throw doubt on the specificity of [^{3}H]imipramine as a selective ligand for the serotonin-uptake site and emphasize the need for more detailed studies of extended antidepressant treatment in which [^{3}H]paroxetine is used as the ligand to characterize the serotonin-uptake site. More recently, 6-[^{3}H]nitroquipazine has also been shown to be a highly specific ligand for serotonin transport sites in rat cortex (Hashimoto and Goromaru, 1991).

Currently, it is unclear how these changes in the low-affinity tricyclic antidepressant sites related to [^{3}H]mianserin recognition sites, which may also play a role in the modulation of serotonergic function in the brain (Brunello et al., 1992). Costa et al. (1983) have hypothesized that, as repeated imipramine and desipramine treatments decrease the density of imipramine-binding sites on serotonergic terminals, the intrasynaptic decrease in the concentration of serotonin triggers a compensatory increase in neuronal firing. These investigators postulate that a cotransmitter, released with serotonin, activates the mianserin-binding sites that are associated with a postsynaptic 5-HT$_2$ receptor site on an interneuron; this could be a mechanism whereby the serotonergic system may be linked to the noradrenergic system.

It would be an oversimplification to conclude that antidepressants relieve the symptoms of depression because they decrease the functional activity of postsynaptic ß-adrenoceptors, an action that also depends on a modification of serotonergic transmission. Although such a hypothesis serves to unify the actions of the disparate types of antidepressants and ECS on the serotonergic and noradrenergic systems, it is not yet possible to say how the antidepressant-induced changes in α_2-adrenergic (U'Prichard et al., 1978), histaminergic and muscarinic (Rehavi and Sokolovsky, 1978), and opiate (Biegon and Samuel, 1980) receptors fit into this scheme.

V. CONCLUSION

The precise mechanism of action of antidepressants still remains an enigma. However, there is increasing evidence that, despite the chemical diversity of the antidepressants, there is evidence that they all bring about adaptational changes in the serotonergic, noradrenergic and, possibly, other neurotransmitter systems (e.g., acetylcholine, GABA, and various neuropeptides such as met-enkephalin). Whether such functional changes are the primary sites of action of antidepressant treatments or a reflection of discrete changes in the activities of various secondary-messenger systems is still uncertain. Thus, the *receptor adaptation hypothesis* of the mode of action of antidepressants brings into question the relevance of their specificity of action on a neurotransmitter system. Clearly, more research needs to be undertaken, not only to substantiate this hypothesis, but also to define more precisely their common site of action.

It is a sobering thought that with one or two exceptions, there is little evidence that the 80 or more compounds in clinical development (Pinder, 1985) will add anything worthwhile to our understanding of depression or in improving the efficacy of treatment of the depressed patient. Perhaps a better understanding of the common mode of action of antidepressants may lead to a more rational development of drugs that combine improved efficacy with fewer adverse side effects.

To conclude on a more optimistic note, the application of the techniques of molecular neurobiology to our understanding of the changes in central neurotransmission that are brought about by the prolonged administration of antidepressants may serve to explain how all such drugs, irrespective of their differences in chemical structure and acute biochemical profiles, correct the abnormal protein synthesis that is ultimately responsible for abnormal neurotransmitter function. By influencing the genetic control of protein synthesis in both the brain and peripheral tissues in which neurotransmitters play a physiological role, antidepressants may now be visualized as bringing about adaptive changes throughout the body and their action not being restricted simply to the brain. It is not without interest that repeated imipramine treatment has been shown to cause a decrease in the modulatory effect of GABA on transmission in the rat vas deferens, an effect that may be due to the action of the antidepressant on the G protein that couples the $GABA_B$–type receptor to the ion channels (Strobel et al., 1989). Such effects are not confined to the GABAergic system alone. Thus chronic, but not acute, administration of desipramine enhances the α_1-adrenoceptor contractile response in rat vas deferens (Finberg and Tal, 1985), whereas the sensitivity of the rat anococcygeal muscle to phenylephrine increases following chronic imipramine treatment (Hong et al., 1986). This suggests that the mechanism of action of antidepressants is similar in both peripheral tissues in the brain.

The decade of the 1970s was largely devoted to an explanation of the mode of action of antidepressants on the concentrations of amines and their metabolites. The 1980s was a decade in which adaptive changes in receptor function was envisaged as important in understanding the action of the antidepressants. Perhaps the 1990s will concentrate our attention on the link between the receptors and their secondary messenger systems. It is always possible that by the year 2000 we shall begin to understand how antidepressants work.

REFERENCES

S. I. Ankier, and B. E. Leonard, Biological aspects of depression: a review of the aetiology, mechanisms of action and clinical assessment of antidepressants, *Int. Rev. Neurobiol., 28*: 183 (1986).

R. C. Arora, and H. Y. Meltzer, Serotonin uptake by blood platelets by schizophrenic patients, *Psychiatric Res., 6*: 327 (1982).

R. C. Arora, and H. Y. Meltzer, Increased serotonin 2 receptor binding as measured by ^{3}H-LSD in blood platelets of depressed patients, *Life Sci., 44*: 725 (1989).

M. Asberg, L. Bertilsson, and D. Tuck, Indoleamine metabolites in the cerebrospinal fluid of depressed patients before and during treatment with nortriptyline, *J. Clin. Pharmacol. Ther., 14*: 277 (1973).

M. Asberg, L. Traskman, and P. Toren, 5-HIAA in the cerebrospinal fluid. A biochemical suicide predictor, *Arch. Gen. Psychiatry, 33*: 1193 (1976a).

M. Asberg, V. A. Ringerger, and F. Sjoqvist, Monoamine metabolites in cerebrospinal fluid and serotonin uptake inhibitors during treatment with chlorimipramine, *Clin. Pharmacol. Ther., 21*: 201 (1976b).

M. Asberg, V. A. Ringberger, P. Sjoqvist, P. Thoren, L. Traskman, and J. R. Tuck, Monoamine metabolites in cerebrospinal fluid and serotonin uptake inhibition during treatment with chlorimipramine, *J. Clin. Pharmacol. Ther., 21*: 2012 (1977).

C. R. Asby, L. A. Carr, C. L. Cook, M. M. Steptoe, and D. D. Franks, Alteration of 5-HT uptake by plasma fractions in the pre-menstrual syndrome, *J. Neural Transm. Gen. Sect., 79*: 41 (1990).

S. P. Banerjee, L. S. Kung, S. J. Riggi, and S. K. Chanda, Development of beta adrenergic receptor subsensitivity by antidepressants, *Nature, 268*: 455 (1977).

M. L. Barbaccia, F. Karoum, and E. Costa, Characterization of the endocoid for imipramine recognition sites, *Endocoids,* H. Lal, F. Labella, and J. Lane, eds., Alan J. Liss, New York, 431 (1985).

S. M. Bayer and E. E. McCoy, A comparison of the 5-HT and ATP content in platelets from subjects with Downs syndrome. *Biochem. Med., 9*: 225 (1974).

A. Biegon, The complex binding of tricyclic antidepressants to rat brain: The case of nortriptyline, *Brain Res., 321*: 347 (1984).

A. Biegon, Characterization and localization of binding sites for tricyclic antidepressants in rat and human brain, *Antidepressants Thirty Years On* (B. E. Leonard and P. S. J. Spencer, eds.), Clinical Neuroscience Publishers, London, 46 (1990).

A. Biegon, and M. Israeli, Localization of the effects of electronconvulsive shock on beta adrenoceptors in the rat brain, *Eur. J. Pharmacol., 123*: 329 (1986).

A. Biegon, and D. Samuel, Binding of a labelled antidepressant to rat brain tissue, *Psychopharmacology, 65*: 259 (1979).

A. Biegon, and D. Samuel, Interaction of tricyclic antidepressants with opiate receptors, *Biochem. Pharmaco., 29*: 180 (1980).

G. V. Born, G. Gragnani, and K. Martin, Long-term effects of lithium on the uptake of 5-hydroxytryptamine by human platelets, *Br. J. Clin. Pharmacol., 9*: 3212 (1980).

P. Blier, C. de Montigny, and Y. Chaput, Electrophysiological assessment of the effects of antidepressant treatments on the efficacy of 5-HT neurotransmission, *Clin. Neuropharmacol., 11*(Suppl. 2): S1 (1988).

D. J. Boullin, and P. A. M. O'Brien, Characterization of receptor mediating 5-HT and catecholamine induced platelet aggregation by alpha and beta blockers, butyrophenones, 5-HT antagonists and chlorpromazine, *Br. J. Pharmacol., 62*: 537 (1971).

L. E. Braddock, P. J. Cowen, J. M. Eliott, S. Fraser, and K. Stamp, Changes in the binding to platelets of 3H-imipramine and 3H-yohimbine in normal subjects taking amitriptyline, *Neuropharmacology, 23*: 285 (1984).

M. S. Briley, S. Z. Langer, R. Raisman, D. Sechter, and E. Zarifian, ^{3}H-imipramine binding sites are decreased on platelets of untreated depressed patients, *Science, 303*: 1209 (1980).

N. Brunello, D. Chuang, and E. Costa, Different synaptic localizations of mianserin and imipramine binding sites, *Science, 215*: 1112 (1982).

N. Brunello, J. Perez, D. Tinelli, A. C. Rovescalli, and G. Racagni, Biochemical and molecular changes in rat cerebral cortex after chronic antidepressant treatment: In vitro and in vivo studies, *Pharmacol. Toxicol., 66*: 112 (1990).

O. S. Brusov, B. S. Beliaeve, A. B. Katasonov, G. P. Zlobina, M. I. Factor, and R. R. Lideman, Does platelet serotonin receptor supersensitivity accompany endogenous depression? *Biol. Psychiatry, 25*: 375 (1989).

J. Butler, and B. E. Leonard, Post-partum depression and the effect of nomifensine treatment, *Int. Clin. Psychopharmacol., 1*: 244 (1986).

D. S. Charney, S. M. Soutwick, P. L. Delgado, and H. H. Krystal, Current status of the ceptor sensitivity hypothesis of antidepressant action, *Pharmacotherapy of Depression* (J. D. Amsterdam, ed.), Marcel Dekker, New York, p. 13 (1990).

S. A. Checkley, Neuroendocrine tests of monoamine function in man: A review of the amine theory and the application to the study of depressive illness, *Psychol. Med., 10*: 35 (1980).

S. Clements-Jewery, The development of cortical beta adrenoceptors subsensitivity in the rat by chronic treatment with trazodone, doxepine and mianserin, *Neuropharmacology, 17*: 799 (1978).

A. Coppen, C. Swade, and K. Wood, Platelet 5-hydroxytryptamine accumulation in depressive illness, *Clin. Chim. Acta, 87*: 165 (1978).

E. Costa, D. M. Chuang, M. I. Barbaccia, and O. Gandolfi, Molecular mechanisms in the action of imipramine, *Experientia, 39*: 855 (1983).

F. T. Crews, and C. B. Smith, Pre-synaptic alpha receptor subsensitivity after long-term antidepresant treatment, *Science, 202*: 322 (1978).

F. J. Crews, A. Camacho, and M. I. Phillips, Cholinergic stimulation of hippocampal pyrimodal cells is inhibited by increasing membrane cholesterol, *Brain Res., 261*: 1255 (1983).

J. A. Cross, and R. W. Horton, Effects of chronic oral administration of the antidepressants, desipramine and zimelidine on rat cortical GABA B binding sites: A comparison with 5HT2 binding site changes, *Br. J. Pharmacol., 93*: 331 (1988a).

J. S. Cross, S. C. Cheetham, M. R. Crompton, C. L. E. Ktona, and R. W. Horton, Brain GABA binding sites in depressed suicide victims, *Psychiatry Res., 26*: 119 (1988b).

B. Davies, D. Sudera, G. Sangella, E. Marchesi-Saviotti, C. Malthias, R. Bannister, and P. Sever, Increased number of alpha receptors in sympathetic denervation supersensitivity in man, *J. Clin. Invest, 69*: 779 (1982).

A. Davis, Molecular aspects of the imipramine receptor, *Experientia, 40*: 782 (1984).

C. De Montigny, P. Blier, and Y. Chaput, Electrophysiologically identified serotonin receptors in the rat CNS: Effect of antidepressant treatment, *Neuropharmacology, 23*: 1511 (1984).

H. M. Emrich, V. Holtt, and W. Kissling, Beta endorphin-like immunoreactivity in cerebrospinal fluid and plasma of patients with schizophrenia and other neuropsychiatric disorders, *Pharmacopsychiat., 12*: 269 (1979).

K. F. Faull, R. B. Holman, G. R. Elliott, and J. D. Barchas, Tryptolines artifacts or reality. A new method of analysis using GC/MS, *beta-Carbolines and tetrahydroisoquinolines,* Alan R. Liss, New York, p. 135 (1982).

R. M. Ferris, B. R. Cooper, and R. A. Maxwell, Studies on bupropion's mechanism of antidepressant action, *J. Clin. Psychiatry, 44*: 74 (1983).

J. P. M. Finberg, and A. Tal, Reduced peripheral pre-synaptic adrenoceptor sensitivity following chronic antidepressant treatment in rats, *Br. J. Pharmacol., 84*: 609 (1985).

J. Fludder, and B. E. Leonard, Chronic effects of mianserin on noradrenaline metabolism in the rat brain: Evidence for a pre-synaptic alpha adrenolytic action in vivo, *Psychopharmacology, 64*: 329 (1979).

J. A. Garcia-Sevilla, Platelet alpha 2 adrenoceptor function in depression and response to drug treatment, *Antidepressants: Thirty Years On* (B. E. Leonard and P. S. J. Spencer, eds.), Clinical Neuroscience Publishers, London, p. 163 (1990).

J. A. Garcia-Sevilla, A. P. Zis, J. C. Selnick, and C. B. Smith, Platelet alpha 2 adrenergic receptors in major depressive disorder, *Arch. Gen. Psychiatry, 38*: 1327 (1981).

C. Gay, S. Z. Langer, H. Loo, R. Raisman, D. Sechter, and E. Zarifan, ^{3}H-imipramine binding to platelets: A state dependent or independent biological markers, *Br. J. Pharmacol., 78*: 57 (1983).

K. Ghose, Biochemical assessment of antidepressive drugs, *Methods in Clinical Pharmacology for the Central Nervous System* (M. Lader and A. Richens, eds.), MacMillan, Basingstoke, England, p. 67 (1982).

D. D. Gillespie, D. H. Manier, E. Sanders-Bush, and F. Sulser, The serotonin/norepinephrine-link in brain II. Role of serotonin in the regulation of beta adrenoceptors in the low agonist affinity conformation, *J. Pharmacol. Exp. Ther., 244*: 154 (1988).

P. J. Goodford, Receptors, spare receptors in other binding sites, *Receptors Again* (J. W. Lamble and A. C. Abbott, eds.), Elsevier, Amsterdam, p. 21 (1984).

P. Gravel, and C. de Montigny, Noradrenergic denervation parents sensitization of rat forebrain neurons to serotonin by tricyclic antidepressant treatment, *Synapse, 1*: 233 (1987).

J. A. Gray, A. Metz, G. M. Goodwin, and A. R. Green, The effects of GABA-mimetic drugs, progabide and baclofen on the biochemistry and function of 5-hydroxytryptamine and noradrenaline, *Neuropharmacology, 25*: 711 (1986).

A. R. Green, and D. J. Nutt, Antidepressants, *Psychopharmacology I, Part I: Preclinical Psychopharmacology* (D. G. Grahame-Smith and P. J. Lowen, eds.), Excerpta Mediea, Amsterdam (1983).

K. Hashimoto, and T. Goromaru, High affinity binding of ^{3}H 6-nitroquipazine to cortical membranes of the rat: Inhibition by 5-hydroxytryptamine and 5-hydroxytryptamine uptake inhibitors, *Neuropharmacology, 30*: 113 (1991).

D. J. Heal, E. M. Hurst, M. R. Prow, and W. R. Buckett, An investigation of the role of 5-hydroxytryptamine in the attenuation of pre-synaptic alpha 2-adrenoceptor mediated responses by antidepressant treatments, *Psychopharmacology, 101*: 100 (1990).

D. Healy, P. A. Carney, and B. E. Leonard, Monoamine related markers of depression, *J. Psychiat. Res., 17*: 151 (1983).

D. Healy, A. O'Halloran, P. A. Carney, and B. E. Leonard, Peripheral adrenoceptors and serotonin receptors in depression, *J. Psychiat. Res., 20*: 345 (1985).

D. Healy, J. Calvin, A. W. Whitehouse, W. White, H. Wilton-Cox, A. E. Theodorou, K. M. Lawrence, R. W. Horton, and E. S. Paykel, Alpha 1-Acid glycoprotein in major depressive and eating disorders, *Journal 20*: 13 (1991).

K. W. Hong, B. Y. Rion, and W. S. Lee, Enhancement of central and peripheral alpha 1 adrenoceptors sensitivity and reduction in alpha 2 adrenoceptor sensitivity following chronic imipramine treatment in rats, *Eur. J. Pharmacol., 29*: 275 (1986).

P. D. Hrdina, Regulation of high and low affinity ^{3}H-imipramine recognition sites in rat brain by chronic treatment with antidepressants, *Eur. J. Pharmacol., 138*: 158 (1987).

P. D. Hrdina, Differences between sodium dependent and desipramine defined ^{3}H-imipramine binding intact human platelets, *Biol. Psychiatry, 25*: 576 (1989).

P. R. Hrdina, B. Foy, and R. J. Summers, Imaging of serotonin uptake sites in brain with 3H-paroxetine: comparison with 3H-imipramine binding, *Antidepressants: Thirty Years On* (B. E. Leonard and P. S. J. Spencer, eds.), Clinical Neuroscience Publishers, London, p. 54 (1990).

P. Huttenen, B. A. Spencer, and R. D. Meyers, Monoamine transmitter release induced by tetrahydro-ß-carboline perfused in hippocampus of the unrestrained rat, *Brain Res. Bull., 15*: 215 (1985).

R. T. Jung, P. S. Shetty, and W. P. James, The effect of refeeding after semi-starvation on catecholamine and thyroid metabolism, *Int. J. Obesity, 4*: 95 (1980).

M. S. Kafka, J. F. Tallman, C. C. Smith, and J. L. Costa, Alpha adrenergic receptors on human platelets, *Life Sci., 21*: 1429 (1977).

M. S. Kafka, A. Wirz-Justice, and D. Naber, Circadian and seasonal rhythms in alpha and beta adrenergic receptors in the rat brain, *Brain Res., 207*: 409 (1981).

I. Kari, P. Peura, and M. M. Airakinsen, Mass fragmentographic determination of tetrahydro-ß-carboline in human blood platelets and plasma, *Med. Biol., 57*: 412 (1979).

K. Kasa, S. Otsuki, M. Iyamamoto, M. Sato, H. Juroda, and N. Ogawa, CSF GABA and homovanillic acid in depressive disorders, *Biol. Psychiat., 17*: 877 (1982).

K. J. Kellar, G. R. Elliot, B. R. Holman, J. Vernikos-Danellis, and J. Barchas, Tryptoline inhibition of serotonin uptake in rat forebrain homogenates, *J. Pharmacol. Exp. Ther., 168*: 619 (1976).

D. A. Kendall, and S. R. Nahorski, 5-Hydroxytryptamine stimulates inositol phospholipid hydrolysis in rat cerebral cortex slices: Pharmacological characterization and effects of antidepressants, *J. Pharmac. Exp. Therap., 223*: 473 (1985).

M. Lampagnani, and G. De Gactano, Comparative effects of ketanserin, a novel serotonin receptor antagonist, on 5-HT induced shape change and 5-HT uptake in rat and human platelets, *Biochem. Pharmacol., 31*: 3000 (1982).

S. Z. Langer, and H. Schoemaker, Effects of antidepressants on monoamine transporters, *Prog. Neuropsychopharmacol. Biol. Psychiatry, 12*: 193 (1988).

K. M. Lawrence, F. De Paermentier, S. C. Cheetha, M. R. Crompton, C. L. E. Katona, and R. W. Horton, Brain 5HT uptake sites labelled with ^{3}H-paroxetine in post-mortem samples from depressed suicide victims, *Br. J. Pharmacol., 98*: 812P (1989).

B. E. Leonard, Current status of the biogenic amine theory of depression, *Neurochem. Int., 4*: 339 (1982).

B. E. Leonard, Neurotransmitter receptors, endocrine responses and the biological substrates of depression: A review, *Hum. Psychopharmacol., 1*: 3 (1986).

B. E. Leonard, The amine hypothesis of depression: A re-assessment, *Biochemical and Pharmacological Aspects of Depression* (K. F. Tipton and M. B. H. Youdim, eds.), Taylor & Francis, London, p. 25 (1989).

B. E. Leonard, Effect of antidepressants on neurotransmission: a common mechanism of action, *Current Aspects of Neuroscience,* Vol. 4 (N. N. Osborne, ed.), MacMillan, Basginstoke, England, p. 205 (1992).

B. E. Leonard, Endocoids in depression: do antidepressants alter endocoids that affect the serotonergic system? *Prog. Neuro-Psychopharmacol. Biol. Psychiat., 17*: 505 (1993).

J. E. Leysen, F. Awontere, L. Kennis, P. M. Laduron, J. Van der Berk, and P. A. T. Janssen, Receptor binding profile of R414681, a novel antagonist at 5HT 2 receptors, *Life Sci., 20*: 1015 (1981).

K. G. Lloyd, F. Thuret, and A. Pilc, Upregulation of GABA B binding sites in rat frontal cortex: A common action of repeated administration of different classes of antidepressants and electroshock, *J. Pharmacol. Exp. Ther., 235*: 191 (1985).

P. Luck, D. P. Milhailides, M. R. Dashwood, M. A. Barradas, P. S. Swever, P. Dandona, and A. Wakeling, Platelet hyperaggregability and increased alpha adrenoceptor density in anorexia nervosa, *J. Clin. Endocrinol. Metab., 57*: 911 (1983).

D. H. Manier, D. D. Gillespie, and F. Sulser, Dual aminergic regulation of central beta adrenoceptors: Effect of atypical antidepressants and 5-hydroxytryptophan, *Neuropharmacology, 28*: 89 (1989).

E. Mann, and S. J. Enna, Neurochemical and behavioural correlates of antidepressant drug action, *Life Sci., 30*: 1653 (1982).

J. O. Marcursson, A. Andersson, and I. Backstrom, Drug inhibitors indicate a single-site model of the 5-HT uptake site/antidepressant binding site in rat and human brain, *Psychopharmac., 99*: 17 (1989).

C. McAdams, F. J. Colohan, J. Brophy, and B. E. Leonard, Alteration by a plasma factor of platelet aggregation and 5HT uptake in depression, *Biol. Psychiat., 32*: 296 (1992).

D. R. McLean, and T. Nihei, Uptake of dopamine and 5-hydroxytryptamine by platelets from patients with Huntington's chorea, *Lancet, 1*: 249 (1977).

D. B. Menkes, M. M. Rasenick, M. A. Wheeler, and M. W. Bitensky, Guanosine triphosphate activation of brain adenylate cyclase: Enhancement by long-term antidepressant treatment, *Science, 219*: 65 (1983).

R. Mishra, A. Janowsky, and F. Sulser, Action of mianserin and zimelidine upon the norepinephrine receptor coupled adenylate cyclase system in brain, *Neuropharmacology, 19*: 983 (1980).

I. Modai, A. Apter, M. Meltzer, S. Tyano, A. Walevski, and Z. Jerushalm, Serotonin uptake by platelets of suicidal and aggressive adolescent psychiatric in-patients, *Neuropsychobiology, 21*: 9 (1989).

S. A. Montgomery, The non-selective effects of selective antidepressants, *Adv. Biochem. Psychopharmacol., 31*: 49 (1982).

D. L. Murphy, C. Donnelly, and J. Moskowitz, Catecholamine receptor function in depressed patients, *Am. J. Psychiatry, 131*: 1389 (1974).

C. B. Nemeroff, R. R. Drishnan, D. G. Blazer, D. L. Knight, D. Benjamin, and L. R. Meyerson, Elevated plasma concentrations of alpha 1 acid glyprotein, a putative-endogenous inhibitor of the tritiated imipramine binding site in depressed patients, *Arch. Gen. Psychiatry, 47*: 337 (1990).

E. J. Nestler, R. Z. Terwiliger, and R. S. Duman, Chronic antidepressant administration alters the subcellular distribution of cyclic AMP dependent protein kinase in rat frontal cortex, *J. Neurochem., 53*: 1644 (1989).

G. S. Omenn, and L. T. Smith, A common uptake system for serotonin and dopamine in human platelets, *J. Clin. Invest., 62*: 235 (1978).

N. N. Osborne, Tricyclic antidepressants, mianserin and ouabain stimulate inositol phosphate formation in vitro in rat cortical slices, *Neurochem. Res., 13*: 105 (1988).

H. R. Olpe, Molecular view of the treatment of depression, *Depression: Molecular and Psychologically Based Therapies—An Integrative View* (J. Korf and L. Pepperlink-Huizen, eds.), T. G. O. Foundation, Drachten, Holland, p. 21 (1982).

J. Overall, L. Holliste, M. Johnson, and V. Pennington, Nosology of depression and differential response to drugs, *JAMA, 195*: 946 (1966).

G. N. Pandey, M. W. Pysken, D. L. Garter, and J. M. Davis, beta-Adrenergic receptor function in affective illness, *Am. J. Psychiatry, 136*: 675 (1979).

S. M. Paul, Serotonin re-uptake sites in platelets and human brain: Clinical implications, Proc. Reg. Symp. World Psychiatr., Assoc. Copenhagen, abstr. 293 (1986).

S. M. Paul, M. Rehavi, and P. Skolnick, Demonstration of specific "high affinity" binding sites for ^{3}H-imipramine on human platelets, *Life Sci., 26*: 953 (1980).

S. M. Paul, M. Rehavi, P. Skolnick, J. C. Ballenger, and F. K. Goodwin, Depressed patients have decreased binding of ^{3}HT-imipramine to the platelet serotonin transporter, *Arch. Gen. Psychiatry, 38*: 1315 (1981).

I. A. Paul, G. E. Ducan, K. R. Powell, R. A. Mueller, T. S. Hong, and G. R. Breese, Regionally specific neuronal adaptation of beta adrenergic and 5-hydroxytryptamine 2 receptors after antidepressant administration in the forced swim test and after chronic antidepressant treatment, *J. Pharmacol. Exp. Ther., 246*: 956 (1988).

J. Perez, D. Tinelli, E. Bianchi, N. Brunello, and G. L. Recagni, cAMP binding proteins in the rat cerebral cortex after administration of selective 5-HT and NE reuptake blockers with antidepressant activity, *Neuropsychopharmacology, 4*: 57 (1991).

S. Peroutka, and S. H. Snyder, Multiple serotonin receptors: Differential binding of ^{3}H-5HT, ^{3}H-LSD and ^{3}H-spiroperidol, *Mol. Pharmacol., 16*: 687 (1979).

F. Petty, and A. D. Sherman, GABAergic modulation of learned helplessness, *Pharmacol. Biochem. Behav., 15*: 567 (1981).

A. Pilc, and S. J. Enna, Supersensitive ß-adrenergic receptors are down regulated in rat brain by mianserin administration, *J. Neural. Transm., 70*: 71 (1987).

A. Pilc, and K. G. Lloyd, Chronic antidepressants and GABA "AB" receptors: A GABA hypothesis of antidepressant drug action, *Life Sci., 35*: 2149 (1984).

R. M. Pinder, Antidepressant drugs of the future, *Psychopharmacology: Recent Advances in Future Prospects* (S. D. Iversen, ed.), Oxford University Press, Oxford, p. 45 (1985).

M. F. Poirier, A. M. Glazin, H. Loo, C. Pimoule, A. Segonacxz, C. Benkelfat, D. Sechter, E. Carifian, H. Schoemaker, and S. Z. Langer, Changes in ^{3}H-5HT uptake and ^{3}H imipramine binding in platelets after clomipramine in healthy volunteers: Comparison with maprotiline and amitriptyline, *Biol. Psychiatry, 22*: 287 (1987).

W. Z. Potter, M. Scheinin, R. N. Golden, M. V. Rudorfer, R. W. Cowdry, H. M. Ctil, R. J. Ross, and M. Linnoila, Selective antidepressants on cerebrospinal fluid. Lack of specificity on norepinephrine and serotonin metabolites, *Arch. Gen. Psychiatry, 42*: 1171 (1985).

M. Rehavi, and M. Sokolovsky, Multiple binding sites of tricyclic antidepressants to mammalian brain receptors, *Brain Res., 149*: 525 (1978).

M. Rehavi, P. Skolnick, B. Hulihan, and S. M. Paul, High affinity binding of ^{3}H-desipramine to rat cerebral cortex: Relationship to tricyclic antidepressant induced inhibition of noradrenaline uptake, *Eur. J. Pharmacol., 70*: 597 (1981).

M. Rehavi, P. Skolnick, M. J. Brownstein, and S. M. Paul, High affinity binding of ^{3}H-desipramine to rat brain: A pre-synaptic marker for NA uptake sites, *J. Neurochem., 38*: 889 (1982).

M. Rehavi, H. Sepcuti, and A. Weizman, Upregulation of imipramine binding and serotonin uptake by estrodiol in female rat brain, *Brain Res., 410*: 135 (1987).

B. L. Roth, T. Nakaki, D. M. Chuang, and E. Costa, Evidence for an endocoid for the $5HT_2$ recognition site, *Prog. Clin. Biol. Res., 192*: 473 (1985).

M. Schachter, D. F. Greaney, G. D. Grahame-Smith, P. Cowen, and J. M. Elliott, Increased platelet membrane ^{3}H-LSD binding in patients on chronic neuroleptic treatment, *Br. J. Clin. Pharmacol., 19*: 453 (1985).

A. A. Schoups, and W. P. De Potter, Species dependence on adaptations of the pre- and post-synaptic serotonergic receptors following long-term antidepressant drug treatment, *Biochem. Pharmacol., 37*: 4451 (1988).

J. A. Scott, and F. J. Crews, Down regulation of serotonin 2, but not of beta-adrenergic receptors, during chronic treatment with amitriptyline is independent of stimulation of serotonin 2 and beta adrenergic receptors, *Neuropharmacology, 25*: 1301 (1986).

M. Scott, H. W. Reading, and J. B. London, Studies on human blood platelets in affective disorder, *Psychopharmacology, 60*: 1431 (1979).

V. Sethy, and D. H. Hodges, Alprazolam in a biochemical model of depression, *Biochem. Pharmacol., 31*: 3155 (1982).

E. G. Shaskin, and S. H. Snyder, Kinetics of serotonin accumulation into slices from rat brain: Relationship to catecholamine uptake, *J. Pharmacol. Exp. Ther., 175*: 404 (1970).

L. J. Siever, M. S. Kafka, S. Targuin, and C. R. Lake, Platelet alpha adrenergic binding and biochemical responsiveness in depressed patients and controls, *Psychiatry Res., 11*: 387 (1984).

P. Skolnick, J. N. Crawley, J. R. Glowa, and S. Paul, beta-Carboline induced anxiety states, *Psychopathology, 17* (Suppl. 3): 52 (1984).

C. B. Smith, J. A. Garcia-Sevilla, and P. J. Hollingsworth, alpha 2 Adrenoceptors in rat brain are decreased after long-term tricyclic antidepressant drug treatment, *Brain Res, 210*: 413 (1981).

S. M. Stahl, and H. Y. Meltzer, A kinetic and pharmacological analysis of 5-hydroxytryptamine transport by human platelets and platelet storage granules: A comparison with central serotonergic neurons, *J. Pharmacol. Exp. Ther., 205*: 118 (1978).

K. Stärke, Regulation of noradrenaline release by pre-synaptic receptor systems, *Rev. Physiol. Biochem. Pharmacol., 77*: 1 (1977).

K. Stärke, M. Gothert, and H. Kilbinger, Modulation of neurotransmitter release by pre-synaptic autoreceptors, *Physiol. Rev., 69*: 864 (1989).

G. H. Strobel, J. B. Calixto, and G. Ballejo, Decreased GABA modulatory effect on rat vas deferens neurotransmission after chronic administration of imipramine, *Cell Mol. Neurobiol., 9*: 469 (1989).

M. F. Sugrue, Current concepts on the mechanisms of action of antidepressant drugs, *Pharmacol. Ther., 13*: 219 (1981).

F. Sulser, Giovanni Lorenzini Foundation Lecture: Antidepressant drug research: Its impact on neurobiology and psychiatry, *Adv. Biochem. Psychopharmac., 31*: 1 (1982).

F. Sulser, Serotonin-norepinephrine receptor interactions in the rat brain: Implications for the pharmacology and pathophysiology of affective disorders, *J. Clin. Psychiatry., 18*: 12 (1987).

F. Sulser, A. J. Janowsky, F. Okada, D. A. Manier, and P. L. Mobley, Regulation of recognition and function of the norepinephrine coupled adenylate cyclase system in the limbic forebrain: Implications for the therapy of depression, *Neuropharmacology, 22*: 425 (1983).

B. E. Suranyi-Cadotte, P. L. Wood, N. P. Nair, and G. Schwarz, Normalization of platelet ^{3}H-imipramine binding in depressed patients during revision, *Eur. J. Pharmacol., 85*: 357 (1982).

S. W. Tang, S. Cheung, A. Strijewski, J. Chudzik, and D. Helmeste, Anti-imipramine antibodies recognize endogenous serotonin uptake and imipramine binding inhibitors, *Psychiat. Res., 34*: 205 (1990).

J. Tuomisto, and E. Tukiainen, Decreased uptake of 5-hydroxytryptamine in blood platelets from depressed patients, *Nature, 262*: 596 (1976).

J. Tuomisto, E. Tukiainen, and U. G. Ahlfors, Decreased uptake of 5-hydroxytryptamine in blood platelet from patients with endogenous depression, *Psychopharmacology, 65*: 141 (1979).

D. C. U'Prichard, D. A. Greenerg, P. F. Sheehan, and S. H. Snyder, Tricyclic antidepressants: Therapeutic properties and affinity for alpha 1-noradrenergic receptor binding sites in the brain, *Science, 199*: 197 (1978).

H. M. van Praag, Depression, suicide and the metabolism of serotonin in the brain, *J. Affective Disor., 4*: 275 (1982).

H. M. van Praag, J. Korf, and J. Puite, 5-Hydroxyindole acetic acid levels in the cerebrospinal fluid of depressive patients treated with probenecid, *Nature, 225*: 827 (1970).

H. M. van Praag, J. Korf, and J. Schut, Cerebral monoamines and depression: An investigation of the probenecid technique, *Arch. Gen. Psychiatry, 28*: 827 (1973).

H. M. van Praag, and S. de Hahn, Central serotonin deficiency is a factor which increase depression vulnerability?, *Acta Psychiatr. Scand. 280* (Suppl.): 86 (1979).

R. C. Veith, R. E. J. Bielski, V. Bloom, J. A. Fawcett, N. Narasimhachari, and R. O. Friedel, Urinary MHPG excretion and treatment with desipramine or amitriptyline prediction of response, effect of treatment and methodological hazards, *J. Clin. Psychopharmacol., 3*: 18 (1983).

J. Vetulani, R. J. Stawarz, J. V. Dingell, and F. Sulser, F., A possible common mechanism of action of antidepressant treatments, *Arch. Pharmacol., 293*: 109 (1976).

Y. C. Wang, G. N. Pandey, and J. Mendels, Platelet adenylate cyclase in depression, *Psychopharmacology, 36*: 291 (1974).

L. P. Wennogle, and L. R. Meyerson, Serotonin uptake inhibitors differently modulate high affinity imipramine dissociation in human platelet membranes, *Life Sci., 36*: 1541 (1985).

P. Willner, *Depression: A Psychobiological Synthesis,* Wiley-Intersciences, New York (1985).

D. T. Wong, and F. P. Bymaster, Subsensitivity of serotonin receptors after long term treatment of rats with fluoxetine, *Res. Commun. Chem. Pathol. Pharmacol., 32*: 41 (1981).

K. Wood, J. Harwood, and A. Coppen, Platelet accumulation of histamine in controls, depressed and lithium treated patients, *J. Affective Disord., 7*: 149 (1984).

K. Wood, C. Swade, M. H. J. Abou-Saaleh, and A. Coppen, Apparent supersensitivity of platelet 5-HT receptors in lithium treated patients, *J. Affective Disord., 8*: 69 (1985).

16

The Neuropharmacology of Anxiety: A Review on the Role of Serotonin

Herman G.M. Westenberg and Johan A. den Boer
Academic Hospital Utrecht, State University of Utrecht, Utrecht, The Netherlands

I. INTRODUCTION

Anxiety disorders have recently become in a state of flux. The delineation of distinct diagnostic entities and the advent of selective pharmacological probes to explore the integrity of neuronal systems in the brain have resulted in a burgeoning of scientific research in this field. Traditionally, benzodiazepines have been the pharmacological treatment of choice for anxiety disorders. Since their discovery in the early 1960s, this class of compounds has been used extensively in clinical practice to treat anxiety states. Accordingly, the entropy of the γ-aminobutyric acid (GABA) system, whose function can be regulated by benzodiazepines, was considered to be an important determinant in the pathogenesis of anxiety. Animal research has highlighted the limbic system as the site that might be pathogenetically involved in anxiety (Gray, 1982). The notion that this brain area is innervated extensively by ascending monoaminergic fibers, has called the serotonergic and noradrenergic systems into play. Moreover, there is clinical evidence to suggest that disturbances in the regulation of serotonin (5-hydroxytryptophan; 5-HT) and norepinephrine (NE) systems are related to anxiety disorders. This chapter sets out to address the role of 5-HT in the pathogenesis of anxiety disorders. Evidence from animal research studies as well as from clinical interventions are assessed from the perspective of neurotransmitter function. Special attention will be paid to the differential role of 5-HT systems in the various symptom domains.

II. THE SEROTONIN SYSTEM

Our knowledge on the 5-HT-containing pathways is rapidly growing. To date, the complexity of the 5-HT neuronal system in terms of morphological characteristics, receptor subtypes, and biochemical linkages is extraordinary. To follow the results of clinical and preclinical studies described in the following, a concise description of the serotonergic system and the current receptor nomenclature is worthwhile.

A. Serotonergic Pathways in the Central Nervous System

The cell bodies of the 5-HT-containing neurons are located preponderantly in the brain stem. From here, ascending and descending fibers innervate virtually all brain regions. The 5-HT-containing cell bodies that give rise to ascending projections are preponderantly housed in the dorsal and median raphe nuclei. Kosofsky and Molliver (1987) have demonstrated in the rat that fibers emerging from the dorsal raphe and the median raphe are morphologically different: those arising from the dorsal raphe nucleus are fine, with small varicosities, whereas those derived from the median raphe nucleus are thick. The morphological differences between the two systems may signify biochemical and functional differences. Thus, Manoumas and Molliver (1988) have shown that fibers from the dorsal raphe nucleus are more likely to be damaged by the neurotoxin, *p*-chloroamphetamine, than those from the median raphe nucleus. Whether this morphological and anatomical differentiation bears any relevance for the pathogenesis and treatment of anxiety is as yet unclear. Although both nuclei appear to innervate overlapping fields, there are also exceptions. Autoradiographic and microdialysis studies reveal that parts of the limbic system, especially the septohippocampal formation, are furnished, for the most part, by projections from the median raphe, whereas the dorsal raphe, in particular its rostral part, innervates with greater density the neostriatum and the thalamus (Bonvento et al., 1992). It is intriguing that projections from the dorsal raphe nucleus parallel those of dopamine to the striatum, whereas ascending projections from the median raphe nucleus match those of norepinephrine to innervate the hippocampus. Both nuclei send their 5-HT projection to the cortex. It is also of interest, that the locus coeruleus (LC), the principal NE-containing nucleus in the central nervous system (CNS), is reciprocally connected to the raphe nuclei. For example, 5-HT neurons in the dorsal raphe nucleus have anatomical connections with the LC (Descarrier and Leger, 1978; Morgane and Jacobs, 1979; Baraban and Aghajanian, 1980). In addition, there are also several functional interactions between the LC and the raphe nuclei. Serotonin appears to have an inhibitory effect on LC firing (Segal, 1979), whereas NE has an excitatory effect on 5-HT activity in the dorsal raphe nucleus (Baraban and Aghajanian, 1980). Another anatomical site where 5-HT–NE interaction may occur is the terminal areas that are innervated by both monoaminergic pathways. Of particular interest is the hippocampus, which receives dense innervation of both systems. Therefore, mutual interactions are also likely to occur in this region. The 5-HT nerve terminals in the hippocampus are endowed with α_2-adrenoreceptors (Göthert et al., 1981; Frankhuyzen and Mulder, 1980), and there are indications of a modulation of the hippocampal 5-HT release by endogenous NE (Feurstein et al., 1985). Lesion studies have suggested a pivotal role of 5-HT in the regulation of the density and function of central ß-adrenoreceptors (Gillespie et al., 1988).

In view of these complex neuronal interactions—the connections described in the foregoing give only a glimpse of all possible interactions—any theory relating a complex behavior, such as anxiety, to a single neuronal substrate would be a reductionistic oversimplification.

B. Serotonin Receptor Heterogeneity

In the last decade, it has also become evident that multiple 5-HT receptors exist in the brain. The cloning of most 5-HT receptors has verified that they are not pharmacological artifacts, but distinct molecular entities that differ in their ability to recognize agonists and antagonists (Julius, 1991). The classification of 5-HT receptors is largely based on binding studies. Currently, four major classes of 5-HT receptors have been identified in the brain: they are designated as 5-HT_1, 5-HT_2, 5-HT_3, and 5-HT_4 receptors. With the exception of the 5-HT_3 receptor, they all belong to the superfamily of G protein-linked receptors. These receptors transduce signals by activiting G proteins, producing relatively slow responses through second messengers. The 5-HT_3 receptor is unique among the 5-HT receptors in that it is a ligand-gated ion channel, producing rapid depolarizing responses, when stimulated. The 5-HT_1 family can be subdivided into at least five different subtypes, all of which appear to be seven transmembrane domain receptors. They are denoted as 5-HT_{1A}, 5-HT_{1B}, 5-HT_{1C}, 5-HT_{1D}, and 5-HT_{1E}. The 5-HT_1 receptors were originally identified by their high affinity for [^{3}H]5-HT. Although the relatively high affinity of the 5-HT_{1C} receptor for 5-HT resulted in its classification as a 5-HT_1-like receptor, subsequent studies have called this classification into question. Unlike the other 5-HT receptors, the 5-HT_{1C} receptor is not negatively coupled to adenylate cyclase. Similar to the 5-HT_2 receptor, stimulation of the 5-HT_{1C} receptor promotes the hydrolysis of phosphoinositides. In addition to this analogy in signal transduction, both receptors also appear to be closely related from a molecular viewpoint; there appears to be a high degree of amino acid sequence homology. These data suggest that the 5-HT_{1C} receptor should be classified as a member of the 5-HT_2 family. The 5-HT_{1A}, 5-HT_{1B}, and 5-HT_{1D} receptors, all are negatively linked to adenylate cyclase activity. The 5-HT_{1E} is a novel 5-HT receptor subtype, also linked to adenylate cyclase, but for which the exact localization and function in the brain is as yet unknown. The 5-HT_{1B} receptor is found only in some rodents and has been suggested to represent the species equivalent of the 5-HT_{1D} receptor of higher species, in which the 5-HT_{1B} receptors are absent (Hoyer and Middlemiss, 1989). This is supported by recent cloning work that has led to a further differentiation of this receptor subtype into a human 5-$HT_{1D\alpha}$ and 5-$HT_{1D\beta}$ site; a closely related rat 5-$HT_{1D\beta}$ clone is identical with the rat 5-HT_{1B} receptor (Hartig, 1992). The 5-HT_4 receptor represents a new receptor subtype for 5-HT (Demuis et al., 1988). As yet, the molecular structure of the 5-HT_4 receptor has not been reported, but pharmacologically it seems to be closely linked to the 5-HT_1 receptors, as it appears to be positively coupled to adenylate cyclase (Bockaert et al., 1978). This multifaceted nature of 5-HT receptors is amazing, considering the limited number of cell bodies present in the brain. It might explain the diversity of behavioral and physiological processes in which 5-HT appears to play a role. It also articulates the necessity for developing selective drugs, because long-standing pharmacological puzzles and confusions can be solved only when the role of individual molecular processes are understood. The effect of this prospect for psychiatry has only begun to be seen, as will be discussed in the following.

C. The Pharmacological Features of Serotonin Receptors

1. *The Serotonin$_1$ Receptor Family*

The 5-HT_{1A} receptors are selectively labeled by 8-hydroxy-2-(di-*N*-propylamino)tetraline (8-OH-DPAT; see Hamon et al., 1990). The distribution of the 5-HT_{1A}-binding sites is well characterized. The 5-HT_{1A} receptor is highly expressed in the hippocampus, the lateral septum, frontal cortex, and dorsal raphe nucleus in rat and human brain (Pazos and Palazios, 1985; Pazos et al., 1986). Direct application of 8-OH-DPAT to the dorsal or median raphe nuclei reduces hippocampal and striatal 5-HT release, whereas direct application into the hippocampus does not (Verge et al., 1985; Hjorth and Sharp, 1991; Bonvento et al., 1992). These findings suggest that 8-OH-DPAT acts at the somatodendritic 5-HT_{1A} autoreceptors at the raphe cell bodies to decrease 5-HT cell firing and hippocampal release of 5-HT. The 5-HT_{1A} receptors in the hippocampus and cortex are thought to be located postsynaptically (Palacios et al., 1987; Hamon et al., 1990). Stimulation of the 5-HT_{1A} receptor on these postsynaptic target cells inhibits hippocampal activity (Andrade et al., 1986; Yocca, 1990) and reduces the glucose utilization as measured by autoradiographic techniques (Grasby et al., 1992). Recently, a new class of drugs, denoted as azapirones, have been developed for this receptor subtype. Compounds of this class, such as ipsapirone, gepirone, and buspirone, all have been found to mimic the effects of 5-HT at the 5-HT_{1A} site and display an anxiolytic profile in animal models of anxiety (see Traber and Glaser, 1987). Analogous to 8-OH-DPAT, these drugs inhibit the neuronal activity in both the raphe neurons and the hippocampal formation (Yocca, 1990). They also attenuate the 5-HT release in hippocampal perfusates when administered systemically (Sharp et al., 1989). In contrast with 8-OH-DPAT, they are considered as partial agonists on the postsynaptic 5-HT_{1A} receptors (Sprouse and Aghajanian, 1988). Despite this knowledge on the pharmacology of azapirones, the mechanism of action underlying their anxiolytic effects in humans remains obscure. The pharmacological effects on 5-HT_{1A} receptors are immediate, but in several brain regions, especially in the dorsal raphe nucleus, they are also temporary, owing to desensitization of the receptors (Blier and de Montigny, 1987; Fanelli and McMonagle-Strucko, 1992). In rat, anxiolytic activity is already seen after acute systemic or local administration in the dorsal raphe nucleus, suggesting that "turning off" 5-HT function is "anxiolytic" in rats (Higgins et al., 1988). In contrast, the anxiolytic effects in humans emerge over several weeks of treatment. This late onset of action in humans, therefore, poses a serious theoretical problem. It has been argued, therefore, that the therapeutic effects of azapirones in humans are mediated by the down-regulation of the somatodendritic autoreceptors in the raphe nuclei. This is a parsimonious explanation, because it does not take into account the acute effects. If this is so, why does acute administration not worsen the symptomatology? Moreover, down-regulation following chronic treatment would only recuperate the normal firing rate. Another possibility is that these compounds are acting through the postsynaptic 5-HT_{1A} receptors. The late onset of action would then be explained by assuming a down-regulation of the postsynaptic 5-HT_{1A} receptors. Electrophysiological studies have revealed, however, that the responsiveness of the postsynaptic 5-HT_{1A} receptors in the dorsal hippocampus is not altered (Blier and de Montigny, 1990). Similar findings were found in autoradiography studies (Suranyi-Cadotte et al., 1990), although desensitization was found in other brain regions (Fanelli and McMonacle-Strucko, 1992). It is also conceivable that the acute effects on the postsynaptic receptors may have been obliterated by acute effects at the presynaptic sites; from a functional point of view, presynaptic and postsynaptic 5-HT receptors have opposite effects. Another possibility for the delayed action in humans would be adaptive changes in other serotonergic or nonserotonergic receptors. The possibility for one 5-HT receptor subtype to modulate the function of another subtype likewise cannot be excluded (Glennon et al., 1991). Interestingly, azapirones have the ability to down-regulate the 5-

HT_2 receptors (Eison and Yocca, 1985), which have also been linked to anxiety, as will be discussed in the next section, but we are faced with yet another problem. Azapirones are partial agonists (Segal et al., 1989); therefore, it is difficult to ascertain whether they are acting as agonists or as antagonists at the postsynaptic 5-HT receptors. Consequently, clinical studies with full agonists and antagonists are required to further our understanding here.

There are as yet no uniquely selective 5-HT_{1B} ligands available for clinical use, although many of the currently used drugs do have affinity for the 5-HT_{1B} site in rodents. Moreover, the significance of these ligands for clinical use is doubtful, as 5-HT_{1B} sites have not been identified in humans. The human analogue of this receptor, the 5-$HT_{1D\beta}$-binding site, exhibits different pharmacological characteristics. Thus far, clinical application of 5-HT_{1D} receptor agonists (e.g., sumatriptan) has been the domain of neurologists to treat migraine. Therefore, these receptor sites will not be further discussed here.

2. *The Serotonin$_2$ Receptor Family*

Members of the 5-HT_2 family of receptors share the ability to stimulate phosphoinositide hydrolysis. This class was originally differentiated from the 5-HT_1 category on the basis of different affinities for [^{3}H]5-HT and [^{3}H]spiperone. The two members of this family, 5-HT_{1C} and 5-HT_2, are both labeled by the antagonists [^{3}H]mesulergine and [^{3}H]mianserin. Neurons that express 5-HT_{1C} are found to be widely distributed in the brain (Julius, 1991). Aside from the choroid plexus, where it was originally discovered, high densities are seen in the hippocampus, particularly in pryamidal neurons in the ventral part of the hippocampus, the posterior thalamic subnuclei, and in other subcortical regions rich in monoaminergic cells, such as the substantia nigra, LC, and raphe nuclei. In general, the cortical labeling is sparse (Harrington et al., 1992). These findings suggest that 5-HT_{1C} receptors are involved in both pre- and postsynaptic serotonergic mechanisms and may serve as autoreceptors in the somatodendritic region. In view of its expression in the periaqueductal gray matter, 5-HT_{1C} receptors are believed to be implicated also in the processing of afferent sensory information and regulation of nociception (Molineaux et al., 1989; Julius, 1991). *m*-Chlorophenylpiperazine (mCPP), the major metabolite of trazodone, has been described as a potent 5-HT_{1C} agonist, but it is by no means a specific ligand. It has affinity for almost all 5-HT-binding sites, and it also potently binds to α_2-adrenoreceptors (Hoyer, 1988; Schoeffler and Hoyer, 1989; Kilpatrick et al., 1987; Hamik and Peroutka, 1989). Particularly noteworthy is its affinity for the 5-HT_3 receptors, to which it binds as strongly as to 5-HT_{1C} sites. However, constants for affinity in vitro do not necessarily reflect activity in vivo. Despite its limited specificity, mCPP is commonly used as probe for the 5-HT function in psychiatric research (Kahn and Wetzler, 1991). Mianserin is a potent antagonist at the 5-HT_{1C} site.

The other member of this family, the 5-HT_2 receptor, shows the highest density in the frontal cortex, but it also occurs in the striatum, nucleus accumbens, and tuberculum olfactorium (Leysen et al., 1985). Little or no labeling has been found in the thalamus, hippocampus, and brain stem (Pazos et al., 1987). The 5-HT_2-binding sites are also expressed in the periphery, including platelets and smooth muscles. They are selectively labeled by [^{3}H]ketanserin. Many antidepressants have high affinity for the postsynaptic 5-HT_2 receptors, and most of them share the ability to cause a gradual down-regulation of 5-HT_2 receptors in rat brain. This feature of antidepressants has long been considered pertinent to the antidepressant efficacy of this class of drugs, but recent findings have called the relevance of this finding into question (see Charney et al., 1991). Ritanserin, a selective 5-HT_2–5-HT_{1C} receptor antagonist, possesses an anxiolytic profile in some animal models of anxiety (Meert and Janssen, 1989) and exerts anxiolytic effects in patients (Cuelemans et al., 1985).

3. *The Serotonin$_3$ Receptors*

Kilpatrick et al. (1988) were the first to demonstrate the presence of this binding site in rat brain. They reported dense labeling in the entorhinal cortex of this species. Subsequent studies revealed the occurrence throughout the brain, including the hippocampus, amygdala, and brain stem. Selective 5-HT_3 antagonists, such as ICS 205-930, MDL 72,222, ondansetron, and zacopride, have been synthesized, and animal tests suggest they will have anxiolytic activity in humans (Tyers et al., 1987; Costall et al., 1988; Rapp and Przegalinski, 1989). As yet, only preliminary reports of clinical trials have appeared, which are not unequivocal (Lader, 1991).

4. *The Serotonin Transporter*

After its release and action on receptors, 5-HT is inactivated by reuptake through a plasma membrane transporter into the presynaptic nerve terminal, where it may be restored in vesicles or metabolized by monoamine oxidase. This uptake site is an important target of action for antidepressants and other psychotropic drugs. An antidepressant-sensitive transporter has recently been cloned from rat brain (Blakely et al., 1991). It appears to be a protein containing 12 transmembrane-spanning zones, structurally related to the GABA, NE, and dopamine (DA) transporters. Selective serotonin-reuptake inhibitors (SSRIs) increase the extracellular levels of 5-HT after brief administration in vivo. Drugs that selectively inhibit the uptake of 5-HT are not only successful antidepressants, but may also have beneficial effects in various forms of anxiety and related disorders, as will be discussed in the clinical section. The delay in onset of antidepressant or anxiolytic action of SSRIs and related compounds is still puzzling. Why does this delay occur when the inhibition of uptake is immediate? One consequence of the increased synaptic level of 5-HT would be activation of the somatodendritic and terminal autoreceptors, leading to a decreased neuronal firing and terminal release of 5-HT. Artigas et al. (1992), who used in vivo brain microdialysis, reported recently that acute systemic administration of fluvoxamine or clomipramine resulted in a significant increase in the extracellular levels of 5-HT in the raphe nuclei, but not in the frontal cortex, suggesting that the expected increase in 5-HT availability in the terminal area is compensated by a diminished impulse flow caused by excessive activation of the somatodendritic or terminal autoreceptors.

In keeping with this finding, electrophysiological findings have revealed that short-term administration of SSRIs leads to a reduction in 5-HT neuronal firing, whereas long-term treatment will restore the normal impulse flow (de Montigny and Aghajanian, 1978; Chaput et al., 1988; Blier et al., 1988). Autoradiographic studies have shown that prolonged treatment with SSRIs may reduce the number of 5-HT_{1A}-binding sites in the dorsal raphe nucleus (Welner et al., 1989). Moret and Briley (1990), studying the in vitro release of 5-HT, found that treatment with citalopram, a novel SSRI, for 21 days also resulted in a down-regulation of the terminal 5-HT autoreceptors in rat brain slices. Desensitization of these autoreceptors would permit these neurons to restore their normal firing rate, resulting in a net gain in efficacy of synaptic signal transduction following long-term treatment. If this reasoning is correct one would predict SSRIs to exert their anxiolytic and antidepressant action by enhancing 5-HT neurotransmission. In keeping with this theory, Chaput et al. (1988) have reported that the response of hippocampal pyramidal cells to activation of the afferent 5-HT fibers in rats was unchanged after acute treatment with fluoxetine or citalopram, but markedly enhanced following chronic treatment with citalopram or zimeldine. Since direct microiontophoretic application of 5-HT did not reveal a heightened responsiveness after chronic treatment, it was concluded, therefore, that SSRIs enhance 5-HT functioning by increasing the amount of 5-HT released per impulse and not by increasing the sensitivity of the postsynaptic 5-HT receptors. Interestingly, short- and long-term administration of gepirone, a 5-HT_{1A} agonist, mimicked the effects of SSRIs (Blier and de Montigny, 1990), suggesting that it possesses similar 5-HT-modifying characteristics. Obviously, processes beyond the 5-HT receptors must also be taken into account when a delayed onset of action is to be explained.

E. Conclusion

The 5-HT system in the brain shows striking diversity and complexity, particularly in terms of receptor heterogeneity and neurochemical coupling to intracellular processes. Moreover, there are indications that the 5-HT system is composed of two parallel systems, which might be functionally different and could, in some instances, innervate corresponding areas. This diversity may explain why such a discrete neuronal system, of which most ascending fibers are housed in two small brain stem nuclei, is involved in such an array of behaviors and physiological processes. There is already abundant evidence that these various functions are mediated through different 5-HT receptor subtypes, of which each has a specific function and distribution pattern. A more complete characterization of the receptors and the genes encoding them, and the development of selective compounds for clinical use, may provide the tools necessary to achieve a more detailed understanding of the events that take place during drug therapy and may enrich our insights in the pathogenesis of the different psychiatric conditions.

The prospect for psychiatry would be not only a better understanding of the disease, but we hope also a greater therapeutic armamentarium.

III. ANIMAL EXPERIMENTS AND SEROTONIN

The growing evidence for the role of 5-HT in anxiety has led to a renewed interest in animal models for anxiety. To examine the wide range of compounds that modify 5-HT neurotransmission, a variety of animal models of anxiety have been employed. In the following section the results of these exercises will be reviewed, but we will begin with a brief description of the commonly used animal models of anxiety.

A. Animal Models of Anxiety

Generally, two main categories of animal models can be distinguished: the conditioned behavior models and the unconditioned behavior models. For a more detailed description see Barrett (1991).

1. *Conditioned Behavior Models*

The conditioned behavior models involve responses developed and controlled by operant-conditioning behavior. The models currently most frequently used are (1) the conflict paradigm, (2) the potentiated startle response, and (3) the periaqueductal gray stimulation.

The Conflict Paradigm. In the conflict model, the animal is conditioned to press a lever to obtain a reward (e.g., food). In the Geller–Seifter version of this model (Geller and Seifter, 1960), lever-pressing following a distinct stimulus (e.g., light) results in the presentation of food and a punishment (e.g., electric shock). Thus, the animal is faced with a conflict between reward and punishment, which will result in a suppressed response. A variety of anxiolytic drugs (e.g., benzodiazepine) consistently produce an attenuation of the behavioral suppression, which is considered to be an indicator for anxiolytic activity in this model. The Vogel conflict model is a variation of this procedure. This test uses water-deprived rats in which licking is suppressed by shocks (Vogel et al., 1971).

The Potentiated Startle Response. A more recently developed test is the fear-potentiated startle response (see Davis, 1988). The startle reflex to a signal (e.g., a loud sound) is potentiated in the presence of a stimulus previously coupled with shock. Benzodiazepines as well as nonbenzodiazepine anxiolytics block the potentiated startle response.

Periaqueductal Gray Stimulation. Focal stimulation of the dorsal part of the periaqueductal gray (DPAG) of the midbrain produces aversive behavioral responses, reflected in animals by fear or flight reactions. The dorsal part of the DPAG belongs to a neuronal system responsible for the behavioral and autonomic expression of defense reaction and for the elaboration of aversive stimuli. The "fear" that can be elicited in animals by electrical stimulation is not dependent on environmental changes, as is true in most conditioned and unconditioned models of anxiety (for review see Graeff, 1990). Anxiolytic drugs raise the threshold for these reactions.

This model has strong face validity for panic disorder, because electrical stimulation in the dorsal midbrain in humans has also been reported to result in strong paniclike reactions (Nashold et al., 1969). Patients with chronically implanted electrodes into the lateral part of the central gray expressed emotional and autonomic reaction that closely resembled a panic attack as defined in the *DSM-III-R* (American Psychiatric Association, 1987), when stimulated.

2. *Unconditioned Behavior Models*

Elevated Plus Maze Test. The elevated plus maze model measures the proportion of entries in the open arms and the time spent on the open arms relative to the total time spent in an elevated maze with intersecting arms, two of which are open and two closed (Pellow et al., 1985; Pellow and File, 1986). An anxiolytic effect is indicated in this model by increases in open-arm entries, without altering the total number of arm entries. A variant of this model is the two-compartment model: a large brightly lit and a small dimly illuminated area.

The Social Interaction Test. The social interaction test measures the effect of drugs on social interaction of rats under levels of high illumination in a novel environment. Anxiolytic drugs, such as the benzodiazepines, increase social interaction under these circumstances, particularly after repeated administration (see File, 1980, 1988).

Other frequently used tests are the distress vocalization test and the defensive burying test (Gardner, 1985; Insel et al., 1986).

3. *General Remarks*

We have not addressed all available animal models of anxiety, and many methodological problems and caveats had to be left undiscussed. The interested reader is referred to the reviews cited in the foregoing. Suffice it to say that each model has specific advantages and disadvantages for clarifying different aspects of anxiety. A general difficulty with most animal models of anxiety is that their face and construct validity is poor. Most studies use the induction of fear as an analogy to human anxiety, and the validation is usually based on their responses to benzodiazepines. Benzodiazepines are considered the treatment of choice in generalized anxiety, but their effects on other anxiety symptoms are either absent or controversial. Hence, extrapolation from animal behavior to anxiety in humans is precarious. Human anxiety can range from normal emotions to clinical syndromes; it can be a component of a physical and mental disorder, but it can also be the central feature of a syndrome. Moreover, anxiety, as a disorder in humans, can be divided into different syndromes. The prevailing animal models of anxiety by no means reflect these different diagnostic entities.

B. Animal Models and Serotonin Neurotransmission

1. *Lesion Studies*

One approach to manipulate 5-HT function is to make selective lesions in 5-HT-containing regions, 5,7-Dihydroxytryptamine (5,7-DHT) and 5,6-DHT are agents toxic to 5-HT neurons. The neurotoxin 5,7-DHT releases punished-responding after injection into the ascending 5-HT pathways at the level of ventral tegmentum and after intraventricular administration (Tye et al., 1977; Lippa et al., 1979). Other investigators, however, have failed to produce a reduction in anxiety following DHT lesions using similar models of anxiety (Commissaris et al., 1981; Thiébot et al., 1984).

Contradictory results have also been observed with other animal models of anxiety. When using the social interaction test, File et al. (1979) did not observe an increase in social interaction after lesioning of the dorsal raphe with 5,7-DHT, whereas Briley et al. (1980) found that intraventricular administration of this neurotoxin resulted in an increase in the ratio of open-arm entries in the elevated plus maze, which is taken as an indication of anxiolytic activity. In part, these disparities might be attributed to the limited specificity of 5,7-DHT to produce 5-HT lesions. Nonserotonergic cell bodies within the raphe nuclei and fibers in the adjacent tegmental nuclei can also be damaged by 5,7-DHT application (Lorens, 1978). A methodological flaw is that 5,7-DHT lesions have a profound effect on appetite (Barofsky et al., 1980). This poses a serious problem, as many of the conditioned behavior models are motivated by appetitive rewards.

In summary, lesion studies suggest, although not consistently, that destruction of 5-HT neurons may result in a behavioral profile resembling anxiolytic activity.

2. *Inhibition of Serotonin Synthesis*

The probability of a close link between 5-HT and anxiety was demonstrated by the pioneering work of Geller and Blum (1970), who found that inhibition of 5-HT synthesis with the tryptophan hydroxylase inhibitor *p*-chlorophenylalanine (pCPA), resulted in an increase in food-motivated, punished behavior in laboratory animals. The effect of pCPA on behavioral suppression could be abolished by the administration of 5-hydroxytryptophan (5-HTP), the immediate precursor of 5-HT, supporting the idea that this effect may result from a decreased 5-HT availability (Geller and Blum, 1970). By and large, studies involving pCPA have yielded more consistent results than studies using 5,7-DHT (Hartman and Geller, 1971; Tye et al., 1979), although negative studies have also been reported (Blakely and Parker, 1973). In the social interaction model, pCPA increased suppressed social interaction, hinting also at an anxiolytic effect of pCPA administration (File and Hyde, 1977).

In summary, studies with pCPA are consistent with the idea that anxiolysis is related to a reduction in 5-HT turnover. Like 5,7-DHT, the findings with pCPA are confounded because administration of this agent causes an increase in food intake and water licking. In view of the nonspecificity of these lesions and the complexity of the 5-HT system, it is difficult to interpret these findings in terms of functional activity.

3. *Nonselective Serotonin Agonists*

If a reduced 5-HT turnover leads to an anxiolytic profile in animal models of anxiety, it is tempting to speculate that the reverse would also be true. Consistent with this idea, File and Lemaitre (1988) found that fenfluramine, a compound that releases 5-HT from its stores and inhibits it uptake, displays anxiogenic features in the social interaction test and the elevated plus maze. 5-Hydroxytryptophan, the indirect 5-HT agonist, produced anxiolytic effects at lower doses, but anxiogenic effects in the higher dose range in a modified Vogel's drinking conflict test (Hjorth et al., 1987). The nonselective 5-HT_1 agonist, mCPP, a compound that has been reported to be anxiogenic in humans, possesses similar characteristics in the conflict model (Kilts et al., 1982) and in the social interaction test (Kennett et al., 1989), whereas in other animal models (e.g., potentiated startle response), it was without effect (Mansbach and Geyer, 1988). Local application of mCPP into the hippocampus was anxiogenic, but injections into the amygdala had no effect on social interaction. The effect of mCPP on social interaction was blocked by three antagonists that share a high affinity for 5-HT_{1C}–5-HT_2 receptors, mianserin, cyproheptadine, and metergoline, but not by the selective 5-HT_2 antagonist, ketanserin, and the 5-HT_{1A}–5-HT_{1B} agonists, cyanopindolol and propranolol. The effects were also blocked by low doses of the 5-HT_3 antagonist ICS 205-930. These findings argue for an anxiogenic action of mCPP mediated through the 5-HT_{1C} receptors. Food-motivated models, such as the conflict test, are hampered because mCPP may reduce food intake in rats (Samanin et al., 1979; Fuller et al., 1981). The results of the social interaction test are likewise confounded by the effect of mCPP on motor activity (Gerson and Baldessarini, 1980). In a recent study, both mCPP and trifluoromethylphenylpiperazine (TFMPP), a 5-HT agonist that exhibits a certain selectivity for 5-HT_{1B} receptors and 5-HT transporter, displayed an anxiogenic profile in the elevated plus maze (Benjamin et al., 1990). Surprisingly, the effects of both agents could be antagonized by the selective 5-HT_{1B} agonist CGS 12066B, suggesting that the in vivo effects of mCPP and TFMPP might be due to an antagonistic effect on the 5-HT_{1B} terminal autoreceptors. Clearly, interactions through other 5-HT receptors with opposing influences on the neurons on which the 5-HT system is impinging, cannot be ruled out. In contrast, both mCPP and TFMPP reduce the effects of electrical stimulation in the DPAG model following acute systemic administration, hinting at an anxiolytic activity in this animal model (Jenck et al., 1989b, 1990a). The antiaversive effects of mCPP could be prevented by pretreatment with mianserin, a 5-HT_{1C} antagonist. The 5-HT_{1C}–5-HT_2 antagonists, ritanserin and metergoline, were anxiogenic, whereas the selective 5-HT_2 antagonist, ketanserin, displayed opposite effects in the same model (Jenck et al., 1990a). In contrast, Schütz et al. (1985) found that local administration of ketanserin did have an effect on aversion when given alone. Microinjections of 5-HT into the dorsal midbrain of rats bearing permanently implanted electrodes, raised the threshold for escape reaction dose-dependently (Schütz et al., 1985). This effect could be antagonized by local application of 5-HT_2

antagonists, such as ketanserin, suggesting that 5-HT plays an inhibitory role in the DPAG-controlled aversion, probably mediated by 5-HT_2 receptors, and that this effect is phasic, rather than tonic. Treatment with 5-HTP agonist, dose-dependently diminishes aversive reactions produced by DPAG stimulation. Electrophysiological data have revealed that ketanserin inhibits the excitatory effects of 5-HT on neurons in the DPAG (Brandao et al., 1991). These findings support the idea of Deakin (1989) that 5-HT_2 mechanisms in the DPAG may mediate panic anxiety in patients with panic disorder (PD).

In summary, the overall picture that emerges from the foregoing cited data is that 5-HT mechanisms are implicated in anxietylike behavior in animals. Yet it is difficult to make any coherence from this collection of data. The direction of the effects, anxiolytic or anxiogenic, depends not only on the model that is being used, but also on the route of administration, as is illustrated by the DPAG data with ketanserin, and on the dose, as is exemplified by the 5-HTP data in the conflict test. Moreover, some animal data are not in agreement with the clinical results obtained with the same compounds in some, but not all, forms of anxiety as will be discussed in the section on clinical data supporting the role of 5-HT in anxiety.

4. *Behavioral Effects of Drugs Acting at Serotonin-1A*

The behavioral effects of 5-HT_{1A} receptor agonists and partial agonists, are summarized in Tables 1–4. Studies with 5-HT_{1A} agonists are complicated because this class of receptors is located both presynaptically, where the agonist exerts an inhibitory effect on 5-HT neurotransmission by "turning down" the firing rate after acute administration, and postsynaptically, where it is assumed to have an enhancing effect on 5-HT function. Generally, data on the effects of 5-HT_{1A} agonists are quite inconsistent. The full agonist 8-OH-DPAT is anxiolytic, anxiogenic, or has no effect in the various animal models (see Table 1 for references). Particularly, the elevated plus maze shows contradictory results. In some studies with this model, 8-OH-DPAT produced anxiogeniclike reactions, whereas other investigators have reported anxiolytic effects with the same model. Anxiolytic effects were also found for 8-OH-DPAT in the social interaction test and the distress vocalization test, but in the DPAG model this compound decreased the threshold for aversive reaction, indicating an anxiogenic activity.

For buspirone, a partial and nonselective agonist, the results are, on the whole, more consistent (see Table 2). Most conflict tests using punishment of drinking have shown an increase in responding, which is considered to predict an anxiolytic effect. However, in almost every experiment in which benzodiazepines were compared with buspirone, the effect of the latter was much smaller. Results in other models were more variable, suggesting either an anxiolytic activity or no effect. Other 5-HT_{1A} partial agonists, such as ipsapirone and gepirone, are also active in several models of anxiety, including the conflict test, the social interaction test, the elevated plus maze, the potentiated startle paradigm, and the two-compartment model (see Tables 3 and 4 for references).

Interestingly, most convincing results suggesting anxiolytic effects in animal tests were obtained in species other than rat or mouse. In pigeons, both buspirone (Barrett et al., 1986; Witkin et al., 1987; Mansbach et al., 1988) and gepirone (Barrett et al., 1986; Mansbach et al., 1988) show unequivocal release of suppression in conflict tests. In two studies in squirrel monkeys, buspirone displayed anxiolytic properties in the conflict test (Geller and Hartmann, 1982; Weissman et al., 1984). In another study with the same species and model, but higher doses of buspirone, the drug was ineffective; at the dos-

Table 1 Effects of 5-HT_{1A}-Agonists in Animal Models of Anxiety: 8-OH-DPAT

Author	Model[a]	Dosage (mg/kg)	Effect[a]	Anxiety[b]
Deacon and Gardner, 1986	GS	0.25	No effect	0
Ketelaars, 1990	GS	1	No effect	0
Carli and Samanin, 1988	Water-lick	0.125–20 in MRN	↓ Suppression	–
Critchey and Handley, 1987	Elevated plus maze	0.015–1.0	↓ In entry ratio	+
Pellow et al., 1987	Elevated plus maze	0.0625–0.25	No effect	
Critchley et al., 1989	Elevated plus maze	0.1	↓ In exploration	
Dunn et al., 1989	Elevated plus maze	0.2	↑ Time open arms	–
Moser et al., 1990	Elevated plus maze	30–150	↓ % Open arm entries	+
Davis et al., 1988	FPS	2.5–10	No effect	0
Mansbach and Geyer, 1988	FPS	0.125–0.5	Blockade	–
Carli and Samanin, 1988	Two-compartment	0.125–2.0	No effect	0
Dunn et al., 1989	SI	0.125–0.25	↑ SI	–
Mos and Olivier, 1990	Separation vocalization	0.1–0.2	↓ In calling	–
Olivier et al., 1990	Four-plate test	1.0–0.4	↑ In crossings	–
Jenck et al., 1989a	DPAG	0.1–1.0	Proaversive	+

[a] GS, Geller–Seifter test; MRN, median raphe nucleus; SI, social interaction; DPAG, Dorsal periaquaductal gray; FPS, fear-potentiated startle.
[b] (+), increase in anxiety; (–), reduction in anxiety; (0), no effect.

ages used in this trial even a decreased response was noted in some animals, hinting at an anxiogenic activity at higher doses. Recently, flesinoxan, a novel 5-HT_{1A} agonist, surpassing buspirone and other azapirones in selectivity and potency, was developed. Flesinoxan seems to induce a typical 5-HT syndrome, which is purported to be mediated by the 5-HT_{1A} receptor (Molewijk et al., 1990), and it also shows high affinity for binding sites labeled by 8-[^{3}H]OH-DPAT. Existing evidence suggests that flesinoxan, in contrast with buspirone, gepirone, and ipsapirone, is a full agonist at the 5-HT_{1A} receptors (Schipper et al., 1990). The behavioral pattern in rats parallels that of 8-OH-DPAT (Ybema et al., 1990). In the conflict test in pigeons, flesinoxan led to a release of suppressed behavior (Barrett et al., 1989a), whereas in the four-plate test and the two-compartment model it was ineffective (Olivier et al., 1990). In a recent study, flesinoxan was reported to reduce separation-induced ultrasonic vocalizations, elicited in rat pups (Mos and Olivier, 1990; Mos et al., 1990). These findings hint at an anxiolytic profile of flesinoxan in some animal models of anxiety.

There are several explanations for the inconsistencies obtained with 5-HT_{1A} agonists in animal models of anxiety. First, buspirone, which has been most extensively studied, is a nonselective 5-HT_{1A} agonist, in that it also possesses dopaminergic activity. It has been demonstrated that buspirone, but not gepirone, increases dopamine synthesis in the

able 2 Effects of 5-HT_{1A}-Agonists in Animal Models of Anxiety: Buspirone

uthor	Model[a]	Dose (mg/kg)	Effect[a]	Anxiety[b]
eismann et al., 1984	Water-lick	0.5–5	↓ Suppression	−
nger et al., 1985	Water-lick	30–100	↓ Suppression	−
son et al., 1986	Water-lick	10	↓ Suppression	−
cCloskey et al., 1987	Water-lick	0.25–1	↓ Suppression	−
ch and Samanin, 1986	Water-lick	0.6, 1.2	↓ Suppression	−
hefke et al., 1989	Water-lick	0.5, 1.2	↓ Suppression	−
oser et al., 1990	Water-lick	0.5–2	↓ Suppression	−
ellow and File, 1986	Elevated plus maze	0.5–20	No effect	0
ellow et al., 1987	Elevated plus maze	4,8	↓ % Time spent in open arm	+
oser, 1989	Elevated plus maze	0.25–2	↓ % Time spent in open arm	+
oser et al., 1990	Elevated plus maze	0.5–2	↓ % Time spent in open arm	+
unn et al., 1989	Elevated plus maze	1	↑ % Time spent in open arm	−
eller and Hartmann, 1982	GS	0.5–7.5	↓ Suppression	−
oldberg et al., 1983	GS	10, 50	No effect	0
oung et al., 1987	GS	30–40	↓ Suppression	−
ile, 1984	SI	0.25, 0.5, 2.5	No effect	0
uy and Gardner, 1985	SI (modified)	5, 10, 20	↑ In SI	−
unn et al., 1989	SI	5, 10	↑ In SI	−
ich and Samanin, 1986	Two-compartment	0.6, 1.2	↑ In BWT	−
ostall et al., 1988	Two-compartment	0.06–2	↑ % Time light area	−
arli et al., 1989	Two-compartment	0.1	↑ In BWT	−
naivi and Martin, 1989	Two-compartment	10, 25, 50	↑ % Time light area	−
ilfoil et al., 1989	Two-compartment	0.1–10	↓ % Time dark side	−
avis et al., 1988	FPS	5, 10	Blockade	−
ehne et al., 1988	FPS	0.6–5	Blockade	−
ansbach and Geyer, 1988	FPS	1.25–5.0	Blockade	−
os and Olivier, 1990	Separation vocalization	0.3–3	↓ In calling	−
livier et al., 1990	Four-plate test	0.1–8	No effect	0

FPS, fear-potentiated startle; BWT, black–white transitions; SI, social interaction; GS, Geller–Seifter test.
(+), increase in anxiety; (−), reduction in anxiety; (0), no effect.

nucleus accumbens (Neisewander et al., 1990). Thus, some of the effects of buspirone might theoretically be explained by its action on dopamine systems. Second, all 5-HT_{1A} agonists show a dose-related decrease in locomotion (Mitman and Geyer, 1989), which might at least partly explain some of the controversial data. Intraperitoneal administration of 5-HT_{1A} agonists, such as 8-OH-DPAT, buspirone, ipsapirone, and gepirone, results in a biphasic response pattern. Moderate doses lead to anxiolytic responses in the elevated plus maze, whereas higher doses appear to be anxiogenic. Third, it has been

Table 3 Effects of 5-HT_{1A}-Agonists in Animal Models of Anxiety: Ipsapirone

Author	Model[a]	Dosage (mg/kg)	Effect[a]	Anxiety[b]
Critchley and Handley, 1989	X-maze	1.0	↑ In exploration	–
Deacon and Gardner, 1986	GS	2.5	No effect	0
Young et al., 1987	GS	5–60	↑ Suppression	–
Fernández-Guasti and López-Rubalcava, 1990	Two-compartment	25, 5	↑ In BWT	–
Davis et al., 1988	FPS	10–40	Blockade at 40 mg/kg	–
Mansbach and Geyer, 1988	FPS	1.0–10	Blockade	–
Moser, 1989	Elevated plus maze	0.025–10	↓ % Open arm entries	+
Pellow et al., 1987	Elevated plus maze	2.5–10	↓ % time open arms	+
Mos and Olivier, 1990	Separation vocalization	0.3–3	↓ In callings	–
Olivier et al., 1990	Four-plate test	0.025, 0.2, 0.3	↑ In Crossings	–

[a] GS, Geller–Seifter test; BWT, Black–white transitions; FPS, fear- potentiated startle.
[b] (+), increase in anxiety; (–), reduction in anxiety; (0), no effect.

shown in several studies that 5-HT_{1A} agonists stimulate appetite, which is a serious flaw in food-motivated behavioral models. Finally, in contrast with animal models of anxiety in which effects are usually seen immediately, these compounds have a delayed onset of action in humans, suggesting that adaptive changes are responsible for the clinical effects of these drugs.

5. *Serotonin$_{1A}$ Agonists: Mechanism of Action*

The mechanism through which these drugs exert their behavioral profiles reminiscent of anxiety is still unclear. Several possibilities, including the stimulation of the somatodendritic 5-HT_{1A} autoreceptors, or stimulation of the corresponding postsynaptic receptors have been proposed. Engel et al. (1984) have reported that the anxiolytic effect of 8-OH-DPAT in the conflict model is reversed after pretreatment with pCPA. The

Table 4 Effects of 5-HT_{1A}-Agonists in Animal Models of Anxiety: Gepirone

Author	Model[a]	Dosage (mg/kg)	Effect[a]	Anxiety[b]
Young et al., 1987	GS	40–80	↓ Suppression	–
Dunn et al., 1989	SI	5–10	↑ In SI	–
Dunn et al., 1989	Elevated plus maze	1–2.5	↑ % time open arm	–
Eison et al., 1986	Water-lick	10	↓ Suppression	–
Barrett et al., 1986	GS (pigeon)	0.1–1.0	↓ Suppression	–
Mansbach et al., 1988	GS (pigeon)	0.1–1.0	↓ Suppression	–

[a] GS, Geller–Seifter test; SI, social interaction.
[b] (+), increase in anxiety; (–), reduction in anxiety; (0), no effect.

authors tentatively attributed this finding to a sensitization of the postsynaptic 5-HT_{1A} receptors. Similar results were obtained in the conflict test (Söderpalm et al., 1989; Söderpalm and Engel, 1990). The biphasic dose–response relation described earlier, might also be explained by assuming a dose-dependent stimulation of pre- or postsynaptic receptors. This idea is consistent with the notion that most 5-HT_{1A} agonists are full agonist on somatodendritic autoreceptors, but mixed agonists–antagonists at hippocampal pyramidal cells. After using the defensive burying paradigm, Fernández-Guasti et al. (1992) recently reported that buspirone and ipsapirone, but not 8-OH-DPAT, produce exactly the same results in 5,7-DHT-lesioned animals as in controls. These data suggest that partial agonists exert their anxiolytic activity through postsynaptic receptors. A confounding factor was that 5,7-DHT by itself produces anxiolytic effects. In contrast, the integrity of the 5-HT system appeared to be essential for the full agonist, 8-OH-DPAT, to exert its anxiolytic activity in this animal model.

6. *Serotonin$_2$ Receptor Antagonists in Animal Models of Anxiety*

As indicated in Table 5, the nonselective 5-HT_2 receptor antagonists, cinanserin, cyproheptadine, methysergide, metergoline, and the mixed 5-HT_{1C}–5-HT_2 antagonist, ritanserin, all showed mixed results in several tests. Generally, their anxiolytic activity is rather weak as compared with benzodiazepines. Stutzmann et al. (1991), who used a selective 5-HT_2 antagonist, RP 62203, and ritanserin in the elevated plus maze, found that RP 62203 dose-dependently increased the number of entries into and the time spent in open arms, whereas ritanserin was ineffective in this study. Moreover, the anxiolytic effects of RP 62203 could be antagonized by the putative anxiogenic FG 7142, at a dose devoid of anxiogenic activity, whereas ritanserin seemed to potentiate this effect. In one study, ritanserin was anxiolytic in the elevated plus maze in animals receiving the drug chronically, but ineffective after acute treatment (Wright et al., 1991), thus correlating with clinical findings (Ceulemans et al., 1985).

The DPAG model reveals rather conflicting data. The mixed 5-HT_2–5-HT_{1C} receptor antagonists, such as cyproheptadine, mianserin, and ritanserin, were anxiogenic, whereas the selective 5-HT_2 receptor blocker, ketanserin, appeared to be anxiolytic in this model. Given that the 5-HT_{1C} agonist mCPP is antiaversive, one might argue that the proaversive effects of the mixed antagonists following acute administration are mediated through the 5-HT_{1C} receptors. As yet, no firm conclusion can be drawn from the currently available animal data concerning the involvement of 5-HT_2 receptors in anxiety.

7. *Serotonin$_3$ Receptor Antagonists in Animal Models of Anxiety*

Information on the anxiolytic activity of 5-HT_3 antagonists is now relatively limited, but ondansetron (GR 38032F), ICS 202-930, and zacopride, all exhibit anxiolytic activity in the two-compartment model (Costall and Nayler, 1992; Kilfoil et al., 1989; Onaivi and Martin, 1989). In the Vogel test, all three were ineffective (Jones et al., 1988; Tyers, 1989), and the social interaction model yielded inconsistent results (Piper et al., 1988; File and Johnston, 1989; Jones et al., 1988; Costall et al., 1989a,b). In the elevated plus maze, ondansetron and BRL 43694 were also ineffective (File and Johnston, 1989). In a recent study, ondansetron did not change 5-HT metabolism in the dorsal raphe nucleus, hippocampus, or amygdala, nor did it affect DA metabolism (Koulou et al., 1990). Ondansetron also induces behavior reminiscent of the 5-HT syndrome in rats. In low doses (2.5 mg/kg), it induces flattened body posture; at intermediate doses, it leads to straub tail and head weaving; whereas at 10 mg/kg it elicits convulsions and death (Hendrie, 1990). Originally 5-HT_3 ligands were developed as peripheral antagonists for

Table 5 5-HT$_2$ Receptor Antagonists in Animal Models of Anxiety

Author	Drug	Model[a]	Dose (mg/kg)	Effect[a]	Anxiety
Winter, 1972	Cinanserin	GS	3–15	No effect	0
Geller et al., 1974	Cinanserin	GS	60	↓ Suppression	–
Cook and Sepinwall, 1975	Cinanserin	GS	15	↓ Suppression	–
Kilts et al., 1981	Cinanserin	Water-lick	56	↓ Suppression	–
Kilts et al., 1982	Cinanserin	Water-lick	10–100	↓ Suppression	–
Peterson and Larssen, 1981	Cinanserin	Water-lick	10–60	No effect	0
Davis et al., 1988	Cinanserin	FPS	10	No effect	0
Graeff, 1974	Cyproheptadine	GS	3–10	↓ Suppression	–
Ketelaars and Bruinvels, 1989	Cyproheptadine	GS	7–10	↓ Suppression on + ↑ extinction	–
Kilts et al., 1982	Cyproheptadine	Water-lick	1–18	No effect	0
Peterson and Larssen, 1981	Cyproheptadine	Water-lick	1–10	No effect	
Davis et al., 1988	Cyproheptadine	FPS	5	No effect	0
Costall et al., 1988	Cyproheptadine	Two-compartment	0.05–10	No effect	0
Jenck et al., 1990a	Cyproheptadine	DPAG	1–10	Proaversive	
Graeff and Schonfeld, 1970	Methysergide	GS	0.3	↓ Suppression	–
Winter, 1972	Methysergide	GS	0.3	↓ Suppression	–
Graeff, 1974	Methysergide	GS	3–10	↓ Suppression	–
Cook and Sepinwall, 1975	Methysergide	GS	1–10	↓ Suppression	–
Kilts et al., 1981	Methysergide	Water-lick	1–10	↓ Suppression	–
Kilts et al., 1982	Methysergide	Water-lick	1–18	No effect	0
Peterson and Larsson, 1981	Methysergide	Water-lick	0.3–3	No effect	0
File, 1981	Methysergide	SI	10–30	No effect	0
Costall et al., 1988	Methysergide	Two-compartment	0.05–10	No effect	0
Leone et al., 1983	Metergoline	GS	0.56	↓ Suppression	–
Kilts et al., 1982	Metergoline	Water-lick	0.25–2	↓ Suppression at 0.7 mg/kg	–
File, 1981	Metergoline	SI	2–4	No effect	0
Pellow et al., 1987	Metergoline	Elevated plus maze	4	↑ % time open arms	–
Costall et al., 1988	Metergoline	Two-compartment	0.05–10	No effect	0
Jenck et al., 1989b	Metergoline	DPAG	0.052–10	Proaversive	+
Ketelaars and Bruinvels, 1989	Ritanserin	GS	20	No effect	0
Colpaert et al., 1985	Ritanserin	Water-lick	25–10	↓ Suppression	–
Critchley and Handley, 1987	Ritanserin	Elevated plus maze	0.025–5.0	↑ Entry ratio	–
Pellow et al., 1987	Ritanserin	Elevated plus maze	0.25–1.0	↓ % Open arms	+
Costall et al., 1988	Ritanserin	Two-compartment	0.05–10	No effect	0
Jenck et al., 1990a	Ritanserin	DPAG	0.1–32	Proaversive	+

[a] GS, Geller–Seifter; FPS, fear-potentiated startle; DPAG, dorsal periaquaductal gray stimulation test; SI, social interaction.
[b] (+), increase in anxiety; (–), decrease in anxiety; (0), no effect.

their potential use in migraine and emesis. Recently, 5-HT_3 antagonists have been proposed as anxiolytics, antipsychotics, and as antiaddictive drugs.

It is unlikely that all these therapeutic claims will be fulfilled in humans. Yet, centrally acting 5-HT_3 antagonists offer an alternative approach to study the pathogenesis of anxiety in relation to 5-HT.

8. *Serotonin-Reuptake Inhibitors*

Although originally developed as antidepressants, SSRIs have received equal attention for their potential use in anxiety disorders, as will be discussed later. Although rather divers in terms of chemical structure, this class of compounds has the common ability to block the 5-HT transporter and to alleviate symptoms of depression and anxiety in humans. Which 5-HT pathways, in what brain area, and which 5-HT receptor subtypes are implicated in the various pharmacological effects of SSRIs are hard to assess. The finding that these compounds have a delayed onset of action suggests that adaptive changes are required for these drugs to become effective.

Antidepressants are ineffective in the conflict test and the drug discrimination model after acute treatment (Mason et al., 1987). While studying the effects of several antidepressants after long-term administration, Commisaris and Fontana (1991) recently reported a gradually developing anticonflict effect, with a latency of onset of 3–5 weeks. The SSRIs have also been reported to exert antiaversive effects in the DPAG model after acute administration. This finding suggests that an increased availability in the DPAG reduces the aversion induced by stimulation (Jenck et al., 1990b). Zimeldine, injected into the midbrain, displayed antiaversive effects that could be antagonized by the mixed 5-HT_{1C}–5-HT_2 antagonist, ritanserin (Audi et al., 1988).

9. *Summary of the Animal Findings*

There is not yet a single model of anxiety that may be said to correspond to a particular type of anxiety disorder in humans, and there are several incongruities in response—anxiolytic in animal models and anxiogenic in humans or vice versa—and drug regimens or acute administration in animals as opposed to chronic administration in clinical studies. In this sense, none of the tests summarized in the foregoing has sufficient validity. Nonetheless, the studies cited, for the most part, strongly suggest the involvement of 5-HT in anxiety. In view of the complexity of the 5-HT system, it is difficult to make any prediction whether an increased or decreased 5-HT function is implicated in anxiety, although lesion studies suggest that diminishing 5-HT function results in a decrease in anxiety.

IV. CLINICAL STUDIES

Recent progress in the field of 5-HT and the advent of novel 5-HT selective drugs with anxiolytic properties in animal models have generated a renewed interest in the role of 5-HT in anxiety disorders. Clinical evidence on the role of 5-HT is mainly derived from treatment studies and challenge paradigms with nonselective drugs. In addition, surrogate measurements in accessible biological samples, including blood, cerebrospinal fluid (CSF), and urine, are employed to assess the functionality of 5-HT systems in the human brain under pathological and normal conditions. This section sets out to address the role of 5-HT in anxiety disorders. Special attention will be paid to the differential role of 5-HT in the various symptom domains.

A. Diagnostic Considerations

Etymologically, *anxiety* means *suffocation, disturbed breathing, or distress,* denoting an association between subjective experiences and bodily sensations. Until the 1960s the term *neurosis* played a dominating role in the clinical description of anxiety, but with the introduction of the *DSM-III* and the *DSM-III-R* (American Psychiatric Association, 1980, 1987), a refinement in the classification has taken place. According to the *DSM-III-R*, anxiety as a disorder can be divided in several main categories, including panic disorder (PD) with and without agoraphobia, generalized anxiety disorder (GAD), social phobia (SP), and obsessive–compulsive disorder (OCD). When anxiety occurs in a paroxysmal fashion, it is called a *panic attack,* the hallmark of PD. Patients with chronic high levels of anxiety that do not have panic attacks are referred to as GAD patients. Social phobia also presents a high degree of anxiety, particularly in situations in which the subject is exposed to the scrutiny of others. Avoidance behavior is generally considered to be a sequela of panic or social anxiety. Anxiety symptoms also undoubtedly feature prominently in some subtypes of OCD, but there is little evidence to support its categorization as an anxiety disorder (Montgomery, 1992). Most data support its perception as a separate diagnostic entity. Of particular interest is the distinction between GAD and PD. This distinction is originally based on the observation that antidepressants, such as imipramine, can block spontaneous panic attacks, whereas, until recently, benzodiazepines were considered to be relatively ineffective against such attacks. Patients with GAD seem to respond best to anxiolytics, such as benzodiazepines (see Westenberg and den Boer, 1993). More recent studies with high-potency benzodiazepines, such as alprazolam, have shown that this class of drugs may also be efficacious in patients with PD, albeit at higher doses than commonly used in GAD.

B. Treatment Studies Supporting the Role of Serotonin

1. *Selective Serotonin-Uptake Inhibitors*

The recognition that antidepressants exert beneficial effects in PD have prompted investigators to evaluate the efficacy of these drugs. The use of antidepressants in the treatment PD originates from the observation of Klein and Fink (1962), who reported that imipramine was effective in anxiety states. The patients treated in this study were rather heterogeneous in their clinical picture, but those patients that now would be classified as suffering from PD, responded favorably to imipramine. In subsequent studies, they provided further evidence that imipramine could prevent panic attacks and that, in most patients, attenuation of panic attacks was ensued by a decrease in other psychopathological dimensions, such as phobic avoidance and anticipatory anxiety (Klein, 1964, 1967). Today, several studies have confirmed the superiority of imipramine over placebo. These studies have been reviewed recently in several articles (see Modigh, 1987); therefore, we will not reiterate all those papers, but rather, address the issue of the pharmacological mechanism underlying this feature. There has been some debate whether effects on NE- or 5-HT-containing neurons define the site at which antidepressants exert the main proportion of their action. Mavissakalian and Perel (1989) have proposed that the efficacy of imipramine in PD may be predominantly due to the serotonergic action of the drug. In a study of PD patients who received imipramine, the plasma imipramine level, but not that of the desmethyl metabolite, correlated significantly with improvement. The parent compound, imipramine, potently inhibits the neuronal uptake of both 5-HT and NE, whereas the metabolite, desmethylimipramine, is a selective NE-uptake blocker.

Thus the antipanic effects of imipramine may be mediated through the 5-HT system.

Studies with SSRIs permit one to dissect and characterize imipramine's mixed effects on these neurotransmitter systems and to explore the role of 5-HT in the pathogenesis of PD. In keeping with the presumed role of 5-HT in the mechanism of action underlying imipramine's effect in PD, beneficial effects were obtained with clomipramine and zimeldine, two selective 5-HT-uptake inhibitors in several open-label studies (Evans et al., 1980; Koczkas et al., 1981; Gloger et al., 1981; Grunhaus et al., 1984). The results of several controlled studies with SSRIs confirm the antipanic efficacy of antidepressants and hint at the involvement of 5-HT (Table 6). There is also evidence that newer drugs, such as fluoxetine, could be effective in PD, but until now only open studies have been published (Gorman et al., 1987; Schneier et al., 1990). By and large, these studies indicate that SSRIs are effective in reducing symptoms of panic and anxiety in patients with PD. Further support for the role of 5-HT in the mechanism of action of antidepressants came from a study with fluvoxamine, which selectively inhibits the uptake of 5-HT, and maprotiline, an antidepressant that has selective effects for the NE transporter (den Boer and Westenberg, 1988). The number of panic attacks and the level of anxiety decreased significantly in patients taking fluvoxamine. In the maprotiline group, there was no significant change in the number of panic attacks and only a slight reduction in anxiety. Subjects in this study were carefully selected, excluding those with concomitant depressive symptoms, to find a "pure" PD sample. Therefore, the data indicate a specific antipanic effect for fluvoxamine, which may be related to its effect on 5-HT systems in the brain. Generally, SSRIs show a latency of 2–4 weeks before the

Table 6 Controlled Studies with Selective 5-HT-Uptake Inhibitors in Panic Disorder

Author	Diagnosis (no. pts)	Treatment	Therapeutic Effect
Evans et al., 1986	PD (25)	ZIM IMI PLAC	ZIM superior to PLA; PLA = IMI
Kahn et al., 1987	PD (35) GAD (7)	5HTP CLOM PLA	CLOM AND 5HTP superior to PLA
den Boer et al., 1987	PD (50)	CLO FLU	CLO = FLU
den Boer and Westenberg, 1988	PD (44)	FLU MAP	FLU superior to MAP
Cassano et al., 1988	PD (59)	CLO IMI	CLO = IMI CLO more rapid onset
Johnston et al., 1988	PD (108)	CLO PLA	CLO superior to PLA
den Boer and Westenberg, 1989	PD (60)	FLU FIT PLA	FLU superior to RIT and PLA

5HTP, 5-hydroxytryptophan; IMI, imipramine; FLU, fluvoxamine; CLO, clomipramine; MAP, maprotiline; RIT, ritanserin; PLA, placebo; PD, panic disorder; GAD, generalized anxiety disorder. Number of patients in parenthesis.

therapeutic effect occurs. In addition, a transient increase in anxiety is seen in most PD patients at the beginning of treatment. This biphasic probile (Fig. 1) suggests that SSRIs display an acute anxiogenic effect that is converted into an anxiolytic effect following extended administration.

Similar anxiogenic effects have been reported for healthy volunteers. When studying the effect of clomipramine on anxiety induced in healthy volunteers by simulated public speaking, Zuardi (1990) found that this antidepressant facilitated the increase in anxiety score. In contrast, benzodiazepines and maprotiline decreased anxiety in this model. It may be tentatively suggested from these findings that the differential effects on 5-HT neurotransmission following short- and long-term administration of SSRIs are responsible for these paradoxical effects. This concurs with experimental data, indicating that brief administration of SSRIs reduces the firing rate of 5-HT neurons, whereas, because of desensitization of the somatodendritic 5-HT_{1A} autoreceptors, an enhanced 5-HT function is seen after repeated administration (de Montigny and Aghajanian, 1978). These data also suggest that stimulation of an as yet unknown subset of 5-HT receptors may underlie the mechanism of action of SSRIs in PD. A selective therapeutic response of SSRIs, as opposed to other antidepressants, such as desimipramine and amitriptyline, has also been demonstrated in OCD (Zohar et al., 1987a; Goodman et al., 1990). Several con-

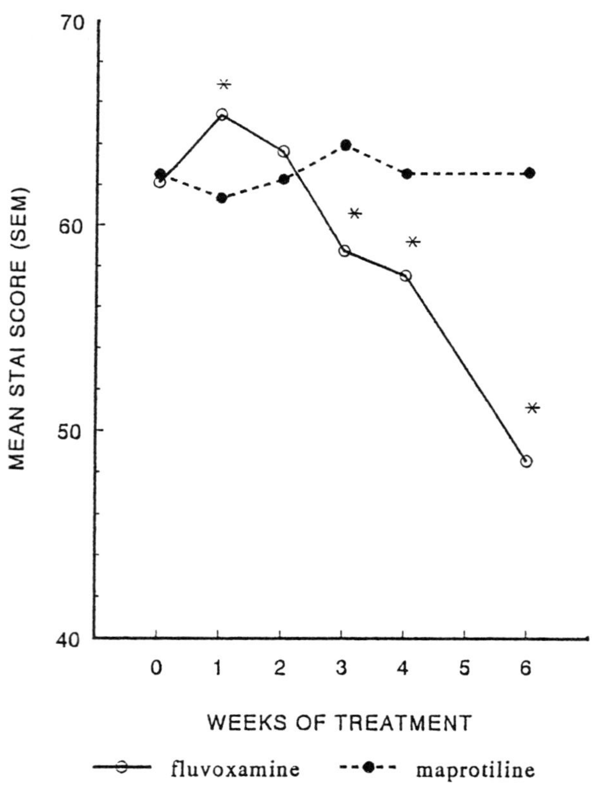

Figure 1 The effect of fluvoxamine and maprotiline in patients with panic disorder as assessed with the State anxiety inventory.
*Significantly different from maprotiline at $p < 0.01$.

trolled studies with clomipramine, and the more selective SSRI, fluvoxamine, all have shown clear evidence of efficacy for these drugs in OCD (Clomipramine Collaborative Study Group, 1991; Goodman et al., 1989, 1990; Jenike et al., 1990; Perse et al., 1987; Cottraux et al., 1990; Fineberg et al., 1992; Montgomery et al., 1990). These findings point toward a role of 5-HT in OCD as well. The influence of NE cannot be ruled out with clomipramine, since this compound has an active noradrenergic metabolite, but the positive results from several controlled studies with fluvoxamine support the assumption that 5-HT is also critical in the treatment of OCD.

Studies with SSRIs in GAD are lacking, but there are indications that patients suffering from social phobia may also respond favorably to SSRIs. Recently, we have demonstrated the efficacy of fluvoxamine on social anxiety (Fig. 2). A clinical relevant improvement was also seen on measures of phobic avoidance and interpersonal sensitivity.

In summary, SSRIs appear to be effective in various anxiety states, most notably in PD and OCD, whereas there is circumstantial evidence for their efficacy in social phobia (den Boer et al., 1992). The effects seem to be specific, namely, not secondary to their antidepressant effects and are probably related to 5-HT functions in the brain.

2. *Effects of Selective Serotonin Agonists*

Clinical evidence that 5-HT may be involved in the GAD is derived mainly from studies with selective 5-HT_{1A} agonists. Studies with buspirone have revealed that this class of compounds possesses beneficial effects in GAD patients (Goldberg and Finnerty, 1979; Schuckit, 1984; Strand et al., 1990; Jacobson et al., 1985; Rickels et al., 1982; Feighner, 1987; Olajide and Lader, 1987; Böhm et al., 1990). Because the anxiolytic

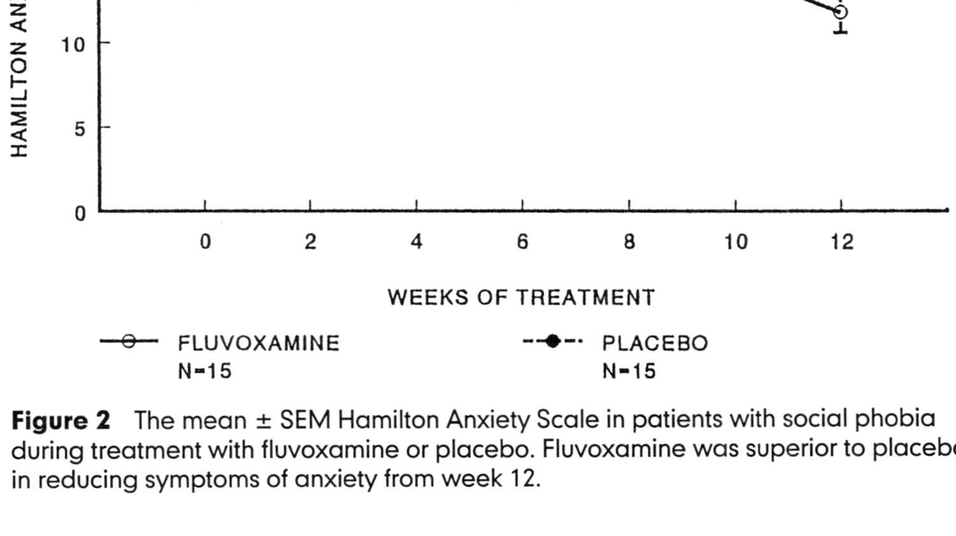

Figure 2 The mean ± SEM Hamilton Anxiety Scale in patients with social phobia during treatment with fluvoxamine or placebo. Fluvoxamine was superior to placebo in reducing symptoms of anxiety from week 12.

effects become apparent only after repeated administration, it is generally assumed that adaptive changes of 5-HT receptors are required to observe clinical relevant effects. As somatodendritic receptors desensitize after prolonged administration, resulting in a recuperation of the normal firing rate, anxiolytic effects might result from activation of the postsynaptic 5-HT_{1A} receptors, rather than from inhibition of 5-HT outflow, resulting from stimulation of the somatodendritic autoreceptors (see Sect. III.B.1). Studies with gepirone and ipsapirone, two relatively selective 5-HT_{1A} agonists, support the notion that 5-HT plays a key role in GAD (Borison et al., 1990; Harto et al., 1988). How full agonists compare with these partial agonists as antianxiety drugs, remains to be seen. Clinical studies with flesinoxan, a compound that approximates 8-OH-DPAT in its affinity for the 5-HT_{1A} receptors, in GAD patients are currently in progress. The clinical findings with azapirones lend credence to animal data predicting anxiolysis, but the delayed onset of action seen in clinical studies, as opposed to the immediate effects in the animal models of anxiety, remains puzzling.

Studies with buspirone in PD are either inconclusive or negative (Schweizer and Rickels, 1988; Sheehan et al., 1988; Pohl et al., 1989; Robinson et al., 1989). In placebo-controlled trials a substantial improvement was seen, but the effect with buspirone was not different from placebo. It cannot be excluded that the huge placebo response seen in these trials may have obscured possible drug effects in PD. Recently, we have investigated the effects of flesinoxan, a 5-HT_{1A} agonist, surpassing buspirone in affinity for this receptor subtype, in PD patients. Patients in this study were treated with flesinoxan and placebo by using a crossover design with a placebo run-in phase (Westenberg et al., 1992). In contrast to our expectations, treatment with 2.4 mg of flesinoxan, a dose that is usually well tolerated by healthy volunteers and GAD patients, resulted in a significant increase in anxiety, rather than a decrease (Fig. 3). In contrast to what is generally seen with SSRIs, this deterioration did not give way to improve-

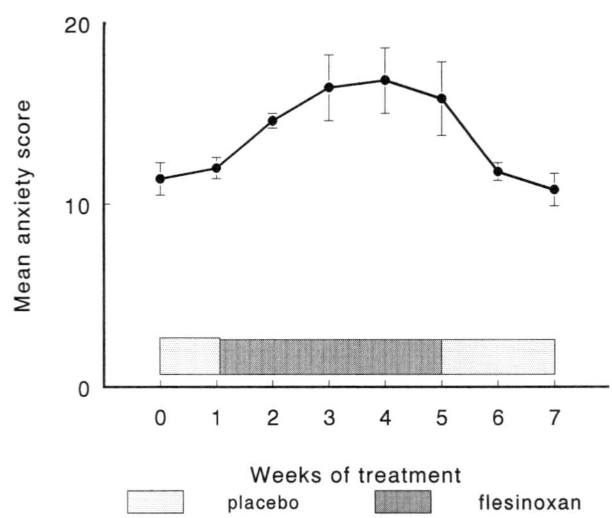

Figure 3 The mean clinical anxiety score in patients with panic disorder treated with 2.4 mg of flesinoxan and placebo. Flesinoxan appeared anxiogenic in this sample.

ment following repeated administration. In a subsequent study in which lower doses were used, flesinoxan was indistinguishable from placebo.

Interestingly, this drug did not increase the frequency of panic attacks. It was anxiogenic, rather than panicogenic, in PD patients. There is as yet only one study with buspirone in OCD. Pato et al. (1991), studying clomipramine and buspirone in a small OCD sample, found that both drugs led to similar improvements on the Yale–Brown Obsessive Compulsive Scale (YBOCS).

In summary, the efficacy of 5-HT_{1A} agonists in GAD is currently the firmest clinical evidence for a role of 5-HT in this condition. The results in PD are puzzling and require further investigation, because they may be a lead to the mechanism of action underlying the paradoxical effects of SSRIs in this condition. The increase in anxiety seen in PD patients contrasts with the results in GAD and suggests a differential role of 5-HT_{1A} receptors in these disorders.

3. *Serotonin Antagonists in the Treatment of Anxiety*

If one reasons from the hypothesis that the effects of SSRIs and other antidepressants in PD may be due to their effect on postsynaptic 5-HT_2 receptors, one would expect selective 5-HT_2 antagonists to be efficacious with a more rapid onset of action in this condition, because of their direct blocking effect on the postsynaptic 5-HT_2 receptors. To validate this hypothesis, den Boer and Westenberg (1990a) performed a placebo-controlled study with ritanserin and fluvoxamine in patients with PD. Clinical studies had indicated that GAD patients might benefit from treatment with ritanserin, suggesting that this receptor antagonist displays anxiolytic activity after prolonged treatment (Ceulemans et al., 1985). The reference drug, fluvoxamine, was significantly superior to placebo on several indexes of anxiety, on the frequency of panic attacks, and on measures of phobic avoidance, but ritanserin had no effect on any of these measures. The outcome of this study suggests that 5-HT_2 antagonists are not efficacious in PD. The presumed supersensitivity of these receptors in PD patients (Kahn et al., 1988), is likewise not corroborated by this study. Whether SSRIs exert their efficacy in PD through 5-HT_2 receptors cannot be excluded. Studies with fluvoxamine and ritanserin or placebo as treatment are required to address this issue.

There is as yet only one small study with ritanserin in OCD (Erzegovesi et al., 1992). Patients in this study were treated with fluvoxamine and received ritanserin or placebo as add-on medication in a double-blind fashion. At the end of the trial, there was a statistically significant difference between the treatment conditions, which was tentatively attributed by the authors to a worsening in the ritanserin group. This finding suggests that the effects of fluvoxamine in OCD can be antagonized by blocking the 5-HT_2 receptors. Whether ritanserin alone also has an effect on the symptomatology in OCD patients is as yet unknown.

Clearly, clinical studies with more selective 5-HT_2 antagonists are required to confirm the differential effects of ritanserin in GAD (anxiolytic), PD (ineffective), and OCD (attenuating the efficacy of antiobsessive drugs).

Much less is known about the clinical effects of 5-HT_3 antagonists in anxiety states. Although animal data have yielded promising results, no conclusive clinical trials have yet been published. In one preliminary report on the efficacy of ondansetron in GAD patients, the efficacy of this putative anxiolytic was difficult to assess owing the high placebo response (Lader, 1991).

C. Challenge Paradigm to Test the Integrity of the Serotonin System

1. *Studies in Panic Disorder*

To elucidate the role of 5-HT, several investigators have used behavioral and neuroendocrine probes to evaluate 5-HT functions in vivo. This paradigm involves the administration of direct- or indirect-acting 5-HT agonists and the measurement of a function allegedly under serotonergic control. The pituitary–adrenal (e.g., the release of cortisol, prolactin, and ß-endorphin) response to 5-HT agonists is commonly used as a marker to assess the functional state of the 5-HT system in humans. Such an approach promises to become increasingly useful as more selective drugs become available for clinical use. Other responses, besides the hormonal response, incude body temperature and behavior. Measurement of the hormonal, physiological, or behavioral effects following administration of 5-HT-selective drugs permits an assessment of the responsivity of the 5-HT system in the brain involved in the effects under investigation. There is extensive pharmacological and neuroanatomical evidence that 5-HT-containing neurons regulate the hypothalamo–pituitary–adrenal (HPA) axis in rats (Fuller, 1990). Serotonin-containing nerve terminals make synaptic contacts with the corticotropin-releasing hormone (CRH)-containing cells in the hypothalamus and direct and indirect 5-HT agonists all increase corticotropin (adrenocorticotropic hormone; ACTH), ß-endorphin, and cortisol release. Another pituitary hormone that is regulated, in part, through 5-HT neurons is prolactin. There is circumstantial evidence that drugs that increase 5-HT function also increase prolactin secretion. With this so-called neuroendocrine strategy, Kahn et al. (1988a) studied the responsivity of 5-HT receptors in PD patients by measuring the cortisol release after administration of mCPP. When given orally (0.25 mg/kg), mCPP induced an augmented cortisol release in PD patients as compared with normal controls and depressed patients. They also found that mCPP increased anxiety in PD patients, but not in healthy controls (Kahn et al., 1988b). From these findings the authors postulated that 5-HT receptors in PD patients might be supersensitive, and that drugs that reduce 5-HT function should be useful therapeutic agents in PD. Anxiogenic effects of mCPP in PD patients were also seen by Klein et al. (1991). Targum and Marshall (1989), who used an oral dose of 60 mg fenfluramine, an indirect 5-HT agonist, found significant greater prolactin and cortisol responses in PD patients than in either depressed patients or healthy controls. The PD patients also revealed a significantly greater anxiogenic response to fenfluramine administration than either depressed patients or healthy controls. These data offer circumstantial evidence for the hypothesis that an impaired 5-HT system must be considered as an important element in the pathophysiology of PD. Other investigators, however, have debated the idea that the 5-HT–HPA interaction is abnormal in PD patients. Charney et al. (1987), using 0.1 mg/kg mCPP intravenously, found similar cortisol and prolactin responses in PD patients and healthy controls. They also reported a similar anxiogenic effect of mCPP in PD patients and controls. Differences in design (dose and route of administration) may account for these discrepancies (Murphy et al., 1989). With prolactin as hormonal probe of 5-HT activity, Charney and Heninger (1986) reported similar increases also in both patients and controls after loading with tryptophan. The validity of the latter test has been questioned by Van Praag et al. (1987), who contend that prolactin release after high doses of trytophan can affect catecholamine as well as 5-HT neurons. It is purported to do so by competing with tyrosine for the same carrier mechanism in the blood–brain barrier, thereby reducing the tyrosine influx into the brain which, in turn, could lead to decreased catecholamine levels. Westenberg and den Boer (1989) evaluated the responsivity of the 5-HT system in PD patients and healthy controls by measuring the neuroendocrine and behavioral concomitants of 5-HTP administration. Cortisol and ß-endorphin plasma levels were used as hormonal probes of the 5-HT responsivity. After an intravenous dose of 60 mg of 5-HTP in combination with 150 mg of carbidopa, a peripheral decarboxylase inhibitor, significant, but similar, increases of both hormones were found in patients and controls. Administration of 5-HTP appeared to decrease, rather than to increase, levels of anxiety in PD patients. Despite overwhelming gastrointestinal side effects, most patients became less anxious by the end of the test. In contrast, controls did not consider 5-HTP administration as a relief; instead, they developed a dysphoric mood, with organic brain syndromelike symptoms. Because the relatively high dose of 5-HTP and the side effects may have obliterated differences in hormonal response, we recently conducted a 5-HTP dose–response study (unpublished results). Administration of 5-HTP in doses ranging from 10 to 40 mg elicited dose-dependent, but similar, rises in cortisol and ß-endorphin in patients with PD and controls. At doses below 40 mg no side effects were reported, supporting the idea that hormonal response was the result of 5-HTP-induced, rather than stress-induced, HPA activity. These findings lend no support to the presumed supersensitivity of central 5-HT systems in PD patients. General problems of the neuroendocrine paradigm are the nonselectivity of the challenge agents used so far and the complexity of the mechanisms controlling the hormones allegedly under 5-HT control. There is considerable pharmacological evidence that activation of either 5-HT_{1A} or 5-HT_2–5-HT_{1C} receptors leads to a stimulation of the HPA axis (Fuller, 1990). In humans, elevated plasma cortisol levels have also been observed after brief administration of selective 5-HT_{1A} ligands, such as ipsapirone and gepirone (Lesch et al., 1990; Rausch et al., 1990). In contrast with mCPP, these selective 5-HT_{1A} ligands induce a blunted response in depressed patients (Lesch et al., 1990), suggesting that these effects may occur through separate pathways. 5-Hydroxytryptamine affects HPA activity through stimulation of the 5-HT release, which may interact with all 5-HT receptor subsets, both pre- and postsynaptically. It has been suggested, however, that the neuroendocrine effects of 5-HTP are mediated through 5-HT_2–5-HT_{1C} receptors, since ritanserin, a 5-HT_2–5-HT_{1C} antagonist, is able to inhibit the 5-HTP-induced cortisol secretion (Lee et al., 1991). The failure of 5-HTP to increase plasma 3-methoxy-4-hydroxyphenylglycol (MHPG), suggest that central noradrenergic activity at least was not affected by 5-HTP administration (Westenberg and den Boer, 1989; den Boer and Westenberg, 1990b).

In summary, the mCPP and fenfluramine findings are intriguing and putatively indicative of an impaired 5-HT function in PD patients. They suggest that an increase in 5-HT activity is positively correlated with anxiety. However, the data just cited do not permit any definite conclusion, because the effects are not unequivocal and were elicited by rather nonselective agents. The data beg for further clinical investigations with more selective 5-HT agonists and antagonists.

2. *Studies in Obsessive–Compulsive Disorder*

The most extensively used pharmacological probe in OCD is also mCPP. Depending on the dose and route of administration, mCPP has produced variable behavioral and neuroendocrine effects in OCD. In one study, oral administration of mCPP (0.5 mg/kg) resulted in increased anxiety and obsessions, compared with controls, but the cortisol response was blunted, and the prolactin response was no different from that of controls (Zohar et al., 1987b). Pigott et al. (1991) have reported significant increases in OCD and anxiety symptoms after oral administration of 0.5 mg/kg mCPP in OCD patients. Pretreatment with metergoline, a nonselective 5-HT antagonist, was able to block the behavioral responses of mCPP. Other investigators, who used the same dose and route of administration, found blunted prolactin responses to mCPP, compared with those of normal controls, but failed to detect different cortisol responses (Hollander et al., 1992). The latter authors also found a worsening of OCD symptoms, but no increase in anxiety. Charney et al. (1988) found blunted prolactin responses to mCPP (0.1 mg/kg intravenously) in female patients, but not in males. In this study no heightened anxiety response was found in OCD patients, and mCPP failed to produce OCD symptoms.

Treatment with fluoxetine, for 12 weeks, diminished the behavioral response to mCPP and normalized the neuroendocrine effects (Hollander et al., 1991). This study suggests that adaptive changes in 5-HT receptor sensitivity had occurred after extended treatment with this SSRI, rendering these subjects less vulnerable to the effects of mCPP.

In one study MK-212, another nonselective 5-HT agonist, produced blunted prolactin and cortisol responses, but did not affect the intensity of the behavioral symptoms (Bastani et al., 1991).

Recently, Lesch et al. (1991a) have studied the effects of ipsapirone in normal controls and drug-free OCD patients. The drug caused rises in plasma ACTH and cortisol levels, indicating that 5-HT_{1A} receptors are involved in controlling the HPA activity, but the responses were no different between patients and controls, suggesting that the 5-HT_{1A} receptor sensitivity is not abnormal. Ipsapirone had no effects on ratings of OCD symptoms. The ability of ipsapirone to induce ACTH and cortisol release was significantly attenuated by pretreatment with fluoxetine, suggesting that a down-regulation of the 5-HT_{1A} receptors controlling HPA activity had taken place (Lesch et al., 1991b). However, no significant relation was found between the attenuation of the 5-HT_{1A}-mediated neuroendocrine responses and the ability of fluoxetine to reduce OCD symptoms, suggesting that the neuroendocrine probe of 5-HT activity reflects the 5-HT function supposedly implicated in the pathogenesis of OCD.

Fenfluramine has also been used in two challenge studies in OCD (Hollander et al., 1992; McBride et al., 1992). In contrast with the findings in PD, fenfluramine did not exacerbate OCD symptoms. Fenfluramine also failed to induce augmented prolactin and cortisol responses in OCD patients, compared with control subjects. In contrast, Hewlett et al. (1992) found blunted prolactin responses in OCD patients when compared with controls after stimulation with fenfluramine.

In conclusion, the challenge data have failed to detect consistent 5-HT dysfunctions in OCD patients. Nevertheless, they are not at variance with the hypothesis drawn from treatment studies that 5-HT systems might play a role in the mechanism of action of SSRIs in OCD.

3. *Studies in Generalized Anxiety Disorders*

To the best of our knowledge, there is currently only one study with mCPP as pharmacological probe in GAD (Germine et al., 1992). In this study, mCPP was reported to augment anxiety and anger ratings in GAD patients, when compared with controls.

D. Surrogate Measures of Serotonin Function

Inferences about 5-HT functions in the brain may also be based on measurements in readily accessible biological fluids, such as blood, urine, and cerebrospinal fluid (CSF). Blood platelets are considered as peripheral markers for some functions of the 5-HT neurons. They share with 5-HT neurons the ability to store and release 5-HT. In contrast with neurons, 5-HT is not synthesized in platelets, but derived from blood. It is taken up into the platelets by a 5-HT-specific transporter, which resembles the transporter in the brain. Platelets also contain other constituents that are found in the brain. Thus, specific high–affinity-binding sites for [^{3}H]imipramine or [^{3}H]paroxetine have been found in brain and platelet membranes (Paul et al., 1980). There is circumstantial evidence that these sites are associated with, but not identical with, the 5-HT-uptake mechanism in both platelets and neurons (Langer et al., 1980). It has been suggested, therefore, that [^{3}H]imipramine binding labels a physiological relevant site that modulates 5-HT reuptake. A reduction in the maximum concentration or density of platelet [^{3}H]imipramine-binding sites has been reported in depressed patients by many investigators (Paul et al., 1981; Raisman et al., 1981; Roy et al., 1987; Innis et al., 1987).

Studies conducted so far in patients with PD do not reveal abnormal [^{3}H]imipramine-binding characteristics (Norman et al., 1986; Innis et al., 1987; Nutt and Fraser, 1987; Schneider et al., 1987; Uhde et al., 1987; Norman et al., 1989). Despite that the number of subjects was relatively small in most studies, it can be concluded that [^{3}H]imipramine binding in PD patients is normal, thereby pointing to a different pathogenesis of PD as opposed to depression. Platelet 5-HT uptake is also considered to share several properties with the presynaptic terminal of 5-HT-containing fibers and, therefore, is used as a peripheral marker of the presynaptic 5-HT function in the brain (Stahl et al., 1982). Platelet 5-HT uptake has been reported to be lower among depressed patients (Tuomisto et al., 1976; Meltzer et al., 1984). In two studies, an augmented maximal uptake rate (V_{max}) and a similar affinity for uptake (K_m) was found in patients with PD relative to healthy controls (Norman et al., 1986, 1989). In contrast, Pecknold et al. (1988) found a reduced V_{max} in patients with PD, whereas den Boer and Westenberg (1990a) found no difference in the platelet kinetics between patients with PD and healthy controls. Another similarity between platelets and the 5-HT system is that they contain 5-HT$_2$-binding sites. While studying peripheral markers of 5-HT activity in PD patients, Butler et al. (1992) found that the density of 5-HT$_2$-binding sites on platelets is elevated and that it remained increased after successful treatment, suggesting that it is a trait marker, rather than a state marker in PD. In contrast, a decrease in [^{3}H]LSD binding, which among others also labels the 5-HT$_2$ sites, on platelets of PD patients was found by Norman et al. (1990).

Measurement of 5-hydroxyindoleacetic acid (5-HIAA), the major metabolite of 5-HT, in CSF has also been used to evaluate brain 5-HT turnover. Several studies have used lumbar CSF 5-HIAA as a marker for 5-HT turnover. Studies in depression have revealed a decrease in CSF 5-HIAA levels in a subgroup of patients (Westenberg and Verhoeven, 1988). There is only one report on CSF 5-HIAA concentrations in PD patients (Eriksson et al., 1991). In this study PD patients did not differ significantly from age- and sex-matched normal controls. If one takes these data together, one may tentatively conclude that these peripheral indexes of 5-HT function do not consistently disclose a 5-HT abnormality in PD. They might point, however, to a neurobiological difference between PD and depression.

Peripheral assessments of the 5-HT system have also been undertaken in OCD patients. By and large, these studies have yielded no consistent results about 5-HT function in OCD. Both reduced and normal [^{3}H]imipramine-binding site densities in OCD, as opposed to control subjects, have been reported (Weizman et al., 1986; Bastani et al., 1991; Black et al., 1990; Kim et al., 1991). However, the coexistence of depression, which is not uncommon in OCD, may explain these disparate findings.

Studies on uptake kinetics are sparse and as yet also controversial (Weizman et al., 1986; Bastani et al., 1991). There are only a few CSF 5-HIAA studies in OCD. In a pioneering study, Thorén et al. (1980) found no gross baseline differences in CSF 5-HIAA levels between patients with OCD and healthy controls. Interestingly, patients who responded to treatment with clomipramine had significantly higher baseline CSF 5-HIAA levels, compared with nonresponders, and amelioration in these patients was positively correlated to the reduction in CSF metabolite levels. Insel et al. (1985) found significant higher 5-HIAA levels in the CSF of OCD patients when compared with controls. These preliminary findings in OCD contrast with the results obtained in depressed patients, in whom the distribution of 5-HIAA in CSF has repeatedly been shown to be bimodal, with a subgroup of depressed patients revealing a diminished metabolite level (see Westenberg and Verhoeven, 1988), and in whom the [^{3}H]imipramine-binding sites, for the most part, are reported to be decreased. These observations are remarkable, considering that a significant proportion of OCD patients may fulfill concomitant *DSM-III-R* criteria for major depression, and OCD and depression tend to appear in the same families.

Surrogate measures of 5-HT in GAD patients are very scanty. In one study, no significant differences in [^{3}H]imipramine binding was found between GAD patients and healthy controls (Schneider et al., 1987).

In summary, peripheral markers do not reveal a coherent picture relative to the 5-HT function in anxiety disorders. The impression emerging from the data is, however, that anxiety and depression manifest themselves differently as far as these peripheral markers of 5-HT are concerned.

V. DISCUSSION

This chapter has reviewed the clinical and animal findings on the role of 5-HT in anxiety. Since the seminal study of Geller and Blum (1970), there is a vast expanding literature relating anxiety to 5-HT. Particularly, the advent of 5-HT-selective drugs and the recent progress in the field of the molecular biology of 5-HT receptors have given strong impetus to research linking 5-HT to psychiatric conditions such as anxiety. The concept that 5-HT might play a role in anxiety is supported by neuroanatomical, neurochemical, electrophysiological, and behavioral findings. Generally, the results from animal and clinical research converge to suggest a role for 5-HT in anxiety, but this overly broad generalization does not take into account the differences in results between animal models of anxiety and clinical trials, nor does it account for the differential effects of these drugs in different forms of anxiety in humans. Interestingly, 5-HT_{1A} agonists are effective in GAD, but not effective or even anxiogenic in PD. Similar differences in response have been reported for the 5-HT_2 antagonist, ritanserin. Animal models of anxiety suggest, for the most part, that anxiety correlates with a decrease in 5-HT function, whereas clinical data are erratic. Challenge studies are usually in keeping with animal data, but treatment studies in humans hint at the reverse; even for a single drug the data look chaotic. For example, mCPP has rather consistently been found to increase anxiety in humans after a single administration, but animal data are less consistent. Based on the social interaction model, some investigators have concluded that mCPP is anxiogenic (Kennett et al., 1989; Whitton and Curzon, 1990), but with the DPAG model, an anxiolytic effect is seen with this compound (Jenck et al., 1989b). This is not an odd example because, for almost every compound, it seems possible to find conflicting data. An important problem with many animal models of anxiety is that they rely on the suppression of ongoing behavior by a conditioned fear of a specific aversive stimulus, which by itself is known to be regulated by 5-HT systems. Therefore, to make any coherence from the collection of data cited in the foregoing is an enterprise that can be performed only at the risk of explaining away the discrepancies. The complexity of the 5-HT system, as outlined in the section on the 5-HT system, and the species differences in receptor subtypes are obvious reasons to explain many disparities.

The paucity of information on clinical effects of specific 5-HT agents makes it impossible to draw firm conclusions about the roles of specific 5-HT subtypes in humans. Disturbances in the balance between the opposing effects of 5-HT receptors should also be considered as an important element. Sex differences found in clinical studies, may be another confounding factor. This phenomenon requires further investigation, since it may be a clue to observed differences in vulnerability between males and females. It is also important to stress, at this point, that a variety of neurotransmitters have already been shown to play a role in anxiety. Because it is unlikely that any one system is crucial, any theory on the neurobiology of anxiety must take into account complex neuronal interaction. In OCD and PD, the most pertinent finding to emerge from the clincial studies relating 5-HT to anxiety is the effect of SSRIs. Although originally developed as antidepressants, these drugs have received equal attention for their potential use in anxiety disorders. The SSRIs have been shown to exert beneficial effects in PD, OCD, and social phobia and, although their efficacy in GAD has not yet been tested, it is plausible to assume efficacy in this condition as well. The picture that emerges from these findings is that SSRIs are globally anxiolytic, irrespective of the syndromal background. However, this need not be true when a particular system, here the 5-HT system, would be involved in the regulation of various behavioral dimensions. Studies relating the effects of selective 5-HT agonists and antagonists may help dissect the various effects of SSRIs. Whether such an undertaking would also shed light on the pathogenesis of anxiety is to be seen, since the efficacy of 5-HT-specific drugs in a particular syndrome does not necessarily imply that it must correct a specific psychopathological dysfunction in that syndrome. Compensatory effects through other pathways, or processes beyond the 5-HT system, must also be considered when pharmacological approaches are being used in the quest for the pathogenesis of anxiety. The negative findings of some challenge studies and surrogate measures, although by no means conclusive, urge restraint. Studies with naturally occurring anxiogenic agents, such as cholecystokinin (CCK) fragments (Bradwejn et al., 1991), and imaging techniques in combination with 5-HT-specific probes may give us a first glimpse at processes that take place during anxiety states. The power of this approach is only starting to be realized.

REFERENCES

American Psychiatric Association, *Diagnostic and Statistical Manual of Mental Disorders,* 3rd ed., APA Press, Washington, D.C. (1980).

American Psychiatric Association, *Diagnostic and Statistical Manual of Mental Disorders,* 3rd ed., revised, APA Press, Washington, D.C. (1987).

R. Andrade, R. C. Malenka, and R. A. Nicoll, A G protein couples serotonin and $GABA_B$ receptors to the same channels in hippocampus, *Science, 234*: 1261 (1986).

F. Artigas, A. Adell, P. Celada, and N. Bel, The raphe nuclei as a preferential target for antidepressant drugs acting on the 5-HT system: In vivo microdialysis studies in freely-moving rats, *Eur. Neuropharmacol., 2*: 276 (1992).

E. A. Audi, J. C. de Aguiar, and F. G. Graeff, Mediation by serotonin of the antiaversive effects of zimelidine and propranolol injected into the dorsal midbrain central gray, *J. Psychopharmacol., 2*: 26 (1988).

F. M. Baraban, and G. K. Aghajanian, Suppression of firing activity of 5-HT neurons in the dorsal raphe by alpha-adrenoreceptor antagonists, *Neuropharmacology, 19*: 355 (1980).

A. L. Barofsky, H. Cannon Grier, and T. K. Pradham, Evidence for regulation of water intake by median raphe serotonergic neurons, *Physiol. Behav., 24*: 951 (1980).

J. E. Barrett, Animal behavioral models in the analysis and understanding of anxiolytic drugs acting at serotonin receptors, *Animal Models in Psychopharmacology* (B. Olivier, J. Mos, and J. L. Slangen, eds.), Birkhäuser Verlag, Basel, p. 37 (1991).

J. E. Barrett, J. M. Witkin, R. S. Mansbach, P. Skolnick, and B. A. Weissman, Behavioral studies with anxiolytic drugs. III Antipunishment actions of buspirone in the pigeon do not involve benzodiazepine receptor mechanisms, *J. Pharmacol. Exp. Ther., 238*:3, 1009 (1986).

J. E. Barrett, S. Gleeson, M. A. Nader, and S. M. Hoffmann, Anticonflict effects of the $5\text{-}HT_{1A}$ compound flesnoxan, *J. Psychopharmacol., 3*: 64 (1989a).

B. Bastani, R. C. Arora, and H. Y. Meltzer, Serotonin uptake and imipramine binding in the blood platelets of obsessive-compulsive disorder patients, *Biol. Psychiatry, 30*: 131 (1991).

D. Benjamin, H. Lal, and L. R. Neyerson, The effects of $5\text{-}HT_{1B}$ characterizing agents in the mouse elevated plus-maze, *Life Sci., 47*: 195 (1990).

D. W. Black, M. Kelly, C. Meyers et al., Tritiated imipramine binding and serotonin uptake in obsessive-compulsive volunteers and psychiatrically normal controls, *Biol. Psychiatry, 27*: 319 (1990).

T. A. Blakely, and L. F. Parker, The effects of *para*-chlorophenylalanine on experimentally induced conflict behavior, *Pharmacol. Biochem. Behav., 1*: 609 (1973).

R. Blakely, H. E. Berson, R. T. Fremeau et al., Cloning and expression of a functional serotonin transporter from rat brain, *Nature, 354*: 66 (1991).

P. Blier, and C. de Montigny, Differential effects of gepirone on presynaptic and postsynaptic serotonin receptors: Single-cell recording studies, *J. Clin. Psychopharmacol., 10*: 13S (1990).

P. Blier, and C. de Montigny, Modification of 5-HT neuron properties by sustained administration of the $5\text{-}HT_{1A}$ agonist gepirone: Electrophysiological studies in the rat brain, *Synapse, 1*: 470 (1987).

P. Blier, C. de Montigny, and Y. Chaput, Electrophysiological assessment of the effects of antidepressant treatments on the efficacy of 5-HT neurotransmission, *Clin. Neuropharmacol., 11*: 1S (1988).

J. Bockaert, A. Demuis, R. Bouhelal et al., Piperazine derivatives including the putative anxiolytic drugs, buspirone and ipsapirone, are agonists at $5\text{-}HT_{1a}$ receptors negatively coupled with adenylcyclase in hippocampal neurons, *Naunyn Schmiedebergs Arch. Pharmacol., 335*: 588 (1987).

C. Böhm, M. Placchi, F. Stallone et al., A double-blind comparison of buspirone, clobazam, and placebo in patients with anxiety treated in a general practice setting, *J. Clin. Psychopharmacol., 10*: 38S (1990).

G. Bonvento, B. Scatton, Y. Claustre, and L. Rouquier, Effects of local injection of 8-OH-DPAT into the dorsal or median raphe nuclei on the extracellular levels of serotonin in serotonergic projection areas in the rat brain, *Neurosci. Lett., 137*: 101 (1992).

R. L. Borison, J. W. Albrecht, and B. I. Diamond, Efficacy and safety of a putative anxiolytic agent: Ipsapirone. *Psychopharmacol. Bull., 26*: 207 (1990).

J. Bradwejn, D. Koszycki, and C. Shriqin, Enhanced sensitivity to cholecystokinin tetrapeptide in panic disorder, *Arch. Gen. Psychiatry, 48*: 603 (1991).

M. L. Brandao, J. A. Lopez-Garcia, and M. H. T. Roberts, Electrophysiological evidence for the involvement of 5-HT_2 receptors in the antiaversive action of 5-HT in the dorsal periaqueductal gray, *Animal Models in Psychopharmacology* (B. Olivier, J. Mos, and J. L. Slangen, eds.), Birkhäuser Verlag, Basel, p. 75 (1991).

M. S. Briley, R. Raisman, D. Sechter, E. Zarifian, and S. Z. Langer, ^{3}H-Imipramine binding in human platelets: A new biochemical parameter in depression, *Neuropharmacology, 19*: 1209 (1980).

J. Butler, A. O'Halloran, and B. E. Leonard, The Galway study of panic disorder II: Changes in some peripheral markers of noradrenergic and serotonergic function in *DSM-III-R* panic disorder, *J. Affective Disord., 26*: 89 (1992).

M. Carli, and R. Samanin, Potential anxiolytic properties of 8-hydroxy-2-(di-*N*-propylamino)tetralin, a selective $serotonin_{1A}$ receptor agonist, *Psychopharmacology, 94*: 84 (1988).

M. Carli, C. Prontera, and R. Samanin, Evidence that central 5-hydroxytryptaminergic neurons are involved in the anxiolytic activity of buspirone, *Br. J. Pharmacol., 96*: 829 (1989).

G. B. Cassano, A. Petracca, G. Perugi et al., Clomipramine for panic disorder: I. The first 10 weeks of a long-term comparison with imipramine, *J. Affective Disord., 14*: 123 (1988).

D. L. S. Ceulemans, M. L. J. A. Hoppenbrouwers, Y. G. Gelders, and A. J. M. Reyntjens, The influence of ritanserin, a serotonergic antagonist, in anxiety disorders: A double-blind placebo-controlled study versus lorazepam, *Pharmacopsychiatry, 8*: 303 (1985).

Y. Chaput, P. Blier, and C. de Montigny, Acute and long-term effects of antidepressant serotonin (5-HT) uptake blockers on the efficacy of 5-HT neurotransmission. Electrophysiological studies in the rat central nervous system, *Adv. Biol. Psychiatry, 17*: 1 (1988).

D. S. Charney, and G. R. Heninger, Serotonin function in panic disorders, *Arch. Gen. Psychiatry, 43*: 1059 (1986).

D. S. Charney, S. W. Woods, W. K. Goodman, and G. R. Heninger, Serotonin function in anxiety, *Psychopharmacology, 92*: 14 (1987).

D. S. Charney, W. K. Goodman, L. W. Price et al., Serotonin function in obsessive–compulsive disorder, *Arch. Gen. Psychiatry, 45*: 177 (1988).

D. S. Charney, P. L. Delgado, L. H. Price, and G. R. Heninger, The receptor sensitivity hypothesis of antidepressant action: A review of antidepressant effects on serotonin function, *The Role of Serotonin in Psychiatric Disorders* (S. L. Brown and H. M. van Praag, eds.), Brunner/Mazel, New York, p. 27 (1991).

Clomipramine Collaborative Study Group, Clomipramine in the treatment of patients with obsessive–compulsive disorder, *Arch. Gen. Psychiatry, 48*: 730 (1991).

F. C. Colpaert, T. F. Meert, C. J. E. Niemegeers, and P. A. J. Janssen, Behavioral and 5-HT antagonists effects of ritanserin: A pure and selective antagonist of LSD discrimination in rat, *Psychopharmacology, 86*: 45 (1985).

L. Cook, and J. Sepinwall, Reinforcement schedules and extrapolations to humans from animals in behavoral pharmacology, *Fed. Proc., 34*: 1889 (1975).

R. L. Commissaris, and D. J. Fontana, A potential animal model for the study of anti-panic treatments, *Animal Models in Psychopharmacology* (B. Olivier, J. Mos, and J. L. Slangen, eds.), Birkhäuser Verlag, Basel, p. 59 (1991).

R. L. Commissaris, W. H. Lyness, and R. H. Rech, The effects of *d*-lysergic acid diethylamide (LSD), 2,5-dimethoxy-4-methylamphetamine (DOM), pentobarbital and methaqualone on punished responding in control and 5,7-dihydroxytryptamine-treated rats, *Pharmacol. Biochem. Behav., 14*: 617 (1981).

B. Costall, and R. J. Naylor, Anxiolytic potential of 5-HT_3 receptor antagonists, *Pharmacol. Toxicol., 70*: 157 (1992).

B. Costall, M. E. Kelly, R. J. Naylor, and E. S. Onaivi, Actions of buspirone in a putative model of anxiety in the mouse, *J. Pharm. Pharmacol., 40*: 494 (1988).

B. Costall, A. M. Domeney, P. A. Gerrard et al., The anxiolytic activities of the 5-HT_3 receptor antagonists GR38032F, ICS-930 and BRL 43694, *Behavioral Pharmacology of 5-HT* (P. Bevan, A. R. Cools, and T. Archer, eds.), Lawrence Erlbaum, Hillside, N.J., p. 383 (1989a).

B. Costall, M. E. Kelly, R. J. Naylor, E. S. Onaivi, and M. B. Tyers, Neuroanatomical sites of action of 5-HT_3 receptor agonist and antagonists for alteration of aversive behaviour in the mouse, *Br. J. Pharmacol., 96*: 325 (1989b).

J. Cottraux, E. Mollard, M. Bouvard et al., A controlled study of fluvoxamine and exposure in obsessive–compulsive disorder, *Int. Clin. Psychopharmacol., 5*: 17 (1990).

M. A. E. Critchley, and S. L. Handley, Effects of the X-maze anxiety model of agents acting at 5-HT_1 and 5-HT_2 receptors, *Psychopharmacology, 93*: 502 (1987).

M. A. E. Critchley, and S. L. Handley, Dorsal raphe lesions abolish effects of 8-OH-DPAT and ipsapirone in X-maze, *Br. J. Pharmacol., 96*: 309 (1989).

M. Davis, The potentiated startle response as a measure of conditioned fear and its relevance to the neurobiology of anxiety, *Anim. Models Psychiatry Disord., 1*: 61 (1988).

R. Deacon, and C. R. Gardner, Benzodiazepine and 5-HT ligands in a rat conflict test, *Br. J. Pharmacol., 88*: 330P (1986).

J. K. W. Deakin, 5-HT receptor subytpes in depression, *Behavioral Pharmacology of 5-HT* (P. Bevan, A. R. Cools, and T. Archer, eds.), Laurence Erlbaum, Hillsdale, N.J., 179 (1989).

C. de Montigny, and G. K. Aghajanian, Tricyclic antidepressants: Long-term treatment increases responsivity of rat forebrain neurons to serotonin, *Science, 202*: 1303 (1978).

A. Demuis, R. Bouhelal, M. Sebben et al., A non-classicial 5-hydroxytryptamine receptor positively coupled to adenylcyclase in the central nervous system, *J. Pharmacol. Exp. Ther., 34*: 880 (1988).

J. A. den Boer, and H. G. M. Westenberg, Effect of a serotonin and noradrenaline uptake inhibitor in panic disorder, a double-blind comparative study with fluvoxamine and maprotiline, *Int. Clin. Psychopharmacol., 3*: 59 (1988).

J. A. den Boer, and H. G. M. Westenberg, Serotonin function in panic disorder: A double blind placebo controlled study with fluvoxamine and ritanserin, *Psychopharmacology, 102*: 85 (1990a).

J. A. den Boer, and H. G. M. Westenberg, Behavioral, neuroendocrine and biochemical effects of 5-hydroxytryptophan administration in panic disorders, *Psychiatry Res., 31*: 267 (1990b).

J. A. den Boer, H. G. M. Westenberg, W. D. J. Kamerbeek et al., Effect of serotonin uptake inhibitors in anxiety disorders, a double-blind comparison of clomipramine and fluvoxamine, *Int. Clin. Psychopharmacol., 2*: 2 (1987).

J. A. den Boer, I. M. Van Vliet, and H. G. M. Westenberg, A double-blind placebo controlled study of fluvoxamine in social phobia, *Clin. Neuropharmacol., 15*(Suppl. 1b): 615 (1992).

L. Descarrier, and L. Léger, Serotonin nerve terminals in the locus coeruleus of the adult rat, *Interactions Between Putative Neurotransmitters in the Brain* (S. Garattini, J. F. Pujol, and R. Samanin, eds.), Raven Press, New York, p. 355 (1978).

R. W. Dunn, R. Corbett, and S. Fielding, Effects of 5-HT_{1A} receptor agonists and NMDA receptor antagonists in the social interaction test and the elevated plus maze, *Eur. J. Pharmacol., 169*: 1 (1989).

A. S. Eison, and F. D. Yocca, Reduction in cortical 5HT_2 receptor sensitivity after continuous gepirone treatment, *Eur. J. Pharmacol., 111*: 389 (1985).

J. A. Engel, S. Hjorth, K. Svensson et al., Anticonflict effect of the putative serotonin receptor agonist 8-hydroxy-2-(di-*N*-propylamino)tetralin (8-OH-DPAT), *Eur. J. Pharmacol., 105*: 365 (1984).

E. Eriksson, P. Westberg, C. Alling et al., Cerebrospinal fluid levels of monoamine metabolites in panic disorder, *Psychiatry Res., 36*: 243 (1991).

S. Erzegovesi, P. Ronchi, and E. Smeraldi, 5-HT-2 receptor and fluvoxamine effect in obsessive–compulsive disorder, *Hum. Psychopharmacol., 7*: 287 (1992).

L. Evans, G. Moore, and J. Cox, Zimeldine—a serotonin uptake blocker—in the treatment of phobic anxiety, *Prog. Neuropharmacol. Biol. Psychiatry, 4*: 75 (1980).

L. Evans, P. Kenardy, and H. Hoey, Effect of a selective serotonin uptake inhibitor in agoraphobia with panic attacks, *Acta Psychiatr. Scand., 73*: 49 (1986).

R. J. Fanelli, and K. McMonagle-Strucko, Alteration of 5-HT_{1a} receptor binding sites following chronic treatment with ipsapirone measured by quantitative autoradiography, *Synapse, 12*: 75 (1992).

J. P. Feighner, Buspirone in the long-term treatment of generalized anxiety disorder, *J. Clin. Psychiatry, 48*(Suppl.): 3 (1987).

A. Fernández-Guasti, and C. López-Rubalcava, Evidence for the involvement of the 5-HT_{1A} receptor in the anxiolytic action of indorenate and ipsapirone, *Psychopharmacology, 101*: 354 (1990).

A. Fernández-Guasti, C. López-Rubalcava, J. Perez-Urizar, and G. Castaneda-Hernandez, Evidence for a postsynaptic action of the serotonergic anxiolytics: Ipsapirone, indorenate and buspirone, *Brain Res. Bull., 28*: 497 (1992).

T. J. Feuerstein, G. Hertig, and R. Jackisch, Endogenous noradrenaline as modulator of hippocampal serotonin (5-HT) release. Dual effects of yohimbine, rauwolscine and corynanthine as a-andrenoceptor antagonists and 5-HT-receptor agonists, *Naunyn Schniedebergs Arch. Pharmacol., 329*: 216 (1985).

S. E. File, The use of social interaction as a method for detecting anxiolytic activity of chlordiazepoxide-like drugs. *J. Neurosci. Method, 2*: 219 (1980).

S. E. File, Behavioral effects of serotonin depletion, *Metabolic disorders of the nervous system* (C. Rose, ed.), Pitman, London, p. 429 (1981).

S. E. File, The neurochemistry of anxiety, *Drugs in Psychiatry*, Vol. 2. (G. D. Burrows, J. R. Morman and B. Davis, eds.), Elsevier, Amsterdam, p. 13 (1984).

S. E. File, How good is social interaction as a test of anxiety? *Anim. Models Psychiatr. Disord., 1*: 151 (1988).

S. E. File, and J. R. G. Hyde, The effects of *p*-chlorophenylalanine and ethanolamine-*O*-sulphate in an animal test of anxiety, *J. Pharm. Pharmacol., 29*: 735 (1977).

S. E. File, and A. L. Johnston, Lack of effects of $5HT_3$ receptor antagonists in the social interaction and elevated plus-maze tests of anxiety in the rat, *Psychopharmacology, 99*: 248 (1989).

S. E. File, and B. J. Lemaitre, L-Fenfluramine in tests of dominance and anxiety in the rat, *Neuropsychobiology, 20*: 205 (1988).

S. E. File, and S. Pellow, The anxiogenic action of a convulsant benzodiazepine: Reversal by chlordiazepoxide and Ro 15-1788 but not by CGS 8216, *Arch. Int. Pharmacodyn. Ther., 271*: 198 (1984).

S. E. File, J. R. G. Hyde, and N. K. Macleod, 5,7-Dihydroxytryptamine lesions of dorsal and median raphe nuclei and performance in the social interaction test of anxiety and in a home-cage aggression test, *J. Affective Disord., 1*: 115 (1979).

N. A. Fineberg, T. Bullock, D. B. Montgomery, and S. A. Montgomery, Serotonin reuptake inhibitors are the treatment of choice in obsessive compulsive disorder, *Int. Clin. Psychopharmacol., 7*(Suppl. 1): 43 (1992).

A. L. Frankhuyzen, and A. H. Mulder, Noradrenaline inhibits depolarization-induced ^{3}H-serotonin release from slices of rat hippocampus, *Eur. J. Pharmacol., 63*: 179 (1980).

W. Fuller, Serotonin receptors and neuroendocrine responses, *Neuropsychopharmacology, 3*: 495 (1990).

Fuller, R. W., H. D. Snoddy, N. R. Mason, and J. E. Owen, Disposition and pharmacological effects of mCPP, *Neuropharmacology, 20*: 155 (1981).

C. R. Gardner, Distress vocalization in rat pups a simple screening method for anxiolytic drugs, *J. Pharmacol. Methods, 14*: 181 (1985).

I. Geller, and K. Blum, The effects of 5-HTP on *para*-chlorophenylalanine (p-CPA) attenuation of "conflict" behavior, *Eur. J. Pharmacol., 9*: 319 (1970).

I. Geler, and R. J. Hartmann, Effects of buspirone on operant behavior of laboratory rats and cynomologus monkeys, *J. Clin. Psychiatry, 43*: 25 (1982).

I. Geller, and J. Seifter, The effects of meprobamate, barbiturates, *d*-amphetamine and promazine on experimentally induced conflict in the rat, *Psychopharmacology, 1*: 482 (1960).

I. Geller, R. J. Hartman, and D. J. Croy, Attenuation of conflict behavior with cinanserin, a serotonin antagonist: Reversal of the effect with 5-hydroxytryptophan and a-methyltryptamine, *Res. Commun. Chem. Pathol. Pharmacol., 7*:1, 165 (1974).

M. Germine, A. W. Goddard, S. W. Woods et al., Anger and anxiety responses to *m*-chlorophenylpiperazine in generalized anxiety disorder, *Biol. Psychiatry, 32*: 457 (1992).

S. C. Gerson, and R. J. Baldessarini, Motor effects of serotonin in the central nervous system, *Life Sci., 27*: 1435 (1980).

D. D. Gillespie, D. H. Manier, E. Sanders-Bush, and F. Sulser, The serotonin/norepinephrine-link in brain. II Role of serotonin in the regulation of beta adrenoceptors in the low agonist affinity conformation, *J. Pharmacol. Exp. Ther., 244*: 154 (1988).

R. A. Glennon, N. A. Darmani, and B. R. Martin, Multiple populations of serotonin receptors may modulate the behavioral effects of serotonergic agents, *Life Sci., 48*: 2493 (1991).

S. Gloger, L. Grunhaus, B. Birmacher, and T. Troudart, Treatment of spontaneous panic attacks with clomipramine, *Am. J. Psychiatry, 138*: 1215 (1981).

H. L. Goldberg, and R. J. Finnerty, The comparative efficacy of buspirone and diazepam in the treatment of anxiety, *Am. J. Psychiatry, 136*: 1184 (1979).

M. E. Goldberg, A. I. Salama, J. B. Patel, and J. B. Malick, Novel non-benzodiazepine anxiolytics, *Neuropharmacology, 22*: 1499 (1983).

W. K. Goodman, L. H. Price, S. A. Rasmussen et al., The efficacy of fluvoxamine in obsessive compulsive disorder: A double-blind comparison with placebo, *Arch. Gen. Psychiatry, 46*: 36 (1989).

W. K. Goodman, L. H. Price, P. L. Delgado et al., Specificity of serotonin reuptake inhibitors in the treatment of obsessive–compulsive disorder: Comparison of fluvoxamine and desimipramine, *Arch. Gen. Psychiatry, 47*: 577 (1990).

J. M. Gorman, M. R. Liebowitz, A. J. Feyer et al., An open trial of fluoxetine in the treatment of panic attacks, *J. Clin. Psychopharmacol., 7*: 329 (1987).

M. Göthert, H. Huth, and E. Schlicker, Characterization of the receptor subtype involved in alpha-adrenoceptor-mediated modulation of serotonin release from the rat brain cortex slices, *Naunyn Schniedebergs Arch. Pharmacol., 317*: 199 (1981).

F. G. Graeff, Tryptamine antagonists and punished behavior, *J. Pharmacol. Exp. Ther., 189*: 344 (1974).

F. G. Graeff, Brain defense systems and anxiety, *Handbook of Anxiety,* Vol. 3, Elsevier, Amsterdam, p. 307 (1990).

F. G. Graeff, and R. I. Schoenfeld, Tryptaminergic mechanisms in punished and nonpunished behavior, *J. Pharmacol. Exp. Ther., 173*: 277 (1970).

P. M. Grasby, T. Sharp, T. Allen et al., Effects of the 5-HT_{1A} partial agonists gepirone, Ipsapirone and Buspirone on local cerebral glucose utilization in the conscious rat, *Psychopharmacology, 106*: 97 (1992).

J. A. Gray, *The Neuropsychology of Anxiety,* Oxford University Press, Oxford (1982).

L. Grunhaus, S. Gloger, and B. Birmacher, Clomipramine treatment for panic attacks in patients with mitral valve prolapse, *J. Clin. Psychiatry, 45*: 25 (1984).

A. P. Guy, and C. R. Gardner, Pharmacological characterization of a modified social interaction model of anxiety in the rat, *Neuropsychobiology, 13*: 194 (1985).

A. Hamik, and S. J. Peroutka, 1-(*m*-Chlorophenyl)piperazine (mCPP) Interactions with neurotransmitter receptors in the human brain, *Biol. Psychiatry, 25*: 569 (1989).

M. Hamon, L. Lanfumey, S. E. Mestikawy et al., The main features of central 5-HT_1 receptors, *Neuropsychopharmacology, 3*: 349 (1990).

M. A. Harrington, P. Zhong, S. J. Garlow, and R. D. Ciaranello, Molecular biology of serotonin receptors, *J. Clin. Psychiatry, 53*(Suppl.): 8 (1992).

P. R. Hartig, Molecular biology of 5-HT_{1d} receptors, *Abstr. 2nd Int. Symp. Serotonin,* Houston, p. 1 (1992).

R. J. Hartmann, and I. Geller, *p*-Chlorophenylalanine effects on a conditioned emotional response in rats, *Life Sci., 10*: 927 (1971).

N. E. Harto, R. J. Branconnier, K. F. Spera, and E. C. Dessain, Clinical profile of gepirone, a nonbenzodiazepine anxiolytic, *Psychopharmacol. Bull., 24*: 154 (1988).

C. A. Hendrie, The 5HT_3 antagonist GR 38032F is highly toxic in DBA/2 mice, *Psychopharmacology, 101*: 429 (1990).

W. A. Hewlett, S. Vinogradov, K. Martin et al., Fenfluramine stimulation of prolactin in obsessive–compulsive disorder, *Psychiatry Res., 42*: 81 (1992).

G. A. Higgins, A. J. Bradbury, B. J. Jones, and N. R. Okley, Behavioral and biochemical consequences following activation of 5-HT_1-like and GABA receptors in the dorsal raphe nucleus of the rat, *Neuropharmacology, 27*: 993 (1988).

S. Hjorth, and T. Sharp, Effect of the 5-HT_{1a} receptor agonist 8-OH-DPAT on the release of 5-HT in dorsal and median raphe-innervated rat brain regions as measured by in vivo microdialysis, *Life Sci., 48*: 1779 (1991).

S. Hjorth, B. Söderpalm, and J. A. Engel, Biphasic effect of *l*-5-HTP in the Vogel conflict model, *Psychopharmacology, 92*: 96 (1987).

E. Hollander, C. DeCarie, R. Gully et al., Effects of chronic fluoxetine treatment on behavioral and neuroendocrine responses to *meta*-chlorophenylpiperazine in obsessive—compulsive disorder, *Psychiatry Res., 37*: 1 (1991).

E. Hollander, C. DeCarie, A. Nitescu et al., Serotonergic function in obsessive–compulsive disorder: Behavioral and neuroendocrine responses to oral *m*-chlorophenylpiperazine and fenfluramine in patients and healthy volunteers, *Arch. Gen. Psychiatry, 49*: 21 (1992).

D. Hoyer, Functional correlates of serotonin 5-HT_1 recognition sites, *J. Receptor Res., 8*: 59 (1988).

D. Hoyer, and D. N. Middlemiss, Species differences in the pharmacology of terminal 5-HT autoreceptors in mammalian brain, *TIPS, 10*: 130 (1989).

R. B. Innis, D. S. Charney, and G. R. Heninger, Differential ^{3}H-Imipramine platelet binding in patients with panic disorder and depression, *Psychiatry Res., 21*: 33 (1987).

T. R. Insel, E. A. Mueller, I. Alterman et al., Obsessive–compulsive disorder and serotonin: Is there a connection? *Biol. Psychiatry, 20*: 1174 (1985).

T. R. Insel, J. Hill, and R. B. Mayor, Rat pup ultrasonic isolation calls: Possible mediation by the benzodiazepine receptor complex, *Pharmacol. Biochem. Behav., 24*: 1263 (1986).

A. F. Jacobson, R. A. Dominguez, B. J. Goldstein, and R. M. Steinbook, Comparison of buspirone and diazepam in generalized anxiety disorder, *Pharmacotherapy, 5*: 290 (1985).

F. Jenck, C. L. E. Broekkamp, and A. M. L. Van Delft, Opposite control mediated by central 5-HT_{1A} and non-5-HT_{1A} (5-HT_{1B} or 5-HT_{1C}) receptors on periaqueductal gray aversion, *Eur. J. Pharmacol., 161*: 219 (1989a).

F. Jenck, C. L. E. Broekkamp, and A. M. L. Van Delft, Effects of serotonin receptor antagonists on PAG stimulation induced aversion: Different contributions of 5-HT_1, 5-HT_2 and 5-HT_3 receptors, *Psychopharmacology, 97*: 489 (1989b).

F. Jenck, C. L. E. Broekkamp, and A. M. L. Van Delft, 5-HT_{1C} receptors in the serotonergic control of periaqueductal gray induced aversion in rats, *Psychopharmacology, 100*: 372 (1990a).

F. Jenck, C. L. E. Broekkamp, and A. M. L. van Delft, The effect of antidepressants on aversive periaqueductal gray stimulation in rats, Eur. J. Pharmacol., 177: 201 (1990b).

M. A. Jenike, S. Hyman, L, Baer et al., A controlled trial of fluvoxamine in obsessive compulsive disorder: Implication for a serotonergic theory, *Am. J. Psychiatry, 147*: 1209 (190).

D. G. Johnston, I. E. Troyer, and S. F. Whitstett, Clomipramine in the treatment of agoraphobic women, *Biol. Psychiatry, 25*: 101 (1988).

B. J. Jones, B. Costall, A. Q. M. Domeney et al., The potential anxiolytic activity of GR38032 F, a 5-HT_3-receptor antagonist, *Br. J. Pharmacol., 93*: 985 (1988).

Julius, D., Molecular biology of serotonin receptors, *Annu. Rev. Neurosci., 14*: 335 (1991).

R. S. Kahn, and S. Wetzler, *m*-Chlorophenylpiperazine as a probe of serotonin function, *Biol. Psychiatry, 30*: 1139 (1991).

R. S. Kahn, H. G. M. Westenberg, W. M. A. Verhoeven et al., Effect of a serotonin precursor and uptake inhibitor in anxiety disorders, a double-blind comparison of 5-hydroxytryptophan clomipramine and placebo, *Int. Clin. Psychopharmacol., 2*: 33 (1987).

R. S. Kahn, G. M. Asnis, S. Wetzler, and H. M. Van Praag, Neuroendocrine evidence for serotonin hypersensitivity in panic disorder, *Psychopharmacology, 96*: 360 (1988a).

R. S. Kahn, S. Welzer, H. M. Van Praag et al., Behavioral indications for serotonin receptor hypersensitivity in panic disorder, *Psychiatry Res., 25*: 101 (1988b).

J. H. Kehne, J. V. Cassella, M. Davis, Anxiolytic effects of buspirone and gepirone in the fear-potentiated startle paradigm, *Psychopharmacology, 94*: 8 (1988).

G. A. Kennett, P. Whitton, K. Shah, and G. Curzon, Anxiogenic-like effects of mCPP and TFMPP in animal models are opposed by 5-HT_{1C} receptor antagonists, *Eur. J. Pharmacol., 164*: 445 (1989).

C. E. J. Ketelaars, Extinction of conflict behaviour in rats, a model which may have predictive value for drugs active in anxiety disorders, Thesis, Rotterdam (1990).

C. E. J. Ketelaars, and J. Bruinvels, The anti-conflict effect of cyproheptadine is not mediated by its 5-hydroxytryptamine antagonistic property, *Life Sci., 44*: 1743 (1989).

T. Kilfoil, A. Michel, D., Montgomery, and R. L. Whiting, Effects of anxiolytic and anxiogenic drugs on exploratory activity in a simple model of anxiety in mice, *Neuropharmacology, 28*: 901 (1989).

G. J. Kilpatrick, B. J. Jones, and M. B. Tyers, Identification and distribution of 5-HT_3 receptors in rat brain using radioligand bindings, *Nature, 330*: 746 (1987).

G. J. Kilpatrick, B. J. Jones, and M. B. Tyers, Identification and distribution of 5-HT_3 receptors in rat brain using radioligand binding, *Nature, 330*: 746 (1988).

C. D. Kilts, R. L. Commissaris, and R. H. Rech, Comparison of anti-conflict drug effects in three experimental animal models of anxiety, *Psychopharmacology, 74*: 290 (1981).

C. D. Kilts, R. L. Commissaris, J. J. Cordon, and R. H. Rech, Lack of central 5-hydroxytryptamine influence on the anticonflict activity of diazepam, *Psychopharmacology, 78*: 156 (1982).

S. W. Kim, M. W. Dysken, G. N. Pandey et al., Platelet ^{3}H-imipramine binding sites in obsessive–compulsive behavior, *Biol. Psychiatry, 30*: 467 (1991).

D. F. Klein, and M. Fink, Psychiatric reaction patterns to imipramine, *Am. J. Psychiatry, 119*: 432 (1962).

D. F. Klein, Delineation of two drug-responsive anxiety syndromes, *Psychopharmacologia, 5*: 397 (1964).

D. F. Klein, The importance of psychiatric diagnosis in prediction of clinical drug effects, *Arch. Gen. Psychiatry, 16*: 118 (1967).

E. Klein, J. Zohar, and F. Geraci et al., Anxiogenic effects of meta-CPP in patients with Panic Disorder—Comparison to caffeine's anxiogenic effects. *Biol. Psychiatry, 30*: 973 (1991).

S. Koczkas, and A. Weissman, A pilot study of the effect of the 5-HT-uptake inhibitor, zimeldine, on phobic anxiety, *Acta Psychiatr. Scand., 290*: 328 (1981).

G. J. Kosofsky, and M. E. Molliver, The serotonergic innervation of the cerebral cortex: Different classes of axon terminals arise from the dorsal and median raphe nuclei, *Synapse, 1*: 153 (1987).

M. Koulu, J. Lappalainen, J. Hietala, and B. Sjöholm, Effects of chronic administration of ondansetron (GR38032F), a selective 5-HT_3 receptor antagonist, on monoamine metabolism in mesolimbic and nigrostriatal dopaminergic neurons and on striatal D_2-receptor binding, *Psychopharmacology, 101*: 168 (1990).

M. H. Lader, Ondansetron in the treatment of anxiety, *Biological Psychiatry,* Vol. 2 (G. Racagni, N. Brunello, T. Fukuda, eds.), Excerpta Medica, Amsterdam, p. 885 (1991).

S. Z. Langer, C. Moret, R. Raisman et al., High affinity ^{3}H-imipramine binding in rat hypothalamus: Association with uptake of serotonin but not norepinephrine, *Science, 210*: 1133 (1980).

M. A. Lee, J. F. Nash, M. Barnes, and H. Y. Meltzer, Inhibitory effect of ritanserin on the 5-hydroxytryptophan-mediated cortisol, ACTH and prolactin secretion in humans, *Psychopharmacology, 103*: 258 (1991).

C. M. L. Leone, J. C. de Aquiar, and F. G. Graeff, Role of 5-hydroxytryptamine in amphetamine effects on punished and unpunished behaviour, *Psychopharmacology, 80*: 78 (1983).

K. P. Lesch, S. Mayer, L. Disslekamp-Tietze et al., 5-HT_{1a} receptor responsivity in unipolar depression. Evaluation of ipsapirone-induced ACTH and cortisol secretion in patients and controls, *Biol. Psychiatry, 28*: 620 (1990).

K. P. Lesch, A. Hoh, J. Disselkamp-Tietze et al., 5-$Hydroxytryptamine_{1a}$ receptor responsivity in obsessive–compulsive disorder, *Arch. Gen. Psychiatry, 48*: 540 (1991a).

K. P. Lesch, A. Hoh, E. M. Schulte et al., Long-term fluoxetine treatment decreases 5-HT_{1a} receptor responsivity in obsessive–compulsive disorder, *Psychopharmacology, 105*: 415 (1991b).

J. E. Leysen, Characterization of serotonin receptor binding sites, *Neuropharmacology of Serotonin* (A. R. Green, ed.), Oxford University Press, London, p. 79 (1985).

A. S. Lippa, P. A. Nash, and E. N. Greenblatt, Preclinical neuropsychopharmacological testing procedures for anxiolytic drugs, *Anxiolytics, Industrial Pharmacology,* Vol. 3 (S. Fielding and H. Lal, eds.), Futura Publishing, New York, p. 41 (1979).

S. A. Lorens, Some behavioral aspects of serotonin depletion depend on method: A comparison of 5,7-dihydroxytryptamine, *p*-chlorophenylanine, *p*-cloroamphetamine, and electrolytic raphe lesions, *Ann. N.Y. Acad. Sci., 305*: 532 (1978).

L. A. Manoumas, and M. E. Molliver, Evidence for dual serotonergic projections to neocortex: Axons from the dorsal and median raphe nuclei are differentially vulnerable to the neurotoxin *p*-chloramphetamine (PCA), *Exp. Neurol., 102*: 23 (1988).

R. S. Mansbach, and M. A. Geyer, Blockade of potentiated startle responding in rats by 5-$hydroxytryptamine_{1A}$ receptor ligands, *Eur. J. Pharmacol., 156*: 375 (1988).

R. S. Mansbach, C. Harrod, S. M. Hoffman et al., Behavioral studies with anxiolytic drugs. V. Behavioral and in vivo neurochemical analyses in pigeons of drugs that increase punished responding, *J. Pharmacol. Exp. Ther., 246*: 114 (1988).

P. Mason, J. Skinner, and D. Luttinger, Two tests in rats for antianxiety effect of clinically anxiety attenuating antidepressants, *Psychopharmacology, 92*: 30 (1987).

M. Mavissakalian, and J. M. Perel, Imipramine dose–response relationship in panic disorder with agoraphobia, *Arch. Gen. Psychiatry, 46*: 127 (1989).

P. A. McBride, M. D. DeMeo, J. A. Sweeny et al., Neuroendocrine and behavioral response to challenge with the indirect serotonin agonist *dl*-fenfluramine in adults with obsessive–compulsive disorder, *Biol. Psychiatry, 31*: 19 (1992).

T. C. McCloskey, B. K. Paul, and R. L. Commissaris, Buspirone effects in an animal conflict procedure: Comparison with diazepam and phenobarbital, *Pharmacol. Biochem. Behav., 27*: 171 (1987).

T. F. Meert, and P. A. Janssen, Psychopharmacology of ritanserin: Comparison with chlordiazepoxide, *Drug Dev. Res., 18*: 119 (1989).

H. Y. Meltzer, M. Lowy, A. Robertson et al., Effect of 5-hydroxytryptophan on serum cortisol level in major affective disorders, *Arch. Gen. Psychiatry, 41*: 391 (1984).

S. M. Mitman, and M. A. Geyer, Effects of 5-HT-1A agonists on locomotor and investigatory behaviors in rats differ from those of hallucinogens, *Psychopharmacology, 98*: 321 (1989).

K. Modigh, Antidepressant drugs in anxiety disorders, *Acta Psychiatr. Scand. 335*(Suppl.): 57 (1987).

H. E. Molewijk, J. A. M. V. D. Heyden, and B. Olivier, The 5-HT_{1A} receptor selectively mediates lower lip retraction in the rat, *Eur. J. Pharmacol., 183*: 1954 (1990).

S. M. Molineaux, T. M. Jessel, R. Axel, and D. Julius, 5-HT_{1C} receptor is a prominent receptor subtype in the central nervous system, *Proc. Natl. Acad. Sci. USA, 86*: 6793 (1989).

S. A. Montgomery, OCD floats free of anxiety, *Eur. Neuropsychopharmacol., 2*: 217 (1992).

S. A. Montgomery, D. B. Montgomery, and N. Fineberg, Early response with clomipramine in obsessive compulsive disorder—a placebo controlled study, *Prog. Neuropsychopharmacol. Biol. Psychiatry, 14*: 719 (1990).

C. Moret, and M. Briley, Serotonin autoreceptor subsensitivity and antidepressant activity, *Eur. J. Pharmacol., 180*: 351 (1990).

P. J. Morgane, and M. S. Jacobs, Raphe projections to the locus coeruleus in the rat, *Brain Res. Bull., 4*: 519 (1979).

J. Mos, and B. Olivier, Separation-induced ultrasounds in rat pups as a model for anxiety disorders: Psychopharmacological profile, *Stress, Biological Rhythms and Psychiatric Disorders* (H. G. M. Westenberg, ed.), De Medicus, Houten, p. 89 (1990).

J. Mos, B. Olivier, and R. V. Oorschot, Behavioural and neuropharmacological aspects of maternal aggression in rodents, Aggressive Beh., 16: 145 (1990).

P. C Moser, An evaluation of the elevated plus-maze test using the novel anxiolytic buspirone, *Psychopharmacoogy, 99*: 48 (1989).

P. C. Moser, M. D. Tricklebank, D. N. Middlemiss et al., Characterization of MDL 73005EF as a 5-HT_{A} selective ligand and its effects in animal models of anxiety: Comparison with buspirone, 8-OH-DPAT and diazepam, *Br. J. Pharmacol., 99*: 343 (1990).

D. L. Murphy, E. A. Mueller, J. H. Hill et al., Comparative anxiogenic, neuroendocrine, and other physiologic effects of *m*-chlorophenylpiperazine given intravenously or orally to healthy volunteers, *Psychopharmacology, 98*: 275 (1989).

B. S. Nashold, Jr., P. W. William, and D. G. Slaughter, Sensations evoked by stimulation in the midbrain of man, *J. Neurosurg., 30*: 14 (1969).

J. L. Neisewander, S. A. McDougalol, S. L. Bowling, and M. T. Bardo, Conditioned taste aversion and place preference with buspirone and gepirone, *Psychopharmacology, 100*: 485 (1990).

T. R. Norman, and D. M. Sartor, Platelet serotonin uptake and ^{3}H-imipramine binding in panic disorder, *J. Affective Disord., 17*: 77 (1989).

T. R. Norman, F. K. Judd, M. Gregory et al., Platelet serotonin uptake in panic disorder, *J. Affective Disord., 11*: 69 (1986).

T. R. Norman, F. K. Judd, K. Gregory et al., High-affinity platelet [^{3}H]LSD binding is decreased in panic disorder, *J. Affective Disord., 19*: 119 (1990).

D. J. Nutt, and S. H. Fraser, Platelet binding studies in panic disorder, *J. Affective Disord., 12*: 7 (1987).

D. Olajide, and M. Lader, A comparison of buspirone, diazepam and placebo in patients with chronic anxiety state, *J. Clin. Psychiatry, 7*: 148 (1987).

B. Olivier, J. Mos, J. V. D. Heyden et al., Flesinoxan; a potent and selective 5-HT_{1a} agonist, *Stress, Biological Rhythms and Psychiatric Disorders* (H. G. M. Westenberg, ed.), De Medicus, Houten, p. 79 (1990).

E. S. Onaivi, and B. R. Martin, Neuropharmacological and physiological validation of a computer-controlled two-compartment black and white box for the assessment of anxiety, *Prog. Neuropsychopharmacol. Biol. Psychiatry, 13*: 963 (1989).

J. M. Palacios, A. Pazos, and D. Hoyer, Characterization and mapping of 5-HT_{1a} sites in the brain of animals and man, *Brain 5-HT_{1a} Receptors* (C. T. Dourish, S. Ahlenius, and P. H. Hutson, eds.), Ellis Horwood, Chichester, p. 67 (1987).

M. Papp, and E. Przegalinski, The 5-HT_{3} receptor antagonists ICS 205-930 and GR 38032F, putative anxiolytic drugs, differ from diazepam in their pharmacological profile, *J. Psychopharmacol., 3*: 14 (1989).

M. T. Pato, T. A. Pigott, J. L. Hill et al., Controlled comparison of buspirone and clomipramine in obsessive–compulsive disorder, *Am. J. Psychiatry, 148*: 127 (1991).

S. M. Paul, M. Rehavi, P. Skolnick, and F. K. Goodwin, Demonstration of high-affinity binding sites for ^{3}H-imipramine on human platelets, *Life Sci., 26*: 953 (1980).

S. M. Paul, M. Rehavi, K. P. Skolnick et al., Depressed patients have decreased binding of tritiated imipramine to platelet serotonin transporter, *Arch. Gen. Psychiatry, 38*: 1315 (1981).

A. Pazos, and J. M. Palacios, Quantitative autoradiographic mapping of serotonin receptors in rat brain. I. Serotonin-I receptors, *Brain Res., 346*: 205 (1985).

A. Pazos, A. Probst, and J. M. Palacios, Serotonin receptors in the human brain, III: Autoradiographic mapping of serotonin-I receptors, *Neuroscience, 21*: 97 (1986).

A. Pazos, A. Probst, and J. M. Palacios, Serotonin receptors in the human brain, IV: Autoradiographic mapping of serotonin-2 receptors, *Neuroscience, 21*: 123 (1987).

J. C. Pecknold, B. Suranyi-Cadotte, H. Chang, and N. P. V. Nair, Serotonin uptake in panic disorder and agoraphobia, *Neuropsychopharmacology, 39*: 917 (1988).

S. Pellow, and S. E. File, Anxiolytic and anxiogenic drug effects on exploratory activity in an elevated plus-maze: A novel test of anxiety in the rat, *Pharmacol. Biochem. Behav., 24*: 525 (1986).

S. Pellow, P. Chopin, S. E. File, and M. Briley, Validation of open:closed arm entries in an elevated plus-maze as a measure of anxiety in the rat, *J. Neurosci. Methods, 14*: 149 (1985).

S. Pellow, A. L. Johnston, and S. E. File, Selective agonists and antagonists for 5-hydroxytryptamine receptor subtypes, and interactions with yohimbine and FG 7142 using the elevated plus-maze test in the rat, *J. Pharm. Pharmacology, 39*: 917 (1987).

T. L. Perse, J. H. Greist, J. W. Jefferson et al., Fluvoxamine treatment of obsessive–compulsive disorder, *Am. J. Psychiatry, 144*: 1543 (1987).

E. N. Peterson, and J. B. Larssen, A water lick conflict paradigm using drug experienced rats, *Psychopharmacology, 75*: 236 (1981).

E. M. Pich, and R. Samanin, Disinhibitory effects of buspirone and low doses of sulpiride and haloperidol in two experimental anxiety models in rats: Possible role of dopamine, *Psychopharmacology, 89*: 125 (1986).

T. A. Pigott, J. Zohar, J. L. Hill et al., Metergoline blocks the behavioral and neuroendocrine effects of orally administered *m*-chlorophenylpiperzine in patients with obsessive–compulsive disorder, *Biol. Psychiatry, 29*: 418 (1991).

D. Piper, N. Upton, D. Thomas, and J. Nicholass, The effect of 5-HT_3 receptor antagonists BRL 43694 and GR 38032 in animal behavioural models of anxiety, *Br. J. Pharmacol., 94*: 314 (1988).

R. Pohl, R. Balon, V. K. Yeragani, and S. Gershon, Serotonergic anxiolytics in the treatment of panic disorder: A controlled study with buspirone, *Psychopathology, 22*(Suppl. 1): 60 (1989).

R. Raisman, D. Sechter, and M. S. Briley, High affinity ^{3}H-imipramine binding in platelets from untreated and treated depressed patients compared to healthy controls, *Psychopharmacology, 75*: 368 (1981).

J. L. Rausch, S. M. Stahl, and R. Hauger, Cortisol and growth hormone responses to the 5-HT_{1a} agonist gepirone in depressed patients, *Biol. Psychiatry, 28*: 73 (1990).

K. Rickels, K. Weisman, N. Norstad et al., Buspirone and diazepam in anxiety: A controlled study, *J. Clin. Psychiatry, 43*: 81 (1982).

D. R. Robinson, R. C. Shrotriya, D. R. Alms et al., Treatment of panic disorder: Nonbenzodiazepine anxiolytics, including buspirone, *Psychopharmacol. Bull., 25*: 21 (1989).

A. Roy, D. Everett, D. Pickar, and S. M. Paul, Platelet tritiated imipramine binding and serotonin uptake in depressed patients and controls: Relationship between plasma cortisol levels before and after dexamethasone administration, *Arch. Gen. Psychiatry, 44*: 320 (1987).

R. Samanin, T. Mennini, A. Ferraris et al., *m*-Chlorophenylpiperazine: A central serotonin agonist causing powerful anorexia in rats, *Arch. Pharmacol., 308*: 159 (1979).

D. J. Sanger, D. Joly, and B. Zivkovic, Behavioral effects of nonbenzodiazepine anxiolytic drugs: A comparison of CGS 9896 and zopiclone with chlordiazepoxide, *J. Pharmacol. Exp. Ther., 232*: 3, 831 (1985).

D. M. Schefke, D. J. Fontana, and R. L. Commissaris, Anti-Conflict efficacy of buspirone following acute versus chronic treatment, *Psychopharmacology, 99*: 427 (1989).

J. Schipper, M. Tulp, H. Sijbesma et al., Preclinical evaluation of flesinoxan as a potential anxiolytic and antidepressant drug, *Eur. J. Pharmacol., 183*: 2059 (1990).

L. S. Schneider, D. Munjack, J. A. Severson, and R. Palmer, Platelet [^{3}H]imipramine binding in generalized anxiety disorder, panic disorder and agoraphobia with panic attacks, *Biol. Psychiatry, 22*: 59 (1987).

F. R. Schneier, M. R. Liebowitz, S. O. Davies et al., Fluoxetine in panic disorder, *J. Clin. Psychopharmacol., 10*: 119 (1990).

P. H. Schoeffler, and D. Hoyer, Interaction of arylpiperazines with $5HT_{1a}$, $5HT_{1b}$, $5HT_{1c}$, and $5HT_{1d}$ receptors: Do discriminatory $5HT_{1d}$ receptor ligands exist? *Naunyn Schneidebergs Arch. Pharmacol., 339*: 675 (1989).

M. A. Schuckit, Clinical studies of buspirone, *Psychopathology, 17*(Suppl. 3): 61 (1984).

M. T. B. Schütz, J. C. de Aquiar, and P. G. Graeff, Anti-aversive role of serotonin in the dorsal periaqueductal grey matter, *Psychopharmacology, 85*: 340 (1985).

E. Schweizer, and K. Rickels, Buspirone in the treatment of panic disorder: A controlled pilot comparison with clorazepate, *J. Clin. Psychopharmacol., 8*: 303 (1988).

M. Segal, Serotonergic innervation of the locus coeruleus from the dorsal raphe and its action on responses to noxious stimuli, *J. Physiol., 286*: 401 (1979).

M. Segal, E. C. Azmitia, and P. M. Whitaker-Azmitia, Physiological effects of selective $5\text{-}HT_{1a}$ and $5\text{-}HT_{1b}$ ligands in rat hippocampus: Comparison to 5-HT, *Brain Res., 502*: 67 (1989).

T. Sharp, S. R. Bramwell, and D. G. Grahame-Smith, $5\text{-}HT_1$ agonists reduce 5-hydroxytryptamine release in rat hippocampus in vivo as determined by brain microdialysis, *Br. J. Pharmacol., 96*: 283 (1989).

D. V. Sheehan, A. B. Raj, K. H. Sheehan, and S. Soto, The relative effiacy of buspirone, imipramine and placebo in panic disorder: A preliminary report, *Pharmacol. Biochem. Behav., 29*: 815 (1988).

B. Söderpalm, and J. A. Engel, Serotonergic involvement in conflict behavior, *Eur. Neuropharmacol., 1*: 7 (1990).

B. Söderpalm, S. Hjorth, and J. A. Engel, Effects of the $5\text{-}HT_{1a}$ receptor agonist and *l*-5-HTP in Montgomery's conflict test, *Pharmacol. Biochem. Behav., 32*: 259 (1989).

J. S. Sprouse, and G. K. Aghajanian, Responses of hippocampal pyramidal cells to putative serotonin $5\text{-}HT_a$ and $5\text{-}HT_b$ agonists: A comparative study with dorsal raphe neurons, *Neuropharmacology, 27*: 707 (1988).

S. M. Stahl, R. D. Ciaranello, and P. A. Berger, Platelet serotonin in schizophrenia and depression, *Serotonin in Biological Psychiatry* (B. T. Ho, ed.), Raven Press, New York, p. 182 (1982).

M. Strand, J. Hetta, A. Rosen et al., A double-blind, controlled trial in primary care patients with generalized anxiety: A comparison between buspirone and oxazepam, *J. Clin. Psychiatry, 51*(Suppl.): 40 (1990).

J. M. Stutzman, B. Eon, F. Darche et al., Are $5\text{-}HT_2$ antagonists endowed with anxiolytic properties in rodents? *Neurosci. Lett., 128*: 4 (1991).

B. Suranyi-Cadotte, S. R. Bodnoff, and S. A. Welner, Antidepressant–anxiolytic interactions: Involvement of benzodiazepine–GABA and serotonin systems, *Prog. Neuropsychopharmacol. Biol. Psychiatry, 14*: 633 (1990).

S. D. Targum, and L. E. Marshall, Fenfluramine provocation of anxiety in patients with panic disorder, *Psychiatry Res., 28*: 295 (1989).

M. H. Thiébot, P. Soubrié, M. Hamon, and P. Simon, Evidence against the involvement of serotonergic neurons in the anti-punishment activity of diazepam in the rat, *Psychopharmacology, 82*: 355 (1984).

P. Thorén, M. Asberg, L. Bertelsson et al., Clomipramine treatment of obsessive–compulsive disorder, II: Biochemical aspects, *Arch. Gen. Psychiatry, 37*: 1289 (1980).

J. Traber, and T. Glaser, 5-HT_{1a} receptor-related anxiolytics, *TIPS, 8*: 432 (1987).

Tuomisto, J., and E. Tukiainen, Depressed uptake of 5-hydroxytryptamine in blood platelets from depressed patients, *Nature, 262*: 596 (1976).

N. C. Tye, B. J. Everitt, and S. D. Iversen, 5-Hydroxytryptamine and punishment, *Nature, 268*: 741 (1977).

N. C. Tye, S. D. Iversen, and A. R. Green, The effects of benzodiazepines and serotonergic manipulations on punished responding, *Neuropharmacology, 18*: 689 (1979).

M. B. Tyers, A review of the evidence supporting the anxiolytic potential of 5-HT_3 receptor antagonists, *Behavioral Pharmacology of 5-HTg* (P. Beven, A. R. Cools, and T. Archer, eds.), Laurence Erlbaum, Hillsdale, N.J. p. 353 (1989).

M. B. Tyers, B. Costall, B. J. Jones et al., The anxiolytic activities of 5-HT_3 receptor antagonists in laboratory animals, *Neurosci. Lett., 29*(Suppl.): 68 (1987).

T. W. Uhde, W. H. Berrettini, P. P. Boy-Byrne et al., [^{3}H]imipramine binding in patients with panic disorder, *Biol. Psychiatry, 22*: 52 (1987).

H. M. Van Praag, C. Lemus, and R. S. Kahn, Hormonal probes of central serotonergic activity: Do they really exist? *Biol. Psychiatry, 22*: 86 (1987).

D. Verge, G. Daval, A. Patey et al., Presynaptic 5-HT autoreceptors on serotonergic cell bodies and/or dendrites but not terminals are of the 5-HT_{1a} subtype, *Eur. J. Pharmacol., 113*: 463 (1985).

J. R. Vogel, B. Beer, and D. E. Clody, A simple and reliable conflict procedure for testing antianxiety agents, *Psychopharmacologia, 21*: 1 (1971).

B. A. Weissman, J. E. Barrett, L. S. Brady et al., Behavioral and neurochemical studies on the anticonflict actions of buspirone, *Drug Dev. Res., 4*: 83 (1984).

A. Weizman, M. Carmi, H. Hermesh et al., High-affinity imipramine binding and serotonin uptake in platelets of eight adolescent and ten adult obsessive–compulsive patients, *Am. J. Psychiatry, 143*: 335 (1986).

S. A. Welner, C. de Montigny, J. Desorches et al., Autoradiographic quantification of serotonin (5-HT_{1a}) receptors following long-term antidepressant treatment, *Synapse, 4*: 347 (1989).

H. G. M. Westenberg, and J. A. den Boer, Serotonin function in panic disorder: Effects of *l*-5-hydroxytryptophan in patients and controls, *Psychopharmacology, 98*: 283 (1989).

H. G. M. Westenberg, and J. A. den Boer, Serotonergic basis of panic disorder, *Psychopharmacology of Panic* (S. A. Montgomery, ed), Oxford University Press, Oxford, p. 91 (1993).

H. G. M. Westenberg, and W. M. A. Verhoeven, CSF monoamine metabolites in patients and controls: Support for a bimodal distribution in major affective disorders, *Acta Psychiatr. Scand., 78*: 541 (1988).

H. G. M. Westenberg, I. M. Van Vliet, and J. A. den Boer, Flesinoxan, a selective 5-HT_{1a} agonist, in the treatment of panic disorder, *Clin. Neuropharmacol., 15*(Suppl. 1b): 60 (1992).

P. Whitton, and G. Curzon, Anxiogenic-like effects of infusing 1-(3-chlorophenyl)piperazine (mCPP) into the hippocampus, *Psychopharmacology, 100*: 138 (1990).

J. C. Winter, Comparison of chlordiazepoxide, methysergide, and cinanserin as modifiers of punished behavior and as antagonists of *N,N*-dimethyltryptamine, *Arch. Int. Pharmacodyn., 197*: 147 (1972).

J. M. Witkin, R. S. Mansbach, and J. E. Barrett, Behavioral studies with anxiolytic drugs. IV. Serotonergic involvement in the effects of buspirone on punished behavior of pigeons, *J. Pharmacol. Exp. Ther., 243*: 970 (1987).

I. K. Wright, M. Heraton, N. Upton, and C. A. Marsden, Comparison of acute and chronic treatment of diazepam and ritanserin in the elevated plus-maze model of anxiety, *New Concepts in Anxiety* (M. Briley and S. E. File, eds.), Macmillan Press, London, p. 277 (1991).

C. E. Ybema, J. L. Slangen, B. Olivier, and J. Mos, Discriminative stimulus properties of flesinoxan, *Pharmacol. Biochem. Behav., 35*: 781 (1990).

F. D. Yocca, Neurochemistry and neurophysiology of buspirone and gepirone: Interactions at the presynaptic and postsynaptic 5-HT_{1a} receptors, *J. Clin. Psychopharmacol., 10*: 6S (1990).

R. Young, A. Urbanic, T. A. Emrey, P. C. Hall, and G. Metcalf, Behavioral effects of several new anxiolytics and putative anxiolytics, *Eur. J. Pharmacol., 143*: 361 (1987).

J. Zohar, and T. R. Insel, Obsessive–compulsive disorder: Psychobiological approaches to diagnosis, treatment, and pathophysiology, *Biol. Psychiatry, 27*: 667 (1987a).

J. Zohar, E. A. Mueller, T. R. Insel et al., Serotonergic responsitivity in obsessive–compulsive disorder, *Arch. Gen. Psychiatry, 44*: 946 (1987b).

A. W. Zuardi, 5-HT-related drugs and human experimental anxiety, *Neurosci. Biobehav. Rev., 14*: 507 (1990).

17

The Clinical Anxiolytic and Antidepressant Efficacy of Drugs with Actions on Serotonin Systems

J. F. W. Deakin
Manchester Royal Infirmary, Manchester, England

I. INTRODUCTION

Two important studies recently emphasized the importance of pharmacotherapy in the treatment and prophylaxis of depression. The National Institute of Mental Health (NIMH) instituted a collaborative research program comparing the efficacy of imipramine, interpersonal psychotherapy, cognitive behavioral therapy, and placebo in the short-term treatment of depression (Elkin et al., 1989). Significant differences between the outcome for imipramine-treated subjects compared with placebo controls were observed, particularly in those with more severe illnesses, for example, defined by a Hamilton depression rating score of 20. Some efficacy for interpersonal psychotherapy, a standardized and operationalized form of psychotherapy, was also demonstrated, but cognitive behavioral therapy had disappointingly small and largely nonsignificant effects. The same rank order of potency was seen in a large-scale trial of the same treatments in the maintenance treatment of depression over a 3-year period (Frank et al., 1990). Approximately 22% of those treated with 200 mg/day of imipramine relapsed, whereas 60–70% of those treated with placebo or with interpersonal psychotherapy, relapsed over the same period. These trials serve to emphasize the importance of pharmacotherapy in the treatment of depression. In addition, the NIMH trial demonstrated the lack of efficacy of any intervention in milder cases of depression. An important task for psychopharmacology in the future is to develop effective treatments for milder illnesses.

The last decade has seen the development of innumerable potential antidepressant and anxiolytic compounds. Many of them are based on the explosion of knowledge concerning mechanisms of serotonin (5-hydroxytryptamine; 5-HT) neurotransmission. This knowledge is outstripping our ability to integrate it into understanding how antidepressants and anxiolytics work and what is wrong with 5-HT mechanisms in anxiety and depression. It is vitally important for advances in these areas to have secure knowledge about therapeutic efficacy of new pharmacological agents. Fortunately, the requirements of the drug-licensing authorities in the United States and in Europe have become increasingly stringent, allowing increasing confidence in the efficacy of licensed agents. Nevertheless, the interpretation of drug trials is very far from being an objective matter. Nearly 20 year ago Morris and Beck (1974) showed that a third of established tricyclic antidepressant drug trials failed to find superiority over placebo. There is thus, on the one hand, the problem of false-negative trial results for which there may be no obvious explanation and, on the other, false-positive trial results.

Other biases and pitfalls need to be borne in mind in the evaluation of efficacy data. For example, there is bias against publishing trials that are negative. Furthermore, trials are often cited as showing efficacy of a new agent, but detailed examination reveals that statistical significance is only achieved on some of the outcome measures. Most trials in depression involve at least three measures of outcome—the Hamilton Depression Rating Scale, global impression of severity, and global impression of improvement—and these measures can be analyzed in those who completed the trial or in those who entered the trial, and these last observations are carried forward. This immediately gives six comparisons. There is rarely a statistical correction for this procedure. Average scores on these outcome measures are usually presented, but this may give a misleading impression of the size of the treatment effect. It is much more important to know the proportion of patients who make a clinically significant improvement under each treatment condition. Fortunately, in recent years, this way of analyzing data has become nearly universal, but it further increases the number of chances of finding statistically significant differences.

Very large multicenter trials probably offer the most compelling evidence for efficacy. One reason is that systematic biases would have to operate in several centers, for a number of investigators, to produce a spuriously significant outcome. One disadvantage of large multicenter trials may be a loss of sensitivity for important differences between established and novel therapeutic agents that become lost in the noise and variability introduced by having many centers. Studies with smaller numbers of patients in a single center, with a small number of investigators, with a similar clinical background and training may thus have a place in evaluation of novel therapeutic agents.

Most researchers now accept that placebo-controlled trials are essential in establishing efficacy of a new agent. This is because alternative methods are indecisive. For example, comparing a new agent with an established agent may show exactly the same rates of improvement, but without a placebo group, there is no certainty that the trial would have shown efficacy of the established agent over placebo. For these reasons, it is generally accepted that the placebo group is essential. An active comparator group establishes whether the trial has produced a false-negative result, should the novel agent appear ineffective compared with placebo.

This chapter provides an overview of the newer antidepressant and anxiolytic agents for which sufficient clinical trial evidence is available for a worthwhile discussion. Some compounds have antidepressant or anxiolyticlike properties in animal behavioral tests, but have not been fully evaluated in humans. For example, there is, as yet, no good trial evidence that ß-agonists or γ-aminobutyric acid (GABA) agonists have clinical efficacy. Such agents will not be discussed.

II. SEROTONIN$_{1A}$

The 5-HT$_{1A}$ agonists were the first major practical product of the explosion of knowledge about 5-HT receptor subtypes of the last 15 years. The first 5-HT$_{1A}$ agonist to be marketed was buspirone, and its major indication is anxiety. However, there is great interest for many other indications in which abnormal 5-HT function has been implicated.

A large number of 5-HT$_{1A}$ agonists have been developed, but most belong to the family of azapirones (e.g., buspirone, gepirone, and ipsapirone). The azapirones all produce a common metabolite 1(2-pyrimidinyl)piperazine (1-IPP) and this is an α_2-antagonist. In addition, some members of this family are dopamine receptor antagonists. At the moment, therefore, it is difficult to know whether the clinical effects of the azapirones are genuinely due to actions at 5-HT$_{1A}$ receptors or whether they are mediated by nonspecific actions. Matters should become clearer with the clinical evaluation of nonazapirone drugs such as flesinoxan and eltoprazine.

A. Mechanism of Action

5-HT$_{1A}$ receptors have pre- and postsynaptic locations. Postsynaptic 5-HT$_{1A}$ receptors are particularly dense in the hippocampus, in a distribution that corresponds to the terminals of the median raphe nucleus (Glaser et al., 1985). 5-HT$_{1A}$ receptor agonists interact with postsynaptic receptors, but they vary in their degree of agonism. Clinically available 5-HT$_{1A}$ agonists are partial agonists and have the ability to stimulate postsynaptic 5-HT$_{1A}$ receptors, but also to block the effects of exogenously applied 5-HT in electrophysiological experiments. Therefore, it is unclear what the effects of clinical doses are on net 5-HT neurotransmission through postsynaptic 5-HT$_{1A}$ synapses. Some recently developed agonists have potent and pure agonist action at postsynaptic sites (e.g., flesinoxan), but there is no available clinical data.

Presynaptic autoreceptors are particularly localized to 5-HT neurons in the dorsal raphe nucleus. All available 5-HT$_{1A}$ agonists are full agonists on the autoreceptor and powerfully suppress the firing of dorsal raphe neurons. There is evidence that tolerance to this effect gradually develops in experimental animals.

The presynaptic actions of 5-HT$_{1A}$ agonists on dorsal raphe neurons and the postsynaptic actions in the terminal areas of the median raphe nucleus offer interesting possibilities to test theories of the neurobiology of depression.

According to one theoretical synthesis (Deakin and Graeff, 1991), 5-HT systems have the general function of mediating adaptive or coping responses to aversive events, but within this framework the different 5-HT subsystems have differentiated functions. Much evidence from animal behavioral studies suggests that projections from the dorsal raphe nucleus mediate anticipatory anxiety and function to guide the organism away from stimuli that predict danger. Such stimuli elicit fear, and this motivates avoidance behavior. It is remarkable that the projections of the dorsal raphe nucleus parallel those of dopaminergic neurons and include innervation of the amygdala and basal ganglia. Both neurotransmitters have powerful effects on locomotion, and it is suggested that the two neurotransmitters mediate avoidance–approach tendencies to incentive stimuli. A further parallelism exists between terminals of the dorsal raphe nucleus and postsynaptic 5-HT$_2$, 5-HT$_{1C}$, and 5-HT$_{1D}$ receptors. In the context of 5-HT$_{1A}$ agonists, it is of considerable interest that they not only suppress activity in presynaptic 5-HT neurons of the dorsal raphe, but also, on chronic administration, lead to a gradual down-regulation of postsynaptic 5-HT_2, 5-HT_{1C} and 5-HT_3 receptors (Eison and Yocca, 1985). These immediate and emergent actions of 5-HT_{1A} agonists would serve to decrease neurotransmission through the putative dorsal raphe nucleus–anxiety mechanism.

The median raphe nucleus has a different terminal distribution, which is mainly cortical and which parallels the distribution of noradrenergic nerve terminals. The concentration of 5-HT_{1A} receptors in the hippocampus has been noted earlier. Deakin and Graeff (1991), after the experiments of Kennett et al. (1985), suggested that the median raphe–5-HT_{1A} system serves to mitigate the behavioral effects of chronic aversive stimuli (stress)—allowing normal behavior to gradually reemerge. It was suggested that depression results from a failure of median raphe–5-HT_{1A} resilience in the face of persistent adversity. Neuroendocrine studies in humans suggests that there is impaired functional neurotransmission through 5-HT_{1A} synapses (Deakin et al., 1990), that these abnormalities are state-dependent (Upadhyaya et al., 1991), that antidepressant drugs share the ability to enhance 5-HT_{1A} neurotransmission (Blier et al., 1987), and that this action is responsible for their efficacy (Delgado et al., 1990).

In summary, from consideration of the normal functions of different 5-HT pathways, morbidy anxiety would result from excessive neurotransmission in projections of the dorsal raphe nucleus through non-5-HT_{1A} receptors, whereas depression is due to impaired functioning mediated by postsynaptic 5-HT_{1A} receptors (a putative mechanism of resilience). Therefore, it is of great interest that the 5-HT_{1A} agonists have actions that would reverse this imbalance. Presynaptic effects would preferentially reduce neurotransmission in dorsal raphe projections, whereas postsynaptic actions of 5-HT_{1A} agonists would tend to restore impaired functioning in the 5-HT_{1A} systems. Such considerations predict efficacy of these agonists in generalized anxiety and in depression.

B. ANXIETY

Major placebo-controlled trials of 5-HT_{1A} agonists in generalized anxiety disorder (GAD) are summarized in Table 1. Rickels et al. (1982) carried out the first major multicenter trial in 212 patients. Diazepam was the active comparator (20–25 mg/day), and there was a placebo group. Both active treatments were effective on all measures. The final Hamilton anxiety score of 15 indicates a degree of residual symptomatology, and the placebo response rate was very small. This suggests that the subjects may have been rather chronic, resistant patients. Nevertheless, 70% of the treatment groups were rated as significantly improved, whereas this applied to only 30% of the placebo treated. Goldberg and Finnerty (1979) made the interesting observation that buspirone and diazepam were significantly superior to placebo in improving ratings of anxiety, but buspirone was superior to both placebo and to diazepam on ratings of depression. Wheatley (1982) failed to find significant differences between buspirone and placebo, and Pecknold et al. (1985) found small treatment effects of buspirone compared with placebo after 3 weeks of treatment, but only on one of the rating scales (Hamilton anxiety).

Ipsapirone has been investigated in generalized anxiety disorder but full descriptions are not available. Kuemmel et al. (1988) briefly described the effects of ipsapirone in 267 patients with GAD. This was a multicenter trial and doses of 2.5, 5, and 7.5 mg three times daily were compared with placebo. Significant drug–placebo differences were seen only for the 5-mg dose. However, all three doses produced very similar degrees of improvement, and there was no sign of a dose–response relation. The treatment ef-

Table 1 5-HT_{1A} **Agonists: Placebo-Controlled Trials in GAD and Related Diagnoses**

Ref. (No. patient)	Results
Goldberg and Finnerty, 1979 (56)	B = D > P (HAMA); B > D = P (HAMD)
Rickels et al., 1982 (212)	B = D > P (all ratings)
Wheatley, 1982 (131)	B = D = P (HAMA) - 3 wk
Pecknold et al., 1985 (60)	D > B = P (HAMA) wk 1 and 2 D = B > P (HAMA) wk 3 and 4 CGI; SCL - NS
Bohm et al., 1990a (20 per group)	B = C > (HAMA; CGI)
Bohm et al., 1990b (20 per group; elderly)	B > P (HAMA; HAMD)
Borison et al., 1990 (7–8 per group)	D > I > P (HAMA)
Kuemmel et al., 1988 (267)	1 > P (HAMA)
Beneke et al., 1988 (123)	1 > P (HAMA; STAI)

Key: B, buspirone; C, clobazam; D, diazepam; I, ipsapirone; P, placebo; HAMA, Hamilton anxiety scores; HAMD, Hamilton depression; VGI, clinical global impression; SCL, Hopkins symptom checklist; NS, not significant.

fect was very small, with a difference of 4 points in the Hamilton anxiety ratings between drug and placebo. The clinical importance of this effect is not likely to be great, although the proportions responding to each treatment are not presented. The same group examined the effects of 2.5–10 mg three-times-daily flexible dosing on symptoms of anxiety in 100 male and female patients. Again, treatment effects were very small (Beneke et al., 1988).

It can be seen that several studies claim efficacy of 5-HT_{1A} agonists in generalized anxiety disorder, but the effect size is small. Two reasons have been advanced for this: a lack of effect in benzodiazepine-experienced patients and a lack of efficacy in panic (see following section).

1. *Serotonin$_{1A}$ Agonists Versus Benzodiazepines*

Several studies find that 5-HT_{1A} agonists produce a slower rate of improvement in symptoms of anxiety compared with benzodiazepines. These differences were significant at weeks 1 and 2 in the trial carried out by Rickels et al. (1988), which compared buspirone with clorazepate. It is clear from these studies that buspirone takes longer to exert anxiolytic effects than the benzodiazepines.

2. *Previous Benzodiazepine Treatment*

Schweizer et al. (1986) reanalyzed data from an earlier trial of buspirone versus clorazepate (Rickels et al., 1982). He made the remarkable observation that 90% of patients who had not previously experienced benzodiazepines showed a significant improvement while taking buspirone. By contrast, only 56% of a group of 39 patients who had previously received benzodiazepines showed a significant improvement. One possibility is that the previously benzodiazepine-treated patients were in a state of withdrawal when entered into the buspirone trial, thereby masking a therapeutic effect. However, the authors tried to reduce the chances of this with a 4-week withdrawal phase before entry into the trial. Schweizer et al. (1986) speculated that benzodiazepine-experienced patients missed the subjective effect when given buspirone and that the failed expectation counteracted the therapeutic effect. However, it seems unlikely that a major, physical anxiolytic effect of buspirone would have been abolished by disappointment at the lack of benzodiazepine-like effect. Furthermore, the lack of a subjective benzodiazepinelike effect of placebo did not diminish the placebo response.

3. *Panic*

Buspirone may not be effective in the treatment of panic attacks. Rickels et al. (1988) found that of seven patients with a previous history of panic who were treated with buspirone, five dropped out. In contrast, nine patients with previous panic attacks who were entered into the clorazepate group all completed the trial. Three trials have examined the effects of buspirone in the treatment of panic disorder, and none has demonstrated superiority over placebo (Sheehan, 1990; Robinson, 1989; Pohl, 1989). Finally, there is anecdotal evidence that buspirone may exacerbate panic.

If true, a lack of effect of 5-HT_{1A} agonists on panic, but efficacy in generalized anxiety disorder has important implications. The finding would suggest that the two conditions are nosologically distinct. Furthermore, it would point to a different role of 5-HT in different types of anxiety (see Deakin and Graeff, 1991).

C. Depression

Fabre (1990) carried out a trial of buspirone against placebo in 140 patients with major depressive disorder and claimed significant superiority at weeks 2, 3, 4, and 6. However, caution is required in interpreting these results since 76 of the patients dropped out before the end of the 8-week treatment trial.

Robinson et al. (1990) carried out a metanalysis of three trials of buspirone against placebo in depression (Table 2). The results of the metanalysis are illustrated in Figure 1. The patients were subdivided according to whether they met *Diagnostic and Statistical Manual of Mental Disorders,* 3rd ed. (*DSM-III*) criteria for melancholia. The significant buspirone—placebo differences were as great in the melancholic subjects as in the nonmelancholic. This is taken as evidence for a genuine antidepressant effect of buspirone, rather than amelioration of anxiety in a depressive illness. However, the effect size is small, with placebo–drug differences of 5 points on the Hamilton depression rating scale. Furthermore, whereas 55% of those treated with buspirone showed significant clinical improvement, so did 32% of those treated with placebo.

Table 2 Trials of 5-HT_{1A} Agonists in Depression

Ref.	Drugs	Patients
Robinson et al., 1990	B > P	418 MDD
Rickels	B > P	153 OP
Fabre	B > P	140 MDD + HAMA > 60% drop-outs
Multicenter	B > P	127
Jenkins et al., 1990	G > P	121 MDD 50% drop-out
Heller et al., 1990	I > P	

Key: See Table 1; I, ipsapirone; G, gepirone; MDD, major depressive disorder; OP, outpatients; IP, inpatients.

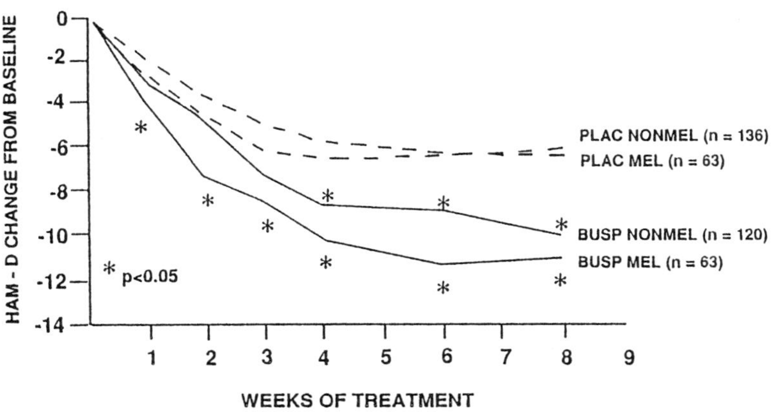

Figure 1 Hamilton depression ratings in patients with depression treated with buspirone or placebo (see Table 2). The patients were subdivided into melancholic and nonmelancholic groups for this analysis. (Redrawn from Robinson et al., 1990.)

Jenkins et al. (1990) have briefly presented the results of a trial of gepirone in major depressive disorder. There were two treatment groups, one receiving 5–45 mg gepirone per day, and another group receiving between 10 and 90 mg. A total of 121 patients entered the intention-to-treat sample, but half dropped out over the 8-week trial. This makes the results almost impossible to evaluate decisively. Hamilton depression ratings declined to a greater extent in the two treatment groups compared with placebo controls, but the difference was only significant when the two active groups were combined. Again, the effect size is small: 4 points on the Hamilton depression rating scale and a 60% improvement rate in those receiving active medication compared with 40% of those taking placebo.

Although the effect size of gepirone in depression appears to be small, it may be genuine. In the foregoing study, those who had improved on gepirone treatment were split into two groups, one of which continued to receive gepirone, and the other was switched to placebo. After 6 weeks, 70% of those who were switched to placebo relapsed, compared with only 30% of the gepirone group.

D. Conclusion

Surprisingly few large-scale placebo-controlled studies of 5-HT_{1A} agonists have been carried out in anxiety and depression. They suggest that there are statistically significant anxiolytic and antidepressant effects of 5-HT_{1A} agonists, but the size of the treatment effect appears to be small. It does seem clear that buspirone has little efficacy in treating panic and may aggravate it.

More studies will be required to elucidate the role of the metabolite 1-PP and of dopamine receptor antagonism in these effects. Indeed, it may be that the metabolite might counteract the therapeutic effect of azapirones (Martin et al., 1989).

III. SEROTONIN$_2$–SEROTONIN$_{1C}$

The main representatives of this class are trazodone, mianserin, and ritanserin. From a theoretical perspective, ritanserin is of the greatest interest because of its selectivity for 5-HT_2–5-HT_{1C} receptors, although it probably has dopamine receptor antagonist actions too. Trazodone is less selective, with weak actions at the 5-HT transporter and at α-receptors. It is metabolized to *m*-chlorophenylpiperazine (mCPP), which is a 5-HT_{1C} agonist with apparent anxiogenic properties in humans. Mianserin's additional actions include α_2-receptor antagonism. The efficacy of mianserin and trazodone have been the subject of an earlier literature and will not be reviewed here.

Many established antidepressant drugs block or down-regulate 5-HT_2 and 5-HT_{1C} receptors. This was proposed as a unified mechanism of action of antidepressants (Peroutka and Snyder, 1980). Deakin (1988) and Deakin and Graeff (1991) suggested that 5-HT^2–5-HT_{1C} antagonism or down-regulation might contribute to the efficacy of antidepressant drugs in reducing symptoms of generalized anxiety, whereas enhancement of 5-HT_{1A} function mediated antidepressant effects. Kahn et al. (1988) has suggested that 5-HT_2–5-HT_{1C} receptors play a crucial role in the mediation of panic. Thus, Deakin and Graeff (1991) predict efficacy of ritanserin in anxiety, with secondary improvement of depression, whereas Kahn predicts efficacy in panic disorder.

The therapeutic profile of ritanserin is thus of critical theoretical importance.

A. Ritanserin in Anxiety

Recent placebo controlled trials of ritanserin in anxiety are summarized in Table 3.

An important early trial was reported by Ceulemans et al. (1985). This trial compared two doses of ritanserin with positive comparator—lorazepam, 4 mg/day. The efficacy of ritanserin appeared to be dose-related and equivalent to lorazepam. This was a short trial, but a significant difference was observed at 2 weeks. In contrast, Pangalila-Ratu Langi and Janssen (1988) failed to find significant superiority of ritanserin over placebo after 2 weeks, but a significant placebo–ritanserin difference was noted by 4 weeks of treatment. A major complication in interpreting this trial is that 10 of 58 patients were excluded because they violated entry criteria, and a further 14 dropped out during the course of treatment. The trial by Hoppenbrouwers et al. (1986a) involved three doses of ritanserin and a diazepam-treated group in an impressively large study. No significant effects of any drug dose was observed. The trial may be criticized because entry criteria were not clearly defined beyond having significant anxiety symptoms. The authors suggest that significant anxiolytic effects of ritanserin might have been obscured by the fact that some 30% of the subjects were withdrawn from benzodiazepines before entry into the trial. However, there is no subsequent analysis of the data to corroborate this.

Pangalila-Ratu Langi and Janssen (1988) investigated the profile of ritanserin's effects in the different symptoms of anxiety. The drug appears to have a particularly marked effect in improving insomnia, tension, lethargy, and depressed mood—the improvements being significant in each. However, on every item patients improved to a greater extent on ritanserin therapy than with placebo. There is no evidence that the improvement was significantly greater on some items than on others. It is clear from many studies that the various symptoms of anxiety and depression are highly intercorrelated, particularly in the neurotic population (Goldberg et al., 1987). Perhaps the most compelling trial of ritanserin in anxiety is that carried out by Waelkens et al. (1984). The trial is not complicated by large numbers of dropouts and a clear-cut significant effect is seen at week 3. The dose used was high—25 mg. The magnitude of the treatment effect is similar to that observed by Ceulemans et al., 1985). However, no formal operational entry criteria were used.

Table 3 Ritanserin Studies in Anxiety

Study	No. of patients	Drug/dose (mg)	Therapeutic evaluation[a]		
			CGI	HAMA	VAMRS
Ceulemans et al., 1985	83	Ritanserin, 10	0.05	0.05	
		Ritanserin, 5	NS	NS	
		Lorazepam, 4	0.05	0.05	
Hoppenbrouwers et al., 1986a	164	Ritanserin, 10	NS	NS	
		Ritanserin, 5	NS	NS	
		Ritanserin, 2.5	NS	NS	
		Diazepam, 10	NS	NS	
Pangalila-Ratu Lanhgi and Janssen, 1988	48	Ritanserin, 10	0.01	0.05	NS
Waelkens et al., 1984	71	Ritanserin, 25	0.001	0.05	

[a] Significant (p) improvements compares with baseline; NS, no significant effect.
Key: CGI, clinical global impression; HAMA, Hamilton anxiety ratings; VAMRS, Visual analog mood-rating scale.

It is difficult to judge the clinical significance of a 7- to 10-point decrease in the Hamilton anxiety rating scale. In the Pangalila-Ratu Langi and Janssen study (1988), about 70% of the patients receiving ritanserin are rated as showing a good or very good improvement, compared with 27% of those taking placebo. Similar effects were claimed by Waelkens et al. (1984). This placebo response rate seems surprisingly small, but nevertheless, these trials suggest that ritanserin has some clinically significant anxiolytic effects.

B. Ritanserin in Mixed Anxiety Depression

Table 4 summarizes studies performed in patients with mixtures of anxiety and depression. The studies by Hoppenbrouwers (1986a,b) were organized by Janssen Pharmaceutical. The inclusion criteria were based on *DSM-III* for generalized anxiety disorder, atypical anxiety, dysthymia, and atypical depression. To ensure adequate levels of anxiety and depression the patients had to score more than 12 points on the Hamilton anxiety rating scale and 15 on the Montgomery–Asberg depression scale. A large number of subjects were treated (232), but by a large number of general practitioners (46). Trends in favor of ritanserin were seen on the symptom-rating scales and on the global severity scales. All three doses of ritanserin were more effective than placebo (p = 0.05). There is no information about withdrawals, clinical feature of the patients, nor details about the treating physicians. However, any systematic bias would have to be very large to produce statistically significant effects of the drug in so many patients.

The studies by Crocq et al. (1988, 1989) again involve numerous outpatients with ill-specific entry criteria. There are too few details to evaluate these trials.

C. Ritanserin in Dysthymia and Minor Depression

Janssen Pharmaceutical confined its trials in depression to minor illness on the basis of an apparent lack of efficacy in open studies with major depression (Table 5). The difficulty in studying lesser degrees of depression is that operational criteria do not exist in *DSM-III* except for the category of the new concept of dysthymia. This is truly a mild depression, but there is a severe entry criterion that the patients have had significant symptoms more or less continuously for 2 years. Because of this criterion for chronicity, only a small percentage of neurotic patients fulfill the criteria for dysthymia.

Two trials were carried out in general practice, and some statistically significant effects were seen with the 20-mg dose (Hoppenbrouwers et al., 1986b; Reyntjens et al., 1986). It is very improbable that rigorous *DSM-III* criteria for dysthymia were applied. Two trials in a University Department in Portugal (Arriaga et al., 1986; Paiva et al., 1987) found statistically significant effects of ritanserin over placebo, but the effect size is small, the results were of borderline statistical significance, and the sample sizes are small. Furthermore, there are no details about patient withdrawals or other features of the design.

Murphy and Checkley (1988) compared placebo and ritanserin (10 mg) in a small trial with 17 patients. They applied rigorous diagnostic criteria for dysthymia and the proportions of male and female subjects were carefully counterbalanced in the two treatment groups. Furthermore, two subtypes of dysthymic patients were present in equal proportions in the two groups (characterological depressives or chronic primary depressives). A female subject dropped out after the first week of treatment with ritanserin because her clinical state deteriorated. Whether or not the patient is included,

Table 4 Summary of Some of the Major Ritanserin Studies in Mixed Anxiety-Depression States

Study	No. of patients	Drug/dose (mg)	Therapeutic evaluation[a]			
			CGI	HAMA	MADS	CBAS
Crocq et al., 1988	121	20	0.01			0.01
		10	0.05			0.05
Crocq et al., 1989	161	10	NS			0.05
		5	NS			NS
Hoppenbrouwers et al., 1986b	55	10	0.05	NS		
Hoppenbrouwers et al., 1989	232	10	0.05	NS	NS	
		5	0.05	NS	NS	
		2.5	0.05	NS	NS	

[a] Significant (p) improvement compared with baseline; NS, no significant effect.

Key: CGI, Clinical global impressions; HAMA, Hamilton anxiety rating; MADS, Montgomery–Asberg Depression Self-Rating Scale; CBAS, Crocq and Bugard Astheno-Depression Scale.

Table 5 Summary of Some Ritanserin Studies in Dysthymia

Study	No. of patients	Drug/dose (mg)	Therapeutic evaluation[a]						
			CGI	HAMA	HAMD	VAMRS	Leeds	VAS	STAI
Arriaga et al., 1986	43	10	0.05		0.05				
Bersani et al., 1988	29	10	0.01	0.01	0.001			0.01	
Hoppenbrouwers et al., 1986c	53	20	0.05		NS				
		10	NS		NS				
Meco et al., 1989[b]	36	10–20	NS	NS	NS			NS	
Murphy and Checkley, 1988	17	10	NS	0.08	0.05				
Paiva et al., 1987	23	10	0.09	NS	NS		0.05	0.05	NS
Reyntjens et al., 1986	93	20	0.05		NS	NS			

[a] Significant (p) improvement compared with baseline; NS, no significant effect.
[b] Significant effects compared with amitriptyline 25–50 mg.
Key: CGI, clinical global impression; HAMA, Hamilton anxiety ratings; HAMD, Hamilton depression ratings; VAMRS, visual analog mood-rating scale; VAS, visual analog scale; STAI, state–trait anxiety inventory.

the end result is similar—a just-significant improvement on Hamilton depression ratings and a borderline trend on Hamilton anxiety ratings for ritanserin-treated patients to do better than those receiving placebo. There were no significant differences on the Carroll rating scale. Although this is a well-designed and carefully executed trial, it cannot be regarded as decisive because of the small numbers and because of the large difference in initial severity scores between the two groups.

In another trial in dysthymia, Bersani et al. (1991) found significant effects of ritanserin against placebo of all ratings. The size of the treatment effect was small, and the improvement in Hamilton depression ratings of 7 points did not approach the 50% reduction that many regard as the definition of a treatment response.

D. The Manchester Neurosis Trial

The Manchester Neurosis Trial was conceived from a theoretical viewpoint (since abandoned by the author; Deakin and Graeff, 1991) which held that mild symptoms of anxiety or depression are highly intercorrelated manifestations of a unitary neurotic syndrome, which encompasses panic disorder (Tyrer, 1985; Goldberg et al., 1987). A standardized clinical interview schedule (CIS; Goldberg et al., 1970) was used to detect significant degrees of anxiety or depression, and this was the sole criterion for entry. Treatment was randomized within clinical subgroups to ensure that the different treatment groups were clinically comparable. Table 6 shows that similar numbers of patients fell into the clinical groups within each treatment group.

One week after interview, patients rated themselves by use of computer-generated Hopkins Symptom Checklist 90 (SCL-90), Spielberger State–Trait Anxiety and Beck Depression Inventory. Treatment began the next day and patients rerated themselves after 7 days of treatment, and all ratings were rated after 4 weeks of treatment. Patients with major depressive disorder were excluded from the trial. Very few patients had symptoms of depression without anxiety, and these subjects were excluded from the analysis.

1. Results

Questionnaire ratings and self-ratings were analyzed by analysis of covariance to adjust the differences in initial scores. Main effects and interactions for clinical group, sex, and treatment were calculated. Table 7 summarizes the significant effects involving drug treatment. Significant interactions between drug and sex and between drug and clinical group were seen on almost every rating scale, and this indicated that the effects of

Table 6 Symptoms of Patients at Entry into the Manchester Neurosis Trial

	Treatment[a]	
Clinical symptom	Placebo	Ritanserin
Anxious	18	14
Anxious + depressed	8	12
Depressed	1	3
Total	27	29
	(12 male, 15 female)	(14 male, 15 female)

[a] Number of patients in each treatment group.

Table 7 Summary of Analysis of Covariance of Treatment Weeks 1-4 of the Manchester Neurosis Trial, Covarying Pretreatment Ratings

	Analysis of covariance[a]		
Therapeutic evaluation	Drug	Drug × sex	Drug × diagnosis
Hamilton Anxiety-Rating Scale		0.06	
Symptom checklist: anxiety		0.02	0.02
State anxiety		0.003	0.1
Trait anxiety	0.04		0.05
Hamilton Depression-Rating Scale			
Beck	0.11	0.05	
Symptom checklist: depression		0.01	0.02

[a] Figures indicate probabilities (p).

ritanserin differed depending on the sex of the subjects and whether they had depressive symptoms or not.

Only one main effect of drug was seen on Spielberger Trait Anxiety. Figure 2 shows the state anxiety ratings improved more in those taking ritanserin than in those taking placebo, and that this effect was seen at week 1. No further effect was seen at week 4. The drug and sex interaction indicated that ritanserin was more effective than placebo, particularly in males. This surprising result is not unprecedented. Gender effects are rarely sought in clinical trials, often because females are preponderant. However, in this trial, roughly equal numbers of the sexes were included. In the Medical Research Council Somatic Therapy Trial (1965), imipramine and phenelzine were effective only in males, compared with placebo, and not in females.

The drug by clinical group interaction indicated that patients with mixed anxiety–depression showed a greater improvement (see Table 7) in most ratings when treated with ritanserin compared with placebo.

The effect size in this trial is small. A 6-point difference in Spielberger Trait Anxiety ratings would not suggest a major therapeutic effect in mixed neurotic outpatients. We speculated that one reason for the small effect size could be due to heterogeneity in the neurotic group. This possibility was suggested by the finding of den Boer and Westenberg (1990) that ritanserin had no effect whatsoever in the treatment of patients with panic disorder and even intensified symptoms on some rating scales, albeit nonsignificantly. For this and for theoretical reasons (Deakin and Graeff, 1991) we retrospectively reanalyzed the Manchester Neurosis Trial, examining treatment effects in those with panic diagnoses and those without. It is clear from Figure 3 that patients with panic diagnoses did significantly less well when taking ritanserin than did those taking placebo. The remaining, nonpanic paitents were diagnostically heterogeneous, and the effect of ritanserin in generalized anxiety disorder could not be evaluated.

E. Efficacy of Ritanserin and Implications

Firm conclusions are not possible on the basis of the available evidence. Ritanserin suffers from not having been the subject of a large-scale multicenter placebo-controlled trial

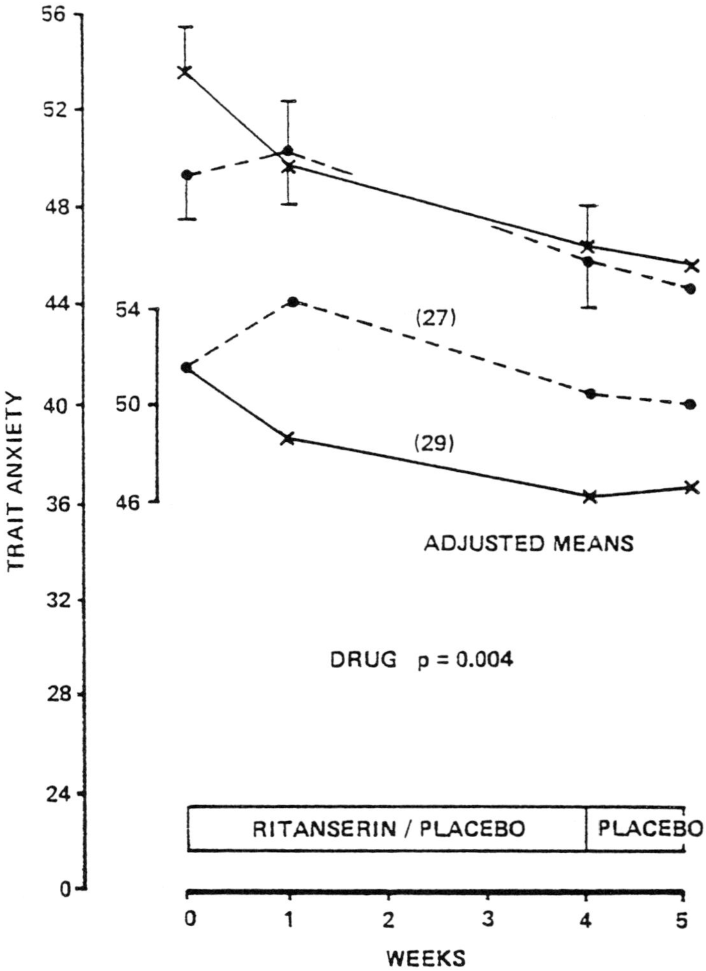

Figure 2 Spielberger trait anxiety scores in the Manchester ritanserin trial. Insert shows means for weeks 1, 4, and 5 covaried for differences in initial scores between placebo and ritanserin treated subjects. Means ± SEM shown.

in major depressive disorder or anxiety. The most consistent findings have been found in trials in patients who have concurrent depressive symptoms.

Ritanserin's effects on anxiety appear to be small and of similar magnitude to the 5-HT_{1A} agonists. As noted earlier, large treatment effects in anxiety trials are rare, even with benzodiazepines (Kahn et al., 1986; Johnstone et al., 1986). Clinical trials in generalized anxiety disorder, especially with a 5-HT_{1A} comparator, would be of considerable interest. It is clear that ritanserin lacks efficacy in panic disorder, and this would appear to be a decisive refutation of Kahn's theory that 5-HT_2–5HT_{1C} down-regulation is the mechanism of action of antidepressants in panic disorder (Kahn et al., 1988).

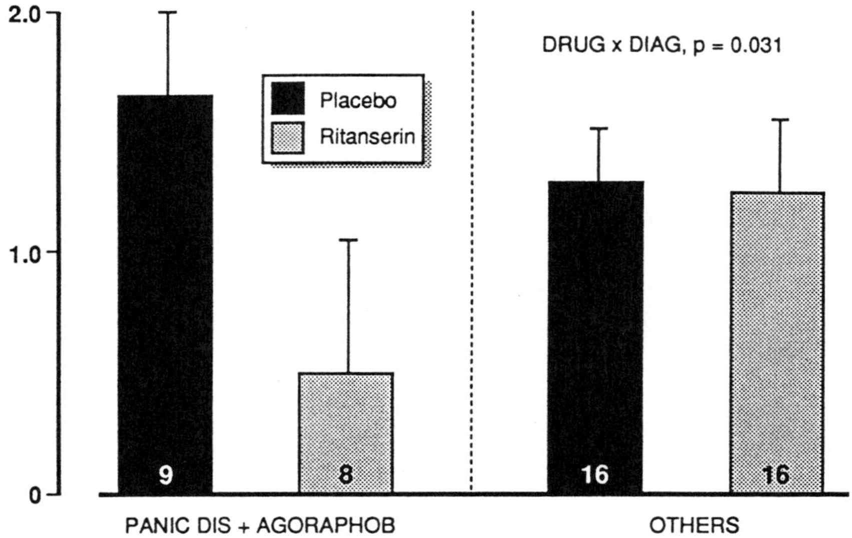

Figure 3 A reanalysis of the Manchester ritanserin trial by ***DSM-III*** panic vs nonpanic diagnosis. The diagnoses were made retrospectively from the case notes. Means ± SEM. (From J. F. W. Deakin, M. Wang, and F. Guimaraes, in preparation.)

IV. SEROTONIN$_3$ ANTAGONISTS

Several very selective 5-HT antagonists have been developed. In preclinical studies, ondansetron, BRL46470, and zacopride have shown anxiolyticlike effects, but somewhat inconsistently. In general, the compounds appear to be active in inhibiting spontaneous forms of anxiety, rather than in tests involving learning. Thus, primates' spontaneous fear reactions to the approach of a human are attenuated by pretreatment with 5-HT$_3$ antagonists. In contrast, the drugs do not appear to be effective in the conflict paradigm—a form of passive avoidance learning (see Costall, 1991 for review).

A further feature of some 5-HT$_3$ antagonists is the unusual dose–response relation. It has been reported that extremely small doses of some 5-HT$_3$ antagonists are effective in animal models of anxiety, but that higher doses lose their efficacy.

Clinical trials are awaited to determine whether these agents have predicted anxiolytic effects. Brief details of a trial of ondansetron versus placebo and a benzodiazepine have been reported, but therapeutic effects were extremely small. Although this has been attributed to a large placebo effect, the final Hamilton anxiety scores suggest there was room for further improvement.

V. SEROTONIN-REUPTAKE BLOCKERS

Several compounds with high affinity for the 5-HT transporter have been developed and marketed. With one or two exceptions, they are devoid of potent effects of functional importance at other neurotransmitter transporters or receptors. The 5-HT-reuptake blockers vary in their pharmacokinetic properties. For example, the half-life of fluoxetine is 52 h and it has a pharmacologically active metabolite that can be detected as long as 2 weeks after last dosing. This has important clinical implications for the treatment of

Table 8 Clinical Pharmacology of Serotonin-Reuptake Inhibitors

Drug	Elimination half-life (h)	Active metabolites	Metabolite elimination half-life (h)	Daily dose (mg)
Fluvoxamine	15	No	15	100–300
Fluoxetine	70	Yes	330	20–80
Sertraline	25	No	NA	50–200
Paroxetine	12–20	No	NA	10–50
Citalopram	33	Yes	?	20–60

overdosage and the commencement of other therapies, such as monoamine oxidase inhibitors after treatment with fluoxetine. The half-lives and metabolism of the 5-HT-reuptake blockers are compared in Table 8.

A. Efficacy

For each of the 5-HT-reuptake blockers listed in Table 9, there is now clear evidence from large multicenter placebo-controlled trials that the agents are superior to placebo in the treatment of depression. It is not yet clear whether the 5-HT-reuptake blockers are more or less effective than other antidepressants in different forms of depression. This is not surprising, as it is far from clear whether there are specific clinical features that predict responsiveness to tricyclic antidepressants and not to placebo.

A literature suggests that electroconvulsive therapy (ECT) is more effective than tricyclic antidepressant drugs in the treatment of delusional depression, whereas the reverse is true for nondelusional depression (Baldwin, 1988; Clinical Research Centre, 1984). The issue has not been investigated with the 5-HT-reuptake blockers. However, there is evidence that initial severity (higher Hamilton depression ratings, for example) predict a greater difference between placebo and active drugs for paroxetine and fluvoxamine (Conti and Dell'Osso, 1989). The same effect for imipramine–placebo differences was noted in the large NIMH study (Elkin et al., 1989). Claims have been made that the 5-HT-reuptake blockers are particularly effective in treating symptoms of anxiety associated with depression and for suicidal ideation (Montgomery, 1992). The claims are

Table 9 Key Trials of 5-HT-Reuptake Inhibitors

	Vs placebo	Vs clomipramine (CLO) or amitriptyline
Fluvoxamine	Cassano et al., 1986	Klok et al., 1981; CLO
Fluoxetine	Cohn and Wilcox, 1985	Young et al., 1987
Sertraline	Reimherr et al., 1990	Reimherr et al., 1990; CLO
Paroxetine	Dunbar et al., 1991	DUAG, 1990; CLO
Citalopram	Mendels et al., 1990[a]	DUAG, 1986; CLO

[a] Abstract only.

based on the early statistical significance of the drug–placebo differences in anxiety and suicidal ideation, whereas other items take 1 or 2 weeks longer to achieve significance. However, all items of depression improve, and no study has carried out the appropriate statistical analysis to show that anxiety or suicidal ideation improve more rapidly than the other items. This would require a drug-by-symptom interaction in an analysis of variance. Reimherr et al. (1984) found "atypical" depressives (Quitkin et al., 1982) responded better when taking fluoxetine than with imipramine, whereas "typical" depressives responded equally well when taking either of the two drugs, with some differences in favor of imipramine.

It is clear that the 5-HT-reuptake blockers generally lack immediate sedative side effects and do not induce weight gain. Nevertheless, it is clear that insomnia is improved by 5-HT-reuptake blockers over a 4- to 6-week period.

B. Comparative Efficacy

Demonstrating that an effective antidepressant drug is more or less effective than existing agents is difficult to establish with certainty, since many patients are required to be confident that any difference observed would be statistically significant. Many trials have compared 5-HT-reuptake blockers with imipramine. For the reasons just mentioned, most trials find no significant differences between the two, but some trials report significant superiority for fluoxetine, fluvoxamine, and paroxetine over imipramine (Feighner and Boyer, 1989; Guelfi, 1983; Bremner, 1984), whereas one or two trials find the reverse (Peselow et al., 1989; Feighner et al., 1989). In comparison with clomipramine and amitriptyline, however, there does seem to be a compelling trend that the symptoms do not resolve as quickly with 5-HT-reuptake blockers. For each of the 5-HT-reuptake blockers, a reasonably well-controlled trial has found statistically significant superiority for the nonselective 5-HT-uptake inhibitors clomipramine or amitryptyline over the selective agent (see Table 9). In other trials, there is a consistent trend for the improvement to be greater in those treated with a nonselective agent.

It can be seen that there is some evidence that the rank order of efficacy of antidepressant drugs in the short-term treatment of depression may be nonselective serotonin 5-HT-uptake inhibitors (clomipramine, amitryptyline) > selective 5-HT-uptake inhibitor > nonselective noradrenaline uptake inhibitor (imipramine). This view is compatible with the anecdotal reports that the antidepressant efficacy of selective 5-HT-uptake inhibitors may be enhanced or potentiated by the addition of a norepinephrine-uptake inhibitor, such as desipramine or lofepramine. Assuming pharmacodynamic interactions are not responsible for such effects, then nonselective 5-HT-uptake inhibitors may be better than selective because they have efficacy against norepinephrine uptake. However, other mechanisms might account for any differences. For example, clomipramine has intrinsic affinity for some postsynaptic 5-HT receptors, including the 5-HT_{1C} and the 5-HT_2 receptor. Deakin (1988) suggested that the shared ability of nonselective agents to antagonize or down-regulate 5-HT_2–5-HT_{1C} receptor functioning might account for some of the therapeutic efficacy—particularly anxiolytic actions (Deakin and Graeff, 1991). Some selective 5-HT-uptake inhibitors also induce a delayed down-regulation of 5-HT_2–5-HT_{1C} receptor binding, but the changes are smaller than with the nonselective agents (Nelson et al., 1989). However, several selective 5-HT-reuptake blockers may act to decrease functional 5-HT_2–5-HT_{1C} neurotransmission by emergent actions on inositol 1,3,4-triphosphate (IP_3) second-messenger mechanisms (Sanders-Bush et al., 1989).

C. Dose-Response Relations

Fixed-dose parallel-group studies have established threshold doses for efficacy for several 5-HT-reuptake blockers, but progressive increases in therapeutic efficacy beyond threshold have not been clearly demonstrated. Indeed, there have been suggestions that there may be an inverted U-shaped dose response relation for fluoxetine (Wernicke et al., 1987; Fichtner et al., 1991; Baldwin, 1991). This is based on anecdotal reports with individual patients in whom a therapeutic effect has disappeared on increasing the dose, to reappear again when the dose was reduced. The parallel-group fixed-dose study of paroxetine is weakly suggestive that higher doses may be slightly less effective than intermediate doses of the drug.

Deakin et al. (1989) suggested that antidepressants work by enhancing 5-HT_{1A} neurotransmission relative to 5-HT_2–5-HT_{1C}, rather than simply enhancing 5-HT neurotransmission globally. It seems possible that intermediate doses might differentially enhance neurotransmission at some 5-HT synapses and not at others, whereas higher doses cause a global enhancement and, thus, less of a therapeutic effect. In keeping with this idea, Martin et al. (1989) found that the efficacy of higher doses of a 5-HT-reuptake blocker in reversing learned helplessness could be restored with the concomitant administration of a 5-HT_2 receptor antagonist. These considerations suggest that 5-HT_2–5-HT_{1C} antagonists might enhance a therapeutic efficacy of selective 5-HT-reuptake blockers in depression. Indeed, it is possible that lithium potentiation of antidepressant efficacy occurs by this mechanism (lithium attenuates the second-messenger response to 5-HT_2–5-HT_{1C} receptor stimulation).

D. Side Effects

The selective 5-HT-reuptake inhibitors lack the anticholinergic and cardiotoxic side effects of tricyclic antidepressant drugs. Furthermore, the selective 5-HT-uptake inhibitors are less likely to cause weight gain. These are the reasons that the 5-HT-reuptake inhibitors constitute a major advance in the treatment of depression (e.g., Cooper, 1988).

Selective 5-HT-reuptake inhibitors have their own side effects. The main problems are nausea, anxiety, and insomnia. The frequency of the side effects depends very much on the method of recording them, but perhaps up to 20% of patients treated with 5-HT-uptake inhibitors may report one or the other of the main side effects. Because these side effects are fewer with 5-HT-reuptake inhibitors than with older nonselective uptake blockers, compliance with treatment is likely to be greater. However, the evidence from controlled clinical trials suggests that dropouts owing to side effects are not, in fact, markedly different between older antidepressant drugs and the selective 5-HT-uptake inhibitors.

Even though anxiety, insomnia, and nausea occur early in therapy and tend to improve after the first 2 weeks, other side effects may emerge significantly more frequently than with placebo during maintenance treatment. These include sweating and anorgasmia. The latter can be successfully treated with the nonselective 5-HT antagonist cyproheptadine before sexual activity.

Reports that fluoxetine released suicidal and aggressive behavior (Teicher et al., 1990) have prompted a careful examination of databases and such fears seem unfounded (Beasley et al., 1991).

E. Efficacy in Other Conditions

1. *Obsessional–Compulsive Disorder*

There is a compelling case that clomipramine is superior to imipramine in the treatment of obsessional–compulsive disorder (OCD). As might be expected, placebo-controlled trials suggest that the selective 5-HT-uptake inhibitors, fluvoxamine and fluoxetine, are also effective (e.g., Goodman et al., 1989). However, the improvement rate is not as great as with depression, and this no doubt reflects the underlying chronicity of a proportion of cases with obsessional–compulsive disorder. Improvement rates of 50–60% were reported in earlier trials with clomipramine, whereas response rates of less than 30% have been reported with the selective 5-HT-uptake inhibitors. This might suggest that clomipramine is somewhat more effective than selective 5-HT-uptake inhibitors, not only as suggested in the foregoing for depression, but also in obsessional–compulsive disorder. However, against this suggestion, some preliminary studies suggest that selective agents may be as effective as clomipramine, but larger comparative studies are needed to establish this point. Furthermore, there is evidence that selective 5-HT-uptake inhibitors, like clomipramine, are superior to norepinephrine-uptake blockers in improving OCD (Goodman et al., 1990).

It is clear that 5-HT-reuptake inhibitors improve the core symptoms of OCD, and that this is not secondary to an antidepressant action of the drugs. Thus, improvement in symptoms of OCD is not proportional to initial severity of depression, and significant efficacy over placebo has been reported in patients without significant symptoms of depression.

2. *Panic Disorder*

There is no doubt that 5-HT-reuptake blockers are effective in the treatment of panic, and it has been most clearly established for the drug fluvoxamine (den Boer and Westenberg, 1990). Compared with a group of subjects treated with placebo or the 5-HT_2–5-HT_{1C} antagonist ritanserin, fluvoxamine-treated subjects showed a progressive reduction in symptoms of panic. There is suggestive evidence that 5-HT-reuptake inhibitors may be more effective than agents with greater effect on norepinephrine-reuptake, such as imipramine and maprotiline (den Boer and Westenberg, 1988). There is no evidence to suggest that the nonselective 5-HT-uptake inhibitor clomipramine is superior to the treatment of panic—there have been no comparative studies.

3. *Eating Disorder*

It is clear that fluvoxamine and fluoxetine decrease the frequency of bingeing in patients with bulimia. However, discontinuation is fairly rapidly followed by resumption of bingeing.

4. *Other Indications*

Impaired 5-HT functioning has been associated with so-called disorders of impulse control, which have been taken to include suicidal behavior, arson, aggression, addictive behavior (alcoholism, drug abuse), and obsessional–compulsive disorder (Linnoila and Virkkunen, 1991). However, these conditions are extremely heterogeneous. Furthermore, inability to restrain impulses does not characterize them all. Patients with obsessional–compulsive disorder, for example, are generally very controlled nonimpulsive individuals. Aggression and drug abuse are not part of the clinical picture of obsessional–compulsive disorder.

Deakin (1992, in press) has suggested that some of the foregoing impulsive behaviors are normally restrained by anticipatory anxiety acquired through the process of socialization. Some forebrain 5-HT systems appear to be concerned with mechanisms of anticipatory anxiety (Deakin and Graeff, 1991), and defective neurotransmission in these pathways may disinhibit such behaviors as aggression, homicide, suicide, and arson.

Drug and alcohol addiction and OCD may, in contrast, be seen as disturbances in mechanisms of learning, resulting in compulsive, rather than impulsive, behavior (Deakin, 1992, in press). Deakin and Graeff (1991) suggested that hippocampal and cortical 5-HT mechanisms may mediate a kind of unlearning, disconnection mechanism, so that responses with an aversive outcome become eliminated from the behavioral repertoire. This mechanism may also be necessary for normal learning and memory (McEntee and Crook, 1991). A failure of this mechanism might thus result in the persistence of abnormal behavior.

These considerations suggest that selective 5-HT-reuptake blockers should be effective in the treatment both of disturbances of the primary drives and of the abnormal acquired drives. Efficacy of 5-HT-reuptake blockers in OCD and eating disorders has already been discussed. There are anecdotal reports of efficacy in gambling, trichotillomania, and paraphilias, but no definitive evidence.

Although there is a literature in animal models of alcoholism that suggests that enhancing 5-HT function might eliminate alcohol-seeking behavior, there is very little clinical evidence that this is so (Thomas, 1991; Tyers and Heyes, 1992; Gill and Amit, 1989). There is a report that nondepressed heavy drinkers reduce their alcohol consumption and were more abstinent during treatment with zimelidine or citalopram (Sellers and Naranjo, 1986). A similar effect of fluoxetine has been reported (Naranjo et al., 1989). However, these are very preliminary studies and more research is needed.

REFERENCES

F. Arriaga, I. Ruiz, E. Lare et al., Ritanserin, an original thymosthenic for the treatment of dysthymia. A double-blind placebo-controlled study, *XVth CINP Congr.*, Abstr. 168 (1986).

B. Baldwin, Delusional and non-delusional depression in late life: Evidence for distinct subtypes, *Br. J. Psychiatry, 152*: 39 (1988).

D. Baldwin, Fluoxetine dose, *Lancet, 338*: 828 (1991).

C. M. Beasley, B. E. Dornseit, and J. C. Bosomworth, Fluoxetine and suicidality: Absence of association in controlled depression trials, *Br. Med. J., 303*: 685 (1991).

M. Beneke, B. Kuemmel, I. Roed, and H. Spechtmeyer, Treatment of anxiety neurosis with ipsapirone, *Psychopharmacology, 96*(Suppl.): 353 (1988).

G. Bersani, F. Pozzi, S. Marini, A. Grispini, A. Pasini, and N. Ciani, 5-HT_2 receptor antagonism in dysthymic disorder: A double-blind placebo-controlled study with ritanserin, *Acta Psychiatr. Scand., 83*: 244 (1991).

P. Blier, C. de Montigny, and Y. Chaput, Modifications of the serotonin system by antidepressant treatments: Implications for the therapeutic response in major depression, *J. Clin. Psychopharmacol., 7*: 245 (1987).

C. Bohm, M. Placchi, F. Stallone, R. E. Gammans, D. R. Alms, R. C. Shrotriya, and D. S. Robinson, A double-blind comparison of buspirone, clobazam, and placebo in patients with anxiety treated in a general practice setting, *J. Clin. Psychopharmacol., 10*: 385 (1990a).

C. Bohm, D. S. Robinson, R. E. Gammans, R. C. Shrotriya, D. R. Alms, A. Leroy, and M. Placchi, Buspirone therapy in anxious elderly patients: A controlled clinical trial, *J. Clin. Psychopharmacol., 10*: 475 (1990b).

R. L. Borison, J. W. Albrecht, and B. I. Diamond, Efficacy and safety of a putative anxiolytic agent: Ipsapirone, *Drug Lit., 26*: 207 (1990).

J. D. Bremner, Fluoxetine in depressed patients: A comparison with imipramine, *J. Clin. Psychiatry., 45*: 414 (1984).

G. B. Cassano, L. Conti, G. Massimetti, F. Mengaii, J. S. Wakelin, and J. Levine, Use of a standardized documentation system (BLIPS/BDP) in the conduct of a multicenter international trial comparing fluvoxamine, imipramine and placebo, *Psychopharmacol. Bull., 22*: 52 (1986).

Clinical Research Centre, Division of Psychiatry, The Northwick Park ECT Trial. Predictors to response to real and simulated ECT, *Br. J. Psychiatry, 144*: 227 (1984).

L. Conti, and I. Dell'Osso, Clinical predictors of response to fluvoxamine, imipramine and placebo, *New Trends Exp. Clin. Psychiatry, 5*: 221 (1989).

T. B. Cohn, and C. Wilcox, A comparison of fluoxetine, imipramine and placebo in patients with major depressive disorders, *J. Clin. Psychiatry, 46*: 26 (1985).

G. L. Cooper, The safety of fluoxetine—an update, *Br. J. Psychiatry, 153*(Suppl. 3): 77 (1988).

B. Costall, and R. J. Naylor, Anxiolytic effects of 5-HT_3 antagonists in animals. *5-HT_{1A} Agonists, 5-HT_3 Antagonists and Benzodiazepines: Their Comparative Behavioural Pharmacology* (R. J. Rodgers and S. J. Cooper, eds.), John Wiley & Sons, Chichester, pp. 133–157 (1991).

L. Crocq, P. Bugard, and P. H. Bourhours, Ritanserin in astheno-depressive patients. A double-blind placebo-controlled study in general practice, *Psychopharmacology, 96*(Suppl.): 329 (1988).

L. Crocq, J. Hoffman, and P. H. Bourhours, Ritanserin in astheno-anxious and astheno-depressive patients, *VIII World Congress of Psychiatry,* Abstr. 1534 (1989).

D. L. S. Cuelemans, M. L. J. A. Hoppenbrouwers, Y. G. Gelders et al., The influence of ritanserin, a serotonin antagonist, in anxiety disorders: A double blind placebo-controlled study versus lorazepam, *Pharmacopsychiatry, 18*: 303 (1985).

Danish University Antidepressant Group (DUAG), Citalopram: Clinical effect profile in comparison with clomipramine. A controlled multicenter study, *Psychopharmacology, 90*: 131 (1986).

Danish University Antidepressant Group (DUAG), Paroxetine: A selective serotonin reuptake inhibitor showing better tolerance, but weaker antidepressant effect than clomipramine in a controlled multicenter study, *J. Affective Disord., 18*: 289 (1990).

J. F. W. Deakin, The neurochemistry of schizophrenia. *Schizophrenia, the Major Issues* (P. E. Bebbington, and P. McGuffin, eds.), Heineman Medical, London (1988).

J. F. W. Deakin, 5-HT antidepressant drugs and the psychosocial origins of depression, BAP Monograph Meeting, Psychopharmacology of Depression, O.U.P. (in preparation, 1992).

J. F. W. Deakin, and F. G. Graeff, 5-HT and mechanisms of defence, *J. Psychopharmacol., 5*: 305 (1991).

J. F. W. Deakin, M. Wang, and F. Guimaraes, Early clinical experience with ritanserin in neurotic patients, *A Clinical Profile of Ritanserin,* ADIS International, Chester, pp. 16–33 (1990).

J. F. W. Deakin, I. Pennell, A. K. Upadhaya, and R. Lofthouse, A neuroendocrine study of 5HT function in depression: Evidence for biological mechanisms of endogenous and psychosocial causation, *J. Psychopharmacol., 101*: 85 (1990).

P. L. Delgado, D. S. Charney, L. H. Price, G. K. Aghajanian, H. Landis, and G. R. Heninger, Serotonin function and the mechanism of antidepressant action: Reversal of antidepressant-induced remission by rapid depletion of plasma tryptophan, *Arch. Gen. Psychiatry, 47*: 411 (1990).

J. A. den Boer, and H. G. M. Westenberg, Effect of a serotonin and noradrenaline uptake inhibitor in panic disorders: A double-blind comparative study with fluvoxamine and maprotiline, *Int. Clin. Psychopharmacol., 3*: 59 (1988).

J. A. den Boer, and H. G. M. Westenberg, Serotonin function in panic disorder: A double-blind placebo-controlled study with fluvoxamine and ritanserin, *Psychopharmacology, 102*: 85 (1990).

G. C. Dunbar, J. B. Cohn, L. F. Fabre, J. P. Feighner, R. R. Fieve, J. Mendels, and R. K. Shrivastava, A comparison of paroxetine, imipramine and placebo in depressed out-patients, *Br. J. Psychiatry, 159*: 394 (1991).

A. S. Eison, and F. D. Yocca, Reduction in cortical $5HT_2$ receptor sensitivity after continuous gepirone treatment, *Eur. J. Pharmacol., 11*: 389 (1985).

I. Elkin, T. Shea, J. T. Watkins, S. D. Imber, S. M. Sotsky, J. F. Collins, D. R. Glass, P. A. Pilkonis, W. R. Leber, J. P. Docherty, S. J. Fiester, and M. B. Parloff, National Institute of Mental Health treatment of depression collaborative research program. General effectiveness of treatments, *Arch. Gen. Psychiatry, 46*: 971 (1989).

L. F. Fabre, Buspirone in the management of major depression: A placebo-controlled comparison, *J. Clin. Psychiatry, 51*: 555 (1990).

J. P. Feighner, and W. F. Boyer, Paroxetine in the treatment of depression: A comparison with imipramine and placebo, *Acta Psychiatr. Scand., 80*: 125 (1989).

J. P. Feighner, W. F. Boyer, C. H. Meredith et al., A placebo-controlled inpatient comparison of fluvoxamine maleate and imipramine in major depression, *Int. Clin. Psychopharmacol., 4*: 239 (1989).

C. G. Fichtner, T. H. Jobe, and B. G. Braun, Does fluoxetine have a therapeutic window? *Lancet, 338*: 520 (1991).

E. Frank, D. J. Kupfer, J. M. Perel, C. Cornes, D. B. Jarrett, A. G. Mallinger, M. E. Thase, A. B. McEachran, and V. J. Grochocinski, Three year outcomes for maintenance therapies in recurrent depression, *Arch. Gen. Psychiatry., 47*: 1093 (1990).

K. Gill, and Z. Amit, Serotonin uptake blockers and voluntary alcohol consumption. A review of recent studies, *Recent Dev. Alcohol., 7*: 225 (1989).

T. Glaser, M. Rath, J. Traber, K. Zilles, and A. Schleicher, A autoradiographic identification and topographical analysis of high affinity serotonin receptor subtypes as a target for the novel putative anxiolytic TV X Q 7821, *Brain Res., 358*: 129 (1985).

D. P. Goldberg et al., Standard psychiatric interview suitable for use in community surveys, *Br. J. Prevent. Soc. Med., 24*: 18 (1970).

H. L. Goldberg, and R. J. Finnerty, The comparative efficacy of buspirone and diazepam in the treatment of anxiety, *Am. J. Psychiatry, 136*: 1184 (1979).

D. P. Goldberg, K. Bridges, P. Duncan-Jones et al., Dimensions of neuroses seen in primary care settings, *Psychol. Med., 17*: 461 (1987).

W. K. Goodman, L. H. Price, S. A. Rasmussen et al., Efficacy of fluvoxamine in obsessive–compulsive disorder, *Arch. Gen. Psychiatry, 46*: 36 (1989).

W. K. Goodman, L. H. Price, P. L. Delgado et al., Specificity of serotonin reuptake inhibitors in the treatment of obsessive compulsive disorder: a comparison of fluvoxamine and desipramine, *Arch. Gen. Psychiatry, 47*: 577 (1990).

J. D. Guelfi, J. F. Dreyfus, P. Pichot et al., A double-blind controlled clinical trial comparing fluvoxamine with imipramine, *Br. J. Clin. Pharmacol., 15*: 411 (1983).

A. H. Heller, M. Beneke, B. Kuemmel, D. Spencer, and N. M. Kurtz, Ipsapirone: Evidence for efficacy in depression, *Drug Lit., 26*: 219 (1990).

M.-L. J. A. Hoppenbrouwers, Y. G. Gelders, G. Vanden Bussche et al., *The effect of benzodiazepine withdrawal on the therapeutic efficacy of a serotonin antagonist (ritanserin) in anxiety,* Clinical Research Report on R55667/5, Janssen Pharmaceutica NV (1986a).

M.-L. J. A. Hoppenbrouwers, Y. G. Gelders, A. J. M. Reyntjens et al., "The control of mood depression by ritanserin, a serotonin S2 antagonist," American College of Neuro-Psychopharmacology Annual Meeting, Washington, D.C. (1986b).

M.-L. J. A. Hoppenbrouwers, G. Vanden Bussche, Y. G. Gelders et al., General well-being improved by ritanserin, a selective serotonin-S2 antagonist in dysthymic patients. A double-blind study vs placebo, *XVth CINP Congr.,* Abstr. 168 (1986c).

S. W. Jenkins, D. S. Robinson, L. F. Fabre, Jr., J. J. Andary, M. E. Messina, and L. A. Reich, Gepirone in the treatment of major depression, *J. Clin. Psychopharmacol., 10*: 77S (1990).

E. C. Johnstone, D. G. C. Owens, C. D. Frith, K. McPherson, C. Dowie, G. Riley, and A. Gold, Neurotic illness and its responses to anxiolytic and antidepressant treatment, *Psycho. Med., 10*: 321 (1986).

R. S. Kahn, D. M. MacNair, R. S. Lipman, L. Covi, K. Rickels, R. Downing, S. Fisher, and L. M. Frankenthaler, Imipramine and chlordiazepoxide in depressive and anxiety disorders. II. Efficacy in anxious outpatients, *Arch. Gen. Psychiatry., 43*: 79 (1986).

R. S. Kahn, G. M. Asnis, S. Wetzler, and H. M. Van Praag, Neuroendocrine evidence for serotonin receptor hypersensitivity in panic disorder, *Psychopharmacology, 96*: 360 (1988).

G. A. Kennett, S. Dickinson, and G. Curzon, Enhancement of some 5-HT-dependent behavioural responses following repeated immobilization in rats, *Brain Res., 330*: 253 (1985).

C. J. Klok, G. J. Brouwer, H. M. van Praag et al., Fluvoxamine and clomipramine in depressed patients: A double-blind clinical study, *Acta Psychiatr. Scand., 64*: 1 (1981).

B. Kuemmel, M. Beneke, G. Krol, G. Schoellnhammer, and H. Spechtmeyer, Ipsapirone in the treatment of generalized anxiety disorder, *Psychopharmacology, 96*(Suppl.): 353 (1988).

M. Linnoila, and M. Virkkunen, Monoamines, glucose metabolism and impulse control, *5-Hydroxytryptamine in Psychiatry: A Spectrum of Ideas* (M. Sandler, A. Coppen, and S. Harnett, eds.), Oxford University Press, Oxford, pp. 258–278 (1991).

W. J. McEntee, and T. H. Crook. Serotonin, memory and the aging brain, *Psychopharmacology, 103*: 143 (1991).

P. Martin, A. M. Laporte, P. Soubrie, S. E. Mestikawy, and M. Hamon, Reversal of helpless behaviour in rats by serotonin uptake inhibitors, *Behavioural Pharmacology of 5-HT* (P. Bevan, A. R. Cools, and T. Archer, eds.), Lawrence Erlbaum, Hillsdale, N.J., pp. 231–233 (1989).

G. Meco, S. Marini, L. Mariani et al., Ritanserin nei disturbi distimci (*DSMIII*): Studio in doppio ceco versus amitiplina, *Progressi in Psichiatria,* Vol. 5 (P. Pancheri and G. C. Reda, eds.), pp. 1299–1307 (1989).

Medical Research Council Clinical Psychiatry Committee, Clinical trial of the treatment of depressive illness, *Br. Med. J., 1*: 881 (1965).

J. Mendels, L. Fabre, and A. Kiev, "A double-blind placebo controlled study of citalopram in manor depressive disorder," 30th Annual Meeting of the New Clinical Drug Evaluation Unit, Florida, May 29–June 1 (1990).

S. A. Montgomery, Suicide and antidepressants, *New Perspectives on the Treatment of Depression* (H. M. van Praag and Y. Lecrubier, eds.), Proceedings of a symposium held in Paris, 28 February 1992, ADIS International, pp. 24–31 (1992).

J. B. Morris, and A. T. Beck, The efficacy of antidepressant drugs, *Arch. Gen. Psychiatry, 30*: 667 (1974).

D. Murphy, and S. A. Checkley, A prevalence study and treatment study of ritanserin in dysthymic disorder, *Psychopharmacology, 96*(Suppl.): 109 (1988).

C. A. Naranjo, E. M. Sellers, K. E. Kadlec, D. V. Woodley-Remus, H. Valencia, P. Sanhueza, and G. Kennedy, Fluoxetine differentially alters consummatory behaviours, *Clin. Pharmacol. Ther., 45*: 171 (1989).

D. R. Nelson, D. R. Thomas, and A. M. Johnson, Pharmacological effects of paroxetine after repeated administration to animals, *Acta Psychiatr. Scand., 80*: 21 (1989).

T. Paiva, F. Arriaga, A. Wauquier et al., Changes in sleep disturbances of dysthymic patients induced by ritanserin, *Proceedings of the International Symposium in Current Trends in Slow Wave Research* (A. Wauquier et al., eds.), Raven Press, New York, pp. 217–234 (1987).

E. A. Pangalila-Ratu Langi, and A. A. I. Janssen, Ritanserin in the treatment of generalised anxiety disorders: A placebo-controlled trial, *Hum. Psychopharmacol., 3*: 207 (1988).

J. C. Pecknold, P. Familamiri, H. Chang, R. Wilson, J. Alarcia, and D. J. McClure, Buspirone: Anxiolytic? *Prog. Neuropsychopharmacol. Biol. Psychiatry, 9*: 639 (1985).

S. J. Peroutka, and S. H. Snyder, Long-term antidepressant treatment decreases spiroperidol-labelled serotonin receptor building, *Science, 210*: 88 (1980).

E. D. Peselow, A.-M. Filippi, P. Goodnick, F. Barouche, and R. R. Fieve, The short- and long-term efficacy of paroxetine HC1: A. Data from a 6-week double-blind parallel design trial vs. imipramine and placebo, *Psychopharmacol. Bull., 25*: 267 (1989).

R. Pohl, R. Balon, V. K. Yeragani, and S. Gershon, Serotonergic anxiolytics in the treatment of panic disorder: A controlled study with buspirone, *Psychopathology, 22*(Suppl. 1): 60 (1989).

F. M. Quitkin, D. Schwartz, M. R. Liebowitz, and J. R. Stewart, Atypical depressives: A preliminary report of antidepressant response and sleep patterns, *Psychopharmacol. Bull., 18*: 78 (1982).

F. W. Reimherr, D. R. Wood, B. Byerley, J. Brainard, and B. I. Grosser, Characteristics of responders to fluoxetine, *Psychopharmacol. Bull., 20*: 70 (1984).

F. W. Reimherr, G. Chouinard, C. K. Cohn, J. O. Cole, T. M. Itil, Y. D. LaPierre, H. L. Masco, and J. Mendels, Antidepressant efficacy of sertraline: A double-blind, placebo- and amitriptyline-controlled, multicenter comparison study in outpatients with major depression, *J. Clin. Psychiatry, 51*(12, Suppl. B): 18 (1990).

A. J. M. Reyntjens, Y. Gelders, M.-L. J. A. Hoppenbrouwers et al., Thymosthenic effects of ritanserin R-55667 a centrally acting serotonin S-2 receptor blocker, *Drug Dev. Res., 8*: 205 (1986).

K. Rickels, K. Weisman, N. Norstad et al., Buspirone and diazepam in anxiety: A controlled study, *J. Clin. Psychiatry., 43* (12, sec. 2): 81 (1982).

K. Rickels, E. Schweizer, I. Csanalosi et al., Long-term treatment of anxiety and risk of withdrawal, Arch. Gen. Psychiatry, 45: 444 (1988).

D. S. Robinson, R. C. Shrotriya, D. R. Alms, M. Messina, and J. Andary, Treatment of panic disorder: Non-benzodiazepine anxiolytics, including buspirone, *Psychopharmacol. Bull., 25*: (1989).

D. S. Robinson, K. Rickels, J. Feighner, L. F. Fabre, R. E. Gammans, R. C. Shrotriya, D. R. Alms, J. J. Andary, and M. E. Messina, Clinical effects of the 5-HT_{1A} partial agonists in depression: A composite analysis of buspirone in the treatment of depression, *J. Clin. Psychopharmacol., 10*: 67S (1990).

E. Sanders-Bush, M. Breeding, K. Knoth et al., Sertraline-induced desensitization of the serotonin 5-HT_2 receptor transmembrane signalling system, *Psychopharmacology, 99*: 64 (1989).

E. Schweizer, K. Rickels, and I. Lucki, Resistance to the anti-anxiety effects of buspirone in patients with a history of benzodiazepine use, *N. Engl. J. Med., 314*: 719 (1986).

E. M. Sellers, and C. A. Naranjo, Therapeutic use of serotonergic drugs in alcohol abuse, *Clin. Neuropharmacol., 9*(Suppl. 4): 60 (1986).

D. V. Sheehan, A. B. Raj, K. H. Sheehan, and S. Soto, Is buspirone effective for panic disorder? *J. Clin. Psychopharmacol., 10*: 3 (1990).

M. Teicher, C. Glod, and J. Cole, Emergence of suicidal preoccupation during fluoxetine treatment, *Am. J. Psychiatry, 1447*: 207 (1990).

R. Thomas, Fluvoxamine and alcoholism, *Int. Clin. Psychopharmacol., 6*: 85 (1991).

P. Tyrer, Neurosis divisible? *Lancet, 1*: 685 (1985).

Tyers, M. B., and A. G. Heyes, 5-HT receptors and addiction, *Central Serotonin Receptors and Psychotropic Drugs* (C. A. Marsden, and D. J. Heal, eds.), Blackwell, Oxford (1992).

A. K. Upadhyaya, I. Pennell, P. J. Cowen, and J. F. W. Deakin, Blunted growth hormone and prolactin responses to L-tryptophan in depression. A state-dependent abnormality, *J. Affective Disord., 21*: 213 (1991).

J. Waelkens, W. De Graeve, H. Duyck et al., *Double-blind comparisons of R55667 and placebo in anxiety and tension states accompanied with somatic symptoms,* Clinical Research Report on R55667/1, Janssen Pharmaceutica NV (1984).

J. F. Wernicke, S. R. Dunlop, B. E. Dornseif, and R. L. Zerbe, Fixed-dose fluoxetine therapy for depression, *Psychopharmacol. Bull., 23*: 164 (1987).

D. Wheatley, Buspirone: Multicentre efficacy study, *J. Clin. Psychiatry, 43*: 92 (1982).

J. P. R. Young, A. Coleman, and M. H. Lader, A controlled comparison of fluoxetine and amitriptyline in depressed out-patients, *Br. J. Psychiatry, 151*: 337 (1987).

18

The Role of Noradrenergic Function in Human Anxiety and Depression

Dennis S. Charney, John H. Krystal, Steven M. Southwick, and Pedro L. Delgado
Yale University School of Medicine, New Haven, Connecticut

I. INTRODUCTION

The brain noradrenergic system has been hypothesized to be involved in numerous brain functions as diverse as learning and memory, sleep, autonomic regulation, and arousal behaviors critical to adaptive functioning of the organism. There is evidence that noradrenergic neurons mediate consumptive behaviors, learned helplessness, and responses to intrinsic and extrinsic danger to the animal.

A variety of psychiatric drugs have important effects on noradrenergic neuronal activity. Many antidepressant drugs sharply block norepinephrine reuptake and reduce ß-adrenergic and α_2-adrenergic receptor function and increase that of the α_1-adrenergic receptor with long-term administration (Heninger and Charney, 1987). A variety of anxiolytic agents, including α_2-receptor agonists, benzodiazepines, and opiates, reduce noradrenergic system responsiveness. Conversely, drugs that increase noradrenergic activity generally have anxiogenic properties (Charney et al., 1990).

These data and others, which will be reviewed in the following, indicate that dysfunction of brain noradrenergic systems may be involved in the pathophysiology and treatment of anxiety and depressive disorders.

II. PRECLINICAL STUDIES OF LOCUS COERULEUS FUNCTION

A major portion of the brain noradrenergic system consists of two main clusters of norepinephrine (NE) cell bodies, the locus coeruleus (LC) and lateral tegmental noradrenergic neurons, from which the axonal system arises to innervate targets throughout the entire neuroaxis (Foote et al., 1983; Moore and Bloom, 1979). The LC sends diffuse projections to brain areas involved in fear or anxiety, such as the thalamus, cerebral cortex, amygdala, hippocampus, and hypothalamus (Davis, 1992; Gray, 1982; LeDoux,

1987). In addition, the LC receives afferent inputs, particularly from the nucleus paragigantocellularis in the ventrolateral rostral medulla, which support a critical role in responses to alterations in both the external and internal environment (Aston-Jones et al., 1992; Svensson, 1987).

Preclinical studies of LC function have led to hypotheses relating activity of the LC and its projections to the neurobiology of human anxiety or fearlike states; the most salient have been conducted in laboratory cats and the stumped-tailed monkey (*Macaca artoides*). Electrical stimulation or activation by yohimbine of the LC in the monkey induces a series of behavioral responses similar to those observed in naturally occurring or experimentally induced fear states (Redmond et al., 1976). Bilateral lesions of the LC decrease the natural occurrence of these behavioral responses in a social group situation and in response to threatening confrontations with humans (Redmond et al., 1972; Huang et al., 1976). Agents that decrease the fucntion of the LC also decrease fearful behavior and partially antagonize the effects of electrical stimulation of the LC in the monkey (Gold and Redmond, 1977). These studies indicated that abnormally high levels of LC activity, causing increased release of norepinephrine at postsynaptic noradrenergic projection sites throughout the brain, may produce some forms of fear or pathological anxiety.

The effect of stressful stimuli on the LC activity has been assessed in freely moving cats. Conditions that are behaviorally activating, but not stressful, such as exposure to inaccessible rats or food, do not increase LC firing. In contrast, stressful and fear-inducing stimuli, such as loud white noise, air puff, restraint, and confrontation with a dog or an aggressive cat, produce a rapid, robust, and sustained increase in LC activity (Abercrombie and Jacobs, 1987a,b; Rasmussen et al., 1986; Levine et al., 1990). Under these conditions, activations are not produced in substantia nigra dopamine neurons (Strecker and Jacobs, 1985) and dorsal raphe serotonin neurons (Wilkinson et al., 1986).

A series of investigations have shown that uncontrollable, but not controllable, stress produces increased responsiveness of LC neurons to excitatory stimulation (Simson and Weiss, 1988a,b). These changes have been associated with α_2-adrenergic autoreceptor subsensitivity, similar to that observed by α_2-receptor blockade. In fact, antagonism of α_2-receptors with idazoxan or yohimbine increases response to excitatory stimuli without altering LC baseline-firing rate. Chronic blockade of opiate, serotonin (5-HT), and γ-aminobutyric acid (GABA) receptors does not appear to influence LC responsiveness (Simson and Weiss, 1988a,b). Consistent with these findings, acute cold restraint stress results in decreased density of α_2-receptors in the hippocampus and amygdala (Torda et al., 1984). The stress-induced increase in norepinephrine turnover is also associated with a decrease in postsynaptic ß-receptor density (Tsuda et al., 1986; U'Prichard and Kvetnansky, 1980; Yocca and Friedman, 1984).

Consistent with these neurophysiological studies of the LC, stress produces regional increases in norepinephrine turnover in the LC and the limbic regions (hypothalamus, hippocampus, amygdala) and cortical regions innervated by the LC. Moreover, it has recently been demonstrated, using intracerebral microdialysis, that immobilization stress, footshock stress, tail-pinch stress, and conditioned fear activate noradrenergic neurons in the hypothalamus and amygdala (Tanaka et al., 1990a,b, 1991; Yokoo et al., 1990).

A parallel activation of LC neurons and sympathetic nerves is produced by noxious stimuli. The LC activation produced by confrontation with a dog is temporally linked to an increase in heart rate and blood pressure, suggesting that LC–NE neurons respond in parallel with sympathetic activation under these conditions. The LC, like sympathetic activity, is highly responsive to various peripheral cardiovascular events, such as alterations in blood volume or blood pressure. Internal events that must be responded to for survival, such as thermoregulatory disturbance, hypoglycemia, blood loss, an increase in PCO_2, or a marked reduction in blood pressure, cause robust and long-lasting increases in LC activity (Morilak et al., 1987a,b,c; Svensson, 1987). There are also visceral influences on LC activity. In rats, distention of the urinary bladder, distal colon, or rectum activates LC neurons (Svensson, 1978). These findings suggest that changes in autonomic or visceral function may result in specific behavioral responses mediated by the brain LC–NE system. Indeed, it has been proposed that the LC–NE system may act as a central analogue of the sympathetic nervous system, with the brain as its end organ (Amaral and Sinnamon, 1977).

The nucleus paragigantocellularis may be involved in simultaneously activating the LC neurons and peripheral sympathetic neurons in response to life-threatening stimuli (Aston-Jones et al., 1992). The LC–NE network may determine whether, under threat, the organism turns attention toward external, sensory stimuli or to internal vegetative events. The system, when functioning normally, may be interpretative and serve to facilitate the planning and execution of behaviors important for survival (Aston-Jones et al., 1992; Svensson, 1987).

III. BEHAVIORAL EFFECTS OF STRESS AND NORADRENERGIC FUNCTION

A. Learned Helplessness

Learned helplessness is a behavioral phenomena in which exposure to uncontrollable stress produces deficits in motivation, learning, and emotion. The behavioral features of helpless animals include psychomotor retardation, loss of appetite, decreased grooming, lack of aggression, elevated cortisol, and sleep disturbance, suggesting analogy to human depressive illness. Several investigators have found particularly large depletions of norepinephrine in the LC region, suggesting that this neurochemical change may mediate the behavioral depression associated with uncontrollable stress. It has been suggested that specific alterations in hippocampal ß-receptors occur with the development of helpless behavior. Learned helplessness phenomena are generally reversed by antidepressant drugs (Weiss and Uhde, 1990).

B. Separation Models

Disruption of social attachment systems frequently leads to the development of grief reactions and, in vulnerable individuals, to clinical depression. Study of the behavioral and neurobiological effects of separation in nonhuman primates has been promoted as an animal model of depression (Henn and McKinney, 1987).

The response to separation is influenced by age, rearing conditions, housing conditions, and treatment with pharmacological agents (e.g., antidepressants). Individual variability in the response to separation can relate to several developmental and neurobiological factors. The noradrenergic system may be involved because animals with reduced levels of cerebrospinal fluid (CSF) norepinephrine at baseline respond to separation with more cuddling and self-directed behaviors. The tyrosine hydroxylase inhibitor, α-methyl-*p*-tyrosine (AMPT), which reduces norepinephrine levels, makes the behavioral responses to separation more severe. The CSF levels of the norepinephrine metabolite 3-methoxy-

4-hydroxyphenylglycol (MHPG) is elevated in peer-only raised monkeys compared with mother-reared monkeys. The CSF MHPG is also increased across repeated separations (Higley et al., 1991; see Willner, 1990 for review).

IV. NEURAL MECHANISMS OF LEARNING AND MEMORY AND NORADRENERGIC FUNCTION

A. Fear Conditioning and Associative Memories

Vivid memories of a traumatic event, physiological reactions, and even flashbacks can be elicited by sensory and cognitive stimuli of many types that have been associated with the original event (Litz and Keane, 1989; McNally et al., 1987). Consequently, patients begin to avoid these stimuli in their everyday life. Classic-conditioning phenomena, which are easily demonstrated in the laboratory, may explain some of these observations. Animals exposed to an emotionally neutral, visual- or auditory-conditioned stimuli (CS) in conjunction with an aversive-unconditioned stimulus (UCS), will subsequently exhibit a conditioned emotional (fear) reaction to the CS in the absence of the UCS. These changes are used to infer that a state of fear has been produced (Davis, 1990). A neural analysis of fear-conditioning in animals, therefore, can be used to examine the mechanisms of how the brain learns and remembers associations of stimuli with traumatic events and may have considerable relevance to our understanding of phobic behaviors.

Numerous paradigms using visual and auditory stimuli have been employed to study the neuroanatomical and neurochemical substrates of fear-conditioning. These investigations have demonstrated fear-conditioning to visual and auditory stimuli is mediated, in large part, by subcortical mechanisms, involving sensory pathways to the thalamus and amygdala (LeDoux et al., 1990). It has been suggested that emotional memories established through thalamoamygdala pathways may be relatively indelible (LeDoux et al., 1989). The neurochemical systems involved in the reduction of the fear-conditioning include the noradrenergic, dopaminergic, opiate, *N*-methyl-D-aspartate (NMDA), and corticotropin-releasing systems (Davis, 1986).

Behavioral paradigms indicate conditioning of noradrenergic neuronal systems may be induced by neutral environmental stimuli previously paired with uncontrollable shock. Neutral stimuli that have been paired with inescapable shock produce increases in brain norepinephrine metabolism and behavioral deficits similar to that elicited by the shock (Cassens et al., 1981). In the freely moving cat, the firing rate of cells in the locus coeruleus are increased by a neutral acoustic stimulus previously paired with an air puff to the whiskers, which also increases firing and is aversive to the cat (Rasmussen et al., 1986). There is also a body of evidence indicating an intact noradrenergic system may be necessary for the acquisition of fear-conditioned responses (Cole and Robbins, 1987; Rasmussen et al., 1986; Tsaltas et al., 1987).

B. Behavioral Sensitization and Noradrenergic Function

Several features of behavioral sensitization may account for the observation that stressors may lead to persistent symptoms of anxiety and depression. Sensitization generally refers to the increase in response magnitude that occurs following repeated administration of a stimulus or shortly following presentation of a different, but stronger, stimulus.

Numerous brain structures and neurochemical systems have been implicated in the behavioral sensitization that occurs following repeated stress. Among the best-studied systems in relation to stress-induced behavioral sensitization is the noradrenergic system.

Limited shock exposure, which does not alter norepinephrine utilization in naive animals, produces increased norepinephrine metabolism that exceeds the rate of synthesis in animals previously exposed to acute uncontrollable shock (Anisman and Sklar, 1978). In chronically shocked animals, reexposure to a shock of lower current than the initial shock produces an increase in turnover, reflecting an increase in norepinephrine release and synthesis (Irwin et al., 1986). A recent study using in vivo microdialysis observed that rats previously exposed to chronic cold stress had enhanced synthesis and release of hippocampal norepinephrine following acute tail-shock stress (Nisenbaum et al., 1992).

Preliminary data indicate that different brain regions are not influenced in the same way by stress reexposure (Irwin et al., 1986). There is an increase in norepinephrine and MHPG levels in both the hypothalamus and hippocampus following stress reexposure. However, hypothalamic norepinephrine increases are associated with reexposure to the primary aversive stimulus (sensitization effect), whereas hippocampal norepinephrine increases are associated with reexposure to environmental cues associated with shock (conditioning effect).

V. STUDIES OF NORADRENERGIC FUNCTION IN ANXIETY DISORDER PATIENTS

Considering the broad functions of the noradrenergic system, abnormal regulation of this system could account for many of the clinical features of anxiety disorders, such as panic disorder and posttraumatic stress disorder (PTSD). Panic disorder and PTSD patients frequently report cardiovascular, gastrointestinal, and respiratory symptoms. Because the LC is responsive to peripheral alterations in the function of these systems, minor physiological changes in these patients may result in abnormal activation of LC neurons and, consequently, panic attacks and flashbacks. These functional interactions may explain the association of anxiety symptoms with tachycardia, tachypnea, hypoglycemia, and visceral and organ distention, as well as the marked sensitivity of panic disorder and PTSD patients to interceptive stimuli. The important role of the noradrenergic system in fear-conditioning may account for the development of phobic symptoms in these patients. Finally, the involvement of noradrenergic neurons in learning and memory may relate to the persistence of traumatic memories in PTSD.

A. Basal Levels of Norepinephrine and Its Metabolites

Increased levels of urine and plasma norepinephine and epinephrine and their metabolites have been reported in healthy subjects following emotional stress (Breggin, 1964; Buchsbaum et al., 1981; Lader, 1974). The symptoms associated with the withdrawal symptoms of opiate abstinence and abrupt tricyclic antidepressant discontinuation include the symptoms of anxiety and have been associated with increases in plama MHPG (Charney et al., 1982a, 1984a).

Plasma epinephrine appears to be elevated in patients meeting *Diagnostic and Statistical Manual of Mental Disorders,* 2nd ed. (*DSM-II*) criteria for anxiety neurosis and *DSM-III* criteria for panic disorder (Cameron et al., 1984; Villacres et al., 1987). The levels of plasma norepinephrine have not been consistently altered in anxiety disorder patients. Catecholamine levels in generalized anxiety disorder patients and controls are similar (Mathew et al., 1982).

Several studies have not found elevated plasma catecholamines following spontaneous or situationally provoked panic attacks (Cameron et al., 1987; Woods et al., 1987). Moreover, plasma and urinary catecholamines (Ballenger et al., 1984; Nesse et al., 1984, 1985), and plasma and CFS MHPG levels in panic disorder patients are generally no different from those of healthy controls (Edlund et al., 1987; Garvey et al., 1987; Lydiard, personal communication 1992; Uhde et al., 1988).

Two studies have found significantly elevated 24-h urine norepinephrine excretion in combat veterans with PTSD, compared with healthy subjects or patients with schizophrenia or major depression (Kosten et al., 1987; Yehuda et al., 1992).

B. Peripheral Noradrenergic Receptor Function

The density and function of platelet α_2-adrenergic receptors have not been consistently abnormal in panic disorder patients (Cameron et al., 1990; Charney et al., 1989a; Nutt and Frazer, 1987; Villacres et al., 1987). The density of platelet α_2-adrenergic receptors is reduced in PTSD, perhaps reflecting adaptive down-regulation in response to chronically elevated levels of circulating endogenous catecholamines (Perry et al., 1987). The relevance of these studies to brain α_2-receptor function is open to question because of the lack of evidence demonstrating that platelet α_2-adrenergic receptors reflect brain α_2-receptor function (Nutt and Frazer, 1987).

Plasma lymphocyte ß-adrenergic receptors are down-regulated in both panic disorder and PTSD (Brown et al., 1988; Krystal et al., 1989). The functional significance of these findings is unclear because the ß-receptors located on lymphocytes are of the β_2-subtype, whereas the β_1-receptor is preponderant in the brain.

C. Peripheral Sympathetic Function

A wide variety of investigations have been conducted to evaluate sympathetic nervous system (SNS) function in panic disorder. These studies have produced markedly divergent findings, yielding no firm consensus on whether a SNS dysfunction exists in panic disorder (Cameron and Nesse, 1988; Freedman et al., 1985; Roth et al., 1992; Stein et al., 1992). For example, panic disorder patients exhibit elevated basal heart rate under laboratory conditions during which anticipatory anxiety is prominent (Roth et al., 1992). However, ambulatory monitoring of heart rate reveals that panic disorder patients do not have higher heart rates than healthy subjects during nonpanic periods (Freedman et al., 1985). Studies of patients during spontaneous or situationally induced panic attacks generally have not demonstrated substantive evidence of SNS hyperactivity as a necessary feature of panic attacks (Stein et al., 1992). Plasma norepinephrine responses to orthostatic challenge are normal in panic disorder patients. A greater heart rate response in panic disorder patients has been observed, but may be due to alterations in vagal tone (Stein et al., 1992).

Most of the early clinical investigations of the pathophysiology of PTSD identified a relation between severe stress exposure, increased peripheral sympathetic nervous system activity, and conditioned physiological and emotional responses (Grinker and Spiegle, 1945; Meakes and Wilson, 1918; Peabody et al., 1918). Since the early 1980s there have been a series of well-designed psychophysiological studies that have further documented heightened autonomic or sympathetic nervous system arousal in combat veterans with PTSD. Combat veterans with PTSD have higher resting mean heart rate and systolic blood pressure, as well as greater increases in heart rate, when exposed to visual and auditory combat-related stimuli, compared with combat veterans without PTSD, patients with generalized anxiety disorder, or healthy subjects (Blanchard et al., 1982, 1986; Kolb, 1984; Malloy et al., 1983; McFall et al., 1990; Orr, 1990; Pallmeyer et al., 1986; Pitman et al., 1987). Furthermore, several psychophysiological studies have found hyperreactive responses to combat-associated stimuli, but not to other stressful noncombat-related stimuli (McFall et al., 1990). These data are consistent with the hypothesis that noradrenergic hyperreactivity in patients with PTSD may relate to the conditioned or sensitized responses to specific traumatic stimuli. Studies evaluating the efficacy of psychotherapeutic techniques emphasizing desensitization to reduce hyperarousal responses to stimuli associated with the psychological trauma represent a current focus of investigation (Boudewyns and Hyer, 1989; Keane et al., 1989).

VI. REGULATION OF NORADRENERGIC FUNCTION IN ANXIETY DISORDERS

A. Yohimbine

The regulation of noradrenergic neuronal function has been examined by determining the behavioral, biochemical, and cardiovascular effects of oral and intravenous yohimbine, an α_2-adrenergic receptor antagonist, in a spectrum of psychiatric disorders, including schizophrenia, major depression (see later), obsessive–compulsive disorder, generalized anxiety disorder, panic disorder, and PTSD (Charney et al., 1984b, 1987, 1989b, 1992; Glazer et al., 1987; Heninger et al., 1988; Price et al., 1986; Rasmussen et al., 1987; Southwick et al., 1993; Uhde et al., 1985). Specific abnormalities have been identified in panic disorder and PTSD. Approximately 65% of panic disorder patients experience yohimbine-induced panic attacks, and these patients have larger yohimbine-induced increases in plasma MHPG than healthy subjects and other panic disorder patients (Charney et al., 1984b, 1987, 1992; Southwick et al., 1992; Uhde et al., 1985). Similar to the panic disorder patients, approximately two-thirds of PTSD patients experience yohimbine-induced panic attacks and, in addition, 40% report flashbacks after yohimbine. As a group, PTSD patients also have greater yohimbine-induced increases in plasma MHPG, sitting systolic blood pressure, and heart rate, than healthy subjects. In the PTSD patients, yohimbine induced significant increases in core PTSD symptoms, such as intrusive traumatic thoughts, emotional numbing, and grief (Southwick et al., 1993). These potentiated responses to yohimbine occurred in panic disorder and PTSD with comorbid major depression. This suggests that patients with so-called mixed panic disorder and depression have abnormalities similar to patients with panic disorder only.

B. Clonidine

A consistent finding in the literature is that the growth hormone rise induced by clonidine is blunted in panic disorder patients (Charney and Heninger, 1986; Nutt, 1986, 1989; Uhde et al., 1989). In a recent investigation, clonidine–growth hormone response was found primarily in the patients who experienced yohimbine-induced panic attacks (Charney et al., 1992). This suggests the diminished postsynaptic α_2-adrenergic receptor function reflected by the blunted clonidine–growth hormone response may relate to presynaptic noradrenergic neuronal hyperactivity.

Several previous investigations observed the clonidine produced greater decreases in plasma MHPG and blood pressure in panic disorder patients than in healthy subjects (Charney et al., 1986, 1992). In the most recent study, the findings were partially replicated. Intravenous clonidine did not result in significant decreases in plasma MHPG in the healthy subjects or the patients who did not experience yohimbine panic attacks. In contrast, clonidine did produce significant decreases in plasma MHPG in the panic disorder patients who experienced yohimbine-induced panic attacks. However, significant decreases in the MHPG response to clonidine were not identified when this subgroup of panic disorder patients were compared with the healthy subjects or the other patients (Charney et al., 1992).

The findings that the abnormal yohimbine-induced increase in plasma MHPG, blunted growth hormone response to clonidine, and significant clonidine-induced decrease in plasma MHPG may be restricted to the panic disorder patients who reported panic attacks following yohimbine administration support the hypothesis that there is a distinct subgroup of panic disorder patients who manifest noradrenergic neuronal dysfunction.

VII. POSSIBLE SITES OF NORADRENERGIC DYSFUNCTION IN PANIC DISORDER AND POSTTRAUMATIC STRESS SYNDROME

The abnormal noradrenergic function observed in panic disorder and PTSD may reflect abnormalities in the LC–NE system at the level of the LC, the LC projection areas, and the interaction of the peripheral sympathetic with the central noradrenergic system. Dysfunction at the LC that produces noradrenergic hyperactivity could be due to decreased functional sensitivity of the α_2-adrenergic autoreceptor or at one or more of the neuronal systems that have regulatory actions on LC activity. Unfortunately, methods have not been developed to directly elevate brain α_2-adrenergic autoreceptor function in humans. The density and function of platelet α_2-adrenergic receptors has not been consistently abnormal in panic disorder patients. However, as noted, the relevance of these studies to brain α_2-receptor function is open to question because of the lack of evidence demonstrating that platelet α_2-receptors reflect brain α_2-adrenergic receptor function.

An alternative explanation for the noradrenergic hyperactivity in panic disorder and PTSD is that excitatory inputs, such as the excitatory amino acids from the nucleus paragigantocellularis to the LC, are increased in function (Aston-Jones et al., 1992). An increase in corticotropin-releasing factor (CRF) secretion is also a prime candidate for an abnormal excitatory input to the LC because of the considerable evidence that CRF has anxiogenic properties (Butler et al., 1990). The brain sites mediating the anxiogenic action of CRF have not been established. However, there is accumulating data that suggest these effects of CRF may be produced by interactions with LC noradrenergic neurons; intracerebroventricular (ICV) infusion of CRF increases norepinephrine turnover in several forebrain areas (Dunn et al., 1987). In a dose-dependent fashion, CRF increases the firing rate of LC–orepinephrine neurons (Valentino and Foote, 1988). Stress, which activates norepinephrine neurons, markedly increases CRF concentrations in the LC (Chappell et al., 1990). Moreover, it has recently been demonstrated that infusion of CRF into the LC produces anxiogenic activity and significant increases in the norepinephrine metabolite 3,4-dihydroxyphenylglycol in forebrain areas, such as the amygdala and hypothalamus (Butler et al., 1990). These data suggest that CRF produces its behavioral-activating and anxiogenic effects, in part, by increasing LC activity. Consequently, it is important to develop clinical paradigms capable of evaluating central CRF activity and the interaction of CRF and noradrenergic function in panic disorder and PTSD patients.

There is abundant evidence implicating the opiate, endogenous benzodiazepine, and serotonin neuronal systems in the development of anxiety and fear. Because each of these systems has inhibitory effects on LC activity it is possible that decreased activity of any one of these systems could account for the increased responsivity to drugs, such as yohimbine, that activate noradrenergic neurons.

Projection areas of the LC are likely to be involved in the enhanced anxiogenic effects of yohimbine in panic disorder and PTSD. The LC projects to most of the brain regions implicated in the pathophysiology of anxiety and fear, including the amygdala, hypothalamus, thalamus, hippocampus, and cerebral cortex. An enhancement of norepinephrine metabolism occurs in these brain areas following a variety of stressful stimuli. It is possible that the behavioral responses to yohimbine in panic disorder are due to increased sensitivity to or abnormal regulation of noradrenergic neurotransmission by terminal α_2-adrenergic autoreceptors in brain structures such as the amygdala.

VIII. TRAUMATIC MEMORIES AND NORADRENERGIC FUNCTION

A striking effect of yohimbine is its ability to increase the severity of the core symptoms associated with PTSD, such as intrusive traumatic thoughts, emotional numbing, and grief. This may be due to the involvement of noradrenergic systems in the mechanisms by which memories of traumatic experiences remain indelible for decades and are easily reawakened by a variety of stimuli and stressors.

Indeed, the strength of traumatic memories may relate to the degree to which certain neuromodulatory systems are activated by the traumatic experience (McGaugh, 1989, 1990). Experimental and clinical investigations have demonstrated that memory processes are susceptible to modulating influences after the information has been acquired. Stimulation of noradrenergic receptors on the amygdala after a learning experience has memory-enhancing effects. Activating the LC–norepinephrine system that projects to the amygdala, by frightening and traumatic experiences may facilitate the encoding of memories associated with the experiences. Moreover, it is possible that reproducing a neurobiological state (noradrenergic hyperactivity in specific brain regions) similar to the one that existed at the time of the memory-encoding can elicit the traumatic memory.

The involvement of noradrenergic neurons in the neural mechanisms of fear-conditioning and behavioral sensitization may relate to the behavioral effects of yohimbine in panic disorder and PTSD. In humans, recrudescence of traumatic memories (e.g., intrusive traumatic thoughts) in response to simple sensory phenomenon, such as specific smells, sounds, and cognitive stimuli circumstantially associated with the original trauma, may occur through fear-conditioning associated with activation of noradrenergic neurons.

The noradrenergic system also appears to be involved in behavioral sensitization, a process that may be related to the initiation and maintenance of certain PTSD symptoms. These data may explain why patients with PTSD and panic disorder who have been exposed to repeated stressors often respond to mild or moderate subsequent stress with exaggerated behavioral and physiological responses (e.g., marked anxiety, panic, and PTSD-specific symptoms) that are more appropriate for emergency situations.

IX. NORADRENERGIC MECHANISMS IN THE ETIOLOGY OF AFFECTIVE DISORDERS

As reviewed, the noradrenergic system appears to serve a global modulatory function in enhancing arousal and orientation to novel or potentially threatening stimuli both intrinsic and extrinsic to the organism. The LC fires in a phasic manner in response to such stimuli and may mediate parallel changes in peripheral sympathetic activity. The LC through its functional interaction with other brain sites, such as the amygdala and cerebral cortex, may attach affect to information from significant internal and external events. Thus, it is possible the noradrenergic system may function as a phasic affective arousal system, which may be abnormally regulated in patients with affective disorders (Siever, 1987). It has been hypothesized the dysphoric hyperarousal symptoms frequently found in depressed patients may relate to increased noradrenergic function, whereas anergic and vegetative symptoms may relate to decreased noradrenergic activity.

A. Basal Levels of Norepinephrine and Its Metabolites

There have been many studies that have measured norepinephrine metabolites in the urine of depressed patients. Early studies of urinary MHPG in depression suggested lower values, particularly in bipolar patients, than in control populations. Subsequent studies have not supported these observations in unipolar patients (see Siever, 1987; Kindler and Lerer 1990 for review). In fact, the largest and best-designed investigation, a multicenter collaborative study, reported no difference in urinary MHPG in both unipolar and bipolar depressed patients compared with normal controls. This study did find increased urinary excretion of the norepinephrine metabolites, vanilly/mandelic acid (VMA) and metanephrine (Davis et al., 1988).

Several investigations have found that plasma norepinephrine concentrations are elevated in unipolar melancholia depression, probably because of increased norepinephrine release (Lake et al., 1982). Depressed patients who are dexamethesone-nonsuppressors may have higher plasma NE than suppressors (Roy et al., 1985). Some evidence exists suggesting that plasma NE is lower in bipolar patients (Siever and Davis, 1985).

Generally, depressed patients have normal plasma MHPG levels. However, there are studies showing that depressed patients have increased variance of plasma MHPG, higher values in bipolar mania, lower values in bipolar depressed, and higher values in some unipolar depressed patients (see Siever and Davis, 1985 for review). The CSF MHPG concentrations may be elevated in mania and agitated states (Agren, 1980; Berger et al., 1980; Koslow et al., 1982; Post et al., 1973; Post and Goodwin, 1980).

There are no consistent alterations in CSF norepinephrine in depressed patients (Christensen et al., 1980; Post et al., 1973; Post and Goodwin, 1980). Sympathetic nervous system function has been assessed in depressed patients by examining the plasma norepinephrine response to orthostasis. The plasma norepinephrine increase on standing is exaggerated in depression (Rudorfer et al., 1985).

B. Peripheral Noradrenergic Receptor Function

Peripheral α_2- and ß-adrenergic receptors have been studied in patients with affective disorders. The awareness that many antidepressants reduce α_2- and ß-adrenergic receptor sensitivity in laboratory animals prompted investigation of these receptors in humans.

Platelet α_2-adrenergic receptor number, as measured by [^{3}H]clonidine (Garcia-Sevila et al., 1983), [^{3}H]dihydroergocryptine (Siever et al., 1984), [^{3}H]epinephrine (Garcia-Sevilla et al., 1987), [^{3}H]*p*-aminoclonidine (Piletz et al., 1990) have been reported to be increased compared with healthy subjects. However, other studies employing [^{3}H]clonidine (Georgotas et al., 1987), [^{3}H]dihydroergocryptine (Wood and Coppen, 1982), [^{3}H]yohimbine, and [^{3}H]rauwolscine (α-yohimbine) (Siever et al., 1986) have revealed no significant difference between healthy subjects and depressed patients.

It has recently been argued that abnormalities of platelet α_2-adrenergic receptors involve an increase in the high-affinity agonist state of the receptor, and only drugs that are likely to label this high-affinity state will demonstrate the abnormality (Garcia-Sevilla et al., 1986, 1990; Piletz et al., 1990). It is postulated that this explains the reasons for the uniform lack of difference in α_2-adrenergic receptor number between depressed patients and healthy subjects, as measured by [^{3}H]yohimbine and other related alkaloids, compared with the more positive results reported for agonists (Garcia-Sevilla et al., 1986).

Studies of platelet α_2-adrenergic receptor responsiveness have been used to assess the conflicting findings in receptor number. However, these studies have also been contradictory, with some studies noting no difference between patients and controls and other studies observing a blunted cyclic adenosine monophosphate (cAMP) response (Kindler and Lerer, 1990; Siever, 1987).

In a recent attempt to further elucidate the relation of platelet α_2-adrenergic receptor number to physiological responsiveness, Garcia-Sevilla et al. (1990) have investigated the α_2-adrenergic receptor-mediated inhibition of platelet adenylate cyclase and induction of platelet aggregation. They found hypersensitive responses to α_2-adrenergic receptor agaonists in drug-free depressed patients who were desensitized following long-term antidepressant treatment.

Measurement of lymphocyte ß-adrenergic receptors has also yielded mixed results, with some authors reporting decreased numbers (Goodwin, 1979) and others reporting no difference (Cooper et al., 1985; Mann et al., 1985) between depressed patients and healthy subjects. On the other hand, the cAMP response to stimulation by ß-adrenergic receptor agonists has led to consistent reports of a blunted response in depressed patients when compared with healthy subjects (Cooper et al., 1985; Ebstein et al., 1988; Goodwin, 1979; Mann et al., 1985; Pandey et al., 1985). There is a dissociation between plama norepinephrine levels and the affinity of agonists for the ß-adrenergic receptor in depressed patients (Buckholtz et al., 1988), in contrast with the normal association between agonist affinity and plasma norepinephrine levels seen in nondepressed populations (Feldman et al., 1983).

C. Postmortem Studies of Receptor Function

Several studies have examined ß-adrenergic receptors in the postmortem brains of depressed patients and individuals committing suicide. The results from these studies have been mixed, with some investigators reporting no difference from controls in ß-adrenergic receptor density (Crow et al., 1984; Kindler and Lerer, 1990). More recent studies employing "drug- and pathology-free" brains and investigating the regional distribution of ß-adrenergic receptors have identified increased ß-adrenergic receptor density in the frontal cortex of violent suicides (Arango et al., 1990; Biegon and Israeli, 1988; Mann et al., 1986). Smaller, but significant, increases have been observed in α_1-receptors. No changes were observed in α_2-receptors using autoradiography of the prefrontal cortex (Arango et al., 1990). Meana and Garcia-Sevilla (1990) found an increase in α_2 receptor density homogenates from an unspecified area of frontal cortex.

X. NEUROPHARMACOLOGICAL CHALLENGE TESTS OF NORADRENERGIC FUNCTION

Virtually all neuroendocrine challenge studies of the noradrenergic system in depression have involved investigations of α_2-adrenergic receptor responsiveness. In an impressive number of studies, the growth hormone response to both oral and intravenous clonidine has been consistently blunted in depressed patients compared with healthy controls. The clonidine-induced decreases in blood pressure and MHPG have, in general, been no different in depressed patients than in healthy subjects (Ansseau et al., 1988; Boyer et al., 1982; Charney et al., 1982b; Checkley et al., 1981, 1984; Matussek et al., 1980; Siever et al., 1982).

Considerable variability in the amount of growth hormone released in response to clonidine exists across both patients and healthy subjects. In an attempt to investigate the underlying reasons for this variability, Eriksson et al. (1988) measured the growth hormone response to guanfacine as well as to growth hormone-releasing hormone (GHRH) in the same subjects. If the mechanisms underlying the variability were related to differences in α_2-adrenoreceptor sensitivity, then the growth hormone response to guanfacine should be different from the response to GHRH. They found a significant correlation between the growth hormone responses to these two agents, suggesting that the variability in the growth hormone response might be due to factors other than α_2-adrenergic receptor responsiveness. For example, there is recent data indicating that a reduction in serotonin function results in a blunting in the GH response to clonidine (Aulakh et al., 1991).

The biochemical, behavioral, and cardiovascular effects of yohimbine have been investigated in depressed patients. Depressed patients demonstrate an increased cortisol and blood pressure response to yohimbine, compared with that of healthy subjects, whereas the plasma MHPG is not significantly different between the two groups of subjects (Heninger et al., 1988).

Amphetamine causes release and blocks reuptake of both norepinephrine and dopamine. It has been used as a neuroendocrine challenge probe of both the norepinephrine and dopamine systems. The growth hormone response to amphetamine is thought to be due to dopamine stimulation of D_2 receptors and norepinephrine stimulation of postsynaptic α_2-adrenergic receptors. The cortisol response appears to be mediated by NE stimulation of postsynaptic α_1-adrenergic receptors.

A blunted growth hormone response to amphetamine in endogenous depressed patients compared with healthy subjects has been reported (Arato et al., 1983; Langer et al., 1975, 1976). However, questions about the interpretations of the blunted growth hormone response have been raised because of the "normal" blunting of this response after menopause and the presence of more postmenopausal women in the patient groups than in the control groups in most studies (Matussek, 1988). Studies investigating the growth hormone response to amphetamine in postmenopausal endogenous depressed patients and matched controls for menopausal status have reported no difference in this hormone response (Halbreich et al., 1982).

The cortisol response to methylamphetamine in depressed patients before and after recovery was reported to be lower in the depressive phase compared with the recovered phase (Checkley and Crammer, 1977). When compared with reactive depressives and other nondepressed psychiatric patients, the cortisol response to methylamphetamine was blunted only by endogenous depressives (Checkley, 1979). In a larger replication using dextroamphetamine, the cortisol response was also diminished in endogenous depressed patients compared with healthy controls (Sachar et al., 1980, 1985). However, when the cortisol response to dextroamphetamine was assessed at 8 AM, rather than the 4 PM time used in the previous studies, no difference was noted between depressed patients and healthy subjects (Feinberg et al., 1981).

Desipramine is a tricyclic antidepressant that is relatively selective as a noradrenergic-reuptake inhibitor, but with significant anticholinergic and antihistaminic effects as well. Single oral doses of desipramine cause a dose-dependent increase in growth hormone and cortisol (Laakman et al., 1977, 1986). The growth hormone response to desipramine is blocked by the nonselective α-adrenergic antagonists, phentolamine, and the α_2-adrenergic antagonist, yohimbine, and potentiated by the nonselective ß-adrenergic antagonist, propranolol, whereas the selective α_1-adrenergic antagonist, prazosin, had no effect, suggesting that at least the growth hormone response to desipramine is mediated by stimulation of postsynaptic α_2-adrenergic receptors (Laakman et al., 1977).

The growth hormone response to desipramine has been reported to be blunted in premenopausal female endogenous depressives (Meesters et al., 1985) and male endogenous depressives (Laakman et al., 1986) compared with healthy subjects. The cortisol response to despiramine has also been blunted in endogenous depressed patients (Asnis et al., 1986).

XI. AN ABNORMALITY IN POSTSYNAPTIC NORADRENERGIC FUNCTION IN DEPRESSION

A synthesis of the studies of noradrenergic function in affective disorder patients suggests that postsynaptic abnormalities may be present in some depressed patients. The most consistent finding here is the blunted growth hormone responses to noradrenergic receptor agonists, such as clonidine, in drug-free depressed patients. Moreover, the failure to identify significant patient–control differences in the growth hormone response to the dopamine agonist, apomorphine (Jimerson, 1987), suggests that this abnormality may be specific to the noradrenergic system and not related to abnormalities in GHRH regulation of growth hormone. Likewise, since the growth hormone response to amphetamine is most likely mediated by the stimulation of postsynaptic dopamine, as well as α_2-adrenergic receptors, it is not surprising to see no patient–control difference with this probe. The blunted cortisol responses to amphetamine and desipramine in depression are also consistent with an abnormality in postsynaptic noradrenergic receptors. The cortisol response to noradrenergic agonists is thought to reflect activation of postsynaptic α_1-adrenergic receptors.

Assessment of postsynaptic ß-adrenergic receptor function in peripheral lymphocytes suggests that an abnormality may exist beyond the receptor level. Wachtel (1989) has postulated that a dysregulation of neuronal second-messenger function is involved in the etiology of affective disorders. This hypothesis suggests that, in depression, there is an imbalance of the major second-messenger systems in the brain, resulting from diminished adenylate cyclase pathway and increased phospholipase C pathway activity, and in mania, the reverse is true (Wachtel, 1989).

A specific presynaptic dysregulation of the noradrenergic system has not been identified. Substantial differences in CSF, plasma, and urinary measures of noradrenergic function have not been identified. Consistent abnormalities in the plasma MHPG responses to clonidine or yohimbine have not been observed.

XII. COMPARISON OF NORADRENERGIC FUNCTION IN PANIC DISORDER AND MAJOR DEPRESSION

As reviewed in detail earlier, there is evidence of noradrenergic dysfunction in both panic disorder and major depression. Both disorders have blunted growth hormone responses to clonidine. However, most often, investigations of noradrenergic function reveal differences between the two disorders. These data are consistent with family studies that indicate panic disorder and major depression are independently transmitted (Weissman et al., 1993)

In some panic disorder patients, there may be an abnormality in the regulation of presynaptic noradrenergic regulation, resulting phasic excessive increases in noradrenergic function. In contrast, presynaptic regulation of noradrenergic function in depression appears to be relatively intact, but postsynaptic noradrenergic function may be reduced. Of interest, despite the differences in noradrenergic function in these two disorders, norepinephrine reuptake inhibitor drugs (e.g., desipramine) are effective for both depression and panic disorder. This indicates that a drug with broad regulatory actions on noradrenergic function can be effective for disorders with different abnormalities in noradrenergic function. It is possible that if specific abnormalities in noradrenergic function can be identified in individual patients with depression or panic disorder then treatment with drugs that are specifically designed to reverse these abnormalities will have a therapeutic effect that is greater in magnitude and more rapid.

ACKNOWLEDGMENTS

Thanks to Evelyn Testa for excellent manuscript preparation. This work was supported by the National Center for Post Traumatic Stress Disorder of the Department of Veterans Affairs.

REFERENCES

E. D. Abercrombie, and B. L. Jacobs, Single-unit response of noradrenergic neurons in the locus coeruleus of freely moving cats. I. Acutely presented stressful and nonstressful stimuli, *J. Neurosci., 7*: 2837 (1987a).

E. D. Abercrombie, and B. L. Jacobs, Single-unit response of noradrenergic neurons in the locus coeruleus of freely moving cats. II. Adaptation to chronically presented stressful stimuli, *J. Neurosci., 7*: 2844 (1987b).

H. Agren, Symptom patterns in unipolar and bipolar depression correlating with monoamine metabolites in the cerebrospinal fluid. I. General patterns, *Psychiatry Res., 3*: 211 (1980).

D. G. Amaral, and H. M. Sinnamon, The locus coeruleus neurobiology of a central noradrenergic nucleus, *Prog. Neurobiol., 9*: 147 (1977).

H. Anisman, and L. S. Sklar, Catecholamine depletion upon reexposure to stress: Mediation of the escape deficits produced by inescapable shock, *J. Comp. Physiol. Psychol., 93*: 610 (1978).

M. Ansseau, Von Frenckell, R. Cerfontaine et al., Blunted response of growth hormone to clonidine and apomorphine in endogenous depression, *Br. J. Psychiatry, 153*: 65 (1988).

V. Arango, P. Ernsberger, P. M. Marzuk et al., Autoradiographic demonstration of increased serotonin 5-HT_2 and ß-adrenergic receptor binding sites in the brain of suicide victims, *Arch. Gen. Psychiatry, 47*: 1038 (1990).

M. Arato, Z. Rihmer, C. M. Banke, and P. Groff, The relationships of neuroendocrine tests in endogenous depression, *Prog. Neuropharmacol. Biol. Psychiatry, 7*: 715 (1983).

G. M. Asnis, C. Z. Lemus, and U. Halbreich, The desipramine cortisol test—a selective noradrenergic challenge (relationship to other cortisol tests in depressives and normals), *Psychopharmacol. Bull., 22*: 571 (1986).

G. Aston-Jones, M. T. Shipley, G. Chouvet, M. Ennis, E. J. Van Bockstaele, V. Pieribone, R. Shiekhattar, H. Akaoka, G. Drolet, B. Astier, P. Charlety, R. Valentino, and J. T. Williams, Afferent regulation of locus coeruleus neurons: Anatomy, physiology and pharmacology, *Prog. Brain Res., 88*: 47 1991).

C. Aulakh, J. L. Hill, C. C. Chiueh, and D. L. Murphy, Functional subsensitivity of serotonin receptors mediating clonidine induced increases in growth hormone in Farom hooded rat strain relative to Wistar rat strain, *Neurosci. Abstr., 17*: 1173 (1991).

J. D. Ballenger, G. A. Peterson, M. Laraia, A. Hudek, C. R. Lake, D. Jimerson, D. J. Cox, C. Trockman, J. R. Shipe, and C. Wilkinson, A study of plasma catecholamines in agoraphobia and the relationship of serum tricyclic levels to treatment response, *Biology of Agoraphobia* (J. C. Ballenger, ed.), American Psychiatric Press, Washington, D.C., p. 27 (1984).

P. A. Berger, K. F. Faull, J. Kilkowski, P. J. Anderson, H. Kraemer, K. L. Davis, and J. D. Barchas, CSF monoamine metabolites in depression and schizophrenia, *Am. J. Psychiatry, 137*: 174 (1980).

A. Biegon, and M. Israeli, Regionally selective increases in ß-adrenergic receptor density in the brains of suicide victims, *Brain Res., 442*: 199 (1988).

E. B. Blanchard, L. C. Kolb, T. P. Pallmeyer, and R. J. Gerardi, A psychophysiological study of post-traumatic stress disorder in Vietnam veterans, *Psychiat. Q., 54*: 220 (1982).

E. B. Blanchard, L. C. Kolb, R. J. Gerardi, P. Ryan, and T. P. Pallmeyer, Cardiac response to relevant stimuli as an adjunctive tool for diagnosing post-traumatic stress disorder in Vietnam veterans, *Behav. Ther., 17*: 592 (1986).

P. A. Boudewyns, and L. Hyer, Psychophysiological response to combat memories and preliminary treatment outcome in Vietnam veteran PTSD patients treated with direct therapeutic exposure, *Behav. Ther., 20*: 245 (1989).

P. Boyer, C. Schaub, and P. Pichot, Growth hormone response to clonidine test in depressive states, *Neuroendocrinol. Lett., 4*: 178 (1982).

P. R. Breggin, The psychophysiology of anxiety: With a review of literature concerning adrenaline, *J. Nerv. Ment. Dis., 109*: 558 (1964).

S.-L. Brown, D. S. Charney, S. W. Woods et al., Lymphocyte beta-adrenergic receptor binding in panic disorder, *Psychopharmacology, 94*: 24 (1988).

M. S. Buchsbaum, G. Muscettola, and F. K. Goodwin, Urinary MHPG stress response personality factors and somatosensory evoked potentials in normal subjects and patients with major affective disorders, *Neuropsychobiology, 7*: 212 (1981).

N. S. Buckholtz, A. O. Davies, M. V. Rudorfer, R. N. Golden, and W. Z. Potter, Lymphocyte beta adrenergic receptor function versus catecholamines in depression, *Biol. Psychiatry, 24*: 451 (1988).

P. D. Butler, J. M. Weiss, J. C. Stout, and C. B. Nemeroff, Corticotropin-releasing factor produces fear-enhancing and behavioral activating effects following infusion into the locus coeruleus, *J. Neurosci., 10*: 176 (1990).

Cameron, O. G., and R. M. Nesse, Systemic hormonal and physiological abnormalities in anxiety disorders, *Psychoneuroendocrinology, 13*: 287 (1988).

O. G. Cameron, C. B. Smith, P. J. Hollingsworth et al., Platelet alpha$_2$-adrenergic receptor binding and plasma catecholamines: Before and during imipramine treatment in patients with panic anxiety, *Arch. Gen. Psychiatry, 41*: 1144 (1984).

O. G. Cameron, M. A. Lee, G. C. Curtis, and D. S. McCann, Endocrine and physiological changes during spontaneous panic attacks, *Psychoneuroendocrinology, 12*: 321 (1987).

O. G. Cameron, C. B. Smith, M. A. Lee, P. J. Hollingsworth, E. M. Hill, and G. C. Curtis, Adrenergic function in anxiety disorders: Platelet alpha$_2$-adrenergic receptor binding, blood pressure, pulse, and plasma catecholamines in panic and generalized anxiety disorder patients and normal subjects, *Biol. Psychiatry, 28*: 3 (1990).

G. Cassens, A. Kurur, M. Roffman, P. Orsulak, and J. J. Schildkraut, Alterations in brain norepinephrine metabolism and behavior induced by environmental stimuli previously paired with inescapable shock, *Behav. Brain Res., 2*: 387 (1981).

P. B. Chappell, M. A. Smith, C. D. Kilts, G. Bissette, J. Ritchie, C. Anderson, and C. B. Nemeroff, Alterations in corticotropin-releasing factor-like immunoreactivity in discrete rat brain regions after acute and chronic stress, *J. Neurosci., 6*: 2908 (1990).

D. S. Charney, and G. R. Heninger, Abnormal regulation of noradrenergic function in panic disorder, *Arch. Gen. Psychiatry, 43*: 1942 (1986).

D. S. Charney, G. R. Heninger, D. E. Sternberg, et al., Abrupt discontinuation of tricyclic antidepressant drugs: Evidence for noradrenergic hyperactivity, *Br. J. Psychiatry, 141*: 377 (1982a).

D. S. Charney, G. R. Heninger, D. E. Sternberg, K. M. Hafstead, S. Giddings, and H. Landis, Adrenergic receptor sensitivity in depression: Effects of clonidine in depressed patients and healthy subjects, *Arch. Gen. Psychiatry, 39*: 290 (1982b).

D. S. Charney, D. E. Redmond, Jr., M. P. Galloway et al., Naltrexone precipitated opiate withdrawal in methadone addicted human subjects: Evidence for noradrenergic hyperactivity, *Life Sci., 35*: 1263 (1984a).

D. S. Charney, G. R. Heninger, and A. Breier, Noradrenergic function in panic anxiety: Effects of yohimbine in healthy subjects and patients with agoraphobia and panic disorder, *Arch. Gen. Psychiatry, 41*: 751 (1984b).

D. S. Charney, S. W. Woods, W. K. Goodman et al., Neurobiological mechanisms of panic anxiety: Biochemical and behavioral correlates of yohimbine-induced panic attacks, *Am. J. Psychiatry, 144*: 1030 (1987).

D. S. Charney, R. B. Innis, R. S. Duman, S. W. Woods, and G. R. Heninger, Platelet alpha$_2$-receptor binding and adenylate cyclase activity in panic disorder, *Psychopharmacology, 98*: 102 (1989a).

D. S. Charney, S. W. Woods, and G. R. Heninger, Noradrenergic function in generalized anxiety disorder. Effects of yohimbine in healthy subjects and patients with generalized anxiety disorder, *Psychiatry Res., 27*: 173 (1989b).

D. S. Charney, S. W. Woods, J. H. Krystal, and G. R. Heninger, Neurobiological mechanisms of human anxiety, *The Biological Basis of Psychiatric Treatment, Progress Basic Clinical Pharmacology* (R. Pohl and S. Gershon, eds.), S. Karger, Basel, p. 242 (1990).

D. S. Charney, S. W. Woods, J. H. Krystal, L. M. Nagy, and G. R. Heninger, Noradrenergic neuronal dysregulation in panic disorder: The effects of intravenous yohimbine and clonidine in panic disorder patients, *Acta Psychiatr. Scand., 86*: 273–282 (1992).

S. A. Checkley, Corticosteroid and growth hormone responses to methylamphetamine in depressive illness, *Psychol. Med., 9*: 107 (1979).

S. A. Checkley, and J. L. Crammer, Hormone responses to methylamphetamine in depression: A new approach to the noradrenaline depletion hypothesis, *Br. J. Psychiatry, 131*: 582 (1977).

S. A. Checkley, A. P. Slade, and E. Shur, Growth hormone and other responses to clonidine in patients with endogenous depression, *Br. J. Psychiatry, 138*: 51 (1981).

S. A. Checkley, I. B. Glass, C. Thompson, T. Corn, and P. Robinson, The GH response to clonidine in endogenous as compared to reactive depression, *Psychol. Med., 14*: 773 (1984).

N. J. Christensen, P. Vestergard, T. Sorenson, and O. J. Rafaelsen, Cerebrospinal fluid, adrenaline and noradrenaline in depressed patients, *Acta. Psychiatr. Scand., 61*: 178 (1980).

B. J. Cole, and T. W. Robbins, Dissociable effects of lesions to dorsal and ventral noradrenergic bundle on the acquisition performance, and extinction of aversive conditioning, *Behav. Neurosci., 101*: 476 (1987).

S. J. Cooper, J. G. Kelly, and D. J. King, Adrenergic receptors in depression: Effects of electroconvulsive therapy, *Br. J. Psychiatry, 147*: 23 (1985).

T. J. Crow, A. J. Cross, S. J. Cooper, J. F. W. Deakin, I. N. Ferrier, M. H. Joseph, F. Owen, M. Poulter, R. Lofthouse, J. A. N. Corsellis, D. R. Chambers, G. Blessed, E. K. Perry, and B. E. Tomlinson, Neurotransmitter receptors and monoamine metabolites in the brains of patients with Alzheimer-type dementia, depression and suicides, *Neuropharmacology, 23*: 1561 (1984).

M. Davis, Pharmacological and anatomical analysis of fear conditioning using the fear-potentiated startle paradigm, *Behav. Neurosci., 100*: 814 (1986).

M. Davis, Animal models of anxiety based upon classical conditioning: The conditioned emotional response and fear potentiated startle effect, *Pharmacol. Ther., 47*: 147 (1990).

M. Davis, The role of the amygdala in fear potentiated startle: Implications for animal models of anxiety, *Trends Pharmacol. Sci., 13*: 35 (1992).

J. M. Davis, S. H. Koslow, R. D. Gibbons, J. W. Maas, C. L. Bowden, R. Casper, I. Hanin, J. I. Javiad, B. S. Chang, and P. E. Stokes, Cerebrospinal fluid and urinary biogenic amines in depressed patients and healthy controls, *Arch. Gen. Psychiatry, 45*: 705 (1988).

A. J. Dunn, and C. W. Berridge, Corticotropin-releasing factor administration elicits a stress like activation of cerebral catecholaminergic systems, *Pharmacol. Biochem. Behav., 27*: 27 (1987).

R. P. Ebstein, B. Lerer, B. Shapira, Z. Shemesh, E. D. G. Moscovich, and S. Kindler, Cyclic AMP second messenger amplification in depression, *Br. J. Psychiatry, 152*: 665 (1988).

M. J. Edlund, A. C. Swann, and C. M. Davis, Plasma MHPG in untreated panic disorder, *Biol. Psychiatry, 22*: 1488 (1987).

E. Eriksson, J. Balldin, G. Lindstedt, and K. Modigh, Growth hormone response to the alpha-2 adrenoceptor agonist guanfacine and to growth hormone releasing hormone in depressed patients and controls, *Psychiatry Res., 26*: 59 (1988).

M. Feinberg, J. F. Greden, and B. J. Carroll, The effect of amphetamine on plasma cortisol in patients with endogenous and nonendogenous depression, *Psychoneuroendocrinology, 6*: 355 (1981).

R. D. Feldman, L. E. Limbird, J. Nadeau, G. A. Fitzgerald, D. Robertson, and A. J. J. Wood, Dynamic regulation of lymphocyte beta adrenergic receptor–agonist interactions by physiological changes in circulating catecholamines, *J. Clin. Invest., 72*: 164 (1983).

S. L. Foote, F. E. Bloom, and G. Aston-Jones, Nucleus locus coeruleus: New evidence of anatomical and physiological specificity, *Physiol. Rev., 63*: 844 (1983).

R. R. Freedman, P. Iani, E. Ettedgui, and N. Puthezhath, Ambulatory monitoring of panic disorder, *Arch. Gen. Psychiatry, 42*: 244 (1985).

J. A. Garcia-Sevila, A. P. Zis, P. J. Hollingsworth, J. F. Greden, and C. B. Smith, Platelet alpha-2 adrenergic receptors in major depressive disorder: Binding of tritiated clonidine before and after tricyclic antidepressant drug treatment, *Arch. Gen. Psychiatry, 38*: 1327 (1981).

J. A. Garcia-Sevilla, P. Guimon, P. Garcia-Vallejo, and M. J. Fuster, Biochemical and functional evidence of supersensitive platelet alpha$_2$-adrenoreceptors in major affective disorder: Effect of long-term lithium carbonate treatment, *Arch. Gen. Psychiatry, 43*: 51 (1986).

J. A. Garcia-Sevilla, C. Udina, M. J. Fuster, E. Alvarez, and M. Casas, Enhanced binding of [^{3}H](–)adrenaline to platelets of depressed patients with melancholia: Effect of long-term clomipramine treatment, *Acta Psychiatr. Scand., 75*: 150 (1987).

J. A. Garcia-Sevilla, D. Padro, T. Giralt, J. Guimon, and P. Areso, alpha$_2$-Adrenoreceptor-mediated inhibition of platelet adenylate cyclase and induction to aggregation in major depression: Effect of long-term cyclic antidepressant drug treatment, *Arch. Gen. Psychiatry, 47*: 125 (1990).

M. J. Garvey, G. D. Tollefson, and P. J. Orsulak, Elevations of urinary MHPG in depressed patients with panic attacks, *Psychiatry Res., 20*: 183 (1987).

A. Georgotas, J. Schweitzer, R. E. McCue, M. Armour, and A. J. Friedhoff, Clinical and treatment effects on ^{3}H-clonidine and ^{3}H-imipramine binding in elderly depressed patients, *Life Sci., 40*: 2137 (1897).

W. M. Glazer, D. S. Charney, and G. R. Heninger, Noradrenergic function in schizophrenia, *Arch. Gen. Psychiatry, 44*: 898 (1987).

M. S. Gold, and D. E. Redmond, Jr., Pharmacological activation and inhibition of noradrenergic activity alter specific behaviors in nonhuman primates, *Neurosci. Abstr., 3*: 250 (1977).

K. Goodwin, Changes in lymphocyte beta-adrenergic receptors in depression and mania, *Psychiatry Res., 1*: 191 (1979).

J. A. Gray, Precis of The neuropsychology of anxiety: An enquiry into the functions of the septo-hippocampal system, *Behav. Brain Sci., 5*: 469 (1982).

R. R. Grinker, and J. J. Spiegle, *Men Under Stress,* McGraw-Hill, New York, p. 219 (1945).

U. Halbreich, E. J. Sachar, G. M. Asnis et al., Growth hormone response to dextroamphetamine in depressed patients and normal subjects, *Arch. Gen. Psychiatry, 39*: 189 (1982).

G. R. Heninger, and D. S. Charney, Mechanism of action of antidepressant treatments: Implications for the etiology and treatment of depressive disorders, *Psychopharmacology: The Third Generation of Progress* (H. T. Meltzer, ed.), Raven Press, New York, p. 535 (1978a).

G. R. Heninger, D. S. Charney, and L. H. Price, alpha-2-Adrenergic receptor sensitivity in depression: The plasma MHPG, behavioral, and cardiovascular responses to yohimbine, *Arch. Gen. Psychiatry, 45*: 718 (1988).

F. A. Henn, and W. T. McKinney, Animal models in psychiatry, *Psychopharmacology: The Third Generation of Progress* (H. Meltzer, ed.), Raven Press, New York, p. 687 (1987).

J. D. Higley, S. J. Suomi, and M. Linnoila, CSF monoamine metabolite concentrations vary according to age, rearing, and sex, and are influenced by the stressor of social separation in rhesus monkeys, *Psychopharmacology, 103*: 551 (1991).

Y. H. Huang, D. E. Redmond, Jr., D. R. Snyder et al., Loss of fear following bilateral lesions of the locus coeruleus in the monkey, *Neurosci. Abstr., 2*: 573 (1976).

J. Irwin, P. Ahluwalia, and H. Anisman, Sensitization of norepinephrine activity following acute and chronic footshock, *Brain Res., 379*: 98 (1986).

D. C. Jimerson, The role of dopamine mechanisms in the affective disorders, *Psychopharmacology: The Third Generation of Progress* (H. T. Meltzer, ed.), Raven Press, New York, pp. 505–511 (1987).

T. Keane, J. Fairbank, J. M. Caddell, and R. T. Zimering, Implosive therapy reduces symptoms of PTSD in Vietnam combat veterans, *Behav. Ther., 20*: 245 (1989).

S. Kindler, and B. Lerer, Norepinephrine and depression: A reappraisal, *The Biologic Basis of Psychiatric Treatment. Progress in Basic and Clinical Pharmacology.* Vol. 3 (R. Pohl and S. Gershon, eds.), S. Karger, Basel, p. 120 (1990).

L. C. Kolb, The post traumatic stress disorders of combat: A subgroup with a conditioned emotional response, *Milt. Med., 149*: 237 (1984).

S. H. Koslow, P. E. Stokes, J. Mendels, A. Ramsey, and R. Casper, Insulin tolerance test: Human growth hormone response and insulin resistance in primary unipolar depressed, bipolar depressed and control subjects, *Psychol. Med., 12*: 45 (1982).

T. R. Kosten, J. W. Mason, E. L. Giller et al., Sustained urinary norepinephrine and epinephrine elevation in posttraumatic stress disorder, *Psychoneuroendocrinology, 12*: 13 (1987).

J. H. Krystal, T. R. Kosten, B. D. Perry et al., Neurobiological aspects of PTSD: Review of clinical and preclinical studies, *Behav. Ther., 20*: 177 (1989).

G. Laakmann, G. Schumacher, O. Benkert, and K. Werder, Stimulation of growth hormone secretion by desimipramine and chlorimipramine in man, *J. Clin. Endocrinol. Metab., 44*: 1010 (1977).

G. Laakmann, K. Zygan, H. W. Schoen et al., Effects of receptor blockers (methysergide, propranolol, phentolamine, yohimbine, and prazosin) on the desimipramine-induced pituitary hormone stimulation in humans. Part I: Growth hormone, *Psychoneuroendocrinology, 11*: 447 (1986).

M. Lader, The peripheral and central role of the catecholamines in the mechanisms of anxiety, *Int. Pharmacopsychiatry, 9*: 125 (1974).

C. R. Lake, D. Pickar, M. G. Ziegler, S. Lipper, S. Slater, and D. L. Murphy, High plasma norepinephrine levels in patients with major affective disorders, *Am. J. Psychiatry, 139*: 1315 (1982).

G. Langer, G. Heinze, B. Reim, and N. Matussek, Growth hormone response to *d*-amphetamine in normal controls and depressive patients, *Neurosci. Lett., 1*: 185 (1975).

G. Langer, G. Heinze, B. Reim, and N. Matussek, Reduced growth hormone response to amphetamine in endogenous depressive patients, *Arch. Gen. Psychiatry, 33*: 1471 (1976).

J. E. LeDoux, Emotion, *Handbook of Physiology–The Nervous System* (V. Mountcastle, F. Plum, S. Geiger, eds.), American Physiology Society, Bethesda, MD. (1987).

J. E. Le Doux, L. Romanski, and A. Xagoris, Indelibility of subcortical emotional memories, *J. Cogn. Neurosci., 1*: 238 (1989).

J. E. Le Doux, P. O. Cicchetti, A. Xagoris, and L. Romanski, The lateral amygdaloid nucleus: Sensory interface of the amygdala in fear conditioning, *J. Neurosci., 10*: 1062 (1990).

E. S. Levine, W. J. Litto, and B. L. Jacobs, Activity of cat locus coeruleus noradrenergic neurons during the defense response, *Brain Res., 531*: 89 (1990).

B. T. Litz, and T. M. Keane, Information processing in anxiety disorders: Application to the understanding of post-traumatic stress disorder, *Clin. Psychol. Rev., 9*: 243 (1989).

P. F. Malloy, J. A. Fairbank, and T. M. Keane, Validation of a multimethod assessment of posttraumatic stress disorders in Vietnam veterans, *J. Consult. Clin. Psychol., 51*: 488 (1983).

J. J. Mann, R. P. Brown, J. P. Halper et al., Reduced sensitivity to lymphocyte beta-adrenergic receptors in patients with endogenous depression and psychomotor agitation, *N. Engl. J. Med., 313*: 715 (1985).

J. J. Mann, M. Stanley, P. A. McBride, and B. S. McEwen, Increased serotonin$_2$ and ß-adrenergic receptor binding in the frontal cortices of suicide victims, *Arch. Gen. Psychiatry, 43*: 954 (1986).

R. J. Mathew, B. T. Ho, D. J. Francis, D. L. Taylor, and M. L. Weinman, Catecholamines and anxiety, *Acta Psychiatr. Scand., 65*: 142 (1982).

N. Matussek, Catecholamines and mood: Neuroendocrine aspects, *Curr. Topics Neuroendocrinol., 8*: 145 (1988).

N. Matussek, M. Ackenheil, H. Hippius et al., Effects of clonidine on growth hormone release in psychiatric patients and controls, *Psychiatry Res., 2*: 25 (1980).

M. F. McFall, M. M. Murburg, G. M. Ko, and R. C. Veith, Autonomic responses to stress in Vietnam veterans with post traumatic stress disorder, *Biol. Psychiatry, 27*: 1165 (1990).

J. L. McGaugh, Involvement of hormonal and neuromodulatory systems in the regulation of memory storage, *Annu. Rev. Neurosci., 2*: 255 (1989).

J. L. McGaugh, Significance and remembrance: The role of neuromodulatory systems, *Psychol. Sci., 1*: 15 (1990).

R. J. McNally, D. L. Luedke, J. K. Besyner, R. A. Peterson, K. Bohm, and O. J. Lips, Sensitivity to stress relevant stimuli in post traumatic stress disorder, *J. Anxiety Disord., 1*: 105 (1987).

J. C. Meakes, and R. M. Wilson, The effect of certain sensory stimulations on respiratory and heart rate in case of "so-called" irritable heart, *Heart, 7*: 17 (1918).

J. J. Meana, and J. J. Garcia-Sevilla, Increased alpha-2 adrenoceptor density in the frontal cortex of depressed suicide victims, *J. Neural Transm., 70*: 377 (1990).

P. Meesters, M. Kerkhofs, G. Charles, C. Decoster, M. Vanderelst, and J. Mendlewicz, Growth hormone response after desipramine in depressive illness, *Eur. Arch. Psychiatry Neurol. Sci., 235*: 140 (1985).

R. Y. Moore, and F. E. Bloom, Central catecholamine neurons systems: Anatomy and physiology of the norepinephrine and epinephrine systems, *Annu. Rev. Neurosci., 2*: 113 (1979).

D. A. Morilak, C. A. Fornal, and B. L. Jacobs, Effects of physiological manipulations on locus coeruleus neuronal activity in freely moving cats. I. Thermoregulatory challenge, *Brain Res., 422*: 17 (1987a).

D. A. Morilak, C. A. Fornal, and B. L. Jacobs, Effects of physiological manipulations on locus coeruleus neuronal activity in freely moving cats. II. Cardiovascular challenge, *Brain Res., 422*: 24 (1987b).

D. A. Morilak, C. A. Fornal, and B. L. Jacobs, Effects of physiological manipulations on locus coeruleus neuronal activity in freely moving cats. III. Glucoregulatory challenge, *Brain Res., 422*: 32 (1987c).

R. M. Nesse, O. G. Cameron, G. C. Curtis, D. S. McCann, and M. J. Huber-Smith, Adrenergic function in patients with panic anxiety, *Arch. Gen. Psychiatry, 41*: 771 (1984).

R. M. Nesse, O. G. Cameron, A. J. Buda, D. S. McCann, C. G. Curtis, and M. J. Huber-Smith, Urinary catecholamines and mitral valve prolapse in panic anxiety patients, *Psychiatry Res., 14*: 67 (1985).

L. K. Nisenbaum, M. J. Zigmund, A. F. Sved, and E. D. Abercrombie, Prior exposure to chronic stress results in enhanced synthesis and release of hippocampal norepinephrine in response to a novel stressor, *J. Neurosci., 11*: 1478 (1991).

D. J. Nutt, Increased central alpha-2 adrenoceptor sensitivity in panic disorder, *Psychopharmacology, 90*: 268 (1986).

D. J. Nutt, Altered alpha$_2$-adrenoceptor sensitivity in panic disorder, *Arch. Gen. Psychiatry, 46*: 165 (1989).

D. J. Nutt, and S. Frazer, Platelet binding studies in panic disorder, *J. Affective Disord., 12*: 7 (1987).

S. P. Orr, Psychophysiologic studies of post traumatic stress disorder, *Biological Assessment and Treatment of Post Traumatic Stress Disorder* (E. L. Giller, ed.), American Psychiatric Press, Washington, D.C. (1990).

T. P. Pallmeyer, E. B. Blanchard, and L. C. Kolb, The psychophysiology of combat-induced post-traumatic stress disorder in Vietnam veterans, *Behav. Res. Ther., 24*: 645 (1986).

G. N. Pandey, P. Sudershan, and J. M. Davis, beta Adrenergic receptor function in depression and the effect of antidepressant drugs, *Acta Pharmacol. Toxicol., 56*: 66 (1985).

F. W. Peabody, H. D. Clough, L. C. Sturgis, J. J. Wearn, and E. H. Thompkins, Effects of injection of norepinephrine in soldiers with "irritable heart," *JAMA, 21*: 1912 (1918).

B. D. Perry, E. L. Giller, and S. M. Southwick, Altered platelet alpha$_2$ adrenergic binding sites in posttraumatic stress disorder, *Am. J. Psychiatry, 144*: 1511 (1987).

J. E. Piletz, A. Halaris, A. Saran, and M. Marler, Elevated ^{3}H-*para*-aminoclonidine binding to platelet purified plasma membranes from depressed patients, *Neuropsychopharmacology, 3*: 201 (1990).

R. K. Pitman, S. P. Orr, D. F. Forgue, J. B. deJong, and J. M. Claiborn, Psychophysiologic assessment of post-traumatic stress disorder in Vietnam combat veterans, *Arch. Gen. Psychiatry, 44*: 970 (1987).

R. M. Post, E. K. Gordon, F. K. Goodwin, and W. E. Bunney, Central norepinephrine metabolism in affective illness: MHPG in the cerebrospinal fluid, *Science, 179*: 1002 (1973).

R. M. Post, and F. K. Goodwin, Approaches to brain amines in psychiatric patients: A reevaluation of cerebrospinal fluid studies, *Handbook of Psychopharmacology,* Plenum Publishing, New York, p. 147 (1980).

L. H. Price, D. S. Charney, A. L. Rubin et al., alpha-2 Adrenergic receptor function in depression: The cortisol release to yohimbine, *Arch. Gen. Psychiatry, 43*: 849 (1986).

K. Rasmussen, D. A. Morilak, and B. L. Jacobs, Single-unit activity of locus coeruleus neurons in the freely moving cat. I. During naturalistic behaviors and in response to simple and complex stimuli, *Brain Res., 371*: 324 (1986).

S. A. Rasmussen, W. K. Goodman, S. W. Woods et al., Effects of yohimbine in obsessive–compulsive disorder, *Psychopharmacology, 93*: 308 (1987).

D. E. Redmond, Jr., Y. H. Huang, D. R. Snyder et al., Behavioral changes following lesions of the locus coeruleus in *Macaca arctoides, Neurosci. Abstr., 1*: 472 (1972).

D. E. Redmond, Jr., Y. H. Huang, D. R. Snyder et al., Behavioral effects of stimulation of the locus coeruleus in the stumptail monkey (*Macaca arctoides*), *Brain Res., 116*: 502 (1976).

W. T. Roth, J. Margraf, A. Ehlers, C. B. Taylor, R. J. Maddock, R. J. Maddock, S. Davies, and W. S. Agras, Stress reactivity in panic disorder, *Arch. Gen. Psychiatry, 49*: 301 (1992).

A. Roy, D. Pikar, M. Linnoila, and W. Z. Potter, Plasma norepinephrine level in affective disorders. Relationship to melancholia, *Arch. Gen. Psychiatry, 42*: 1181 (1985).

M. V. Rudorfer, R. J. Ross, M. Linnoila, M. A. Sherer, and W. Z. Potter, Exaggerated orthostatic responsitivity of plasma norepinephrine in depression, *Arch. Gen. Psychiatry., 42*: 1186 (1985).

E. J. Sachar, G. Asnis, R. S. Nathan, U. Halbreich, M. A. Tabrizi, and F. S. Halpern, Dextroamphetamine and cortisol in depression, *Arch. Gen. Psychiatry, 37*: 55 (1980).

E. J. Sachar, J. Puig-Antich, N. D. Ryan et al., Three tests of cortisol secretion in adult endogenous depression, *Acta Psychiatr. Scand., 71*: 1 (1985).

L. J. Siever, Role of noradrenergic mechanisms in the etiology of the affective disorders, *Psychopharmacology: The Third Generation of Progress* (H. T. Meltzer, ed.), Raven Press, New York, p. 493 (1987).

L. J. Siever, and K. L. Davis, Overview: Toward a dysregulation hypothesis of depression, *Am. J. Psychiatry, 142*: 1017 (1985).

L. J. Siever, T. W. Uhde, E. K. Silberman et al., Growth hormone response to clonidine as a probe of noradrenergic receptor responsiveness in affective disorder patients and controls, *Psychiatry Res., 6*: (1982).

L. J. Siever, M. S. Kafka, T. R. Insel, C. R. Lake, and D. C. Murphy, Effect of clorgyline administration on human platelet alpha-adrenergic receptor binding and platelet cyclic AMP responses, *Psychiatry Res., 9*: 37 (1984).

L. J. Siever, T. W., D. L. Jimerson, C. R. Lake, I. J. Kopin, and D. L. Murphy, Indices of noradrenergic output in depression, *Psychiatry Res., 1*: 59 (1986).

P. E. Simson, and J. M. Weiss, Altered activity of the locus coeruleus in an animal model of depression, *Neuropharmacology, 1*: 287 (1988a).

P. E. Simpson, and J. M. Weiss, Responsiveness of locus coeruleus neurons to excitatory stimulation is uniquely regulated by alpha-2 receptors, *Psychopharmacol. Bull., 24*: 349 (1988b).

S. M. Southwick, J. H. Krystal, C. A. Morgan, D. Johnson, L. M. Nagy, A. Nicolau, G. R. Heninger, and D. S. Charney, Abnormal noradrenergic function in post-traumatic stress disorder, *Arch. Gen. Psychiatry 50*: 266–274 (1993).

M. B. Stein, M. E. Tancer, and T. W. Uhde, Heart rate and plasma norepinephrine responsivity to orthostatic challenge in anxiety disorders, *Arch. Gen. Psychiatry, 49*: 311 (1992).

R. E. Strecker, and B. L. Jacobs, Substantia nigra dopaminergic unit activity in behaving cats: Effect of arousal on spontaneous discharge and sensory evoked activity, *Brain Res., 361*: 339 (1985).

T. H. Svensson, Peripheral, autonomic regulation of locus coeruleus noradrenergic neurons in brain: Putative implications for psychiatry and psychopharmacology, *Psychopharmacology, 92*: 1 (1987).

M. Tanaka, A. Tsuda, H. Yokoo, M. Yoshida, Y. Ida, and H. Nishimura, Involvement of brain noradrenaline system in emotional changes caused by stress in rats, *Ann. N.Y. Acad. Sci., 16*: 159 (1990a).

T. Tanaka, H. Yokoo, A. Tsuda, and M. Tanaka, Stress increased hypothalamic noradrenaline release studied by intracerebral dialysis method, *Neuroscience, 16*: 293 (1990b).

T. Tanaka, H. Yokoo, K. Mizoguchi, M. Yoshida, A. Tsuda, and M. Tanaka, Noradrenaline release in the rat amygdala is increased by stress: Studies with intracerebral microdialysis, *Brain Res., 544*: 174 (1991).

T. Torda, R. Kvetnansky, and M. Petrikova, Effect of repeated immobilization stress on rat central and peripheral adrenoceptors, *Stress: The Role of Catecholamines and Other Neurotransmitters* (E. Usdin, R. Kvetansky, and J. Axelrod, eds.), Gordon & Breach, New York, p. 691 (1984).

E. Tsaltas, J. A. Gray, and M. Fillenz, Alleviation of response suppression to conditioned aversive stimuli by lesions of the dorsal noradrenergic bundle, *Behav. Brain Res., 13*: 115 (1987).

A. Tsuda, M. Tanaka, Y. Ida, S. Tsujimaru, I. Ushijima, and N. Nagasaki, Effects of preschock experience on enhancement of rat brain noradrenaline turnover induced by psychological stress, *Pharmacol. Biochem. Behav., 24*: 115 (1986).

T. W. Uhde, P. P. Roy-Byrne, B. J. Vittone, J. P. Boulenger, and R. M. Post, Phenomenology and neurobiology of panic disorder, *Anxiety and the Anxiety Disorders* (M. Tuma, ed.), Lawrence Erlbaum, Hillsdale, N.J., p. 557 (1985).

T. W. Uhde, R. T. Joffe, D. C. Jimerson, and R. M. Post, Normal urinary free cortisol and plasma MHPG in panic disorder: Clinical and theoretical implications, *Biol. Psychiatry, 23*: 575 (1988).

T. W. Uhde, M. G. Stein, B. J. Vittone et al., Behavioral and physiological effects of acute and chronic clonidine in panic disorder, *Arch. Gen. Psychiatry, 46*: 170 (1989).

D. U'Prichard, and R. Kvetnansky, Central and peripheral adrenergic receptors in acute and repeated immobilization stress, *Catecholamines and Stress: Recent Advances* (E. Usdin, R. Kvetnansky, and I. J. Kopin, eds.), Elsevier, Amsterdam, p. 299 (1980).

R. J. Valentino, and S. L. Foote, Corticotropin-releasing hormone increases tonic but not sensory-evoked activity of noradrenergic locus coeruleus neurons in unanesthetized rats, *J. Neurosci., 8*: 1016 (1988).

E. C. Villacres, M. Hollifield, W. J. Katon, W. C. Wilkinson, and R. C. Veith, Sympathetic nervous system activity in panic disorder, *Psychiatry Res., 21*: 313 (1987).

H. Wachtel, Dysbalance of neuronal second messenger function in the aetiology of affective disorders: A psychophysiological concept hypothesising defects beyond first messenger receptors, *J. Neural Transm., 75*: 21 (1989).

S. R. B Weiss, and T. W. Uhde, Animal models of anxiety, *Neurobiology of Panic Disorder* (J. C. Ballenger, ed.), Alan R. Liss, New York, p. 1 (1990).

M. M. Weissman, P. Adams, J. Lish, P. Wickramaratne, E. Horwath, D. S. Charney, S. W. Woods, E. Leeman, and E. Frosch, The relationship between panic disorder and major depression: A new family study, *Arch. Gen. Psych.,* in press.

L. O. Wilkinson, E. D. Abercrombie, and B. L. Jacobs, Environmental stress and activity of dorsal raphe serotonergic neurons in the freely moving cat, *Soc. Neurosci. Abstr., 12*: 1134 (1986).

P. Willner, Animal models of depression: An overview, *Pharmacol. Ther., 45*: 425 (1990).

K. Wood, and A. Coppen, $alpha_2$ Adrenergic receptors in depression, *Lancet, 1*: 1121 (1982).

S. W. Woods, D. S. Charney, C. A. McPherson, A. H. Gradman, and G. R. Heninger, Situational panic attacks: Behavioral, physiological, and biochemical characterization, *Arch. Gen. Psychiatry, 44*: 365 (1987).

R. Yehuda, S. M. Southwick, E. L. Giller et al., Urinary catecholamine excretion and symptoms in Vietnam combat veterans. *J. Nerv. Ment. Dis. 180*: 321–325 (1992).

F. D. Yocca, and E. Friedman, Effect of immobilization stress on rat pineal beta-adrenergic receptor-mediated function, *J. Neurochem., 42*: 1427 (1984).

H. Yokoo, M. Tanaka, M. Yoshida, A. Trsuda, T. Tanaka, and K. Mizoguchi, Direct evidence of conditioned fear-elicited enhancement of noradrenaline release in the rat hypothalamus assessed by intracranial microdialysis, *Brain Res., 536*: 305 (1990).

19

Antidepressive Drugs for Treatment of Anxiety Disorders—and Vice Versa

Peter Tyrer
St. Mary's Hospital Medical School, St. Charles Hospital, London, England

Jonathan Tyrer
University of Sheffield, Sheffield, England

I. A HISTORICAL INTRODUCTION

In Chapter 1 of this book the many changes that have taken place in psychiatric views of anxiety and depression have been outlined. It is important to appreciate that many of these changes developed from treatment. As soon as any treatment is perceived as being specific, or at least preferentially indicated, for anxiety or depression, then there is greater reason for separating these moods and normalizing their description as distinct disorders. The apparent continuous reform of the classification of anxiety, depression, and neurotic disorders in the last 30 years has, at least partly, been fueled by the introduction of new drugs, or of new specifications for old ones. Among the arguments used for the introduction of new diagnoses is evidence suggesting differences in treatment response.

The best example of this is represented by the work of Klein who, more than any other person, has been responsible for introducing the diagnosis of panic disorder into current classifications. Before this time there was a loose distinction between the two major conditions of *anxiety neurosis* and *depressive neurosis*. This was accompanied by the expectation that those patients with anxiety neurosis would be treated by psychological techniques, such as relaxation and rest together with sedative drugs (initially the barbiturates, followed by meprobamate and the benzodiazepines), whereas depression was normally treated with antidepressant drugs.

Klein threw a spanner into this admittedly imperfect working model by demonstrating, initially in a paper with Max Fink in 1962, and subsequently in a separate paper (Klein, 1964), that severe anxiety, primarily in the form of panic, was specifically helped by treatment with the antidepressant drug, imipramine. Clinical observation suggested to Klein that the improvement in symptoms must be related to the effect of imipramine on the core symptoms of the panic attack, and he subsequently suggested that antidepressants such as imipramine "blocked" the panic attack in a manner analogous to a drug, such as a ß-adrenoceptor-blocking drug, preventing tachycardia in the presence of high levels of circulating catecholamines.

In particular, Klein was convinced that the improvement could in no way be related to a direct effect of the drug on depressive symptoms. By doing this, he departed significantly from the views of many other clinical psychiatrists and diagnosticians of this time. In the years following the introduction of antidepressants it became commonplace for prescribers to conclude that all patients who responded to antidepresant drugs had a form of depressive disorder. Thus the concept of *atypical depression* was born, a concept that has never been a satisfactory diagnostic entity (Paykel et al., 1983) and which, in its most absurd form, was described in the Italian literature as *depressione sine depressione.* This description allowed the diagnosis of all psychiatric disorders as depression if the clinician so desired. As the demonstration of the efficacy of antidepressants was one of the most exciting developments of the 1960s, it was perhaps hardly surprising in retrospect that so many clinicians went around "discovering" how many of their patients with a wide range of psychiatric symptoms were, in effect, suffering from a depressive illness because they had responded to imipramine or amitriptyline.

Klein went one step further in identifying panic as the symptom that was improved specifically by imipramine. He suggested that generalized background anxiety was not helped by antidepressants and, therefore, was fundamentally different from panic. In a series of eloquent articles and presentations he convinced the psychiatric community in the United States that panic disorder deserved to be recognized as a condition independent of anxiety neurosis. He succeeded, and so in 1980, with the publication of the *Diagnostic and Statistical Manual of Mental Disorders,* 3rd ed. (DSM-III), panic disorder appeared for the first time as a separate diagnosis. In changing the classification of *anxiety neurosis,* it was necessary to identify another form of *nonpanic anxiety*. This subsequently became the diagnosis of generalized anxiety disorder. Klein maintained that this exercise of what he termed "pharmacological dissection" with imipramine helped to distinguish two forms of anxiety that were not previously thought of as separate conditions. Indeed, in the original identification of anxiety neurosis as a separate diagnostic disorder, described so well by Freud in 1894, panic was one of the key symptoms of anxiety neurosis. Freud's description of panic attacks, both nocturnal and diurnal, has hardly been bettered, indicating that the many changes in classification of anxiety that have taken place recently have followed much more from the introduction of newer treatments than from any change in clinical observation of the primary conditions.

If this separation had been carried out cleanly and unequivocally, there would be no need for this chapter. Each mental disorder would have its own specific treatments that would not overlap significantly with any other. Klein's original observation would have been extended so that certain drug treatments were specific for panic, others for generalized anxiety disorder, and yet others for the diagnosis of dysthymia and major depressive episode.

Unfortunately, as we all know in clinical practice, the distinction has not been made cleanly, partly because of two issues. The first is that of comorbidity and overlap of different diagnoses. *Comorbidity* is a term that has become extremely popular in research circles in the United States, but that has little meaning to the clinical practitioner. It describes "any distinct additional clinical entity that has existed or that may occur during the clinical course of a patient who has the index disease under study" (Feinstein, 1970). Comorbidity is noted most with anxiety and depression, but is marked throughout the nonpsychotic disorders. Where it may be used inappropriately is when two alleged "diseases" are, in fact, the same condition and, hence, apparent comorbidity is actually indicative of a common disorder. In practice, this can lead to difficulties in interpreting the situation in which anxiety symptoms improve with a specific treatment for depression, or vice versa. This could mean that the treatment is also effective in anxiety disorders (if the principle of comorbidity is accepted) or that the anxiety symptoms are part of the single condition that comprises both anxiety and depressive symptoms (if the concept of a single disorder with overlapping symptomatology is accepted).

The second issue, which has featured prominently in the North American literature, but hardly at all in Europe, is the primary–secondary distinction of anxiety and depressive symptoms. There are strong arguments for considering the chronology of anxiety and depression as important in classification because of differences in response to treatment and outcome in primary mood disturbance and that which is secondary to medical or other psychiatric disorder (Woodruff et al., 1967; Winokur et al., 1990). This has not been examined adequately in specific studies of drug efficacy in anxiety and depression, but deserves to be.

In this review the extent to which treatment apparently underlines diagnosis will be discussed by listing the evidence of efficacy for each of the antidepressive drugs in the anxiety disorders and following this with other evidence, usually less well-documented, that antianxiety drugs can be effective in depressive disorders. Wherever possible the diagnostic groups will be discussed in terms of the newer classification. Thus, generalized anxiety disorder, panic disorder, and phobias will be discussed separately under the heading of anxiety disorders, and dysthymic disorder and major depressive episode will be discussed under the heading of depressive disorders. Because obsessive–compulsive disorders are included among the anxiety disorders, they will also be mentioned briefly.

The term *depressive neurosis,* currently a synonym for dysthymia, will also be incorporated into the review. Because there is no evidence that any antianxiety drugs are effective in the severe forms of depressive illness (depressive psychosis, melancholia), this diagnosis will not be discussed. However, its very absence shows that at least one depressive disorder is sufficiently distinct to be considered a diagnostic and treatment entity. In each example, Klein's policy of pharmacological dissection will be followed. When there is evidence that the improvement in symptoms could have been a consequence of changes in other symptoms, apart from the main ones discussed by the authors, this will be mentioned. For this reason, many of the old studies are suspect because they did not have the diagnostic criteria that protect more recent studies from criticism.

In evaluating published studies, it is often difficult to come to firm conclusions when contradictory data emerge from controlled trials. One common technique of combining the findings is that of metanalysis, whereby data from many different studies are combined and the effect size of each treatment calculated. This technique has been used in evaluating psychotherapy in particular (Smith and Glass, 1977). It is really satisfactory only when the researcher has all the data available for the comparisons, including published and unpublished data, when this is available in raw form, and when the treatment designs of the different studies are similar enough for data combination. In these comparisons, we have used a new approach in which the validity of the findings from each study is determined using a scale, the clinical validity index (CVI), which is then used to compare the combined results of studies using the statistics of randomization (Tyrer and Tyrer, 1992) (Table 1).

Table 1 Clinical Validity Index (CVI) for Comparing Results of Controlled Clinical Trials

Factor	Absent	Present	Uncertain
	Initial score for each trial is 1 from which the scores below are added		
Representative population	−0.1	+0.1	0
Appropriate entry criteria	−0.1	+0.1	0
Randomized allocation	−0.1	+0.1	0
Adequate sample size	−0.1	+0.1	0
Dropout rate less than 20%	−0.1	+0.1	0
Bias-free assessments	−0.1	+0.1	0
Sound design and measurements	−0.1	+0.1	0
Good statistics/interpretation	−0.1	+0.1	0
Good account of methodology	−0.1	+0.1	0
Independence of investigators	−0.1	+0.1	0

Maximum CVI = 2.0; minimum CVI = 0.
Source: Tyrer and Tyrer, 1992.

II. ANTIDEPRESSANTS IN ANXIETY DISORDERS

A. Tricyclic Antidepressants

1. *Agoraphobia and Panic*

It is reasonable to start with panic disorder and agoraphobia, as this fits in with the chronological development of the subject. According to *DSM-III* conventions, agoraphobia is a common outcome of panic because fear of having a panic attack in vulnerable situations often leads to secondary avoidance and the development of phobias. Comparison of patients with panic disorder with those who have agoraphobia with panic shows great similarity (Thyer et al., 1985) and so the two conditions can be considered together.

Klein's early studies were with imipramine, and this has become the benchmark drug for comparisons. Imipramine is among the less sedative of the antidepressants and inhibits the reuptake of norepinephrine and serotonin similarly (Iversen and Mackay, 1979); therefore, it is well placed to be a comparison drug. Subsequent studies have shown that other tricyclic antidepressants are very similar in efficacy to imipramine; hence, these are not included here.

The main studies of imipramine in panic disorder and agoraphobia with panic are illustrated in Table 2. Apart from one study (Marks et al., 1983), all these showed clear superiority of imipramine over placebo control, and comparison of CVIs indicated that these differences were highly significant.

Improvement is normally delayed for between 2 and 4 weeks (and so is clearly not a direct effect of the sedative anticholinergic and antihistaminic effects of imipramine) and is often dramatic. Consequently, it is wise to warn the patient about the likely delay in onset of therapeutic effects and to emphasize the need for regular drug ingestion. The dosages required vary greatly and it is difficult to give clear recommendations. In the United States "adequate" doses of imipramine are much higher than in Europe, and for the treatment of panic attacks over 150 mg/day is recommended (Liebowitz, 1988).

Table 2 Controlled Trials of Imipramine in Agoraphobia and Panic Disorders

Author	*n*	Design	Duration (wk)	Results	Clinical validity index (CVI)
Trials showing superiority of imipramine					
Sheehan et al., 1980	57	Imipramine, placebo, and phenelzine	12	Imipramine and phenelzine both superior to placebo; phenelzine superior to imipramine for phobic avoidance	1.4
Zitrin et al., 1980	76	Imipramine and in vivo exposure compared with placebo	26	Imipramine groups superior to placebo	1.6
Zitrin et al., 1983	218	Imipramine, behavior therapy, supportive therapy, placebo	26	Imipramine superior to placebo in agoraphobics	1.6
McNair and Kahn, 1981	57	Imipramine and chlordiazepoxide	8	Imipramine superior for panic and depression symptoms	1.3
Telch et al., 1985	37	Imipramine, exposure, no exposure, placebo	26	Imipramine groups superior to placebo with exposure and to imipramine and placebo without exposure	1.4
Cross-national Collaborative Study, 1992	500	Alprazolam, imipramine, and placebo	8	Alprazolam and imipramine superior to placebo; delayed efficacy of imipramine	1.6
		Total scores for trials showing imipramine superior to placebo			8.9
Trials showing no difference between imipramine and placebo					
Marks et al., 1983	45	Two-by-two design with imipramine, placebo, and relaxation	28	No significant difference between imipramine and placebo	
		Total scores for trials showing imipramine equivalent to placebo			1.1

Conclusion: Imipramine greatly superior to placebo. Probability of imipramine being superior to placebo ($p < 0.0001$).

Consequently, the study carried out by Marks et al. (1983) is considered suspect in the United States (but probably not in Europe) because the mean doses taken were lower than 150 mg at most times in the study (124 mg at week 6, 158 mg at week 14, and 110 mg at week 26), even though plasma drug levels were within the acceptable range for efficacy.

It also must be acknowledged that some patients appear to respond to very low doses. Thus, according to Klein and his colleagues:

> Some patients (10–20% of those with panic disorder) are amazingly sensitive to the medication. Those who react to 25 mg of imipramine as if it were a strong stimulant, by intense tension and insomnia, can be successfully treated by lowering the dose to what seem to be completely absurd homeopathic levels, such as 3 mg daily. (Klein et al., 1980, p. 564).

It is surprising that more attention has not been paid to dosage requirements of imipramine and other antidepressants in anxiety disorders, although it has been acknowledged by Klein's group for many years, in that in their research studies dosages are gradually built up from very low levels. Nevertheless, the assumption commonly made that dosage needs to be increased steadily to relatively high levels has not been tested, and there have been no studies investigating whether there may be a therapeutic "window" of dose and plasma levels associated with antianxiety response. The experience we have had of antidepressants in depressive disorders in this subject is confusing and not particularly helpful, but we are likely to have learned something from past mistakes and, with better technology, it should be possible to gain knowledge that will allow useful advice to be given to the clinician.

Although imipramine is clearly superior to placebo in treating panic and agoraphobia, it does not mean that it is a specific antianxiety drug. In Table 3 the equivalent trials of the closely related drug, clomipramine, in obsessive–compulsive disorder are analyzed, with virtually identical results. There has been continued argument over whether these results indicate that clomipramine is a specific antiobsessional drug or merely treats the depressive symptoms that are common in obsessive–compulsive disorders (Marks, 1983; Mavisskalian et al., 1985). As anxiety is a common and therapeutically important element in obsessional disorders (Wolpe, 1958), it is reasonable to at least entertain the hypothesis that it acts primarily by reducing anxiety symptoms.

Because one accepts that antidepressants are superior to placebo in panic and agoraphobia does not mean that they are preferred drug treatments for these disorders. The important comparisons are with established treatments. Unfortunately, there are very few adequate comparisons of standard antianxiety treatments and antidepressants in panic disorder and agoraphobia. Only alprazolam, which was specifically introduced as a treatment for panic disorder, has been tested satisfactorily.

These comparisons have shown only one study in which an antidepressant, imipramine, was superior to a benzodiazepine (McNair and Kahn, 1981). All other studies with alprazolam have showed no differences in efficacy, but a quicker onset of action with the benzodiazepine. The comparison of CVIs shows no differences between the two drug classes (Table 4). Alprazolam has been the most intensively studied of the benzodiazepines in panic (Ballenger et al., 1988). As might be expected from pharmacological principles, alprazolam is rapid in action in panic, but after 4 weeks of treatment there is little to choose between the two drugs (Cross-national Collaborative Study, 1992).

Table 3 Comparison of Controlled Trials of Clomipramine in Obsessive-Compulsive Disorder

Author	n	Design	Duration (wk)	Results	Clinical validity index (CVI)
Thoren et al., 1980	24	Clomipramine, nortriptyline, placebo	5	Clomipramine superior to placebo	1.4
Montgomery et al., 1980	14	Clomipramine, placebo (crossover)	4	Clomipramine superior for compulsive thoughts, but not rituals	1.1
Marks et al., 1980	40	Two-by-two comparison of clomipramine, placebo exposure and relaxation	38	Clomipramine better than placebo, but not for the least-depressed patients	1.4
Ananth et al., 1981	20	Clomipramine and amitriptyline	4	Clomipramine superior for depressive, obsessive, and anxiety symptoms	1.2
Insel et al., 1983	13	Clomipramine and clorgyline (crossover)	6	Clomipramine superior to clorgyline	1.0
Flament et al., 1985	19	Clomipramine, placebo	5	Clomipramine superior to placebo	1.1
Mavissakalian et al., 1985	12	Clomipramine and placebo	12	Clomipramine generally superior to placebo	1.1
Volavka et al., 1985	19	Clomipramine and imipramine	12	Clomipramine superior to placebo for obsessional and mood symptoms	1.0
Insel et al., 1985	22	Desipramine, clomipramine, and zimeldine (crossover)	5	No difference between zimeldine and desipramine, but patients were later treated with clomipramine and responded	1.3
		Total score for trials showing clomipramine superior to placebo			10.6
Rapoport et al., 1980	9	Clomipramine, placebo, desipramine, (crossover)	5	No difference between active drug and placebo	1.3

Conclusion: Clomipramine greatly superior to placebo. Probability of clomipramine being superior to placebo ($p < 0.0001$).

Table 4 Controlled Trials of Imipramine Versus Benzodiazepines in Agoraphobia and Panic Disorders

Author	n	Design	Duration (wk)	Results	Clinical validity index (CVI)
Trials showing superiority of antidepressant over benzodiazepine					
McNair and Kahn, 1981	57	Imipramine and chlordiazepoxide	8	Imipramine superior for panic and depression symptoms	1.3
Trials showing equivalent efficacy of antidepressant and benzodiazepine					
Sheehan et al., 1984	115	Alprazolam, phenelzine, imipramine, placebo	10	All active drugs better than placebo, but no differences among them	1.3
Rizley et al., 1986	26	Alprazolam, imipramine	12	No overall differences, but alprazolam quicker-acting	1.1
Charney et al., 1986	47	Alprazolam, imipramine, trazodone	8	No differences between alprazolam and imipramine, both superior to trazodone	1.4
Cross-national Collaborative Study, 1992	500	Alprazolam, imipramine, and placebo	8	Alprazolam and imipramine superior to placebo; delayed efficacy of imipramine	1.6

Conclusion: No difference in efficacy between imipramine and benzodiazepines in agoraphobia and panic disorder. Probability of antidepressant being superior to benzodiazepine ($p > 0.05$).

However, there is some recent evidence from further analysis of the Cross-national Collaborative Study that imipramine is more effective in panic associated with respiratory symptoms (e.g., shortness of breath, choking, smothering sensations), and alprazolam is more effective in nonrespiratory panic (Briggs et al., 1993). If this work is confirmed, it would represent one of the few good examples of Klein's pharmacological dissection; but we have had false dawns before.

Other Antidepressants. The results from a study of tricyclic antidepressants may not be transferable to antidepressants as a whole. There are hints from several studies that both monoamine oxidase inhibitors and selective reuptake inhibitors of serotonin (5-HT) are somewhat more effective than the original tricyclics in treating panic, agoraphobia, and social phobias.

Monoamine oxidase inhibitors have not been compared adequately with tricyclic antidepressants, apart from one major study (Sheehan et al., 1980) that showed that phenelzine was marginally superior to imipramine for some phobic symptoms and work adjustment. However, another important study by Liebowitz and his colleagues (1984) in atypical depression suggested that phenelzine was more effective than imipramine in reducing "interpersonal sensitivity," a core feature in social phobias, and Liebowitz and his colleagues are currently extending this work further in the treatment of social phobia.

On present evidence, one can conclude that monoamine oxidase inhibitors are at least as effective in the treatment of anxiety disorders as tricyclic antidepressants and possibly more so when phobic symptoms are preponderant (Tyrer and Shawcross, 1988). There are also suggestions, which although powerfully put are not a substitute for adequately controlled studies, that monoamine oxidase inhibitors are highly effective in obsessive–compulsive disorders (Jain et al., 1970; Jenike et al., 1982). They need to be compared with other antidepressants in this condition also.

Selective 5-HT-reuptake inhibitors may also have an important place in the treatment of anxiety and panic disorders, as well as in obsessive–compulsive conditions. Clomipramine, although a tricyclic antidepressant, is also a selective 5-HT-reuptake inhibitor (Iversen and Mackay, 1979), and it has been suggested that its efficacy in obsessive–compulsive disorders (see Table 3) is related to its uptake blockade specificity.

den Boer and Westenberg (1988) found that the selective 5-HT-reuptake inhibitor, fluvoxamine, was somewhat more effective than the selective norepinephrine-reuptake inhibitor, maprotiline, in treating panic disorder, and there is support for this view from Evans et al. (1986), who found zimeldine to be more effective than imipramine and placebo in a trial cut short by the withdrawal of zimeldine from open prescription.

The hypothesis that panic disorder might be associated with supersensitivity of postsynaptic 5-HT_2 receptors was tested by den Boer and Westenberg (1990) by comparing the efficacy of fluvoxamine and ritanserin, a 5-HT_2 receptor antagonist, and essentially disproved, as ritanserin was a much less effective treatment than fluvoxamine. The mechanism of action, therefore, remains uncertain but there is now sufficient suggestion of the superiority of selective 5-HT-reuptake inhibitors over conventional antidepressants to justify full formal comparison of their use across the range of anxiety disorders.

2. *Generalized Anxiety Disorder*

In Klein's original work, imipramine was not effective in treating generalized or anticipatory anxiety, although the evidence for this was anecdotal instead of being based on formal comparisons in the different diagnoses. However, this conclusion can be questioned in view of the results of later studies. These suggest that antidepressants are not only more effective than placebo in generalized anxiety, but are, in many instances, superior to conventional antianxiety drugs, such as the benzodiazepines, provided that they are given for 4 weeks or longer (Tables 5 and 6).

The evidence for the superiority of antidepressant therapy over benzodiazepines in generalized anxiety disorder shown in Table 6 suggests that antidepressant effects are somewhat stronger than in panic disorder (see Table 4), but it will be noticed that alprazolam does not feature in Table 6. The possible implications of this are discussed in the next section.

III. ANTIANXIETY DRUGS IN DEPRESSIVE DISORDERS

The literature on this subject is much more sparse than the equivalent "mismatch" for antidepressants. Early open clinical studies at the dawn of the benzodiazepine era suggested that these drugs might have some antidepressant activity (e.g., Bowes, 1960; Hines, 1960), but later controlled studies with benzodiazepines in the 1960s and early 1970s showed no evidence of any significant antidepressive effects of these compounds (Greenblatt and Shader, 1974). A review of all the available literature up to 1978 revealed that of 20 double-blind, controlled studies of antidepressants and antianxiety drugs in depressive illness (Schatzberg and Cole, 1978) showed only one (Raskin et al., 1974) in which a benzodiazepine, diazepam, was superior. This study, which we have estimated to have a clinical validity index of 0.8, used phenelzine as the comparison antidepressant in a dosage and population (inpatients) that was subsequently realized to be inappropriate (Tyrer, 1979); thus, it is not surprising that diazepam was superior. Because the antidepressant was superior to the benzodiazepine in 10 of the other 19 studies, the findings are unequivocal; benzodiazepines in conventional dosage, although equal or superior to other sedative–hypnotic drugs in the treatment of anxiety, are inferior to antidepressants in the treatment of depression. This does not imply that they necessarily lack antidepressant properties, as there have been no satisfactory placebo-controlled studies demonstrating inefficacy, and as 9 of the 20 studies cited by Schatzberg and Cole showed no difference in efficacy, these findings at least hint at antidepressant action.

The only other study in which a benzodiazepine has been shown to be superior to an antidepressant is that by Tiller et al. (1989). Diazepam was compared with a new reversible monoamine oxidase inhibitor, moclobemide, in a double-blind, sequential trial in which patients with mixed depressive diagnoses were paired and treated with increasing doses of diazepam (15–45 mg/day) or moclobemide (150–450 mg/day). After 4 weeks of treatment (but not later than 8, diazepam was superior to moclobemide. The authors concluded that benzodiazepines may "be safe, well-tolerated antidepressants for atypical depression, and more appropriate than conventional antidepressants" (Tiller et al., 1989, p. 488).

There are several inadequacies about this study, including diagnosis, design, and selection criteria, that make this conclusion questionable (Douzenis et al., 1990; O'Shea, 1990), and our clinical validity index is only 0.4. However, there is one important is-

Table 5 Summary of Trials of Antidepressant Versus Placebo in Generalized Anxiety Disorder

Author	n	Design	Duration (wk)	Results	Clinical validity index (CVI)
Antidepressant superior to placebo					
Johnstone et al., 1980	240	Amitriptyline, diazepam, and placebo	4	Amitriptyline superior to placebo generally in both anxious and depressed patients	1.3
Kahn et al., 1986	223	Imipramine, chlordiazepoxide, and placebo	8	Imipramine superior to placebo	1.3
Total score for trials showing antidepressants superior to placebo					
Antidepressant equivalent to placebo					
Tyrer et al., 1988	201	Dothiepin, diazepam, and placebo; cognitive and behavior therapy, self-help	10	Dothiepin no better than placebo, but patients on placebo had more additional treatments	1.5
Rickels et al., 1974	108	Amitriptyline and placebo	4	Amitriptyline superior to placebo for depression, but no clear-cut benefit for anxiety symptoms	0.9
Total scores for trials showing antidepressants equivalent to placebo					

Conclusion: Some superiority of antidepressants over placebo. Probability of antidepressant being superior to placebo ($p < 0.01$).

Table 6 Summary of Trials of Antidepressants Versus Benzodiazepines in Generalized Anxiety Disorder

Author	n	Design	Duration (wk)	Results	Clinical validity index (CVI)
Antidepressant superior to benzodiazepine					
Kleber, 1979	53	Desipramine and diazepam	4	Desipramine superior to diazepam	1.0
Johnstone et al., 1980	240	Amitriptyline and diazepam	4	Amitriptyline superior to diazepam generally in both anxious and depressed patients	1.3
Kahn et al., 1986	223	Imipramine, chlordiazepoxide, and placebo	8	Both active drugs superior to placebo, imipramine superior to chlordiazepoxide after 4 weeks	1.3
Tyrer et al., 1988	201	Dothiepin, diazepam and placebo; cognitive and behavior therapy, self-help	10	Diazepam inferior to all other treatments, including dothiepin	1.5
		Total score for trials showing antidepressant superior to benzodiazepine			5.1

Conclusion: Significant superiority of antidepressants over benzodiazepines. Probability of antidepressant being superior to benzodiazepine ($p < 0.001$).

sue raised that may be of relevance, that of dosage. The one benzodiazepine specifically alleged to have antidepressant activity is alprazolam (Rickels et al., 1982, 1985; Feighner, 1983) and in these studies, in which alprazolam was compared with conventional antidepressants and found to be of similar efficacy, alprazolam was given in doses equivalent to about 45 mg of diazepam, much higher than those recommended for the treatment of anxiety in clinical practice. Therefore, it is possible that in higher doses benzodiazepines may have antidepressant activity.

Unfortunately, the diagnostic dissection allowed by the many studies that have been carried out with antidepressants in anxiety is not possible with antianxiety drugs in depression. Dysthymia has not been treated with benzodiazepine in formal studies, and a study of treatment of the more severe depressive disorders with benzodiazepines would probably fail to pass the scrutiny of any respectable ethical committee.

IV. A RECONCILING HYPOTHESIS

How can the results of these studies be interpreted? Any explanation has to take account of the efficacy of tricyclic antidepressants across the range of anxiety and depressive disorders (with the possibility that monoamine oxidase inhibitors and some of the newer antidepressants are even more effective in this group), possible differential response in diagnoses dependent on dosage, and the comorbidity of anxiety, depression, and other neurotic disorders.

Hudson and Pope (1990) suggest on the basis that clinical response is similar to that of major depression in panic disorder, bulimia, obsessive–compulsive disorder, and some forms of somatization and attention deficit disorders, that all these conditions should be considered as part of the same group of *affective spectrum disorder*. This has some merit, but is perhaps too all-embracing. An alternative strategy that we have already shown as a failure (Paykel et al., 1983) is to consider the anxiety disorders that respond to antidepressants as *atypical depression*. This extends the boundaries of depression too far and creates a large heterogeneous group that has no common depressive features.

The large degree of overlap between anxiety and depressive disorders could also explain the findings. As it is so common to have significant depression in anxiety disorders and vice versa, it could still be possible for antianxiety drugs to treat anxiety symptoms only and lead to improvement, and similarly for antidepressant drugs and depressive symptoms.

The explanation we favor is, like Hudson and Pope's suggestion, a diagnostic one. This suggests that most patients with anxiety and depression can be separated into two groups on the basis of the severity of their symptoms. After severe depression (melancholia) is excluded, those with a double disorder who have more severe symptoms have the *general neurotic syndrome,* whereas those with minor symptoms have *cothymia* (Tyrer, 1985, 1989). If they have single-mood pathology, then an appropriate diagnostic term can be chosen for them from existing diagnoses, but it is likely that these conditions will be much fewer than the combined mood disorders. Of these syndromes, panic and generalized anxiety disorder can be considered distinct, if necessary, but in clinical terms, they differ mainly in severity. Severe anxiety will always lead to episodes of panic, mild anxiety much less so. The attribution of a single syndrome implies that at different times there will be variation in the prominence of different symptoms. Anxiety, depression, or panic are dominant at different times, but this will not necessarily alter treatment, although when both moods are prominent simultaneously joint treatment may be appropriate. This model still allows the possibility of pure anxiety and depressive syndromes at the extremes (Fig. 1); they doubtless exist, but in clinical practice they account for less than 5% of the total with anxiety and depressive syndromes.

In choosing drug treatment the time scale of therapy is very important. If treatment is expected to continue for longer than 1 month (which is the norm in the general neurotic syndrome), then an antidepressant is the treatment of choice, the selection of which is determined more by anticipated unwanted effects than any other criterion, although relative efficacy is becoming increasingly prominent in making the choice. If drug treatment is considered necessary for a short time only (e.g., for a patient who prefers and is receiving psychological treatment, but who is temporarily in great distress because of symptoms), then an antianxiety drug for a matter of days only is preferable.

To some extent, dosage of drugs is determined by the severity of the disorder. The more severe the symptoms, the higher the dosage of both antianxiety and antidepressant drugs. This suggestion is supported by differential dosage of benzodiazepines in panic and generalized anxiety disorder [which has led to the suggestion that generalized anxiety disorder is a "milder form of the same biological illness, panic disorder" (Sheehan and Raj, 1990, p. 72)], but not yet in the depressive disorders. The main problem with the use of benzodiazepines and other sedative-hypnotic drugs in high doses for long periods is the risk of dependence. Although there are many who feel that the risk of dependence is either overstated or an acceptable risk in the more handicapped patients, I cannot personally justify my conscience in choosing this therapeutic route until all other therapeutic interventions have failed. However, there are others who consider the toxicity of antidepressants in overdose as a much more serious risk than benzodiazepine dependence.

Nevertheless, once treatment becomes long-term, the advantages of antidepressants usually exceed those of benzodiazepines. They are more effective over time, and there

```
Anxiety        Mixed anxiety-depression     Depression

|__________________________________________________|

Benzodiazepines  Benzodiazepines/        Antidepressants
 (low dose)      antidepressants          (? low dose)
      |                 |                       |
+-----+--------------------------------------+--+---+
|GAD  |          Cothymia                  |DYS     |
+-----+------------------------------------+--------+
|PANIC| General neurotic syndrome          |MDE     |
+--+--+----------------+-------------------+-+------+
   |                   |                     |
Benzodiazepines   Antidepressants          Tricyclic
 (high dose)    (with possible preference antidepressants
                for MAOI's or 5-HT
                selective reuptake
                inhibitors)
```

Figure 1 A model for diagnosing and treating anxiety and depression with psychotropic drugs: DYS, dysthymia; GAD, general anxiety disorder; MDE, major depressive episode.

is no significant tolerance to their therapeutic effects. It is these pharmacological issues, and the related ones of drug interactions and unwanted effects that determine the choice of treatment to a much greater extent than whether anxiety or depression predominates at any one time. For more "pure" depression, I personally still prefer the tricyclic antidepressants, on the grounds that their efficacy has yet to be adequately equaled or surpassed, the choice ranging between lofepramine at one extreme (low toxicity, low sedation) to trimipramine at the other (high sedation).

The importance of this model is that both new and old drugs in anxiety and depression are not shackled in diagnostic fetters too early in their life. Unfortunately, marketing policy tends to demand such "pigeon-holing," and there are many examples of the errors committed as a result. The labeling of monoamine oxidase inhibitors as *antidepressants* is one clear example, which almost led to their therapeutic demise before they were found to have marked effects in anxiety, obsessional, and phobic disorders. Moclobemide seems to be going down the same cul de sac of depression only, although, as cited earlier, the antianxiety value of the selective 5-HT-reuptake inhibitors is now being appreciated and voices raised against their restricted antidepressant use (Healy, 1991).

In a 100-year's time our current preoccupation with distinguishing anxiety from depression in a myriad different ways will probably be looked on with wry amusement; I hope by then we will have a proper explanation of the mechanisms of neurotic disorder that allow such amusement to be justified.

REFERENCES

J. Ananth, J. Pecknold, N. Van Den Steen, and F. C. Engelsmann, Double-blind comparative study of clomipramine and amitriptyline in obsessive neurosis, *Prog. Neuropsychopharmacol.*, *5*: 257 (1981).

J. C. Ballenger, G. D. Burrows, R. L. DuPont, et al., Alprozolam in panic disorder and agoraphobia: results from a multicenter trial. I. Efficacy in short-term treatment, *Arch. Gen. Psychiatry, 45*: 413 (1988).

H. A. Bowes, The role of Librium in an out-patient psychiatric setting, *Dis. Nerv. Syst.*, *21*(Suppl.): 20 (1960).

A. C. Briggs, D. D. Stretch, and S. Brandon, Subtyping of panic disorder by symptom profile, *Br. J. Psychiatry, 163*: 201 (1993).

Cross-national Collaborative Study: Second Phase Investigators, Drug treatment of panic disorder: Comparative efficacy of alprazolam, imipramine and placebo, *Br. J. Psychiatry, 160*: 191 (1992).

J. A. den Boer, and H. G. Westenberg, Effect of a serotonin and noradrenaline uptake inhibitor in panic disorder: A double-blind comparative study with fluvoxamine and maprotiline, *Int. Clin. Psychopharmacol.*, *3*: 59 (1988).

J. A. den Boer, and H. G. M. Westenberg, Serotonin function in panic disorder: A double blind placebo controlled study with fluvoxamine and ritanserin, *Psychopharmacology, 102*: 85 (1990).

D. S. Charney, S. W. Woods, W. K. Goodman, et al., Drug treatment of panic disorder: the comparative efficacy of imipramine, alprazolam and trazodone, *Clin. Psychiatry, 47*: 580 (1986).

A. Douzenis, N. Gene-Cox, and K. Kho, Is diazepam an antidepressant? *Br. J. Psychiatry, 156*: 279 (1990).

L. Evans, J. Kenardy, P. Schneider et al., Effect of a selective serotonin uptake inhibitor in agoraphobia with panic attacks: A double-blind comparison of zimeldine, impriamine and placebo, *Acta Psychiatr. Scand.*, *73*: 49 (1986).

J. P. Feighner, G. C. Aden, L. F. Fabre, K. Rickels, and W. T. Smith, Comparison of alprazolam, imipramine, and placebo in the treatment of depression, *J. Am. Med. Assoc., 249*: 3057 (1983).

A. Feinstein, The pre-therapeutic classification of comorbidity in chronic disease, *J. Chronic Dis., 23*: 455 (1970).

M. F. Flament, J. L. Rapoport, C. J. Berg, W. Sceery, C. Kilts, B. Mellstrom, and M. Linnoila, Clomipramine treatment of childhood obsessive–compulsive disorder: A double-blind controlled study, *Arch. Gen. Psychiatry, 42*: 977 (1985).

S. Freud, On the grounds for detaching a particular syndrome from neurasthenia under the description "anxiety neurosis," *Complete Psychological Works,* Vol. 3 (trans. J. Strachey, 1962), Hogarth Press, London, pp. 85–117 (1895).

D. J. Greenblatt, and R. I. Shader, *Benzodiazepines in Clinical Practice,* Raven Press, New York (1974).

D. Healy, The marketing of 5-hydroxytryptamine: Depression or anxiety? *Br. J. Psychiatry, 158*: 737 (1991).

L. R. Hines, Methaminodiazepoxide (Librium): A psychotherapeutic drug, *Curr. Ther. Res., 2*: 227 (1960).

J. I. Hudson, and H. G. Pope, Jr., Affective spectrum disorder: Does antidepressant response identify a family of disorders with a common pathophysiology? *Am. J. Psychiatry, 147*: 552 (1990).

T. R. Insel, E. A. Mueller, I. Alterman, M. Linnoila, and D. L. Murphy, Obsessive–compulsive disorder and serotonin: Is there a connection? *Biol. Psychiatry, 20*: 1174 (1985).

T. R. Insel, D. L. Murphy, R. M. Cohen, I. Alterman, C. Kilts, and M. Linnoila, Obsessive–compulsive disorder: A double-blind trial of clomipramine and clorgyline, *Arch. Gen. Psychiatry, 40*: 605 (1983).

L. L. Iversen, and A. V. P. Mackay, Pharmacodynamics of antidepressant and antimanic drugs, *Psychopharmacology of Affective Disorders* (E. S. Paykel and A. Coppen, eds.), Oxford University Press, Oxford, pp. 60–90 (1979).

V. K. Jain, R. P. Swinson, and J. G. Thomas, Phenelzine in obsessional neurosis, *Br. J. Psychiatry, 117*: 237 (1970).

M. A. Jenike, O. S. Shurman, N. H. Cassem et al., Monoamine oxidase inhibitors in obsessive–compulsive disorder, *J. Clin. Psychiatry, 4*: 131 (1983).

E. C. Johnstone, D. G. Cunningham Owens, C. D. Frith et al., Neurotic illness and its response to anxiolytic and anti-depressant treatment, *Psychol. Med., 10*: 321 (1980).

R. J. Kahn, D. M. McNair, R. S. Lipman, L. Covi, K. Rickels, R. W. Downing, S. Fisher, and L. M. Frankenthaler, Imipramine and chlordiazepoxide in depressive and anxiety disorders: II. Efficacy in anxious out-patients, *Arch. Gen. Psychiatry, 43*: 79 (1986).

R. J. Kleber, A double-blind comparative study of despiramine hydrochloride and diazepam in the control of mixed anxiety/depression symptomatology, *J. Clin. Psychiatry, 40*: 165 (1979).

D. F. Klein, Delineation of two drug-responsive anxiety syndromes, *Psychopharmacologia, 5*: 397 (1964).

D. F. Klein, and M. Fink, Psychiatric reaction patterns to imipramine, *Am. J. Psychiatry, 119*: 432 (1962).

D. F. Klein, R. Gittelman, F. Quitkin, and A. Rifkin, *Diagnosis and Drug Treatment of Psychiatric Disorder: Adults and Children,* 2nd ed., Williams & Wilkins, Baltimore (1980).

M. R. Liebowitz, Imipramine in the treatment of panic disorder and its complications, *Psychiatr. Clin. North Am., 8*: 37 (1985).

M. R. Liebowitz, A. J. Fyer, J. M. Gorman et al., Tricyclic therapy of the *DSM-III* anxiety disorders: A review with implications for further research, *J. Psychiatr. Res., 22*(Suppl. 1): 7 (1988).

M. R. Liebowitz, A. J. Fyer, J. M. Gorman, R. B. Campeas, and D. P. Sandberg, Tricyclic therapy of the DSM-III anxiety disorders: a review with implications for further research, *J. Psychiatr. Res. (suppl.1), 22*: 7 (1988).

M. R. Liebowitz, F. M. Quitkin, J. W. Stewart, P. J. McGrath, and W. Harrison, Phenelzine v imipramine in atypical depression: a preliminary report, *Arch. Gen. Psychiatry, 41*: 669 (1984).

I. M. Marks, Are there anti-compulsive or anti-phobic drugs? Review of the evidence, *Br. J. Psychiatr., 140*: 338 (1983).

I. M. Marks, R. S. Stern, D. Mawson, J. Cobb, and R. McDonald, Clomipramine and exposure for obsessive–compulsive rituals, *Br. J. Psychiatry, 136*: 1 (1980).

I. M. Marks, S. Grey, S. D. Cohen et al., Imipramine and brief therapist-aided exposure in agoraphobics having self-exposure homework: A controlled trial, *Arch. Gen. Psychiatry, 40*: 153 (1983).

M. R. Mavissakalian, S. M. Turner, L. Michelson, and R. Jacob, Tricyclic antidepressants in obsessive–compulsive disorder: Anti-obsessional or antidepressant agents? *Am. J. Psychiatry, 142*: 572 (1985).

D. M. McNair, and R. J. Kahn, Imipramine compared with a benzodiazepine for agoraphobia, *Anxiety: New Research and Changing Concepts* (D. F. Klein and J. G. Rabkin, eds.), Raven Press, New York, pp. 69–80 (1981).

S. A. Montgomery, Clomipramine in obsessional neurosis: A placebo controlled trial, *Pharm. Med., 1*: 189 (1980).

B. O'Shea, Is diazepam an antidepressant? *Br. J. Psychiatry, 156*: 279 (1990).

E. S. Paykel, R. R. Parker, P. R. Rowan, B. M. Rao, and C. N. Taylor, Nosology of atypical depression, *Psychol. Med., 13*: 131 (1983).

J. Rapoport, R. Elkins, and E. Mikkelsen, Chlorimipramine in adolescents with obsessive–compulsive disorder, *Psychopharmacol. Bull., 16*: 61 (1980).

A. Raskin, J. G. Schulterbrandt, N. Reatig, T. D. Crook, and D. Odle, Depression subtypes and response to phenelzine, diazepam and a placebo: Results of a nine hospital collaborative study, *Arch. Gen. Psychiatry, 30*: 66 (1974).

K. Rickels, J. P. Feighner, and W. T. Smith, Alprazolam, amitriptyline, doxepin and placebo in the treatment of depression, *Arch. Gen. Psychiatry, 42*: 134 (1985).

K. Rickels, I. Csanalosi, H. R. Chung, W. G. Case, A. Pereira-Ogan, and R. W. Downing, Amitriptyline in anxious–depressed outpatients: A controlled study, *Am. J. Psychiatry, 131*: 25 (1974).

R. Rizley, R. J. Kahn, D. M. McNair, and L. M. Frankenthaler, A comparison of alprazolam and imipramine in the treatment of agoraphobia and panic disorder, *Psychopharmacol. Bull., 22*: 167 (1986).

A. F. Schatzberg, and J. O. Cole, Benzodiazepines in depressive disorders, *Arch. Gen. Psychiatry, 35*: 1359 (1978).

E. Shammas, Controlled comparison of bromazepam, amitriptyline, and placebo in anxiety–depressive neurosis, *Dis. Nerv. Syst., 38*: 201 (1977).

D. V. Sheehan, and A. Raj, Benzodiazepine treatment of panic disorder, *Handbook of Anxiety,* Vol. 4 (R. Noyes, Jr., M. Roth, and G. D. Burrows, eds.), Elsevier, Amsterdam, pp. 169–206 (1990).

D. V. Sheehan, J. B. Claycomb, and O. S. Surman, Comparison of phenelzine, imipramine, alprazolam and placebo in the treatment of panic attacks and agoraphobia, *Presented at Annual Meeting of American Psychological Association.* (1984).

D. V. Sheehan, J. Ballenger, and G. Jacobsen, Treatment of endogenous anxiety with phobic, hysterical, and hypochondriacal symptoms, *Arch. Gen. Psychiatry, 37*: 51 (1980).

M. L. Smith, and G. V. Glass, Meta-analysis of psychotherapy outcome studies, *Am. Psychol., 32:* 752 (1977).

M. J. Telch, W. S. Agras, C. B. Taylor, W. T. Roth, and C. C. Gallen, Combined pharmacological and behavioral treatment for agoraphobia, *Behav. Res. Ther., 23*: 325 (1985).

P. Thoren, M. Asberg, B. Cronholm, L. Jornestedt, and L. Traskman, Clomipramine treatment of obsessive–compulsive disorder: A controlled clinical trial, *Arch. Gen. Psychiatry, 37*: 1281 (1980).

B. A. Thyer, J. Himle, G. C. Curtis, O. G. Cameron, and R. M. Nesse, A comparison of panic disorder and agoraphobia with panic attacks, *Compr. Psychiatry, 26*: 208 (1985).

J. Tiller, I. Schweitzer, K. Maguire, and B. Davies, Is diazepam an antidepressant? *Br. J. Psychiatry, 155*: 483 (1989).

P. Tyrer, N. Seivewright, S. Murphy, et al., The Nottingham study of neurotic disorder: comparison of drug and psychological treatments, *Lancet, ii*: 235 (1988).

P. Tyrer, Clinical use of monoamine oxidase inhibitors, *Psychopharmacology of Affective Disorders* (E. S. Paykel and A. Coppen, eds.), Oxford University Press, Oxford, pp. 159–178 (1979).

P. Tyrer, Neurosis divisible? *Lancet, 1*: 685 (1985).

P. Tyrer, *Classification of Neurosis,* John Wiley & Sons, Chichester, (1989).

P. Tyrer and C. Shawcross, Monoamine-oxidase inhibitors in anxiety disorders, *J. Psychiatr. Res. (Suppl. 1) 22*: 87 (1988).

P. Tyrer, and J. Tyrer, Comparing the quality of data from several clinical trials, *Br. J. Psychiatry, 160*: 126 (1992).

J. Volavka, F. Neziroglu, and J. A. Yaryura-Tobias, Clomipramine and imipramine in obsessive–compulsive disorder, *Psychiatry Res., 14*: 83 (1985).

G. Winokur, The concept of secondary depression and its relationship to comorbidity, *Psychiatr. Clin. N. A., 13*: 567 (1990).

J. Wolpe, *Psychotherapy by Reciprocal Inhibition,* Stanford University Press, Stanford, Calif. (1958).

R. Woodruff, G. Murphy, and M. Herjanic, The natural history of affective disorders: 1—Symptoms of 72 patients at the time of index hospital admission, *J. Psychiatr. Res., 5*: 255 (1967).

C. M. Zitrin, D. F. Klein, and N. G. Woerner, Treatment of agoraphobia with group exposure in vivo and imipramine, *Arch. Gen. Psychiatry, 37*: 63 (1980).

C. M. Zitrin, D. F. Klein, N. G. Woerner, and D. C. Ross, Treatment of phobias. 1. Comparison of imipramine hydrochloride and placebo, *Arch. Gen. Psychiatry, 40*: 125 (1983).

20

Immune Function in Depression and Anxiety

Ziad Kronfol
University of Michigan Medical Center, Ann Arbor, Michigan

I. INTRODUCTION

A decade or two ago very little was known about possible interactions between the central nervous system (CNS) and the immune system. Neuroscientists were concerned primarily with ways the central nervous system accomplishes activities such as perception, memory, sensorimotor coordination, and autonomic regulation. Immunologists, on the other hand, dealt with ways the immune system achieves the distinction of material between self and nonself, as well as the protection against invading microorganisms and possibly cancer. These two systems were seen as operating independently of each other, with no need or venue for intercommunication.

Two decades of intensive research by investigators in widely diverging fields have resulted in the discovery of the existence of strong links between the central nervous system and the immune system. The evidence comes from work done by experts in such disciplines as physiological psychology, psychiatry, neurology, anatomy, microbiology, immunology, pharmacology, epidemiology, and oncology. From these and related fields, a new discipline was born. It is called *psychoneuroimmunology*. Although still in its infancy, this discipline is already having an influence on our understanding of pathophysiological mechanisms in infection and cancer, and is providing new tools to explore psychopathological pathways in schizophrenia and depression.

This chapter will be devoted to an overview of recent developments in psychoneuroimmunology, with special emphasis on immune function in depression and anxiety disorders. I will start with a review of the effects of stress on the immune system, followed by examples of central nervous system–immune interactions. I will then review key evidence in support of an immunological mechanism in depression and anxiety.

II. STRESS AND THE IMMUNE SYSTEM

A. Preclinical Studies

There has recently been a serious effort among immunologists and neuroscientists alike to investigate the role of behavioral stress and neural mechanisms in the regulation of the immune system. Several review articles have summarized different aspects of the work in this area (Riley, 1981; Stein et al., 1985). The general scheme has been one of the following: (1) comparing morbidity and mortality rates with specific immune-related disorders in stressed and nonstressed animals; (2) stressing animals and comparing specific immune measures in the stressed animals and nonstressed controls; (3) studying the effects on the immune system of neural or hormonal manipulations that are usually involved in the stress response.

In a series of experiments, Rasmussen (1969) showed that experimental stress could increase the susceptibility of mice to infection with a variety of microorganisms, such as herpes simplex virus, poliomyelitis virus, and Coxsackie B virus. Similar experiments by other investigators revealed that experimental stress could also alter susceptibility to infection with bacteria and parasites. Riley (1981), on the other hand, studied the effects of stress on tumor growth in animals. He and his co-workers have injected two groups of animals with a cancer-promoting virus, and subjected one group to rotational stress, while keeping the other group "unstressed." They found that the tumors grew larger and faster in the stressed group, resulting in greater morbidity and mortality among the stressed animals. Other investigators have obtained similar results, but have also indicated that factors such as timing of the stressor or control over the stressor were crucial if tumor enhancement was to be obtained (Sklar and Anisman, 1979; Sklar et al., 1981). The effects of stress on animal models of autoimmune disorders have also been investigated. It has thus been shown that the severity of experimental allergic encephalomyelitis, an autoimmune disease of the central nervous system, and the course of adjuvent arthritis, a possible analogue of rheumatoid arthritis, could be altered by stressful manipulations in the rat.

An association between stressful manipulation and an increased risk for immune-related disorders, even when present, does not necessarily prove that immune dysregulation is the culprit. Stress, it has been argued, could lead to illness through entirely different mechanisms, such as malnutrition or altered physical activity. Researchers, therefore, had to design experiments with stress as the independent variable and various immune measures as dependent variables. Monjan and Collector (1977) used a sound device to stress mice. They measured blastogenic activity of spleen cells and found an initial decrease in this immune measure compared with controls, followed by an increase in the same measure. They concluded that stress alters immune function and that both immune suppression and immune enhancement can accompany stress. Keller et al. (1981) used random electrical foot shock as their stress paradigm. They found that stressed animals showed a decline in spleen cell responses to mitogen stimulation and that this decline was proportional to the severity of the stressor. Other investigators have shown that control over the stressor was also an important factor, since animals learning to escape the shock did not show the same degree of immunosuppression (Laudenslager et al., 1983).

In a somewhat-related series of experiments, Ader and Cohen (1975) have shown that principles of behavioral conditioning could be applied to the immune response. More specifically, they have shown that a neutral stimulus, not known to possess immunological properties (conditioned stimulus) can be made to similarly affect the immune response following pairing with a stimulus with specific immunological properties (unconditioned stimulus). Here again, the mechanisms underlying conditioned immune responses are unknown, but are thought to involve hormones and neurotransmitters that underlie the conditioning process.

B. Clinical Studies

The relation between stressful life events and medical illness has been the subject of numerous research investigations (Weiner, 1977). Whereas the bulk of the existing literature seems to support the notion that stressful events can affect a person's general state of health, there is little agreement on possible mechanisms underlying such associations. Investigators have initially suspected the autonomic nervous system, and later, the endocrine system in playing major roles in such changes. More recently, a great deal of interest has been shown in the possibility that stress-related changes in the immune response may play a role in the etiology of such disorders.

The effects of human stress on specific immunological measures have received considerable attention. Although different types of human stressors have been studied, the most widely investigated have been the stress of medical student examinations and the stress of bereavement. In studying the relatively mild stressor of medical school examination, Dorian et al. (1982) measured in vitro lymphocyte proliferation in psychiatric residents before and after their Oral Fellowship Examination and found a reduction in lymphocyte responses the morning before the examination, particularly among "highly stressed" candidates. Jemmott and colleagues (1983) took repeated measures of the rate of secretion of salivary immunoglobulin A in dental school students and found the rate of secretion to be significantly lower during periods of high academic stress. In a series of experiments addressing the effects of medical student examinations on the immune system, Kiecolt-Glaser et al. (1984) have identified a variety of subtle immunological changes present on the morning of the examination day (stress) compared with nonexamination days (baseline). These immunological changes include decreases in natural killer (NK) cell activity, interferon production, and percentage of peripheral blood leukocytes expressing the interleukin-2 receptor (IL-2R). The same group of investigators has shown that some of these differences (e.g., IL-2R) can be traced back to the level of gene expression, since levels of IL-2R mRNA were also decreased at the time of the examination (Glaser, 1990).

The effects of a more severe form of stress, the stress of bereavement, on immune regulation have also been investigated. Bartrop et al. (1977) compared lymphocyte response to mitogen stimulation in a group of bereaved subjects and normal controls. They found a reduced response to mitogen stimulation in the bereaved group. The two groups did not otherwise differ in the number of T and B cells, serum immunoglobulin levels, the presence of autoantibodies, and delayed hypersensitivity skin testing. These studies were later replicated by Schleifer et al. (1983), who showed lymphocyte function to decline following bereavement and to gradually normalize over a period of several months, compared with prebereavement baseline values. Other studies, presently underway, are seeking to establish a link between stressful events, immune impairment, and disease susceptibility. Results of such studies will determine the clinical implications of what, until now, has been mostly descriptive and correlational.

III. CENTRAL NERVOUS SYSTEM–IMMUNE INTERACTIONS

If it is now well established, as presented in the previous section, that stress affects the integrity of the immune response, mechanisms underlying this association ought to be sought. In this section, therefore, I will briefly review anatomical, physiological, and pharmacological evidence of interactions between the central nervous system and the immune system. Data in this field are rapidly growing; consequently, I will be somewhat selective, leaving it to the reader to expand knowledge in any particular area of choice.

A. Anatomical Relations

The immune system comprises tissues, organs, and cells loosely connected to each other. The thymus, the spleen, and regional lymph nodes are organs of the immune system. Bone marrow, liver, and skin possess specialized tissue dealing with immune phenomena. Blood cells comprise neutrophils, lymphocytes, and monocytes, that are also responsible for immune functions. Although this system is internally regulated in a highly complex way, recent evidence suggests that the immune system is also regulated by the nervous system. Williams et al. (1981) have shown that the thymus, the spleen, and the lymph nodes are innervated by the autonomic nervous system and, therefore, receive sympathetic or parasympathetic nerve fibers. Those fibers can be seen around blood vessels, but also branch inside the parenchyma. Electronic microscopy pictures show sympathetic nerve varicosities in apposition to the membranes of mast cells and lymphocytes. Furthermore, receptors for acetylcholine and catecholamine have also been identified on the cell surface of lymphocytes (Singh et al., 1979). Researchers have also shown that autonomic manipulation, such as chemical sympathectomy or epinephrine administration, can alter the immune response.

Conversely, the brain may also be the site of important immunoregulatory activities. Microglia are known to play a role similar to macrophages in other organ systems. Specific parts of the brain (e.g., anterior hypothalamus) are important for the integrity of the immune response. Lesions in the anterior hypothalamus of guinea pigs suppress spleen lymphocyte responses to mitogen stimulation (Keller et al., 1980). Lesions in the same area also protect animals from lethal anaphylaxis (Stein et al., 1976). There are also data from several groups suggesting that cerebral laterality is associated with immune regulation. Lesions in the left cerebral cortex of rodents were associated with a decline in spleen lymphocyte responsiveness to mitogens, whereas lesions in the right cerebral cortex were associated with an enhancement in these responses (Renoux et al., 1983).

B. Physiological Relations

Different parts of the brain are involved, in some as yet unclear way, in the integrity of the immune response. This section will deal more specifically with regulatory and feedback mechanisms between the neuroendocrine and immune systems.

I have already alluded to the fact that stress affects the integrity of the immune response. This was initially attributed to the effects of cortisol, an immunosuppressive hormone. Riley (1981) has shown that many effects of stress on the immune system in an animal model could be mimicked by corticosterone. Keller et al. (1983), on the other hand, have shown that the immunosuppressive effects of stress in an animal model can still be observed even after the animal had undergone adrenalectomy and, therefore, was unable to secrete corticosterone. The same group of investigators (Keller et al., 1988) have continued with the same strategy to investigate the effects of hypophysectomy on stress-induced immunomodulation. Their results underscore the complexity of these interactions and reveal that different pituitary hormones are involved, with both enhancing and inhibitory influences on the immune system.

There is also growing evidence that immune challenges could interfere with neurophysiological regulation. Besedovsky and colleagues (1977) have shown an increase in firing rates of neurons of ventromedial nuclei in the rat hypothalamus after antigenic stimulation. More recently, several studies have shown that infusions of interleukin-1 (IL-1) could lead to activation of the hypothalamic–pituitary–adrenal (HPA) axis in vivo, and that IL-1 can stimulate the release of corticotropin-releasing hormone (CRH) from the hypothalamus (Sapolsky et al., 1987). There is also evidence, although still somewhat controversial, that under certain conditions, lymphocytes can synthesize and release stress hormones, such as corticotropin (adrenocorticotropic hormone; ACTH), and endorphins (Blalock, 1989).

C. Pharmacological Relations

Once it has been established that the central nervous system and the immune system are constantly communicating with each other, the next question becomes what language do they use. In this section, I will briefly review the effects of neurohormones and neurotransmitters on specific immune functions, and mention some recent literature alluding to the effects of cytokines on neural and behavioral regulation.

For decades, it has been known that corticosteroids affect the traffic of leukocytes (Dougherty and White, 1943). More specifically, it is well documented that adrenal extracts are associated with an increase in the number of circulating neutrophils and a decrease in the numbers of circulating lymphocytes, monocytes, and eosinophils. In fact, before the accurate measurement of levels of glucocorticoids by modern laboratory techniques, a rough estimate of glucocorticoid activity was indirectly made by obtaining a blood eosinophil count.

More recently, corticosteroids have been found to play an important role in immune regulation. Specifically, corticosteroids have been associated with several immunoregulatory activities, including a decrease in the number of CD3 lymphocytes (T cells) and, particularly, the CD4 subtype (T helper cells), a decrease in mitogen-induced lymphocyte proliferation and natural killer cell activity, and a decline in cytokine production (Slade and Hepburn, 1983; Nair and Schwartz, 1984). Whereas early research in psychoneuroimmunology tended to attribute to cortisol many of the effects of stress on the immune system, more recent studies have shown that cortisol is by no means unique in possessing such properties (Kronfol et al., 1986). Most hypothalamic–pituitary–adrenal axis hormones, including CRH, ACTH, the endorphins, and the enkephalins, are now known to play a role in immune regulation. Furthermore, whereas the effects of cortisol have generally been described as being immunosuppressive, some of the other hormones (e.g., ß-endorphin) seem to possess immunoenhancing properties (Froelich and Bankhurst, 1984; Keller et al., 1988).

Although hormones of the HPA axis have often been implicated in mediating the interactions between the brain and the immune system, particularly those induced by stress, recent research indicates that other hormones, pertaining to other physiological axes, also play important roles. In particular, the hypothalamic–pituitary–thyroid axis, and the hypothalamic–pituitary–gonadal axis have both been shown to interact with the immune system. Thyroxine, for instance, has been shown to enhance specific immune measures (Ahlqvist, 1976). Testosterone has in general been immunosuppressive (Grossman, 1985). Other hormones, such as insulin, vasopressin, and growth hormone, also possess immunoregulatory properties. Prolactin has recently been shown to stimulate several immune functions. Many of these hormones seem to work in concert. For example, profound immunoregulatory changes occur during pregnancy, partly to protect the fetus from being rejected and partly to allow the mother to remain healthy during her pregnancy. Since many of these hormones are dysregulated during pregnancy, it is reasonable to assume that the net effect on the immune system will have to depend on the interplay of these hormones and their physiological properties (Ahlqvist, 1981).

Hormones, however, are not the only mediators between the brain and the immune system. Neurotransmitters, such as epinephrine, norepinephrine, serotonin, and acetylcholine, also seem to possess immunoregulatory properties. The net effect on the immune system, however, is complex and dependent on a multitude of factors. The effect of norepinephrine, for instance, seems to vary with the dose, the duration, the specific receptor(s) being stimulated, feedback regulatory mechanisms, and other hormones or neurotransmitters being stimulated by norepinephrine (Hall and Goldstein, 1981).

Whereas most of the interactions between the brain and the immune system seem to be mediated by hormones or neurotransmitters secreted by the nervous system, recent evidence suggests that cytokines, which are immunoregulatory substances that are produced and secreted by immune cells, may also possess properties that may, in some way, make them act like neurotransmitters. Interleukin-1 (IL-1), for instance, seems to act at the level of the hypothalamus to increase the secretion of CRH, which in turn activates the whole HPA. Interleukin-1 also seems to play a role in temperature regulation and sleep induction (Dinarello, 1989). Although little is known about the brain origin of IL-1, its synthesis and release, IL-1 immunoreactive fibers, particularly dense in certain regions of the hypothalamus and arcuate nucleus, have been identified (Breden et al., 1988). More research in this area is certainly needed, particularly now that newer cytokines are being discovered on a regular basis.

IV. THE PSYCHOIMMUNOLOGY OF DEPRESSION AND ANXIETY

A. The Psychoimmunology of Depressive Disorders

1. *Rationale*

The last one or two decades have witnessed an explosion of research related to the psychobiology of the affective disorders. Details of this are to be found in other parts of this book. Rationale for studies investigating the integrity of the immune response in affective disorders, however, has been based on three major assumptions: (1) depression is associated with an increased risk of immune-related disorders, such as infection, autoimmune disorders, and cancer; (2) stress, which is commonly associated with depression, has been shown to interfere with immune regulation; and (3) the pathophysiology of depression, although still not completely elucidated, seems to include dysregulation in neurotransmitter and hormone systems, notably affecting the hypothalamus and other parts of the limbic system. These assumptions will be briefly discussed here:

Depression and Immune-Related Disorders. Two thousand years ago, the Greek scientist Galen noted that "melancholic" women were more likely than "sanguine" women to develop cancer of the breast. These observations have recently been tested with modern scientific research methods. According to Bahnson (1980), patients who are likely to develop cancer suffer from loneliness and hopelessness stemming from deprived early childhood experiences. Their personality is marked by rigidity and inhibition, and the excessive use of denial and repression. Other investigators have also underscored the notions of suppressed anger, helplessness, and lack of emotional expression as characteristic of the so-called cancer-prone personality. There has also been a good deal of research concerning the association between depression and the risk of cancer. The results, however, have been inconsistent. Kerr and colleagues (1969) and Whitlock and Siskind (1979) found an increased mortality rate caused by cancer in depressed patients. These findings, however, have been disputed by Evans and associates (1974) and Tsuang and co-workers (1980), who found no such increases in cancer mortality in the depressed patients they investigated. These, however, have been mostly retrospective studies. In a large epidemiological prospective study of 2020 middle-aged employees who were given the Minnesota Multiphasic Personality Inventory (MMPI) and were followed-up for 17 years for the development of cancer, Shekelle et al. (1981) found a significant association between death from cancer and elevated depression scores on the MMPI. These data suggest, but do not necessarily establish, an association between depression and the risk of cancer.

In addition to cancer, researchers have also inquired about a possible association between depression and infectious diseases. The data here are not as rigorous as for cancer. Most of the work has centered around a possible association between stressful life events and infectious diseases, such as infectious mononucleosis or herpes simplex. Few studies have attempted to establish a link between depression and the risk of infection in general. There are also isolated reports of an association between depression and infection with a specific agent, such as the herpes simplex virus (Cappel et al., 1978).

Allergy and autoimmune disorders are other examples of diseases with faulty immunoregulatory mechanisms. There have also been reports of an association between depression and autoimmune disorders (Freeman et al., 1964). A survey of psychological symptoms in a dermatological clinic, carried out by Preston (1969), revealed that as many as 70% of patients suffering from eczema and as many as 84% of patients with chronic urticaria were depressives. Matussek and associates (1983), on the other hand, found higher frequencies of allergic disorders among "monopolar endogenous depressives," but not among other forms of depression. There are also reports of associations between depression, on the one hand, and rheumatoid arthritis and thyrotoxicosis, on the other.

In summary, numerous reports have been published over the last few years suggesting a possible association between immune-related disorders and depression. The data, however, have been rather soft, hinting more toward a possible role for psychosocial and emotional factors in general as cofactors in the etiology of these disorders, rather than establishing a specific etiological link between depression per se and a specific medical illness.

Stress and the Immune System. The effects of stress on the regulation of the immune system have already been reviewed in previous sections of this chapter. The argument here is that since stressful life events are associated with depression, and since stressful life events can impair immune function, it therefore is reasonable to expect an association between depression per se and impairment in immune regulation. Evidence related to the association between depression and immune function will be presented later.

Neuropharmacology and Neuroendocrinology of Affective Disorders. As is evident from other chapters in this volume, there has recently been a real explosion of research in the neuropharmacology and neuroendocrinology of the affective disorders. The reader is referred elsewhere for details of these findings (Goodwin and Jamison, 1990). What is important from the perspective of the psychoimmunologist is that many of the hormones and neurotransmitters that have been shown to be dysregulated during a depressive episode do affect the regulation of the immune response. As discussed earlier, both norepinephrine and serotonin, neurotransmitters postulated to play major roles in the pathophysiology of depression, are now known to possess regulatory activities on functions of immune cells. More specifically, both norepinephrine and serotonin activate membrane receptors on the surface of immune cells and, hence, modulate their functions. The net effect, however, seems to be related to the dose, duration, specific receptor(s) involved, and so on. The same can also be said about hormones, many of which are known to be dysregulated during depression. In particular, HPA activation, which frequently occurs during the acute phase of depression, results in the secretion of excessive amounts of ACTH, ß-endorphin, and cortisol, all of which affect the integrity of the immune response. Again, the net effect on the immune system depends on the interplay of these and other hormones or neurotransmitters.

2. Immune Studies in Depression

Immune studies in depressive illness began appearing in the literature in the early 1980s. A recent review is provided by Stein and coauthors (1991). The earlier studies were rather simple. Immune measures were limited to one or two immune tests. The most common tests were leukocyte enumeration, lymphocyte subtyping, and lymphocyte responses to mitogenic stimulation. Kronfol et al. (1984) compared peripheral leukocyte counts in a group of 177 unmedicated depressives and 178 unmedicated schizophrenics. Compared with the schizophrenic controls, depressed patients showed a significant increase in the concentration of neutrophils and significant decreases in the concentrations of lymphocytes, monocytes, and eosinophils. Although adrenal steroids were not measured in these patients, the authors noted that the blood cell picture in the depressed group was consistent with higher levels of glucocorticoids.

As the technology for the functional subtyping of lymphocytes was developing, several studies examined the proportions of different lymphocyte subsets among depressed patients and compared them with normal controls. Most studies seem to indicate that the percentages of different lymphocyte subtypes (including the T cells, the B cells, the T helper cells, and the T suppressor cells) are not significantly different between depressed patients and normal controls (Kronfol and House, 1989). A study by Evans and colleagues (1992) indicates that the number of NK cells may be decreased in depressed patients compared with control groups.

Functional immune assays have also been compared between depressed patients and matched controls. The most commonly used assay was lymphocyte response to mitogen stimulation, a crude assay of lymphocyte reactivity to nonspecific stimuli. Kronfol et al. (1983) first reported a decrease in mitogen-induced lymphocyte proliferation in depressed patients compared with controls. These findings have been replicated by most, although not all, independent investigators. The reason for the discrepancy is unclear. Differences in patient population, choice of controls, and assay techniques account for at least some of the discrepancy.

A more specific and perhaps more relevant functional immune assay is natural killer cell activity. The NK activity is involved in host defenses against viral-infected cells and possibly against cancer. Most studies comparing NK activity in depressed patients and normal controls have found NK activity to be significantly impaired in the depressed group (Kronfol et al., 1989). This finding, at least according to the study of Evans et al. (1992), seems to be more common among males and may be related to a decrease in the number of circulating NK cells. There have also been reports of an association between immune impairment, age, and the severity of depression (Schleifer et al., 1989). Some of these associations, however, need further clarification.

The association between immune impairment and HPA activation in depression has received considerable attention. Kronfol and House (1989) have shown that, although the traffic of circulating leukocytes (notably neutrophilia on the one hand, lymphocytopenia and monocytopenia on the other), was associated with increased levels of glucocorticoids, impaired lymphocyte mitogenic activity was not. Similar findings concerning NK activity have been obtained by Irwin et al. (1990). The role of other hormones in inducing immune dysregulation, notably CRH, ACTH, and ß-endorphin, need to be further investigated.

In summary, immune studies performed to date on patients with affective disorders mark only the beginning of an exciting new chapter in the psychobiology of depression. Even though several findings have been independently replicated, others have not. Furthermore, although reports of immune dysregulation in depressed patients may shed some light on psychobiological pathways in the pathophysiology of depression, they do not necessarily imply immunodeficiency in these patients. Whereas some of the reports indicate statistically significant differences with normal controls, the clinical significance of these findings remain largely undetermined. More research is certainly needed to address many of these fascinating, yet very complex, issues.

B. The Psychoimmunology of Anxiety

Although there are probably as many compelling reasons to conduct immunological investigations in anxiety-disordered patients as there are in patients with major depression, there have been very few immune studies of anxiety disorders published. The reasons for this are not very clear. At least in the United States, biological research in affective disorders has generally outpaced biological research in other psychiatric disorders. This, however, has only been true during the 1970s and early 1980s. The late 1980s and the 1990s have witnessed a revival of interest in the psychobiology of various psychiatric disorders, particularly schizophrenia and anxiety disorders. Although major advances have been made in the epidemiology, genetics, and neuropharmacology of the anxiety disorders, there are, as yet, no reports of a systematic immunological assessment of subjects with anxiety disorders.

The rationale for conducting immune studies in patients with anxiety disorders is in many ways similar to that advanced for the study of depressive illness. Many of the arguments raised in favor of a postulated immune dysregulation in depressive illness could equally be raised to justify immune studies in anxiety disorders. Stressful life events are often associated with symptoms of anxiety and depression, and any association with immune impairment could as well be related to the anxiety symptoms as to the depression. Furthermore, anxiety disorders are also associated with autonomic and neuroendocrine dysregulation. This will ultimately result in the dysregulation of neurotransmitter or neurohormone mechanisms. These neurotransmitters and neurohormones will, in turn, affect the regulation of the immune system.

Reports of an association between anxiety symptoms and immune dysregulation are rare and often misleading because of the presence of confounding variables such as stress or other psychiatric symptoms. Baker et al. (1985), for instance, noted an association between levels of anxiety in medical students and the proportion of helper T lymphocytes. First-year medical students reported a higher level of subjective anxiety than second-year controls. They also had a significant increase in the proportion of helper T lymphocytes.

Reports of immune function studies in patients with anxiety disorders are even more difficult to find. Published reports are very preliminary, sketchy, or incomplete. There are, however, several published abstracts addressing this issue. Schleifer et al. (1990) initially reported that the number of peripheral blood lymphocytes and lymphocyte subsets (T cells, B cells, NK cells, T helper, and T suppressor) were not significantly different between patients with panic disorder and matched controls. They did, however, note that lymphocyte responses to the mitogens concanavalin A (Con-A) and pokeweed mitogen (PWM) appeared lower in the panic disorder patients. Keller et al. (1991) compared several immune measures in patients with major depression and matched controls. Although no significant difference was noted, a subgroup of patients with major depression and history of simultaneous panic disorder showed increased immunocyte number and function compared with their controls. Their final reports are patiently awaited to clarify these discrepancies.

V. CONCLUSION

The relations between the brain and the immune system are now firmly established. I have briefly reviewed some of the anatomical, physiological, and pharmacological evidence supporting those interactions. I have also presented an overview of the basic and clinical implications, in particular, the effects of stress on immune function, and the possible role of mood states and stressful life events in the multifactorial etiology of immune-related disorders such as infection, allergy, autoimmune diseases, and cancer. I have also alluded to recent evidence suggesting that products of the immune system, particularly certain cytokines, can influence neuroendocrine secretion and behavioral regulation. This is a rapidly evolving field, with new knowledge being generated at a very fast rate.

With this broad perspective in mind, it is evident that the immunology of specific psychiatric disorders constitutes only a small branch of the vast field of psychoneuroimmunology. While interesting and important questions have been raised, particularly concerning possible immunological dysfunction in patients with major depression, the answers have been sketchy and sometimes inconsistent. Even when a specific immune aberration, such as decreased NK activity, has been confirmed by several laboratories, such a finding does not necessarily imply that depressed patients are more susceptible to infection or cancer. To answer this question, a different type of longitudinal epidemiological study, combining both psychological and immunological measures, should be conducted over relatively long periods. Similarly, the mechanism(s) by which NK activity might be impaired in depressed patients defies any simple or quick answer. The time has come for careful studies in the psychoneuroimmunology of selected psychiatric disorders, including depression and anxiety, to be conducted. These should incorporate objective diagnostic assessment, careful selection of controls, adequate sample size, state-of-the-art immunological techniques, a longitudinal design, prospective assessment of health variables, and perhaps, most importantly, the formulation of specific plausible hypotheses. Only then can we expect definitive answers to some of the most pressing questions.

ACKNOWLEDGMENTS

This work was supported in part by USPHS grants MH42988 and AA07378. The author also thanks Cathy Schleif for secretarial assistance.

REFERENCES

R. Ader, and N. Cohen, Behaviorally-conditioned immunosuppression, *Psychosom. Med., 37*: 333 (1975).

J. Ahlqvist, Endocrine influences on lymphatic organs, immune responses, inflammation and autoimmunity, *Acta Endocrinol. (Suppl.), 206* (1976).

J. Ahlqvist, Hormonal influences on immunologic and related phenomena, *Psychoneuroimmunology* (R. Ader, ed.), Academic Press, New York, p. 355 (1981).

C. Bahnson, Stress and cancer: The state of the art, *Psychosomatics, 21*: 975 (1980).

G. H. Baker, M. S. Irani, N. A. Byrom, N. M. Nagvekar, R. J. Wood, J. R. Hobbs, and D. A. Brewerton, Stress, cortisol concentrations and lymphocyte subpopulations, *Br. Med. J., 290*: 1393 (1985).

R. Bartrop, L. Lazarus, D. Luckhurst, L. Kiloh, and R. Penny, Depressed lymphocyte function after bereavement, *Lancet, 1*: 834 (1977).

H. Besedovsky, E. Sorkin, D. Felix, and H. Haas, Hypothalamic changes during the immune response, *Eur. J. Immunol., 7*: 325 (1977).

J. E. Blalock, A molecular basis for bidirectional communication between the immune and neuroendocrine systems, *Physiol. Rev., 69*: 1 (1989).

C. Breden, C. Dinarello, and C. Saper, Interleukin-1 immunoreactive innervation of the human hypothalamus, *Science, 240*: 321 (1988).

R. Cappel, F. Gregoire, L. Thiry, and S. Sprecher, Antibody and cell-mediated immunity to herpes simplex virus in psychotic depression, *J. Clin. Psychiatry, 39*: 266 (1978).

C. Dinarello, Interleukin-1 and its biologically related cytokines, *Adv. Immunol., 44*: 153 (1989).

B. Dorian, D. Garfinkel, G. Brown, A. Shore, D. Gladman, and E. Keystone, Aberrations in lymphocyte subpopulations and function during psychological stress, *Clin. Exp. Immunol., 50*: 50 (1982).

T. Dougherty, and A. White, Influence of adrenal cortical secretion on blood elements, *Science, 98*: 367 (1943).

D. Evans, J. Folds, J. Petitto, R. Golden, C. Pedersen, M. Corrigan, J. Gilmore, S. Silva, D. Quade, and H. Ozer, Circulating natural killer cell phenotypes in men and women with major depression: Relation to cytotoxic activity and severity of depression, *Arch. Gen. Psychiatry, 49*: 388 (1992).

N. Evans, J. Baldwin, and D. Gath, The incidence of cancer among patients with affective disorders, *Br. J. Psychiatry, 124*: 518 (1974).

E. Freeman, B. Feingold, K. Schlesinger, and F. Gorman, Psychological variables in allergic disorders: A review, *Psychosom. Med., 26*: 543 (1964).

C. Froelich, and A. Bankhurst, The effect of ß-endorphin on natural killer cytotoxicity and antibody dependent cellular cytotoxicity, *Life Sci., 35*: 261 (1984).

R. Glaser, S. Kennedy, W. Lafuse, R. Bonneau, C. Speicher, J. Hillhouse, and K. Glaser, Psychological stress-induced modulation of interleukin 2 receptor gene expression and interleukin 2 production in peripheral blood leukocytes, *Arch. Gen. Psychiatry, 47*: 707 (1990).

F. Goodwin, and K. Jamison, *Manic-Depressive Illness,* Oxford University Press, New York (1990).

C. Grossman, Interactions between the gonadal steroids and the immune system, *Science, 227*: 257 (1985).

N. Hall, and A. Goldstein, Neurotransmitters and the immune system, *Psychoneuroimmunology* (R. Ader, ed.), Academic Press, New York, p. 475 (1981).

M. Irwin, T. Patterson, T. Smith, C. Caldwell, S. Brown, J. C. Gillin, and I. Grant, Reduction of immune function in life stress and depression, *Biol. Psychiatry, 27*: 22 (1990).

J. Jemmott, J. Borysenko, D. C. McClelland, R. Chapman, D. Meyer, and H. Benson, Academic stress, power motivation, and decrease in secretory rate of salivary secretory immunoglobulin A, *Lancet, 1*: 1400 (1983).

S. Keller, M. Stein, M. Camerino et al, Suppression of lymphocyte stimulation by anterior hypothalamic lesions in the guinea pig, *Cell. Immunol., 52*: 334 (1980).

S. Keller, J. Weiss, S. Schleifer, N. Miller, and M. Stein, Suppression of immunity by stress: Effects of a graded series of stressors on lymphocyte stimulation in the rat, *Science, 213*: 1397 (1981).

S. Keller, J. Weiss, S. Schleifer, N. Miller, and M. Stein, Stress-induced suppression of immunity in adrenolectomized rats, *Science, 221*: 1301 (1983).

S. Keller, S. Schleifer, A. Liotta, R. Bond, N. Farhoody, and M. Stein, Stress-induced alterations of immunity in hypophysectomized rats, *Proc. Natl. Acad. Sci. USA, 85*: 9297 (1988).

S. Keller, A. Andreoli, C. Taben, M. Rabacus, and P. Maran, "Immunity and depression: Role of cortisol and prolactin," Society of Biological Psychiatry, Annual Meeting, New Orleans, Abstr. 192 (1991).

T. Kerr, K. Shapiro, and M. Roth, The relationship between premature death and affective disorders, *Br. J. Psychiatry, 115:* 1277 (1969).

J. Kiecolt-Glaser, W. Garner, C. Speicher, G. Penn, J. Holliday, and R. Glaser, Psychosocial modifiers of immunocompetence in medical students, *Psychosom. Med., 46*: 7 (1984).

Z. Kronfol, and J. D. House, Lymphocyte mitogenesis, immunoglobulin and complement levels in depressed patients and normal controls, *Acta Psychiatr. Scand., 80*: 142 (1989).

Z. Kronfol, J. Silva, J. Greden, S. Dembinski, and R. Gardner, Impaired lymphocyte function in depressive illness, *Life Sci., 33*: 241 (1983).

Z. Kronfol, R. Turner, H. Nasrallah, and G. Winokur, Leukocyte regulation in depression and schizophrenia, *Psychiatry Res., 13*: 13 (1984).

Z. Kronfol, J. D. House, J. Silva, J. Greden, and B. J. Carroll, Depression, urinary free cortisol excretion and lymphocyte function, *Br. J. Psychiatry, 148:* 70 (1986).

Z. Kronfol, M. P. N. Nair, J. Goodson, K. Goel, R. Haskett, and S. Schwartz, Natural killer cell activity in depressive illness: A preliminary report, *Biol. Psychiatry, 26*: 753 (1989).

M. Laudenslager, S. Ryan, R. Drugan, R. Hyson, and S. Maier, Coping and immuno-suppression: Inescapable but not escapable shock suppresses lymphocyte proliferation, *Science, 221*: 568 (1983).

P. Matussek, D. Agerer, and G. Seibt, Allergic disorders in depressive patients, *Compr. Psychiatry, 24*: 25 (1983).

A. Monjan, and M. Collector, Stress-induced modulation of the immune response, *Science, 196*: 307 (1977).

M. P. N. Nair, and S. A. Schwartz, Immunomodulatory effects of corticosteroids on natural killer and antibody-dependent cellular cytotoxic activities of human lymphocytes, *J. Immunol., 132:* 2876 (1984).

K. Preston, Depression and skin disease, *Med. J. Aust., 1*: 326 (1969).

A. Rasmussen, Emotions and immunity, *Ann. N.Y. Acad. Sci., 164*: 458 (1969).

G. Renoux, K. Biziere, M. Renoux, J. M. Guillaumin, and D. Degenne, A balance brain asymmetry modulates T cell-mediated events, *J. Neuroimmunol., 5*: 227 (1983).

V. Riley, Psychoneuroendocrine influences on immunocompetence and neoplasia, *Science, 212:* 1100 (1981).

R. Sapolsky, C. Rivier, G. Yamamoto, P. Plotsky, and W. Vale, Interleukin-1 stimulates the secretion of hypothalamic corticotropin-releasing factor, *Science, 238*: 522 (1987).

S. Schleifer, S. Keller, M. Camerino, J. Thornton, and M. Stein, Suppression of lymphocyte stimulation following bereavement, *JAMA, 250*: 374 (1983).

S. Schleifer, S. Keller, R. Bond, J. Cohen, and M. Stein, Major depressive disorder and immunity: Role of age, sex, severity, and hospitalization, *Arch. Gen. Psychiatry, 46*: 81 (1989).

S. Schleifer, S. Keller, B. Scott, and J. Vecchione, "Lymphocyte function in panic disorder," Society of Biological Psychiatry, Annual Meeting, New York, Abstr. 58 (1990).

R. Shekelle, W. Raynor, A. Ostfled, D. Garron, L. A. Bieliauskas, S. C. Liu, C. Maliza, and O. Paul, Psychological depression and 17-year risk of death from cancer, *Psychosom. Med., 43*: 117 (1981).

U. Singh, D. Millson, P. Smith, and J. T. Owen, Identification of ß-adrenoreceptors during thymocyte ontogency in mice, *Eur. J. Immunol., 9*: 31 (1979).

L. Sklar, and H. Anisman, Stress and coping factors influence tumor growth, *Science, 205*: 513 (1979).

L. Sklar, V. Bruto, and H. Anisman, Adaptation to the tumor-enhancing effects of stress, *Psychosom. Med., 43*: 331 (1981).

J. Slade, and B. Hepburn, Prednisone-induced alterations of circulating human lymphocyte subsets, *J. Lab. Clin. Med., 101*: 479 (1983).

M. Stein, R. Schiavi, and M. Camerino, Influence of brain and behavior on the immune system, *Science, 191*: 435 (1976).

M. Stein, S. Schleifer, and S. Keller, Immune disorders, *Comprehensive Textbook of Psychiatry* (H. Kaplan and B. Sadock, eds.), Williams & Wilkins, Baltimore, p. 1206 (1985).

M. Stein, A. Miller, and R. Tretsman, Depression, the immune system, and health and illness, *Arch. Gen. Psychiatry, 48*: 171 (1991).

M. Tsuang, R. Woolson, and J. A. Fleming, Causes of death in schizophrenia and manic-depression, *Br. J. Psychiatry, 136*: 239 (1980).

H. M. Weiner, *Psychobiology and Human Disease,* Elsevier North Holland, New York (1977).

F. Whitlock, and M. Siskind, Depression and cancer: A follow-up study, *Psychol. Med., 9*: 747 (1979).

J. Williams, R. Peterson, P. Shea, J. Schmedtje, D. C. Bauer, and D. Felten, Sympathetic innervation of murine thymus and spleen: Evidence for a functional link between the nervous and immune systems, *Brain Res. Bull., 6:* 83 (1981).

21

Stress Responsive Neurohormones in Depression and Anxiety

David Michelson and Philip W. Gold
National Institute of Mental Health, National Institutes of Health, Bethesda, Maryland

I. INTRODUCTION

Over the past decade, our understanding of the brain's endocrine functions has increased dramatically. A growing body of knowledge has begun to delineate the variety of roles played by central and peripheral hormones in regulating behavioral and affective states, and to characterize abnormalities of hormonal function associated with psychiatric illness. In this chapter we will try to describe our current understanding of neuroendocrine function in anxiety and depressive syndromes, with particular reference to stress responsive neurotransmitters. Our central premise is that these elements form part of a specific system, activated in the face of stress, and becoming maladaptive in both anxiety and depressive disorders through persistent or recurrent dysphoric arousal (Gold et al., 1988a,b).

In health, arousal is an adaptive response to a variety of stimuli. It is an integral component of the stress response (the organism's capacity to handle disturbances in its homeostasis), and can be understood as a state of heightened readiness to respond to (usually external) stimuli. Changes characteristic of arousal include alertness, vigilance, focused attention, inhibition of vegetative functions, such as feeding or sleep, and peripheral changes that tend toward increasing immediately available energy. The subjective experience of arousal can be pleasurable (e.g., the excitement induced by sexual stimuli), dysphoric (an apprehensive response to a feared event or situation), or affectively neutral (the heightened attention of a challenging but nonthreatening situation).

In anxiety disorders, the state of dysphoric, apprehensive arousal becomes fixed, sometimes as a response to specific stimuli (e.g., phobias), sometimes without obvious stimuli ("free-floating anxiety"), or occurs unpredictably and unrestrainedly (as in panic disorders). There is not generally a primary disturbance of mood or self-perception, and it is typically the arousal itself that the patient identifies as responsible for his or her discomfort.

Depressive disorders also involve maladaptive and dysregulated states of arousal. The discomfort experienced by depressed patients, however, is not perceived by the patient as a consequence of hyperarousal per se (although in some, hypoarousal may be a primary complaint), and a disturbance of mood is a requirement of the diagnosis. Patients with classic melancholic depression experience extreme, unremitting states of arousal, with diffuse anxiety and loss of normal neurovegetative functions, such as sleep, appetite, and sexual drive. Melancholia is typically characterized by a preoccupation with disturbing internal stimuli and self-referential, negativistic ideas, and the anxiety of melancholic depression differs experientially from generalized anxiety in that it is usually attached to the self and is experienced as guilt, shame, or worthlessness. Some patients have an increase in motor activity and are often described as having an *agitated depression,* whereas others appear to become so internally preoccupied that they are unresponsive to their environment and exhibit marked psychomotor retardation (*Diagnostic and Statistical Manual of Mental Disorders,* 3rd ed., revised; *DSM-III-R,* 1987). Depression can also present without a disturbance of neurovegetative functions (nonmelancholic depression); such patients' primary symptoms are persistent, unrelenting sadness and dysphoric mood, and an inability to take pleasure or interest in the world about them (DSM-III-R, 1987). In this sense, such patients share with melancholically depressed patients a restriction of the capacity to respond to external stimuli. Functions that are relatively less cognitively or affectively based, such as sleep, appetite, and libido, one might say soma, as opposed to psyche), however, are relatively preserved. Still other depressed patients suffer from persistent feelings of listlessness and anergia; often they feel chronically fatigued, have increased appetites and gain weight, and are hypersomnic. Although such patients share with melancholically depressed patients an inability to respond in any full way to the outside world, they do not show the pathological hyperarousal characteristic of melancholia. Rather, these patients seem basally underaroused. Interestingly, patients often identify the stimulus to this state of hyperresponsivity, as with, for example, rejection hypersensitivity.

Conceptualized in this way, understanding both anxiety and depression involves understanding the biology and endocrinology of arousal and, more generally, the stress response. In the following sections, we shall review the phenomenology and biology of the generalized stress response and present data about the role of the effectors of the generalized stress response in both the clinical and biochemical manifestations of major depression and anxiety and as potential substrates for antidepressant and anxiolytic agents.

II. THE GENERALIZED STRESS RESPONSE

Living organisms are constantly balancing intrinsic and extrinsic disturbing forces to maintain a dynamic equilibrium. The counteracting and reestablishing forces required for this task include a complex repertoire of molecular, cellular, physiological, and behavioral responses, and involve a substantial portion of our cellular machinery. Stress can be understood as a state of dysharmony, or threatened homeostasis (Chrousos and Gold, 1992). Disturbing force or threats to homeostasis are *stressors,* and physical or cognitive reactions that attempt to counteract the effects of the stressors to reestablish homeostasis are *adaptive responses.*

Both physical and emotional stressors evoke central and peripheral responses that act to preserve homeostasis. Centrally, pathways mediating arousal, vigilance, focused attention, and appropriate regression are facilitated, whereas pathways that serve vegetative functions such as sleep, feeding, and reproduction are inhibited. Peripheral adaptation occurs principally through glucocorticoids, which promote a redirection of energy and provide feedback to restrain the central effectors of the stress response (Munck et al., 1984). A successful adaptative response depends not only on responding quickly to appropriate stimuli, but also on being inhibited by counterregulatory elements that prevent an overresponse.

Because this response is both essential for survival and remarkably consistent, it has been suggested that a dedicated system has evolved that is specific and constitutes a generalized stress response. The identification of some of the biochemical effectors of the stress response and the central loci responsible for producing and releasing these substances has begun to substantiate this hypothesis. Two important components of the generalized stress response, the function of which will be described in the following, are corticotropin-releasing hormone (CRH); (Munck et al., 1984) and the locus coeruleus–norepinephrine system (Foote et al., 1980).

A. Corticotropin-Releasing Hormone

The corticotropin-releasing hormone (CRH) and the locus coeruleus-norepinephrine (LC–NE) autonomic nervous system are two of the principal components of the generalized stress response. CRH is a 41-amino acid peptide. Although its presence had been hypothesized for many years, it was not until 1981 that Vale et al. elucidated the sequence of this elusive releasing factor. Over the past decade the physiology of CRH has become increasingly well understood.

Although the paraventricular nucleus (PVN) of the hypothalamus contains the highest concentration of CRH in the brain, it is also synthesized in a variety of extrahypothalamic locations, including Barrington's nucleus in the brain stem (adjacent to the locus coeruleus), the central nucleus of the amygdala, and the cerebral cortex (Swanson et al., 1983). The CRH receptors are located in disparate brain regions, including areas apparently lacking CRH nerve terminals and cell bodies, suggesting a parasynaptic mode of information processing (Swanson et al., 1983; Herkenham, 1987). These anatomical data provide a context for the observation that the intraventricular administration of CRH to the rat produces a series of coordinated physiological and behavioral events, adaptive during stressful situations. These include activation of the pituitary–adrenal axis and the sympathetic system, facilitation of pathways subserving vigilance, cautious avoidance, anxiety, and inhibition of pathways subserving vegetative functions such as growth, reproduction, and feeding (Brown et al., 1982; Sutton et al., 1982; Britton et al., 1982; Sirinathsinghji et al., 1983; Rivier and Vale, 1984).

B. The Locus Coeruleus–Norepinephrine System

The other system most prominently involved in mediating arousal (and in disorders involving arousal) is the catecholaminergic (primarily noradrenergic) system. In the brain the largest collection of noradrenergic neurons is located in a region of the dorsolateral pons known as the locus coeruleus (LC). There is a large body of evidence connecting the LC with many brain processes involved in arousal. The LC receives many inputs; these include a dense network of CRH terminal fields, compatible with data that the LC-firing rate increases markedly following the iontophoretic application of CRH (Valentino et al., 1983).

The LC not only receives input from CRH neurons, but sends afferent projections to CRH neurons as well, particularly those in the parvocellular component of the PVN. We have shown that NE is a potent stimulus to CRH release from rat hypothalamic explants (Calogero et al., 1988a,b).

In addition to the PVN and other hypothalamic nuclei, the LC sends an extraordinarily dense network of fibers to virtually every cortical neuron, to the amygdala, and to the hippocampus. The LC also projects to the nucleus accumbens where noradrenergic inputs activate mesocortical and mesolimbic dopamine systems.

The CRH system and the LC–NE system seem to participate in a complex, reverberatory loop in which excitement of one component activates the other, and both act widely throughout the brain and peripherally to mediate the physiological and behavioral changes associated with arousal. Because this chapter is primarily concerned with endocrine aspects of anxiety and depression, LC function will not be explored in detail, but it is important to keep in mind that CRH and related hormones do not act independently of the LC–NE system.

C. The Hypothalamic–Pituitary–Adrenal Axis

Corticotropin-releasing hormone was first isolated as the principal secretagogue for the anterior pituitary hormone corticotropin (adrenocorticotropin; ACTH). In the hypothalamus, CRH is synthesized principally in the parvocellular region of the paraventricular nucleus and is released from nerve terminals that constitute the median eminence into hypophyseal portal blood. At the anterior pituitary, acting through the second-messenger system, cyclic AMP (cAMP), it stimulates cleavage of proopiomelanocortin, the precursor molecule of ACTH, ß-endorphin, and melanin-stimulating hormone (α-MSH), and the release of ACTH. Corticotropin is a 39-amino acid peptide that acts at the adrenal cortex to release cortisol, the primary peripheral stress hormone. In turn, cortisol acts at both the hypothalamus and the pituitary to inhibit the release of CRH and ACTH, respectively. Although CRH is the principal stimulus to ACTH release, other hormones are also important. Arginine vasopressin (AVP) possesses ACTH-releasing properties and acts synergistically with CRH to promote pituitary–adrenal activation. Other neurohormones such as angiotensin and cholecystokinin (CCK) also possess ACTH-releasing properties.

The discovery of CRH has led to many studies exploring its potential relevance to the hypercortisolism of melancholia and Cushing's disease. The prominent behavioral effects of CRH also led to investigation of its potential role in the behavioral syndromes associated with these and related disorders.

III. STRESS RESPONSIVE, AROUSAL-PRODUCING NEUROENDOCRINE AND NEUROTRANSMITTER SYSTEMS IN THE SYNDROMES OF MAJOR DEPRESSION

Depression is a syndromal illness that presents in several different ways and that likely has more than one cause. It can occur once or recurrently, and recurrences can be a series of depressive episodes (unipolar affective illness) or alternations between manic and depressive states (bipolar affective illness) (Gold et al., 1988a). The signs and symptoms of depressive illness point to several aspects of hypothalamic dysfunction. Depressed patients can experience disturbances in appetite (either anorexia or hyperphagia), can sleep too little or too much, often have decreased libido, hypothalamic amenorrhea, and an apparent phase advance of rapid eye movement (REM) sleep and body temperature rhythms. These striking changes in homeostasis are highly suggestive of neuroendocrine dysregulation and have made investigations in this area a principal focus of research efforts in depression (Gold et al., 1988b).

A. Melancholia

The classic form of major depression is melancholia, a consistent association of symptoms that includes insomnia (typically difficulty falling asleep or early-morning awakening), anorexia and weight loss, decreased libido, and a diurnal variation in mood. The clinical picture of melancholia best illustrates the concept that major depression is not a state of emotional and cognitive inactivation. Indeed, the hallmark of melancholic depression is an intensely painful arousal and an obsessional preoccupation with personal inadequacy and the inevitability of loss. In this sense, melancholia can be understood as an organized state of anxiety focused on self-representation and experienced as inappropriate guilt and self-contempt (Gold et al., 1988a). Recent data indicate that melancholia, similar to other forms of major depression, tends to be a recurrent illness, with episodes that become more frequent over time.

Pathological activation of the hypothalamic–pituitary–adrenal (HPA) axis in melancholic depression is the most consistent and widely investigated biological abnormality in psychiatry (Sachar et al., 1970; Carroll et al., 1976). Several types of measures have been used to demonstrate activation of the HPA axis in melancholic depression. Studies sampling blood over 24-h periods have shown elevation of plasma cortisol in patients with melancholic depression with preservation of a circadian rhythm. Measurements of urinary free cortisol are also elevated. Melancholic depressed patients tend not to suppress cortisol secretion in response to the long-acting synthetic glucocorticoid, dexamethasone.

Three lines of evidence suggest that hypercortisolism in major melancholic depression reflects a defect at or above the hypothalamus resulting in the hypersecretion of CRH. First, plasma ACTH responses to synthetic ovine CRH are attenuated in major depression, indicating that the pituitary corticotroph cell is appropriately restrained by the negative-feedback effects of elevated glucocorticoids (Gold et al., 1984; Gold et al., 1986). Second, normal controls given a continuous infusion of CRH have a pattern and magnitude of hypercortisolism consistent with that seen in depression (Schulte et al., 1985). Third, CRH in the cerebrospinal fluid (CSF) of depressed patients correlates positively with indexes of pituitary–adrenal activation (Roy et al., 1987). In addition, recently obtained preliminary data from the continuous sampling of lumbar CSF for 30 h indicates that depressed patients secrete an increased number of CRH pulses into the CSF, and that CSF CRH levels range from normal to elevated over the course of a day (M. Kling, unpublished observations). Consistent with this data, in single-sample CSF studies we found normal CSF CRH levels in depressed patients, and other groups have reported a range of normal to elevated levels of CRH in the CSF of patients with major depression (Nemeroff et al., 1984).

The normal responsiveness of the pituitary corticotroph cell to the negative feedback of glucocorticoids in patients with depression could account for the failure of depressed patients to show the physical stigmata of profound hypercortisolism. In depressed patients, unlike Cushing's disease patients, any centrally mediated rise in plasma ACTH and cortisol secretion would lead to a secondary glucocorticoid restraint of the corticotroph cell with a fall in the plasma levels of cortisol. In such a feedback-regulated system, it is less likely that the kind of sustained hypercortisolism typical of Cushing's disease could supervene.

Increased secretion of CRH may contribute not only to the hypercortisolism of major depression, but also to other aspects of this hyperaroused state. Hypothalamic CRH is released not only at the median eminence, but also through projections into numerous areas of the brain including the floor of the third ventricle for secretion into the CSF (Swanson et al., 1983). Moreover, extrahypothalamic CRH cell bodies and terminal fields are located throughout the CNS, especially in close association with the central autonomic system, the LC, and in many periventricular locations (Swanson et al., 1983). As yet, it is unknown whether hypothalamic and extrahypothalamic CRH are released in parallel. Nevertheless, this distribution of CRH within and beyond the boundaries of the hypothalamus provides an anatomical context for the observation that CRH can simultaneously activate and coordinate a series of metabolic, cardiovascular, and behavioral responses that are adaptive during threatening or stressful situations. In the rat, the intracerebroventricular administration of CRH leads not only to activation of the pituitary–adrenal axis, but also to activation of the sympathetic nervous system (Brown et al., 1982), and to several behavioral changes characteristic of the stress response and melancholia. These include increased context-dependent changes in motor activity, decreased feeding, hypothalamic hypogonadism, and decreased sexual behavior. In larger doses, CRH produces behavioral effects that can be construed as anxiogenic, including hyperresponsiveness to acoustic startle, decreased exploration in an open field, and enhancement of conditioned fear (Swerdlow et al., 1986).

The cause of CRH hypersecretion in depression remains unknown. In vitro studies show that norepinephrine, serotonin, and acetylcholine are potent stimuli to the CRH neurons, whereas γ-aminobutyric acid (GABA), the opiates, CRH, ACTH, and glucocorticoids are inhibitory (Calogero et al., 1988a–d).

The activation of the CRH system in melancholic depression is also associated with a concomitant activation of the LC–NE system. Direct assay of norepinephrine and mass spectroscopic assay of the norepinephrine metabolite 3-methoxy-4-hydroxyphenylglycol (MHPG) have shown normal or increased levels of CSF norepinephrine, increased plasma levels of norepinephrine, and increased CSF and urinary levels of MHPG (Post et al., 1984; Wyatt et al., 1971). Successful responses to antidepressant medications, even those that do not act principally on the norepinephrine system, are consistently associated with decreases in CSF and plasma MHPG (Campbell et al., 1979). These clinical data are consistent with preclinical data indicating that monoamine oxidase inhibitors and tricyclic antidepressants decrease the firing rate of the LC and reduce the level of norepinephrine metabolites in the brain, and that tricyclics and electroconvulsive treatment (ECT) down-regulate corticol ß-receptors, which are thought to mediate the arousal-producing effects of norepinephrine (Nyback et al., 1975; Murphy et al., 1986; Sulser et al., 1978).

Several lines of data indicate that the CRH and norepinephrine systems mutually reinforce each other's functional activity. Valentino has shown that the direct application of CRH onto locus coeruleus neurons in awake, free-ranging rats markedly increases the LC-firing rate, and we have shown that the intracerebroventricular administration of CRH significantly enhances glucose utilization in the LC (J. Perini, unpublished data).

Conversely, norepinephrine is a potent stimulus to the in vitro release of CRH (Calogero et al., 1988a), whereas propranolol attenuates the arousal-producing effects of centrally administered CRH. Recent data show that the central administration of a CRH antagonist significantly diminishes nitroprusside-induced increases in the firing of the LC. The idea that the CRH and LC–NE systems are activated in concert during episodes of major depression and that there is a possible functional relation between them is supported by a significant positive correlation in patients with depression between the levels of CRH and norepinephrine and its metabolites in the CSF (Roy et al., 1987a).

Many hypothetical models have been advanced to account for the mechanism of action of tricyclic antidepressants and other agents effective in the treatment of melancholic depression, and none of these are mutually exclusive. We have recently demonstrated that chronic (2 months) administration of tricyclic antidepressants to rats causes a significant decrease in the expression of CRH mRNA in the paraventricular nucleus of the hypothalamus and of tyrosine hydroxylase mRNA in the locus coeruleus. These findings were associated with a significant decrease in the expression of type 1 glucocorticoid receptor mRNA in the hippocampus, which is thought to be a principal restraining element of the PVN CRH system (Brady et al., 1991). These data support the notion that melancholic depression reflects a generalized stress response that has escaped its usual glucocorticoid-mediated counterregulation.

B. Atypical Depression

The pathological hyperarousal of melancholic depression represents the classic and perhaps best described of the syndromes of major depression. In contrast to this state of intense arousal, however, is the inactivation characteristic of certain nonmelancholic depressions commonly referred to as "atypical." In many ways, this syndrome seems to be the antithesis of melancholic depression. The melancholic symptoms of anorexia and early-morning awakening contrast with the hyperphagia and hypersomnia of atypical depression. Intense anxiety about self and the ruminative preoccupations with the inevitability of loss characteristic of melancholia are, in patients with atypical depression, more muted and complaints are often of passivity, anergia, and apathy (Gold et al., 1988a).

The syndrome of atypical depression often crosses the boundaries of classic psychiatric illnesses to include such disorders as Cushing's disease, hypothyroidism, seasonal affective disorder, and chronic fatigue syndrome. We have advanced preliminary data suggesting that each of these disorders may be associated with hyposecretion of CRH and hypothesize that this may be reflected clinically in the lethargy and fatigue that are the primary manifestations of the depressive syndromes associated with these disorders.

C. Cushing's Disease

Depression can be the first symptom of Cushing's disease, often preceding the onset of the physical stigmata of hypercortisolism by months or years. Work in our group, however, showed that the hypercortisolism of melancholia—in contrast with that of Cushing's disease—reflects a CNS rather than a pituitary defect. The fact that patients with Cushing's disease experience depressions, the features of which usually include lethargy, fatigue, and hypersomnia and not the hyperarousal classically associated with melancholia (M. Kling et al., unpublished observations), suggested that Cushing's disease might serve as a model for atypical depression. In particular, if the CRH neuron in Cushing's disease, in contrast to that in melancholia, was suppressed, rather than activated, it would provide an important clue to the pathophysiology of atypical depression.

Several lines of data have suggested that this is indeed true. Patients with Cushing's disease show pronounced adrenal insufficiency after successful resection of ACTH-secreting tumors; this could reflect either suppression of residual pituitary corticotrophs by long-standing hypercortisolism or suppression of the hypothalamic CRH neuron. That it is the hypothalamic CRH neuron which is suppressed was suggested by data that post-operative Cushing's patients could generate attenuated, but measurable, plasma ACTH responses to exogenous CRH. This is consistent with an intact pituitary that has been understimulated by a suppressed hypothalamic CRH neuron for an extended period (which is appropriate in the setting of unrestrained ACTH and cortisol driven by an ACTH-secreting adenoma) (Gold et al., 1986). The case for a central adrenal insufficiency following surgery was further supported by data suggesting that the plasma ACTH response to exogenous CRH in postoperative patients with Cushing's disease can be enhanced by several days of priming with synthetic CRH, compatible with the idea of a pituitary corticotroph unprimed by endogenous CRH for an extended period (G. P. Chrousos et al., unpublished observations). Further evidence is found in the fact that patients with Cushing's disease have a profound decrease in the secretion of CRH into the CSF (Kling et al., 1991). Complementary to these data showing hypofunction of the CRH neuron in Cushing's disease, preliminary studies suggest that these patients also have decreased function in the LC–NE system, indicated by a significant reduction of CSF MHPG levels in patients with this disorder (M. A. Kling and P. W. Gold, unpublished observations). The weight of available evidence in this illness thus points to a depression with a pattern of inactivation that is associated with diminished hypothalamic secretion of CRH.

Although Cushing's disease provided the initial model for exploring the pathophysiology of atypical depression, evidence is now accumulating from other sources to support and expand the hypothesis that atypical depressions associated with inactivating symptoms are associated with suppression of central arousal-producing mechanisms.

D. Hypothyroidism

Patients with hypothyroidism often complain of depression associated with lethargy, fatigue, and hypersomnia. Although the direct effect of the hypothyroidism may, in itself, be important, we have advanced several lines of data suggesting that experimentally induced hypothyroidism in rats is associated with a central CRH deficiency and pituitary–adrenal insufficiency (Kamilaris et al., 1992). Hypothyroid rats show diminished basal plasma ACTH and corticosterone secretion, decreased CSF corticosterone levels, a signifiant reduction in adrenal weight, and diminished plasma cortisol responses either to ACTH itself or the ACTH released during stimulation with CRH, interleukin-1a, or during hypoglycemic stress. Hypothyroid rats also show decreased expression of CRH mRNA in the PVN, decreased PVN CRH content, and decreased CRH release from hypothalamic organ cultures in response to KCl and a variety of secretagogues. Preliminary data also suggest that patients with hypothyroidism have a reduction in evening basal plasma cortisol levels and responses to exogenous CRH, suggestive of a possible central CRH deficiency (Kamilaris et al., 1992). Although further work remains to be done, the data are intriguing in suggesting the notion of a depressive syndrome that is inactivating in nature and associated with inadequate central secretion of CRH.

E. Seasonal Affective Disorder

The depression of seasonal affective disorder is characterized by hyperphagia and hypersomnia. Although patients with this disorder show normal or slightly reduced 24-h basal corticosteroid secretion, there is a significant attenuation and delay in the ACTH response to exogenously administered ovine CRH (Vanderpool et al., 1991). This delayed pattern is similar to that described in patients with central adrenal insufficiency secondary to trauma or tumor (Schulte et al., 1984) and in patients with Cushing's disease postoperatively (the pituitary corticotroph is inappropriately unresponsive in the setting of hypocortisolemia). This contrasts with the response seen in melancholic depression (the pituitary corticotroph is appropriately restrained by sustained hypercortisolemia; Gold et al., 1986). A subtle or subclinical deficiency of CRH in patients with seasonal affective disorder could contribute to the lethargy and hypersomnia they experience, again buttressing the concept of an inactivating depression associated with centrally mediated hypoactivity of the HPA axis.

F. Chronic Fatigue Syndrome

A subtle central adrenal insufficiency also seems to be present in some patients with the chronic fatigue syndrome. Patients with this disorder show significant reduction in 24-h total excretion of urinary free cortisol and in basal evening total and free cortisol concentrations. In association with these findings, patients with the chronic fatigue syndrome show an exaggerated plasma cortisol response to low doses of ACTH, but a blunted response to high ACTH doses (Demitrack et al., 1991). These data are compatible with intact adrenal glands that have been persistently understimulated and that, as a result, have become hypersensitive to low levels of circulating ACTH, but unable to respond fully to maximal stimulation on the basis of atrophy. Similar to the seasonal affective disorder patients and the postoperative Cushing's patients, and despite the presence of hypocortisolism, patients with the chronic fatigue syndrome show a significant blunting of the plasma ACTH response to synthetic CRH (40). In addition to the possible consequences of a deficiency of an arousal-producing neurohormone (CRH), the lethargy and fatigue of the chronic fatigue syndrome could also reflect basal hypocortisolism per se, which is known to be associated with fatigue states. Other manifestations of the chronic fatigue syndrome (which can include arthralgias, myalgias, feverishness, and increases in titers of a variety of viral antigens) could also reflect this subtle adrenal insufficiency.

IV. PANIC DISORDER

Anxiety is ubiquitous in psychiatric disorders. One illness that would seem to provide an ideal model for studying anxiety and anxious arousal is panic disorder, with its episodic and relatively bounded attacks of severe anxiety. The explosive quality associated with an acute panic attack suggests paroxysmal activation of the CRH and LC–NE systems. However, clinical studies in patients during lactate-induced panic attacks have shown only a moderate activation of the sympathetic nervous system and little if any evidence of pituitary–adrenal activation. There are, however, several lines of circumstantial evidence suggesting that CRH might play a role in panic disorder, despite the absence of dramatic pituitary–adrenal responsiveness during acute episodes, and that suggest a hypothetical model accounting for both CRH hypersecretion and pituitary–adrenal quiescence.

A. Exercise

Treadmill exercise results in dose-dependent increases in ACTH, cortisol, and NE responses, and plasma lactate concentrations during exercise correlate positively with the degree of pituitary–adrenal activation (Luger et al., 1987). To explore whether this pituitary–adrenal activation is mediated by activation of the CRH neuron, we assessed the effects of lactate (in concentrations equivalent to those measured in our subjects during exercise) on the release of CRH from in vitro rat hypothalami. In this paradigm, lactate produced a dose-dependent increase in CRH release, with the maximal stimulatory dose equal to the highest levels achieved during exercise stress (A. E. Calogero et al., unpublished observations). These data suggest that the well-documented phenomenon of exercise and lactate-induced panic may occur by activation of the CRH neuron. Our data that introcerebroventricular administration of CRH increases the LC glucose utilization rate, and other studies showing CRH-induced activation of the LC further strengthen the notion of CRH as a major component of exercise- and lactate-induced panic.

B. Pituitary Adrenal Function in Panic Disorder

Patients with panic disorder show an attenuated ACTH response to exogenous CRH, despite the apparent absence of chronic hypercortisolism that could restrain the pituitary corticotroph cell in its response to CRH (Roy-Byrne et al., 1986). In contrast to patients with major depression, these patients did not show an exaggerated adrenocorticol response to the ACTH released during CRH stimulation. This finding indicates that patients with panic disorder do not have the adrenal hypertrophy that occurs in depressed patients as a consequence of chronic ACTH stimulation. Although we cannot definitively account for the blunted ACTH response to CRH in patients with panic disorder in the absence of sustained hypercortisolism, we speculate that this might reflect hyporesponsiveness of the pituitary corticotroph cell to CRH during the course of an acute panic attack (i.e., a restricted ability to respond to sudden, intense stimulation). In the light of Munck's hypothesis that the principal role of glucocorticoid secretion during stress is to restrain the adaptive responses from overshooting, such a defect could play a permissive role in the explosive and uncontained anxiety seen during an acute panic attack. Alternatively, the blunted plasma ACTH response to CRH in patients with panic disorder could reflect negative-feedback effects of a sudden elevation of cortisol secretion in patients with panic disorder because of an exaggerated response to the novelty of the experimental situation.

The lack of evidence of chronic hypercortisolism in panic disorder is compatible with the episodic, explosive nature of this illness. The eucortisolism of panic disorder would provide the context for an explosive discharge of the CRH neuron, because the relative lack of cortisol restraint on the CRH neuron would permit profound activation. A graphic example of this concept is the phenomenon of relaxation-induced panic, in which panic attacks occur unpredictably. Presumably, such attacks occur preferentially when the

CRH system is relatively quiescent and unrestrained by high cortisol levels and, thus, is vulnerable to a marked upward excursion in functional activity.

C. Pharmacological Evidence

Pharmacological data also circumstantially support the idea that CRH is hypersecreted in patients with panic disorder. The three classes of agents most effective in treating panic disorder (tricyclic antidepressants, monoamine oxidase inhibitors, and benzodiazepines) significantly inhibit either CRH mRNA expression in the PVN of the rat hypothalamus or hypothalmic pituitary adrenal function (Brady et al., 1991; Brady et al., 1992; Kalogeras et al., 1990).

V. A POSSIBLE ROLE FOR STRESS–RESPONSIVE NEUROENDOCRINE ELEMENTS IN SUSCEPTIBILITY TO ILLNESSES ASSOCIATED WITH INFLAMMATORY AND AFFECTIVE COMPONENTS

The evidence for depressive syndromes associated with undersecretion of CRH has opened up exciting new lines of research, since in addition to its behavioral effects, CRH also has a better-known and better-characterized role as a central nervous system element recruited by the peripheral immune system to counterregulate the immune response by inducing glucocorticoid secretion.

The possible functional significance of the negative-feedback loop between the immune and central nervous systems was demonstrated by Sternberg, who showed that increased susceptibility to inflammatory disease [e.g., streptococcal cell wall (SCW)-induced arthritis in the Lewis (LEW/N) rat] was related to a defect in the response of the CRH neuron to a variety of inflammatory triggers, resulting in deficient pituitary–adrenal activation and a loss of glucocorticoid-mediated restraint of the immune response. These triggers included not only SCW, but also IL-1α and serotonin agonists such as quipazine. Sternberg also demonstrated that the relative arthritis resistance of F344/N rats compared with LEW/N rats was related to their intact HPA axis responses to these same inflammatory triggers (Sternberg et al., 1989a,b). Physiological replacement doses of corticosteroids (dexamethasone) in LEW/N rats significantly suppressed the severity of the arthritis in this arthritis-susceptible strain, whereas suppression of the HPA axis in F344/N rats with the corticosteroid receptor antagonist RU 486 led to development of severe systemic inflammation and arthritis in response to SCW in this otherwise inflammatory disease-resistant strain. Interruption of the F344/N HPA axis at the level of serotonin stimulation with the serotonin antagonist LY53857 was also associated with development of arthritis (Sternberg et al., 1989b). Thus, whether present on a genetic basis, as in LEW/N rats, or on a pharmacological basis, as in RU486-treated F344/N rats, interruptions of the HPA axis are associated with susceptibility to inflammatory disease. In a series of additional studies, Sternberg demonstrated that the deficient ACTH and corticosterone responses in LEW/N rats were likely to be secondary to a profound defect in regulation of CRH biosynthesis and secretion, rather than to a defect in the CRH peptide itself (Sternberg et al., 1989b).

Sternberg and her colleagues also explored whether the relative hypoactivity in LEW/N and hyperactivity of the CRH neuron in F344/N rats could be associated with behavioral differences in these strains (Sternberg et al., 1992). These studies revealed behavioral differences as well as differences in neuroendocrine responses to behavioral stressors in LEW/N and F344/N rats, consistent with their relative hypo- and hyper-CRH responsiveness: LEW/N rats exposed to a variety of behavioral stresses, including swim stress, restraint, or ether stress, exhibit profoundly blunted plasma ACTH and corticosterone responses to these stresses compared with F344/N rats. In open-field studies, LEW/N and F344/N rats show differences in behavior consistent with their respective deficient or increased CRH responses to the new environment of the open field. Behavioral assessment of LEW/N and F344/N rats after intracerebroventricular administration of CRH indicated that LEW/N rats were more sensitive to the behavioral effects of low-dose CRH than were F344/N rats, a finding consistent with chronic undersecretion of CRH in LEW/N rats. These studies thereby identify the CRH neuron as a central nervous system element, responding to peripherally generated inflammatory mediators, which plays a dual role in the rat during the stress of injury or inflammation. The first of these is an immunological role, recruiting the pituitary–adrenal axis to counterregulate the immune response; the second is a behavioral role—to engender cautious restraint that tends to prevent further exposure to injury during the stress of injury or inflammation.

These data provide provocative new evidence that points to the possibility of a unitary etiology for the mixture of physiological and depressive symptoms reported in certain inflammatory and immune disorders. The corresponding defective behavioral and HPA axis responses to behavioral stressors of LEW/N rats suggest that both susceptibility to inflammatory disease and nonadaptive behavioral responses to stress are associated with the same underlying neuroendocrine defect. The reported excess of depressive symptoms in illnesses, such as rheumatoid arthritis, may thus not only have to do with the stress of a chronic illness, but also with dysregulation or deficiencies in CRH secretion (Sternberg et al., 1989a,b, 1992).

REFERENCES

L. S. Brady, P. W. Gold, M. Herkenham et al., The antidepressants fluoxetine, idosoxan and phenelzine alter corticotropin releasing hormone and tyrosine hydroxylase mRNA levels in rat brain: Therapeutic implications, *Brain Res., 572*: 117 (1992).

L. S. Brady, H. J. Whitfield, R. J. Fox et al., Long-term antidepressant administration alters corticotropin-releasing hormone, tyrosine hydroxylase and mineralocorticoid receptor gene expression in rat brain. Therapeutic implications, *J. Clin. Invest., 87*: 831 (1991).

D. R. Britton, G. Koob, J. Rivier et al., Intraventricular corticotropin releasing factor enhances behavioral effects of novelty, *Life Sci., 31*: 363 (1982).

M. R. Brown, L. A. Fisher, J. Spiess et al., Corticotropin releasing factor: Actions on the sympathetic nervous system and metabolism, *Endocrinology, 111*: 928 (1982).

A. E. Calogero, W. T. Gallucci, G. P. Chrousos et al., Catecholamine effects upon rat hypothalamic corticotropin-releasing hormone secretion in vitro, *J. Clin. Invest, 82*: 839 (1988a).

A. E. Calogero, W. T. Gallucci, G. P. Chrousos et al., Interaction between GABAergic neurotransmission and rat hypothalamic corticotropin release hormone secretion in vitro. Theoretical and clinical implications, *Brain Res., 463*: 28 (1988b).

A. E. Calogero, W. T. Gallucci, R. Bernardini et al., Effect of cholinergic agonists and antagonists on rat hypothalamic corticotropin releasing hormone secretion in vitro, *Neuroendocrinology, 47*: 303 (1988c).

A. E. Calogero, W. T. Gallucci, P. W. Gold et al., Multiple feedback regulatory loops upon rat hypothalamic corticotropin-releasing hormone secretion: Potential clinical implications, *J. Clin. Invest., 82*: 767 (1988d).

Calogero, A. E., Bernardini, R., A. N. Margioris et al., Effects of serotonergic agonists and antagonists on corticotropin releasing hormone secretion by explanted rat hypothalami, *Peptides, 10*: 189 (1989).

I. C. Campbell, D. C. Murphy, D. W. Gallagher et al., Neurotransmitter-related adaptation in the central nervous system following chronic monoamine oxidase inhibition, *Monoamine Oxidase: Structure, Function, and Altered Functions* (T. P. Singer, R. W. Von Korff, and D. L. Murphy, eds.), Academic Press, New York, pp. 517–530 (1979).

B. J. Carroll, G. C. Curtis, B. M. Davies et al., Urinary free cortisol excretion in depression, *Psychol. Med., 6*: 43 (1976).

G. P. Chrousos, and P. W. Gold, The concepts of stress and stress system disorders, *JAMA, 267*: 1244 (1992).

M. A. Demitrack, J. K. Dale, P. W. Gold et al., Evidence for impaired activation of the hypothalamic–pituitary–adrenal axis in patients with chronic fatigue syndrome, *J. Clin. Endocrinol. Metab., 73*: 1224 (1991).

Diagnostic and Statistical Manual of Mental Disorders (*DSM-III-R*), Prepared by the Work Group to Revise *DSM-III* of the American Psychiatric Association, American Psychiatric Association, Washington, D.C., 1987.

S. L. Foote, G. Ashton-Jones, and F. E. Bloom, Impulse activity of locus coeruleus neurons in awake rats and monkeys is a function of sensory stimulation and arousal, *Proc. Natl. Acad. Sci. USA, 77*: 3033 (1980).

P. W. Gold, G. P. Chrousos, C. Kellner et al., Psychiatric implications of basic and clinical studies with corticotropin releasing hormone, *Am. J. Psychiatry, 141*: 619 (1984).

P. W. Gold, D. L. Loriaux, A. Roy et al., Responses to corticotropin releasing hormone in the hypercortisolism of depression in Cushing's disease. Pathophysiologic and diagnostic implications, *N. Engl. J. Med., 314*: 1329 (1986).

P. W. Gold, F. K. Goodwin, and G. P. Chrousos, Clinical and biochemical manifestations of depression: Relation to the neurobiology of stress. Part I, *N. Engl. J. Med., 399*: 348 (1988a).

P. W. Gold, F. K. Goodwin, and G. P. Chrousos, Clinical and biochemical manifestations of depression: Relation to the neurobiology of stress. Part II, *N. Engl. J. Med., 319*: 371 (1988b).

M. Herkenham, Mismatches between neurotransmitter and receptor localizations in brain: Observations and implications, *Neuroscience, 23*: 1 (1987).

K. T. Kalogeras, A. E. Calogero, T. Kuribayashi et al., In vitro and in vivo effects of the traizolobenzodiazepine alprazolam on hypothalamic–pituitary–adrenal function: Pharmacologic and clinical implication, *J. Clin. Endocrinol. Metab., 70*: 1462 (1990).

T. C. Kamilaris, E. O. Johnson, M. A. Smith et al., Effects of short- and long-duration hypothyroidism on the rat hypothalamic–pituitary–adrenal axis: In vivo and in vitro evidence for a central CRH deficiency, *Endocrinology*, (in press; 1992).

M. A. Kling, A. Roy, A. R. Doran et al., Cerebrospinal fluid immunoreactive corticotropin-releasing hormone and adrenocorticotropin secretion in Cushing's disease and major depression: Potential clinical implications, *J. Clin. Endocrinol. Metab., 72*: 260 (1991).

A. Luger, P. Dester, S. B. Kyle et al., Acute hypothalamic–pituitary–adrenal responses to the stress of treadmill exercise: Physiologic adaptations to physical training. *N. Engl. J. Med., 316*: 1309 (1987).

A. Munck, P. M. Guyre, and N. J. Holbrook, Physiological functions of glucocorticoids in stress and their relation to pharmacological actions, *Endocr. Rev., 5*: 25 (1984).

D. L. Murphy, C. Aulukh, and N. Garrick, How antidepressants work: Some continuing conclusions based on clinical and laboratory studies of the long term consequences of antidepressant drug treatment, *Antidepressant and Receptor Functions* (D. L. Murphy, ed.), Chichester, John Wiley & Sons, pp. 106–125 (1986).

C. B. Nemeroff, E. Wilderlov, G. Bissette et al., CSF concentrations of corticotropin releasing factor-like immunoreactivity in depressed patients, *Science, 226*: 1342 (1984).

H. V. Nyback, J. R. Walter, G. K. Agarjanian et al., Tricyclic antidepressants: Effects on the firing rate of brain noradrenergic neurons, *Eur. J. Pharmacol., 32*: 302 (1975).

R. M. Post, D. C. Jimerson, J. C. Ballenger et al., Cerebrospinal fluid norepinephrine and its metabolites in manic depressive illness, *Neurobiology of Mood Disorders* (R. M. Post and J. C. Ballenger, eds.), Williams & Wilkins, Baltimore, pp. 539–553 (1984).

C. Rivier, and W. Vale, Influence of corticotropin releasing factor on reproductive functions in the rat, *Endocrinology, 114*: 914 (1984).

A. Roy, D. Pickar, M. Linnoila et al., Cerebrospinal fluid corticotropin releasing hormone in depression: Relationship to noradrenergic function, *Psychiatry Res., 20:* 229 (1987a).

A. Roy, D. Pickar, S. M. Paul et al., CSF corticotropin releasing hormone in depressed patients and normal control subjects, *Am. J. Psychiatry, 144*: 641 (1987).

P. P. Roy-Byrne, T. W. Uhde, R. M. Post et al., The CRH stimulation test in patients with panic disorder, *Am. J. Psychiatry, 143*: 896 (1986).

E. J. Sachar, L. Hellman, D. K. Fukushima et al., Cortisol production in depressive illness: A clinical and biochemical clarification, *Arch. Gen. Psychiatry, 23*: 289 (1970).

H. Schulte, G. P. Chrousos, P. W. Gold et al., Continuous administration of synthetic ovine corticotropin releasing hormone in man: Physiological and pathophysiological implications, *J. Clin. Invest., 175*: 1781 (1985).

M. H. Schulte, G. P. Chrousos, P. C. Avgerinos et al., The corticotropin-releasing hormone stimulation test: A possible aid in the evaluation of patients with adrenal insufficiency, *Clin. Endocrinol. Metab., 58*: 1064 (1984).

D. J. S. Sirinathsinghi, L. H. Rees, J. Rivier et al., Corticotropin releasing factor is a potent inhibitor of sexual receptivity in the female rat, *Nature, 305*: 232 (1983).

E. M. Sternberg, J. M. Hill, G. P. Chrousos et al., Inflammatory mediator-induced hypothalamic–pituitary–adrenal axis activation is defective in streptococcal cell wall arthritis-susceptible Lewis rats, *Proc. Natl. Acad. Sci. USA, 86*: 2374 (1989a).

E. M. Sternberg, W. S. Young, Jr., R. Bernardini et al., A central nervous defect in biosynthesis of corticotropin-releasing hormone is associated with susceptibility to streptococcal cell wall induced arthritis in Lewis rats, *Proc. Natl. Acad. Sci. USA, 86*: 4771 (1989b).

E. M. Sternberg, J. R. Glowa, M. A. Smith et al., Corticotropin releasing hormone related behavioral and neuroendocrine responses to stress in Lewis and Fischer rats, *Brain Res., 570*: 54 (1992).

F. Sulser, J. Ventulani, and D. L. Mobley, Mode of action of antidepressant drugs, *Biochem. Pharmacol., 27:* 257 (1978).

R. E. Sutton, G. F. Koob, M. LeMoal et al., Corticotropin releasing factor produces behavioral activation in the rat, *Nature, 297*: 331 (1982).

L. W. Swanson, P. E. Sawchenko, J. Rivier et al., Organization of ovine CRF immunoreactive cells and fibers in the rat brain: An immunohistochemical study, *Neuroendocrinology, 36*: 165 (1983).

N. R. Swerdlow, M. A. Geyer, W. Vale et al., Corticotropin releasing factor potentiates acoustic startle in rats: Blockade by chlordiazepoxide, *Psychopharmacology, 88*: 147 (1986).

R. J. Valentino, S. L. Foote, and G. Ashton-Jones, Corticotropin releasing factor activates noradrenergic neurons of the locus caeruleus, *Brain Res., 270*: 363 (1983).

J. Vanderpool, N. Rosenthal, G. P. Chrousos et al., Evidence for hypothalamic CRH deficiency in patients with seasonal affective disorder, *J. Clin. Endocrinol. Metab., 72*: 260 (1991).

R. J. Wyatt, B. Portnoy, D. J. Kupfer et al., Resting plasma catecholamine concentrations in patients with depression and anxiety, *Arch. Gen. Psychiatry, 24*: 65 (1971).

22

Neuropeptide Alterations in Affective and Anxiety Disorders

Rachel Yehuda
Mount Sinai School of Medicine and Bronx Veterans Affairs, New York, New York

Charles B. Nemeroff
Emory University School of Medicine, Atlanta, Georgia

I. INTRODUCTION

Neuropeptides, molecules comprising two or more amino acids linked by peptide bonds, function as important chemical messengers. More than 50 neuropeptides have now been isolated and sequenced. Neuropeptides are heterogeneously distributed in the peripheral and the central nervous system (CNS) and exert multiple actions as hypothalamic hypophysiotropic hormones, as neuromodulators, and often, as neurotransmitters. As knowledge accrues concerning the various roles of individual neuropeptides in modulating behavior, it has become increasingly clear that many of these substances may have relevance to particular psychiatric disorders. This chapter will summarize preclinical and clinical studies that have implicated neuropeptide alterations in the pathophysiology of depression and anxiety and will further explore how the findings, in the aggregate, have enhanced our understanding of the relation between affective and anxiety disorders. We will begin by examining the rationale for studying neuropeptides in depression and anxiety, and by describing the research strategies that have been employed for exploring the role of neuropeptides in these disorders.

II. RATIONALE FOR EXPLORING NEUROPEPTIDE MODULATION IN AFFECTIVE AND ANXIETY DISORDERS

One of the primary reasons to study neuropeptide activity in affective and anxiety disorders is that these substances modulate the activity of hormones and neurotransmitters that have already been implicated in these disorders. As such, the study of neuropeptides allows a more precise understanding of the dysregulation of neuroendocrine and neurotransmitter systems that may be closer to the primary "source" of the biological defect.

For example, neuroendocrine abnormalities in depression and anxiety disorders have been repeatedly demonstrated in the hypothalamic–pituitary–adrenal (HPA) axis and the hypothalamic–pituitary–thyroid (HPT) axis (Butler and Nemeroff, 1990; Yehuda et al., 1991a, 1991b, 1993a; Pihoker and Nemeroff, in press). Because the primary physiological control of anterior pituitary hormone secretion is mediated by releasing and release-inhibiting neuropeptides in the hypothalamus (for further review, see Nemeroff, 1991), it has become particularly relevant to study the neuropeptide systems that may ultimately regulate neuroendocrine alterations in psychiatric illness.

Similarly, the study of neuropeptides in affective and anxiety disorders is important because of findings of altered monoamine neurotransmission in these disorders. The observation that neuropeptides are widely distributed throughout the CNS, with each peptide showing a unique distribution pattern, has revealed that, in addition to their actions as releasing factors, neuropeptides act as neuromodulators or neurotransmitters within the CNS. Many of the classic monoamine neurotransmitter systems implicated in psychiatric illness, such as norepinephrine, dopamine, and serotonin, either innervate, or are innervated by, neuropeptides. The demonstration of colocalization of neuropeptides and neurotransmitters (Nemeroff and Bissette, 1986; Hokfelt et al., 1984) has provided additional anatomical evidence for the interaction of neuropeptides and neurotransmitters.

A third impetus for studying neuropeptides in psychiatric illness is that neuropeptides are densely concentrated (with and without colocalized neurotransmitters) in brain regions thought to be involved in the pathogenesis of major psychiatric disorders and, when exogenously administered, produce effects that may be related to psychiatric symptoms. For example, intraventricular injection of certain neuropeptides in laboratory animals produces profound behavioral effects that resemble signs and symptoms of certain psychiatric disorders. As such, some neuropeptides may be depressant or anxiogenic substances in and of themselves. This hypothesis has begun to be tested by measuring basal concentrations of peptides in plasma, cerebrospinal fluid (CSF), and tissues of depressed and anxious patients, and also by examining the effect of various neuropeptides on depressive and anxiety symptoms. These and other strategies for studying the role of neuropeptides in psychiatric disorders are further described in Section III.

III. CURRENT STRATEGIES FOR EVALUATING A SPECIFIC ROLE FOR NEUROPEPTIDES IN PSYCHIATRIC DISORDERS: PRECLINICAL AND CLINICAL STUDIES

A. Preclinical Studies

Preclinical studies have been useful in providing the basis for our understanding of neuropeptide interactions with other brain neuroregulators. Specifically, by injecting the peptide of interest into the brains of laboratory animals, it has been possible to study the effects of the peptide on other neurotransmitter hormonal systems and behavior, and to begin hypothesis-testing the type(s) of alterations that may be present in specific clinical disorders.

B. Clinical Studies

Three types of human studies have been performed to date: (1) postmortem studies in which the concentration of neuropeptides and neuropeptide receptors are measured, (2) studies measuring the concentration of peptides in biological fluids such as CSF and plasma, and (3) studies measuring behavioral or biological changes following administration of neuropeptides (i.e., challenge tests). Each of these studies has produced valuable information; however, owing to methodological constraints, no one approach has allowed any definitive conclusions to be drawn concerning neuropeptide alterations in human disease.

The major advantage of postmortem studies is the ability to sample peptides directly in brain tissue. However, the total concentration of peptide reflects the amount of peptide in both the nonreleasable and releasable pools and, therefore, may occasionally represent a relatively static measure. Furthermore, there are many methodological problems in studying postmortem samples. In addition to problems, such as differences in postmortem decay and other neurochemical confounds and standardization of cause of death, it is often difficult to obtain valid clinical information concerning the relation between peptide alterations and severity of illness. However, it has been possible to measure the number and affinity of neuropeptide receptors in postmortem tissue of patients, as will be described in the following.

In living humans, it has been possible to obtain an estimate of neuropeptide activity by measuring the concentration of a particular neuropeptide in the CSF. The concentration of peptide in the CSF is thought by some, but not all, investigators to accurately reflect extracellular fluid concentrations in brain and, therefore, has an advantage over studies measuring the amount of peptide in tissue. However, although CSF concentrations provide an overall estimate of brain neuropeptide availability, these measures lack information concerning the regional source of the neuropeptide measured.

Another strategy for studying the role of neuropeptides in affective and anxiety disorders has been to administer neuropeptides, or neuropeptide agonists or antagonists, to patients and measure subsequent neuroendocrine, and possibly, behavioral changes. Even though these studies often provide interesting information, it is problematic to make assumptions about what is happening in the brain based on peripheral, rather than central, administration of neuropeptides.

IV. CORTICOTROPIN-RELEASING FACTOR IN DEPRESSION AND ANXIETY DISORDERS

Corticotropin-releasing factor (CRF) is a 41-amino acid neuropeptide that is localized primarily in the parvocellular region of the paraventricular nucleus (PVN) of the hypothalamus (Olschowka et al., 1982). This neuropeptide was originally discovered by Saffran and Schally in hypothalamic extracts (1955) and was sequenced 25 years later by Vale and his colleagues (1981). Corticotropin-releasing factor is the major physiological regulator of corticotropin (adrenocorticotropic hormone; ACTH), ß-endorphin, and other proopiomelanocortin (POMC)-derived peptides from the pituitary gland (Rivier et al., 1982; Donald et al., 1983; Rock et al., 1984), and it also acts as a neurotransmitter in several extrahypothalamic brain areas (Smith et al., 1986). Immunohistochemical and radioimmunoassay studies have shown that CRF is heterogeneously distributed in both hypothalamic and extrahypothalamic brain regions, including the forebrain (frontal cortex, amygdala, stria terminalis; Swanson et al., 1983; Sawchenko and Swanson, 1985; Fellman et al., 1982; Merchenthaler, 1984) and brain stem (e.g., locus coeruleus, parabrachial nucleus; Chappell et al., 1986; Merchenthaler, 1984; Swanson et al., 1983). The heterogeneous extrahypothalamic distribution of CRF receptors has been demonstrated both by autoradiographic and radioligand-binding techniques (De Souza et al.,

1984, 1985a,b; Millan et al., 1987). It is partly because of its extrahypothalamic distribution in limbic areas that regulate emotionality, that CRF has been hypothesized to play a role in the pathogenesis of anxiety and affective disorders (Nemeroff, 1991).

A. Preclinical Evidence Implicating Corticotropin-Releasing Factor in the Pathophysiology of Depression and Anxiety

There are several lines of evidence that support a role for CRF in the pathophysiology of affective and anxiety disorders. First is the observation that intraventricular administration of CRF induces behaviors in animals that resemble symptoms of depression and anxiety. For example, intracerebroventricular injections of CRF to rats cause a decreased food intake (Britton et al., 1982, 1986b; Krahn et al., 1986; Morley and Levine, 1982; Gosnell et al., 1983), decreased sexual behavior (Sirinathsinghji, 1985, 1987; Sirinathsinghji et al., 1983), increases in locomotor activity (Britton et al., 1986a,b; Sutton et al., 1982; Tazi et al., 1987), and disruptions in normal sleep. These behavioral alterations have been suggested to be analogous to the *Diagnostic and Statistical Manual of Mental Disorders,* 3rd ed., revised (*DSM-III-R*) criteria for major depression of weight loss, decreased libido, psychomotor agitation, insomnia, and depressed mood, respectively (Nemeroff, 1991).

Anxiety-related behaviors in response to intraventricular CRF include an increased startle response (Swerdlow et al., 1986), increased psychomotor agitation in familiar environments (Britton et al., 1986a,b; Sutton et al., 1982; Tazi et al., 1987), decreased exploratory behavior (Berridge and Dunn, 1986; Lee et al., 1987), and increased freezing (Britton et al., 1982; Berridge and Dunn, 1986, 1987) in novel environments (Britton et al., 1982; Sutton et al., 1982) in rats. Sympathoadrenal activation similar to that observed in anxiety disorders such as posttraumatic stress disorder (Kosten et al., 1987; Yehuda et al., 1990a,b, 1992b) is also enhanced following intracerebroventricular injection of CRF. Specifically, CRF injection increases both brain noradrenergic turnover (Dunn and Berridge, 1987) and peripheral epinephrine and norepinephrine secretion, and results in increased heart rate and blood pressure (Brown, 1986; Brown et al., 1982; Fisher et al., 1982, 1983; Lenz et al., 1987). Many of the anxiety-related behavioral effects of CRF can be reversed by clinically effective anxiolytics, such as chlordiazepoxide (Britton et al., 1985; Dunn and File, 1987). Furthermore, the ß-adrenergic antagonist propranolol can reverse CRF-stimulated increases in anxiety in response to conditioned emotional stress (Cole and Koob, 1988).

A second line of evidence supporting a role for CRF in affective and anxiety disorders is that CRF exerts activity in brain areas throught to be directly involved in the pathophysiology of these disorders. For example, CRF increases the neuronal-firing rate of noradrenergic neurons (Valentino and Foote, 1987; Valentino et al., 1983), as well as epinephrine turnover (Butler et al., 1990) after microinjection in the locus coeruleus. Noradrenergic neurons in this region mediate behavioral activation to stress and have been implicated in the pathophysiology of both affective and anxiety disorders (Redmond and Huang, 1979; Svensson, 1987). The finding that CRF increases noradrenergic neuronal firing in this region suggests that CRF may mediate neuroendocrine and behavioral arousal in response to stress. Furthermore, it is possible that alterations in locus coeruleus activity in affective and anxiety disorders may, in part, be secondary to increased CRF secretion. Indeed, there is support from preclinical studies that CRF neuronal systems are altered in the rat brain following both acute and chronic stress; in fact, CRF concentrations are significantly increased in the locus coeruleus after stress (Chappell et al., 1986). Because noradrenergic projections from the locus coeruleus innervate many brain areas in the forebrain, it is anatomically plausible that increased noradrenergic activation in response to CRF hypersecretion could be involved in the pathophysiology of affective and anxiety symptoms in humans.

B. Clinical Data Supporting a Role for Corticotropin-Releasing Factor in the Pathophysiology of Depressive and Anxiety Disorders

Behavioral and biological data concerning the effects of CRF in animals clearly support the hypothesis that increased CRF synaptic availability may occur in affective or anxiety disorders. In addition to preclinical evidence for this hypothesis, it is rendered plausible by the already well-established biological findings of increased hyperactivity of the HPA axis in depressive disorder and increased activation of the locus coeruleus in anxiety disorders (i.e., specifically, panic disorder and posttraumatic stress disorder), that both phenomena are mediated by CRF.

That hyperactivity of the HPA axis occurs in approximately 40–60% of patients with major depressive disorder has been one of the most venerable findings in biological psychiatry. This hyperactivity is manifested by increased basal plasma cortisol concentrations (Sachar et al., 1973), increased urinary free-cortisol excretion (Carroll et al., 1976), and a decreased number of lymphocyte glucocorticoid receptors (Gormley et al., 1985; Whalley et al., 1986). Responses of depressed patients to hormonal challenge have also been consistent with the notion of hypercortisolemia. Depressed patients show a high rate of cortisol nonsuppression in response to dexamethasone (Carroll et al., 1981; Evans and Nemeroff, 1983) and a blunted ACTH response to exogenously administered CRF (Gold and Chrousos, 1985; Gold et al., 1976; Amsterdam et al., 1987; Lesch et al., 1988; Kathol et al., 1989; Kilts et al., 1987) (discussed in greater detail later). Overproduction of hypothalamic CRF could contribute to the increased activity of the HPA axis in major depression.

The CRF concentrations in the CSF have now been measured in several separate studies. Although measurements of peptide concentrations alone are insufficient to determine if changes in synthesis, storage, or release are present, they probably represent alterations in the activity of peptide-containing neurons or of altered clearance. In particular, CSF CRF concentrations are thought to reflect CRF released directly from the brain (Post et al., 1982). Nemeroff and his colleagues (1984) were the first to report significantly increased CRF-like immunoreactivity in depressed patients compared with healthy subjects, schizophrenics, and demented patients. Subsequently, in five additional studies, the finding of increased CSF CRF concentrations in depressed patients has been confirmed (Arato et al., 1986; Banki et al., 1987; France et al., 1988; Widerlov et al., 1988a; Risch et al., 1991). Furthermore, Nemeroff et al. (1991) determined that the elevation in CSF CRF concentration in depression is most likely state-dependent. The CSF CRF concentrations were measured in depressed patients before and after a series of electroconvulsive therapy (ECT) treatments. Whereas depressed patients showed an elevated CSF CRF before ECT, CSF CRF concentrations were decreased 24 h after their final ECT treatment. Roy et al. (1987) and, subsequently, Kling et al. (1991) have not been able to replicate the increased CRF CSF concentrations; however, this group did report that CRF concentrations were positively correlated with other indexes of HPA axis activity, such as dexamethasone nonsuppression (Roy et al., 1987). Differences in the lumbar puncture techniques, sampling methods, and most importantly, patient populations, probably account for at least some of the discrepancies between laboratories.

Although the findings of increased CSF CRF concentrations in depression are of considerable interest and clearly suggest a role for central neuronal CRF overactivity in affective disorders, it is important to recognize that CSF measures represent a relatively crude sampling of overall brain CRF function. Thus, these CSF measures, in and of themselves, are not informative in localizing the specific CRF neural circuits that may be responsible for the increased CSF CRF in depression. For example, the proportion of CSF CRF that derives from extrahypothalamic CRF-containing neurons is unclear. However, when CSF and plasma concentrations have been sampled simultaneously, there is a marked CSF–plasma dissociation, suggesting that CSF CRF concentrations are not greatly influenced by peripheral plasma CRF (Post et al., 1982). Another potential limitation of the CSF CRF–sampling method is that CSF CRF concentrations do not provide information about the concentration of CRF directly reaching the anterior pituitary gland. However, Widerlov et al. (1986) reported that drug-free depressed patients had higher plasma CRF concentrations than healthy controls. In contrast with CSF CRF measurements, plasma CRF measurements are thought to reflect secretion from hypothalamic CRF neurons terminating in the median eminence. The finding of increased plasma CRF concentrations support a role for increased hypothalamic CRF secretion in major depression. However, increased plasma CRF concentrations were not observed in a study by Charlton et al. (1986). It is of paramount importance to recognize the technical difficulty associated with measurement of CRF in plasma. For example, both the Widerlov et al. (1986) report and the Charleton et al. (1986) report appeared before discovery of the CRF-binding protein that is present in plasma and brain.

Further verification of increased CRF in major affective disorders has come from postmortem studies of CRF receptor density in suicide victims. Suicide victims represent one population for examining CRF in depression because depression is a major determinant of suicide (Van Praag, 1985; Yehuda et al., 1988), and more than 50% of completed suicide victims are patients with major depressive disorder. Nemeroff et al. (1988) demonstrated a 23% decrease in CRF receptor number in the frontal cortex of 26 suicide completers compared with 28 control subjects.

There are as yet no published studies that have examined CSF CRF concentrations in patients with anxiety disorders. Given the plethora of preclinical information suggesting that CRF in the locus coeruleus can mediate anxiety-related symptoms (discussed earlier), it is plausible to hypothesize that CSF CRF concentrations in generalized anxiety, panic, or posttraumatic stress disorder (PTSD) patients would be increased, especially when patients are symptomatic. Data from CRF infusion studies in PTSD have tended to support the idea of increased CRF secretion in anxiety disorders. Studies with the CRF stimulation test in affective and anxiety disorders are described in the following section.

C. Corticotropin-Releasing Factor Challenge Studies in Major Affective and Anxiety Disorders

The CRF challenge strategy has been employed in the study of depression, primarily as a tool to investigate the mechanisms responsible for the hypercortisolemia commonly observed in this disorder. When administered at a dose of 1g/kg, CRF produces a robust ACTH and cortisol response in normal humans (Schuemeyer et al., 1984). In drug-free patients with major depressive disorder, the ACTH response to CRF is attenuated. This phenomenon has now been demonstrated in several studies (Gold et al., 1984; Holsboer et al., 1984; Gold and Chrousos, 1985; Amsterdam et al., 1987; Lesch et al., 1988; Kathol et al., 1989; Krishnan et al., 1991). Even though the exact mechanism leading to the blunted pituitary response in depression is unknown, the current best explanation for this phenomenon is that the attenuated ACTH secretion is a result of a decreased pituitary responsiveness to CRF caused by long-term hypersecretion of CRF from the median eminence and resultant down-regulation of anterior pituitary CRF receptors.

A second explanation that has been invoked to explain the blunted ACTH response to CRF is that of an increased negative-feedback inhibition of the pituitary, secondary to abnormally high circulating cortisol levels (Lowy et al., 1989). Although the blunted ACTH response to CRF plausibly could be secondary to hypercortisolemia, recent findings cast doubt on this theory. Von Bardeleben and Holsboer (1989) and Krishnan et al. (1991) found that depressed patients, unlike normal controls, continue to exhibit an ACTH and cortisol response to CRF if pretreated with high doses of dexamethasone. An increased ACTH response to CRF was also observed in depressed patients treated with metyrapone (which eliminates the negative-feedback of corticosteroids by inhibiting cortisol synthesis) (Lisansky et al., 1989). If the blunted pituitary–adrenal response to CRF occurred because of hypercortisolemia and increased negative-feedback, pretreatment with dexamethasone should have abolished ACTH and cortisol responses to CRF. Thus, the blunted ACTH response to CRF in depression likely reflects pituitary desensitization secondary to hypothalamic CRF hypersecretion.

In patients with panic disorder (Roy-Byrne et al., 1990) and posttraumatic stress disorder (Smith et al., 1989), the ACTH response to CRF is also blunted. However, the mechanisms underlying this effect are likely to be distinct from the mechanism described in the foregoing for major depressive disorder, primarily because patients with panic disorder and posttraumatic stress disorder are not chronically hypercortisolemic. In panic disorder, cortisol secretion has been reported to be normal (Liebowitz et al., 1985) as well as increased (Goldstein et al., 1987); however, the cortisol-response to dexamethasone has consistently been reported to be normal (Goldstein et al., 1987; Bridges et al., 1986; Curtis et al., 1982; Faludi et al., 1986; Lieberman et al., 1983; Roy-Byrne et al., 1985; Sheehan et al., 1986). In PTSD, recent evidence suggests that there may be an enhanced negative feedback of the HPA axis characterized by lower ambient cortisol levels and increased sensitivity of the pituitary gland (Yehuda et al., 1990b, 1991a, 1991b, 1993) that is reflected in low-baseline urinary cortisol excretion (Mason et al., 1986; Yehuda et al., 1990b), an increased number of lymphocyte glucocorticoid receptors (Yehuda et al., 1991a), and an exaggerated inhibitory cortisol response (i.e., supersuppression) to dexamethasone (Yehuda et al., 1993). In panic disorder and PTSD, the attenuated ACTH response to CRF in the absence of hypercortisolemia may be due to hyperresponsitivity of the pituitary gland to cortisol, resulting directly from an increased number of glucocorticoid receptors on the adenohypophysis.

Further studies examining glucocorticoid receptors in anxiety and affective disorders are clearly warranted to determine the extent to which major depression and anxiety disorder are similar in HPA axis abnormalities. Specifically, studies examining both plasma and CSF CRF concentrations would shed light on this issue. An increased CSF

CRF concentration in both panic disorder and posttraumatic stress disorder would be consistent with the anxiogenic effects of the peptide in the brain, primarily at the locus coeruleus. Conversely, plasma CRF concentrations in both of these disorders might be expected to be normal or subnormal to those observed in normal subjects and depressed patients.

VI. SOMATOSTATIN IN AFFECTIVE AND ANXIETY DISORDERS

A hypothalamic inhibitor of growth hormone release was isolated in crude form by Krulich et al. (1968), and somatostatin was subsequently isolated and sequenced in 1973 (Brazeau et al., 1973). Over the last two decades, evidence has been accumulating that supports a neuromodulatory role for this tetradecapeptide. Somatostatin is widely distributed in the brain, with high concentrations in the median eminence (Patel et al., 1979; Van Leeuwen et al., 1979), limbic system, cerebral cortex, hippocampus, and hypothalamus (Krisch, 1981). Somatostatin receptors have also been localized in discrete brain structures (Leroux and Pelletier, 1984; Tran et al., 1985). Following iontophoretic application of somatostatin in various brain regions, both inhibitory and excitatory neuronal effects have been observed (Delfs and Dichter, 1983; Dodd and Kelly, 1978; Olpe et al., 1980) suggesting that this peptide may function as a neurotransmitter. Furthermore, somatostatin alters the turnover of several neurotransmitters, as well as inhibits the secretion of several hormones (Reichlin, 1983; McCann, 1982).

A. Relevance of Preclinical Studies of Somatostatin to Depression

Intracerebrovascular injection of somatostatin to rats results in the disruption of behaviors in rats that may be relevant to depression. Typically, however, the relation between somatostatin administration and the behavior is biphasic. For example, central somatostatin administration affects locomotor activity, with low doses stimulating and high doses inhibiting locomotion (Rezek et al., 1977). Similarly, low doses of somatostatin are associated with decreased feeding behavior, whereas high doses are associated with increased feeding (Aponte et al., 1984; Lotter and Woods, 1977; Rezek et al., 1976). Somatostatin both decreases (Havlicek et al., 1976; Rezek et al., 1976) and increases (Danguir, 1986) sleep. The biphasic nature of the behavioral responses to somatostatin are interesting because major depressive disorder may be characterized as either classic or atypical, with the latter characterized by psychomotor agitation, weight gain, and hypersomnia. Other behaviors affected by somatostatin may also be relevant to depression. For example, somatostatin appears to affect cognitive behavior in rats. Impaired cognitive function, most notably in the area of memory disturbances, is common in major depressive disorder. Somatostatin injection has been associated with enhanced learning and the reversal of learning deficits, whereas somatostatin depletion, using cysteamine, diminishes cognitive performance (Vecsei et al., 1984; Walsh et al., 1985).

B. Clinical Data Supporting a Role for Somatostatin in Depression

Several groups have now reported significant decreases in CSF somatostatin concentrations in drug-free depressed patients, compared with normal controls (Gerner and Yamada, 1982; Rubinow, 1983; Black et al., 1986; Sunderland et al., 1987; Bissette et al., 1986; Davies et al., 1988). In most of these studies, the decrease in CSF somatostatin levels was state-dependent. For example, Agren and Lundqvist (1984) demonstrated significantly lower CSF somatostatin concentrations in a group of depressed patients studied at the peak of their depression, compared with patients studied 2 months after their depression peaks. Rubinow et al. (1986) reported that depressed patients in the euthymic state had CSF somatostatin concentrations comparable with those of normal controls. Interestingly, Charleton et al. (1988) did not observe differences in somatostatin concentration or somatostatin receptor binding in postmortem tissue of depressed patients compared with normal controls. A decreased concentration of somatostatin, and an accompanying increase in receptor number would be consistent with the low CSF concentrations of this peptide observed. Indeed, in Alzheimer's dementia, the reduced CSF concentrations of somatostatin (Bissette et al., 1986) are accompanied by a reduced cortical concentration of somatostatin (Davies et al., 1988).

The extent to which alterations in somatostatin secretion represent one of the major pathophysiological processes in affective disorders is an area that requires further investigation. Somatostatin does inhibit stimulated ACTH secretion (Heisler et al., 1982; Petraglia et al., 1986) as well as stress-induced CRF secretion (Brown et al., 1984) and, therefore, decreased somatostatin availability could contribute to the hypercortisolemia observed in major depression. In fact, decreased CSF somatostatin concentrations have been associated with dexamethasone nonsuppression in some (Doran et al., 1986), but not all (Agren and Lundqvist, 1984; Bissette et al., 1986), studies of depressed, schizophrenic patients (Doran et al., 1986), Alzheimer's patients (Serby et al., 1986), and patients with anorexia nervosa (Kaye et al., 1988). The lack of diagnostic specificity of low CSF somatostatin concentrations for depression as illustrated by the similarly low levels of somatostatin observed in Alzheimer's disease, schizophrenia, and anorexia nervosa (Gerner and Yamada, 1982; Bissette et al., 1986; Rubinow et al., 1983), coupled with the observation that hypercortisolemia can, in and of itself, decrease CSF somatostatin levels (Wolkowitz et al., 1987; Kling et al., 1991), and confound efforts to assess the exact role of this tetradecapeptide in the pathophysiology of major depressive disorder.

Studies of somatostatin in depression can potentially contribute to our understanding of the pathophysiology of affective disorders relative to its relation to anxiety disorders, regardless of whether this peptide is directly involved in the etiology of major depressive disorder. In contrast to the universal findings of decreased CSF somatostatin concentrations in depressed patients, the concentration of this peptide appears to be normal in panic disorder (Vecsei and Widerlov,1988; Pitkanen et al., 1989). Thus, preclinical and clinical studies of this peptide, especially its relation to other neuromodulatory peptides (such as CRF), may allow elucidation of separate pathophysiological mechanisms of affective and anxiety disorders.

VII. VASOPRESSIN IN AFFECTIVE AND ANXIETY DISORDERS

Vasopressin is a nonapeptide that has diverse actions both as a hormone and as a neuromodulator. This neuropeptide is synthesized primarily in the supraoptic (SON) and paraventricular nuclei (PVN) of the hypothalamus, and is released through separate pathways directly into the neurohypophyseal system (Morris et al., 1987;), anterior lobe of the pituitary and the spinal cord (Swanson and Sawchenko, 1980), third ventricular near the median eminence (Robinson and Zimmerman, 1973), and other brain areas, including the olfactory nucleus and pineal gland (Buijs, 1987). Vasopressin is also synthesized in other brain areas, such as the suprachiasmatic nucleus (Vandesande et al., 1975), the bed nucleus of the stria terminalis (Sofroniew, 1983), and the locus coeruleus, amygdala, and dorsomedial hypothalamus (Caffe and Van Leeuwen, 1983; Caffe et al., 1985). Other authors have provided an extensive review of vasopressin localization, synthesis, and release within the CNS (McDonald and Krishnan, 1991; Buijs, 1987).

A. Hormonal and Neuromodulatory Effects of Vasopressin: Potential Relevance of Preclinical Studies to Depression

The various hormonal effects of vasopressin are mediated in the periphery by distinct pathways. The primary hormonal actions of vasopressin are to regulate fluid and electrolytic balance, particularly under conditions of dehydration. Vasopressin acts primarily in the kidney to maintain body fluids at a constant osmolarity and volume (Valtin, 1987). However, this hormone is also a potent vasoconstrictor in the systemic circulation (Altura, 1977) and acts to increase blood pressure in dehydrated states (Cowley and Liard, 1987). Additional hormonal effects of vasopressin include stimulation of glucagon release and a direct action in the liver to promote glycogenolysis and gluconeogenesis (Spruce et al., 1985; Helms 1977).

Vasopressin is also involved in the regulation of HPA axis activity. Vasopressin both potentiates the effects of CRF and stimulates ACTH release directly from the pituitary (Hedge and Huffman, 1987). Modulation of vasopressin synthesis and release by glucocorticoid negative-feedback has also been demonstrated in both animals (Wolfson et al., 1985) and humans (Ahmed et al., 1967). Evidence that vasopressin release of pituitary ACTH is distinct from its effect on hypothalamic CRF release has more recently been provided (Widerlov et al., 1989).

In the last several years, there has been a growing focus on the CNS effects of vasopressin. Specifically, the finding that vasopressin can directly increase the firing rate of hippocampal neurons has suggested that this peptide may also function as a neurotransmitter (Muhlethaler and Dreifuss, 1982). Furthermore, several investigators have observed behavioral effects of vasopressin, primarily on learning and memory processes. In a series of elegant studies, DeWied and his colleagues (1965, 1975) demonstrated that vasopressin depletion, induced either by neurohypophysectomy or present in the Brattleboro rat (i.e., a rat strain that lacks vasopressin owing to a genetic defect), is associated with a slower extinction of avoidance behavior, a phenomenon reversed by vasopressin administration. Vasopressin injections into limbic areas, such as the hippocampal dentate gyrus, produce enhanced memory consolidation of avoidance behaviors (Kovacs et al., 1977).

B. Clinical Studies of Vasopressin in Affective Disorders

Studies in humans have tended to support the idea that vasopressin may be involved in improving memory and learning (reviewed by Jolles, 1987). Because memory alterations and other cognitive deficits occur in affective illness, a role for vasopressin in affective disorders was postulated many years ago (Gold and Goodwin, 1978). The hypothesis that vasopressin may be involved in the pathophysiology of affective disorders has also been supported by the fact that, in addition to effects on cognition and memory, the peptide also modulates other CNS processes altered in affective illness, such as pain sensitivity, circadian rhythmicity, and rapid eye movement (REM) sleep (Gold and Goodwin, 1978).

Evidence supporting a role for vasopressin in depression came from two lines of investigation. First, is the observation that vasopressin, at least partially, improves memory and other depressive symptoms in affective disordered patients (Gold et al., 1979). Second, are studies showing that CSF concentrations of vasopressin are reduced in patients with nonpsychotic bipolar depression (Gold et al., 1981, 1983b; Gjerris et al., 1985a). The decrease in vasopressin appears to be state-dependent. Because CSF vasopressin is believed to be distinct from vasopressin released from PVN and SON neurons into the hypophyseal–portal systems (Ang and Jenkins, 1982), the foregoing finding implicates central vasopressin pathways in affective disorders.

There is also evidence that certain peripheral vasopressin pathways may be altered in affective disorders. Gold et al. (1983b) measured plasma vasopressin in response to systemic saline injections in affectively disordered patients. The results of this saline "challenge" test indicated that depressed bipolar patients showed a decreased plasma vasopressin secretion compared with patients with bipolar manic disorder (Gold et al., 1983b). Consistent with this finding, Laruelle et al. (1990) observed significant differences in plasma levels of vasopressin neurophysin in depression. However, it is likely that only certain peripheral vasopressin pathways are involved in mediating this effect and specifically, that vasopressin neurons involved in the regulation of the HPA axis are not involved. The effects of vasopressin in potentiating CRF and in directly stimulating ACTH release from the pituitary, for example, would not be consistent with Gold and associates' findings. Therefore, the findings suggest that only some peripheral pathways may be altered.

The role of vasopressin in affective disorder may prove to be indirect. For example, Gold and his colleagues have suggested that alterations in vasopressin may be linked with catecholamine alterations in affective disorder (Gold and Goodwin, 1978). Furthermore, the specificity of the finding of decreased vasopressin concentrations in affective disorder is unclear. There is evidence, for example, that CSF concentrations of vasopressin are reduced in schizophrenia (van Kammen et al., 1981). A role for vasopressin in the pathophysiology of anorexia nervosa and bulimia nervosa has also been hypothesized (Gold et al., 1983a). No data now exist concerning vasopressin secretion in anxiety disorders.

VIII. THYROTROPIN-RELEASING HORMONE IN DEPRESSION AND ANXIETY DISORDERS

Thyrotropin-releasing hormone (TRH) was the first hypothalamic-releasing hormone to be isolated and characterized (Bowers et al., 1970; Burges et al., 1970). This tripeptide is found in high concentration in the hypothalamus, but is also found in substantial quantities in other brain regions (Jackson and Reichlin, 1974; Oliver et al., 1974; Winokur and Utiger, 1974). It is released from nerve terminals in the median eminence of the hypothalamus and transported from the primary plexus of the hypothalamohypophyseal portal system to the anterior pituitary gland where it results in the increased synthesis and release of thyrotropin-stimulating hormone (TSH). The anterior pituitary hormone, in turn, stimulates the synthesis and release of the major thyroid hormones triiodothyronine (T_3) and thyroxine (T_4). In addition to exerting their well-described metabolic effects, T_3 and T_4 feed directly back to the adenohypophysis and hypothalamus to partially regulate the synthesis and release of TRH and TSH (Griffiths, 1985).

A. Evidence for an Antidepressant Effect of Thyrotropin-Releasing Hormone

Even before the extrahypothalamic localization of the neuropeptide was discovered, Plotnikoff et al. (1972) demonstrated CNS-mediated behavioral effects of TRH. In this study, TRH was injected intraperitoneally into mice that had been pretreated with a monoamine oxidase inhibitor. The TRH produced a significant enhancement of the spontaneous motor activity observed following administration of L-3,4-dihydroxyphenylalanine (L-dopa) and a monoamine oxidase inhibitor. Importantly, the behavioral effects of TRH in this paradigm occurred even in mice that had previously undergone hypophysectomy, suggesting that the motor-enhancing effects of this peptide were mediated by the CNS, rather than by the pituitary–thyroid axis.

Subsequently, two reports suggested an antidepressant effect of TRH in drug-free depressed patients. Kastin et al. (1972) and Prange et al. (1972) reported that administration of a bolus of TRH produced a rapid and significant improvement in depressive symptomatology. This effect, however, was short-lasting. Itil et al. (1975) also reported improvement in motivational deficits in depressed patients and demonstrated concurrent activation of electroencephalographic (EEG) patterns similar to those observed with antidepressants. Most studies, however, failed to demonstrate significant antidepressant effects of TRH.

B. Thyrotropin-Releasing Hormone Alterations in Major Depressive Disorder

In light of the possibility raised by the foregoing studies that TRH may have antidepressant effects, it is certainly of interest that the CSF concentration of this peptide is *increased* in depressed patients (Kirkegaard et al., 1981; Banki et al., 1988). These results, therefore, suggest CNS hypersecretion of TRH in major depressive disorder.

Hypersecretion of TRH in depressed patients should not be surprising because TRH hypersecretion may result in TRH receptor down-regulation in the anterior pituitary thyrotrophs, and is theoretically consistent with the blunted TSH response to TRH that is seen in approximately 25% of depressed patients (Loosen, 1985; Loosen and Prange, 1982). Although no actual correlations between CSF TRH concentrations and the TSH response to TRH have been observed in depression, such a relation was recently observed in alcoholic patients (Adinoff et al., 1991).

Interestingly, there is a subset of depressed patients that show the opposite response to TRH administration (i.e., an exaggerated TSH response; Gold et al., 1982; Extein et al., 1981; Nemeroff et al., 1985). This response is seen in about 10–15% of depressed patients and is consistent with the idea that a proportion of depressed patients exhibit subclinical hypothyroidism.

Why some depressed patients exhibit an attenuated response to TRH, whereas others show an exaggerated response, remains unclear. What is clearly needed is a longitudinal study of depressed patients in which hypothalamic–pituitary–thyroid axis testing could be conducted over time to determine whether patients exhibiting an exaggerated response to TRH in time become TSH blunters.

C. Thyrotropin-Releasing Hormone Alterations in Anxiety Disorders

A blunted TSH response to TRH has been observed in some panic disorder patients (Roy-Byrne et al., 1986; Gillette et al., 1989). However, in one of these studies, the blunted TSH response to TRH in panic was present only in patients with concurrent major depression (Gillette et al., 1989). Another study suggested that, in the absence of clinically overt thyroid disease, the TSH response to TRH is normal in panic disorder (Stein and Uhde, 1988).

A normal TSH response to TRH has also been observed in PTSD (Kosten et al., 1990). In fact, 36% of the subjects appeared to show an exaggerated response to TRH. Because TSH blunting in depression may result from norepinephrine hyposecretion, Kosten et al. (1990) hypothesized that the normal TSH response to TRH they observed may have resulted from norepinephrine hyperactivity in this disorder. Clearly, the blunted TSH response to TRH may serve to differentiate between anxiety and affective disorders.

IX. ß-ENDORPHIN IN DEPRESSION AND ANXIETY DISORDERS

One of the major reasons for an interest in opiates in depression and anxiety disorders was the observation that opiates may have antidepressant effects. The mood-elevating effects of opium, for example, were described centuries ago. Kraepelin recommended this treatment for depressed patients as early as 1905. More recent studies also suggested an antidepressant effect of ß-endorphin. ß-Endorphin is an opioid peptide localized in subcortical structures of the brain, including limbic and hypothalamic areas (Khachaturian et al., 1985), and in the anterior pituitary. In earlier open studies Kline et al. (1977) and Angst et al. (1979) reported significant improvement in depressed patients following intravenous ß-endorphin administration. These findings were substantiated by Catlin et al. (1980) and Gerner et al. (1980) in controlled trials. Others could not confirm these findings, and it is unclear if intravenously administered ß-endorphin even enters the brain (see Nemeroff and Bissette, 1986, for a comprehensive review of these studies). Although opiates are not practically useful treatments for depression because of their dependence–addictive nature or liability, such studies have been informative in suggesting a role of endogenous opiates in depression. The observation that the opiate antagonist nalaxone does not affect mood (Davis et al., 1977; Emrich et al., 1979; Terenius et al., 1977), has weakened the hypothesis of an opiate modulation of depression. However, in two studies, that used very high doses, Cohen et al. observed increases in anxiety in normal controls (1983) and an augmentation of symptom severity in depressed patients (1984).

Studies of CSF ß-endorphin immunoreactivity in depression and anxiety disorders have, by and large, yielded inconclusive results for a role of this peptide in these disorders. Most studies (Black et al., 1986; Pickar et al., 1982; Davis, 1982; Naber et al., 1981; Garber and Sharp, 1982; France and Urban, 1991) have revealed normal CSF concentrations of ß-endorphin in depressed patients. However, an early study reported an increased concentration of ß-endorphin in CSF (Terenius et al., 1976), whereas another showed a correlation between CSF ß-endorphin levels and depression in patients with chronic pain (Almay et al., 1978). There is one report showing increased CSF ß-endorphin concentrations in panic disorder patients (Pitkanen et al., 1989).

ß-Endorphin is also present in large concentrations in the pituitary, and it can readily be measured in plasma. This peptide shares the same precursor molecule (proopiomelanocortin) with ACTH and is thought to be under a physiological regulation similar to that of ACTH (Guillemin et al., 1977). Studies of plasma ß-endorphin in depression are particularly interesting in light of the controversy concerning the origin of hypercortisolism in this disorder. If the abnormality resulting in hypercortisolemia is of central origin, as suggested by many investigators, plasma levels of ß-endorphin should be increased in depression. However, if hypercortisolism in depression is mediated by pituitary ACTH secretion, ß-endorphin levels would not necessarily be expected to correlate with other HPA axis measures. Interestingly, although most all studies have clearly shown evidence for HPA hyperactivity in major depressive disorder, plasma ß-endorphin has not been consistently altered in this disorder. Some investigators have shown increased concentrations (Risch 1982; Genazzani et al., 1984; Karkkainen et al., 1987), whereas others have found normal concentrations (Cohen et al., 1984; Alexopolous et al., 1983; Daly et al., 1987; Maes et al., 1990a) of this peptide.

Although baseline concentrations of plasma ß-endorphin have not produced definitive information, recent studies have suggested that measurement of ß-endorphin levels after dexamethasone administration may enhance our understanding of HPA dysfunction in depression and, ultimately, may be more specific indexes of HPA abnormalities in depressed patients than postdexamethasone cortisol levels (Maes et al., 1990a,b). In one study, postdexamethsone cortisol levels were significantly correlated with postdexamethasone ß-endorphin levels (Maes et al., 1990b). More recently, Young et al. (1991) measured ß-endorphin–ß-lipotropin secretion in response to hydrocortisone sodium succinate infusion to characterize glucocorticoid fast-feedback mechanisms in major depressive disorder. Depressed patients did not show the normal rise in ß-endorphin–ß-lipotropin secretion in response to hydrocortisone infusion, suggesting an absence of glucocorticoid fast-feedback mechanisms in major depression. Fast-feedback is believed to involve hypothalamic and hippocampal brain centers, rather than the pituitary; thus, the findings suggest a role for central regulation of glucocorticoid fast-feedback in depression.

X. CHOLECYSTOKININ IN DEPRESSION AND ANXIETY DISORDERS

Cholecystokinin (CCK), in a 33-amino acid, containing gut–brain peptide, also exists in tetrapeptide and octapeptide forms. Long known as a gastrointestinal peptide, CCK was discovered to exist in the CNS (Beinfeld, 1983; Vanderhaegen et al., 1975). It has now been localized in several brain regions, including the cerebral cortex, amygdala, and hippocampus (Roberts et al., 1982; Reeve et al., 1984) and, importantly, is colocalized with other neurotransmitters, particularly, dopamine in the midbrain (Hokfelt et al., 1980).

Although earlier studies focused on a role for CCK in satiety, nociception, and schizophrenia, recent evidence suggests that this peptide may be involved in anxiety disorders. Preclinical studies have shown that microiontophoretic application of both CCK-8 and CCK-4 results in electrophysiological excitation in several brain regions and these effects are reversed by benzodiazepines (Bradwejn and de Montigny, 1984, 1985; Bouthillier and de Montigny, 1988). Administration of CCK into the amygdala produced anxiety in behavioral paradigms (Hendrie and Dourish, 1990).

Studies of humans have suggested that CCK-4 produces symptoms of anxiety (de Montigny, 1989) and actual panic attacks (Bradwejn et al., 1990, 1991) in both normal controls and panic disorder patients. Panic disorder patients are unusually susceptible to the anxiogenic effects of this peptide. The induction of panic by CCK-4 injection was 100% for panic disorder patients, compared with 50% for controls. It remains to be determined whether endogenous CCK neuronal activity is abnormally altered in panic disorder as well as the extent to which an enhanced sensitivity to the anxiogenic effects of CCK is specific to this psychiatric disorder.

Currently, there is no evidence that CCK may be altered in affective disorders; several studies have reported normal CSF concentrations of CCK in depression (Gjerris et al., 1984, 1985b; Gerner and Yamada, 1982). However, there are as yet no published studies of the effect of CCK on psychiatric symptoms in depressed patients. Studies examining the effects of CCK injection in depressed patients, as well as studies of CSF CCK in anxiety-disordered patients are needed to clarify the role of this peptide in the pathogenesis of anxiety or depression.

XI. NEUROPEPTIDE Y IN DEPRESSION AND ANXIETY DISORDERS

Neuropeptide Y (NPY) is a 36-amino acid peptide that has been isolated relatively recently (Tatemoto and Mutt, 1980). This peptide is localized in large concentrations in the peripheral (Lundberg et al., 1982) as well as central (Adrian et al., 1983) nervous system. Specifically, the greatest concentrations of NYP exist in the hypothalamus, limbic areas, brain stem nuclei, and cortex.

The primary functions of hypothalamic NPY appear to be in regulating hormonal secretion (Kalra and Crowley, 1984), circadian rhythm (Albers et al., 1984), and food intake (Levine and Morley, 1984). The colocalization of NPY and other neuropeptides and neurotransmitters, such as somatostatin and norepinephrine (for review, see Allen and Bloom, 1986; McDonald, 1991), in brain regions such as the locus coeruleus, has further suggested that this neuropeptide may be involved in modulating a wide variety of behaviors relevant to psychiatric illness.

Preclinical studies have demonstrated behavioral effects of centrally administered NPY related to both depression and anxiety. In particular, intracerebroventricular NPY injection produces sedation (Fuxe et al., 1983; Heilig and Murison, 1987) that may be related to anxiolytic actions (Heilig et al., 1989).

Human studies have produced conflicting findings concerning NPY alterations in psychiatric illness. To date, two studies have examined NPY concentrations in CSF. Widerlov et al. (1988b) reported that the concentration of this peptide was reduced in patients with depression. Berrettini et al. (1987) failed to replicate this finding. Future studies of NPY in depressed and anxious patients seem warranted.

XII. SIMILARITIES AND DIFFERENCES BETWEEN NEUROPEPTIDE ALTERATIONS IN AFFECTIVE AND ANXIETY DISORDERS

After reviewing the evidence for peptide alterations in depression and anxiety, it is interesting that many of the peptide differences observed in depression have also been observed in anxiety. However, it is striking that not all peptides that are altered in depression are altered in anxiety, and vice versa. Given this observation, that both similarities and differences appear to exist between the two groups of disorders, the study of neuropeptides may allow us to ultimately address the extent of which affective and anxiety disorders share a common pathophysiology, and the extent to which they are pathophysiologically distinct. The available data are illustrated in Table 1.

There has been much speculation concerning the possibility of a shared etiology or pathophysiology between depressive and anxiety disorders (Butler and Nemeroff, 1991; Yehuda et al., 1991a). This is supported primarily by studies documenting an unusually high comorbidity and symptom overlap between the two disorders. To the extent that there are specific biological alterations present in affective and anxiety disorders, one might argue for their distinctness. Furthermore, despite the observation that some neuropeptides produce symptoms consistent with both depression and anxiety disorders, the lack of a consistent profile of neuropeptide alterations in these two disorders may suggest important pathophysiological differences between them. When a specific peptide is altered similarly in affective and anxiety disorders, rather than suggesting that the two disorders share common etiological mechanisms, this finding may explain the high incidence of comorbidity between depressive and anxiety disorders.

An important point borne out from studies of neuropeptides in psychiatric disorders is that disorders may share a common neuroendocrine alteration and still be pathophysiologically distinct. For example, CRF may be increased in both affective and anxiety disorders, but in different locations, and for different reasons. Ultimately, more sophisticated neuropeptide and neuroendocrine studies may provide some important keys for these issues.

Table 1 Summary of Findings Concerning Neuropeptide Alterations in Depression and Anxiety Disorders

Neuropeptide	Depression	Panic	PTSD
CRF			
[CSF]	↑	Unknown	Unknown
Stimulation test	↓ ACTH	↓ ACTH	↓ ACTH
Somatostatin			
[CSF]	↓	Normal	Unknown
Vasopressin			
[CSF]	↓	Unknown	Unknown
IV administration	↑ Memory	Unknown	Unknown
TRH			
[CSF]	↑	Normal	Unknown
Stimulation test	↓TSH[a]	Normal	↑ TSH
β-Endorphin			
[CSF]	Normal	↑	Unknown
CCK			
[CSF]	Normal	Unknown	Unknown
IV administration	Unknown	↑ Panic	Unknown
NPY			
[CSF]	↓	Unknown	Unknown

[a] The response to TRH is also increased in a small subset of depressed patients.

The differences between major depressive disorder and posttraumatic stress disorder have been documented in studies of the HPA axis (Yehuda et al., in press,a). An interesting question that arises concerns the similarities between posttraumatic stress disorder and other anxiety disorders, such as panic disorder. There is evidence to suggest similarities between panic disorder and posttraumatic stress disorder in noradrenergic dysregulation. For example, Southwick et al. (1991) reported an increased frequency of panic attacks in both panic disorder and PTSD patients following intravenous infusion of the α_2-antagonist yohimbine. A subset of PTSD patients also reported experiencing flashbacks during the yohimbine infusion. Conversely, the robust findings of enhanced sensitivity of the HPA negative-feedback system in PTSD has not been observed in studies of panic disorder. However, interestingly, panic disordered patients appear to have "normal" pituitary–adrenal response in some aspects (i.e., hypercortisolemia does not appear to be a major neuroendocrine abnormality in panic disorder). However, similar to posttraumatic stress disorder, panic patients show a blunted ACTH response to CRF. Thus, it may be that studies employing methods targeted specifically toward elucidating hypersensitivity of the HPA axis (i.e., studies employing the low-dose dexamethasone suppression test and studies of basal glucocorticoid receptor activity), may indeed show that PTSD and other anxiety disorders are related but are distinct pathophysiologically from major depressive disorder. Furthermore, the findings of neuropeptide alterations in panic disorder suggest that CSF and plasma neuropeptide measurements, wherever possible, should be employed in the study of the biology of posttraumatic stress disorder.

XIII. FUTURE STRATEGIES FOR FURTHER EXPLORING NEUROPEPTIDE ALTERATIONS IN PSYCHIATRIC ILLNESS

Neuropeptide systems are relevant to the study of psychiatric disorders because they are neurotransmitters in many CNS neurons. It is possible, given the methodological limitations of peptide studies to date, that in later years we will consider the studies reviewed in this chapter quite primitive. However, regardless of our current inability to precisely measure neuropeptide neuronal activity and modulation of specific behaviors and symptoms in humans, it is striking that clear reproducible differences in neuropeptide modulation between depressed patients, anxious patients, and normal controls have been observed, even in the relatively rudimentary examinations that have been performed to date and, furthermore, that preclinical data examining the effect of neuropeptides on behavior have often correctly predicted the direction of neuropeptide alterations in almost every instance.

Clearly, future peptide research will be significantly enhanced by technological advances that may help overcome some of the current methodological limitations. An important future direction is in the development of methods for measuring the turnover of neuropeptides. At the present time it is not possible to reliably measure neuropeptide turnover in either humans or animals. It is, however, theoretically possible to obtain estimates of brain neuropeptide biosynthesis. Although this can be achieved with in situ hybridization techniques with complementary DNA (cDNA) probes to visualize or biochemically measure mRNA in microscopic sections of the brain, such techniques have not yet been applied to human studies.

Another future direction is in the development of pharmacological neuropeptide agonists and antagonists that permeate the blood–brain barrier. In particular, nonpeptide lipid-soluble agonists or antagonists that have high affinity for peptide receptors would be useful for examining the effect of peptides on behavior. The development of neuropeptide agonists and antagonists could potentially be employed to study neuropeptide receptors by brain-imaging techniques. Such tools would permit direct testing of hypotheses concerning a role for neuropeptides in anxiety and affective disorders.

ACKNOWLEDGMENTS

Supported in part by NIMH MH-42088, MH-46791 (Dr. Nemeroff), and MH-49536 (Dr. Yehuda).

REFERENCES

B. Adinoff, C. B. Nemeroff, G. Bisette et al., Inverse relationships between CSF TRH-concentrations and the TSH response to TRH in abstinent alcoholics, *Am. J. Psychiatry 148*: 1586 (1991).

T. E. Adrian, J. M. Allen, and S. R. Bloom, Neuropeptide Y distribution in human brain, *Nature, 306*: 584 (1983).

H. Agren, and G. Lundqvist, Low levels of somatostatin in human CSF mark depressive epiodes, *Psychoneuroendocrinology, 9*: 233 (1984).

A. B. J. Ahmed, B. C. George, C. Gonzalez-Auvert et al., Increased plasma arginine vasopressin in clinical adrenocorticol insufficiency and its inhibition by glucosteroids, *J. Clin. Invest., 46*: 111 (1967).

H. E. Albers, C. F. Ferris, S. E. Leeman, and B. D. Goldman, Avian pancreatic polypeptide shifts hamster circadian rhythms when microinjected into the suprachiasmatic region, *Science, 223*: 833 (1984).

G. S. Alexopolous, C. E. Inturrisi, R. Lipman et al., Plasma immunoreactive ß-endorphin levels in depression, *Arch. Gen. Psychiatry, 40*: 181 (1983).

J. M. Allen and S. R. Bloom, Neuropeptide Y: A putative neurotransmitter, *Neurochem. Int., 8*: 1 (1986).

B. G. L. Almay, F. Johansson, L. von Knorring et al., Endorphins in chronic pain: I. Differences in CSF endorphin levels between organic and psychogenic pain syndromes, *Pain, 5*: 153 (1978).

B. M. L. Altura, Comparative cellular and pharmacologic actions of neurohypophyseal hormones on smooth muscle, *Fed. Proc., 36*: 1,840 (1977).

J. D. Amsterdam, G. Maislin, A. Winokur et al., Pituitary and adrenocortical responses to the ovine corticotrophin-releasing hormone in depressed patients and healthy volunteers, *Arch. Gen. Psychiatry, 44*: 775 (1987).

V. T. Y. Ang and J. S. Jenkins, Blood–cerebrospinal fluid barrier to arginine-vasopressin, desmopressin and desglycinamide arginine-vasopressin in the dog, *J. Endocrinol., 93*: 319 (1982).

J. Angst, V. Auenrieth, F. Brem et al., Preliminary results of treatment with ß-endorphin in depression, *Endorphins in Mental Health Research* (E. Usdin, W. E. Bunney, and N. S. Kline, eds.), Oxford University Press, New York, pp. 518–528 (1979).

G. Aponte, P. Leung, D. Gross et al., Effects of somatostatin on food intake in rats, *Life Sci., 35*: 741 (1984).

M. Arato, C. M. Banki, C. B. Nemeroff et al., Hypothalamic–pituitary–adrenal axis and suicide, *Psychobiology of Suicidal Behavior* (J. J. Mann and M. Stanley, eds.), New York Academy of Sciences, New York, pp. 263–270 (1986).

M. Arato, C. M. Banki, G. Bissette et al., Elevated CSF CRF in suicide victims, *Biol. Psychiatry, 25*: 355 (1989).

C. M. Banki, G. Bissette, M. Arato et al., CSF corticotrophin-releasing factor-like immunoreactivity in depression and schizophrenia, *Am. J. Psychiatry, 144:* 873 (1987).
C. M. Banki, G. Bissette, M. Arato, and C. B. Nemeroff, Elevation of immunoreactive CSF TRH in depressed patients, *Am. J. Psychiatry, 145*: 1526 (1988).
M. C. Beinfeld, Cholecystokinin in the central nervous system: A minireview, *Neuropeptide 3*: 411 (1983).
C. W. Berridge, and A. J. Dunn, Corticotrophin-releasing factor elicits naloxone sensitive stress-like alterations in exploratory behavior in mice, *Regul. Peptides, 16*: 83 (1986).
C. W. Berridge, and A. J. Dunn, A corticotrophin-releasing factor antagonist reverses the stress-induced changes of exploratory behavior in mice, *Horm. Behav., 21*: 393 (1987).
W. H. Berrettini, A. R. Doran, J. Kelsoe et al., Cerebrospinal fluid neuropeptide Y in depression and schizophrenia, *Neuropsychopharmacology, 1*: 81 (1987).
G. Bissette, E. Widerlov, H. Walleus et al., Alterations in cerebrospinal fluid concentrations of somatostatin-like immunoreactivity in neuropsychiatric disorders, *Arch. Gen. Psychiatry, 43*: 1148 (1986).
O. M. Black, H. T. Ballantine, Jr., D. B. Carr et al., ß-Endorphin and somatostatin concentrations in the ventricular cerebrospinal fluid of patients with affective disorder, *Biol. Psychiatry, 21*: 1077 (1986).
A. Bouthhillier and C. de Montigny, Long-term benzodiazepine treatment reduced neuronal responsiveness to cholecystokinin: An electrophysiological study in the rat, *Eur. J. Pharmacol., 151*: 135 (1988).
C. Y. Bowers, A. V. Schally, D. S. Schalach et al., Activity and specificity of synthetic thyrotropin-releasing hormone in man, *Biochem. Biophys. Res. Commun., 39*: 352 (1970).
J. Bradwejn, and C. deMontigny, Benzodiazepines antagonize cholecystokinin-induced activation of rat hippocampal neurons, *Nature, 312*: 363 (1984).
J. Bradwejn, and C. deMontigny, Effects of PK 8165, a partial benzodiazepine receptor agonist, on cholecystokinin-induced activation of hippocampal pyramidal neurons: A microiontophoretic study in the rat, *Eur. J. Pharmacol., 112*: 415 (1985).
J. Bradwejn, D. Koszycki, and C. Shriqui, Enhanced sensitivity of cholecystokinin tetrapeptide in panic disorder: Clinical and behavioral findings, *Arch. Gen. Psychiatry, 48*: 603 (1991).
J. Bradwejn, D. Koszycki, and G. Meterissian, Cholecystokinin tetrapeptide induces panic attacks in patients with panic disorder, *Can. J. Psychiatry, 35*: 83 (1990).
F. Brambilla, A. R. Genazzani, F. Facchinett et al,. ß-Endorphin and ß-lipotropin plasma levels in chronic schizophrenia, primary affective disorders and secondary affective disorders, *Psychoneuroendocrinology, 6*: 321 (1981).
P. Brazeau, W. Vale, R. Burgus et al., Hypothalamic polypeptide that inhibits the secretion of immunoreactive pituitary growth hormone, *Science, 197*: 77 (1973).
M. Bridges, V. K. Yeragani, J. M. Rainey et al., Dexamethasone suppression test in patients with panic attacks, *Biol. Psychiatry, 21*: 853 (1986).
D. R. Britton, M. Varela, A. Garcia, and M. Rosenthal, Dexamethasone suppresses pituitary–adrenal but not behavioral effects of centrally administrated CRF, *Life Sci., 38*: 211 (1986c).
D. R. Britton, G. F. Koob, J. Rivier, and W. Vale, Intraventricular corticotropin-releasing factor enhances behavioral effects of novelty, *Life Sci., 31*: 363 (1982).
K. T. Britton, J. Morgan, J. Rivier et al., Chlordiazepoxide attenuates response suppression induced by corticotropin-releasing factor in the conflict test, *Psychopharmacology, 86*: 170 (1985).
K. T. Britton, G. Lee, R. Dana, et al., Activating and "anxiogenic" effects of corticotropin releasing factor are not inhibited by blockade of pituitary–adrenal system with dexamethasone, *Life Sci., 39:* 1281 (1986a).
K. T. Britton, G. Lee, W. Vale et al., Corticotropin-releasing factor (CRF) receptor antagonist blocks activating and anxiogenic actions of CRF in the rat, *Brain Res., 369*: 303 (1986b).

M. R. Brown, L. A. Fisher, J. River et al., Corticotropin-releasing factor: Effects on the sympathetic nervous system and oxygen consumption, *Life Sci, 30*: 207 (1982).

M. Brown, Corticotropin-releasing factor: Central nervous system sites of action, *Brain Res., 399*: 10 (1987).

M. R. Brown, C. Rivier, and W. Vale, Central nervous system regulation of adrenocorticotropin secretion: Role of somatostatin, *Endocrinology, 114*: 1546 (1984).

R. M. Buijs, Vasopressin localization and putative functions in the brain, *Vasopressin: Principles and Properties* (D. M. Gash and G. J. Boer, eds.), Plenum Press, New York, pp. 91–116 (1987).

R. Burges, T. E. Dunn, D. Desideris et al., Characterization of ovine hypothalamic hypophysiotropic TSH-releasing factor, *Nature, 226*: 321 (1970).

P. D. Butler, and C. B. Nemeroff, Corticotropin-releasing factor as a possible cause of comorbidity in anxiety and depressive disorders, *Comorbidity of Mood and Anxiety Disorders* (J. D. Maser and C. R. Cloninger, eds.), American Psychiatric Press, Washington, D.C., pp. 413–438 (1990).

P. D. Butler, J. M. Weiss, J. C. Stout, and C. B. Nemeroff, Corticotropin-releasing-factor produces fear-enhancing behavioral activation effects following infusion into the locus coeruleus, *J. Neurosci., 10*: 176 (1990).

A. R. Caffe, and R. W. Van Leeuwen, Vasopressin-immunoreactive cells in the dorsomedial hypothalamic region, medial amygdaloid nucleus and locus coeruleus of the rat, *Cell Tissue Res., 233*: 23 (1983).

A. R. Caffe, F. W. Van Leeuwen, R. M. Buijs et al., Co-existence of vasopressin, neurophysin and noradrenaline immunoreactivity in medium-sized cells of the locus coeruleus and subcoeruleus in the rat, *Brain Res., 338*: 160 (1985).

B. J. Carroll, G. C. Curtis, D. M. Davies et al., Urinary free cortisol excretion in depression, *Psychol. Med., 6*: 43 (1976).

B. J. Carroll, M. Feinberg, J. F. Greden et al., A specific laboratory test for the diagnosis of melancholia, *Arch. Gen. Psychiatry, 38*: 15 (1981).

D. H. Catlin, D. A. Gorelick, R. H. Gerner et al., Clinical effects of ß-endorphin infusions, *Advances in Biochemical Psychopharmacology,* Vol. 22, *Neural Peptides and Neuronal Communication* (E. Costa and E. M. Trabucchi, eds.), Raven Press, New York, pp. 465–472 (1980).

P. B. Chappell, M. A. Smithe, C. D. Kilts et al., Alterations in corticotropin-releasing factor-like immunoreactivity in discrete rat brain regions after acute and chronic stress, *J. Neurosci., 6*: 2908 (1986).

B. G. Charleton, C. Wright, and A. Leake, Somatostatin content and receptors in the cerebral cortex of depressed and control subjects, *J. Neurol. Neurosurg. Psychiatry, 51*: 719 (1988).

B. G. Charleton, A. Leake, N. Ferrier et al., Corticotropin releasing factor in plasma of depressed patients and controls, *Lancet, 1*: 161 (1986).

M. R. Cohen, R. M. Cohen, D. Pickar et al., High dose naloxone infusions in normals: Dose-dependent behavioral, hormonal, and physiological responses, *Arch. Gen. Psychiatry, 40*: 613 (1983).

M. R. Cohen, D. Pickar, I. Extein et al., Plasma cortisol and ß-endorphin immunoreactivity in nonmajor and major depression, *Am. J. Psychiatry, 141*: 628 (1984).

B. J. Cole, and G. F. Koob, Propranolol antagonizes the enhanced conditioned fear produced by corticotropin-releasing factor, *J. Pharmacol. Exp. Ther., 247*: 902 (1988).

A. W. Cowley, and J. F. Liard, Cardiovascular actions of vasopressin, *Vasopressin, Principles and Properties* (D. M. gash and G. J. Boer, eds.), Plenum Press, New York, pp. 389–434 (1987).

G. C. Curtis, O. G. Cameron, and R. M. Nesse, The dexamethasone suppression test in panic disorder and agoraphobia, *Am. J. Psychiatry, 139*: 1043 (1982).

R. J. Daly, P. F. Duggan, P. J. Bracken et al., Plasma levels of ß-endorphin in depressed patients with and without pain, *Br. J. Psychiatry, 150*: 224 (1987).

J. Danguir, Intracerebroventricular infusion of somatostatin selectively increases paradoxical sleep in rats, *Brain Res., 367*: 26 (1986).

P. Davies, R. Katzman, and R. D. Terry, Reduced somatostatin-like immunoreactivity in cerebral cortex from cases of Alzheimer's disease and Alzheimer senile dementia, *Nature, 288*: 279 (1988).

G. C. Davis, W. E. Bunney, E. G. de Fraites et al., Intravenous naloxone administration in schizophrenia and affective illness, *Science, 197*: 74 (1977).

G. C. Davis, M. S. Buchsbaum, D. Naber et al., Altered pain perception and cerebrospinal endorphins in psychiatric illness, *Ann. N.Y. Acad. Sci., 398*: 2421 (1981).

J. R. Delfs, and M. A. Dichter, Effects of somatostatin on mammalian cortical neurons in culture: Physiological actions and unusual dose response characteristics, *J. Neurosci., 3*: 1176 (1983).

C. DeMontigny, Cholecytokinin-4 tetrapeptide induces panic-like attacks in healthy volunteers: Preliminary findings, *Arch. Gen. Psychiatry, 46*: 511 (1989).

E. B. DeSouza, Corticotropin-releasing factor receptors in the rat central nervous system: Characterization and regional distribution, *J. Neurosci., 7*: 88 (1987).

E. B. De Souza, M. H. Perrin, T. R. Insel et al., Corticotropin-releasing factor receptors in rat forebrain: Autoradiographic localization, *Science, 224*: 1449 (1984).

E. B. De Souza, T. R. Insel, M. H. Perrin et al., Corticotropin-releasing factor receptors are widely distributed within the rat central nervous system: An autoradiographic study, *J. Neurosci., 5*: 3189 (1985a).

E. B. De Souza, T. R. Insel, M. H. Perrin et al., Differential regulation of CRF receptors in anterior and intermediate lobes of pituitary and brain following adrenalectomy in rats, *Neurosci. Lett., 56*: 121 (1985b).

D. De Wied, The influence of the posterior and intermediate lobe of the pituitary and pituitary peptides on the maintenance of a conditioned avoidance response in rats, *Int. J. Neuropharmacol., 4*: 157 (1965).

D. DeWied, B. Bohus,. van Wimersma, and T. B. Griedanus, Memory deficit in rats with hereditary diabetes insipidus, *Brain Res., 85*: 152 (1975).

J. Dodd and J. S. Kelly, Is somatostatin an excitatory transmitter in the hippocampus? *Nature, 273:* 674 (1978).

R. A. Donald, C. Redekopp, V. Cameron et al., The hormonal actions of corticotropin-releasing factor in sheep: Effect of intravenous and intracerebroventricular injection, *Endocrinology, 113*: 866 (1983).

A. Doran, R. D. Rubinow, A. Roy et al., CSF somatostatin and abnormal response to dexamethasone administration in schizophrenic and depressed patients, *Arch. Gen. Psychiatry, 43*: 365 (1986).

A. J. Dunn, and C. W. Berridge, Corticotropin-releasing factor administration elicits a stress-like activation of cerebral catecholaminergic systems, *Pharmacol. Biochem. Behav., 27*: 685 (1987).

A. J. Dunn, and S. E. File, Corticotropin-releasing factor has an anxiogenic action in the social interaction test, *Horm. Behav., 21*: 193 (1987).

L. E. Eiden, The cell biology of the peptidergic neuron: An overview, *Neuropeptides in Psychiatric and Neurologic Disorders* (C. B. Nemeroff, ed.), Johns Hopkins University Press, Baltimore, pp. 1–7 (1988).

H. M. Emrich, C. Cording, S. Piree et al., Actions of naloxone in different types of psychoses, *Endorphins in Mental Health Research* (E. Usdin, W. E. Bunney, and N. S. Kline, eds.), Oxford University Press, New York, pp. 352–360 (1979).

D. L. Evans, and C. B. Nemeroff, Use of the dexamethasone suppression test using *DSM-III* criteria on an inpatient psychiatric unit, *Biol. Psychiatry, 18*: 505 (1983).

I. Extein, A. L. C. Pottash, and M. S. Gold, Relationship of thyrotropin-releasing hormone test and dexamethasone suppression test abnormalities in unipolar depression, *Psychiatry Res., 4*: 49 (1981).

G. Faludi, M. Kasko, A. Perenyi et al., The dexamethasone suppression test in panic disorder and major depressive episodes, *Biol. Psychiatry, 21*: 1008 (1986).

D. Fellman, C. Bugnon, and A. Gouger, A Immunocytochemical demonstration of corticoliberin-like immunoreactivity (CLI) in neurons of the rat amygdala central nucleus (ACN), *Neurosci. Lett., 34*: 253 (1982).

L. A. Fisher, J. Rivier, C. Rivier et al., Corticotropin-releasing-factor: Central effects of mean arterial pressure and heart rate in rats, *Endocrinology, 110*: 2222 (1982).

L. A. Fisher, G. Jesson, and M. R. Brown, Corticotropin-releasing-factor: Mechanisms to elevate mean arterial pressure and heart rate, *Regul. Peptides, 5*: 153 (1983).

R. D. France, and B. J. Urban, Cerebrospinal fluid concentrations of ß-endorphin in chronic low back pain patients: Influence of depression and treatment, *Psychosomatics, 32*: 72 (1991).

R. D. France, B. Urban, K. R. R. Krishman et al., CSF corticotropin-releasing factor-like immunoreactivity in chronic pain patients with and without major depression, *Biol. Psychiatry, 23*: 86 (1988).

K. Fuxe, L. F. Agnati, A. Harfstrand et al., Central administration of neuropeptide Y induces hypotension, bradyapnea, and EEG synchronization in the rat, *Acta Physiol. Scand., 118*: 189 (1983).

A. R. Genazzani, F. Petraglia, F. Facchinetti et al., Opioid plasma levels in primary affective disorders: Effect of desimipramine therapy, *Neuropsychobiology, 12*: 78 (1984).

R. H. Gerner, and T. Yamada, Altered neuropeptide concentrations in cerebrospinal fluid of psychiatric patients, *Brain Res., 238*: 298 (1982).

R. H. Gerner, D. H. Catlin, D. A. Gorelick et al., beta-Endorphin: Intravenous infusion causes behavioral change in psychiatric patients, *Arch. Gen. Psychiatry, 37*: 642 (1980).

G. M. Gillette, J. C. Garbutt, and D. E. Quade, TSH response to TRH in depression with and without panic attacks, *Am. J. Psychiatry, 146*: 743 (1989).

A. Gjerris, O. J. Rafaelsen, P. Vendsborg et al., Vasoactive intestinal polypeptide decreased in cerebrospinal fluid in atypical depression, *J. Affective Disord., 7*: 325 (1984).

A. Gjerris, M. Hammer, P. Vendsborg et al., Cerebrospinal fluid vasopressin—changes in depression, *Br. J. Psychiatry, 147*: 696 (1985a).

A. Gjerris, O. J. Rafaelson, A. S. Sorensen et al., Cholecystokinin and other neuropeptides in the cerebrospinal fluid in psychiatric disorders, *Nord. Psykiatr. Tidsskr., 39*(Suppl. 11): 45 (1985b).

P. W. Gold, G. Chrousos, C. Kellner et al., Psychiatric implications of basic and clinical studies with corticotropin-releasing factor, *Am. J. Psychiatry, 141*: 619 (1984).

P. W. Gold, and P. Chrousos, Clinical studies with corticotropin-releasing factor: Implications for the diagnosis and pathophysiology of depression, Cushing's disease and adrenal insufficiency, *Psychoneuroendocrinology, 10*: 401 (1985).

P. W. Gold, and F. K. Goodwin, Vasopressin in affective illness, *Lancet, 1*: 1233 (1978).

P. W. Gold, H. Weingartner, C. Ballenger et al., Effects of *l*-desamino-8-*p*-arginine vasoprsessin on behavior and cognition in primary affective disorder, *Lancet, 2*: 992 (1979).

P. W. Gold, F. K. Goodwin, R. M. Post, and G. L. Robertson, Vasopressin function in depression and mania, *Psychopharmacol. Bull., 17*: 7 (1981).

M. S. Gold, A. L. C. Pottash, and I. Extein, "Symptomless" autoimmune thyroiditis in depression, *Psychiatry Res., 6*: 261 (1982).

P. W. Gold, W. Kaye, G. L. Robertson et al., Abnormalities in plasma and cerebrospinal-fluid arginine vasopressin in patients with anorexia nervosa, *N. Engl. J. Med., 308*: 1117 (1983a).

P. W. Gold, G. L. Robertson, J. C. Ballenger et al., Neurohypophyseal function in affective illness, *Psychopharmacol. Bull., 19*: 426 (1983b).

P. W. Gold, D. L. Loriaux, A. Roy et al., Responses to corticotropin-releasing hormone in the hypercortisolism of depression and Cushing's disease, *N. Engl. J. Med., 314*: 1329 (1986).

S. Goldstein, U. Halbreich, G. Asnis et al., The hypothalamic–pituitary–adrenal system in panic disorder, *Am. J. Psychiatry, 144*: 1320 (1987).

G. J. Gormley, M. T. Lowy, A. T. Reder et al., Glucocorticoid receptors in depression: Relationship to the dexamethasone suppression test, *Am. J. Psychiatry, 142*: 1278 (1985).

B. A. Gosnell, J. E. Morley, A. S. Levine, A comparison of the effects of corticotropin-releasing factor and sauvagine on food intake., *Pharmacol. Biochem. Behav. 19*: 771 (1983).

E. C. Griffiths, Thyrotrophin releasing hormone: Endocrine and central effects, *Psychoneuroendocrinology, 10*: 225 (1985).

R. Guillemin, T. Vargo, J. Rossier et al., ß-Endorphin and adrenocorticotropin are secreted concomitantly by the pituitary gland, *Science, 197*: 1367 (1977).

V. Havlicek, M. Rezek, and H. Friesen, Somatostatin and thryotropin releasing hormone: central effect on sleep and motor system, *Pharmacol. Biochem. Behav., 4*: 455 (1976).

V. Havlicek, M. Rezek, L. Leybin et al., Analgesic effect of cerebral ventricular administration of somatostatin (SRIF), *Fed. Proc., 36*: 363 (1977).

G. A. Hedge, and L. J. Huffman, Vasopressin and endocrine function, *Vasopressin, Principles and Properties* (D. M. Gash and G. J. Doer, eds.), Plenum Press, New York, pp. 435–476 (1987).

M. Heilig, and R. Murson, Intracerebroventricular neuropeptide Y suppresses open field and home cage activity in the rat, *Regul. Peptide, 19*: 221 (1987).

M. Heilig, B. Soderpalm, J. A. Engel, and E. Widerlov, Centrally administered neuropeptide Y (NPY) produces anxiolytic-like effects in animal anxiety models, *Psychopharmacology, 98*: 524 (1989).

S. Heisler, T. Resisine, V. Hook et al., Somatostatin inhibits multireceptor stimulation of cyclic AMP formation and corticotropin secretion in mouse pituitary tumor cells, *Proc. Natl. Acad. Sci. USA, 79*: 6502 (1982).

D. A. Helms, Short-term hormonal control of hepatic carbohydrate and lipid catabolism, *FEBS Lett., 80*: 237 (1977).

C. A. Hendrie, and C. T. Dourish, Anxiolytic profile of the cholecystokinin antagonist devazepide in mice, *Br. J. Pharmacol., 99*(Suppl.): 138 (1990).

T. Hokfelt, J. F. Rehfeld, L. Skirboll et al., Evidence of coexistence of dopamine and CCK in meso-limbic neurons, *Nature 285*, 476 (1980).

T. Hokfelt, B. J. Everitt, T. Theodorsson-Norheim et al., Neurotensin and NPT-like immunoreactivities in central catecholamine neurons, *Neuropharmacology and Central Nervous System: Theoretical Aspects* (E. Usdin, A. Carlsson, and A. Dahlstron, eds.), Alan R. Liss, New York, pp. 231-237 (1984).

F. Holsboer, U. von Bardeleben, A. Gerken et al., Blunted corticotropin and normal cortisol responses to human corticotropin-releasing factor in depression, *N. Engl. J. Med., 311*: 1127 (1984).

T. M. Itil, C. D. Patterson, N. Polvan et al., Clinical and CSN effects of oral and intravenous thyrotropin-releasing hormone, *Psychopharmacol. Bull., 1*: 29 (1975).

I. M. D. Jackson, and S. Reichlin, Thyrotropin-releasing hormone (TRH): Distribution in the hypothalamic and extrahypothalamic brain tissue of mammalian and submammalian chordates. *Endocrinology 95*: 854 (1974).

J. Jolles, Vasopressin and human behavior, *Vasopressin: Principles and Properties* (D. M. Gash and G. J. Boer, eds.), Plenum Press, New York, pp. 549–578 (1987).

S. P. Kalra, and W. R. Crowley, Norepinephrine-like effects of neuropeptide Y on LH release in the rat, *Life Sci., 33*: 1173 (1984).

J. Karkkainen, T. Laatikainen, H. Naukkarinene et al., Plasma endogenous and dexamethasone suppression test in depression, *Psychiatry Res., 21*: 151 (1987).

A. J. Kastin, D. S. Schalch, R. H. Ehrensing et al., Improvement in mental depression with decreased thyrotropin response after administration of thyrotropin-releasing hormone, *Lancet, 2*: 740 (1972).

R. G. Kathol, R. S. Jaeckle, J. F. Lopez, and W. H. Meller, Consistent reduction of ACTH responses to stimulation with CRH, vasopressin and hypoglycemia in patients with major depression, *Br. J. Psychiatry, 155*: 468 (1989).

W. Kaye, D. R. Rubinow, H. Gwirtsman et al., CSF somatostatin in anorexia nervosa and bulimia: Relationship to the hypothalamic-pituitary-adrenal cortical axis, *Psychoneuroendocrinology, 13*: 265 (1988).

H. Khachaturian, M. E. Lewis, M. K. Shafer, and S. J. Watson, Anatomy of CNS opioid systems, *Trends Neurosci., 8*: 111 (1985).

C. D. Kilts, G. Bissette, K. R. R. Krishnan et al., The preclinical and clinical neurobiology of corticotropin-releasing factor (CRF), *Hormones and Depression* (U. Halbreich, ed.), Raven Press, New York, pp. 297–311 (1987).

C. Kirkegaard, J. Faber, L. Hummer et al., Increased levels of TRH in cerebrospinal fluid from patients with endogenous depression, *Psychoneuroendocrinology, 4*: 227 (1979).

N. S. Kline, C. H. Li, H. E. Lehmann et al., beta-Endorphin induced changes in schizophrenic and depressed patients, *Arch. Gen. Psychiatry, 34*: 111 (1977).

M. A. Kling, A. R. Doran, D. R. Rubinow et al., The cerebrospinal fluid neurohormonal milieu in Cushing's disease, major depression and normal volunteers: Pathophysiologic and diagnostic relevance, *J. Clin. Endocrinol. Metab., 72*: 260 (1991).

T. R. Kosten, J. W. Mason, E. Giller et al., Sustained urinary norepinephrine elevation in posttraumatic stress disorder, *Psychoneuroendocrinology, 12*: 13 (1987).

T. R. Kosten, V. Wahby, E. Giller, and J. Mason, The dexamethasone suppression test and thyrotropin-releasing hormone stimulation test in posttraumatic stress disorder, *Biol. Psychiatry, 28*: 657 (1990).

G. L. Kovacs, L. Vecsei, G. Szabo et al., The involvement of catecholaminergic mechanisms in the behavioral action of vasopressin, *Neurosci. Lett., 5*: 337 (1977).

D. D. Krahn, B. A. Gosnell, M. Grace et al., CRF antagonist partially reverses CRF and stress-induced effects on feeding, *Brain Res. Bull., 17*: 285 (1986).

B. Krisch, Somatostatin-immunoreactive fiber projections into the brainstem and spinal cord of the rat, *Cell Tissue Res, 217*: 531 (1981).

K. R. R. Krishnan, J. C. Ritchie, D. Reed et al., CRF stimulation test results before and after dexamethasone in depressed patients and normal controls, *J. Neuropsychiatry Clin. Neurosci.,* (in press; 1991).

L. Krulich, A. P. S. Dhariwal, and S. M. McCann, Stimulatory and inhibitory effects of purified hypothalamic extracts on growth hormone release from rat pituitary in vitro, *Endocrinology, 83*: 783 (1968).

M. Laruelle, A. Seghers, S. Goffinet et al., Plasmatic vasopressin neurophysin in depression: Basic levels and relations with HPA axis, *Biol. Psychiatry, 27*: 1249 (1990).

E. H. Y. Lee, Y. P. Tang, and C. T. Chai, Stress and corticotropin-releasing factor potentiate center region activity of mice in an open field, *Psychopharmacology, 93*: 320 (1987).

H. J. U. Lenz, A. Raedler, H. Greten, and M. R. Brown, CRF initiates biological actions within the brain that are observed in response to stress, *Am. J. Physiol., 252*: 34 (1987).

P. Leroux, and G. Pelletier, Radioautographic localization of somatostatin-28 binding sites in the rat brain, *Peptides, 5*: 503 (1984).

K. W. E. Lesch, R. Ekman, G. Lauz et al., delta Sleep-induced peptide response to human corticotropin-releasing hormone (CRH) in major depressive disorder: Comparison with CRH-induced corticotropin and cortisol secretion, *Biol. Psychiatry, 24*: 162 (1988).

A. S. Levine, and J. E. Morley, Neuropeptide Y: A potent inducer of consummatory behavior in rats, *Peptides, 5*: 1025 (1984).

J. A. Lieberman, R. Brenner, M. Lesser et al., Dexamethasone suppression test in patients with panic disorder, *Am. J. Psychiatry, 140*: 917 (1983).

M. R. Liebowitz, J. M. Gorman, A. J. Fryer et al., Lactate provocation of panic attacks II: Biochemical and physiological findings, *Arch. Gen. Psychiatry, 42*: 709 (1985).

J. Lisansky, G. T. Peake, R. J. Strassman et al., Augmented pituitary corticotropin response to a threshold dosage of human corticotropin-releasing hormone in depressives pretreated with metyrapone, *Arch. Gen. Psychiatry, 46*: (1989).

P. T. Loosen, The TRH-induced TSH response in psychiatric patients: A possible neuroendocrine marker, *Psychoneuroendocrinology, 10*: 237 (1985).

P. T. Loosen, and A. J. Prange, Serum thyrotropin response to thyrotropin-releasing hormone in psychiatric patients: A review, *Am. J. Psychiatry, 239*: 405 (1982).

E. C. Lotter, and S. C. Woods, Somatostatin decreases food intake, *Diabetes, 26*(Suppl. 1): 358 (1977).

M. T. Lowy, G. J. Gormley, A. T. Reder et al., Immune function, glucocorticoid receptor regulation and depression, *Depressive Disorders and Immunity* (A. H. Miller, ed.), APA Press, Washington, D.C., pp. 105–134 (1989).

J. M. Lundberg, L. Terenius, T. Hokfelt et al., Neuropeptide Y (NPY)-like immunoreactivity in peripheral noradrenergic neurons and effects of NPY on sympathetic function, *Acta Psychiatr. Scand., Suppl., 335*: 51 (1982).

M. Maes, M. P. Jacobs, E. Suy et al., An augmented escape of ß-endorphins to suppression by dexamethasone in severely depressed patients, *J. Affective Disord., 18*: 149 (1990a).

M. Maes, M. Vanderwoude, C. Schotte et al., A revised interpretation of post-dexamethasone ACTH and cortisol in unipolar depressed females, (1990b).

J. W. Mason, E. L. Giller, T. R. Kosten et al., Urinary free cortisol levels in posttraumatic stress disorder patients, *J. Nerv. Ment. Dis., 174*: 145 (1986).

S. M. McCann, Physiology and pharmacology of LHRH and somatostatin, *Annu. Rev. Pharmacol. Toxicol., 22*: 491 (1982).

J. K. McDonald, NPY and related substances, *CRC Crit. Rev. Neurobiol., 4*: 97 (1988).

I. Merchanthaler, Corticotropin-releasing factor (CRF)-like immunoreactivity in the rat central nervous system. Extrahypothalamic distribution, *Peptides, 5*: 53 (1984).

M. A. Millan, A. B. A. Samra, P. C. Wynn et al., Receptors and actions of corticotropin-releasing hormone in primate pituitary gland, *J. Clin. Endocrinol. Metab., 64*: 1036 (1987).

J. E. Morley, and A. S. Levine, Corticotropin releasing factor, grooming and digestive behavior, *Life Sci., 31*: 1459 (1982).

J. F. Morris, D. B. Chapman, and H. W. Sokol, Anatomy and function of the classic vasopressin-secreting hypothalamo-neurohypophysical system, *Vasopressin: Principles and Properties* (D. M. Gash and G. J. Boer, eds.), Plenum Press, New York, pp. 1–90 (1987).

M. Muhlethaler, and J. J. Dreifuss, Vasopressin excites hippocampal neurons, *Nature, 296*: 749 (1982).

D. Naber, D. Pickar, R. M. Post et al., Endogenous opioid activity and ß-endorphin immunoreactivity in CSF of psychiatric patients and normal volunteers, *Am. J. Psychiatry, 138*: 1427 (1981).

C. B. Nemeroff, Clinical significance of psychoneuroendocrinology in psychiatry: Focus on the thyroid and adrenal, *J. Clin. Psychiatry, 50*: 13 (1989).

C. B. Nemeroff, *Psychoneuroendocrinology,* Current Concepts, The UpJohn Company, Kalamazoo, Michigan (1990).

C. B. Nemeroff, The neurobiology of neuropeptides: An introduction, *Neuropeptides and Psychiatric Disorders* (C. B. Nemeroff, ed.), American Psychiatric Press, Washington, D.C., pp. 3–14 (1991).

C. B. Nemeroff, and G. Bissette, Neuropeptides in psychiatric disorders, *American Handbook of Psychiatry* (P. A. Berger and H. K. H. Brodie, eds.), Basic Books, New York, pp. 64–110 (1986).

C. B. Nemeroff, and D. L. Evans, Thyrotropin-releasing hormone (TRH), the thyroid axis, and affective disorder, *Ann. N.Y. Acad. Sci., 553*: 304 (1989).

C. B. Nemeroff, E. Widerlov, G. Bissette et al., Elevated concentrations of CSF corticotropin-releasing factor-like immunoreactivity in depressed patients, *Science, 226*: 1342 (1984).

C. B. Nemeroff, J. S. Simon, J. T. Haggerty et al., Antithyroid antibodies in depressed patients, *Am. J. Psychiatry, 142*: 840 (1985).

C. B. Nemeroff, E. Widerlov, G. Bissette et al., Reduced corticotropin-releasing factor binding sites in the frontal cortex of suicides, *Arch. Gen. Psychiatry, 45*: 577 (1988).

C. B. Nemeroff, G. Bissette, H. Akil, and M. Fink, Neuropeptide concentrations in the cerebrospinal fluid of depressed patients treated with electroconvulsive therapy: Corticotropin-releasing factor, ß-endorphin and somatostatin, *Br. J. Psychiatry, 158*: 59 (1991).

C. Oliver, R. L. Eskay, N. Ben-Jonathan et al., Distribution and concentration of TRH in the rat brain, *Endocrinology, 96*: 540 (1974).

H. R. Olpe, V. J. Balcar, H. Bittinger et al., Central actions of somatostatin, *Eur. J. Pharmacol., 63*: 127 (1980).

J. A. Olschowka, T. L. O'Donhue, and G. P. Meuller, The distribution of CRF-like immunoreactive neurons in rat brain, *Neuroendocrinology, 35*: 305 (1982).

Y. C. Patel, K. Hoyte, and J. B. Martin, Effects of anterior hypothalamic lesions on neurohyophysial and peripheral tissue concentration of somatostatin in the rat brain, *Endocrinology, 195*: 712 (1979).

F. Petraglia, F. Facchinetti, G. D'Ambrogio et al., Somatostatin and oxytocin infusion inhibits the rise of plasma ß-endorphin, ß-lipoprotein and cortisol induced by insulin hypoglycemia, *Clin. Endocrinol., 24*: 609 (1986).

D. Pickar, D. Naber, R. M. Post et al., Endorphins in the cerebrospinal fluid of psychiatric patients, *Ann. N. Y. Acad. Sci., 398*: 399 (1982).

C. Pihoker, and C. B. Nemeroff, The role of corticotropin-releasing factor in the pathophysiology of anxiety disorders, *Biology of Anxiety Disorders. Recent Developments* (Hoehn Series Progress in Psychiatry), APA Press (in press).

A. Pitkanen, U. Lepola, A. Ylinen, and P. J. Rickkinen, Somatostatin and ß-endorphin levels in cerebrospinal fluid of nonmedicated and medicated patients with epileptic seizures, *Neuropeptides, 13*: 9 (1989).

N. P. Plotnikoff, A. J. Prange, G. R. Breese et al., Thyrotropin releasing hormone: Enhancement of DOPA activity by a hypothalamic hormone, *Science, 178*: 417 (1972).

P. M. Post, P. Gold, D. R. Rubinow et al., Peptides in cerebrospinal fluid of neuropsychiatric patients: An approach to central nervous system peptide function, *Life Sci., 31*: 1 (1982).

A. J. Prange, I. C. Wilson, P. P. Lara et al., Effects of thyrotropin-releasing hormone in depression, *Lancet, 1*: 999 (1972).

D. E. Redmond, Jr., and Y. Huang, Current concepts. II: New evidence for a locus coeruleus–norepinephrine connection with anxiety, *Life Sci., 25*: 2149 (1979).

J. R. Reeve, V. E. Eysselein, H. Walsh et al., Isolation and characterization of biologically active and inactive cholecystokinin octapeptide from human brain, *Peptides, 5*: 459 (1984).

S. Reichlin, Somatostatin, *Brain Peptides* (D. T. Krieger, M. J. Brownstein, and J. B. Martin, eds.), John Wiley & Sons, New York, pp. 711–752 (1983).

S. Reichlin, I. M. D. Jackson, L. E. Seyler, and Y. Grimm, Regulation of the secretion TRH and LHRH, *Frontiers in Neurology and Neuroscience Research* (P. Seeman and G. M. Brown, eds.), University of Toronto Press, Toronto, pp. 48–59 (1900).

M. Rezek, V. Havlicek, K. R. Hughes et al., Cortical administration of somatostatin (SRIF): Effects on sleep and motor behavior, *Pharmacol. Biochem. Behav., 5*: 73 (1976).

M. Rezek, V. Havlicek, K. R. Highes et al., Behavioral and motor excitation and inhibition induced by the administration of small and large doses of somatostatin into the amygdala, *Neuropharmacology, 16*: 157 (1977).

S. C. Risch. Beta-endorphin hypersecretion in depression: Possible cholinergic mechanisms, *Biol. Psychiatry, 17*: 1071 (1982).

S. C. Risch, D. S. Janowsky, L. L. Judd et al., The role of endogenous opioid systems in neuroendocrine regulation, *Psychiatr. Clin. North Am., 6*: 429 (1983).

S. C. Risch, R. J. Lewine, R. D. Jewart et al., Relationship between cerebrospinal fluid peptides and neurotransmitters in depression, *Central Nervous System Peptide Mechanisms in Stress and Depression* (S. C. Risch, ed.), American Psychiatric Press, Washington, D.C., pp. 93–103 (1991).

C. Rivier, J. Rivier, and W. Vale, Inhibition of adrenocorticotropic hormone secretion in the rat by immunoneutralization of corticotropin-releasing factor, *Science, 218*: 377 (1982).

G. W. Roberts, P. L. Woodhams, J. M. Polak, and T. S. Crow, Distribution of neuropeptides in the limbic system of the rat, the amygdaloid complex, *Neuroscience, 7*: 99 (1982).

A. G. Robinson, and E. A. Zimmerman, Cerebrospinal fluid and ependymal neurophysin, *J. Clin. Invest., 52*: 1260 (1973).

J. P. Rock, E. H. Oldfield, H. M. Schulte et al., Corticotropin-releasing factor administered into the ventricular CSF stimulates the pituitary–adrenal axis, *Brain Res., 323*: 365 (1984).

A. Roy, D. Pickar, S. Paul et al., CSF corticotropin-releasing hormone in depressed patients and normal control subjects, *Am. J. Psychiatry, 144*: 641 (1987).

P. P. Roy-Byrne, L. M. Bierer, and T. W. Uhde, The dexamethasone suppression test in panic disorder: Comparison with normal controls, *Biol. Psychiatry, 20*: 1237 (1985).

P. Roy-Byrne, T. W. Uhde, R. M. Post et al., The corticotropin-releasing hormone stimulation test in patients with panic disorder, *Am. J. Psychiatry, 143*: 896 (1986).

D. R. Rubinow, Cerebrospinal fluid somatostatin and psychiatric illness, *Biol. Psychiatry, 21*: 341 (1986).

D. R. Rubinow, P. W. Gold, R. M. Post et al., CSF somatostatin in affective illness, *Arch. Gen. Psychiatry, 40*: 409 (1983).

E. J. Sachar, L. Hellman, Roffwarg et al., Disrupted 24-hr patterns of cortisol secretion in psychotic depression, *Arch. Gen. Psychiatry, 28*: 19 (1973).

M. Saffron, and A. V. Schally, Release of corticotropin by anterior pituitary tissue in vitro, *Can. J. Biochem. Physiol., 33*: 408 (1955).

P. E. Sawchenko, Adrenalectomy-induced enhancement of CRF and vasopressin immunoreactivity in parvocellular neurosecretory neurons: Anatomy, peptide, and steroid specificity, *Neuroscience, 7*: 1093 (1987).

P. E. Sawchenko, and L. W. Swanson, Localization, colocalization and plasticity of corticotropin-releasing factor immunoreactivity in rat brain, *Fed. Proc., 44*: 221 (1985).

H. Schuemeyer, P. W. Avgerinos, W. T. Gold et al., Human corticotropin releasing factor dose response and time course of ACTH and cortisol secretion in man, *J. Clin. Endocrinol. Metab., 59*: 1103 (1984).

M. Serby, S. B. Richardson, B. Rypma et al., Somatostatin regulation of the CRF–ACTH–cortisol axis, *Biol. Psychiatry, 21*: 971 (1986).

D. V. Sheehan, J. B. Claycomb, O. S. Surman et al., Panic attacks and the dexamethasone suppression test, *Am. J. Psychiatry, 140*: 1063 (1986).

D. J. S. Sirinathsinghji, Modulation of lordosis behavior in the female rat by corticotropin releasing factor, ß-endorphin and gonadotropin releasing hormone in the mesencephalic central gray, *Brain Res., 336*: 45 (1985).

D. J. S. Sirinathsinghji, Inhibitory influence of corticotropin releasing factor on components of sexual behavior in the male rat, *Brain Res., 407*: 185 (1987).

D. J. S. Sirinathsinghji, L. H. Rees, J. Rivier et al., Corticotropin-releasing factor is a potent inhibitor of sexual receptivity in the female rat, *Nature, 305*: 232 (1983).

M. A. Smith, G. Bissette, T. A. Slotkin et al., Release of corticotropin-releasing factor from rat brain regions in vitro, *Endocrinology, 118*: 1997 (1986).

M. A. Smith, J. Davidson, J. C. Ritchie et al., The corticotropin-releasing hormone test in post-traumatic stress disorder, *Biol. Psychiatry, 26*: 349 (1989).

M. V. Sofroniew, Morphology of vasopressin and oxytocin neurons and their central and vascular projections, *The Neurohypophysis: Structure Function and Control Progress in Brain Research* (B. A. Cross and G. Leng, eds.), Elsevier, Amsterdam, pp. 101–113 (1983).

S. M. Southwick, J. H. Krystal, and D. S. Charney, Yohimbine in PTSD, *APA New Res. Abstr., 143*: (1991).

B. A. Spruce, A. J. McCulloch, J. Burd et al., The effect of vasopressin infusion of glucose metabolism in man, *Clin. Endocrinol., 22*: 463 (1985).

M. B. Stein, T. N. Uhde, Routine screening of thyroid indices in patients with panic attacks. *J. Clin. Psychiatry, 49*: 204 (1988).

R. E. Sutton, G. F. Koob, M. LeMoal et al., Corticotropin releasing factor produces behavioral activation in rats, *Nature, 297*: 331 (1982).

T. H. Svensson, Peripheral, autonomic, regulation of locus coeruleus noradrenergic neurons in brain: Putative implications for psychiatry and psychopharmacology, *Psychopharmacology, 92*: 1 (1987).

L. W. Swanson, and P. E. Sawchenko, Paraventricular nucleus: A site for the integration of neuroendocrine and autonomic mechanisms, *Neuroendocrinology, 31*: 410 (1980).

L. W. Swanson, P. E. Sawchenko, J. Rivier, and W. W. Vale, Organization of ovine corticotropin-releasing factor immunoreactive cells and fibers in the rat brain: An immunohistochemical study, *Neuroendocrinology, 36*: 165 (1983).

N. R. Swerdlow, M. A. Geyer, W. W. Vale, and G. F. Koob, Corticotropin-releasing factor potentiates acoustic startle in rats: Blockade by chlordiazepoxide, *Psychopharmacology, 88*: 147 (1986).

T. Sunderland, D. R. Rubinow, P. N. Tsariot et al., CSF somatostatin in dementia, elderly depression and age-matched controls, *Am. J. Psychiatry, 144*: 1313 (1987).

K. Tatemoto, and V. Mutt, Isolation of two novel candidate hormones using a chemical method for finding naturally occurring polypeptides, *Nature, 285*: 417 (1980).

A. Tazi, N. R. Swerdlow, M. LeMoal et al., Behavioral activation by CRF: Evidence for the involvement of the central forebrain, *Life Sci., 41*: 41 (1987).

L. Terenius, A. Wahlstrom, and J. Agnen, Nalaxone treatment in depression: Clinical observations and effects on CSF and endorphins and monoamine metabolites, *Psychopharmacology, 54*: 31 (1977).

V. T. Tran, G. R. Uhl, D. C. Petty et al., Autoradiographic localization of somatostatin receptors in rat brain, *Eur. J. Pharmacol., 101*: 307 (1985).

W. Vale, J. Speiss, C. Rivier et al., Characterization of a 41-residue ovine hypothalamic peptide that stimulates secretion of corticotropin and ß-endorphin, *Science, 213*: 1394 (1981).

R. J. Valentino, and S. L. Foote, Corticotropin-releasing factor disrupts sensory responses of brain noradrenergic neurons, *Neuroendocrinology, 45*: 28 (1987).

R. J. Valentino, S. L. Foote, and G. Aston-Jones, Corticotropin-releasing factor activates noradrenergic neurons of the locus coeruleus, *Brain Res., 270*: 363 (1983).

H. Valtin, Physiological effects of vasopressin on the kidney, *Vasopressin Principles and Properties* (D. M. Gash and G. J. Boer, eds.), Plenum Press, New York, pp. 369–388 (1987).

J. J. Vanderhaegen, P. Lofstra, and G. Vierendeels, Cholecystokinin in the central nervous system and neurohypophysis, *Peptides, 2*: 81 (1981).

R. Vandesande, K. Dierick, and J. DeMey, Identification of the vasopressin–europhysin producing neurons of the rat suprachiasmatic nuclei, *Cell Tiss. Res., 156*: 377 (1975).

D. P. Van Kammen, R. N. Waters, P. Gold et al., Spinal fluid vasopressin, angiotensin I and II, beta-endorphin and optiod activity in schizophrenia: A preliminary evaluation, *Biological Psychiatry* (C. Perris, G. Struwe, and B. Jansson, eds.), Elsevier North-Holland, Amsterdam, pp. 339–344 (1981).

F. W. Van Leeuwen, C. Deraay, D. R. Swaab et al., The localization of oxytocin, vasopressin, somatostatin, and luteinizing hormone releasing hormone in the rat neurohypophysis, *Cell Tiss. Res., 202*: 189 (1979).

H. M. Van Praag, Biological suicidal research: Outcome and limitations, *Biol. Psychiatry, 21*: 1305 (1985).

L. Vescei, and E. Widerlov, Brain and CSF somatostatin concentrations in patients with psychiatric or neurological illness: An overview, *Acta Psychiatr. Scand., 78*: 657 (1988).

L. Vecsei, C. Kiraly, I. Bollok et al., Comparative studies with somatostatin and cysteamine in different behavior tests on rats, *Pharmacol. Biochem. Behav., 21*: 833 (1984).

J. Von Bardeleben, and F. Holsboer, Cortisol response to a combined dexamethasone–human corticotropin-releasing hormone challenge in patients with depression, *J. Neuroendocrinol., 1*: 485 (1989).

T. J. Walsh, D. F. Emerich, A. Winokur et al., Intrahippocampal injection of cysteamine depletes somatostatin and produces cognitive impairments in the rat, *Soc. Neurosci. Abstr., 11*: 621 (1985).

L. J. Whalley, N. Borthwick, D. Copolov et al., Glucocorticoid receptors and depression, *Br. Med. J., 292*: 859 (1986).

E. Widerlov, C. Wahlestedt, R. Hakanson, and R. Ekman, Altered brain neuropeptide function in psychiatric illnesses—with special emphasis on NPY and CRF in major depression, *Proceedings 15th C.I.N.P. Congr. Clin. Neuropharmacol., 9*[Suppl. 4]: 572 (1986).

E. Widerlov, G. Bissette, and C. B. Nemeroff, Monoamine metabolites, corticotropin-releasing factor, and somatostatin as CSF markers in depressed patients, *J. Affective Disord., 14*: 99 (1988a).

E. Widerlov, L. H. Lindstrom, C. Wahlested, and R. Ekman, Neuropeptide Y and peptide YY as possible cerebrospinal fluid markers for major depression and schizophrenia, respectively, *J. Psychiatry Res., 22*: 69 (1988b).

E. Widerlov, R. Ekman, L. Jensen et al., Arginine vasopressin, but not corticotropin releasing factor, is a potent stimulator of adrenocorticotropic hormone following electroconvulsive treatment, *J. Neural Transm., 75*: 101 (1989).

A. Winokur, and R. D. Utiger, Thyrotropin-releasing hormone regional distribution in rat brain, *Science, 185*: 265 (1974).

B. Wolfson, R. W. Manning, L. G. Davis et al., Colocalization of corticotropin releasing factor and vasopressin mRNA in neurons after adrenalectomy, *Nature, 315*: 59 (1985).

O. M. Wolkowitz, D. R. Ruvinow, A. Breier et al., Prednisolone decreases CSF somatostatin in healthy humans: Implications for neuropsychiatric illness, *Life Sci., 41* 1929 (1987).

R. Yehuda, S. M. Southwick, J. W. Mason et al., Neuroendocrine aspects of suicidality, *Endocrin. Metab Clin. North Am., 17*: 83 (1988).

R. Yehuda, S. M. Southwick, B. D. Perry et al., Hypothalamic–pituitary–adrenal and noradrenergic interactions in PTSD, *Biological Assessment and Treatment of PTSD* (E. Giller, ed.)., *Progr. Psychiatry,* APA Press, Washington, D.C. (1990a).

R. Yehuda, S. M. Southwick, G. Nussbaum et al., Low urinary cortisol excretion in patients with PTSD, *J. Nerv. Ment. Dis., 178*: 366 (1990b).

R. Yehuda, M. T. Lowy, S. M. Southwick et al., Lymphocyte glucocorticoid receptor number in post-traumatic stress disorder, *Am. J. Psychiatry, 149*: 499 (1991b).

R. Yehuda, S. M. Southwick, J. Krystal, D.S. Charney, J. W. Mason, Enhanced suppression of cortisol following dexamethasone administration in combat veterans with posttraumatic stress disorder and major depressive disorder, *Am. J. Psychiatry, 150*: 83 (1993).

R. Yehuda, E. L. Giller, S. M. Southwick et al., Hypothalamic–pituitary–adrenal dysfunction in posttraumatic stress disorder, *Biol. Psychiatry 30*: 1031 (1991a).

R. Yehuda, S. M. Southwick, X. Ma et al., Urinary catecholamine excretion and severity of symptoms in PTSD, *J. Nerv. Ment. Dis. 180*: 321–325 (1992b).

E. A. Young, R. F. Haskett, V. Murphy-Weinberg et al., Loss of glucocorticoid fast feedback in depression, *Arch. Gen. Psychiatry, 48*: 693 (1991).

23

Benzodiazepines, Benzodiazepine Receptors, and Endogenous Ligands

Willy Haefely
F. Hoffmann–La Roche, Ltd., Basel, Switzerland

I. INTRODUCTION

In the mid-1950s Leo Sternbach, medicinal chemist in the laboratories of Hoffmann-La Roche in Nutley, New Jersey, synthesized compounds of a new class of chemicals characterized by the bicyclic nucleus benzo-1,4-diazepine. One of these, chlordiazepoxide, in a broad pharmacological screening performed under the direction of Lowell O. Randall, was found to have interesting sedative, anticonvulsant, and muscle relaxant activities, combined with remarkably low acute toxicity. Clinical studies confirmed the pharmacological profile, and chlordiazepoxide was launched in 1960 as an anxiolytic–sedative drug under the trade name Librium (1,2). Extensive structural variation of this prototype compound led over the subsequent three decades to the worldwide launch of about 50 drugs commonly termed *benzodiazepines* (3). This term implies similarities with chlordiazepoxide in chemical structure as well as in the pharmacological profile and, more recently, in the mechanism of action (i.e., the interaction with a defined molecular target, the benzodiazepine receptor; BZR). The term benzodiazepine is ambiguous because, as will be shown in this chapter, compounds with a benzodiazepine structure and acting at the BZR can differ quite markedly in their pharmacological profile and because compounds with a nonbenzodiazepine structure (e.g., cyclopyrrolones, triazolopyridazines, imidazopyridines, ß-carbolines) can interact with the BZR in a way similar to true benzodiazepines. The term *BZR ligands* will be used here to include all chemicals interacting with this receptor, irrespective of their activity.

In the mid-1970s the efforts to identify the mechanism of action of benzodiazepine tranquilizers, using γ-aminobutyric acid (GABA), resulted in the demonstration that these compounds interacted very selectively with the distinct type of synaptic transmitter system in the central nervous system (CNS) (4,5). Although these initial studies clearly showed that benzodiazepines required the presence of GABA in synapses for exerting their effect, the precise site of action (at the GABAergic neuron itself or at the GABA receptive neuron) could not be pinpointed. In 1977, using tritiated diazepam as radioligand, the postulated specific high-affinity-binding sites were discovered in the CNS (6–9). Overall, inhibition of radioligand binding correlated well with pharmacological activity of the benzodiazepines studied, strongly suggesting that these binding sites represented the primary site of action (i.e., the benzodiazepine receptors). Binding sites for benzodiazepines were found in the CNS as well as in peripheral tissues; however, these two classes of BZ-binding sites differed clearly from each other by their affinity for ligands (7). The terms *central* and *peripheral BZR*s were coined, giving rise to ambiguities that will be dealt with later.

The ability to label BZR reversibly and irreversibly (10) with radioligands was instrumental in the further elucidation of its function and structure. About 1980, a new type of BZR ligand was found, of which flumazenil is the prototype (11,12). These ligands have no, or only a negligible, effect of GABAergic transmission and the effect of exogenous GABA; however, they selectively and competitively antagonize the effects of classic benzodiazepines. Accordingly, the latter were called agonists and the former antagonists of the BZR. At the same time, in the search for possible endogenous ligands of the BZR, ß-carboline 3-carboxylic acid derivatives were identified that not only antagonized the effects of agonists, but by themselves reduced the effect of GABA and $GABA_A$ receptors and exhibited a pharmacological profile that is the exact mirror image of the agonist profile (13–15, see 16). The term *inverse agonists* of the BZR was proposed (16) and is now in common use.

Binding of ligands to the BZR was found to be modulated by GABA (17), and BZR colocalized with GABA-binding sites (18), suggesting a close functional interaction between the $GABA_A$ receptor and the BZR. This functional connection between the two receptors turned out to be based on a tight physical coupling, as the solubilization and isolation of the BZR resulted in the copurification of the $GABA_A$ receptor channel complex (19–23). From partial sequence information of the purified protein complex two cDNAs were cloned that encode two homologous proteins, called subunits α and ß (24). The ectopic coexpression of the corresponding cRNAs in Xenopus oocytes resulted in the membrane incorporation of a receptor channel complex responding to GABA with a chloride flux as expected of a $GABA_A$ receptor channel. The GABA-induced chloride gating of this recombinant protein complex was modulated by barbiturates, but inconsistently by benzodiazepines (24). Schofield and collaborators (24), therefore, proposed that the $GABA_A$ receptor chanel was a heterooligomeric complex consisting of α- and ß-subunits, the latter containing the binding site for GABA and the former the binding site for benzodiazepines. This provided a structural basis for the earlier hypothesis that the BZR is an integral part of the $GABA_A$ receptor channel and functions as an allosteric modulatory site of the $GABA_A$ receptor channel complex. This proposed structure of the $GABA_A$ receptor channel, with its integral BZR, is correct in principle, but rapidly turned out to be much more complicated in reality. About 15 different subunit forms have now been identified that are encoded by distinct genes. Posttranscriptional processing leads to additional variants. This provides the potential for multiple combinatorial assemblies of $GABA_A$ receptor channels and explains earlier evidence for receptor heterogeneity (25,26). Recent research has focused on studying the expression of the different subunit genes in various cells and the investigation of the function of ectopically expressed subunit compositions. It is still unknown how many native receptor channel forms exist and what their exact subunit composition is. These open questions are of obvious relevance for the physiology and pharmacology of $GABA_A$ receptor channels.

The radioligand assay has been used over the past 15 years to search for putative endogenous ligands that might affect the function of the BZR in normal or pathological situations (27). A completely unexpected recent finding was the presence in humans, animals, and plants of various compounds, with a benzodiazepine structure and affinity for the BZR (28). It thus appears that none of us can avoid having "natural" benzodiazepines in the body.

II. THE GABAERGIC SYSTEM

Because the BZR is an integral part of all or of most $GABA_A$ receptors (29), understanding the effects of BZR ligands at cellular and system levels (30–33) requires a basic knowledge of the structure and function of the GABAergic system (34).

The GABAergic neurons can be visualized in tissue slices by two specific properties; namely, their specific uptake of radiolabeled GABA by a plasma membrane carrier and the presence of the enzyme glutamic acid decarboxylase (GAD), which forms GABA from its immediate physiological precursor, glutamic acid, and that can be identified by specific antibodies. GABA itself can also be visualized immunocytochemically. Considerable information is available on the topography of GABAergic neurons. These neurons are present in all areas of the CNS in various densities. The GABAergic projection neurons occur primarily in the cerebellum (all cerebellar Purkinje neurons are GABAergic and convey the cerebellar cortical output to deep cerebellar and brain stem nuclei) and in the striatrum, where they represent a major output system to the substantia nigra and to the thalamus as well as in the substantia nigra, which they connect with the thalamus and the tectal area. The greatly preponderant number of GABAergic neurons, however, are interneurons involved in the local regulation of neuronal activity (Fig. 1). A few GABAergic neurons have been found in the intestinal tract. Many GABAergic neurons contain a cotransmitter (peptides or monoamines) for which the function is not yet known. The GABAergic system is the most important inhibitory system of the brain, where about one-third of all synapses are thought to be GABAergic. The vital importance of the GABAergic system is most easily demonstrated by the effect of GABA receptor blockers: they increase neuronal activity throughout the CNS, resulting dose-dependently in increased alertness, anxiety, muscular spasms, seizure activity, and death. Apparent paradoxical effects of GABA antagonists, in particular after local administration, are readily explained by the fact that GABAergic neurons are arranged in series in some CNS areas (i.e., some GABAergic neurons innervate other GABAergic neurons). This gives rise to inhibition or disinhibition of the downstream neuron in the series, and the GABAergic efficacy of the upstream neuron increases or decreases, respectively.

The GABA released from GABAergic neurons can act on two classes of GABA receptors on the postsynaptic or target neuron as well as on the terminals of the releasing neuron itself (autoreceptors). These two classes of receptors, called $GABA_A$ and $GABA_B$ (35) receptors (Fig. 2), can be clearly separated by their affinity for several agonists (e.g., muscimol versus baclofen) and antagonists (e.g., bicuculline versus phaclofen), their structure, their allosteric modulation, and their signal transduction mechanism (36). Since the $GABA_A$ receptor is the more important functionally and the only one con-

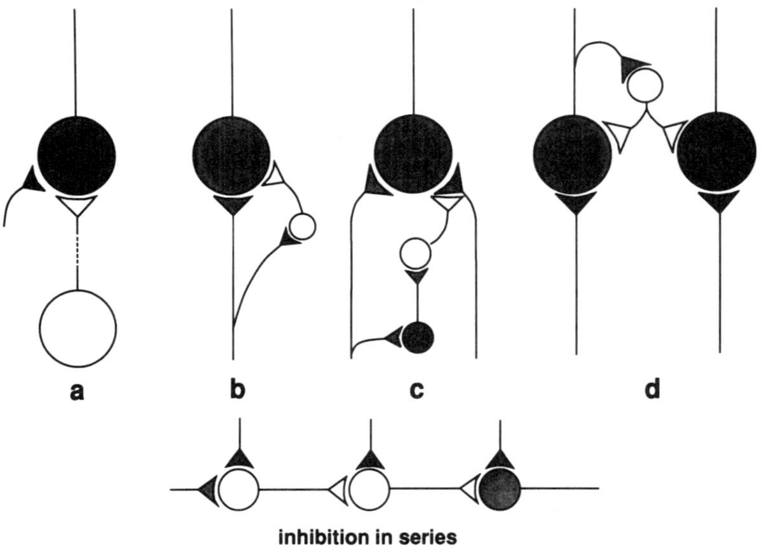

Figure 1 Some characteristic neuronal circuits containing a GABAergic neuron. GABAergic neurons are indicated by open symbols, excitatory neurons by filled symbols. (a) GABAergic projection neuron; (b) and (c) feed-forward inhibition (postsynaptic inhibition in b and presynaptic inhibition in c; (d) feedback inhibition. Bottom circuit contains two GABAergic neurons in series.

	$GABA_A$	$GABA_B$
Common agonist	GABA	GABA
Common antagonist	-	-
Selective agonist	Muscimol	Baclofen
Selective antagonist	Bicuculline	Phaclofen
Transducer	Anion channel	GTPase (G protein) AC ↓ Ca^{2+} current ↓ K^+ current ↑
Allosteric modulatory sites	Benzodiazepines Barbiturates Steroids General anesthetics Convulsants	?

Figure 2 Characterization of $GABA_A$ and $GABA_B$ receptors.

nected with BZR, this chapter is restricted to the $GABA_A$ receptor, although the $GABA_B$ receptor is a molecular target for interesting drugs.

The GABAergic neurons innervate neurons of all neurotransmitter phenotypes, albeit with different intensity. It is clear, therefore, and very important to keep in mind when progressing from the molecular and cellular level to the more complex levels of circuits, of networks, and of the entire CNS, that interfering with GABAergic neurotransmission can, in principle, alter the activity of any neuron system of the CNS, the actual change in the activity of a neuron being determined by the ongoing activity of GABAergic afferents, but also by the other synaptic inputs.

III. THE $GABA_A$ RECEPTOR CHANNEL STRUCTURE AND FUNCTION

A. General Module Structure

The $GABA_A$ receptor channel is a member of a family of ligand-regulated ion channels, to which the nicotinic cholinoceptor, the glycine receptor, the $serotonin_3$ (5-HT_3) receptor, and probably still others (e.g., the *N*-methyl-D-aspartate [NMDA]-type receptor for excitatory amino acids) belong (37). This family is characterized by the ligand recognition and binding sites being an integral part (a subunit) of the channel complex; that is, no coupling molecules, such as G-proteins (guanosine nucleotide-binding proteins) are required in the interaction between the ligand-binding protein (receptor) and the effector complex (ion channel). The signal transduction is initiated by the binding of the ligand to the receptor subunit, which results in a conformational change of the receptor molecule. This conformational transition in the receptor molecule (*interdomain communication*) may be sufficient by itself or induces secondarily a conformational change in other subunits of the supramolecular complex (*intersubunit interaction*) to alter the spatial arrangement of the constituents of the complex. This results in the opening of the pore formed by the circular pseudosymmetric disposition of the subunits. The best-studied member of this family, the nicotinic cholinoceptor of the muscle endplate, is a heteropentamer [i.e., a complex of five subunits (two α, two ß, and one γ) held together by noncovalent forces. In analogy to this receptor, the other members, including the $GABA_A$ receptor channel, are presumed to be heteropentameric complexes, too (Fig. 3).

B. Subunits of the $GABA_A$ Receptor Channel

The existence of three types of subunits (α, ß, γ) of the $GABA_A$ receptor channel is now well established, and two more have been described (24,38). Their molecular mass is between 50 and 60 kDa, and the number of amino acid residues ranges between 423 and 521 (38).

The primary structure reveals sequence homology of 30–40% between the subunit types and predicts a characteristic topology (24,38) (Fig. 4). There are four domains of about 20 amino acids, each characterized by a high hydrophobicity. These domains are likely to form α-helices and to perpendicularly span the lipid bilayer of the plasma membrane. They are labeled transmembrane domains TM_1 to TM_4, according to their position in the $NH_{2\text{-}4}$ to COOH-terminal direction within the polypeptides. The NH_2-terminal part upstream of TM_1 is located in the extracellular space. This large ectodomain contains two to three potential *N*-glycosylation sites and a highly conserved ß-loop, stabilized by a disulfide bridge. Short stretches connect the first TMs, and a larger intra-

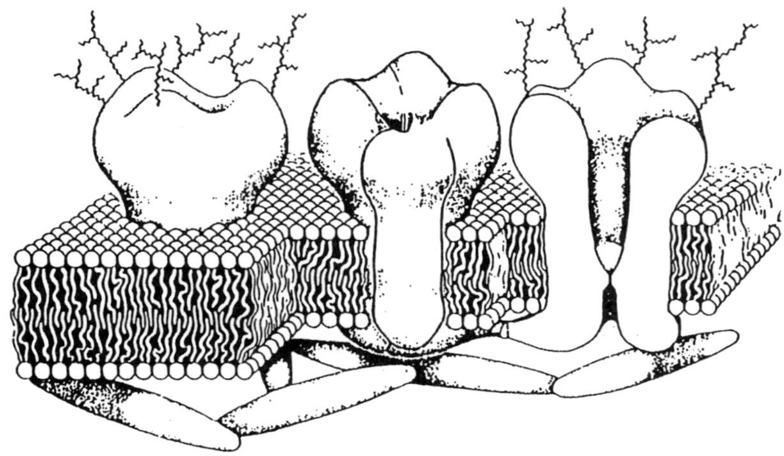

Figure 3 Schematic model of the $GABA_A$ receptor channel embedded in the plasma membrane, with presumed pentameric structure in analogy to the nicotinic cholinoceptor. The trees indicate the carbohydrate chains. The receptor may be in contact with cytoskeletal components (bottom).

cellular domain connects TM_3 and TM_4. The short COOH-terminus is located extracellularly. The subunit types show a high sequence homology in their TM domains, but differ considerably in the intracellular loop connecting TM_3 and TM_4. A consensus sequence for phosphorylation by protein kinase C is present in this loop of the ß-subunit type, and a consensus sequence for tyrosine phosphorylation occurs in the γ_2-subunits. In analogy to the nicotinic cholinoceptor, the $GABA_A$ receptor channel formed by five subunits (heteropentamer) is thought to be arranged in a pseudosymmetrical way around the axis of the central pore (see Fig. 4). Each subunit would be anchored in the plasma membrane by the cluster of its four TM domains. One helix domain of each of the five clusters of TM stretches is assumed to form the wall of the channel pore. The stretches of the subunits located just outside of the TM_1 domain, and likely to form the outer mouth of the channel, are rich in positively charged residues, consistent with the anion-selectivity of the $GABA_A$ receptor pore; corresponding sites in the subunits of the nictonic cholinoceptor are negatively charged, in fitting with the cation-selectivity of this receptor pore. Channel-gating and its allosteric modulation depend on subunit composition, as shown by the study of ectopically expressed recombinant receptor types in the Xenopus oocyte or mammalian cell lines (see following).

Ectopic expression studies in Xenopus oocytes, which normally do not express the $GABA_A$ receptor, have shown that a single subunit type (α or ß) can form a homooligomeric receptor channel that responds with a very poor chloride flux to GABA application (except the subunit of a retinal GABA receptor) (39) and that is positively modulated by pentobarbital (40). Expression of the rat $ß_1$-subunit alone resulted in a chloride channel that was open in the absence of GABA and that could be closed by picrotoxin (41). Cotransfection with cRNAs encoding an α- and a ß-subunit apparently gives rise to a heterooligomeric complex responding to GABA in a similar, but not identical, manner to native receptors. Such γ-subunit-less recombinant receptors show modu-

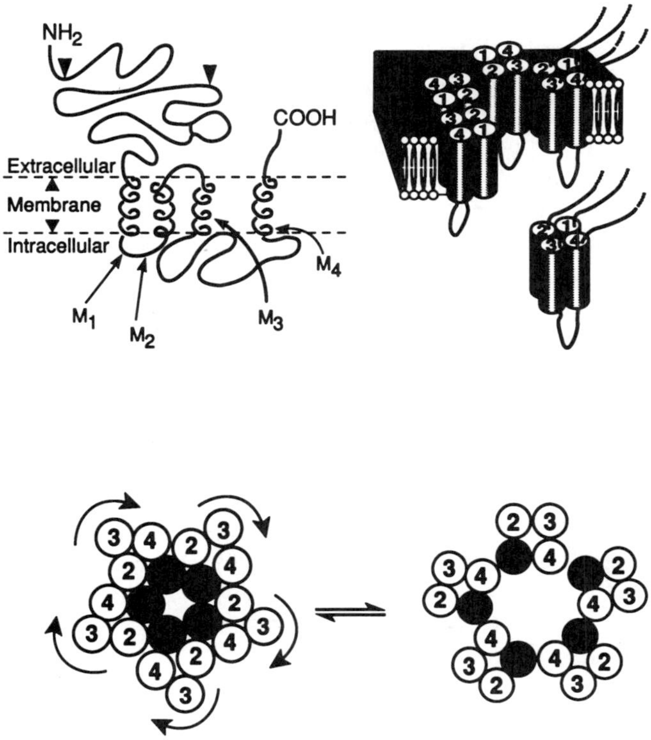

Figure 4 Schematic topology of the $GABA_A$ receptor channel: Top left: assumed subunit topology. TM, transmembrane stretches. Arrowheads indicate putative glycosylation sites. Top right: The five clusters of transmembrane stretches (cylinders) anchor the pentameric receptor channel complex in the plasma membrane. Bottom: Possible transition between channel-closed and channel-open forms by rotation of the subunits.

lation of their GABA response by barbiturates and selected steroids; however, no consistent modulation by BZR ligands (42). Modulation by the latter ligands requires the presence of a ß-subunit in the heterooligomer (see following).

The recently cloned subunits ρ_1 and ρ_2 (39,43) seem to form a type of $GABA_A$ receptor, which differs in many respects from the $GABA_A$ receptors found throughout the CNS, by having a higher affinity for GABA, being insensitivity to bicuculine and BZR ligands, and occurring in the retina and other parts of the visual system (44,45). This type may be considered the postulated $GABA_C$ receptor (46).

C. Binding Sites for γ-Aminobutyric Acid and Allosteric Modulators

The three-dimensional structure of the $GABA_A$ receptor channel is not yet known. Therefore, we can only speculate on the location, shape, and residue composition of the presumed binding pocket for GABA, and other $GABA_A$ receptor agonists, as well as isosteric $GABA_A$ receptor antagonists (i.e., antagonists acting at the GABA-binding area). In view of the hydrophilicity of GABA, this site is likely to be on the ectodomain and readily accessible from the extracellular space (Fig. 5). Although several findings point to the ß-subunits as the subunit carrying the GABA-binding site (47), it is possible that other subunits also contain such a site, or at least contribute to forming the binding area, possibly located at or close to an interphase between subunits (47a,48a).

The $GABA_A$ receptor channel contains, in addition to the recognition site for GABA and its isosteric antagonists, various sites through which different chemicals can modulate the channel-gating function of GABA (see Fig. 5). These sites are clearly different from the GABA-binding site, but can affect, at an unknown distance (intra- and intermolecularly), the affinity of the latter for GABA or influence the conformational transition induced in one or more subunits by GABA and that underlie the channel gating. The best known of these allosteric sites is the BZR, which is located, at least partially, on α-subunits (49). Other allosteric sites exist for barbiturates and related compounds, for a spectrum of convulsants (e.g., picrotoxin and so-called cage convulsants) (50,51), for distinct steroids (52–54), but also for volatile general anesthetics (55) and, possibly, for alcohols (see 56). Most of these allosteric modulators of the $GABA_A$ receptor channel are rather hydrophobic compounds. Their binding sites are, therefore, likely to be hydrophobic pockets, perhaps accessible through the membrane lipid bilayer.

D. Structural Heterogeneity or Polymorphism of the γ-Aminobuteric $Acid_A$ Receptor Channel

Soon after the initial cloning of an α- and a ß-subunit (24,57), it became clear that each of these two, as well as the later discovered γ-subunit, occur as multiple structural variants or isoforms (42,57–72).

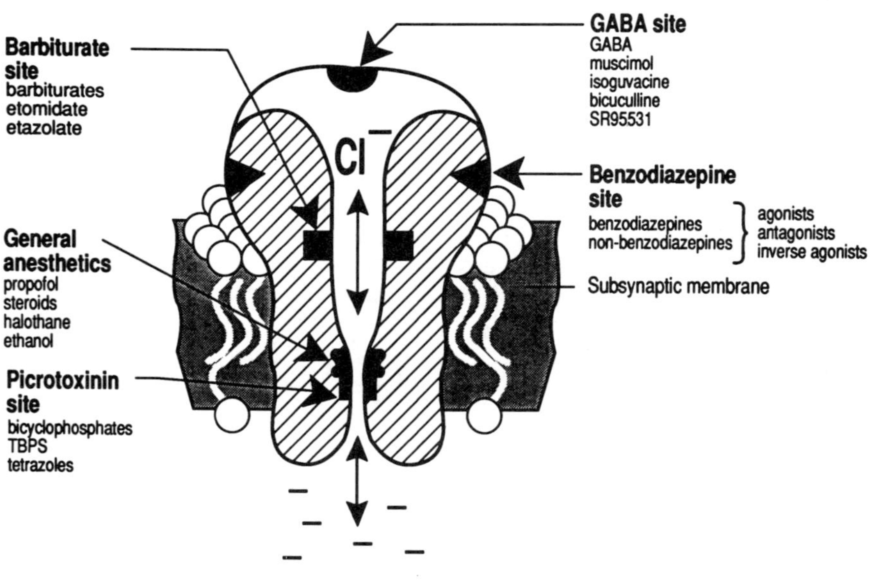

Figure 5 Schematic diagram of the $GABA_A$ receptor channel with the various ligand-binding sites.

Currently, six variants of the α-subunit (α_1–α_6), four of the ß-subunit, three of the γ-subunit, and two of the δ-subunit are known (43,73,74). Subtype variants have a high (over 70%) sequence homology among themselves. These variants are encoded by distinct genes. The genomic organizations of the entire genes for the murine δ-subunit (65) and of the chicken β_4-subunit (75) have been analyzed and found to be very similar. There are nine exons and highly conserved intron–exon boundary positions. The human gene for the α_2-subunit is located on chromosome 4, the α_1 gene is on chromosome 5, the δ-subunit on chromosome 1 (65), and α_3 gene on the X-chromosome (76), and ρ_1 and ρ_2 genes on chromosome 14 (43). Additional variants are likely to be found that derive from posttranscriptional modifications (alternative splicing, mRNA editing) (64,77). A similar situation is known for the nicotinic cholinoceptor, which shows subunit polymorphism in function of cell type, developmental stage, and exogenous influences (e.g., innervation of the skeletal muscle by motor neurons).

A considerable literature is accumulating on the regional expression of the various subunit variants in the CNS and peripheral tissue based on in situ hybridization, histochemistry, and immunohistochemistry (see, e.g., 78–88).

With the currently identified subunit variants of the $GABA_A$ receptor channel, assuming a pentameric structure and allowing for all combinatorial assemblies, several thousands of compositions of this receptor are theoretically possible. In reality, this number is probably rather small. The determination of the composition of native receptors will be very difficult, in particular, if a given neuron should be able to express and assemble receptors composed of different subunits and subunit variants (89,90). Restricted information obtained from ectopically expressed receptors indicate that the subunit variant composition may affect GABA receptor affinity, channel conductance, and kinetics, as well as intensity and direction of allosteric modulation.

The type of subunit α variant primarily appears to determine the affinity of the BZR for various ligands; however, the presence of a γ-subunit is a prerequisite for the expression of allosteric modulation by BZR ligands. Posttranslational modifications of the receptor, for example, phosphorylation and glycosylation (91), may be further determinants of the affinity.

In recent investigations, several $GABA_A$-benzodiazepine receptors of different subunit composition, obtained by the injection of mRNA coding for distinct subunits into Xenopus oocytes or mammalian cell lines, have been studied with radioligand binding and electrophysiological techniques (40,42,48a,61–63,67,74, 92, 93–110). Several characteristic pharmacological signatures have been discovered. There is one caveat to these studies: it is not known with which stoichiometry the products of the injected mRNAs were assembled in the membrane. It will be interesting to compare this information from recombinant receptor variants with characteristics of native variants, once these became known.

E. Classification of γ-Aminobutyric Acid$_A$–Benzodiazepine Receptor Subtypes

The high number of subunit variants of the $GABA_A$ receptor channel now identified (90,111,112), allows, in principle, the formation of multiple combinations, thus creating a large putative spectrum of $GABA_A$ receptor subtypes.

The composition of these receptors may be ontogenetically regulated, resulting in a changing receptor phenotype during the development of the CNS (113–115). Neurons may differ in their $GABA_A$ receptors according to neurotransmitter phenotype or regional localization (116). Individual neurons may express preferentially or exclusively one receptor type, or express various types. It is possible that expression of subunit variants, their intracellular targeting, processing, and aggregation into obligomers are affected by exogenous factors (e.g., chronic exposure to ligands or pathological states of the CNS; 117).

Recent studies with recombinant receptors, mainly in the Xenopus oocyte system, have provided interesting insight into the relation between receptor composition and functional properties (sensitivity to GABA, channel conductance, channel kinetics, allosteric modulation). However, it should be remembered that the number of native receptor types is unknown and that none of the putative native receptor types has yet been characterized for subunit composition. It is totally unknown how relevant the physiological and pharmacological differences between putative receptor subtypes are in reality.

The triazolopyridazine CL 218,872 was one of the first nonbenzodiazepines found to bind specifically to the BZR. In vitro, the compound exhibited higher affinity for BZR in the cerebellum than in other brain areas. CL 218,872 was originally thought to have anticonvulsant and anticonflict activity, without producing sedation. This behavioral and binding profile was suggested to reflect a preferential activation of a subtype of BZR, coined BZR I (118–120).

The hypothesis that BZR I (preponderant in cerebellum) mediates anticonvulsant and antianxiety effects, whereas BZR II (preponderant in cortex and hippocampus) is responsible for sedative activity, is no longer tenable. CL 218,872, which has not been investigated in humans, is a partial BZR agonist (e.g., 121) and loses its discriminating affinity for receptor subtypes in vivo. Other compounds were later found to bind preferentially to the presumed BZR I, in particular zolpidem and alpidem (122,123); however, their profiles of activity do not differ significantly from full agonistic benzodiazepines, which have similar affinity for the presumed BZR I and BZR II. The issue of BZR subtypes has recently been reviewed (124).

Recent studies with ectopically expressed recombinant $GABA_A$ receptors have identified several subunit compositions that seem to determine BZR I and BZR II characteristics (66,94). The use of the brain regional distribution of binding sites for a variety of radioligands labeling different sites on the $GABA_A$ receptor has led to the proposal of four receptor subtypes (51). One receptor subtype, expressed almost exclusively by granule cells of the cerebellum and that contains the α_6 subunit (67a), impresses mainly in autoradiograms (125). It does not recognize most BZR ligands, but binds the partial inverse agonist Ro 15-4513 (126). No specific functions for this receptor subtype has yet been identified.

This well-documented subunit heterogeneity of the $GABA_A$ receptor calls for a meaningful and convenient classification. In principle, it could be based on physiological and pharmacological properties (pharmacological signature) or on the structural composition (structural signature). It does not seem to be of any help to propose a new classification and nomenclature (122) prematurely; rather, it would appear prudent to await the structural elucidation of distinct native receptor phenotypes. It is quite possible that the structural multiplicity of receptors results in only a very few, if any, receptor subtypes with pharmacologically relevant distinct properties.

IV. ALLOSTERIC MODULATION OF THE γ-AMINO-BUTYRIC-ACID$_A$ RECEPTOR CHANNEL BY LIGANDS OF THE BENZODIAZEPINE RECEPTOR

The BZR was among the first drug receptors that were identified as allosteric modulatory sites on receptors for a neurotransmitter. In the meantime, other neurotransmitter receptors have been found to be subject to allosteric modulation by endogenous compounds and by xenobiotics (e.g., the NMDA receptor for excitatory amino acids), and more such receptors will undoubtedly be identified in the future. However, the BZR is still of unmatched importance and interest, because of the broad spectrum of therapeutic activities it is able to mediate and because it is still unique in its ability to exert modulation in the two opposite directions.

Indeed, the BZR responds to three classes of ligands (Fig. 6), with fundamentally different properties (127–135). *Agonists* of the BZR are agents that induce positive allosteric modulation of the $GABA_A$ receptor channel function, *inverse agonists* induce negative allosteric modulation, and *BZR antagonists* bind to the BZR without modulating the $GABA_A$ receptor channel function; however, they competitively antagonize the effects of agonists as well as inverse agonists. Adapting to this particular situation the core concept of molecular pharmacology, which explains ligand regulation of receptor function by two properties of ligands, affinity and intrinsic efficacy, BZR agonists, in-

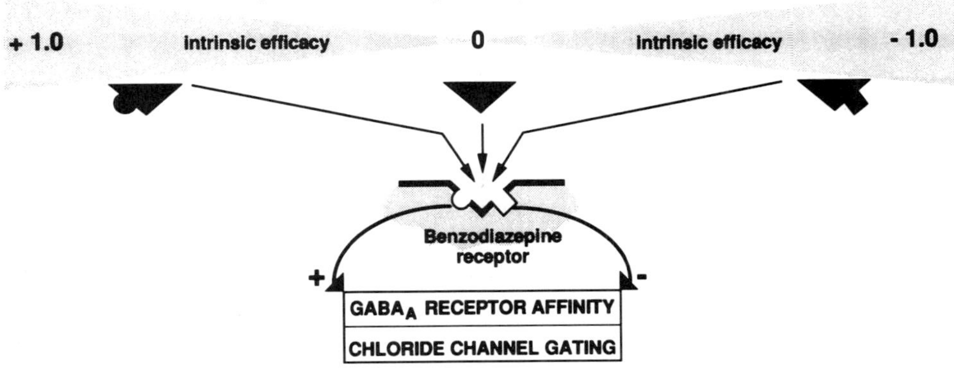

Figure 6 Spectrum of benzodiazepine receptor ligands, with full agonists on the left (intrinsic efficacy +1.0), full inverse agonists on the right (intrinsic efficacy −1.0), pure competitive antagonists in the center (intrinsic efficacy 0), and partial agonist in between. The examples shown all have the benzodiazepine nucleus. A very simplistic diagram illustrates why ligands binding to the benzodiazepine receptor can positively or negatively modulate the GABA receptor channel function, or fail to do so.

verse agonists, and antagonists are ascribed high-positive, high-negative, and zero intrinsic efficacy, respectively. *Intrinsic efficacy* is the inherent property of a ligand to induce or to stabilize, after forming a reversible, noncovalent, binary ligand–receptor complex, a conformational state of the receptor that acts as a stimulus for signal transduction.

The simplest model to explain the concept of intrinsic efficacy of ligands of the $GABA_A$ receptor channel is the two-state model of receptor–channel conformation. The model has to be used at two levels of complexity.

In a first step, we consider the regulation of gating of the $GABA_A$ receptor channel by the GABA-binding site in the absence of modulation by other sites. The receptor–protein complex is assumed to exist in either of two energetically favored conformations: (1) the *active conformation* characterized by the channel-open form and the GABA-binding site in a higher-affinity form for GABA; and (2) the *inactive conformation* corresponding to the channel-closed form and lower-affinity state of the GABA-binding site. In the absence of GABA, the equilibrium between the two states is thought to be strongly toward the inactive conformation (i.e., spontaneous openings of the channel are extremely rare events). When GABA has access to the receptor, it binds preferentially to the receptor channel complex in its active conformation, thereby stabilizing this conformation and shifting the conformational equilibrium toward the open state; channel-opening events now occur frequently. The GABA antagonists, such as bicuculline, can be thought of as preferring the binding site in its inactive form, stabilizing it, and reducing the chance for GABA to bind to the active form. Intrinsic efficacy can be viewed as the ability of a ligand to preferentially bind to one of the conformational states, high-intrinsic efficacy (of $GABA_A$ receptor agonists), meaning high preference for the active conformation, low-intrinsic efficacy (of $GABA_A$ receptor antagonists), no preference for this conformation. The existence of partial agonists of the $GABA_A$ receptor is explained by their less-marked distinction of the two states.

On a higher level of complexity, the $GABA_A$ receptor channel can be assumed to oscillate between two substates of the active form that differ in their affinity for GABA and their tendency to adopt the channel-open or channel-closed form (Fig. 7). The higher-affinity substate would be coupled with one conformation of the BZR, the lower-affinity substate with another conformation. As for the two main states of the $GABA_A$ receptor channel, we can look at the two substates as the *active* and *inactive* states, the former coinciding with the $GABA_A$-binding site in its higher-affinity state. We have to assume that the two substates are in an equilibrium at which they occur with similar probability. The GABA-binding site in the absence of a BZR ligand would then, on the average, be in an intermediate state of affinity. The explanation for the existence of three classes of BZR ligands modulating the function of the GABA-activated $GABA_A$ receptor channel assumes that agonists (such as diazepam) of the BZR have a higher affinity for the active (positive modulatory) state of the BZR. Accordingly, they would shift the $GABA_A$ receptor into a higher-affinity state, with the result that the receptor–channel complex becomes more sensitive to GABA. Conversely, inverse agonists of the BZR have a higher affinity for the inactive (negative modulatory) state of the BZR. They would stabilize this state and shift the equilibrium of the two substates of the open form toward the lower-affinity state, reducing the effect of GABA. Antagonists of the BZR, such as flumazenil, can then be considered as ligands that do not discriminate between the BZR in the two states, binding to both equally well without, thereby, shifting the equilibrium of the substates and, hence, not modulating the effect of GABA; however, antagonizing the effects of both BZR agonists and inverse agonists by inhibiting their

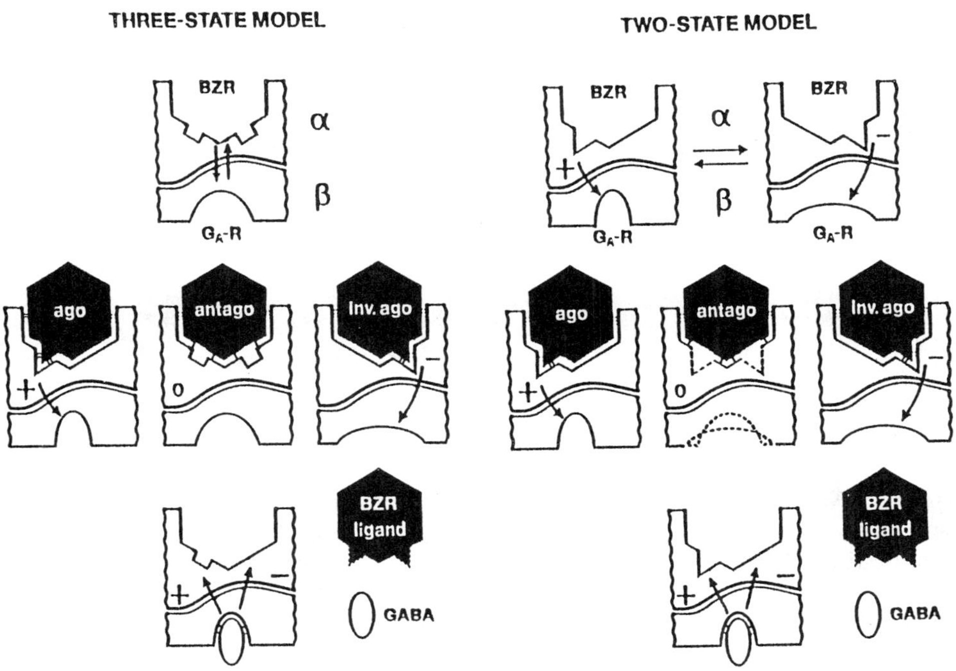

Figure 7 Schematic diagrams to explain the bidirectional modulation of the $GABA_A$ receptor channel function by the allosteric benzodiazepine receptor. Left the induced fit model; right the two-state model. The benzodiazepine-binding site and the GABA-binding site are shown as binding pockets on two different subunits, of which only fragments are depicted.

access to the respective states. As at the level—the GABA-binding site—the two-state model explains the intrinsic efficacy of ligands of the BZR: a lower degree of discrimination between the two states determines partial agonists and partial inverse agonistic activity. The conformational equilibrium inherent to the two-state model also explains why inverse agonists have been found for the BZR, but not for the $GABA_A$ receptor. In the latter, the equilibrium is far in favor of the channel-closed form (Fig. 8). Hence, inverse agonist at the GABA-binding site (i.e., ligands with high preference for the closed state) would not be recognized as such, even if they existed, because they cannot induce a "more-closed" channel. They would appear as antagonist-like compounds, with truly zero intrinsic efficacy (i.e., no discrimination between the states and, therefore, producing no shift in the equilibrium). The BZR allows for agonists (positive modulators) as well as for inverse agonists (negative modulators) because the conformational equilibrium of this modulatory site probably permits it to oscillate continuously at a similar rate between the two sites.

The two-state model used in the foregoing to treat $GABA_A$ and BZR function assumes the spontaneous oscillation between states and assumes that ligands "select" and stabilize preexisting conformations. An alternative model of the BZR function assumes the existence of three states (16), the normal unliganded one being neutral (i.e., lacking modulatory influence on the $GABA_A$ receptor). This model considers agonists as ligands able

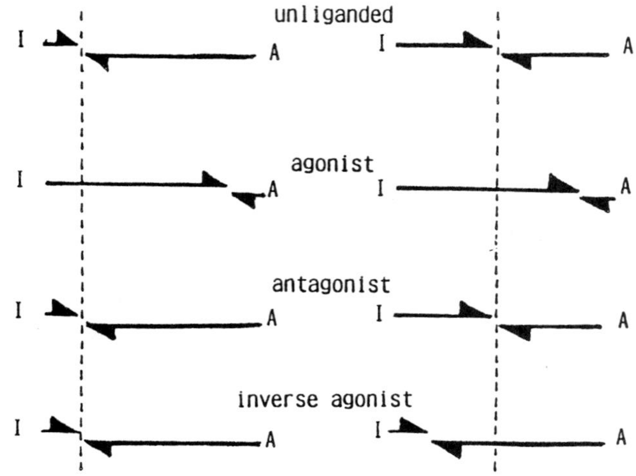

Figure 8 Diagram, based on a two-state model, to explain the absence and presence, respectively, of bidirectional activation of the GABA-binding site and benzodiazepine receptor. The left vertical row illustrates the equilibrium (vertical dashed line) between the inactive (I) or channel-closed coformation and the active (A) or channel-open conformation of the GABA receptor in the absence of allosteric modulation. The GABA agonists shift the equilibrium toward the channel-open conformation; antagonists do not alter the equilibrium, inverse agonists (if they exist) cannot shift the equilibrium farther to the left and, therefore, cannot be distinguished from antagonists. The right vertical row illustrates the situation with the allosteric modulatory benzodiazepine receptor. The equilibrium is shown to be in the middle between the negative modulatory (I) and the positive modulatory (A) conformation. Agonists and inverse agonists can shift the equilibrium (or setpoint) to the right and left, respectively.

to induce ("induced fit"), and not to select, a positive modulatory conformation, and inverse agonists as inducers of a negative modulatory form. Pure antagonists would bind to the neutral conformation as it exists in the absence of a ligand (see Fig. 7).

The intrinsic efficacy of BZR ligands can be assessed only indirectly by comparative procedures. The most obvious way is to study the effects of BZR ligands on dose–response curves for GABA, taking as $GABA_A$ receptor channel function the GABA-induced chloride conductance measured electrophysiologically on single neurons or the GABA-induced changes in the excitability of neuronal populations (e.g., spontaneous or evoked firing, dorsal root potentials). Alternatively, GABA-induced chloride flux can be measured using ^{35}Cl. Figure 9 illustrates schematically the alterations of GABA dose–response curves by BZR ligands. Agonists and partial agonists produce a leftward shift, the intensity of which is dose-dependent, and the maximal shift is a measure of the intrinsic efficacy. Most importantly, BZR agonists and partial agonists produce an apparent increase of the potency of GABA, but do not increase the maximum effect achieved with GABA (in other words, GABA's efficacy). Antagonists have no or only negligible effects on GABA activity, and inverse partial and full agonists shift the GABA dose–response curve to the right and decrease its maximum. Figure 10 shows the

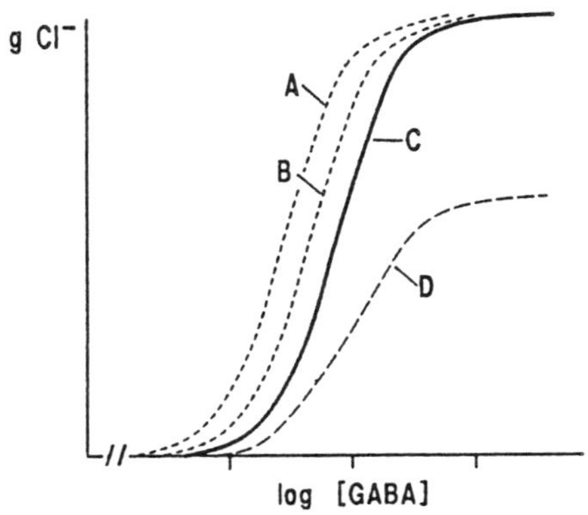

Figure 9 Schematic dose–response curve of GABA for induction of chloride permeability of a neuron in the absence of modulatory agents (C), in the presence of maximally effective concentrations of a full (A) and partial agonist (B), and in the presence of an inverse agonist (D).

maximal potentiation or depression of GABA-induced chloride influx into rat brain membrane vesicles by a series of BZR ligands.

The peak positive or negative modulatory activity of BZR ligands, as assessed by methods just described, is probably best termed *intrinsic activity* as originally used (136). This intrinsic activity is the result of the intrinsic efficacy (an inherent property of the ligand) and factors specific for a given biological test system, the most important being receptor reserve for a given effect (i.e., the density of receptor-binding sites and the

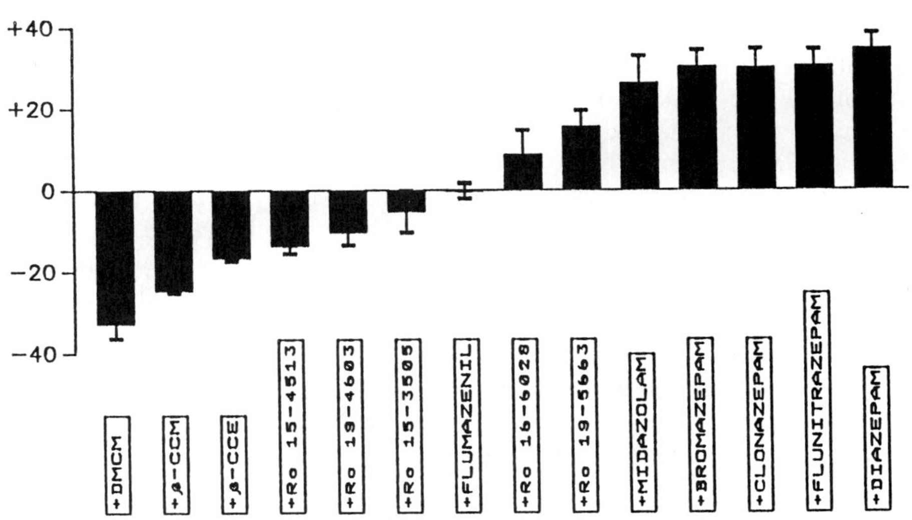

Figure 10 Modulation by various benzodiazepine receptor ligands of 10 μM GABA-induced ^{35}Cl-flux into rat brain synaptosomes. Negative and positive allosteric modulation by the highest effective concentration of the ligands is indicated in percentage change of flux by GABA alone. (From Ref. 207.)

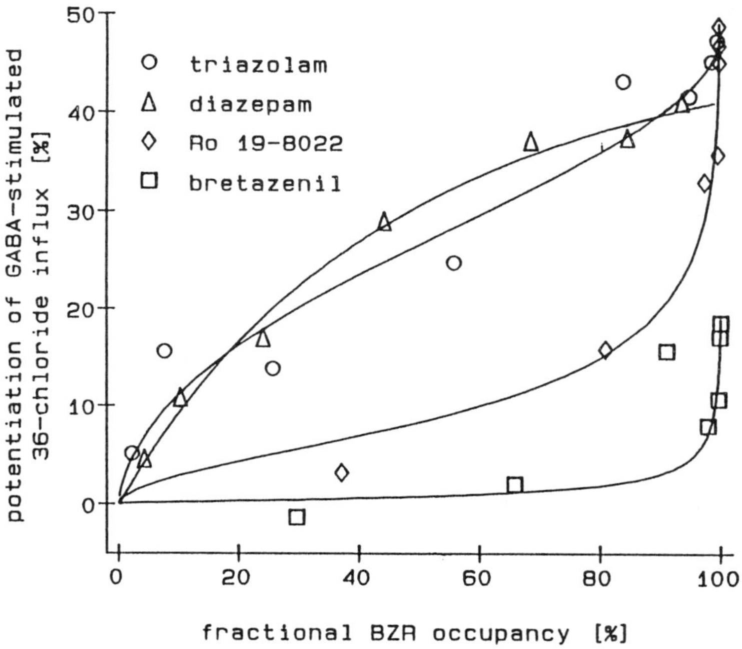

Figure 11 Correlation of benzodiazepine receptor occupancy with potentiation of GABA-induced ^{36}Cl influx into rat cerebral cortex membrane vesicles. Receptor occupancy was measured by inhibition of [^3H]flumazenil binding. (From. Ref. 137.)

degree of receptor–effector coupling). *Intrinsic efficacy* can be defined as the ratio of fractional effect (i.e., effect in percentage of the maximal obtainable one) to fractional receptor occupany (i.e., percentage occupation of available receptors) in a given test system. The smaller the fractional receptor occupancy required to obtain a given magnitude of effect, the higher is the intrinsic efficacy. To obtain more accurate estimates of the intrinsic efficacy of BZR ligands it is, therefore, advantageous to determine both fractional receptor occupancy and fractional effect (137,138). This can be done in vitro as well as in vivo (Fig. 11).

Estimates of the intrinsic efficacy of BZR ligands can also be derived from the study of the effect of GABA on BZR ligand binding. This is possible because GABA receptor (GABA-binding site) and BZR (binding site for BZR ligands) show mutual allosteric modulation. Thus, in the presence of GABA or a GABA mimetic, the binding of BZR agonists is increased, that of antagonist unaffected, and that of BZR inverse agonist decreased (17,139). Binding of BZR partial agonists and partial inverse agonists is less affected by agonist occupation of the GABA-binding site.

More difficult to assess for technical reasons, but nevertheless clearly demonstrated, is the increase by BZR agonists of the affinity of the $GABA_A$ receptor for GABA (140).

V. OTHER ALLOSTERIC MODULATORY SITES ON THE γ-AMINOBUTYRIC $ACID_A$ RECEPTOR

In addition to the BZR, the $GABA_A$ receptor channel contains several other binding sites for endogenous or exogenous ligands that mediate positive or negative allosteric modulation of the receptor channel function. Sites for barbiturates and related agents (38,50), anticonvulsants (noncompetitive or allosteric GABA antagonists; 141), endogenous and synthetic steroids (52–54,142–144); volatile (55,144) and intravenous (145,146) general anesthetics and, probably, alcohols (56a) exist. They are less well-characterized than the BZR. None of them has yet been clearly shown to mediate bidirectional modulation like the BZR. One important difference between some of these modulatory receptors and BZR is that barbiturates, steroids, general anesthetics, and alcohols can, in addition to increasing the apparent potency of GABA (shift of its dose–response curve to the left) also increase, at high concentrations, the maximum effect of GABA or even open the $GABA_A$ receptor channel in the absence of GABA. This is probably not achieved by a direct binding to the GABA-binding site itself, although it can be blocked by the competitive GABA antagonist bicuculline, but may result from a massive allosteric induction of the $GABA_A$ receptor-open conformation.

Ro 5-4864, the convulsant *p*-chloro derivative of diazepam, is a ligand of the mitochondrial BZR (see later discussion). In addition, there is evidence that this atypical benzodiazepine binds somewhere on the $GABA_A$ receptor channel to modulate channel function. This binding site is clearly not identical with the classic high-affinity BZR (143).

VI. MODULATION OF BENZODIAZEPINE RECEPTOR LIGANDS OF CENTRAL NERVOUS SYSTEM FUNCTIONS

Transmission at individual GABAergic synapses is modulated by BZR ligands in essentially the same way as the effect of exogenously applied GABA; that is, agonists and partial agonists increase the apparent potency of GABA or increase the sensitivity of target neurons to GABA to a varying intensity, full or partial inverse agonists depress GABAergic synaptic transmission, and pure antagonists fail to affect GABAergic transmission, but antagonize the positive or negative modulatory effect of agonistic or inverse agonistic BZR ligands (32,33).

To understand the effect of BZR ligands on complex neuronal activities of the CNS, it is imperative to consider the following facts:

First, GABAergic neurons do not act as major pathways conveying sensory or motor information. Rather, they modulate information processing at all levels of relay and integrative steps primarily by preventing overexcitation of probably all neurons, at least in the brain. Pharmacological modulation of GABAergic transmission is, therefore, capable of affecting virtually all CNS functions.

Second, the magnitude of the modulatory influence of BZR ligands on GABAergic synaptic transmission will depend on the actual synaptic concentration of GABA in any individual synapse and, hence, on the spatial and temporal activity of GABAergic neurons, as well as on the excitatory state of individual neurons. The positive and negative modulation by agonistic BZR ligands, therefore, will never be of the same magnitude at all GABAergic synapses. Regional and global effects of these ligands will accordingly differ quite markedly as a function of background neuronal activity.

Third, saturation of BZR in the CNS by even full agonists fails to abolish overall neuronal activity of the CNS because their peak potentiation of GABA is moderate (two- to threefold shift of the GABA dose–response curve) and because reduction of excitatory neuron activity, in turn, reduces activation of GABAergic neurons and, hence, the synaptic concentration of GABA, the effect of which can be allosterically modulated. These latter two mechanisms account for the excellent tolerance of potent BZR agonists that hardly affect other targets at BZR-saturating doses.

VII. PLASTICITY OF THE γ-AMINOBUTYRIC ACID$_A$–BENZODIAZEPINE RECEPTOR

Extended exposure to BZR agonists can result in tolerance to at least part of their therapeutic effects and to physical dependence. A great deal of research has aimed at revealing the molecular changes underlying tolerance and physical dependence and withdrawal (e.g., 147–152). In principle, these phenomena could be due to receptor desensitization (reduced affinity or reduced signal transduction) or to receptor up- or down-regulation (increased or decreased density of receptor channel molecules as a result of altered expression or lifetime). A decreased density of BZR has been described after long-term treatment of animals with BZR agonists; however, this phenomenon has been contested repeatedly or has varied considerably in quantitative terms. Receptor gene transcription is being investigated with specific subunit probes now available (153–155). Measurements of receptor turnover (synthesis internalization, recycling) have been initiated. Desensitization of the GABA$_A$ receptor is a likely basis for tolerance and physical dependence. The GABA$_A$ receptor channel is very prone to rapid desensitization by GABA, even in the absence of allosteric modulators (i.e., neurons exposed to GABA for fractions of a second become less responsive to the neurotransmitter; 156). This desensitization is accelerated by BZR agonists—not surprisingly, as they enhance the potency of GABA. There is increasing evidence for an impaired signal transduction, that is, coupling between GABA binding and channel opening and its allosteric modulation (150,151). This uncoupling does not appear to occur at all GABA$_A$ receptor channels to the same extent. No change in the GABA-induced chloride uptake has been found (152). A loss of the normal potentiating action of BZR full agonists on GABA-induced chloride flux and an enhanced inhibitory effect of inverse agonists after subchronic treatment with full agonists have been described, together with a cross-tolerance to phenobarbital and ethanol (152). Of great heuristic and, possibly, therapeutic interest is the finding that a BZR antagonist is capable of almost immediately reversing GABA$_A$ receptor desensitization (150,152). The symptoms of acute withdrawal in physically dependent individuals are fully consistent with a state of reduced GABA$_A$ receptor channel function. Overall, there are still marked contradictory findings in this area of research that remain to be resolved.

The function of the GABA$_A$ receptor appears to change according to the phosphorylation state (103,157–161). In view of the complex networks of protein kinases and phosphatases, receptor function may critically depend on past and ongoing signal transduction in neurons.

VIII. NATURAL AND ENDOGENOUS LIGANDS OF THE BENZODIAZEPINE RECEPTOR

The discovery of BZRs immediately raised the question of whether endogenous ligands (compounds synthesized within or outside the brain) were acting as physiological or pathological ligands of this modulatory site. The problem is of particular interest because an endogenous ligand could act as either positive modulator (agonist) or negative modulator (inverse agonist) of the GABA$_A$ receptor channel. A considerable amount of investigation has been devoted to solving the question. The current state of knowledge can be summarized as follows.

The existence of endogenous ligands cannot be deduced from the activity of exogenous BZR ligands; that is, exogenous ligands do not simply act as mimetics or antagonists of (agonistic or inverse agonistic) endogenous ligands (27). Exogenous ligands produce the same effects in experimental situations that exclude the presence of endogenous ligands as in in situ situations during which such compounds could be available to interact with the receptor.

On the other hand, compounds of low (nonpeptidic) and high molecular mass (peptidic) have been discovered in the brain and extracerebral tissues on the basis of their inhibitory interaction with the binding of radioligands of the BZR. Inosine, hypoxanthine, and nicotinamide (162) have such a low affinity that they are unlikely to affect the BZR in situ. β-Carboline-3-carboxylic acid esters (13,14) are probably not synthesized in the body. The peptide diazepam-binding inhibitor (DBI) and its putative proteolytic fragments also reveal unusual low affinity for being neuroactive peptides, and their interaction with the BZR in vivo has not been shown beyond any doubt. Diazepam-binding inhibitor and its processing products bind to the BZR, the peripheral BZR, and to a yet ill-defined allosteric site on the $GABA_A$ receptor different from that of the classic BZR (163,164). DBI occurs in extracerebral tissues and seems to act as an inhibitor of insulin and somastatin release in the pancreas (165–178).

It recently came as a great surprise when ligands of the BZR were identified that were undoubtedly benzodiazepines, among them diazepam, in animal and human tissues (28,179–197). These compounds are normally present in too low concentrations to be effective at the BZR; however, they were increased in patients and animals with liver failure and hepatic encephalopathy (198). Interestingly, arousal and cognitive functions improved transiently in a proportion of patients with hepatic encephalopathy in response to the BZR antagonist flumazenil (199). These BZs are unlikely to be synthesized in animal and human tissues, but are probably microbial or plant products. Biosynthetic pathways for their formation have been proposed (200). Their increase in hepatic insufficiency may result from increased absorption, decreased metabolic inactivation, or release from hepatic stores. We should probably better refer to them as natural BZR ligands, than as endogenous ligands or endozepines.

IX. GLIAL AND EXTRACEREBRAL γ-AMINOBUTYRIC $ACID_A$–BENZODIAZEPINE RECEPTORS

The $GABA_A$ receptors exist on sympathetic ganglion cells, adrenal medullary cells (201,202), beta cells of the pancreas (203), as well as on neurons of the enteric plexus and intestinal smooth muscle. Modulation of these receptors by BZR ligands has been reported, but appears to be less consistent than on central neurons. The composition of these extracerebral $GABA_A$ receptor channels is not yet established. In spite of the broad use of BZR ligands in therapy, effects that could be accounted for by modulation of these peripheral $GABA_A$ receptor channels have not been identified. The source of GABA and the conditions under which these receptors could be regulated by GABA are also unknown.

Glial cells in culture have functional $GABA_A$ receptors. They are modulated by BZR ligands in a way that is different from those of neurons (204,204a). A possible effect of these ligands on glial function in situ remains to be shown.

X. THE SO-CALLED PERIPHERAL (MITOCHONDRIAL) BENZODIAZEPINE RECEPTORS

In the early studies on specific receptors for BZs that used tritiated diazepam, high-affinity–binding sites were found in peripheral tissues, in particularly high density in kidney, adrenal gland, and testes (7,205,206). The various ligands showed a very different rank order of affinity for the sites in the CNS and in the periphery (7). Although diazepam had similar affinity for both sites, clonazepam did not bind to the peripheral site; the same was later found for flumazenil (207). These sites were unfortunately called peripheral BZR, a misnomer, as they are also present in the CNS. They are clearly not part of the $GABA_A$ receptor channels and, since they are located preferentially, if not exclusively, in the mitochondrial membrane (206,208), they are also referred to as mitochondrial BZR. They are briefly mentioned here because they are sometimes confused with the $GABA_A$ receptor-coupled "central" BZR.

Characterization of the binding protein from mitochondrial membrane led to the identification of an 18-kDa protein, the cDNA of which was cloned (209–211). This protein was proposed to be involved in the transport of cytosolic cholesterol to the mitochondrial inner membrane where it is metabolized to steroids (212,215). Two other proteins, of 30 and 32 kDa, also binding ligands of the mitochondrial BZR, were recently identified as the adenine nucleotide carrier and the voltage-dependent anion channel (VDAC), respectively (216). These authors propose that the mitochondrial BZR is a complex of three associated proteins, a steroid carrier (an essential component of the steroid biosynthetic machinery), the VDAC, and an adenosine nucleotide carrier (through which porphyrins and ATP enter the mitochondria). This complex function may explain the reported effects of ligands of the mitochondrial BZR on steroidogenesis (217) and mitochondrial respiration (205,218–220) (by providing ATP and porphyrin for the biosynthesis of cytochrome). The in vivo relevance of the ligand effects observed in vitro is not yet clear (221), and the characterization of ligands of the mitochondrial BZR as agonists and antagonists is still confusing. The peptide diazepam-binding inhibitor (DBI) and its processing products have been proposed to regulate the mitochondrial BZR (214). A hypothetical connection between the $GABA_A$ receptor-coupled BZR and the mitochondrial receptor has been made by proposing that ligands of the latter may stimulate biosynthesis of neuroactive steroids in the CNS, which then could modulate the $GABA_A$ receptor channel through its allosteric modulatory site for steroids. The antiproliferative and cell-differentiating activity of a series of BZ derivatives (222,223) cannot, as originally thought, be ascribed to peripheral BZR (224). Effects of ligands of the peripheral BZR on immune cells (e.g., 225) remain to be explained. The existence of still another BZR of low affinity (226) remains to be confirmed.

There is increasing interest in the mitochondrial BZR of glial cells in brain morphology and imaging. Increases in glial cells (gliosis) and, possibly, activation of glia (227) can easily be measured using high-affinity ligand of the mitochondrial BZR.

Recently, a cDNA has been cloned that codes for a 36-kDa polypeptide that copurifies with the $GABA_A$ receptor channel complex on a BZ affinity column (228). The predicted primary structure shows high homology with the VDAC of human B lymphocytes. It is presently unclear whether this VDAC is coupled to the $GABA_A$ receptor in vivo.

XI. FUTURE DEVELOPMENTS OF BENZODIAZEPINE RESEARCH

Because of the immense number of investigations performed over the past 15 years and some fortunate properties of the ligands of the $GABA_A$–benzodiazepine receptor, drugs acting through the BZR are presently the best understood centrally active agents. Yet, many questions remain unanswered.

Current research focuses on the molecular biology of the $GABA_A$–BZR and on the discovery and development of BZR ligands with superior therapeutic properties.

A difficult task will be the identification of the subunit composition of native $GABA_A$ receptor channels, the determination of the number of receptor subtypes and their localization in the CNS. Subunit-specific antibodies (229) and high-resolution technology are required. These characteristics may not be static, but subject to plasticity. The factors determining this multiplicity will have to be clarified. It is not yet clear how the three-dimensional structure of a membrane-anchored oligomeric receptor channel complex can be analyzed. However, this is necessary to learn more about the different ligand-binding sites and the ways ligands bind (49) and induce changes in charge distribution and conformation of the receptor.

Once the structures of native receptors are known, their pharmacology (ligand discrimination) can be determined. Do subtypes confer pharmacologically relevant differences? How can such differences possibly affect the activity profile of drugs on complex CNS functions? The available restricted information predicts small interspecies differences in the primary structure of receptor subunits. How important are these differences in functional terms?

Benzodiazepine receptor ligands have innumerable applications in therapy. In spite of their extraordinary safety, one would like to design compounds that are more tailor-made for the various indications and that have greatly reduced drawbacks, such as the induction of tolerance and physical dependence. In principle, two approaches may be chosen. One is the search for ligands with marked discrimination between receptor subtypes. This approach is based on the hypothesis that distinct receptor subtypes would be localized in a way such that $GABA_A$ receptor modulation would be permitted only on the synapses required for desired therapeutic effects. It is by no means obvious that nature does us this favor. The second approach has already resulted in exciting new ligands. It is based on the fact, already known for other receptors, that partial (low-efficacy) agonists can differ drastically from full agonists in their pharmacological profile (135,230). Bretazenil is such a compound that seems to have greatly reduced intrinsic efficacy at various BZR subtypes (110) and has greatly reduced sedative activity and physical dependence liability (232–234).

Partial inverse agonists with the appropriate trace of negative intrinsic efficacy were shown in animal and human studies to increase alertness and cognitive function. They deserve more attention for the treatment of cognitive dysfunctions. On the other hand, the use of such drugs (e.g., Ro 15-4513; 126) to treat alcoholism, does not look promising.

The BZR is one of several allosteric modulatory sites on the $GABA_A$ receptor channel. Projects are under way that aim at novel ligands on these sites (e.g., the site on which certain steroids act). Future work will show whether other such allosteric modulators of the $GABA_A$ receptor will possess superior properties over the BZR ligands.

The origin of natural benzodiazepines in the body, which make of all of us involuntary benzodiazepine users, is not yet clear. What are the major natural sources? Which are the factors that produce accumulation of these compounds in hepatic insufficiency and, possibly, in other pathological situations? New findings will undoubtedly lead to more questions.

REFERENCES

1. L. H. Sternbach, The benzodiazepine story, *Prog. Drug Res., 22*: 229 (1978).
2. W. Haefely, Alleviation of anxiety—the benzodiazepine saga, *Discoveries in Pharmacology* (M. J. Parnham and J. Bruinvels, eds.), Elsevier Science Publishers, Amsterdam, p. 269 (1983).
3. W. Haefely, E. Kyburz, M. Gerecke, and H. Möhler, Recent advances in the molecular pharmacology of benzodiazepine receptors and in the structure–activity relationship of their agonists and antagonists, *Adv. Drug. Res., 14*: 165 (1985).
4. W. Haefely, A. Kulcsàr, H. Möhler, L. Pieri, P. Polc, and R. Schaffner, Possible involvement of GABA in the central actions of benzodiazepines, *Adv. Biochem. Psychopharmacol., 14*: 131 (1975).
5. E. Costa, A. Guidotti, and C. C. Mao, Evidence for the involvement of GABA in the action of benzodiazepines: Studies on rat cerebellum, *Adv. Biochem. Psychopharmacol., 14*: 113 (1975).
6. H. B. Bosman, R. Case, and P. Di Stefano, Diazepam receptor characterization: Specific binding of benzodiazepines to macromolecules in various brain areas of the rat brain, *FEBS Lett., 82*: 368 (1977).
7. C. Braestrup, and R. F. Squires, Specific benzodiazepine receptor in rat brain characterized by high-affinity (^{3}H)diazepam binding, *Proc. Natl. Acad. Sci. USA, 74*: 3805 (1977).
8. H. Möhler, and T. Okada, Properties of ^{3}H-diazepam binding to benzodiazepine receptors in rat cerebral cortex, *Life Sci., 20*: 2101 (1977).
9. H. Möhler, and T. Okada, Demonstration of benzodiazepine receptors in the central nervous system, *Science, 198*: 849 (1977).
10. M. K. Battersby, J. G. Richards, and H. Möhler, Benzodiazepine receptor: Photoaffinity labeling and localization, *Eur. J. Pharmacol., 57*: 277 (1979).
11. W. Hunkeler, H. Möhler, L. Pieri, P. Polc, E. P. Bonetti, R. Cumin, R. Schaffner, and W. Haefeley, Selective antagonists of benzodiazepines, *Nature, 290*: 514 (1981).
12. W. Haefely, and W. Hunkeler, The story of flumazenil, *Eur. J. Anaesthesiol.*, [Suppl.],2: 3 (1988).
13. C. Braestrup, M. Nielsen, and C. E. Olsen, Urinary and brain ß-carboline-3-carboxylates as potent inhibitors of brain benzodiazepine receptors, *Proc. Natl. Acad. Sci. USA, 77*: 2288 (1980).
14. C. Braestrup, R. Schmiechen, G. Neef, M. Nielsen, and E. N. Petersen, Interaction of convulsive ligands with benzodiazepine receptors, *Science, 216*: 1241 (1982).
15. M. Nielsen, and C. Braestrup, Ethyl ß-carboline-3-carboxylate shows differential benzodiazepine receptor interaction, *Nature, 286*: 606 (1980).
16. P. Polc, E. P. Bonetti, R. Schaffner, and W. Haefely, A three-state model of the benzodiazepine-receptor explains the interactions between the benzodiazepine antagonist Ro 15-1788, benzodiazepine tranquilizers, ß-carbolines, and phenobarbitone, *Arch. Pharmacol., 321*: 260 (1982).
17. J. F. Tallman, J. W. Thomas, and D. W. Gallager, GABA-ergic modulation of benzodiazepine binding site sensitivity, *Nature, 288*: 609 (1978).
18. J. R. Unnerstall, M. J. Kuhar, D. L. Niehoff, and J. M. Palacios, Benzodiazepine receptors are coupled to a subpopulation of γ-aminobutyric acid (GABA) receptors: Evidence from a quantitative autoradiography, *J. Pharmacol. Exp. Ther., 218*: 797 (1981).

19. P. Schoch, and H. Möhler, Purified benzodiazepine receptor retains modulation by GABA, *Eur. J. Pharmacol., 95*: 323 (1983).
20. P. Schoch, B. Häring, B. Takacs, H. Stähli, and H. Möhler, A GABA/benzodiazepine receptor complex from bovine brain: Purification, reconstitution and immunological characterization, *J. Receptor Res., 4*: 189 (1984).
21. E. Sigel, and E. A. Barnard, A γ-aminobutyric acid/benzodiazepine receptor complex from bovine cerebral cortex. Improved purification with preservation of regulatory sites and their interactions, *J. Biol. Chem., 259*: 7219 (1984).
22. E. Sigel, and E. A. Barnard, A γ-aminobutyric acid/benzodiazepine receptor complex from bovine cerebral cortex. Improved purification with preservation of regulatory sites and their interactions, *J. Biol. Chem., 259*: 7219 (1984).
23. E. Sigel, E. A. Stephenson, C. Mamalaki, and E. A. Barnard, A γ-aminobutyric acid/benzodiazepine receptor complex of bovine cerebral cortex: Purification and partial characterization, *J. Biol. Chem., 258*: 6965 (1983).
24. P. R. Schofield, M. G. Darlison, N. Fujita, D. R. Burt, F. A. Stephenson, H. Rodriguez, L. M. Rhee, J. Ramachandran, V. Reale, T. A. Glencorse, P. H. Seeburg, and E. A. Barnard, Sequence and functional expression of the $GABA_A$ receptor shows a ligand-gated receptor super-family, *Nature, 328*: 221 (1987).
25. W. Sieghart, and M. Karobath, Molecular heterogeneity of benzodiazepine receptors, *Nature, 286*: 285 (1980).
26. W. Sieghart, Multiplicity of $GABA_A$ benzodiazepine receptors, *Trends Pharmacol. Sci., 10*: 407 (1989).
27. W. Haefeley, Endogenous ligands of the benzodiazepine receptor, *Pharmacopsychiatria, 21*: 43 (1988).
28. J. D. Rothstein, W. Garland, G. Puia, A., Guidotti, R. J. Weber, and E. Costa, Purification and characterization of naturally occurring benzodiazepine receptor ligands in rat human brain, *J. Neurochem., 58*: 2102 (1992).
29. P. Schoch, J. G. Richards, P. Häring, B. Takacs, C. Stähli, T. Staehelin, W. Haefely, and H. Möhler, Co-localization of $GABA_A$ receptors and benzodiazepine receptors in the brain shown by monoclonal antibodies, *Nature, 314*: 168 (1985).
30. W. Haefely, L. Pieri, P. Polc, and R. Schaffner, General pharmacology and neuropharmacology of benzodiazepine derivatives, *Handb. Exp. Pharmacol., 55/II*: 13 (1981).
31. W. Haefely, P. Polc, L. Pieri, R. Schaffner, and J.-P. Laurent, Neuropharmacology of benzodiazepine: Synaptic mechanisms and neural basis of action, *The Benzodiazepines: From Molecular Biology to Clinical Practice* (E. Costa, ed.), Raven Press, New York, p. 21 (1983).
32. W. Haefely, and P. Polc, Electrophysiological studies on the interaction of anxiolytic drugs with GABA-ergic mechanisms, *Anxiolytics: Neurochemical, Behavioral and Clinical Perspectives* (J. B. Malick, S. J. Enna, and H. I. Yamamura, eds.), Raven Press, New York, p. 113 (1983).
33. W. Haefely, and P. Polc, Physiology of GABA enhancement by benzodiazepines and barbiturates, *Benzodiazepine/GABA receptors and Chloride Channels: Structural and Functional Properties* (R. W. Olsen and J. C. Venter, eds.), Alan R. Liss, New York, p. 97 (1986).
34. A. Stelzer, $GABA_A$ receptors control the excitability of neuronal populations, *Int. Rev. Neurobiol., 33*: 195 (1992).
35. N. G. Bowery, $GABA_B$ receptors and their significance in mammalian pharmacology, *Trends Pharmacol. Sci., 10*: 401 (1984).
36. J. Bormann, Electrophysiology of $GABA_A$ and $GABA_B$ receptor subtypes, *Trends Neurosci., 11*: 112 (1988).

37. E. A. Barnard, M. G. Darlison, and P. H. Seeburg, Molecular biology of the $GABA_A$-receptor: The receptor/channel superfamily, *Trends Neurosci., 10*: 502 (1987).
38. F. A. Stephenson, The $GABA_A$ receptors: Structure and function, *Curr. Aspects Neurosci., 3*: 177 (1991).
39. G. R. Cutting, L. Luc, B. O'Hara, L. M. Kasch, D. Donovan, S. Shimack, S. E. Antonarakis, U. B. Guggino, G. R. Uhl, and H. H. Kazazian, Cloning of the GABA rHO_1 cDNA: A novel GABA subunit highly expressed in retina, *Proc. Natl. Acad. Sci. USA, 88*: 2673 (1991).
40. D. B. Pritchett, H. Sontheimer, C. M. Gorman, H. Kettenmann, P. H. Seeburg, and P. R. Schofield, Transient expression shows ligand gating and allosteric potentiation of $GABA_A$ receptor subunits, *Science, 242*: 1306 (1988).
41. E. Sigel, R. Baur, P. Malherbe, and H. Möhler, The rat $ß_1$-subunit of the $GABA_A$ receptor forms a picrotoxin-sensitive anion channel open in the absence of GABA, *FEBS Lett., 257*: 377 (1989).
42. D. B. Pritchett, H. Sontheimer, B. D. Shivers, S. Ymer, H. Kettenmann, P. R. Schofield, and P. H. Seeburg, Importance of a novel $GABA_A$ receptor subunit for benzodiazepine pharmacology, *Nature, 338*: 582 (1989).
43. G. Cutting, S. Curristin, H. Zoghbi, B. O'Hara, M. Seldin, and G. Uhl, Identification of a putative GABA receptor subunit r_2 cDNA and colocalization of the genes encoding r_2 and r_1 to human chromosome Gg 14-21 and mouse chromosome 4, *Genomics,* (in press; 1992).
44. A. Nistri, and L. Sivilotti, An unusual effect of γ-aminobutyric acid on synaptic transmission of frog tectal neurons in vitro, *Br. J. Pharmacol., 85*: 917 (1985).
45. L. Sivilotti, and A. Nistri, Pharmacology of a novel effect of γ-aminobutyric acid on the frog optic tectum in vitro, *Eur. J. Pharmacol., 164*: 205 (1984).
46. G. A. R. Johnston, Multiplicity of GABA receptors, *Benzodiazepine/GABA Receptors and Chloride Channels. Receptor Biochemistry and Methodology,* Vol. 5 (R. W. Olsen and J. C. Venter, eds.), Alan R. Liss, New York, p. 57 (1986).
47. S. O. Caslotti, F. A. Stephenson, and E. A. Barnard, Separate subunits for agonist and benzodiazepine binding in the γ-aminobutyric $acid_A$ receptor oligomer, *J. Biol. Chem., 261*: 15013 (1986).
47a. M. Bureau, and R. W. Olsen, γ-Aminobutyric acid/benzodiazepine receptor carries binding sites on both two major peptide subunits, *Biochem. Biophys. Res. Commun., 153*: 1006 (1988).
48. M. Bureau, and R. W. Olsen, Multiple distinct subunits of the γ-aminobutyric acid-A receptor protein show different ligand-binding affinities, *Mol. Pharmacol., 37*: 497 (1990).
48a. E. Sigel, R. Baur, S. Kellenberger, and P. Malherbe, Point mutations affecting antgonist affinity and agonist dependent gating of $GABA_A$ receptor channels, *EMBO J., 11*: 2017 (1992).
49. F. A. Stephenson, M. J. Duggan, and S. Pollard, The γ_2 subunit is an integral component of the γ-aminobutyric acid-A receptor but the α_2 polypeptide is the principal site of the agonist benzodiazepine photoaffinity labeling reaction, *J. Biol. Chem., 265*: 21160 (1990).
50. R. W. Olsen, and A. J. Tobin, Molecular biology of $GABA_A$ receptors, *FASEB J., 4*: 1469 (1990).
51. R. W. Olsen, R. T. McCabe, and J. K. Wamsley, $GABA_A$ receptor subtypes: Autoradiographic comparison of GABA, benzodiazepine, and convulsant binding sites in the rat central nervous system, *J. Chem. Neuroanat., 3*: 59 (1990).
52. M. D. Majewska, N. C. Harrison, R. D. Schwartz, J. L. Baker, and S. M. Paul, Steroid hormone metabolites are barbiturate-like modulators of the GABA receptor, *Science, 232*: 1004 (1986).
53. N. L. Harrison, M. D. Majewska, J. W. Hanington, and J. L. Baker, Structure–activity relationship for steroid interaction with the gamma-aminobutyric acid-A receptor complex, *J. Pharmacol. Exp. Ther., 241*: 346 (1987).

54. K. W. Gee, M. B. Bolger, R. E. Brinton, H. Coirini, and B. S. McEwen, Steroid modulation of the chloride ionophore in rat brain: Structure–activity requirements, regional dependence and mechanism of action, *J. Pharmacol. Exp. Ther., 246*: 803 (1988).
55. M. Nakahiro, J. Z. Yeh, E. Brunner, and T. Narahshi, General anesthetics modulate GABA receptor channel complex in rat dorsal root gangling neurons, *FASEB J., 3*: 1850 (1989).
56. K. A. Wafford, D. M. Burnett, T. V. Dunwiddie, and R. A. Harrison, Genetic difference in the ethanol sensitivity of $GABA_A$ receptors expressed in xenopus oocytes, *Science, 249*: 291 (1990).
56a. F. F. Weight, Cellular and molecular physiology of alcohol actions in the nervous system, *Int. Rev. Neurobiol., 33*L: 289 (1992).
57. C. Mamalaki, F. A. Stephenson, and E. A. Barnard, The $GABA_A$/benzodiazepine receptor is a heterotetramer of homologous α and ß subunits, *EMBRO J., 6*: 561 (1987).
57a. M. Hirouchi, R. Kawano, T. Katagivi, Y. Takahashi, and K. Kuriyama, Nucleotide and deduced amino acid sequences of the $GABA_A$ receptor α-subunit from human brain, *Neurochem. Int., 15*: 33 (1989).
58. F. A. Stephenson, M. J. Duggan, and S. D. Lasalotti, Identification of the α_3 subunit in the $GABA_A$ receptor purified from bovine brain, *FEBS Lett., 243*: 358 (1984).
59. B. D. Shivers, I. Killisch, R. Sprengel, H. Sontheimer, M. Köhler, P. R. Schofield, and P. H. Seeburg, Two novel $GABA_A$ receptor subunits exist in distinct neuronal populations, *Neuron, 3*: 327 (1989).
60. S. J. Lolait, A.-M. O'Carroll, K. Kusano, J. M. Muller, M. J. Brownstein, and C. C. Mahan, Cloning and expression of a novel rat $GABA_A$ receptor, *FEBS Lett., 246*: 145 (1989).
61. P. R. Schofield, D. B. Pritchett, H. Sontheimer, H. Kettenmann, and P. H. Seeburg, Sequence and expression of human $GABA_A$ receptor α_1- and $ß_1$ subunits, *FEBS Lett., 244*: 361 (1989).
62. S. Ymer, A. Draghun, M. Köhler, P. R. Schofield, and P. H. Seeburg, Sequence and expression of a novel $GABA_A$ receptor a subunit, *FEBS Lett., 258*: 119 (1989).
63. S. Ymer, P. R. Schofield, A. Draghun, P. Werner, M. Köhler, and P. H. Seeburg, $GABA_A$ receptor ß-subunit heterogeneity: functional expression of cloned cDNA's, *EMBRO J., 8*: 1665 (1989).
64. P. Whiting, R. M. McKernan, and L. I. Iversen, Another mechanism for creating diversity in γ-aminobutyrate type A receptors: RNA splicing directs expression of two forms of γ_2 subunit, one of which contains a protein kinase C phosphorylation site, *Proc. Natl. Acad. Sci. USA, 87*: 9966 (1990).
65. B. Sommer, A. Poustka, N. K. Spurr, and P. H. Seeburg, The murine $GABA_A$ receptor α-subunit gene: Structure and assignment to human chromosome 1, *DNA Cell Biol. 9*: 561 (1990).
65a. M. Khrestchatisky, A. J. MacLennan, M.-Y. Chiang, W. Xu, M. B. Jackson, N. Brecha, C. Sternini, R. W. Olsen, and A. J. Tobin, A novel α subunit in rat brain $GABA_A$ receptors, *Neurons 3*: 745 (1989).
66. D. B. Prichett, and P. H. Seeburg, γ-Aminobutyric $acid_A$ receptor α_5-subunit creates novel type II benzodiazepine receptor pharmacology, *J. Neurochem., 54*: 1802 (1990).
67. P. Malherbe, A. Draghun, G. Multhaup, K. Beyreuther, and H. Möhler, $GABA_A$-receptor exposed from rat brain α- and ß-subunit cDNAs displays potentiation by benzodiazepine receptor ligands, *Mol. Brain Res., 8*: 199 (1990).
67a. K. Kato, Novel $GABA_A$ receptor α-subunit is expressed only in cerebellar granule cells, *J. Mol. Biol., 214*: 619 (1990).
68. W. Wisden, A. Herb, H. Wieland, K. Keinänen, H. Lüddens, and P. H. Seeburg, Cloning, pharmacological characterization and expression pattern of the rat $GABA_A$ receptor α_4 subunit, *FEBS Lett., 289*: 227 (1991).
69. A. N. Bateson, R. J. Harvey, W. Wisden, T. A. Glenclose, A. A. Hicks, S. P. Hunt,

E. A. Barnard, and M. G. Darlison, The chicken $GABA_A$ receptor α_1 subunit: cNDA sequence and localization of the corresponding mRNA, *Mol. Brain Res., 9*: 333 (1991).

70. M. Khrestchatisky, A. J. MacLennan, N. J. K. Tillakaratne, M.-Y. Chiang, and A. J. Tobin, Sequence and regional distribution of the mRNA encoding the α_2 polypeptide of rat γ-aminobutyric $acid_A$ receptors, *J. Neurochem., 56*: 1717 (1991).

71. A. Herb, W. Wisden, H. Lüddens, G. Puia, S. Vicini, and P. H. Seeburg, The third gamma subunit of the gamma-aminobutyric acid type A receptor family, *Proc. Natl. Acad. Sci. USA, 89*: 1433 (1992).

71a. D. Wilson-Shaw, M. Robinson, C. Gambarana, R. E. Siegel, and M. Sikula, A novel subunit of the $GABA_A$ receptor identified using the polymerase chain reaction. *FEBS Lett., 284*: 211 (1991).

72. D. Wilson-Shaw, M. Robinson, C. Gambarana, R. E. Sigel, and J. M. Sikula, A novel ξ gamma subunit of the $GABA_A$ receptor identified using the polymerase chain reaction, *FEBS Lett., 284*: 211 (1991).

73. D. R. Burt, and G. L. Kamatchi, $GABA_A$ receptor subtypes: From pharmacology to molecular biology, *FASEB J., 5*: 2916 (1991).

74. P. H. Seeburg, W. Wisden, T. A. Vendoorn, D. B. Pritchett, P. Werner, A. Herb, H. Lüddens, R. Sprengel, and B. Sakmann, The $GABA_A$ receptor family: Molecular and functional diversity, *Cold Spring Harbor Symp. Quant. Biol., 55*: 29 (1990).

75. A. Lasham, E. Vreugdenhil, A. N. Bateson, E. A. Barnard, and M. G. Darlison, Conserved organization of γ-aminobutyric $acid_A$ receptor genes: Cloning and analysis of the chicken β_4-subunit gene, *J. Neurochem., 757*: 352 (1991).

76. V. J. Buckle, N. Fujita, A. S. Ryder-Cook, J. M. J. Deny, P. J. Barnard, R. V. Leto, P. R. Schofield, P. H. Seeburg, A. N. Bateson, M. G. Darlison, and E. A. Barnard, Chromosomal localization of $GABA_A$ receptor subunit genes: Relationship to human genetic disease, *Neuron, 3*: 647 (1989).

77. A. N. Bateson, A. Lasham, and M. G. Darlison, γ-aminobutyric $acid_A$ receptor heterogeneity is increased by alternative splicing of a novel ß-subunit gene transcript, *J. Neurochem., 56*: 1437 (1991).

78. K. Fuchs, D. Adamiker, and W. Sieghart, Identification of α_2 and α_3-subunits of the $GABA_A$-benzodiazepine receptor complex purified from the brain of young rats, *FEBS Lett., 261*: 52 (1990).

79. D. Benke, S. Mertens, A. Trzeciak, D. Gillessen, and H. Möhler, Identification of the γ_2-subunit in native $GABA_A$-receptors in brain, *Eur. J. Pharmacol., 189*: 337 (1990).

80. D. Benke, S. Cicin-Sain, S. Mertens, and H. Möhler, Immunochemical identification of the α_1- and α_3-subunits of the $GABA_A$ receptor in rat brain, *J. Receptor Res., 11*: 407 (1991).

81. D. Benke, S. Mertens, A. Trzeciak, D. Gillessen, and H. Möhler, $GABA_A$-receptors: Association of the γ_2-subunit with the $\beta_{2/3}$ subunits, *J. Biol. Chem., 266*: 4478 (1991).

82. D. Benke, S. Mertens, A. Trzeciak, D. Gillessen, and H. Möhler, Identification and immunohistochemical mapping of $GABA_A$ receptor subtypes containing the δ-subunit in rat brain, *FEBS Lett., 283*: 145 (1991).

83. A. D. Buchstaller, D. Adamiker, K. Fuchs, and W. Sieghart, *N*-Deglycosylation and immunological identification indicates the existence of ß-subunits isoforms of the rat $GABA_A$ receptor, *FEBS Lett., 287*: 27 (1991).

84. A. D. Buchstaller, K. Fuchs, and W. Sieghart, Identification of α_a, α_2- and α_3-subunits isoforms of the $GABA_A$ benzodiazepine receptor in the rat brain, *Neurosci. Lett., 129*: 237 (1991).

85. A. J. MacLennan, N. Brecha, M. Khrestchatisky, C. Sternini, N. J. K. Tillikaratne, M.-Y. Chang, K. Anderson, M. Lai, and A. J. Tobin, Independent cellular and ontogenetic expression of mRNAs encoding three α polypeptides of the rat $GABA_A$ receptor, *Neuroscience, 43*: 369 (1991).

86. W. Wisden, D. J. Laurie, H. Mouyer, and P. H. Seeburg, The distribution of 13 $GABA_A$ receptor subunit mRNAs in the rat brain. I. Telencephalon, diencephalon, mesencephalon, *J. Neurosci., 12*: 1040 (1992).
87. D. J. Laurie, P. H. Seeburg, and W. Wisden, The distribution of 13 $GABA_A$ receptor subunit mRNAs in the rat brain. II. Olfactory bulb and cerebellum, *J. Neurosci., 12*: 1063 (1992).
88. E. Persohn, P. Malherbe, and J. G. Richards, Comparative molecular neuroanatomy of cloned $GABA_A$ receptor subunits in the rat CNS, *J. Comp. Neurol., 326*: 193 (1992).
89. R. W. Olsen, M. H. Bureau, S. Endo, and G. Smith, The $GABA_A$ receptor family in the mammalian brain, *Neurochem. Res., 16*: 317 (1991).
90. H. Lüddens, and W. Wisden, Function and pharmacology of multiple $GABA_A$ receptor subunits, *Trends Pharmacol. Sci., 12*: 49 (1991).
91. P. M. Sweetman, and J. F. Tallman, Regional differences in brain benzodiazepine receptor carbohydrates, *J. Pharmacol. Exp. Ther., 29*: 299 (1986).
92. L. A. C. Blair, E. S. Levitan, J. Marshall, V. E. Dionne, and E. A. Barnard, Single subunits of the $GABA_A$ receptor form channels with properties of the native receptor, *Science, 242*: 579 (1988).
93. E. S. Levitan, P. R. Schofield, D. R. Burt, L. M. Rhee, W. Wisden, M. Köhler, N. Fujita, H. F. Rodriguez, S. Stephenson, M. G. Darlison, E. A. Barnard, and P. H. Seeburg, Structural and functional basis for $GABA_A$ receptor heterogeneity, *Nature, 335*: 76 (1988).
94. D. B. Pritchett, H. Lüddens, and P. H. Seeburg, Type I and type II $GABA_A$–benzodiazepine receptors produced in transfected cells, *Science, 245*: 1389 (1989).
95. D. B. Pritchett, and P. H. Seeburg, γ-Aminobutyric acid type A receptor point mutation increases the affinity of compounds for the benzodiazepine site, *Proc. Natl. Acad. Sci. USA, 88*: 1421 (1991).
96. G. Puia, M. R. Santi, S. Vincini, D. B. Pritchett, P. H. Seeburg, and E. Costa, Difference in the negative allosteric modulation of g-aminobutyric acid receptors elicited by 4¢-chlorodiazepam and by a ß-carboline-3-carboxylate ester: A study with natural and constituted receptor, *Proc. Natl. Acad. Sci. USA, 86*: 7275 (1989).
97. G. von Blankenfeld, S. Ymer, D. B. Pritchett, H. Sontheimer, M. Ewert, P. H. Seeburg, and H. Kettenmann, Differential benzodiazepine pharmacology of mammalian recombinant $GABA_A$ receptors, *Neurosci. Lett., 115*: 269 (1990).
98. P. Malherbe, E. Sigel, R. Baur, E. Persohn, J. G. Richards, and H. Möhler, Functional characteristics and sites of gene expression of the α_1, β_1, γ_2-isoform of the rat $GABA_A$ receptor, *J. Neurosci., 10*: 2330 (1990).
99. H. Möhler, P. Malherbe, A. Draghun, and J. G. Richards, $GABA_A$-receptors: Structural requirements and sites of gene expression in mammalian brain, *Neurochem. Res., 15*: 199 (1990).
100. S. Ymer, A. Draghum, W. Wisden, P. Werner, K. Keinänen, P. R. Schofield, R. Sprengel, D. B. Pritchett, and P. H. Seeburg, Structural and functional characterization of the γ_1 subunit of $GABA_A$/benzodiazepine receptors, *EMBO J., 9*: 3261 (1990).
101. E. Sigel, R. Baur, G. Trube, H. Möhler, and P. Malherbe, The effect of subunit composition of rat brain $GABA_A$-receptors on channel function, *Neuron, 5*: 703 (1990).
102. T. W. Verdoorn, A. Draghum, S. Ymer, P. H. Seeburg, and B. Sakmann, Functional properties of recombinant rat $GABA_A$ receptors depend upon subunit composition, *Neuron, 4*: 919 (1990).
103. E. Sigel, R. Baur, and P. Mahlerbe, Activation of protein kinase C results in down-regulation of different recombinant $GABA_A$channels, *FEBS Lett., 291*: 150 (1991).
104. S. Vicini, Pharmacologic significance of the structural heterogeneity of the $GABA_A$ receptor–chloride channel complex, *Neuropsychopharmacology, 4*: 9 (1991).
105. G. Puia, S. Vicini, P. H. Seeburg, and E. Costa, Influence of recombinant γ-aminobutyric

acid$_A$ receptor subunit composition on the action of allosteric modulators of γ-aminobutyric acid-gated U$^-$ currents, *Mol. Pharmacol., 39*: 691 (1991).
106. M. Masotti, J. L. Schlichting, M. D. Antonacci, P. Giusti, M. Memo, E. Costa, and A. Guidotti, γ-Aminobutyric acid$_A$ receptor heterogeneity in rat central nervous system: Studies with clonazepam and other benzodiazepine ligands, *J. Pharmacol. Exp. Ther., 256*: 1 (1991).
107. S. Shimada, G. Cutting, and G. R. Uhl, γ-Aminobutyric acid A or C receptor? γ-Aminobutyric ρ_1 receptor RNA induces bicuculine-, barbiturate-, and benzodiazepine-insensitive g-aminobutyric acid response in Xenopus oocytes, *Mol. Pharmacol., 41*: 683 (1992).
108. F. Knoflach, K. H. Backus, T. Giller, P. Malherbe, P. Pfimlin, H. Möhler, and G. Trube, Pharmacological and electrophysiological properties of recombinant GABA$_A$ receptors comprising the α_3, β_1 and γ_2 subunits, *Eur. J. Neurosci., 4*: 1 (1992).
109. F. Knoflach, T. Rhyner, S. M. Kellenburger, V. Drescher, P. Malherbe, E. Sigel, and H. Möhler, The γ_3-subunit of the GABA$_A$ receptor confers sensitivity to the benzodiazepine receptor ligands, *FEBS Lett., 293*: 191 (1991).
110. G. Puia, I. Ducic, S. Vicini, and E. Costa, Molecular mechanisms of the partial allosteric modulatory effects of bretazenil at γ-aminobutyric acid type A receptor, *Proc. Natl. Acad. Sci. USA, 89*: 3620 (1992).
111. P. R. Schofield, B. S. Shivers, and P. H. Seeburg, The role of receptor subtypes diversity in the CNS, *Trends Neurosci., 13*: 8 (1990).
112. H. Lüddens, I. Killisch, and P. H. Seeburg, More than one alpha variant may exist in a GABA$_A$/benzodiazepine receptor complex, *J. Receptor Res., 11*: 535 (1991).
113. A. Eichinger, and W. Sieghart, Postnatal development of proteins associated with different benzodiazepine receptors, *J. Neurochem., 46*: 173 (1986).
114. C. Gambarana, R. Pittman, and R. E. Siegel, Developmental expression of the receptor α_1 subunit mRNA in the rat brain, *J. Neurobiol., 21*: 1169 (1990).
115. P. Botolin, M.-R. Santi, M. Memo, E. Costa, and D. R. Grayson, Distinct development patterns of expression of the rat α_1, α_5, γ_{2S} and γ_{2L} GABA$_A$ receptor subunit mRNAs in vivo and in vitro, *J. Neurochem., 59*: 62 (1992).
116. J. M. Séquier, J. G. Richards, P. Malherbe, G. W. Price, S. Matthews, and H. Möhler, Mapping of brain areas containing RNA homologous to cDNA's encoding the α- and ß-subunits of the rat GABA$_A$ receptor, *Proc. Natl. Acad. Sci. USA, 85*: 7815 (1988).
117. M. Memo, P. Bovolin, E. Costa, and D. R. Grayson, Regulation of γ-aminobutyric acid$_A$ receptor subunit expression by activation of *N*-methyl-D-aspartate-selective glutamate receptors, *Mol. Pharmacol., 39*: 599 (1991).
118. C. A. Klepner, A. J. Lippa, D. I. Benson, M. C. Santo, and B. Beer, Resolution of two biochemically and pharmacologically distinct benzodiazepine receptors, *Pharmacol. Biochem. Behav., 11*: 457 (1979).
119. R. F. Squires, D. I. Benson, c. Braestrup, J. Coupet, C. A. Klepner, V. Myers, and B. Beer, Some properties of brain specific benzodiazepine receptors: New evidence for multiple receptors, *Pharmacol. Biochem. Behav., 10*: 825 (1979).
120. A. S. Lippa, K. M. Garrett, B. Tabakoff, B. Beer, L. P. Wennogle, and L. R. Meyerson, Heterogeneity of brain benzodiazepine receptors: Effects of physiological conditions, *Brain Res. Bull., 14*: 189 (1985).
121. V. de la Sayette, C. Chavoix, E. Brouillet, P. Hantraye, M. Kumimoto, M. Khalili-Varesteh, B. Guibert, C. Prenant, and M. Maziére, In vivo benzodiazepine receptor occupancy by CL 218,872 visualized by positron emission tomography in the brain of the living baboon: Modulation by GABA-ergic transmission and relation with anticonvulsant activity, *Exp. Brain Res., 83*: 397 (1991).
122. S. Z. Langer, and S. Arbilla, Limitations of the benzodiazepine receptor nomenclature: A proposal for a pharmacological classification as omega receptor subtypes, *Fundam. Clin. Pharmacol., 2*: 159 (1988).
123. J. Benavides, B. Peny, A. Dubois, G. Penault, E. Morel, B. Zivkovic, and B. Scatton,

In vivo interaction of zolpidem with central benzodiazepine (BZD) binding sites (as labeled by ^{3}H-Ro 15-1788) in the mouse brain. Preferential affinity of zolpidem for the ω_1 (BZD_1) subtypes, *J. Pharmacol. Exp. Ther., 245*: 1033 (1988).

124. A. Dobler, and I. L. Martin, Multiple benzodiazepine receptors: No reason for anxiety, *Trends Pharmacol. Sci., 13*: 76 (1992).
125. H. Lüddens, D. B. Pritchett, M. Köhler, I. Killisch, K. Keinänen, H. Monyer, R. Sprengler, and P. H. Seeburg, Cerebellar $GABA_A$ receptor selective for a behavioural alcohol antagonist, *Nature, 346*: 648 (1990).
126. E. P. Bonetti, W. P. Burkard, M. Gabl, W. Hunkeler, H.-P. Lorez, J. R. Martin, H. Möhler, W. Osterrieder, L. Pieri, P. Polc, J. G. Richards, R. Schaffner, R. Scherchlicht, P. Schoch, and W. Haefely, Ro 15-4513: Partial inverse agonisms at the BZR and interaction with ethanol, *Pharmacol. Biochem. Behav., 31*: 733 (1989).
127. W. Haefely, The biological basis of benzodiazepine actions, *The Benzodiazepines Current Standards for Medical Practice* (D. E. Smith and D. R. Wesson, eds.), MTP Press, Lancaster, p. 7 (1985).
128. W. Haefely, Structure and function of the benzodiazepine receptors, *Chimia, 41*: 389 (1987).
129. W. Haefely, Benzodiazepines, *Int. Anestesiol. Clin., 26*: 262 (1988).
130. W. Haefely, Pharmacology of the allosteric modulation of $GABA_A$ receptors by benzodiazepine receptor ligands, *Allosteric Modulation of Amino Acid Receptors: Therapeutic Implications* (E. A. Barnard and E. Costa, eds.), Raven Press, New York, p. 47 (1989).
131. W. Haefely, Benzodiazepine receptor and ligands: Structural and functional differences, *Benzodiazepines: Current Concepts* (I. Hindmarch, G. Beaumont, S. Brandon, and B. E. Leonard, eds.), John Wiley & Sons, Chichester, p. 1 (1990).
132. W. Haefely, The $GABA_A$-benzodiazepine receptor: Biology and pharmacology, *Handbook of Anxiety, Vol. 3: The Neurobiology of Anxiety* (G. D. Burrows, M. Roth, and R. Neyes, eds.), Elsevier, Amsterdam, p. 165 (1990).
133. W. Haefely, Comparative pharmacology of benzodiazepine receptor ligands with differing intrinsic efficacy, *Transmitter Amino Acid Receptors: Structures, Transduction and Models for Drug Development* (E. A. Barnard and E. Costa, eds.), Thieme, New York, p. 91 (1991).
134. J. G. Richards, P. Schoch, and W. Haefely, Benzodiazepine receptors: New vistas, *Semin. Neurosci., 3*: 191 (1991).
135. C. R. Gardner, Pharmacological profiles in vivo and benzodiazepine receptor ligands, *Drug. Dev. Res., 12*: 1 (1988).
136. E. J. Ariens, *Molecular Pharmacology,* Academic Press, New York (1964).
137. M. Facklam, P. Schoch, and W. Haefely, Relationship between benzodiazepine receptor occupancy and potentiation of $GABA_A$-stimulated chloride flux in vitro of four ligands of a differing intrinsic efficacies, *J. Pharmacol. Exp. Ther., 261*: 1106 (1992).
138. M. Facklam, P. Schoch, E. P. Bonetti, F. Jenck, J. R. Martin, J.-O. Moreau, and W. Haefely, Relationship between benzodiazepine receptor occupancy and functional effects in vivo of four ligands of differing intrinsic efficacies, *J. Pharmacol. Exp. Ther., 261*: 1113 (1992).
139. T. M. De Lorey, and G. B. Brown, γ-Aminobutyric $acid_A$ receptor pharmacology in rat cerebral cortical synaptoneurosomes, *J. Neurochem., 58*: 2162 (1992).
140. D. R. Bristow, R. Moratalla, and I. L. Martin, Flunitrazepam increases the affinity of the $GABA_A$ receptor in cryostat-cut rat brain sections, *Eur. J. Pharmacol., 184*: 335 (1990).
141. A. Concas, M. Sena, E. Sanna, and G. Biggio, (^{35}S)*t*-Butylbicyclophosphoro thionate binding: A biochemical trial to identify allosteric modulators of γ-aminobutyric $acid_A$ receptors, *Transmitter Amino Acid Receptors: Structure, Transduction and Models for Drug Development* (E. A. Barnard and E. Costa, eds.), Thieme, New York, p. 77 (1991).
142. N. C. Lan, J.-S. Chun, D. Belelli, D. B. Pritchett, P. H. Seeburg, and K. W. Gee, A steroid recognition site is functionally coupled to an expressed $GABA_A$–benzodiazepine receptor, *Eur. J. Pharmacol., 188*: 403 (1990).

143. N. C. Lan, D. L. Johnson, and K. W. Gee, Identification and characterization of two novel modulatory sites on the gamma-aminobutyric $acid_A$ receptor–ionophore complex, *Transmitter Amino Acid Receptors: Structure, Transduction and Models for Drug Development* (E. A. Barnard and E. Costa, eds.), Thieme, New York, p. 129 (1991).
144. E. J. Moody, P. D. Suzdak, S. M. Paul, and P. Skolnick, Modulation of the benzodiazepine/γ-aminobutyric acid receptor chloride–channel complex by inhalation anaesthetics, *J. Neurochem., 51*: 1386 (1988).
145. J. J. Lambert, C. Hill-Venning, J. A. Peters, N. C. Stungess, and T. G. Hales, The action of anesthetic steroids on inhibitory and excitatory amino acid receptor, *Transmitter Amino Acid Receptors: Structure, Transduction and Models for Drug Development* (E. A. Barnard and E. Costa, eds.), Thieme, New York, p. 219 (1991).
146. M. S. Langley, and R. C. Heel, Propofol: A review of its pharmacodynamic and pharmacokinetic properties and use as an intravenous anaesthetic, *Drugs, 35*: 334 (1988).
147. L. G. Miller, W. R. Galpern, D. J. Greenblatt, M. Lumbin, and R. I. Shader, Chronic benzodiazepine administration. IV. A partial agonist produces behavioral effects without tolerance or receptor alterations, *J. Pharmacol. Exp. Ther., 254*: 33 (1990).
148. D. O. Ngur, H. C. Rosenberg, and T. H. Chiu, Modulation of GABA-stimulated Cl-flux by a benzodiazepine agonist and an "inverse agonist" after chronic flurazepam treatment, *Eur. J. Pharmacol., 176*: 351 (1990).
149. D. J. Roca, G. D. Schiller, L. Friedman, I. Rozenberg, T. T. Gibbs, and D. H. Farb, γ-Aminobutyric $acid_A$ receptor regulation in culture: Altered allosteric interactions following prolonged exposure to benzodiazepines, barbiturates, and methylxanthines, *Mol. Pharmacol., 37*: 710 (1990).
150. D. W. Gallager, R. J. Marley, and T. D. Hernandez, Biochemical and electrophysiological mechanisms underlying benzodiazepine tolerance and dependence, *The Biological Basis of Drug Tolerance and Dependence* (J. A. Pratt, ed.), Academic Press, London, p. 44 (1991).
151. L. G. Miller, and D. J. Greenblatt, Neurochemistry of the benzodiazepines, *Drugs of Abuse and Neurobiology* (R. R. Watson, ed.), CRC Press, Boca Raton, p. 175 (1992).
152. A. M. Allan, L. D. Baier, and X. Zhang, Effects of lorazepam tolerance and withdrawal on $GABA_A$ receptor-operated chloride channels, *J. Pharmacol. Exp. Ther., 261*: 395 (1992).
153. C. Heninger, N. Saito, J. F. Tallman, K. M. Ganett, M. P. Vitek, R. S. Duman, and D. W. Gallager, Effects of continuous diazepam administration on $GABA_A$ subunit mRNA in brain, *J. Mol. Neurosci., 2*: 101 (1990).
154. I. Kang, and G. Miller, Decreased $GABA_A$ receptor subunit mRNA concentrations following chronic lorazepam administration, *Br. J. Pharmacol., 103*: 1285 (1991).
155. P. Montpied, A. L. Morrow, J. W. Karanian, E. I. Ginns, B. M. Martin, and S. M. Paul, Prolonged ethanol inhalation decreases γ-aminobutyric $acid_A$ receptor α-subunit mRNAs in the rat cerebral cortex, *Mol. Pharmacol., 39*: 157 (1991).
156. K. Krnjevic, Desensitization of GABA receptors, *GABA- and Benzodiazepine Receptors* (E. Costa, ed.), Raven Press, New York, p. 111 (1981).
157. A. Stelzer, A. R. Kay, and R. K. S. Wong, $GABA_A$ receptor function in hippocampal cells is maintained by phosphorylation factors, *Science, 241*: 339 (1988).
158. E. Sigel, and R. Baur, Activation of protein kinase C differentially modulates neuronal Na^+, Ca^{2+}, and γ-aminobutyrate type A channels, *Proc. Natl. Acad. Sci. USA, 85*: 6192 (1988).
159. P. M. Sweetman, J. Lloyd, P. Gallombardo, R. T. Malison, D. W. Gallager, J. F. Tallman, and E. J. Nestler, Phosphorylation of the $GABA_A$/benzodiazepine receptor α subunit by a receptor-associated protein kinase, *J. Neurochem., 51*: 1274 (1988).
160. E. F. Kirkness, C. F. Bovenkirk, T. Veda, and A. J. Turner, Phosphorylation of γ-aminobutyrate (GABA) benzodiazepine receptors by cyclic AMP-dependent protein kinase, *Biochem. J., 259*: 613 (1989).

161. M. D. Browning, M. Bureau, E. N. Dudek, and R. W. Olsen, Protein kinase C and cAMP-dependent protein kinase phosphorylate the ß-subunit of the purified $GABA_A$ receptor, *Proc. Natl. Acad. Sci. USA, 87*: 1315 (1990).
162. H. Möhler, P. Polc, R. Cumin, L. Pieri, and R. Kettler, Nicotinamide in a brain constituent with benzodiazepine-like actions, *Nature, 278*: 563 (1979).
163. K. W. Gee, R. E. Brinton, and B. S. McEvan, Regional distribution of Ro 5-4864 binding site that is functionally coupled to the γ-aminobutyric acid/benzodiazepine receptor complex in rat brain, *J. Pharmacol. Exp. Ther., 244*: 379 (1987).
164. D. M. Turner, D. W. Sapp, and R. W. Olsen, The benzodiazepine alcohol antagonist Ro 15-4513: Binding to a $GABA_A$ receptor subtype that is insensitive to diazepam, *J. Pharmacol. Exp. Ther., 257*: 1236 (1991).
165. A. Guidotti, C. M. Forchetti, M. A. Corda, D. Konkel, C. D. Bennett, and E. Costa, Isolation, characterization and purification to homogeny of an endogenous polypeptide with agonist action on benzodiazepine receptor, *Proc. Natl. Acad. Sci. USA, 80*: 3531 (1983).
166. H. Alho, E. Costa, P. Ferrero, M. Fujimoto, D. Csenza-Murphy, and A. Guidotti, Diazepam-binding inhibitor. A neuropeptide located in selected neuronal populations of rat brain, *Science, 229*: 179 (1985).
167. P. W. Gray, D. Glaister, P. H. Seeburg, A. Guidotti, and E. Costa, Cloning and expression of cDNA for human diazepam binding inhibitor, a natural ligand of an allosteric regulatory site of the γ-aminobutyric acid type A receptor, *Proc. Natl. Acad. Sci. USA, 83*: 7547 (1986).
168. H. Marquardt, G. J. Todaro, and M. Shoyab, Complete amino acid sequences of bovine and human endozepines, *J. Biol. Chem., 261*: 9727 (1986).
169. P. Ferrero, M. R. Santi, B. Conti-Tronconi, E. Costa, and A. Guidotti, Study of an octadeca neuropeptide derived from diazepam binding inhibitor (DBI): Biological activity and presence in rat brain, *Proc. Natl. Acad. Sci. USA, 83*: 827 (1986).
170. E. Costa, and A. Guidotti, Neuropeptide as cotransmitters: Modulatory effects at GABAergic synapses, *Psychopharmacology: The Third Generation of Progress* (H. Y. Meltzer, ed.), Raven Press, New York, p. 425 (1987).
171. C. Ferrarese, H. Alho, A. Guidotti, and E. Costa, Colocalization and corelease of GABA and putative allosteric modulators of GABA receptor, *Neuropharmacology, 26*: 1011 (1987).
172. Z. Chen, B. Agerberth, K. Gell, M. Andersson, V. Mutt, C-G. Ostenson, S. Efendic, J. Barros-Söderling, B. Persson, and H. Jörnvall, Isolation and characterization of porcine diazepam-binding inhibitor, a polypeptide not only of cerebral occurrence but also common in intestinal tissues and with effects on regulation of insulin release, *Eur. J. Biochem., 174*: 239 (1988).
173. M. L. Barbaccia, E. Costa, and A. Guidotti, Endogenous ligands for high-affinity recognition sites of psychotropic drugs, *Annu. Rev. Pharmacol. Toxicol., 28*: 451 (1988).
174. E. Slobodyansky, A. Guidotti, C. Wambebe, A. Berkovich, and E. Costa, Isolation and characterization of a rat brain triakontatetraneuropeptide, posttranslational product of diazepam binding inhibitor: Specific action at the Ro 5-4864 recognition site, *J. Neurochem., 53*: 1276 (1989).
175. G. P. Owens, A. K. Sinha, J. M. Sikala, and W. E. Hahn, Sequence and expression of the murine diazepam binding inhibitor, *Mol. Brain Res., 6*: 101 (1984).
176. A. Guidotti, H. Alho, A. Benkovich, D. H. Cox, C. Ferrarese, E. Slobodansky, M. R. Santi, and D. Wambebe, DBI processing: Allosteric modulation at different GABA/benzodiazepine receptor subtypes, *Allosteric Modulation of Amino Acid Receptors: Therapeutic Implications* (E. A. Barnard and E. Costa, eds.), Raven Press, New York, p. 104 (1989).
177. C.-G. Ostenson, B. Ahren, S. Karlsson, E. Sandberg, and S. Efendic, Effects of porcine diazepam-binding inhibitor on insulin and glucagon secretion in vitro from the rat edocrine pancreas, *Regul. Peptides, 29*: 143 (1990).

178. A. Guidotti, Role of DBI in brain and its posttranslational processing products in normal and abnormal behavior, *Neuropharmacology, 30*: 1425 (1991).
179. L. Sangameswaran, and A. L. De Blas, Demonstration of benzodiazepine-like molecules in the mammalian brain with a mononclonal antibody to benzodiazepines, *Proc. Natl. Acad. Sci. USA, 82*: 5560 (1985).
180. L. Sangameswaran, H. M. Fales, P. Friedrich, and A. L. De Blas, Purification of a benzodiazepine from bovine brain and detection of benzodiazepine like immunoreactivity in human brain, *Proc. Natl. Acad. Sci. USA, 83*: 9236 (1986).
181. J. Wildmann, J. Niemann, and H. Mattai, Endogenous benzodiazepine receptor agonist in human and mammalian plasma, *J. Neural Transm., 66*: 151 (1986).
182. J. Wildmann, H. Möhler, W. Vetter, U. B. Ranalder, K. Schmidt, and R. Maurer, Diazepam and *N*-desmethyl-diazepam are found in rat brain and adrenal and may be of plant origin, *J. Neural Transm., 70*: 383 (1987).
183. J. Wildmann, W. Vetter, U. B. Ranalder, K. Schmidt, R. Maurer, and H. Möhler, Occurrence of pharmacologically active benzodiazepines in trace amounts in wheat and potato, *Biochem. Pharmacol., 37*: 3549 (1988).
184. A. L. De Blas, and C. Sotela, Localization of benzodiazepine-like molecules in the rat brain. A light and electron microscopy immunocytochemistry study with an anti-benzodiazepine monoclonal antibody, *Brain Res., 413*: 285 (1987).
185. A. L. De Blas, D. Pank, and P. Friedrich, Endogenous benzodiazepine-like molecules in human, rat and bovine brain studied with a monoclonal antibody to benzodiazepines, *Brain Res., 413*: 275 (1987).
186. K. D. Mullen, W. B. Mendelson, J. V. Martin, M. L. Barrett, and E. A. Jones, Could an endogenous benzodiazepine ligand contribute to hepetic encephalopathy? *Lancet, 1*: 457 (1988).
187. K. D. Mullen, K. M. Szanter, and K. Kaminsky-Russ, "Endogenous" benzodiazepine activity in physiological fluids of patients with hepatic encephalopathy, *Lancet, 2*: 81 (1990).
188. J. H. Medina, C. Pena, M. Piva, A. C. Paladini, and E. De Robertis, Presence of benzodiazepine-like molecules in mammalian brain and milk, *Biochem. Biophys. Res. Commun., 152*: 534 (1988).
189. J. H. Medina, C. Pena, M. Levi de Stein, C. Wolfman, and A. C. Paledini, Benzodiazepine-like molecules, as well as other ligands for the brain benzodiazepine receptors are relatively common constituents of plants, *Biochem. Biophys. Res. Commun., 165*: 547 (1989).
190. C. C. Lian, L. S. Liu, J. Y. Hibbard, and J. Y. Wu, Purification and characterization of a benzodiazepine-like substance from mammalian brain, *Neurochem. Res., 14*: 345 (1989).
191. J. D. Rothstein, G. McKhann, P. Guarnei, M. L. Barbacia, A. Guidotti, and E. Costa, Hepatic encephalopathy and cerebrospinal fluid content of diazepam binding inhibitor (DBI), *Ann. Neurol., 26*: 57 (1988).
192. M. Olasmaa, J. D. Rothstein, A. Guidotti, R. J. Weber, S. M. Paul, S. Spector, M. L. Zeneroli, M. Baraldi, and E. Costa, Endogenous benzodiazepine receptor ligands in human and animal hepatic encephalopathy, *J. Neurochem., 55*: 2015 (1990).
193. M. Moesmaa, A. Guidotti, E. Costa, J. D. Rothstein, M. E. Goldman, R. J. Weber, and S. M. Paul, Endogenous benzodiazepine in hepatic encephalopathy, *Lancet, 1*: 491 (1989).
194. A. S. Basile, S. H. Gamaral, E. A. Jones, and P. Skolnick, $GABA_A$ receptor complex in an experimental model of hepatic encephalopathy: Evidence for elevated levels of an endogenous benzodiazepine receptor ligand, *J. Neurochem., 53*: 1057 (1989).
195. A. S. Basile, L. Pannell, T. Jaouni, S. H. Gammal, H. M. Fales, E. A. Jones, and P. Skolnick, Brain concentration of benzodiazepines are elevated in an animal model of hepatic encephalopathy, *Proc. Natl. Acad. Sci. USA, 87*: 5263 (1990).
196. E. Unsold, D. R. Krishna, C. Fischer, and U. Klotz, Detection of desmethyldiazepam and diazepam in brain of different species and plants, *Biochem. Pharmacol., 38*: 2473 (1989).

197. E. Unsold, C. Fischer, E. Rothemund, and U. Klotz, Occurrence of "natural" diazepam in human brain, *Biochem. Pharmacol., 39*: 210 (1990).
198. A. S. Basile, L. Pannell, T. Jaouni, S. H. Gammal, H. M. Fales, E. A. Jones, and P. Skolnick, Brain concentration of benzodiazepines are elevated in an animal model of hepatic encephalopathy, *Proc. Natl. Acad. Sci. USA, 87*: 5263 (1990).
199. P. Ferenci, G. Grimm, S. Meryn, and A. Gangl, Successful treatment of portal–systemic encephalopathy by the benzodiazepine antagonist flumazenil, *Gastroenterology, 96*: 240 (1989).
200. G. Bringmann, A. first biosynthetic proposal for the in vivo formation of naturally occurring diazepam-like 1,4-benzodiazepines, *J. Neural Transm., 88*: 77 (1992).
201. K. Kataoka, Y. Gutman, A. Guidotti, P. Panela, J. Wroblewski, D. Cosenza-Murphy, J. Y. Wu, and E. Costa, Intrinsic GABAergic system of adrenal chromaffin cells, *Proc. Natl. Acad. Sci. USA, 81*: 3218 (1984).
202. J. Bormann, and D. E. Clapham, γ-aminobutyric acid receptor channels in adrenal chromaffin cells: A patch clamp study, *Proc. Natl. Acad. Sci. USA, 82*: 2168 (1985).
203. P. Rorsman, P.-O. Berggren, K. Bokvist, H. Ericson, H. Möhler, C.-G. Östenson, and P. A. Smith, Glucose inhibition of glucagon secretion involves activation of $GABA_A$—receptor chloride channels, *Nature, 341*: 233 (1989).
204. J. Bormann, and H. Kettenmann, Patch clamp study of γ-aminobutyric acid receptor Cl^- channels in cultured astrocytes, *Proc. Natl. Acad. Sci. USA, 85*: 9336 (1988).
204a. H. Kettenmann, Properties of (gamma-aminobutyric acid)$_A$ receptors in glial cells, *Transmitter Amino Acid Receptors: Structures, Transduction and Models for Drug Development* (E. A. Barnard and E. Costa, eds.), Thieme, New York, p. 37 (199[illegible]).
205. R. R. H. Anholt, Mitrochondial benzodiazepine receptors as potential modulators of intermediary metabolism, *Trends Pharmacol. Sci., 12*: 506 (1986).
206. A. Verma, and S. H. Snyder, Peripheral type benzodiazepine receptors, *Annu. Rev. Pharmacol. Toxicol., 29*: 307 (1989).
207. J. G. Richards, H. Möhler, and W. Haefely, Benzodiazepine binding sites: Receptors or acceptors? *Trends Pharmacol. Sci., 3*: 233 (1982).
208. S. H. Snyder, A. Verma, and R. R. Trifiletti, The peripheral-type benzodiazepine receptor: A protein of mitochondrial outer membranes utilising porphyrins as endogenous ligands, *FASEB J., 1*: 282 (1987).
209. K. L. Antkiewicz-Michalnk, A. Guidotti, and K. E. Krueger, Molecular characterization and mitochondrial density of recognition site for peripheral-type benzodiazepine ligands, *Mol. Pharmacol., 34*: 272 (1988).
210. K. L. Antkiewicz-Michalnk, A. G. Mukhin, A. Guidotti, and K. E. Krueger, Purification and characterization of a protein associated with peripheral-type benzodiazepine binding sites, *J. Biol. Chem., 263*: 17317 (1988).
211. R. Sprengel, P. Werner, P. H. Seeburg, A. G. Mukhin, M. R. Santi, D. R. Grayson, A. Guidotti, and K. E. Krueger, Molecular cloning and expression of cDNA encoding a peripheral-type benzodiazepine receptor, *J. Biol. Chem., 264*: 20415 (1989).
212. A. G. Mukhin, V. Papadopoulos, E. Costa, and K. E. Krueger, Mitochondrial benzodiazepine receptors regulate steroid biosynthesis, *Proc. Natl. Acad. Sci. USA, 86*: 9813 (1989).
213. V. Papadopoulos, A. G. Mukhin, E. Costa, and K. E. Krueger, The peripheral-type benzodiazepine receptor is functionally linked to Leydig cell steroidogensis, *J. Biol. Chem., 265*: 3772 (1990).
214. V. Papadopoulos, A. Berkovich, and K. E. Krueger, The role of diazepam binding inhibitor and its processing products at mitochondial benzodiazepine receptors: Regulation of steroid biosynthesis, *Neuropharmacology, 30*: 1417 (1991).
215. K. E. Krueger, and V. Papadopoulos, The peripheral-type benzodiazepine receptor: Cell biological role and pharmacological significance, *Transmitter Amino Acid Receptors: Struc-*

ture, Transduction and Models for Drug Development (E. A. Barnard and E. Costa, eds.), Thieme, New York, p. 153 (1991).

216. M. W. McEnery, A. M. Swansons, R. R. Trifiletti, and S. H. Snyder, Isolation of the mitochondrial benzodiazepine receptor: Association with the voltage-dependent anion channel and the adenine nucleotide carrier, *Proc. Natl. Acad. Sci. USA, 89*: 3170 (1992).

217. K. Yanagibashi, Y. Ohno, N. Nakamichi, T. Matsui, K. Hayashida, M. Takamura, K. Yamada, S. Ton, and M. Kawamura, Peripheral-type benzodiazepine receptors are involved in the regulation of cholesterol side chain cleavage in adrenocorticol mitochondria, *J. Biochem. (Tokyo), 106*: 1026 (1989).

218. A. Verma, J. S. Nye, and S. H. Snyder, Porphyrins are endogenous ligands for the mitochondrial (peripheral-type) benzodiazepine receptor, *Proc. Natl. Acad. Sci. USA, 84*: 2256 (1987).

219. J. D. Hirsch, C. F. Beyer, L. Malkowitz, B. Beer, and A. L. Blumer, Mitochondrial benzodiazepine receptors mediate inhibition of mitochondrial respiratory control, *Mol. Pharmacol., 35*: 157 (1989).

220. J.-C. Larcher, J.-L. Vayssiere, F. J. Le Marquer, L. R. Cordeau, P. E. Keane, A. Bachy, F. Gros, and B. P. Croizat, Effects of peripheral benzodiazepines upon O_2 consumption or neuroblastoma cells, *Eur. J. Pharmacol., 161*: 197 (1989).

221. M. Gavish, Y. Katz, S. Bar-Ami, and R. Weizman, Biochemical, physiological, and pathological aspects of the peripheral benzodiazepine receptor, *J. Neurochem., 58*: 1589 (1992).

222. J. K. T. Wang, J. I. Morgan, and S. Spector, Benzodiazepines that bind at peripheral sites inhibit cell proliferation, *Proc. Natl. Acad. Sci. USA, 81*: 753 (1984).

223. J. K. T. Wang, J. L. Morgan, and S. Spector, Differentiation of Friend erythroleukaemia cells induced by benzodiazepines, *Proc. Natl. Acad. Sci. USA, 81*: 3770 (1984).

224. A. M. C. Gorman, G. B. O'Beirne, C. M. Regan, and D. C. Williams, Antiproliferative action of benzodiazepines in cultured brain cells is not mediated through the peripheral-type benzodiazepine acceptor, *J. Neurochem., 53*: 849 (1989).

225. H. Bessler, R. Weizman, M. Gavish, I. Notti, and M. Djaldetti, Immunomodulatory effect of peripheral benzodiazepine receptor ligands on human mononuclear cells, *J. Neuroimmunol., 38*: 19 (1992).

226. W. C. Taft, and R. J. De Lorenzo, Micromolar affinity benzodiazepine receptor regulate voltage-sensitive calcium channels in nerve terminal preparations, *Proc. Natl. Acad. Sci. USA, 81*: 3118 (1984).

227. Y. F. Oh, J. W. Francis, G. J. Markelonis, and T. H. Oh, Interleukin-1-ß and tumor necrosis factor-α increase peripheral-type benzodiazepine binding sites in cultured polygonal astrocytes, *J. Neurochem., 58*: 2131 (1992).

228. M. H. Bureau, M. Khrestchalisky, M. A. Heeren, E. B. Zambrowicz, H. Kim, T. M. Grisan, M. Colombini, A. J. Tobin, and R. W. Olsen, Isolation and cloning of a voltage-dependent anion channel like M_r 36,000 polypeptide from mammalian brain, *J. Biol. Chem., 267*: 8679 (1992).

229. J. Zezula, K. Fuchs, and W. Sieghart, Separation of α_1, α_2, and α_3 subunits of the $GABA_A$–benzodiazepine receptor complex by immunoaffinity chromatography, *Brain Res., 563*: 325 (1991).

230. W. Haefely, J. R. Martin, and P. Schoch, Novel anxiolytics that act as partial agonists at benzodiazepine receptors, *Trends Pharmacol. Sci., 11*: 452 (1990).

231. W. Haefely, E. P. Bonetti, M. Facklam, F. Jenck, J. R. Martin, J.-L. Moreau, J. G. Richards, and P. Schoch, Partial agonists of benzodiazepine receptors for the treatment of epilepsy, sleep and anxiety disorders, *Adv. Biochem. Psychopharmacol., 47*: 379 (1992).

232. J. R. Martin, L. Pieri, E. P. Bonetti, R. Schaffner, W. P. Burkard, R. Cumin, and W. Haefely, Ro 16-6028: A novel anxiolytic acting as a partial agonist at the benzodiazepine receptor, *Pharmacopsychiatry, 21*: 360 (1988).

233. J.-L. Moreau, F. Jenck, L. Pieri, P. Schoch, J. R. Martin, and W. Haefely, Physical dependence induced in DBA/2J mice by benzodiazepine receptor full agonists, but not by the partial agonist Ro 16-6028, *Eur. J. Pharmacol., 190*: 269 (1990).
234. J. W. Mandema, M. T. Kuck, and M. Danhof, In vivo modeling of the pharmacodynamic interaction between benzodiazepine which differ in intrinsic efficacy, *J. Pharmacol. Exp. Ther., 261*: 56 (1992).

24

A Review of the ß-Carboline Abecarnil: An Anxiolytic with Dual Mechanisms of Action at Central γ-Aminobutyric Acid$_A$ Receptor Sites

Rosemary C. Bischoff, D. N. Stephens, S. McDonald, T. Duka, and Rainer Dorow
Schering AG, Berlin, Germany

I. INTRODUCTION

Anxiety disorders are among the most common mental disorders diagnosed in clinical practice. Goldberg and Bridges (1987), with use of a structured interview schedule, found that 15.8% of new patients presenting to their general practitioner fulfilled the diagnostic criteria for generalized anxiety disorder [*Diagnostic and Statistical Manual of Mental Disorders,* 3rd ed., revised (*DSM-3-R;* American Psychiatric Association, 1987)].

The pharmacotherapy of choice for anxiety disorders are the benzodiazepines. They are effective antianxiety agents, differing only in their pharmacokinetic properties, their side effect profile, dependency potential, and cost. Some of the reasons benzodiazepines are among the most widely prescribed medications in the world are that they have a wide margin of safety, almost no lethality when taken alone in overdose, and are effective in psychiatric disorders as well as anxiety symptoms associated with a vast range of somatic, psychiatric, and situational disorders.

On the negative side, the benzodiazepines produce a range of side effects that are mainly dose-related. The most common (tiredness and drowsiness) are most troublesome during the first weeks of treatment. Benzodiazepines may release aggression and inhibit motor functions. Judgment, memory, and motor coordination may also be impaired. Additional disturbing adverse characteristics include that tolerance may develop, withdrawal effects occur, and there is the potential for dependency. Many of the problems are associated with the discontinuation of benzodiazepine medication. A study by Rickels et al. (1988) showed that 40% of patients abruptly switched from long half-life benzodiazepines to placebo after 6 months of treatment were unable to tolerate being drug-free and returned to their treatment. The symptoms of the benzodiazepine discontinuation syndrome can range from mild dysphoria, insomnia, sweating, tremor, and muscle cramps, to major problems, such as convulsions. However, the elimination half-life of the compound is thought to play a major role in the appearance of discontinuation symptoms after shorter-term use, especially when benzodiazepines are taken as hypnotics. Short-lived compounds give rise to most problems. The misuse of benzodiazepines by patients who begin to take high doses of the compounds appears to occur relatively seldom. A further problem, however, which has become more apparent in recent years in Europe as well as the United States, is the nonmedical abuse potential of benzodiazepines, often taken in combination with other substances of abuse.

In the light of these problems, new drugs have been sought that have equal efficacy to, but fewer problems than, the benzodiazepines. The first approach has been to look at compounds with an entirely different mechanism of action. One such agent is buspirone, an approved antianxiety agent binding to serotonin $(5\text{-HT})_{1A}$-receptors. This drug does not cause sedation or functional impairment and has little potential for abuse, but it can take up to 2 weeks or longer to have a beneficial effect and has unpleasant side effects, such as nausea and dysphoria. Furthermore, Schweizer and Rickels (1986) reported that the benzodiazepine-withdrawal syndrome may arise when buspirone is given to patients whose benzodiazepine treatment was terminated abruptly, owing to a lack of cross-tolerance between the two treatments. This might have added to the impression of several clinicians that buspirone is ineffective in the treatment of general anxiety disorder (GAD). Other serotonergic agents in clinical development are gepirone, ondansetron, and ipsapirone. The second pharmacological approach has been to stay with the benzodiazepine receptor, which has proved its value clinically, but to search for agents with more selective therapeutic efficacy. The theoretical basis for these endeavors is the idea that it may be possible to dissociate the broad spectrum of effects, desirable or otherwise, that characterize the known ligands of the receptors. Two approaches have been employed to achieve this. The first entails the use of compounds acting as partial agonists. Such compounds possess less efficacy than full agonists in facilitating the effects of γ-aminobutyric acid (GABA), either because of a partial effect at the receptor, or because, in a population of receptors, they may possess equal affinity for both agonist and antagonist conformations, thereby achieving an agonist effect at only a proportion of the receptors. Since a full potentiation of GABAergic inhibition by such substances does not take place, even at full receptor occupancies, those benzodiazepine effects requiring high levels of GABAergic inhibition (e.g., sleep-induction) are not induced by such partial agonists. Furthermore, as Figure 1 illustrates, the dose–response relation is shallower than for a full agonist, so that a greater separation of doses giving rise to different effects is also possible. An example of such a compound, which has been tested clinically by Merz (1984), is the benzodiazepine, bretazenil.

A second approach to producing a selection action with benzodiazepine receptor ligands is to exploit the discovery of receptor subtypes. Although pharmacological evidence for benzodiazepine receptor subtypes (BZ1 and BZ2) has been available for some years, it is only recently that molecular biology has revealed the panoply of possible subtypes of the central GABA_A–benzodiazepine receptor complex and that neurobiology has succeeded in demonstrating a heterogeneous distribution of subtypes in mammalian brain. If one assumes that the various properties of benzodiazepines are mediated by actions in different brain regions, or at different sites within a given region, it should be possible to achieve a separation of such effects by designing drugs acting at subtypes of the receptor and, indeed, it appears from work done by Pritchett et al. (1989) that the pharmacological suggestion of two subtypes of BZ receptor also has a basis in the structural differences of receptor subtypes.

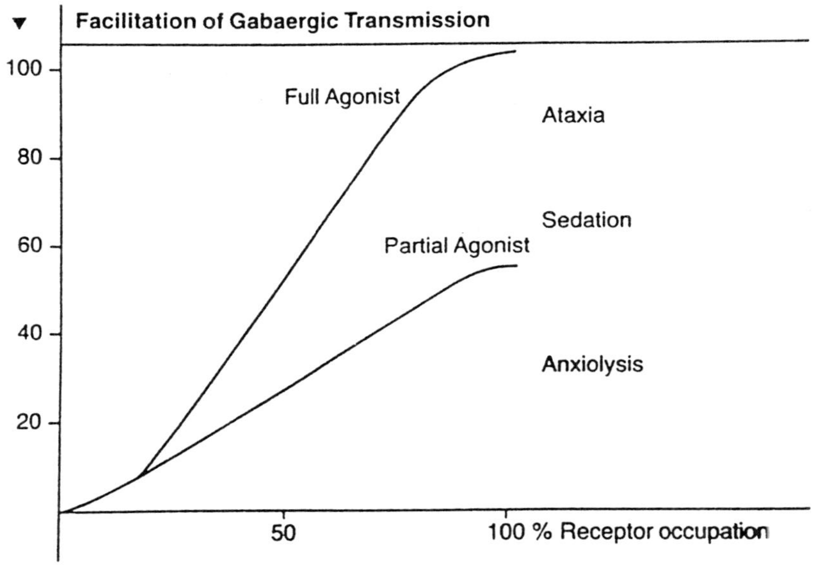

Figure 1 Schematic presentation of the relation between benzodiazepine receptor occupation and pharmacological efficacy of full or partial agonists. According to experimental experience, the different pharmacological effects of benzodiazepine receptor ligands require different receptor occupations and, thus, different levels of activation of the GABA system. Partial agonists have a shallower occupation–effect relation, allowing a better separation of the pharmacological effects, with weak partial agonists never achieving significant GABA facilitation, even at full-receptor occupations to induce sedation.

An example of a compound that acts at selective receptor sites that came on to the market recently is alpidem. The claims that this compound is significantly different from the benzodiazepines clinically are now hard to evaluate, as no studies appear to have as yet been carried out that use the drug for longer than 6 weeks.

This chapter will describe pharmacological and very early clinical work on a new compound, abecarnil, which is thought to combine both these modes of action.

II. ABECARNIL

Abecarnil is a ß-carboline-3-carboxylic acid ester derivative with a high affinity for central benzodiazepine receptors. Figure 2, illustrating work by Stephens et al. (1990), shows that abecarnil is approximately ten times more potent than diazepam in displacing [^{3}H]lormetazepam from cortical membranes, and that whereas the affinity of diazepam for the [^{3}H]lormetazepam-labeled binding sites is enhanced 2.8-fold in the presence of 30 μM muscimol, the affinity of abecarnil for these receptors is enhanced only 1.24-fold in the presence of the $GABA_A$ agonist. This observations suggest that abecarnil may be acting as a partial agonist at these sites.

Biochemical pharmacological data from the same authors on the ability of abecarnil to enhance the binding of [^{35}S]TBPS to its binding site associated with the chloride chan-

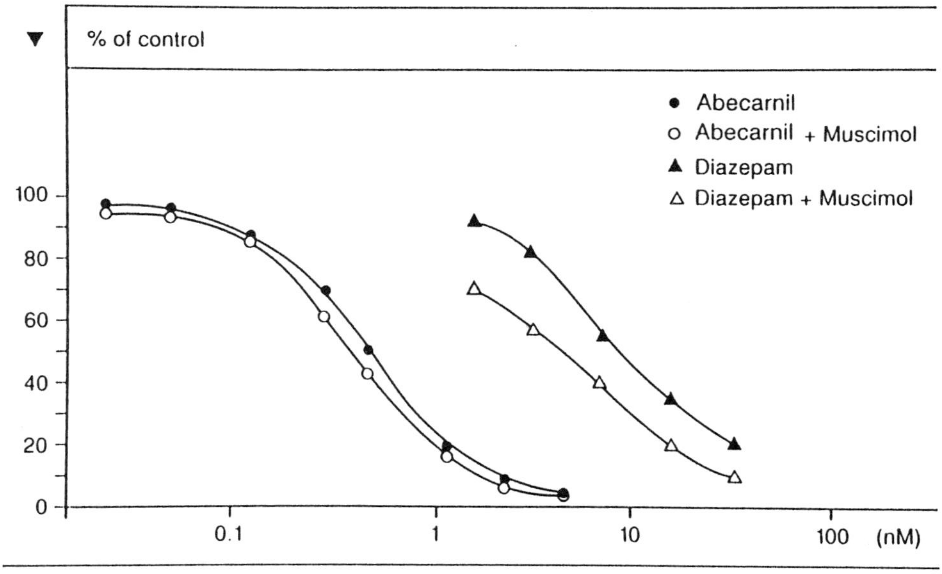

Figure 2 Displacement by abecarnil and diazepam of [^{3}H]lormetazepam binding from rat cortical membranes. Incubation was carried out at room temperature either in the presence of 50 μM bicuculline (to ensure an absence of GABA), or in the presence of 30 μM muscimol. Displacement of [^{3}H]lormetazepam by diazepam was strongly, and by abecarnil, weakly enhanced in the presence of the GABA agonist. (From Stephens et al., 1992)

nel showed that abecarnil enhanced binding of [^{35}S]TBPS to cortical membranes 1.37-fold at 20 min (nonequilibrium conditions). The corresponding value for diazepam was 1.39. These values also indicate an agonistic action of abecarnil, but here it is comparable with that of diazepam.

II. PHARMACOLOGY OF ABECARNIL AND PARTIAL AGONISTIC MECHANISM OF ACTION

In animal pharmacology, Stephens et al. (1990) and Turski et al. (1990) found that abecarnil has a selective action in that the compound is active in several tests predictive of anxiolytic and anticonvulsant activity, whereas in tests of motor coordination, abecarnil, in contrast with diazepam, showed no or only weak activity. The interpretation of these results in terms of partial versus selective activities of the compound is complex. In a test of anxiolytic activity employing mice, the four-place test, abecarnil was about eight times as potent as diazepam in releasing punished exploratory behavior (MED 0.1 vs 0.78 mg/kg, i.p.), although in binding studies in the mouse, abecarnil was only 1.7 times more potent than the benzodiazepine.

Figure 3, from the work of Stephens et al. (1990), compares the effect of abecarnil with diazepam in a water-lick conflict test in rats (Petersen and Buus-Lassen, 1981), revealing that, in this model, abecarnil was about five times more potent than diazepam. Table 1 shows the proportion of central benzodiazepine receptors occupied by abecarnil and diazepam at their minimal effective doses (MED) in the lick-suppression test, as well

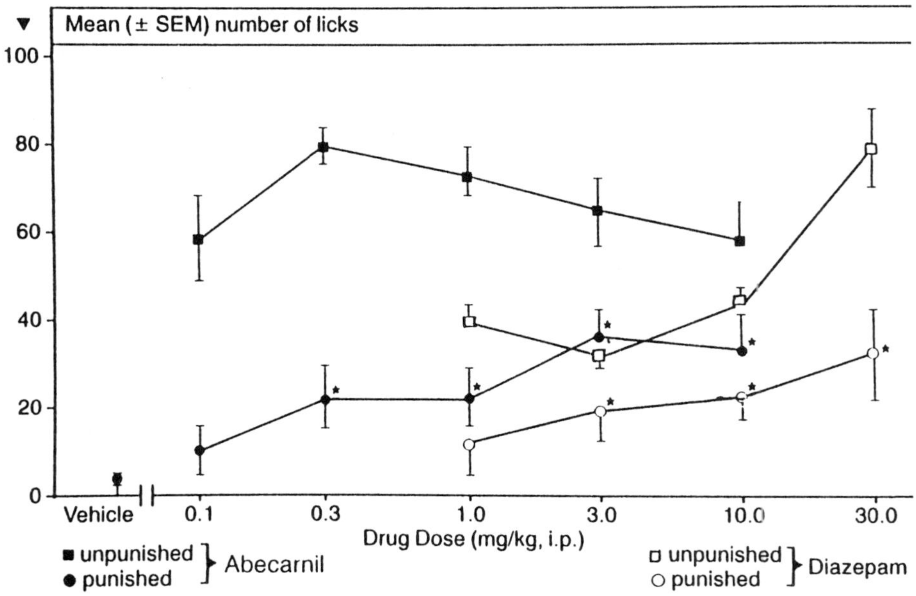

Figure 3 Effect of abecarnil and diazepam on licking behavior of thirsty rats. The rats were 48-h water-deprived and trained to lick at a water spout. Every 30th lick was punished by a 0.4 mA shock to the tongue. *Indicates a significant enhancement of licking rate (t-test, $p < 0.05$). (From Stephens et al., 1990)

as some other tests. Surprisingly, abecarnil needed to occupy a smaller proportion of receptors than diazepam to achieve its anxiolytic effect in the lick-suppression test, a result that is most easily explained by abecarnil possessing a selective action at a subpopulation of receptors responsible, among other things, for its action in this test. Abecarnil was also found by the same authors to be unexpectedly potent in terms of receptor occupation in antagonizing the penthylenetetrazole discriminative stimulus, a test also often interpreted as a measure of anxiolytic activity (Shearman and Lal, 1978; see

Table 1 Fractional Receptor Occupation (Forebrain) at MED or ED_{50} Values in Tests of Anxiolytic Activity or Motor Impairment

	Diazepam		Abecarnil	
	Effective dose	% Receptor[a] occupation	Effective dose	% Receptor occupation
Rat				
Waterlick (MED)	3	50	0.3	21
PTZ cue antagonism (ED_{50})	0.5	14	0.04	4
Exploratory motility (ED_{50})	0.4	12	1.0	48
Mouse				
4-Plate test (MED)	0.78	28	0.1	8
Chimney test (ED_{50})	1.46	33	>100	>99

[a] $\% \text{ receptor occupancy} = \dfrac{100}{(ED_{50}/\text{dose} + 1)}$.

Andrews and Stephens, 1990). Thus, in certain measures of anxiolytic activity, abecarnil may behave as a full agonist, whereas in tests of muscle relaxant activities it appears to act as a partial agonist.

Figure 4 shows that for a series of compounds acting at the $GABA_A$ receptor complex, including several benzodiazepines, potency in the four-plate test (predictive of anxiolytic activity) correlates highly with potency in impairing the ability of mice to escape from a chimney (a measure of motor coordination). Abecarnil (ZK 112119), and two other ß-carbolines, ZK 91296 and ZK 95962, in contrast with benzodiazepines, do not induce an impairment of muscle coordination in the chimney test in mice. Indeed, when given together with a dose of a benzodiazepine, lormetazepam, chosen to impair muscle coordination in 100% of mice tested, all three ß-carbolines antagonized the ef-

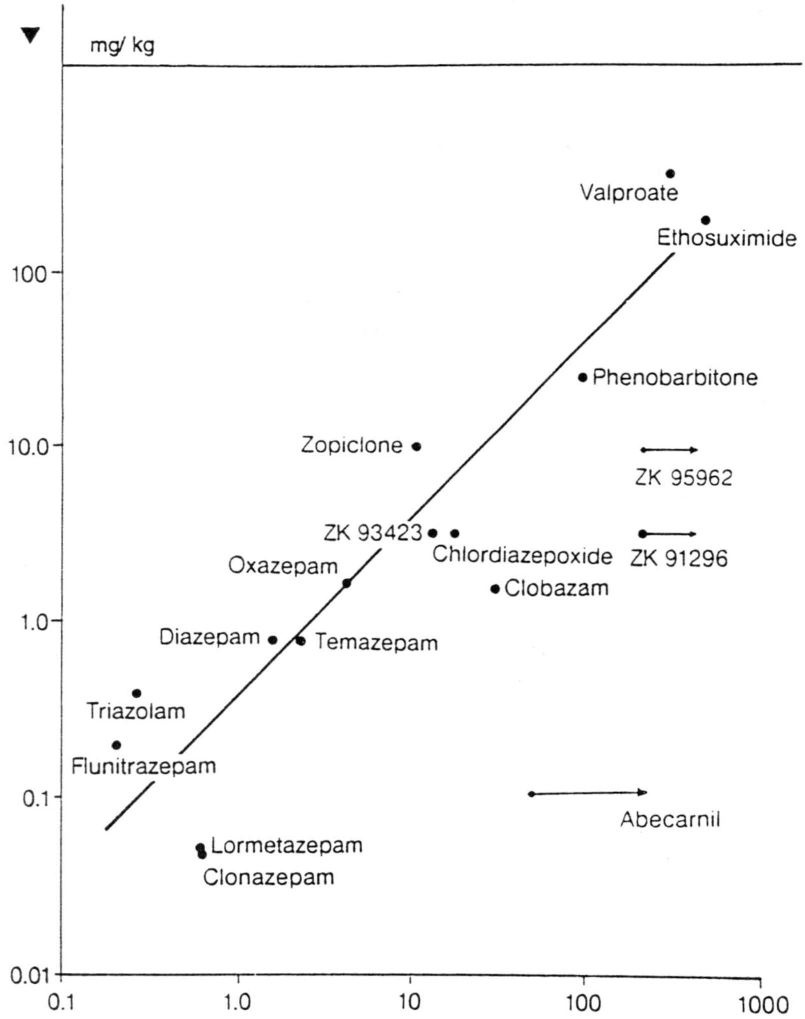

Figure 4 Correlation of the potencies of substances in the four-plate test of anxiolytic activity and chimney test of ataxia in mice.

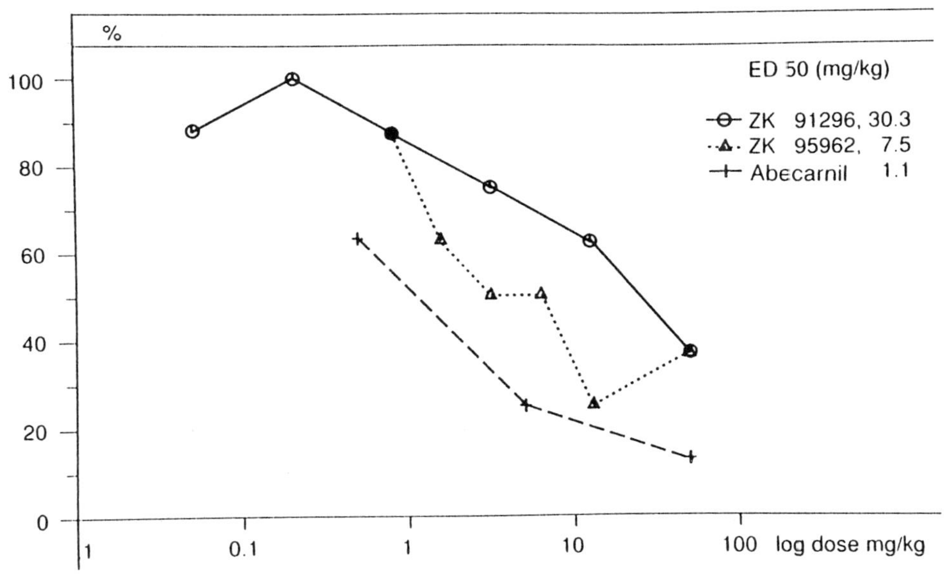

Figure 5 Antagonism of the ataxic effect of lormetazepam by the ß-carbolines abecarnil, ZK 91 296, and ZK 95 962.

fect of the benzodiazepine, in a dose-dependent fashion (Fig. 5). This ability of compounds to exert agonist-like effects in one test and antagonist-like effects in another is classically explained by the postulation that they act as partial agonists at central benzodiazepine receptors.

Figure 6 compares the effects of abecarnil and diazepam in another test relating to muscle coordination. Electromyographic (EMG) activity of the gastrocnemius–soleus muscle of rats was increased by treating the animals with etorphine (20 μg/kg, i.p., given 10 min before the experiment), and the ability of diazepam and abecarnil to reduce the enhanced activity was compared. Diazepam reduced EMG activity in a dose-dependent manner, the minimal effective doses being 2 mg/kg, i.p.; abecarnil at doses up to 100 mg/kg had no effect. In contrast with the results obtained in the chimney test, however, abecarnil was not able to antagonize the muscle relaxant effects of diazepam.

That abecarnil neither exerted effects of its own, nor antagonized the effects of diazepam, is more difficult to reconcile with a partial agonist explanation and the simplest interpretation might be that abecarnil possesses a low-affinity for those benzodiazepine receptors that are important for the muscle relaxant effects of diazepam in this test.

A. Selectivity of Receptor Binding

The pattern of results just described has encouraged us to look for atypical-binding profiles of abecarnil. The most direct way of approaching this, using [^{3}H]abecarnil, is technically difficult because of the high lipophilicity of abecarnil, resulting in very high levels of nonspecific binding, and a weak signal/noise ratio in studies of displaceable binding to receptors. For this reason, we have been limited to studies of the ability of abecarnil to displace [^{3}H]benzodiazepines from different brain regions. In common with other ß-carbolines, abecarnil shows a slightly higher potency in displacing [^{3}H]flumazenil

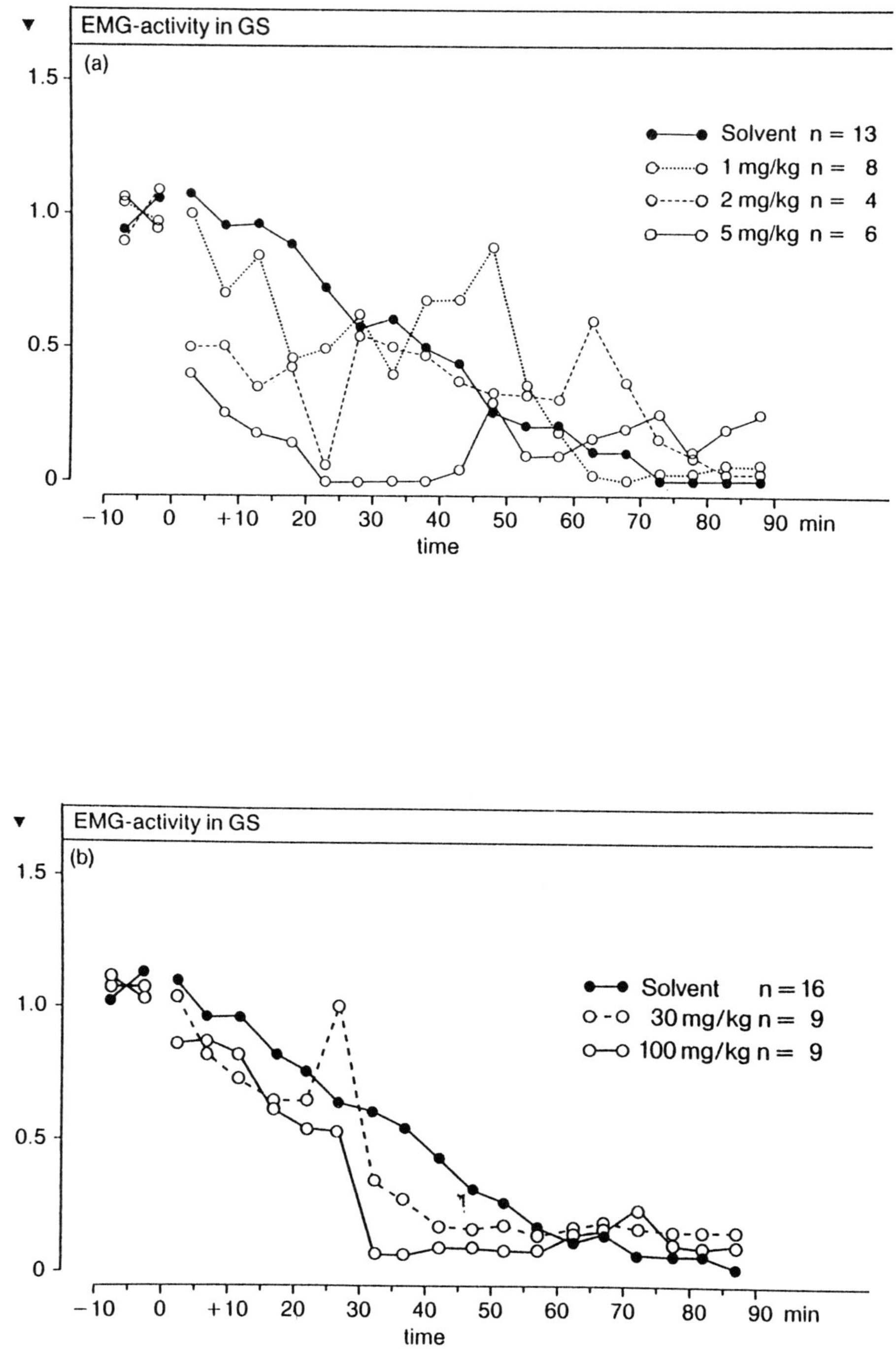

Figure 6 Time course of action and dose relation of (a) abecarnil and (b) diazepam on electromyographic (EMG) activity in the gastrocnemius muscle of rats treated with etorphine. The abscissa indicates normalized EMG (resting activity = 1); $^{*}p < 0.05$; $^{**}< 0.01$; $^{***} < 0.005$

Table 2 K_i **Values (nM) for the Displacement of (^{3}H)-Flumazenil Binding to Rat Brain Membranes in GABA-Free Conditions**

	Experiment 1[a]			Experiment 2[b]	
Drug	Cortex	Striatum	Cerebellum	Cerebellum	Spinal
Diazepam	47 (5.4)	48 (4.0)	60 (4.0)	110 (3.3)	130 (4.4)
Abecarnil	0.31 (1.4)	0.83 (2.3)	0.53 (1.6)	0.24 (1.9)	1.3 (2.6)
Zolpidem	150 (5.7)	360 (6.6)	94 (5.0)		
CL 218872	510 (2.0)	970 (2.1)	410 (2.3)		
β-CCE	0.75 (0.4)	0.98 (0.6)	0.48 (0.5)	2.6 (0.6)	13 (0.6)

Values in parentheses indicate GABA ratio values (ratio of K_i in presence of GABA to K_i in GABA-free condition).

[a] Experiment 1 at room temperature. GABA-free condition ensured by 30 μM bicuculine.
[b] Experiment 2 at 37°C. GABA-free 100 μM bicuculine. GABA rich = 100 μM GABA.
Source: Stephens et al., 1992.

from its binding sites in rat cerebellar membranes compared with cerebral cortex or striatal membranes. Although this is suggestive of a preference of abecarnil for the BZ1-type receptors, the differences in the affinities for the different brain regions is not as great as that found for the BZ1-selective ligands CL 218,872 or zolpidem (Table 2; experiment 1).

Table 2 also shows the results from another experiment comparing the affinity of abecarnil with that of other ligands for [^{3}H]flumazenil-labeled binding sites in cerebellum and spinal cord membranes (Stephens et al., 1992). In this experiment, the benzodiazepine diazepam showed affinities similar to cerebellum and spinal cord membranes, whereas abecarnil and the inverse agonist ß-carboline, ß-CCE, showed a fivefold higher affinity for cerebellar sites. Taken together, these results suggest that the benzodiazepines are unselective in binding to benzodiazepine receptors in different brain regions, whereas abecarnil possesses its lowest affinity for spinal cord receptors, an intermediate affinity for striatal and cerebellar membranes, and its highest affinity for cortical sites.

Although this observation is consistent with the good separation of the anxiolytic and sedative–ataxic side effects of abecarnil, it does not fully explain the lack of muscle relaxant effects reported earlier, since even in spinal cord, abecarnil possesses a higher receptor affinity than diazepam. Table 2 also shows the GABA ratios of the four substances in cerebellum and spinal cord; the low GABA ratio of abecarnil suggesting partial agonism in both brain regions, contributing to abecarnil's lack of muscle relaxant activity.

The results summarized here indicate that abecarnil may be selective for certain subpopulations of benzodiazepine–GABA receptor, and that its intrinsic efficacy at those receptors for which it has a preferential affinity may be variable; data from anxiolytic tests suggest that abecarnil acts as a full agonist in occupying a smaller proportion of receptors than diazepam at equieffective doses. On the other hand, abecarnil's lack of effects on motor coordination and muscle tone can be explained only partly by a selective-binding profile, abecarnil's ability to antagonize the effects of a full agonist in a test of ataxia in the mouse (see Fig. 5), suggesting partial agonistic activity in the spinal cord.

Interestingly, such a mixed profile of differing affinities for different receptor subtypes, as well as evidence for a mixed full agaonist–partial agonist profile at different subtypes has also been found in studies of abecarnil's action at recombinant receptors (Pribilla et al., in press).

B. Dependency Potential in Animal Models

Both the preferential-binding profile and the partial agonist character would predict that abecarnil might show superiority to benzodiazepines in terms of dependence potential following long-term treatment and abuse liability. Animal data strongly suggest that this is true.

Abecarnil has been compared with various benzodiazepines in several animal models of precipitated and spontaneous withdrawal, employing mice (Steppuhn et al., submitted), rats (Emmett-Oglesby et al., submitted), dogs (Löscher et al., 1992), and baboons (Sannerud et al., in press). In all these models, abecarnil has shown markedly reduced or absent dependence potential. In work of our own (Steppuhn et al., submitted), mice were treated for 21 days with abecarnil or diazepam given daily as a depot in sesame oil to ensure equivalent kinetics and levels of receptor occupation. During a subsequent 3-week withdrawal period, the mice were monitored electrophysiologically for convulsant episodes in hippocampal and cortical electroencephalograms (EEG), for enhanced EMG activity, and for behavioral signs of increased anxiety. Diazepam showed signs of withdrawal in all three measurements, whereas abecarnil showed no withdrawal signs during the 21-day withdrawal period: Taken together these reports suggest that abecarnil has a markedly reduced dependence potential relative to benzodiazepines. Furthermore, abecarnil over a wide dose range did not support self-administration in baboons, although triazolam was self-administered at high rates (Sannerud et al., in press).

Thus, possibly as a result of a combination of partial agonist activity, and selectivity for receptor subtypes, abecarnil appears to possess a pharmacological profile different from the benzodiazepines, being anxiolytic, without major side effects, and showing a lack of activity in certain animal models of dependence and abuse.

III. SAFETY, PHARMACOKINETICS, AND PRELIMINARY PHARMACOLOGICAL PROFILE IN HEALTHY VOLUNTEERS

The safety, tolerability, and pharmacokinetics as well as pharmacodynamic aspects of abecarnil were assessed in two Phase I studies (single and a multiple [over 7 days] dose) in healthy volunteers (Duka et al., 1989; Krause et al., 1990, 1991). Additionally, the interaction between abecarnil and the benzodiazepine receptor antagonist flumazenil has been studied (Duka et al., 1990). Table 3 indicates treatment and measurement schedule.

The drug was found in all studies to be safe and well tolerated; although after 20- and 40-mg single application and after 20 mg t.i.d. and 30 mg t.i.d., CNS depressant effects were observed or reported. The most frequent were dizziness, unsteady gait, and lack of concentration. No drowsiness or severe sedation was reported or observed. A dissociation was found between sedation, as measured by the visual analog scale [bipolar millimeter scale with the poles sleepy (0 mm) and alert (100 mm)] to perform the digit symbol substitution test (DSST), a psychomotor task. In the DSST, subjects are presented with a series of digits and asked to copy symbols coded to the digits 1–9 as able 3 Treatments and Measurements Schedule[a]

	Single dose	Multiple dose	Interaction study
		Treatments	
	Abecarnil in escalating doses of 1, 5, 10, 20, 40 mg or placebo	Abecarnil in escalating doses of 5, 10, 20, 30 mg t.i.d. (at days 2–6 of treatment)	Abecarnil 20 mg; 2 h later flumazenil either 0.3 or 0.9 or 2.7 mg or placebo i.v.
easurements		Time schedule	
dverse reactions	Pre to 24-h posttreatment	Day 0–9	Pre to 24 h after abecarnil
fety	Pre to 22-h posttreatment	Day 0–9	Pre to 24 h after abecarnil
AS	Pre 1.5, 3.5, 5.5, 24 h posttreatment	Day 0–9; 1.5 h posttreatment	Pre, 3 h after abecarnil
SST	Pre 1.5, 3.5, 5.5, 24 h posttreatment	Day 0–9, 1.5 h posttreatment	Pre, 3 h after abecarnil
ctograph			Pre, 2.5 h after abecarnil

n the multiple dose study a single dose was administered on day 1, three doses daily on days 2–6 and a single dose on day 7. ne day before treatment day (day 0) and 1 day after the last treatment (day 8) as well as on day 1 and 7, afternoon and ening, and on day 9, morning, subjects received single-blind placebo. Day 0 was used as baseline stage.

quickly and as correctly as possible. In both studies (Fig. 7; Tables 4 and 5), abecarnil impaired performance in DSST, but did not induce sedation as measured by the visual analog scale.

This preliminary profile of the pharmacological effects of abecarnil in healthy humans may indicate a partial or specific agonist activity and further support data from animal studies (Stephens et al., 1990; Turski et al., 1990).

In the interaction study between abecarnil and flumazenil, abecarnil, again in a high dose of 20 mg in combination with placebo, and 20 mg in combination with 0.3, 0.9, or 2.7 mg of flumazenil was found to be safe and well tolerated. Figure 8 shows the results of actograph measurements (balance test). In this test the movements of the subject to maintain balance were recorded through a moving platform as vertical power changes. The increase in the deviations from 0 line induced by abecarnil combined with placebo (indicative of unsteadiness) were antagonized by the high dose of flumazenil. Figure 9 shows DSST performance from the same study. The impairment seen after abecarnil combined with placebo was not antagonized by any of the three doses of flumazenil.

Flumazenil was able to antagonize the effects of abecarnil on actograph (balance-test) measured 30 min after flumazenil administration only in high doses; it did not antagonize the effects of abecarnil on DSST (60 min after flumazenil administration). Failure of flumazenil in the low doses (0.3 mg or 0.9 mg) to antagonize the CNS effects of a high dose of abecarnil (20 mg) indicates that this dose probably leads to a high concentration of the substance at the receptor site. Failure of flumazenil, even in the high dose (2.7 mg), to antagonize the impairments induced by abecarnil in the DSST performance may be due to the short half-life of flumazenil.

Pharmacokinetic evaluations revealed that peak concentrations on day 1 were reached at about 2 h for the two lower doses and about 2.6 h after the higher doses. Steady state

(a)

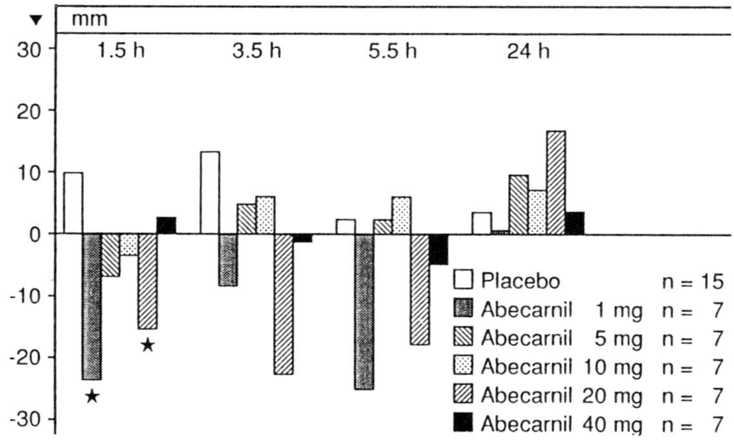

(b)

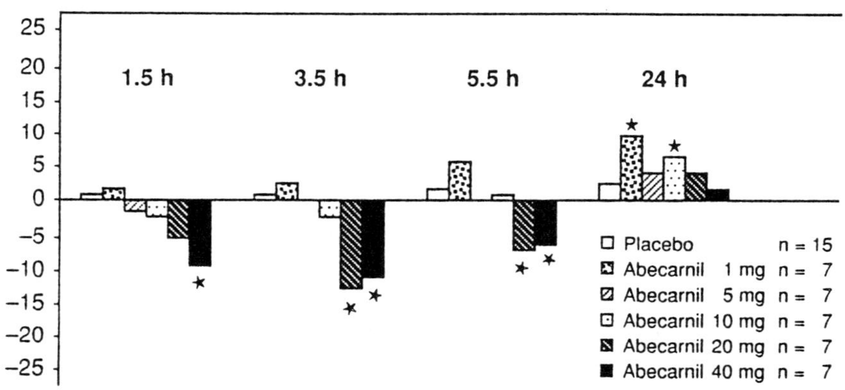

Figure 7 Self-rating changes (a) VAS and (b) DSST performance change after different abecarnil treatments; values above 0 indicate subjective feelings of alertness for VAS and improvement for DSST, and below 0 of sleepiness for VAS, and impairment for DSST. No differences were found in the baseline values between the treatment groups; $*p < 0.05$.

was achieved after 1 day of multiple dosing. There was also a dose-proportional increase in C_{max} and area under the curve (AUC) values. The terminal half-life was in a range of 5–7 h and was not affected either by dose or by single versus multiple administration.

In summary, single and multiple dose Phase I studies in healthy volunteers established maximum dosage levels and dosing guidelines for the initial dose-finding study with patients. Single doses up to 40 mg and multiple doses up to 90 mg/day revealed safety-related findings that are typical of other similarly acting anxiolytic compounds (e.g., dizziness, tiredness, and unsteady gait).

It is not now possible to say whether the doses chosen for these studies are of relevance for the clinical use of the compound. The very early dose-finding study by

Table 4 Visual Analogue Scale

	Treatments[a]				
Days of treatment	Placebo (n = 12)	15 mg/d (n = 7)	30 mg/d (n = 7)	60 mg/d (n = 7)	90 mg/d (n = 7)
Day 1	2.8 ± 16.4	−4.3 ± 13.5	1.7 ± 9.7	−11.4* ± 11.5	2.0 ± 25.3
Day 7	1.9 ± 14.6	−4.0 ± 13.4	4.9 ± 17.0	−23.0 ± 31.4	−7.4 ± 16.9

[a] Values given are differences of means ± SD (mm) obtained on days 1 and 7 of treatment from baseline values (day 0). Values above 0 indicate subjective feelings of alertness, and below 0 of sleepiness.
$*p < 0.05$ vs placebo.

Table 5 Digit Symbol Substitution Task

	Treatments[a]				
Days of treatment	Placebo (n = 12)	15 mg/d (n = 7)	30 mg/d (n = 7)	60 mg/d (n = 7)	90 mg/d (n = 7)
Day 1	0.3 ± 5.1	−7.0 ± 2.5	−2.0 ± 5.4	−15.1* ± 11.4	−20.4 ± 6.0
Day 7	9.8 ± 5.6	5.3 ± 5.7	5.0 ± 4.1	0.6* ± 8.8	−1.4 ± 7.4

[a] Values given are differences of means ± SD (number of correct answers) obtained on days 1 and 7 of treatment from baseline values. Values above 0 indicate improvement, below 0 impairment of performance.
$*p < 0.05$ vs placebo.

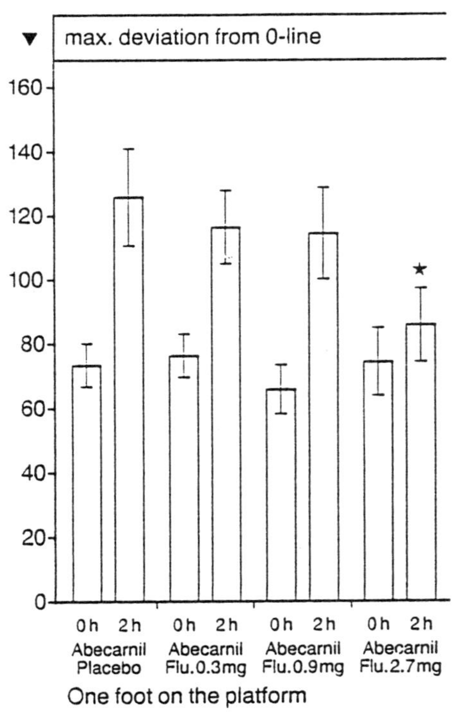

Figure 8 Maximum deviations from 0 line as given on the actograph before and after different treatment combinations; $*p < 0.007$. Flu, flumazenil.

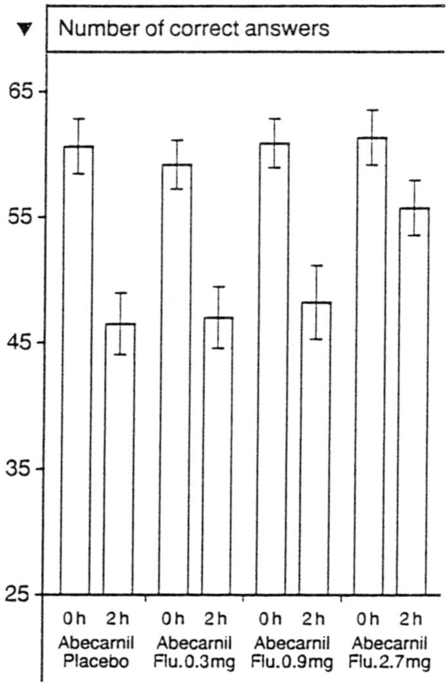

Figure 9 Number of correct answers in DSST are given before and after different treatment combinations. Flu, flumazenil.

Ballenger and colleagues (1991), described in the next section, would seem to indicate that the optimal therapeutic dose may lie considerably lower than the doses studied here.

IV. FIRST DOSE-FINDING STUDY IN ANXIETY PATIENTS

This controlled, double-blind trial of abecarnil in GAD patients was the first application of a ß-carboline, a new chemical entity, in patients. The following brief review of results and the conclusions are based on the evaluations of results from the 129 outpatients diagnosed according to the American Psychiatric Association (1987) DSM-III-R. The main objective of this study was to establish the tolerability and safety margins of abecarnil in high doses and to examine the effects of abrupt discontinuation. A further objective was to provide preliminary evidence of efficacy of abecarnil as assessed by the Hamilton anxiety rating scale and the clinical global impression scale.

The duration of the study was 5 weeks, consisting of a 1-week screening period, a 3-week double-blind treatment period, plus a 1-week single-blind placebo period (abrupt discontinuation). Patients were randomized to receive either 15–30 mg/day abecarnil (high dose) or placebo, or 7.5–15 mg/day (medium dose) abecarnil or placebo, or 3–9 mg/day (low dose) abecarnil or placebo. All doses were given three times daily. A fixed-dose regimen was used for the first week and doubled for the next 2 weeks (forced titration). In the 3–9 mg/day group, the dosage was doubled after the first week and further increased to 9 mg/day in the third week. In the event that the patient could not tolerate the dose increase, the investigators had the option of reducing the daily dosage.

An analysis was performed on 129 patients ($n = 34$ for the high-dose group; $n = 35$ for the medium-dose group; $n = 32$ for the low-dose group; and $n = 28$ for the placebo group).

Patients' characteristics were as follows: the mean age was 45; 60% men, 95% Caucasian, 57% married, 63% college educated. Most patients had mild to moderate levels of anxiety with a current episode of anxiety of 1.5–5 years. The onset of anxiety was 9–16 years previously.

Of those who entered and received at least one dose of study medication, 65% (22) in the high-dose group completed the double-blind treatment period, 89% (31) completed treatment in the medium-dose group, 97% (31) completed treatment in the low-dose group, and 93% (26) completed treatment in the placebo group. The mean daily dose in the high-dose group was 13.7 mg in the first week, 20.2 mg in the second, and 21.4 mg in the third week. In the medium-dose group it was 6.6 mg in the first week and 12.0 mg in the second and third week. In the 3–9 mg dose group the mean daily dose was 2.9 mg/day in the first week, 5.5 mg/day in the second, and 7.7 mg/day in the third week. The mean number of capsules taken in the placebo group was 2.8 in the first week, 5.5 for the second week, and 6.4 for the third week.

The primary reason for discontinuation in the high-dose group ($n = 10$) was adverse events. In the medium-dose group one patient discontinued owing to adverse reactions. There were no dropouts because of adverse reactions in the low-dose group.

Safety as assessed by physical examinations, vital signs, ECGs and laboratory tests showed no clinically relevant changes. Several central nervous system (CNS) adverse events were reported in the high-dose group. (Because of this, the original dosage schedule had been amended to allow for two lower dosage ranges, i.e., medium dose and low dose, instead of the originally planned dosage increase of 30–60 mg/day and 60–90 mg/day). The most *frequent* adverse event, drowsiness, appeared to be dose-related. The most *prominent* adverse events reported during the double-blind treatment period in the high-dose group were drowsiness (81%), equilibrium loss (26%), and confusion (24%); in the medium-dose group they were drowsiness (51%), fatigue (17%), and coordination difficulty (14%); in the low-dose group, they were drowsiness (31%) and fatigue (12%), and in the placebo group they were drowsiness (14%) and dizziness (11%). Insomnia, the most frequent side effect in the single-blind placebo period, was reported by 38% of the patients in the high-dose group and 29% of the patients in the medium-dose group.

Efficacy was assessed by the Hamilton anxiety rating scale (HAS) and the clinical global impression scale (CGI). Abecarnil given in the low-dosage range was significantly superior to placebo at the $p < 0.05$ level (two-tailed) intent-to-treat analysis of covariance for the following key variables: both items on the CGI—overall severity (week 3) and global improvement (weeks 2 and 3), the HAS total and psychic factor (week 2). In addition, the low dose was significantly superior to placebo in the percentage of patients who showed at least 50% improvement in the HAS total at week 3 (after showing borderline superiority to placebo in week 2). By this criterion 61% of the patients were categorized as treatment successes, compared with only 30% in the placebo group.

Abecarnil in the medium-dose range was significantly superior to placebo for the key variable, HAS total (week 2). For the insomnia item of the HAS, all three abecarnil groups were significantly superior to placebo at every weekly evaluation during the double-blind treatment (Fig. 10).

During the single-blind placebo (drug withdrawal) period, there were no significant differences between the low-dose group and placebo after abrupt discontinuation for any

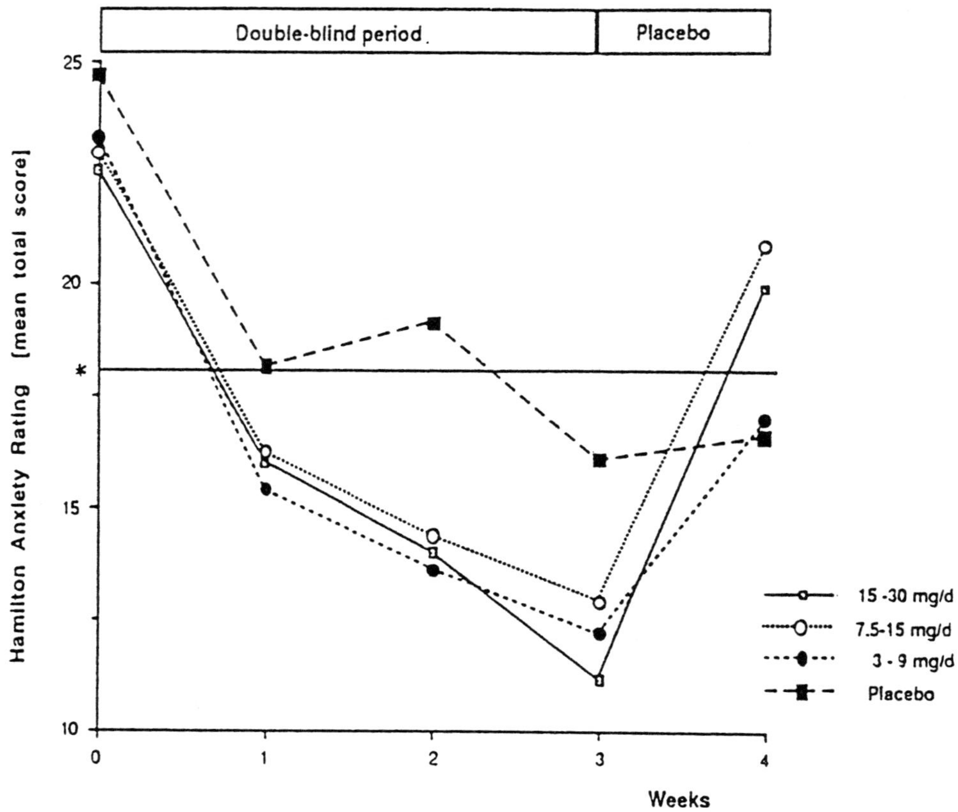

Figure 10 Hamilton anxiety rating scale: total mean score at each week (intent-to-treat pool observed cases analysis). *Inclusion criterion for the study was a score of 18 or more.

of the key variables. However, under the placebo treatment there was loss of efficacy in the two groups previously treated with the higher doses of abecarnil.

In summary, this first dose-finding study of abecarnil demonstrated a dose range that is both safe and efficacious. The 3- to 9-mg/day dosage not only showed efficacy superior to placebo, but also had an acceptable adverse reaction profile, both during treatment and, perhaps most importantly, after abrupt withdrawal of medication. For the two higher dose ranges, adverse reactions in some patients given 15–30 mg/day would preclude the use of starting doses as high as 15 mg/day; the 7.5–15 mg/day dose, although more efficacious, still caused adverse reactions at 15 mg/day, which reduced its usefulness.

The results of this trial have been reported in full by Ballenger et al. (1991).

The positive outcome of this study is especially notable given the constraints placed on the design, the fact that it was a multicenter study, the small size of the treatment groups, and the high placebo response. This first dose-finding study of abecarnil resulted in the selection of a dose range for further trials, designed to test clinically the very promising results obtained to date.

ACKNOWLEDGMENT

We thank the many colleagues from our respective departments who have kindly provided the data on which this chapter is based.

REFERENCES

American Psychiatric Association, *Diagnostic and Statistical Manual of Mental Disorders,* 3rd ed., revised, American Psychiatric Press, Washington, D.C. (1987).

J. S. Andrews, and D. N. Stephens, Drug discrimination models in anxiety and depression, *Pharmacol. Ther., 47*: 267 (1990).

J. C. Ballenger, S. McDonald, R. Noyes, K. Rickels, N. Sussman, S. Woods, J. Patin, and J. Singer, The first double-blind, placebo-controlled trial of a partial benzodiazepine agonist abecarnil in generalized anxiety disorder, *Psychopharmacol. Bull., 27*: 171 (1991).

T. Duka, B. Schütt, R. Dorow, S. McDonald, W. Krause, and K. Fichte, ß-Carboline anxiolytic: Phase 1 single and multiple dose studies to establish safety, tolerability and drug effects, *Eur. J. Clin. Pharmacol., 36*(Suppl.): A48 (1989).

T. Duka, B. Schütt, T. Mager, R. Dorow, S. McDonald, and H. Ott, Abecarnil, a ß-carboline anxiolytic: Phase I studies to establish safety, tolerability and drug effects, *CINP, Abstr., 1*: 147 (1990).

M. W. Emmett-Oglesby, D. Lytle, and S. A. English, Abecarnil used to treat benzodiazepine withdrawal, *β-Carbolines: From Molecular Biology to the Clinic* (D. N. Stephens, ed.), Springer, Heidelberg (in press).

D. Goldberg, and K. Bridges, Screening for psychiatric illness in general practice, *J. R. Coll. Gen. Pract., 37*: 15 (1987).

W. Krause, T. Duka, and H. Matthes, Pharmacokinetics and biotransformation of the anxiolytic abecarnil in healthy volunteers, *Xenobiotica, 21*: 763 (1991).

W. Krause, B. Schütt, and T. Duka, Pharmacokinetics and acute toleration of the ß-carboline derivative abecarnil in man, *Arzneimittelforschung, 40*: 529 (1990).

W. Löscher, and D. Hönack, Withdrawal precipitation by benzodiazepine receptor antagonists in dogs chronically treated with diazepam or the novel anxiolytic and anticonvulsant ß-carboline abecarnil, *Naunyn-Schmiederbergs Arch. Pharmacol.,* (1992).

W. A. Merz, Partial benzodiazepine agonists; initial results in man, *Clin. Neuropharmacol., 7*(Suppl. 1) (1984).

E. N. Petersen, and J. Buus Lassen, A water lick conflict paradigm using drug experienced rats, *Psychopharmacology, 75*: 236 (1981).

I. Pribilla, R. Huba, and H. H. Schneider, Abecarnil displays full or partial agonism at different recombinant $GABA_A$ receptor subtypes, *β-Carbolines: From Molecular Biology to the Clinic* (D. N. Stephens, ed.), Springer, Heidelberg (in press).

D. B. Pritchett, H. Lüddens, and P. H. Seeburg, Type I and type II $GABA_A$-benzodiazepine receptors produced in transfected cells, *Science, 245*: 1389 (1989).

K. Rickels, E. Schweizer, and I. Csanalosi, Long-term treatment of anxiety and risk of withdrawal, *Arch. Gen. Psychiatry, 45*: 444 (1988).

C. Sannerud, N. A. Ator, and R. R. Griffiths, Behavioral pharmacology of abecarnil in baboons: Self-injection, drug discrimination and physical dependence, *Behav. Pharmacol.,* (in press).

E. Schweizer, and K. Rickels, Failure of buspirone to manage benzodiazepine withdrawal, *Am. J. Psychiatry, 143*: 1590 (1986).

G. T. Shearman, and H. Lal, Discriminative properties of pentyelenetetrazole in the rat, *Stimulus Properties of Drugs: Ten Years of Progress* (F. C. Colpaert and J. A. Rosencrans, eds.), Elsevier, Amsterdam (1978).

D. N. Stephens, H. H. Schneider, W. Kehr, J. S. Andrews, K.-J. Rettig, L. Turski, R. Schmiechen, J. D. Turner, L. H. Jensen, E. N. Petersen, T. Honore, and J. B. Hansen,

Abecarnil, a metabolically stable, anxioselective ß-carboline acting at benzodiazepine receptors, *J. Pharmacol. Exp. Ther., 253*: 334 (1990).

D. N. Stephens, and W. Kehr, ß-Carbolines can enhance or antagonize the effects of punishment in rats, *Psychopharmacology, 85*: 143 (1985).

D. N. Stephens, L. Turski, M. Hillmann, J. D. Turner, H. H. Schneider, and M. Yamaguschi, What are the differences between abecarnil and conventional benzodiazepine anxiolytics, *Advances in Biochemical Psychopharmacology* (G. Biggio, A. Concas and E. Costa, eds.), Raven Press, New York (1992).

K. Steppuhn, H. H. Schneider, L. Turski, and D. N. Stephens, Long term treatment with abecarnil does not induce dependence in mice, (submitted).

L. Turski, D. N. Stephens, L. H. Jensen, E. N. Petersen, B. S. Meldrum, S. Patel, J. Bondo Hansen, W. Loescher, H. H. Schneider, R. Schmiechen, and S. H. Autoren, Anticonvulsant action of the ß-carboline abecarnil; studies in rodents and baboon, *Papio papio, J. Pharmacol. Exp. Ther., 253*: 344 (1990).

25

Anxiety, Depression, and Personality: Neurophysiological and Clinical Data

Dragan M. Svrakic and C. Robert Cloninger
Washington University School of Medicine, St. Louis, Missouri

I. INTRODUCTION

Recent advances in neurotransmitter biology, neuroanatomy, and personality theory and measurement have converged to suggest that normal and deviant personality may reflect heritable variations in neurochemical functions. For example, neurochemically coded distributed neural networks have been hypothesized to determine biases underlying normal motivated behavior (Cloninger, 1987a). Likewise, personality disorders have been postulated to reflect extreme variations in monoamine activity and consequent susceptibility to deviant moods, learning styles, and maladaptive behaviors (so called trait-vulnerability) (Sollof, 1990).

Cloninger and colleagues (1992) have recently developed a comprehensive psychobiological model of personality, which is based on a synthesis of concepts and data from various disciplines, ranging from behavior genetics and cognitive neuroscience to theology and insight meditation. This model distinguishes temperament and character in an attempt to integrate biogenetic, environmental, and phenotypic aspects of normal and deviant personality development and structure. The temperament factors are prominent early in childhood and are determined about equally by genetic influences and environmental influences specific to each individual (Heath et al., 1992); in contrast, the character factors are also heritable, but they mature in adulthood and appear to be influenced by social learning and familial environmental factors (Cloninger et al., 1992). In brief, the model defines behavioral, clinical, genetic, and neurophysiological aspects of four temperament dimensions called *novelty seeking, harm avoidance, reward dependence,* and *persistence* (Cloninger, 1987a; Cloninger et al., 1992). In addition, the model defines three dimensions of character, called *self-directedness, cooperativeness,* and *self-transcendence,* in terms of three major levels of identification of the self-concept as an autonomous individual (self-directedness), as an integral part of human society (cooperativeness), and as an integral part of the universe (self-transcendence). The Tridimensional Personality Questionnaire (TPQ), a 100-item, self-report, true–false questionnaire was developed to measure the three temperament dimensions of novelty-seeking, harm avoidance, and reward dependence (Cloninger, 1987a). The composition of the TPQ questions was guided by the specific learning characteristics typical of each of the dimensions (Cloninger, 1987a). Recently, the Temperament and Character Inventory (TCI) (Cloninger, 1992) was developed to measure all seven temperament and character dimensions (Table 1). The TCI includes most of the TPQ questions for the temperament scales, plus additional questions evaluating the character dimensions.

Each of the higher-order dimensions of temperament and character consists of several lower-order traits. In a large sample of Australian twins, Heath et al. (1992) showed that

Table 1 TCI Scales and Subscales

I. Temperament

Novelty seeking (NS) (40 items)
- NS1: exploratory excitability vs stoic rigidity (11 items)
- NS2: impulsiveness vs reflection (10 items)
- NS3: extravagance vs reserve (9 items)
- NS4: disorderliness vs orderliness (10 items)

Harm avoidance (HA) (35 items)
- HA1: worry and pessimism vs uninhibited optimism (11 items)
- HA2: fear of uncertainty (7 items)
- HA3: shyness vs gregariousness (8 items)
- HA4: fatigability vs vigor (9 items)

Reward dependence (RD) (24 items)
- RD1: sentimentality (10 items)
- RD3: attachment vs detachment (8 items)
- RD4: dependence vs independence (6 items)

Persistence (RD2) (8 items)

II. Character

Self-directiveness (S) (44 items)
- SD1: responsibility vs blaming (8 items)
- SD2: purposefulness vs lack of goal direction (8 items)
- SD3: resourcefulness vs inertia (5 items)
- SD4: self-acceptance vs self-striving (11 items)
- SD5: congruent second nature (12 items)

Cooperativeness (C) (42 items)
- C1: social acceptance vs social intolerance (8 items)
- C2: empathy vs social disinterest (8 items)
- C3: helpfulness (9 items)
- C4: compassion vs revenge (10 items)
- C5: principled vs self-serving (9 items)

Self-transcendence (ST) (33 items)
- ST1: self-forgetful vs self-conscious (11 items)
- ST2: transpersonal identification (9 items)
- ST3: spiritual acceptance (13 items)

Total: 226 items

one component of the original reward dependence dimension (i.e., persistence) is inherited independently from other aspects of temperament. In this chapter we focus primarily on the neurophysiological and clinical aspects of the temperament dimensions of novelty seeking, harm avoidance, and reward dependence because these have been confirmed to be most important in relation to anxiety, depression, and personality disorders. In addition, we discuss to some extent the role of character in determining the presence or absence of personality disorders.

II. BIOLOGICAL AND NEUROPHYSIOLOGICAL BACKGROUND OF TEMPERAMENT

One of the most robust findings in personality research is that most of the differences between individuals in temperament can be accounted for by three major dimensions. The most prominent tridimensional models of temperament are those of Eysenck (1967), Cloninger (1987a), Tellegen (1985), and Gray (1982). Some of these models (e.g., Tellegen, 1985; Eysenck, 1967) were derived factor-analytically and, therefore, do not describe behavior beyond observable phenotypic traits. Gray considered biological determinants, but has not developed a psychometrically satisfactory assessment instrument. The major difficulty in mapping variation in personality to its underlying etiological processes arises because factor analysis can determine only the minimal number of distinguishing personality traits, not their underlying causative factors (Cloninger, 1987a).

However, biological and genetic studies do permit a choice among alternative ways of summarizing personality and temperament traits. For example, Gray (1982) noted that drugs that reduce scores on neuroticism, such as alcohol or benzodiazepines, also reduce scores on measures of introversion. This suggests that neuroticism and extraversion probably share biological determinants. Still, factor-analytically derived phenotypic models (Eysenck, 1967, in particular) assume that neuroticism and extraversion are independent personality dimensions.

Studies of the genetic structure of personality also provide many clues about the underlying causal structure of personality. Phenotypic models (Eysenck, 1967; Tellegen, 1985; Costa and McCrae, 1985) do not take into account that the observed personality structure may differ from the underlying biogenetic structure because, in addition to genetic factors, learning and environmental factors also influence phenotypic variation. For example, the genetic factors for sociability and impulsivity were shown to be different (Eaves and Eysenck, 1975). Still, they are regarded by Eysenck as components of a single phenotypic trait—extraversion (Eysenck and Eysenck, 1985). Likewise, Heath and Martin (1990) showed that psychoticism is not genetically unitary. On the other hand, in addition to being heritable, the temperament dimensions of novelty seeking, harm avoidance, and reward dependence were also shown to be *genetically homogeneous and independent* (Heath et al., 1992).

Novelty seeking is viewed as a heritable bias in the activation or initiation of behaviors such as frequent exploratory activity in response to novelty, impulsive decision-making, pursuit of and approach to potential rewards, quick loss of temper, active avoidance of frustration, and escape from punishment, accompanied by a particular pattern of physiological arousal, such as increased heart rate and decreased tolerance for pain or other kinds of punishment (Cloninger, 1987a).

Individuals high in novelty seeking are curious, exploratory, fickle, easily bored, impressionistic, impulsive, extravagant, enthusiastic, disorderly, unconventional, quick-tempered, evasive, deceptive. Low novelty seeking persons are content, quiet, rigid, patient, methodical, reflective, frugal, reserved, orderly, regimented, slow-tempered, stoical, forthright, honest.

Harm avoidance is defined as a heritable bias in the inhibition or cessation of behaviors, and is manifest, on one hand, as pessimistic worry in anticipation of future problems and, on the other hand, as passive avoidant behaviors such as fear of uncertainty, shyness, and rapid fatigability. Individuals high in harm avoidance are cautious, worrying, pessimistic, restrained, fearful, shy, fatigable, asthenic. Low harm avoidant persons are confident, carefree, optimistic, risk-taking, bold, outgoing, energetic, vigorous.

Reward dependence is defined as a heritable bias in the maintenance or continuation of ongoing behaviors. This temperament dimension derives from a tendency to respond intensely to signals of reward (e.g., verbal signals of social approval, sentiment, and succor), and to maintain or resist extinction of behavior that has previously been associated with rewards or relief from punishment. Reward dependence reflects needs for intimacy, overachievement, conformity to peer pressure, sensitivity to loss or rejection, ambition, reward seeking in response to frustration, and proneness to sympathetic sentiment. *Persistence,* defined as perseverance despite frustration and fatigue, has been shown to be genetically independent of reward dependence, defined as sentimentality, social attachment, and dependence on approval. Individuals who are high in reward dependence are also sentimental, socially sensitive, tender-hearted, dedicated. In contrast, individuals who are low in reward dependence do respond to practical rewards, such as money, but are insensitive to verbal signals of social reinforcement and quickly become indifferent and terminate activities or relations that are no longer gratifying. These persons are also practical, insensitive, cold-blooded, detached.

The underlying dimensions of temperament and the psychometric properties of the TPQ have received empirical support with normative samples (Cloninger et al., 1991), clinical samples (Brown et al., 1992; Freedland et al., 1991), and cross-cultural surveys (Svrakic et al., 1991; Takeuchi et al., 1990).

The following two facts are relevant to the dimension of the biological background of temperament traits. First, most personality models (e.g., Tellegen, 1985; Eysenck, 1967; Cloninger, 1987a), postulate a close functional association between major temperament traits and three "hardwired" emotions (i.e., anger, fear, love, or attachment) shared by humans and many other animals. We discuss this topic in more detail later in the chapter. Second, the tridimensional genetic structure of personality has been replicated many times in many different cultures (e.g., Svrakic et al., 1991; Takeuchi et al., 1990). Apparently, temperament traits have a biological background that not only goes beyond the level of sociocultural differences, but is shared by all higher animals.

As noted by Cloninger (1991), to approach temperament from a neurobiological perspective, the following two observations should be helpful:

1. Nieuwenhuys (1985) has pointed out that the extent of the limbic system corresponds well to the widespread distribution of the three principal monoamines—dopamine, serotonin, and norepinephrine. The monoaminergic projections from specific nuclei in the brain stem represent widespread distributed networks that are involved in many opponent processes regulating adaptation to experience.
2. Cloninger (1987a) has noted that available neurobehavioral studies suggest that each specific monoaminergic network has a major modulatory role in only one of the three putative systems of behavioral activation, maintenance, and inhibition.

Moreover, Cloninger (1987a) postulates a close functional relation between novelty seeking, harm avoidance, and reward dependence, and these three brain systems: novelty seeking with the brain system for activation; harm avoidance with the brain system for inhibition; and reward dependence with the brain system for maintenance of behavior.

In this chapter, we present only a very brief review of neuroanatomical and biochemical networks (also referred to as brain systems) that underlie the temperament dimensions of harm avoidance, novelty seeking, and reward dependence. (For more details on this topic, see Cloninger 1987a, 1991.) It should be emphasized that the literature on the relation between specific psychological or behavior dimensions and specific neurophysiological functions is extensive. The following literature review is, to some extent, selective to highlight major points.

A. Behavior Activation System and Novelty Seeking

Dopaminergic cell bodies in the midbrain receive inputs from several sources and then project impulses to the forebrain, thereby acting as the final common pathway for the behavioral activations system (Wise, 1980; Fowles, 1980). More informatively, the behavioral activation system primarily involves dopaminergic cell bodies in the ventral tegmentum with their projections to the striatum, nucleus accumbens, and frontal and limbic cortex (Cloninger, 1987a, 1991). Low basal dopaminergic activity is associated with frequent exploratory activity, more intense responses to novel stimuli and high novelty seeking (Cloninger, 1987a).

This is supported by clinical and laboratory data (also summarized in Cloninger, 1991).

1. Spontaneous exploratory behavior by mammals in a novel environment depends on integrity of mesolimbic dopaminergic projections, particularly from the ventral tegmental area to the nucleus accumbens (Iversen, 1977).
2. Dopaminergic activation of D_2 receptors in the nucleus accumbens increases exploratory locomotor activity in response to novel stimuli (Mogenson et al., 1980), as well as to appetitive and predatory approach behavior (Al-Khatib et al., 1987).
3. Self-stimulation with electrodes at sites of dopaminergic neurons is rapid and is accompanied by marked locomotor activation and positive reinforcement of eliciting behaviors in mammals and by reports of subjective experience of pleasure and satisfaction in humans (Wise, 1980; Routtenberg, 1978; Heath, 1964).

Clinical pharmacological data also support the postulated association between novelty seeking and low basal dopaminergic activity.

1. Attention deficit disorder (high novelty seeking—low dopamine activity) is responsive to dopamine agonists, such as amphetamine or methylphenidate (Cloninger, 1986).
2. Hysteroid dysphorics are high in novelty seeking (i.e., they are impulsive and seek sensations). The traits are responsive to monoamine oxidase inhibitors (MAOIs), which increase dopaminergic, serotonergic, and noradrenergic activity; but not to tricyclic antidepressants (TCAs), with serotonergic and noradrenergic, but no dopaminergic effects (Liebowitz, 1987).
3. Persons with histrionic personality disorder (PD) manifest high novelty seeking (low dopaminergic activity), high reward dependence (low noradrenergic activity),

and low harm avoidance (low serotonergic activity). Histrionic persons particularly benefit from MAOIs because of the general increase in activity of all the monoamines.

4. Chronic dopamine blockade seems to produce apathetic, amotivational states. There may be levels of dopamine activity that are too low to support any exploratory behavior or incentive function, since the approach to even novel stimuli would not be reinforced. At the other end of the spectrum, excessive dopaminergic states, whether natural or drug-induced, may render everything interesting or novel, as seen in mania (Liebowitz, 1987).

High novelty seeking is positively associated with the likelihood of initiating use of drugs that stimulate dopaminergic activity, such as amphetamines, low doses of ethanol, or cigarette smoking (Pomerleau et al., 1992; Cloninger, 1987b). In contrast, individuals who are susceptible to Parkinson's disease (which is a dopamine-dependent disorder) are less likely to become smokers (Shahi and Moochhala, 1991) and are also lower in novelty seeking, but not other temperament traits (Menza et al., 1990).

B. Behavior Inhibition System and Harm Avoidance

The behavior inhibition system primarily involves the limbic system, including the septohippocampal system, the Papez circuit, the prefrontal cortex, as well as the ascending monoaminergic and cholinergic pathways that innervate these forebrain structures (Gray, 1982). Cloninger (1987a) postulates a close functional association between high basal serotonergic activity, fast passive avoidance learning, and harm avoidant behaviors (such as anticipatory worry, pessimism, and fatigability).

This hypothesis is supported by clinical and laboratory data (also summarized in Cloninger, 1991):

1. Ascending serotonergic projections from the dorsal raphe nuclei to the substantia nigra inhibit nigrostriatal dopaminergic neurons and are essential for passive avoidance learning, that is, conditioned inhibition of activity by signals of punishment, frustrative nonreward, or uncertainty about safety (Thiebot et al., 1984).
2. The effects of antianxiety drugs in humans are strongly correlated with their effects on passive avoidance learning in rodents (Sepinwall and Cook, 1980), which depends on inhibition of serotonergic neurons in the dorsal raphe (Thiebot et al., 1984).
3. In humans, serotonergic activity, as measured by cerebrospinal concentration of its metabolites, is lower in individuals who are extreme risk-takers than in those who are harm-avoidant (Brown et al., 1979; Banki and Arato, 1983; Linnoila et al., 1983).
4. In rodents, activation of the serotonergic projections consistently leads to inhibition of behaviors, whether the inhibition is motivated by unconditioned punishment (Anisman, 1978), unconditioned rewards (Jacobs, 1972), or conditioned signals of punishment and nonreward (Gray, 1982).
5. Negative-feedback circuits moderate the opposing influences of serotonergic and catecholaminergic projections. In particular, the habenular–interpeduncular complex maintains a tonic facilitation of serotonergic activity and inhibition of dopaminergic activity (Nishikawa and Scatton, 1985; Nishikawa et al., 1986). In turn, the activity of the habenular–interpeduncular complex is regulated by a long negative-

feedback circuit in which an ascending serotonergic projection from the superior central nucleus activates S1 receptors in the medial and posterior septal nuclei, thereby inhibiting an excitatory septohippocampal cholinergic projection to the habenular–interpeduncular complex.

Clinical pharmacological data most convincingly support the postulated association between harm avoidance and high basal serotonergic activity.

High basal serotonergic activity seems to determine high harm avoidance in obsessive–compulsive disorder (OCD). It is well established that OCD responds to serotonin-reuptake blockers (clomipramine, fluoxetine, fluvoxamine). Extended application of these drugs suppresses serotonergic system activity toward more normal levels (Liebowitz, 1987). Cerebrospinal fluid (CSF) findings show high basal serotonergic activity in OCD patients who respond to serotonin-reuptake blockers, and normalization of serotonin activity following long-term treatment (the treatment suppresses serotonin activity, presumably by reducing postsynaptic serotonin sensitivity) (Cloninger, 1988).

C. Behavior Maintenance and Reward Dependence

The behavior maintenance system primarily involves neurons in the dorsal bundle arising from the locus coeruleus in the pons. Ascending noradrenergic pathways project to hypothalamus and limbic structures, including the amygdala, septum, and hippocampus, and then branch throughout the entire neocortex (Cloninger, 1987a, 1991). Low basal noradrenergic activity is associated with more intense responses to rewards and better maintenance (resistance to extinction) of rewarded behavior (i.e., reward dependence, (Cloninger, 1987a, 1991).

This is supported by clinical and laboratory data (also summarized in Cloninger, 1991):

1. Norepinephrine release leads to an increased signal/noise ratio in its postsynaptic targets, thereby allowing relevant or important stimuli to stand out from irrelevant stimuli (Aston-Jones, 1985).
2. In humans, short-term reduction of norepinephrine release by acute intake of the a_2-presynaptic agonist clonidine selectively impairs paired associative learning, particularly the acquisition of novel associations (Frith et al., 1985).
3. The ability of arginine vasopressin to enhance memory when injected immediately after a learning trial and to maintain previously acquired behavioral tolerance to the antianxiety effects of alcohol depends on the integrity of the dorsal noradrenergic bundle (Kovacs et al., 1979; Hoffman et al., 1983).
4. In rhesus monkeys, individuals with low basal noradrenergic activity at rest show severe depressivelike responses to social separation (Kraemer et al., 1984).
5. Long-term partial reduction of norepinephrine release in the forebrain by partial destructive lesions of the locus coeruleus or its dorsal bundle has been reported to increase postsynaptic sensitivity to norepinephrine, increased resistance to extinction of previously rewarded behavior, and improved responses to conditioned signals of relief of punishment in two-way active avoidance task in rodents (Gray, 1982). However, initial reports of resistance to extinction have not been replicable (Trevor Robins, personal communication); likewise, persistence appears to be independent of other aspects of reward dependence, such as sentimentality and social attachment (Cloninger, 1992).

Clinical pharmacological data supporting the association between reward dependence and low basal noradrenergic activity are limited relative to the cited data for harm avoidance and novelty seeking.

1. Abstinent alcoholics with reward dependent traits have been demonstrated to have low basal norepinephrine turnover (Borg et al., 1983).
2. In humans, short-term reduction of norepinephrine release by acute infusion of the α_2-presynaptic agonist clonidine selectively impairs paired associative learning, particularly the acquisition of novel associations (Frith et al., 1985).

It is critical to recognize that the genetic independence of the three neuroadaptive systems described here does not mean that they each operate separately. Each of the monoaminergic systems receives input from a variety of sources and, in turn, distributes its output in a widespread fashion. In other words, the widespread distribution of each monoaminergic projection system defines a complex distributed network coordinating the dynamic interaction of many structures and involving a wide variety of other neurotransmitters and neuromodulators (Cloninger, 1991).

Quite similar to what is proposed here, Brown and colleagues (see Chap. 13) suggest that disordered norepinephrine metabolism may be related to the psychopathological dimension of hedonic function or the ability to experience pleasure; disordered dopamine metabolism may be more directly related to the mobilizing and directing of the goal-directed behaviors or an incentive system; whereas dysregulation of serotonin function may be related to anxiety.

Despite such general agreements, we are still far away from a neurophysiological "atlas" of specific behaviors. First, most of the presented findings and hypotheses are yet to be clinically tested. Second, recent advances in neurotransmitter biology show the complexity of neurotransmission systems in the brain. Multiple types and subtypes of receptors and neurotransmitters have been discovered. Consequently, our ideas about specificity of drug action and specificity of neurotransmission have changed and are likely to continue to change.

Nonetheless, it seems useful to formulate models of personality based on known relations between specific behaviors, specific neurotransmitters, neurotransmitter receptors, and signal transduction pathways. Clinical and neurobiological testing (and the corresponding revisions) of such models may provide answers to etiopathogenetic questions about personality and behavior per se, and for emotionality, motivation, and mood disorders. In the remainder of this chapter we present psychometric data that provide an interesting picture of the relation between temperament, normal and pathological mood states, and mood traits.

III. MOOD STATES AND PERSONALITY

Despite extensive efforts, the relation between personality and normal and pathological mood states (the latter are also called affective disorders) has not been explained completely. Instead, various interpretations of this relationship have been suggested (e.g., Wetzel et al., 1980; Charney et al., 1981; Akiskal et al., 1983; Widiger, 1989; Phillips et al., 1990). In brief, personality has been postulated to be a precursor of affective disorders, a chronic complication of affective disorders, a contributor to affective disorders (i.e., personality factors outline life events resulting in deviant moods), a modifier of affective disorders (i.e., personality changes the age of onset, the symptomatic expression, or the prognosis of mood disorders), a dimension orthogonal to affective disorders (suggesting that personality and affective disorders are independent from each other), an attenuated form of affective disorders (i.e., a less severe clinical expression of the same disorder), or a phenotypically independent expression of a diathesis common to both personality disorders and affective disorders.

The diverse interpretations of the relation between affective disorders and personality derive partly from the conceptual and methodological problems the field faces. For example, even when valid measures of personality in affective disorders are obtained, there remains the question of elucidating their relevance to the pathogenesis of deviant moods (Akiskal et al., 1983). The issue of causality is best addressed in studies in which subjects at high risk for mood and/or anxiety disorders are assessed before the onset of these disorders and then followed through a period of psychiatric risk. Prospective studies, however, are difficult to accomplish in the clinical population. Personality is usually evaluated after the onset of affective disorders, when the state–trait effect interferes with reliable conclusions (Akiskal et al., 1983). Also, personality disorders and pathological mood states can be interwoven to the extent that no meaningful distinction between them can be made (Widiger, 1989), as implied in the concepts of characterological depression (Akiskal et al., 1980) and depressive personality (Chodoff, 1972).

On the other hand, it has been generally accepted that affective states, especially anxiety and depression, tend to change scores on personality tests. However, studies relying on Eysenck's personality model have yielded inconsistent results. Some authors report that depression and anxiety increase neuroticism and reduce extraversion (Boyce et al., 1989), whereas others show that mood and anxiety states change only neuroticism (Liebowitz et al., 1979; see Davidson et al., 1985, for review). Still others (Davidson et al., 1985) suggest that high neuroticism scores may not reflect personality features in depressed or anxious persons because 19 of the 24 neuroticism items appear in the Hamilton depression scale, and 12 in the Hamilton anxiety scale. As we will show later in this chapter, Cloninger's (1992) model of temperament and character is more specific relative to the relation of personality to mood and anxiety states.

The effect of anxiety states on personality measures has been less well studied than that of depression. Anxiety was shown to correlate highly with neuroticism (Bianchi and Ferguson, 1977). Reich et al. (1986) studied patients with agoraphobia and panic disorder and found that state anxiety, like depression, is a possible confounding factor in personality measurement.

Clearly, the data suggest that studies evaluating the relation between mood and personality, both in psychopathology and in the general population, may improve our conceptualization of this relation.

A. Empirical Data

We (Brown et al., 1992) analyzed the relation of temperament, as defined by Cloninger (1987a), and mood and anxiety, as measured by the Beck depression inventory (BDI) and the Karolinska personality scales. The Karolinska scales used measure somatic and psychic anxiety, muscular tension, social desirability, monotony avoidance, and impulsivity (Schalling et al., 1973). In addition, we interviewed the subjects by the tridimensional inventory of personality style (TIPS), a semistructured interview that evaluates novelty seeking, harm avoidance, and reward dependence on a 7-point scale (Cloninger, 1987a). The subjects were retested after 3–6 months.

This study showed that mood and anxiety affect personality domains differentially. Most aspects of temperament, particularly the dimensions of novelty seeking and reward dependence, were essentially independent from current mood and anxiety states. In contrast, the harm avoidance scores in depressed and anxious psychiatric patients were much higher than those in the general population, pointing to a potential diagnostic or screening use of the TPQ in mood and anxiety states. Moreover, harm avoidance was related highly to mood and anxiety states. This is illustrated in Table 2.

Harm avoidance correlated highly positively with the BDI (0.64), psychic anxiety (0.77), somatic anxiety (0.61), and muscular tension (0.51), and negatively with monotony avoidance (–0.43). Novelty seeking and reward dependence were not related to mood and anxiety states. Reward dependence was related weakly to the Karolinska personality scale of monotony avoidance, and novelty seeking to the Karolinska personality scales of inpulsivity and monotony avoidance, as predicted by Cloninger (1987a). Similar trends characterized the subscales.

The correlation matrix of changes in personality and mood states and anxiety after 3–6 months are summarized in Table 3.

Changes in the harm avoidance scale and its subscales were related highly to changes in psychic and somatic anxiety, muscular tension, impulsivity, and depression (0.25). In contrast, changes in novelty seeking and reward dependence were largely unrelated to changes in mood and anxiety states.

In this depressed sample, the test–retest coefficients for novelty seeking (NS), reward dependence (RD), and harm avoidance (HA) were 0.84, 0.78, and 0.51, respectively. In contrast, in the general population, the test–retest reliability for NS, RD, and HA were 0.76, 0.70, and 0.78, respectively (Cloninger et al., 1991). Clearly, the harm avoidance dimension is more stable than the other two temperament dimensions in the general population, but becomes less stable in depressed and anxious subjects.

The correlations between self-report (TPQ) and interview (TIPS) assessment of the three temperament dimensions were high (range from 0.76 to 0.78), pointing to a high agreement between self-report and the rater's assessment of the harm avoidance dimension. Thus, the observed change in harm avoidance is unlikely to be an artifact (i.e., it is unlikely that, owing to depression, the subjects evaluated their actually unchanged harm avoidance dimension in a biased way).

The observed high correlations between harm avoidance and depression and anxiety do not reflect that the former is simply a measure of the latter, because results strikingly similar to those observed in depressed psychiatric patients also characterized clinically euthymic subjects. More informatively, a sample of 86 college students (none of the subjects reported any physical or mental disorder) completed the TPQ and the Profile of Mood States (POMS-bi) (Lorr and McNair, 1984, 1988). Again, harm avoidance and its subscales were related highly to mood states (i.e., to the negative poles of the scales measuring subclinical negative moods, e.g., depressed, tired, confused, unsure, anxious). Novelty seeking and reward dependence were unrelated to the POMS-bi mood states (Svrakic et al., 1992). Therefore, the data show that the harm avoidance temperament trait tends to covary with clinical depression and anxiety and subclinical negative moods. In other words, harm avoidance captures the pessimistic and fearful part of personality and temperament, which is more or less pronounced in everyone.

Both the likelihood that relatively large portions of personality may be independent from mood and anxiety states and the likelihood that some precisely delineated personality domains covary with mood and anxiety brings us a step closer to the understand-

Table 2 Correlations Between Measures of Personality, Mood States, and Anxiety (N = 50)

	NS	NS1	NS2	NS3	NS4	RD	RD1	RD2	RD3	RD4	HA	HA1	HA2	HA3	HA4
BDI	0.05	−0.32	0.15	0.08	0.27	0.04	0.12	0.26	−0.25	−0.02	0.64^{a}	0.56^{a}	0.36^{b}	0.25	0.55^{a}
SA	0.08	−0.16	0.17	0.22	0.00	0.021	0.37^{b}	0.37^{b}	−0.10	−0.06	0.61^{a}	0.56^{a}	0.41^{a}	0.30	0.43^{a}
PA	0.04	−0.33	0.23	0.13	0.11	0.07	0.26	0.30	−0.24	0.00	0.77^{a}	0.66^{a}	0.53^{a}	0.54^{a}	0.45^{a}
MA	0.34^{b}	0.66^{a}	0.17	0.06	0.01	0.30	−0.01	0.17	0.43^{a}	−0.07	−0.43^{a}	−0.15	−0.22	−0.40^{a}	−0.43^{a}
MT	0.23	−0.17	0.31	0.38^{b}	0.14	0.11	0.22	0.27	−0.12	−0.06	0.51^{a}	0.45^{a}	0.24	0.28	0.41^{a}
I	0.67^{a}	0.40^{a}	0.70^{a}	0.43^{a}	0.30	0.12	−0.08	−0.00	0.19	0.12	−0.13	−0.19	−0.14	−0.07	0.01
SD	−0.14	−0.04	−0.00	0.00	−0.36^{b}	0.09	0.22	0.10	−0.00	−0.08	−0.08	−0.14	−0.11	−0.11	−0.03

^{a} < 0.005;
^{b} < 0.01

NS, novelty seeking; NS1, exploratory excitability vs stoic rigidity; NS2, impulsiveness vs reflection; NS3, extravagance vs reserve; NS4, disorderliness vs regimentation. HA, harm avoidance; HA1, anticipatory worry vs uninhibited optimism; HA2, fear of uncertainty vs confidence; HA3, shyness with strangers; HA4, fatigability and asthenia vs vigor. RD, reward dependence; RD1, sentimentality vs insensitiveness; RD2, persistence vs irresoluteness; RD3, attachment vs detachment; RD4, dependence vs independence. BDI, Beck Depression Inventory; SA somatic anxiety; PA, psychic anxiety; MA, monotony avoidance; MT, muscular tension; I, impulsivity; SD, social desirability.

Table 3 Correlations Between Changes in Measures of Personality, Mood, and Anxiety ($N = 41$)

	ΔNS	ΔNS1	ΔNS3	ΔNS3	ΔNS4	ΔRD	ΔRD1	ΔRD2	ΔRD3	ΔRD4	ΔHA	ΔHA1	ΔHA2	ΔHA3	ΔHA4
ΔBDI	−0.13	−0.36[a]	0.18	0.01	0.05	0.00	−0.04	−0.00	−0.09	0.20	0.25	0.36[a]	−0.05	0.30	0.32[a]
ΔSA	−0.13	−0.25	−0.02	−0.00	0.04	−0.15	−0.03	0.02	−0.31[a]	−0.05	0.34[a]	0.35[a]	−0.09	0.47[c]	0.34[a]
ΔPA	−0.24	−0.37[b]	−0.07	0.12	−0.12	0.15	0.08	0.32[a]	−0.23	0.16	0.54[c]	0.44[c]	0.15	0.52[c]	0.44[c]
ΔMA	0.18	0.33[a]	−0.07	0.12	−0.12	0.01	0.03	0.20	−0.16	−0.10	−0.09	0.11	−0.25	0.12	−0.19
ΔMT	−0.14	−0.42[b]	0.01	0.26	−0.07	−0.10	0.06	−0.09	−0.27	0.21	0.46[c]	0.40[b]	0.01	0.52[c]	0.40[b]
ΔI	0.29	0.36[b]	0.07	−0.05	0.16	0.29	0.18	0.42[c]	0.10	−0.20	−0.35[a]	−0.31[a]	−0.16	−0.26	−0.32[a]
ΔSD	−0.08	−0.06	−0.09	−0.01	0.00	0.00	0.13	0.21	−0.24	−0.12	0.02	0.03	−0.16	0.18	−0.01

[a] < 0.05;
[b] < 0.01;
[c] < 0.005.

NS, novelty seeking; NS1, exploratory excitability vs stoic rigidity; NS2, impulsiveness vs reflection; NS3, extravagance vs reserve; NS4, disorderliness vs regimentation. HA, harm avoidance; HA1, anticipatory worry vs uninhibited optimism; HA2, fear of uncertainty vs confidence; HA3, shyness with strangers; HA4, fatigability and asthenia vs vigor. RD, reward dependence; RD1, sentimentality vs insensitiveness; RD2, persistence vs irresoluteness; RD3, attachment vs detachment; RD4, dependence vs independence. BDI, Beck Depression Inventory; SA, somatic anxiety; PA, psychic anxiety; MA, monotony avoidance; MT, muscular tension; I, impulsivity; SD, social desirability; Δ, change.

ing of the relation of personality to mood and anxiety states. We suggest that it is the systematic state-dependence of harm avoidance (i.e., its sensitivity to mood and anxiety states) that can provide useful information about this relation. The harm avoidance temperament trait may reflect variation in serotonergic activity and the behavior inhibition system that includes the septohippocampal system, serotonergic projections from the raphe nuclei, and cholinergic projections from the frontal neocortex from ventral tegmental area and basal nucleus of Meynert (Cloninger, 1987a, p. 576). In other words, the observed changes in harm avoidance reflecting changes in normal and pathological mood states point to specific neuroanatomical areas and neurochemical processes that determine motivational aspects of behavior and may be useful in future studies of mood traits, normal and pathological mood states, personality disorders, and personality.

IV. MOOD TRAITS AND PERSONALITY

Emotionality, temperament, and personality are closely related and difficult to separate for observation and study. For example, *personality* is defined as individual differences in motivated behavior and emotionality (Cloninger, 1987a). Likewise, *temperament* is defined as early developing personality traits (Buss and Plomin, 1984) observable as individual differences in emotionality, sociability, and activity, or simply as emotionality (Goldsmith, 1987).

The concepts of emotionality and personality overlap from a neuroadaptive perspective as well. First, Panksepp (1982) maintained that key emotions arise ultimately from "hardwired" neural circuits in the limbic brain that facilitate diverse and adaptive behavioral and physiological responses to major classes of environmental challenges. The circuits, and their corresponding emotions, arose early in mammalian brain evolution and remain similar in humans and other mammals. These "basic" emotions are considered critical motivational phenomena that have had adaptive function at all evolutionary levels (Izard, 1977). Quite similar to this concept of key emotions, Cloninger (1987a) describes temperament in terms of three independent, heritable, and stable dimensions, reflecting basic emotions generated by hardwired circuits in the limbic brain (Cloninger, 1987a). In addition to understanding emotions as being tied to specific brain structures, Cloninger's (1987a) model postulates that emotionality critically influences learning processes, motivated behavior, and adaptation to the environment. Phenomenologically, temperament and emotionality closely correspond to each other (Table 4).

Table 4 Correspondence Between Personality and Emotionality

Personality dimension	Characteristic emotional traits: High scorer	Characteristic emotional traits: Low scorer
Novelty seeking	Quick-tempered, excitable, curious, enthusiastic, exuberant, easily bored	Slow-tempered, stoical, uninquiring, inexuberant, unenthusiastic, tolerant
Reward dependence	Loving, sensitive, warm, dedicated, depressed if separated	Unfriendly, insensitive, cool, irresolute, indifferent if alone
Harm avoidance	Fearful, doubtful, timid, dismayed, disgusted, fatigable	Relaxed, self-assured, bold, daring, dauntless, vigorous

As shown in Table 4, key temperament dimensions can be systematically associated with basic mood traits: novelty seeking with anger and impulsivity; reward dependence with love—attachment; and harm avoidance with fear and anxiety. In accord with this close correspondence between temperament and emotionality, authors see personality as deriving from basic emotions (Tellegen, 1985), or define individual differences as reflecting differences in patterns of discrete emotions across individuals (Izard, 1977), or consider emotions as central-organizing axes for personality (Malatesta, 1988).

The assumed stable and significant functional association between biogenetic dispositions to specific moods and observable personality traits is supported by neuroanatomical and neurophysiological data. For example, both prenatal and postnatal developmental regressive changes in neurons, resulting in structural reorganization of neuronal circuits in frontal, temporal, and limbic cortical areas, may form the basis for integration and maturation of most complex features of personality, which are organized around a set of enduring behavioral and emotional dispositions (Carlson et al., 1988, review this subject in detail).

It has been repeatedly shown that a limited number of emotions portray individual differences in adults and children (Izard, 1977; Lang, 1985; Tellegen, 1985; Maziade et al., 1986). In addition, three to four discrete emotions are consistent across many cultures (Ekblad, 1988; Olendick et al., 1989). In deviant behaviors, personality disorders seem to reflect behavioral expression of a limited number of deviant emotional types; that is, cold–aloof, fearful, and impulsive—dramatic (Widiger et al., 1987). Likewise, *DSM-III-R* (APA, 1987) relates only three deviant emotional types in children (aggressive, avoidant, and detached) to adult personality disorders.

A. Empirical Data

The data presented so far support the hypothesis that enduring emotional traits critically determine both normal and deviant personality development and contour. In what follows, we analyze the relation between personality dimensions assessed by the temperament and character inventory (TCI) (Cloninger, 1992), and enduring moods (i.e., mood traits) assessed by the multiple affective adjective checklist, revised (MAACL-R; trait form) (Zuckerman and Lubin, 1985).

The sample and the results of this study are presented in detail in Svrakic et al. (1992a). In brief, the MAACL-R measures five lower-order mood traits (anxiety, depression, hostility, positive affect, and sensation seeking), reflecting two higher-order mood dimensions of dysphoria (comprising anxiety, depression, and hostility) and positive affect–sensation seeking. The version of the TCI used in this study had only two character scales (i.e., self-directedness and cooperativeness), in addition to the three temperament scales of novelty seeking, harm avoidance, and reward dependence. The MAACL-R (trait form), with five mood dimensions, seemed appropriate for a study addressing the issue of the relation between enduring moods and five personality dimensions assessed by the TCI.

We used a computer to administer the MAACL-R. A sentence remaining subjects to describe the way they "generally feel" appeared on the screen simultaneously with adjectives describing mood traits. This was intended to reduce the effect of current mood states on the subjects' assessment of his or her enduring moods.

Mood traits and personality dimensions manifested a meaningful and predictable relation in this study. Table 5 presents the correlations between the TCI personality traits and the MAACL-R mood traits.

Table 5 Correlations Between MAACL-R and TCI Scales (× 100)

	Host SenSk	Anx	Depr PosAff		
NS1	11	31[c]	−03	−05	08
NS2	27[c]	−08	19	18	−22[c]
NS3	04	00	00	16	09
NS4	18	05	−08	02	−11
NS	23[c]	09	04	13	−06
HA1	15	−34[b]	61[a]	44[a]	−47[a]
HA2	−12	−47[a]	36[b]	24[c]	−27[c]
HA3	05	−37[b]	35[b]	17	−26[c]
HA4	00	−45[a]	24[c]	28[c]	−28[c]
HA	04	−53[a]	54[a]	39[a]	−44[a]
RD1	−01	−02	13	22[c]	16
RD2	00	18	−19	−19	01
RD3	−20[c]	10	−01	−07	31[c]
RD4	−27[c]	−18	15	−06	06
RD	−20[c]	07	02	00	27[c]
RD134	−21[c]	00	10	07	28[c]
SD1	−31[c]	29[c]	−48[a]	−57[a]	35[b]
SD2	−17	39[a]	−40[a]	−40[a]	27[c]
SD3	−21[c]	39[a]	−47[a]	−37[a]	29[c]
SD	−29[c]	42[a]	−54[a]	37[a]	
C1	−39[a]	01	−17	−06	09
C2	−46[a]	17	−26[c]	−24[c]	29[c]
C3	−41[a]	−01	−11	−10	19
C	−56[a]	09	−24[c]	−19	26[c]

[a] < 0.0001;
[b] < 0.001;
[c] < 0.05; significant correlations underlined.
N = 100. NS, novelty seeking; NS1, exploratory excitability; NS2, impulsiveness; NS3, extravagance; NS4, disorderliness. HA, harm avoidance; HA1, worry/pessimism; HA2, feeling of uncertainty; HA3, shyness; HA4, fatigability. RD, reward dependence; RD1, sentimentality; RD2, persistence; RD3, attachment; RD4, dependence. SD, self-directedness; SD1, responsibility; SD2, purposefulness; SD3, resourcefulness. C, cooperativeness; C1, social acceptance; C2, empathy; C3, helpfulness. Host, hostility; SenSk, sensation seeking; Anx, anxiety; Depr, depression; PosAff, positive affect.

Novelty seeking correlates with hostility (0.23), reward dependence is positively related to positive affect (0.27), and negatively to hostility (–0.20), and harm avoidance is related to anxiety (0.54) and depression (0.39), and negatively to sensation seeking (–0.53) and positive affect (–0.44). This pattern matches theoretical predictions (Cloninger, 1987a). For the TCI character dimensions, the self-directedness scale is related to sensation seeking (0.42), positive affect (0.37), depression (–0.56), anxiety (–0.54), and hostility (–0.29). The cooperativeness character dimension is related to positive affect (0.26) and to hostility (–0.56). Similar trends were observed for the TCI subscales.

In accord with the foregoing, harm avoidance, novelty seeking, and reward dependence were predicted by anxiety, hostility, and positive affect, respectively. The self-directedness scale was predicted by low depression primarily, and the cooperativeness scale and its subscales inversely by hostility (Table 6).

Cloninger (1986) defined a conceptual framework for explaining individual differences in personality that underlie susceptibility to chronic somatic and chronic psychic anxiety. According to this conceptual framework, repeated exposure to an aversive stimulus with a warning signal leads to acute anticipatory anxiety, whereas repeated exposure to an aversive stimulus without a warning signal leads to a long-term sensitization or chronic anxiety. The unpredictability of aversive stimuli or the unreliability of warning signals can arise in either of two general ways. Either extreme hypovigilance (observable in high novelty seeking–low harm avoidance persons), or extreme hypervigilance (observable in high harm avoidance–low novelty seeking persons), leads to unreliable assessment of risk, such that an individual cannot identify safe situations accurately. Individuals with chronic cognitive anxiety have an *obsessional* information-processing style, characterized by hypervigilance and extreme sensitivity in recognizing contingent relationships and perceiving potential danger (Cloninger, 1986). In contrast, individuals with chronic somatic anxiety have a *histrionic* or *hysterical* information-processing pattern characterized by hypovigilance, distractibility, and difficulty recognizing temporal or contingent relationships (Cloninger, 1986). Individuals with histrionic cognitive patterns tend to seek novelty, which is adaptive for them by increasing vigilance and perceptual sensitivity. Individuals with obsessional cognitive pattern tend to avoid novelty because exposure to unfamiliar settings and stimuli is maladaptive for them. They seek routine, familiar, ritualized behavior, which is adaptive for them by reducing vigilance (Cloninger, 1986).

A similar framework for explaining individual differences in personality that underlie susceptibility to specific types of depression has not been formulated. However, our data suggest that, in addition to being closely related to susceptibility to anxiety, harm avoidance may be a risk factor for depression as well. Traditionally, depression has been considered an example of the hypofunction of the serotonergic system. Yet, the postulated association of high basal serotonergic activity with harm avoidant behaviors does not necessarily contradict the hypothesis that harm avoidance stands behind one's susceptibility to depression. As noted in Chapter 13, "originally the serotonin hypothesis of depression proposed a hypofunction of this system, subsequent research made it unclear whether the serotonin dysfunction in depression was related to hypofunction or hyperfunction of this system."

Table 6 Partial Regressions of the TCI Scales on the MAACL Mood Scales

	Harm avoidance	Reward dependence	Novelty seeking	Self-directiveness	Cooperativeness
Hostility			05[c]		(−) 31[a]
PosAffect		07[b]			
SensSeek	(−) 19[a]			06[a]	
Anxiety	29[a]			(−) 06[b]	
Depression				(−) 31[a]	
Multiple R2	48[a]	07[b]	05[c]	43[a]	31[a]

[a] < 0.0001;
[b] < 0.01;.
Tf c < .005.
PosAffect, positive affect; SensSeek, sensation seeking. Minuses denote negative (inverse) relations.

In addition, depression and anxiety are almost always comorbid. For example, Hamilton (1989) found anxiety in 97% of melancholic patients, and Kim (1979) found psychic anxiety in 97% and somatic anxiety in 98% of depressed subjects. Cross-sectionally, pure anxiety states without depressive admixtures are more commonly observed in the clinic than the reverse (Hamilton, 1983). However, when the two disorders are examined longitudinally, anxiety, followed by depression, is more common than the reverse (Kendell, 1974). Therefore, Cloninger's conceptual framework for explaining personality factors underlying susceptibility to chronic somatic and chronic psychic anxiety holds for at least some types of depression, especially depression secondary to chronic anxiety syndromes.

V. CONCLUSION

In this chapter we focused on neurophysiological and clinical aspects of the relation between temperament traits, anxiety states, and mood traits. It has been suggested recently that monoamine dysfunctions may be better related to certain behavior dimensions (normal or deviant), rather than to psychiatric diagnoses. For example, Brown et al. (see Chap. 13) point to difficulties in formulating a unifying theory to explain the etiopathogenesis of depression through the dysfunction of any single neurotransmitter. They suggest that serotonin, norepinephrine, and dopamine dysfunctions may be better related to certain psychopathological dimensions, rather than to depression itself.

Available data suggest that harm avoidance and various syndromes of depression and anxiety have many common clinical, psychometric, and neurophysiological features. In contrast, other dimensions of temperament seem largely unrelated to these syndromes.

Further studies should incorporate both nosologic diagnosis and evaluation of monoaminergic dysfunction along harm avoidance, reward dependence, or novelty seeking, or any other psychological and behavior dimensions (e.g., aggression, impulsivity, violence; see Chap. 13). This may have critical nosological and treatment implications. As we have shown in this chapter, inherited variation in neurochemical activity may determine dispositions to certain moods and learning styles. In other words, deviant personality traits are postulated to reflect heritable variations in some basic neurochemical functions interfering with a person's ability to regulate affects and cognition, and to control impulses. Therefore, enduring personality changes may follow drug-induced changes of dispositions to moods and learning styles. When directed toward the deepest level of personality (i.e., neurochemical systems mediating dispositions to mood and learning), medication may harmonize the dispositions; this, in turn, can change the perception of, the approach to, and the adaptation to the environment.

However, not every person with extreme temperament dimensions requires treatment. The temperament dimensions are approximately normally distributed in the general population, with most people having intermediate values. On the other hand, many persons high in novelty seeking may be well-adapted researchers, fighter pilots, or explorers, many persons high in harm avoidance may be well-adapted bookkeepers or environmentalists, and many persons high in reward dependence may be well-adapted and reliable friends, wives, and husbands. In other words, deviant personality is a relative, context-dependent concept.

If extreme variants of temperament traits are not necessarily deviant, what then makes some people maladjusted personality disorders? The answer is: their character. According to our data, only when accompanied by deviant character traits, extreme temperament traits qualify as maladjusted personality disorders. We (Svrakic et al., 1992b) have found significant negative correlations between the character dimensions of self-directedness and cooperativeness and the number of symptoms for all types of personality disorder. In fact, low scores on character dimensions are a common denominator that indicates the presence or absence of personality disorder. In addition to being uniformly related to low character scores, the number of symptoms for individual personality disorders is specifically related to a combination of high or low scores on the temperament scales of novelty seeking, harm avoidance, and reward dependence. Therefore, specific combinations of high or low temperament dimensions define the clinical subtype for individual personality disorders.

Temperament dimensions may be responsive to psychopharmacology and behavioral intervention, whereas character traits may be more responsive to cognitive, existential, and psychodynamic forms of psychotherapy. However, it is likely that any changes in temperament will be reflected in character and vice versa. This suggests that psychotherapy and pharmacotherapy are equally important and synergistic in the treatment of disorders of personality, anxiety, and mood.

ACKNOWLEDGMENT

Supported in part by grant MH31302 from the National Institute of Mental Health, grants AA07982 and AA08028 from the National Institute of Alcoholism, and a grant from the John D. and Catherine T. MacArthur Foundation Mental Health Research Network on the Psychobiology of Depression.

REFERENCES

H. S. Akisal, S. L. Rosenthal, and R. F. Haykal, Characterologic depression, *Arch. Gen. Psychiatry, 37*: 777 (1980).

H. S. Akiskal, M. A. Hirschfeld, and B. I. Yerevanian, The relationship of personality to affective disorders. A critical review, *Arch. Gen. Psychiatry, 40*: 801 (1983).

I. M. Al-Khatib, M. Fujiwara, K, Iwasaki, Y. Kataoka, and S. Ueki, The role of brain catecholamines in the exhibition of muricide induced by nucleus accumbens lesions and the effect of antidepressants in rats, *Pharmacol. Biochem. Behav., 26*: 351 (1987).

H. Anisman, Neurochemical changes and stress, *Psychopharmacology of Aversively Motivated Behavior* (H. Anisman and G. Bignami, eds.), Plenum Press, New York (1978).

APA, *Diagnostic and Statistical Manual for Mental Disorders,* 3rd ed., revised, American Psychiatric Association Press, Washington, D.C. (1987).

G. Aston-Jones, Behavioral functions of locus coeruleus derived from cellular attributes, *Physiol. Psychol., 13*: 118 (1985).

C. M. Banki, and M. Arato, Amine metabolites, neuroendocrine findings, and personality dimensions as correlates of suicidal behavior, *Psychiatry Res., 10*: 253 (1983).

S. Benjaminsen, Primary non-endogenous depression and features attributed to reactive depression, *J. Affective Disord., 3*: 245 (1981).

G. N. Bianchi, and G. N. Ferguson, The effect of mental state on EPI scores, *Br. J. Psychiatry, 131*: 306 (1977).

S. Borg, H. Kvandle, D. Mossberg, P. Valverius, and G. Sedvall, Central nervous system noradrenaline metabolism and alcohol consumption in man, *Pharmacol. Biochem. Behav., 18*(Suppl.): 375 (1983).

P. Boyce, D. Hadzi-Pavlovic, G. Parker et al., Depressive types and state effects on personality measures, *Acta Psychiatr. Scand., 81*: 197 (1989).

G. L. Brown, F. K. Goodwin, J. C. Ballenger, P. F. Goyer, and L. F. Major, Aggression in humans correlates with cerebrospinal fluid amine metabolites, *Psychiatry Res., 1*: 131 (1979).

S. Brown, D. M. Svrakic, T. R. Przybeck, and C. R. Cloninger, The relationship of personality to mood and anxiety states: A dimensional approach, *J. Psychiatr. Res., 26*: 197 1992).

A. Buss, and R. Plomin, *Temperament: Early Developing Personality Traits,* Lawrence Erlbaum, Hillsdale, N.J. (1984).

M. Carlson, F. Earls, and R. Todd, The importance of regressive changes in the development of the nervous system: Towards a neurobiological theory of child development, *Psychiatr. Dev., 1*: 1 (1988).

D. S. Charney, C. J. Nelson, and D. M. Quinlan, Personality traits and disorder in depression, *Am. J. Psychiatry, 138*: 1601 (1981).

P. Chodoff, The depressive personality: A critical review, *Arch. Gen. Psychiatry, 11*: 666 (1972).

C. R. Cloninger, A unified biological theory of personality and its role in the development of anxiety states, *Psychiatr. Dev., 3*: 167 (1986).

C. R. Cloninger, A systematic method for clinical description and classification of personality variants: A proposal, *Arch. Gen. Psychiatry, 44*: 573 (1987a).

C. R. Cloninger, Neurogenetic adaptive mechanisms in alcoholism, *Science, 236*: 410 (1987b).

C. R. Cloninger, A unified biosocial theory of personality and its role in the development of anxiety states: A reply to commentaries, *Psychiatr. Dev., 2*: 83 (1988).

C. R. Cloninger, Brain networks underlying personality development, *Psychopathology and the Brain* (B. J. Carroll and J. E. Barrett, eds.), Raven Press, New York, pp. 183–208 (1991).

C. R. Cloninger, *The Temperament and Character Inventory,* Washington University School of Medicine, Department of Psychiatry, PO Box 8134, St. Louis, MO, 63110 (1992).

C. R. Cloninger, T. R. Przybeck, and D. M. Svrakic, The Tridimensional personality questionnaire: US normative data, *Psychol. Rep., 69*: 1047 (1991).

C. R. Cloninger, D. M. Svrakic, and T. R. Przybeck, A psychobiological model of temperament and character, *Arch. Gen. Psychiatry* (in press).

P. Costa, and R. McCrae, *The NEO Personality Inventory Manual,* Psychological Assessment Resources, Odessa, FL (1985).

J. Davidson, R. Miller, and R. Strickland, Neuroticism and personality disorder in depression, *J. Affective Disord., 8*: 177 (1985).

L. Eaves, and H. J. Eysenck, The nature of extraversion: A genetical analysis, *J. Pers. Soc. Psychol., 32*: 102 (1975).

S. Ekblad, Influence of child rearing on aggressive behavior in a transcultural perspective, *Acta Psychiatr. Scand., 344*(Suppl.): 133 (1988).

H. J. Eysenck, *The Biological Basis of Personality,* Charles C Thomas, Springfield, IL (1967).

H. J. Eysenck, and M. W. Eysenck, *Personality and Individual Differences: A Natural Science Approach*, Plenum Press, New York (1985).

K. E. Freedland, R. M. Carney, R. J. Krone, L. J. Smith, M. W. Rich, G. Eisenkramer, and K. C. Fisher, Psychological factors in silent myocardial ischemia, *Psychosom. Med., 53*: 13 (1991).

D. Fowles, The three arousal model: Implications of Gray's two factor learning theory for heart rate, electrodermal activity, and psychopathy, *Psychophysiology, 17*: 87 (1980).

C. D. Frith, J. Dowdy, I. N. Ferrier, and R. J. Crow, Selective impairment of paired associate learning after administration of a centrally-acting adrenergic agonist (clonidine), *Psychopharmacology, 87*: 490 (1985).

H. Goldsmith, Roundtable: What is temperament? Four approaches, *Child Dev., 58*: 505 (1987).

J. A. Gray, *The Neuropsychology of Anxiety,* Oxford University Press, New York (1982).

M. S. Hamilton, The clinical distinction between anxiety and depression, *Br. J. Clin. Pharmacol., 15*(Suppl. 2): 165S (1983).

M. Hamilton, Frequency of symptoms in melancholia (depressive illness), *Br. J. Psychiatry, 154*: 201 (1989).

R. G. Heath, *The Role of Pleasure on Behavior,* Harper & Row, New York (1964).

A. Heath, and N. Martin, Psychoticism as a dimension of personality: A multivariate test of Eysenck and Eysenck's psychoticism construct, *J. Pers. Soc. Psychol., 58*: 111–121 (1990).

A. Heath, C. R. Cloninger, and N. Martin, Testing a model for the genetic structure of personality, (submitted; 1992).

P. L. Hoffman, C. L. Melchior, and B. Tabakoff, Vasopressin maintenance of ethanol tolerance requires intact brain noradrenergic systems, *Life Sci., 32*: 1065 (1983).

S. D. Iversen, Brain dopamine systems and behavior, *Handbook of Psychopharmacology,* Vol. 8 (L. L. Iversen, S. D. Iversen, and S. H. Snyder, eds.), Plenum Press, New York (1977).

C. Izard, *Human Emotions*, Plenum Press, New York (1977).

B. L. Jacobs, Amygdala unit activity as a reflection of functional changes in brain serotonergic neurons, *Serotonin and Behavior* (J. Barchas and E. Usdin, eds.), Academic Press, Nwe York (1972).

R. E. Kendell, The stability of psychiatric diagnosis, *Br. J. Psychiatry, 124*: 352 (1974).

K. I. Kim, CLinical study of primary depressive symptoms. Part III, *Neuropsychiatry, 16*: 46 (1979).

G. L. Kovacs, B. Bohus, and. D. H. G. Versteeg, Facilitation of memory consolidation by vasopressin: Mediation by terminals of the dorsal noradrenergic bundle? *Brain Res., 173*: 73 (1979).

G. W. Kraemer, M. H. Ebert, C. R. Lake, and W. T. McKinney, Cerebrospinal fluid measures of neurotransmitter changes associated with pharmacological alteration of the despair response to social separation in rhesus monkeys, *Psychiatry Res., 11*: 303 (1984).

P. Lang, The cognitive psychophysiology of emotion, *Anxiety and Anxiety Disorders* (H. Tuma and J. Masser, eds.), Lawrence Erlbaum, Hillsdale, NJ, pp. 131–170 (1985).

M. R. Liebowitz, Discussions arising from: Cloninger C.R. A unified biosocial theory of personality and its role in the development of anxiety states, *Psychiatr. Dev., 4*: 377 (1987).

M. R. Liebowitz, F. Stallone, D. K. Dunner, and R. F. Fieve, Personality features of patients with primary affective disorder, *Acta Psychiatr. Scand., 60*: 214 (1979).

M. Linnoila, M. Virkkunen, M. Scheinin, A. Nuutila, R. Rimon, and F. K. Goodwin, Low cerebrospinal fluid 5-hydroxyindoleacetic acid concentration differentiates impulsive from non-impulsive violent behavior, *Life Sci., 33*: 2609 (1983).

M. Lorr, and D. McNair, *Manual Profile of Mood States—Bipolar Form,* EDITS, San Diego (1984/1988).

C. Z. Malatesta, The role of emotions in the development and organization of personality, *Neb. Symp. Motiv., 36*: 1 (1988).

M. Maziade, P. Boutin, R. Cote et al., Empirical characteristics of the NYLS temperament in middle childhood: Congruities and incongruities with other studies, *Child Psychiatry Hum. Dev., 17*: 38 (1986).

M. A. Menza, N. E. Forman, H. S. Goldstein, and L. I. Golbe, Parkinson's disease, personality, and dopamine, *J. Neuropsychiatry Clin. Neurosci., 2*: 282 (1990).

G. J. Mogenson, D. L. Jones, and C. Y. Yim, From motivation to action: Functional interface between the limbic system and the motor system, *Prog. Neurobiol., 14*: 69 (1980).

R. Nieuwenhuys, *Chemoarchitecture of the Brain,* Springer Verlag, Berlin (1985).

T. Nishikawa, and B. Scatton, Inhibitory influences of GABA on central serotonergic transmission: Involvement of the habenulo-raphe pathways in the GABAergic inhibition of ascending cerebral serotonergic neurons, *Brain Res., 331*: 81 (1985).

T. Nishikawa, D. Fage, and B. Scatton, Evidence for, and nature of, the tonic inhibitory influence of habenulointerpeduncular pathways on cerebral dopaminergic transmission in the rat, *Brain Res., 373*: 324 (1986).

T. Olendick, N. King, and R. Frary, Fears in children and adolescents: Reliability and generalizability across gender, age, and nationality, *Behav. Res. Ther., 27*: 19 (1989).

J. Panksepp, Toward a general psychobiological theory of emotions, *Behav. Brain Sci., 5*: 407 (1982).

K. A. Phillips, J. G. Gunderson, R. M. A. Hirschfeld et al., A review of depressive personality, *Am. J. Psychiatry, 147*: 830 (1990).

C. S. Pomerleau, O. F. Pomerleau, K. A. Flessland, and S. M. Basson, Relationship of tridimensional personality questionnaire scores and smoking variables in female and male smokers, *J. Subst. Abuse, 4*: 143 (1992).

J. Reich, R. Noyes, W. Coryell, and T. W. O'Gorman, The effect of state anxiety on personality measurement, *Am. J. Psychiatry, 134*: 760 (1986).

A. Routtenberg, The reward system of the brain, *Sci. Am., 239*: 154 (1978).

D. Schalling, B. Gronholm, M. Aberg, and S. Espmark, Ratings of psychic and somatic anxiety indicants; interrater reliability and relations to personality variables, *Acta Psychiatr. Scand., 49*: 353 (1973).

J. Sepinwall, and L. Cook, Mechanism of action of the benzodiazepines: Behavioral aspects, *Fed. Proc., 39*: 3021 (1980).

G. S. Shahi, and S. M. Moochhala, Smoking and Parkinson's disease—a new perspective, *Rev. Environ. Health, 9*: 123 (1991).

P. Sollof, What's new in personality disorders?: An update on pharmacologic treatment, *J. Pers. Disord., 4*: 233 (1990).

D. M. Svrakic, T. R. Przybeck, and C. R. Cloninger, Further contribution to the conceptual validity of the unified biosocial model of personality: US and Yugoslav data, *Compr. Psychiatry, 32*: 195 (1991).

D. M. Svrakic, T. R. Przybeck, and C. R. Cloninger, Emotional states and personality traits, *J. Affective Disord., 24*: 217 (1992).

D. M. Svrakic, T. R. Przybeck, C. Whitehead, and C. R. Cloninger, Emotional traits and personality dimensions, *Arch. Gen. Psychiatry* (in press).

D. M. Svrakic, C. Whitehead, T. Przybeck, and C. R. Cloninger, Differential diagnosis of personality disorders by the seven factor model of temperament and character, *Arch. Gen. Psychiatry* (in press).

M. Takeuchi, A. Yoshino, M. Kato, Y. Ono, and T. Kitamura, "Reliability and validity of the Japanese version of the tridimensional personality questionnaire (TPQ) among university students," International Conference on Psychiatric Diagnosis, Tokyo, Japan, September 5–7 (1990).

A. Tellegen, Structures of mood and personality and their relevance to assessing anxiety, with an emphasis on self-report, *Anxiety and the Anxiety Disorders* (A. H. Tuma and J. Maser, eds.), Lawrence Erlbaum, Hillsdale, NJ, pp. 681–706 (1985).

M. H. Thiebot, M. Hammon, and P. Soubrie, Serotonergic neurons and anxiety relation behavior in rats, *Psychopharmacology of the Limbic System* (M. R. Trimble and E. Zarifian, eds.), Oxford University Press, New York, pp. 164–174 (1984).

R. D. Wetzel, C. R. Cloninger, B. Hong, and T. Reich, Personality as a subclinical expression of the affective disorders, *Compr. Psychiatry, 21*: 197 (1980).

T. A. Widiger, The categorical distinction between personality and affective disorders, *J. Pers. Disord., 3*: 77 (1989).

T. A. Widiger, T. Trull, S. Hurt et al, A multidimensional scaling of the *DSM II* personality disorders, *Arch. Gen. Psychiatry, 44*: 557 (1987).

R. A. Wise, Action of drugs of abuse on brain reward system, *Pharmacol. Biochem. Behav., 13*: 213 (1980).

M. Zuckerman, and B. Lubin, *Manual for the MAACL-R,* Educational and Industrial Testing Service, San Diego (1985).

Index

About the Editors

JOHAN A. DEN BOER is an Associate Professor of Clinical and Biological Psychiatry in the Department of Biological Psychiatry at the State University of Utrecht, The Netherlands. The author or coauthor of nearly 150 professional papers, book chapters, and abstracts, he is President of the Interdisciplinary Society of Biological Psychiatry (The Netherlands) and a member of the International Society of Neuroendocrinology and the British Association of Psychopharmacology, among other organizations. Dr. den Boer received the M.D. degree (1982) from the State University of Utrecht, The Netherlands, and the Ph.D. degree (1988) in psychiatry from the State University of Utrecht, The Netherlands.

J. M. Ad SITSEN is a Professor of Clinical Pharmacology in the Medical Faculty at the State University of Utrecht, The Netherlands, and head of the Section on Central Nervous System Drugs in the Medical Research and Development Unit at Organon International BV, Oss, The Netherlands. He is the editor or coeditor of two books and the author of numerous professional papers on pharmacology, clinical pharmacology, and the clinical trials of psychotropic drugs. A member of the European College of Neuropsychopharmacology, the British Pharmacological Society, and the American Society of Clinical Pharmacology and Therapeutics, among other organizations, Dr. Sitsen received the Pharm.D. degree (1970), the Ph.D. degree (1972) in medicinal chemistry, and the M.D. degree (1980) from the State University of Utrecht, The Netherlands.